MANSTEIN

MANSTEIN

HITLER'S GREATEST GENERAL

MUNGO MELVIN

Weidenfeld & Nicolson

LONDON

First published in Great Britain in 2010
by Weidenfeld & Nicolson

An Hachette UK company

3 5 7 9 10 8 6 4 2

Cartography © Barbara Taylor, 2010

A CIP catalogue record for this book
is available from the British Library.

ISBN 978 0 297 84561 4

Typeset by Input Data Services Ltd,
Bridgwater, Somerset

Printed and bound in the UK by
CPI Mackays, Chatham, ME5 8TD

The Orion Publishing Group's policy is to use papers
that are natural, renewable and recyclable products and
made from wood grown in sustainable forests. The logging
and manufacturing processes are expected to conform
to the environmental regulations of the country of origin.

Weidenfeld & Nicolson

The Orion Publishing Group Ltd
Orion House
5 Upper Saint Martin's Lane
London WC2H 9EA

www.orionbooks.co.uk

Contents

List of Maps

Author's Note on Spellings and Military Terminology

In writing this book, I have attempted to follow the many conventions of formulation and style common in both general and military writing, but have risked diverging from them when it seemed sensible to do so. In Central and East European place names, for example, I have used historical German and Russian titles rather than the modern Ukrainian, and apologize to my Ukrainian friends for doing so. Hence I refer to Lemberg (German) or Lvov (Russian) but not Lviv (Ukrainian). Within Russian, I have dropped the soft sign Russian ь normally rendered in English as an apostrophe. So I use Sevastopol, not Sevastopol', and Kharkov, rather than either Khar'kov (Russian) or Kharkiv (Ukrainian). For consistency, not least to provide commonality with David Glantz's scholarship, I use the Russian *Dnepr* rather than the Ukrainian Dnipro or German Dnieper for that great river; similarly, *Dnestr* rather than either Dnister (Ukrainian) or Dneister (German).

In the nomenclature of large formations, from the German I translate *Heeresgruppe* as 'army group', but retain '*Front*' for a Soviet group of armies. I use 'Eleventh' when referring to a German army and '64th', for example, when describing a Soviet one. I retain the Roman number of a German corps (such as Manstein's LVI), but use an Arabic one for an equivalent Soviet formation. I use the specific term 'Panzer' for a German armoured unit and 'Tank' for a Soviet one. These distinctions may appear a trifle pedantic, but they make a complex battle narrative between German and Soviet forces easier to follow. For a general description of the symbols used in the maps, see the general key below Map 1. Where more explanation is required, see the specific keys on the following maps.

Prologue

'I pay tribute before the whole German people to the heroic achievements of the troops fighting under your command.' Adolf Hitler[1]

After four weeks of hard pounding, the guns fell silent on 1 July 1942 over the once mighty citadel and naval base of Sevastopol. As the clouds of dust and acrid smoke lifted, an eerie stillness descended over the battered town and port. Although some isolated pockets of the Red Army continued to resist fanatically for a few days more, the last major Soviet bastion on the Crimea had fallen to the invading German and Rumanian forces. For over eight months the veteran troops of Colonel General Erich von Manstein's Eleventh Army had invested the seemingly impregnable fortress, purportedly the strongest in the world, whose capture had become for Hitler as much a matter of political prestige as a military object.[2] The great siege had ended with a spectacular feat of German arms, one last great – gasping – triumph for Germany during the Second World War before the crushing debacle at Stalingrad, six months later.

The ferocious struggle for Sevastopol remains – in the West at least – a dimly recalled event, a dark and distant chapter in the German–Soviet conflict so large in scale and desperate in nature that it continues to defy modern imagination. Manstein, the victor, is almost as forgotten as the campaign of nearly seventy years ago. The final attack of June 1942, with all the heavy artillery and close air support that the Wehrmacht could put at his disposal, only just succeeded.[3] Losses on both sides had been horrendous. And for the Germans, the bloody battles for the city would prove a dramatic episode in an ultimately unsuccessful war. Of the victory hard won in July 1942, by May 1944 all had been lost and the Crimea abandoned. On 1 May 1945, Stalin announced that brave Sevastopol, along with Leningrad, Moscow and Stalingrad, was to become a 'hero-city' of the Soviet Union.

The summer of 1942 marked the high-water mark in Germany's fortunes in the Second World War. In the Western Desert, Colonel General Erwin Rommel had captured the stronghold of Tobruk on 21 June, and the British Eighth Army was in headlong retreat towards Egypt and the Nile. For the Allies, the prospects looked equally grim in the Soviet Union. In recent months on the Eastern Front, Soviet armies near Leningrad, Kharkov in the Ukraine and on the Kerch peninsula on the Crimea had all been defeated decisively. As Manstein savoured his crowning success at Sevastopol, the main weight of the German Army in the East – under the aegis of Operation BLUE – was beginning its overly ambitious summer offensive towards the Caucasus and its economically crucial oilfields that would lead to the fatal distraction and climactic battle of Stalingrad. Despite incurring over a million casualties since the start of Operation BARBAROSSA on 22 June 1941, Hitler's hopes of smashing Bolshevism in the summer of 1942 were still high, if not unduly optimistic.[4]

In the meantime, Germany could celebrate another splendid victory. It earned Erich von Manstein, at the age of 54, his field marshal's baton: the zenith of his career. Preceded by a triumphant fanfare, Berlin radio broadcast a special communiqué announcing the fall of Sevastopol. Shortly after, Hitler's warm congratulatory message clattered over the teleprinter link to the Eleventh Army's forward command post at the Tatar settlement of Yukhary Karales, now called Zalesnoe, 20 kilometres due east of Sevastopol:

> To the Commander-in-Chief of the Crimean Army,
> Colonel-General v. Manstein,
>
> In grateful appreciation of your exceptionally meritorious services in the victorious battles of the Crimea, culminating in the annihilation of the enemy at Kerch and the conquest of the mighty fortress of Sevastopol, I hereby promote you Field-Marshal. By your promotion and the creation of a commemorative shield to be worn by all ranks who took part in the Crimean campaign, I pay tribute before the whole German people to the heroic achievements of the troops fighting under your command.
>
> ADOLF HITLER[5]

The largely self-contained campaign on the Crimea in 1941–42 had proved a bitter and costly fight, in many senses a microcosm of the much wider, total war waging between Germany and the Soviet Union that stretched from the Barents Sea in the Arctic north to the Black Sea in the south. Whilst German personnel and *matériel* losses continued to mount, the capability of the Red Army was on the increase – quantitatively if not yet qualitatively – despite the grievous damage it had suffered thus far in fighting a 'sacred war' (*sviashchennaya voyna*) in defence of Mother Russia.[6]

In stark contrast with the First World War, when most of Germany's military effort was directed and expended on the Western Front, from June 1941 onwards the *decisive* campaign was fought in the East. It was here that Manstein wrestled to contain the Red Army's growing offensive power and argued with Hitler about the conduct of operations from Stalingrad onwards. As multiple Soviet *fronts* (groups of armies) threatened to engulf the German southern wing, he demanded repeatedly freedom of manoeuvre to conduct counterstrokes on a vast, operational scale in order to unbalance, then bring the Russian juggernaut to a halt and defeat it. As Manstein remarked, however, this approach was inconsistent with the supreme commander's 'way of thinking [that] conformed more to a mental picture of masses of the enemy bleeding to death before our lines than to the conception of a subtle fencer who knows how to make an occasional step backwards in order to lunge for the decisive thrust'.[7]

The Field Marshal argued with the Führer so persistently that he was dismissed as an army group commander at the end of March 1944. Throughout his career, Manstein was an assertive subordinate and self-assured commander. Although relations remained cordial for the most part, there was certainly no love lost between him and Hitler, which was painfully obvious to all involved. As the crises mounted on the Eastern Front, which shifted inexorably westwards, and Germany's defeat appeared increasingly inevitable, on 10 January 1944 *Time* magazine enquired provocatively whether Manstein would 'play the Teutonic Pétain' – and betray his head of state.[8] He did not. Although his retort to a member of the resistance that 'Prussian field marshals do not mutiny' is probably a fiction, it neatly represents his position.[9] Even though Manstein opposed Hitler's catastrophic decision-making, unlike Claus, Graf von Stauffenberg, he would not go for the kill. Ultimately, he failed in a doomed personal contest that saw Hitler's implacable will trump reasoned military judgement. On his farewell from Headquarters Army Group South, Manstein's intensely loyal staff presented him with an oil painting by a Dutch master of two fighting cocks (the *Hahnenkampf*), symbolizing poignantly his combative relationship with the Führer.[10] No other general served Hitler so well whilst disputing his military decisions so consistently.

Today, despite his impressive military record, Manstein remains a highly controversial figure. No German barracks bears his name: any such link would unleash a storm of political protest. Since the Second World War, and more particularly over the last thirty years, there has been a distinct historiographic trend to cast senior figures such as

Manstein in a bad light, and to brand the Wehrmacht as a criminal organization.[11] Of course, the less than favourable aspects of his career demand close scrutiny, bearing in mind that he was brought in front of a British military court in 1949. Amongst seventeen charges of war crimes, he was accused of 'deliberately and recklessly disregarding his duty' by failing to ensure the humane treatment of Soviet prisoners of war, large numbers of whom died or were handed over to units of the German *Sicherheitsdienst* (SD) to be killed. Equally damning was the alleged involvement of his army in the widespread shootings of partisans, in support of the mass extermination of Jews by *Einsatzgruppe* D and in the conduct of brutal 'scorched earth' policies. Although Manstein was acquitted on eight charges, he was found guilty on nine, resulting in a sentence of eighteen years' imprisonment, subsequently reduced to twelve on confirmation.

After the fighting ends, apart from the quest for justice or retribution, it is perhaps inevitable that the ensuing analysis of causes and outcomes continues in an undeclared war of reputations. The first battle to be fought in the resulting peace, if one prevails, is that of the memoirs: the reappraisal of past events and personalities seen through the eyes of the principal surviving participants. Military history written through the perspective of the commanders involved can rarely be objective. To expect otherwise would be naive. War, to recast Clausewitz, remains the province of egos, as well as the familiar realms of danger, physical exertion, suffering and chance. Whilst it is the job of the military historian rather than the participant to bring distance and objectivity to bear, without the views of those directly involved in the making of events, any history would lack colour and authenticity.[12]

After the Second World War, both the victorious and the vanquished offered their memoirs to a curious and impatient public trying to understand what had happened, and to learn how decisions that had affected the lives of millions of men and women had come to be made. If the writers of such works were already well-known figures, then interest in their reminiscences and opinions was assured. Of the Western Allied military commanders, Bradley (*A Soldier's Story*), Eisenhower (*Crusade in Europe*) and Montgomery (*The Memoirs*), all contributed highly readable 'how I won the War' accounts, with their arguments about each other enhancing their readers' interest and hence sales.[13] On the Soviet side, descriptions of war became the instruments of state propaganda as much as outlets for personal point-scoring as exemplified by polemical collections such as *Battles Hitler Lost* and heavily edited individual works from the likes of Marshal Zhukov and General Chuikov.[14]

Unsurprisingly, the Germans had to approach their memoirs from a different perspective, that of the losing side. Amongst the best-known and accessible works are those of Guderian (*Panzer Leader*), Kesselring (*A Soldier's Record*) and Manstein (*Lost Victories*).[15] All three accounts fed assiduously the myth of a 'clean' and invincible Wehrmacht whose hard-won tactical successes were thrown away through strategic shortcomings, not only in terms of insufficient national resources, but more significantly through the political and military errors of Adolf Hitler.

Manstein's autobiography is in many ways the most illuminating of the genre, as much for what it does *not* say as for what it does. He devotes a huge amount of attention to operational and strategic issues, and, not unnaturally, to his eminent role in these. Within the wider context of Germany's wars of aggression and crimes against humanity, however, the reader will search in vain for any specific description of the Holocaust, or for any detailed account of the widespread actions of Germany's armed forces (and not just the SD or formations of the *Waffen* SS) against prisoners of war and subject peoples under occupation. This, after all, was not Manstein's purpose. Had Hitler only accepted the advice of his generals, he maintained, then the outcome of the war might have been quite different. The obvious limitation of this self-serving rationalization is a simple one: a good number of Hitler's senior generals, including himself, were happy enough to support the regime – one that offered them success and glory – until the tides of war turned against Germany. By then, and notwithstanding the various plots against the Führer, argu-ably it was too late to prevent further disaster and to halt the steep decline towards Germany's defeat.

Writing in the 1950s, General Siegfried Westphal, evaluating fellow officers of the General Staff, declared that Manstein 'possessed the greatest strategic and general military gifts. Forward-looking, always full of new, good, and often brilliant ideas, and organizer of genius, a difficult subordinate and a generous superior, he was always in the front rank when the interests of the Army were at stake'.[16] It is reported that Marshal of the Soviet Union Rodion Yakovlevich Malinovsky said: 'We considered the hated von Manstein our most dangerous opponent. His technical mastery of every, and I mean every, situation was unequalled. Things would perhaps have gone much worse for us if every general in the German Wehrmacht had possessed his stature.'[17] The British historian Liddell Hart regarded Manstein as the 'ablest of all the German generals', based on his 'superb strategic sense'.[18]

Somewhere between the operationally gifted commander, respected by friends and foes alike, and the individual, whom modern critics vilify on account of his association with war crimes, lies the 'real' Manstein.[19] Of all the major commanders of the Second World War, to date he has not been the subject of a full-scale biography in English.[20] Such a work is long overdue. Whilst Manstein's many accomplishments on the battle-field represent an obvious focus of interest, his complex interaction with the Führer and seemingly ambivalent attitude to Hitler's criminal regime provide an equally rich seam of enquiry, as does the Field Marshal's character and personality.

This book describes Manstein's life and career, highlighting his various achievements in the Second World War and documenting his numerous attempts to influence and moderate Adolf Hitler's decision-making. It is not necessary to identify with Hitler and fascism to express a favourable opinion on Manstein's operational prowess.[21] Far from it: Manstein was neither an active supporter of Hitler nor a member of the Nazi Party. Indeed, an essential line of investigation is to determine the nature of his loyalty to the Führer, and to examine the extent of his association with those involved in the failed assassination attempt of 20 July 1944.

More specifically, this biography sketches Manstein's roots, childhood and youth; it describes his formative years during the First World War, the Weimar Republic and the rise of Nazism, documenting his service in the Reichswehr and the new Wehrmacht; and concentrates on his performance in various command and staff positions in the Second World War. Thereafter, his confinement as a British prisoner of war and his subsequent trial, sentence and custody are explored. By way of an epilogue, the book examines the Field Marshal's historical legacy in his memoirs, and his role as a senior mentor to the German Armed Forces (the Bundeswehr) during its foundation in the mid 1950s.

In an historic and heroic sense, the pursuit of victory defines the prime role of a military commander. Yet the military genius required to achieve such a result is elusive: it rests on a rare and harmonious blend of experience, intellect and temperament.[22] Manstein demonstrated such qualities, becoming a much-respected master of manoeuvre. To under-stand his generalship, it is necessary to appreciate the making of the man, his personal strengths and weaknesses. His character was moulded through his Prussian family tradition, class and military education. His unrivalled competence in the Second World War was based on his thorough grounding as a young officer serving in mainly staff positions on the Eastern and Western Fronts during the Great War. He then served as a company and battalion commander during the turbulent Reichswehr years. All these experiences helped fashion Manstein the soldier.

In many respects, as an aristocratic Prussian general staff officer, Manstein was bound to view the world after the First World War and the Versailles '*Diktat*' of 1919 in a similar way to that of a then obscure former Bavarian Army corporal, plebeian Adolf Hitler. If they both felt that Germany had been 'stabbed in the back', there could not have been a greater contrast between two individuals in upbringing and attitude. They were forced to confront and deal with each other over twenty years later. Their co-operation and conflict at the intersections of military strategy and operational art did much to determine the outcome of the Second World War, first on the Western and subsequently on the Eastern Front, for better and for worse.

If there is one dominant theme of this analysis, then it is the exploration of the complex relationship between a commander-in-chief and his head of state. Under the supreme test of war, a collision between political will and professional military opinion may well result, as in Manstein's case. Whatever the basic cause of such discord, and whether in a dictatorship or a democracy, almost inevitably it is the senior officer who must depart. Whether dismissed or resigned, he must then reflect on his conscience and record.

Manstein's career illuminates the inevitable tensions in trying to make inadequate military means match overambitious political ends, particularly if they are fundamentally flawed and ideologically driven. The pressure to conduct warfare in an unrestrained way produced calamitous effects and unimaginable suffering on the Eastern Front. The enduring lessons are as relevant today in quite different global circumstances as they were seventy years ago. War, after all, is just as much about the clash of ideas and peoples as their armed forces. Hence senior military commanders need an understanding of not only the operational methods, tactics and technologies that serve them, but also the wider political, economic and social ramifications of war. Appreciating the perceptions and reactions of populations at home and abroad, and in meeting honestly the requirement to resource sufficiently any necessary campaigns, should never be separated from the planning and conduct of operations. Authors of contemporary policies and strategies ignore these basic truths at their peril, as they do the constraints of international law.

1

Son of Prussia

'A clever but very serious young man.'
Martha von Sperling-Manstein

Family and Early Life

Erich Fritz von Lewinski, named Manstein, was born in 1887, a year of
birth he shared with none other than the British soldier Bernard Law
Montgomery. Both learned their trade in their nations' general staffs
during the First World War, became noted tutors of staff and trainers of
men and won great victories in the Second World War; both earned their
field marshal's batons in the process and wrote controversial memoirs
afterwards, remaining contentious figures thereafter; both forged their
nations' post-war armies in their mould: such were their enduring
legacies.

Manstein's and Montgomery's characters also exhibited further
similarities: critical of others, to many their very self-confidence
bordered on conceit. Their well-organized and highly capable staffs,
however, were intensely loyal. Unsurprisingly, notwithstanding their
exceptional military abilities, both Manstein and Montgomery managed
to annoy their diverse superiors with uncommon regularity, a trait, it
must be observed, rather more apparent in the latter. That said, there
was little else in common between the aristocratic Prussian officer's
son – born to serve the German Kaiser – and the son of a modest Anglo-
Irish parson, who took the King's commission. Patrician Manstein, on
the losing side, became a convicted war criminal; in his opinion, and
that of many others, a victim of 'victors' justice'. Humbler Montgomery,
in birth if not in attitude, on the winning side, was feted as a national
hero. They never met despite Manstein's best efforts at the war's end
to surrender personally to Montgomery on the Lüneburg Heath in
early May 1945.[1]

Fifty-eight years earlier in the small Thuringian town of Rudolstadt,
a curious telegram arrived from Berlin: 'Today a young boy is born for
you. Mother and child well. Best wishes. Helene and Lewinski.' This

brief communication announced the birth of baby Erich on 24 November 1887, the tenth son of Eduard Julius Ludwig von Lewinski (1829–1906) and fifth child of his second wife Helene, née von Sperling (1847–1910).[2] Before Erich's birth his mother had arranged for her childless younger sister Hedwig (1852–1925) to adopt the baby if it were a boy. This sort of pragmatic pact seemed to run in the family: previously Hedwig, married to Georg von Manstein (1844–1913), had adopted Martha, the young daughter of her recently deceased brother and naval officer Erich von Sperling (1851–89).

The Lewinski, Manstein and Sperling families had strong aristocratic roots and were proud of their long, loyal service to the Prussian Crown, producing officers in every generation. A particularly notable exemplar was General Christoph Hermann von Manstein (1711–57), who had fought with distinction against the Austrians during the Seven Years War. Despite being blamed – somewhat unfairly – for the Prussian defeat at Kolin (18 June 1757), he was judged generously by Frederick the Great in his assessment of Prussian generals as 'très bon'.[3]

The royal connection was maintained in the latter half of the eighteenth century when a lieutenant colonel von Manstein served as 'Generaladjutant von der Infanterie' to King Frederick William II, acting as an equerry who handled the sovereign's military correspondence.[4] Manstein's grandfather Albrecht Gustav (1805–77) commanded the 6th Prussian Division in the wars of 1864 against Denmark and 1866 against Austria. During the Franco-Prussian War of 1870–71, he commanded IX (Schleswig-Holstein) Corps, distinguishing himself particularly at the battles of Gravelotte and Le Mans. The city of Altona (now part of Hamburg) made him a freeman in 1872. So the Manstein name in the final quarter of the nineteenth century had at least local, if not regional, fame: the 84th Infantry Regiment stationed in Schleswig was called the 'Mansteiner'. Schleswig still has its Mansteinstrasse today, as do Berlin and Hamburg.

Military traditions ran as deeply in the Manstein family as they did generally in Wilhelmine Germany. On retirement, Albrecht Gustav von Manstein was presented by his grateful corps with a commemorative dagger. Engraved with the battle honours Düppel, Alsen, Königgrätz, Gravelotte, Orléans and Le Mans it represented a gazetteer of the most famous actions of Prussia's wars of unification. Following the example of his forefathers, Manstein carried the memento throughout his career. His natural father Lewinski served on the Prussian staff in the wars of 1864, 1866 and 1870–71, retiring as a general of artillery in 1895.[5] His maternal grandfather Major General Oskar von Sperling (1814–72) was chief of staff of the Steinmetz and Goeben armies during the Franco-Prussian War. Meanwhile, the brothers of his adoptive mother were all officers. Hedwig's younger sister Gertrud von Sperling (1860–1914) had married in 1879 no less a catch than Paul von Beneckendorff und von Hindenburg (1847–1934), the victor of Tannenberg and national hero of the First World War, and late Reich president between 1925 and 1934. With all these close military connections, as Manstein himself remarked, it was 'little wonder that he had wished to become a soldier from an early age'.[6]

The family in which Erich grew up was relatively well to do. Although the Mansteins had lost their landed estates in East Prussia several generations before, both his grandfathers (Manstein and Sperling) had received substantial grants from the German parliament (the Reichstag) in recognition of their meritorious service in the Franco-Prussian War. So the family, if not uncommonly rich, enjoyed a certain status and financial independence. Manstein's adoptive father was a Prussian officer of the old school. And yet his strictness, maintained his son, albeit moderated by a dry humour, disguised a fundamentally kind heart. Hence Erich von Manstein appears to have enjoyed a genuinely close family life. He knew and accepted his position as an adoptive child, enjoyed the tender affection of his adoptive mother in particular, whilst retaining a link to his natural parents through visits to Schloss Burgwitz-Trebnitz in Silesia.

Manstein records that he was surrounded by love and happiness on both sides of his family, natural and adoptive, and he enjoyed a close relationship with Martha (1884–1956), three years his elder. The warmth of feeling was mutual: Martha von Sperling-Manstein's memoirs portray a picture of genuine sisterly love and deep affection, of happy if not halcyon childhood times together at home and on holiday. Within the family, Erich was known throughout his life as 'Erli'; his early attempts to say Martha came out as 'Atta', a nickname that stuck. Both children called their adoptive parents 'father' (using the more familiar *Väterchen* rather than *Vater*) and 'mother' (*Mütterchen* rather than *Mutter*) as opposed to uncle or aunt.

The majority of aristocratic families had at least one son in the army, bound by oath and tradition to the Prussian king and German Kaiser. Manstein's character reflected the norm found in a close-knit circle of Prussian military families, in which duty, honour, obedience and a sense of responsibility for others were all dominant virtues. Such qualities also reflected the sober, no-nonsense German-Prussian work ethic in which Manstein was brought up. As he later mused, his heart lay in the vast, if not often monotonous landscape of northern Germany, in the quiet forests and lakes of the Mark [Brandenburg], Pomerania and Prussia, in the German seas, in the wide expanse of the eastern plain and in the mighty brick [church] domes of the north that, like castles, watch over the east.[7]

Young Manstein was a bright, temperamental and somewhat tender child, who despite his conventional family upbringing, resented the dumb authority of school. Whereas he accepted the word of his family and of his adoptive father in particular, 'encouraged' by the occasional punishment, he was argumentative and difficult at times with his peers and teachers alike. Not being a physically strong youngster, he tended to live on his wits. He was forthcoming and lively enough in class but not particularly industrious. Unsurprisingly, his school reports reflected the familiar refrain: 'with more application ought to do much better'. We see here also the origins of Manstein, who in his own words was in later life 'not a simple or easy subordinate', wishing to discuss and debate an issue on its merits rather than accepting a matter 'because it is so'.[8]

Manstein, as he later freely admitted, could often appear 'cool and sharp in tone', attributes that did not always engender him to others.[9] As a result, and particularly to those who did not know him well, Manstein could be regarded as a cold and unfriendly individual. Only the moderating influence of his wife, his dear Jutta-Sibylle von Loesch whom he married in 1920, he declared, helped suppress his 'tendency to egotism' – another uncanny similarity to Montgomery.[10]

Manstein's early school years were spent in the successive garrison towns of his adoptive father, who served in the Prussian-controlled lands of eastern, northern and western Germany. These included Rudolstadt in the minor principality of Schwarzburg-Rudolstadt within the modern-day federal state of Thuringia; in Schwerin, the capital of the former Grand Duchy of Mecklenburg-Schwerin; and, latterly, in Strasbourg in Alsace. Following the Franco-Prussian War, with the German accession of the French provinces of Alsace and Lorraine, Strasbourg had become Strassburg in Elsass-Lothringen, a Reichsland or imperial territory.

The Strasbourg of Manstein's childhood remained very much a militarized frontier city, housing the best part of an army corps, on account of its geostrategic situation and mixed Franco-German history and heritage. His father commanded the 132nd Prussian Infantry Regiment, with its headquarters in the citadel. In later life Manstein was to stress Strassburg's origins as a free city of the German Reich, which had been rudely interrupted by nearly two hundred years of French rule, following

Louis XIV's seizure of the city in 1681. When Manstein attended the Lyceum in Strasbourg between 1894 and 1899, if the historic tensions between the French and German-oriented populations did not erupt frequently in the classroom or on the streets, they smouldered on none the less never far below the surface.

Manstein looked back on his early years in Strasbourg with many fond memories of his family life. Inside his parents' villa at the Schiltigheimer Tor, his most treasured possessions (and top wish for birthday or Christmas presents) were his prized Heinrichsen tin soldiers, with whom he fought many a battle on the dining-room table. But a healthy young lad could not stay indoors all the time. His sister recorded a typical episode of their childhood days together:

> On 24 November, Erli's birthday, we could still play outside without our coats, oblivious of winter. We were really proud that on such special days, [father's] regimental band would often give a recital. However, we had to go forward to the circle of bandsmen and thank the bandmaster. I would have preferred to have hidden myself when our big Newfoundlander began to howl at the beginning of the music. I grabbed him ... by his collar lead, and we both gave our thanks: I for the concert; the dog for its conclusion.

Strasbourg's fortifications provided a magnet for young Erich's curiosity and enthusiasm for all things military. The city's defences were held to be impregnable, so strong that *even* the Prussians could not breach them during the war of 1870–71! Martha recalled that her precocious brother would frequently drag around a bemused escorting lieutenant through the casements and magazines, pumping him full of detailed questions.[11]

In his adult life Manstein was imbued with a deep sense of the culture and history of Strasbourg, with its striking medieval centre crowned by its world-famous Gothic cathedral. For him, Strassburg and Elsass (Alsace) exemplified the enduring sore between France and Germany that had brought such misery to these two great nations in three recent wars. In 1958, one year after the signing of the Treaty of Rome, Manstein suggested that Strasbourg should become the capital city of the European Community.[12] He had already called for European unity in his unpublished work 'Der Weg zum Weltfrieden' ('The Way towards World Peace'), written in a British prisoner-of-war camp between 1946 and 1948.[13] Prophetic words indeed: whilst Brussels represents today the economic and political hub of the European Union, the European Parliament also sits in Strasbourg for twelve plenary sessions a year.[14] It is of no coincidence that the headquarters of the modern-day Eurocorps, a symbol of European military integration, is stationed in that city.

Manstein's pleasant schoolboy days in Strasbourg were cut short by a new stage of life, which turned out as his first step in a long and distinguished military career. His adoptive father Georg retired from the Prussian Army in the autumn of 1899, and after a brief stay over the winter in Berlin, his parents embarked on a series of journeys at home and abroad. Young Erich needed education and a home, so at the beginning of the new school year after the Easter of 1900, at the tender age of 12, he entered the Royal Prussian Cadet Corps. This step very much matched his personal wishes and those of his father. For the first two years of military education he was sent to the junior cadet school at Plön in Holstein prior to spending his last four years at Prussia's senior cadet institution (*Hauptkadettenanstalt*) at Gross-Lichterfelde in Berlin.

As a young cadet housed in Plöner Schloss, Manstein undertook a busy regime of classes, gymnastics and sport, completing his Lower and Upper Third years of secondary education (the *Unter-* and *Obertertia*).[15] Plön also acted as a school for the royal princes. During Manstein's time there, Prince Oskar of Prussia was also a pupil, although his education was conducted on a largely separated basis. Whilst Manstein was not selected to sit with the prince during his special private tutorials, he none the less attended a demonstrably royal institution, which helped set the tone of his subsequent military education and service at court.

Although now a cadet, Manstein was still a young lad who went home during his long vacations. In 1900 he spent one last idyllic summer holiday with Martha at the Baltic fishing village of Ahrenshoop, which later became a famous seaside resort. She recalled Erli's arrival that year:

> He appeared in his cadet uniform, which was far too big for him, his tender neck disappearing into a stiff collar. Mother was quite aghast at his appearance – whilst he was so proud of his royal tunic. Despite his protestations she made him change immediately into a sailor suit, and only the reminder that sailors of the Imperial Navy wore such uniforms calmed him down.[16]

In comparison with provincial Plön, Gross-Lichterfelde was a much larger and grander establishment, which at its peak in the 1900s housed over 1,600 cadets. With royal support, the institution had moved on to its sprawling new site in south-west Berlin in 1878.[17] Although it housed 14- to 18-year-olds, in many respects Gross-Lichterfelde represented Germany's equivalent of Sandhurst or West Point in inculcating the enduring officer ethos of serving to lead. The majority of the German Army's future stars in the Second World War were educated there, including Gerd von Rundstedt who had undergone cadet training twelve years before Manstein.[18] Manstein completed a full period of education at Gross-Lichterfelde, gaining his *Abitur*, as he would have done in a civilian *Realgymnasium*.[19] Hence he was qualified to study for a degree. But Manstein followed the norm by direct entry into the field army on completion of his cadetship: a university education was equally uncommon in the Prussian Army at the time as it was in the British, French or United States armies.[20]

Life as a cadet was physically and mentally hard, occasionally if not systemically brutal, and deliberately designed to be so in the manner of a British public school or American military institute of the same period. Apart from the formal academic instruction and physical training, other aspects of a junior cadet's 'education' were left in the hands of the senior cadets, who, when appointed as under officers, performed the roles of company commanders, prefects and dormitory monitors. Whilst the German public's perception of the cadet schools was poor on account of recurring tales of harassment, bullying and corporal punishment, it would appear that the vast majority of individuals who survived the Spartan system benefited from their education, and saw things rather more positively. Heinz Guderian, who followed in Manstein's footsteps to Gross-Lichterfelde in 1903, recalled: 'When I remember my instructors and teachers from these formative years it is with emotions of deep gratitude and respect. Our education in the cadet corps was of course one of military austerity and simplicity. But it was founded on kindness and justice.'[21]

The cadets valued the sense of camaraderie and comradeship. For his part, Manstein looked back on the strong team spirit (*Korpsgeist*) between cadets that arose from their similar backgrounds, the families of officers or civil servants (*Beamte*). He maintained that such homogeneity represented 'what every army needs', despite the hidden risk of uniformity.[22] Common standards and values such as a sense of duty, obedience and responsibility were all drilled into cadets such as Manstein. Self-discipline, self-control and the ability to overcome fear through personal pride were all prized qualities, and especially, 'learning to keep a stiff upper lip'. The latter quality, Manstein remarked, was the same one that made 'British colleges' so famous in Germany.[23]

As Manstein came from a well-connected aristocratic family he was entitled to be selected as a page of the royal court during his time as a cadet. He described his various page duties with great pride, his account tinged unmistakably with sentimentality for the regal pomp and ceremony that was lost irretrievably with the abdication of the German

Kaiser in November 1918. The whole complex apparatus and pageantry of court, the colourful uniforms, music and dance, arcane orders of chivalry and strictly enforced rules of precedent all impressed the young Manstein. This was a captivating world of glitter and glamour for an aspiring man of his class, rubbing shoulders with royalty, senior military figures and the diplomatic corps in the grand state rooms of the Berliner Schloss.

Manstein acted as both a *Hofpage*, a handsome boy who provided a decorated background presence in the staterooms of court, and in an even more privileged status, as a *Leibpage* or personal escort. In the case of a lady, he would carry the train of her ballgown. Undoubted highlights of royal page duty were the splendid weddings, grand balls, state dinners and investitures in orders such as that of the 'Knights of the Black Eagle'. Manstein did not seem to spare a critical thought for such events, nor indeed consider their exorbitant cost.[24] Yet he was neither in the position nor remotely inclined to question the requirements of the German Kaiser and King of Prussia. 'Firm in loyalty' (*In Treue fest*) was, after all, the personal motto given to him by his adoptive father.

Despite the pleasant distractions of page duties at the royal court, Manstein's education proceeded apace. At the end of his fourth year at Lichterfelde (the *Oberprima*) he passed his *Abitur* with a respectable 'good'. This result, Manstein noted, was but 'to the amazement of some his teachers'.[25] He had already demonstrated an ability to pass examinations without excessive stress; his calmness under pressure in his later career would do much to enhance his military reputation.

There were cultural diversions too: on occasions he accompanied his sister to the theatre in Berlin. Martha recalled him (then a tall, slim youth of 16 years old) on one such excursion to see a performance of *Faust* as a 'clever but very serious young man, following Goethe's text word for word to check that nothing – on account of the afternoon performance – had been left out'.[26] Manstein's attention to detail would become legendary, be it for the military or for more mundane family matters.

Entry into the Guards

On completion of his time as a cadet at Gross-Lichterfelde, Ensign (*Fähnrich*) Manstein joined the prestigious 3rd Prussian Foot Guards, a regiment in which his uncle Hindenburg had served. Indeed, this close family connection provided the rationale for his entry. In his first year in the army proper (1906), Manstein undertook a period of specialist instruction at the royal military school in Engers am Rhein near Neuwied, north of Koblenz, before returning to his parent regiment in Berlin. He was promoted to second lieutenant on 27 January 1907, his commission being backdated to 14 June 1905.

Life as a young subaltern in an élite Prussian Guards unit was certainly not all one elegant social whirl, although living in Berlin had its obvious attractions. Manstein's first responsibility at regimental duty was to train contingents of new recruits, which involved not only ceremonial duties but also the vital tactical skills of shooting and field craft. His soldiers, mainly volunteers drawn from across Prussia, were of a quality higher than the conscripts of the regional line infantry. The military training year followed a well-worn pattern of drill and exercising at company, battalion and regimental level, culminating with larger-scale autumn manoeuvres involving divisions and army corps. So Manstein had ample opportunity to get to know the young men in his charge through exercises on nearby training areas such as the Döberitz Heath, as well as performing on the Tempelhof parade ground, where the Kaiser's splendid reviews were held every spring and autumn. Yet, as Manstein stressed, the Guards were combat troops first and foremost, and 'parade drill was an additional burden' as opposed to a primary task.[27]

Manstein described his mess life in some detail. At the time, the *Offizierskasino* represented, as it still does today in the British Army, the centre of regimental life and tradition. So guest nights celebrating famous battle honours such as the storming of the Düppel entrenchments (18 April 1864), the battle of Königgrätz (3 July 1866), the famous assault of the Guards at St Privat (18 August 1870) and, of course, the Kaiser's birthday (27 January 1859) were all important events in the regimental calendar. Former officers and wider friends of the regiment were invited back to such commemorations and to the monthly dining-in nights, broadening the company and lending gravitas to the occasion. On being invited to become an officer of the regiment, an individual would remain on the books as an honorary mess member on posting or retirement: the wider regimental family looked after its own.

Senior officers (whether still serving or not) were expected to look after and guide their juniors in an unofficial mentoring role. Serving in Berlin or in nearby Potsdam offered keen, young Guards officers such as Manstein the additional advantage of attending specialist lectures and undertaking private study in preparation for entry into the General Staff, thus improving career possibilities.[28] Talking shop in the officers' mess, however, was frowned on – young officers were expected to have wider cultural tastes and interests. Recreational sport was one of them. Manstein made good use of his regiment's two sailing yachts, cruising on summer Sundays on the pretty lakes of the upper Spree near Berlin. In addition, he had to exercise his horse Frechdachs (Cheeky Little Thing) regularly.

Serving in an army at peace, Manstein also had extended periods of leave to enjoy; accordingly, he travelled widely throughout Germany, the Baltic and to Switzerland. At the end of September 1908, he undertook a particularly interesting four-week journey by train and steamer to Turkey, Greece and Italy. The opportunity for an extended vacation arose through his close personal friendship with a fellow subaltern, Wilhelm Dietrich (Dico) von Ditfurth, whose father was a German instructor of the Turkish Army in Constantinople. The Ditfurths had invited Manstein, along with a mutual friend Gebhard von Bismarck, to come out to stay with their son. Apart from their adventures as tourists sampling the exotic delights of the bazaar and inspecting architectural charms such as the Hagia Sophia, Manstein and his two comrades were able to extend their military education whilst abroad. Invited to view an exercise of the Turkish Guard Corps, he noted that the troops displayed considerable enthusiasm and their officers (many of whom had been trained by Germans) also made a 'good impression'.[29]

On their return to Germany the happy trio voyaged through the Mediterranean, visiting Greece and Athens briefly, and then spending a week in Italy, taking in Messina, Naples, Capri, Pompeii and Rome.[30] This extensive 'grand tour' represented one of Manstein's most cherished memories of his youth. Not only had he got to know himself and his closest friends better, but he had also learned something of the wider world outside Berlin and Germany. Whilst such broadening of horizons through foreign travel is taken for granted today, a century ago it represented an exceptional opportunity for a young German officer. In Manstein's case it was one evidently well taken.

Within Germany, 1910 marked the fiftieth anniversary of the founding of 3rd Prussian Foot Guards. Manstein recalled that thousands of former officers and guardsmen came to Berlin to watch the grand parade and to take part in the celebrations, a proud and misty-eyed day for all involved. For Manstein, as for thousands of other young officers in the German and other armies, regimental duty created bonds of close comradeship and friendship that were to last for life, survival in war, of course, permitting. Apart from Ditfurth and Bismarck, Manstein's regimental chums also included his cousin, Hindenburg's son Oskar, who was a regular visitor to the Manstein family. Few, if any, who enjoyed those carefree pre-war days could have imagined the catastrophe that was to engulf Europe in the late summer of 1914.

During the first half of 1910, Manstein was detached to the Military Gymnastics Institute in Wünsdorf, south of Berlin, prior to becoming adjutant of the fusilier battalion of 3rd Foot Guards in July 1911. He served successfully in that capacity until his entry into the War Academy (*Kriegsakademie*) in Berlin for general staff training in the autumn of 1913. Meanwhile, his professional talents were becoming all apparent: his battalion commander, Lieutenant Colonel von Schulzendorff, described him on departure as 'the best adjutant I've ever had'.[31]

Into the General Staff

Before the First World War, no other army in the world enjoyed the tradition, prestige and reputation of the German General Staff. The creation of the great Prussian military reformers Gneisenau and Scharnhorst in the early nineteenth century, it had come to international renown through the spectacular Prussian-German successes during the wars of 1864, 1866 and 1870–71. By way of contrast, the United States and British General Staffs were not set up until 1903 and 1906 respectively.

Under the steady guidance of Moltke the Elder, its long-serving chief from 1857 to 1888, the General Staff had developed into two branches. The Great General Staff (*Grosser Generalstab*), housed in Berlin, had a simple strategic function: to prepare the concentration and deployment of forces for war. At the operational and tactical levels, members of the Field General Staff (*Truppengeneralstab*) planned and executed operations in army, corps and divisional staffs. In this manner, unity of purpose and commonality of method was achieved within an imperial army that apart from the Prussian mass contained substantial contingents from Saxony and Bavaria. Amongst the General Staff's roles at this level was the ironing out of the idiosyncrasies of the individual royal commanders.

The operational effectiveness of German armies in the latter half of the nineteenth century had benefited enormously through good organization, detailed preparation and realistic training as much as any technological advantage on the battlefield. General staff branches for railways and cartography developed timetables and maps in great thoroughness to facilitate deployment (*Aufmarsch*). Doctrine in the form of field service regulations was written to provide a unifying framework of understanding for the employment (*Einsatz*) of troops on operations. In addition, the duties of the staff were set out in detailed handbooks, which were of such quality that the new British General Staff copied them.[32]

Meanwhile, past wars were studied rigorously in order to glean lessons for the future. All this professional activity supported a German Army that had not fought – unlike those of Britain, Japan and Russia – any major campaign or war since its defeat of France in 1871, excepting its involvement (along with other Western powers) in suppressing the Boxers in China (1900–01) and its brutal subjugation of the Hereros and Hottentots in German South-West Africa (1904). Yet no one could accuse Germany generally or Prussia specifically of neglecting its military. Far from it, the largest and most professionally organized and trained army in Europe had long prepared for a large-scale war, and was keen to show its mettle in combat.

After attendance at the War Academy, the professional understanding and competence of members of the General Staff were developed through exercises, war games and staff rides. Manstein was later to benefit from, and contribute greatly to, such activities. No other nation at the time competed in the scope and rigour of such training.[33] The staff ride, in particular, became a key event in the military calendar to examine new operational plans and test the commanders and staffs entrusted with their execution. It was said of von Moltke the Elder's successor but one, Field Marshal Alfred Count von Schlieffen, that he would set tactical problems to his subordinates on Christmas Eve and expect their solutions on Boxing Day.[34] Schlieffen, best remembered for his famous plan to defeat France in one massive turning movement around Paris, was an avid student of military history. He was intrigued by Hannibal's spectacular destruction of the Roman Army in 216 BC through encirclement at Cannae and believed he had discovered the Holy Grail of military success. His 'Cannae' thesis was to become a piece of operational dogma, a striking case study in the abuse of military history that remained a *Leitmotiv* of German operational thought for another generation.[35] Whilst Hannibal had won the famous battle of annihilation through better leadership and tactics, the Romans with superior strategic means, including greater resources of manpower and not least maritime power, had won the Second Punic War, a lesson that the Germans forgot to their cost in two world wars.

Manstein entered a three-year course at the Royal Prussian War Academy (*Königlich Preussische Kriegsakademie*) in Berlin on 5 October 1913. Entry followed a highly competitive selection procedure designed to identify young officers with the character, intellect, industry and potential to make them thoroughly reliable and flexible 'commanders' assistants' (*Führergehilfen*). The specific object of the training was the 'initiation of a limited number of qualified officers of all arms into the higher branches of the military science, so as to deepen and widen their knowledge, and to clear and sharpen their military judgement'.[36] Such was the rigour of the assessment and examination regime that only 20 per cent of the initial entry would complete the full three years at the War Academy.

By the time Manstein joined the academy in central Berlin, housed in an elegant building wedged between Unter Den Linden and the parallel Dorotheenstrasse, the institution had lost some of its original character as a military university. In 1910 the proportion of non-military subjects in the syllabus had been dropped from 50 to 36 per cent, and much of the remaining material became optional.[37] Although it retained its rich historical tradition, the academy had become more a junior staff college in the process, albeit one in the heart of a capital city, and whose teaching faculty included professors from Berlin universities.

Manstein's year had 168 officers.[38] Whilst he was not the youngest course member (that privilege belonged to his famous classmate Heinz Guderian, one year his junior), it was significant that the German Army would train an officer for three years in his mid to late twenties when other armies such as the British would spend less time at a later age. A military education at the War Academy was a formative experience and investment for life. Although Manstein completed only one year of his general staff training before the outbreak of war, his professional military education thereafter was completed 'on the job' in a variety of assignments designed to test and to extend his capabilities. Apart from Guderian, another notable member of the 1913 entry was Erich Hoepner, Manstein's immediate superior as commander of the Fourth Panzer Group during the invasion of the Soviet Union in the summer of 1941. He became a prominent member of the opposition to Adolf Hitler and was put to death following the failure of the 20 July plot to assassinate the Führer in 1944.

Manstein did not describe his War Academy days whatsoever in his memoirs, which in view of his later appointments in the General Staff, including those involving professional military education, is surprising. Likewise, he devoted little attention to documenting his career during the First World War, as he was but a 'small wheel in a big business'.[39] None the less, it is possible to sketch a brief summary of his general staff training and wartime career from other sources.

Mandatory courses in tactics and military history formed the core of the syllabus in each of the three years; general staff duties were added in the third. Manstein would also have taken classes in weaponry, fortifications, military survey, military law and transportation. Hence the bulk of the instruction was operationally focused. There were several surprising omissions in the syllabus, which reflected a traditional German-Prussian aversion to studying personnel, intelligence or logistic matters in any depth. Apart from general history, which was obligatory, a student would have opted to study either a block of science (mathematics, physics and physical geography) or a mixed block of general geography and a language (French, Russian, Polish or English). In total there were twenty-five hours of formal instruction during the working week in the first and second years, allowing the remainder of the time to be devoted to private study and sport. Course members were expected to keep a healthy mind and body, notwithstanding the obvious diversions of Berlin.[40]

A further enduring weakness of the German General Staff educational system before the First and Second World Wars was its emphasis on tactical and operational level matters to the near exclusion of wider strategic study. This was to lead to successive generations of technically superb senior and middle-ranking officers, generally more proficient than their enemies, but who none the less had been denied the opportunity to learn about the crucial interdependence of all three instruments of national power: diplomatic, economic and military.[41] Whilst it could be argued that higher-level strategy was not suitable curriculum material for a lieutenant, there was no subsequent opportunity for such formal education in the career of a general staff officer other than attendance at specific training events such as war games and staff rides, which were pitched at the operational level.

In Manstein's case, his informal education continued after the First World War when he became a tutor of the General Staff. Throughout his military career he broadened his general knowledge by extensive study of both military and non-military material; his extensive personal library is vivid testament to this. In consequence he was an extraordinarily well-read individual. His particular cultural interests were confirmed by one of his aides-de-camp (ADC) during the Second World War. Writing of their service together in France, Rudolf Graf recalled:

> In my opinion, Field Marshal von Manstein possessed a very good sense and empathy for art. On all the journeys that I was allowed to take part in, he took every opportunity to visit cathedrals, galleries, museums and castles. I was always amazed by his comprehensive knowledge of French history, as well as architecture, painting and the fine arts.[42]

Ironically, Manstein was as much an autodidact in this respect as his future supreme commander, Hitler, was in matters of higher command.

The First World War

As the storm clouds gathered over Europe during the fateful summer of 1914, Manstein and his contemporaries from the War Academy were undertaking attachments to units and formations of the field army. This was a routine event and integral to the course of study, balancing theory and practice, giving students an opportunity to learn about different branches of the army and to gain staff experience by working in head-quarters at various levels. Following the German mobilization on 2 August 1914, all students were ordered to return to their parent arm and unit. Reporting back to Berlin, Manstein was appointed adjutant of the 2nd Guards Reserve Infantry Regiment of the 1st Guards Reserve Division. In consequence, he was to experience fierce fighting on both the Western and Eastern Fronts over the next three months before he was severely wounded in action in Poland.

Manstein did not record his feelings at the time, but it would be reasonable to suppose that he followed the mood of the army and nation, confident of a quick victory through the triumph of German arms against the French and Russian foe. As he went off to war, his mother wrote to him: 'My dear child, place these lines on your heart, for they will take care of you and protect you. In these lines lies my whole rich and great love for you, my Erli, and my and Father's blessing. . . . March proudly under our dear Kaiser's flag.'[43] Manstein carried this talisman in his breast pocket for the rest of the war.

Germany violated Belgian neutrality on 4 August 1914 and began to besiege Liège, whose capture would enable the right wing of the German Army to swing round Flanders into France. The 1st Guards Reserve Division, part of the Prussian Guards Reserve Corps under the command of General of Artillery Max von Gallwitz, did not take part in the first two weeks of battle. Its first major action was the storming of the Belgian fortress at Namur, guarding the confluence of the rivers Sambre and Meuse. The corps was part of Colonel General Karl von Bülow's Second Army, which together with First (to its right) and Third Armies (to its left) formed part of the great sweeping arm of envelopment that pivoted round Metz. German war planners since Schlieffen left office in 1905 had assumed that if Germany did not invade Belgium the French would, and if such an act would draw Britain into the war its potential on land would not amount to much.[44] Meanwhile, believing a strong right wing would mean a weak German centre, the French commander-in-chief, General Joseph Joffre, ordered a twin offensive into the Ardennes and Lorraine following the false logic and unrealistic objectives of the pre-war Plan XVII.

To a young lieutenant marching off to his first campaign and war, and for tens of thousands like him amongst all the armies involved, such strategic and operational level considerations hardly mattered. Local tactical success, however, did and duty called. Manstein's regiment first saw action on 19/20 August 1914 at the small town of Andenne on the march up the north bank of the river Meuse from Liège to Namur. French and Belgian rearguards hotly contested the probing German spearheads before retiring, leaving a confused and volatile situation in their wake.

German forces in Belgium were already on edge due to the alleged actions of *francs-tireurs* (*Freischärler*) in impeding their advance, particularly on the line of march through urban areas. From the evidence available, it is not possible to determine how many members of 2nd Guards Reserve Regiment were involved in the shooting of over two hundred Belgian civilians in the town, only one of several atrocities reflecting the cruel pattern of German frightfulness (*Schrecklichkeit*) that so enraged the Allies and neutral countries that first summer of war.[45] As adjutant, and right-hand man and operations officer to the regimental commander, it would be surprising if Manstein had not been made aware of the incident. Since he devoted such little space in his memoirs to describing his experiences during the First World War, it would be unfair to single out this event as a conscious act of omission. Yet in view of his experiences during the Second World War and subsequent trial and sentence as a war criminal, it has to be said that an enduring feature of the German Army from 1870 to 1945 was its harsh reaction against armed resistance by civilian populations.

The same heavy and 'super-heavy' guns, including a 420-mm siege howitzer (the famous 'Big Bertha') that had pounded Liège into submission (4–16 August), were employed in supporting the German attack on Namur's ring of outlying forts and its impressive central citadel. The Belgian 4th Infantry Division was expected to hold out until relieved by elements of the French Fifth Army under General Charles Lanrezac. As so often happens in war, such careless optimism was confounded by the unexpected actions of the enemy for the Germans pounced, attacking simultaneously over the Sambre at Charleroi and over the Meuse south of Namur. Thus poor Lanrezac was fixed, mentally and physically: the combined threat from two German armies (Second and Third respectively) prevented him from dispatching more than a token brigade to aid the beleaguered Belgian garrison. After three days of exceptionally heavy bombardment (21–23 August), even the reinforced concrete of the famous military engineer Brialmont began to shake and crumble. With the German penetration at Charleroi, the Belgians decided to evacuate Namur just as the forts were about to fall, the last capitulating on 25 August. On top of a worsening situation to the north and east, the loss of Namur prompted Lanrezac to order a general withdrawal from the Sambre to avoid 'another Sedan', recalling Napoleon the Third's humiliating surrender there to the Prussians on 2 September 1870. Meanwhile, to his left, Field Marshal Sir John French's British Expeditionary Force was retiring in good order after its plucky stand at Mons on 24 August 1914 against two corps of Colonel General Alexander von Kluck's First Army.

Whether Manstein observed techniques at Namur that were to help him nearly twenty-eight years later at the siege of Sevastopol must remain a matter of conjecture. It suffices to say that by 24 August, after twenty days of war, the 'Battle of the Frontiers' had been decided in Germany's favour but at a considerable price of men, and, as crucially, of time. Meanwhile on the Eastern Front, the Germans' heavy casualties (particularly at Gumbinnen near the border on 20 August) and the growing threat from the Russian advance into East Prussia with two armies pitched against the German Eighth Army had rattled the German High Command (the *Oberste Heeresleitung* (OHL)). When the Chief of the General Staff, General Helmuth von Moltke the Younger, lost confidence in the ability of Eighth Army to hold the Russian offensive, on 26 August he ordered the transfer of two army corps from the Western to the Eastern Front. The Guards Reserve Corps was one of these reinforcing formations, which otherwise would have been available for employment at the crucial First Battle of the Marne (6–10 September 1914) when the British and French armies counterattacked, slamming the Schlieffen Plan into reverse gear and thereby dashing at a stroke German dreams of a quick decisive victory.

In East Prussia, the commander of Eighth Army, General Maximilian von Prittwitz und Gaffron, had lost his nerve as the Russians continued their advance. He was replaced by the 67-year-old Field Marshal Paul von Hindenburg, plucked out of retirement so hurriedly from his elegant villa in Hannover that he possessed no modern field grey uniform.[46] To assist him as chief of staff was one of the rising stars of the army, Erich Ludendorff, fresh from making his name by his daring capture of Liège's citadel. Meanwhile, having marched back to Aachen on 31 August, Manstein's regiment was entrained the next day and deployed eastwards, completing its new concentration east of Elbing by 3/4 September 1914.

As a result, it arrived too late to take part in the battle of Tannenberg (26–31 August) and the spectacular destruction of Samsonov's 2nd Army. It went into action between Allenburg and Wehlau to the north of Lake Mauer in the First Battle of the Masurian Lakes (9–14 September) against Rennenkamp's 1st Army.[47] Whilst the decisive action at Tannenberg established the reputations of Hindenburg and Ludendorff, sent to restore the situation in the East, their subsequent success at the Masurian Lakes served to confirm it.

There was no time for Manstein's regiment to recuperate as 1st Guards Reserve Division was redeployed yet again to take part in the German Ninth Army's offensive from Upper Silesia into Poland to the river Vistula. On 28 September 1914 the division started its advance of 300 kilometres, to the vicinity of Warsaw. Although the march to the Vistula was a tactical success, its operational impact proved short-lived. Several strategic factors now came into play to assist the Russians, which were a portent of similar events that occurred on the Eastern Front during the Second World War. First, although the Russians had suffered grievously in East Prussia, their losses did not represent a mortal blow as so many reserves of manpower, however badly equipped and led, remained. Secondly, with Japan Britain's ally and therefore security assured in the Far East, reinforcements could be brought in from Siberia. Thirdly, there was sufficient operational space for both sides on the Eastern Front to manoeuvre in move and counter-move, for which it was now the Russians' turn to act. Fourthly, German overconfidence – manifested in the form of long, exposed and thinly held flanks – could be punished. Accordingly, the Russian High Command, the *Stavka*, sought opportunities for launching a new offensive on a grand scale involving the North-Western and South-Western *Fronts*. Thus the German advance into Poland looked increasingly precarious, particularly if co-operation between German forces and her Austro-Hungarian allies on the southern flank broke down, as it indeed began to. So the stage was set for a major counterattack to eliminate the German Ninth Army and as much of the Austro-Hungarian First Army as possible.

In the event, in the face of superior Russian forces, the Ninth Army, including the ad hoc 'Woyrsch' Corps, which encompassed 1st Guards Reserve Division, conducted an orderly withdrawal. It was during the course of this retrograde manoeuvre – a retreat in any other name – that Manstein was severely wounded, removing him from regimental duty and leading to his subsequent duty on the General Staff. In a rare personal vignette, Manstein described the incident of 17 November 1914 as his division established a defensive position on the Upper Silesian frontier:

We expected an attack by the enemy, two Caucasian corps, the Czar's élite troops, who were pushing hard forward. Into this situation on 16 November 1914 burst the news of Mackensen's victory at Kutno. Every regiment was ordered to form a pursuit detachment and to advance the very same night. I asked my regimental commander, Oberst von Cramer, for permission to take part. He snarled in agreement. However, the radio orders proved illusory. The Russians weren't contemplating retreat. Thus our battalion ran into an enemy position at Katowice, which we attempted to attack. When Major von Bassewitz, the standard-bearer and I had almost reached the [enemy] trench, the Russians charged us at the bayonet. During the ensuing hand-to-hand struggle, I took a shot that floored me. My adversary, also hit, fell on top of me. A second shot paralysed me.

Manstein, struck down in the left shoulder and left knee, was carried back to the German lines. His regimental commander greeted him with the immortal words 'That'll teach you'.[48] Evacuated to Germany, his recovery and rehabilitation in the military hospitals at Beuthen and Wiesbaden took six months.[49] In this first period of war, Manstein was decorated with the Iron Cross Second Class for bravery in action.

On release from nursing care and following convalescent home leave, on 17 June 1915 Manstein joined the headquarters staff of Tenth Army on the Eastern Front under the command of General Max von Gallwitz, in whose corps he had served previously. His first staff position was 'assistant' general staff officer to the Ia – the principal general staff officer and chief of operations – where he learned at first hand the complex business of planning and co-ordinating operations at army level. He remained in this function for over a year, taking part in the great German summer offensive between July and September 1915 that conquered much of northern Poland and Lithuania, and then in Eleventh Army's attack in October 1915 from Hungary over the Danube into Serbia. These battles were followed by a winter campaign that culminated with the occupation of Montenegro and Albania. Meanwhile, Manstein was promoted to captain on 24 July 1915.

By April 1916 Manstein was back on the Western Front, where the German major offensive at Verdun on the right (east) bank of the Meuse had been under way since 21 February. Gallwitz's staff formed a special Headquarters 'West Meuse' for an attack up the left of the river. There Manstein witnessed several bloody battles of attrition, including the

desperate fights for the Le Morte-Homme ridge (the 'Dead Man' or
'*Toter Mann*'). Over the last year he had observed Gallwitz carefully in
three campaigns, gaining, he recalled, 'an insight into the requirements
of the high command in the planning and conduct of the offensive battle'
from one of Germany's most able commanders of the First World War.[50]

On 1 August 1916 Manstein was posted as the Ib (general staff officer
for supply) in the new army headquarters staff of General Fritz von
Below. His new chief of staff was none other than Colonel Friedrich
('Fritz') von Lossberg, who gained the reputation within the Kaiser's
army as one of its most talented tacticians, the 'Lion of Defence'. His
standing was so high that he was shuffled from one threatened army
sector to the next as the 'Fireman of the Western Front'.[51]

Albeit from the comparative safety of an army command post,
Manstein exchanged the hell of Verdun for an equally unpleasant one at
the Somme. Rather than organizing an attack, Manstein's new headquarters was struggling to contain a combined British-French offensive
between July and November 1916. Despite the deep scar left on the
British national psyche, the battle of the Somme did succeed in weakening the German Army significantly. So much so, that the German
High Command ordered a strategic withdrawal over the winter of 1916–
17 to the *Siegfried-Stellung*, better known in Britain as the Hindenburg
Line.

Following the Somme, Manstein witnessed the remarkable transformation of the German Army between autumn 1916 and spring 1917
through the adoption of a new flexible doctrine, the *Principles of Command
in the Defensive Battle in Position Warfare*. By abandoning the former rule
that 'ground must be held at all costs', the Germans adopted a much
more flexible defensive system of depth designed to force the attacker to
expend himself whilst the defender preserved his strength.[52] Although
he never specifically commented on this new approach, there is little
doubt that Manstein was considerably influenced by it in the Second
World War: one of his hallmarks in army group command on the Eastern
Front was his 'elastic defence'.

A particular incident during the spring of 1917 appears as a defining
moment in Manstein's early career. In the aftermath of the failed French
Nivelle offensive during the Second Battle of the Aisne, Kaiser Wilhelm
II visited the headquarters of First Army in Rethel (50 kilometres south-
west of Sedan). As a young general staff officer, Manstein was privileged
to witness the briefing given by General von Below. The commander-
in-chief described recent operations, in which the French had suffered
grievous losses without achieving a decisive breakthrough, and observed

that several heights seized by the French could not be recaptured in immediate counterattack. Manstein described what happened next, adding his reflections on the scene:

> The Kaiser chipped in: 'They'll be retaken of course.' General von Below calmly ignored this remark. We [the staff] were all quite clear that the words of the Supreme Warlord could not, and would not, have any consequences. The Army did not have any forces available for a counter-attack, and would not receive them anyway from the High Command for such a purpose. Even if tactically successful, such an attack would not justify the expected sacrifice. The fact that an order, expression of will, or even the actual words of the Monarch could be so easily ignored made me realize the extent to which the Kaiser had already given up real power. For any young officer brought up to believe in the inviolate nature of a regal command, this revelation came as a great shock.[53]

What Manstein omitted to state in his memoirs was the fact that *any* commander-in-chief might find himself in a comparable situation in which he has a duty to ignore an inappropriate order, which incidentally, if carried out, would have been against the spirit of the new defensive doctrine. Twenty-five years on, his relations with Adolf Hitler during the Second World War were to take him into that very difficult grey zone of reconciling personal responsibility to his command with loyalty and deference to the national command authority. Manstein learned an important lesson here, as he was later to take many a leaf out of von Below's book in dealing with the Führer. Yet there was one vital dif-ference: whereas the Kaiser had become increasingly irrelevant to the higher direction of war by 1917, Hitler continued to hold absolute sway over his generals to the end.

After serving just over a year in von Below's headquarters on the Western Front, Manstein returned to the East on 1 October 1917 as Ia (equivalent at this level to chief of staff) of the 4th Cavalry Division stationed in Riga. On 16 November he reported to his mother that 'it's always raining here and not much is happening. The Russians are on the other side of the Düna [the river Dvinsk] and they are waving white flags.'[54] A month later, an armistice between Germany and Russia came into effect and peace negotiations commenced shortly afterwards. Leon Trotsky, the Bolshevik People's Commissar for Foreign Relations, however, stormed out of the peace talks on 10 February 1918. On 18 February, the Central Powers repudiated the armistice in response. The military consequence was the German occupation of the former Russian provinces of Livland (roughly corresponding to Latvia today) and

Estonia to 'safeguard their independence from Bolshevist Russia', in which operation Manstein's division took part.

On 3 March, Lenin was obliged by force of circumstance to concede even harsher terms than those demanded during the earlier negotiations, enshrined in the crippling Treaty of Brest-Litovsk. It resulted in Russia's Bolshevik government renouncing all claims to Finland, the new Baltic states (Estonia, Latvia and Lithuania), Belarus, Poland, the Ukraine, the Crimea and several districts in the Caucasus.[55] The enforced peace on the Eastern Front allowed Germany to transfer forty-four divisions to the West in the spring of 1918, including Manstein's, prior to mounting a final all-out offensive to defeat the British and the French and so end the war before America's growing military power could be brought to bear.

Manstein was posted on 4 May 1918 to the 213th Infantry Division under command of Major General von Hammerstein. As an 'attack division', his new formation had received special training in 'storm tactics' for offensive operations as opposed to a normal 'trench' infantry division only deemed capable of holding the line.[56] Manstein witnessed the final Reims offensive in July 1918 that was fought to a standstill, the final gamble of Ludendorff's series of six major operations that year, which ended with the culmination and exhaustion of the German Army on the Western Front. Whereas the previous offensives had scored some tactical and even some momentary operational success, the net result of the stupendous German effort in 1918 was strategic failure.[57] During the earlier '*Görz*' operation between 27 May and 18 June, for example, 213th Division had achieved a notable breakthrough west of Reims in penetrating the French line by no less than 17 kilometres in five days. Yet the cost in men had been extremely high: not including the missing, Hammerstein's division lost 85 officers and 3,143 men either killed or wounded in action, a third of its strength over a period of three weeks.[58] With stretched supply lines, mounting casualties on this scale, and a lack of fresh mobile reserves, the Germans could not convert tactical penetration – however spectacular in terms of distance gained – into *decisive* operational manoeuvre, let alone realize a strategic victory.

Meanwhile, Manstein had simpler concerns from time to time. Writing to his mother on 25 July 1918, for example, he requested that she send him toothpaste and tobacco, adding laconically, 'things haven't quietened down here yet, therefore there is still much to be done. At the moment we're back to fighting defensive battles for a change, which is not so pleasant.'[59] The French counterattack of 18 July (which included two American divisions) in the Second Battle of the Marne was followed by the British counter-offensive of 8 August 1918 at Amiens, two black days for the German Army.[60] As one historian has observed, the Reims operation involved many German officers who were to come to later prominence during the Second World War. Gerd von Rundstedt was a corps chief of staff; apart from Manstein, divisional staffs included such famous names as Walther Model, Ewald von Kleist, Hasso von Manteufel and Erwin von Witzleben.[61]

The tide of war had finally turned. By August 1918 the Allies were advancing across the Western Front with new vigour. Not only were better combined arms tactics, including very effective artillery, tank and air support, yielding important operational successes, but also the presence and growing fighting power of the American forces had tilted the military strategic balance firmly in the Allies' favour. In contrast, the German Army was spent. With shortages of men, supplies, equipment and training, and with Spanish influenza depleting the ranks, all hope of winning the war evaporated.

As Ernst Jünger recalled, Allied propaganda leaflets extolling 'the wonderful life to be had in British prisoner-of-war camps' were sufficiently threatening for the German High Command to reward their collection at 30 pfennigs apiece.[62] For Germany, the war was lost, whether or not the home front collapsed. This was the harsh reality that Manstein and millions of other Germans would have to face, even though many were to deny after the war that their army had in fact been defeated in the field.

With a naval mutiny, and no military or diplomatic options left open, hunger taking its toll and civil unrest increasing at home, the Kaiser was forced to abdicate on 9 November 1918. He had accepted advice that his army would no longer follow him. Although the German Army had not been annihilated by a decisive battle (that which von Schlieffen had aimed to inflict on Germany's enemies), since August it had been pushed back steadily towards the homeland in a series of battles that may not be as remembered today as either the Verdun or the Somme, but were none the less as hard-fought and bloody. The Germans' heady, optimism of the spring had been extinguished in the power of the Allied counter-offensives of the late summer and autumn, and by the increasingly depressing news from home.

The twin punch of defeat and deprivation delivered a crippling psychological shock to Germany's army and people. It comes as no surprise, therefore, that Manstein gave far more detail in his memoirs about the traumatic experiences of armistice, the long march home and revolution in the final months of 1918 than about the military successes he had witnessed during the previous spring and summer. Hence it is surely no exaggeration to state that his career thereafter was shaped as much by the *outcome* of the First World War as by his conduct in it. In any event, he was much wiser for his experience.

2

A Rising Star: The Reichswehr Years

'The whole future of warfare appears to me to lie in the employment of mobile armies, relatively small but of high quality ...' General Hans von Seeckt[1]

Homeward Bound

As the First World War on the Western Front drew to a close in November 1918, Manstein's division was concentrated on the French industrial centre of Sedan, a quickly forgettable place but for its rich military past. The 213th Infantry Division had taken part in a number of hard-fought defensive battles, including one against the American 1st Infantry Division, the 'Big Red One', during the Argonne-Meuse offensive.[2] When the armistice of 11 November came into effect the Meuse had become the German front line. Sedan, where Moltke the Elder had won on 2 September 1870 a famous victory against Napoleon III, now witnessed German defeat.

Within the town, order and discipline broke down. The German conscripts were tired, hungry and demoralized, wanting to return home. They found temporary distraction in alcohol, which was available in copious quantities. Its lure was such that Manstein recorded the 'entrances to the wine cellars had to be dynamited in an effort to stop troops getting to the drink'.[3] More seriously, revolutionary thinking within the ranks had to be quashed. The high command decided – in a pragmatic manner – to channel soldiers' concerns through the chain of command. Hence the corps orders to 213th Infantry Division on 11 November contained the apparently contradictory instructions: 'The discipline of troops is to be secured by all means, [and] in accordance with the direction received from the OHL [Army High Command], soldiers' councils are to be established in companies, batteries and squadrons on the basis of a free vote of officers and men.'[4] Military authority was soon re-established: there was neither the time to rest nor to contemplate defeat. In order to meet the strict Allied timetables for disengagement and retirement to the east of the Rhine, 213th Division had to start its long homeward journey without delay.[5]

Manstein's precise hand was in all the detailed staff work involved. His instructions, however, had to be reproduced on the backs of maps and on pages torn from old exercise books, such was the shortage of paper at that time in the German Army. The division's march route took in Luxembourg, Trier, the Moselle valley, then striking east over the forested Hunsrück to cross the Rhine at Rüdesheim to enter Frankfurt am Main 'as on a victory parade'.[6] That the German Army had managed to return home in such good order, ably organized by the General Staff at all levels, blessed with unseasonably good weather, all added to the myth of an undefeated force – to some extent restoring the confidence of the troops in their leadership. As one prominent historian of the period noted, although 'revolutionized', the German 'military machine remained practically intact'.[7]

On entry into Frankfurt, Manstein was deeply moved by the 'sight of a city bedecked in flags and by the cheers and garlands of a welcoming population'. Unfortunately, the discipline of the troops was soon undermined, as he recalled, by 'revolutionary propaganda'. Naturally enough, all the soldiers wanted to be home by Christmas, but this was an impossible feat. Just as the regiments were about to entrain for their home stations, new orders required 213th Division to march on to Bad Kissingen, 100 kilometres further to the east, and remain stationed there until the beginning of January 1919. Unsurprisingly, this sudden change of plan did not go down at all well. En route, the divisional engineer battalion mutinied briefly: 'only the denial of food supplies brought it quickly back under command'.[8]

Manstein, meanwhile, now had time enough to ponder on the defeat, revolution and abdication of Wilhelm II, and the resulting impact on Germany and its people. Chancellor Prince Max von Baden had announced the Kaiser's abdication in Berlin on 9 November 1918, but the formal proclamation 'renouncing for all time claims to the throne of Prussia and to the German imperial throne' was not published until the 30th. For officers such as Manstein, the wording of the remainder of Wilhelm II's brief note of abdication was of existential significance:

> At the same time I release all officials of the German Empire and of Prussia, as well as all officers, non-commissioned officers and men of the navy and of the Prussian army, from the oath of fidelity which they have tendered to me as their Emperor, King and Commander-in-Chief.
>
> I expect of them that until the re-establishment of order in the German Empire they shall render assistance to those in actual power in Germany,

in protecting the German people from the threatening dangers of anarchy, famine and foreign rule.[9]

Thus Manstein's early career as an officer in a royal army came to an abrupt end. As a self-confessed monarchist, he had to switch his allegiance from an individual, the Kaiser, to the collective: Germany and its people.

For members of the Prussian Army, Manstein observed, their personal bond to their king meant that Wilhelm II's abdication did not just signal a new form of government. Rather, it represented the 'collapse of their [entire] world'. The solemn oath of loyalty, suggested Manstein, went far beyond any mere political or ethical link: 'It perhaps can only be explained by the German term *Gefolgstreue* (personal allegiance)'.[10] So Manstein, together with many tens of thousands of professional officers, had now to confront the harsh reality of the new Weimar Republic. The German Army's loyalty would need to be transferred from the person of the monarch to the state (*Reich*) and people (*Volk*) – abstract expressions that would take on a deeper and darker symbolism under National Socialism in the years to come, and ultimately, to a personal allegiance to Hitler.

Consequences of the Treaty of Versailles

Manstein survived the bloodletting of the First World War, having spent the majority of the war years as a junior member of the General Staff, serving in headquarters rather than at regimental duty. From the perspective of the German Army, it made eminent sense to employ the younger – even partially trained – members of a thinly spread General Staff in this manner, exploiting their brainpower, rather than risking their muscle and scarce talents in leading storm-troopers. Hence Manstein's contribution to the war effort was more cerebral than heroic. Whilst he had not had the opportunity to demonstrate exceptional valour in battle as a *Frontkämpfer* to gain the coveted Pour le Mérite (the Blue Max), in the manner of Erwin Rommel and Ernst Jünger, Manstein's record was none the less meritorious, including the award of the Iron Cross (First and Second Classes), and of the Knight's Cross with Swords of the Royal Prussian Order of Hohenzollern.[11]

The German Army was also wise enough to acknowledge that competence and experience in formation staff work would provide a sounder foundation for future high command than time spent in the trenches, whatever the military and social cachet of frontline duty. As a result, although Manstein had not completed his general staff training in August 1914, his wide wartime experience at divisional, corps and army level had given him an excellent grounding and practical eye for the organization and handling of troops, which more than compensated for the missing two years of military education at the *Kriegsakademie*.[12]

After the First World War, Manstein would next see active service as chief of staff of an army group during the German invasion of Poland in September 1939. In the intervening twenty-one years, he and his countrymen were confronted with the consequences of the Treaty of Versailles that concluded the First World War. Under the terms of the Treaty, Germany was forced to accept blame for starting the war; pay reparations to the Allies; abandon its overseas territories and colonies; return Alsace and Lorraine to France; cede large tracts of territory on its eastern border to Poland; and to accept severe restrictions on its armed forces, with the Rhineland becoming a demilitarized zone. The German Army was limited to 100,000 officers and men, conscription was banned, and its famous General Staff was to be disbanded. Amongst its establishment of 4,000 officers, Manstein was retained in the new German armed forces, the Reichswehr, which consisted only of the army and navy, as an air force was banned under the Treaty.[13] Furthermore, Germany was not allowed armoured vehicles, heavy artillery, aircraft or submarines. Finally, Germany was only to be invited to join the new League of Nations when it had demonstrated its peace-loving credentials.

The head of the German military delegation at the peace conference of Versailles was General Hans von Seeckt, who had risen to prominence as an exceptionally capable chief of staff at army and army group levels on the Eastern Front since 1915. In December 1917 he became chief of staff to the Ottoman Field Army, but even his extraordinary powers of organization in that theatre could not 'salvage the unsalvageable'.[14] None the less his reputation was secure as a master of operational manoeuvre and of coalition warfare: in many ways he became a role model for younger generations of general staff officers such as Manstein. Although not an elegant figure with his 'thin, red, turkey neck, his inscrutable face and its inevitable monocle', he had an overpowering intellectual stature. A military genius, he possessed the rare gift of planning for the long term.[15]

When von Seeckt took over in July 1919 as the first chief of the *Truppenamt* (Troop Office), the disguised successor to the Great General Staff, he initiated a comprehensive study of lessons from the past war and a programme to rewrite the army's doctrine. In March 1920 he became *Chef der Heeresleitung* (Chief of Army Command), and thus remained the institutional head of the German Army until he resigned in October 1926. He was very much the father of the Reichswehr as an élite professional army: his formative ideas on doctrine, training and organization shaped its development for seven years.

All this activity was achieved under the watchful eyes of an Allied Control Commission that monitored the activities of the German Army for any breach of the Treaty, including any use of the banned technology. Although a conservative in many respects who hankered after the traditions of the Prussian-German Army, von Seeckt was a creative thinker on tactical matters, a not particularly abundant quality amongst the chiefs of European armies between the two world wars. But he was certainly no democrat: he despised the Weimar Republic and kept the army distant from politics and the population. By making the organization 'apolitical', he safeguarded the Reichswehr from undesired left-wing influence and ensured that it remained right wing and undemocratic in perception and outlook.

Such was the context of Manstein's service between the Kaiser's abdication and Hitler's rise to power. In this volatile period of political and economic turmoil, Manstein got married, started a family and, through his clearly discernible professional qualities, became a rising star in the German Army. His memoirs of this period provide a fascinating perspective of life in Germany during the troubled years of the fatally flawed Weimar Republic.

Germany's many internal tensions were matched by a surfeit of external threats. The risk of foreign intervention served as a constant reminder of the inherent vulnerability of the Reich and the requirement to develop a modern force to defend its sovereignty. The loss of lands to Poland was a bitter consequence of the past war. As Manstein commented pithily on the exclusion of part of his father-in-law's estates on the Silesian/Polish border, 'The Poles could have no claim on this area whether on historical or ethnic grounds, let alone [denying] the German-speaking population to decide for themselves.'[16]

Manstein's views on Poland were by no means extreme or atypical. There was no sense of German collective guilt following the First World War.[17] In his eyes and in those of millions of other Germans, the Versailles Treaty, signed under duress, was a shameful '*Diktat*'. That Germany, which had expected to win the war, should now be threatened by inconsequential powers such as Poland, was never accepted by the nationalists who formed a large proportion of the German population. Such trenchant feeling later formed the fertile ground for National Socialism that triumphed through popular vote over communism. Back in 1922, von Seeckt had declared that: 'Poland's existence is intolerable, incompatible with the survival of Germany. It must disappear, and it will disappear through its own internal weakness and through Russia – with our assist-ance.... With Poland falls one of the strongest pillars of the Treaty of Versailles, the preponderance of France.'[18] Such forthright views were not confined to the military. That same year, under the title *Wille, Macht und Schicksal* (*Will, Power and Fate*), Professor Max Lenz of Hamburg University wrote in defiance of history: 'We had to suffer the greatest humiliation, the greatest and most unbearable ignominy at the hands of the Poles ... these Samaritans who never were able to create anything out of their own strength ... That we shall never forgive or forget.'[19]

Meanwhile, Manstein's career after the end of the First World War had begun to develop: slowly at first, but his obvious talents of intellect and industry ensured that he was advanced into staff positions of growing responsibility. On the demobilization of 213th Division, Manstein returned to Berlin in January 1919. He attempted to join his old unit, 2nd Guards Reserve Regiment, from which he had departed – wounded in action – in November 1914. The General Staff (not yet disbanded), however, had other ideas. He was posted to Magdeburg to assist in the raising of volunteer units of former soldiers, collectively termed the *Freikorps* (Free Corps), which were used by the government not only to fight in Poland and in the Baltic states, but also to suppress the far left and communist opposition within Germany. In the words of one critical historian, the *Freikorps* represented a 'band of ultra-reactionary and vicious enemies of democracy'.[20] Not surprisingly, in parts of Germany there was also violent opposition to these freebooters. In the province of Saxony, for example, there was little official support for the *Freikorps* so Manstein, restless as ever for demanding employment, secured a new posting with the *Grenzschutz Ost* (Frontier Defence East), charged with maintaining the integrity of Germany's border with Poland.

On joining the staff of Frontier Defence Command (South) in Breslau (now Wrocław in Poland) in February 1919, Manstein found a confused situation, to say the least. The principal military task was to prevent further westward expansion by the Poles, who had already seized much of the ethnically mixed Prussian province of Posen (now Poznań) through a popular uprising. There were more local difficulties too. The civilian authorities in Silesia were suspicious of the military (as in Saxony) and the troops contained a good number of malcontents. Of the famed Prussian 'order', there was precious little in evidence. Yet the Germans held the upper hand during the sporadic fighting with Polish 'armed bands', which continued to flare up along the disputed border areas in 1919. Plans for the recapture of all lost territory in Posen through surprise attack were made, but any such large-scale military intervention would have triggered an angry response from the Western Allies.

Matters came to a head with the conclusion of the Versailles peace conference in July 1919, at which the Allies accepted the Poles' territorial claims. Germany found herself again in crisis: whether to accede to or refuse the terms of a treaty that required the loss of much of the provinces of Upper Silesia, Posen and West Prussia. East Prussia was cut off from the rest of Germany, and isolated Danzig declared a 'free' city. What upset many Germans as much as the amputation of historic lands (some 13 per cent of Germany's pre-war territory) was – in their eyes – the manifest unfairness of an imposed treaty whose harshness had exceeded their worst fears.

Under the threat of Allied invasion and prolongation of the blockade, after much tense discussion and debate, the German delegation at Versailles felt compelled to sign the Treaty. Added to this external pressure was widespread internal division, exploited by the left and the communists, which for the German right confirmed the 'stab in the back' (*Dolchstoss*) legend. General Wilhelm Groener, First Quartermaster General (Deputy Chief of the General Staff), had declared on the eve of the armistice that 'the army stands splendidly; the poison comes from home', whilst the socialist President Friedrich Ebert had greeted returning Guards units in Berlin, declaring: 'We welcome you back home with joyful hearts, the enemy did not defeat you.'[21] In this manner the German people were fed the dangerous myth that the Kaiser's army had marched home undefeated. Whilst the new Reichswehr was being formed, the most potent military force in Germany at the time became the motley collection of *Freikorps*.

Whether, as Manstein insinuated, the threat of French occupation with 'black [colonial] troops forming their spearheads', provided the ultimate intimidation in forcing Germany's hands at Versailles or not remains unproven.[22] Its claims that it had laid down arms on 11 November 1918 on the basis of President Woodrow Wilson's Fourteen Points, and none other, hardly formed a strong and sustainable negotiating position. Memories of the Germans' grossly unfair treatment of the Russians at Brest-Litovsk were far too recent for that. The revengeful French demanded compensation for their huge losses through excessive reparations, a precedent set by none other than Germany in 1871.

Many within the German military, including Manstein, were inclined to view acceptance of the *Diktat* as a profound mistake despite the contemporary political, economic and military realities. Whilst grand strategy and political subtlety were never the German General Staff's forte, speculation as to what would have happened had the Treaty been more generous to Germany had a seductive quality. Whether, in consequence, there would have been no rise of Hitler and thus no Second World War, as Manstein suggested in his memoirs, surely stretches this line of counter-factual reasoning.[23] Whether there remained sufficient international discord to spark another major conflict in Europe *without* Hitler and his fellow Nazis remains one of the big 'what-ifs' of twentieth-century history.

In the summer of 1919, Manstein's spell of duty on the eastern border came to an end. After a short interlude in Berlin, he was posted in August 1919 to Kassel to join the newly formed *Gruppenkommando* II. This was one of two army-level headquarters, whose principal responsibility was to draw down the German Army from 500,000 men into its new structure of seven infantry and three cavalry divisions. Working under the direction of the chief of staff, General Fritz von Lossberg, under whom he had served at the Somme, Manstein was closely involved in the transformation of what was termed the 'Provisional Reichswehr' from its interim to its final 'Treaty' organization. In this restructuring, the German Army was keen to preserve as much combat power as it could. The aim throughout was to maintain combat units at the expense of those with supporting roles, which entailed relying on civilian organizations to perform repair and transportation functions. In this manner, military logistic expertise could be hidden from Allied view within commercial concerns. Such an approach was but one small manifestation of evasion of the terms of the Treaty, which became increasingly sophisticated in the 1920s as the Germans tried to outwit the Allied Control Commission.

In Kassel, meanwhile, Manstein observed the ripples of the abortive Kapp Putsch. General Freiherr Walther Lüttwitz plotted with Dr Wolfgang Kapp to overthrow the democratically elected Reich government under the Social Democrat Chancellor Gustav Bauer. Two *Freikorps* brigades, including the Marine Brigade Ehrhardt awaiting disbandment on the Döberitz training area outside Berlin, were designed to provide the military muscle. Notwithstanding the fact that the government had fled the capital to Stuttgart, the muddled revolution of 13 March 1920 failed to take root in Berlin in the face of a general strike. Throughout Germany, the mass of the Reichswehr – on von Seeckt's orders – declined either to lend any support to, or, equally, to intervene against, the rebel forces.

Events in Kassel threatened to turn sour when a huge, menacing crowd gathered in front of the *Gruppenkommando*, believing the military based there to be co-conspirators. Manstein and his colleagues were 'completely surprised' by the turn of events unfolding in Berlin. That day, he recorded, officers could only move about freely when armed for self-protection, such was the mounting tension in 'socialist Kassel'.[24] As it became clear that the putsch in Berlin was failing, the sceptical crowd eventually dispersed.

Manstein devoted considerable space in his memoirs to analysing the implications and consequences of Kapp's failed attempt to seize power. He was convinced that Kapp and von Lüttwitz had acted with patriotic motives, and not in the pursuit of personal motives. He recorded that Freiherr von Hammerstein-Equord, then on Lüttwitz's staff, explained that his father-in-law mounted the putsch 'to save the Reich at the last moment'. Whatever the case, Manstein admitted to some regard for Kapp, noting that the troops stationed in the east of the Reich (where most territory was lost in consequence of the Treaty of Versailles) and the majority of the population there were sympathetic to his cause.[25]

A Silesian Marriage

Aged 31 at the end of the First World War, Manstein was still a bachelor, a not uncommon circumstance for an officer of his age and class. Of his four natural and adoptive parents, only his adoptive mother, Hedwig, was still alive. Whilst hunting with his kinsmen the von Coellns in Diechslau, Silesia, in early January 1920, Manstein met his future wife, Fräulein Jutta-Sibylle von Loesch. She was a slightly built, dark-haired girl of 19 years, delicate physically but of strong character. It must have been true love at first sight, for the pair became engaged within three days on 10 January. They married exactly five months later on 10 June 1920 in Lorzendorf in *Kreis* (county) Namslau. Manstein's spouse was the only daughter of landowner and reserve captain of cavalry Arthur von Loesch and his wife Amaly, née von Schack. By all accounts, the wedding was an elegant and traditional affair with the *Gutshaus* (more a squire's country seat than a simple farmhouse) of his parents-in-law lovingly bedecked with massed flowers, the wedding party all gaily dressed in full military pomp and civil finery.

For several generations the von Loesch family had farmed in Silesia and owned property in the Silesian capital of Breslau. Following the end of the First World War, economic recovery was barely getting under way. Soon this part of central Europe was affected by a frontier dispute that threatened the new peace. Of Arthur von Loesch's three estates in

Namslau (Lorzendorf, Hennersdorf and Butschkau), the latter was lost when the new German–Polish frontier line came into effect in the summer of 1920. Manstein had married into a conservative, well-established and well-meaning Christian family, who, through their good social works on behalf of their employees, he claimed, 'were the exact opposite of the biased propaganda image of Prussian Junkers'.[26] According to Manstein, Arthur von Loesch's benign paternalism included building a settlement for his workers and funding the construction of an orphanage. This rural idyll was to remain intact until shattered by the sudden arrival of the Red Army in January 1945, when Silesia was occupied and lost irrevocably to Germany.

The Mansteins' marriage was quickly blessed with two offspring. Daughter Gisela was baptised on their first wedding anniversary in 1921; their first son, Gero, was born a year later on New Year's Eve. Accordingly, he was given the second name of Sylvester (the German equivalent of the Scottish Hogmanay). A second son, Rüdiger, followed seven years later in 1929. Whilst both Gisela and Rüdiger survived the Second World War, Gero was killed in action as a young officer whilst serving in his father's old division (the 18th Infantry) on the Eastern Front in October 1942.[27]

There is no doubt that the Mansteins' marriage was very close, and that they depended greatly on each other. If his uncle Paul von Hindenburg had spared but one glib acknowledgement for his wife Gertrud, describing her as his 'best friend and comrade',[28] Manstein was much more generous in extolling the virtues of his own wife, dedicating his memoirs to Jutta-Sibylle. His admiration is striking:

> Whatever life may yet bring us, the love of my wife has overcome all sorrows and difficulties. She was the dearest mother to our children that can be imagined. But her love and willingness to help did not just extend to us or the wider family. Anyone who came to her found understanding for his or her needs, and received help as far as it was in her gift. Yet she did not claim anything for herself. She was always prepared to suppress her own wishes in order to improve our and others' lives.[29]

Frau Manstein was a considerable asset to her husband. As an endearing hostess she became quite famous, for the Mansteins socialized and entertained well, whether in Kolberg, Berlin or later on in Liegnitz.[30] She also had a kind ear for those who sought advice, and she helped quietly behind the scenes whenever she could. During the Second World War she looked after not only her own children, but also fostered several others too. At her husband's war crimes trial in

Hamburg in 1949 she appeared every day in the courtroom to give him moral support.

Manstein's happy marriage was a sure beacon to him over the next forty-six years, helping him overcome the many vicissitudes of war and peace, including the long years of separation during the Second World War, subsequently as a prisoner of war (1945–49) and then as a convicted man (1949–53). So when it came to writing his memoirs, whilst Manstein did not expect his readers to agree with all of his actions, opinions and judgements, he appealed to them to respect one matter above all: the pen-picture of his wife. Exemplary of so many other German wives and mothers who had endured so much, Jutta-Sibylle von Manstein was, he said, 'loving, brave and faithful'.[31] As a couple, the Mansteins strove to fulfil their wedding promise: 'God is love. Whoever lives in love lives in God, and God in him.' (1 John 4.16)

Company Command

Manstein was appointed on 1 October 1921 as officer commanding the sixth company of the Reichswehr's 5th (Prussian) Infantry Regiment, a formation of 2nd Infantry Division. The sub-unit, which carried on the tradition of the former Prussian 5th Foot Guards, was barracked in the small town of Angermünde in Brandenburg, lying approximately halfway between Berlin and Stettin (now the Polish city of Szczecin). Manstein, unconsciously emulating Dr Johnson's famous jest that 'the noblest prospect which a Scotchman ever sees is the high road that leads him to England!', declared that the 'finest feature of the town was the train station as a means of departure'.[32] His cutting observation, as he conceded, was a trifle unfair. The town had a pretty medieval centre and an attractive setting, surrounded by the forests and lakes of the Uckermark.

Angermünde had housed a Prussian garrison since 1694, and in the 1880s a new barracks had been erected in the Schwedterstrasse. In comparison with racy Berlin of the early 1920s, the town with a modest population of about 5,000 souls – '*typische Kleinstadt*' as the Germans would say – had many comic diversions of German provincial life. The town guard society, for example, played a central role in upholding local traditions and in fostering close civil-military relations. It was chaired by the rather earnest and eccentric Herr Gott. As a distinguished veteran of 1871, Manstein recounted, he was 'allowed to wear the uniform of his old regiment, the Lifeguard-Hussars'.[33] Whilst Hauptmann Manstein might have tired of the society's lengthy meetings – at which the Prussian-German bureaucratic predilection for detailed points of procedure would exhaust the most patient – he bore this particular chore with reasonably good cheer.

From a professional standpoint, however, Manstein was lucky to enjoy a good deal of autonomy in his sub-unit command. Whilst his battalion commander was in Prenzlau, some 40 kilometres distant or just under an hour away by car, both his regimental and divisional commanders were based in Stettin, some two hours away. Despite the threat of routine visits and inspections, such isolation fuelled Manstein's independent way of doing business, which chimed with the times.

During his tour of command in Angermünde, he was able to develop his leadership skills and training methods. In exercises he stressed the need for commanders at all levels to think (*Denken*) and to act (*Handeln*) as necessary without always seeking prior authority. At unit level, inculcating this approach was essentially a practical matter, fostered predominantly through practical field training as opposed to instruction in the classroom. One of Manstein's company officers, Lieutenant Franz von Gaertner, recalled in his memoirs of the Reichswehr years that at Angermünde 'three days a week were devoted to marches and tactical exercises, one day on the rifle range with one day remaining for barracks duties'.[34] Notwithstanding his upbringing in 3rd Foot Guards and his present company's historical traditions, Manstein did not waste his soldiers' time on excessive drill, spit and polish: tactical competence in the field was far more important than any precision on parade.

Manstein's self-styled approach to running his company was pure *Auftragstaktik* (mission command): a philosophy of command based on informing a subordinate *what* he has to achieve without prescribing *how*. Manstein's method also served an underlying purpose: if the German Army were ever to expand again, as indeed it might, it needed a sound, broad stock of confident leaders capable of exhibiting initiative. It required soldiers, as well as non-commissioned and commissioned officers, who not only could think for themselves at their own level, but also were capable of taking the job of their superiors with minimum preparation. Thus, once his subordinates had learned a task, Manstein let them get on with it, largely unsupervised.

Exploiting a loophole in the Treaty of Versailles, German units had retained a far greater proportion of non-commissioned officers to private soldiers than strictly necessary, which meant that such leadership training could rest on a sure foundation.[35] This benign state of affairs very much supported the creative concept of von Seeckt, who had stressed 'quality not quantity': under his inspirational leadership he created an army 'not of mercenaries, but of leaders'.[36] In this manner the *Führerheer* became a reality. Von Seeckt's intentions from high command were reinforced by enlightened junior leaders such as Manstein and Rommel.

Despite the forced intimacy of the trenches, the Kaiser's army had seen a considerable gulf between the officer corps and the conscripts in the ranks, notwithstanding the social levelling involved through the granting of commissions to non-commissioned officers in the field. Now, under von Seeckt, unit commanders were instructed to improve the quality of living and working accommodation and, crucially, to draw the best out of each volunteer under their command. The aim was to develop a much closer bond of comradeship than in the former imperial army without in consequence sacrificing military authority and discipline. In this respect the Reichswehr was becoming a thoroughly modern volunteer army, able to recruit and select 8,000 bright and fit young men each year for twelve years' service.

Within his company, Manstein was at pains to develop his principal subordinates, recognizing that their mutual understanding provided the basis of tactical success. This was an enduring objective, and one which he refined subsequently at battalion and divisional command. As he noted after the war:

> My aim was not only to train my soldiers well, and particularly so in their battlefield skills, but also to bring on a core of junior leaders, who would become section and platoon commanders on any expansion of the army. I believe that I succeeded in achieving this during my two years as a company commander. When one talks so much about team-work today, and that it must form the foundation of military training and activity on the battlefield, this idea was already realized in our time. Then the basic team was a machine-gun or rifle section, whose composition remained permanent.[37]

Furthermore, as Manstein stressed, there was no place for 'breaking personalities'.[38] Moreover, setting the 'right tone' between the leaders and the led, between older and younger generations of soldiers, was vitally important to the health of the unit. Whilst neither Manstein personally nor the Reichswehr generally was unique in highlighting this matter, such an approach was ahead of its time in comparison with other European armies, and in stark contrast to the negative image of brutality to its own ranks that the Wehrmacht earned for itself during the Second World War.

Von Seeckt was acutely aware of the numerical and technical inferiority of the Reichswehr, but noted that 'greater mobility, better training, superior use of terrain and constant night operations offer partial substitutes' for modern weapons.[39] Under his vigorous direction a new Army Regulation 487, *Command and Combined Arms Battle*, was researched and written by a committee of subject matter experts.[40] Amongst the key tenets of this new doctrine, was the requirement for commanders (and particularly subordinate ones) to make timely decisions, to seize the initiative (very much Manstein's approach) and to undertake offensive action. Together with its successor publication of 1933, Army Regulation 300, this body of doctrine formed the basis of much of the German Army's general tactical competence and frequent success throughout the Second World War.[41] So in looking ahead to the requirements of a future war, if starved of modern technology and weapons such as tanks and aircraft, the Reichswehr could at the very least embrace the latest thinking in methods of command and in combined arms tactics. In this manner, and long before the German Army fielded its own armoured forces, the foundations of a mobile approach to warfare were being established in doctrine and in training programmes. Here indeed was fertile ground in which the roots of Blitzkrieg were established.[42]

Manstein had other responsibilities apart from training his men. His period of company command coincided with Germany's extreme inflation crisis, when the value of the Reichsmark plummeted. He records that money at the end of the month always seemed to run short for his soldiers, a not uncommon experience in other times and in other armies. As the months of 1923 unfolded, however, the Reichsmark lost value on a daily basis. Members of the regimental pay staff were often late and lacking in money when making their appearance in Angermünde. So much so that Manstein was forced on at least one occasion to borrow cash or arrange credit on their behalf from local shopkeepers. Evidently, this was an officer who cared deeply about his troops.[43]

The experienced company commander sought to improve his soldiers' welfare in barracks, including giving them the maximum freedom in the way they arranged their accommodation. He left it up to the members of each section of eight men to determine for themselves whether the two rooms allocated should be divided equally between them or split between living and sleeping accommodation, a flexibility of choice that was well ahead of its time. He also encouraged weekend leave, realizing it was better for his troops to return home or relax in Berlin rather than remain idle in Angermünde.

Tutor of the General Staff

As a general staff officer, Manstein's period of duty at company command was cut short to the minimum obligatory period of two years. Hence in October 1923 he was posted back to the staff in what was to become a significant, if not pivotal, stage in his career, lasting four years. Although still a captain, he was entrusted with the tutoring of aspirant general staff officers. Although the General Staff as an institution was banned under the terms of the Treaty of Versailles, von Seeckt was determined to maintain its disciplined and harmonized way of thinking (*Generalstabsmentalität*) through education and practice. In terms of organization, the *Truppenamt* (Troop Office) within the Reichswehr ministry in Berlin replicated the work of the former Great General Staff, whilst individual general staff officers were disguised as 'commanders' assistants' (*Führergehilfen*) or 'command staff officers' (*Führerstabsoffiziere*).

After the First World War, the *Kriegsakademie* had been forced to close its doors in Berlin. So with its usual ingenuity, the Reichswehr had found an effective solution: taking the trainers to the trainees rather than the other way around. Instead of attending the War Academy, the trainee general staff officers undertook a four-year course of instruction. The first two years involved part-time academic study at the regional military district headquarters (*Wehrkreiskommando*), accompanied by a rigorous home reading and study programme. This was followed with a third, practical, year serving as a trainee staff officer on one of the divisional staffs. The final, academic, year was spent in Berlin in the Reichswehr ministry, working under the intense supervision of selected members of the *Truppenamt*. On average, only a third of the original trainees completed the full programme.[44] Against any international comparison, the German Army in the 1920s possessed one of the most advanced general staff training systems in the world (the other being the Soviet Union's), yet its throughput was limited. The lack of experienced general staff officers became only too apparent when the army expanded rapidly in the mid 1930s.

Not surprisingly, the Reichswehr posted some of its very best officers to act as general staff training instructors. Each military district headquarters had three general staff tutors on its books. Manstein spent a year as one in *Wehrkreiskommando* II in Stettin. Because he could find no suitable accommodation in that city, he was forced by dint of circumstance to remain with his family (a wife with two very young children under 3 years old) in Angermünde. Therefore, he had to make a daily round trip of 200 kilometres, on what he could afford to pay, a fourth class rail ticket. His attempts to obtain due recompense through a claim for 'residence to place of duty' travel not only failed, but his formal complaint in response also earned him a stern rebuke from von Seeckt. It manifested in a week's house arrest and a two-year delay to Manstein's formal accreditation into the General Staff that was only rectified when he became its vice-chief in 1936, some thirteen years later.[45] So much for von Seeckt's enlightened policies when it came to dealing with one 'little captain's' rights and concerns.[46] If a modernist in military thought, he remained an old-fashioned Prussian traditionalist at heart, particularly when it came to upholding the rigid authority of the army's high command.

After his first year as a trainer-cum-tutor in Stettin, Manstein was posted to an equivalent position in Dresden in *Wehrkreiskommando* IV, much to his and his family's delight. The 'Florence on the Elbe' was a city that the Mansteins enjoyed living in, despite its high property prices. Compared with unsophisticated Angermünde, the vibrant capital of Saxony had much to offer. Dresden's pleasing landscape, impressive architecture and rich cultural life made it a keenly sought posting. Later, in wartime, the city became a haven for those escaping the advancing Red Army until the bombing of 13–14 February 1945. As Manstein noted after the war, 'Unfortunately, the senseless barbarity in 1945 turned it into a city of ruins and demanded countless casualties from a population swelled with refugees.'[47]

During his period (1923–27) in Dresden, Manstein threw his heart and soul into his work teaching military history and tactics, learning, as he freely admitted, as much as his students did in the process. Any honest military instructor or member of the directing staff of a command and staff college appreciates this fundamental truth: successful teaching not only requires knowledge, it also demands insight and understanding, intelligently and inspiringly conveyed. Mentoring his small groups of young general staff officers gave him great personal satisfaction, adding considerably to his own professional development. There were other compensations too: general staff training involved a good amount of travel in the form of staff rides around Saxony and Germany as a whole. These trips were not all work. After a day out in the fresh air studying tactical problems, convivial stops in *Gasthöfen* (country inns) brought some lighter moments over a glass of wine or beer, and a chance to chew the fat over some particular issue, military or otherwise. Occasionally, there was also the opportunity to take a short cultural break: one of Manstein's most pleasant memories of this period was attending a Mozart festival in the park of Würzburg's famous Residenz, the stunning creation of the master architect, Balthasar Neumann.[48]

Furthermore, Manstein managed to find the time to learn Spanish during his free hours in Dresden. Having entered and won an army essay competition on the subject of the *Führerheer*, his reward was a ministerial travel grant that allowed him to take his wife on a summer holiday to Spain. The Mansteins toured Andalusia and Catalonia, savouring those regions' culture and architecture. Yet the Reichswehr's monetary largesse was limited. As cash was short, apart from their brief sojourns in Madrid and Barcelona, they stayed in 'primitive guesthouses', but in this manner got to know directly the 'life and bustle of the local population [far] better than a globetrotter'.[49]

From October 1927 to August 1929 Manstein served as general staff officer to 'Infantry Commander IV' (another Reichswehr disguise appointment) in Magdeburg. Effectively he was chief of staff to a shadow divisional commander, General Rudolf Krantz, who was responsible for training three infantry regiments and an engineer battalion. Manstein, perhaps for the first time since his regimental duty before the First World War, was under-challenged. But none the less he acknowledged that he learned a lot from his time supporting Krantz, particularly from observing his personal style of command. Yet after the rich cultural life and bright sights of Dresden and, most recently, Spain, life in drab Magdeburg (excepting its magnificent cathedral) must have felt dull in comparison. In career terms, too, he had reason to become somewhat frustrated with his future prospects: promotion came very slowly during the Reichswehr years, even for members of the élite General Staff.

Manstein became a major only on 1 February 1928, aged 40, having served no less than thirteen years as a captain. His daughter Gisela recalled the 'deep pride and joy in the family', when he was at last promoted to field rank; as a major her father was 'now someone'.[50] In comparison, Montgomery was already a lieutenant colonel at the end of the First World War. The distinction is not trivial: whereas in the British Army the appointment drove the rank (and still does today), in the German Army advancement in rank followed a complex system of time served and relative seniority, tempered by performance.

Working in the Ministry

On conclusion of his tour in Magdeburg, on 1 October 1929 Manstein was posted to Berlin to join the *Truppenamt*, housed within the Ministry of War in the Bendlerstrasse. For any talented general staff officer, a tour 'in the Ministry' is almost inevitable if he is to succeed in his profession. An officer in such a position should gain an understanding of the complexities of military-political relations and in the practicalities of military strategy when the means available do not necessarily match the desired political ends. These enduring realities applied to German staff officers 'driving desks' in Berlin during the Reichswehr years. Manstein's appointment was as one of three section heads within 'T1', the first directorate of the *Truppenamt*, corresponding to the Operations and Plans Division of a modern general or joint staff. As such, it was responsible for dealing with the organization and command of the German Army, and its potential employment in preserving the integrity of the Reich, protecting it from either external or internal threats.

Manstein's section had two main tasks. The first was to act as the operational planning staff to the Chief of the Army;[51] the second responsibility was to prepare war games and staff rides that provided a training focus and stimulus for schooling commanders and general staff officers at the operational level. Both functions played to Manstein's emerging strengths: his rare appreciation for strategic and operational matters, combined with an outstanding ability as a planner. For three years he was able to develop his understanding and reputation, building close, if not on occasion tense, working relationships with his subordinates, colleagues and superiors. Manstein was lucky at this formative stage of his career to have two exceptionally capable general staff officers working for him who both had outstanding careers thereafter.

The first was Adolf Heusinger, who became chief of operations of the Army High Command (OKH) during the Second World War, and subsequently the first General Inspector of the Bundeswehr in 1957. Heusinger, ten years Manstein's junior, was the product of a recent general staff training scheme (1927–30), and after Manstein, was regarded as one of the finest upcoming brains of the General Staff. Writing long after the Second World War, Heusinger admitted: 'My initial time under Manstein was very difficult. I was confronted with completely new tasks in an operational level framework which I hadn't worked in before. Additionally, I met in Manstein a superior spirit, a man who worked exceptionally quickly . . . and demanded the same from his subordinates.' Thus Heusinger found that Manstein was 'not always comfortable' to work for. But having spent a few months in the Ministry learning the ropes, he went on to work 'enthusiastically' for his demanding superior for several years.[52]

Manstein's other principal subordinate was Josef Kammhuber, who later as a Luftwaffe general created the first integrated air defence system of wartime Germany that bore his name.[53]

Manstein had a particularly close professional relationship with the Chief of Army Command, General Baron Kurt von Hammerstein-Equord. They had a common regimental background, having served together in 3rd Foot Guards before the First World War, along with Kurt von Schleicher (later chancellor at the end of the Weimar Republic). In Manstein's opinion, Hammerstein-Equord was one of the cleverest persons he had ever met, but he was not one for detailed staff work.[54] Manstein maintains that the catch-phrase 'field regulations are for the dim' stemmed from him, implying that the good – as opposed to an *average* – officer had no need for such intellectual props. If Manstein is to be believed, this supposition is ironic noting that none other than Hammerstein-Equord signed off Army Regulation 300 *Truppenführung* (Command and Control of Armed Forces) in 1933, arguably one of the most important doctrine publications ever written.[55]

One suspects that Manstein, a 'natural' in tactics and in operational art, held a similarly acute opinion on the value of doctrine, for he never mentions its importance again in his memoirs. Perhaps this very understatement reflects the fact that tactical and operational level understanding was a *sine qua non* for advancement to the highest ranks in the German Army, in which there was no place for the gifted amateur, whatever his class, social connections or sporting interests. Professional ability was demanded and developed from the lowest to the highest levels; trainers and the trained were kept in focus by a unifying spirit and doctrine in which inter-arm rivalries were kept in check.

Later on, however, as the part mechanization of the army took place, strains would appear between the 'modernizers', such as panzer enthusiast Heinz Guderian, and the more traditional thinkers such as Ludwig Beck, who became Manstein's mentor. Yet in one very important respect the German Army built and maintained a clear lead over other Western European armies: in its 'combined arms' thinking, in which infantry, cavalry (to become armoured troops) and artillery, together with supporting arms such as engineers, worked harmoniously on the battlefield.[56] This tactical concept widened into joint co-operation between land and air forces in the form of close air support, a priority area of development for the new German Luftwaffe.

Getting Round the Treaty of Versailles

One of Manstein's first responsibilities in the Army Office was to explore how to expand the German Army beyond its 100,000-men limit in order to provide a more credible means to defend the Reich. This was a major challenge as all mobilization measures were banned under the Treaty. When Manstein assumed office, a draft plan existed to add sixteen infantry divisions to the existing seven, together with the three cavalry divisions.[57] The mobilization planning work previously had been the responsibility of *Truppenamt* T2 (Army Organization) with Lieutenant Colonel Wilhelm Keitel (later chief of the Wehrmacht High Command, 1938–45) as the lead desk officer. If reservists and veterans from the First World War were to be recalled to the colours, there was neither enough *matériel* to equip all twenty-one infantry divisions, nor a simple method to effect such structural change. In addition to the Treaty limits, internal political, social and economic constraints reduced the army's freedom of action. At the time, Germany's unemployment was approaching three million as the economic depression caused by the Wall Street Crash of 24 October 1929 began to hit Germany hard. Further spending on the armed forces inevitably took second place to what Keitel called 'the outrageous increases in unemployment benefit'.[58]

Manstein left no comment on such budgetary or political matters. He went on to solve the apparently insoluble problem of arming a hypothetical expanded army. By drawing on reserve stocks of weapons, combing through all the establishment tables and identifying how numbers of support weapons could be reduced, he made the figures work. He then designed a larger structure: on mobilization each existing infantry regiment (and, in turn, each division) would spawn two new ones. To achieve this expansion, however, a good deal of existing planning would need to be reworked. Overcoming institutional resistance to change in a ministry is never easy, but Manstein's plan was approved, overturning much of Keitel's work in the process. It brought him considerable kudos, fresh into his new job. That said, he gave little credit to the work of T2 or of Keitel in preparing the ground so thoroughly beforehand.

In his memoirs, Manstein was quite open about the fact that expanding the army breached the terms of the Treaty. As an imposed '*Diktat*', for him and most Germans it had no *moral* force; it was to be renounced at the first available opportunity. Manstein rationalized the requirement to achieve 'the most primitive form of security' on the grounds that

Germany, whether it faced its potential enemies Czechoslovakia, France and Poland singly or in combination, was numerically inferior.[59]

In addition to the plan to expand the army, other measures were considered necessary to improve Germany's defences. The first was the organization of the Border Protection Force on the frontiers with Czechoslovakia and Poland. This amounted to no fewer than thirty – largely static – volunteer units of regimental (equivalent to a weak brigade) strength, each supported by a light artillery detachment. Manstein, however, was not too complimentary about their military value in the event of foreign invasion, comparing them (embracing the terminology of the Hague Convention) with a 'people, who on the approach of the enemy, take to arms; stand under organized military command; and observe the rules and conventions of war'.[60]

A second development in the period 1931–32 was the plan to erect fortifications on Germany's eastern borders. The greatest assessed threat came from Poland, whose practice mobilizations along the frontier with East Prussia had begun to rattle Germany. Which one would be the precursor to invasion? As fortifications along the border were banned under the Treaty, Manstein argued for the erection of a strong redoubt within the hinterland of East Prussia – the so-called Heilsberger Triangle – that would buy time for an effective German defence to be developed in the face of superior Polish forces. *Reichsminister* Wilhelm Groener approved Manstein's plan and work soon started on erecting wire and anti-tank obstacles and in constructing concrete bunkers. Such defences represented a foretaste of Germany's subsequent and much more extensive fortifications on the Oder–Warthe Line, which protected Berlin from direct Polish attack, and the more famous Siegfried Line (*Westwall*) on the French border.

The most significant change, however, which Manstein underplayed in his memoirs, was the development of new weapons such as tanks and aircraft in close co-operation with the USSR, in clear breach of the Treaty, along with plans to increase the overall production of armaments and to establish a small air force.

All these initiatives *preceded* Hitler's accession to power in January 1933. Together, they provided a sure foundation for the subsequent expansion of land and air forces. Although Manstein did not go into any detail, the early work undertaken by the Reichswehr proved of immense value to Hitler when he forced a hectic pace of expansion and rearmament between 1933 and 1939.

Foreign Travels

In 1931 and 1932, Manstein was privileged to undertake several foreign trips that gave him valuable insights into the people and armed forces of some of Germany's potential enemies, including their leading military personalities. The first was to Czechoslovakia in 1931 to view the autumn manoeuvres. Despite the protest of the Polish authorities, who objected to Germany establishing a military mission in Prague, the visit went ahead. There was no such 'mission', of course, but the incident was typical of the febrile state of German–Polish relations.

Manstein spent his visit in the company of a group of foreign military attachés, which he described in his usual caustic manner. He noted that the number of medals any attaché wore was in inverse proportion to the military value of his nation! Of the British attachés he met on this trip and elsewhere, he observed: 'They had an impressive knowledge of the country they were accredited to. When dealing with the leading personalities of a nation, they displayed an affected nonchalance, carrying a riding whip even at the most formal of occasions.'[61] In contrast, the American attaché in Prague displayed 'an amazing openness in talking about his impressions of what he had been shown'. Of the manoeuvres themselves, Manstein noted that whilst the camouflage of units was good, otherwise the tactical handling of troops was 'only average, if not mediocre'. He described the heterogeneous composition of the Czechoslovakian Army as a distinct weakness, noting that 'units from the German, Hungarian and Slovakian minorities were hardly likely to fight for the state with any enthusiasm'.[62]

The Soviet Union and Germany had cemented 'normal relations' in the Treaty of Rapallo in 1922, which was followed up by the Treaty of Berlin in 1926. Although the initial drivers for this diplomatic engagement were political and economic, Soviet–German military relations also blossomed. Close co-operation in new tactics and technology was to mutual advantage. From the mid 1920s the Reichswehr developed aircraft, tanks and chemical weapons, all banned to Germany under the Treaty of Versailles, in secret centres established in Soviet territory. The Red Army also profited from this research and development, as it did from German general staff training and visits to the Reichswehr.

Manstein's first visit to the Soviet Union took place in September 1931 when he accompanied General Adam on a fact-finding trip. Although not mentioned by Manstein in his memoirs, Keitel and Colonel Walther von Brauchitsch (then head of T4, later to become commander-in-chief of the German Army in 1938) were also members of the German delegation.

Hosted warmly by officers of the Red Army, the German guests made a series of visits to economic and military installations in Moscow, Kharkov (including its newly constructed tractor works) and Kiev. Soviet hospitality was excellent throughout, with a good deal of old-fashioned Russian culture such as ballet and opera thrown in for good measure.

Here Manstein, then a middle-ranking general staff officer, had a golden opportunity to meet some of the leading personalities of the Red Army, some of whom were either purged by Stalin in his rounds of show trials and summary executions in 1936–39, whilst others survived to fight during the Second World War. Some of his most revealing vignettes concern the later marshals of the USSR, Voroshilov, Budenny and Tukhachevsky.

Soon after arriving in Moscow, Manstein was a dinner guest of Kliment Yefremovich Voroshilov (1891–1972), the Commissar for War. Although Voroshilov's apartment in the Kremlin was well appointed, Manstein found that the number of rooms 'was modest for a man of his position'. Whilst he formed the impression that 'those at the top of the Bolshevist regime still led a simple life', the meal that Voroshilov offered his German guests 'was sumptuous'. The *zakuska* (hors d'oeuvres) alone lasted two hours. Manstein seemed surprised that the wives of the senior Russian officers ate at the same table, but enjoyed their charming company none the less. Not speaking any Russian, he could only converse with the wife of the then Chief of the Soviet General Staff, General Aleksandr Ilyich Yegorov, who spoke good French. In one of Manstein's rare recorded opinions of the opposite sex, he described this particular fair lady of Moscow as the 'only strikingly elegantly dressed wife' present. No doubt Madame Galina Antonovna Yegorova's fine wardrobe reflected her 'glamorous profession as a film actress'.[63]

For the debonair, moustachioed heroic cavalry commander of the Civil War, Semyon Mikhailovich Budenny (1883–1973), whom he met again in 1932, Manstein had less time, describing him as a 'primitive old warhorse'. In the spring of 1942, as commander-in-chief of the North Caucasus Direction, Budenny opposed Manstein whilst fighting on the Crimea but Stalin later removed him from this post. Sparing no scorn, writing after the war, Manstein observed that Budenny's military knowledge garnered from his War Academy days 'obviously did not suffice to make him suitable for high command', but noted that unlike practically all the other generals, he did not 'always follow the facial expression of the commissars'.[64] So he had at least one virtue after all.

In comparison with Voroshilov and Budenny, perceptively Manstein described Mikhail Nikolayevich Tukhachevsky (1893–1937) in a rather more positive fashion:

> Without doubt the Deputy War Commissar was an interesting personality. He had served in the royal guards, but that had not prevented him from becoming a revolutionary. He appeared to me as an equally clever but inconsiderate individual. Although he was keen on the technical co-operation with the Reichswehr – with an emphasis of taking much and giving as little as possible – his sympathies seem to lie with the French, as much as a Soviet commander was allowed to have such.[65]

Ironically, Tukhachevsky was accused by Stalin of having sympathies with the Germans, but their differences were far more fundamental than that, for the Soviet leader feared him as an innovative and independently minded thinker. Manstein did not allude in his memoirs to the fact that Tukhachevsky, a former Chief of the General Staff, was head of the Red Army's Technology and Armament Department. As an exceptionally gifted operational theorist and modernizer, he was the principal author of the ground-breaking Provisional Field Regulations of 1936. Accused falsely of collaborating with (as opposed to the reality of warning about) Hitler's Germany, he was shot by firing squad on Stalin's orders, brave Budenny being amongst the military tribunal that had condemned him. Nazi Germany was fortunate not to have to contend with Tukhachevsky during the Second World War.[66]

On their return, on behalf of the German delegation, General Adam thanked Voroshilov for the splendid hospitality they had received. Their senior Soviet host responded in early 1932, writing:

> I was very happy to hear of your satisfaction with your visits during your stay in our country. General, please accept my deepest gratitude for your comments on the training and current state of the Red Army. As these comments come from a representative of a friendly country and a distinguished military expert, they represent considerable value to me.[67]

Less than ten years later Nazi Germany attacked the Soviet Union, resulting in the most devastatingly brutal and costly conflict the world has ever seen. Perhaps this tragic development stands as a pertinent reminder of the harsh fact that international relations can swing violently within a decade, or much shorter. Today's new friends, for all their alluring charm, can become our enemies again.

Together with a description of his second journey to the Soviet Union in 1932, Manstein's account of the 1931 trip provides valuable context to his wartime memoirs of the battles he fought on the Eastern Front ten years later. During his two visits Manstein had an excellent opportunity to observe the Red Army and to learn the geography of the areas over which he was later to campaign. The value of this exposure, which cut a number of ways, would only become apparent in retrospect. Manstein formed some harsh judgements of the Soviets, which led him later to underestimate the military potential of the Red Army, and specifically to disparage the quality of decision-making by its senior commanders. After the Second World War, he criticized the Soviet military as 'an incompetent high command and a lack of a sense of individual responsibility, based on the totalitarian system, insufficient work in the staffs, inadequate initiative displayed at the lower levels of command and by the soldiers themselves all contributed to the defeats of the first [war] years'.

Reflecting on the painful 'lost victories' experienced on the Eastern Front, Manstein declared bitterly:

> At the outbreak of war there was no German numerical superiority, only a partial one in equipment. Certainly, Soviet commanders learnt during the war. But at the end of the day, their successes were predominantly due to their overwhelming superiority in numbers, quite apart from errors made by the supreme German command. When the odds stand at 5:1, or even 7:1, then there is no place left for military art. The Soviet commanders possessed blood and iron in sufficient quantities to obviate largely the need for the art of command.[68]

Whereas Hitler had no direct personal knowledge of the Soviet Union prior to the German invasion of June 1941, many of his principal advisors, including the later field marshals Brauchitsch, Keitel and Manstein, certainly did.

Apart from writing down the military capabilities of the Red Army during the planning of the invasion of the Soviet Union, the Germans compounded this error by underestimating their future opponent's economic potential. Manstein and Keitel should have known better. In a contemporaneous note to his father following the 1931 trip, Keitel, for example, made many accurate observations of the USSR. He highlighted: 'The immense expanse of space; the availability of all thinkable raw materials, pre-requisites of an independent economy; the unshakeable belief in [industrial] development and the Five Year Plan; work is being carried out at full speed.' Surely Keitel, Brauchitsch and Manstein had seen enough to deduce the burgeoning economic and military capability of the Soviet Union?[69]

As later chapters will narrate, in common with Hitler and other senior

Wehrmacht commanders, Manstein was unable to predict the extent to which the Red Army and its leaders would learn from their early failures. They failed to appreciate that the Soviet armed forces would outfight their German opponents at the strategic and operational levels of war, for all their obvious tactical shortcomings in the execution of their sound combined arms doctrine. It was not solely about feeding overwhelming numbers of formations into battle, as Manstein maintained. He over-looked the fact that the Russians understood and applied superior oper-ational art in achieving their great victories. Yet he was hardly alone in his flawed assessment following the Second World War. Even into the early 1980s, at the height of the Cold War, former Wehrmacht octo-genarian generals such as Hermann Balck and Friedrich von Mellenthin would lecture their eager and gullible United States Army audiences on the strengths and weaknesses of the Red Army. The latter declared on one occasion: 'Believe us, they are masses and we are individuals. That is the difference between the Russian soldier and the European soldier.'[70] Perhaps so, but quantity, as Lenin remarked so famously, has a 'quality of its own'.

Following Manstein's second trip to the Soviet Union in 1932, during which he observed the Red Army's autumn manoeuvres in the Caucasus and spent some further time in Moscow, he was due a new appointment. A return to regimental duty and battalion command beckoned. For the first time in his career since joining 3rd Foot Guards over twenty-five years before, Manstein stated where he wanted to serve next. His elder son Gero, a delicate lad, suffered from acute asthma and sea air seemed to do him good. So Manstein requested a tour in Pomeranian Kolberg on the Baltic coast. His preference of posting was granted: the Manstein family never regretted this choice.

3

Serving Under Hitler

'There was much in the new regime that to us, and to the mass of the population, did not appeal.'[1] Erich von Manstein

Battalion Command

Kolberg (now Kołobrzeg in Poland), lying at the mouth of the Persante River, is an elegant resort on the Baltic, a jewel of the Pomeranian coastline. Its claim to fame is as much historical as geographical. Whilst Bismarck quipped famously that 'the whole of the Balkans is not worth the healthy bones of a single Pomeranian musketeer', defending the north Prussian homeland, including Kolberg, indeed was.[2] The town had long been an important royal fortress and had a special claim on German national sentiment by virtue of its valiant defence against the French in 1807. One of the most bizarre ironies of Hitler's Third Reich was the lavish production of the film *Kolberg*, which portrayed the joint struggle of its garrison and townsfolk to withstand the siege.[3] No expenses were spared in making *Kolberg* during the war years 1943–44: over ten thousand troops, which would have been far better employed at the front, were used as extras. When the revised film finally was released to German cinemas on 30 January 1945, the twelfth anniversary of Hitler's coming to power, it was already far too late to uplift popular morale. The defeats and enormous losses on all fronts had made it clear to all but the most fanatical of Nazis that the war was lost. Incredibly, a copy of the film was even parachuted into the Atlantic fortress of La Rochelle, whose beleaguered garrison was still holding out. History does not record the impact of this action, but it must go down as one of the most futile gestures of the entire war.

On 1 October 1932, Manstein assumed command of the *Jäger* (light infantry) battalion of the Reichswehr's 4th Infantry Regiment in Kolberg. In his famous war memoirs, *Defeat into Victory*, Field Marshal Slim recorded that the best commands were 'a platoon, battalion, division and an army'.[4] The same was true for Manstein, who whilst serving in a vastly different military culture and environment, valued particularly his appointments at these levels. Battalion command proved a welcome break from the routine of general staff work in Berlin. As a unit commanding officer he again had direct personal contact with soldiers; there was no more rewarding responsibility, he maintained, than 'turning German youths into competent men who loved their fatherland.'[5]

Manstein admired greatly his trusty light infantrymen, professional soldiers who were of a 'dependable country stock and whose forefathers had served Germany well in past wars'. The light infantry battalion attracted recruits of high quality with a good school education, many of whom would later be going into forestry. And foresters' sons, Manstein noted, 'were dependable soldiers'. What he did not reflect in his memoirs, however, was the Reichswehr policy of concentrating recruiting in rural areas in order to minimize undesirable socialist thinking creeping in from the big cities. Manstein was fortunate, too, in having a highly capable and widely respected regimental commander, Colonel Adolf Strauss, who went on to command Ninth Army during the campaign in the West in 1940. Their professional relationship was sound and mutually supporting; Manstein clearly admired him. As at company command, Manstein was given his head and he relished the opportunity to train his men in his own fashion. As any good commanding officer in every first-class army would state, his 'men's pride in their battalion was indeed matched by his pride in them'.[6]

Manstein and his family were delighted by their posting to Kolberg, which had many attractions apart from the military. They rented a house close to the beach, and in the summer months they were to spend the majority of their free time near or in the water. His daughter Gisela recalls: 'Father used to take Gero and me for barefoot morning runs along the beach, summer or winter. Only in very bad weather would we stay at home for some indoor exercises.'[7] Manstein kept himself fit through light athletics and swimming, and he rode out as much he could, including supporting his own battalion hunt on the local training area. He would retain these sporting interests throughout the Second World War, exercising whenever he had the opportunity, not necessarily to his immediate staff's delight.

The Manstein family much enjoyed the company and warm hospitality of the local minor aristocracy, who, augmented by the wealthy from Pomerania and Silesia, gathered for the 'season' in Kolberg each August on conclusion of the busy summer holidays. As one local wit put it, 'The Pomeranian aristocracy escaped from their ancient forests, their amber-decorated wives to the fore, in order to throw themselves into the sea.'[8] An added attraction in August was the annual horse show. All in all,

Manstein concluded that: 'The Kolberg years were – alongside my time as a lieutenant in the Guards – the most pleasant and carefree of my military career.'⁹ Presumably he did not intend any irony in that remark, but it is none the less surprising. His tour of duty of the Baltic coast was surely overshadowed by events in Berlin and Germany as a whole, culminating with Hitler's accession to power as chancellor on 30 January 1933.

Whilst Manstein enjoyed his period of battalion command, the German economic situation was becoming more desperate and the political situation ever more volatile. Hitler had made his initial breakthrough in the parliamentary elections of 14 September 1930 when his National Socialist German Workers Party (NSDAP) achieved 107 seats, a ninefold jump from twelve. The world depression had driven German unemployment to six million by early 1932. Although the National Socialists became the biggest party in the Reichstag election of 31 July 1932, winning 230 out of 608 seats, they had failed to gain a majority. A state of constitutional crisis and uncertainty continued until Hindenburg appointed Hitler chancellor on 30 January 1933 with the Reichswehr's tacit support.¹⁰

Kolberg was not spared the impact of the 'national revolution', which the National Socialists brought about once they had been elected as the majority party in the Reichstag during the last federal election of the Weimar Republic on 5 March 1933. Only six days previously the Reichstag building had burned down. At that time Manstein's battalion was shooting on the ranges at the Döberitz training area. By strange coincidence, one of his non-commissioned officers (an unnamed *Oberjäger*), on leave in Berlin at the time, just happened to walk by the Reichstag and was the first to report the building ablaze on the evening of 27 February. He later received a reward from the German government for his initiative.¹¹ The Reichstag fire turned out to be one of the pivotal events in the establishment of Nazi Germany. It led directly to the Reichstag Fire Decree issued on the strength of opposing a supposed Communist terror that nullified many of the civil liberties of the German population, including the suppression of any opposition to Hitler and elimination of a free press.

Following the elections of 5 March, one of the first acts of the reaffirmed National Socialist government was the Enabling Law of 24 March 1933, which was approved with an overwhelming vote. Together with the Fire Decree, this law led to the dismantling of parliamentary democracy and, as Manstein noted, 'opened the way to Hitler's dictatorship'.¹² A 'legal state' had ceased to exist at popular wish.

Manstein recorded a couple of incidents in 1933 that highlighted the radical changes that were now sweeping German society and affecting the Reichswehr alike. The first involved a visit by the new minister-president of Prussia, Hermann Göring, to a party rally in Kolberg. From Berlin came an order to provide a guard of honour for the event, a remarkable break from German military tradition in that such a guard hitherto would have been reserved for visiting heads of state, and not employed for party political purposes. According to Manstein, he and his Reichswehr colleagues in Kolberg saw the order as a blatant example of the Minster of Defence's (General Werner von Blomberg) kowtowing to the Party, and set out to circumvent it as best they could on parade. Instead of the guard commander reporting to Göring, he reported instead to the regimental commander (Colonel Strauss), who then invited the portly bigwig from Berlin to accompany him inspecting *his* troops. Yet in taking this small step of opposition to the creeping politicization of the army, Manstein may have made an enemy in Goring, for their mutual antipathy was to grow from this time on, albeit not evidently so until Manstein gained high command during the Second World War.[13]

The second matter, which affected urban rather more than rural life, was the growing number of attacks against the Jews. Manstein described these as having a 'particularly repulsive effect in such a small town as Kolberg'. One particular case came to his attention. It concerned the senior doctor of the local children's home, a former medical officer who had earned an Iron Cross First Class during the First World War. As a 'half-Aryan', he was being hounded out of his job by the local Nazis. Strauss and Manstein intervened and the doctor kept his post for the time being, and he continued to be invited to the officers' mess – much to the annoyance of the local Party officials.[14]

Opposition to the anti-Semitic measures being introduced throughout Germany during 1933 was not widespread within the German Army. Some honour was restored at national level when the Reich president complained to Hitler about the discrimination being shown to Jewish war veterans. Hindenburg wrote: 'If they were worthy of fighting and bleeding for Germany, they must be considered worthy of continuing to serve the Fatherland in their profession.' Hitler replied cynically that: 'One of the major reasons why the old Prussian state was such a clean one was that the Jews were granted only a very limited access to the civil service. The officer corps kept itself almost entirely pure.'[15] In other words, the army was hardly in a position to complain about anti-Semitism when it had itself condoned such institutional discrimination. With minor modifications the anti-Semitic laws were enacted: German officials and soldiers henceforth were required to prove their Aryan forebears. Whether Manstein had anything to do with his uncle's failed intervention remains unknown, but he was to act on behalf of former Jewish officers in his next general staff appointment. The life of the Jewish communities across Germany became worse, exposed to insensibility or intimidation at best, violent assaults or even murder at worst.

In the meantime, frictions were already appearing between the Reichswehr and the SA, the *Sturm-Abteilung*, the National Socialists' private army of brown-shirts, run by Ernst Röhm. Fights broke out in Kolberg between soldiers of Manstein's battalion and the local SA, whose thuggish elements were getting out of control, the only pleasing aspect of which, as he recorded dryly, was that the 'SA-men and not his light infantrymen took a beating'.[16] Further tensions arose at an official level when the army was ordered by Blomberg to detach personnel for training the SA, which did nothing to improve relationships. Manstein must have spoken for many Germans after the Second World War when he recorded – albeit with retrospective judgement – his impressions of that time:

> ... there was then a widely held view that Hitler knew nothing of the mistakes, *faux pas* or even the misdeeds of his people, and that he would certainly not approve of them, were he to find out. This was a deception that held throughout Germany for a long time. Looking back it is odd, that we soldiers, who put great store on a commander being responsible for the behaviour of his subordinates, did not apply this test to Hitler. We believed that we could not apply the same rule to politicians as was a matter of course in our own military profession.[17]

Yet who was denying what and deceiving whom? Manstein, as a serving officer, was never a member of the NSDAP. Along with many millions of other Germans, however, he was in some respects a tacit supporter of Hitler certainly to the outbreak of the Second World War and – in all probability – for at least a couple of years into it.

National Socialism was a supremely popular ideology: Hitler was elected democratically; the vast majority of the German people, spanning the working, middle and much of the upper classes, not least captains of industry, supported him. So strong was the sense of a long-sought relief from economic misery and political disorder and a feeling of national reawakening, skilfully manipulated by Goebbels' insidious and unscrupulous propaganda machine, that it obscured any collective moral outrage at the government's actions.

It is one thing in hindsight to criticize the *inactions* of people living in a totalitarian state, it is quite another to offer effective resistance oneself in such circumstances. For those used to freedom, enjoying an independent press and democracy today, it is only too easy to condemn the millions then who were blindly passive in the face of the abuses of Nazism. Not that the excesses were public, for the 'truth' is not necessarily a whole one: it is often what people want to see. That said, the fear of physical violence, losing one's job, inhuman imprisonment and, ultimately, execution was very real: estimates vary as to the numbers of Social Democrats, Communists and other opposition elements rounded up in 1933, but the generally accepted figure is at least 100,000. These political prisoners were the first inmates of the German concentration camps, not the Jews.

At the same time, Manstein did not describe the *Gleichschaltung*, the mandatory 'co-ordination' of German society, in which 'almost every aspect of political, social and associational life was affected, at every level from the nation to the village'.[18] Whilst peripheral Kolberg proved no sanctuary from this all-embracing process, it is perhaps significant that Manstein underplayed the darker side of National Socialism of the time, including the ruthless – to become boundless – violence and widespread contempt of life and property. In any personal memoirs, it is often the case that what is *not* said often has as much significance as that stated: Manstein's are no exception. The sad fact remains that much of the German population adulated and supported Hitler; many in the military proved no exception. Manstein's own position was ambiguous if not contradictory: as a devout Christian he had a profound sense of human dignity, hence his complete disdain for much of what the Nazi thugs did on the streets. But as nationalist and patriot he was all for the strong and confident *Reich* that Hitler so seductively promised.

Military District Chief of Staff

On 1 February 1934, Manstein was posted back to Berlin to become the chief of staff of *Wehrkreiskommando* III, having been promoted to colonel on 1 December the previous year. Manstein's request to remain in Kolberg for at least the usual (for a general staff officer) two years in battalion command was turned down by the then Chief of Army Command, General Kurt Freiherr von Hammerstein-Equord, who held it essential that his protégé gain wider experience for future employment in higher positions of the General Staff. As Manstein took up his new position, the previous commander of the *Wehrkreis*, General Werner

Freiherr von Fritsch, took over from Hammerstein-Equord in the newly titled post of Commander-in-Chief of the German Army. In his place came General Erwin von Witzleben, whom Manstein knew well from their time working together as general staff tutors in Dresden. Apart from his personal qualities, Manstein respected his boss especially because he delegated – a pleasant position for a highly competent chief of staff to 'run the shop', enjoying the full confidence of his commander. Later a prominent member of the resistance against Hitler, Witzleben was executed following the failed coup of 20 July 1944.

One notable individual served within Manstein's staff: Colonel Hans Graf von Sponeck, the chief of operations. He was later to serve under Manstein as a divisional and corps commander in the Crimea in 1941–42; his tragic end is described later.

Within Germany there was an internal reckoning to come in the meantime. The criminal activities of the SA and its street gangs had become ever more brash and unsettling to both the army and the population at large, risking not only civic order but also compromising the role of the police and army. Relations between the army and the SA had worsened in recent months, culminating with Röhm's outrageous demands that the army provide trained men for his organization. A showdown was fast approaching and Hitler felt forced to act.

On 28 February 1934, Hitler summoned the heads of the Reichswehr and leaders of the SA and the SS to a meeting in the Reichswehr ministry on the Landwehr canal in Berlin. All were gathered in the Ministry's large conference room. This was the first time that Manstein had seen, and heard, the Führer at close hand. He recorded that Hitler did not make a strong impression on him, but recalled the speech in sufficient detail to remember Hitler's objective of freeing the Reich from the 'shackles of Versailles'. The preconditions for reaching this benign state of affairs included having 'a united people and external security guaranteed by military rearmament'. Manstein also noted Hitler's ideas about achieving the necessary living space (*Lebensraum*) for the German people. Perhaps most significant for Manstein at the time was Hitler's firmly stressed view that the Wehrmacht (the new collective title of Germany's armed forces had yet to be adopted formally) was, and would remain, the 'sole bearer of weapons of the nation'.[19] No doubt this was a carefully aimed shot across the bows of the SA, if not a highly visible moral boost for the army. Curiously, Manstein did not record Hitler setting out the military consequences of his expansionist foreign policy. To achieve the necessary living space, Hitler had declared, 'Short decisive blows against the West, then against the East could therefore become necessary.'[20]

This remarkable portent of future war would haunt Germany for the
next eleven years.

The Jewish Question

Manstein's personal position on the National Socialist policies with
regard to the treatment of the Jewish population in Germany is a complicated one, marked by compromise and contradiction. He appeared to
be opposed to the introduction of a ban on the employment of Jewish
officers in the Armed Services, famously documented in a formal letter
to General Ludwig Beck, the chief of the *Truppenamt* in 1934, written
just after he assumed his position of chief of staff of *Wehrkreiskommando*
III in Berlin. His intervention appears to be the only recorded instance
of protest against the application of the so-called Aryan Paragraph prohibiting Jews from becoming or remaining civil servants, a restriction
which also applied to the military.[21] Closer examination of Manstein's
letter of 21 April 1934 and his enclosed memorandum (a lengthy typewritten document), however, reveals a rather more equivocal stance on
the fate of the Jews in Germany.[22]

So what had driven Manstein to write his outspoken démarche? He
had received a letter from a young second lieutenant from his old
Kolberg battalion, whom he regarded particularly highly on account of
his 'character, conviction and ability'. In his covering letter to Beck,
Manstein made clear that he was not just concerned about this particular
regrettable case (involving the retrospective enforcement of the Aryan
Paragraph), but rather about the wider question of how the officer corps
should stand in the matter.

Manstein's memorandum begins starkly with the statement 'Let it be
assumed that the requirement for pure Aryan descent and marriage in
the Wehrmacht' since 30 January 1933 is 'an absolute matter of course for
the future'. He confined his subsequent remarks only to 'the retrospective
application of the Aryan Paragraph to long-serving soldiers', although
his covering letter had expressly included in its gambit those non-Aryan
veterans who had taken part in the First World War. Manstein's hard
line continued with 'nobody disputes the fact the professions of judges,
lawyers and doctors were flooded with Jews and half-Jews', and that a
'rigorous cleansing' was required, but he questioned the need for this
action to be extended to the military with such a small proportion of
Jews.

Manstein's principal objection to the measure was based on the assertion that the soldier's profession is like no other: the individual must be

prepared to lay down his life for his country. If a soldier was prepared year-long to make the ultimate sacrifice, he should not be suddenly told 'you're no longer [fit to be] a real German'. Secondly, Manstein objected vociferously to the political pressure being exerted on the army, complaining that 'we are capitulating to those anti-military people who are agitating against the army and are deliberately making the false accusation that the army and its officer corps is composed of Jews'. Thus, all things considered, any purging action, which was 'urgently required in other professions', was not required in the army.

In sum, Manstein felt that the honour of the officer corps was being put at risk by the application of the Aryan Paragraph. 'Now is the moment', he declared, 'when we must show that we in the army not only talk about comradeship, but we can make it really happen.' Further, he noted, 'the order that the Aryan Paragraph should be applied within the Wehrmacht has been issued and cannot be reversed in the normal course of things. But it has already achieved its desired effect on the mass of the population.' He argued that henceforth the officer corps alone should be the sole judge as to whether a non-Aryan officer should be permitted to continue to serve. Therefore Manstein suggested that the following tests should be applied:

1. Has the officer consistently shown himself to be a pure-blooded German in his conviction and behaviour?
2. Is the officer corps certain that the officer concerned – from a fraction of foreign blood – possesses no characteristics of a foreign race that could influence his basic Aryan attitude in a foreign-raced manner?
3. Does the officer corps continue to believe that the officer concerned remains suitable as a fully fledged German Army officer?

If there were positive answers to all three questions, then Manstein proposed that any missing birth certificate could be replaced by a declaration of honour by the officer corps.

Manstein's letter, although approved by Witzleben, and signed off by both Beck and Fritsch, led to no changes whatsoever in the treatment of Jews or part-Jews in the German military. General von Blomberg, the Reich Minister for War, even considered taking disciplinary action against Manstein for his impertinence. In retrospect, his protest was naive. It was inconceivable that Hitler would have changed his mind on the basis of a solitary colonel in the General Staff objecting. With no further opposition forthcoming, the matter was quietly dropped.

Manstein had shown significant moral courage in opposing the anti-Aryan clause when the remainder of the Wehrmacht had remained silent.

It has been suggested that 'he dressed up his protest in terms that were intended to leave no doubt as to his ideological soundness'.[23] This interpretation may well be valid: to have dissented further from the government line would have led to professional suicide. There is also good evidence to suggest that Fritsch and Beck shielded him, as a highly promising general staff officer, from any censure. In any event, his career was unaffected.[24] As we shall see later, however, Manstein's position appeared to have changed subtly by the time of his public eulogy of Hitler's policy on the Führer's fiftieth birthday on 20 April 1939. During the early, successful war years, some of Manstein's language with regard to the Jews – in particular his use of the term 'Bolshevist-Jewish system' in connection with the USSR – was largely indistinguishable from the standard rhetoric of the regime itself. In the meantime, he had expressed his sense of moral outrage at the *application* of the law, rather than posing any fundamental opposition to the racist policies that prompted it.

Yet there was also a much wider, equally important issue at stake: Manstein had sounded a prophetic warning note about the acquiescence of Germany's armed forces under political pressure on the vital matter of military honour. As he wrote, 'If we betray today a small element of our principles, tomorrow people will demand the heads of others! ... A violation of the ethical arena will definitely revenge itself.'[25]

The Röhm Affair

Tension between Germany's armed forces (particularly within the army) and the SA continued to mount during the first half of 1934. Hitler began to fear – or perhaps, more accurately, to manufacture a fear – of a coup against him. Whilst Röhm certainly had uttered treasonable comments about Hitler, the extent to which he had planned a putsch remains open to academic debate. The real significance of the matter lies in the manner in which Hitler turned the situation skilfully to his advantage, eliminating at a stroke both the threat from the SA, ingratiating himself with the armed forces and placing them under his protection. At that time he manipulated the legitimate concerns of the army about the SA and the threat posed to its members. In his memoirs, Manstein claimed that he feared for his own life during the period immediately *before* the Night of the Long Knives of 30 June 1934 when Hitler struck. The SA had posted machine-gunners in a nearby house to threaten the *Wehrkreiskommando* headquarters building, and Manstein armed himself night and day with a pistol for self-defence. His concern was such that he sent his wife and children down to his wife's family estate in Silesia to get them safely out of the way with a suitable cover story. As Gisela Lingenthal remembers, 'It was so unlike Father to take us out of school, but he told us that we needed to assist with the fruit-picking and of course we welcomed an extended summer holiday in Lorzendorf.'[26]

Manstein states that he had no advance warning of Hitler's move, but it remains a fact that elsewhere in Germany the army supported the police action in decapitating the SA, which indicates a measure of joint planning. Manstein's reactions to the killings, including those of General and Frau von Schleicher and of General von Bredow as well as Röhm and his cronies, were mixed. On the one hand he supported the suppression of the SA as it represented a latent, if not real, threat to the internal security of the German state, and with that came the associated risk of a second revolution, and all that would entail. For Röhm's demise, Manstein offered no regrets: as a flagrant homosexual he belonged in prison.[27] If this condemnation sounds harsh and bigoted today, we must judge Manstein by the prevailing mores, and his was a typical and representative point of view when he wrote his memoirs in the mid 1950s. On the other hand, Manstein condemned the brutal method involved in the suppression of the SA, signalling beyond all doubt the end of the rule of law in Germany.

The murder of Kurt von Schleicher, the retired soldier, minister and ex-chancellor, aroused Manstein's anger. They had served together in the same Guards fusilier battalion between 1907 and 1910, when Schleicher was adjutant. Manstein had succeeded him in that post and the two had remained in regular contact, dining together in the officers' mess of 3rd Foot Guards in Berlin. Although there is no evidence that Manstein remained in close touch with Schleicher after the First World War, he had none the less lost a comrade.

In the immediate aftermath of 30 June, Manstein had expected some reaction from Blomberg. He was not aware of the Minister of Defence's acquiescence, if not complicity, in the affair. When none resulted, he requested that his superior, Witzleben, speak to General von Fritsch.[28] In the same manner, Manstein claims that Fritsch asked Blomberg to confront Hitler, but he refused. Allegedly, Schleicher had been conspiring with France but no concrete evidence was ever produced to substantiate this accusation, however plausible it might have appeared. Blomberg even went so far as to forbid senior army officers from attending Schleicher's funeral; Manstein left no indication as to whether – in a defiant gesture – he joined the sole general who did, the recently retired Hammerstein-Equord. Whilst Hitler had assumed personal responsibility for his actions, the army's leaders had either supported him or failed to intervene to protect life, including that of its own.

The subsequent concerns of the generals came to nothing except for a 'declaration of honour' made on behalf of their murdered comrades: it amounted to little more than the army purging its conscience. In view of the space that Manstein accorded in his memoirs (no fewer than nine pages) to Schleicher, there is a distinct sense of tragedy and remorse in his comrade's fate. Manstein concluded: 'Schleicher was mistaken in his political estimation of National Socialism generally and in Hitler in particular. But he was prepared to fight [for his country] and fell as a patriot by the hand of those – whom we now know today – who led Germany into such misfortune.'[29]

That the army's leadership had failed to act was duly noted by the Führer as a sign of weakness. To have expected the Reichswehr to ride against the tide of public opinion at the time would have demanded a degree of prescience as to the likely future course of events and a volume of collective moral courage that was not available. Without doubt, Hitler's standing within the army and in the population at large rose as a result of 30 June – the threat to public order had been eliminated. Yet popularity hardly legitimizes a dictatorship. Along with many other officers, Manstein was summoned to the Reichstag session held in the Kroll Opera House on 13 July 1934 to hear Hitler's explanation of events. Unsurprisingly, much of his self-serving, two-hour speech was aimed at explaining the decision to act so decisively against the SA and at unifying the country behind him. But if his listeners – bearing in mind that no fewer than thirteen members of the Reichstag had just been murdered – expected some apology or atonement, they were disappointed.

Hitler gave one of his most bloodcurdlingly bravura performances, including: 'I gave the order to shoot the most guilty of this treason, and I further gave the order to burn down to the raw flesh the ulcers of our internal well-poisoning and the poisoning from abroad.'[30] Manstein did not recall this particularly venomous passage but remembered Hitler declaring dramatically that in the event of his project failing, he would reach for his pistol as he could not bear to live.[31] Only with hindsight can we judge just how ironic Hitler's prophetic words turned out to be, coming to fatal fruition in his Berlin bunker on 30 April 1945.

The Death of Hindenburg

Shortly after the disposal of Röhm, public attention in Germany turned to the death of Hindenburg and its aftermath. The venerable field marshal and Reich president had passed away on 1 August 1934. For the members of the Reichswehr, Hindenburg's death meant the loss of their commander-in-chief, who personified a continuity of military tradition from the Kaiser and the Royal Prussian Army. Manstein had seen his aged uncle twice in 1934 before his physical condition declined rapidly during the early summer. One occasion was a purely family affair but the other was a formal concert evening held at the President's palace in Berlin. Manstein was astounded by the old field marshal's ability then to recall all his guests' names. Even more surprising to him, however, was the public goodwill that Hindenburg displayed to Hitler. For his part, the Führer was demonstrably respectful to the President.[32] Their relationship had not always been so harmonious. When Hitler first met Hindenburg on 10 October 1931, the latter had treated him with barely disguised contempt, keeping him standing. He was singularly unimpressed by Hitler's political views too, considering he might be good enough for a minister of posts, but certainly not as a chancellor.[33] As late as 27 January 1933, just three days before Hitler took power, Hindenburg had declared that he 'had no intention of making that Austrian corporal either Minister of Defence or Chancellor of the Reich'.[34]

Eighteen months later and Hindenburg was dead; a long shadow was cast over the nation. Hitler determined to exploit the funeral for his own purposes, transferring it from the deceased's estate at Neudeck (expressly going against the late President's wishes, who desired to be laid beside his wife) to the Tannenberg memorial in East Prussia in order to extract the maximum propaganda effect for film and radio. Manstein joined family, former regiment and the German nation to honour Hindenburg. He was impressed by the occasion, carried out with full pomp and circumstance. Even Hitler's impromptu speech (his adjutant having mislaid the prepared one) did not spoil the dignified ceremony, although Manstein – and no doubt many others present – was surprised that the Führer should commend Hindenburg to enter Valhalla. As the field marshal's coffin was borne into its final resting place in the memorial's tower, the majestic march of 3rd Foot Guards was played, perhaps for the very last time on a state occasion.[35]

Germany had lost a president and gained unexpectedly a new one, for Hitler had neatly combined the presidency with the chancellorship. This dramatic and highly significant constitutional change came into effect after Hindenburg's death. Henceforth Hitler was to be addressed as Führer and *Reichskanzler*. Although there was neither public discussion nor political debate on the issue in the Reichstag, Hitler scored a triumph in the subsequent referendum that confirmed his new status. The other

surprise was addressed to all members of the German armed forces who,
at the suggestion of the ever compliant Blomberg, were required on 2
August 1934 to make a solemn oath. Every officer and man of the
Reichswehr had to declare: 'I swear by God this sacred oath, that I will
yield unconditional obedience to the Führer of the German Reich and
Volk, Adolf Hitler, the Supreme Commander of the Wehrmacht, and,
as a brave soldier, will be ready at any time to lay down my life for this
oath.'[36]

Hence 2 August 1934 sealed Hitler's accession to supreme power.
After the Second World War, Manstein observed that the members of
the Reichswehr had no alternative but to make such an oath.[37] Yet the
consequences were to prove dire: it bound the Wehrmacht to support
Hitler through thick and thin, regardless of the reckless path along which
he took Germany. From a soldier's perspective, however, to break an
oath would be to cast out all military virtue, the very foundation of
military life, a crisis of conscience that those wishing to oppose Hitler
would have to overcome. For the majority, including officers such as
Manstein, the oath represented a convenient excuse not to act. His later
mentor and Chief of the General Staff (1936–38) General Ludwig Beck,
for example, who as a colonel had celebrated the election result of 14
September 1930 in his artillery regiment's officers' mess, was heard to
remark that 2 August 1934 represented the 'darkest day of my life'.[38] As
the military leader of the opposition, Beck attempted to take his own life
when the plot of 20 July 1944 failed. After bungling shooting himself,
he was polished off by a sergeant.

Meanwhile, the Reichswehr had already come to terms with Hitler
before Hindenburg's death. Hitler took a great interest in the army and
was keen to be kept well informed of technical developments to improve
its fighting power. Manstein recalled one visit by the Führer to an
exercise laid on by Military District III on the Zossen training area,
south of Berlin. Amongst the equipment on display were experimental
models of the first light tanks, which at this stage of development were
only tracked chassis without turrets and guns. In mock combat with
elements of 9th Cavalry Regiment, a number of horses took fright at
these strange devices, and 'because the tank decks were open, the out-
raged riders attacked the defenceless drivers with their sabres'. More
seriously, Manstein observed how skilfully Hitler mixed with the officers
over breakfast, adeptly adjusting his manner and tone to his audience,
speaking 'objectively, clearly and with moderation'.[39]

The reintroduction of general conscription on 16 March 1935 came
as a complete surprise to both Witzleben and Manstein. It was Hitler's

idea, too, to enlarge the army from its Treaty of Versailles limit of seven infantry divisions to a new structure comprising twelve army corps with a total of thirty-six divisions in one phase of expansion. As an expert in this area, Manstein would have preferred to have seen a staged increase in the size of the army through a tripling of the establishment to twenty-one divisions first, for which he had already done the detailed planning some years before. As Manstein observed, conscription and the rapid increase in the size of the army changed its character. New recruits (among them members of the Hitler Youth) reflected the new political, National Socialist, order and outlook in society.

Meanwhile, the pace of modernization of equipment was also breathtaking, with the introduction of the new panzer formations and, within the infantry divisions, the incorporation of heavy artillery and anti-tank units. Newly raised army battalions and regiments were split again to form the basis of yet new ones. Simultaneously, the Luftwaffe was being established, drawing off experienced officers to fill its ranks and demanding huge financial and technical investment.

So the army had its hands full. Thus, according to Manstein, it failed to keep an eye on political developments within Germany.[40] Do such circumstances justify Manstein's view? Whilst the Reichswehr had a tradition of being apolitical, as long as any threat came from the right (as the Kapp Putsch had shown), its senior leadership had been intriguing in the politics of the Reich, especially during the running political crises of 1932–33. At the same time, the National Socialist influence on the army had become pervasive, reflecting its impact on German society as a whole. There seems little doubt that the German military relished expansion and mechanization. This collective betterment was matched by greatly improved individual career prospects across all ranks in comparison with the slow, dead man's shoes promotion system of the old Reichswehr.[41]

Back into the General Staff of the Army

Colonel Manstein was a direct beneficiary of, and major actor in, the army's rapid enlargement. On 1 July 1935, as a colonel, he was appointed Chief of the Operations Branch of the Army General Staff. He held this post until 1 October 1936 when he was advanced to become *Oberquartiermeister* I (First Quartermaster General) in the rank of major general. De facto, he became Vice-Chief of the General Staff and right-hand man to General Beck. In so doing, Manstein had followed in the footsteps of Gustav von Wietersheim in both appointments. They were plum jobs in the army, bringing him into the heart of its strategic planning and centre of influence at a time when Hitler's foreign and rearmament policies were advancing Germany towards war. Manstein supported directly not only Beck but also the commander-in-chief (Colonel General von Fritsch). So his career was now in the sharp ascendant; he had been promoted from colonel to major general in just under three years, there being no intermediate rank of brigadier general in the German Army at that time, and having skipped the normal colonel's appointment of regimental commander in the process.

When Manstein took up post in 1935, the 'restraining shackles of the Treaty of Versailles' had already been broken, and General Beck had already remodelled the former *Truppenamt* into a Great General Staff along traditional Prussian lines in the spirit of his illustrious predecessors Moltke the Elder and Alfred von Schlieffen.[42] But, as Manstein noted, there was now a crucial development in the military command structure that had undermined the position of Chief of the General Staff. Whereas in the Kaiser's time the 'Chief' had enjoyed an immediate right of access to the head of state, now the *Reichskriegsminister* (Minister of War) – also Commander-in-Chief of the Wehrmacht – and the Commander-in-Chief of the army stood in between. That aside, the newly re-established General Staff of the army had expanded from the five branches of the former *Truppenamt* into thirteen, grouped into four divisions, each under an *Oberquartiermeister* (OQ).

As a section chief in 1935, Manstein was lucky to have three brilliant staff captains working for him: Siegfried Westphal, Henning von Tresckow and Bernhard von Lossberg, the son of the famous First World War general. Manstein's close association with Tresckow, later a prominent member of the resistance against Hitler, stemmed from this period. Westphal recorded that on reporting for duty on 1 August 1935, he was received by Colonel von Manstein 'in the friendliest manner' and informed immediately that he was to form a new staff section under his personal direction to consider 'organization, equipment and training' matters from an operational level perspective. In this manner, Manstein was able to influence the rest of the General Staff, keeping an independent line. The two went on to work closely together for over three years. In his memoirs, Westphal sung his chief's praises:

> [He] was a pleasant man, a military genius. He demonstrated that in every position during the Second World War. He worked unbelievably quickly; impatiently, he couldn't stand long presentations. He was a generous superior officer, a complete gentleman, but an uncomfortable subordinate. He didn't have too many friends amongst his peers. This was

also due to the fact that he didn't tend to expend much effort in trying to convince them … I learned much from him, and never heard an unfriendly word from him.

In sum, he felt that Manstein was the 'outstanding figure of the German General Staff'.[43]

In 1936, as OQ I, responsible for operations, Manstein was the *primus inter pares* amongst his three fellow quartermaster generals: Rudolf Schmidt (OQ II – supply), Carl-Heinrich von Stülpnagel (OQ III – intelligence) and Franz Halder (OQ IV – training). Apart from war plans, his own responsibilities included army organization, fortifications, mapping and, not least, technical research and development.

Once again, Manstein had a bunch of talented subordinates, including Colonel Erik Hansen, his successor as chief of operations, who later served as a well-trusted commanding general of LIV Army Corps within Eleventh Army in the Crimea. Another notable branch chief was the highly ambitious Colonel Walther Model, responsible for technical development, whom Manstein described as 'a live wire full of new ideas'.[44] During the Second World War, Model advanced from divisional to army group commander, taking over from Manstein in Army Group South in April 1944. As a master of the solid, tactical defensive battle rather than bold operational manoeuvre, he was much trusted by Hitler.

Manstein's most important role in both his appointments in the General Staff during the years 1935–38 was war planning. His account of his involvement in this prime strategic function is of considerable historical interest. It sheds important light on that period, highlighting the tension that arose between certain elements of the army's senior leadership (principally Beck) and Hitler, as the Führer propelled his country towards war. When undertaking planning, whether at the strategic, operational or tactical levels, the first two factors to be evaluated normally are the ground and enemy forces. Strange as it may now appear, long after the inter-war years and the Second World War, Germany felt itself surrounded by potentially aggressive neighbours. Between the two world wars, Poland, France and Czechoslovakia were all viewed with deep suspicion. Hence, as we have seen, the priorities for the Reichswehr under von Seeckt had been to disguise and preserve as much fighting power as possible under the Treaty of Versailles limits for the defence of the Reich and to develop secret new weapon such as tanks and aircraft in the Soviet Union.

Manstein had played a major role in the development of the army whilst serving in the *Truppenamt*. Even with Hitler's accession to power, the main focus of war planning remained defensive in design. Certainly up to 1938 the Wehrmacht was in no shape to fight an offensive war on any grand scale against a major opponent such as France. During his time in the Army General Staff, Manstein was concerned primarily with developing *defensive* deployment plans. That said, in March 1936 he was involved in planning the reoccupation of the Rhineland. Two years later, he had a key role in preparing the military support to the *Anschluss* (the union with Austria), which came about whilst he was taking over as a divisional commander.

With the signing of the German–Polish non-aggression agreement of 26 January 1934, the major perceived threat to Germany's security remained France. For the eventuality of a French invasion, deployment plan 'Red' was developed in 1935/36. Apparently unaware of the predominantly French defensive mentality – expressed in unmistakably concrete terms through the construction of the Maginot Line – the Germans assumed that their opponents would launch an offensive towards the middle Rhine between Karlsruhe and Mainz. How the attack would develop thereafter was open to several possible sequels. In one, it was presumed that the French would continue their offensive by breaking through between the Odenwald and the Black Forest to link up with Czech troops advancing from Bohemia, thus splitting southern Germany from the north. As likely, Manstein considered, was a French main effort north of the river Main with a thrust into the 'heart of the Reich', and a potential turning movement towards the north in order to envelop the Ruhr area.[45] Manstein considered a French offensive through Belgium towards the lower Rhine as less probable. In response, the German plan foresaw three strong armies holding the French on the Rhine, whilst guarding the borders with Poland and Czechoslovakia with a weak army each, augmented by the Border Security Force East. As the Germans war-gamed this scenario, they convinced themselves that in the case of a French attack, the Czechs would grasp the opportunity to launch a major offensive themselves against Germany rather than await the outcome of a battle on the Rhine. For the eventuality of a major Czech attack, deployment plan 'Green' was developed, which saw the mass of the German Army concentrating on their eastern foe first, whilst standing guard on an economy-of-effort basis against France in the west.

So what should we make of such planning? Taking an historical perspective, there was nothing extraordinary in the fact that the German Army was planning how to fight and win a continental war on one or more fronts. Since Moltke the Elder's day, the General Staff had investigated the operational modalities of switching forces from one front to another, exploiting Germany's internal lines of communication based on an extensive rail network, built for this purpose as much as for economic development. Manstein maintained that, at the prevailing state of German military expansion and rearmament, all military opinion pointed to the necessity of '*avoiding* war for years to come'. Furthermore, 'Any war for Germany – on account of her central position [in Europe] – would bring the danger of a multi-front war, which in view of the experiences of the First World War, should be avoided at all costs'.[46] He stressed repeatedly in his memoirs that both the deployment plans 'Red' and 'Green' were only designed by the Army General Staff to meet and counter the possibility of foreign attack, and had absolutely nothing to do with Hitler's expansionist plans first revealed to the Wehrmacht's leadership in 'November 1937'. Manstein was no doubt alluding here to Hitler's meeting with his principal military and foreign policy advisors recorded in the infamous Hossbach Memorandum.

The facts point otherwise. Hitler had already given advance notice of his intentions with the publication of his two-volume polemic *Mein Kampf* in 1925 and 1927. In successive speeches before and after he came to power on 30 January 1933 he had warned that Germany would need to expand its living space for her people. On 3 February 1933, for example, he had informed the army district commanders that: 'I set myself the deadline of six to eight years to exterminate Marxism completely. The army will be able to conduct an active foreign policy, and the goal of expanding the living space of the German people will be achieved with arms – the objective would probably be in the East.' Three years later in his memorandum on the Four-Year Plan, drawn up in the summer of 1936, Hitler declared that: 'If we do not succeed in developing the German Wehrmacht without delay into the first army of the world in its training, and in the drawing up of units, in its armament and above all in its spiritual education, Germany will be lost.' The message that the Wehrmacht should conduct 'the historic life struggle of the peoples' was unequivocal: the German armed forces were not designed to stand around 'in being' to deter future enemies but rather to take the fight to them. Why else was the German economy running at such breakneck speed to transform each service both quantitatively and qualitatively into effective military instruments, with 'an army capable of waging a decisive offensive war'?[47]

Additional evidence that brings Manstein's account into some doubt comes from no lesser source than Blomberg, who stated on 24 June 1937 in his 'Order for the Uniform Preparations of the Wehrmacht' that 'Germany did not have to reckon with an attack from any direction.'[48] It scarcely seems credible that Manstein, as the German Army's senior planner, remained in the dark for so long about the realities of Hitler's aggressive policies and the associated future employment of the Wehrmacht. Further, in his analysis of the potential war plans of foreign powers Manstein made a classic mistake in crediting the Reich's potential opponents with a strategic opportunism and operational virtuosity that was far more German in spirit and design than French or Czechoslovak. When one takes into the account the successive German deployments into the Rhineland, Austria, the Sudetenland and then the rest of Czechoslovakia, Manstein was being narrowly accurate when he stated that the first real (in the sense of formal deliberate planning) offensive deployment plan was developed in 1939 under Hitler's direction for the attack on Poland under the codename 'White'.[49]

By 1937, war planning assumed an initial posture of strategic defence, but on secondary fronts such as Czechoslovakia, the 'battle was to be waged offensively'.[50] Manstein was deeply involved in the planning and conduct of the German Army's staff rides to refine and test war planning. Such exercises were also designed to develop the participants' practical understanding of handling large bodies of troops (corps and armies). Using both real and imaginary scenarios, the classical tactical factors of terrain, forces, time and space were all considered.

Despite the harmonization of military thought generated through common education and doctrine, there is always scope for professional disagreement during training and operations. Heusinger, then a general staff officer of 11th Division in Allenstein, East Prussia, recalled a war game in the winter of 1936 that Manstein had planned on behalf of General Beck. The senior general present was General Walther von Brauchitsch, the regional corps commander. At the final discussion, Brauchitsch's solution did not correspond to Manstein's. From this time on, according to Heusinger, there was a 'latent contradiction between Brauchitsch and Manstein', which had 'consequences for Manstein and later for the conduct of the war'.[51]

It was indeed the legitimate work – and core business – of a general staff to prepare for war, focusing on defending the homeland. The traditional German concept of defence, based on winning a decisive battle through operational manoeuvre, required a blend of offensive and defensive tactical actions. Despite the hubris that was to conflate operational level thinking with military strategy during the Second World War, German generals in the mid 1930s were more realistic in their aspirations. After all, the full potential of mechanized forces had yet to be demonstrated. Yet the traditional German overconfidence and instinctive disregard for an enemy's capabilities were never far away. The 1935 *Truppenamt* staff ride, for example, had involved the study of a counter-offensive against Czechoslovakia aimed at the destruction of the Czech Army. Manstein had provided Beck with a cautionary note for his closing address: 'The prospects for a quick, decisive operation against the enemy must be regarded as really questionable for various reasons.' As Beck's biographer has noted, the majority of the participating generals and general staff officers on this occasion had 'come to considerably more optimistic solutions'.[52]

A winning *campaign*, however, could involve several battles, which would require the appropriate number of reinforcing troops and logistic support. Thus, the real indicator of preparation for an offensive war lies not in operational level study and training alone but rather in the establishment of sufficient forces, equipment and stocks to embark on an offensive strategy in pursuit of foreign policy objectives. It needs opportunity and political will – and ultimately decision – as well as military capabilities. In Hitler's case it was 'opportunistic will', banking on intimidating his opponents with a combination of bluff and mailed fist. The necessary financial and *matériel* resources for any war of duration are enormous, and represent a massive drain on an economy. Hence the decision to gear up a nation for wars of aggression is much more a political and economic act than a military one. Germany's Four-Year Plan of 1936 provided the launch pad for just such an expansionist policy, requiring the German Army to be fully operational and prepared for war within four years.

By early 1940 the German Army had swelled to 102 divisions with over 2.6 million men – hardly a defensive force, as it had already shown in a convincing manner its offensive capabilities in Poland in September 1939, the first Blitzkrieg. Yet, if we are to believe Manstein, the high command of the German Army was thinking in purely defensive terms until the spring of 1939, when Hitler ordered the necessary preparations to be made for the invasion of Poland.[53]

Technical Developments

The name of Heinz Guderian probably more than any other is associated with the creation of the German armoured forces that were to play such a prominent role in securing Germany's early victories and, subsequently, in delaying its inevitable defeat during the Second World War. Together, the siren-screeching Ju82 Stuka dive-bomber and the menacing mass of the Mark IV main battle tank of the German Army remain iconic symbols of Blitzkrieg. Yet the development of Germany's armoured forces (the *Panzerwaffe*) rested as much on tactical and operational innovations as on technical developments.

Manstein was at pains to point out in his memoirs that notwithstanding Guderian's energy, fighting spirit and considerable achievements as 'creator of the armoured troops', he was not alone in understanding the potential of armour. Although there were indeed conservative elements in the German Army, the General Staff was not one of them.[54] This view contradicts conventional wisdom. Guderian, echoed by his very sympathetic biographer, had stated that Beck was one of the principal 'obstructors' of the new armoured force. Reflecting faithfully his subject's opinion, Kenneth Macksey observed pithily that Beck:

> represented the focal point of wholescale resistance by those influential members of the General Staff who remained unconvinced of the viability of the new weapons and systems – be they tanks, aircraft or the new Wehrmacht Central [Armed Forces] Staff with its challenge to the old supremacy of the General Staff. Guderian was not being unfair when he remarked, after 1945, that this type of general '... dominated the Army General Staff and pursued a personal policy which ensured that the leading General Staff positions in the Central Branch were always occupied by men of their own way of thinking.[55]

One could deduce that Manstein was typical of those being accused of being obstructive by Guderian. After the Second World War, Manstein made much of his criticisms of the Wehrmacht staff organization, but he also set out his own defence of the General Staff in relation to the development of armoured forces. Following Guderian's lead, he also credited a positive influence from the pioneering British trials and the works of Major General J. F. C. Fuller and Captain B. H. Liddell Hart. Modern historiography rightly casts some doubt on the impact of Liddell Hart's writing in Germany, as there is considerable evidence to suggest that he prompted both Guderian and Manstein after the war to highlight his own role. As we shall see later, Liddell Hart supported Manstein during his period of detention as a prisoner of war, his war crimes trial and subsequent imprisonment, and was intimately involved in the publication of the English edition of Manstein's wartime memoirs, *Lost Victories*.[56]

Returning to German developments before the Second World War, Manstein's role as head of the operations division and then First Quartermaster in the General Staff required him to explore the operational level employment of self-contained armoured corps and armies, which at that time did not exist. This experimental investigation was undertaken with the usual German thoroughness through the medium of the army staff rides in the period 1935–37, during which Manstein supported the Chief of the General Staff. Manstein acknowledged freely that Beck was inclined to pour cold water on Guderian's successes, but that 'lay in the former's nature to weigh up carefully the pros and cons rather than to take risks'.[57] Yet, as Manstein stressed, the German Army possessed at the outbreak of war in September 1939 no less than four active panzer divisions (a fifth was being improvised), four 'light' divisions and four motorized infantry divisions for operational employment.[58] Certainly, his claim that this armoured force was way ahead of all other armies is true in comparison with the Polish, French and British, but was characteristically wide of the mark if he had been minded to reflect on Soviet developments up to this date.

Meanwhile, where Guderian and Manstein did differ in approach was in the role of armour in supporting infantry formations. Based on his experience of the First World War, Manstein (and the General Staff more widely) recognized the urgent requirement to restore the offensive potential of the infantry in the face of the defensive power of the machine gun. Whilst supporting the need for the strongest affordable contribution by armoured forces, restrictions on *matériel* dictated that the mass of the German Army must remain one based primarily on infantry divisions. Further, when Beck hesitated to risk all on the new armoured formations it was at a time when the tactical value of tanks was evident, but the shock effect of their operational level employment in deep operations had yet to be demonstrated.

Manstein understood that if that potential were to be realized fully, then it made sense to improve the fighting power of the infantry in order to conduct mobile operations as well. He agreed with Guderian that it was not worthwhile (and here he diverged from Beck) forming heavy armoured brigades to accompany the infantry in attack. If they were to be established alongside the panzer corps, then Germany could only afford a very small number of them. In this regard, the German Army did not follow the British route of developing independent armoured or tank brigades to provide direct tactical support to infantry divisions.[59] For most of the Second World War, German armour remained concentrated in its panzer (and, later, the motorized panzer grenadier) divisions. Rather, the infantry divisions should contain new armoured fighting vehicles – the 'storm artillery' composed of assault guns.

If Guderian is regarded as the creator of the German armoured force, then Manstein deserves greater recognition for his role in developing the storm artillery.[60] Although designed primarily as an infantry support weapon, the same equipment was developed subsequently with the introduction of a long-barrelled high velocity gun as a highly effective source of anti-tank defence. During the First World War, once a tactical breakthrough had been achieved in the enemy's first defences, the main difficulty lay in bringing up the horse artillery across cratered terrain in sufficient time in order to sustain the attack into the depth of the enemy's position and to the break-out beyond. Manstein saw the answer to this problem in developing armoured self-propelled guns based on a tank chassis that would accompany the infantry in attack and suppress enemy machine-gun nests and local artillery. Hence if the assault gun were to become the weapon of choice to achieve the 'break-in' and 'break-through' battles, 'break-out' and exploitation were to remain the preserve of the tank.

Manstein produced a paper on storm artillery in the autumn of 1935. In so doing he faced a wall of opposition from artillery, armour and anti-tank experts alike. It did not help either that the senior leadership of the German Army at the time was composed of self-assured artillerymen. Beck, for one, declared: 'Well, my dear Manstein, this time you have shot wide of the mark.'[61] With Fritsch he was to have more luck, drawing the commander-in-chief's attention to the fact that the artillery could now resume its historical role in taking a direct part in the battle rather than just providing indirect fire. Apparently this appeal to the sense of honour of a former horse gunner convinced Fritsch, as did Manstein's suggestion that the new weapon should be manned by the artillery rather than by the infantry. So 'cap-badge' competition, often the crippling bugbear of the British Army of the time and long after, also played an important role in the German Army. Despite its pride in the professional objectivity of its General Staff, which endures today, the history of the storm artillery demonstrates that sometimes inter-arm pride and rivalry can have a paradoxically beneficial outcome.

With the support of Fritsch, the German Army pressed ahead with the research and development of the storm artillery with remarkable speed, bearing in mind the parallel demands of the new armoured troops. Manstein was well supported by the Chief of Army Procurement, General Karl Becker, who developed the first prototype based on the chassis of a Mark II armoured fighting vehicle mounted with a short 75-mm gun, the lack of a rotating turret distinguishing the 'assault gun' from a tank. Field trials of the first equipments were undertaken in the winter of 1937/38 and combined arms exercises in 1938/39.[62] By the autumn of 1937, Fritsch had signed the order for the production of sufficient assault guns based on the chassis of the Mark III tank to equip all active infantry divisions with a storm artillery detachment of three batteries of four guns initially (which was raised subsequently to six), by the autumn of 1939.[63] In addition, each of the new panzer divisions were meant to receive a detachment, and the reconnaissance detachments of the infantry, panzer, light and motorized infantry divisions a platoon of assault guns each.

These ambitious plans were never realized. As Manstein recorded bitterly after the war, after Fritsch and he had left office in early 1938, the new commander-in-chief, Colonel General von Brauchitsch, cancelled the order. It would appear that this was a 'realism' economy measure rather than reflecting any change in doctrine. The fact was that the German Army was expanding at a rate faster than the rate of procurement for heavy weaponry would allow. Thus only six assault-gun batteries were raised and trained in the first half of 1940, and only four of these independent sub-units were employed in the French campaign. They proved themselves on operations and doubts as to their value were overcome.[64] Production of assault guns increased steadily thereafter and detachments of three batteries each were established, as Manstein had foreseen four years before. These units were treated as army troops and were subordinated to a corps or division on a case by case basis.

The storm artillery – better known as either an assault gun or tank-destroyer, reflecting its double function – performed well in combat. As Manstein was able to confirm during his campaign in the Crimea, it represented a valuable and flexible weapon system. Cheaper than a tank to produce, the assault gun provided a dependable and welcome means of fire support and anti-tank defence. Hence Manstein was surely right to be proud of his role in identifying the operational requirement and making the case for it, and vehemently so. After the Second World War on his release from imprisonment, Manstein was a regular guest of honour at various military unions, not least those of the storm artillery at Karlstadt am Main.[65]

4

At the Very Centre of Power

*'My career in the General Staff... qualified me to become subsequently
Chief of the General Staff.'* Erich von Manstein[1]

Family Life in Berlin

Life in Berlin in the mid 1930s brought its own pressures and compensations. Although he was busy working in the War Ministry, Manstein appreciated the attractions of living in the capital city (*Reichshauptstadt*). As a father of three children he was keen to give his family the best possible social environment. In 1936 he bought an attractive villa in Faradayweg, near the Thielpark, in the elegant suburb of Dahlem in the south-west of the city. The house had recently belonged to Elisabeth Bergner, a famous Jewish actress who had fled to London.[2] The Mansteins had now become established, reflecting his background, position and rank. Whilst their neighbours indeed may have been 'upper class with a sprinkling of film stars and wealthy financiers',[3] they could afford to support a comfortable, but certainly not extravagant life. There were many house guests too: daughter Gisela recalls self-invited family members from the country making frequent use of the place to stop over in Berlin. 'We soon got used to that, but on one occasion, I even had to sleep in the bath!'[4]

As a major general, Manstein earned nearly 1,200 Reichsmark a month, a respectable amount, ten times the average of an industrial worker.[5] He had a batman (*Bursche*) provided by the army, and the Mansteins could afford to employ two domestic servants from Silesia, a cleaning maid and a cook. The three children were well settled in local schools. His wife Jutta-Sibylle did not have any paid employment and as an officer's, let alone a general's wife, was not expected to. This military-social norm reflected the traditional view of an army wife, whose job was to support her husband, to entertain, to bring up the family and to provide charitable support. Only in exceptional circumstances was it considered suitable that an officer's wife should work. As such, a German officer's family life differed in little respect from that common in the

American, British or French armies of the period, and for at least one generation thereafter.

Although it coincided with the National Socialist credo that a woman's place was to look after 'children, kitchen and church' (*Kinder, Küche und Kirche*), the Mansteins and thousands of other German military families would have been appalled to think that their lifestyle was mandated in such a politicized manner. Frau Manstein had become a member of the NSDAP, but her husband, as a serving officer, could not and was required to remain apolitical. She did so, according to her surviving son, 'in order to protect her husband', who was 'well known for his reticence towards the Party and the regime'.[6] Manstein made a point of not discussing contemporary military matters with the family. When the Mansteins entertained, generously but not lavishly, a suitably eclectic mix of military and civilian guests was invited; the dinner table conversation was steered towards cultural rather than political affairs.

That said, the Mansteins were typical of the majority of the German population that still saw much good in the Führer and his government at that time. Manstein declared in Hamburg in 1949 that he had hoped that National Socialism would 'succeed in bridging the gap between the working class and middle classes'.[7] After the 'revolution' of 30 January 1933 and the shock of the Röhm crisis and its bloody aftermath in the summer of 1934, two years later the expanding economy, powered by Germany's rapid rearmament and civil reconstruction, had reduced unemployment by over two million. The occupation of the Rhineland on 7 March 1936 had passed off peacefully without a shot being fired, despite the fears of the military. Germany seemed at ease with itself. With the XIth Olympic Games being held that summer in Berlin, and the need to present an acceptable face to the rest of the world, even the public humiliation and mistreatment of the Jews had been abated on Hitler's orders. The common feeling of *Volksgemeinschaft* (meaning the belonging together as a national people rather than community spirit) was genuine enough; the terrible dangers that lay ahead were far from sight and mind.

For Manstein, meanwhile, there was a mass of work to be completed in the War Ministry. His portfolio was wide, and, as deputy to Beck, he supervised the day-to-day dealings of the Army High Command. Accordingly, he had to work long hours: his younger son, Rüdiger, a 7-year-old in 1936, barely recalls seeing his father when the family lived in Berlin except on Sundays and during holidays.[8] In contrast, his daughter remembers much more of her father at the time, and felt that he regulated carefully his time in the office, leaving punctually at five o'clock so that he 'could come home for an hour's rest in the evening'.[9] From time to time, however, Manstein did have to bring his work home. In the summer of 1937, for example, he drafted a memorandum on high command during a holiday with his wife and elder son Gero, then aged 15, when staying in the Black Forest town of Freudenstadt. That said, although his career took priority, Manstein divided carefully duty and home-life, finding relaxation in his various hobbies: classical music (particularly Mozart), architecture and history, foreign languages and gardening. As Gisela Lingenthal recalls, 'Father never talked about his job. That was taboo.'[10]

Further Foreign Travels

Manstein's duty commitments were not confined to Berlin or visiting headquarters and exercises throughout Germany. Following the pattern of Reichswehr visits that he had participated in some years before, Manstein undertook a series of trips abroad representing the Army High Command and General Staff. As on previous occasions, he had many fond memories of these foreign sojourns that gave him an opportunity to gauge the military value of potential allies and to learn something of their life and culture.

In August 1936, for example, Manstein was a guest of the Italian Army at the royal manoeuvres held in the vicinity of Naples. Mussolini himself took part, and greeted his international guests on the first day, and King Victor Emmanuel joined on the second. Manstein recorded his astonishment at the bizarre manner in the way the exercise developed, during which *Il Duce* called on various contingents to sing and interrupted the military activities with various, some apparently unscheduled, visits, including to a monastery, to a sports event and even to the theatre. Of the manoeuvres themselves, Manstein felt that they had 'nothing in particular to offer'. Whereas he conceded that the convoy discipline of the motorized troops was good, as were the camouflage measures, the tactical training on show 'did not match the German standard' and the Italian tanks he saw had 'neither sufficient armour nor armament'.[11] There was no opportunity, moreover, to view the development and dissemination of orders within or between headquarters, which to an expert trainer such as Manstein would have given him a clue as to the efficiency of the Italian Army's system of command. On conclusion of the manoeuvres, after a splendidly pompous parade in the presence of the King, there was time for some rest and recuperation. Manstein managed to visit Capri, climb Vesuvius, inspect the ruins of Pompeii, bathe on the beach at Ischia and take a short stay in Rome, which he had last visited as a young lieutenant before the First World War: not bad for government work. Yet an impoverished Manstein complained that he had hardly enough cash in hand to pay a tip because of German currency controls.

He recorded his impressions of his time in Italy. Albeit written over twenty years later, and with the usual benefit of hindsight, his comparison of the relationship of the military to the fascist regimes in Italy and Germany, and his estimate of Mussolini's character, remain of historical note. Manstein observed that Italian officers, even senior ones, 'lived in fear of Mussolini' and did 'everything to avoid his disapproval'.[12] However, his claim that he could not recall any circumstance of such overzealousness by German officers in the presence of Hitler, excepting a few in his most intimate circle who were fully submissive intellectually, rings a little hollow. In this respect, perhaps Manstein made the honourable mistake of assuming that his uncompromising attitude to the Führer was typical. His observations of Mussolini, however, surely captured the man. The *Duce* had a dominating personality and possessed great style. He understood how to adjust his manner masterfully to the occasion at hand, 'able to present himself sometimes as dictator and at other times as a kind host or good chap'. In comparison with Hitler, Mussolini appeared more human. Yet Manstein could not prevent himself from remarking that the Italian leader:

> ... wanted to bring up his people, despite their poverty and zest for life, in the manner of the ancient Romans, and to build a new Roman Empire. But, unlike Hitler increasingly, he did not associate the destiny of his people with himself. Mussolini overestimated the powers of his people, but he never abused the trust and heroism of his people in the manner of Hitler. Attributes, that said, which are not as strongly evident as they are with us Germans.[13]

Manstein summed up bluntly what many Germans would have thought at the time. In contrast with field marshals Kesselring and Rommel, however, he had little to do with the Italian armed forces during the Second World War, save witnessing the collapse of its Eighth Army in early 1943 on the Eastern Front.

During the following year (1937), Manstein attended the autumn manoeuvres of the Hungarian and Bulgarian armies. In Hungary, General von Schwedler, the Chief of the German Army Personnel Office,[14] and he were hosted very well, as were their fellow Italian and Austrian guests. Manstein was greatly impressed by the professionalism

of the Hungarian troops and recorded that their officer corps displayed –
more evidently so than in other armies – 'a chivalrous view of soldiering',
and one in which 'we grew up and safeguarded from the royal [Prussian]
army to bring into the present time'. Two prominent Hungarians took
part in the exercise: Field Marshal Grand Duke Joseph and the Regent,
Admiral Horthy. Manstein was entertained by the latter in his castle in
Budapest. 'Who would have thought', Manstein later remarked, that
Horthy would 'become [my] daily bridge partner in the witnesses' prison
at Nuremberg' in 1946.[15] No doubt the two aristocrats played many a
chivalrous game together. Whether they reflected on the fates of their
two countries, and on the reasons for their meeting in such strained
circumstances, remains unknown. Such are the ironies of war.

Manstein's account of his trip to Bulgaria contains much fascinating
detail of military and geographical interest but sheds little additional
light on understanding what made him tick or the military potential of
that country. When he returned to Berlin he had little clue that his time
serving as 'Number 2' in the German High Command and General Staff
was drawing to a close. Whilst he had buried himself in his work, whether
it be writing operational studies or dealing with questions of command
and control, he had made himself unpopular with some elements in
Berlin over the last couple of years. He was no friend of the newly
established Wehrmacht staff. Manstein was to be dismissed from post in
February 1938, along with many others in one of Hitler's biggest purges
of the generals. In the meantime, the two issues in which he had differed
from the Wehrmacht High Command (and through it, indirectly with
Hitler) – how to expand the army in peacetime and how to regulate the
command of Germany's armed forces in war – were coming to a head.
Manstein, ever outspoken, had developed his own, very clear, ideas as
to how Germany's armed forces should be developed. His undoubted
professional expertise in this area was to be reaffirmed twenty years
later when he became a specialist military advisor to the West German
government.

Expanding the Army

From the very start of Germany's military expansion, which Manstein
took as the introduction of general conscription, there was a fundamental
difference in approach between Hitler and the Army High Command.
Hitler, to use a modern idiom, was concerned primarily with impressing
on the world Germany's new strength in the 'shop window' for political
purposes. Thus he was interested, as Manstein recounted, in a rapid

expansion 'of the numbers of soldiers and in the number of divisions' and in demonstrating 'the modernity of their armament'.[16] In this narrow regard, Hitler differed little from Churchill, who was often frustrated by the inability of the British Army in the Second World War to generate, train, deploy and sustain a sufficiently large field force.[17] Although Manstein conceded after the war that Hitler had offensive plans from the very beginning, he held that they were long kept secret from the army. Thus a big question arises: at what stage should the German senior military leadership have deduced the real nature and purpose of Hitler's plans? One of the central charges laid against the German High Command at Nuremberg, at which Manstein became one of the principal defence witnesses, rested on this matter. It is hardly surprising, then, that his memoirs of the period before the Second World War reflect his earlier explanations of the differences between Hitler and the Army High Command. His aim throughout was to implicate the former and to exonerate the latter.

Manstein represented the Army High Command view that it was self-evident that the army had to have an offensive capability, but only in the context of conducting a defensive war. Further, as one might expect, Manstein stressed that the command wanted to 'do solid work'. Specifically, 'the morale, education and training of the troops were more important than numbers alone'.[18] In other words, to use a modern doctrinal approach, the expansion of an army should have a firm base, reflecting not only the tangible physical, but also the intangible moral and the conceptual components of fighting power. Yet for all Hitler's close interest in modern weaponry, Manstein was at pains to point out that with the notable exception of the tracked assault gun, all the major items in the army's equipment programme were already in development before the Führer came to power. Manstein criticized Hitler for not recognizing the potential of rocketry and for blocking its development for years, but did not state the consequences. In any case, it remains doubtful whether the V-weapons (*Vergeltungswaffen*) such as the V2 rocket, could have been introduced any earlier, such were the scientific and technological challenges to be overcome.

When reflecting on the conduct of operations during the war, Manstein's comments on the sustainability of the army in terms of providing sufficient stocks of munitions and holding appropriate reserves of trained personnel seem well justified. In comparison with the Western Allies, in particular, the German Army was not so well provided for logistically. According to Manstein, Hitler did not take the General Staff's requirements in this area seriously. The proof of the pudding was the crisis following the first few months of campaigning in Russia, when ammunition stocks of the principal artillery piece, the light howitzer, ran very short. Even the ammunition supply for the infantry failed, a state of affairs 'that had never come about during the First World War'.[19] Manstein failed to point out that the demand for ammunition is a function of the intensity of combat. That stocks ran low during the attack on the Soviet Union had many other contributory factors, not least the difficulty of bringing forward supplies over extended, exposed and difficult lines of communication.

All in all, Manstein maintained that a balanced expansion of the German Army would have taken until 1942 to complete, and that was the opinion of the high command before the war. Even then it would have been able to fight only a 'defensive war', the nature of which Manstein omitted to expand on. As revealed in the infamous Hossbach Memorandum, in which Hitler's principal adjutant, Colonel Friedrich Hossbach, recorded a secret session of the Führer with his foreign minister (Konstantin Freiherr von Neurath) and senior military advisors (Blomberg together with the heads of the armed services) on 5 November 1937, Hitler had conceded that the Wehrmacht would not be fully ready for war until 1943–45. But he was frustrated by the negative attitude of his generals none the less. It was at this meeting that Hitler set out unequivocally his expansionist policies, including the need to use force in order to create sufficient *Lebensraum* (living space) for the German people, and his attitude towards Austria and Czechoslovakia.[20]

Manstein saw the difference of views between Hitler and the Army General Staff as a continuing and worsening cause of friction, to which the establishment of the intermediary staff OKW only added. Writing after the war, he felt that the cautionary, if not apprehensive, view of Beck and the General Staff was neither contradicted by the stunning victory in Poland nor by the rapid defeat of France. Specifically:

> The successes in Poland were only possible because the Western Allies for quite incomprehensible reasons did not exploit the opportunity that was then open to them. One could not imagine before the war that the French Army command would prove so helpless in the face of the German offensive in the West, and that the resistance of France would collapse so quickly.[21]

Manstein might have added that the triumphs in Poland and France led to the fateful overestimation of German capabilities in attacking the Soviet Union, where the lack of *matériel* and personnel resources (ammunition, fuel, equipment and manpower) became a critical constraint on the German Army's operations. Yet Hitler was not alone in his hubristic assessment of the Wehrmacht's capabilities: after the fall of France in June 1940 it was endemic within the German High Command.

Meanwhile, back in 1935–39, the army was growing apace, and at a rate that disturbed Beck in particular, who argued for a more gradual expansion. Apart from the many organizational challenges, including the difficulties in providing the necessary trained manpower, equipment and infrastructure, he saw a distinct risk of Germany (or rather Hitler) provoking war with its new-found military strength. Although plans for increasing the size of the army had predated Hitler's coming to power in 1933, they had rested on building up the force progressively to achieve the long-standing target of twenty-one divisions in *war*. The distinction between the organization and strength of a peacetime army (*Friedensheer*) and that of wartime (*Kriegsheer*) was important. In December 1933, the decision had been taken to create a peacetime army of twenty-one divisions within four years, but Hitler demanded that this be brought forward to one year (in other words by the end of 1934), which Fritsch and Beck managed to delay until the autumn of 1935. This modified plan was overtaken by events. When Hitler declared his intention out of the blue in March 1935 that Germany would possess an army of thirty-six divisions grouped in twelve army corps, it had been based on a study by the *Truppenamt* that a wartime army of sixty-three to seventy-three divisions would need thirty to thirty-six divisions in peace. Again, there was a difference in view as to how quickly these targets could be achieved. The Army High Command was thinking in terms of 1941 at the earliest, not least because of the time it would take, within the 36-division total, to complete the partial mechanization of the army, which required the raising of the new panzer and motorized infantry divisions and the establishment of the necessary corps and army troops.

For all Hitler's pressure, the peacetime strength (520,000) of the 36-division army in October 1936 was still short of nearly 100,000 men of its establishment.[22] It was none the less an impressive achievement: the army had grown more than fivefold in less than four years and preparations had been made for creating a much bigger field force in war.[23] As new demands came, old schemes had to be either thrown away or modified extensively; fully revised structures and basing plans had to be drawn up. Manstein was at the very centre of this detailed staff work, and, largely unrecorded by history, his talents helped create the army that Hitler was later to employ and abuse. Simply put, the foundation of much of the German Army's early successes in the Second World War

lay in Manstein's organizational genius as much as in the operational
ideas he later brought to bear, and for which he is much more readily
remembered.

Questions of High Command

Apart from the expansion of the army, one of the matters that agitated
Beck and Manstein the most during the period 1936–38 was the question
of the high command of Germany's armed forces in peace and war. The
establishment of the Armed Forces Office (*Wehrmachtamt*) in 1935 had
begun to undermine the authority of the Army High Command,
although at this stage the army commander-in-chief (Fritsch) and the
Reichswehr minister and commander-in-chief of the armed forces
(Blomberg) worked harmoniously together. The new Luftwaffe under
Göring became a competitor for attention and resources, and pursued
its own agenda of rapid development, stressing throughout loyalty to
Hitler. But the main object of Manstein's unease, building on similar
concerns expressed previously by Beck, was how high command in war
would be exercised. His focused presentation and stalwart defence of a
single service point of view has some echoes today in the American,
British and German armed forces, which, with various degrees of success,
have had to overcome the services' prejudice and adopt 'joint' structures
at the military strategic and operational levels of command.

Manstein's paper, 'Organization of the Command of the Wehrmacht',
written in the summer of 1937, was designed to inform the Chief of
the General Staff (Beck) and the commander-in-chief (Fritsch) in their
discussions with Hitler, Blomberg and the central Wehrmacht staff.[24]
His main thesis was that if Germany, a continental power, were bound
to conduct war primarily on land, then the army, as the principal armed
service, should be responsible primarily for the planning and execution
of operations. Thus it made compelling sense to the author that the
army's commander-in-chief should chair a supreme military council
(*Oberster Kriegsrat*) that would provide the necessary strategic direction
and guidance to the armed forces. Such a body would also have an
important co-ordinating function between the Services, without delving
into the detail of each. Specifically, the [joint] Reich Chief of the
General Staff would be the 'advisor to the Commander-in-Chief of the
Wehrmacht [the Führer] for the command of the armed forces in war....
To ensure the unity of the strategic direction of war and the command
of the army, the Reich Chief of General Staff would be at the same time
the commander-in-chief of the army.'[25]

A supporting consideration that informed the formulation of the paper, which Manstein reflected in his memoirs, was that it was not possible under the conditions of modern war for one man or one office to undertake two functions at the same time: first, military *command* in war (the drawing up and execution of strategic and operational plans); and, secondly, the *organization* of the nation for war.[26] What Manstein meant in the latter role was the strategic requirement to identify, organize and employ sufficient personnel and *matériel* in order to achieve the nation's war objectives. This area of activity, resourcing the armed forces, according to Manstein, should be the job of a defence minister, and that there should be a clear division of responsibility between him and the Reich Chief of the General Staff, who would be responsible for strategic and operational planning. Manstein acknowledged that there would be a potential for conflict between the two (with the minister providing the *means* and the chief determining the *ways* of war) that could only be resolved by the nation's political leader directing, confirming or adjusting the strategic *ends* in order to reflect the political or economic factors at play.

Personalities impinged as much on policies in Hitler's Germany as they do on modern states today. Manstein noted after the war that the Army High Command viewed Blomberg as 'hardly the man ... who would stand up to Hitler with sufficient determination'.[27] Further, in his view, he was not a strong enough character to guarantee a co-ordinated approach to the command of the three armed Services, and in particular, to impose his will on Göring, who did largely as he pleased. In addition, there were doctrinal differences emerging between the German Army and the Luftwaffe. In the mid 1930s, the German Air Force was pursuing a strategy of 'operational air war' (*operativer Luftkrieg*) in which once air superiority had been achieved, air power should be directed at attacking the war potential of an enemy and the morale of its people. As Manstein later remarked, this was exactly the unsuccessful strategy that the British–American air forces followed until well into 1944. The Army High Command believed that victory would only result from the defeat of the enemy's armed forces by joint action between all components of the Wehrmacht, and this should be the first step in the successful conclusion of a war, a typically Clausewitzian viewpoint.

Manstein's principal opponent in advancing his case was an army officer: General of Artillery Wilhelm Keitel, chief of the Armed Forces Office. Rather than supporting the army's position, he advised Blomberg to strengthen the competence and power of the joint Wehrmacht as opposed to the Army General Staff. Hitler was inclined to do this in any case as he was frustrated by what he perceived as the timidity of the army's senior leadership and its old-fashioned way of thinking. The opportunity to transform Keitel's office into the German Armed Forces High Command (*Oberkommando der Wehrmacht* (OKW)) came in February 1938 with the removal of Blomberg and Fritsch. For all his criticism of that command, Manstein enjoyed a good working relationship with [Colonel] Alfred Jodl, head of the Armed Forces Operations Staff. Manstein recalls him observing: 'The big problem is that the stronger personalities are in OKH. If Fritsch, Beck and you were in OKW, you would think otherwise.'[28]

Writing the paper in 1937 also gave Manstein good cause to reflect on the competencies required in high command, as opposed to a senior position on the staff, which he would have to demonstrate himself within the following five years. It remains instructive to observe Manstein's thinking after the war on this matter, with the personality of Blomberg in mind. Manstein wrote:

> For a commander, understanding, knowledge and experience are essential prerequisites. Deficiencies in these qualities can to some extent be made good by a chief of staff, provided the commander is willing to follow his advice. More importantly, the commander must possess character and a human soul. These qualities alone bring him the resolution to withstand the inevitable crises in war. In addition to professional ability, they provide the basis for daring decisions in difficult situations. Finally, the confidence of troops that the commander leads is based primarily on the steadfastness of his character.

By Manstein's analysis, Blomberg would not pass this test of high command. On numerous occasions, he had failed to demonstrate sufficient moral courage in standing up to Hitler. Yet his dismissal would leave the German armed forces, and the army in particular, in an even worse position, as the events of early 1938 would confirm.

In retrospect, Manstein's 'high command' paper was doomed from the outset by a combination of personal and institutional inter-service opposition. The heads of the air force and navy (Göring and Raeder respectively) were set dead against it, as was Keitel. Above all, Hitler saw it as an 'army' attack against his authority. On 13 June 1938 in the wake of the Sudeten crisis, the Führer decided on a top-level command structure that made the OKW a joint staff, but its 'chief' in the person of Keitel was given neither the authority of a commander-in-chief nor of a chief of staff. Its planning and co-ordinating authority over the

German armed services was limited. As a result, OKW never became a 'joint general staff' of the Reich that its title might suggest. In so doing, Hitler created the conditions for the chaotic command set-up that plagued the planning and conduct of operations during the Second World War.[29]

The Blomberg–Fritsch Crisis

1938 brought a totally unexpected change to the command structure of Germany's armed forces and to Manstein's career. The New Year had started in a routine enough fashion. Manstein spent the last week of January representing the Army High Command at a war game of the military district headquarters in Königsberg (now Kaliningrad) in East Prussia. Colonel General Gerd von Rundstedt, then commander of Group 1 (an army group equivalent), under whose command the military district lay, was the senior officer present. On the conclusion of the exercise, Manstein accompanied Rundstedt on the train journey back from Königsberg to Berlin, a mutually convenient and simple courtesy. For Manstein, however, the drama began to unfold when Rundstedt confided suddenly that Beck had summoned him to return to Berlin as a 'matter of urgency', but had given no further details. Rundstedt went on to say that he suspected that the business had something to do with War Minister Field Marshal Werner von Blomberg's very recent marriage but could not offer any further explanation.

The mystery deepened when the two generals arrived at Berlin's Friedrichstrasse station on the morning of 31 January and were met by Beck personally. Beck and Rundstedt departed promptly by staff car, leaving the trusty Manstein standing behind. Back in the War Ministry the next morning on 1 February, Beck apologized for his odd behaviour and explained there was a nasty intrigue running concerning Blomberg and Fritsch, but could not say anything more at this stage, having been pledged to secrecy. Manstein, for the moment, was still left very much in the dark.[30]

As the first days of February unfolded, however, Manstein became a close but not intimate witness to the sensational crisis that developed, a scandal that shook Germany, the Wehrmacht and the German Army. Within a week, both Blomberg and Fritsch had been disgraced and forced to resign. In addition to the removal of both principals, many other generals were either retired or transferred, Manstein included, in a grand reshuffle of military and political appointments that also embraced the dismissal of von Neurath.[31]

Blomberg, a widower aged 60, had become infatuated with a typist in the War Ministry, a certain Fräulein Erna Gruhn, less than half his age. He had served the Führer well during the previous five years, believing his main task lay in drawing the Wehrmacht into National Socialism. His loyalty to the regime had been amply demonstrated during the Röhm crisis in the summer of 1934 when he had failed, as Manstein noted critically, to intervene on behalf of Generals von Schleicher and von Below during that affair. The Führer had rewarded Blomberg's fealty with promotion to field marshal in 1936 and the award of the NSDAP gold medal in the same year. He had remained a safe pair of hands until his quite unexpected and seemingly totally out-of-character love affair. Suspecting nothing untoward, Hitler and Göring blessed the union personally by appearing as witnesses at the War Minister's civil marriage ceremony on 12 January 1938.

Unfortunately, it turned out shortly afterwards that Blomberg's new wife not only came from humble origins but, far more shockingly, was also of dubious virtue. The seedy revelations that she was a former prostitute and now pregnant, brought dishonour to the German Army and its officer corps; more crucially, it disappointed and embarrassed Hitler personally. It did not help matters that Gruhn's former colleagues spilled the beans in the press, and no honourable German officer could bring himself to address her as 'Frau Feldmarschall'. Blomberg had no leg left to stand on as he had broken his own Wehrmacht regulation concerning marriage, which required expressly that 'the bride should have a stainless reputation, should be upright and loyal to the state, and belong to a respectable and loyal family'.[32] Whether Heinrich Himmler or his equally objectionable subordinate, Reinhard Heydrich, had failed deliberately to warn Hitler of the risks entailed in Blomberg's class-cutting relationship with a 'girl of the people' remains unproven, as does whether there was indeed a long-standing and carefully orchestrated conspiracy to remove both him and Fritsch. Yet it was rather odd, as Manstein observed, that in what had become a police state the record of a woman such as Gruhn had not been brought to light.[33] Not for nothing, one might add, was the German euphemism for a lady of the night a 'woman under police supervision', a standing task of the *Sittenpolizei* (moral police or vice squad).

The fact remains that when Blomberg resigned on 27 January 1938, it left Hitler with somewhat of a quandary as to finding a suitable successor. The position was both political and military, combining a ministerial appointment with command of Germany's armed forces. Hitler did not want an ambitious political crony such as Göring, also commander-in-chief of the Luftwaffe, who had his covetous eye on the post, occupying such an important office of state or position of supreme command. Nor did he want an assertive and authoritative soldier such as Fritsch, Blomberg's widely supposed natural successor, who enjoyed the respect and loyalty of the German Army. According to Manstein, there was never much trust or mutual confidence in any case between Hitler and Fritsch. Whether Fritsch's concerns over Hitler's foreign policy, as alluded to in the Hossbach Memorandum of the previous November (about which Manstein denied any knowledge until after the war), played a dominant role in his downfall remains doubtful. Pre-calculated move or not, ever the opportunist, Hitler seized the moment to appoint himself as commander-in-chief of the Wehrmacht and chose Keitel to become his chief of staff, or, more precisely, Chief of the German Armed Forces High Command (*Oberkommando der Wehrmacht* (OKW)). Keitel was a protégé and colleague of Blomberg, who had appointed him to be head of the Armed Forces Office of the War Ministry on 1 October 1935. A more recent family connection existed through the engagement of Blomberg's youngest daughter Dorle (short for Dorothee) to Keitel's eldest son Karl-Heinz in January 1938.[34]

The manner in which Hitler selected Keitel tells it all. Blomberg recalled the scene to his up-and-coming subordinate Walter Warlimont, who became deputy chief of the OKW operations staff under Alfred Jodl. According to Warlimont's record, having failed to receive a nomination for the chief of OKW staff, Hitler asked Blomberg: 'What's the name of that general who's been in your office up to now?' The latter replied, 'Oh, Keitel; there's no question of him; he's nothing but the man who runs my office.' Seizing on this straight away Hitler said at once: 'That's exactly the man I'm looking for.'[35]

Although Keitel paid with his life at Nuremberg on 16 October 1946, he was never a commander or war leader in his own right and was condemned from his first day in office to perform the role of a willing manager and chief scribe of the Führer's business. So loyal to his master did Keitel become that he was nicknamed 'Lackeitel', an irreverent play on his surname and *Lakei*, the German word for 'lackey'. This demeaning description, however, belies Keitel's impressive administrative and organizing skills. Although Keitel remained in post until the downfall of the Third Reich, surviving Hitler's increasing animosity and disdain, he never gained the respect of the high commands of the German Navy, Army or Air Force. In his own words, 'as Chief of Staff under Hitler, one had a position which was impossible.... Really I was Chief of Staff without responsibility and without knowing what Hitler really wanted, and without being told by him.'[36]

Manstein had little time either for Keitel or his office, noting after the war, that: 'From its very inception Hitler had relegated OKW to the status of a military secretariat. In any case, its chief, Keitel, would not have been in the least capable of advising Hitler on strategy.'[37] Indeed, Manstein showed no sympathy for someone who conducted so much of Hitler's dirty work. Their mutual antipathy was long-standing in any case. As staff officers serving together in the *Truppenamt* in the early 1930s, they had had serious professional differences over mobilization plans. Manstein had proven then that he was an equally capable general staff officer, if not Keitel's intellectual superior. So was it a bitter and envious Keitel who had schemed together with Göring to force Hitler to dismiss Manstein in March 1944? Perhaps this was not so in Keitel's case. In his memoirs written shortly before his death, Keitel stressed that he attempted on no less than three occasions to convince Hitler to appoint Manstein as commander-in-chief of the army, 'first of all in the autumn of 1939 before the campaign in the West; secondly in December 1941 as Brauchitsch departed; and for the third time in September 1942 when Jodl and I came into conflict'.[38] The fact remains that not only Manstein but also history as a whole has been unkind to Keitel, who perhaps deserved a better fate than the hangman's rope at Nuremberg.

Meanwhile, Fritsch was the innocent victim of an insidious plot. Falsely accused of being a homosexual, and against all protestations to the contrary on his word as an officer and gentleman, on 3 February 1938 he was forced to resign. Although his complete lack of guilt was confirmed in a subsequent military court of honour chaired by Göring, he was not reinstated as commander-in-chief of the army. By this time, his removal remained convenient to Hitler as his more compliant successor, General Walther von Brauchitsch, was already in office. As a token measure of rehabilitation, Fritsch was appointed *Chef* (honorary colonel) of the 12th Artillery Regiment. He retired quietly to rural life on the Lüneburg Heath, occupying a spacious country house, Achterberg, south-west of Dorfmark, where he had enjoyed many a pleasant leave whilst still serving.[39] Attempts by Beck and Brauchitsch to gain a complete and public exoneration of Fritsch during 1938 came to naught. Fritsch joined his regiment at the outbreak of the Second World War, accompanied it to Poland and fell in action on 22 September 1939 outside Warsaw. By a curious irony, Manstein, who always admired Fritsch, sought refuge in Achterberg towards the war's end in 1945.

Returning to the early afternoon of 4 February 1938, Manstein was summoned along with other senior officers to the Chancellery to hear Hitler's explanation of his actions over Blomberg and Fritsch. As usual, the Führer gave a cleverly constructed and lengthy discourse of self-justification, which Manstein described in surprising detail.[40] Although we should treat Manstein's retrospective account written twenty years after the event with some caution, it none the less serves to illustrate the moral dilemma in which he and his colleagues sat at the time. Hitler articulated his concerns about the impact of the double affair on Germany's reputation, painting himself as the principal victim. As Manstein noted bitterly about Blomberg's fall from grace:

> None of those present could escape the impression that Hitler's deep disappointment, which he had suffered through the behaviour of the former commander-in-chief of the Wehrmacht, whom he had promoted to field marshal, was genuine, and that his indignation was justified. In particular, we army generals had to accept that the failure of the highest-ranking member of the officer corps was a stigma that now tainted us. What a feeling of humiliation that the politician Hitler could now appear as the guardian of the Wehrmacht's honour.[41]

On top of all this came the scandalous accusation against Fritsch. Manstein was convinced that none of the admirals or generals present believed one word of it. Those who knew him, described him as a 'gentleman through and through'. Manstein, the junior general present, was so incensed by Hitler's description of the case that he felt moved to challenge the Führer and shout out that it was all one big, infamous lie. But a dramatic exchange between the two, on this occasion, did not come about. Manstein justified his inaction as the 'triumph of convention and common sense over the instinct which I should have followed'. He, like many others, felt lamed by the Blomberg case. Further, as he declared, 'it was not a lack of moral courage, as is so often claimed, that kept our mouths shut at that moment. Rather, it demonstrated the defencelessness of honourable people in the face of a piece of nastiness that lay well beyond our powers of imagination.'[42] Keitel, however, recalled distinctly that Manstein made the sole intervention, 'asking whether a "Chief of the General Staff of the Wehrmacht" could be created, to which Hitler instantly responded, "The way would be open at the appropriate time"'.[43]

Whatever the truth of this event, Hitler, according to some historians, was expecting some opposition or at least a request for clarification from the generals on 4 February. The fact that there was none apart from Manstein's confirmed the triumph of the dictator, 'who had out-manoeuvred, defeated, humiliated and dragooned the German Army'.[44]

There were much worse indignities to come, and many more of them.

The German public was first made aware of Hitler's decisions through a special radio announcement made in the late evening of 4 February 1938; the written text was published the next day.[45] Manstein already knew his fate before Hitler announced the purge of senior posts. He recalls being informed by Beck either the afternoon before or during the morning of 4 February about the principal moves that affected the army.[46] Beck told Manstein that he was being replaced by his colleague General Franz Halder and that his future appointment would be commander of the 18th Infantry Division in Liegnitz. Beck assured Manstein that he had absolutely nothing to do with this development and that he had not even been consulted. So why was Manstein being moved on in such a manner? Although he was liable for a command posting in due course, he had not yet completed his tour as First Quartermaster and deputy to the Chief of the General Staff. Manstein believed that Hitler, who hardly knew him, was not the instigator. But both Blomberg and Keitel knew Manstein not only as a loyal assistant of Fritsch and Beck, but also as a robust champion of OKH's claim to command operations in war over that of OKW's. In other words, he was, and not for the last time, proving an awkward subordinate, whose presence was becoming uncomfortable to the chain of command.

According to Manstein, his suspicions were confirmed by Keitel's own actions several days later. Apparently, Beck had summoned Keitel to his office and asked for an explanation as to why Manstein was being posted without prior consultation. An argument must have ensued for Beck showed him the door (literally) and in his haste to make a safe exit, Keitel left a note in the Chief of the General Staff's office, on which all the personnel changes were listed. Not only was Manstein's name on it, but also Beck's! Against the latter's name was placed a question mark and a note: 'Future Group Commander, successor Halder'.[47] This was a remarkably prescient forecast of future events: when Beck resigned in August that year over the Sudeten crisis, he was indeed replaced by Halder as chief. Beck had the notable honour of being the only German general who resigned voluntarily from Hitler's National Socialist regime.

Manstein felt with some justification that he was an unlucky victim of circumstance. As much as he looked forward to divisional command, he regretted the 'painful separation from my highly respected superiors and mentors, Colonel General Baron von Fritsch and General Beck.'[48] Further, it appeared that he would have to abandon the general staff career stream. As only a traditional Prussian general staff officer such as Manstein could feel, he was bitter that the possibility of assuming the famous position that Moltke, Schlieffen and Beck had held was now extinguished.[49] Yet it is difficult to feel unduly sympathetic to Manstein's sense of pathos at this stage of his career. He went on to thrive at command as opposed to general staff positions at every level from division to army group, and in any case was overdue a return to duty with troops. Having not commanded a regiment, it was high time that he got 'back to the front' as a divisional commander. More fundamentally, experience at formation command did not necessarily exclude future employment as Chief of the General Staff. Far from it, it would also increase Manstein's future employability.

Manstein's family viewed the impending move to Liegnitz and Silesia with mixed feelings. Although sad to be leaving their smart house in Berlin, Jutta-Sibylle looked forward, for the first time in her married life, to living in her home province of Silesia and seeing more of her wider family. It was she, according to daughter Gisela, who tried to cheer up her husband with a description of what Liegnitz had to offer. Referring to the Baedeker guide, she read out: 'Liegnitz, dormitory town at the foot of the *Riesengebirge*, a mountain range on the German/Czech border' – pausing dramatically – 'not worth a stop.' Manstein replied sadly: 'You see, I told you so.' Her deeply depressed father, according to Gisela Lingenthal, 'swore never to go back to the Ministry, and in fact never to return to Berlin at all.'[50]

In the event, Manstein was not able to assume his new appointment in Liegnitz at the end of February 1938 because an international crisis required him to remain temporarily at his post in the War Ministry. Hitler had decided that the time was now ripe for his desired union with Austria and was manufacturing the conditions for it. The *Anschluss* was to prove one of the Führer's greatest political triumphs: the military intervention, in which Manstein had the major role in the planning, turned out to be another of Hitler's bloodless wars of flowers (*Blumenkriege*).

Union with Austria

With a heavy heart, Manstein handed over his post as First Quartermaster to General of Artillery Franz Halder, who had just been promoted from lieutenant general. The disparity in rank between the two must have rubbed salt into the wound of his dismissal as he would have to wait until 1 April 1938 before his promotion to lieutenant general. Manstein's departure led to a rather odd situation. Whereas he had given Halder the key to his office safe, said a curt '*Auf Wiedersehen*' and promptly walked out, the Chief of the General Staff then insisted that he should continue working in the OKH for a transitional period. Beck wanted him to remain at his side in order to brief the new army commander-in-chief, Colonel General Walther von Brauchitsch, on deployment plans, the expansion of the army, the construction of border defences and, notwithstanding the aftermath of Blomberg and Fritsch, on matters of high command. This arrangement, of course, made some sense, as Manstein represented the 'corporate memory' and it allowed Halder to be party to these discussions as well.

Manstein was still stuck in Berlin when Beck, deputizing for an absent Brauchitsch, was summoned by Hitler to appear in the Chancellery at eleven o'clock on the morning of Monday, 7 March 1938. The object of concern appeared to be Austria. Beck decided to take Manstein with him (Halder's whereabouts that day are not recorded) for this rare meeting with the Führer, who received them cordially, together with Keitel, fresh in his new post. Manstein recalled that Hitler felt compelled to deal with Austria on the matter of union with Germany immediately and to act before the plebiscite of the Austrian people, due on 13 March, took place. Hitler considered that the Austrian Federal Chancellor, Schuschnigg, had been bounced into agreeing the vote; any result would not necessarily be a 'fair' reflection of popular wishes. The Führer believed that the Austrian people would welcome German intervention and considered the risks of any involvement by other foreign powers to be negligible, with the possible exception of Italy. Whilst Hitler's objective in pre-empting a democratic vote might not have gone his own way, Manstein professed in his memoirs to be thoroughly convinced by the Führer's analysis, which was borne out by subsequent events. Manstein noted that this meeting represented the first occasion on which he had met Hitler, speaking as a 'sober politician' as opposed to a populist speaker. In such a small circle, perhaps Manstein, like so many others before and after him, had come under his seductive spell momentarily.[51]

After his summing up of the geopolitical situation, Hitler asked for an estimation of the forces required for an invasion of Austria, adding that, under all circumstances, it must take place in the early hours of Saturday, 12 March 1938. Many a senior officer's breath would have been taken away by the enormity of the decision, the attendant risks involved and, above all, by the pressure of time to plan and conduct such a major operation. That morning, Hitler was doubly fortunate in dealing with the two best operational brains of the German Army. After a short discussion with Manstein, Beck replied on the spot with the following recommendation. Assuming that neither the Austrian Army nor the population would oppose the invasion, sufficient forces would be required in order to deter any moves by either the Czechs or Italians. A weak, symbolic German force might encourage them to participate or to impose conditions on Germany. Beck then recommended that the two Bavarian infantry corps (VII and XIII), together with the 2nd Panzer Division, should be grouped together under a provisional army headquarters for the mission. Hitler agreed this advice, directing later that his regimental-sized personal bodyguard, the SS *Leibstandarte Adolf Hitler*, should take part, together with an armoured corps headquarters.

The difficult part of the discussion came in convincing Hitler of the need to give the army sufficient warning time. Few politicians have any real understanding of the practical implications of alerting, mobilizing, preparing and deploying troops, let alone their employment. It is a senior officer's duty to explain implacably the force requirements to achieve the mission and to insist on a timely political decision, a contentious matter that remains highly relevant today. On this occasion Hitler proved no exception to the rule and had to be persuaded that even a partial mobilization, with all the political risks involved, had to be carried out to ensure that sufficient troops would be ready at the right place and time. Hitler was not convinced when Beck added that the mobilization order would need to be issued by 16.00 hours that very afternoon.[52]

Beck and Manstein returned straight away to the War Ministry in the Bendlerstrasse. There was not a second to waste in the drafting of the mobilization and deployment order. Unfortunately, there was little contingency planning for this eventuality to fall back on, save an incomplete and untested staff study, 'Case Otto', which presumably had inspired Beck's and Manstein's considerations with Hitler. Therefore, all the necessary detail had to be thought through afresh under enormous time pressure. Astonishingly, Manstein and his colleagues completed the order in time. Hitler's confirmation, however, was required before the signal message could be issued via the German Army's highly efficient teleprinter system. Recognizing the urgency of the matter, Hitler did not dilly-dally on this occasion, as he was to do many times subsequently, greatly to the frustration of Manstein and other senior commanders during the Second World War. To the relief of Beck and Manstein, and all the mobilization planners, the Führer's approval was received at 16.30 hours, still just in time to issue the deployment order.

The operation went off smoothly with some minor glitches in the warning of the divisions concerned, and some much more embarrassing breakdowns affecting the armoured troops on their march to Vienna.

According to Manstein, the German Army learned a lot from the part-mobilization and deployment into Austria. Problems in command and logistic support were put right in time for Hitler's next foreign excursion into the Sudetenland that summer. Few other armies in the world at that time or since would have been in a position to improvise and deploy such a force so quickly, albeit it did not have to fire a shot in combat. Whilst the *Anschluss* bringing Austria *heim ins Reich* (home into Greater Germany) remained one of Hitler's most daring political actions, much of its success rested on the organizational capabilities of the German General Staff, an accolade for Manstein and his planners.

For Beck, however, the ease with which Hitler had achieved union with Austria – completely on his terms – was distinctly worrying. What would be his next target? An invasion of Czechoslovakia, or threat of one, would surely bring about a general war in Europe, for which Germany was not ready. Ironically, Beck's and Manstein's cool and accurate advice to Hitler on 7 March 1938 had fuelled the Führer's risk-taking and adventurism.

Without his trusty assistant, Beck set himself the task of dissuading Hitler from pursuing any further foreign ambitions, a forlorn but not futile objective. Manstein had one further task before he could take up his post in Liegnitz. He accompanied Brauchitsch to Vienna to investigate how the Austrian Army should be incorporated into the German. Manstein proposed that a branch of the General Staff be established in Vienna, and that Austria's seven brigades be organized into four divisions.

On return from Vienna, Manstein was able to wind up all his remaining business in Berlin and move, finally, to Liegnitz.

5

To War Again

*'The question is not one of the justice of our cause, but
exclusively of victory.'* Adolf Hitler, 21 August 1939

Silesian Command

On 31 March 1938, Manstein assumed command of the 18th Infantry
Division in Liegnitz. His tour of duty lasted for seventeen months until
the Wehrmacht's mobilization just prior to the German invasion of
Poland on 1 September 1939. Strangely, he devoted relatively little space
in either of his memoirs, which overlap at this point of his career, to
describing the formation he led. He concentrates rather on narrating
strategic developments such as the German annexation of the Sudetenland, Hitler's occupation of the remainder of Czechoslovakia and the
approaching war with Poland. Family and other sources provide sufficient background material to fill the gap.[2]

Manstein took over from Lieutenant General Hermann Hoth, who
had commanded the division since October 1934.[3] The military destinies
of these two generals were later intertwined when Hoth, as an army
commander, served in Manstein's army group on the Eastern Front
during the climactic battles of Stalingrad and Kursk (1942–43). Back in
the spring of 1938, Manstein found himself in a delicate situation whilst
his predecessor was still waiting to take up his new appointment as
commanding general of XV Army Corps (Motorized). Whilst Hoth
remained with his family in Liegnitz until further notice in a rented
apartment, accommodation had to be found for his successor. Due to a
change of housing policy, Manstein was entitled to an official service
residence. As none suitable could be found at short notice, he moved
into temporary digs.

For some unexplained reason, Manstein determined to take his
daughter with him to Liegnitz, whilst leaving the rest of the family in
Berlin. Gisela ended up as the only girl in a boys' *Gymnasium* and
completed her *Abitur* at 17, a rare feat. Eventually, the Mansteins were
able to move into an elegantly refurbished villa in the Holteistrasse near

the centre of town. Manstein's daughter recalls fondly its 'large garden with fruit trees and an adjoining stable for two horses'.[4] She went on early morning rides with her father during 1938, and on occasion accompanied him to military sporting and associated social events, including the annual Hubertus hunt. By this time, Manstein had sold his house in Berlin. If this decision was discussed with his wife, it was a matter not aired with his daughter and elder son, who both wished to retain a home in the capital. Their father determined, however, to make a complete break from Berlin.

Once Jutta-Sibylle had decorated and furnished her new family home, she asked Frau Hoth to come round. It led to an amusing episode that casts fresh light on Manstein's character. Gisela explains:

> As Father hated ladies' tea parties, Mother had invited Frau Hoth on a day that he was due to be away on a tour of inspection of the Czech border ... We went down to tea ... and as we entered Father's adjoining study, we saw him just arrived and still in his coat, obviously in a bad mood and very much annoyed about his trip for some reason. Mother went to calm him down and said 'Fine, that you're back home now, but I've invited Frau Hoth for tea today.' 'For God's sake, that's all I need now,' Father responded, and at that very instant none other than Frau Hoth appeared in front of him. Our new maid Trudel had forgotten to announce her. It was a terrible moment – I wanted to vanish – but a smiling Frau Hoth came over to Father and explained that her husband would react in exactly the same way. From that day on, she belonged to the very small group of women that he respected and conversed with.[5]

As a result of this incident, the Mansteins and Hoths became friends. Gisela got to know the Hoths' only son, Jochen, of similar age, who attended the same *Gymnasium* and became a 'really good chum'.

Manstein now had his hands full getting to know his new division and putting it through its paces. Although the German Army put great store on decentralized command, this was tempered by the divisional commander's duty to control the efficiency and state of training of his subordinate formations and units. As Manstein had many visits and inspections to carry out, he was on the road for much of the time.

The 18th Infantry Division, one of three major formations in VIII Army Corps commanded by his old friend Ernst Busch, was spread out widely over Lower Silesia in seven garrison towns. Manstein's area of responsibility was a triangular zone bounded in the north by Grünberg (now Zielona Gora in Poland); Breslau (Wrocław) in the south-east; and Görlitz in the south-west. Apart from Liegnitz that housed the divisional headquarters, 51st Infantry Regiment (formerly the Kaiser's Royal Grenadiers[6]) and 18th Artillery Regiment, the principal garrisons were Glogau on the Oder and Görlitz on the western (Lausitzer) Neisse, in which the bulk of 54th and 30th Infantry Regiments respectively were based. Apart from these four large regiments, Manstein also commanded the divisional machine-gun, anti-tank, engineer, signals, medical and supply battalions; in all about 17,000 men, 5,000 horses, 1,000 motor vehicles and 500 motorcycles.[7]

Although Hoth had handed over to Manstein a well-trained formation, its new commander described 18th Infantry Division as 'by no means ready' for war. Several battalions had yet to be fully manned and the divisional artillery regiment still lacked its heavy gun detachment. Despite, or perhaps because of these challenges, Manstein noted it was 'a great joy to stand at the head of this division, supported by first-class commanders and a well-organized staff run by the excellent Major von Strachwitz, the first general staff officer.'[8] As was to become his practice as a corps commander in 1940–41, Manstein focused on training his own divisional headquarters and subordinate formation staffs, and deploying his troops into the field. As a historian of the division observed, Manstein 'could build on a solid foundation, and above all, school the officer corps in war games and exercises'.[9] Not surprisingly, the division made regular use of the extensive Neuhammer (Świętoszów) training area on its doorstep, lying to the south-east of Sagan (Żagan).

Manstein did not provide any detail as to the training regime he imposed, but evidently he enjoyed the experience and was proud of what he achieved. He recalled that 'Silesia had produced good soldiers from time immemorial, so the military education and training of new units was a rewarding task'. He noted further:

> [From] the beginning of April 1938 I [was] able to devote myself entirely to my job as a divisional commander. It was a particularly satisfying task – even more satisfying in those years than at any other time – but it called for every ounce of one's energy, since the expansion of the army was still far from complete. The continual formation of new units entailed a constant reorganization of those already in existence, while the speed of rearmament, and especially the attendant growth of both the officer and non-commissioned officer corps, meant that the most exacting demands were made on commanders at all levels if we were to fulfil our aim of creating inherently stable and highly trained troops who would guarantee the security of the Reich.[10]

What Manstein forgot to mention in his memoirs was that the German

Army was now growing to such a size that it posed a threat to *other* nations' sovereignty.

At this stage of his career on the eve of the Second World War, despite his banishment from the centre of power in Berlin to Silesia, Manstein was not immune to political influence and propaganda. On one notable occasion, at least in what was destined for public as opposed to private consumption, he was outspoken in his support of Hitler. On the Führer's birthday on 20 April 1939, Manstein addressed his troops on parade. The next day, the local newspaper, the *Liegnitzer Tageblatt*, reported his words:

> Soldiers, comrades! Today, the Wehrmacht and the whole German people commemorate the 50th birthday of our Führer and give our admiration and thanks, in love and faithfulness, to our supreme commander. On this day we thank God that he gave the German people this great son, keeping his hand on this brave front-line soldier during all the storms of the World War, protecting his life during the years of the struggle and blessing his conduct as Führer so clearly. We commemorate the way in which our Führer has led us over the past six years: from the division of centuries to the unity of all Germans, out of deepest poverty to work and bread, from powerlessness to security; from shame and inability to greatness! We remember the deeds of the Führer, which represent milestones on the path to our Great German Reich: Rhineland, German-Austria, Sudetenland, Bohemia and Moravia, Memelland.
>
> When the German people thank the Führer today, then it is because he has led us on the path to peace. But let us remind ourselves that he took this path as a fighter and soldier. We vow to match his soldierly abilities with all our strength: in the never-ending love of our people, in our resolute belief in Germany, in brave action, tough determination and in our total commitment for our Reich! When it appears as if an opposing world wishes to put walls around Germany in order to prevent our Führer from completing his work, so we vow today to him: we shall protect his work despite all challenges and carry out his will, wherever he leads us! Let our vow on this 50th birthday of our Führer be heard across the whole world: Adolf Hitler, our great Führer, *Sieg Heil*![11]

So what should we make of Manstein's remarks? Significantly, he did not make any reference whatsoever to this event in his memoirs: it would have hardly helped his carefully crafted reputation as a critic of Hitler, albeit his opposition was primarily on military grounds rather than political. It remains unclear whether Manstein believed in what he was saying at the time. Was he just doing his duty, or was he reflecting the popular mood?

Detailed research by the German historian Roland Kopp has shown that the Wehrmacht chain of command mandated garrison commanders to address their soldiers in barracks on the morning of Hitler's birthday. Holding a subsequent parade in public, potentially involving thousands of spectators, was entirely optional. Kopp investigated no less than 280 events: Manstein was amongst the vast majority (a ratio of four out of five) of German commanders who made such speeches on that day. What he said, moreover, was not particularly unusual as a comparison with twenty-eight texts reproduced by Kopp makes clear.[12] Manstein implies in his memoirs that he admired much in Hitler at the time. Specifically, he observed that:

> Hitler appeared as the saviour who overcame the deadly danger of Bolshevism and unemployment in Germany. Notwithstanding the brutal methods, he banished the threatening spectre of civil war and at the same time opened the possibility of bridging the gap which had divided the working and middle classes up to then. The Wehrmacht witnessed the reclamation of its prime responsibility – and was able at last to meet it: to act as the shield of the Reich from external danger.[13]

Amongst the military, Manstein was hardly alone in such thinking.

The Sudeten Crisis and Beck's Opposition to Hitler

Hitler was not content with his success in annexing Austria in the spring of 1938. Other ethnic German populations were still, in his view, being denied the chance to join the Greater German Reich. His eyes turned in particular to the German-speaking part of western Czechoslovakia, the Sudetenland. As ever, Hitler had both political and military options in mind.

During the summer of 1938 Manstein was detached from divisional command to act as chief of staff of Twelfth Army, commanded by Colonel General Wilhelm Ritter von Leeb. This army was foreseen as the principal force to deploy to the Bavarian-Czech border and then to occupy the Sudetenland. Preparations for the operation were already entrusted to a small planning staff led by Colonel (in General Staff) Günther Blumentritt. At one of his meetings with Blumentritt and Leeb, Manstein recalls hearing about a paper written by Beck, which set out his concerns about Hitler's foreign policy that was destined to bring about an 'unwinnable war' for Germany. Although Manstein states that he did not see this document, now known as the Beck Memorandum, he was aware of Beck's intention to resign and strove to prevent it.

In fact, Beck had written several critical memoranda on policy matters in recent months.[14] The stimulus for his campaign of letters was a realization that Hitler had aggressive intentions against Czechoslovakia that could bring Britain and France into conflict against Germany, a war which the nation was not yet ready to fight. His first memorandum of 5 May 1938, in which he had stated that Germany could not hope to win against a coalition stronger than itself, was followed by another on 29 May in response to a speech by Hitler to his generals the previous day. Whilst Beck agreed that Germany required *Lebensraum* and needed a speedy resolution of the Czech question, he concluded that in the event of intervention by 'supporting powers' (meaning Britain and France), 'a successful campaign against the Czechs could be won, but Germany would lose the war'.[15]

A third memorandum dated 3 June containing more military technical detail for the benefit of Brauchitsch was followed by a fourth on 16 July, Beck's last attempt to change the course of German foreign and security policy. In his final 'Memorandum to the Commander-in-Chief on the military hopelessness of a war against Czechoslovakia', Beck called on the 'Supreme Commander of the Wehrmacht' to 'stop the preparations for war' and 'to postpone a forceful solution of the Czech question until the military conditions had changed sufficiently'. In a supplementary speaking note written the same day, Beck appealed to 'all upright and serious German men in positions of responsibility' to adopt 'all imaginable means and ways to prevent a war against the Czech [state]', the consequence of which must 'lead to a world war, that would mean the *finis Germaniae*'. Further, the military obedience of the highest commanders of the Wehrmacht has a limit at the point where their knowledge, conscience and sense of responsibility forbid the execution of a command. If their advice and warnings in such a situation are not listened to, they have the right and duty to the people and to history to resign from their posts.'[16] Beck would shortly feel compelled to do so in order to give a lead to others.

On 21 July 1938, Manstein wrote a lengthy memorandum to Beck.[17] Whilst avoiding any discussion of the political situation, he argued again for a review of the high command of Germany's armed forces, an old hobby horse of both his and Beck's. In presenting his technical arguments for such a change, Manstein seems to have missed the vital point that it was Hitler's *policies* – rather than any inadequacies in the top military structure – that were driving Germany to war. Beck was arguing from a strategic standpoint that Manstein did not share. None the less he observed loyally to Beck that:

No successor to you, General, would have the same position, such respect or authority as you enjoy, General, in order to achieve the necessary unity [of military command] by this or any other way. The army does not possess anyone who can match your ability and strength of character to replace you, who would be in a position to master in a similar manner the difficult military tasks that face us today. I trust that you will not take offence, General, from my openness, as my words do not reflect a cheap politeness, rather an inner conviction.[18]

Thus Manstein's support for Beck was conditional.[19] Whilst he advised him to remain in post, he also encouraged him to rid himself of the burden of strategic responsibility – a matter solely for the political leadership – and play a full part in securing military success against Czechoslovakia.

Curiously, Manstein omitted to reflect this latter, equally important, aspect of his appeal in his memoirs. For Beck, however, the impression that his brilliant, former assistant had resigned himself to operational thinking and obedience to the political leadership rather than recognizing that the General Staff – in the personification of its chief – had a duty to express a strategic view must have been disappointing.[20] Indeed, their relationship drifted thereafter. On 31 July Beck prepared a written reply to Manstein intimating that he was no longer able to accept the responsibility of serving in such circumstances, stating it was already 'too late' to effect change. In the event, the letter was not sent as its contents were communicated verbally to Manstein when he met Beck in Berlin on 9 August.[21] Presumably (for Manstein leaves no record of this exchange) the Chief of the General Staff informed him then that Brauchitsch had held a meeting with senior army commanders on 4 August, at which the memorandum of 16 July was read out. Disappointingly, Brauchitsch had declined to face down Hitler and Germany's senior generals remained unquestioningly loyal.

As a result, Beck felt, and was indeed, isolated in the army. Despite some anxieties about the increasing likelihood of war, his active opposition to Hitler's policies was largely a solo effort although a few individuals, including his successor Halder, were scheming quietly in the background. Beck and others of like mind, however, were not representative of the German military élite, including officers such as Manstein, which preferred collectively by tradition and personal inclination to leave politics to the politicians. Hence there were no mass resignations in the manner that Beck had wished. Yet Hitler would appear to have been unnerved temporarily by Beck's démarche. The

Führer sought, therefore, to convince the armed forces, and especially the German Army, whose corporate spirit in the form of its General Staff he resented so particularly, of the soundness of his policy.

On return from summer leave spent on the North Sea island resort of Sylt, Manstein was summoned to a conference on 10 August in Hitler's Alpine retreat at Berchtesgaden.[22] Hitler's purpose in holding this meeting was to bring the army round to his way of thinking. Rather than inviting the commanders-in-chief, or troublesome individuals such as Beck, he directed that the chiefs of staff of the armies destined to take part in any operation against Czechoslovakia should attend. Manstein was amongst this group. He believed he had seen through Hitler's design: faced with opposition from the army's high command, he surmised that the Führer thought he would have an easier time convincing a younger generation of generals of his policies.

After greeting his guests and showing off the breathtaking panorama view over the Alps from his grand reception room in the Berghof, Hitler invited the generals to breakfast. Manstein sat next to him: this was the first occasion in which he had an opportunity to discuss matters at close hand with the Führer. He found the usually loquacious German leader 'deep in his thoughts', 'in no way forthcoming' and 'difficult to engage'.[23] Not wanting to raise political or military matters, Manstein ventured to introduce an alternative topic into the conversation. Having recently attended an exhibition of German art in Munich, he volunteered his opinion on several paintings to Hitler.[24]

Manstein left a detailed account of the Führer's two-hour-long speech on the Czechoslovakian situation. He noted Hitler's exposition of the prevailing political scene in Europe and the increasing subjugation of the German minority, and the latent threat of the Czechs as a potential enemy in a variety of circumstances. The real significance of the occasion, according to Manstein, lay not in what Hitler told his listeners, but rather in how he reacted to indirect criticism in the following discussion period. He described the scene:

> Whilst Hitler was trying to alleviate our concerns [about the risks of military moves against Czechoslovakia] through counter-argument, he suddenly exploded when General [Gustav] von Wietersheim, the designated chief of staff of the army due to defend the western border, raised the issue of the *Westwall*. Wietersheim's declaration (which accorded with that of his commander-in-chief, General Adam) that the *Westwall* was by no means strong enough to hold a French attack with the weak forces then available put Hitler into a scarlet rage. The drift of his reply was that

the *Westwall* would indeed be proof against any enemy for an extended duration if only the generals were as brave as the musketeers.[25]

As Manstein observed, Hitler never again gave his generals another opportunity for such a frank and robust exchange of views. The enduring moral is clear: when a political leader stops listening to his senior military advisors, then he alone must accept full responsibility for any resultant failure.

The deployment of German forces to the Czech border went off smoothly. As a result of the Munich Agreement signed on 29 September, the Czechs capitulated the next day without a fight and on 1 October yielded the Sudetenland to Germany. Naked military force had changed internationally recognized borders. Despite this violation, there was indeed briefly 'peace in our time', as the British prime minister Neville Chamberlain declared infamously on his return to London from meeting Hitler. But the poor Czechs (not represented at Munich) had been duped in favour of British and French appeasement of Germany. Betrayed, they lost the majority of their industry as well as their formidable border defences in consequence.

As temporary chief of staff of Twelfth Army, Manstein recorded that the German Army's march across the border on 1 October 1938 was met by a 'rapturous reception' by the local Sudeten German population.[26] In addition to his own observations, it is likely that he was informed by reports from members of 18th Division, which took part in the operation, led again by Hoth. Once the Sudetenland was occupied, however, there remained 'nothing more exacting to do than supply the troops'.[27] As this was not a matter that required his operational expertise, Manstein requested permission to return to his command. What he did not appear to know then, however, was that at the very time of the Munich conference, Halder had been planning a military putsch against Hitler in order to prevent a war in Europe.

Manstein maintains that he first heard about Halder's plans when he was confined in the witnesses' prison at Nuremberg in 1945–46. In close collaboration with General Erwin von Witzleben and Colonel Hans Oster, Halder had designed a march on Berlin by reliable German Army formations under trusted commanders, including 23rd Infantry Division and its 9th Infantry Regiment, from Potsdam, to seize power from Hitler. But the order to move against the government never came. Whether such an audacious enterprise would ever have succeeded remains highly doubtful, notwithstanding that 'German resistance against Hitler was at its most intense in August and September 1938' in the opinion of the noted German historian Golo Mann.[28] Sadly for Germany and Europe, military opposition against the Führer could never be mobilized effectively then or subsequently, for neither the strength of the army nor the mass of the people was ever behind it.

In the event, the Munich Agreement had taken all the wind out of Halder's sails. A peaceful solution to the Sudeten crisis removed both the rationale for and any motivation in a military revolt against Hitler. So the plan came to naught. Manstein, reflecting after the war, doubted the coup's chances of success in any case. He did not think it possible to have led German troops against Hitler or, indeed, to find officers in the German Army in 1938 that 'were prepared to take up arms against their supreme commander and to whom they had made an oath of loyalty'. Rather, 'It took the terrible developments up to 1944', he declared, 'before officers – every one of whom must be regarded as honourable – could bring themselves to attempt the removal of the head of state.'[29] After all, as Mann observed, the generals' profession was 'to make war, not play politics, far less to bring down their own government'. Further, 'the German generals never learned this art and never practised it: it was not in their tradition'.[30]

After the occupation of the Sudetenland, Manstein resumed normal peacetime duties in Liegnitz. Hitler's march on Prague on 15 March 1939 and the illegal seizure of rump Czechoslovakia was conducted by German motorized troops. Yet the occupation of that country led to some contradiction in Manstein's thinking after the Second World War over the rights of nationalities. In his memoirs, he noted that as a result of Munich, Czechoslovakia – a state that had been created at Versailles 'disregarding the right of self-determination' – had failed in his view (in other words: to resist effectively) when first seriously tested. How could such a state construct survive, he observed, 'in which one national group, whose population was less than a half of the whole, suppressed three other nationalities, whose tribal-brothers (Stammesbrüder) formed the populations of the neighbouring states?'[31]

Hence, in Manstein's view, a multi-ethnic Czechoslovakia did not deserve to survive as a nation state. He was not to predict that it divided amicably by means of a 'velvet divorce' nearly sixty years later into the separate Czech and Slovak Republics. Whereas Manstein could see nothing wrong in the incorporation of the Sudetenland into the German Reich, dissolving the parent state was a step too far. As he reflected: 'Hitler's actions towards the remainder of Czechoslovakia, his abandonment of the moral, legal right of self-determination damaged not only other powers, but also the German people with the worry that he would attack across other frontiers. The danger of war hung thereafter over Europe.'[32] Indeed it did. Not one veiled hint of such concern appeared in his long-forgotten speech of 20 April 1939 in Liegnitz. Manstein's memory after the Second World War was stunningly precise on most occasions, but conveniently selective on others.

After Germany's creation of the 'Protectorate of Bohemia and Moravia' and the client state of Slovakia, driving a cart and horse through the Munich Agreement, it should have been clear to the majority of educated people in Germany that the Western Powers would now have to take fresh stock of Hitler. The general euphoria over another successful 'war of flowers' and the public adulation of the Führer disguised the fact that the rules of the game in Europe were changing. Although he had out-manoeuvred the military opposition with yet another bloodless triumph, Hitler's luck in avoiding armed conflict was beginning to evade him. Peace in Europe was fast running out. The thousands of reservists across Germany, who had been recalled briefly to the colours on two separate operations in Czechoslovakia, would soon return for a much longer and deadlier test, from which a great many would not return.

Prelude to the Polish Campaign

Throughout the first seven months of 1939 Manstein was able to concentrate his efforts in preparing his troops for war, wherever and whenever it would come. In addition to training, elements of his division were seconded to construction duties on the eastern frontier with Poland, strengthening the *Ostwall*. Manstein had been responsible for some of the earlier planning for this frontier defence, when Poland was seen as a real threat to Germany's security. Now such activity was all part of a grand strategic deception plan, as Hitler's next object was an offensive against Poland. Months of fruitless diplomacy in 1939 to bring about a peaceful resolution of Germany's claims (reversing the Treaty of Versailles) for the return of Danzig and guaranteed road and rail links to East Prussia had convinced the Führer that a military solution was necessary. As the German political pressure mounted, inevitably so did the Polish reaction, at the cost of the German minority within Poland. Viewed as intolerable oppression from Berlin, this was all welcome grist to the German propaganda mill.

Meanwhile, planning for Operation Plan WHITE against Poland had been initiated some months before in the spring of 1939. A fast-moving campaign involving two army groups, including strong armoured and air forces, was foreseen for the invasion of Germany's eastern neighbour.

On mobilization and deployment against Poland, Manstein was pre-
assigned as chief of staff of Headquarters Army Group South under
Colonel General Gerd von Rundstedt. To plan the operations of this
army group, in the early summer of 1939 a small staff team, *Arbeitsstab
Rundstedt*, had been set up in Berlin under the direction of Colonel
Günther Blumentritt.[33]

There was a good professional relationship between Manstein and
Rundstedt. If not in awe of him, Manstein respected his senior highly
and enjoyed working with him. He recalled:

> As an exponent of operational art he was brilliant – a talented soldier who
> grasped the essentials of any problem in an instant. Indeed, he would
> concern himself with nothing else, being supremely indifferent to minor
> detail. He was a gentleman of the old school – a type, I fear, which is now
> dying out, but which once added a delightful variant to life.[34]

Rundstedt's outstanding ability was confirmed by Westphal, who noted
that during the staff rides of the mid 1930s, which Manstein and he had
planned and co-ordinated on behalf of the commander-in-chief, General
Fritsch, 'Generals Rundstedt, Ritter von Leeb, von Bock and Halder
stood out without competition at the top.'[35]

Manstein and Blumentritt had already worked closely together in
Headquarters Twelfth Army during the Sudetenland operation. Their
respect was mutual. The former described his relationship with his
junior partner as one of 'the closest confidence'; Blumentritt described
Rundstedt's chief of staff as 'the energetic, able and impulsive Lieutenant
General von Manstein'.[36]

On 19 August 1939, Rundstedt and Manstein were instructed to
attend a conference held by Hitler at Obersalzberg in two days' time.
The next day they drove from Liegnitz to Linz, staying overnight there
with Manstein's farming brother-in-law, Friedrich von Loesch, completing their journey the next morning. At the Berghof, all the army
group and army commanders, together with their chiefs of staff and the
naval and air force commanders, had assembled to hear Hitler's address.
As Manstein observed pithily in his memoirs, 'he was not going to let
the occasion turn into open discussion after his experience with the
chiefs of staff the previous year'. Before Hitler arrived to speak, Göring
appeared 'garbed as if he had been invited to a masked ball in a soft-
collared white shirt, worn under a green jerkin adorned with big buttons
of yellow leather' with 'his paunch girded by a sword belt of red leather
richly inlaid with gold, at which dangled an ornamental dagger'. For
Manstein, this was hardly appropriate dress for a conference that had so

serious a purpose. Such was his personal disdain for Göring that he whispered to his colleague Lieutenant General Hans von Salmuth, the designated chief of staff of Army Group North, 'I suppose the Fat Boy's here as a strong-arm man?'[37]

Commenting after the war, Manstein implied that this particular speech by Hitler was used unfairly as prosecution evidence during the International Military Tribunal at Nuremberg. Manstein tried to set the record straight in his account but in so doing merely added to the controversy surrounding it. He recalled that whilst Hitler was 'absolutely determined to bring the German–Polish question to a head at this time, even at the price of war', at the same time he was not convinced that the Western Powers would oppose him.[38] Hitler's audience, however, appeared not so sure, although accounts differ.

Halder, for one, noted that Hitler stressed 'countermoves by Britain and France must be expected'. More ominously, the Führer went on to declare: 'We are not setting out just to reach a specific line or establish a new frontier, but rather we seek the annihilation of the enemy, which we must pursue in ever new ways.' For special emphasis Halder underlined one of Hitler's remarks: 'The question is not one of the justice of our cause, but exclusively of achieving victory.' He also recorded Hitler requiring of his generals: '[Be] harsh and remorseless. We must all steel ourselves against humanitarian reasoning!'[39]

Whether Hitler's aggressive language, including demanding the wholesale destruction of Poland, did indeed mean that he resolved to annihilate its people, Manstein doubted, for 'nothing he had said could give us any hint of how he was to treat the Poles later on.'[40] The biggest surprise to him, however, was the Führer's trump card in disclosing the impending conclusion of a non-aggression treaty with the Soviet Union (the Molotov–Ribbentrop Pact), which was signed in the early hours of 24 August. As a footnote to this conference, Manstein denied categorically in his memoirs that Hitler said anything about his only fear being 'a last-minute offer of mediation from some pig-dog (*Schweinehund*) or other'. The fact remains that this remarkable comment remains enshrined in the German official history of the Second World War.[41]

Hitler was 'impressed by his talk to the generals', according to his army adjutant, Major Gerhard Engel. Whilst he prided himself on his ability to grasp what effect his words had on an audience, the Führer felt it 'was different with the older officers, they adopted a staring, mask-like expression which betrayed nothing. That was how it had been today.'[42] These senior officers, however, were not sure, even at this late stage, whether Germany was heading for war or not. Would not Britain and France back down again, mused Manstein in his memoirs, for the pact with the Soviet Union had 'rendered Poland's position hopeless from the start'.[43] So it all could have turned out as yet another of Hitler's elaborate bluffs.

On departing Berchtesgaden Manstein returned home to Liegnitz for a day's leave, 'a measure of inner disbelief', he claimed, 'in the likelihood of an imminent outbreak of war'.[44] Although Manstein says that his recollections of Hitler's speech at the Berghof are consistent with the summarized account rendered by OKW war diarist Helmuth Greiner, the latter's description makes it clear that Hitler *did* intend to make war against Poland. Why else would Hitler reportedly state that 'it was of great importance to test the new German Wehrmacht in a limited conflict before it came to general reckoning with the victorious powers of the world war'? Furthermore, the Führer believed that 'proof of the Wehrmacht's capabilities would be of considerable significance for the armed forces themselves and for their public reputation'.[45]

As Germany mobilized for war, Manstein headed for Army Group South's field location to join Rundstedt.[46] His headquarters had commandeered part of the Seminary of the Holy Cross near the old Silesian fortress town of Neisse, on the eponymous eastern river, now the Nysa Kłodzka, close to the Slovakian border. Not only did the brothers of the Steyler Mission remain at their ecclesiastical and training duties, but both Blumentritt and Manstein reported that the 'worldly-wise' abbot joined Rundstedt and his staff for deep discussions over several evening meals. Apparently, he entertained the commander and his senior staff with his accounts of the 'self-sacrificing work of the missionaries in distant parts of the globe'. Whether such clerical tales of derring-do did in fact provide a 'welcome distraction' from the 'burning problems which the immediate future presented', as Manstein claims, remains open to question. Surely the ever increasing likelihood of war in Europe must have come up in conversation.[47]

Poland's strategic position was precarious. It was outnumbered by superior German armed forces in both quantity and quality, and its own geography played against it. Poland's army in peacetime comprised thirty infantry divisions together with one mountain, eleven cavalry and two motorized brigades. In addition, there were up to ten infantry divisions' worth of reserve regiments, which would be called up on mobilization, and a mixed bag of frontier and home defence units of varying quality. In comparison with the German Luftwaffe, the Polish Air Force was completely outclassed.

Poland was surrounded on all sides (see Map 1). A German attack could be developed from the north from East Prussia, from the west out of Pomerania and Silesia, or from the south from Slovakia, or by any combination of these axes. The Soviet Union posed an additional threat from the east. Excepting the Carpathian Mountains in the south, Poland enjoyed no natural frontiers and possessed no modern fortifications on any front. Immediate military support from either Britain or France was not possible. But the brave Poles were determined to defend their homeland and the ensuing German campaign, the first Blitzkrieg, was hard-fought on both sides.

To face a German invasion, the Poles had grouped the bulk of their land forces into seven 'named' armies that covered the northern, western and southern frontiers, whilst retaining only a small central reserve on the Vistula in the area Modlin-Warsaw-Lublin. A small group of forces east of the river Bug could do no more than screen the border with the Soviet Union.

Manstein devoted considerable space in his memoirs to an assessment of Poland's strategic position in 1939. In his view, the Polish deployment, 'aimed as it was at covering everything, including the forward province of Poznań, was bound to bring defeat'. The only option for Poland was to 'hold out until an offensive by the Western Powers compelled the Germans to withdraw the mass of their forces from the Polish theatre'. A strategic response based on playing for time would have depended, in his view, on protecting the Polish Army from operational encirclement through German manoeuvre from the northern and southern flanks. It would also have required fighting a delaying battle in the west, retaining the bulk of Polish forces in central Poland to face the Germans' main offensive from Silesia. In sum, there 'was nothing for it but to plan the really decisive defence as far back as the Bobr-Narew-Vistula-San (or Dunajec) line, and merely to fight for time anywhere forward of this'.[48]

As ever, such a retrospective analysis is informed by observation of the course of events, but Manstein was right to state that Poland could only be saved by the Western Powers. In September 1939, the only army on the continent that could have attacked Germany with sufficient combat power was the French, with a paper strength on mobilization of over a hundred divisions. In the event, France declined to mount a general offensive, launching an ineffectual attack into the Saarland. Thus Poland's fate was secured. The British Expeditionary Force of only four divisions (initially) deployed to France was of minimal strategic value and scarcely of any operational significance at this opening stage of the Second World War.

Germany deployed two armies in Army Group North to attack from Pomerania and East Prussia (Third and Fourth Armies respectively). The main effort was established in Army Group South. Rundstedt was due to attack with two armies launching from central and Upper Silesia (Eighth and Tenth) and a third from the Upper Silesian industrial region, eastern Moravia and western Slovakia (the Fourteenth). In total, the German Army fielded forty-two regular divisions against Poland: twenty-four infantry, three mountain, four motorized infantry, six armoured and four 'light' (mechanized). In addition, ten reserve divisions took to the field. The *Waffen* SS, not yet a serious competitor to the army for men and weaponry, contributed the Führer's bodyguard, *Leibstandarte Adolf Hitler*, a motorized regiment. In terms of equipment, the Germans mustered 3,600 armoured vehicles and 1,929 aircraft against the Polish totals of 750 and 900 respectively.

To guard the western frontier, Germany deployed forty-six infantry divisions, of which only eleven were fully trained. There was no man-oeuvre force available because all the Wehrmacht's mobile formations were deployed on the eastern border of the Reich for the invasion of Poland.[49]

Army Group South's plan, reflecting OKH's requirement for 'quick offensive action' in order to 'maintain the initiative against the enemy', was developed as follows. Specifically, the army group was ordered, 'by advancing from Silesia, and "by concentrating strong forces (Tenth Army)" between Wieluń and Zawiercie, to attack in the direction of Warsaw and to seize the Vistula above and below the capital.' By this means, and in close co-ordination with the operations of Army Group North, 'the bulk of the Polish Army was to be encircled whilst still west of the Vistula.'[50] This key operational idea underpinned the German plan of campaign, which rested on the deep penetration by mobile forces – particularly by the panzer and light (mechanized) divisions – in close conjunction with powerful air support to smash the Polish defences and to pre-empt the committal of their reserves.

To undertake its mission whilst achieving the maximum amount of surprise and momentum along a broad front of over 300 kilometres, Army Group South placed no less than twenty-five divisions of its three armies in its first operational echelon, retaining only eight divisions as either army or army group reserves. Such a disposition of forces reflected a well-calculated risk in the planning that presumed a solid but badly organized and poorly equipped enemy such as the Poles, although the lack of fresh German reserves did cause some tense moments during the campaign.

Later in the Second World War, the German Army made a bad habit out of its early successes, albeit conditioned by an overall lack of forces, by putting far too much effort forward at the front. Whether in attack or defence, for all their tactical ability, the Germans failed to develop adequate operational let alone strategic depth, precisely the same errors made by the Poles and the French in 1939 and 1940 respectively.

Army Group South's eventual scheme of manoeuvre required that the relatively weak Eighth Army of five divisions advance towards Łódź as quickly as possible and at the same time protect the northern flank of its southern neighbour, Tenth Army. The latter army, the army group's *main effort* with thirteen divisions, including seven mobile (armoured, light or motorized), was required to make a rapid thrust to the Vistula, engaging the Polish forces in its wake. Meanwhile, Fourteenth Army of twelve divisions, including three mobile, was to advance into West Galicia, and to encircle the Polish grouping of forces in the vicinity of Krakow.[51]

The First Blitzkrieg

Hitler's invasion of Poland commenced with a false start. The deployment order of 25 August for an attack at 04.30 hours the next day was rescinded just in time to prevent leading reconnaissance units and other motorized elements from crossing the frontier. The mobilization, however, was not cancelled and it continued to run. To the military, such extraordinary action could only be explained in terms of giving diplomacy – reinforced by a mailed fist – one last chance. For the troops concerned, the deployment was presented as 'grand manoeuvres under combat conditions', with both training and live ammunition being carried.[52]

Hitler's hesitant hand-brake 'stop' turned into a final galloping 'go' on 1 September, with an H-hour of 04.45 hours. In so doing the German Army gained an additional six days' time to mobilize, ensuring a greater degree of security in the west and unity of effort in the east. That first morning of the Second World War, tension mounted in Rundstedt's army group headquarters. Manstein observed that for a higher formation staff such as his own, 'the moment of attack marks the beginning of a period of waiting that is charged with suspense and anxiety'. Furthermore, and this is a point equally valid today, 'subordinate formations quite rightly dislike getting inquiries about the progress of a battle, which they are liable to interpret as a sign of nervousness'. 'Consequently,' he concluded, 'it is better just to sit and wait.'[53] Manstein and his operations staff were soon busy enough with the monitoring of the operational situation, co-ordinating the actions of three subordinate armies with the Luftwaffe's Fourth Air Fleet and directing the flow of reserves to feed the army group's unfolding scheme of manoeuvre as necessary.

Despite the pressure of staff work in the monastery, Manstein still found the time to write to his wife, starting a pattern of regular correspondence throughout the war that gives many clues to his views on events, whether political or military, and on personal family matters. On 1 September he wrote: 'Now the die is cast. Early this morning we crossed all along the frontier.... It's a grand decision of the Führer in view of the attitude of the Western Powers up till now. His offer to solve the Polish question was so obliging, that England and France – if they really wanted peace – should have pushed Poland into accepting.' Having been able to visit his old division the day before, he added, 'it was touching to see the staff so pleased when I suddenly appeared. Now the lads are in battle.'[54] Three weeks later, on a trip with Rundstedt, he witnessed 18th Division again in combat. With pride, Manstein recorded meeting his successor: 'Cranz told me it was a pleasure to command such a well-trained division in war, which I can well believe, but it was also a joy to hear.'[55]

Back on the first day of war, the German Army and Luftwaffe scored operational and tactical surprise, achieving their initial objectives, including much damage to the Polish Air Force. Although there was fierce fighting in the air and in the border areas, the Poles were pushed back steadily. The German ground offensive appeared to develop into a pursuit, particularly in Army Group South's sector. Strong elements of the Polish Army, however, had yet to be engaged so there was always the possibility of counterattack. On 3 September, Manstein reflected on the first two days of battle and considered potential enemy intentions. He concluded that 'the opponent has only committed part of his forces so far and does not intend to defend in the vicinity of the border ... and could attempt to concentrate forces forward of the San-Vistula line'. He then described the threats to the exposed flanks of the advancing armies, not least to the Eighth, but stressed the need to press home the army group's attack quickly 'in order to destroy the enemy with all means west of the Vistula'.[56] Within a week, Manstein's foresight was rewarded with the biggest and most bitterly fought engagement of the campaign.

On a personal front, Manstein soon entered into a daily routine, which he described to his wife:

I get up at 6.30, plunge into the water [for a swim], into the office by 7.00. Morning reports, coffee, then work or trips with R[undstedt].

Midday, field kitchen here. Then half an hour break. In the evening after supper, which we eat together with the general staff officers as at lunch, the evening reports come in. And so it goes on to 11.30.[57]

One of the first spectacular actions of the war had been the encirclement of the Polish forces in the Radom pocket over the period 8–14 September by elements of Tenth Army. This success was followed by the bigger battle at the Bzura, in which the northern flank of Eighth Army came under heavy attack from the Polish Poznań and Pomorze Armies. As Manstein recalled, the situation that looked critical to Eighth Army on 10 September, 'offered us the chance of winning a big victory, since strong enemy forces had now been committed to a battle west of the Vistula, and this, if the right actions were taken on our side, would end in their destruction'.[58]

The Germans employed elements of no less than six corps from Eighth, Tenth and Fourth Armies in order to encircle the Polish forces and prevent their break-out to the south and east towards Warsaw. It required the intervention of Headquarters Army Group South directly into the close management of the battle in order to redeploy and co-ordinate the employment of air and land forces in a well-orchestrated manner. Manstein was now in his element orchestrating on behalf of Rundstedt a fast-moving fight (8–19 September), in which the German flexibility of ground manoeuvre in close conjunction with offensive air support was shown to best advantage.

The result of the battle of the Bzura, the 'biggest self-contained action' of the campaign, was the defeat of 'nine Polish infantry divisions, three cavalry brigades and elements of ten further divisions'. As Manstein reflected, if this engagement did not 'measure up in actual results to the big battles of encirclement fought in Russia later on, it was still the largest of its kind to date'. Moreover, '[The battle] was not one which could be planned from the outset through penetration of the enemy front by powerful tank formations, but arose from counter-moves made on the German side when the enemy's own actions unexpectedly gave us our big opportunity.'[59] His conclusion exemplified the flexible method of command, based on seizing the initiative by adept operational level decision-making, which he was later to master against the Red Army. The ability to conduct such a sophisticated but very much improvised manoeuvre, as opposed to the execution of a set-piece plan, rested on the capacity of well-trained subordinate commanders and troops to switch their effort from one place to another at the right time to achieve a decisive effect.

Throughout the campaign, Manstein continued to write home regularly. In one of these letters he described: 'Yesterday, I was travelling with R[undstedt]. An endless journey on awful roads, many destroyed bridges and shot-up villages. Unfortunately there wasn't the time to get right up to the front. Sometimes it's really difficult just to sit at the back.' The realities of war and memories returned a few days later when Manstein drove down the road he had marched in 1914. 'I got out at the place', he noted, 'where I was wounded. I thought then my chances of getting away were pretty slim. A peculiar sensation after 25 years to be back in a war, and to stand there again. A feeling that underlines one's thanks to God.'[60]

At the Bzura, Manstein had mastered his first operational crisis since the First World War. The campaign, however, was not yet over. Following the Soviet invasion of eastern Poland on 17 September 1939 and the establishment of the demarcation line on the Vistula, Hitler pressed for an early capture of Warsaw. He ordered that the Polish capital should be taken by the end of the month; earlier German attempts to seize it off the line of march on 8 and 16 September had been repulsed, incurring heavy losses to the attackers.

Manstein recorded that Army Group South did not wish 'to become involved in a battle inside Warsaw' because this 'would inevitably have caused extraordinarily high losses both to the attacking troops and the civil population'. Accordingly, Eighth Army, tasked with securing the city, was ordered to invest the 'fortress area'. Warsaw would be 'compelled to surrender by a combination of artillery bombardments and air raids, or if these did not produce results, by a food and water shortage'. Manstein was at pains to point out that:

> Army Group H.Q. had successfully opposed an earlier wish of Hitler's to have the city bombed by the Luftwaffe, our argument then that no air raid at that particular juncture would have had a direct bearing on, or in any way benefited, military operations. In the present instance, however, these same reasons served to justify bombardment.[61]

In fact, Warsaw had been under heavy air attack since the war began. Not surprisingly, many of the city's inhabitants had little desire to tempt their fate on its capture and tried to make their way towards the German ring of encirclement. On 24 September, Halder noted Manstein's report:

> Masses of refugees streaming westward towards our lines. Order to shoot has been given for the night. If the refugees are allowed to leave, it would be impossible to starve out the city. Moreover, the city's garrison would

be enabled to take full advantage of the opportunities for street fighting, with all its inevitable complications. A decision must be made.[62]

It came on 25 September ('Inferno Sunday') when the Germans extended their air attacks and shelling against the outer fort and important supply centres to the city centre and other urban areas.[63] The next day leaflets were dropped warning the garrison and local population that the bombardment would be intensified and calling on its occupants to surrender. Manstein omitted to mention that Warsaw was hit by a fresh storm of artillery fire and air strikes and that a twenty-hour truce to spare the local population was also turned down by the Germans.

As the screw was tightened on the Polish capital, on 25 September Army Group South was blessed by a visit by Hitler. Manstein described the event to his wife:

> We were out all day because the Führer was here.... Rundstedt and Reichenau briefed him. He was very impressed and happy about the scale of [our] successes. We then took him close up to the ring of encirclement round Warsaw, just as the bombardment and an attack on a suburb got under way.... The Führer flew off after a very cordial farewell.... On the journey, it was nice to see how the soldiers rejoiced everywhere as the Führer drove past. They ran up [to the road] from far away: every face shone. By the way, the war here appears to be more or less over.[64]

The Germans' massive artillery and air attack destroyed the city's water supply and caused very heavy casualties amongst the civilian population (25,800 dead and approximately 50,000 wounded) in its smashed city blocks. Although the Warsaw Army could have fought on, with Soviet intervention and the inactivity of the Western Allies Poland's strategic position was hopeless, as was that of her capital city.

At noon on 27 September, as Rundstedt and Manstein visited again 18th Division whilst storming one of Warsaw's outlying forts, they heard that the Polish garrison intended to capitulate. Later, Manstein confided in his wife, 'We are very glad about this result, which spares us much blood. To attack into a sea of houses is a nasty business.' He then reflected on the campaign thus far. 'I am very content and certainly proud (internally) about the success of our army group. One couldn't hope for more.'[65]

On 1 October, German forces entered the city and the Warsaw Army tramped out into captivity and an uncertain future. The next day, Rundstedt took the salute at a march past of German troops, including 18th Division, who filed through the 'completely destroyed' city centre. 'It was a great joy', Manstein wrote, 'to see my old division marching into Warsaw, something I had always wished for.'[66] Despite that triumph and their successes over the past four weeks, he was very unhappy with the news that his army group headquarters was to remain in Poland. Hitler had appointed von Rundstedt as Commander-in-Chief East on 3 October, placing him in command of the German forces of occupation. The old general was likewise very unimpressed by this new mission.

Headquarters Army Group North had received orders to redeploy to the Western Front. Manstein did not disguise his disappointment. Because Army Group South, in his view, had undertaken the lion's share of the fighting in Poland, he felt that his headquarters should have received the new mission. Neither he nor Rundstedt had any desire whatsoever to play any future role in occupied Poland, perhaps aware of the suffering already experienced by the Polish people, and conscious that far worse might come. Blumentritt hints at this, recording that 'Party Gauleiters entered the land and, as during the campaign there had already been sharp differences in opinion between Rundstedt and these gentry, every effort was made to get away from Poland.'[67] Manstein agreed. He felt it 'appeared scarcely attractive to play the occupying power with an administration which would be run by a prominent member of the party'.[68] He meant here none other than the infamous Hans Frank, who would later assume the position of Governor General of Poland.

When Hitler returned on 5 October with the Third Reich's top military leaders for a victory parade in Warsaw, Manstein made it clear that he did not want to remain in Poland for long. He lobbied OKH hard for a change in the command structure, and made the point to Halder's deputy, Carl-Heinrich von Stülpnagel, First Quartermaster for Operations, that any campaign in the west would need more than one army group headquarters. Whatever his personal wishes, Manstein's professional advice was appropriate. OKH reviewed their plans accordingly. To his, Blumentritt's and Rundstedt's delight, Colonel Adolf Heusinger of the OKH operations staff visited their headquarters on 15 October 1939 and gave them the good news: they were to establish a new army group headquarters at Koblenz in the west.[69]

The Polish campaign proved to be a stunning and triumphant feat of German arms. In his memoirs, Manstein glossed over any military shortcomings that had been exposed, let alone describing the immediate fate of the Polish people and the suffering that the population experienced then or subsequently during the Second World War. Rather, he used the opportunity to extol the virtues of the German armed forces:

The new Wehrmacht had passed its first test with flying colours. So far, even the army staff had been able to act without interference from outside; the military commanders had retained full authority of command; the troops had had a purely military battle to fight, and for that reason it had still been possible to fight chivalrously.[70]

In his strategic analysis, Manstein was correct to state that the Germans were 'bound to win this campaign' provided two conditions pertained: first, that Germany would have to accept a 'very high degree of risk in the west in order to have the necessary superiority in the east'; and secondly, that the 'Western Powers did not in any way exploit this risk to render timely aid to the Poles'.[71] Whilst the gamble may have been worth taking in the short term, the greater danger of a world war with France and the British Empire had now transpired, as Beck had forewarned. In the meantime, so long as military operations could be kept short in both reach and duration, the German way of war would triumph.

At the operational level, the German system of command had shown its agility, as demonstrated by Army Group South's swift reaction to the crisis at the Bzura – converting a dangerous tactical setback into operational victory. This very virtuosity, in which Manstein and Rundstedt excelled, masked the lack of reserves.[72] The risk-taking involved, whilst justified against the Poles, was a virtue that was to backfire later in the attack against the Soviet Union.

Although the campaign became Hitler's first '*Blitzsieg*' (lightning victory), subsequently elevated to the status of a '*Blitzkrieg*' (lightning war) – combat particularly associated with the new technologies of tank and aircraft – the revolution in warfare that it appeared to represent was as much operational in nature. The German conquest of Poland reflected doctrine and concepts that had been developed in the course of many years of map exercises, staff rides, trials and formation exercises between the wars, albeit the field training with troops had been conducted on a much smaller scale.

Whether German troops at the tactical level had fought chivalrously in Poland as Manstein maintained is now hotly disputed. By the time of the International Military Tribunal at Nuremberg (1945–46), there was already a considerable amount of evidence that pointed to widespread criminal behaviour by members of the German security forces. That much of the Polish intelligentsia and Jewish population were singled out for eradication is a matter of historical fact. What remains a focus for detailed research is the extent to which crimes were carried out by the

German Wehrmacht as opposed to SS or SD units, or before the handover from the military to the civilian administration on conclusion of the campaign. The historian Ian Kershaw has described an 'orgy of atrocities' by the SS, in which the 'need to sustain good relations with the Wehrmacht initially restricted the extent and arbitrariness of the shootings'.[73] Oliver von Wrochem, author of a highly critical study of Manstein, writes: 'In many places Wehrmacht soldiers ran amok; according to estimates, 16,000 [civilians] died as a result of executions. Particularly in the area of Army Group South it came to massacres and maltreatment of prisoners of war during and after the regular hostilities.'[74] Ten years later, Manstein would have to answer three charges of war crimes in Poland.

An Important Postscript

In the English version of *Lost Victories*, many of Manstein's personal reminiscences were cut out in order to shorten the book. The consequence is that the English-speaking reader sees rather more of Manstein as the cold military technician, and rather less of the man touched by the many vicissitudes, including the human losses, of war. Manstein took the trouble to mention *in memoriam* three individuals who died as a result of the Polish campaign.

The first to whom he paid special tribute was Colonel General Freiherr von Fritsch, who as the honorary colonel of 12th Artillery Regiment, returned from retirement to fight alongside his men. He fell in action on 22 September 1939 outside Warsaw and was given a state funeral on 26 September in Berlin. Manstein had heard that as Fritsch had made his farewell to Beck on the outbreak of war, he had remarked, 'I cannot carry on my life as now.' His death wish was met: as he lay dying, he told the aide-de-camp attending to his wounds, 'Don't bother, it's not worth it.'[75]

Manstein's greatest personal loss was the death of his oldest and closest friend, Colonel Wilhelm Dietrich von Ditfurth, a fellow cadet at Plön and Lichterfelde, and comrade officer in 3rd Foot Guards. The two served together as general staff officers during the First World War at the battle of the Somme and remained in touch when Ditfurth acted as personal mentor to the sons of the German Crown Prince. After the First World War, the families kept in close contact. *Onkel* Dico was a regular visitor to the Manstein home. Manstein stated that his friend was 'one of the most likable and kind men I ever knew. He was very mature, clever and open to everything beautiful and good.'[76] Ditfurth fell at the head of his motorized infantry regiment at the battle of Radom.

The other personal blow was the death of his brother-in-law, Konrad von Loesch, the eldest brother of Jutta-Sibylle. As a reserve cavalry captain (*Rittmeister*) of a reconnaissance detachment he was struck down by a shot in the spinal cord during the battle of the Bzura on 9 September. He succumbed to his wounds in March 1940 whilst being treated in the famous Charité hospital in Berlin. His loss, Manstein recorded, 'hit us all badly, but particularly my wife, who only one year younger, had grown up with him'.[77]

There was one further exclusion in the description of the Polish campaign in *Lost Victories*. As an apparently trivial incident concerning a female visitor to the army group headquarters, its significance was probably overlooked in translation. On 12 September, a film director appeared unannounced in the headquarters (now at Lublinitz), together with a camera team in tow. Manstein described the elaborate costume of the 'elegant partisan' in some detail, noting her quaint 'tunic, breeches and soft high boots', with 'a pistol hung on her leather belt', and her 'close-combat equipment was supplemented by a knife stuck in her boot, Bavarian style'.[78] But he did not reveal, for some reason, her name. Perhaps Manstein surmised that the identity of the individual, the talented propagandist of the Third Reich, would have been clear to the vast majority of his readers. Leni Riefenstahl had made the world-famous films of the Nuremberg Rallies (*Sieg des Glaubens* and *Triumph des Willens*) and the 1936 Berlin Olympics (*Olympia*). She was now in charge of the Special Riefenstahl Film Unit (*Sonderfilmtrupp Riefenstahl*).

Manstein cautioned her from making a dangerous trip to the front, but she insisted on continuing her journey in order to film the fighting. His intelligence officer (the Ic), Major Rudolf Langhaeuser, came up with the bright idea of sending her on to Headquarters Tenth Army under the command of General Walther von Reichenau, whom she knew well. So off she went, but soon reappeared back at the army group headquarters in a distressed state. By pure coincidence, she and her crew had witnessed on 12 September 1939 the shooting of a crowd of Polish Jews in the market square of the small town of Końskie in central Poland and had fled the scene in a state of shock. Riefenstahl subsequently denied seeing the crime herself, but claimed to have heard about it shortly after it happened.[79] In any event, she resigned in protest from her new-found role as a war reporter.

In recounting this incident, Manstein stressed that it had resulted from a 'senseless outburst of shooting because of the nervousness of an anti-aircraft gun officer, who reached the square just as an unfounded panic erupted there.' The officer responsible for this crime was court-martialled immediately and sentenced to a loss of rank and several years' imprisonment. 'A sign', he underlined, that the army chain of command 'took severe action in such cases.' Manstein went on to note that this firm approach was later rendered ineffective for 'Hitler withdrew the army's jurisdiction in cases that involved the civil population' by the beginning of the campaign in Russia.[80] He credited Reichenau with pressing the charge of manslaughter. Wrochem, one of Manstein's greatest critics, asserts that the case only went to court following Riefenstahl's personal intervention with Hitler. The lieutenant concerned received a lenient one-year sentence, which was subsequently quashed.[81]

Whatever the truth of the matter, this incident is remarkable because it is the only war crime whatsoever that Manstein recounts in his memoirs. When it came to his trial in Hamburg in 1949, three of the seventeen charges laid against him were on account of alleged crimes within the area of responsibility of Army Group South. Suffice it to say at this stage, he was found *not guilty* on these counts. In fact, Manstein did not mention even in passing other, much larger atrocities that were committed by German forces in Poland, or for that matter, anywhere else during the war. So the reader of *Lost Victories* in translation is not alerted to that fact, except for a short explanation of the infamous Commissar Order.[82]

Some in the military chain of command took a stand at the time and objected to what was going on. Principal among these was Colonel General Johannes Blaskowitz, who wrote a stinging illustrated memo-randum to the Army High Command on the illegal, murderous actions of the SD and police units. When it was presented to Keitel, he refused to acknowledge it and forbade any such intervention in the future.[83] Engel records that on 18 November 1939 the report was seen by Hitler, who 'lashed out furiously against [the] "infantile attitude" in Army High Command. The war couldn't be run with Salvation Army methods.'[84] This should have come as no surprise. Hitler had already told Keitel a month before that the Wehrmacht should consider itself lucky to be relieved of responsibilities of civil administration in Poland.[85]

A striking conclusion comes from no lesser source than the German official history: '... the fact that the Wehrmacht was able to keep the initiative from the start [of the campaign] was a vital prerequisite of its subsequent successes'. Manstein was to take a full part in these, but one can find nothing in his memoirs even remotely resembling that history's final comment:

An equally important consequence of the Polish campaign was that National Socialist Germany now had the opportunity for an almost unrestricted exploitational and racist policy which, in its inhumanity, surpassed the imagination of most Germans. The Wehrmacht which had gone to war willingly if not enthusiastically, relying on the political leadership and its seemingly justified demands against Poland, had created the prerequisites of an occupation policy that ran counter to international law, an occupation policy which it often watched helplessly and which attracted to it the odium of shared responsibility. Its general passiveness, soon to find a consistent continuation in its unprotesting surrender of the administration of occupied Poland, could not therefore – in spite of the need to differentiate – acquit it of shared guilt for the conditions which now came into being.[86]

Manstein would insist consistently after the Second World War that the Wehrmacht had fought a 'clean war' in this and in subsequent campaigns, a claim that has now been thoroughly discredited.[87] His oral evidence at Nuremberg on 12 August 1946 that 'we, together with our soldiers, conducted the war in a military manner' should be seen in this light.[88]

6

Architect of Victory

'The man is not to my liking, but he knows something
about [how] to get things done.' Adolf Hitler

Preview: Breakfast with Hitler

On 17 February 1940 in Berlin there occurred a simple, unassuming event that changed the course of world history. Manstein journeyed to the *Reichshauptstadt*, the capital city of the Third Reich, to breakfast with Adolf Hitler. That day would turn out to be extremely auspicious for both: the outcome of their meeting would help shape the German conduct of the war in the West.[2] If Hitler accepted Manstein's novel plan of attack, the fate of France, Belgium and Holland was surely sealed. Yet as Manstein strode up the wide entrance steps from the Vossstrasse and entered Hitler's extravagantly imposing new Chancellery, designed by Albert Speer, it must have been a bittersweet moment. Damned by his critics within the *Oberkommando des Heeres* (OKH), the Army High Command, this was Manstein's golden opportunity to advance his personal point of view directly with the Führer. It was the painful experience of most German senior officers to be so enthralled by Hitler that they would often fluff their lines and fail to press home their case. Manstein, never one to suppress a personal opinion based on professional insight, was determined to speak up. He was to do so here and on many subsequent occasions with Hitler, particularly during a later period of the war when serving as an army group commander on the Eastern Front (1942–44).

Manstein had been informed on 27 January that he would shortly assume command of XXXVIII Army Corps in Stettin, 200 kilometres north-east of Berlin. This move amounted to dismissal from his post as chief of staff of Army Group A, with its headquarters in Koblenz. Manstein had departed the ancient Rhine city on 9 February for a period of leave at home in Liegnitz pending his assumption of corps command. In most armies, a transfer from a staff to a senior command function would be extremely welcome to any rightfully ambitious officer with designs on the highest ranks. But Manstein was a product of the Prussian general staff system in which a 'chief' had the authority and duty to originate and direct the planning in his own right, as well as on behalf of his commander. Being chief of staff of a group of armies poised to mount the most powerful offensive of the war to date was indeed no ordinary staff position. And Manstein, as we shall see, was no ordinary soldier.

Manstein's determined efforts to secure the high command's agreement to his extraordinary sickle-cut (*Sichelschnitt*) plan incurred the displeasure of both of the commander-in-chief, Colonel General Walther von Brauchitsch and Colonel General Franz Halder, the German Army Chief of the General Staff.[3] Although he desired a field command, in many respects Manstein had wished to remain in Koblenz under Colonel General Gerd von Rundstedt, the commander of Army Group A. This happy partnership of arms had already proved itself in the Polish campaign: an apparently ideal combination of a relaxed 'hands-off' commander with an energetic and highly competent chief of staff. Rundstedt, in a similar manner to Field Marshal Harold Alexander, relieved the tedium of high command with a passion for reading crime novels. In so doing they amused their more than competent staffs by trying to disguise their innocent distractions.

Whilst Rundstedt was certainly more than a distant figurehead, Manstein represented the principal intellectual stimulus and driving force. Thus the Rundstedt–Manstein partnership resembled that of Hindenburg and Ludendorff of the previous war. But whereas the latter duumvirate was able to impose a collective will on the Kaiser, neither Rundstedt nor Manstein – together or separately – ever achieved the same degree of influence on Hitler other than on some exceptional occasions. 17 February 1940 was one such event.

Meanwhile, Manstein's banishment to command an infantry corps based in Stettin, a military backwater, was certainly no consolation prize. Halder had resolved to remove the irritant chief of staff in Koblenz from planning his 'private war' and to replace him with someone more compliant with the high command's way of thinking.[4] But if this act of constructive dismissal was designed to condemn Manstein to military oblivion, it failed spectacularly. Hitler had more than an inkling of Manstein's operational idea, and was already thinking along similar lines in some respects. At this early stage of the war, Hitler's intuitive political feel, his uncanny grasp of the strategically possible, was still holding – as was his predilection for the innovative and unconventional opening, as evidenced by his close involvement in the planning of the spectacular *coup de main* on the Belgian fort of Eban Emael on 10 May 1940.

During the previous autumn, the debate over the evolution of the campaign plan had raged between Headquarters Army Group A, OKH, *Oberkommando der Wehrmacht* (OKW), the German Armed Forces High Command, and the Führer himself. It had proved a bitter clash of ideas, egos and professional jealousies so typical of Nazi Germany, but one not entirely unknown in other military cultures. From Manstein's perspective, the haggling over the campaign plan must have seemed at times more challenging than the subsequent manoeuvre on the battlefield. His bitter feelings about his tenure as chief of staff at Koblenz are summed up poignantly in his description of this period as the 'winter of discontent'. Whether it would be followed as in Shakespeare's *Richard III* by a 'glorious summer' remained to be seen.

Against this background, it hardly surprises that Manstein's crucial meeting in Berlin in the *Reichskanzlei* (Chancellery) was born of subterfuge. Hitler's chief adjutant and personal staff officer, Colonel Rudolf Schmundt (later a lieutenant general who died of injuries received during the assassination attempt on Hitler at Rastenburg on 20 July 1944), was well aware of the tensions over the planning, and the resulting friction between Manstein and OKH. One of Manstein's most gifted and trusted general staff officers, Lieutenant Colonel Henning von Tresckow, had invited his old friend Schmundt down to Koblenz previously and the two had tramped many a long walk in the surrounding countryside discussing future operations. Tresckow went on to become the youngest major general of the German Army and, heavily implicated in the resistance to Hitler, committed suicide after the failure of the plot to kill the Führer in July 1944.

Returning to 1940, Manstein had used the Tresckow connection to influence Schmundt.[5] When he reported his observations of Headquarters Army Group A's thinking to Hitler, the Führer expressed interest in seeing Manstein. But a way had to be found to invite the general to Berlin without incurring the suspicion of OKH.[6] Manstein's posting provided the ideal cover. Along with four other newly appointed corps commanders and a divisional commander, one Erwin Rommel, Manstein was ordered to attend a working breakfast.[7] Manstein noted in his diary:

> Reported to the Führer with the others. Breakfast followed. [He displayed] amazing knowledge over military-technical innovations in all states. Afterwards I was detained for an hour to discuss operations. I presented the essentials of our memorandum to OKH. Had full agreement. Indeed an astonishing convergence of thinking from the same points of view that we had represented right from the beginning.[8]

Manstein's post-war memoirs were rather less effusive with respect to Hitler. Before the private session in Hitler's study, the Führer had discussed the implications of the *Altmark* incident over breakfast. The capture of the German supply ship by the British destroyer HMS *Cossack* within Norwegian territorial waters the previous day (16 February) provoked Hitler into a long discourse about the inability of 'small states to maintain their neutrality'. These were prophetic words indeed as Germany invaded Norway based on that flimsy pretext without warning on 6 April 1940, and would fall on Luxembourg, Belgium and the Netherlands a month later.[9]

Immediately after the meeting of 17 February, Manstein wrote a detailed memorandum for the benefit of his former headquarters, setting out the key points of the discussion. His principal observation was:

The *aim of the offensive in the West* must be to *bring about a decision on land* [emphasis as in original]. For the limited objectives given in the present deployment order, the defeat of largest possible enemy groupings in Belgium and the seizure of parts of the Channel coastline, the political and military stakes are too high. The goal must be the final victory on land. Operations must therefore be directed [immediately] towards achieving a final decision in France, and the destruction of French resistance.[10]

In a nutshell, he summed up what *Sichelschnitt* was all about: seeking a strategic decision through a novel operational method that would play to German strengths and exploit the weaknesses of her enemies.

At the heart of any campaign plan lies a fundamental 'operational idea', which provides the intellectual foundation and framework of any subsequent operations plan. Its design reflects the anticipated reactions of the enemy as much as the actions of friendly forces. As such it is much more than an opening gambit: far rather, the *outcome* is determined and realized through move and counter-move, playing greatly to the psychology of the parties involved. Though military science is required to calculate the forces required in time and space, the overall conception is above all a creative activity, the operational art. Operational ideas have an elusive quality: the successful ones are the mark of military genius that reflects a complex and rare blend of experience, intuition and understanding. Manstein's name will forever be linked to his audacious plan for the defeat of Allied forces in Flanders and France. Like many great concepts, it had a difficult and painful gestation. As the later Field Marshal remarked, 'Hard work and endeavour must always confront the ordinary mortal before he attains his goal. No ready-made works of art can spring from his brain as did Pallas Athene from the head of Zeus.'[11]

An Operational Idea is Born

We must now return to Manstein's work in Koblenz during the autumn of 1939. On 24 October 1939 the staff took up quarters in the fashionable Hotel Riesen-Fürstenhof overlooking the Rhine, and took over the headquarters building of the 34th Division close to the Deutsches Eck, the confluence of the Moselle and the Rhine. The elegant hotel and the beautiful surrounding area were all very familiar to him: he had received some of his formative education before the First World War in the Prussian military school housed within the baroque palace at Engers, some 10 kilometres to the north. As he noted at the time, 'In Engers, close by, I learned tactics. I would have scarcely believed then that I would apply such learning here as chief of an army group. But thank goodness the dreams of youth soar higher.'[12]

Manstein had little time to dwell on such private memories or to indulge in *Kaffee und Kuchen* in the many pleasant Rhine cafés, for despite the prevailing *drôle de guerre* there was serious business to be done. He had already started to think long and hard about the coming offensive in the West during an extended car journey from Liegnitz to Koblenz, drafting a personal appreciation, which he recorded on 24 October in his war diary.

In his estimate of the situation, he considered carefully the pros and cons of Germany launching an immediate offensive. On the plus side, Manstein cited that the 'longer one waited, the stronger the English would become, and the Belgians and the French would have more time to develop their fortifications.' Amongst the many factors that spoke for delaying the attack was the likelihood of bad weather that would impede the employment of Germany's motorized formations. In that case, as he observed, 'our trump card would be missing'. In terms of the enemy, a decisive factor 'could be the undoubtedly low appetite for war amongst the French population, and in any final consideration, within its army'. Manstein saw advantage in provoking France to launch its own offensive. In the case of a German attack, however, 'the French soldier will fight for the "sacred ground of France" as he has always done'. The best outcome would involve luring French and British forces into neutral Belgium, perhaps having to fight their way in and so dissipating effort. Hence from a military viewpoint, on balance everything appeared to indicate that Germany should attack 'when we are fully ready to, and at a time of year that would facilitate our trump card, and not least when we can force our opponents to march into Belgium'. Manstein also sensed that the German Army's offensive power would grow more quickly than the enemy's defensive capability initially and hence there would be a narrow window of advantage in slipping – but not for too long – the coming offensive.

As to *how* to attack, Manstein was quite clear as to the requirement: 'One must only employ the decisive offensive power of the Army in the pursuit of <u>decisive</u> success.'[13] Furthermore,

> it should be clear that this [success] can not be achieved alone through the destruction of parts of the enemy's armies and in gaining a chunk of the [Channel] coast. Forcing a complete decision on land against England and France is questionable at the moment as the prerequisite conditions in terms of command arrangements and of [sufficient] forces have yet to be achieved, excepting the [special] case of a refusal of the French soldier to fight. Above all, from the directives of OKH, however, it would appear that there is not the will to 'go' for a big victory. The belief in one is lacking. That's what makes it so bad![14]

That autumn the war plans were refined continuously as the operation was delayed successively. Bad weather was not the only cause; profound disagreements within the German military chain of command, and between that and Hitler as its political (and increasingly military) director, hampered planning.

Before making any further assessment of Manstein's personal role in the development of the campaign plan codenamed Operation YELLOW, Germany's strategic position in 1939–40 must be reviewed. After the stunning successes in Poland and subsequent ones in the West, the myth of Blitzkrieg emerged, fuelled by contemporary German propaganda and subsequently by a flood of post-war books and films. Modern historical research, however, has determined that Blitzkrieg was not a strategic concept that had been conceived before the war despite the demonstrations of German military prowess between 1939 and 1941. Although it appeared to be a fundamentally new way of making war, it was as much an operational improvisation based on sound tactics on the ground, effective close air support and good leadership as any original strategic approach. Neither the apparently invincible blending of armour, infantry, artillery and combat engineers into combined arms, nor the joint co-ordination of air and ground forces makes for a successful strategy. Manstein's oft-quoted ability as a 'strategist' is itself based on a fundamental misunderstanding of the role of military strategy, of its linkages to the wider instruments of national power including the economic resources to conduct war and the gearing between its three levels: strategic, operational and tactical. If tactics form the steps from which operational leaps are assembled, a coherent strategy must shape and chart the guiding path.[15] Manstein was first and foremost an '*Operateur*', a genius at the *operational* level.

A national or 'grand' strategy seeks to balance the overall aims or *ends* with the military and other *means* available by determining the most appropriate *ways* of prosecuting a security and defence policy and, if deemed necessary, of conducting war. A state's options for evolving such a policy are governed by its geostrategic position in which its geography, population and economic potential must be compared with that of its neighbours, whether friend or foe, and, in turn, with their allies. The German experience in two world wars demonstrates that no amount of tactical or operational virtuosity on the battlefield can make up for inherent strategic military, political and economic weaknesses. Likewise, the apparent advantage of operating on interior strategic lines, allowing the switching of forces between the Western and Eastern Fronts, cannot compensate for an overall lack of military resources, as events of the First World War had shown.

Conversely, tactical or even operational level setbacks can be overcome by the application of strategic military power, *provided* there remain sufficient time, space and forces to stabilize the situation such as to prevent outright defeat. Thus the side that appears to gain the upper hand in the initial stages of a war may be defeated subsequently through the application of superior strategic resources including armament production, typically but not necessarily on a coalition basis, and with the adoption (and refinement as necessary) of tactical and operational methods perhaps observed in one's enemies. Germany was never in a position to effectively neutralize Britain's sea power, her prize strategic asset. Further, as we shall see later, the Soviet Union was able to withstand (just) the German attack of June 1941, which culminated at the gates of Leningrad and Moscow in December. Yet the Red Army did not reach Berlin on the return match until April 1945. The Soviet Union, even west of the Urals, had the strategic depth and national resources that both Poland and France lacked.

In both world wars Germany sought *operational* solutions to its self-imposed strategic dilemma: how to win wars as quickly as possible before its opponents on two fronts recovered sufficiently to turn the scales. Although Manstein provided the original solution for the defeat of France, he was no *grand* strategist in the manner of his erstwhile mentor, Colonel General Beck, who had foreseen the possibility of eventual defeat if Hitler embroiled Germany in a world war. There was, as the noted German military historian Klaus-Jürgen Müller has pointed out, a 'malicious irony' in this: the fundamental idea for the victory in the coming campaign in the West came from none other than Manstein, a general of the Beck school.[16] It appeared, but never proved, to be a war-winner.

The strategic problem facing Germany in autumn 1939 was political, economic and military in nature. On the one hand, would Britain and France throw in the towel after Poland's defeat? Could further armed conflict be averted? Indeed, Hitler had pledged in his speech to the Reichstag in Berlin on 6 October 1939, no doubt for the benefit of both his foreign and domestic audiences, his determination to avoid war whilst holding out a prospect of an international conference to settle Europe's peace and security problems, and to respect the neutrality of Belgium and the Netherlands in any case.[17]

If an offensive campaign were to be required, any significant delay would benefit Britain and France more than Germany as their war economies were being built up and their defences improved. Despite an OKH study that had indicated that the German Army would not have sufficient strength to penetrate the Maginot Line until 1942, Hitler did not accept the caution of his generals as a brake on offensive action. Hitler was determined to defeat France (and so Britain) before Stalin intervened in the East, breaking their pact. As in 1914, Germany chose to seek victory first in the West. If Hitler had misjudged the political resolution of the Western Allies in not seeking an accommodation with Germany, he did not overestimate their limited military capabilities. Sensing French and British weakness, he decided to attack. Thus if the strategic end (to seek a decision in the West) was now fixed, the question was to find the appropriate operational way to achieve it with the tactical means and limited economic resources already to hand.

Whilst Germany attacked Poland, the French Army had mobilized and deployed to its defensive positions, including manning the Maginot Line that stretched from Luxembourg in the north to the Swiss border in the south. Facing the Belgian frontier in anticipation of a German attack were the four armies of the First Group of Armies, joined by the British Expeditionary Force – initially of two corps (just four divisions). In May 1940, a total of ninety-two divisions were able to meet the German offensive, including five motorized infantry, five light cavalry, three light mechanized and three armoured divisions – the latter raised in the first quarter of 1940.[18] In the meantime, the British had expanded its field army in France to three corps (nine infantry divisions and a tank brigade) with a separate division (51st (Highland)) serving alongside the French in the Saar. That said, this second British Expeditionary Force in a generation represented a far less significant contribution to the Allied cause than in 1917–18 when no less than four armies (sixty divisions) of the British Empire had served on the Western Front. Meanwhile, the German Army had continued to expand over the winter of 1939–40 to 157 divisions, of which ninety-three (including ten panzer divisions) were employed on 10 May 1940 for the offensive in the West.[19]

Once victory had been assured in Poland the previous September, OKH planned initially what appeared superficially as a rerun of the Schlieffen Plan of 1914. The main effort of the attack lay in a sweeping envelopment through northern Belgium towards the Channel coast. Manstein raised objections to it primarily from an operational as opposed to a strategic perspective. The distinction here is important: whilst Manstein sought better operational *ways* to achieve the desired victory, other generals opposed the strategic *ends* of an offensive war, and later, the crimes that were involved in its prosecution. In the autumn of 1939 the principal posts in OKH were filled by those who were against conducting any war in the West. These included Brauchitsch, Halder and Carl-Heinrich von Stülpnagel.[20] Manstein, however, formed no active part of any political or military opposition aimed at unseating or killing Hitler at this – or indeed at any other – stage of the war.

Despite his contemporary and subsequent reputation as a strategist, an image polished skilfully in his memoirs, Manstein's professional forte was fundamentally that of operational art. Simply put, his outstanding ability lay in the planning of major operations and campaigns, and not of wars themselves. Yet the distinction is crucially important. If Manstein was more capable than either Montgomery or Patton, he was not a grand strategist in the manner of the Briton, Field Marshal Alan Brooke (later, Viscount Alanbrooke) or the American, General George C. Marshall, who served their nations' chiefs of staff committees so adroitly.

Manstein also appeared to understand his limitations at the strategic level, noting the inherent challenges when dealing with Hitler:

> Whenever Hitler perceived he was not making any impression with his opinions on operational matters, he immediately produced arguments from the political or economic sphere. Since he had knowledge of the political situation or economic circumstances which a front-line commander did not possess, his arguments on such matters were generally irrefutable. As a last resort all one could do was to insist that if Hitler did not agree to the proposals or demands presented to him, things would turn out badly from a military point of view leading to even worse political and economic repercussions.[21]

The future field marshal inspired confidence through his sheer competence at planning at the operational level, and his associated skill in the handling of higher formations. Most senior officers suffer fools badly, and Manstein proved no exception. In his case, however, it would be unfair to conclude that his outstanding military intellect triumphed over his rather blunt character.

Life with Manstein was often hard going, but not without its big compensations and little idiosyncrasies. On 31 October 1939, for example, he wrote home admitting that his most recent attempt to accompany his work with recordings of 'good chamber music' in order to escape 'the marches and the imbecilic dance music pouring out on the radio when the inconsequential news is not on' had failed as before. 'If we allow this type of propaganda and entertainment to go on any longer', he complained to Jutta-Sibylle, 'we'll all end up shaking our legs about.'[22]

He attracted an intensely loyal personal staff precisely on account of his clear views and steadfastness in crisis. His thoughts and actions commanded widespread respect well beyond his area of responsibility. In any event, the strategic outcome of his operational idea was the defeat of France, Belgium and the Netherlands, and the eviction of British forces from continental Europe within a *blitz* campaign of six weeks' duration. This was no small feat by any measure, and one not matched in immediate strategic effect by a Western Allied general against German forces during the whole of the Second World War, Eisenhower, Montgomery and Patton included. In terms of mastery of the operational art, Manstein had no peers outside the Soviet Union. Yet, as we shall see later, events on the Eastern Front during 1941–44 against the likes of Marshal of the Soviet Union Zhukov would test Manstein to his limits.

Meanwhile, returning to 1939, Hitler's Directive No. 6 for the Conduct of the War, dated 9 October, set out the purpose of the offensive in the West as:

> ... to defeat as much as possible of the French Army and of the forces of the allies fighting on their side, and at the same time to win as much territory as possible in Holland, Belgium, and Northern France, to serve as a base for the successful prosecution of the air and sea war against England and as a wide protective area for the economically vital Ruhr.[23]

In turn, OKH published its draft operational order on 19 October. Whilst on a short home leave before travelling to Koblenz, on the 21st Manstein had collected a copy of the OKH plan at the Army General Staff's wartime headquarters at Zossen, south of Berlin. Thus he was able to start his personal analysis without delay, and was assisted sub-sequently by his small team of planners, including Blumentritt.

At that time, a distraction played on Manstein's mind that reveals a little, arguably justified, personal vanity. He was hanging on news of the operational honours list from the Poland campaign. As is so often the case, those who consider themselves – perhaps unwisely – to be well deserving, may turn out empty-handed. Manstein hoped for a *Ritterkreuz* (Knight's Cross) but was disappointed. He took out his frustration on his diary: 'Despite two nominations by R[undstedt], I'm not on [the list].... I'm used to disappointments in recent years.... Certainly, after the troops, fame is earned by the commander. But I would like to believe that my responsibility was big enough: I alone suggested the operations and wrote the orders.'[24] To his wife, he wrote:

> In any event it remains a fact that the great successes of the army group have proved insufficient to recognize the contribution of the chief of the general staff. It would appear that the motto 'be more than you appear' is being applied more than ever. Based on this treatment, I'm thinking about applying for a command. I've got no desire to stay in a position that is treated as second-class.[25]

Manstein had little time to ponder further on his future. Shortly after the army group staff's arrival in Koblenz, a revised plan from OKH dated 29 October arrived. The main effort of the German attack remained being carried out by Army Group B to the north, in other words on the *right* wing of the German Army. The distinctions between the two plans are fine ones, but suffice it to say that Manstein had already drafted on 31 October a critical response to be directed to Brauchitsch under Rundstedt's signature.[26]

Manstein's personal efforts to amend the campaign plan amounted to no less than six memoranda sent up the chain of command. Although he had made a considerable nuisance of himself, the German general staff system encouraged the use of the formal think-piece (*Denkschrift*) as a means to consider and promote operational ideas. The British official military history is mistaken in suggesting that Rundstedt was the ori-ginator of *Sichelschnitt*.[27] Perhaps the author did not appreciate that, under the German general staff system, a chief of staff had the authority to originate thinking on behalf of his commander and to communicate directly to the chief of staff in the next higher echelon of command.[28]

Following their successful partnership in Poland, Manstein's relationship to von Rundstedt matured during the autumn of 1939. If Rundstedt remained a little distant to his chief of staff, the not insignificant age gap of twelve years was bridged to a certain extent by their mutual respect. There was no sense of the frostiness that was to accompany their later years together as British prisoners of war. During their time together in Koblenz, Manstein made some efforts to get closer to his commander. He accompanied Rundstedt on several of his daily walks along the Rhine promenade, failing in the process to convince his commander of the merits of investing in a proper winter coat rather than relying on a thin rubber macintosh. Already 65 years old in 1940, Rundstedt was a tough old warrior; his Spartan training as a cadet in the 1880s served him well in later years, including his detention as a British prisoner of war.

Brought out of retirement in 1938, Rundstedt served the entirety of the Second World War, albeit with a couple of breaks when sacked twice by Hitler, and on two occasions being recalled to duty. Like Manstein, Rundstedt was no Nazi. As traditional monarchists brought up to serve the Kaiser, both disliked Hitler, his entourage and regime. Manstein should have known better than to have enticed Rundstedt to visit a front cinema that included a showing of Goebbels' weekly film review. The elderly, but certainly not yet senile commander, was not at all impressed by such banal propaganda and commented disparagingly throughout. For his part, Manstein was pleased that his boss's pithy asides were not overheard.[29]

The commander-in-chief's personal manner also took some getting used to. 'The good Rundstedt', Manstein confided to his wife in early November, 'sometimes swears rather too much.' Exactly a month later, the old boy was at it again: 'Yesterday evening he was swearing so much that I went off to bed without any further ado.' So what had irritated Rundstedt so much? Manstein explained:

> [His frustration] often concerns matters that he could change, if he were to get out more and deal with them. I've now ordered that a visit programme is to be organized for him that will concentrate on all those things that fret him. First of all it will achieve wonders, and secondly, he'll have something positive to occupy himself with. You know what works with [difficult] children: 'distract'![30]

It is doubtful that Manstein as an army group commander would ever have succumbed willingly to any such well-meaning therapy organized by his chief of staff.

It was the planning of the coming offensive that dominated both Rundstedt's and Manstein's thoughts and actions, rather than their working relationship. From a modern perspective, when one looks at the German operational design at this stage of the war in more detail, there is scant evidence to support the propaganda-driven, popular images of Blitzkrieg. Surprisingly, there is little prominence given to the role of the new armoured forces, the *Panzertruppe*, or of the air force (Luftwaffe), which had both shown their worth in Poland. Manstein based his objections to the OKH planning largely on its unoriginal scheme of manoeuvre in terms of the standard German operational metrics of forces, time and space, together with the need to achieve surprise and, vitally, to deceive the enemy as to the real intention of the campaign. He was thus careful to couch his arguments in broadly traditional terms, without overplaying his hand with respect to the anticipated combined shock effect of the *Panzertruppe* and Luftwaffe acting in close unison. Their potential in playing a decisive role in the West became more appreciated as planning proceeded.

Rundstedt's letter of 31 October 1939 to the commander-in-chief of the German Army reveals as much the operational insight of his own chief of staff as his own personal professional acumen. From this day onwards Rundstedt and Manstein fought a determined crusade for a new campaign plan, in which their unified aim was to switch the main effort of the German offensive from Army Group B to A, in other words to their area of responsibility. Their motivation for this change of emphasis would not appear to have been driven by any pursuit of personal prestige, in the manner that would later bedevil the planning and conduct of certain German, Soviet and Anglo-American operations. Rather, following the lead of Rundstedt, Manstein's approach was ever strictly professional (*sachlich*). His arguments at this stage and later on in the war were presented in a terse third person singular without embellishment, a cold, compelling logic typical of his general staff schooling and tradition.

If the OKH strategic concept only offered the prospect of a '*Teilsieg*', a 'partial solution', towards victory in the West, then it demanded revision and Manstein knew what was required. Specifically, Army Group A observed:

> It is possible that an early success will be gained over Belgium and the Franco-British forces forward-deployed there. However, the overall success [of the campaign] will not depend on this initial outcome, but rest rather on whether a wider overall success can be achieved in striking and *destroying* the enemy forces in Belgium and north of the Somme *altogether*, and not only in attacking them frontally. Additionally, and sooner or later, a French counterattack from the south or south-west must certainly be contained.[31]

On this basis, two complementary strands of Manstein's integrated operational idea emerged: first, the envelopment of all Allied forces north of
the Somme (having drawn a considerable proportion into Belgium);
secondly, the defeat of any counter-move by French operational or
strategic reserves (see Map 2).

Manstein's creative genius lay in understanding that both objectives
could be achieved in one bold manoeuvre, what became later known as
the *Sichelschnitt*. If the German forces could traverse the Ardennes, break
through the French defences and cross the river Meuse quickly enough,
they should be able to develop sufficient momentum to exploit across
the plain of Picardy to reach the deep objective of the Channel coast
before the Allies would be able to react sufficiently. Deception would be
achieved by telegraphing a main attack in the north (Army Group B) –
waving 'the Matador's Cloak' in Liddell Hart's retrospective analogy.
Simultaneously, the unexpected axis and strength of the main effort in
the centre (Army Group A), directed at achieving crossings of the Meuse
on the fifth day of the offensive in the vicinity of Sedan, would garner
surprise. Only strong armoured forces could yield such an extraordinary
result, together with concentrated close air support.[32] Thus Manstein,
ever the chess player, sought a decision as much based on the distraction
and anticipated reaction of the Allies as on Germany's opening gambit.
It was this dynamic and largely intuitive approach that distinguished him
from the more mechanistic thinking of the majority of his opponents
and colleagues. Yet he too, later, was to be the subject of successful Soviet
deception on the Eastern Front based on inadequate intelligence.[33]

Manstein's principal concern remained the threat of a French counterattack from the south, and particularly one involving the armoured
reserves concentrated in the vicinity of Reims. Such were the stakes:
decisive strategic gain could not be achieved without incurring appreciable operational risk. As he wrote, 'The risk, but also the opportunity
of [realizing] a great success, and one magnified if the enemy reinforces
his north wing, lies with Army Group A.'[34] As ever, the expertise lay in
calculating it and, above all, in converting theory into practice.

Manstein and Rundstedt recognized the intrinsic problem in realizing
their scheme of manoeuvre: a lack of forces. From their point of view,
the ends, ways and means calculus would not balance unless their army
group were to be reinforced. Hence much of the subsequent correspondence and ensuing argument between Army Group A and OKH
concerned two very closely related issues: first, about the intended object
and method of attack and, secondly, over the requirement for reinforcements. With only Twelfth and Sixteenth Armies in Army Group A, there

were insufficient forces to undertake the required operational tasks. Hence Manstein argued not only for a third army, but also for significant bolstering of the existing two.

Rundstedt's three demands (drafted as ever by Manstein and his busy planning staff) were: first, to shift the main effort of the German offensive in the West from the north to the centre, forming a powerful southern arm of attack; secondly, to propel on this axis strong motorized forces to 'strike in the back' of the Allied forces expected in northern Belgium; and thirdly, to employ an army offensively to defeat the anticipated French counterattack from the south. OKH, however, did not accept the ambitious scheme of manoeuvre presented by Army Group A. During a visit to Koblenz on 3 November, Brauchitsch dismissed the request for additional troops with 'Yes, if (only) I had the forces available.'[35] From Manstein's perspective, this statement confirmed that, at best, the army commander-in-chief had not concurred with the operational arguments, or, perhaps rather more worryingly, had not understood them. From now on, the personal rift between them deepened. It would have consequences for Manstein's career.

In early November 1939 there was considerable despondency in Koblenz amongst the commander, chief of staff and operations staff of Army Group A. To be ignored by a superior headquarters at any time is a very awkward business, but it represents a particularly tiresome state of affairs when planning and conducting operations. This sense of frustration became acute when a summary of operational intentions sent by Army Group A to OKH on 6 November remained unanswered. OKH surprised the staff in Koblenz on 12 November, however, with a signal stating that Hitler had ordered a group of mobile troops to be formed within the army group. Based on Guderian's XIX Corps, it comprised: 2nd and 10th Panzer Divisions, a motorized division, the *Leibstandarte* and the Infantry Regiment *Grossdeutschland*, an élite army motorized formation.[36] The initial task of the new mobile group was twofold:

> To defeat mobile enemy forces deployed into southern Belgium, and thereby lighten the task of Twelfth and Sixteenth Armies; and to gain a surprise hold of the west bank of the Meuse at, or south-east of, Sedan and so set the conditions for the continuation of operations, particularly in the event that the armoured formations allocated to Fourth and Sixth Armies fail to fulfil their promise.[37]

So what had caused Hitler to direct OKH to provide these reinforcements? In his memoirs, Manstein ascribes this welcome development to the possible influence of his friend Colonel General

Ernst Busch, commander-in-chief of Sixteenth Army, who was well aware of the army group's thinking. He had recently presented his operational planning in person to Hitler and so the idea of an armoured thrust through the Ardennes may have come up in discussion then. In view of Busch's later scepticism about the plan, some doubt must remain on this possibility. Alternatively, as Manstein conceded – rather generously perhaps in view of their later tense relationship – Hitler himself may have recognized the opportunity presented by such a manoeuvre.[38] Manstein observed:

[Hitler] had a keen eye for the art of the tactically possible and spent much time brooding over maps. He may have spotted that a crossing over the Meuse was most easily achieved at Sedan, whereas the armoured forces of the Fourth Army would encounter much more difficult going further downstream. He may also have recognized that a crossing at Sedan would represent a promising spot (in the sense of an opening [sic] of the Meuse-line for the south flank of Army Group B) and wished – as ever – to pursue all tempting objectives simultaneously.[39]

Guderian, commander of XIX Corps, meanwhile, was none too pleased about the dispersal of the armoured forces, which broke his famous maxim '*Klotzen, nicht Kleckern*' ('Clout, don't dribble'). He came round to Manstein's thinking when asked for his advice about the going for armour in the Ardennes and the possibility of crossing the Meuse in the vicinity of Sedan. As we have seen earlier, Manstein also knew the lie of the land intimately, having taken part in the German defensive battles in Champagne in the spring of 1917, in the Reims offensives in May and July of 1918, and having fought with the 213rd Infantry Division in the Sedan area during that autumn.

Guderian had attended a general staff war school at Sedan in early 1918 and thus was able to confirm on the basis of a detailed map study and his personal recollections from twenty-one years before that 'the operation that [Manstein] had planned could in fact be carried out'. But Guderian attached a very significant proviso: 'A sufficient number of armoured and motorized divisions must be employed, if possible, all of them.'[40] This was welcome grist to Manstein's mill: not only did he have the supporting evidence from Germany's leading proponent of armoured warfare, but also he knew that Hitler listened to Guderian's advice. It should be recalled that Guderian and Manstein both attended the War Academy in Berlin in 1913, and although not close friends on intimate '*Du*' terms, their mutual respect, bordering on admiration, is evident from their memoirs. After the war, Manstein declared graciously:

'Ultimately it was [Guderian's] élan which inspired our tanks in their dash round the backs of the enemy to the Channel coast.'[41]

Despite the reinforcement of XIX Corps and Guderian's personal encouragement, Manstein remained unimpressed with OKH. On 21 November, Brauchitsch and Halder visited Army Group A's headquarters in Koblenz, along with the commander of Army Group B, Colonel General Fedor von Bock. In addition, the army commanders of both army groups were present, who were later invited to speak. Although an army group chief of staff, and with a lot to say, Manstein was not.

Undeterred by this personal slight, Manstein and his planning staff then refined their proposals for the coming offensive, including a carefully argued case for yet additional forces, in a memorandum released later on 21 November. As its more detailed successor of 6 December, this document would stand muster today in a command and staff college as a cogently formulated and succinctly articulated appreciation (or 'estimate') of the situation.[42] In broad terms, the army group's *initial* intent was based on achieving surprise by attacking through the Ardennes; driving through Luxembourg at best speed; breaking through the Belgian frontier fortifications before the French had time to organize an effective defence; and then defeating the French forces in southern Belgium. This major operation, it was planned, would set the conditions for both the continuation of the main attack beyond the Meuse west to the estuary of the Somme and the creation of an active offensive front to the south. More importantly, the surprise generated by the unanticipated axis of advance should be compounded by the unexpected tempo of attack. As the Allies found to their cost, the very speed of the German offensive was astonishing, if not bewildering, and was to have a paralysing effect on decision-making. Manstein's greatest contribution was not in planning the preliminary operation to the Meuse, but rather in calculating what was required to achieve decisive success *beyond* it – into the operational and strategic depth of northern France.

Notwithstanding the day-to-day pressures as a busy chief of staff in Koblenz, Manstein still found the time to write regularly to Jutta-Sibylle, reflecting on personal and other family matters. As with many bright individuals frustrated at particular stages of their careers, he was prone to speculate on past events. He observed:

[In many respects,] it is depressing that I didn't take over from Beck. Perhaps I would have managed to have manoeuvred OKH into a better position over matters of high command than it appears to be currently. I believe I would have achieved this through displaying greater initiative than Ha[lder], and by being more disposed to making early positive proposals rather than expressing concerns. But it remains questionable whether I would have succeeded.[43]

One can have some sympathy with Manstein's position. From a subordinate's perspective there's only one thing worse than having a less capable commander than you: if he's not even bright enough to recognize the fact and to utilize your talents to best advantage. Nevertheless, whatever one may find to criticize in Rundstedt, he was shrewd enough to give Manstein the freedom to advance his own ideas for the benefit of the army group and for the campaign as a whole. That was Rundstedt's prime legacy during the development of the campaign plan: he facilitated his chief of staff rather than the other way about. Within the German Army this rather odd arrangement could be made to work: in an Allied one it would be unthinkable.[44]

Returning to the planning of the offensive, OKH remained unbending despite Headquarters Army Group A's memorandum of 21 November. For the moment, Halder was still hindering any fresh thinking. Although Manstein was unsighted on the matter, Hitler by this date was already considering reinforcing Guderian's corps, if required. There was not yet a conscious desire to adjust the focus of attack from north to centre (Army Group B to A), but rather an implicit acknowledgement that the main effort might have to be switched if Army Group B were not to make as rapid progress as anticipated. Thus the Führer wanted to ride both horses and to back the emerging winner once the campaign was well under way – or as Manstein described it graphically, 'following the hare'.[45] Good in theory but hard in practice: a very real difficulty lies in achieving this kind of flexibility within the land environment. Once an initial deployment is set, armoured forces rarely can be rushed around the battlefield quickly enough to give substance to a newly designated main effort at the operational level. Switching air power (and now combat aviation) is often the only effective method.

In his next memorandum of 6 December, Manstein displayed his full powers of military estimation, requesting the necessary forces if Army Group A were to fulfil the operational promise that shone so brightly in his mind. A new army (the Eighteenth) was needed to advance through southern Belgium and then to thrust towards the lower Somme to attack into the rear of the enemy forces that were likely to engage Army Group B.[46] A second army (the Twelfth) was required for committal in a southwesterly direction to defeat offensively any French counterattack. A third army (the Sixteenth), as previously envisaged, would cover the deep southern flank between the northern end of the main Maginot Line westwards towards Sedan.[47]

Manstein set out his case for a grand total of forty divisions, including an army group reserve of four. Significantly, even at this advanced stage of planning, he requested only two corps of armoured and motorized troops (XIX and XIV Corps respectively). Whilst this represented the potential to build a main effort with Army Group A, it hardly constituted a concentration of a sufficiently large grouping of mobile troops to bring about the intended psychological shock effect on the Allies.

The key to gaining the necessary operational surprise was the rapid appearance of armour in strength at the Meuse and its undiminished impetus thereafter. However, the clear majority of the German mobile troops (including eight out of ten panzer divisions and two of the four motorized infantry divisions) remained with Army Group B under Manstein's submission. The *Sichelschnitt* had yet to acquire its required cutting edge. The distribution of the armoured and motorized forces remained unchanged under Manstein's next proposal of 18 December. It is thus abundantly clear that whatever Guderian's advice as to concentrating these forces to form a clear *Schwerpunkt* (main effort), for some reason it had not been followed through.

The rationale for Manstein's hesitation in demanding sufficient mobile forces to execute his plan is unclear, and is not explained in his memoirs. Perhaps he could not bring Rundstedt round to appreciating their potential, or he felt the time was not yet ripe to call for their subordination to Army Group A. In any event, Manstein did not call unequivocally for sufficient additional armour despite implying the requirement. Guderian, for his part, complained about Rundstedt's lack of understanding of armoured warfare rather than that of Manstein. Indeed, Manstein under Beck's direction had investigated the employment of panzer corps and even panzer armies during the general staff rides of 1935–36 and in the planning of Operation GREEN undertaken in 1937 prior to the invasion of Czechoslovakia the following year.[48]

In Manstein's own words in January 1940, Army Group A was still being denied the necessary armour that 'must [come] *under command from the outset* if there were to be any chance of achieving surprise in southern Belgium and driving around the enemy in the direction of the Somme estuary'.[49] It's now clear that he was already thinking in terms of grouping a greater number of panzer divisions than hitherto within Army Group A, and most probably had this in mind all the while since discussing the matter with Guderian. As the expert military historian Karl-Heinz Frieser has pointed out, Manstein was only able 'to shed his diplomatic self-restraint' during the meeting with Hitler. He demanded 'strong Panzer [forces] or none at all'.[50] Critically, the fact remains that following the events of 17 February, sufficient armoured forces *were* switched from Army Group B to Army Group A.

War-gaming the Plan

In the meantime, other events had been conspiring to bring about a shift of operational direction. The disclosure of part of the German campaign plan (the so-called Mechelen incident) had represented a serious lapse in operations security. On 10 January, a Major Reinberger of 7th Airborne Division was flying in bad weather from Münster to Cologne in a Fieseler Storch liaison aircraft. Against regulations, he had carried on his person the operation order of First Air Fleet. His pilot got lost, ran out of fuel and made a forced landing in Belgium. Although Reinberger tried to burn the document, at least part of it remained intact and fell into Belgian hands.[51] Whilst there was no immediate change of plan, the German High Command could not dismiss the possibility of their intentions being made known to the Allies.

Brauchitsch visited Koblenz again on 25 January to attend a conference at Headquarters Army Group A that included the subordinate army commanders. Manstein presented once again his ideas, declaring that the insertion of XIX Corps alone through the Ardennes represented a half-measure, which would not achieve the desired success at Sedan. However, Brauchitsch refused to release the follow-on XIV Motorized Corps from the OKH reserve to Army Group A. Thus there would be no change of main effort until operations were under way, indicating to Manstein that the potential compromise of the plan had not yet caused a fundamental change in the thinking of the high command. Whether the professional disagreement between Brauchitsch and Manstein turned into a bitter argument bordering on insubordination, as has been suggested, remains to be substantiated.[52] In any event, Manstein's posting followed two days later – hardly a coincidence.

Before he left Koblenz, Manstein organized a war game on 7 February for Army Group A. The *Kriegsspiel* had long been a tool of the Prussian (then German) General Staff to develop and refine operational plans, rehearsing move and counter-move.[53] During the play, it was observed that Guderian's XIX Corps attacking alone over the Meuse at Sedan would prove problematical, to say the least. More armoured forces would be required. Manstein gained the impression that Halder, who was observing the game, 'was at last beginning to realize the validity of our standpoint'. Significantly, Halder noted in his diary:

> I think there is no sense in the armoured corps attacking alone across the Meuse on [the] fifth attack day. No later than [on the] third attack day, OKH must be able to decide whether it wants to launch a concerted attack across the Meuse or let the army groups slug it out on their own.[54]

This war game marked Manstein's formal farewell from Headquarters Army Group A. On the conclusion of the exercise, Rundstedt thanked his departing chief of staff in the presence of all the participants. Manstein was deeply moved by this friendly gesture, recording in his memoirs:

> [Von Rundstedt's] choice of words on this occasion reflected all the kindness and chivalry of that great commander. It was a further source of satisfaction to me that the two army commanders of our Army Group, Generals Busch and List, as well as General Guderian, not only deplored my removal but were genuinely dismayed by it.[55]

Rundstedt left no record of this event, but Guderian wrote generously of Manstein's departure:

> Manstein ... aroused such animosity in the High Command that he was appointed commanding general of an Infantry Corps. He requested that he at least be given a Panzer Corps: his request was not granted. As a result our finest operational brain took the field as a commander of a corps in the third wave of attack, though it was largely due to his brilliant initiative that the operation was to be such an outstanding success.[56]

Manstein departed Koblenz on 9 February for a short home leave at Liegnitz prior to assuming command of XXXVIII Army Corps. On 13 February, Major General Alfred Jodl, Chief of Operations of OKW, recorded in his diary that Hitler wished to review plans for the offensive in the West. Jodl gave the Führer a report that highlighted the opportunity of achieving surprise by attacking at Sedan.[57] As previously noted, Halder had been coming round to the idea of generating a main effort with sufficient armoured forces within Army Group A. The war game in Koblenz had provided a major a change of heart: professional objectivity was beginning to triumph over his personal antipathy for Manstein.

On 14 February, Halder observed a second war game, held at Headquarters Twelfth Army at Mayen, during which the mounting strains between the participants became increasingly apparent. He recorded that 'Guderian and von Wietersheim plainly show lack of confidence in success.... The whole tank operation is planned wrong!' Meanwhile, the commander of Twelfth Army, Colonel General Wilhelm List, was 'endeavouring to find new patterns of teamwork between armour, air force, and the conventional arms'.[58] Guderian's account of the war game confirms the tense nature of the discussions and the widening split opening up between him and more conservative thinkers who insisted that the infantry divisions needed to catch the armour up before forcing the Meuse. He criticized Rundstedt who did not have 'any clear idea about the potentialities of tanks, and declared himself in favour of the more cautious solution'. Guderian's exasperation was exemplified by 'Now was the time when we needed Manstein!'[59]

The German Army was surely exceptionally lucky to enjoy the twin talents from the War Academy class of 1913, who had worked closely together in the planning of the sickle-cut manoeuvre. Sadly, this happy partnership was not to be repeated. Manstein and Guderian went on to clash over the planning for the battle at Kursk in the summer of 1943, as we shall see later. It was significant that the German Army (and later the Red Army) paid enormous attention to war-gaming in a manner that was not replicated by the Western Allies at this stage of the war. Whilst the Germans investigated extensively and rehearsed diligently their plans (and that of their opponents) in the spring of 1940, the Allies did not. Montgomery, for one, complained about 'a faulty command set-up' and observed that,

> G.H.Q. of the B.E.F. had never conducted any exercises, either with or without troops, from the time we had landed in France up to the day active operations began in May 1940. The need for wireless silence was given as an excuse; but an indoor exercise on the model could easily have been held. The result was a total lack of any common policy or tactical doctrine throughout the B.E.F.; when differences arose these differences remained, and there was no firm grip from the top.[60]

There could not have been a greater contrast between the German Army and its opponents in the West in terms of organization and style of command. Despite the many personal and professional differences that surfaced during the planning and execution of the operation, the Germans had at the very least a common purpose, a unifying doctrine and associated training regime that was singularly absent in the Allies.[61] This common framework of military understanding, far more than any particular technological advance, augmented by a clear determination and will to fight, and a readiness to accept casualties, provided the backbone of the German success in the campaign. Victory did not come about solely due to the incompetence of their enemies.

For the majority of Hitler's generals, the coming campaign in the West offered ideal opportunities for recognition and advancement. In contrast, the future prospects appeared less promising for Manstein, given his relatively humble role in training an infantry corps in the East. Required to become largely a spectator in the campaign's first act, Operation YELLOW, he was lucky enough to gain a virtuoso role in the second, leading his corps in Operation RED, the completion of the defeat of France. Meantime, he had one important task to perform before assuming command of his corps: to meet Hitler in Berlin.

As we have already seen, the working breakfast at the *Reichskanzlei* on 17 February 1940 afforded Manstein the opportunity to brief Hitler on his operational idea and associated scheme of manoeuvre. By all accounts, the Führer was enthused by Manstein's suggestions, including the proposed employment of 'strong armoured forces'. By this time, Halder was already working out the details required to put Manstein's ideas into practice and to give them greater substance by providing more armour for Army Group A. After the war, he was to dispute Manstein's essential contribution in challenging OKH's original design and in proposing a new plan. In an interview of 1967, whilst praising Manstein's military prowess – particularly on the Eastern Front – Halder maintained that 'The plan for the French campaign – as it was executed – did not come from him.'[62] This view can be easily refuted: the fact that Halder claimed Manstein's idea as his does not lend him any credibility. Success, as they say, has many fathers whilst failure has few.

In agreeing with Manstein, Hitler overcame temporarily his personal distaste of an old-style Prussian general staff officer in favouring the brilliantly unconventional operational idea. That Manstein's plan to encircle the entire Allied northern wing along the Channel coast, which OKH (in reality, his rival Halder) had considered absurd and dangerous, now coincided with his own instinct to switch the main effort to the southern arm of attack merely confirmed the superior military judgement of the Führer to his professional military advisors. Much as Hitler liked to live the myth that this brilliant idea was his (in a similar manner to Halder), there was an important distinction between Manstein's far-reaching *operational level* plan in pursuit of a strategic outcome and Hitler's purely *tactical* inclinations towards Sedan.[63]

There can be little doubt that the Führer's discussions with Jodl and Schmundt on 13 February had already primed his coincidental thinking about Sedan as the easiest place to cross the Meuse. In contrast, Manstein, as Frieser has rightly pointed out, was 'thinking all the way to the Channel Coast'. Hence if Manstein shares with Halder and Hitler the credit for the adoption of *Sichelschnitt* in its final form, the original operational concept was very much his alone. As General Graf von Kielmansegg has made perfectly clear: 'The idea was entirely and totally Manstein's.'[64] Halder's contribution thereafter from March to May 1940, whilst Manstein remained banished in Stettin, lay in defending the new plan against all objections.

7

A Glorious Summer

'Our hard-hit opponent was no longer able to offer anything more than localized and temporary resistance in the open field.' Erich von Manstein

A Frosty Start

Pleasant courtesies were still observed at this stage of the war. Following his private meeting with the Führer on 17 February 1940, Manstein was escorted politely out of the *Reichskanzlei* by two of Hitler's adjutants, Colonel Rudolf Schmundt and Major Gerhard Engel. One might reasonably expect that Manstein would have been well satisfied: he had managed to brief Hitler on his operational plan. He did not appear, however, to have been particularly elated by the result, knowing that he had no decisive role to play in the coming offensive. Engel recorded that Manstein 'complained about the OKH and said that his ideas were nothing new there. In gratitude he had been given an infantry corps, and this to a man who had begged for a panzer corps. Halder would not now be able to oppose it. With Beck this had been rather different.'[2] So the decision to post Manstein away from the coming action stood.

Manstein proceeded as ordered from Berlin to Stettin. Three weeks earlier, on 27 January 1940, Headquarters XXXVIII Army Corps had begun to form up in Cambrai barracks. In accordance with standard German practice (and that of the Western Allies) a corps headquarters (*General Kommando*) was not responsible for a fixed grouping of forces.[3] Thus Manstein's primary concern in early 1940 was to train his own headquarters and the corps signals unit. He accomplished this through a series of six map and command post exercises run over as many weeks from February to April.

The brand-new corps commander had thought well ahead about the potential employment of his force, anticipating with uncanny accuracy its eventual role in France. The opening scenario for Exercise 4, for example, reflected 'wide stringing out of the corps caused by an attack over a river; the difficulties of this form of combat, particularly for logistics, [and] the separation of supporting from fighting troops'. This

was precisely the situation he was to confront in June at the obstacles of
the Somme, Seine and Loire. The sixth map exercise considered river
crossing operations again.[4] On the conclusion of a demanding test
deployment and field training exercise, the corps headquarters was
declared operational on 5 April 1940, no mean feat. Apart from Manstein,
much of the credit for this performance must go to his energetic Chief
of the General Staff, Colonel Arthur Hauffe, together with his well-
drilled and confident staff.

On the orders of OKH, from March to early May, Manstein and
members of his headquarters inspected five new infantry divisions that
were being raised in this region of Germany, Pomerania and in the newly
incorporated province of Warthegau, now in north-west Poland.[5] One
of the formations that Manstein visited in the very cold March of 1940
was 197th Infantry Division, which was exercising in the area around
Posen (Poznań). Friedrich Wilhelm von Mellenthin, a bright and confident young major of the General Staff, was serving as the Ia, the
division's chief of staff.[6] In his memoirs, he described a chance meeting
with Manstein during the winter of 1939/40 and provided an ironic
anecdote to the general's subsequent visit to the division:

> Whilst travelling by train to the East, I bumped into Lieutenant General
> von Manstein – the Chief of Staff of Army Group A on the Western
> Front – at a Berlin railway station. In his brash manner, he quipped:
> 'Mellenthin, what are you up to in Warthegau [the newly conquered
> province in western Poland], when it's just about to get going in the West?'
> ... to my amazement he was the commanding general who inspected our
> division several weeks later. At the end of the visit, which passed off
> excellently, I stood next to Manstein alone and could not stop myself
> from pointing out: 'Well, General, it all turns out rather differently from
> what one thinks!'[7]

Contrary to the popular Anglo-American clichéd view of straight-faced,
humourless Germans, there was indeed a place for good-natured rapport
within the German Army, and particularly one between members of the
General Staff in which a common education and upbringing counted
much more than military rank. One cannot imagine Montgomery or
Bradley being engaged in such an open manner by a much more junior
officer unless he was an aide-de-camp (ADC).

In his memoirs, however, Manstein skips over the spring of 1940 in a
couple of paragraphs, neither bothering to name the formations he
visited nor mentioning his own staff, in stark contrast to the detailed
descriptions of events and personalities he gives later on in the Second

World War. Fortunately, his senior ADC of the period, Hauptmann Rudolf Graf, left a condensed but none the less useful record. It offers an interesting perspective of Manstein preparing himself as a commander in barracks: 'In general, we saw him only at briefings and at mealtimes. Most of the time he remained by himself in his room, where – I later found out – he worked intensely on his maps and military writings until late into the night.'[8]

Manstein's personal account only bursts into life on 10 May 1940, when he learns of the start of the German offensive in the West. Such was the level of secrecy surrounding the launch of the campaign that he first heard on the radio that operations were under way. Whilst the corps commander was at home in Liegnitz on a short leave over Whitsun, his ADC was getting married that very day. In the evening, Headquarters XXXVIII Corps was ordered to move south-west to Braunschweig (Brunswick), and later to Düsseldorf, where the headquarters of Army Group B was located. The freshly married Graf joined his commander there, after a compressed honeymoon of only two days. Such hard luck is part of military life.

Development of the Campaign Plan

Whilst the first phase of the campaign in France and the Low Countries (Operation YELLOW) was very much Manstein's creation, once Army Chief of Staff Franz Halder belatedly had grasped his operational idea, he had reinforced Army Group A with sufficient forces to enable it to achieve the decisive success that Manstein had envisaged. Key to realizing the full potential of the *Sichelschnitt* plan was the *operational level* employment of the seven panzer and three motorized infantry divisions grouped within Army Group A. The mass of these divisions was concentrated in General of Cavalry Ewald von Kleist's panzer group, an ad hoc and experimental grouping with a status midway between a corps and an army. It was equipped with a total of 1,222 tanks, representing half the total German armoured strength. Within this group, Guderian's XIX and Lieutenant General Hans Reinhardt's XXXXI Panzer Corps formed the hardened tip of an armoured lance, followed by General of Infantry Gustav Anton von Wietersheim's XIV Motorized Corps.[9] In addition, General of Infantry Hermann Hoth's XV Panzer Corps was subordinated directly to Colonel General Hans-Günther von Kluge's Fourth Army, employed on the right (northern) flank of the army group.[10]

Kleist's mobile group of ten divisions had the sequential tasks of breaking through the French defences on the Meuse and then continuing the attack into the depth of the enemy. It had to be strong enough to achieve both without loss of momentum, whilst risking enemy air attack and overstretching its own logistic support. This was a revolutionary departure from conventional military practice. The French would have expected to see infantry formations, with massive artillery preparation and support, attacking to set the necessary conditions for a break-out and subsequent exploitation by armoured forces (the Montgomery method at El Alamein over two years later in October 1942). It was this inversion of contemporary military thinking and the substitution of air power for artillery that so surprised the French Army at all levels, and that which caused considerable strain within the German Army between the modernists such as Guderian and more conservative thinkers such as Rundstedt.

Without the bold imagination, clarity of thought and guiding influence of Manstein, the commander and staff of Army Group A had begun to doubt the viability of the *Sichelschnitt* campaign plan in general and specifically to question the wisdom of employing the armour in such an unproven, experimental manner. Karl-Heinz Frieser's detailed research contained in his unsurpassed study of the German campaign in the West, *The Blitzkrieg Legend*, has confirmed that Manstein's successor Lieutenant General Georg von Sodenstern was the centre of such orthodoxy. Within two weeks of his taking over from Manstein, on 22 February 1940 he submitted his concerns formally to Rundstedt:

> I am not convinced that even the reinforced panzer and motorized units will manage to force the crossing over the Meuse with the kind of breadth that is necessary for operational purposes. Yes, I doubt, to begin with, that they be in a position to cross the Meuse River even only here and there, holding the bridgeheads thus gained until the following infantry divisions would be able to make room for an operational exploitation featuring the necessary breadth and depth.... But even if that should come off successfully, the panzer and motorized units by that time will be so 'exhausted' that sending them deep into the enemy rear areas will no longer offer any chances of success.[11]

Sodenstern reinforced his criticisms in a more detailed paper on 5 March, raising several pertinent points on the difficulties of the approach through the Ardennes; the likelihood of encountering French delaying forces forward of the Meuse; the dangers of air attack and likely traffic chaos on the march routes; and most crucially, doubting whether the 'infantry-weak' panzer divisions would be in sufficient shape to force the crossings, let alone be available to mount an operational level attack into the enemy's depth.[12] This conservative evaluation confirms that Sodenstern's thinking was more akin to Ludendorff's predominantly tactical-operational level methodology of the First World War than Manstein's radical operational-strategic design in the Second.

Unfortunately for the Allies, such internal criticism within the German chain of command was countered effectively by the combination of Halder, Kleist and Guderian. As a result, the *Sichelschnitt* plan was executed with sufficient strength, surprise and tempo to catch the French off guard at the Meuse, and was to keep the Allied forces unbalanced thereafter to the Channel coast. The plan worked *because* it was so daringly unconventional, exploiting inherent systemic weaknesses in French force structures, command and control, and above all, in will and morale. Further, as Liddell Hart later observed, the more the Allies pushed into northern Belgium, the greater the possibility of German success in the south – the dynamic of the revolving door.[13] Had Sodenstern, rather than Manstein, been the chief of staff of Army Group A during the autumn of 1939 then it is surely inconceivable that the German Army would have developed such an original plan of attack. Yet without the determination and skill of corps commanders such as Guderian, Hoth and Reinhardt, and the bravery and élan of the troops under their command, no such stunning success as that achieved in May 1940 would have occurred. The Luftwaffe, too, contributed greatly to the German success, although its losses in equipment and crews proved heavy.

Above all, it was Halder, previously the arch-critic of Manstein and his daring plan, who from mid February 1940 had taken on the mantle of the freshly converted. In the absence of Manstein, he developed *Sichelschnitt* into its final form and overruled Sodenstern's and others' objections. As Halder impressed on Bock, who remained unconvinced of the outcome of the plan until Guderian's breakthrough at Sedan on 13 May: 'Even if the operation had only a ten percent chance of success, I would stick by it. It alone will lead to the enemy's annihilation.'[14]

Meanwhile, another rising star came into prominence during the spring of 1940. Within a couple of months, Kleist's exceptionally energetic chief of staff Colonel Kurt Zeitzler organized from scratch the panzer group, for which there was neither conceptual nor historical precedent, and neither doctrine nor detailed procedures available. At the same time, Kleist and Zeitzler had to contend with the bureaucratic frictions of the infantry armies in whose areas of responsibility the mobile divisions were concentrated. Zeitzler went on to become army chief of staff in succession to Halder in September 1942, and in consequence Manstein would have much to do with him later on in the war.[15]

Spectator to Sichelschnitt

As military history was being made in the Ardennes and at the Meuse in 1940, Manstein was condemned, in his own words, to act as a bystander for the first couple of weeks of the campaign, whilst Guderian raced to the Channel. As operations developed with increasing tempo, he moved his corps headquarters progressively further westwards. He even found the time for some military tourism, inspecting the Belgian fort of Eban-Emael, which had fallen to German glider-borne infantry and combat engineers on 10/11 May. Placed under command of Army Group A on 16 May, he took the opportunity to visit his former headquarters (now deployed forward from Koblenz to Bastogne) the next day. Although warmly received by Rundstedt and Sodenstern, one suspects that the occasion was not without a little chagrin for Manstein.

At Rundstedt's headquarters he learned that his corps headquarters was to be resubordinated to List's Twelfth Army. Whilst the attacks of both army groups were progressing well, concerns about the threat to the ever-extending southern flank of Army Group A had mounted. These fears proved unfounded as there was no French operational level shock grouping poised to mount such a counterattack.

By employing its Seventh Army – including three of Frances's precious mobile divisions – on the extreme left flank of the Allied line and subsequently splitting up the central reserve of three heavy armoured divisions concentrated in the Reims area, the French High Command had managed to dissipate all its operational and strategic reserves. The careful husbanding of reserves for employment at the decisive point in time and space to achieve operational or strategic effect is one of the principal tasks of a senior commander. Without such reserves at his disposal, or a plan to create fresh ones from less threatened areas, such a commander is in danger of becoming irrelevant. The German armed forces had gained the operational, and arguably the strategic, initiative within a week of their campaign in the West, but the increasingly promising situation was not as clear to the high command at the time as it may now appear in retrospect.

Rundstedt had already imposed a temporary halt on the armoured divisions on the morning of 16 May, which was confirmed by Hitler who came to Headquarters Army Group A the next day, intervening directly for the first time in the operational execution of the campaign. Rundstedt had forbidden any movement – except for advance elements – west of the line Beaumont–Montcornet.[16] From his point of view, this order was primarily a precautionary measure, designed to provide time for the

infantry divisions to catch up. Hitler was worried more about the possibility of a large-scale French counterattack – and the risk of a resulting
setback that could have unfortunate political and psychological consequences. So rather than pressing on with the advance to the Channel,
Hitler appeared more concerned about establishing a secure line of
defence along the river Aisne, in the area around Laon, and, later, the
Somme.[17] Stopping movement along the 'panzer corridor' – literally in
its tracks – would not necessarily improve its protection; its very flank
security came from its forward momentum.

Notwithstanding the startling successes of the campaign thus far, the
German High Command was far from euphoric, with views diverging
as to how operations should be developed. Whilst there was nervousness
at Army Group A, which chimed with Hitler's nagging concerns, Halder,
keeping his cool, was frustrated increasingly by the failure to consummate
a great victory. In turn, his sentiments were shared by many of the army
corps and division commanders involved. Despite the deployment of
significant forces to protect the southern flank, the spectre of a major
French counterattack continued unduly to unnerve Hitler until after the
fall of Dunkirk. As both Manstein and Halder observed, Hitler appeared
to mistrust his own luck, lacking confidence in the *Sichelschnitt* campaign
plan as a whole, whilst overestimating the powers of recovery of the
French and remaining concerned – not without some justification –
about the state of German armoured forces. An exasperated Halder
recorded on 17 May:

> Rather unpleasant day. The Führer is terribly nervous. Frightened by his
> own success, he is afraid to take any chance and so would rather pull the
> reins on us. Puts forward the excuse that it is all about his concern for
> the left flank! Keitel's telephone calls to army groups on behalf of Führer
> and Führer's personal visit to AGp. B have caused only bewilderment and
> doubts.[18]

Manstein was no longer in a position to influence such considerations,
and from the tone of his memoirs, he seemed to regret the fact. Required
to shepherd the forward movement of Second Army, in the second
echelon, his operational level expertise was hardly taxed by organizing
what was essentially an administrative road movement exercise.[19]

None the less this task represented an important contribution to the
campaign, ensuring that fresh infantry formations were fed continuously
into the offensive – and to guard the flanks – as the German advance
rolled steadily westwards to the Channel. The members of Manstein's
staff, moreover, were rushed off their feet. Graf recorded that the

'headquarters was on the go day and night. All available personnel – including the operations, personnel, intelligence and supply officers – were deployed to important crossroads and junctions in support of traffic regulation teams.'[20] Whether Manstein's corps headquarters had been specially chosen by OKH for this crucial task, as his staff suspected, cannot be proven. Nevertheless, much of the success of *Sichelschnitt* depended on it.

In *Lost Victories*, Manstein devoted a considerable amount of space to discussing the impact of the high-level decision-making during this opening week of the campaign, highlighting the bad precedent set in allowing Hitler to override the professional military judgement of the Chief of the Army General Staff: 'It is now apparent that Hitler, though not bold enough to accept a temporary risk on the southern flank of the German offensive, was already claiming the right to exercise a personal and detailed control of army operations.'[21]

Manstein would not appear to have appreciated that Rundstedt had also played a significant part in the halt process on 17 May 1940, which lost at least a day's march in the armoured advance to the Channel coast. Luckily for the Allied forces, they would get further respite when the German armour was prevented from advancing quickly towards Dunkirk as a result of the British counterattack at Arras on 21 May and the subsequent German halt order of 24 May, which imposed a two-day freeze on armoured movement.

Forward elements of Guderian's corps, the motorized infantry of 2nd Panzer Division, had already reached the Channel coast at Noyelles, north-west of Abbeville, during the early hours of 21 May, the twelfth day of the campaign. Later that day, the predominantly British counterattack at Arras had failed tactically, but had induced a sense of operational crisis within the German chain of command quite out of proportion to the opposing forces involved. It resulted in a transitory paralysing effect: in consequence, the advance of the German armour was halted, albeit temporarily.[22] Guderian had given his divisions the Channel ports as their objectives on 22 May: 2nd Panzer to Boulogne, 1st Panzer to Calais and, crucially, 10th Panzer Division to Dunkirk. As a result of the events at Arras, however, the latter division remained held back as a superfluous reserve in Kleist's Panzer Group. The capture of Boulogne took three days and the defiant defence of Calais by the British 30th Brigade Group lasted to the morning of 26 May. In the meantime, French forces continued to hold out heroically in Lille, which fixed elements of several German divisions that would otherwise been able to attack or pursue the withdrawing British and French troops. Thus Allied forces gained an unexpected breathing space.

Meanwhile, the leading divisions of Army Groups A and B were closing in on the ever-narrowing pocket held by the Belgian Army, the BEF and elements of the French First, Seventh and Ninth Armies. Surely the hammer (Army Group B) would soon strike the anvil (Army Group A), smashing everything in between.[23] By the evening of 24 May, with the German armour astride the river Aa at Gravelines on the coast, less than 15 kilometres from the town centre of Dunkirk, British and French forces had yet to withdraw in any strength into the comparative security of the Dunkirk perimeter.

Manstein's corps headquarters was still hard at work. On 21 May it had no fewer than twelve divisions under command for movement. Three days later, the corps war diarist recorded: 'The advance to the west continues to be conducted ruthlessly. It all depends on feeding as many divisions as possible into the tube to the Channel coast, in order to be armed against all enemy attempts to break through from the south and north.'[24] With the surrender of Belgian forces on 28 May, the apparent entrapment of the BEF at Dunkirk and the defeat of French forces north of the Somme and Oise, Manstein's *Sichelschnitt* plan, suitably developed by Halder, was fulfilling all its promise: a strategically decisive German victory was not just in the air – it appeared there all but for the final taking.

The Fight for the Somme Crossings

Manstein had no part to play in the high drama playing out at Dunkirk. As a corps commander, his task was guarding his allotted sector of the southern flank on the lower Somme and then preparing for the subsequent major operation to complete the defeat of France (Operation RED). It was indeed ironic that Manstein's first involvement in combat during the campaign was to defend the German bridgeheads at Abbeville and Amiens, when he himself had sought to secure the southern flank through *offensive means*. As we have seen, Manstein had envisaged a complete army (of up to twelve divisions) crossing the lower Somme to disrupt any counterattack force and to prevent the establishment of defensive positions. Although there were no significant operational level reserves available, British and French forces none the less mounted determined attempts to seize the Somme crossings, ranging in scope from battalion to multi-divisional, largely disjointed, attacks. At the same time, with the German High Command's focus on Dunkirk, the French

Army in record time had managed to develop strong fortifications along the Somme, Oise and Aisne, which together formed the Weygand Line. France's last effective line of defence would shortly be tested by the full weight of the German Army and Air Force.

The fight for the Somme crossings (27 May–4 June) represented the only occasion during the Second World War when units of the British Army faced German forces under Manstein's direct command. For this reason, he never caught the British public's imagination during the Second World War in the manner of Rommel. On 20 May, the scratch British garrisons of Abbeville and Amiens had been swept aside by Guderian's 2nd and 1st Panzer Divisions.[25] These German formations had been relieved in place by 2nd Motorized and 9th Panzer Divisions then under command of Wietersheim's XIV Corps. As Manstein assumed responsibility for the bridgeheads on the morning of 27 May, 57th and 9th Infantry Divisions were arriving to take over the defence. Slick German battle drills ensured no confusion, even in the midst of battle.

When Wietersheim handed over, he told Manstein confidently that he did not 'anticipate any large-scale enemy activity'. These were indeed 'famous last words' for within an hour reports came in that both bridgeheads were under heavy armoured attack: it turned out to be a day of crisis. Manstein records that at Amiens 'several heavy French tanks were knocked out', and at Abbeville, the British lost a 'total of thirty British light and medium tanks'.[26] The Allied attack on 27 May was conducted by a potentially very powerful combination of British and French forces, involving 2nd and 3rd Armoured Brigades of the recently disembarked 1st (British) Armoured Division and elements of 2nd and 5th French Light Cavalry Divisions. The operation failed dismally. As the official British History records:

> Co-operation with the French divisions was ineffective, and close mutual support almost non-existent.... The German hold on the Somme and on their bridgeheads had not been disturbed, and in using cruiser tanks unsupported by artillery and infantry to attack prepared defences we had heavy losses. Sixty-five had been put out of action by the enemy, though some were recovered; fifty-five had mechanical breakdowns for there had been little opportunity for maintenance since they had landed and hurried forward into battle.[27]

Characteristically, Manstein's tactical response to these bothersome attacks was to launch a corps-level counterattack himself, but Fourth Army Headquarters forbade any such aggressive manoeuvre. Whilst 1st

(British) Armoured Division reorganized and took no further part in the fight for the Somme crossings until 4 June, the French struck again on 28 May. General de Gaulle's heavy 4th Armoured Division attacked on 29 and 30 May but failed to dislodge Manstein's divisions from their bridgeheads.[28] Desperate Allied attempts continued. On 4 June, 51st (Highland) Division, the Composite Regiment of 1st Armoured Division (formed from the remnants of two badly mauled armoured brigades) and elements of the French 31st Infantry and 2nd Armoured Divisions assaulted in vain the Abbeville bridgehead, incurring heavy losses.

The Germans had shown on the Somme that they were the masters of an integrated defensive battle. Manstein had been in his element, as his ADC described:

> Every day at dawn our commanding general drove out with his trusty driver – Sergeant Nagel – to visit the forward troops in order to gain a personal view of the situation and assess their morale. He used every opportunity to speak with the infantry in combat right at the front, and especially to enquire as to their concerns. The soldiers were always receptive and gave their opinions frankly. Our commanding general always liked a cheerful answer much more than any obsequious deference.[29]

The fighting had proved fast and furious. Within 2nd Motorized Division, on 27 May an anti-tank gunner called Hubert Brinkforth had accounted for nine of the British tanks destroyed at Huppy, 10 kilometres south-west of Abbeville, in a dramatic twenty-minute action. In recognition of this deed, he was immediately promoted to corporal and Manstein made his first commendation for a Knight's Cross on behalf of a private soldier.[30]

On the British side, the need to develop combined arms tactics to defeat effective German anti-tank defences was lost entirely in the British lessons study, the *Bartholomew Report*. The bloody price of such unprofessional neglect would be paid time and again in the Western Desert.[31] There was also a darker side to the defence of the Somme line. An entry in the war diary of Manstein's corps headquarters noted without further comment: 'In Amiens ten hostages were shot as a result of repeated and widespread acts of sabotage.'[32] It was turning out to be not such a 'clean' war after all.

The Final Act

On 5 June, the German Army and Air Force launched powerful assaults over the Somme at dawn, heralding the start of the fresh offensive. For the Wehrmacht, this second phase of the campaign represented no stroll in the park. On some occasions, and particularly during the defence of the Somme, the French stood firm and fought hard, and typically in a much more coherent and determined manner than during the initial phase of the fighting. Defences were organized in greater depth and French morale recovered temporarily. None the less, German force of arms in the air and on land prevailed.

When outnumbered by the Allies on 10 May, Germany had been forced to rely on operational level surprise and an associated disorientating speed of advance, smooth air-to-land co-operation and sound tactical competence in conducting a combined arms battle. By the beginning of June the scales of war had now turned decisively in Germany's favour. With the Belgian and Dutch surrenders, the elimination of the French First, Seventh and Ninth Armies, and the expulsion of the majority of British forces from the Continent, the German Army in the West of 104 divisions (with nineteen held in reserve) faced a much depleted and disorganized French opponent of sixty-six divisions, together with the two principal remaining British formations (51st (Highland) and 1st Armoured Divisions). If one adds the proven superiority of German air and armoured forces, the outcome of Operation RED was certain.

It was thus a matter of 'when' rather than 'if' a final decision in the West would be achieved. If it is remarkable that the Germans enjoyed in June 1940 such a quantitative and qualitative lead, it is even more striking when one considers that this would be the *last* time in the Second World War (with the possible exception of operations conducted in the early summer of 1941 in the Balkans) that such an overwhelming advantage on this scale would occur. Never again would German forces attack with such a decisive victory so well within their grasp. Equally notable was the administrative agility of the German Army in its reorganization and redeployment between the two phases of the campaign, and the assured close support of the Luftwaffe. This was surely the German Wehrmacht at the height of its fighting power, logistic flexibility and operational superiority.

The German operational plan saw Army Group B due to assault over the Somme on 5 June, Army Group A over the Aisne on 9 June and Army Group C to attack on order. Army Group B formed the right wing of the German attack with the Fourth, Sixth, Eighteenth and Ninth Armies, together with Kleist's panzer group (XIV and XVI Corps) attacking to the east of Amiens. Army Group A's attack involved the Second, Twelfth and Sixteenth Armies, with Guderian's newly constituted Panzer Group (XXXIX and XXXXI Corps) forming the main striking force.

On 15 June Army Group C attacked with First and Seventh Armies. Such was the confidence of OKH that the Army Groups A and B had divergent axes. As a result of the unexpectedly tough French opposition to von Kleist's Panzer Group south and east of Amiens in the first four days of its attack, it was redeployed further east on to a parallel axis to Guderian's. The net result was that no fewer than four mobile corps attacked in a south-easterly direction, the inner arm (Guderian) wheeling east on approaching the Swiss border, entrapping – in conjunction with Army Group C's attacks – approximately 500,000 men of the French Third, Fifth and Eighth Armies in the Lorraine pocket, its eastern limit formed by the Maginot Line. The result was the practical manifestation of Manstein's second operational idea, the sequel to *Sichelschnitt* – achieving the envelopment and destruction of the remainder of the French Army with a powerful right hook.

Manstein's account of his attack within Fourth Army's operation over the Somme on 5 June 1940 and subsequent pursuit of the defeated French as far as the Loire River over the following two weeks reads as one of the most exhilarating and personally rewarding periods of his military career (see Map 3) His fast-moving narrative of operations is interspersed by a more philosophical commentary on command, coloured by descriptions of a flying visit to the cathedral at Le Mans and the various châteaux he stayed in – not forgetting to add some anecdotal details of their recently departed owners.

Employing his three infantry divisions as if they were fully motorized formations, Manstein advanced as quickly as Hoth's XV Panzer Corps on his right flank. Throughout this operation, Manstein showed that he could handle a corps in a determined, flexible and bold manner. Despite his service throughout the First World War and the recent defence of the Somme bridgeheads, this was his first opportunity to command a significant body of troops in a fast-flowing battle of manoeuvre.[33] For this reason alone, it is worth recording the operation in some detail. The XXXVIII Corps consisted of three 'standard' infantry divisions, 6th (Westphalian), 27th (Swabian) and 46th (Sudeten), which were predominantly foot- and horse-powered formations.[34] This was the reality for the bulk of the German Army during the Second World War, in which armoured and motorized formations formed only a small proportion. But each of these infantry divisions was capable of forming a motorized forward detachment (*Vorausabteilung*), which Manstein used to mimic the aggressive tactics of the fully mobile armoured and motorized formations. The necessary motor vehicles were drawn from three sources: the divisional anti-tank, reconnaissance and engineer battalions.

Once a breakthrough of the Somme defence line had been achieved, it was these forward detachments that set the pace of the ensuing pursuit, racing ahead in motor cycles and 'soft' wheeled road transport without regard to open flanks, probing the paths of least resistance and attempting to 'bounce' one water obstacle after the next. To use the terminology of later theorists of manoeuvre warfare, this was 'reconnaissance-pull' demonstrated to optimum effect. The trick was to find a gap in the enemy's defences and to press on regardless, drawing on support from the rear as quickly as it could be brought up.

Manstein's immediate and potentially most difficult task in this second phase of the campaign was to force a crossing over the river Somme. His corps remained subordinated to Kluge's Fourth Army, deployed on the right flank of the German Army anchored on the Channel coast. On the Somme line, II Corps had assumed responsibility for the Abbeville bridgehead. Reinforced by 11th Motorized Infantry Brigade, this corps was to attack parallel to the coastline. In the centre came Hoth's XV Panzer Corps, Fourth Army's main effort, which included Rommel's 7th Panzer Division. Manstein's corps (XXXVIII) was next in line, the left-hand major formation of Fourth Army. To Manstein's own left was Wietersheim's XIV Corps, initially operating in the Sixth Army's zone of attack, poised to break out of the Amiens bridgehead.

Tightly sandwiched in between XV and XIV Corps, Manstein's front was only 20 kilometres wide.[35] The sectors for his two attacking divisions (46th and 27th) were narrower in accordance with German doctrine.[36] As ever, the realities of the terrain and the nature of the enemy's defences would influence the planning and conduct of any assault river-crossing operation rather more than the adoption of any strict staff college template. Manstein described the ground facing his corps, which was far from ideal:

> While the high ground on our own side undulated gently down towards the Somme and had no woods to provide any effective cover, the southern banks rose steeply and gave the enemy an ample view of our jumping off positions. However, the actual valley of the river, which was only a few hundred yards wide, concealed the two opposing front lines from each other by virtue of the numerous thickets at the water's edge. On the southern side – still within the valley – were several villages, notably Breilly, Ailly and Picquigny, which the enemy appeared to have occupied in strength. Like most French villages, they had massive houses and walls

that offered excellent strong points to any defender. Up on the high ground behind the steep southern bank, in the rear of the enemy's defence zone, there were more villages and a number of sizeable woods affording the enemy useful centres of resistance and cover for his artillery.[37]

The crossing of the Somme began at dawn on 5 June 1940. In view of the difficult terrain and the enemy forces facing him – 13th (Alsatian) Division and 5th (North African) Colonial Division – Manstein had elected to mount his attack without prior artillery preparation in order to gain the maximum amount of tactical surprise. Both 27th and 46th German Divisions made successful crossings whilst 6th Division was held uncommitted in a second echelon of attack.

Unlike the demoralized soldiers of 55th Division who had fled in the face of Guderian's crossing of the Meuse at Sedan on 13 May, the French forces opposing Manstein fought hard, clinging on to their fortified villages and well-prepared positions on the heights. Manstein flattered his enemy with, to modern tastes, an undiluted racist compliment:

> The enemy fought bravely – the negroes with their characteristic blood-thirstiness and contempt for human life, the Alsatians with the toughness one had to expect from this Alemanic people, who had furnished Germany with so many good soldiers in World War I. It was really tragic to meet these German [sic] lads as foes in the present fighting.[38]

None the less, the German attacks proceeded well and by the evening of 5 June, Manstein's corps had achieved sufficient depth for his artillery to be brought over the Somme. On his flanks, the neighbouring corps had not made so much progress. To the west, XV Corps was held up initially by a determined French resistance, with Rommel's 7th Panzer Division fighting hard for the key road through Quesnoy-sur-Araines.[39] Manstein makes no mention of such activity on his immediate right flank. Indeed, Rommel's name does not appear in his memoirs whatsoever. To the east, XIV Corps had run into a minefield south of Amiens and in consequence its attack was redirected on a south-south-easterly axis of advance, diverging from Manstein's corps. Within XXXVIII Corps, 27th and 46th Divisions had taken their objectives – the high ground to the south of the Somme, which dominated the valley, 'though not without heavy losses'.[40]

At the end of a day's combat after a successful assault river crossing, a soldier's natural response is to consolidate and to prepare a newly won bridgehead for defence. Tired troops, however well trained, have to be forced to dig in. In some circumstances, however, this is exactly the wrong action. If resistance is light or if orders demand, the attack should be continued without delay. Lieutenant Colonel Hermann Balck had made a name for himself during the night of 13/14 May by dragooning his weary troops of 1st Motorized Infantry Regiment (1st Panzer Division) to seize and exploit beyond Point 301, south of the Meuse at Frénois, near Sedan, sensing that the French defences were crumbling to his front. Balck had summed up his steely approach with an enduringly perceptive remark: 'What is easily done today, can cost streams of blood tomorrow.'[41]

The same situation occurred less than a month later at the Somme, albeit at commanding general level. During the early hours of 6 June, Manstein had driven out to the command post of 46th Division and, finding everyone 'still half asleep after the strenuous events of the previous day', pressed on to its forward regiments. Sensing a lack of enemy activity to his front, Manstein drove in his *Kübelwagen* (the German wartime equivalent of the Willis Jeep developed from the Volkswagen people's car) into the village of Oissy,[42] and finding it undefended, returned to inform the commander of the infantry regiment responsible for its capture, suggesting 'that he should do his own reconnaissance in future'.[43]

This minor tactical vignette, which Manstein clearly took great pride in describing, serves a number of purposes. He declared that sometimes a commander has to 'set a drastic example' if the circumstances demand. Secondly, and this perhaps gives some clue as to Manstein's personality and leadership style, he felt this action was necessary as 'the fighting troops did not know me yet'. German Army doctrine was clear on this matter:

> The example and bearing of officers and other soldiers who are responsible for leadership has a decisive effect on the troops. The officer, who in the face of the enemy displays coolness, decisiveness, and courage, carries his troops with him. He also must win their affections and earn their trust through his understanding of their feelings, their way of thinking, and through selfless care for them.[44]

During the Second World War, Manstein failed to gain the public reputation, bordering on adulation, that Guderian and Rommel both enjoyed as being particularly close to their front-line troops. Thus he was never accorded a popular soubriquet such as the former's *schnelle Heinz* or the latter's *Wüstenfuchs* (desert fox). On the Allied side, Montgomery was known universally as 'Monty', Eisenhower as 'Ike'. Their names if not their faces were recognized by the soldiers under their command. Noting these examples from the Second World War, it is surely hard to subscribe to Wavell's view that 'modern generals are hardly known to the large armies they command'.[45] If a successful general's fame precedes his presence on the battlefield, that reputation must be won in the first place.

There may be some truth in the view that Manstein appeared as a rather remote figure when serving as an army group commander (1942–44). As a corps commander in France, and later in the Soviet Union leading successively both a corps and an army (1941–42), Manstein needed no lessons in the requirement to keep up with troops in contact and to feel their pulse in combat. Notwithstanding the introduction of more effective communications, the exercise of command today – particularly at the tactical level – may still require the presence of the commander at a critical time and place to take charge at the decisive point. Manstein recorded with pride that his second ADC, Lieutenant von Schwerdtner, and his young driver, Sergeant Fritz Nagel, showed great enthusiasm in this minor scouting task. In this manner, Manstein indicated that he had a loyal team working closely for him. When Nagel was killed two years later just prior to the final assault on the Soviet fortress of Sevastopol, Manstein's personal remorse was clear enough.

Meanwhile, on the Somme, the French forces had yet to crack and run as they had done at the Meuse. They were pushed back slowly but steadily, prompting the XXXVIII Corps war diarist to give grudging acknowledgement: 'The enemy continues to resist tenaciously and defends stubbornly in the villages and woods, even if he is enveloped deeply.'[46] But given enough pressure, the dam would break. On 6/7 June, Manstein moved his headquarters forward again, positioning it close behind his attacking divisions: it was imperative to maintain a close eye on the battle as a break-out beckoned. As he remarked, 'The field commander whose reaction here is to wait for unimpeachable intelligence reports to clarify the situation has little hope of being smiled upon by the Goddess of War.'[47]

Pursuit to the Loire

By 8 June, after four days of hard fighting, it became clear that the French, having failed to hold the German attack over the Somme, might attempt to contest the next major water obstacle, the Seine, with renewed vigour. For Manstein, it was self-evident that crossings over that river had to be seized before the enemy had a chance to organize an effective defence. Achieving early and deep penetration of the French positions, the operation was evolving from attack (*Angriff*) to pursuit (*Verfolgung*), which needs to be conducted relentlessly – driven hard to the 'last breath of man and beast'.[48]

Although the leading elements of his corps were still some 70 kilometres from the Seine that evening, Manstein gave orders for his ad hoc motorized forward detachments to press on immediately in order to achieve crossings on the 9th, with the divisional main bodies of the infantry regiments and the horse-drawn artillery to follow at their best rate of march to reach the river *on the same day*.[49] The 6th Division (which by now had relieved 27th Division and had distinguished itself meantime in the fighting on 7 June for Poix, 28 kilometres south-west of Amiens) was directed to cross at Les Andelys, and 46th Division at Vernon. The divisional commanders knew that the problem of assaulting the French Seine line would be greatly eased if they could capture the bridges intact. In simple terms, however strenuous a forced march in the heat of high summer would prove, the potential tactical gain would be worth all the pain. Thus a high tempo of operations remained of the essence.

Manstein had also impressed on his command that this was an occasion for swift action from an operational level perspective. If the lower Seine could be crossed without delay, the French defence of Paris would be unhinged. The XXXVIII Corps (and likewise his neighbouring formations) would envelop and thus outflank the French, who would be forced to withdraw to avoid being trapped in Paris and its environs. Hence a favourable opportunity to exploit to the Seine had to be seized immediately. Manstein was already beginning to show that he could not only plan a large-scale manoeuvre, achieving a position of advantage with respect to the enemy, but also execute one in confident style. Every apprentice needs the time and place to refine his handiwork – the 'assault march to the Loire' provided him with the ideal test-bed to become a true master of his profession.

His divisions duly achieved what was asked of them and on 9 June reached the Seine. The 6th Division found the bridge at Les Andelys already blown, but by the afternoon was preparing to assault over the river and to develop its crossing with pontoon equipment. The 46th Division fared less well, having started three hours' late on its march and its divisional commander having lost communications with his forward detachment. Such are the very real frictions of war. None the less, by the early evening elements of 46th Division had closed up to the river, coming under heavy machine-gun fire from the opposite bank. Manstein directed in person that the division was to start crossing that night.

Ideally, Manstein needed fresh mobile forces to press home his attack over the Seine and continue the pursuit without delay. The 27th Division remained in the second echelon, trailing 46th Division, on the left axis of the corps' advance. He had been allocated a fourth division, 1st Cavalry, from Fourth Army reserve, but with an important string attached – it was only to be committed to cover the army's deep left flank on the river Oise. That said, although Manstein would have preferred to have committed fresh formations to the pursuit south of the Seine, his extended eastern flank remained threatened by French armour. On 11 June, 1st Cavalry Division repelled a strong tank attack there. Hence, Kluge's judgement as army commander was justified on this occasion, but Manstein refused to concede the point, calling again for the release of this division for employment south of the Seine in order to reinforce success. Manstein proved here, as on many future occasions, as difficult a subordinate as Guderian. Kluge held to his previous decision: he switched 1st Cavalry Division from XXXVIII to I Corps in the army's second echelon. It remained responsible for guarding the Oise flank.

So Manstein had to continue his operation with his existing corps of three infantry divisions. He had learned a valuable lesson in higher command that tactical considerations may need to be subordinated to the operational level good. None the less, the normally ungenerous Halder noted in his diary some 'very cheering developments in Fourth Army sector. Under very good leadership it has established itself firmly in the part of Rouen north of the Seine [and] has seized Les Andelys with forces under von Manstein's command'.[50]

The assault river crossings of the Seine on 9/10 June 1940 were not without incident. Although the French did not contest them in such a determined manner as at the Somme, the German pontoon bridges at Les Andelys and Vernon came under intense French artillery fire and were struck by aircraft of the Royal Air Force. Attacks by RAF Battles of the Advanced Air Striking Force and Blenheims of Bomber Command disrupted crossings and temporarily put the bridge at Vernon out of action. This air interdiction explains in part why it took two days for XXXVIII Corps, including 27th Division, to cross the river. However, in stark contrast with the 43rd (Wessex) Division of the XXX (British) Corps, which crossed the Seine near the same point in the opposite direction on 30 August 1944, the Germans possessed only limited military engineering support.[51]

Although Manstein's corps was the first of Fourth Army to achieve a foothold south of the Seine, his troops remained isolated and exposed to further air and ground attack. On 11 and 12 June, 46th Division (his forward left formation) was attacked by strong armoured forces. Manstein considered, as he had done during the Somme bridgehead battles, that the best solution was to attack in such circumstances, 'keeping hard on the enemy's heels'.[52] His view had been informed by captured enemy documents that indicated a large-scale withdrawal was being planned. Hardly had he issued orders for a full-blown corps attack with three divisions, than Manstein received an important visitor, the commander-in-chief of Fourth Army. Senior officers in all armies seem to have the knack of arriving at an awkward time and place for their subordinates. Kluge proved no exception: he was concerned that the restless Manstein would press on without regard to his neighbouring corps. From a Fourth Army perspective, there was some realignment and reorganization to be achieved, which Manstein failed to credit. Rommel's division had reached the Seine near Rouen in the early hours of 8 June, but Kluge had wheeled the entire XV Corps north-westwards (and elements of the following II Corps) towards the Channel coast in order to entrap XI Corps of the French Tenth Army withdrawing from the Somme. Manstein was now left on his own at the exposed southern tip of Fourth Army.

The result of Rommel's rapid diversion from the Seine was the capture of two brigades of 51st (Highland) Division at Saint-Valéry-en-Caux. Cut off by 7th Panzer Division, Major General Victor Fortune had failed in his attempt to reach Le Havre. After an unequal fight on the perimeter of the town on 11 June, Fortune and his men 'waited all night on the beach' for evacuation but none came. Fog had prevented the Royal Navy from approaching the shore. Pre-empted by the surrender the next day of the French IX Corps, under whose orders 51st Division was serving, Fortune had no option but to lay down his arms to Rommel by mid morning.[53] There was to be no repeat of Dunkirk on this tragic occasion: in total, over 20,000 British and French troops were captured.

Meanwhile, Manstein was preparing to advance beyond the Seine in force in pursuit of the disorganized and retreating French and British troops. At 21.00 hours on 12 June, his headquarters reported to Fourth Army that 'three divisions stood south of the Seine'.[54] The critical, and urgent, decision that arose was to determine the limit of exploitation for the corps. Manstein wished to press on without further delay, anticipating Hitler's Directive No. 15 of 14 June:

> Enemy forces on the lower Seine and in the Paris area will be vigorously pursued by the advance of the right flank of the Army along the coast towards the Loire estuary and by a turning movement from the Chateau-Thierry area towards the Loire above Orléans. Paris will be occupied in force as soon as possible.[55]

Kluge appeared to agree in principle but felt he had to await the receipt of fresh operational objectives from higher command. Despite his caution, he did permit a limited advance of 20 kilometres beyond the Seine as far south as the line Evreux–Pacy.

On 14 June, Brauchitsch visited Headquarters XXXVIII Corps. Manstein recorded no impression of any residual personal tension. But matters remained strictly formal: whilst noting the successes of XXXVIII Corps to date, Brauchitsch did not let on anything about future intentions. Visits from senior commanders can have their uses in informing higher-level decision-making. And so it proved: during the very next day (the 15th) Kluge informed Manstein that the Fourth Army objective was now Le Mans, 130 kilometres to the south-west – in other words, more than halfway to the Loire. Manstein needed no reminder from his army commander that the pursuit needed to be conducted relentlessly without conforming to flanking formations. Maintaining a high tempo of operations remained essential if the momentum gained thus far were to be sustained expeditiously.

On 16 June, Manstein's troops experienced their last hard fighting of the campaign on the line La Ferté-Vidame–Senoches–Châteauneuf-en-Tymerais. By evening they had broken through the enemy, including elements of the 1st, 2nd and 3rd Light Mechanized Divisions that had been evacuated from Dunkirk and reinserted at Brest. From now on the pace of the pursuit accelerated and the objectives deepened. Manstein was ordered to detach 46th Division (it later returned) to I Corps that was following up on his left flank. The two forward corps of Fourth Army (XXXVIII *left*; XV *right*) were ordered to secure bridgeheads over the Loire. On 18 June, one of Manstein's infantry regiments marched 78 kilometres in the oppressive summer heat whilst a motorized forward detachment under Colonel Lindemann pressed on west of Le Mans.[56]

Manstein managed to catch up with Lindemann on 19 June, having motored 50 kilometres 'without seeing a single German soldier'. Observing considerable numbers of demoralized French troops, including a complete artillery detachment that had surrendered, the disintegration of the French Army was increasingly apparent to him. Before he reached Lindemann, however, Manstein undertook a personal diversion to Le Mans, where his grandfather had made a victorious entry seventy years before, and visited its 'magnificent cathedral'. How Manstein found the time for such excursions and to visit charming châteaux such as the 'splendidly furnished' Bonnétable – 'next to the Loire castles … probably the most impressive building of its kind I came across in France' – where he stayed during the night of 18/19 June, remains to be explained.[57]

Manstein was not the only German commander to mix a heady cocktail of culture with the bloody business of conflict during that campaign. After all, the Germans have the saying 'to live like God in France'. From Rundstedt to Rommel, the preferred location for a German army or army group headquarters in France was a château, where command could be exercised effectively in appropriate style, and, as importantly, where the staff and supporting troops could be accommodated, fed and protected. In contrast, Montgomery's tented camps were a model of austerity, as were most German field headquarters on the Eastern Front. That situation, however, reflected military necessity rather than free choice.

The fighting was not quite over. When Manstein reached Lindemann at Le Lion d'Angers, 22 kilometres north-west of Angers, he found the Germans bogged down in the face of accurate French tank and machine-gun fire. Once again he intervened at the lower tactical level in order to get the stuck advance moving again. Notwithstanding the direct and indirect fire support he received from a motorized artillery battery, Lindemann had failed to dislodge the enemy holding the bridge over the Mayenne. Manstein went forward and determined that apart from the immediate vicinity of the bridge, the enemy was not in much strength, if at all. He then urged a company commander to swim across downstream from the bridge and offered to accompany him. So encouraged by their corps commander, the company then stripped off and struck out for the far bank without loss, and so secured the bridge from the rear. This very minor, yet not so untypical, engagement had cost a number of German dead on the approaches to the bridge and eight hours' delay. Once the forward detachment was across, Manstein returned to his command post that had been moved up during the course of the day. But as soon as he had done so, he sent his senior ADC, Graf, back to Lindemann with strict instructions to cross the Loire that night.

Despite the German Army's well-deserved reputation for *Auftragstaktik* (mission command) in which decision-making was decentralized as far as practicably possible, engendering local initiative, there remained limits on the freedom of action any commander could enjoy. German doctrine noted wisely that 'Independence of spirit must not become arbitrariness. By contrast, independence of action within acceptable boundaries is the key to great success.'[58] During both phases of the campaign, there had been unwelcome interventions at higher levels that had caused various temporary halts to operational manoeuvre. At the tactical level, however, the challenge was as much to get stalled manoeuvre going again, often when troops were dog-tired. In the manner of

Lenin, who is supposed to have remarked, 'Trust is good, control is better', Manstein had known instinctively when to keep a close eye on his subordinates, but without over-constraining them. His treatment of Lindemann proved no exception. According to Manstein, when Graf reached Lindemann's forward detachment, he found a heap of weary soldiers just about to settle down and snatch some well-deserved rest. Armed with his commanding general's clear intent, Graf spurred them into action and then proceeded to direct the first boat across the Loire.[59] With aides of that rare quality, commanding generals are truly blessed.

Manstein seemed to enjoy the company of young officers such as Graf and Schwerdtner, who acted as his personal assistants and 'directed telescopes' in the manner of those employed by Napoleon, von Moltke and Montgomery. This was to become a hallmark of Manstein's command style during the war. With increasing rank, a commander has insufficient time on operations to visit every formation or unit under his command, nor can he always rely on the chain of command for timely information. With situation reports being passed via several layers of military bureaucracy, inevitably there is some delay and the potential risk of vital details being left out. Thus sometimes a commander needs to have a set of dependable and discreet 'eyes and ears' (and even a voice) which he can deploy to a critical spot, give instructions on his behalf and then report back. Manstein employed this system to its full potential, insisting that he had assistants of the right quality to perform such a demanding role, who needed to understand the context and purpose of his operations.

By 19 June, Manstein's divisions were approaching the last of the three major French rivers they would have to cross: the Loire. They kept up a furious pace with the infantry regiments marching daily between '60 and 70 kilometres in the scorching heat'.[60] The corps war diary recorded:

> The pursuit of the enemy is being continued with minimal resistance. According to prisoners' statements, the French Army appears to be dissolving. Despite the exceptional effort required, it is therefore the task of the corps to approach the Loire as quickly as possible in order to deny the enemy sufficient time to build up a deliberate defence.[61]

One senses Manstein's pen here, determined to push his troops to their absolute limits in order to exploit the situation.

His corps was evidently well up to the challenge, but getting very tired. During the night of 19/20 June, the forward detachments of 6th and 27th Divisions crossed the Loire at Ingrades and Chalonnes respectively. French resistance had all but collapsed but Manstein's troops were by now exhausted. 'The pursuit continues inexorably', the corps war diarist noted, but complained: 'However, we must soon have an opportunity to put boots and horseshoes into order. Up till now, there's been no possibility of any break or rest.'[62] By 22 June both forward divisions had completed their passage over the Loire and 46th Division had closed up. The next day, Manstein's corps heard the welcome news that an armistice had been signed; the campaign was over.

Assessment

Following the formal cessation of hostilities, Manstein issued an Order of the Day, thanking his divisions for their sacrifice, bravery and performance. From the successful attack over the Somme, they had undertaken a highly successful pursuit of 500 kilometres without the benefits of armour or motorization, a military feat that should earn the name of an 'assault march to the Loire'. Whilst Manstein exaggerated slightly his point about a lack of mobile troops, his infantry regiments indeed had marched on their feet during the summer's heat in just over two weeks, achieving an average of over 30 kilometres per day – which would put many an army to shame, equalling the performance of the Roman legions. For an infantry corps, the operation proved an exceptional achievement, for which Manstein was honoured with the award of the Knight's Cross on 19 July. Meanwhile, his promotion to General of Infantry on 1 June had passed without ceremony during the action at the Somme.

The events of May and June 1940 had demonstrated Manstein's outstanding abilities as an operational level planner and a battlefield tactical commander. His brilliant *Sichelschnitt* manoeuvre – developed by Halder and Hitler – had brought unprecedented military success to Germany. The German command system during the campaign was not perfect by any means, but the Allies' inherent weaknesses and mistakes in battle had contributed significantly to the German victory. Yet the German advantage was predominantly a qualitative one, based on a highly imaginative operational plan executed with superior tactics and with powerful air support, and, in the case of *Fall Gelb*, not one based on superiority in numbers. The Germans' high morale and determined will to fight also proved a major contributor to their success, an ideological factor often overlooked in the retrospective analysis after the Second World War.[63] Notwithstanding the failure to exploit the situation at Dunkirk and to destroy the BEF, in just six weeks the German Army and Air Force had destroyed the armed forces of the Netherlands,

Belgium and France and evicted the British from mainland Europe.

From the assault over the Somme, fighting south to the Seine and pressing on to the Loire, Manstein had employed his corps in an aggressive and determined manner. Whilst he had a well-trained, energetic and highly effective headquarters staff, he also pushed himself hard, working throughout the day and well into the night. His method of command was simple. On return from a busy day visiting subordinate formations and units, often starting at dawn, he would return normally to his headquarters between 20.00 and 21.00 hours. Then he would share his experiences and impressions with members of his staff, receiving in return an update from his chief of staff. He would then give his direction for the next day, normally contained in a corps operations order. Before it could be issued, however, he and the staff had to wait for the army order and check everything was consistent with the higher intent. It was Hauptmann Graf's job to present the corps order to Manstein for his signature, an event which rarely happened before 23.00 hours. He recalled the typical routine:

> When I entered the room of the commanding general, almost always he sat bending over the maps covering his area of responsibility in order to study with a magnifying glass every fold of the ground and every particular terrain feature. If he required any changes to the orders, one realized that most of the time he had an exact knowledge of the ground conditions. In addition, he sat often at his own typewriter, which he always had with him, in order to type material himself. Admittedly, it wasn't clear exactly what he wrote, but it transpired that he was working on his personal war diary, which would later find expression in his books.[64]

Between 05.00 and 06.00 hours the next morning, Manstein would receive the early morning reports of any activity over the night period. After giving any necessary direction he would then be back on the road. He thrived on such a hectic pace of activity, and survived on less than five to six hours' sleep. There was no 'early to bed' regime as demanded by Montgomery.

Although the circumstances were different, whether serving on the General Staff or in a command position, Manstein showed certain similar characteristics. Confident in his own competence and judgement, he was happy to drive either an idea or his forces to the limit. Germany was indeed lucky to enjoy such talent, but the very operational success achieved sowed the seeds of its later defeat.

Militarily, it can be argued that Germany had an easy victory with the defeat of Belgium, France and the Netherlands, and the expulsion of

British forces from the Continent. Economically, it had to gear up to the needs of total war and was not to peak in armaments production until 1944. Meanwhile, however, the German armed forces began to assume an aura of invincibility. Having achieved so much for comparatively little loss, overconfidence began to infect the normally sober minds of the General Staff. More dangerously, such hubris was even more evident in Hitler, whose thoughts were already turning east. Following on from the earlier success of Blitzkrieg in Poland, the campaign for France would haunt Germany on the Eastern Front from 1941 to the end of the War. So ultimately, the startling success in France was indeed a *victory lost*, which masked inherent weaknesses in German strategic capabilities. In the Soviet Union major deficiencies in intelligence, manpower and equipment would all be severely punished. Setting aside the excursions into the Balkans, never again would the Germans have it so good or so easy on a large-scale campaign.

In the meantime, the Royal Air Force was to administer a sharp rebuke over Britain's skies during the long hot summer of 1940. Underestimating one's future enemies is often the unintended consequence of past military success. Hitler, aided and abetted by the pliant high commands of the OKW and of the single services, was to make history in the process and to condemn himself and his people to destruction over the next four years of war. One could do well to recall that he was neither the first nor the last national leader to do so.

8

From France to Russia

'It is the inspiration and the wish of all the troops to sweep all difficulties out of the way, and put England to rout.' XXXVIII Corps War Diary

Sojourn on the Loire

A commander is served by the staff, as are the troops subordinated to him. An experienced staff anticipates the commander's requirements and understands his preferences. Whilst Manstein's divisions were forcing the Loire, on 19 June 1940 his camp commandant had requisitioned the imposing castle of Serrant, a jewel amongst the famous moated châteaux of the Loire.[1] Manstein enjoyed dwelling amidst such grandeur, marvelling at the sumptuous decoration whilst admiring the 'wonderful library' and 'magnificent staircase', and not least the state bedroom in which he rested, together with its adjoining 'and equally splendid dressing room'.[2] Ironically, his billet in Serrant in the high summer of victory of mid June 1940 proved his most comfortable until his flight to the grand Weissenhaus in Schleswig-Holstein in late April 1945 during the dying days of the Third Reich, and subsequent detention there under the authority of the occupying British Army.

In the meantime, the French armed forces had surrendered. As Manstein noted, 'The wheel had turned. The road from Compiègne 1918 to Compiègne 1940 had been a long one. Where would it take us from here?'[3] It then looked as if the war would surely end: only Britain remained undefeated. For Manstein and his troops, however, it would prove but a pleasant interlude.

Shortly after the armistice came into effect on 25 June 1940, Headquarters XXXVIII Corps was ordered eastwards to the middle reaches of the Loire and stationed near Sancerre. This was not a popular move. Manstein and his staff exchanged elegant and historic Serrant for a smaller, modern and tasteless pile built for the Cointreau family. Expressing contempt for the 'parvenu mentality of the owner', he scorned in particular a poorly executed portrait of the crowned heads of Europe that included the Kaiser, Queen Victoria and old pater Cointreau, brandishing a glass of his own sweet orange liqueur.[4] Of the world-famous beverage, Manstein, who enjoyed a good burgundy, left no comment. The offending picture was removed. To downgrade the standard of accommodation is one matter but to upset the fine sensibilities of any aristocratic senior officer is surely to risk such retribution, whether physical or literary.

The historian Alistair Horne observed prettily that 'the first summer days after the armistice indeed seemed like a halcyon time of insouciant rapture.'[5] On the cessation of hostilities, however, Manstein's troops were not given much time to relax after their recent exhortations. As in any army, the best way to maintain discipline is to keep soldiers busy. In XXXVIII Corps there was no exception to this rule, as its war diarist made clear:

> The quiet after the armistice is being used to remove all defects that have arisen, and to restore military uniformity within the troops which had got into a rather disorderly state. March battalions [of battle casualty replacements] are arriving in order to bring the divisions back up to strength. Drill, weapon training, riding and sport prevent any waning of the fighting power of the Corps.[6]

In addition, there were externally imposed tasks, including taking over responsibility for organizing and guarding prisoner-of-war camps. There was also a special place reserved for military tradition and ceremonial. During the late evening of 26 June, for example, Manstein attended a beating retreat laid on by one of his engineer units; the next day, he took part in a church parade for his headquarters.[7]

One of the corps commander's biggest headaches, however, was to secure sufficient guards of honour in the big *Wehrmachtsparade* being held in Paris to commemorate Germany's victory. Manstein was distinctly unimpressed with the original allocation of only one unit, the 740th Artillery Battalion. A fine gunner outfit no doubt, but it was not integral to any of the three divisions that had fought under his command during the recent weeks. As recorded in the war diary, the commanding general 'set all connections in motion in order to achieve that each division would provide at least one detachment'.[8] The final outcome of the dispute is not recorded.

Despite the many urgent tasks of recuperation and reconstitution that faced the German Army, and not least coping with the hundreds of thousands of French prisoners of war and displaced persons, there would be time soon enough for the victors to savour the pleasures of France. Manstein was at pains to record the 'impeccable behaviour' of the

German occupying troops at this stage of the war, noting further that 'nothing happened to disturb our relations with the civil population during my six months in France'. He declared that looting was strictly prohibited and that any offenders were severely punished. In so doing, he echoed other Wehrmacht officers' statements in this regard, such as that from Siegfried Westphal who had maintained that 'the good discipline of the German Army of 1940, which the French themselves have acknowledged, ensured that cases of this sort were rare'.[9]

Without testing the veracity of such observations, they contributed in the 1950s none the less to the myth of a 'clean' German Army untainted by the repression and excesses more usually associated with the *Waffen* SS. The forced deportations of French workers to the munitions factories in Germany and of the French Jews to the extermination camps in Poland had yet to come. More generally, the French population suffered humiliation and depravation. As Max Hastings has reminded us, 'The German wartime occupation of France was one of the most traumatic experiences to befall a European nation in modern times.' It is now too easy to forget the 'horrors of fraternal strife, collaboration, betrayal, sacrifice and resistance'.[10]

Significantly, Manstein did not make any such bold claims about the good behaviour of troops under his command in the Soviet Union. That, after all, turned out to be a quite different kind of war, with a degree of mutual brutalization and inhumanity the belligerents of the recent campaign in France could scarcely imagine.[11] In stark contrast to the later privations and dangers of soldiering on the Eastern Front, Manstein's rose-tinted view of France – unencumbered by any experience of the ferocious fighting in Normandy in 1944 – must have been shared by the vast majority of those serving there in the German armed forces in 1940:

> I suppose everyone tended to fall under the spell of that blessed land, with its beautiful scenery and wealth of monuments to an ancient culture – to say nothing of the delights of a famous cuisine. And the things that were still to be had in the shops! Admittedly our purchasing power was limited, as only a percentage of a man's pay was issued in occupation currency. This regulation was strictly enforced where the army was concerned, thereby imposing a check on the natural urge to go shopping – a thing most desirable for Wehrmacht prestige. Still, one had enough to make an occasional trip to Paris and pass the day savouring the charm of that city.[12]

Meantime, Hitler in his habitually immodest manner had declared the newly won campaign as the 'most glorious victory of all time'.[13] Such confident hyperbole must have appeared justified to many observers, whether at home or abroad. So much so that OKH considered the disbandment of some army infantry divisions and planned the conversion of others to an armoured or motorized role.[14]

Manstein's headquarters was tasked with supervising a number of divisions preparing to undertake the transformation process. Hardly had this work got under way when Manstein's pleasant sojourn on the Loire was cut short. Along with many more senior commanders, he was summoned to Berlin to attend the Reichstag session in the Kroll Opera House on 19 July 1940, at which Hitler announced the end of the campaign in the West. The Führer praised the achievements of the commanders concerned, announced a list of promotions and went on to warn that the great British Empire would be destroyed by the war, which was never his intention, adding almost as an afterthought:

> In this hour I feel it my duty before my conscience to launch once again an appeal for reason on England's part. I believe I am qualified to do this, not because I ask for something as the defeated party, but rather as the victor I speak for common sense. I see no grounds for the continuation of this conflict.[15]

In his description of Hitler's speech, Manstein made little detailed comment on Hitler's political posturing and cryptic peace offering to Britain, giving instead a detailed critique of the promotions.[16] The Führer had elevated Göring to Reich Marshal and promoted twelve army and Luftwaffe generals to field marshal.[17] Of the German Army generals so favoured, Manstein criticized Keitel (Chief OKW) as undeserving, for he 'had held neither a command nor the post of a Chief-of-Staff'. Although Manstein begrudged neither Brauchitsch, who had won the two campaigns of Poland and France, nor his former army group commander, Rundstedt, for receiving such advancement, he considered that the status of the field marshal rank had been undermined by the promotion of so many generals at one time: 'Natural as the German people found it to honour meritorious soldiers, we army men felt the distinctions now bestowed overstepped the bounds of necessity both in character and scope.' Manstein went on to list three traditional grounds for promotion to field marshal: 'to have led a campaign in person, to have won a battle or to have taken a fortress'.[18]

As we shall see later, Manstein was promoted to field marshal on 1 July 1942 on the successful completion of the conquest of the Crimea, culminating with the capture of Sevastopol by his Eleventh Army, thus meeting neatly his own conditions.

Preparing for Operation SEA LION

On the day of the Reichstag session of 19 July, Manstein was informed that his corps headquarters was to move to the Channel coast and to prepare for the invasion of England, Operation *Seelöwe* (SEA LION). Hitler had already given his initial planning direction for the operation on 1 July 1940 and, following various OKW and single service staff studies, issued on 16 July his Directive No. 16, *Preparations for a Landing Operation against England*. Hitler declared:

> As England, in spite of her hopeless military situation, still shows no sign of willingness to come to terms, I have decided to prepare, and if necessary to carry out, a landing operation against her. The aim of this operation is to eliminate Great Britain [*das englische Mutterland*] as a base from which the war against Germany can be continued, and if it should be necessary, to occupy the country completely.[19]

It is widely supposed that neither Hitler nor the German armed forces had considered any requirement to invade the United Kingdom until after the Fall of France in June 1940.[20] This view is partially correct. Whilst no detailed contingency planning for a landing on the British shore had been undertaken, the German Army and Navy had looked at the possibility of an invasion *before* 10 May 1940.

Significantly, there was no integrated joint, OKW-led planning as had been the case in the invasion of Denmark and Norway. For Britain, each of the Services had undertaken, largely on the initiative of its respective chief of staff, its own broad analysis and then compared notes. The original OKH staff study (codenamed 'North West') of 13 December 1939, and one quite different from that adopted in the summer of 1940, envisaged a landing on the English east coast between the Wash and the Thames, supported by air landing and parachute operations. Yet the results of the various German staff studies before May 1940 led to one key prerequisite for success: the need for 'absolute air superiority'. This prime condition was required to ensure both the elimination of the Royal Air Force and the Royal Navy as a threat to the escorting ships and to the landing force itself. Otherwise, 'a combined operation with a landing in England as its object must be rejected'.[21]

Once Hitler's Directive No. 16 had been issued, the original target date set for the invasion was mid August, but it later slipped to the third week of September. To the German Navy, in particular, it appeared an almost insurmountable challenge as it lacked both transports and escorts. In the summer of 1940, the Germans did not enjoy the luxuries of time and resources (particularly in terms of maritime and logistic support) that the Allies possessed four years later in the planning and preparation for Operation OVERLORD. Nor had Germany the opportunity to rehearse in the manner of the Allies' landings in North Africa, Sicily and mainland Italy, where amphibious tactics, techniques and procedures were painstakingly developed. Everything was being conducted at break-neck speed, testing German technical ingenuity and organizational cap-abilities to their limits. In comparison with the more generous planning time given prior to the invasions of Poland, France and the Soviet Union, it was a hard task indeed to forge a highly interdependent, inter-service plan for an invasion of Britain in four weeks from mid July 1940, let alone to develop specialist equipment for the landing and to train with it. A wide separation of German headquarters compounded the dif-ficulties in co-ordinating the efforts of the army, navy and air force, ironically a mistake the Allies made three years later when planning Operation HUSKY, the invasion of Sicily, in July 1943.

In late July 1940, XXXVIII Corps moved to elegant Le Touquet-Paris-Plage, a coastal resort of choice for France's social élite between the wars. It was evident that neither Manstein nor his staff had lost a penchant for comfortable living for the headquarters was established in the famous Royal Picardy hotel. When opened in 1930 with its 500 bedrooms (all en-suite), 50 apartments, 120 lounges, swimming pool and fitness centre, it was advertised as the largest and most luxurious hotel in the world. It was so big, Graf recalled, that the corps headquarters occupied only two of its nine floors. Manstein, however, lived separately in a 'beautiful cottage, which belonged to a French shipping magnate and was very tastefully furnished'.[22]

Meanwhile, detailed planning as a result of Hitler's directive was already well under way. The starting conditions for the invasion of Britain were now very different from those pertaining in the autumn of 1939. Although little had been done to construct or adapt the necessary trans-portation means for the crossing as a result of indecision before and after May 1940, the German Army and Air Force were otherwise in good shape, proven in battle and of high morale. Whilst all the ports from the north of Norway to the south of France theoretically were available to the German Navy, it could not hope to recover from the crippling losses (especially in destroyers) it had suffered at the hands of the Royal Navy during the battle for Norway. Furthermore, the Royal Air Force, which already had showed its mettle above Dunkirk, remained to be defeated.

In the course of the summer of 1940 the German Army developed two plans for the invasion of Britain. The first and more ambitious of these foresaw an extensive set of landings across a broad front on the English south coast.[23] A grand total of forty-one divisions would have landed in four waves, supported by approximately 2,500 aircraft of the Luftwaffe. To put this force into context, it would have faced fewer than ten British or Canadian divisions out of a total of twenty-two defending the entire United Kingdom, with under 1,000 combat aircraft of the Royal Air Force. The British divisions' state of equipment and training ranged from poor to just adequate. But the German superiority in numbers and quality was of no accord unless the landings on the southern English coast could be assured. Even for the ever resourceful German Army and its combat engineers the Channel was, after all, a rather too wide stretch of water to cross without significant air and maritime support. Whilst the Luftwaffe was confident as to its ability to achieve air superiority, the *Kriegsmarine* remained doubtful of its capability to project and protect such large forces across the Straits of Dover, let alone the wider English Channel, in the face of the combined opposition from the Royal Navy and Royal Air Force.

Taking into account the German Navy's severe and detailed objections to its initial plan, OKH issued on 30 August 1940 a new operational instruction that reduced the number of assaulting divisions to a more realistic figure of nine during the first wave, albeit that five of these could only be landed in part (see Map 4). The Sixteenth Army (XIII and VII Corps), forming Army Group A's main effort, was to land between Folkestone and Hastings and, as initial objectives, to capture Dover (with the support of 7th Parachute Division) and secure a bridgehead up to 15 kilometres in depth. Simultaneously, landing on the Sussex coast, Ninth Army (Manstein's XXXVIII and General Walther Heitz's VIII Corps) was to seize an area of similar depth between Bexhill and Worthing.[24] In the second wave, two further infantry divisions would be landed, along with four panzer and two motorized divisions. This would be followed by a third wave of six infantry divisions, with two divisions from Sixth Army and three further divisions from the OKH reserve forming a general reserve or fourth wave. Even this more modest plan involved thirty divisions.

Air support of the invasion would have been provided by Field Marshal Albert Kesselring's *Luftflotte* 2 and Field Marshal Hugo Sperrle's *Luftflotte* 3, co-operating with the Sixteenth and Ninth Armies respectively. Apart from reconnaissance, German air power was tasked with providing direct air support to the landing forces; prevention of interference by the Royal Navy and the Royal Air Force; and the interdiction of British Army reserves moving towards the landing zones.[25]

The German Navy's plan for SEA LION was focused on two tasks: protection of the transport of the German Army across the Channel, and providing the necessary crews and command and control for the crossing. There were simply not enough ships available to offer naval gunnery support for the landings themselves. The main weight of the German maritime force would have been deployed on the western flank of the Channel, involving the *Kriegsmarine's* remaining ten destroyers (the other ten had been sunk off Norway) and twenty motor torpedo boats, whilst protection of the north-eastern flank would have been entrusted to thirty torpedo boats. These deployments would have been supported by mine-laying and submarine operations. The few remaining larger naval units, including four cruisers accompanied by light forces and transport ships, would have conducted a feint against the British east coast codenamed 'Autumn Journey' (*Herbstreise*), designed to create the impression of the main German assault there whilst conveying the idea that operations in the Channel constituted a large-scale deception.

Although Manstein had no hand in the strategic or operational level planning of SEA LION, his role as commander of one of the four corps planned to land in the first echelon was not insignificant. During the summer of 1940, he and his staff were immersed in preparations for the invasion. His headquarters also assumed responsibility for a Sixteenth Army training school at Le Touquet set up to develop embarking and disembarking techniques on the adapted Elbe and Rhine barges that would form the principal transportation means to cross the Channel. As the Germans established belatedly, such an undertaking was considerably more complex than a large-scale assault river-crossing operation, itself one of the most difficult tasks for an army formation to conduct. Because of limitations to shipping, only two-thirds of each division of Ninth Army could be transported in the first wave, thus putting a premium on getting the assaulting infantry ashore as quickly as possible and obtaining the most effective air and naval support. Gaining an initial lodgement on a hostile shore manned by a competent defensive force remains the most challenging aspect of any amphibious operation, as the bloody affairs at Dieppe on 19 August 1942 and at Omaha Beach on 6 June 1944 were to demonstrate later on in the war.

Ironically, the Germans did not appreciate in the summer of 1940 that Britain was already developing landing craft for attacking German-occupied continental Europe. Under Churchill's personal direction, the 'apparatus of counter-attack' was being forged: by October 1940, trials of the first Landing-Craft Tank (L.C.T.) were under way.[26] Meanwhile, the Germans were developing their own models, adapting various barges and ferries, and with typical technical ingenuity, were even researching futuristic designs for high-speed hydrofoils. In addition, they were already testing light amphibious tanks (*Schwimmpanzer*) and heavier submersible models (*Unterwasserpanzer*), preceding the introduction of American duplex-drive (DD) Sherman tanks that were employed to mixed success during the Normandy landings.[27] For SEA LION, Manstein's corps would have been supported by one of the four available battalions of amphibious and submersible tanks. The *Unterwasserpanzer* were to find employment in the Soviet Union, including the crossings of the river Bug in June 1941.

In making up shortfalls in time and *matériel*, the German Army and Navy continued to improvise and train hard throughout the late summer of 1940. Despite the inevitable delays and other setbacks, an entry in the war diary of XXXVIII Corps for 1 August 1940 recorded:

> Preparations for the task have immediately commenced. Exercises are carried out on land and sea. Everything is new; everything must first be contrived and tested. Every unit must strive to advance the work with its own ideas. The inventive spirit is absolutely necessary to solve the many problems. It is the inspiration and the wish of all the troops to sweep all difficulties out of the way, and put England to rout.[28]

Such confidence was a trifle exaggerated. The corps headquarters quitted the Royal Picardy hotel, presumably due to air attacks, and moved inland to Flixecourt, a small commune between Abbeville and Amiens, a far less obvious target.

During August 1940, designated assault units and formations such as Manstein's divisions undertook amphibious training along the Channel coast from Ostend to Cherbourg. Yet no amount of training, let alone enthusiasm or energy, could make up for the fact that there were no specialist landing craft available such as those being developed by the Royal Navy and by the United States Marine Corps. Powered assault boats and inflatable rafts, the stock equipment of the German Army engineers, were only suitable for employment in the final run in to shore, weather and sea conditions permitting. They could not carry ashore more than the small bodies of men required as initial landing parties. So apart from a motley collection of fishing trawlers and motor boats, all hopes rested on the modified Elbe and Rhine barges – poor substitutes at best for proper landing craft. The barges were adapted to incorporate disembarkation ramps in yards across north-west Germany and the Low Countries. After the conversion process, the barges had to be towed to the Channel, vulnerable to air attack during transit, and then concentrated in a limited number of Channel ports, where they were exposed to further attack by the Royal Air Force. By no stretch of the imagination could such craft be considered fit for purpose in anything but the most benign of seas (state two and under). If the crossing could not be attempted before mid October 1940, the next opportunity would come in May 1941.

Despite the delays in the conversion process and the disruptive air attacks, the numbers of converted barges rose steadily during August and the first two weeks of September. Training with them, however, was not always that successful. Many a soldier got an unexpected cold bath as the ersatz landing craft were beached inexpertly. Yet the invasion forces needed to practise under realistic conditions and become skilled in new techniques. Commanders and staffs had also to learn on the job, as no one in the Wehrmacht had ever considered planning, let alone conducting, such a large-scale amphibious operation. Manstein kept himself abreast of all tactical and technical developments, visiting his troops regularly and assessing their state of preparation. As his ADC recalled, 'We were always amazed at the speed in which the commanding general mastered new, not very familiar material, and by the passion with which he tackled the matter.'[29] Despite all the challenges, Manstein noted that 'all personnel showed the utmost keenness (*Feuereifer*) in training for their unaccustomed task, and we were convinced that, like everything else, it could be mastered in due course.'[30]

Morale, Manstein maintained, remained high. Whilst professional opinions differed within the German military as to the chances of success for SEA LION, Graf confirmed that Manstein 'beamed confidence' throughout. For the troops, training by the sea in the summer had its usual compensations: messing about in boats may have been hard work but was surely preferable to the grinding tedium of occupation guard duties. Not surprisingly, Manstein and his personal staff took regular swims in the Channel. On one occasion, by failing to recognize the incoming tide, he nearly lost his precious Mercedes staff car on the beach.[31] He identified in the process a valuable lesson about the need to compensate for the rise and fall of the tides in any landing operation.

In the face of an opposed landing and an undefeated Royal Navy and Royal Air Force, was German confidence justified? Within XXXVIII Corps, Manstein's 34th Infantry Division, sailing from Boulogne, was planned to land in the vicinity of Bexhill, whilst 26th Division, embarking at Etaples, was due to come ashore at Pevensey Bay, east of Eastbourne, the site of William the Conqueror's unopposed landing on 28 September 1066.

The tempo of preparations for the coming invasion picked up markedly in September 1940. There was a mass of detail to deal with, much of it new, such as loading tables for boats and ferries, which kept the corps and subordinate headquarters extremely busy. As the corps war diarist noted on 10 September, 'After numerous conferences, warning orders and drafts, the first operation order is being written for the "England" operation.' Inspections and visits kept both staffs and troops on their toes. On the 12th of the same month, for example, Field Marshal von Brauchitsch arrived at Flixecourt. 'The Corps and especially 26th Division have been preparing for days', the diarist noted, 'but the exercise cannot be run on the intended scale due to the shortage of naval craft'.[32]

In September 1940, Manstein would have been opposed by Lieutenant General A. F. A. N. ('Bulgy') Thorne's XII Corps and elements of the newly formed Local Volunteer Force, later to be termed the Home Guard. The three divisions of this British corps were now strung out along the coasts of Kent and East Sussex, with little depth to their positions and lacking strong reserves. The corps would have had to take the brunt of the entire German army group attack of two armies comprising elements of nine divisions in the first wave, excluding elements of two airborne divisions, making it larger than the Allied D-Day attack on Normandy. Unlike the Royal Air Force fighting for its survival, XII Corps' defences fortunately were never tested.

Meantime, despite the best efforts of the Luftwaffe, Germany could not achieve air supremacy over Southern England and the Channel. As Halder noted on 14 September after a review of preparations for the attack on Britain:

1. Successful invasion means victory, but it is predicated on complete air domination.
2. Bad weather has so far kept us from seizing complete mastery of the air.
3. All other factors have been worked out as desired.

More significantly, he recorded 'Decision: Operation SEA LION is not going to be called off yet', indicating growing doubts within the German High Command.[33] Not only had the Royal Air Force's fighters triumphed in the Battle of Britain, but also its less spectacular bombers had inflicted serious damage on the German invasion fleet, particularly on raids against the Channel ports of embarkation during mid September.

Hitler postponed his confirmatory decision to invade from 14 September to 17 September, which would have given the required ten days' notice for an invasion on 27 September. After the signal failure of the Luftwaffe on 15 September to defeat the Royal Air Force, Hitler then postponed the invasion on 17 September 1940 until further notice – 'bis auf weiteres'.

Manstein's corps, however, was not stood down: training continued, despite indications from the chain of command that the likelihood of any landing operation was diminishing fast. On 7 October, the corps war diary reflected this obvious contradiction without further comment, noting on the one hand that 'the prospects for the execution of "Sea Lion" are getting ever less', but on the other, 'preparations must continue inexorably'.[34] That morning Manstein galloped across the sands to inspect a unit embarkation exercise at Le Touquet, and conducted a similar ride the next day to visit the headquarters of 254th Division to discuss matters of its employment. In this manner, he was determined to keep physically fit and mentally active for the task that lay ahead.

With the shortening autumn days and worsening sea conditions drawing near, and with no immediate prospect of winning the air war over England, a final decision to abandon launching SEA LION in 1940 was taken by Hitler just a few days later on 12 October.

British morale remained high despite the Luftwaffe's switch of focus from defeating the Royal Air Force to bombing cities. Whilst London may have burned during the Blitz, nothing could alter the fundamental fact that the essential preconditions for SEA LION were not met. Simply put, neither the German Navy nor Air Force could guarantee a relatively safe passage across the Channel for the German Army's landing force, and under Churchill's leadership the British were determined to fight on regardless. In retrospect, it remains doubtful whether Hitler's heart was ever really in the operation – he probably understood the risks involved as well as anybody in the German High Command. In a grand strategic sense, he wanted to avoid incurring any military setback that would have had grave political consequences. If Britain could not be forced to submit directly, an indirect way must be found.

Manstein's Strategic Review

Rather curiously, Manstein failed to give much operational, tactical or technical detail of Operation SEA LION in his memoirs. His extensive commentary on the planned invasion was primarily strategic in scope.[35] It is worth reviewing as it indicates Manstein's understanding of the difficulties the German Wehrmacht faced and his appreciation of the other options open to Germany at the time. Manstein's analysis starts with the surprising claim that Germany and Britain should have settled their differences:

> It is the tragedy of that brief period in which the fate of Europe was settled for so many years to come that neither side sought any means of coming to terms on a common-sense basis. What is certain is that Hitler would have preferred to avoid a life-and-death struggle with the British Empire because his real aims lay in the east.[36]

Whereas Manstein was no doubt largely correct in his appraisal of Hitler's ulterior motives, his assessment of the British government, people and national character is less convincing. Whilst he admired 'that admirable tenacity of the British which impels them to go through with any struggle they have embarked on', he criticized their 'inability to discern an even worse system' than Hitler and his regime, declaring that 'British eyes were blind to ... the might which the Soviet Union had attained and the dangers inherent in its dedication to the idea of world domination'.[37] Yet to most Britons, to exchange the potential threat of Soviet global domination with the reality of Europe under Hitler was hardly an inviting prospect.

Although Manstein had travelled, as we have seen, to the Ottoman Empire in his youth before the First World War, to Czechoslovakia, Italy, Spain and the Soviet Union between the wars, and had fought in France during both, he had never toured Britain. He only 'visited' as a prisoner of war between 1946 and 1948. Hence his observations of British politics were all second-hand at best. His judgement of Churchill, in particular, strikes an odd chord: '[He] was probably too much of a fighter. His mind was too exclusively concerned with battle and ultimate victory' to see beyond the defeat of Germany 'into the political future'.[38] Such criticism of the man who forecast the Iron Curtain and who called for Europe's unification is hardly convincing.

Considering Britain's determination not to bow to Hitler's Germany, Manstein concluded that there was no practical alternative but for the war to continue. The issue thus became not so much 'what next', but rather *how* to achieve Britain's defeat. Manstein advanced three broad strategic courses of action open to Germany after the Fall of France: to strangle Britain by cutting off its supply lines; to remove its power base in the Mediterranean; and to invade the British Isles.[39] Manstein did briefly consider a fourth option of a strategic air war (at the time, German usage was *operativer Luftkrieg*), but he rejected it as an unfeasible course of action on the grounds that the Luftwaffe possessed inadequate means to prosecute it. The fifth option of isolating Britain by defeating the Soviet Union first was the course that Hitler decided on *after* the failure to set adequate conditions for SEA LION.

In Manstein's view, blockading Britain into submission would have only been realistic had Germany possessed sufficient submarines and long-range aircraft, and even aircraft carriers. In the summer of 1940, none of these means was available. The Luftwaffe would have required sufficient 'mastery of the skies' to stop the RAF from attacking the German U-boats, and at the same time ought to have been powerful enough to attack not only Britain's shipping and port infrastructure, but also its production centres for aircraft for a sustained period.

Turning to the 'Mediterranean' option, Manstein considered that cutting this vital lifeline of empire would have represented a serious but not necessarily fatal blow for Britain. The long route around the Cape of Good Hope provided an alternative strategic line of communication to the Middle East and India. The employment of concentrated German air power in the Mediterranean did prove very damaging to Britain in 1941/42, but the failure to mount a serious attempt to capture Malta squandered much of this effort, which, in Manstein's view, was a 'cardinal error'.[40] Equally importantly, a German concentration of effort in the Mediterranean would have drawn in so many forces, that, in his opinion, the Soviet Union could have been tempted to enter the war against Germany.

Manstein's survey concluded with a detailed analysis of the invasion of Britain.[41] He acknowledged that the conquest of the British Isles would not necessarily have meant the complete defeat of the empire. With the support of the dominions, Churchill's government would have fought on. But it would have made *defeating* Germany incomparably more difficult, if not impossible. From a military perspective, an invasion of Britain would 'undoubtedly have been the right solution' *provided* it offered the prospect of success.[42] Further, Manstein pointed out that whilst Germany did not possess the absolute air and maritime supremacy in the summer of 1940 that the Allies enjoyed in June 1944 on Operation OVERLORD, it does not necessarily mean that SEA LION would have failed.

Manstein was right to identify the two essential strategic preconditions for a successful invasion: first, the operation needed to be conducted at the earliest possible date; and secondly, the German armed forces needed to neutralize the Royal Air Force and the Royal Navy in the Channel and its approaches.[43] In turn, the imperative of time was twofold in nature: the earlier the crossing, the less preparation time Britain would have for reconstituting its forces and building its defences; and secondly, the greater the chances of good weather and favourable sea conditions. Had Germany been better prepared, and invaded Britain in June 1940 immediately following Dunkirk or the Fall of France, the results could have been catastrophic for Britain.

In the final part of his analysis, Manstein developed his views on Hitler's policy with regard to Britain and the Soviet Union. Fundamentally, he declared, 'there can hardly be any doubt that Hitler always wished to *avoid a contest with Britain and the British Empire*'.[44] Moreover, if the British Empire were to be destroyed, either the United States, Japan or the Soviet Union rather than Germany would profit. Following this reasoning, Hitler's policy towards Britain did make some sense. Further, if the Führer did not wish to confront Britain, and had not expected such an easy victory over France, SEA LION was leading him down a strategic path that conflicted with his political outlook.

What Manstein found particularly 'disastrous' was the fact that Hitler's concept 'encountered no sympathy in Britain'.[45] If Britain had to be invaded, Hitler understood the grave risks involved. Likewise, if the invasion were to fail, the military and, above all, the political consequences were of enormous significance. Whilst the Wehrmacht would be weakened, Germany's military power would not be impaired irreparably. Far more importantly, a spectacular failure would damage Hitler's prestige at home and abroad. But in failing to confront such risks, Manstein concluded that Hitler 'committed *his big error of judgement*'. More specifically, Hitler missed a unique opportunity to strike a decisive blow: 'The longer the war with Britain dragged on, the greater the danger threatening the Reich in the east must become.'[46]

Looking back at events of seventy years ago, from an operational perspective perhaps SEA LION might just have scored some success, provided the strategic conditions for such an attack permitted – which manifestly they did not. Whether Manstein's preferred course of action might have led to a climactic air battle over the Channel, whether the invasion fleet would have survived determined air and maritime interdiction, and whether the Germans would have gained a sufficient lodgement on the seashores of Kent and Sussex against a desperate defence on land, must be left to war-gamers.[47]

Manstein's upbeat assessment of SEA LION was made fifteen years after the event. Having contributed so imaginatively to the planning of the defeat of France, one might well ask why such an able and creative general did not submit his operational and strategic views to the German

High Command during the summer of 1940. After all, as chief of staff of Army Group A he had pestered OKH regularly from October 1939 to his dismissal in February 1940. In the summer of 1940 Manstein commanded an army corps, then very much a tactical unit of military employment. Between him and OKH were two levels of command: army and army group. The simple answer was that he had his hands full in training his divisions and other units.

As for Manstein's views on Germany's strategy for the Mediterranean, his later wartime experience, in almost continuous service on the Eastern Front from 22 June 1941 until his dismissal on 31 March 1944, no doubt shaped his judgements. He regarded the Mediterranean as a wasteful sideshow, and, as we shall see later, resented the decision to divert German forces from the Eastern Front to Italy when the Allies landed in Sicily on 10 July 1943, as the battle of Kursk neared its fateful climax. Whereas the Mediterranean theatre of operations was vital to Britain, it was not for Germany – except to prop up its lame partner Italy.[48]

In a footnote (literally) to his description of Operation SEA LION, Manstein managed to stir up a minor controversy about the German plan for an invasion of Britain when the English edition of his memoirs was published in 1958.[49] Had Britain been invaded, Manstein observed purely hypothetically that three issues might have arisen: whether the British population would have continued to resist; whether a government would have been found to sign a capitulation; and whether the means could have been found to feed the British population.[50]

In its carping review of *Lost Victories* on 25 May 1958, the *Sunday Dispatch* was incensed by the latter matter, particularly in view of Manstein's comment that Belgium had survived German occupation during the First World War. The comparison clearly offended the national pride of the *Sunday Dispatch* reviewer who condemned Manstein the man, and his memoirs, with a contemptuously jingoistic swipe: 'For 13 years the silence – and humility – of defeat have been wearing thin. This week they crack. A book goose-steps into Britain which fanfares the German defence of "why we lost the war" with the bombast of a Teutonic trumpet-call.'[51]

Other reviewers were rather more generous in their assessment of Manstein's work. But his views on SEA LION struck a raw nerve at the time, when memories of Dunkirk, the Battle of Britain and the Blitz were all relatively fresh in the British public's mind. It is perhaps also true that but for an accident of geography, Britain too would have succumbed to Nazi Germany. In 1958, the experiences of the summer of 1940 were rather too close for comfort. German generals such as

Manstein would have formed the first cohort of that regime's military governors. It might have turned out as benign an occupation as that of France in 1940, or as miserable as that had become by 1944. The level of collaboration or the extent of opposition by the British people is difficult to predict. It is reasonable to assume, however, that the majority of the population would have tried to get on quietly with their own lives: any active resistance would have been met with harsh German retribution, as in France and even more punitively so in the Soviet Union.

Preparing for Operation BARBAROSSA

In Manstein's view, defeating Britain's 'sword on the continent', as the Soviet Union appeared to Hitler, would prove an alternative but, ultimately, far more dangerous strategic approach than the invasion of the United Kingdom. But Hitler distrusted the motives of Stalin, and feared an attack from that quarter. Following their partition of Poland in September 1939, Germany and the Soviet Union were now facing each other across an uneasy fault line dividing Central Europe: these totalitarian powers were bound to clash with seismic results. Soviet troop levels were already increasing behind the new common frontier. From a socioeconomic standpoint, Hitler believed that the required living space and associated resources including agriculture, industry and oil for the German people lay only in the East. From his perspective, war between Germany and the Soviet Union was inevitable. Thus, according to Manstein, Hitler was forced to 'eliminate the Soviet Union by a *preventive war*' when there was no effective enemy remaining on the Continent (meaning either Britain or France).[52] The result was the German invasion of the Soviet Union: Operation BARBAROSSA.

Manstein had long wished to command an armoured corps. Although he had earned recognition during the French campaign with the award of the Knight's Cross, he wished to prove himself further as a practitioner of manoeuvre, conscious perhaps of the fame already attached to illustrious names such as Guderian and Rommel. After months of relative inactivity over the winter of 1940/41 on the Channel coast, Manstein's professional ambition was realized. He bade farewell to XXXVIII Corps at the end of February and returned to Germany to assume command on 15 March 1941 of a newly established formation, LVI Army Corps (Motorized), in Bad Salzuflen in eastern Westphalia. Although not yet titled a panzer corps, his new command would at last enable him to lead a combination of panzer and motorized infantry divisions in battle.[53]

Manstein's new corps was subordinated to Fourth Panzer Group within the area of operations of Army Group North. Deep operational manoeuvre – one of the hallmarks of Blitzkrieg – was to colour the opening phase of the campaign. Although an infantryman, Manstein was well qualified and strongly recommended for such a command. Following his departure from Ninth Army in France, he had received a glowing appraisal from the commander-in-chief, Colonel General Adolf Strauss (Manstein's regimental commander in Kolberg), who described his precocious subordinate as 'exceptionally clever' with a 'very agile mind, energetic and single-minded'. Manstein had 'proved an outstanding commander in battle, and equally so as an educator and trainer of the divisions subordinated to him after operations'. Overall, his performance over the last year was 'outstanding'; consequently Strauss recommended him for future 'command of a large motorized formation and an army'.[54]

Although Manstein had been instrumental in forging the triumphant invasion plan in the West, he was excluded from influencing the operational design of Hitler's fateful march east, in which the Führer aimed to 'crush Soviet Russia in a rapid campaign'.[55] Manstein records that he did not see any of the detailed planning until 'very late', and as far as he could recall, that was 'some time in May 1941'.[56] As a mere corps commander, he was not one of the group of senior officers (about 100 all told, including the army group and army commanders with their chiefs of staff) who were briefed by Hitler on 30 March 1941 in the New Reich Chancellery in Berlin about the coming campaign. Whether he was informed as to the detailed contents of the Führer's address is unknown, but it would be surprising if he had not been by the end of April, for Hitler had set out not only his geostrategic ambitions in the East, but also his policies with regard to the conduct of the war there. Halder's notes are explicit: the war against Russia involved 'extermination of the Bolshevist commissars and of the Communist intelligentsia'. Further, 'this war will be very different from the war in the west. In the east, harshness today means lenience in the future. Commanders must make the sacrifice of overcoming their personal scruples.'[57]

What Manstein certainly did receive was direction from the level of command above him. At the beginning of May 1941, orders from Headquarters Fourth Panzer Group under the signature of Colonel General Erich Hoepner stated:

[The war against Russia] is the old fight of the Germans against the Slavs, the defence of European culture against the Moscovite-Asiatic flood, the repulsion of Jewish Bolshevism. The goal of this fight must be the destruction of contemporary Russia and therefore it must be conducted with enormous violence. Every combat action, in its conception and conduct, must be governed by the iron will to pitiless and complete annihilation of the enemy. In particular there is to be no mercy for the carriers of the current Russian-Bolshevik system.'[58]

In common with other major formations, Manstein's orders of 12 June 1941 to his divisions included as an annex the OKW 'Guidelines for the Conduct of Troops in Russia'. The tone of this document was equally unambiguous. It declared that 'Bolshevism is the mortal enemy of the National Socialist German people. This corrupt world view and its supporters warrant Germany's struggle. This battle demands ruthless, energetic and drastic measures against Bolshevik agitators, guerrillas, saboteurs and Jews, as well as the complete elimination of all resistance, both active and passive.'[59] From such language, it was self-evident that the coming campaign was ideologically driven and German troops were to be indoctrinated in its true purpose.

As Manstein's divisions made their final preparations for battle, they were briefed by their commanders on the nature of the conflict that lay ahead and what special conditions applied. Following his address to senior officers on 30 March 1941, Hitler had directed that normal military legal procedures were to be suspended in the coming campaign. On his behalf, Field Marshal Keitel in his capacity as Chief OKW issued instructions on 13 May that removed any protection for civilians caught up in the fighting and gave special safeguards for the German troops conducting it. As the British Deputy Judge Advocate General summed up in connection with Manstein's war crimes trial, the 'Barbarossa Jurisdiction Order' provided that: 'Offences by enemy civilians were to be withdrawn from court-martial procedure, franc-tireurs relentlessly liquidated, suspected elements to be brought before an officer, on whose decision depended whether they were to be shot, and collective forcible measures were to be taken against localities where treacherous attacks [sic] were made.'[60] In this manner, the Jurisdiction Order forecast the true nature of Hitler's war in the East, setting it firmly on a predetermined, ideologically motivated, murderous path.

The better known but equally illegal Commissar Order of 6 June 1941 was a specific measure designed to eliminate the representatives of the hated Bolshevist political system embedded in Soviet society and its army. The infamous order was justified on the grounds it was to be expected that the political commissars would be responsible for 'hateful, gruesome and inhumane treatment' of German prisoners. German troops were to be clear that the 'protection and care of the commissars in accordance with international law was false'; and that the 'instigators of barbaric, Asiatic methods of combat' were none other than the political commissars. They were to be 'dealt with with weapons'; in other words, they were to be shot out of hand.[61]

Manstein's views on the Commissar Order are revealing for they demonstrate his inner conflict on the issue, bordering on a denial that it was unjust. On the one hand, he considered, even after the war, that the Soviet political commissars were, *without being soldiers*,

> fanatical fighters, but fighters whose activities could only be regarded as illegal according to the traditional meaning of warfare. Their task was not only the political supervision of Soviet military leaders but, even more, to instil the greatest possible degree of cruelty into the fighting and to give it a character completely at variance with the traditional conceptions of soldierly behaviour.[62]

On the other, he acknowledged that 'an order like the *Kommissarbefehl* was utterly unsoldierly. To have carried it out would have threatened the honour of our fighting troops but also their morale.'[63] Setting aside the moral and legal arguments, the most pragmatic approach was to evade implementing the order as far as possible. As Manstein observed, '[it] simply incited the commissars to resort to the most brutal methods and to make their units fight on to the end.'[64]

Within LVI Corps, the Commissar Order was distributed by word of mouth and discussed.[65] Manstein stated in his memoirs that he refused to implement the order within his command, and that he notified his superiors accordingly. Whilst there is no direct evidence to the contrary apart from one ambiguous report on 9 July 1941 of four commissars being shot, it is perhaps revealing that Manstein made no mention of opposing the Commissar Order in his personal correspondence.[66] In fact, in a letter to his wife of 20 July 1941, he put down much of the Red Army's tenacity to it being 'driven by its political commissars'.[67]

In the meantime, had Manstein been able to advise Hitler on the coming campaign as he had done in February 1940, there is no reason to believe that the final outcome of the war on the Eastern Front would have been any different. Hitler's decision to confront Stalin was exceptionally ill-considered, as was the counsel he received from his senior military advisors. There is little doubt that Stalin's purges, the Red Army's poor performance against the Finns the previous winter and

not least the Wehrmacht's stunning successes in the West had led to
dangerous over-optimism all-round.

As Manstein noted *after* the war, the essential strategic preconditions
for a successful campaign against Stalin's Soviet Union did not exist.
In his opinion, a cardinal failure was Hitler's underestimation of the
'strength of the Soviet state system, its sources of strength and the
fighting power of the Red Army'. If it had been possible to defeat the
Soviet Union militarily in one swift campaign, Manstein argued, then
this result would only have come about had there been an inner
collapse of the Soviet system. Hitler's repressive policies in the occupied
areas in the East (about which, unsurprisingly, Manstein consistently
failed to mention his own, albeit *indirect*, contribution) prevented this
from happening. Indeed, Manstein's post-war claim that such policies
'pursued through his Reich Commissioners and Security Service (S.D.)'
were 'in complete negation of the efforts of the military authorities'
looks extremely thin today in the light of the considerable evidence
to the contrary.[68]

Secondly, in Manstein's view, the lack of a 'common strategic concept
shared between Hitler and the military high command (OKH)' bedevilled the planning and conduct of the campaign. Hitler gave too high
a priority to political and economic objectives such as Leningrad, the
industrialized region of the Donets Basin (Donbas) in the eastern
Ukraine and the oilfields of the Caucasus, rather than concentrating on
the defeat of the Red Army, which OKH envisaged would mass in front
of Moscow.[69] In fact, Stalin had deployed initially a major proportion of
his forces, including the majority of his newly re-established mechanized
troops, into the Ukraine, which he feared (rightly) that Hitler coveted.[70]

Manstein's retrospective assessment, of course, was informed by hindsight; his memoirs here need to be treated with caution accordingly. But
he was surely correct in stating that the final plan of attack into the
Soviet Union represented a dangerous 'dispersion of military effort on
the flanks', with thrusts through the Baltic states towards Leningrad
(Army Group North) and into the Ukraine to Kiev (Army Group South),
rather than concentrating on the central axis through White Russia
towards Moscow (Army Group Centre). Hence, as one of the foremost
military studies of the Great Patriotic War has stated, 'from its inception,
Operation BARBAROSSA contained the danger of dissipating the German
effort in a vain attempt to seize everything simultaneously'.[71] Despite
the employment of four 'Panzer Groups' (later to be retitled Panzer
Armies), each containing two or more motorized corps of two to four
mobile divisions, in the vastness of the theatre of operations there was

not enough armour and air support to be decisive everywhere, and insufficient enabling logistic wherewithal.[72]

In this basic mismatch between political ambitions and military realities, the German Supreme Command failed. Hitler's decision to invade the Soviet Union was a grand strategic error, the enormity of which was masked initially by the opening tactical triumphs of German air and land operations and by well-orchestrated combined arms action, and not least through the incompetence of their opponents in that 'first period of war'. So began the fateful campaign: it proved to be an historical blunder greater than Napoleon's in 1812.

9

Panzer Corps Commander

'I have always taught that one must take a risk, and naturally I take one now. After all, I am commander of a mobile corps!' Erich von Manstein[1]

Prelude to Battle

Although the signs of an impending German attack on the Soviet Union were becoming all too clear by the early summer of 1941, Stalin refused to believe that Hitler would commit himself to such a risky undertaking. So he opted for a strategic compromise between preparing for war by a covert, partial mobilization whilst attempting, almost at any cost, to preserve the peace. Hence the Soviet leader sought to avoid provoking Hitler and continued to dispatch valuable goods to Germany until the very day of the invasion. Meanwhile, German intelligence under-estimated consistently the size of the Soviet armed forces and their capacity to expand on mobilization.[2]

The Red Army's precautionary deployment (which Hitler saw as a confirmation of impending attack) was a further compromise: one that tried to maintain a forward defence poised for a counter-offensive and one echeloned in depth, a task made all the harder by the simultaneous reinforcement and a root-and-branch structural reorganization of units. Stalin's purges of the officer corps in the late 1930s and associated weaknesses in command, control and communications compounded the Red Army's difficulties, as would the Luftwaffe's rapid achievement of air supremacy on the outbreak of hostilities.

Facing Army Group North were Soviet formations stationed within the Baltic Special Military District, under command of Colonel General F. I. Kuznetsov. This largely administrative grouping became the North-Western *Front* (an army group equivalent) on the outbreak of war, with 8th and 11th Armies (each with a collocated mechanized corps) already deployed forward close behind the Lithuanian–German border. The 27th Army was held nearly 400 kilometres to the rear astride the Latvian–Estonian–USSR tri-border area. In addition, the *Front* had 5th Airborne Corps at its disposal. As war started, only one of the two mechanized corps (the 3rd) had received its first allocation of about one hundred of the brand-new medium T-34 and heavy KV-1 tanks, which were much better armed and armoured than German models.[3] German intelligence had failed to give any warning of the new threat: Manstein was very fortunate that Reinhardt's corps ran into strong elements of the Soviet 3rd Mechanized Corps rather than his.

Writing after the war, Manstein viewed the Soviet dispositions of June 1941 as primarily defensive rather than offensive in nature. As the Red Army 'could have closed up and become capable of going over to the attack', however, it constituted a deployment 'against every contingency'.[4] Such strategic matters aside, following the launch of Operation BARBAROSSA it would become clear very quickly that fierce counterattacks were part and parcel of Red Army doctrine, however inexpertly conducted at this stage of the war. In addition, tenacious Soviet defensive tactics, including the ambushing of German columns on the march, would soon characterize the campaign, as would the onset of partisan operations against lines of communication.

Spearheading Army Group North's attack from East Prussia into the Baltic states, Fourth Panzer Group was required to advance as quickly as possible on Leningrad or, as many Germans still called it, St Petersburg (see Map 5). On this axis, the army group's initial task was to seize crossings over the river Daugava (Dvina) opposite and below the town of Daugavpils (Dvinsk). On the left flank, Colonel General Georg von Küchler's Eighteenth Army marched up the Baltic coast towards Riga. On the right, Sixteenth Army, commanded by Colonel General Ernst Busch, advanced on Kaunas (Kovno).[5]

Fourth Panzer Group's plan saw parallel attacks by General of Armoured Troops Hans-Georg Reinhardt's XXXXI Army Corps (Motorized) on the left with four divisions, including two panzer and one motorized infantry, and by Manstein's LVI Corps on the right with 8th Panzer, 3rd Motorized Infantry and 290th Infantry Divisions. Hoepner retained the motorized SS *Totenkopf* (Death's Head) Division in reserve, available to reinforce the corps making the most progress. Manstein's corps was ordered to break out in an easterly direction from the forest area north of the river Memel (Neman) and east of Tilsit (Sovetsk) to gain the main road to Daugavpils north-east of Kaunas, whilst Reinhardt's corps headed for Jēkabpils (Jakobstadt).

On Sunday, 15 June 1941, Manstein left home in Liegnitz (having attended a war game in Prague the previous Friday) and arrived back in his corps concentration area between Insterburg (Chernyakhovsk) and Tilsit, both lying in the present-day Kaliningrad *Oblast* of the Russian

Federation. His first port of call on the 16th was to present his objections about Fourth Panzer Group's task organization over the head of Hoepner to the army group commander, Field Marshal Wilhelm Ritter von Leeb.

Common to realizing both the army group's and panzer group's plans was the rapid seizure of the bridges over the river Daugava to open up the main axis towards Leningrad. As Manstein described it, the advance of Fourth Panzer Group would become 'a race to see which of the two corps could reach [it] first'.[6] He resolved to 'be the winner' despite the fact that his rival sister corps had two panzer divisions – together with four reinforcing battalions of artillery rather than one – in anticipation of relatively greater enemy resistance. Manstein refuted this logic and argued that as *his* corps was likely to encounter a weaker enemy in depth, where it would gain comparatively greater success, the panzer group main effort should be placed with him rather than with Reinhardt.[7]

Leeb demurred and upheld Hoepner's original plan, perhaps mindful of the fact that Reinhardt, having been employed recently in the Balkans, was the more experienced commander of the two. Manstein returned disappointed to his corps and attended a war game of 290th Infantry Division that afternoon. But his disagreement of opinion with Hoepner was significant. Although fellow members of the War Academy class of 1913, infantryman Manstein did not see eye-to-eye with cavalryman Hoepner for the rest of the campaign. As the divisions of LVI Corps found the going harder and the opposition much tougher the further they advanced into Russia, Manstein became increasingly frustrated with his superior's handling of the situation, an argument conducted in a 'battle of letters', to which we shall return later.

On 18 June, four days before the attack on the Soviet Union, Manstein took the opportunity to make a round of visits, including to Headquarters Sixteenth Army to have breakfast with his old friend Ernst ('Papa') Busch, and then on to meet his elder son Gero, who was serving as a soldier in the 18th Infantry, then a motorized division in Guderian's Third Panzer Group. His journey that morning had taken him to Allenburg (now Russian Druzhba) and the memorial of 2nd Guards Reserve Regiment, in which he had served as a young officer in the action at the river Alle during the First Battle of the Masurian Lakes in September 1914. This was surely a poignant moment, as was certainly his time later on that day with Gero chatting, sunbathing and going for a swim. Manstein found his boy 'cheerful and fit' and noted later in his diary that it was a 'great joy to find the youngster so fresh'.[8] To see his elder son so at ease in uniform, and obviously in the best of health, must have been very welcome after all the years of coping with Gero's severe asthma.

Manstein's divisions were now making final preparations for the attack. To maintain operational security, 8th Panzer Division had been brought up from Prague by train at the last possible safe moment, arriving in the Insterburg concentration area on 17/18 June. The constrained space in the corps assembly area, tucked in immediately behind the German frontier just north of the Neman, meant that Manstein could only employ 290th Infantry Division (*left*) and 8th Panzer Division, reinforced with a regiment from 3rd Motorized Division (*right*) in the initial assault. He kept the balance of 3rd Motorized in hand south of the river. The assaulting divisions moved into their forward assembly areas under cover of the short summer nights of 19/20 and 20/21 June.[9]

At 13.00 hours on Saturday, 21 June, Manstein's corps was notified that the attack on the Soviet Union would commence the next morning. Hoepner's order of the day appealed to the soldiers of Fourth Panzer Group: 'Tomorrow we join the great battle which we must fight against Bolshevik slavery in order to preserve the German people and our descendants. I place my trust in your military ability and spirit of daring. Through you we shall win. Let the Lord God be with you!'[10] Manstein declined to add a further exhortation.

Into Battle: Operation BARBAROSSA

Hitler's war against the Soviet Union started at 03.05 hours precisely on 22 June 1941, the 129th anniversary of Napoleon's invasion of Russia. Having cleared the thinly held Soviet forward positions with little difficulty, Manstein's troops were soon faced with a more elaborately constructed defensive belt based on pillboxes, a foretaste of what was to meet them later on at the Stalin Line on the former Russian frontier. There was no time to pause: it was essential to maintain the momentum of the advance if the bridges over the Daugava were to be seized intact.

Manstein had the advantage of knowing the local terrain well from the First World War. He had appreciated beforehand that the intermediate gorge of the Dubissa River represented a serious obstacle and could form the backbone of the Soviet defence. Hence it was imperative to pre-empt this possibility by seizing the crossing at Airogola, 80 kilometres from the frontier, on the first day of battle, a tall order indeed. A forward detachment of Major General Erich Brandenburger's 8th Panzer Division achieved this vital first step by the evening of the 22nd. Manstein knew that he had to press on to Daugavpils without regard to flanking formations, taking huge risks in consequence.

So turned out the first day of an altogether quite different and decidedly more brutal war. Shortly before midnight, Manstein recorded in his personal war diary 'an endless, arduous drive in dust and over poor tracks to the 8th Panzer Division', then 'back to [my] command post in the forest at 23.00; no tent, no food'.[11] The pleasant domestic comforts of campaigning in France the previous summer must have seemed a distant memory. He soon accustomed himself, however, to sleeping under canvas in some isolated woodland bivouac, sharing a tent with his dashing young cavalry ADC, Lieutenant 'Pepo' Specht.

Manstein earned his spurs as a panzer corps commander pushing his divisions forward through the unforgiving forests and swamps of the Baltic states and north-western Russia. There were seldom viable routes available to enable enemy strong points to be out-flanked by manoeuvring cross-country. This was the 'real Russia' which after two weeks of operations, he described to his wife as 'an interminable expanse, with meagre cultivation, miserable villages, terrible roads, unimaginable dust and water that at best can be used for washing'.[12]

It was not only the difficult terrain of his area of operations that imposed new and unwelcome challenges. Manstein also narrated that his troops had found the 'gruesomely mutilated bodies' of a reconnaissance patrol, which had been cut off during the first day of campaign.[13] Specht and he resolved then never to let themselves fall alive into the hands of this particular enemy, who did not appear to observe the rules of war. Indeed, Manstein's orders to his own command prior to the operation had given due forewarning: 'Extreme caution and strictest attention is required towards all members of the Red Army, including those captured, because underhand fighting methods are to be expected.'[14] Not that the German forces employed in the invasion of the Soviet Union behaved well either; far from it. They committed by design horrendous crimes, particularly on the civil populations of White Russia, Ukraine and of Russia itself. The scale and character of the Second World War had changed profoundly with the onset of combat on the Eastern Front.

At this opening stage of the campaign, Manstein was given his head by the panzer group and army group commanders. So he drove his divisions forward at a furious pace. By the third day (26 June), his corps, facing little resistance, was plunging deep into the enemy's rear, leaving its left (west) neighbour (XXXXI Corps) far behind, stuck on the Dubissa. He was lucky that his corps had not run into any T-34 or KV-1 tanks, which were now giving the panzer divisions of Reinhardt's corps so much trouble.[15] On the deep right (south-western) flank, the infantry divisions of X Corps (Sixteenth Army) had no chance of catching up yet. So both Manstein's flanks and lines of communication were wide open, 'a gradually worsening situation', he noted with characteristic understatement.'[16] Unhelpfully, he received ambiguous guidance from higher command, being warned of the risks involved in continuing the advance, but was given no specific orders as to what to do.

So Manstein was left to decide for himself. A cautious commander in similar circumstances would have paused in order to consolidate whilst neighbouring troops were brought up to secure the flanks. Yet he had no truck with such 'tidy battle' staff-college solutions. He resolved to push on regardless, recording his decision in the best tradition of German *Auftragstaktik* (mission command):

> We have not beaten the Russians, for they are withdrawing. It is difficult to judge whether this is according to plan or whether they are totally surprised. We hope the latter. In any event I now know what it means to take responsibility as a commander. I have always taught that one must take a risk, and naturally I take one now. After all, I am commander of a mobile corps![17]

Manstein's risk-taking paid off handsomely for 8th Panzer Division seized both the vital road and rail bridges over the Daugava at Daugavpils on the morning of 26 June, just before they were about to be blown by the sappers of the retreating Red Army. This remarkable *coup de main* was complemented by 3rd Motorized Division seizing further crossings the next day.

In just over four days, Manstein's corps had forced a stunning feat of arms, striking deep over a distance of almost 400 kilometres in a breathless 'panzer drive' through Lithuania into Latvia. By comparison, this rate of advance far exceeded anything accomplished in the French campaign. What made it more impressive was that it had been achieved with relatively few casualties – for the tempo of the attack had provided LVI Corps with its own security. Manstein put down his startling success moreover to the quality of his troops and the fact that the 'name of "Dünaburg" [Daugavpils] had been foremost in the mind of every officer and man'.[18]

Manstein's corps was now perched in a precarious, over-extended position. The nearest friendly troops were 100–150 kilometres to the rear. Enemy air raids on the bridges intensified but ran into a wall of flak (on one day the Soviets lost sixty-four aircraft). The Soviet 21st Mechanized Corps under Major General D. D. Lelyushenko mounted determined counterattacks. Manstein recalled: 'Before long we were having our work cut out to beat off the attacks [the enemy] launched on the northern bank of the Dvina with an armoured division in support, and at a number of points the position became quite critical.'[19] On 29 June the quartermaster section of the corps headquarters was struck close to his forest command post, and Manstein, having just departed, was lucky not to have been caught up and killed in this hit-and-run engagement.[20]

It remains a moot point whether Manstein in this situation should have pressed on with the attack, but he was ordered to hold his present position by Hoepner, who wished to ensure that XXXXI Corps was also in a position to advance beyond the Daugava. The outstanding question was in which direction: north-east to Leningrad or south-east to Moscow?

When the panzer group commander flew to Headquarters LVI Corps on 27 June to discuss future intentions, Hoepner was 'at a loss as to what was required', according to Manstein. As he noted, 'One might reasonably expect the commander of a whole panzer group to be in the picture about future objectives, but that was obviously not the case.'[21] There was indeed no love lost between these two generals. In the event, Manstein was ordered to expand his bridgehead over the Daugava and to mark time by waiting for XXXXI Corps and the left wing of Sixteenth Army to conform. Hitler, ever with an eye for the beckoning tactical opportunity, on 27 June desired 'to throw the whole weight of Armoured Group Hoepner on Dvinsk'. Whilst this reflected Manstein's local opinion, on this occasion the Führer had not pressed his point with OKH.[22] Was there any alternative course of action worth pursuing? Manstein conceded that the 'further a single panzer corps – or indeed the entire panzer group – ventured into the depths of the Russian hinterland, the greater the hazards became'.[23] It was also true that any delay favoured the Soviet defenders who were able to reorganize and reinforce particularly threatened sectors.

For his part, Hoepner was also aggravated by the enforced wait on the Daugava between Jēkabpils and Daugavpils. As is so often the case, tension between two particular levels of command is replicated elsewhere in the military hierarchy. Whilst Manstein cursed Hoepner, the panzer group commander in turn blamed Army Group North and the ponderous actions of Sixteenth and Eighteenth Armies for the muddled situation they were in. In a frank note – bordering on the disloyal to his superior – Hoepner wrote on 1 July to his two subordinate corps commanders, confirming that the objective was Leningrad:

> The Army Group commander is strongly influenced by the thought that
> the Panzer Group alone is not in a position to break the enemy resistance

between [the] Düna [Daugava] and Leningrad, and is taking measures to bring up the [Infantry] Armies close to the Panzer Group. In this manner our freedom of manoeuvre will be limited. The Panzer Group must break away from the [Infantry] Armies in order to generate its true form in fast, agile, penetrating operations. Provided we can secure quickly the area south-east of Pskov, it is certain that we will be destined to break through to Leningrad. Let this objective fire our spirits![24]

So Hoepner tried to motivate his force but without, crucially, indicating how Leningrad was to be assaulted and on what axes it should be approached. With which corps, for example, would the main effort lie? This open question continued to bedevil Manstein's relations with Hoepner, and his with von Leeb. As critically, the *Panzergruppe* had already outrun its supply chain by the fourth day of campaign.[25]

Lack of clarity as to the future conduct of operations, coupled with a chronic underestimation of the transport capacity required to sustain over three million men in the field, was systemic within the German chain of command at the time. Neither Army Group North nor OKH had determined yet the final scheme of manoeuvre for this critical stage of the campaign. On 2 July, Halder acknowledged that there 'seem to be certain differences in von Leeb's and Hoepner's views of what the next moves should be'. He added that they 'depended on our directives, which have not yet been given, but are due now'.[26]

In retrospect, German hesitation at the Daugava, for all Manstein's best efforts, Hoepner's frustration and Halder's belated design, exacerbated by a catastrophic logistic situation, generated as much a moral as a physical recovery in the Soviet defence. The resulting six-day pause in German offensive operations provided a vital respite to the inexperienced North-Western *Front* command, which began to regain its balance after the initial shock of 22 June 1941. The comparison with the crossing of the Meuse in May 1940 is telling: would France have fallen had Guderian's armour waited sedately at Sedan for the infantry to catch up for an equivalent period? Surely not. As Manstein remarked bitterly, a 'panzer drive' such as the one his corps conducted to Daugavpils 'inevitably generates confusion and panic in the enemy communications zone; it ruptures the enemy's chain of command and makes it virtually impossible for him to co-ordinate his counter-measures. These advantages had now been waived as a result of Fourth Panzer Group's decision – however commendable its motives – to consolidate ...'[27]

Manstein's view corresponded to the Soviet theory of deep battle, put into such successful practice later on in the war, when the tide had turned in the Soviet Union's favour. Within the Red Army, 'shock groups' were formed to achieve a breakthrough of the enemy's front whilst 'mobile groups' were designed to exploit rapidly into the depth of the enemy's rear to cause the inevitable physical and psychological collapse of his system of defence by rendering his counter-moves irrelevant.[28]

In the meantime, German exponents of armour such as Heinz Guderian and Hermann Hoth (commanding the Third and Second Panzer Groups respectively), together with Reinhardt and Manstein in Fourth Panzer Group, were demonstrating how to manoeuvre their forces to best operational effect. In today's doctrine this 'manoeuvrist approach' is explained as one that focuses on defeating the enemy rather than on seizing ground. Its aims are to shatter the cohesion of one's opponent by applying strength against weakness, always looking to grasp the initiative by seeking and exploiting ruthlessly tactical opportunities as they arise. With the technology available in the 1940s, to make such an approach work, commanders needed to position themselves well up behind their leading formations whilst remaining in radio contact with their main headquarters. Manstein was an accomplished practitioner of such 'forward command', having developed his personal style in France the previous summer.

Forward Command

Manstein's method of command in LVI Corps is instructive for it informs us as much about the realities of war as the application of military doctrine. His own account is valuable in highlighting the essence of forward command, an active style of leadership that puts an emphasis on the commander going forward to view – and, if necessary, to direct personally – the action rather than waiting passively for news of it from a command post in the rear. As he observed, if the commander 'waited too far back for reports from his forward units, decisions would be taken much too late and all kinds of chances would be missed'. Further, as Manstein had experienced in France, and now again in Russia, on the conclusion of an engagement it is often 'necessary to counteract the only natural phenomenon of battle fatigue and to instil new life into the men'. In a similar manner to Patton, Manstein felt that 'higher commanders should show themselves as often as possible to the front-line troops'.[29] In this approach he gave due regard to the moral component of fighting power, noting that a 'senior commander must not only be the man who perpetually has demands to make in the accomplishment of his mission; he must be an ally and a comrade as well'. Additionally, the commander 'himself derives fresh energy from [such] visits to the fighting troops'.

One suspects Manstein looked back with due pride and considerable emotion on his time as a panzer corps commander for he eulogized his troops, who were often 'more confident and optimistic than I had been led to suspect'. At the front, and there are many pictures to confirm this approach when he became subsequently an army commander, he would stop, smoke a cigarette and speak to his troops quite informally. These were the precious moments of command in which Manstein 'never failed to encounter that irrepressible urge to press on, that readiness to put forth that very last ounce of energy, which are the hallmarks of the German soldier'.[30]

Manstein also knew full well that an effective commander needs to keep his feet on the ground and cannot forever rush around chasing the action and risk outstripping his communications in the process. Hence he was very conscious of the requirement for sound organization and continuity of command. His hard-won personal experience commanding XXXVIII and LVI Corps was clear enough. Whilst the headquarters administrative and logistics branch needed to remain static for a few days at a time in order to keep combat supplies flowing smoothly, the commanding general and his operations branch 'had to move their tactical headquarters forward once or even twice a day if they were to keep in touch with the mechanized divisions'. Corresponding to Montgomery's later practice in the British Army, Manstein declared that the only way to keep a headquarters mobile 'is to cut the tactical staff to a minimum – always a salutary measure where command is concerned', and 'to do without any of the usual comforts'.[31]

A commander's headquarters is only as good as the personnel who man it, and Manstein was blessed with a highly competent staff at LVI Corps. By his own admission, he relied heavily on his chief of staff, Colonel Harald Freiherr von Elverfeld, 'a cool, high-minded and never-failing counsellor', and on his 'highly-spirited and talented' chief of operations (the Ia), Major Detleffson, whom Manstein's surviving son, Rüdiger, recalls being described as 'a really cheeky chap'. Manstein was equally impressed by the head of his intelligence section (the Ic), Major Guido von Kessel, and was supported well by his 'indefatigable quarter-master', Major Kleinschmidt, and by the head of his adjutant-general's branch (the IIa), Major Ado von der Marwitz, an old friend from his Engers and Kolberg days.[32] Of his supporting artillery and engineer commanders, let alone his air liaison staff, Manstein left no mention.

Manstein's daily routine in the Soviet Union reflected the pattern he had developed during the French campaign. After hearing the morning updates and giving any necessary direction in his corps headquarters, he would leave as soon as possible to conduct a visit to a division, returning at midday, and if time permitted, see another formation in the afternoon. Meanwhile, his chief of staff would remain in the tactical headquarters. This system of flexible forward command was only feasible if the corps commander and his headquarters were able to stay in close touch with each other. Thus Manstein in his *Kübelwagen* was accompanied invariably by a radio vehicle, manned by his dependable signals officer, Willy Kohler (later a major in the General Staff), and for security, often by an armoured car.[33]

Forward command was not without its inherent frustrations and dangers. Within the first three weeks of operations in the East, Manstein was complaining on 12 July about the 'unending midges, heat and dust'. Once the fine summer weather turned at the end of August, travelling on Russian dirt roads became a lengthy undertaking. On 2 September, Manstein recorded that he took no less than eight hours to travel 30 kilometres and had to be pulled out of the mud no fewer than eight times by a gun tractor of an SS unit ('fine lads', he noted), finally having to be towed home. Earlier in the campaign, on 3 July, Manstein was caught in heavy artillery fire whilst out on the road, an incident in which his driver, Sergeant Fritz Nagel, was wounded. Back at his 'Tactical HQ', less than two weeks later, two bombs fell within 50 metres of his tent during the night of 15 July, a very near miss indeed. On 8 September, Manstein was equally lucky to walk away unscathed from a mine strike that seriously damaged his staff car. All in all, Manstein had an eventful time commanding a corps well forward, allowing him more often than not to gauge the morale and capability of his troops at the critical, often decisive, point.[34]

Running Disagreements with Higher Command

If a mobile corps strikes deeply into the enemy's hinterland, it runs the risk of being attacked into its flanks, and, at worst case, of being encircled, and thereby face destruction. The deeper the penetration, the more likely that the enemy – given sufficient forces held in depth – will isolate the attacking force and defeat it in detail. This unwelcome, and to a large extent predicted, state of affairs affected LVI Corps in mid July 1941, when it was encircled briefly by the Red Army. Whilst Manstein managed to extricate himself from that particular predicament, he felt throughout that month that Hoepner was not giving him appropriate tasks. A clever subordinate such as Manstein proved to be a difficult one to handle, as the differences on paper between the two expose all too clearly.

On 2 July, Fourth Panzer Group resumed its advance from the Daugava. Whilst Manstein held the bridges at Daugavpils, the crossing downstream at Jēkobpils had been destroyed. So a new bridge had to be constructed there, all requiring precious time. In the light of this circumstance, for some reason Hoepner had not switched one of XXXXI Corps' two panzer divisions to LVI Corps (Manstein had suggested the closer of the two, 6th Panzer), but had allocated it the SS *Totenkopf*. Each of the corps now had three 'fast' divisions: both moved off on parallel axes in the direction of Ostrov, but progress was uniformly slow in the face of dogged resistance by the Red Army. The panzer group was now approaching the Stalin Line, believed to be heavily fortified and defended. With this in mind, Hoepner decided to swing LVI Corps round to the east in order to out-flank a presumed enemy armoured grouping in the vicinity of Pskov. As Manstein had forecast, 8th Panzer and 3rd Motorized Divisions ran into extremely swampy ground and made little headway, whilst the *Totenkopf* found the going relatively better but encountered a fierce enemy defence, and took heavy casualties.

Manstein offered an interesting perspective on the *Waffen* SS, based largely on his experience of the *Totenkopf*, 'one of the best' SS divisions he encountered during the war. Although this particular motorized formation displayed good march discipline, and 'always showed great dash in the assault and was steadfast in defence', it suffered excessive losses through lack of training and inexperience, equally evident amongst its officers and non-commissioned officers. Such was his concern that Manstein requested that the division's headquarters be reinforced with an experienced general staff officer to supervise its planning. Whilst there was no lack of valour, this particular formation often missed favourable opportunities, requiring it to fight repeated actions, causing a spiral of further casualties. So much so that within ten days of the launch of Operation BARBAROSSA, the three infantry regiments of the *Totenkopf* had to be collapsed into two. None the less, Manstein paid considerable respect to the fighting men of the SS, despite their political leadership, declaring:

> In no circumstances must we forget, however, that the *Waffen* SS, like the good comrades they were, fought shoulder to shoulder with the army at the front and always showed themselves as courageous and reliable. Without doubt a large proportion of them would have been only too glad to be withdrawn from the jurisdiction of a man like Himmler and incorporated into the army.

He felt, however, it was 'an inexcusable mistake to set them up as a separate military organization', which 'in general paid a toll of blood incommensurate with its actual gains'.[35]

Within a week of hard but unrewarding efforts to force a new route of advance, LVI Corps returned to its original axis. The enemy armoured grouping at Pskov, meanwhile, had proved a 'phantom in Hoepner's imagination', according to Manstein. The attempt to envelop the town had cost the fruitless foray into the swamp, all, in turn, a consequence of the 'false deployment from the beginning [of the operation] with a strong left instead of a right wing'.[36] That said, Hoepner may have been influenced by poor higher-level intelligence and earlier concerns about the whereabouts and intentions of an 'Armoured Group Pskov', however misplaced. Halder, for example, had commented on this group – falsely presumed to be 1st Mechanized Corps – on both 24 and 25 June.[37]

In any event, by 9 July the panzer group was concentrated in the vicinity of Ostrov. Although the trophy bag of destroyed enemy formations and captured equipment was growing daily, Leningrad remained a long way off, over 300 kilometres to the north-north-east. In this situation, Manstein argued for a 'rapid, direct and uniform advance' on that city as it 'offered the best chance not only of effecting its quick capture but also of cutting off the enemy forces retreating into Estonia before the Eighteenth Army'. Once again he was to be disappointed for he was ordered to manoeuvre off the main road to Luga (now reserved for XXXXI Corps) and advance cross-country in a north-easterly direction through Porkhov and Novgorod to Chudovo in order to 'cut the line of communications between Leningrad and Moscow at the earliest opportunity'.[38]

The result was a divergence of axes of the two armoured corps and a consequent dissipation of their overall striking power; SS *Totenkopf* had in any case reverted to panzer group reserve by this stage. Manstein's frustrations grew on 14 July when Hoepner ordered XXXXI corps to move north-westwards in order to block enemy forces retiring through Narva on the Baltic coast before the advancing Eighteenth Army. Manstein put pen to paper and set out his views in a forceful manner to his superior:

> The shift of the operational main effort of the Panzer Group to its left wing in the area west of the Pleskau-Petersburg [Pskov-Leningrad] road inevitably makes the task for LVI Corps more difficult ... In the face of 3 weeks of continuous march and combat, as well as losses, and the [resulting] greatly reduced attacking power of the corps, I consider a

reinforcement of the right wing of the Panzer Group is required. There-fore I propose the formation of an attack group, whose task will be to cut the line of communications between Petersburg and Moscow. The group should consist of LVI Corps, including the S.S.T. Division, and I Army Corps.

He proposed further that his two remaining divisions (8th Panzer and 3rd Motorized) should be given a rest day – the first of the campaign – that would also allow I Corps sufficient time to close up. He also pointed out that a mixture of mechanized and infantry divisions 'would guarantee the earliest success, as far as the terrain permitted the generation of attacking power'.[39] Hoepner was unconvinced, replying equally formally the next day that 'as the enemy resistance on the left flank currently was less than on the right', he would 'concentrate the mass of the Panzer Group more in a northerly direction in order to make possible still the breakthrough towards Leningrad'. He rejected Manstein's idea as to building a special attack group because 'it would take 3–4 more days; represent a new operation going beyond the current framework [of operations] and leave XXXXI Corps on its own'. However, Hoepner applied to Army Group North for I Corps to be brought up to protect the panzer group's exposed right flank, conceding Manstein's point that the right wing of the group needed strengthening. None the less he did not release the *Totenkopf* Division to LVI Corps, which Manstein had specifically requested. Finally, he granted the possibility of a rest day for Manstein's tired divisions with 'I leave it to you'; adding that whereas the overall advance of the panzer group could be delayed, 'it cannot be brought to a stand-still'.[40]

Meanwhile, the tactical situation worsened markedly for Manstein's corps even before he had received Hoepner's reply – 15 July turned out to be an 'evil day'. The 8th Panzer Division had advanced through Soltsy, about 40 kilometres east of Lake Ilmen, and was strung out between the Mshaga and Shelon rivers. Red Army units (believed to be substantially more than corps strength) under the command of Lieutenant General N. F. Vatutin, chief of staff of the North-Western *Front*, launched a series of powerful attacks into the flanks of 8th Panzer Division and cut its line of communications. Headquarters LVI Corps, located in the panzer division's rear echelons on the Shelon, west of Soltsy, was likewise isolated. As if matters could not get any worse, 3rd Motorized Division to the north was attacked simultaneously by superior enemy forces. A considerable part of LVI Corps was now encircled. For a critical few

days, 8th Panzer Division had to be resupplied with small arms ammunition and bread by air.

LVI Corps estimated it was fighting two tank and a number of rifle
divisions, with strong artillery and air support. In fact, it had been
attacked by the reinforced 11th Army as part of a *Stavka*-directed
counterstroke known as the Soltsy-Dno Offensive.[41] Zhukov made much
of this Soviet action in his memoirs, declaring 'Caught unawares, the
enemy turned tail and began a hasty withdrawal. In hot pursuit, the 11th
Army inflicted heavy losses on the enemy troops. Were it not for the help
of the approaching 16th German Army, von Manstein's 56th Mechanized
Corps [*sic*] would have been totally annihilated.'[42]

Eventually, 8th Panzer Division managed to break out through Soltsy
to the west. The 3rd Motorized Division was able to disengage and
regroup, having beaten off 'no less than seventeen successive attacks'.
The corps' main supply route was reopened by SS *Totenkopf*, which had
been put back under Manstein's command for this purpose. By 18 July,
'the crisis was as good as over' and LVI Corps concentrated around Dno,
having lost ground but remaining as an intact fighting force. In addition,
I Corps (11th and 21st Infantry Divisions) from Sixteenth Army closed
up towards Dno, making Manstein's position once again secure.

Having mastered his first big crisis during the war, Manstein's confidence remained unchecked. Yet the setback at Soltsy was of operational
significance: it had cost Army Group North valuable time, perhaps up
to three weeks, and the chance to unify the two motorized corps of
Fourth Panzer Group for a concentrated attack towards Leningrad was
lost yet again.[43] A small consolation prize was the fact that the Soltsy-
Dno operation had cost the Red Army dear. Sixteenth Army had salvaged
from a courier aircraft a letter signed by Marshal of the Soviet Union
K. Ye. Voroshilov, commander of the newly established North-West
Strategic Direction (responsible, *inter alia*, for the North-Western
Front), which confirmed that 'very substantial elements of the Soviet
armies had been wiped out', referring specifically to the action at Soltsy.[44]

Manstein's actions and demeanour during the temporary crisis as his
corps was surrounded are informative. On the one hand, the calm
general – a self-assured master of manoeuvre – continues to think clearly
about the battle that lies ahead, still arguing the point with Hoepner
about the future employment of the panzer group. On the other, entries
in his personal war diary reflect the real pressure that he was under; had
he taken a risk too far on this occasion? On 16 July, in a letter to Hoepner,
Manstein argued no longer that his corps should be reinserted on to the
Luga–Leningrad main road (his earlier request), but rather that it should

join XXXXI Corps east of Narva and that the panzer group should be employed together in the attack on Leningrad, exploiting the four good available approach routes. Manstein had at last realized that the main Luga–Leningrad road – lined with dense forests and deep swamps for the most part – was a trap to armoured forces, for he could not manoeuvre his divisions effectively from it.[45]

Meanwhile, at the height of the 'encirclement crisis' on 17 July, it was becoming clear to him that he would have to order 8th Panzer Division to break out and regroup to the west. In other words, his corps would need to retire under enemy pressure to avoid destruction. During this stressful situation Manstein was disappointed with his chief of staff's reaction on learning that the enemy had again broken in. He noted: 'E. [Elverfeldt] announces this [development] with a doleful expression and waits for me to comment. As I am just about to make the decision to pull back, unfortunately it is no moral support whatsoever when E. only puts on a sad face.'[46] To the benefit of both individuals, however, this appeared to be an uncharacteristic, isolated incident, as there are no further such critical entries in Manstein's diary.

Manstein's concerns about Hoepner's leadership continued unabated. In addition, he was alarmed increasingly by the steadily mounting battle casualties, particularly amongst his infantry battalions. On 22 July, Manstein complained once again to his superior about the difficulty of the terrain his corps was forced to fight in, stressing that it 'could not be more unsuitable'. In the 'large tracts of bush, woods and swamp', he maintained, 'our superiority in artillery cannot be fully brought to bear', and 'the terrain demands an intense employment of infantry', which the 'fast' divisions are not capable of. In four weeks of combat up to 20 July, the three mechanized divisions had suffered nearly 6,000 casualties (262 officers and 5,682 non-commissioned officers and men). His appeal that Hoepner should approach Army Group North to get LVI Corps re-deployed into more suitable terrain 'that reflects the capability of mobile troops', remained unanswered.[47] Manstein gave away no military secret by writing to his wife that 'the happy time, when one could advance deeply each day, has passed for the time being'.[48]

When the panzer group commander visited Headquarters LVI Corps on 25 July, and was briefed in person by Manstein on the situation highlighting that 'with this attrition of forces, we cannot go on as we are', Hoepner apparently 'did not know what he should do'. In such circumstances Manstein's frustration appeared complete. He noted that day: 'the dispersion of forces and the totally impossible terrain will bring the advance on Petersburg to a final stop'. But all was not gloom, for he had received some welcome personal news on the same day as Hoepner's visit. He learned that his son Gero was well (15 July) and had been made a non-commissioned officer: 'At last something nice in the depression of the recent days', he confided to his diary.[49]

When Lieutenant General Friedrich Paulus, *Oberquartiermeister* I (Vice-Chief of the General Staff) from OKH visited LVI Corps on 26 July, Manstein had some vent for his mounting frustrations over the command of the panzer group. The event was significant for two reasons. First, Manstein could explain his present difficulties with Paulus, one of the principal military authors of BARBAROSSA, and through him as Halder's deputy, seek to influence a change in operational if not strategic direction. Manstein argued for the withdrawal of the entire panzer group and its redeployment in a thrust against Moscow, thus building a strategic main effort for the decisive battle to come. On the other hand, if Leningrad were to remain an attainable objective, then his corps 'must be saved for the final thrust on the city'. The best thing to do in order to achieve a quick success, Manstein continued, would be to 'concentrate the whole Panzer Group up north in the area east of Narva, whence it could drive straight for the city'.[50] Although Paulus 'entirely agreed' with Manstein's proposals, which Halder – based on reporting that evening from Paulus – appeared to support, nothing substantial came of them.[51] The second significant aspect of the discussion between Manstein and Paulus was that this was the last recorded occasion that they met face-to-face before the tragedy of Stalingrad unfolded late in 1942, when Paulus, commanding Sixth Army, came under command of Manstein's Army Group Don.

Over the next couple of weeks, Manstein's corps battled up the sole main road towards Luga and Leningrad. In addition to the natural obstacles, the Red Army began to reinforce these heavily through very extensive mine-laying and massive demolitions. As a result, the fighting became slow and costly. In the meantime, LVI Corps had been reorganized, with Manstein having to release 8th Panzer Division to Fourth Panzer Group (and then to Army Group North) for anti-partisan operations, whilst receiving the newly arrived SS Police Division, a poor exchange indeed. The SS *Totenkopf* had remained with Sixteenth Army at Lake Ilmen, so Manstein retained only one mobile formation, 3rd Motorized Infantry, together with the worn-out 269th Infantry Division.

Manstein viewed the coming battle for Luga with concern, estimating that a frontal attack on that well-defended town would demand a heavy toll on his troops. So, notwithstanding the inherent difficulty of the terrain, he designed a surprise double envelopment – with the potential to become an encirclement – for which he needed significant reinforcement. With the SS Police and 269th Divisions attacking from the south and south-west, he planned that 3rd Motorized Division, supported by elements of XXVIII Corps, should cut off Luga from the east and north-east, whilst 8th Panzer Division would attack from the west. The icing on the cake would be provided by 36th Motorized Division completing the encirclement ring to the north-west of the town. If this operation succeeded, Manstein promised Hoepner optimistically on 31 July, 'then the middle sector of the enemy front south-west of Petersburg would not only be broken but destroyed, and thus the way would lay open' to Leningrad.[52]

On 1 August, Manstein was to be disappointed yet again by Hoepner's half-hearted response. Whilst the panzer group commander concurred with his assessment of the enemy situation and considered the encirclement of Luga to be 'desirable', neither 8th Panzer Division nor 36th Division could be made available for the operation. But Manstein was not a subordinate to give up easily. He submitted revised proposals on 2 and 3 August, both, however, to no avail. In the event, a much diluted attack on Luga was postponed repeatedly until 10 August. It was still in progress when Manstein was given a new mission: his headquarters and 3rd Motorized Division were at last to join up with XXXXI Corps in the north for the assault on Leningrad. Much to Manstein's chagrin, 8th Panzer and SS *Totenkopf* Divisions remained in their present roles, another unwelcome example of the dispersion of effort that had characterized the campaign thus far. As Manstein commented bitterly in his memoirs, Guderian's famous maxim '*Klotzen, nicht Kleckern*' ('Clout, don't dribble!') was not being followed at all, and all his efforts to retain the three mobile divisions to fight together as a panzer corps had proved unsuccessful.[53]

None the less, Manstein in mid August 1941 was still quietly confident of success, but was beginning to realize that the campaign was getting harder and could well last into the winter. Writing to his wife on 14 August, he felt that 'here with us on the northern wing, it looks as if the "Russians" are at the end of their tether; it's also going well in the south at present. But Stalin can still withdraw to Siberia, then admittedly without the possibility of undertaking anything decisive.'[54] Yet the Red Army was a long way from being defeated for it fought back with dogged determination and supreme sacrifice. Privately, Manstein was also beginning to modify his views on his opponents. In an earlier letter (30 July 1941), for example, he had conceded to his wife, 'our propaganda paints the Russians in a very black manner. The fact is that they are not always so cruel. Yesterday a soldier came through who had been captured; he was well-treated until he escaped.'[55] Throughout his correspondence there is a tacit acknowledgement that whilst he was involved in a terrible war, he must, as a soldier, simply get on with it.

Defeating the Staraya Russa Offensive

At noon on 15 August 1941, LVI Corps was relieved in place at Luga by L Corps under the command of General of Cavalry Georg Lindemann, an old friend of Manstein's from the First World War. Manstein then set out straight away on a gruelling eight-hour drive to his new headquarters location at Lake Samro, 200 kilometres to the north. On arrival he received fresh orders from Headquarters Fourth Panzer Group to turn around and go under command of Sixteenth Army in order to restore the situation south of Lake Ilmen where 'X Corps was almost encircled by 5–6 Soviet divisions at Staraya Russa'. Manstein admitted to a 'fit of rage' in his diary that evening, for not only had he been denied 8th Panzer Division for operations towards Leningrad, but also it was now not even available for the new 'fire-brigade' mission. The next day, he drove 260 kilometres in thirteen hours to Dno, to receive orders from Colonel General Busch at Headquarters Sixteenth Army. The very welcome news on arrival that Gero was fine and had been decorated with the Iron Cross First Class helped him overcome his seething anger of recent days.[56]

Manstein's concerns were matched at Headquarters Fourth Panzer Group, whose war diary reflects growing frustration in the conduct of the campaign. The sudden orders to detach LVI Corps had 'crashed in like a bomb'. Just at the very moment when the group was poised to reinforce its left flank with Manstein's corps for the final attack on Leningrad, this formation was dragged away to support Sixteenth Army on the right. The war diarist gave full vent to his commander's feelings: 'The Panzer Group must give up its reserve because neither the Sixteenth Army nor the Army Group have created one in order to deal in time with their flank security. That's high command!'[57]

Sixteenth Army was at the receiving end of the *Stavka*-directed Staraya Russa offensive operation. Once again Lieutenant General N. F. Vatutin had been called on to organize an ambitious operational level counter-stroke. It was aimed not only at pre-empting the final German advance on Leningrad but also 'driving a corridor' between Army Groups North and Centre in the area of Soltsy–Staraya Russa–Dno, south-west of Lake Ilmen. Whilst the newly formed 48th Army was directed from Novgorod, north of Lake Ilmen, to attack I (German) Corps, another newly formed Soviet army (the 34th, described mistakenly by Manstein as the 38th), supported by the 11th and 27th, would mount the main attack south of Lake Ilmen on the Staraya Russa–Dno axis. The Soviet offensive, initially due to begin on 3–4 August, was postponed to the 12th. Whereas the southern attack by 34th Army achieved early success against X (German) Corps, which it pushed back and almost enveloped from the south and west, the attack on the northern axis by 48th Army never got off the ground. It had been forced to defend Novgorod, which was lost through German attack on 16 August.[58]

Manstein's counterattack – with just two motorized divisions and a supporting flank protection force (an ad hoc brigade, Group Lieb) – was designed not only to relieve X Corps but also to destroy the Soviet 34th Army by rolling up its southern flank from the west. By 18 August, Manstein had deployed his force by concealed moves into carefully camouflaged forward assembly areas ready to strike the next day. The attack opened with the desired and essential surprise. With very effective Stuka close air support for the first time in the campaign from Colonel General Wolfram von Richthofen's specialist ground attack force, VIII Air Corps, Manstein's divisions overwhelmed a superior enemy in difficult, sandy terrain. In close conjunction with X Corps, which went over to the offensive, LVI Corps decisively defeated 34th Army, reaching the river Lovat, south-east of Staraya Russa, on 22 August.

The resounding tactical success was very welcome to Manstein and his two divisions. Their booty was considerable, including 12,000 prisoners, 246 guns and 141 tanks. Manstein was even able to celebrate on the evening of 21 August by eating wild duck for dinner, shot by pistol (whose is not recorded!). None the less, the *Stavka* had again imposed considerable delay on Army Group North by its offensive, and although the Red Army had been once again defeated, it could make up its depleted numbers much more easily than the Wehrmacht.[59]

After an all-too-brief pause on the Lovat, Manstein's corps joined Sixteenth Army in a slow easterly advance rather than in a bold pursuit to the south of Lake Ilmen. Not only was the enemy resistance increasing, but also by the end of the month heavy rains came and the roads turned fast to mud. All this increased the strain on the troops, and after two months in almost continuous action, LVI Corps was tiring and wearing out very quickly. On 29 August, Manstein wrote to Busch pointing out that his two motorized infantry divisions had enjoyed hardly a proper rest day since the beginning of the campaign, that their equipment was worn out and their casualties to date were considerable (SS

Totenkopf: 4,800; 3rd Motorized: 3,500). Accordingly, he requested a decent period of rest, reconstitution and maintenance, and the allocation of 'at least one panzer division', preferably the 8th Panzer, so that LVI Corps could regain its fighting power. To underline his point, Manstein remarked that without a panzer division his corps 'remained a torso'; moreover, its absence in recent combat had resulted in the enemy not being 'completely destroyed in the pursuit' as it should.[60]

In his response to Manstein's report, Busch was sympathetic to his subordinate's valid concerns, but uncompromising in meeting them. There was no prospect of receiving 8th Panzer Division at the present as it was engaged elsewhere. Busch also appreciated 'that the fighting power of all the divisions of LVI Corps, in line with all the other divisions of the Army, is considerably reduced'. But then came the crunch: 'However, I am convinced that all the divisions of the Army, and indeed all the divisions of LVI Corps, are quite clear about the fact that a rest period is not possible' due to the insufficiency of forces to meet the tasks given. That said, Busch provided Manstein's corps with two reinforced infantry regiments and held out the prospect of future operations involving armoured forces towards Demyansk.[61]

Undeterred, Manstein appealed next to Lieutenant General Kurt Brennecke, chief of staff of Headquarters Army Group North, in a personal letter. He did not mince his words, complaining that his corps had been 'badly handled since the start of the campaign'; that it had 'always been employed in the worst terrain conditions'; and that 'my single panzer division was taken away just at the point when success beckoned at Luga'. Finally, he asked Brennecke to do what he could to bring about 'a sensible employment of LVI Corps', properly structured, with 8th Panzer Division back in the fold.[62] Notwithstanding all his protestations, Manstein's wishes were not met during his remaining time of command.

Over the following ten days Manstein's unrested corps slogged on through the rain and mud, overcoming stiffening enemy resistance to force a crossing over the river Pola and then pushing south-eastwards 'to a point just short of Demyansk'. On 12 September Manstein received orders that his headquarters with 3rd Motorized Division would shortly come under command of Ninth Army in Army Group Centre.[63] Late that very evening, whilst playing bridge in his tent with a couple of members of his staff, he received a surprise phone call from Busch.

'Are you standing or sitting?' his old friend enquired. Manstein immediately thought the worst but Busch proceeded to read out a signal from OKH: 'General of Infantry von Manstein is to move immediately to

Army Group South in order to assume command of Eleventh Army.'
Manstein was 'speechless with joy', he recorded, 'finally the army
command I've longed for, and on top of that, in a nice area'.[64]

Assessment

Manstein's advancement to army command was richly deserved. In two
quite separate campaigns, he had proved an accomplished corps commander. Whilst in France he had forced a pursuit from the Somme to
the Loire, meeting little significant opposition after the first couple of
days; fighting in the Baltic states and in Russia was much tougher all
round. In the opening three months of Operation BARBAROSSA, he had
demonstrated a clear ability to command well forward, to motivate and
manoeuvre his corps in difficult terrain against a tenacious enemy and
to recover calmly from temporary setbacks. Whether in attack or in
defence, in pursuit or in withdrawal, Manstein was able to maintain
throughout the integrity of his command, displaying a fine judgement
as to the art of the possible. Amongst the many battles he fought in
command of LVI Corps, his bold 'panzer drive' to the Daugava during
the first four days of campaign and his counterattack at Staraya Russa in
mid August 1941 stand out as masterfully conducted operations.

The only fly in the ointment during this period of near continuous
combat, linked closely to his frustrations over the misemployment of his
corps, was his poor relationship to his superior, Colonel General
Hoepner. It was a classic and inevitable confrontation between an
awkward, gifted subordinate and a hesitant, probably over-promoted
superior (to be fair, there are such conflicts in most armies). Hoepner's
appraisal of the precocious Manstein is revealing, for it indicates the
tension between the two. In the normal clipped tones of a German
military *Beurteilung*, he described his subject as a 'lively, self-willed,
personality. Intelligent, creative mind with a high standard of general
military education and sensible operational views.' Praise indeed, but
then came the rub: 'he still lacks sufficient experience in the practical
command of a mobile corps'. Recalling that Hoepner had commanded
such a formation in France without achieving the notable distinction,
say, of either Guderian or Hoth, and had led his panzer group in Russia
to no decisive effect, Manstein must have found this cutting assessment
harsh and unjust. Unfortunately, he left no record of his true feelings on
receipt of the galling appraisal, but his running criticism of Hoepner's
handling of his two corps tells its own story.

In terms of future potential, Hoepner declared Manstein as 'suitable for employment "one-up"' – a faint endorsement. Fortunately, Hoepner's report had no bearing on Manstein's future career, and it is significant that the additional comments made by Busch were very much more positive, praising Manstein's role in defeating the Soviet Staraya Russa offensive in particular. On the back of the same report, von Leeb, the army group commander, described Manstein as 'an ambitious, passionate commander with lots of ideas which he carries out capably. Suitable for army command.'[65] Manstein's following year in the Crimea, crowned by his capture of Sevastopol and promotion to field marshal, would indeed more than confirm this rather lacklustre assessment.

Manstein's talents as a field commander, as opposed to those of a senior general staff officer, were recognized rather late. In the Prussian-German military tradition there was no great distinction between the two, as it was assumed that a high-flying general staff officer was equally capable of commanding: his education, training and development was directed precisely to that purpose. Sometimes, however, the system got it wrong: Paulus stands as a notable example of a gifted general staff officer far less suited to higher command. That said, there was little of the institutional prejudice against those with outstanding staff ability and intellectual curiosity that characterized other armies such as the British. Above all, Manstein's rare abilities at the operational level, complementing his proven tactical expertise, marked him out as highly suited for command of an army and an army group over the next two and a half years.

Meanwhile, over the first three months of campaign, Manstein's corps, exploiting at best speed, had set the pace for Army Group North. Despite the hard-won successes, however spectacular in terms of enemy formations destroyed and prisoners taken, setbacks and disappointment were soon to haunt Hitler's confident, all-conquering Wehrmacht. What Germany needed most urgently in the late summer of 1941 was a sober military strategist to advise the Führer, pointing out the harsh realities of an over-ambitious campaign against the Soviet Union. Neither Keitel nor Halder proved a suitable foil to Hitler. Whether Manstein would be given the opportunity to fill either of their positions remained to be seen.

10

The Campaign in the Crimea

'We had the best and brightest commander-in-chief, who enjoyed our complete trust and deepest veneration.' Dietrich von Choltitz[1]

Taking over the Eleventh Army

The German military philosopher Carl von Clausewitz wrote that danger is 'part of the friction of war', observing that 'chance makes everything more uncertain'.[2] At 12.30 hours on 12 September 1941, luck ran out for the commander of the German Eleventh Army, Colonel General Eugen Ritter von Schobert, when his Fieseler Storch light aircraft landed on a Russian minefield and burst into flames.[3] He and his pilot were killed instantly. By that evening, Hitler had appointed Schobert's successor. Over the next ten months Manstein captured swiftly most of the Crimea, skilfully thwarted determined Soviet attempts to liberate it during the winter of 1941/1942, and consummated his conquest in mid-summer with the capture of Sevastopol.[4] As he noted, the campaign deserves attention for 'it is one of the few cases where an army was still able to operate independently in a segregated theatre of war, left to its own devices and free from interference from the Supreme Command.'[5]

On the afternoon of 17 September 1941, Manstein arrived at his new headquarters in Nikolayev, a Soviet naval base at the mouth of the southern Bug.[6] First and Second Panzer Groups had just encircled Marshal of the Soviet Union Budenny's South-Western *Front* defending Kiev, resulting in the loss of four Soviet armies comprising forty-three divisions, an unmitigated disaster for the Red Army.[7] Notwithstanding such spectacular success, Eleventh Army had slogged all the way from the Rumanian–Soviet border. Progress had been slow, casualties high and supply lines increasingly stretched. Having just led a motorized corps in the forests of northern Russia, Manstein was now responsible for an *infantry* army on the open steppe of the southern Ukraine – 'ideal tank country', as he remarked – with no armour in support.[8]

Whereas Schobert had been a 'hands-off' commander, Manstein was soon in the thick of all operational planning.[9] Before his arrival, his reputation for clear thinking had preceded him. The chief of staff, Colonel Hans Wöhler, advised in a staff conference: 'Don't be afraid of the new commander-in-chief. He is a friend of relaxed conversation.' Coincidentally, the preceding war diary entry stated, 'it is not worthy of an officer to witness shootings of Jews'.[10] Manstein was entering a different type of war yet again in Army Group South.

Manstein was again blessed with an extraordinarily capable staff, including Colonel Theodor Busse, head of the operations section. A solid, bespectacled and operationally gifted general staff officer, he became a lifelong friend. In the intimate working environment of a busy operational headquarters, Manstein's clipped manner appeared abrasive. Busse confided with his former commander's defence lawyer, Reginald Paget, that during the first few weeks, he 'hated [Manstein's] guts' and 'never left his presence without smarting'. He went on:

> But in spite of myself I admired his amazing grasp. Then one day, late in the evening, he sent for me and said: 'Busse, I realise that you are the hardest worked member of my staff. I hate to ask you this, but will you look through these papers and see if you can find any possible grounds upon which I can spare these men?' ... From that point onwards I saw von Manstein in a new light. Beneath his icy exterior there was a kindly, indeed an emotional humanity.[11]

In dealing with cases of cowardice, Manstein suspended a court-martial sentence of death for four weeks with the agreement of the soldier's regimental commander. If the condemned 'redeemed himself in action during this time', Manstein quashed the sentence; 'if he failed again, it was carried out'. Of all the men he dealt with in this way, 'only one went over to the enemy. All others either proved their worth or died like true soldiers in the heavy fighting in the east.'[12]

The situation facing Eleventh Army in mid September 1941 was unenviable. Although numerically superior Soviet forces (9th and 18th Armies) to its front were in retreat, they retained considerable residual fighting power. Worse still, Manstein had assumed the poisoned chalice of a double mission, which would lead inexorably to the dissipation of his forces on two divergent axes. Striking east, he had to advance along the northern shore of the Sea of Azov towards Rostov-on-Don whilst tasked simultaneously to turn south to capture the Crimea as a 'special priority'.

At first sight, the Crimea appeared a diversion. From a strategic perspective, however, its seizure had much to commend it. On 12 August 1941, Army Group South was ordered by Hitler to 'occupy the Crimean

Peninsula, which is particularly dangerous as an enemy air base against the Rumanian oilfields'.[13] Nine days later, the Führer gave further directions. 'The most important aim to be achieved before the onset of winter', he wrote, 'is not the capture of Moscow' but, rather, 'to seize the Crimea and the industrial and coal mining area of the Donets Basin, and to cut off the Russian oil supply from the Caucasus'.[14]

To control operations on both his eastern and southern fronts, on 21 September Manstein established a forward headquarters in a collective farm at Askania Nova on the dry Tavriya Steppe.[15] Frequent Soviet air attacks had delayed this move.[16] Once a favourable air situation had been achieved, Manstein was able to visit his corps and divisional commanders more freely. He confided to Paget: 'My tactical decisions were influenced greatly by the morale of the particular units that would have to carry them out.' Busse confirmed: 'When the Field-Marshal talked to the troops they always felt that they could do what he asked.'[17]

The peculiar geography of the Crimean peninsula favours strongly the defender (see Map 6). Separating the Crimea from the Ukrainian mainland is the Lazy Sea (Zatoka Syvash), a stretch of seawater, mudflats and salt marsh that forms a 30-kilometre western extension to the Sea of Azov. The shallow Syvash was not suitable for a major amphibious operation: Manstein's army had nothing more substantial than his combat engineers' assault boats.

From the north there are three potential avenues of approach to the Crimea. In the north-west lies the Perekop, with a road and railway running through a slender tongue of twisted land at the head of the Ishun isthmus. Historically, this was the principal gateway to the Crimea with its ancient bulwark, the Tatar Ditch, still posing a formidable obstacle to movement in 1941. To the north-east, the Chongar peninsula of southern Ukraine is linked to the Crimea by the isthmus at Salvako, and then by the causeways and bridges carrying the main railway line and road from Kiev and Melitopol over the Syvash to Dzhankoi and Simferopol. Forcing a corps attack axis through a gap only 2 kilometres wide and then over the causeways would have been suicidal. Rightly it was discounted in Manstein's planning as being 'quite useless'.[18] Slightly further to the east lay one final approach route at Genichesk, separated by a short stretch of water from the Arabat, itself a very narrow neck of land that stretched nearly a hundred kilometres south-east to the Kerch peninsula. It, too, was unsuitable for developing a major attack.

So only the Perekop offered any realistic prospect for Manstein's entry into the Crimea, albeit by frontal assault. Once the isthmus had been breached, the northern two-thirds of the Crimea, consisting of open steppe, terrain particularly suitable for armoured operations, lay ripe for rapid exploitation. To the south and east of Simferopol lies the Crimean mountain chain that towers above the southern and south-eastern coastline.[19]

On taking over, Manstein commanded the following German forces: XXX Corps under General of Infantry Hans von Salmuth; XXXXIX Mountain Corps under General of Infantry Ludwig Kübler; and LIV Corps under General of Cavalry Erik Hansen.[20] A separate infantry division (the 50th) was split between supporting the Rumanians at Odessa and being 'partly engaged mopping up the Black Sea Coast'.[21] Of the Axis forces under command, the Third Rumanian Army comprised a mountain and a cavalry corps, each of three brigades – the equivalent of a further two divisions of uncertain capability.

The first operational decision that Manstein faced was to determine how to pursue the enemy towards the east *and* to capture the Crimea: should these tasks be conducted simultaneously or sequentially? As he noted critically, it was a decision that 'was really the responsibility of the Supreme Command'.[22] Forcing the Perekop was too difficult to be left to the single corps (LIV) assigned already for this task. The 51st Separate Army under Colonel General F. I. Kuznetsov had recently assembled three militia divisions for its defence and three more were on the way; the total Soviet force on the Crimean peninsula would soon amount to twelve rifle and four cavalry divisions, of mixed quality.[23] In any case, as Manstein concluded, 'a stubborn defence by even three enemy divisions would probably suffice to deny LIV Corps access to the Crimea or at least cause it considerable losses in the fight through the Isthmus'.[24]

The terrain between Perekop and Ishun, lying 30 kilometres south-east, which narrows to 3 kilometres in width, had been thickened with strong field defences. At Perekop, the first zone of defence incorporated the Tatar Ditch. In depth, the Soviets had constructed a second main zone of defence linking the salt lakes and the new town of Krasnoperekopsk (Red Perekop), built in the 1930s to commemorate the Red Army's famous victory there over the White Russians in 1920. These natural and manmade obstacles, when combined with the local Soviet superiority in the air – for the Luftwaffe could not be strong everywhere on the Eastern Front – demanded a 'hard and exhausting struggle' by Eleventh Army.

Manstein needed reinforcements if any breakthrough were to be converted into exploitation and pursuit: the only source now was his two corps pressing eastwards (XXX and XXXXIX). To attempt both operations simultaneously would result in neither objective being achieved, so Manstein decided to give initial priority to the Crimea over Rostov-on-Don. In breaking in at Perekop, he reinforced LIV Corps as best he could with all available army artillery, anti-aircraft and engineer units, and feinted operations from the Chongar peninsula. He brought up 50th Division to reinforce LIV Corps and warned XXXXIX Mountain Corps to 'conquer the Crimea quickly after the breakthrough' had been achieved.[25]

Notwithstanding the anticipated difficulties, such was Manstein's optimism that he tasked the *Leibstandarte*, in conjunction with other motorized elements of the army, to act as a fast mobile group to pursue the retreating enemy to Sevastopol and capture the city. To substitute the troops drawn from his eastern front, he placed the Rumanians, reinforced by German troops, in a thinly manned defensive line on the steppe approximately 100 kilometres east of the Dnepr bend. In so doing he took a big, albeit calculated, risk. It represented the 'price that had to be paid if we were to avoid attempting the capture of the Crimea with inadequate forces'.[26]

Storming the Perekop and the Battle of Azov

A deliberate attack – one with detailed preparation – as opposed to one conducted hastily off the line of march can favour either the attacker or defender depending on the relative build-up of resources on both sides, particularly in terms of fire support. A frontal attack such as the one conducted by Manstein's army at Perekop, against a determined enemy in a prepared defensive position may result, as German Army doctrine noted, 'in long, obstinate fighting for dominance'.[27] And so it turned out. When LIV Corps attacked on 24 September 1941 it achieved an initial, extremely hard-fought penetration to the Tatar Ditch. On the 26th, 73rd Division stormed the obstacle as described by a young officer:

> At 04.40 hours, therefore before dawn, divisional artillery concentrated its fire on the regimental breakthrough axis. Under cover of the barrage infantry troops worked themselves forward until they were close to the Tatar Ditch. At 04.50 the artillery support was lifted. In unison, infantry and engineers rushed forward traversing the northern edge of the ditch, sliding and slipping down into the channel, at some places twenty metres deep, climbing up the far side and breaking into and seizing the enemy positions.[28]

During the next night, LIV Corps, reinforced by the *Leibstandarte*, began to break through south-west of Armiansk, and prepared to mount an attack past the Ishun lakes. But, as Manstein noted, 'the fruit of this hard-won victory, the final break-out into the Crimea, could still not be plucked'.[29] Since 26 September, the Soviet 9th and 18th Armies, twelve divisions reinforced with strong tank units, had been mounting increasingly threatening attacks on Third Rumanian Army. By the morning of the 27th, Soviet forces had forced a penetration in the north between XXXXIX Corps heading for the Perekop (which Manstein turned back) and the Rumanians. An alarming 15-kilometre 'hole' suddenly appeared in his eastern line of defence.

On 28 September, within XXX Corps' sector to the south-east, the situation became yet more critical. Manstein was now obliged to act decisively in order to maintain the integrity of his army. Although he did not close down his attacks at Ishun immediately, it became evident soon enough that LIV Corps was exhausted and that he must divert fresh forces to meet the new threat. In any case, the German High Command – 'on the Führer's orders' – had intervened unhelpfully by reserving the *Leibstandarte*, Manstein's only fully mobile formation, for employment with First Panzer Group for the intended thrust to Rostov-on-Don.[30]

By counterattacking with XXXXIX Corps, together with elements of 50th and 22nd Divisions and the *Leibstandarte* drawn from Perekop, Manstein was able to stabilize the situation on 29 September. It had proved a close-run affair. To stiffen resolve, he established a small tactical headquarters at Nish Segorosi close 'to the danger spot'. As he remarked, such action

> is always an expedient measure in times of crisis, if only because it prevents subordinate staffs from pulling out early and making a bad impression on the troops. On the occasion in question it was particularly appropriate in view of the tendency of many Rumanian headquarters staffs to change their locations prematurely.[31]

His concern about his allies was born of experience. On at least one occasion, he had found it necessary to rally the Rumanians in person, finding 'their commanders' staff cars pointing west with their engines running'.[32]

But it required more than Manstein's mere presence to win the battle. Following urgent requests, Army Group South finally ordered von Kleist's First Panzer Army on 1 October to advance into the rear of the Soviet grouping (9th and 18th Armies). This envelopment from the north and further hard fighting by Eleventh Army attacking east to capture Melitopol decided the battle of the Sea of Azov. Total Soviet losses by 10 October amounted to 106,362 prisoners, 212 tanks and 672 artillery pieces. In retrospect, Manstein believed that his army could have been driven back to the Dnepr had the Soviet counter-offensive been better planned and led. As one historian observed, 'it was a victory pulled from the brink of disaster'.[33]

Although never one for dramatic gestures, Manstein thought the action worthy of recognition. He issued an order of the day on 4 October 1941:

> Soldiers of the 11th and 3rd Rumanian Army!
> You can be proud of your achievements when attacking as well as in defence against the enemy assault, which you have brought about through loyal comradeship-in-arms. We remember our comrades who gave their lives and blood, whose sacrifice has set us on the path to final victory.[34]

The stunning success also brought Manstein his first mention during the Second World War in the daily *Wehrmachtsberichte* (reports of the Wehrmacht) on 11 October 1941.[35]

The battle caused a necessary rethink in the German High Command. At last, the impracticability of Eleventh Army conducting two simultaneous operations was recognized. Manstein retained XXX and LIV Corps for the Crimean operation, some five and two-third divisions, for a third of 50th Division was still employed in the vicinity of Odessa. Conquering the Crimea and then mounting an operation over the Strait of Kerch on to the Kuban peninsula and the Caucasus still figured prominently in OKH's thinking. Manstein applied to Army Group South for the 'immediate release of a corps of three divisions for the Crimea', and called for increases in air support.[36] Although he received Headquarters XXXXII Corps with 24th and 132nd Infantry Divisions, it remained to be seen whether such reinforcements would guarantee the 'complete clearance of the Crimea'.[37] As he predicted, the Soviet Supreme Command would rather abandon Odessa than lose Sevastopol.

Over the period 2–16 October, the Red Navy evacuated the Coastal Army from Odessa and reinforcements began to flow into Sevastopol and into other smaller ports of the western Crimea, exacerbating Manstein's problems. Although some Soviet shipping was lost, neither the Luftwaffe nor the *Kriegsmarine* had sufficient forces to interdict this sea line of communication effectively. As a result, Soviet land and naval forces had pulled off a remarkable operation on the scale of Dunkirk, evacuating some 300,000 military and civilian personnel without significant loss.

When Manstein resumed his offensive at Ishun on 18 October, six German divisions were soon faced by 'eight Soviet rifle and four cavalry divisions'. Even allowing for a significant overestimation of the enemy, his forces hardly dominated. The LIV Corps eventually assaulted the Ishun position with 22nd, 46th and 73rd Infantry Divisions. Initial progress was excruciatingly slow and extremely costly. True, Manstein was able to mass his army's artillery but this could not offset the Soviet air superiority over the battlefield. He recalled:

> The salt steppes of the isthmus, flat as a pancake and bare of vegetation, offered no cover whatsoever to the attacker. Yet the air above them was dominated by the *Soviet* Air Force, whose fighters and fighter-bombers dived incessantly on any target they could find. Not only the front-line infantry and field batteries had to dig in: it was even necessary to dig pits for every vehicle and horse behind the battle zone as protection against enemy aircraft. Things got so bad that anti-aircraft batteries no longer dared to fire in case they were immediately wiped out from the air.[38]

Such was Manstein's mounting concern about the lack of air support that he wrote on 20 October to General Sodenstern, chief of staff of Army Group South, arguing for a 'drastic concentration of the Luftwaffe' to defeat the enemy air force, to destroy the Soviet artillery and to give his weakened infantry the necessary 'moral uplift in the attack'. Further, he requested 'at least one mobile armoured formation' to block the road between Simferopol and Sevastopol in order to cut off retreating Soviet forces.[39]

Manstein's diary entry for 22 October reveals that he even considered calling off his offensive once he had forced the Ishun position in order to 'bleed the Russians in counter attacks' and to allow the concentration of Fourth Air Fleet to keep the Russian Air Force at bay. He decided to press on, noting 'how often have I taught that one should not throw away victory five minutes too early'.[40] With the arrival of the *Mölders* fighter wing (*Jagdgeschwader* 52), local air superiority by day was achieved by 26 October.

Meanwhile, Manstein had become increasingly alarmed by the declining fighting power of his force, a recurring feature of the campaign. The commander of a 'particularly good division' (73rd Infantry) had reported on two occasions that week that his formation could 'do no more'. 'This was the hour', he wrote after the war, 'that usually comes sooner or later in such a contest, when the outcome of the battle is on the razor's edge. It was the hour that must show whether the will of the attacker to exert himself to the very limit of physical endurance is stronger than that of the defender to go on resisting.'[41] Manstein's soldiers were made of stern stuff: their opponents cracked first on 28 October. The German pursuit into the Crimea could now begin.

Exploitation into the Crimea

With the departure of the *Leibstandarte*, Manstein did not have any obvious means immediately available to exploit the situation by plunging into the Crimea before the Soviets could recover. So he employed an old device he had used before with XXXVIII Corps in France. He assembled a forward detachment comprising the reconnaissance battalion of 22nd Infantry Division, a reinforced Rumanian motorized regiment and sundry other German motorized troops.[42] Manstein tasked this ad hoc mobile group under Colonel Heinz Ziegler to drive hard south towards the river Alma. On 31 October, Ziegler's force cut the road between Sevastopol and Simferopol, capturing the Crimean capital the next day.

Heavy rain slowed down the pursuit by Manstein's infantry divisions, as did determined Soviet rearguard actions. The German High Command, however, was delighted with Manstein's achievements. Brauchitsch congratulated him on 30 September, signalling his 'best wishes and full recognition for the outstanding performance of the command and the troops in the breakthrough into the Crimea'. Manstein, however, had more pressing concerns, noting acerbically, 'I would have much preferred to have received a panzer division.'[43]

On 30 October, he set out his proposed intent in a typically carefully argued estimate to Headquarters Army Group South. He assessed that his opponent had two courses of action open: either to hold the southern Crimea as a firm base for maritime and air operations; or, if too weak to achieve this, to split his forces, directing the mass to Sevastopol and the remainder to Kerch. Manstein considered the most attractive option for Eleventh Army was to pursue the retreating 51st Separate Army to Kerch. He hoped this would tempt Soviet forces out of the mountains and provoke a general engagement on open ground to German advantage away from Sevastopol's fortifications.

Manstein had presumed here a degree of operational sophistication that his opponents were not yet capable of. He conceded 'that it is unlikely that the enemy would decide on such an operation. Probably he would only win time to prepare Sevastopol for defence.' Hence Manstein decided to focus his main effort against the anticipated Soviet concentration between Simferopol and Sevastopol, and to cut off any retreat into the fortress city. At this stage he did not plan to attack the enemy grouping at Kerch until sufficient forces could be released from Sevastopol.[44] But the unexpected tenacity and resilience of the Soviet forces confounded this approach: whilst Kerch fell to Manstein's forces on

16 November – only to be recaptured by the Red Army at the end of December 1941 and lost again in mid May 1942 – Sevastopol held out until 1 July 1942.

On 1 November, having received endorsement for his plans from Headquarters Army Group South, Manstein confirmed his scheme of manoeuvre. Two corps, LIV and XXX, with a total of four divisions, were tasked to take Sevastopol, whilst XXXXII Corps with three German divisions, together with the Rumanian Mountain Corps, was to press eastwards towards Kerch.

Meanwhile, the Soviet command structure on the Crimea was in disarray although Russian troops were retreating in reasonably good order. On 30 October, Major General Ivan Efimovich Petrov, commander of the Coastal Army that had been redeployed from Odessa, called a council of war at Ekibash, a small settlement 40 kilometres north of Sevastopol. According to one of his subordinate commanders, Colonel I. A. Laskin, Petrov declared:

> there is unofficial information that Colonel General Kuznetsov has been dismissed from commanding the Crimean armed forces and the 51st Army. The situation here is changing quickly and not to our advantage. . . . We have two options, two ways to go: either to Sevastopol, to the main Navy base of the Black Sea Fleet so that we can defend the city and the base together with the Fleet; or we can go to the Kerch Peninsula to join the 51st Army and establish the defence there.[45]

Petrov consulted his divisional commanders and then announced his decision that the Coastal Army would retreat to Sevastopol.

Despite Manstein's best efforts, his forces were far too dispersed over the southern Crimea to prevent the Coastal Army from breaking through to Sevastopol either over the mountains or escaping along the coastal road from Alushta and Yalta. In the race against time to reach the city, the Soviets just managed to forestall any German attempt to seize Sevastopol off the line of march. Eleventh Army would now need more time to bring up the troops, heavy artillery and ammunition required for a deliberate operation. The heady optimism of the first two weeks of November, reflected in Halder's comment that 'good progress has been made in the Crimea, but it will take a few more days before we have cleared out the last enemy', was to be confounded by the tenacity of the Soviet defence and by the onset of winter.[46]

Until the main railway line to Simferopol (and onwards to the army's principal off-loading point at Bakhchisarai) was reopened in January 1942, all combat supplies were hauled over the Crimea's poor roads, most of which were unpaved. In contrast, the Red Navy still controlled the Black Sea, providing a vital lifeline to the population and the Soviet forces in Sevastopol. In 1941 the first snow on the Crimea fell early on 9 November, followed by continuous 'hopeless rain' as Manstein recorded on 11 November, that turned all German routes into muddy tracks that 'brought everything to a halt'.[47] With the onset of the Russian *rasputitsa* (literally, the time without roads) any chance of a swiftly conducted assault on Sevastopol disappeared. The worsening weather and declining daylight favoured the Soviet defenders. Petrov's men used the precious time to reinforce their fortifications with well-camouflaged bunkers, wire entanglements, mines, machine-gun posts and field-gun positions.

As Manstein's divisions struggled forward towards Sevastopol and Kerch, and fought off determined attacks by partisans in the mountains, Headquarters Eleventh Army established itself in and around Simferopol. Whilst the administrative branch (Ib with specialist logistics staffs) remained in the city, Manstein with his operations and intelligence sections (Ia and Ic respectively), 'found very suitable accommodation in one of the new schools built by the Soviets' in Sarabus.[48] Manstein shared a small farmhouse nearby with his chief of staff, living in 'a modest room' with only 'a bed, a table and a chair, a stool for the wash-bowl to stand on, and a few clothes-hooks'. Neither he nor his staff believed 'in indulging in comforts which the ordinary soldier had to do without'.[49]

For his office, Manstein used a classroom heated by two improvised stoves. As in all armies, when operations become static, the dampening hand of 'routine' administration returns to dominate the life of a headquarters. According to Paget, Manstein 'hated paper work and rarely read papers that were put before him. He expected his officers to report concisely upon their contents and then he initialled the papers to indicate that they had been reported on.'[50] So perhaps there was some truth in Manstein's comments after the war that he could not remember reading various documents, and perhaps even the more incriminating ones.

Intermittent Soviet air raids on the nearby Sarabus airfields caused some disruption to staff work. Manstein was on the road most of the time visiting his subordinate formations, not without its attendant dangers. For the majority of his front-line troops, the daily threat and personal demands of combat remained immense. Although Eleventh Army had conquered all of the Crimea by 16 November 1941 except for the heavily fortified area around Sevastopol, frequent partisan ambushes meant that no road movement was safe from attack, and particularly so in the mountains.

Winter is always hard for the soldier: the German *Landser* manning the half-ring of circumvallation around Sevastopol faced not only enemy artillery fire and air attack, but also debilitating living conditions. As the historian of 22nd Division noted bitterly:

> It was not all that cold, but the storms from the sea and the wet snow made life in the front line a misery. Clothing was completely insufficient: many soldiers did not have a coat; far fewer still had gloves or head protection. On top of this came the physical exhaustion; [in this condition] even light wounds could lead to death.[51]

OKH had made no effective preparations for a winter campaign in the Soviet Union. Manstein did what he could do for his troops, but his army was at the very end of an extremely long and thin supply chain, which had no redundancy.

The lack of troops made it even more difficult to give soldiers in the hollowed-out infantry companies the urgent rest and recuperation they needed. Across his seven infantry divisions, losses up to 7 November from combat and sickness, including jaundice, amounted to nearly 40,000 men. Despite receiving almost 16,000 replacements, Eleventh Army was still approximately 25 per cent short of its establishment. The opening stages of the campaign in the Crimea had also proved very costly in Russian blood. German intelligence estimates put Soviet military losses since 18 October 1941 as 100,000, of which three-quarters were prisoners of war.[52] For the civilian population of the Crimea, however, there were yet thousands of casualties to come.

The First Defence of Sevastopol

In Nakhimov Square (named after the famous nineteenth-century Russian admiral) in central Sevastopol stands a monolithic Soviet memorial to the city's heroic defence during the Second World War. Its rough but evocative sculpture depicts a brave granite-faced defender deflecting two enemy bayonets, yet succumbing to a third, symbolizing the Soviet perspective that Sevastopol had experienced three major assaults, not just the two described in German accounts, including Manstein's. In his prize-winning biography of Petrov, *The Commander*, Vladimir Karpov attempts to put the record straight. He described the unsuccessful German attacks on Sevastopol in early November, and then detailed the major operation to seize the city later that month – a month that Manstein preferred to 'forget', according to Karpov, because of German failures.[53] For the citizens of the city, the

Great Patriotic War had started suddenly nearly five months earlier.

At the outbreak of war, Sevastopol (meaning the 'magnificent city') was shining gem of the Soviet Union with its elegant streets, gleaming public buildings, extensive defences, warehouses and dockyards. An officer of the Black Sea Fleet recorded:

> It was a wonderful Crimean evening; ... all the streets and boulevards in the city were lit. The white houses were bathed in light, the clubs and theatres beckoned the sailors on shore leave to come inside. There were crowds of sailors and local people, dressed in white, packing the city's streets and parks.[54]

This peaceful calm was soon shattered with the shrill wail of the air-raid sirens and the exploding bombs of the German attack. That German night raid for all its planned surprise, however, did not amount to much: the Black Sea Fleet was not seriously damaged. Soviet Naval Command in Moscow had sensed something was up and warned the fleet headquarters in Sevastopol. Its commander, Vice-Admiral F.S. Oktyabrsky, blackened the city and his ships just in time in the early hours of 22 June 1941 before the German planes struck. Despite some hesitation by anti-aircraft units to open fire, he reported to Moscow that the 'German attack had been beaten off'.[55]

Thereafter, daily life in the city went on largely undisturbed for nearly four months until the Crimea's defence was punctured at Ishun-Perekop by Manstein's army. By mid October Sevastopol was overflowing with tens of thousands of civilian refugees, soldiers and marines transported from Odessa. On 7 November 1941, the Soviet High Command appointed Oktyabrsky as overall commander of the Sevastopol Defence Region[56] with Petrov in command of the land forces. By mid November, the Soviet outpost 'line' of forward positions was 44 kilometres long.[57] Divided into four sectors, the region was designed to contain forty-two battalion-sized defensive areas, incorporating a complex of forts, air and coastal defence batteries, anti-tank ditches and field fortifications such as bunkers and trenches exploiting the difficult terrain to the utmost.[58] The fortress area (see Map 7) was far from complete by Manstein's main attack in December 1941.

From a Soviet perspective, the first determined German assault on Sevastopol started on 11 November – one day after Petrov's Coastal Army had reconcentrated to defend the city. In contrast to his subsequent attempts to seize Sevastopol (December 1941 and June 1942), Manstein's main avenue of approach was in the south-east, along the coastal route from Yalta to Sevastopol, following the line of the old Vorontsov road of Crimean War fame, which intersected the famous Balaklava battlefield and led up and over the Sapun Gora heights towards the city. In 1941 this area was guarded by the troops of the first and second defensive sectors, who were tasked to hold the hills around Balaklava and the vital ground around the settlement of Kamary (now Oboronnoe) at all costs.

Manstein's XXX Corps, reinforced by 22nd Infantry Division, undertook repeated attacks during the period 11–21 November with heavy air support. The Soviet defence was equally ferocious and casualties mounted rapidly on both sides; on 15 November, a single Russian regiment (the 514th) lost 400 men alone. Petrov understood well the significance of the danger facing him, declaring that day:

> The situation at Balaklava has become critical. The enemy has seized Height 212.1, the last before Balaklava. We must recapture the heights, for they are key positions on this axis. Should we succeed, then the entire enemy grouping in the area of Balaklava will fall into a trap. At the same time we [must] reinforce the defence of the whole southern sector. In addition we must attack the enemy's flank.[59]

Soviet troops duly counterattacked on 20 November, securing Kamary after several attempts.

After this bitter struggle, both sides were exhausted and dug in. The front lines drawn there at the end of that month were occupied until June 1942 when Manstein launched his final offensive to capture Sevastopol. Although he devoted next to no space in his memoirs to the earlier battles on this front, he did concede briefly that his enemy 'had been able to hold his own here when 105 [German] Infantry Regiment achieved its bold capture of the Balaklava Fort in autumn 1941'. As he observed, 'penetration to this chain of fortified summits was rendered all the more difficult by the fact that one hill always flanked the next'.[60] No wonder that the Soviet defence was so effective.

Bolsheviks, Jews, Partisans and Prisoners of War

Few war crimes charges against Manstein after the Second World War had such weight as those concerning the treatment of the Soviet prisoners of war and Jews in the Crimea. Out of a total of seventeen charges brought against him in 1949, no fewer than eleven related to alleged crimes committed by German forces within the area of responsibility of Eleventh Army from September 1941 onwards.[61] An account of Manstein's trial and its outcome is given in a later chapter, but the context of his infamous order of 20 November 1941 (erased from history in his memoirs) warrants explanation here.

By the autumn of that year it had become clear that German lines of communication in rear areas across the whole of the Eastern Front were vulnerable to attack. Isolated detachments of the retreating Red Army fought on until they were destroyed or surrendered. But many Soviet soldiers remained undetected to form the nucleus of mixed military and civilian armed units – organized by Marshal Voroshilov's Partisan Directorate – that continued to harass the German rear areas across the Eastern Front. The Crimea proved no exception: its southern mountains provided a safe haven for partisans until the Soviet liberation in May 1944. Because the Germans never conceded their irregular opponents any combatant status, the fighting between the occupying force and the partisans defending their homeland was especially vicious: no quarter was given on either side.

On 10 October 1941, Field Marshal Walther von Reichenau, commander-in-chief of the Sixth Army, issued his infamous order titled 'Conduct of Troops in the Eastern Territories'. He stated that the 'most essential aim of war against the Jewish-Bolshevistic system is a complete destruction of their means of power and elimination of the Asiatic influence from European culture'. More specifically, 'if isolated partisans are found using firearms in the rear area of the army drastic measures are to be taken', code presumably for 'they are to be shot'. Reichenau's order, described by the Führer as 'excellent', was forwarded to the other armies in the East on 28 October, with the appending 'request to issue corresponding instructions on the same lines if this has not already been done'. So it can be assumed – but not proved – that the Reichenau order arrived at some stage in early November in Manstein's headquarters. For all its bigotry, there is a certain irony – if not contradiction – in Reichenau's thinking. Although he had been an ardent supporter of Hitler and anti-communist in the 1930s, he was none the less only a recent convert to violent anti-Semitism. At the same time, he had become openly critical of Hitler's policies and was against the German attack on the Soviet Union. Once the campaign started, however, he had co-operated with the *Einsatzgruppen* (special action groups), the notorious death-squads of the SS. But he also called for the raising of ethnic Ukrainian and White Russian divisions in the fight against communism, which Hitler opposed although he needed as many additional forces as he could obtain.[62]

Apart from the Reichenau order with its 'invitation' from the high command, there was another, more local, impetus for Manstein's staff to prepare something similar for distribution within Eleventh Army. On 19 November, the headquarters war diarist recorded: 'Throughout the day conspicuously lively partisan activity. Marching columns and ammunition convoys on the main supply routes have been attacked by machine-gun fire, sometimes with artillery.' All march movements that day, however, 'ran generally to plan'.[63] A shortage of troops prevented the securing of the lines of communication and so the partisan problem would remain. The army intelligence and security branch presented an order to the commander-in-chief – an incident that Manstein could not recall after the war – and asked him on 20 November to sign up to one of the most damning documents presented in prosecution evidence at the International Military Tribunal at Nuremberg and subsequently at his own trial at Hamburg.[64]

Manstein stated at Nuremberg on 10 August 1946 that 'this order escapes my memory entirely', claiming:

> I had to write and read a large number of reports and if I forgot this order, a fact which I admit, it is not surprising. I only know that this order, at any rate, as opposed to the Reichenau order, very strongly emphasizes the demands which I made for decent behaviour on the part of my soldiers. That, after all, is the important point.[65]

In fact, on 20 November Manstein worked in his headquarters drawing up plans for the crossing of the Strait of Kerch, Operation WINTER GAME, having consulted the commanding general of XXXXII Corps in Feodosia on the subject the previous day. Neither the army war diarist nor Manstein mentions the order of 20 November in their respective records.[66]

In sentiment and tone, Manstein's order follows that from Reichenau in condemning the Jews and partisans, and in calling for harsh action against both, but in contrast to its model adds some important constraints on the actions by troops against the civilian population. The first part of the order reminds its readers:

> Since 22 June, the German People has been involved in a life and death struggle against the Bolshevik system. This struggle is not being carried out against the Soviet Armed Forces alone in the established form laid down by European rules of warfare. Behind the front, too, the fighting continues. Partisan snipers dressed as civilians attack individual soldiers and small units try to disrupt our re-supply by sabotage with mines and hellish devices. . . . Jewry is the middleman between the enemy in the rear and the remains of the Red Army and the Red leadership still fighting. . . .

The Jewish Bolshevik system must be wiped out once and for all and should never again be allowed to invade our European living space.... The soldier must appreciate the necessity for the harsh punishment of Jewry, the spiritual bearer of Bolshevik terror. This is also necessary to pre-empt all uprisings, which are mostly plotted by Jews.

Taken alone, the intent here seems unequivocal: Manstein's troops appear to be given carte blanche to ignore the rules of war, to take the hardest possible action against partisans and to repress the Jewish population of the Crimea in particular. Significantly, no mention is made of the independent *Einsatzgruppe* D, commanded by Hans Ohlendorf, which prosecuted a policy of racial liquidation on the Crimea. The SS squads carried out a number of horrendous 'cleansing actions' against the Jews, most notably in Simferopol, where it is alleged that on one occasion over 10,000 were murdered.[67] In the western outskirts of the city, amongst a scrap of scruffy parkland leading off from Marshal Zhukov Street, an extensive monument to the 'many thousands killed' reminds visitors today of Simferopol's tragic past.

The second part of Manstein's order, often overlooked, strikes in contrast a tone of moderation:

... Voluntary co-operation in the rebuilding of the occupied country is an absolute necessity for the achievement of our economic and political aims. The just treatment of all non-Bolshevik sections of the population, some of whom have for years fought heroically against Bolshevism, is a prerequisite. Rule over this land brings with it the obligation to achieve, to be hard on oneself and to put personal interests last. The behaviour of every soldier is being constantly watched. It either makes hostile propaganda impossible or provides ammunition for it. If, on the land, the soldier takes the farmer's last cow, his breeding pig, his last chicken or his seed-corn, then no revitalising of the economy can be achieved.

Manstein then adds a very important point, which has an enduring character, surely relevant for contemporary counter insurgency operations: 'With every action, it is not the immediate result that is important. All actions must therefore be considered for their long-term effect.' In other words, the value of any tactical action must be balanced against the likely and desired operational or strategic outcomes. Further, 'Respect for religious practices, especially of the Mohammedan Tatars must be insisted upon.' Manstein attempted to drive a wedge between the Russian and the Tatar populations on the Crimea. To a large extent, the latter ethnic group regarded the Germans as liberators. The tragedy of the Tatars is that they backed the wrong side and paid for it in blood. Following the Soviet recapture of the Crimea in May 1944, Stalin ordered the mass deportation of the 'traitorous' Tatars to central Asia. It is estimated that hundreds of thousands died either on the journey there or on arrival.

For the record, the concluding part of Manstein's order called for: 'The self-assured, not arrogant bearing of all soldiers; restraint towards prisoners and the opposite sex; no wasting of food.' Finally, the order declared that the toughest action is to be taken 'against licence and self-interest; against degeneration and indiscipline; against any affront to soldierly honour'. Notwithstanding the moderation of the second part, the first section appears damning. So what was Manstein's purpose in signing what might appear at first sight to be a contradictory order? In his evidence at Nuremberg, he tried to explain its context and his position:

> I did not write the order at all myself. Very probably the order was shown to me in draft and then I signed it. If the first part mentions the fight against the system and the extermination of the system as well as the fight against the Jews as the supporters, in the last analysis it had its proper justification. But all that has nothing to do with the fact that Jews were to be exterminated. They were to be excluded, and the system was to be removed. That is the point that matters:[68]

As a major part of his research into Manstein's war crimes, the German academic Oliver von Wrochem has analysed the order of 20 November 1941 and its context in detail. He has unearthed substantive evidence indicating that Headquarters Eleventh Army was closely involved in the planned liquidation of Jews and partisans on the Crimea, of which Manstein consistently denied any knowledge, shedding considerable doubt on the veracity of his statements after the war on the matter.[69]

At Nuremberg, Manstein's counsel posed a most important question: 'How do you explain the fact that the murder of 90,000 Jews could have escaped your attention?' The court eagerly awaited an answer: the Field Marshal was ready with a reply:

> These 90,000 Jews who were mentioned were not murdered in my zone of command. As [the witness] Ohlendorf has stated, his zone reached from Cernauti, that is, from the Carpathians to Rostov [-on-Don]; that is approximately 1,200 kilometres long and probably 300 to 400 kilometres broad. In this huge zone not only the 11th Army was operating, but also

the 1st Armoured Army,[70] and the 3rd and 4th Romanian Armies, that is to say four armies; and these 90,000 persons who are supposed to have been murdered in the course of a year are therefore distributed over a wide area, of which only a small portion was occupied by the 11th Army in the Crimea.

As will be explained later, the prosecution at Manstein's trial in 1949 attempted to demonstrate that he not only was aware of the killings, but also had done nothing to stop them. It suffices to say at this stage that Manstein was found *not guilty* on the most serious charges relating to the murders of Jews, gypsies, communists and partisans.[71]

Sevastopol – The First Major Assault

In his appreciation of the middle of November, Manstein considered carefully the lie of the land around Sevastopol. Although he did not admit it, the failure of XXX Corps to achieve any notable success whatsoever in the Balaklava area during the earlier attacks must have weighed heavily on his mind. In reviewing the terrain, he gave more emphasis to alternative axes of attack. The approaches to the Soviet outer defensive perimeter appeared *comparatively* more open in the northern sector from the Belbeck valley south towards Sevastopol Bay (also termed Severnaya Bay, the Northern Bight). The eastern sector contained rougher terrain still with almost impenetrable gorges, thickets of rough scrub and woodland and rocky outcrops. To the south-east, the mountains and hills rising from the Black Sea coast made the approaches very difficult. Significantly, a lack of good access roads (apart from the main coastal route) hindered the bringing up of supplies here – particularly artillery ammunition – to any attacking force. In any case, the dominating ground of the Sapun Gora gave the defenders good observation over the Crimean War battlefield of Balaklava, including its famous north and south 'valleys', making this avenue even more challenging as recent combat had shown.

Manstein took all these geographical matters into consideration in formulating his plan for the capture of Sevastopol. Equally important, however, were the factors of time and forces available, and not least the nature of the enemy and its defences. The 'more quickly he could attack', he noted, 'the less time the enemy would have to organize his defence, and therefore the greater the chance of success'.[72] His able opponent, Petrov, had already shown a remarkable degree of improvisation in strengthening the Soviet defences in recent weeks. Taking into account

Soviet maritime superiority, Manstein focused his attack on the northern and north-eastern approaches to Sevastopol, rather than from the east and south-east, in reversal of the Allied plan of 1854.

Notwithstanding the density of the Soviet fortifications to the north of the city, Manstein placed his main effort here with LIV Corps (22nd, 50th, 132nd Infantry Divisions and the recently arrived 24th Infantry, together with the mass of his artillery). The XXX Corps (72nd and 170th Infantry Divisions (the latter from Kerch) with a Rumanian mountain brigade) mounted a fixing and diversionary attack in the south. Manstein planned to redeploy his 73rd Infantry Division from Kerch as well to reinforce LIV Corps, leaving XXXXII Corps with only one division (the 46th) to guard the eastern peninsula. He directed the Rumanian Mountain Corps to combat the partisans in the mountains. Only a Rumanian cavalry brigade, a handful of coastal defence batteries and a mixed bag of units drawn from the combat divisions and rear area services guarded the long and vulnerable Crimean coastline.

The outbreak of winter and ensuing logistic problems continued to bedevil Eleventh Army's preparations for the attack. On 17 November, Manstein's chief supply officer (*Oberquartiermeister*) Colonel Friedrich Wilhelm Hauck reported that four out of five railway locomotives south of the Dnepr were immobilized by severe frosts; likewise 50 per cent of road transport was out of use. On some days, Eleventh Army had to make to do with only one or two trainloads of supplies per day. In consequence, 'supplies only met current demands; building up of stocks for the attack on Sevastopol was not possible'.[73]

Manstein postponed his assault on the city to 27 November and then again to 17 December. The continuing delays were not pleasing to the German High Command. In his directive No. 39 of 8 December 1941, Hitler had ordered the Eastern Front to abandon full-scale offensive operations on account of 'the severe winter weather which has come surprisingly early'. Within 'the framework of generally defensive operations', however, a number of 'special tasks' were set out, including the Crimea: 'Sevastopol will be captured as soon as possible.'[74] So the pressure on Manstein to gain a quick victory was all too clear, and one deduced by Petrov. With a parallel battle of Moscow in mind, the Soviet general is alleged to have declared: 'We will keep Sevastopol and hold the powerful 11th Army. That is a great help too.'[75]

Manstein's frustrations on the eve of attack increased when he was ordered on 17 December to release 73rd and 170th Infantry Divisions to reinforce First Panzer Army after its embarrassing setback at Rostov-on-Don.[76] He was able to convince the new commander-in-chief of

Army Group South, Field Marshal Reichenau, to retain the 170th. Much to Manstein's chagrin, the 73rd was redeployed. This meant that he could now only employ four rather than five divisions for the main assault on Sevastopol from the north.

The first major attempt to seize Sevastopol by deliberate attack lasted two terrible winter weeks and failed with heavy losses. Owing to concentrated artillery support, initial gains had been scored in the attack sectors of 22nd and 132nd Divisions. But '50th and 24th Divisions were not making any real progress', Manstein recalled, 'in the extraordinarily difficult mountain country, parts of which were overgrown in almost impenetrable bush.' With insufficient air support, poor weather and limited daylight, Manstein's divisions burned themselves out against a well-entrenched enemy. He realized that the 'heavy fighting for the pill-boxes, which the enemy defended with stubborn determination' was 'sapping the strength of our troops, and the severe cold to which they were henceforth exposed taxed their energies to the utmost'.[77] Soviet air strikes and heavy-calibre artillery fire added to the lengthening casualty lists. One of the Soviet coastal batteries, which the Germans called the 'Maxim Gorki I', with its two armoured turrets mounting a pair of 30.5-cm (12-in) guns apiece, appeared invulnerable to air, artillery and assault gun-attack: its devastating fire broke up many a German assault. Even for the highly rated 22nd (Lower Saxony) Division, the price of its success in clearing the Belbeck valley and its deep but isolated penetration south towards Sevastopol proved too much.

Although the 22nd Division's 'vanguard' 16th Infantry Regiment under Colonel Dietrich von Choltitz managed to force its way into Fort Stalin during the night of 30/31 December, marking the high-water point of the attack, company strengths were now as low as ten to twenty men. Although the enemy 'was fought-out and his will weakened', the divisional history maintained, 'indescribable enemy artillery fire had brought our troops to the end of their strength. An intact regiment could have won the Severnaya Bay by the last day of the year.'[78] Any sober analysis of the situation would indicate that this was wishful thinking.

Manstein had left his attack too late and now had no further forces available to finish the task. In any case, the Soviets had already landed large groups of forces at Kerch and Feodosia (on 26 and 29 December 1941 respectively), forcing him to suspend the assault on Sevastopol and order a withdrawal north to the Belbeck valley. In Soviet eyes, the German general, 'seized with impotent fury', was denied the honour of presenting Hitler with the 'Christmas present' of Sevastopol. The gallant defenders' success represented 'a very good New Year present' to 'the [Soviet] country and people'.[79]

Whether the December 1941 assault would have succeeded had Manstein had another division available must be doubted. He might have been tempted to continue the attack at further heavy loss for another day or two, perhaps three, but the Soviet defence of Sevastopol at the turn of 1941/42 was simply too strong to be overcome without much heavier fire support. For all the blood spent for little obvious tactical, let alone scant operational level benefit, German confidence began to ebb worryingly.

Outstanding field commanders such as Choltitz felt that far too much was being asked of their brave men to little effect. He asked to be relieved. Manstein found the time during the middle of one of his worst crises during the Second World War to visit 16th Infantry Regiment. Choltitz recalled his commander-in-chief expressing 'in moving words his thanks for the bravery of our troops'.[80] Manstein sent the physically and mentally exhausted regimental commander – one of his best – back to Germany on sick leave.[81] The Eleventh Army had suffered over 8,500 casualties between 17 and 31 December, quite unsustainable in the circumstances.

Manstein was so concerned about the collapsing morale of his army that he wrote on 7 January 1942 to his formation commanders, acknow- ledging the impact of the decision to break off the attack on Sevastopol and the suspension of leave, quite apart from the debilitating effects of 'losses, exhaustion, vermin and the demands of winter'. In consequence, he requested that his subordinates boost their soldiers' spirits by making clear:

> Every man must understand that this battle is all about the survival of our nation and its future. However, here in the Crimea as elsewhere, only victory, whether in defence or attack, determines the fate of the individual. Every man must be clear that capture means death, and that every with- drawal endangers his comrades. The feeling that everyone fights for each other must be held high. [Furthermore,] the enemy is not better off – rather worse. . . . For the most part, we're no longer dealing with Russians, but rather with men pressed into the war from the subjugated peoples of the Caucasus. . . . But we know for what [cause] we are fighting. What the Russian soldier can tolerate, the German soldier can endure better![82]

The best cure for demoralized troops is to rest, reinforce and retrain them and then put them back into action. Manstein's soldiers – in common with German units all along the Eastern Front – had little respite that bitter winter of 1941/42. The divisions of Eleventh Army held on with grim determination, as did their opponents.

Mastering the Winter Crises

The Soviet landings on the Kerch peninsula in late December 1941 were but a part of the much wider 'Stalin offensive' launched across the whole Eastern Front. Following the Red Army's success in forcing back Army Group South from Rostov-on-Don to the Mius River at the end of November, the *Stavka* ordered the Transcaucasus *Front* to regain a 'foothold on the Crimea' and then to liberate it. The *Front*'s 44th and 51st Armies, in close co-operation with the Black Sea Fleet, mounted the Kerch–Feodosia amphibious operation aimed at seizing the Kerch peninsula and relieving Sevastopol through the destruction of the German Eleventh Army.[83]

Manstein wrote disparagingly about the 'brutal will' of Stalin, which found expression in the ruthless manner in which Russian troops were expended.[84] Whatever they lacked in tactical finesse and operational skills at this stage of the Second World War, Soviet forces certainly made up for such shortcomings with immense effort, exploiting the Red Navy's control of the Black Sea. The scale, multiplicity and sequencing of the Soviet attempts to recapture the peninsula threatened Manstein to such an extent that only his personal agility in redeploying his scarce forces to the right place just in the nick of time saved his army on a number of occasions. His mastery of what appeared at times to be a hopeless situation during the winter of 1941– 42 saw the commander of Eleventh Army displaying steadfastness in adversity and resolution in response. His intuition, initiative and improvisation in dealing with a succession of crises earned him grudging respect from his superiors and opponents alike.

The landings at Kerch by elements of the Soviet 51st Army could not have come at a worse time for Manstein as Eleventh Army was fully stretched. His main effort remained the capture of Sevastopol, the assault of which involved six out of his seven German infantry divisions. At Kerch only the sole German division of XXXXII Corps (46th Infantry), together with the 8th Rumanian Cavalry Brigade and a motorized regiment, was available to respond. According to Manstein's account and Eleventh's Army war diary, the corps commander, Lieutenant General Hans Graf von Sponeck, wished to evacuate the Kerch peninsula and withdraw to a defensive position at its neck at Parpach (now Yachminne), where any Soviet offensive could be sealed off most economically.

Manstein disagreed fundamentally with his subordinate's assessment fearing (rightly as it turned out) that once the Soviet forces had made a strong lodgement on the Crimea, expelling them would be exceptionally difficult, requiring a major counter-offensive operation. So he ordered Sponeck to 'hurl the [enemy] back into the sea' whilst 'he was still off-balance after his landing'.[85] Meanwhile, on 28 December, and again on the 30th, he ordered Hansen's LIV Corps to continue its attack on Sevastopol. Anticipating further Soviet landings on the eastern coast, Manstein ordered two Rumanian mountain brigades to move to Feodosia, and recalled 213rd Infantry Regiment (a reinforced regimental group of the departed 73rd Infantry Division) to deploy there as well. Notwithstanding the fact that counterattacks by 46th Division on 27 and 28 December had managed already to eliminate most of the Soviet landing forces, Sponeck requested again permission to withdraw. Manstein refused once more.[86]

The subsequent landings at Feodosia on 29 December by two divisions of the Soviet 44th Army were opposed initially by light German forces (principally 46th Army Engineer Battalion recuperating after heavy fighting at Sevastopol) as Manstein's planned reinforcements had yet to arrive. This new development, together with continuing pressure at Kerch, appeared to threaten the integrity of XXXXII Corps to such an extent that Sponeck decided on his own initiative to withdraw from the Kerch peninsula to Parpach. What appeared to have tipped the situation in his mind was a report of a landing of further Soviet forces on the coast north-east of Feodosia, who threatened to turn northwards and cut off the Kerch peninsula, isolating XXXXII Corps in the process.

Looking at the whole of the campaign on the Crimea, 29 December 1941 appears to be one of the most critical days of all for Manstein, the impact of which was recognized elsewhere.[87] Halder, for example, noted laconically in his diary: 'A very bad day! ... [Sponeck] has immediately been removed from his post, but the damage done can hardly be repaired.'[88]

Sponeck maintained to his death (he was murdered on Himmler's orders on 23 July 1944) that he had taken the correct action in ordering the withdrawal of 46th Division. In retrospect, Manstein appeared to agree to some extent. As a result of the events of 29 December 1941, he had wanted to replace Sponeck with General of Infantry Franz Mattenklott, the former commander of 72nd Infantry Division, rather than having him court-martialled.[89] Manstein was neither informed of the date of the court martial nor given the opportunity of making a formal representation on his former subordinate's behalf. On 23 January

1942, Sponeck was sentenced to death on account of negligent disobedience in the field. A month later, Hitler commuted the sentence to six years' 'fortress arrest'.[90]

Meanwhile, the operational situation continued to worsen for the Germans. On 4 January 1942, Manstein formulated an uncharacteristically pessimistic assessment, writing that the 'current situation of the Eleventh Army is the consequence of it being too weak since the beginning of the campaign for the tasks given to it'. Therefore, 'it has expended its strength to a far greater degree than other armies, and as a result has not been able to complete its final task, the capture of Sevastopol'. Turning to the enemy:

> The opponent is not attempting to achieve a partial objective, the relief of Sevastopol; rather, he is seeking a decision, the destruction of Eleventh Army, through which he can open the path into the deep flank of the Army Group. He masters the sea and without doubt possesses [sufficient] forces in the Caucasus, which he could use for landing operations at other places. He will do this, and should he succeed, fix all the forces of the Army.

Manstein then considered the risks of enemy landings on the southern and western coasts, predicting rightly that further amphibious operations would follow. He observed further:

> The situation of the Eleventh Army on the Crimea should be viewed differently from that of the other armies standing on a continuous Eastern Front. Even a deep penetration by the enemy [elsewhere] will run its course under the winter weather conditions. Here there is a relatively high chance of being completely cut off. This is not only a big risk for the Army, but taking a wider view, represents one for the whole front. In this circumstance it really depends on destroying the enemy's eastern [Kerch–Feodosia] grouping, and thereby restoring a reasonably safe situation. To achieve this aim, the Army must concentrate all the forces that it can make free for this task.

In concluding his estimate, Manstein reached an atypical low in his confidence in the ability of his army to rise to the occasion, making a prophetic point: 'Whether the forces of the Army are sufficient for a quick and decisive attack against the enemy grouping at Kerch–Feodosia is not certain. If we don't achieve a complete success here, then further landings by the enemy could make the situation untenable at short notice and then not recoverable.'[91]

Manstein's concerns were well founded. Whilst reinforcing their existing bridgehead at Feodosia, Soviet troops landed on 5 January 1942 at Eupatoria on the western coast. Here Germans were not only being opposed by regular Soviet troops but also by armed 'partisans' in civilian clothing. After two days of intense combat, the town was again in German hands. A description of the action is omitted from the English version of Manstein's memoirs. Its aftermath represents no credit to German arms: it took two German infantry regiments, a reconnaissance battalion and an engineer battalion to master the situation in vicious house-to-house fighting. Not only were 1,200 'partisans' in civilian clothing summarily executed, but also 150 Red Army prisoners of war were shot out of hand.[92]

After liquidating the opposition in Eupatoria, Manstein eliminated enemy forces at Feodosia. Meanwhile, the Soviets strengthened their hold of the Kerch peninsula by bringing reinforcements over the ice-road from Kuban. During the limited hours of daylight and in frequent periods of bad weather, the Luftwaffe was unable to interdict Soviet lines of communication. Manstein possessed insufficient forces to mount an effective counter-offensive to regain Kerch. Fortunately, the Soviet 51st Army had not pursued 46th Division at the year's end with any vigour. Nor had the 44th Army attempted to cut it off. This twin fortune allowed the shattered German division to reach the Parpach isthmus by a series of forced marches, albeit having lost much of its heavy equipment, including artillery.

In military affairs generally, and in commanders' memoirs in particular, it is not unusual to justify one's own lack of achievement by exaggerating the strength of the opponent. The British over admiration of Rommel, the 'Desert Fox', used to mask systemic weaknesses during the campaign in North Africa until the arrival of Montgomery, is a case in point. In his account of the winter crises, however, Manstein observed critically of his opponent:

> Had the Soviet commander [Kozlov] pressed home his advantage by pursuing 46 Division really hard from Kerch and thrusting relentlessly after the Rumanians as they fell back from Feodosia, the fate of the entire Eleventh Army would have been at stake. As it happened, he did not know when to take time by the forelock. Either he did not realize what a chance he had, or else he did not venture to seize it.[93]

There is little doubt that by failing to exploit vigorously from their bridgeheads at Kerch and Feodosia, the Soviets had missed a golden opportunity to defeat Manstein's army. Had they been able to capture and hold the main rail and road hubs at either Dzhankoi or Simferopol, so severing the Germans' logistic jugular, then Eleventh Army's fate would have been sealed. Thus it is hard not to agree with Karpov's swingeing assessment: 'If the command of the newly formed Crimean *Front* had acted with the same determination as the Sevastopol defenders, its success would have been complete. For unknown reasons, however, it was incredibly sluggish and failed to mount a decisive offensive. Even Manstein was puzzled by that.'[94]

At the beginning of 1942, Kozlov was under intense pressure from Stalin, who directed him on 5 January: 'You have been given the military and civilian ships, you have the force, and the weather will become better. I ask you not to postpone any more and to begin the operation no later than 12 January.'[95] Soviet command on the Crimea, however, remained ponderous.

Despite his enemy's lack of initiative, the odds facing Manstein in his attempt to recapture Feodosia looked unpromising. On 14 January he wrote 'that it was the most difficult decision to risk an attack with three weak divisions and insufficient artillery, without the armour which will not be present for another 4–5 days, with questionable *Stuka* support, all in bad weather … but it is the last chance…. One must take the risk. Let God help us!'[96] Although the operation (15–18 January) ran unexpectedly well, Manstein was unable to exploit his success and recapture the Kerch peninsula in its wake.[97] On 19 January both his corps commanders involved reported that their divisions could not continue. Not only did Eleventh Army lack the necessary reinforcements, including the requested armoured units and additional air support, but the Soviets had continued to reinforce their troops at both Kerch and Sevastopol.

Although he did not receive any fresh German troops until the spring, Manstein drew on further Rumanian forces (18th Infantry Division) and the local Tatar population. To protect their villages from attacks by the partisans, he had ordered the raising of 'self-protection companies'.[98] In addition, over 2,000 Tatar volunteers were incorporated into German front-line infantry companies as much-needed riflemen.[99]

Other matters at the beginning of 1942 were to distract Manstein. His hopes of advancement had been raised through the strong reassurance of confidence that he had received on 16 January from Hitler's chief adjutant, Schmundt:

> in the recent critical weeks, the Führer has often thought about employing you, General, in other places where the situation is critical. That would certainly have occurred had the Führer not had the impression that

no other than you could master the difficult situation on the Crimea. Therefore the Führer will not set about any changes [in command] until the danger to the Crimea is removed.[100]

On 30 January Manstein observed in his diary that Rommel had been promoted to colonel general, but noted in disappointment 'nothing for us of course'. He would have to wait until 6 March for his promotion, which he acknowledged on that day without further comment.

Meanwhile, on 27 February 1942, the recently established Soviet Crimean *Front*, consisting of 44th, 47th and 51st Armies (each the strength of a reinforced German corps) on the Kerch peninsula together with the Coastal Army at Sevastopol, mounted a series of concerted attacks against the German positions in both locations. For Eleventh Army it was 'touch and go' for a couple of weeks as Manstein did not have any reserves in hand to employ – he was fully committed on both fronts. Once again Manstein set out his case for reinforcements to Headquarters Army Group South by dint of cool estimation and clear explanation of the situation facing him. Without exaggeration, he declared that if he were to remain unreinforced in this critical situation, there was a very real possibility of losing the Eleventh Army *and* the Crimea. In his judgement, he needed urgent reinforcements in the form of two panzer divisions and very strong air support in order to defeat the inevitable enemy offensive and, when the time was right, to counter-attack.[101]

In the event, OKH mustered two newly raised formations (22nd Panzer and 28th Light Infantry Divisions) to assist Eleventh Army.[102] Meanwhile, Soviet attacks battered away tirelessly at the German positions at Parpach throughout late February and March. A German counter-attack on 20 March by XXXXII Corps failed in large part due to the 'new armoured division' running straight 'into a Soviet assembly area in the early-morning mist'. Manstein, an experienced trainer of troops, conceded that it had been premature to employ a new unit in this fashion before it had been put through 'its paces in exercises with its parent formation'.[103] But in view of the fragility of the German defence at Parpach, Manstein had little choice other than to commit the green division into battle immediately. Although it proved inexpert in its first combat, 22nd Panzer Division achieved some success, none the less, by disrupting yet another Soviet attack.

With the arrival of 28th Light Division, the German defenders were able over the period 9–11 April to beat off the final Soviet offensive by 44th and 51st Armies. It involved, according to Manstein, 'between six and eight rifle divisions ... supported by 160 tanks'.[104] Having banked this significant defensive success, Manstein could now look forward to dealing offensively with the enemy groupings at Kerch and Sevastopol. As ever, the German High Command pressed him impatiently for early and decisive action.

The Recapture of the Kerch Peninsula – Operation BUSTARD HUNT

Hitler's Directive No. 41 of 5 April 1942 set out the strategic rationale and operational intentions for the German summer offensive of 1942 under the nickname Operation BLUE. The Führer's overall intent was to capture Leningrad in the north, to hold in the centre and to concentrate 'all available forces' on the main operations in the southern sector in order to 'secure the Caucasian oilfields'. Before the principal blow of this new campaign could be launched, preliminary operations had to be conducted, including a 'mopping-up operation in the Kerch peninsula on the Crimea and the capture of Sevastopol'.[105]

Manstein had already determined that he needed to destroy the main threat to his army – presented by the Soviet grouping on the Kerch peninsula – before he attempted to assault Sevastopol again. The enemy at Kerch 'could be given no time to recover from the losses of his abortive attacks. Sevastopol would have to be shelved until the Soviet forces on the Kerch peninsula had been wiped out.'[106] Before the arrival of the two reinforcing formations, he had only seven German infantry divisions plus a regiment under command. Whereas he could only count on retaining 22nd Panzer Division for the recapture of the Kerch peninsula, he hoped that 28th Light Division would remain attached to his army until completion of the campaign in the Crimea.

In the face of the Soviet strength at Kerch (according to German estimates amounting to seventeen rifle divisions, three rifle brigades, two cavalry divisions and four independent armoured brigades[107]), Manstein was forced to be inventive in order to mitigate his enemy's considerable numerical superiority. In addition to reinforcements, he needed to design an imaginative plan of attack and required a degree of good luck in the form of a poorly conducted Soviet defence, which on previous experience at Sevastopol could not be counted on.

Manstein called on his allies again for further assistance. His staff had put together an extensive visit programme (3–6 April 1942) for Marshal Antonescu. Employing all his charm and diplomacy whilst escorting the Rumanian leader, Manstein gained promises of additional Rumanian forces: 10th and 19th Infantry Divisions together with 8th Cavalry

Brigade, the latter now redesignated a division without any increase in strength. Notwithstanding these welcome reinforcements, Manstein still faced an uphill struggle in achieving the appropriate force ratios for breaking into the main Soviet defence, let alone breaking *out* beyond to exploit eastwards towards Kerch. Once again he had to take further risk in stripping forces back from the Sevastopol front to the absolute minimum required to invest the fortress.

On 17 April, Manstein was summoned to discuss future operations with Hitler. It was his first such meeting since briefing the Führer in Berlin in the *Reichskanzlei* on his proposals for the campaign in the West, over two years previously. Hitler sent his own transport aircraft, a specially adapted Focke-Wulf 200 *Condor* maritime reconnaissance bomber, to pick him up at Simferopol and take him to the Führer's Headquarters – the *Wolfschanze* (wolf's lair) – at Rastenburg in East Prussia. Shortly after arriving that afternoon, Manstein had a private session with Field Marshal Keitel, who 'looked really old'.[108]

During the conference with Hitler, Manstein presented his plan to destroy the enemy on the Kerch peninsula prior to capturing the fortress of Sevastopol. He stressed that he needed reinforcements to guarantee a successful outcome to both operations. The Führer's response was 'whilst he could not give [further] divisions', he could provide 'the strongest [possible] support of the Luftwaffe and in *matériel* assistance'.[109] Manstein's overall impression of the interchange with Hitler was positive: the Führer 'listened attentively to what I had to say and fully agreed with Eleventh Army's view on the manner in which to conduct both the Kerch offensive and the assault on Sevastopol. He made not the least effort to interfere in our plans, or, as was so often the case later on, to ramble off into endless recitations of production figures.'[110]

Taking advantage of the loan of Hitler's aircraft, Manstein flew to Liegnitz the next day for a lightning stop-over, his first visit home since taking over command of Eleventh Army seven months before. In a rare, touching personal comment, he recorded in his diary, 'it is always so nice to see one's sweetheart'. On the return overnight flight to the Crimea, Gero accompanied him; together they toured Simferopol on 19 April. Manstein noted, 'it was a great joy to have the boy with me for once.'[111]

After his elder son's departure on 20 April, Manstein returned to the normal hectic pace of army command with a busy round of visitors and inspections. The commander of VIII Air Corps, Colonel General Wolfram von Richthofen, together with the chief of staff of the Luftwaffe, Colonel General Hans Jeschonnek, appeared on the 21st. Hitler was as good as his word in providing additional air support; VIII Air

Corps represented the strongest ground attack force in the Luftwaffe and was commanded by one of its most capable leaders. The meeting between Manstein and Richthofen, one historian observed, 'went surprisingly well, despite the potential for a major ego clash between these two brilliant but conceited personalities'. For his part, Richthofen noted in his diary that evening, 'Manstein was surprisingly mellow and accommodating. He understands everything. It was extremely uplifting.'[112] Despite the odd frictions between them, Manstein conceded that his air force colleague 'was certainly the most outstanding Luftwaffe leader we had in World War II. ... I remember [his] achievements and those of his Air Corps with the utmost admiration and gratitude.'[113]

Manstein inspected the Sevastopol and Kerch fronts prior to the visit of the army group commander, Field Marshal von Bock, on the 28th. On 3 May, Manstein was back at Headquarters XXX and XXXXII Corps, along with Richthofen, to discuss the impending offensive. When bad weather delayed the arrival of air reinforcements, the start of the attack was put back successively to 8 May.

From an operational level perspective, Manstein had to devise a scheme of manoeuvre that would play to his strengths and exploit his enemy's weaknesses. On the ground, he was outnumbered by at least two to one, hardly a promising starting condition for an offensive. An attack across a broad front against the Soviets' forward position at the isthmus of Parpach, 18 kilometres wide, might well push the defenders back towards their rear position at the Tatar Ditch, but would not lead to a decisive outcome. The shape of the Soviet's forward-leaning defence, however, offered an opportunity to envelop a substantial part of the principal enemy grouping, 51st Army, contained in the northern sector. Between the settlement of Koi Assan (now Vladyslavivka) and the Syvash Sea, the Soviet line bulged 10 kilometres to the west; south of the town the defences ran directly down to the Black Sea coast. If Manstein could achieve a substantial penetration in this area, defended by 44th Army, he would then be able to lunge into 51st Army's weak southern flank and rear. Having won sufficient freedom of manoeuvre, the lead elements of Eleventh Army could then exploit eastwards as quickly as possible towards Kerch, destroying 47th Army – located in the Soviet rear – in the process.

To achieve any prospect of success, Manstein's plan required a good degree of surprise, deception and, above all, tempo in attack. In the north, Manstein simulated a principal axis with VII Rumanian and XXXXII Corps to fix 51st Army. He placed his *real* main effort with XXX Corps (50th Infantry, 28th Light, 132nd Infantry and 22nd Panzer

Divisions) against 44th Army in the south, with orders to swing the armoured division to the north around the rear of the 51st Army. By this scheme of manoeuvre he aimed to defeat both forward Soviet armies before finishing off the third held in depth. In order to give further substance to this main effort, Manstein concentrated the mass of his artillery and focused the close air support of VIII Air Corps in the south. In addition, 170th Infantry Division, 231st Infantry Regiment and 8th Rumanian Cavalry Division stood by to reinforce XXX Corps on orders. Finally, Manstein devised an amphibious operation to land an infantry battalion by assault boats in an attempt to turn the southernmost flank of the Parpach position, a trick he was to use again on a larger scale nearly two months later during the final stages of the assault on Sevastopol.

As Manstein readily admitted in his memoirs, the viability of his plan depended on achieving two conditions: first, making the enemy believe for as long as possible that the 'decisive attack would come in the north until it was too late for him to back out of the trap or to throw his reserves into the southern sector'; and secondly, 'the speed with which XXX Corps – and in particular 22 Panzer Division – carried out the northward thrust.'[114]

Manstein's unexpected 'below the belt' blow hitting the Soviet defence very hard under the 'bulge' was greatly facilitated by the incompetence of the Soviet command in both the planning and conduct of its defensive battle. Without demeaning Manstein's and Eleventh Army's considerable achievement, inexcusable failures by the Crimean *Front*'s commanders contributed significantly to their own defeat. A great share of the blame for this incompetence must go to Kozlov and his advisors.[115]

Despite some short delays, on 8 May 1942 Eleventh Army attacked the Soviet Parpach position. Although the amphibious operation miscarried, XXX Corps forced the anti-tank obstacle and 'shattered the enemy's southern wing'. It was, however, as Manstein reflected, 'no easy battle', for the defenders fought hard.[116] The 22nd Panzer Division then attacked on 9 May. Notwithstanding enemy counterattacks with tank units, and heavy rain on 10 May that slowed down movement and restricted air support, German armour reached the northern coast on 11 May, 'bottling up some eight enemy divisions as it went'.[117] On the extreme southern flank, Brigade Group Grodeck broke into the enemy's rear areas and advanced eastwards with such rapidity that the Soviet defenders were unable to react in time to block its path.

In a blatantly self-serving effort to deflect impending and certain criticism, one of the *Stavka* representatives sent to supervise the Soviet defences, Commissar of First Rank L. Z. Mekhlis, signalled Stalin on

8 May blaming Kozlov for the mess the Soviet forces on the Kerch peninsula were in. The supreme warlord would have none of this, replying:

> You are adopting the strange position of detached observer who accepts no responsibility for the affairs of the *Krimfront*. That is a very comfortable position, but is one that absolutely stinks. On the Crimean Front, you – you – are no detached onlooker but a responsible representative of the *Stavka*, responsible for all the successes and failures and obliged to correct errors by the command on the spot. You along with the command are responsible for the fact that the left flank of the Front is wretchedly weak. If 'the whole situation pointed to the fact that tomorrow the enemy will attack', and you did not take all possible measures to repulse him, limiting yourself to passive criticism, then the worse for you.

Calamity indeed struck and the Soviet command structure never recovered from the first day of the German attack. As one historian observed aptly, 'Manstein *versus* Mekhlis was no match: disaster rolled with terrifying speed upon the Crimean Front.'[118]

As the Soviet commanders continued to flounder, letting down their hard-pressed and out-fought troops, on the fourth day of battle Manstein ordered a general pursuit. On 16 May, the town of Kerch fell to 170th Infantry Division and 213rd Infantry Regiment. Significant Soviet resistance continued, however, in the local Adzhimushkai stone quarries, caves and catacombs, where fanatical stay-behind parties, according to Soviet accounts, 'waged a heroic fight' until the end of October 1942.[119]

In retrospect, Manstein had achieved the seemingly impossible. He claimed in his memoirs that the battle had cost the Soviet forces no less than '170,000 prisoners, 1133 guns and 258 tanks', declaring proudly that a 'true battle of annihilation had been fought to a victorious finish'.[120] Indeed it had, representing one of his greatest triumphs that owed much to his personal operational virtuosity and tactical skill, earning him on 19 May 1942 yet another mention in the *Wehrmachtsberichte*.[121] Total German casualties were less than 8,000.

There were other factors at play, however, that had helped bring about this spectacular success. In contrast with the battle of the Perekop the previous autumn, Manstein had been assured by Hitler of effective air support from the outset of the operation. He rightly gave full tribute to the decisive role played by German air power during the battle. Richthofen's VIII Air Corps had provided the promised 'air-to-surface' support to devastating effect. It had flown between 1,000 and 2,000 sorties per day before the diversion of key units to Kharkov (to help counter Marshal Timoshenko's major offensive to capture that city), and between 300 and 800 thereafter, which represented no mean effort.[122] Far from it, the destruction of forward defences during the opening stages of the operation and the disruption of the command and control of Crimean *Front*'s subordinate field headquarters and command posts by precision attack throughout was considerable, generating much of the Soviet paralysis in response to the Germans' truly joint and multinational offensive.

The success of such co-operation between air and land forces was indeed a good omen for Manstein's ultimate challenge on the Crimea: the long-awaited capture of Sevastopol. Whereas Manstein and Richthofen enjoyed Hitler's praise for a job well done, Stalin took quick revenge on the incompetent commanders of the Crimean *Front*, the odious Mekhlis rightly included, who were lucky to escape with demotions rather than losing their heads.

But perhaps Operation BUSTARD HUNT had been a little too easy. It had proved a 'lop-sided victory', which had 'confirmed German confidence in their own abilities and their contempt for the abilities of the Soviets'.[123] The assault on Sevastopol against a skilled and determined defence would turn out to be a far bloodier affair, a portent of yet worse to come at Stalingrad.

Sevastopol – Planning the Second Major Assault, Operation STURGEON CATCH

As in the previous autumn and early winter, Manstein was confronted by the same geographical difficulties in mounting an assault on Sevastopol over broken ground, regardless of his chosen avenue of approach. In the meantime, however, the Soviet defenders under the irrepressible Petrov and his troops had continued to reinforce that very same terrain with additional field fortifications. They had extended methodically gun and tank positions in all four defensive sectors and sowed the intervening fields of fire with new – unmarked – minefields. Balancing that distinctly negative development, Manstein was at last assured of a much greater density of artillery and air support than previously, his two main trumps. Further, the longer hours of daylight and the better weather were to his advantage. For his soldiers, however, the burning summer heat with 40-degree highs was oppressive. Most significantly, there would soon come a time when his fighting power was no longer sufficient to complete the capture of the fortress city and naval base. Then much, if not all, of the sacrifice to date would have been in vain.

Manstein determined that Eleventh Army's main axis of attack should again be in the north because the going there was 'far easier' than in the southern part of Sevastopol's defences, although the 'enemy fortifications were undoubtedly stronger and more numerous' above Severnaya Bay than to its east and south. He also calculated that artillery and air power could be more effectively employed here. A further deliberation was the need to 'gain command of the harbour at the earliest possible date' to prevent enemy movement and resupply, noting the Luftwaffe's limited capability to interdict the sea lines of communication. He could ill afford to neglect attacking elsewhere as the Soviet defender not only needed to be fixed in place to facilitate his main attack, but also had to be defeated as a fighting force. Therefore, as in the previous December, a supporting attack was to be launched with the aim of gaining the Sapun position 'on both sides of the roads leading from the south coast and Balaklava to Sevastopol'.[124]

Manstein, together with his operational and logistics staffs, had thought hard about the Sevastopol operation, and had planned well ahead for it. A crucial precondition for success was the requirement to stockpile sufficient artillery ammunition and air munitions for the attack. In addition, orders had to be issued in good time to allow the subordinate corps, divisions and regiments to prepare for their specific roles in the operation. Eleventh Army's warning order in preparation for Operation STURGEON CATCH was distributed on 14 May 1942, during the height of the reconquest of the Kerch peninsula. This good practice illustrates the old maxim at the operational level that planning for the subsequent battle must be completed before the current action is concluded.

In fixing the date of the attack, Manstein had to balance carefully the need to maximize the amount of artillery and ammunition available against the likelihood that VIII Air Corps' concentrated support on the Crimea could only be of *limited* duration as it would be needed soon to support Army Group A's main offensive into the Caucasus. He knew that time was not on his side as he had already experienced the 'flexing' of air power to meet the Soviet Kharkov offensive in May 1942 during BUSTARD HUNT.

Eleventh Army's scheme of manoeuvre (see Map 7) was similar to that adopted in December 1941. Again, the main attack was to be conducted by LIV Corps (132nd, 22nd, 50th and 24th Infantry Divisions in line from west to east) in the northern sector. Its initial task was to break into the heavily fortified zone and capture the high ground immediately north of the eastern end of Severnaya Bay, mounting a supporting attack on its left wing to take the heights of Gaitany and the ground immediately to its south-east. Domination of this key terrain would facilitate a subsequent, supporting attack by the Rumanian Mountain Corps further south. Its 18th Infantry Division would assist the southern wing of LIV Corps whilst its 1st Mountain Division supported the northern wing of its southern neighbour, XXX Corps.

Manstein's second German corps was required to mount a large-scale attack directed towards the Sapun Gora. To take this objective it would have to penetrate and clear a path through the Soviet outer defensive zone based on the strong points such as 'North Nose', 'Chapel Mount' and the village of Kamary (Oboronnoe), the scene of such vicious fighting in November 1941, and 'eliminate the flanking fire from the rocky heights of Balaklava in the south'.[125] Whilst 72nd Infantry Division would launch its attack astride the main road to Sapun Gora, 28th Light Division would mount a supporting operation to clear the Balaklava hills. Meanwhile, 170th Division would be retained initially as corps reserve. Applying Manstein's intent, the commander of XXX Corps, Lieutenant General Maximilian Fretter-Pico, was in no doubt about the need for drive and energy in the attack, demanding in his orders: 'I expect every commander to exploit every possible success through daring and quick action.'[126]

A major challenge facing Manstein was how to deny – as far as he could – his intentions to his perceptive opponent. His ability to do so was extremely limited. Petrov had already fought off two attacks on Sevastopol, and knew how Eleventh Army operated. Further, the lie of the land and the Axis forces' dispositions telegraphed that another major assault most probably would take place in the north.[127]

It is doubtful, however, whether any of Manstein's deception measures had any beneficial effect. A German intelligence report of 14 June, one week into the main ground offensive, estimated that no less than forty out of a total of seventy-five enemy battalions within the Sevastopol Defence Region were securing the fortress area north of Severnaya Bay, exactly where Eleventh Army's primary objective lay. The order of battle of the Coastal Army, which Manstein's intelligence branch had estimated accurately from a combination of signals intelligence, captured documents and the interrogation of prisoners, consisted of six rifle divisions, a dismounted cavalry division and three marine infantry brigades.[128]

In the face of these opposing forces, the difficult terrain and extensive defences, Manstein knew that there would be no short cuts that summer in assaulting a fortress as strong as Sevastopol. It could only be captured through the flexible combination of 'joint fires' – to use a contemporary military idiom – of air and artillery power to prepare and to support a determined (and potentially costly) infantry attack, assisted by assault engineers. Apart from one separate German tank battalion (which contained both conventional tanks and new remotely controlled, tracked demolition devices), an improvised company of captured Soviet T-34s and a limited number of assault guns, he had no substantial armoured forces – let alone specialist armoured engineer equipment – to smash his way into the city.[129]

Likewise, there was no scope for any fancy manoeuvre. Manstein expressly forbade his forces to get involved in 'hopeless forest fighting'.[130] This was going to be a set-piece battle, with inevitable attrition on both sides. Therefore he gave special attention to the artillery preparation phase of the attack (2–6 June), writing out a detailed four-page instruction himself. He set out its purpose as:

> In combination with the Luftwaffe, to break the morale of the enemy; by extending the bombardment to leave him uncertain as to the timing of our infantry assault; to destroy strong or particularly important fortifications or supply bases; by enticing enemy guns to fire to enable the destruction of a part of his artillery before the infantry attack.[131]

The concentration and weight of artillery support available for the June 1942 attack on Sevastopol was unprecedented for the German Army in any campaign and was not to be repeated during the Second World War. In total, Manstein massed over 611 guns in 208 batteries on a 36-kilometre front, the equivalent of 17 barrels per kilometre. In the assault sectors, the density was much higher, but as he noted, it did not achieve the ratio of over 200 per kilometre attained by the Red Army later on in the war. Supplementing the artillery were 754 mortar tubes and rocket launchers of the *Nebeltruppe* (chemical/smoke troops).[132] In addition, there were two super-heavy 60-cm 'Karl' mortars, and the biggest artillery piece ever employed, the 80-cm-calibre 'Dora' cannon firing from Bakhchisarai. This 'monster', as Manstein described it, had been developed to bombard the Maginot Line in France, but had not been ready in time. Impressive as a technical achievement, he remarked, Dora's effectiveness 'bore no relation to all the effort and expense that had gone into making it'.[133]

So the stage was set for the forthcoming battle. A few days before the attack, Manstein was struck by misfortune. Following a visit to XXX Corps' headquarters on the southern coast, he had undertaken a reconnaissance on an Italian E-boat towards Balaklava to 'ascertain how much of the coastal road, up which the whole of the corps' reinforcements and supplies must pass was visible from the sea and liable to come under observed bombardment from that quarter'.[134] On the return passage, the vessel was engaged by two Soviet fighters off Yalta. One of the Russian pilots recorded the action:

> I swooped down, caught the boat in the sight and pulled the triggers. The white deck of the boat turned red with blood. Dark figures rushed about and collapsed on the deck. Wood splinters flew into the waves. Bringing the aircraft out of the dive, I looked back: the cannon and machine guns of the supporting aircraft were hitting the target.[135]

In this bloodbath, in which seven out of sixteen on the boat were either killed or wounded, Manstein was extremely lucky to have escaped unscathed. Tragically, his driver since 1938, Sergeant Fritz Nagel, was mortally wounded. For Manstein, the loss was profound, for 'throughout the years he had been a devoted comrade and in time had become a real friend'.[136] At the graveside, Manstein's eulogy could have been said for thousands of Nagel's comrades-in-arms. In paying personal tribute, the army commander spoke:

> For more than five years as my driver and loyal companion you have sat next to me at the steering wheel of our staff car. Your certain eye, your steady hand, have taken us through many countries and over many thousands of kilometres. There has never been a harsh word between us. Together we have seen many good things, and together we have experienced the main actions and the victories of the campaigns. Last year you were wounded at my side; now a deadly bullet has struck you. In the years of daily life and great events we became friends. The bond of friendship that connected us cannot be cut by the treacherous bullet that hit you.[137]

Manstein bade farewell to his driver in the German cemetery near Yalta. Apart from losing his favourite ADC, 'Pepo' Specht, and elder son Gero four months later, Nagel's death hit him hardest during the war.

The Final Attack on Sevastopol

Between 2 and 7 June, massed German artillery and aircraft of VIII Air Corps pounded the city of Sevastopol and its defences for five days of intense preparatory fires that aimed to paralyse the Soviet defenders. Laskin, one of the four sector commanders, recalled:

> German aircraft were in the air above our positions all day long. We could not hear their engines in the continuous thunder of guns and shell

explosions. Groups of bombers following in rapid succession looked like countless flocks of fantastic black birds. A whirlwind of fire was raging at all our positions.... More than 1,000 guns and mortars were firing simultaneously at our narrow fourth defence sector and about 100 bombers were raining bombs upon us.[138]

Meanwhile, Manstein and his operations team moved to a forward command post at Yukhary Karales (now Zalesnoe), a Tatar village nestling in a picturesque, narrow limestone gorge 20 kilometres east of the centre of Sevastopol. Close by, the Germans established an observation post at Point 473.4 on the rounded Yel Burun summit, near the cave city of Cherkess-Kermen.

Manstein and his staff climbed up to their vantage point during the night of 6/7 June 1942 to view the imminent attack. It was a rare opportunity in the Second World War for an army commander to view most of his battlefield. H-Hour was due at 03.00 hours but the Soviet defenders had got wind of this time through interrogation of prisoners of war. Petrov launched a pre-emptive artillery strike five minutes before in an attempt to catch the German infantry exposed in their jumping-off positions, having seen through Manstein's deception measures. According to Karpov, the intensity of German artillery fire and bombing raids in different sectors had indicated 'the direction of the main German thrust, [which would] be undertaken in the fourth sector defended by Laskin's division and Potapov's brigade, while the secondary strike would be dealt along the Yalta highway in the south'.[139]

After the first few days of fighting, casualties on both sides were horrendous with commanders and soldiers alike exhausted and their units completely spent. But for all the pressure on Petrov's men, the German attack appeared to have culminated by the third day. Manstein's memoirs paint an heroic picture: ' ... The spirit of the German soldier – all his courage, initiative, and self-sacrifice contending with the dogged resistance of an opponent whose natural elements were the advantage of terrain and the tenacity and steadfastness of the Russian soldier reinforced by the iron compulsion of the Soviet system.'[140]

In fact, the German army commander was in deep trouble: he had failed to achieve any surprise whatsoever in the opening of his attack and the anticipated daily objectives were not met anywhere. Simply speaking, he needed not only additional troops but had also, as a matter of urgency, to integrate all elements of his assault force to much better overall effect if the bid to capture Sevastopol were to have a chance of success.

Manstein noted on 8 June the lack of overall progress in 'exploiting the effect of the massed artillery fire and the Luftwaffe immediately and fully'. Professional as ever, he sought quickly to integrate lessons from the first day of the attack. He ordered a number of measures to improve artillery support to the attacking infantry and re-emphasized the primary tasks for air strikes: 'suppression of enemy batteries, in so far that the corps artillery is not in a position to achieve this; and direct support of the attack through Stuka [dive-bombers]', whose shock effect was to be realized immediately before the break-in battle and applied to the direct front of the infantry.[141] This was close air support at its most dangerous proximity to his own troops, with all the attendant risks of what we now describe as 'blue-on-blue' friendly fire.

On 9 June, Manstein requested Halder to release 46th Infantry Division from Kerch to reinforce the assault on Sevastopol. He argued again that he required five rather than four divisions for the northern axis of attack, each of these having lost already here 'at least 1,000 men' in the face of the 'extraordinary difficulties of the terrain, the tenacity of the enemy, the strength of his fortifications and his forces', which had been reinforced, according to prisoners of war, 'by the 9th Marine Brigade'.[142] Eventually, Manstein was able to exchange the burnt-out regiments of 132nd Infantry Division with the relatively fresh formations of the 46th. Following further requests, OKH authorized the release of three infantry regiments, followed by an additional two, which arrived later on in the battle.[143] Such was the pressure on him that he even agreed to resubordinate his only army reserve, the reconnaissance battalion of 22nd Division, to LIV Corps.

In the interim, the divisions of this corps tore deeply into the fortified zone at heavy cost, with Fort Stalin falling on 13 June to 16th Infantry Regiment, with Choltitz again at its head. There was justice in that coup, for the same unit had been forced to withdraw from the fort during the abortive winter offensive. By 17 June, the outer ring of forts in the north had been captured, including the vaunted 'Maxim Gorki I' armoured battery by elements of 132nd Division. But it would take until the 21st before LIV Corps could clear the final approaches to Severnaya Bay. In the south, the supporting attack was facing similar difficulties. Even so, XXX Corps was able to 'drive a wedge into the advance positions' in front of the Sapun Gora feature, if not yet pierce it.[144]

Manstein was concerned about the indifferent performance of the Rumanians, some of whose commanders were hesitant, if not inept in his assessment. Matters came to a head on 22 June when he wrote to the Rumanian corps commander demanding an explanation as to why his corps had not attacked as ordered on the previous day. Dissatisfaction increased when the commander of the German liaison team, Colonel Freiherr von Nagel, complained that the Rumanian corps commander 'sabotaged every German order, and the limited success of 1st Rumanian Mountain Division was down to the incompetence of the corps and divisional commanders'. So Manstein drove to the Rumanian Corps headquarters on 23 June and questioned the commander on his conduct. He followed up this intervention on the 28th with a visit to the headquarters of 1st Rumanian Mountain Division, where he raised further concerns about the 'inadequacies of command', reminding the divisional commander of the need to guarantee co-operation between infantry and artillery.[145]

Throughout the battle zone, the Soviet defence was more stubborn than expected: German and Rumanian losses continued to escalate accordingly. Manstein was keen to see for himself the conditions his commanders and troops were facing in order to gauge morale and to inform his decision-making. On his extended battlefront visits of mid June he learned that the average rifle company strength was now 20–30 men.[146] Within a week's fighting, LIV Corps had lost on average 2,275 men *per division*. Manstein knew that any future success depended on sustaining the fighting power of his infantry. Yet the much-needed close-in armoured support was very thinly spread: across the army front there were typically only twenty-four assault guns operational each day.[147]

From his frequent visits to the front line, it is clear that Manstein was no armchair general of popular caricature. Evidence from war diaries undermines claims by some commentators that he sought the comfortable life.[148] Neither did Manstein forget the fact that the soldier in the van of the attack carries the greatest physical burden in battle. On 23 June he awarded the Iron Cross First Class to the company commander who had stormed the Maxim Gorki I battery, presenting the Second Class medal to the assault troop commander.

Despite the tenacity of the Soviet defence, after two weeks of the most bitter and intense combat Manstein's troops had captured the outer fortified zone on the northern front by the morning of 26 June. On fighting their way through that area, they had encountered fanatical resistance. In the underground storage sites, driven into the cliffs overlooking Severnaya Bay, and in the railway tunnel near Inkerman, Soviet troops, including thousands of civilians taking shelter there, refused to surrender. Political commissars blew the cliff down to block one of the cavern entrances and so buried thousands under rock rather than yield to the attacking force. To the south, XXX Corps threw 170th Infantry Division into the fight and made some further gains towards the Sapun position. The 1st Mountain Division redeemed the honour of the Rumanian Corps by at last making some solid progress. For Petrov's Coastal Army, meanwhile, the losses had likewise mounted. By 22 June, Manstein's troops had taken nearly 12,000 prisoners and German engineers had made safe over 65,000 Soviet mines that had been scattered across the battlefield.

Notwithstanding his soldiers' hard-won gains, Manstein had to decide whether to press on with the assault as the fighting power of his army was diminishing daily: his divisions had suffered on average a further 2,000 losses each. Even Hitler, following closely the progress of the German regiments inching their way towards Sevastopol on a specially produced 1:25,000 scale map, updated daily, began to question the wisdom of the attack – given the priority that needed to be accorded to the main summer offensive towards the Caucasus. Once again, the overall lack of air power in the East was becoming acute: fighter-bomber cover over the advancing Army Groups A and B was thinning alarmingly. On 7 June, the Führer had already raised concerns about the level of air support to Eleventh Army. He had made it clear then that 'if the attack does not succeed, then it must be abandoned and the fortress besieged. A reinforcement of the Luftwaffe in order to force a decision is out of the question.' In any case, there has never been 'so much heavy and effective artillery as that provided for [the attack on] Sevastopol'.[149] Hitler, for once, was not unreasonable in his assessment: VIII Air Corps reported on 14 June 1942 – to cite a typical day – that no fewer than 803 aircraft were in action, of which 625 were fighters or dive-bombers.

In view of the sacrifice already made at Sevastopol, there was an understandable determination after two weeks of heavy fighting to press on almost whatever the odds, a dangerous mind-set that would return to haunt the German High Command at Stalingrad in the autumn. The question whether the German Army could afford to keep substantial forces stationed on the Crimea – not only to contain Sevastopol for a further prolonged period, but also to thwart any future Soviet landings – had yet to be answered. On balance, the benefits of destroying the enemy grouping at Sevastopol, denying it as a future base to the Red Navy and freeing up as many troops as possible for employment elsewhere, were accepted.

On 27 June Manstein confirmed his decision to launch a final attack on the city. He had toyed with the idea of shifting the main effort from the north to the south-east, but it was simply not possible to move the artillery and ammunition stocks in time without running the risk of a substantial operational pause ensuing, which would give the Soviet defenders much needed respite. So the principal thrust remained on the axis of LIV Corps.

Manstein's plan for capturing the city of Sevastopol was novel. In the south, a strong supporting attack – simulated on a broad front – was to seize the Sapun Gora ridge. The main attack rested on an amphibious operation across the 1,000-metre-wide Severnaya Bay in assault boats, the attendant risks of which were self-evident to the troops of 22nd and 24th Infantry Divisions given this task. He faced considerable opposition from his subordinates for what appeared to be a foolhardy venture. To give him and his staff due credit, however, Eleventh Army had issued a week before a timely warning order for the 'continuation of the attack in the inner fortress area'.[150]

Undaunted by his failure to achieve initial surprise on 7 June, Manstein tried again to deceive the Soviet defenders, stressing the importance of disguising the preparations for the crossing of the bay 'with all means'. Amongst a number of deception measures, artillery fire was not to concentrate on the intended attack sectors in the days before the attack, and if possible, there would be no artillery preparation before H-Hour. Further, the bringing forward of assault boats was to be delayed for as long as possible. Specifically, their passage 'over the Belbek [river] was only to happen at night'.[151] Manstein's memoirs contain a stirring description of the crossing of Severnaya Bay, which unhinged the 'dreaded Sapun position':

> a tremendous tension gripped everyone connected with the operation. In order to blanket all noise from the northern shore, VIII Air Corps kept up an incessant air raid on the city. The whole of the artillery stood by to begin a murderous bombardment of the clifftops on the southern shore the very moment any fire from there showed ... But everything remained quiet on the other side.... At one o'clock the first wave from 22 and 24 Divisions pushed off and headed for the opposite shore.... by the time the enemy defences on the cliffside went into action our sturdy grenadiers had gained a firm foothold.[152]

The unqualified success of the operation, which in audacity and dash resembled Wolfe's scaling of the Heights of Abraham at Quebec in 1759, was much to the relief of Manstein and his troops.

The final days of the German assault on Sevastopol can be summarized quickly enough as Soviet resistance – for all its heroism in the preceding weeks of battle – crumbled in the face of German superiority in the air and powerful concentric attacks on land.

As LIV Corps crossed Severnaya Bay and secured its southern shore and Inkerman at its eastern end, XXX Corps launched its attack on the Sapun Gora defences. The reinforced 170th Infantry Division attacked unexpectedly on a very narrow front with massed artillery and air support. It managed to pierce the Soviet positions and then turned neatly to roll them up, allowing 72nd and 28th Divisions to close up. All three divisions then continued the attack on 29 June towards the city, manoeuvring to envelop it to its south towards the Chersones peninsula. Meanwhile, 4th Rumanian Mountain Division set about 'flushing the defence system round Balaklava from the rear', taking 10,000 prisoners of war in the process. As Manstein noted, following the successful crossing of Severnaya Bay and the seizure of the Heights of Inkerman by LIV Corps, together with the penetration of the Sapun position by XXX Corps, 'the fate of Sevastopol was sealed'.

The screw turned further and history in some ways repeated itself with the capture of the defensive positions on the Malakoff Hill – the scene of so much bitter fighting during the Crimean War. Now German forces could threaten the city centre directly. In 1855 the French capture of Fort Malakoff had precipitated a Russian evacuation of the city and withdrawal northwards across Severnaya Bay, an escape option not open in 1942. Manstein was concerned that the Soviet defenders would 'make a last stand behind Sevastopol's perimeter defences and finally in the city itself'. To avoid even more friendly force losses, he resorted to a massive artillery and air strike in order to show the enemy 'that he could not expect to extract a further toll of blood from us in house-to-house fighting'.[153]

So 1 July 1942 began with an exceptionally heavy bombardment. Sensing the inevitability of defeat, surviving elements of the Coastal Army began to pull back from the city during the previous night, planning to stage a 'final last stand' on the Chersones peninsula and hoping that the Red Navy would evacuate as many as possible. Although Manstein did not know it at the time, Soviet command in the city had begun to break down in a confused scramble to escape. But for the bulk of the troops, the order to abandon Sevastopol had come too late. There was confusion at the top and no comparison whatsoever with the orderly evacuation from Odessa. By the time that large-scale operations finished on the Crimea, no fewer than 90,000 Soviet soldiers, marines and naval personnel went into German captivity, 30,000 from the Chersones peninsula alone. The fighting was not quite over, for resistance continued at the Maxim Gorki II battery a week beyond its declared capture on 4 July. More ominously, the partisan problem in the Crimean Mountains remained until the end of the German occupation.

Aftermath and Assessment

For all the decorations or honours a commander can receive, there is no higher accolade than the admiration of his troops. In any final analysis, there is nothing better than success for breeding confidence. Whilst Manstein was no charismatic and self-publicizing leader in the mould of Rommel, his soldiers none the less respected him enormously. As a frequent visitor to front-line units, he was certainly no distant figure despite the unfair and unsubstantiated slur of château-generalship. His subordinate commanders knew that they could raise legitimate concerns to him without censure and receive clear direction and guidance in response. Choltitz wrote:

> We had the best and brightest commander-in-chief, who enjoyed our complete trust and deepest veneration; a man whom every soldier at the front knew; one who was concerned about his soldiers' hardships and engaged personally to find remedies for them. And if it was not his way to make himself popular with the troops, every individual knew of his high degree of human conviction with regard to his own soldiers, as well as against the enemy and his civilian population. ... Without exaggeration I can add that every soldier felt personally decorated by his promotion.[154]

Manstein displayed generalship of a high order during the campaign. He not only knew the tactical battle well, but he also understood how to fight at the operational level, balancing one risk against another, and taking pragmatic and timely decisions after due consultation and deliberation. In offensive operations he showed imagination and boldness whilst in defence he remained serenely calm under pressure. All round, he proved to be a confident and resolute commander, who had learned to outfight his often disorganized and numerically superior opponents by more agile command.

But he was by no means infallible. With the benefit of hindsight, his greatest mistake was to allow his forces to become too widely dispersed during the initial exploitation phase into the Crimea in late October and throughout November 1941. Analogous to the situation before he punched through the Perekop–Ishun positions, when he grappled with two missions in two divergent directions, he allowed himself to order two main axes of pursuit in following the Soviet forces into Sevastopol and Kerch simultaneously. After he failed to take Sevastopol off the line of march in consequence, he then showed a much firmer hand. He played his few remaining cards wisely in first containing the Soviet

Kerch–Feodosia operation, and then by destroying the enemy grouping at Kerch in Operation BUSTARD HUNT.

Throughout, Manstein was compelled to fight with insufficient forces. By the beginning of 1942 it was clear to him that the 'current situation of the Army is the result of being too weak for the tasks it has been given, right from the beginning of the campaign'. Some six months *before* the capture of Sevastopol he was forced to acknowledge that his divisions were being consumed 'at a far faster rate than in other armies'.[155]

Taking a wider strategic perspective, Manstein's eventual victory in the Crimea in the summer of 1942 was a Pyrrhic affair for the German war effort in the East as a whole, not only in terms of personnel and *matériel* losses, but also in *time*, valuable time that Germany could ill afford to waste in excursions off the main effort. Although the last three months of the campaign witnessed exemplary co-operation between German air and land forces, the failure to blockade Sevastopol effectively by air and sea (accepting that the German Navy was in no position to insert warships larger than E-boats into the Black Sea) was a critical weakness in operational design and execution. The lack of German maritime support condemned Manstein to an exhausting campaign of attrition. Of 'joint manoeuvre' there was precious little on the German side in stark contrast to the sustained Soviet naval supply effort and widespread amphibious operations.

For all the valour shown on both sides in the battle of Sevastopol, was the human sacrifice involved worth it? The key operational question at the beginning of the campaign remained at its end: having invested Sevastopol, would the resources required for its capture have been better employed elsewhere? The German official history records that there were nearly 25,000 German casualties during the assault of June–July 1942 and rightly questions whether the likely cost of isolating the city rather than capturing it (three to four German divisions, according to Manstein) would have been more than outweighed by the savings in time, effort, *matériel* and blood.[156] The Rumanians also fought hard, despite Manstein's criticism of their officer corps.

For all the spectacular massed artillery and concentrated close air support, the losses, particularly amongst skilled junior non-commissioned officers and young officers within the infantry and assault engineers, could not be easily replaced. Thus it remains debatable whether the glory of capturing Sevastopol was worth this toll in Axis blood. Taking the complete campaign on the Crimea, the German casualties were higher still, although no reliable official statistics are available. Perhaps the point is brought home by a visit to the new German central military cemetery at Goncharnoe on the Sevastopol–Yalta road, which has space enough in its sombre grounds for over 40,000 dead.

Manstein's record over the treatment of prisoners of war and of the local civilian population remains hotly disputed. At the very least, his was an act of omission in failing to control or intervene in the murderous activities of *Einsatzgruppe* D in the Crimea rather than one of commission. Whilst there is considerable evidence indicating co-operation between Headquarters Eleventh Army and the *Einsatzkommandos*, there is little substantiation of Manstein's knowledge or personal involvement.

Many of the Soviet dead are buried at the war memorial and cemetery near the Sapun Gora. Petrov, whose skill in defending both Odessa and Sevastopol tied down very significant Axis forces, survived and went on to become a *front* commander. Yet amongst Stalin's generals he remains a largely forgotten figure for all his contribution to the Soviet war effort. Manstein only footnoted him; he deserved greater recognition as a skilled opponent whose steadfast denial of Sevastopol during a 300-day siege fixed and bled white an entire German Army.

11

The Vain Struggle for Stalingrad

'Stalingrad is to be held with all means.' Adolf Hitler

Rumania to Leningrad

Mopping-up operations on the Crimea did not require the presence of a German field marshal. After ten months in command of Eleventh Army, an exhausted Manstein needed a break. He had an offer of leave he was anxious to take up. During Marshal Antonescu's visit following the recapture of the Kerch peninsula in May 1942, the Rumanian leader had invited him to holiday in the Carpathians once Sevastopol had fallen. Manstein's last act on the Crimea, a victory celebration on 4 July held at the Livadia Palace in Yalta, was rudely interrupted by a Soviet air-raid, a potent reminder that the war was far from over. After flying back home the next day to Liegnitz, Manstein then travelled on to Rumania towards the end of the month for some rest and recuperation, accompanied by his wife and elder son Gero, who was recovering from scarlet fever.

Whilst his family vacation gave him a welcome respite from command, it took on many aspects of a state visit, used for propaganda purposes to reinforce German–Rumanian relations. Manstein was treated as a most distinguished foreign guest and given everywhere a warm reception. It was the only time, he recalled, that 'he had been received with such honour and protected so carefully', noting with faint modesty that 'one has to get used to' such preferential treatment, for 'it is more comfortable to be a normal traveller'.[1]

An undoubted highlight of Manstein's stay was a visit to the German minority population in Siebenbürgen (Transylvania). In the pictures of a smiling, newly promoted field marshal relaxing amongst his hosts and family, there is no trace of the recent discord over the conduct of combined operations in the Crimea on which Manstein had often taken his Rumanian allies to task. Basking in his recent success and enjoying generous hospitality throughout, this happy Rumanian interlude represented a personal high point of the war, coincident with German strategic fortunes overall. As the Red Army withdrew under heavy German pressure towards Stalingrad and the Caucasus, in North Africa the British Eighth Army was forced back to the 'final' El Alamein position guarding Cairo and the Nile. Victory seemed to beckon in both theatres of war.

On 12 August 1942 Manstein returned to the Crimea. On previous planning, he expected that Eleventh Army would conduct Operation BLÜCHER to force a crossing of the Strait of Kerch in support of Army Group A's drive south from Rostov-on-Don. Army Group B's focus, meantime, had become Stalingrad. It had been intended that this city and the Caucasus would be sequential objectives in that order but Hitler, ever overconfident of success after less than a month of summer campaign, had fresh ideas. In his directive of 23 July 1942, he concluded prematurely that 'the broad objectives outlined by me for the southern flank of the Eastern Front have largely been achieved'. Although he conceded with uncanny prescience that 'the enemy will probably defend [Stalingrad] tenaciously', Army Group A was still ordered to head for the Baku oilfields on the Caspian coast. At the same time, the original plan to employ Manstein's army towards the Caucasus was dropped in favour of supporting Army Group North's capture of Leningrad 'by the beginning of September' in Operation NORDLICHT.[2]

Hitler had fixed in his mind that Manstein, proven as a master of siege warfare, could replicate in the north his startling success at Sevastopol. Yet such was the pressure on German resources that three more of Manstein's battle-tested divisions were diverted to other tasks, leaving him with only Headquarters LIV and XXX Corps with a total of four divisions and his heavy siege artillery for employment at Leningrad.[3] Manstein very much regretted the break-up of his veteran army, describing it as 'deplorable'. He was surely right to point out that 'mutual acquaintanceship and the trust that comes of fighting hard battles together are factors of the utmost importance in war and should never be disregarded'.[4] One of the great strengths of the German Army, however, was the flexibility it derived from common doctrine, organization and training. Under the unit principle (*Einheitsprinzip*) standardized units (companies, battalions, regiments, divisions) could be attached or detached as required without any loss of tactical integrity.[5]

Of more fundamental concern to Manstein was the likely consequence of diverting Eleventh Army away from the main effort of the German Army's offensive that summer. It was on the southern wing of the Eastern Front that the decisive battles for the Caucasus and Stalingrad were to be fought. 'This was a task', Manstein maintained categorically, 'for which we could never be too strong.'[6] Events proved him right. Once again, Hitler's predilection for attempting far too much with too little and splitting German resources on widely divergent axes (such as those of Army Groups A and B) came to the fore. It was another example of an over-ambitious design of campaign leading to a completely under-resourced plan. By the summer of 1942 the Soviet armed forces were by no means beaten: they were being reinforced at a far faster rate in men and *matériel* than their opponents. The Germans underestimated this trend consistently.

On 24 August 1942 Manstein visited Hitler's forward headquarters (codenamed *Werwolf*) hidden in the dense pinewoods of Stryzhavka outside Vinnitsa in the western Ukraine. He had come to discuss future intentions with Halder but became an unfortunate witness to one of the Führer's final tirades against his hapless Army Chief of the General Staff. Halder had already made it clear to Manstein that he had disagreed with Hitler over his military strategy in the south, and opposed the proposed operation against Leningrad. The focus of the Führer's scorn on this particular occasion lay in his criticism of Ninth Army's defence of the exposed Rzhev salient of Army Group Centre. A fuse must have blown in the normally servile Halder for he 'emphatically contradicted' Hitler during their midday conference, pointing out the realities of the situation. It provoked a furious response from the Führer.[7] Highly embarrassed, Manstein left the undignified scene in the map-room, and 'remained away till Hitler calmed down'. He took the opportunity to speak to Major General Rudolf Schmundt, the Führer's head of personnel, and advised him 'either Hitler must listen to his Chief-of-Staff of the Army and show him at least the respect that was his due, or Halder must take the only course remaining open to him'.[8]

Halder was dismissed four weeks later on 24 September 1942 – replaced by the zealous General of Infantry Kurt Zeitzler, previously chief of staff at von Rundstedt's Headquarters Army Group D in France. In the stifling heat and poisonous atmosphere of *Werwolf*, Manstein had just experienced a bitter foretaste of what was to come from now on in dealing with the Führer.

It would appear that Manstein had yet to develop a profound scepticism of Hitler, for he had enjoyed pretty much a free hand on the Crimea and been advanced recently to field marshal. Much later, he provided a devastating critique of Hitler in his memoirs, a magisterial analysis of the Führer's strengths and weaknesses. This discourse did much to serve the writer's purpose in painting a convincing narrative of Hitler's consistent strategic misdirection.[9] But it was only on the basis of his experience as an army group commander that Manstein was able to condemn an interfering Hitler for his want of 'military ability based on experience' and his lack of 'all sense of judgement'.[10]

Such was Manstein's enduring loyalty (at least publicly) and faith in Germany's 'cause' – and in the inevitability of final victory or at least in achieving a stalemate – that he was slow to recognize the chronic flaws in Hitler's character and decision-making, and not least in Germany's overall strategic weakness against the Soviet Union and the Western powers. Privately, Manstein was by now quick to criticize Hitler, referring to him disrespectfully amongst his utterly dependable army group staff as 'Effendi', an obsolete Turkish rank equivalent to a lieutenant.[11] In any critical analysis, however, he failed to address two fundamental matters. First, was anybody in Germany in a position to stand up to Hitler; and secondly, had not the German military high command failed collectively to do so since 1933? To apportion all the blame for Germany's defeat on Hitler is as perverse as to give him sole credit for all her earlier victories. By the summer of 1942 – even before the great debacles at El Alamein and Stalingrad – the Führer distrusted his generals and they increasingly him. One close witness at the time recalled him describing 'the entire body of senior commanders' as being 'intellectually conceited and incapable of learning or seeing the wood for the trees'.[12] Disliking any expression of contrary opinion to the point of incandescent rage, he now removed himself as much as possible from the company of the generals he so despised, refusing even to dine with them.

Manstein's evaluation of Hitler as a supreme commander set the scene for his description of the doomed struggle to save the Sixth Army at Stalingrad, and his renewed attempts to obtain operational freedom of manoeuvre then and thereafter. One particular area that Manstein highlighted was Hitler's lack of risk taking. Here he distinguished carefully between the Führer's proven track record in political opportunism and his aversion to taking military risks, which Manstein highlighted in two ways. He complained about Hitler's lack of understanding of the need to conduct operations, particularly defensive ones, 'elastically'. Such an approach required a willingness to surrender 'conquered territory', which Hitler consistently opposed. Secondly, in Manstein's view, Hitler never really grasped the 'rule that one can never be too strong at the crucial spot, that one may even have to dispense with less vital fronts or accept the risk of radically weakening them in order to achieve a decisive aim'.[13] In retrospect, the errant diversion of Eleventh Army to Leningrad was but a further operational symptom of this strategic malaise. Simply put, the Führer failed to grasp the fact that the essential

corollary of concentration of force in one place was the need to econo-
mize effort elsewhere. But Hitler feared denuding 'secondary fronts or
subsidiary theatres in favour of the spot where the main decision had to
fall, even when a failure to do so was palpably dangerous'.[14] By this way
of analysis, Manstein's readers are alerted to the powerful constraints
under which he operated: any success gained was therefore far the greater
for them.

Meanwhile, by 27 August 1942 Manstein's headquarters had moved
north to Leningrad. Ambitious plans to attack to link up with the Finns
and to 'raze Leningrad to the ground' were immediately pre-empted by
a major Soviet offensive launched the same day by the Volkhov *Front*
under General Kirill Meretskov south of Lake Ladoga. The 'Sinyavino
Operation', involving 8th and 2nd Shock Armies, achieved some initial
success, and threatened to break the German ring around Leningrad.[15]
In particular, 2nd Shock Army's attack, directed on a westerly axis
between the southern shore of the lake and the town of Mga, appeared
acutely dangerous. This development was sufficiently worrying for
Hitler to telephone Manstein directly during the afternoon of 4 September, bypassing Headquarters Army Group North in the chain of
command. The Führer promptly ordered him to 'restore the situation
by offensive action'.[16] So instead of launching the major assault on
Leningrad, Eleventh Army was employed as a fire brigade to master a
local crisis, which soon turned into a major battle with a month of heavy
fighting.

For the German High Command, the failed Soviet offensive to relieve
Leningrad and the earlier operations directed against Army Group
Centre, together with the presence of strong strategic reserves retained
in the vicinity of Moscow, all served to reinforce the mistaken impression
that a major counter-offensive was unlikely at Stalingrad.[17] Soviet deception measures (*maskirovka*) were becoming increasingly sophisticated, a
significant development in military capability, which the Germans failed
to appreciate. It was a trend set to continue as German intelligence staffs
failed consistently to distinguish between the real and dummy axes of
enemy attack.

Whilst the battle at Lake Ladoga raged, the main German offensive
in the south appeared to Manstein to 'be petering out in the Caucasus
and at the gates of Stalingrad'.[18] He was correct in his assessment.[19]
Although Sixth Army had penetrated the city on the west bank of the
Volga by the beginning of September, it was never completely secured.
Under the fresh and ruthless leadership of Lieutenant General Vasily
Ivanovich Chuikov, the Soviet 62nd Army fought back doggedly. The

battle soon degenerated into vicious hand-to-hand combat in factory, house, cellar and sewer, which the Germans described aptly as the war of rats (*Rattenkrieg*).

By early autumn 1942 the German Army had shot its bolt on the southern wing of the Eastern Front. It had culminated operationally if not strategically in that any further forward progress, whether in the windswept high Caucasus or in the smashed city blocks of Stalingrad, was no longer worth the candle against stiffening Soviet resistance. Stalin had recently issued his famous 'Not one step backwards' Order No. 227 on 29 July 1942, declaring:

> To retreat further means to doom yourself and with it to doom our Motherland.... Not one step backwards! This must now be our main slogan. It is necessary steadfastly, to the last drop of blood to defend each position, each metre of Soviet territory, to hold every patch of Soviet soil, and to hold it as long as possible.[20]

The order then spelled out punishments for disobedience and imposed iron discipline. Military penal units (*shtrafnie voinskie podrazdeleniya*) on the German model were introduced, together with a Soviet innovation. 'Blocking detachments' (*zagradotryadi*) were deployed behind the main forces to prevent weak units and individuals from withdrawing.[21] Moreover, Stalin had ample reserves available to throw into the fight for *his* city, formerly Tsaritsyn, where, according to a leading biographer, in 1918 'he had gained his confidence as a man of action, learned how to govern by terror, won Lenin's trust and Trotsky's hatred'.[22] Twenty-four years later, the death-struggle for the city on the Volga epitomized the clash of two totalitarian regimes, in which no quarter was given on either side.

In the fighting from September to November 1942, any modest tactical advantage gained by German forces in Stalingrad was completely out of proportion to the enormous *matériel* and personnel costs involved. Superficially, it looked like a re-run of the siege of Sevastopol. But for the Soviet defenders there was a new spirit, and crucially, the battle was developing to their operational advantage, desperate as the tactical conditions in the city must have appeared at the time. Chuikov's rock-steady chief of staff, Major General Nikolai Ivanovich Krylov, who had escaped from the Crimea, compared his previous experience with Stalingrad: 'There, our force was melting away, while here it was replenished. There was a lot in common. [However,] it seemed to us sometimes as if we were still continuing the same battle. But we did not feel doomed, like we did in Sevastopol.'[23]

The employment of Manstein's four remaining divisions of Crimean veterans would not necessarily have made any appreciable difference to the outcome of the battle; it would have merely added to the butcher's bill. Had a *reinforced* Eleventh Army supplemented the Axis armies guarding the exposed flanks, or been retained in depth, say, at the confluence of the Donets and the Don, as a powerful operational level reserve, then perhaps the outcome at Stalingrad might have been different. Such a genial solution would have required Hitler not only to have abandoned his dream of capturing Leningrad beforehand, but it would have also meant concentrating fresh German troops in the south that were simply not available at the time, and could not have been supplied easily in any case.

None the less, more could have been achieved within the existing force levels had operations been co-ordinated better between Army Groups A and B, and across the whole of the Eastern Front. What was lacking, as Manstein argued, was a unified military command structure for the decisive southern wing, if not 'some modification of the Supreme Command'. Hitler would have none of it. 'From no other quarter', claimed Manstein, 'was the inadequacy of his military leadership ever put to him quite so bluntly.'[24] Having assumed command directly of Army Group A, following his peremptory sacking of Field Marshal List on 9 September 1942, the Führer was hardly in the mood to concede any authority. Although he had indicated to Manstein that he would appoint him as the new commander-in-chief of this army group should he leave Vinnitsa, this vague promise was quietly forgotten.[25]

The evidence points to Hitler having very mixed feelings about Manstein. Keitel's memoir offers an interesting perspective on their relationship. When Brauchitsch departed as commander-in-chief of the army in December 1941, to be replaced by the Führer himself, Keitel had proposed that Jodl should take over from Halder as Chief of the Army General Staff. Further, he suggested that Manstein become the 'Armed Forces Chief of the General Staff' with 'a new definition of his duties vis-à-vis myself as the Chief of the High Command'. Although, according to Keitel, Hitler apparently did not reject the proposal out of hand, he had determined to keep both Jodl and Halder in their present positions, considering the latter as 'honest, loyal, reliable and obedient'. In Keitel's opinion, 'great though Hitler's regard for Manstein was, he feared him to a degree; he feared his independent ideas and strength of personality'.[26] This assessment is confirmed by Halder, who recalled the Führer describing Manstein in the following terms: 'Whilst he has a genial brain, he has too independent a character.'[27]

All subsequent attempts to change the command structure on the Eastern Front failed because Hitler was not prepared to relinquish direct control of operations. Manstein's hopes had been raised when the well-connected Lieutenant Colonel Henning von Tresckow, still a close friend of Schmundt, got to know about what was under discussion.[28] On 13 December 1941 he had written to Manstein urging him to 'demand an [appointment] at [Chief] OKW level and don't be satisfied with one at OKH'. Although Tresckow 'had good grounds' to believe such a move was in the offing, unfortunately for Manstein, none came.[29] So he remained in command of Eleventh Army.

The second opportunity for advancing Manstein's case came in September 1942 when Hitler decided to part with Halder. Keitel maintains that he 'energetically championed General von Manstein as Halder's successor'. Hitler, however, 'again rejected my proposal, this time with the excuse that he could not spare him from his present command'. Presumably Hitler had in mind here Manstein's role in the Leningrad operation. Interestingly, Keitel then proposed Paulus whom the Führer also refused, saying that he intended him to take over from Jodl 'after the battle of Stalingrad'.[30] In the event, Zeitzler took over from Halder and Manstein was not reassigned until appointed in November 1942 commander-in-chief of Army Group Don.

The Soviet Encirclement of Stalingrad

Meanwhile, the Red Army was biding its time for launching a major counter-offensive. The German Sixth Army's exposed position at Stalingrad, compounded by weakly guarded flanks, offered an enticing possibility for mounting an encirclement operation on a grand scale. Defeating the Axis grouping at Stalingrad was only the first of a series of ambitious operational blows designed to wrest the strategic initiative irrevocably from the Fascist invader. Stalin approved Operation URANUS designed to destroy enemy forces in the Stalingrad area, which was to be followed by Operation SATURN, aimed at eliminating *all* the Axis forces in the southern Soviet Union (in other words, Army Groups A and B in their entirety).

In parallel, Operation MARS was to be directed against Army Group Centre in an effort to push in the Rzhev salient, force the commitment of German reserves and inflict as much damage as possible. Although the eventual failure of MARS – largely airbrushed out of Soviet historical accounts – was eclipsed by the spectacular successes of URANUS and SATURN, the latter in scaled-down form, it was very much more than a distraction operation.

Operation URANUS was a 'classic' encirclement (see Map 8). Credit for its brilliant design must not only go to the *Stavka* representatives Colonel Generals (later Marshals) G. K. Zhukov and A. M. Vasilevsky, but also to the talented Colonel General N. F. Vatutin, the 41-year-old commander of the South-Western *Front*. The northern attacking arm, striking to the south-east, comprised formations of his *Front*, including 5th Tank and 21st Armies, supported by 65th Army of the Don *Front*. Their role was to envelop Third Rumanian Army and to isolate Sixth Army. On the Germans' southern flank, the other wing of the Soviet encirclement was formed by 51st and 57th Armies of General A. I. Eremenko's Stalingrad *Front*, attacking westwards through Fourth Rumanian Army. Both thrusts were designed to meet in the vicinity of Kalach-on-Don, 75 kilometres west of Stalingrad.[31] A crucial ingredient of the Soviet plan required the Red Air Force to establish local air superiority over Stalingrad and its approaches, for which purpose the 8th Air Army was reinforced with the latest aircraft.[32]

So did German Army intelligence observe the Soviet build-up and deduce Stalin's most probable and most dangerous intentions? By the end of the war, *Fremde Heere Ost* (FHO – Foreign Armies East) had a deservedly poor reputation. It had failed consistently to predict the timing, axis and strength of Soviet counter-offensives. Its shortcomings over Stalingrad were amongst its greatest, and had, with the possible exception of the destruction of Army Group Centre in June 1944, the worst strategic consequences for Germany. On 29 August 1942 FHO had concluded that the 'Russian Army was indeed weakened, but was not at all beaten', and warned ominously that 'its command had many possibilities to mount operational level attacks against the Wehrmacht and its allies'.[33] Ironically, Hitler had recognized more precisely the inherent risk of leaving the Don flank so weakly guarded in the drive towards Stalingrad. As early as 16 August 1942, he had expressed his concern, alluding to the spectacular Bolshevik victory over White Russian forces in 1920, based on a map that Halder had found.[34] On that occasion, the 'Red' forces had crossed the upper Don near Serafimovich (160 kilometres north-west of Stalingrad) and then thrust south-westwards towards Rostov-on-Don.

Whereas FHO assessed that the concentration of forces in the vicinity of Serafimovich in the late summer of 1942 was a possible preliminary to an offensive against Army Group Centre, Hitler rightly saw the latent danger for Army Group B, having pushed its exposed head – Sixth Army – into the fatal noose of Stalingrad. As one leading historian has noted, 'Hitler's fears were premature, but his predictions were surprisingly accurate.'[35] But there is an enormous difference between deducing correctly a possible enemy intention and taking the appropriate measures to deal with it. Hitler's precautionary deployment of 22nd Panzer and 298th Infantry Divisions into the area behind the Italian Eighth Army was woefully insufficient to cover the waxing operational, let alone strategic, risk. So whilst the coming Soviet counter-offensive was not an absolute surprise, its ambitious scale and resultant effect certainly were.

As the Soviets prepared to mount the Stalingrad 'strategic offensive operation', Manstein was struck hard with two personal tragedies. The first was the loss of his favourite ADC, Lieutenant Pepo Specht, who died in a crash-landing of a Fieseler Storch on the way to join his new regiment. When Manstein buried him on 25 October 1942, it was 'a sad blow to everyone, most of all myself'. Immediately after the funeral Manstein flew to Vinnitsa to receive his field marshal's baton from Hitler. Thinking of Specht, Manstein wrote, 'What a thrill it would have given him to have been on this flight.'[36]

Hitler received his guest on 26 October with more than due courtesy, being 'exceptionally charming', Manstein recalled.[37] The Führer went on to praise the performance of the Eleventh Army at Lake Ladoga, which must have given Manstein considerable satisfaction, extending his reputation as a 'winning commander'. Seizing the opportunity for a frank exchange of views with Hitler, he expressed his concerns about the hollowed-out state of the German infantry after a year and more of intense fighting on the Eastern Front. Regiments were going into battle under-strength and were getting ever more worn out as a result because the flow of casualties was not being made good by sufficient numbers of battle casualty replacements. What particularly annoyed Manstein was the recent establishment of the twenty-two Luftwaffe 'field divisions', for which no fewer than 170,000 men had already been made available. Whilst he appreciated that these formations could well contain 'first-class soldiers', where, he asked, were they to 'obtain the vital combat experience for fighting in the East'? Equally validly he questioned, 'From where was the "Luftwaffe" going to find the necessary divisional, regimental and battalion commanders?' Manstein must have spoken for many in the Wehrmacht by stating that this development was 'sheer nonsense'. Hitler declined to give way on the issue as he had no stomach to upset Göring, who was not prepared, as Manstein recalled, 'to hand over "his" soldiers, reared in the spirit of National Socialism, to an army which still had chaplains and was led by officers steeped in the traditions of the Kaiser'.[38]

Curiously, Manstein did not record Hitler's concerns about the worsening operational situation and the build-up of Soviet forces on the Don, particularly those detected in the Serafimovich bridgehead. Other sources indicate that Hitler told him of 'an especial danger' that existed between Voronezh and Stalingrad.[39] It was Hitler's intention to bolster up the Axis forces (Second Hungarian, Eighth Italian and Third Rumanian Armies) on the exposed northern Don flank with some of the first of the unproven Luftwaffe field divisions, which, as predicted, would count for little in heavy combat against Soviet armour. It remains open to speculation why Manstein did not recount Hitler's disquiet about the growing threat to Sixth Army. For all the Führer's failings, perhaps he did not want to credit Hitler with having any anticipation of the impending disaster. Possibly it suited Manstein's record to imply that Hitler was solely responsible for military miscalculation rather than stating that FHO had been repeatedly in error over Soviet intentions. Yet Hitler was not able to convert his uncanny intuition into an effective response. For the moment, he considered the best course of action was to press on with the capture of Stalingrad, now as much a political as any military objective. History repeated itself when he assessed intuitively that the Allies would land in Normandy as opposed to Pas de Calais in the summer of 1944, but then failed to reinforce sufficiently German defences there.

The second disaster struck Manstein soon after his meeting with Hitler at Vinnitsa. Gero Manstein was killed in action on 29 October 1942 whilst serving as a second lieutenant in the 51st Panzer Grenadier Regiment of his father's old division. He had last seen his son at Head-quarters Sixteenth Army whilst visiting his friend Busch on 18 October, accompanied by Specht. Heartbroken, the field marshal buried his elder son on the shore of Lake Ilmen on the 31st. He had fallen, as so many, 'like the brave soldier he was'. In one of the most moving passages of his war memoirs, Manstein described his loss:

> There was not a single flaw in this boy's make-up. Modest, kind, ever eager to help others, at once serious-minded and cheerful, he had no thought for himself, but knew only comradeship and charity. His mind and spirit were perpetually open to all that is fine and good. It was his heritage to come from a long line of soldiers; but by the very fact of being an ardent German soldier he was at once a gentleman in the truest sense of the word – a gentleman and a Christian.[40]

After the funeral, Manstein spent a few days in Liegnitz to console his wife and family. It was indeed 'the hardest blow that could have befallen my dear wife, myself and our children'.[41]

Cool professional as he was, Manstein took a long time to get over Gero's death. A month later, according to Richthofen, he was still grieving and in a 'poor mental state'. His bereavement added further to the stress of taking over army group command with a near impossible mission – saving Sixth Army at Stalingrad. As Germany faced its worst crisis to date during the Second World War, Manstein had become 'desperate about the decisions made at the top'.[42] On 27 November 1942, Colonel von Mellenthin, who had last seen the Field Marshal in much better times in March 1940, reported in to Headquarters Army Group Don prior to assuming his post as chief of staff of XXXXVIII Panzer Corps. He was struck by 'how old' the army group commander now looked.[43] Yet if any Wehrmacht general was going to pull a surprise operational rabbit out of a malformed strategic hat, it was surely only Manstein at the very top of his form, and not one weighed down so heavily by personal remorse. During the Stalingrad episode, arguably he bore a burden far greater than any other German general during the entire war, and withstood far more sustained enemy pressure than any Western Allied one.

In early November Headquarters Eleventh Army moved to Vitebsk and was placed under command of Army Group Centre in anticipation of countering an expected Soviet offensive. All hopes of resurrecting the Leningrad operation were long forgotten. As Manstein remarked, there was 'nothing of importance' to report during this brief interlude in this relatively quiet sector whilst the fate of Sixth Army and elements of Fourth Panzer Army was sealed at Stalingrad.[44]

On 19 November, the Red Army launched URANUS. The now usual firestorm of tube and rocket artillery heralded the South-Western *Front*'s assault in the icy mist. The attack of the Stalingrad *Front* followed a day later. In both sectors Soviet tanks scattered the over-extended Rumanian troops in the snow. The two armoured pincers snapped shut at Sovietskii, 20 kilometres south-east of Kalach, during the late afternoon of 23 November, completing the ring of encirclement. The resulting pocket, 50 kilometres from east to west and 40 from north to south, contained twenty-two German and Rumanian divisions, amounting to more than a quarter of a million men.[45]

Without doubt, it was one of the neatest such operations of the Second World War, meticulously planned, its preparations well concealed in the open steppe, and executed audaciously. At the 'two points of penetration strong Soviet tank forces had immediately pushed through in depth', commented Manstein ruefully, 'just as we had taught them to do'.[46] It was an operational feat that the Western Allies failed to match nearly two years later in Normandy, when the Falaise Pocket entrapping the German Fifth Panzer and Seventh Armies was not fully sealed due to an incomplete link-up conducted with insufficiently strong armoured forces, the consequence of hesitant and disjointed Allied command.

Hitler had divined too late the full measure of the Soviet counter-offensive. But it was not his only strategic concern, for the crisis at Stalingrad had come quickly on the heels of Rommel's defeat at El Alamein and the landing of Allied forces on the North African littoral near Casablanca, Oran and Algiers on 7/8 November 1942. His spontaneous reaction was to reinforce North Africa against Rommel's advice. Just at the time when the Eastern Front needed reinforcements most, 250 transport aircraft and over 80,000 men were sent to Tunisia by OKW to the despair of OKH. Richthofen's Fourth Air Fleet was stripped of combat aircraft, depriving Army Groups A and B of close air support and the ability to interdict effectively the lines of march and supply of any Soviet counter-offensive. Altogether, it was another crass example of Hitler's dissipation of the Wehrmacht in support of secondary arenas. The failure to concentrate scarce military resources in the East, the critical theatre of operations, would cost Germany dear in the war against the Soviet Union. So whatever decisions the Führer made over the coming months, he never accepted the simple truth that his air and ground forces were impossibly overstretched, and he would not accept sensible counsel from anybody to change course.

On 8 November, during a rabble-rousing speech in a Munich beer cellar, Germany's leader had proclaimed himself to his old comrades as the 'master of Stalingrad'.[47] More recent history informs us that politicians of whatever particular persuasion are often prone to announce prematurely 'their' military successes and to ignore any cautionary professional advice to the contrary in the process. Hitler proved no exception in this regard. Once a fatal error is made there can often be no turning back, as his remarks of 12 December 1942 bear witness:

> We should under no circumstances give this [Stalingrad] up. We won't get it back once it's lost. And we know what that means.... We can't replace the stuff we have in there. If we abandon it, we abandon the whole purpose for the campaign. To think that I will come back here next time is madness ... We won't come back here, so we can't leave. There has been too much bloodshed to do this.[48]

Although inflexible and intemperate, Hitler was not a complete fool.

Three weeks before, when the alarming threat to Sixth Army had finally sunk in on the launch of the Soviet offensive, he had finally seen the need to impose a new command structure (Army Group Don) to save Stalingrad, even if he did not have the reserves available to achieve it.

General Heusinger recalled that the Führer resolved at his evening briefing on 22 November 1942 to 'insert a new army group headquarters on both sides of Stalingrad, as originally foreseen for Antonescu'. Moreover, 'the best man for the job is Manstein'.[49] In fact, some two days earlier, as recorded in the very first entry in the Army Group Don War Diary, made at 12.30 hours on 20 November 1942, Headquarters Eleventh Army received a warning order from Zeitzler 'for a new task in the area of Army Group B'. During the early hours of the 21st more specific orders came from OKH. 'Field Marshal von Manstein with the staff of Eleventh Army is to assume command of Fourth Panzer Army, Sixth Army and Third Rumanian Army as Army Group Don' and to 'bring the enemy attacks to a standstill and recapture the positions previously occupied'.[50]

In Manstein's emerging view of the situation it was becoming clear that Hitler and OKH had not yet fully understood the acute risk of Sixth Army being encircled and all that implied for the integrity of the entire southern wing of the Eastern Front.[51] He was the one commander on whom so many Germans in Stalingrad rested their hopes. '*Haltet aus, Manstein haut uns raus*' ('Hold on, Manstein will get us out') was the soldiers' cry in Sixth Army.[52]

Rarely in history has any commander assumed so much responsibility in such dire straits and been damned to failure for all his efforts. It was to prove Manstein's supreme military and moral test of the Second World War.

The Poisoned Chalice

Manstein's decision-making over Stalingrad remains highly contentious. His account in *Lost Victories* of his attempts to save Sixth Army has attracted more criticism than any other passage by far.[53] Many survivors and commentators felt that he had shifted too much blame on to the unfortunate Paulus, and that he had sacrificed cynically hundreds of thousands of men by his refusal to disobey Hitler's 'no surrender' orders. Furthermore, should Manstein have ordered Paulus to break out immediately? Should he not have visited the pocket himself to assess the situation? Did he ever, in fact, give the final order to break out? Thereafter, once all hope of a successful relief operation had passed, should he not have ordered the surrender of the troops in Stalingrad in order to limit any further loss of life? An additional, hotly disputed, matter is Manstein's claim that he was not fully in the chain of command with respect to Sixth Army because Hitler and OKH gave orders directly to Paulus. Whilst accepting that a detailed consideration of such issues would constitute a book in its own right to join the burgeoning literature on Stalingrad, this account attempts to examine Manstein's perspective and reasoning.

When his headquarters in Vitebsk received orders from OKH on 20 November, Manstein was not present as he was visiting a subordinate formation (LIX Corps). Although he had been called back immediately, his train had hit a mine laid by partisans and his return was delayed to the next morning. None the less, he had already completed an initial estimate of the situation affecting Sixth Army. Through his highly competent assistants (Chief of General Staff General Friedrich Schulz, Chief of Operations Colonel Theodor Busse) he had advised Zeitzler by signal that the 'employment of forces amounting to an army in strength would be required to restore the situation in the area of Army Group B'. Critically, Manstein cautioned that these forces should not be employed prematurely 'before their assembly was fully complete', and that further troops would be required.[54] His assessment was accurate and borne out by subsequent events, but he was optimistic if he thought sufficient reinforcements could be made available in time.

The consequences of the lack of any true German operational reserves in the East, or of any significant strategic ones held elsewhere, were now becoming all too apparent. OKH could only release a slow dribble of formations, initially amounting to a corps headquarters, and two divisions each of infantry and armour. Although he did not detail his precise requirements at the time, Manstein needed at the very least a fresh panzer army, with a balanced mix of twelve to sixteen fully manned and equipped panzer and infantry divisions, if he were to have any realistic chance of saving Sixth Army, let alone restoring a firm front at Stalingrad and repelling further Soviet attacks.[55] Unluckily and tragically for General Paulus and his rapidly waning army, fighting, freezing and, starving in that city, sufficient forces were never at hand for mounting an effective relief effort.

In the event, Manstein was promised additional troops amounting in total to four panzer and four infantry divisions (one a mountain unit) and three Luftwaffe field divisions, the latter of dubious fighting power, in two operational groupings. Within Fourth Panzer Army, Head-quarters LVII Panzer Corps (transferred from Army Group A together with the weak 23rd Panzer Division), a full-strength 6th Panzer Division from the West, and 15th Luftwaffe Field Division, were planned to arrive in the area of Kotelnikovo by 3 December. To the north-west, in the sector of Third Rumanian Army, a new ad hoc grouping, Army Detachment Hollidt, consisting of three infantry divisions (62nd, 294th and 336th), XXXXVIII Panzer Corps (11th and 22nd Panzer Divisions), 3rd Mountain Division and two Luftwaffe divisions (7th and 8th), was due to become operational on the Upper Chir River around 5 December 1942.[56] By any rigorous analysis of the relative force ratios, these reinforcements were insufficient for the task, even if the Red Army kindly obliged by inaction, which of course it did not.

Already, on 21 November, Manstein saw the acute danger of the forces in Stalingrad being encircled. Accordingly, he sent a signal to Headquarters Army Group B requesting it 'to check whether and when a formation each of Fourth Panzer and Sixth Armies, best grouped under a corps command on the line Kalach–Nizhne Chirskaya, could be made available for employment towards the west'.[57] Manstein was never able to discover whether Sixth Army received this instruction. Even had it been executed, it would have been far too late for Soviet armour captured the vital Don bridge at Kalach on 22 November, cutting the main German supply route.

Shortly before Manstein prepared to move to Novocherkassk, 35 kilometres as the crow flies north-east of Rostov-on-Don, to establish his new army group headquarters, his new ADC had reported for duty on 18 November 1942. Lieutenant Alexander Stahlberg was a member of a long-established, typically conservative and rich Prussian family of the old school. He had moved seamlessly within the highest political and military circles, having worked in the secretariat of Vice-Chancellor von Papen in 1933 before entering the 6th (Prussian) Cavalry Regiment in 1935 to avoid joining the Nazi Party. He had fought in France, Flanders and in northern Russia, and had been selected for general staff training. He was identified by his cousin, Henning von Tresckow, as a suitable medium to entice Manstein into joining the resistance against Hitler. Remaining by his field marshal's side to the end of the war, Stahlberg's memoirs provide a series of valuable insights into Manstein's demeanour and decision-making.

Right from the start, the relationship between commander-in-chief and new ADC was cordial and courteous, but never overfamiliar. Stahlberg recalled that on their first meeting his new boss – dressed informally in his habitual white linen uniform jacket, cigar in hand – offered him the job on the following terms: 'If you like, we'll give each

other a try.' The junior officer accepted immediately. Manstein then
explained: 'You will be my constant companion; you will be present at
all my conversations; you will take brief minutes of our daily doings, in
so far as they are important. You will listen to my telephone conversations, write for me and keep my files, both the military and some
of the private ones.' Stahlberg took to Manstein, 'a gentleman', for he
'was a superior entirely to my taste. I was to work for a man of real
consequence, who honoured me with the greatest trust.'[58] For his part,
the Field Marshal described his ADC as his 'faithful assistant ... in all
personal matters'.[59]

Prior to establishing Headquarters Army Group Don and taking over
German and Rumanian forces in the Stalingrad sector, Manstein and his
operations staff needed to be briefed by Headquarters Army Group B in
Starobelsk. Very poor weather prevented Manstein from flying south so
he and his staff were compelled to travel all the way to Novocherkassk
in his armoured command train, entailing a lengthy journey of nearly
2,000 kilometres strung out over five days.[60] It was not without
incident. Having steamed out of Vitebsk at 18.00 hours on 21 November,
Russian partisans soon struck again. The train had to reverse back to the
town whilst the destroyed track was repaired, delaying their departure
to 08.00 hours the next morning, a typical example of the inevitable
friction of war and the growing threat to German lines of communication.

Later on the 22nd, Manstein broke his journey at Smolensk to receive
a situation update from the commander-in-chief of Army Group Centre,
Field Marshal Günther von Kluge. Kluge and his chief of staff, General
Otto Wöhler (formerly of Headquarters Eleventh Army), waited on
the platform as Manstein's train chugged in. They boarded Manstein's
carriage and briefed him and his staff. The news about the operational
situation was grim enough but worse soon came. Kluge gave the new
army group commander some friendly advice about Hitler's propensity
to meddle in tactical business, even down to battalion level. 'Be warned,'
he minded, 'the Führer ascribes the survival of the Eastern Army during
the great crisis last winter, not to the morale of our soldiers and all our
hard work, but exclusively to his own skill.' Whilst Kluge was speaking,
Stahlberg observed Manstein closely: 'His face twitched once or twice,
but he was silent.'[61]

As Manstein's military train trundled southwards at a best speed of
30–50 kilometres per hour, despite the inevitable pressures of the situation, there was some time for Manstein and Stahlberg to get to know
each other.[62] During this and subsequent rail journeys, the pair listened

to classical records on Manstein's portable gramophone player, his only luxury excepting fine cigars and the odd brandy. Mozart was the Field Marshal's favourite composer: he liked especially piano concertos and opera. The two also fought each other at chess. Stahlberg recalled that his commander, on balance the better player, 'always played an attacking game and enjoyed mating me with all the pieces on the board'. Confounded that Stahlberg did not play bridge, Manstein put him on an immediate crash course under the tutelage of three junior staff officers.[63]

Early in the morning of 24 November 1942, Manstein celebrated his 55th birthday with his officers. In response to Major General Schulz's brief speech, the Field Marshal said a few words of thanks. An astonished Stahlberg noted that 'he was by no means a good speaker and that he did not open up in the presence of a number of people'. On reflection, 'he exerted an influence, even a certain fascination, in a small, familiar circle, and most of all à deux'.[64] In common with many well-educated, highly intelligent men, and for all his razor-sharp military intellect, Manstein was an essentially shy and sensitive individual with absolutely none of the bullying bravado of the Nazi German officer so often crudely caricatured on stage and film.

Following Manstein's arrival in Starobelsk towards 09.00 hours later that morning, Colonel General Maximilian Baron von Weichs and the staff of Army Group B, including the chief, Lieutenant General Georg von Sodenstern, offered a truly dismal overview of the situation. They were convinced that Sixth Army's position was 'hopeless', and that it must 'break out immediately'.[65] This estimate was based on the assumption (a very realistic one, as it turned out) that it could not be resupplied by air with the necessary ammunition, fuel and food. For Hitler, OKH and the Luftwaffe (and shortly Headquarters Army Group Don), the two crucial issues were whether the Sixth Army could indeed be reprovisioned by air, and when should it break out, if at all.

When Operation URANUS commenced on 19 November, Hitler was ensconced in his Alpine retreat, the Berghof at Obersalzberg, separated from Zeitzler and OKH in East Prussia. With the second arm of the Soviet attack erupting on 20 November, he finally grasped the extreme gravity of the situation. He initiated Manstein's appointment and considered the prospects of resupplying Sixth Army by air. As Göring was unavailable to attend to brief him, supposedly 'too busy' on other duties, he summoned the Luftwaffe chief of staff, Colonel General Hans Jeschonnek. Recalling that the air force had supplied 100,000 men in the Demyansk pocket for several months during the previous winter, he gave Hitler an impromptu assurance that the Luftwaffe would be able to repeat such a feat, despite the fact that the situation at Stalingrad was very different. If it had taken a force of almost 500 Ju52s to guarantee 150 being available each day to transport no more than 300 tonnes, then delivering Sixth Army's needs (approximately 750 tonnes) would not be possible, given that the Luftwaffe was already fully stretched in meeting its current commitments, not least those in the Mediterranean.

Hitler, in accepting Jeschonnek's over-hasty advice, as one expert has pointed out, was not thinking yet of 'an airlift of the Demyansk scale or duration'. The Führer 'still thought that Manstein would soon break the encirclement and restore the southern front'. Hence 'Sixth Army would only need to be supplied by air in the meantime'. Göring's subsequent reassurance made at the Berghof on 22 November before he had an opportunity to check his chief of staff's advice or confer with the air commanders on the spot, 'who were unanimous . . . in their belief that the air force could not supply the entire Sixth Army', merely strengthened Hitler's resolve. On the afternoon of the previous day (21 November), he had ordered Paulus to stand firm and fight 'despite the danger of temporary encirclement'. If necessary, the garrison troops of 'Fortress Stalingrad', as it was now termed, 'will hold out all winter and I shall relieve them by a spring offensive'.[66]

Although Sixth Army's minimum daily supply requirement was revised downwards to 500 tonnes, even this reduced target figure was never achieved. The whole idea of the air bridge was far-fetched for it ignored the limited capacity of the Luftwaffe both in the air and in terms of its ground organization, failed to take account of the poor winter weather and factored out any effective interdiction by the Red Air Force. Although the distances from the principal air bases (Tatsinskiy and Morozovsk) to Stalingrad's main airfields (Gumrak and Pitomnik) were modest by modern standards (300 and 240 kilometres respectively), realistically no transport crew could fly more than two sorties a day at best. There were never enough aircraft available. At the start of the operation the Luftwaffe managed to assemble about 200 Ju52 transports and 100 Heinkel 111 converted bombers, far short of the 1,000 needed. Thereafter, losses exceeded reinforcements. Neither of these types could carry more than 2 tonnes, a ridiculously small amount in comparison with today's large military transport aircraft such as the Boeing C-17 Globemaster III, which can carry up to 70 tonnes over 4,000 kilometres.

Over the period 25 November 1942 to 11 January 1943, a total of 3,196 sorties achieved an average daily supply rate of only 104.7 tonnes. The only salvation was that 24,910 wounded were evacuated in the process. The collective advice of all the local air commanders, that an aerial resupply of Sixth Army was impractical, was proven to be correct. As one eyewitness described it, 'the requirements of 300, 500 and even 600 tonnes sank in snow drifts, in mist, and then in the terrible icy cold and in fatal crashes caused by the weather and enemy action'.[67] So every day the surrounded army remained in Stalingrad the weaker it became, and every day's delay in launching a relief operation made it less likely that it could assemble sufficient strength to break out towards the relieving force. These were the cold, irrefutable facts that condemned Sixth Army. Neither Manstein nor any other commander could save it unless a miracle happened. Hitler had manoeuvred himself into a position from which he could not extract himself, having nailed his political colours to the shattered mast of Stalingrad.

Most accounts of the battle agree that the critical day for deciding whether Sixth Army should stay put in the pocket or attempt to break out was 24 November 1942. This was the defining moment of crisis during which Manstein – not yet in command – conferred with Weichs at Starobelsk, and by which time Hitler had returned to his *Wolfschanze* headquarters near Rastenburg, East Prussia, with Zeitzler close at hand at OKH at Mauerwald near Angerburg. Between 22 and 24 November the principal commanders and advisors concerned had been largely out of touch, at the very worst possible time. To cap it all, Göring had left Obersalzberg to go absent in Paris on an art-hunting expedition in blatant dereliction of duty.

Excepting Manstein, the consensus of the senior army and air force generals in the East was that Paulus should break out immediately. At this crucial juncture, the commander of Sixth Army dithered: the best time to act was before the Red Army could consolidate its inner and outer rings of encirclement.[68] Manstein, perhaps not yet fully aware of the catastrophic threat facing the entire southern flank of the Eastern Front, and thinking that adequate reserves were being assembled in time for a viable relief operation, feared that Sixth Army would not be in a position to break out without assistance. *Provided* a sufficient level of air supply could be established, a very big and dangerous assumption, he considered it best to delay any order to break out until a properly orchestrated relief operation could be launched. With this in mind, Manstein sent the following signal to Paulus at 13.00 hours on 24 November 1942:

> [I] assume command of Army Group Don on 26.11. We will do all we can to get you out. In the meantime, it is imperative that [Sixth] Army, whilst holding firm on the Volga and North fronts in accordance with

the Führer's order, stands by strong forces as soon as possible, in order to force a supply route towards the south-west if necessary, at least temporarily.[69]

Manstein's order did not seal the fate of Sixth Army. It was doomed well beforehand by being exposed so recklessly at Stalingrad with such weakly defended flanks. The risk was compounded by the Germans' lack of any ready operational reserve available to restore the situation in the event of a Soviet counter-offensive. That said, Hitler may well have latched on to Manstein's initial assessment and reinforced his conviction that Sixth Army should remain *in* Stalingrad, rather than fighting its way *out*, with terrible consequences.

With the benefit of hindsight, Manstein may have appeared unduly confident of his abilities on arrival at Starobelsk. He had been thrust at minimal notice into a position of enormous responsibility in order to salvage the situation where others (Hitler, OKH and the commander and staff of Army Group B) had failed previously. Although responsibility must always rest with the commander, he may also have been unduly influenced by his chief of operations, the phlegmatic Busse, who encouraged Manstein with his customary remark: 'It's a bad business, Sir, but we'll manage somehow.'[70] After all, had they not mastered together the various crises on the Crimea during the previous winter?

The fact remains that Manstein was in a dangerously and uncharacteristically overconfident disposition on that critical day of 24 November. Crucially, he did not appear to appreciate fully the limited capability of the Luftwaffe at that time. Although he had phoned Richthofen, commander of Fourth Air Fleet, on the 24th, their first meeting to discuss the situation was not until the morning of 27 November. His advice to Manstein was that the Luftwaffe could not deliver any more than 300 tonnes per day to Stalingrad. In fact, it only approached this figure once during the seventy-day operation. So his reliance on the third-hand assertions of Göring about the potential capacity of the airlift was extremely ill-judged, bordering on the naive. He later explained his gullibility: 'That Göring would commit the supreme frivolity of promising an adequate airlift, and thereafter not even do everything to achieve the necessary minimum, was something no soldier could foresee.'[71]

Notwithstanding the impracticality of any airlift, the precise object of the relief of Stalingrad was neither clear to, nor agreed by, everyone concerned in the chain of command. Was it to save Sixth Army or to secure Stalingrad? Shortly after giving his instructions to Paulus on

24 November, Manstein telephoned OKH to give his recommended course of action. It diverged from that of Weichs and his staff in that it delayed any order for break-out, still based on the assumption that sufficient air supply could be assured.[72]

Of all the judgements he made during the Second World War, Manstein's recommendation that Sixth Army should not break out immediately is one of the most controversial. A recent historian has strongly criticized him, suggesting that his misplaced optimism was driven by his ambition 'to pull off an operational masterpiece and be seen as the "Saviour of Stalingrad"'.[73] Paulus's biographer is equally critical, advancing the view that Manstein was driven by the requirement to 'restore the situation' rather than by the necessity of saving Sixth Army. He also reinforces the point that Manstein's advice to OKH that Paulus should not immediately break out pulled the rug from under those opposed to Hitler's 'stand fast' on the Volga.[74]

In fact, Manstein's detailed diary entries over this critical period confirm that he had agonized over the fate of Sixth Army, and was under no illusions whatsoever as to the perilous position of the troops trapped in Stalingrad and to the criticality of air supply for their survival. Whilst on the train from Starobelsk to Novocherkassk, he recorded on 25 November: 'Overnight, I've thought long and hard about whether it was right not to accept the proposal of Army Group [B] in demanding an immediate breakout as a last salvation. I'm convinced that this was right.' He then set out his reasoning, including the view that Hitler would not have agreed to an immediate break-out; he considered that the Führer would only agree to it if demanded as a 'last resort'. As significantly, such were the challenges of winter weather, superior enemy forces and very limited combat supplies, Manstein doubted the capability of Sixth Army to extract itself without external support. He concluded:

A break-out in the current circumstances is dependent on aerial resupply and co-operation with forces from outside [the ring], and assumes an enormous effort on the part of the [chain of] command and the troops involved. If the air supply succeeds, as does the deployment of relief forces, then remaining in place is preferable, temporarily. If these preconditions are not met, then only an attempt at breaking-out remains. . . . In any event, there can hardly be a worse situation to be in.

As an after-note, he considered that the only realistic window for Sixth Army to have broken out without external assistance had already passed – '20–22 November, if at all possible'. And, finally, he stressed that the 'prestige of Stalingrad' is 'not a factor for me in the slightest'.[75]

As a matter of record, Manstein did not assume full command of his army group until 08.00 hours on 27 November 1942, *some six days* after being warned of his new appointment and *four days* since the Soviets had encircled Stalingrad. It became readily apparent that far more than just the fate of Sixth Army was at stake. Manstein was required to take into account the enemy pressure on, and the resulting actions of, his neighbouring army groups: 'A', to the south in the Caucasus; and 'B', to the north, with an alarming gap of 300 kilometres in between. If there was ever a time when the Eastern Front needed a Joint Commander-in-Chief '*Ost*' to co-ordinate the whole military air and ground effort in the East, then this was it. Only one commander could assess where he should accept safely some risk in one sector of the front in order to concentrate sufficient force to take decisive action elsewhere. Despite the supposed authority of OKH over the army groups, in practice forces were released from one to another only with great reluctance, and often far too late.

Hitler hoped forlornly that Stalingrad, once relieved, would remain a firm lodgement on the Volga for which so much German blood and not least his political reputation had been spent. According to his army adjutant, Major Gerhard Engel, in discussion on 26 November 1942 the Führer rejected Manstein's grand design to pull back Sixth Army and withdraw 'perhaps as far as the Dnieper, accumulate reserves, and then begin [a] new flank operation from the north down to the [Black] Sea'. Hitler 'turned it all down' for it 'would be seen as weakness', and have an 'intolerable effect on Germany's allies'. As for Manstein, he had 'good ideas operationally', but 'in view of the overall situation they were more grey theory'.[76]

The remainder of the train ride south (24–26 November) brought back fleetingly some happier memories for the Field Marshal. As he recalled in his memoirs, he had 'travelled down the same line to Rostov to attend the manoeuvres of the Red Army in the Caucasus' in 1932 with 'all sorts of interesting impressions' lying ahead of him. Ten years later, in the middle of a desperate total war, he contemplated the situation, 'the gravity of which my staff and I had no illusions. Time and again our thoughts went out to our beleaguered comrades at Stalingrad.'[77]

Manstein eventually reached Novocherkassk, the former capital city of the Don Cossacks, at 13.30 hours on 26 November. As he recorded in his diary the next day, 'There are only two courses open. One is to fight on to the last bullet as the Führer has ordered. The other would be to break-out at a desired time when the [necessary] forces and means are still available, in co-operation with external relief [forces].'[78] This was indeed the crux of the issue: could he convince Hitler and Paulus of the need to break out when the time came? Yet far worse could come: '... looking at the overall situation, consider the courses open to the Russians against the Italians and in exploiting the gap between us and Army Group A, should Sixth Army be destroyed. So now it's not only about Sixth Army ... but rather whether we can hold the southern wing during the winter.'[79] The integrity of the entire Eastern Front was at stake.

The next morning, Manstein's brand-new army group headquarters was fully operational by 08.00 hours, no mean feat of signals and staff organization. With his ADC and orderlies in tow, he moved into a former tsarist villa, a structure worthy of Catherine the Great's famous Prince Potemkin. Aristocratic Stahlberg recalled that 'its fittings no longer bore any relation to the external façade; one could not have imagined more primitive furnishings'. Stranger still, 'two soldiers ... short, friendly Cossacks, with huge Russian fur caps, but in German uniforms guarded the entrance steps.[80]

Whilst the savage fighting in the cauldron of Stalingrad continued unabated only 200 kilometres away, there was no time to dwell on such niceties. Early that first evening in Novocherkassk (18.35 hours) on the 26th, Manstein received a long hand-written report from Paulus in response to his signal of 24 November. The commander of Sixth Army described recent events and explained that he had received no orders or information from a higher level 'for the past thirty-six hours', and that he was confronted with the choice of either remaining in his present position – so complying with the orders issued to him – or 'breaking through to the south-west'. Further, in the case of the second option he had requested from the Führer 'freedom to take such a final decision if it should become necessary', to which he had received no direct reply. Paulus stressed that he had requested this authority to 'guard against issuing the only possible order in that situation too late', and that he would only give such an order 'in an extreme emergency' and asked Manstein to accept his word for this. He went on to state that the 'airlift of the last three days has brought only a fraction of the calculated minimum requirement (600 tonnes = 300 Ju daily)', but felt that 'the army can hold out for a time'. But the most remarkable, and telling, remark was Paulus's final one: 'Allow me to say, *Herr Feldmarschall*, that I regard your leadership as a guarantee that everything possible is being done to assist Sixth Army. For their part, my commanders and gallant troops will join me in doing everything to justify your trust.'[81]

In Army Group Don's war diary, which contains a summary of Paulus's letter, there is no reference to any reply by Manstein, presumably because he soon intended to fly into Stalingrad. In any case, he had received more precise information on Sixth Army's supply situation from Major General Wolfgang Pickert, commander of 9th Flak Division and senior Luftwaffe officer in Stalingrad, which indicated that Paulus was not in a position to move for lack of fuel. So this was surely a matter for urgent clarification. A break-out, however, was never on the Führer's agenda. Zeitzler instructed Manstein accordingly on the morning of 28 November that 'Stalingrad is to be held with all means'.[82]

That same day Manstein sent his chief of staff into Stalingrad to establish the situation there and to inform Sixth Army of his plans for the relief operation. This act remains one of Manstein's most serious misjudgements of the war, for he alone, as an army group commander-in-chief, had a personal responsibility for his principal subordinate. Only by flying into Stalingrad could he discuss and explain his intentions without any risk of misinterpretation and see for himself the rapidly worsening conditions in the pocket. His later explanation that he had 'resolved to fly into the pocket and talk to Paulus' but then had accepted advice from Schulz and Busse to the contrary, rings rather hollow. He justified this decision on the grounds that he might be detained in Stalingrad for a couple of days; being away for that time was 'inadmissible in view of the tense situation and the need to keep OKH constantly aware of the Army Group's views'.[83]

Manstein's argument holds little water, for once in the city he would have enjoyed assured communications with his own headquarters and with OKH. Thus there is little doubt that he could have remained abreast of the admittedly very fluid operational situation when visiting Sixth Army. Manstein needed to meet Paulus urgently in order to discuss procedures for initiating a break-out in fraught circumstances, and potentially against the Führer's orders. Had Manstein given an assurance to his subordinate that he, as army group commander, would assume full personal responsibility for such a decision, then it is reasonable to suppose that Paulus might have reacted more flexibly during the relief operation.

Whatever the practicalities, it was Manstein's military duty to gauge the situation in Stalingrad for himself. Quite simply, he needed to speak to Paulus and his corps commanders face to face. In his obsequious letter of 24 November, the commander of Sixth Army had already indicated his deference to Manstein and his dependence on his superior's ability to master the situation. In turn, the Field Marshal knew that Paulus, a weak and compliant character who had never led a major formation in battle until assuming command of an army, would hesitate under pressure. Whether Manstein agonized over the matter is not recorded, but it is safe to assume that he did not discount the need to see Paulus lightly. In a letter to his wife on 14 February 1943, some twelve days after the German surrender, he set out his views, subsequently confirmed in his memoirs:

> In fact, I wanted to [fly in], but declined in view of the weather situation. It was always questionable whether one could have flown back on the same day, and I could not afford to stay there for two days. Right from the beginning, I wasn't just worried about Stalingrad but had wider concerns. Schulz, Busse and Eismann were each there on one occasion. I would have liked to have been for 'moral' reasons, but it just didn't work out. Even Paulus requested that I should not come.[84]

There can be little doubt that Manstein's record would have been much the finer had he visited Sixth Army in Stalingrad, even once, and not sent a series of representatives in lieu.[85]

The Abortive Relief Operation

Manstein's attack to rescue the entrapped Axis forces in Stalingrad was almost bound to fail. Russian strength, the weakness of the German relieving force and Sixth Army's inability to break out all combined to make it a desperate venture. None the less, he had to make the effort. Within a week of being warned off for army group command, he had completed his first plan on 28 November. It was made on the assumption that LVII Corps would be ready for employment by 3 December and the Hollidt Group (particularly its mobile element of XLVIII Panzer Corps) six days later. Manstein intended to conduct the relief operation with both attack groups. Whilst LVII Corps advanced north-eastwards from the area of Kotelnikovo, XLVIII Corps would thrust eastwards from the Middle Chir River towards Kalach. Sensing the urgency of the situation, he considered attacking with only LVII Corps, should Sixth Army's position deteriorate to such an extent that it could hold out no longer. Crucially, the co-operation of Paulus's army 'by attacking in a south-westerly direction in any event was essential', based on the 'concentration of mobile reserves drawn from the front, potentially by shortening the line on the Volga'.[86]

It is abundantly clear from this reasoning that Manstein never thought that he would have sufficient striking power to relieve Stalingrad *without* Sixth Army launching its own attack to link up with the relieving force. This is a crucial consideration often missed in other accounts of the battle. With Hitler forbidding any voluntary surrender of ground, a vital prerequisite to give Paulus the necessary freedom of manoeuvre, and Sixth Army's inherent weakness, the conditions for the relief operation were exceptionally challenging, to say the least. It could be argued that they were *never* going to be met. This predicament had already been recognized by General Seydlitz-Kurzbach within the pocket, who had urged his fellow corps commanders to break out immediately in order to avoid certain catastrophe. Inevitably, such realism could quickly turn defeatist in outlook.

In contrast, Manstein remained positive but was forced to bide his time whilst he waited for his relief forces to be assembled for a complex and extremely risky operation. Unflappable Busse, Manstein's alter ego on his staff, may have continued to contribute a degree of complacency. In any event, it was compounded by his chief of staff, who had just returned from Stalingrad with a surprisingly positive message. According to General Schulz, there was 'no immediate danger to Sixth Army having overcome the first days of crisis. The constant supply flights and the successful air combat by our fighters over the pocket contribute to cement confidence and morale.'[87] This was a fool's paradise, for Sixth Army was withering quickly on the vine whilst Russian interceptors and massed anti-aircraft artillery exacted a steady toll of German transport aircraft.

Schulz had in fact spent most of his brief visit in Stalingrad discussing the situation with Paulus's overconfident chief, Schmidt, and had only the time for a brief meeting with the army commander. So Manstein could not accurately judge – even at third hand – what Paulus's likely reaction would be to his orders to break out. This was a fatal and tragic omission, underlining the view that Manstein was irresponsible in not confronting Paulus directly. A telephone call to congratulate him on his promotion to colonel general on 30 November, and all the subsequent conversations at a distance, however lengthy, could never make up for the failure to meet him in Stalingrad. Manstein acknowledged after the war that whilst Paulus 'was probably a better-trained tactician and a clearer thinker, it looked as if his Chief-of-Staff was the stronger personality of the two'.[88] Knowing this relationship, he should have flown in at the first opportunity or, failing that, certainly on 18 December rather than sending that day his chief of intelligence, Major Eismann, as the relief force neared Stalingrad. As we shall see, this was the critical moment when Manstein should have ordered Paulus in person to break out.

During the evening of 1 December 1942, Manstein issued his Directive No. 1 for Operation WINTERGEWITTER (WINTER TEMPEST), the relief of Sixth Army (see Map 9). As he recalled in his memoirs: the 'crux of the matter' was that 'the maximum risk had to be accepted if we were to bring our comrades of Sixth Army a chance of salvation'.[89] His revised plan saw elements of Fourth Rumanian Army covering the right flank of Fourth Panzer Army, which was to attack on 8 December with LVII Corps (6th and 23rd Panzer Divisions with the newly established 15th Luftwaffe Field Division) and XLVIII Panzer Corps, detached from Army Detachment Hollidt (336th Infantry, 11th Panzer and 7th Luftwaffe Field Divisions). In addition, 17th Panzer Division was being brought up, but not yet released by Hitler and OKH to Army Group Don. Meanwhile, Sixth Army was to concentrate all available armoured forces ready to break out and link up with Fourth Panzer Army.[90]

In war the enemy always has a vote, and heavy Soviet attacks continued to wear down Sixth Army. More worryingly, OKH and Army Group Don saw the increasing possibility of another major Soviet offensive operation being launched towards Rostov-on-Don. This would aim at cutting off not only Manstein's command but also Army Group A, still fixed, largely immobile, in the North Caucasus. In fact, *Stavka* was planning Operation SATURN to achieve just that result.[91] So Manstein was faced with a dilemma, should he conserve his modest striking power – that contained in the two corps being assembled for the relief of Stalingrad – to parry any new Soviet offensive, or should he continue to employ them as intended in WINTER TEMPEST? He felt he could attempt only one of the two possible courses of action. Hitler (and hence OKH) wanted to have it both ways by holding the weak 17th Panzer Division as a 'strategic reserve'. This procrastination delayed its release to either XLVIII or LVII Panzer Corps. So once again the failure to husband sufficient reserves overall and then to insert them at the decisive point – in this case none other than the relief of Stalingrad – marked the confused German decision-making at the time.

From first principles of operational design, Manstein needed to furnish the relieving force with the necessary combat power to thrust towards Stalingrad and, simultaneously, protect it from the inevitable Soviet counterattack. Bearing in mind the enemy's dispositions in between (strong elements of at least three armies), this would have required a full-scale German counter-offensive at army group level.[92]

The reality was that Manstein only had a fraction of the forces required at his disposal. It remained to be seen whether either elements of XLVIII Corps or 17th Panzer Division could be made available to join the attack.

That meant that Colonel General Hoth, commander of Fourth Army, apart from weak supporting Rumanian forces (two corps in name only), had LVII Panzer Corps solely for this vital operation. Of that corps, only one major formation, 6th Panzer Division, was at full war establishment with about 160 tanks and assault guns. So Sixth Army's only hope of rescue – and at that a very slender one indeed – rested largely on the offensive power of this fresh unit supported by the very much weaker 23rd Panzer Division, a 'division' in name only with its twenty serviceable tanks. As one critical commentator would have it, 'the Germans mounted an effort that for spectacular futility is reminiscent of the Charge of the Light Brigade in 1854'.[93]

Before Manstein could launch the relief attempt the situation for Army Group Don as a whole deteriorated considerably as a result of renewed Soviet pressure. During early December 1942, he juggled forces in meeting one crisis after another, struggled vainly for timely decisions and requested urgent reinforcements from higher command. Yet he often appeared at his best when the situation was at its most dire, as the campaign in the Crimea had proved. No amount of operational level talent, however, could change the strategic facts.

Outside the Stalingrad pocket, where Sixth Army continued to beat off repeated assaults, the main Soviet threat was directed towards the thinly held front on the Lower Chir River. Attacks by 5th Tank Army were defeated at heavy cost. An enemy breakthrough here, in Manstein's analysis, would 'have cleared the way to the Morozovsk and Tatsinskiy airfields ... as well as to the Donets crossings and Rostov'. In the face of a determined Soviet onslaught that started in this sector on 4 December, he felt he had no choice 'but to agree that XLVIII Corps' (whose reinforcing 11th Panzer and 336th Infantry Divisions had now arrived) should be employed to 'bolster up the front'. Under the famous Balck-Mellenthin partnership (respectively commander and chief of staff equivalent), 11th Panzer Division's tactical successes as a 'veritable fire-fighter, dashing from one spot to the next every time the thin screen of alarm units threatened to collapse', could not hide the fact that Manstein's operational freedom of action was extremely limited.[94] The Red Army continued to call the shots.

The biggest constraint, and one that endured until Stalingrad fell, was Hitler's refusal to evacuate the city on prestige grounds, even if a viable land corridor could be established to Sixth Army. Manstein disagreed fundamentally, 'convinced as ever that this was entirely the wrong solution and that it was essential to become operationally mobile again if disaster were to be avoided'.[95] The words 'operationally mobile' neatly sum up his philosophy of manoeuvre, in which defensive operations needed to be conducted 'elastically' in order to set the conditions for a decisive counter-offensive. This approach was never to Hitler's taste; with some exceptions forced by circumstance, he was inclined to view every step back as a probable defeat rather than as a potential preliminary to victory.

Even if Manstein had obtained the 'operational freedom' he desired in December 1942, it would have been to no effect without the necessary forces for mounting the relief operation. With Army Detachment Hollidt (principally XLVIII Corps) no longer in position to attack, everything rested on reinforcing Fourth Panzer Army's LVII Panzer Corps. This was his only uncommitted force. As he remarked bitterly in his memoirs, anyone 'could see that [it] was not going to reach Stalingrad with only 6 and 23 Panzer Divisions'.[96] Manstein was unsuccessful in either extracting III Panzer Corps from Army Group A or finding a way to release 16th Motorized Infantry Division, which covered the deep exposed northern flank of First Panzer Army. Neither did he receive any further reinforcements from OKH, which continued, on Hitler's instruction, to withhold 17th Panzer Division. His mounting frustration at his poor hand was suppressed in a calmly worded estimate of the situation on 9 December, which concluded prophetically, even assuming that a relief operation were to be successful:

> The corollary of any decision to keep Sixth Army at Stalingrad must therefore be the decision to fight this battle through to a completely decisive ending. This will necessitate: (i) providing Sixth Army with extra forces to maintain its defensive capacity ... ; (ii) reinforcement of the adjoining [Allied] fronts; ... launching a decisive offensive as soon as our own forces permit. Whether the forces required can be made available and brought into action at short notice is not for me to judge.[97]

Without sufficient forces being made available to mount an effective relief operation in the first place, however, it was a complete illusion to talk of holding on to Stalingrad, let alone staging a full-scale counter-offensive. One suspects that Manstein knew this as he wrote his estimate, but he felt he must make the attempt all the same.

A detailed account of the relief operation is given by the commander of 6th Panzer Division, Major General Erhard Raus, who offers a stirring description of German superiority in combined arms tactics.[98] For all his formation's hard-won success, neither he nor his corps or army commander, nor indeed the army group commander, could improve the operational level odds that were so heavily stacked against them. On a fine winter's day, 12 December 1942, the relief attack was finally launched from the bridgehead at dawn. With all the limited artillery and air support that could be brought to bear, the two divisions (in combat power worth less than one and a half) of General of Panzer Troops Friedrich Kirchner's LVII Panzer Corps stormed across the monotonous brown steppe astride the main railway line towards Stalingrad, some 130 kilometres distant. Notwithstanding the short hours of daylight, the relief force made surprisingly good progress initially but soon ran into superior Soviet forces.[99]

With the launch of Fourth Panzer Army's attack towards Stalingrad, the operational initiative passed briefly to Manstein. *Stavka* representative Vasilevsky, who had drawn up the ambitious plan for Operation SATURN, was forced to concede that 'his priority mission of preventing [the] German relief of Stalingrad might be in jeopardy if he did not act'. Abandoning the deep objective of Rostov-on-Don, the modified Operation LITTLE SATURN required the South-Western *Front* to conduct a shallower envelopment of the Italian Eighth Army and Army Detachment Hollidt by attacking to the south-east towards Morozovsk rather than to the south. Most worryingly for Manstein, however, Vasilevsky diverted a fresh army to assist 51st and 57th Armies in blocking and defeating LVII Panzer Corps.[100] As fate would have it, the odds worsened considerably when General Rodion Yakovlevich Malinovsky's élite 2nd Guards Army, 'one of the best-equipped and most formidable of the Red Army, with its five rifle corps and a mechanized corps', came into action straight off the line of march in a snowstorm.[101] Meanwhile, Operation LITTLE SATURN had commenced on 16 December. The Italian Eighth Army was ripped asunder by the attacks of the South-Western *Front*'s 1st and 3rd Guards Armies, supported by 5th Tank Army and the Voronezh *Front*'s 6th Army.

There was one, all too brief, glimmer of fortune in the attempt to relieve Stalingrad. Notwithstanding increasing enemy resistance and worsening weather, Raus's spearhead reached the Mishkova at dawn on 19 December, having achieved a slender penetration of 80 kilometres. With the capture of an intact crossing at the village of Bolshaya-Vasilevka, 6th Panzer Division's bridgehead – in truth more a toe-prod than a foothold – was now only 50 kilometres from Sixth Army's closest troops. Inevitably, 6th Division's spearheads, short of fuel and ammunition, came under immediate and furious Soviet tank assault.[102] Some German observers in Stalingrad claimed to see gun flashes from the relief force, but 'close' was not near enough for Sixth Army.

The 17th Panzer Division, released finally to LVII Panzer Corps, attacked on 17 December on 6th Panzer's left flank. It, too, reached the Mishkova but could not force a crossing under increasing enemy pressure. This weak formation, despite the energetic and inspiring leadership of General Frido von Senger und Etterlin, later famous for his stalwart defence of Cassino in 1944, had only thirty operational tanks. So it stood no chance of restoring momentum to the stalled relief operation, stuck on the Mishkova in fierce blizzards. As Senger und Etterlin observed bitterly after the war, 'what I had feared at the start of the relief operation had now come to pass. The Russians had no intention of allowing one weak corps to rob them of their great victory at Stalingrad.'[103] Manstein was not yet willing to abandon the relief operation, although renewed Soviet attacks on the Chir threatened to unhinge his entire army group.

For the soldiers entrapped in Stalin's city, the brief period 18–23 December 1942 provided the only ray of hope since the chance to break out a month before had been squandered through Paulus's passivity and Hitler's 'iron will' to stand firm. As Manstein described it, the 'moment for which we had longed since take-over [of Army Group Don], when the approach of relief forces would offer Sixth Army its chance to break free, had arrived'.[104] This was now the only possible opportunity for executing the planned link-up since the encirclement. Accordingly, on 18 December Manstein requested authority from Hitler via Zeitzler to order Sixth Army to break out. The full text, reproduced in his memoirs, contains his two key demands:

> [A]s LVII Panzer Corps by itself obviously cannot make contact with Sixth Army on the ground, let alone keep a corridor open, I now consider a break-out to the south-west to be the last possible means of preserving at least the bulk of the troops and the still mobile elements of Sixth Army.
>
> The breakthrough, the first aim of which must be to make contact with LVII Panzer Corps on about the Yerik Mishkova, can only take place by forcing a gradual shift of Sixth Army towards the south-west and giving up ground sector by sector in the north of the fortress area as this movement progresses.[105]

At Hitler's headquarters that evening, the situation was discussed again but no decision was made. Engel recorded:

> M[anstein] again requested break-out by Sixth Army. Only way to maintain link to Stalingrad [sic] and so save the greater part of the army. Mood is depressed. F[ührer] turned down break-out once more despite desperate plea by Z[eitzler]. Very angry telephone calls from Busse and

also von M[anstein], since all [reserves] have been directed to join Army
Group B, now on the move, in order to plug the gap by the Italians.[106]

Thus Manstein's signal remained unanswered: Sixth Army stayed put.
The criticality of the situation was not lost on the Red Army, however.
It increased the intensity of its attacks on LVII Corps, whose exposed
position became more tenuous by the hour. To make matters far worse,
Manstein was forced to pull back 6th Panzer Division over the next few
days in order to restore the situation on the Chir front, the integrity of
which was threatened again by the erupting LITTLE SATURN offensive.

Manstein's account of the events of 19 December 1942 and the following week remains controversial, particularly in relation as to whether
he did in fact give Paulus a *clear* order to break out in defiance of Hitler.
A key matter of dispute arises over the wording of the Army Group
Don's order of 19 December, 18.00 hours. The first part (Paragraph 2)
was clear enough: 'Sixth Army is to begin its "Winter Tempest" attack
as early as possible. Be prepared to advance beyond Donskaya Tsaritsa if
necessary in order to link up with LVII Corps in order to get the [supply]
convoy through.' The 'Winter Tempest' attack refers here to Sixth
Army's contribution to its *own relief* by breaking out to the south-west
in order to meet the advance elements of Fourth Panzer Army. Confusion
then crept in with a subtly different requirement (Paragraph 3):

> Development of the situation may make it necessary to extend the mission
> in Paragraph 2 up to the [river] Mishkova. Codeword 'Thunderclap'. In
> this case the aim is likewise to link up with LVII Corps quickly with
> armour in order to get the convoy through, and then, by covering the
> flanks on the lower Karpovka and Chervlenaya, to bring the Army forward
> to the Mishkova simultaneously with a sector-by-sector evacuation of the
> fortress area. Circumstances may demand that Operation 'Thunderclap'
> immediately follows the 'Winter Tempest' attack.[107]

Manstein's order can be criticized on several grounds. First, his intent
is not at all clear: what exactly does he require Paulus to do, and by
when? Knowing that Sixth Army was not in a position to concentrate
sufficient force in the south-west of the pocket in order to break out
without economizing effort elsewhere, which could only be achieved by
a partial, if not full, simultaneous evacuation of the 'fortress area' (as
implied by the extended attack under 'Thunderclap'), he has given Paulus
a mission that could not be executed if Hitler's stay-put orders were to
be obeyed to the letter. Secondly, as army group commander, he has
given no specific direction to Fourth Panzer Army for the benefit of

LVII Corps, nor requested the Luftwaffe to surge either its transport of fuel into the pocket or its interdiction of Soviet forces prior to, and during, the initial, most decisive phase of the operation, the speedy link-up with LVII Corps. Thirdly, he did not address how the 50-kilometre gap was to be closed, when Sixth Army had already reported that it had fuel for only 30 kilometres.

Whether Sixth Army could have evaded destruction remains hotly disputed: it could risk annihilation either on the open steppe or within Stalingrad, a Hobson's choice. Schmidt, for one, maintained long after the war that there was never any real possibility of a successful break-out.[108] Whatever, Paulus failed to order his army to move and Manstein declined to press the point. By the end of December, LVII Panzer Corps was beaten back to its line of departure by superior Soviet forces. So the only relief attempt, on which all hopes rested, had failed: the agony of Stalingrad would continue until the beginning of February 1943.

In any final analysis, the deciding issue was not any lack of clarity in Manstein's orders, but rather the impossibility of the task. If Stalingrad was not the Field Marshal's finest hour, the troops of the relieving force and the crews of the Luftwaffe had done their very best. Their gallantry, as of the German forces encircled in the city, was not in doubt. Meanwhile, the coming and inevitable Soviet victory on the Volga, derived from their heroic defensive battle and stunning counterattack, would be richly deserved.

12

A Brief Glimpse of Victory

*'By the end of the winter campaign the initiative was back in German hands,
and the Russians had suffered two defeats.'* Erich von Manstein[1]

Martyrdom on the Volga

In war, it is often glibly said that 'fortune favours the bold'; whether the
bold actually deserve or receive such benefit is seldom questioned.[2] By
late December 1942, any last luck had run out for the German Sixth Army
in Stalingrad, as it had done so for the Soviet defenders of Sevastopol six
months earlier. Common to these two sieges was the remarkable courage
and stoicism of the troops involved. But the results of both battles showed
that no amount of risk-taking or individual valour displayed at the tactical
level could alter necessarily the overall operational and strategic odds.
Nations who send their sons and daughters into overexposed outposts
abroad would do well to remember this, as many conflicts since the
Second World War, including those in Indo-China, Iraq and Afghani-
stan, have demonstrated amply.

Manstein dedicated his account of Sixth Army's 'martyrdom on the
Volga' to the 'German soldiers, who starved, froze and died there'.
Noting the unlikelihood of any monument being erected to commemorate their sacrifice, he declared eloquently, 'the memory of their
indescribable suffering, their unparalleled heroism, fidelity, and devotion
to duty will live on long after the victors' cries of triumph have died away
and the bereaved, the disillusioned and the bitter at heart have fallen
silent'.[3] His moving paean for the dead was prompted by the famous
epigram of Simonides, dedicated to the brave Spartans who fell to a man
at Thermopylae: 'Go tell the Spartans, you who read: We took their
orders, and here lie dead.'[4]

For all their fortitude, was the sacrifice of over 225,000 men from the
twenty German and two Rumanian divisions and supporting troops
worth it? What had it achieved? The lost battle of Stalingrad resulted
in an unprecedented catastrophe for Hitler. Worse than the defeat a
year earlier at Moscow, it had far more severe political and military

consequences. If the losses of the Rumanian Third and Fourth Armies smashed on either side of Stalingrad are included, together with the complete collapse of the Italian Eighth Army on the Upper Don and the subsequent defeat of the Hungarian Second Army in January 1943, then the Soviet winter counter-offensive was nothing less than a strategic disaster for the Axis cause. It showed all interested powers, including Germany's allies and 'concerned' neutrals such as Turkey, that the Third Reich had severely overreached itself and could never hope to win against the Soviet Union.

Furthermore, the net result of the Soviet counter-offensive at Stalingrad and subsequent operations in its winter campaign was the removal of the surviving Axis contingents from the Eastern Front and the evacuation of German forces from the Caucasus. Although the Red Army had suffered terrible losses in making these gains, everything Hitler hoped for in Operation BLUE had vanished. His fantasy of crossing over the southern Russian frontier and advancing to the Middle East and Iran remained just that – a vain dream devoid of all reality.

The only operational benefit of Sixth Army's 'martyrdom' was that it had tied down so many Soviet forces for so long, and that Operation SATURN had been downgraded to LITTLE SATURN. Had the Germans lost Rostov-on-Don, the prime terrain objective of SATURN in December 1942, then Army Group A, and particularly a large chunk of First Panzer Army, could not have escaped destruction. Despite Manstein's and Zeitzler's constant urging, Hitler's permission to start this urgently required withdrawal from the Caucasus (and at this stage only a partial one at that) came characteristically late on 29 December 1942 in 'response to the insistence of Don Army Group'.[5] None the less, Stalin was unable to inflict in full measure his intended mortal blow on the German Army in the East, the *Ostheer*.[6] Army Groups A and Don survived to fight another day notwithstanding the grievous loss of Sixth Army, Germany's strongest. As we shall see, Manstein managed to stabilize the southern wing of the front and the Soviet winter offensive was brought to a halt in March 1943 in spectacular fashion, offering a brief glimpse of victory. Yet nothing could disguise the harsh fact that the destruction of so many Axis forces (the equivalent of no less than fifty-five divisions) in the meantime had 'fundamentally changed the situation to the detriment of Germany and her allies'.[7] The strategic balance had now shifted in favour of the Soviet Union and its Western allies.

For the German people, moreover, there was no way of disguising the magnitude of the catastrophe at Stalingrad and the psychological blow it represented. Too many soldiers' letters had reached the homeland for it to be brushed aside as a mere setback. Goebbels had tried to counter anguish and defeatism in his famous speech of 18 February 1943 at the Berlin *Sportpalast*, declaring 'total war'.[8] The strategic truth, however, had already been drawn on the battlefield. Marshal Zhukov, even stripping away the bombastic tone of his memoirs, hit the nail on the head when he explained the 'causes of the German debacle' and the Soviets' 'epoch-making victory':

> [The] failure of all Hitlerite strategic plans for 1942 was due to an underestimation of the forces and potentialities of the Soviet State, the indomitable spirit of the people. It also stems from an over-estimation by the Nazis of their own forces and capabilities. [Secondly,] utilization of the surprise factor, correct selection of the directions of the main effort, accurate detection of weak points in the enemy defences led to the defeat of the German troops in the operation[s] codenamed URANUS, SMALLER SATURN [and] RING.

Zhukov could not avoid listing a number of other contributory factors, not least the 'Party and political work conducted by the Military Councils … and commanders', 'who fostered in soldiers confidence and bravery, and encouraged mass heroism on the battlefield'.[9]

For both sides, there was as much a psychological as any physical turning point. Germany's offensive operations had culminated. In view of the Soviet superiority, the only option available was to switch to a strategic defence. How aggressively it could be conducted at the operational level would depend on the time, space and forces available, and above all, on the skill of its commanders. As Manstein was soon to show, the Red Army could still be defeated in the field.

In the meantime, the final agony of Stalingrad is briefly told. In the grand scheme of the Second World War, it is tempting to describe the German defeat on the Volga in terms of a 'decisive point'. Although such vocabulary is valid in any strict, detached, military analysis of campaign, it obscures the irrefutable fact that the battle was a human disaster. Manstein was surely right, therefore, to remind his readers:

> The death-struggle of Sixth Army, which began around the turn of the year [1942–43], is a tale of indescribable suffering. It was marked not only by the despair and justified bitterness of the men who had been deceived in their trust, but even more by the steadfastness they displayed in the face of an undeserved and inexorable fate, and by their high degree of bravery, comradeship and devotion to duty, and by their calm resignation and humble faith in God.[10]

None the less, it is perfectly appropriate to examine Hitler's and Manstein's decision-making during the last few, debilitating weeks of the Sixth Army: after all, the fate of so many thousands of soldiers rested on their political and military leaders.

By late December 1942, the combat power of the encircled troops in Stalingrad had diminished dramatically. On the 26th, when only 70 tonnes of supplies were flown into the pocket, Paulus reported that 'bloody losses, cold, and inadequate supplies have recently made serious inroads on divisions' fighting strength'. Moreover, it was 'no longer possible to execute [a] break-out unless [a] corridor is cut in advance and [my] Army [is] replenished with men and supplies'. So Paulus was in no doubt as to the nature of the impending disaster. He concluded his report with a plea: 'radical measures [are] now urgent'.[11] None was available.

Back at Hitler's headquarters in East Prussia, the mood had turned to one of frustration and resignation for there was nothing now that could save Sixth Army. As Engel recorded, 'here [is] deepest depression. Nearly everybody had been hoping against hope that P. [Paulus] would take the risk and try to break out against his orders.' However unrealistic the prospect, he felt that the army commander 'could have got out with the bulk of his men, albeit at a high cost in material'. Yet the fact remained that 'Nobody knows what should be done next at Stalingrad.' In the face of unfolding events he was powerless to change, the Führer had turned 'very quiet', and was 'almost never seen except at daily situation conferences and to receive reports'.[12]

By the end of the year, Hoth's Fourth Panzer Army had been pushed back to its line of departure, then further west still towards Rostov-on-Don. Building on the success of the Stalingrad counter-offensive, the Soviet Middle Don operation had sealed Sixth Army's fate. As Zhukov noted accurately, the encircled German force 'had no prospect of relief, stocks had run out, troops were on starvation rations, hospitals were packed, and the death rate from injury and disease was steep. The end was in sight.'[13]

On 9 January 1943, following instructions by the supreme command in Moscow, the Soviet Don *Front* presented Sixth Army with a surrender ultimatum. The demand was summarily rejected the same day by Paulus on Hitler's orders. Manstein did not defer. Perhaps tilting at the obvious criticism after the war, he went to considerable lengths in his memoirs to explain why, in his view, a capitulation on this date would not have been appropriate. His rather banal comments that, 'if every Commander-in-Chief were to capitulate as soon as he considered his position hopeless, no one would ever win a war' and 'even in situations apparently quite bereft of hope it has often been possible to find a way out in the end' provided little justification. What mattered far more was the operational rationale for sustaining the struggle in Stalingrad at such high human cost. The critical consideration, therefore, which he stressed repeatedly, was the fate of the entire southern wing of the German Army on the Eastern Front. So Manstein was on safer ground when he stated:

> this in turn brings us to the crucial point which justifies Hitler's order to refuse to capitulate and also barred the Army Group from intervening in favour of such action at that particular time. No matter how futile Sixth Army's continued resistance might be in the long run, it still had – as long as it could conceivably go on fighting – a decisive role to fulfil in the overall strategic situation. It had to try to tie down the enemy forces opposing it for the longest possible space of time.[14]

Strictly speaking, he was right in his assessment. Sixth Army's prolonged and heroic stand on the Volga continued to fix seven armies of Rokossovsky's Don *Front*, powerful forces which otherwise could have been employed elsewhere to 'telling effect'.[15] That said, the conduct of war ought never to be reduced to the moves of an elaborate chess game: the humanitarian imperative to end a lost battle and so prevent any further loss of life must at some stage take precedence over military considerations.

Manstein maintained to his deathbed the deeply held conviction that Germany was not doomed to defeat as a result of Stalingrad. One of his central themes in *Lost Victories* is that it would have been possible to have come to some sort of draw, however illusory that view might now appear. For all his professional military capabilities, Manstein was not a politically astute man. In propounding his solution, he failed to appreciate the utter determination of Stalin and the Soviet people not only to free their sacred Motherland (*Rodina*), but also to punish the Fascist invaders and render the aggressor incapable of mounting a war of conquest ever again. He also underestimated the strength of feeling against Germany held by the Western Allies, who at the Casablanca conference (14–24 January 1943) had demanded unconditional surrender.

It would be far too simple, however, to dismiss out of hand Manstein's perspective that 'in those days it was by no means certain that Germany was bound to lose the war in the military sense'.[16] Accepting that the military is but one instrument of national power, in early 1943 Germany had yet to realize the full potential of its war economy: that would take another year under Albert Speer's best efforts.[17] Furthermore, despite its huge losses on the Eastern Front, the Wehrmacht still had considerable reserves of men and equipment, much of it being squandered in the totally futile defence of Tunisia or dissipated to little benefit in other peripheral theatres such as Norway or the Balkans. The fundamental issue Manstein raised was whether a military stalemate could have been brought about, and if, in turn, it would have caused 'a similar state of affairs in the political field'. He felt a 'draw' 'would have been entirely within the bounds of possibility if the situation on the southern wing of German armies could in some way have been restored'.[18] All his efforts during and following the disaster at Stalingrad were aimed at achieving that one objective – staving off defeat – as opposed to the pursuit of ultimate victory.

In the weeks that followed Sixth Army's defiant refusal to capitulate, the Soviet forces slowly but surely pushed in the German defence. Operation RING, designed to reduce the pocket, was prosecuted with ruthless ferocity. Throughout this period, bad weather and heavy fighting continued to hinder aerial resupply. Freezing and worn out, German troops fought on: the sapping starvation of the survivors accelerated, as did the appalling suffering of the injured and wounded. Manstein was not immune to the human misery involved, observing that it was but 'a cruel necessity of war which compelled the [German] Supreme Command to demand that one last sacrifice of the brave troops of Stalingrad'.[19]

Within Stalingrad, the situation worsened steadily and losses mounted alarmingly. The bread ration was cut from 200 to 100 grams a day; after all the horses had been slaughtered, the dogs came next. When the airfields at Pitomnik and Gumrak were lost on 12 and 22 January respectively, the inevitable end drew much closer: no supplies in; no wounded out. The start of a series of concentrated Soviet blows to liquidate the German hold of the city centre began on 22 January. On 24 January, Paulus signalled: 'Fortress can be held for only a few days longer. Troops exhausted and weapons immobilized as a result of non-arrival of supplies. Imminent loss of last airfield will reduce supplies to a minimum. No basis left on which to carry out mission to hold Stalingrad.'[20] He requested permission to break out in small organized groups. In response, he received a stark message 'Re break-out: Führer reserves right of final decision.' It never arrived.[21]

By this late stage, Manstein had realized the futility of any further sacrifice in Stalingrad and pressed Hitler hard to give Paulus permission to enter into surrender negotiations. The Führer refused point-blank. That same day (24 January 1943), the Soviets had broken through the last remaining coherent front and split the German forces in the city into three smaller segments. Within a week, Paulus (promoted to field marshal to encourage him not to fall into the hands of the Russians alive) and his immediate staff had surrendered at their final command post, the Univermag department store in Red Square.

In one of those great ironies of history, it was Colonel Ivan Andreevich Laskin, a hero of the defence of Sevastopol and now chief of staff of the 64th Army, who arranged the cessation of hostilities in Stalingrad. The guns fell silent on 2 February when the last defenders of XI Corps in the northern pocket gave up. No fewer than 90,000 Germans were captured of which only 5,000 came back to their Fatherland. Although the fighting had stopped, cold, disease and malnutrition in Stalingrad was soon replicated in Soviet prisoner-of-war camps; only the very strongest and exceptionally lucky pulled through.

Manstein had done his very best to relieve Stalingrad. When that attempt failed for lack of forces, he felt compelled by military logic, and in accordance with Hitler's instructions, to require Sixth Army to fight on. Perhaps somewhat belatedly, he had urged the Führer to agree to its surrender when the airlift was broken and when any further resistance was no longer justified on military grounds. Of the German leader's role, Manstein wrote:

> It was certainly to Hitler's credit that he accepted responsibility unre-
> servedly and made no attempt whatever to find a scapegoat. On the other
> hand, we are confronted by his regrettable failure to draw any conclusions
> for the future from a defeat for which his own errors of leadership were
> to blame.[22]

One consequence of Stalingrad was the temporary loosening of Hitler's micro-control of operations in early 1943. It led to timely evacuations from the exposed Demyansk and Rzhev salients that forestalled Soviet blows and created much needed reserves. Manstein also exploited this situation in stabilizing the southern wing of the Eastern Front by the end of March. Without gaining sufficient freedom to manoeuvre, it is doubtful whether he would have achieved anything like the fleeting operational success he gained.

Extracting any flexibility from the Führer, however, drained him. His mounting frustration over Hitler's way of war caused him to consider tendering his resignation on several occasions. When Hitler denied him urgent reinforcements for Fourth Panzer Army, he wrote to Zeitzler on 5 January 1943 asking to be relieved of command:

Should these proposals not be approved and this headquarters continue to be tied down to the same extent as hitherto, I cannot see that any useful purpose will be served by my continuing as commander of Army Group Don. In the circumstances it would appear more appropriate to replace me by a sub-directorate of the kind maintained by the Quartermaster-General.[23]

Hitler refused his request. Matters came to a head again towards the end of the month with the Führer's rejection of his demand to allow Sixth Army to surrender. His principal subordinates again advised him against resignation. His 'closest collaborator' Busse, according to Manstein's account, is recorded saying in late 1942: 'If I had not kept begging him [Manstein] to stay for the troops' sake, he'd have chucked the job back at Hitler long ago.'[24]

Notwithstanding his stated desire to step down, Manstein was probably right in his assertion that Hitler would not have accepted his resignation. The Führer tolerated and needed him for another year. The army group commander had further professional ambitions in any case. He knew that he was well qualified to take over from either Zeitzler or Keitel, or to assume overall command of the Eastern Front. This was a view shared by many of Germany's generals who criticized the conduct of operations. Hermann Balck, for example, commented in his diary on 17 February 1943 that 'the solution generally desired throughout the Army' is for 'Manstein to assume as Commander-in-Chief East'.[25]

Of more enduring interest are Manstein's comments *against* military resignation. He concluded that a senior commander 'is no more able to pack up and go home than any other soldier'. Furthermore, 'the soldier in the field is not in the pleasant position of a politician, who is always at liberty to climb off the band-wagon when things go wrong or the line taken by the Government does not suit him. A soldier has to fight where and when he is ordered.'[26] True enough for a politician in a democracy, but dictators such as Hitler are not in the habit of standing down: they either die of natural causes or come to a premature, violent end.

In early 1943, Manstein faced fighting some very difficult battles with Hitler in order to prevent any further disintegration on the southern wing as a result of renewed Soviet attacks. He had been wrestling with this problem since his assumption of command. With Stalingrad soon to fall, resolution of this issue became ever more urgent. It all revolved around securing a more coherent command of the Wehrmacht and the Eastern Front.

Important Visitors as Stalingrad Falls

By 26 January 1943, Headquarters Army Group South had established itself in Taganrog, a port on the Sea of Azov. That afternoon, Manstein received three visitors: Major General Rudolf Schmundt, Hitler's principal adjutant; General Erich Fellgiebel, his old '*Duz*' friend from their days serving together in Dresden during the 1920s; and Major Claus Schenk Graf von Stauffenberg, whom he met for the first time. The latter was a general staff officer in the organization section of the Army Staff based in Berlin. Eighteen months later, on 20 July 1944, he placed the bomb that nearly killed Hitler. The declared purpose of Stauffenberg's present visit, authorized by Zeitzler, was to discuss the raising of Russian volunteer units. If his real reason was to sound out Manstein as a potential supporter of the resistance, he was to depart disappointed.

By an alliterative play on names, Taganrog can be associated with Tauroggen in Lithuania, where a convention was signed in 30 December 1812 between Prussian and Russian forces, prompting the Prussian uprising against French occupation in the Wars of Liberation. Stauffenberg is alleged to have mentioned pointedly the word 'Tauroggen' in conversation. Was there a deliberate ambiguity here? Surely Stauffenberg was not encouraging any overture to the Russians. Far rather, was he not trying to appeal to the Field Marshal's sense of loyalty to his country in bringing about a change in political course?

What was said in private conversation between Manstein and Stauffenberg may never be known: the meeting has taken on almost a legendary status in the history of the military opposition to Hitler. Without doubt, Stahlberg's extensive record – based on what he recalled, forty years after the event, through a half-open door – has fed the story of a violent argument between the two about whether the Führer should relinquish supreme command, and forcibly so.[27]

The facts are that each of Manstein's visitors was entered into the headquarters log for separate office calls. The Field Marshal only left a very brief note of his guests in his private war diary, without making clear who was present:

> Schmundt came with Fellgiebel and Stauffenberg. Long conversation during which I try to make clear the requirement for a uniform command structure for the Wehrmacht and one in which the Führer will take on a Chief of the General Staff whom he really trusts. I stress most emphatically that any idea that the Führer should give up command of the army

is completely mistaken: first of all he would never do it, and secondly, because everything is bound up in trust in his person.[28]

There is no hint here whatsoever that any *coup d'état* against Hitler was discussed, as Peter Hoffmann has suggested in his *History of the German Resistance*.[29] That said, Manstein would have been extremely foolhardy to have committed all that was discussed in his private conversations to his diary.

What Manstein didn't mention is that he did have a second, private, session with Stauffenberg *after* having received Schmundt and the others. This is unclear in Stahlberg's account, who suggests that they were alone during their first meeting. Hans Breithaupt has offered a credible explanation of what happened. One of Manstein's staff officers, Raban Freiherr von Canstein, met with his chief, Colonel Eberhard Finckh, and Stauffenberg later that evening.[30] His recollection of Stauffenberg's immediate feedback from the conversation with the Field Marshal is that Manstein had stressed the impracticalities of any changes to Germany's political leadership. Internally, 'it would be too soon for the German people'; externally, it was now 'too late' with the recent Allied declaration at Casablanca of 'unconditional surrender'.[31]

Stauffenberg left empty-handed. The next day Manstein wrote to his wife, confiding cryptically:

> Yesterday Schmundt and Fellgiebel were here and also a Graf Stauffenberg. I had a very long discussion with Schmundt, from which I hope perhaps something will emerge. The others came with their worries as if I could provide them with remedies. The trust is always very touching, but how should I change things that are not within my power and possibility?[32]

On 27 January, Manstein had another discussion with Schmundt and Fellgiebel that went over much the same ground of the previous day. 'Fellgiebel wanted me to press myself on the Führer as Chief of the General Staff,' he noted in his diary. But he rejected this approach: 'A posting there only makes sense if I am called to that appointment, and accorded sufficient trust which is a necessary condition for the acceptance of any operational level proposals.'[33]

Manstein refused to act: from his perspective – with Stalingrad doomed – he had to remain focused on saving the southern wing of the Eastern Front. On the day that Sixth Army surrendered, he comforted his wife, writing that her concern about 'many in Stalingrad being disappointed in me' was 'really of no importance'. 'It may be', he continued, 'that many placed their hopes in me. Some even wrote to me, stating that if anyone was going to pull it off, it would be me.' Yet he conceded that the relief could not have succeeded: 'And I don't believe I could have changed matters for the better: you can be reassured of that.' Two days later, he wrote again about the fall of Stalingrad. Declining to comment about the failure of the relieving force to link up or Sixth Army's inability to break out, he placed the blame primarily on the poor weather, which had prevented the Luftwaffe from flying sufficient combat and supply sorties. 'This, and other [contributing] factors, lay outside my sphere of influence.'[34]

Rival Plans

By any reckoning, the strategic situation facing the German Army was dire. With the destruction of the Hungarian Second Army and the remnants of the Italian Eighth Army of Army Group B in mid January 1943 on the Upper Don River, Soviet forces had managed to create a significant gap below the German Second Army defending the Voronezh sector. Far to the south, Army Group A was being pushed north-westwards to Rostov whilst Manstein's army group, specifically his Fourth Panzer Army, struggled to keep open the crossing over the Don. Meanwhile, the rest of his force (Army Detachment Hollidt and the Fretter-Pico Group) was fighting a delaying action back to the middle Donets as the Red Army advanced towards Voroshilovgrad (now Lugansk).

To their opponents it appeared that the entire southern wing of the Eastern Front was about to collapse, or already in such a state. Not unnaturally in this context, optimism mounted on the Soviet side. As one expert analyst of the period has researched, *Stavka* now pondered plans to accelerate the offensive and force German forces back to the Dnepr River line and perhaps even beyond.' More specifically (see Map 10),

> Between 20 and 23 January the *Stavka* approved two plans for operations which it hoped would achieve that aim. The first, codenamed Operation 'Skachok' (Gallop), sought to liberate the Donbas region and drive German forces across the Dnepr River. The second, codenamed Operation 'Zvezda' (Star), aimed at liberating Kharkov and pushing German forces as far as possible to the west. The two *front* operations would occur simultaneously with final Soviet preparations to reduce the Stalingrad pocket. Elsewhere on the Eastern Front the Soviets launched supporting offensives.[35]

In attempting to exploit as much momentum as possible from their successes to date and resulting German weakness, the *Stavka* ordered that these fresh offensives should be conducted without any operational pause. The *fronts'* armies, corps and divisions received few if any replacements and had no time to re-equip or restock. A further limitation was that there were no significant operational reserves available, other than what could be released from Stalingrad once it capitulated. Soviet numerical superiority, however, was still guaranteed in both operations.

Operation GALLOP (also known as the Donbas Operation) was spearheaded by Vatutin's South-Western *Front* with support from the Voronezh and Southern *Fronts* to the north and south respectively. Operation STAR (the Kharkov–Kursk Operation) was the sole responsibility of General F. I. Golikov's Voronezh *Front*. GALLOP was launched on 29 January, whilst STAR followed five days later. Manstein, of course, did not have any detailed knowledge of Soviet planning but he had discerned *Stavka's* broad intentions easily, for their plan was 'obvious enough'. He feared that the German southern wing would be cut off and pushed back against the Sea of Azov or the Black Sea. In his view, this opening had been offered by the German Supreme Command 'on a silver platter'. Had the Soviets exploited this opportunity, the 'fate of the entire Eastern Front would have been sealed sooner or later'.[36] Thus the key strategic question boiled down to whether the Soviets would succeed in trapping Army Groups A and Don, or would Manstein be able to avert such a disaster?

At this critical stage of the war and his career, Manstein faced multiple challenges that educed his most inspirational leadership. Whilst he countered Soviet offensive operations with the limited options available, he confronted Hitler repeatedly in order to extract the necessary decisions and resources to enable his plans. In his memoirs, he described activities in this period as distinct 'phases'. Caution is required in using this term as it suggests that there was a coherent campaign plan into which these phases neatly fitted. There was not. Rather, the successive 'phases' were used by Manstein in his narrative to facilitate his retrospective analysis of events.

As it became clear that Stalingrad could not be held and Sixth Army would be lost, Manstein realized there was a way in which, against all the odds, 'a grave crisis could have been turned into victory'. His operational idea was based on surrendering territory and enticing Soviet forces to over-extend themselves into an area of his choosing. When their offensive had culminated, at the critical time and place he would then unleash a counter-offensive that would strike at an exposed flank, catching them off-balance. This backhand blow (*Schlagen aus der Nachhand*) would be effected by withdrawing from the Caucasus, Lower Don, Donets and potentially as far west as the Lower Dnepr. The forces saved by shortening the front would be concentrated into an area somewhere around Kharkov, and then employed in an 'envelopment operation with the aim of pushing our pursuer back against the sea and destroying him there'.[37] In a sudden, powerful transition from the defensive to the offensive, Manstein was emulating what Clausewitz described graphically as 'the flashing sword of vengeance'.[38]

This basic operational concept, although never executed on the ambitious scale he conceived, provided the intellectual stimulus for his counterattacks in February and March 1943 that stabilized the southern wing of the Eastern Front until the summer. Had he been given the freedom to plan and execute this scheme of manoeuvre on a larger scale, involving all the forces of Army Groups A, B and Don, then he might just have prevented German defeat on the Eastern Front. Although he promoted his views to OKH on two occasions, once in early January and again in March 1943, Hitler never approved this bold, undoubtedly hazardous, operation. Relinquishing all the ground captured at such heavy loss during the summer campaign of 1942 went against the German leader's instincts; in any case, a vision of a counterblow constructed in this manner lay beyond his operational understanding. Therefore Manstein was forced by events to improvise operations along these lines rather than following any elegantly formulated campaign plan. Much of what he decided and directed was extemporized under extreme enemy and time pressure, whilst taking huge risks, and prising decisions out of Hitler at the last safe moment, and sometimes beyond that.

In the face of the Führer's trenchant opposition to any voluntary withdrawal, particularly if the region concerned – such as the Don basin – had industrial benefit to the Reich, Manstein was only able to achieve a partial solution to his grand design. It involved building up defensive shoulders on the northern and southern flanks, holding firm to the Kharkov area and the Mius position respectively, drawing the enemy into a funnel-shaped void in between, whilst 'leapfrogging' his mobile forces from east to west in order to generate sufficient striking power for his counterblow between the Donets and the Dnepr.[39] Concentrating the necessary air and land forces to achieve this joint scheme of manoeuvre was a perilous enterprise. It was all conducted in the midst of winter, with limited road and rail capacities, when Soviet forces were attacking continuously and threatening to pre-empt Manstein's moves.

Manstein's counterstroke proved a masterpiece of operational and logistic design, and in the integration of air and land forces. There is hardly a better example of such a manoeuvre available in the Second World War. Hence it became a popular topic for general staff study and debate within the United States Army and the Bundeswehr, as it appeared to offer a useful approach (if not a patent solution) in dealing with Soviet offensive superiority during the Cold War.[40] The British general (later field marshal) Sir Nigel Bagnall also drew inspiration from Manstein's elastic method of mobile defence during the mid 1980s in revising successively the operational approaches of the 1st (British) Corps and NATO's Northern Army Group in Germany.[41]

To gain a full appreciation of Manstein's daunting problem and novel solution, it is useful to consider the classic operational factors of *forces*, *space* and *time*.

After the loss of Sixth Army and the four Axis armies, the Germans were significantly outnumbered. In his memoirs, Manstein makes much of this fact: at the end of March 1943 he had thirty-two divisions at his disposal in Army Group South (formerly Don) whilst facing no fewer than '341 enemy formations, consisting of rifle divisions, armoured or mechanized brigades, and cavalry divisions'.[42] Thus he could claim that he was outnumbered by as much as 7:1 overall, even taking into account the lower average combat strengths of Soviet formations in comparison with their German counterparts. More recent expert research has shown this figure to be an exaggeration. For example, the overall correlation of forces during Operation GALLOP was initially only 2:1 in infantry and 4:1 in tanks to the Soviet advantage.[43] That said, Soviet doctrine aimed at achieving much higher local superiorities, often seeking and achieving as much as 10:1 in critical breakthrough sectors. As ever, great care needs to be exercised in comparing numbers as the fighting power of a force rests also on the *quality* of its equipment, logistics, doctrine, training and command. At this stage of the war and beyond, for all the strategic and operational constraints they were operating under, the majority of German forces could still count on being *tactically* superior to their enemies, whether Soviet, British or American.

The area of the rival Soviet and German operations in the first three months of 1943 was vast, even excluding the area south of Rostov-on-Don to the Caucasus. From Kharkov in the north to the Sea of Azov in the south is approximately 700 kilometres; from the big Don bend in the east to the Lower Dnepr and the crossings at Dnepropetrovsk and Zaporozhye in the west is over 400 kilometres. It includes the important coal- and steel-producing region of the Donets Basin (the Donbas) and the cluster of smog-filled cities around Donetsk (formerly Stalino). The river Donets transects the area, flowing in a generally south-easterly direction till it joins the Don 100 kilometres north-east of Rostov. West of the Donets, the smaller river Mius flows south directly into the Sea of Azov near Taganrog. In overall extent, this immense combat zone was approximately 280,000 square kilometres, representing roughly the eastern half of Ukraine's land mass, or an area larger than that of the United Kingdom but not quite the size of Poland.[44]

Manstein did not have much time to play with as decisions from Hitler came invariably either late or too late. A prime example was the much-deferred matter of withdrawing First Panzer Army from the Caucasus. Overall, he had to contend with the fact that he only had limited time available until the spring thaw came towards the end of March that rendered most movement near to impossible. What alarmed Manstein primarily was the possibility of Soviet forces seizing the Dnepr crossings and the vital Don bridge at Rostov in the meantime and so dislocating his planned counter-manoeuvre. Zaporozhye on the Lower Dnepr lay 420 kilometres from the enemy front at Kasankaya on the Don. To make his point, he compared this potential Soviet operational bound with his panzer march of four days in June 1941 from Tilsit to Dvinsk at the head of LVI Corps. He had fought then 'against opposition that was certainly tougher than anything the Italian or Hungarian Armies could offer on the Don'.[45]

Questions of Command and Manoeuvre

Manstein's ability to realize his plan to hold, then defeat, the Soviet offensive between the Donets and the Dnepr rested on gaining the maximum freedom of manoeuvre from Hitler whilst at the same time preserving that for his subordinate formations. Much of the enduring benefit of Manstein's *Lost Victories*, other than its intrinsic historical value, lies in his analysis of the challenges of operational command. Although the context, scale and scope of operations in contemporary conflicts are greatly different from those which Manstein directed, there is still considerable merit in reflecting on his writing today. Hence those responsible for the planning and conduct of major combat operations at large formation level (corps and echelons above) should have much to learn from his practical advice, borne from hard-fought experience.

Manstein maintained that the basis of his success in early 1943 lay in the adherence by army and army group commanders and staffs to two well-established German imperatives of command, namely: 'conduct operations in a mobile and elastic manner'; and, secondly, 'give commanders at all levels as much scope for initiative and independence as possible'. These long-established German principles, he stressed, were 'greatly at variance with Hitler's way of thinking'. Indeed, the Führer 'repeatedly sought to meddle in the operations of subordinate head-quarters by issuing specific orders of his own'.[46] Perhaps for the benefit of members of the newly formed Bundeswehr as much for the general reader, Manstein elaborated on the second principle. He described what the British now term Mission Command (*Auftragstaktik* and Mission Orders in German and American usage respectively), building on his earlier remarks on the subject.[47]

It is worth quoting Manstein at some length in order to characterize the historical German art of command that he fought so hard to maintain during the war, although ultimately unsuccessfully because of Hitler's outright opposition to such flexible methods:

> It has always been the particular forte of German command to grant wide scope to the independence of subordinate commanders – to allot them *missions* which leave the method of execution to the discretion of the commander concerned. From time immemorial – certainly since the days of Moltke the Elder – this principle has distinguished Germany's military from that of other armies. The latter, far from giving the same latitude to subordinate commanders at the tactical and operational levels, have always tended to prescribe, by means of long and detailed instructions, the way orders should be carried out or to make tactical action conform to a specific template.[48]

In contrast, the German method, in Manstein's professional view:

> ... is really rooted in the German character, which – contrary to all the nonsense talked about 'blind obedience' – has as a strong streak of individuality and – possibly as part of its Germanic heritage – finds a certain pleasure in taking risks. The granting of such independence to subordinate commanders does, of course, presuppose that all members of the military hierarchy are imbued [in flesh and blood] with certain tactical or operational principles. Perhaps only the School of the German General Staff could have produced this consistency of outlook.[49]

One might take issue today with the view that Mission Command can only be exercised by Germans. None the less, the willingness to take calculated risks – not rash gambles – within a given framework of allo-cated authority marks this particular style of command. It is one that requires entrusted, independently minded commanders who are keen to grasp the initiative, acting purposefully whilst following their superior commanders' broad intentions.

Manstein remained open to the possibility that the senior commander may have to intervene in the command of lower echelons. Not all subordinates are equally capable, for example, and there are specific occasions that require more detailed orders than others. But he warned against 'over-command' expressly, noting the 'more complex the situation and the smaller the forces with which he has to manage, the more [the commander] is tempted to meddle in the business of his subordinates'. Such interference from above was one of Manstein's pet hates. Likewise, he advised against offering unaccountable 'off-the-record "advice"' to subordinate headquarters because it 'kills all initiative and hides responsibility'.[50]

Within his own army group headquarters, Manstein maintained that he and his staff only intervened in the operations of subordinate armies when it was imperative to do so. His record is good in this regard. In comparison, overdirection from Hitler (and OKH on his instructions) was commonplace. Even more frustrating was Hitler's 'dilatoriness in the taking of urgently needed decisions'.[51] To get around this problem, Manstein and his staff made recourse to an old trick. They would report that unless an OKH directive was received by a certain date or time, they would act anyway at their own discretion. Whether such behaviour improved mutual understanding and trust between his headquarters and OKH in the long term, he was careful to omit.

Some senior commanders find fault in neighbouring formations, particularly if their own plans are adversely affected by others' inaction. Manstein was particularly critical of Army Group A's slow disengagement from the Caucasus. Accepting that Hitler had delayed the necessary decision until 29 December 1942, by the end of January 1943, First Panzer Army had yet to cross the Don at Rostov and form up in the Middle Donets as required in the 'leapfrog' plan. By way of small consolation, the northern half of this army had come under his command on 27 January, facilitating urgent co-ordination with Fourth Panzer Army and Army Detachment Hollidt. In direct reference to his southern neighbour, Manstein felt that headquarters and troops tend to get too fixed and comfortable in their defensive positions, and particularly so in winter, a 'hardening up process which inevitably sets in whenever mobile operations degenerate into static warfare'. He strongly condemned the result: 'troops and formation staffs lose the knack of quickly adapting themselves to the changes which daily occur in a war of movement.'[52]

In such a war, with few fixed lines and plenty of gaps for an enterprising enemy to exploit, no headquarters remains invulnerable to either ground or air attack. On 7 January 1943, for example, the situation looked alarming for the commander and staff of Army Group Don at Novocherkassk. A weak Soviet force appeared 20 kilometres away on the northern bank of the Don when Cossack troops and customs and border police guarding that stretch of the river had melted away. The enemy was dispatched by a scratch tank force drawn from a nearby armoured workshop, led by a captain on Manstein's staff: a simple but nevertheless effective expedient in the heat of battle.[53]

There is a surely a contemporary lesson here for armed forces. Whereas in peacekeeping (and even in counterinsurgency operations), it is perfectly sensible to erect and maintain static headquarters and troop locations, the same is not necessarily the case in major combat operations. All units – whether combat or logistic – and formation headquarters (at least their 'forward' elements) must be capable of moving quickly and efficiently. In this regard, Manstein practised what he preached. Enemy pressure and the unfolding of his operational plan required the successive moves of his army group headquarters westwards from Novocherkassk to Taganrog on 12 January, followed on the 29th with a further move to Stalino. Only on 12 February did he and his staff occupy their 'final' headquarters location near the Dnepr crossing at Zaporozhye.

Wrangling with Hitler

All the much vaunted German flexibility of command at the tactical and operational levels was of little utility if the overarching strategy and command structure were defective. Under Hitler's leadership, from mid-summer 1941 onwards, they were. Nothing that Manstein could do would alter that basic truth. Although he was never able to face down Hitler on matters of grand strategy, being less informed on political and economic matters, he was none the less determined to fight his corner on matters of military strategy and of high command. There were two major occasions in February 1943 when he raised both, closely related, critical issues with the Führer. The first opportunity came on the 6th of that month.

Since the failure to relieve Stalingrad, there had been no relief for Manstein and his hard-pressed forces. His subordinate commands (First and Fourth Panzer Armies, and Army Detachment Hollidt) had yet to reach their planned locations: respectively on the Middle Donets, held ready between the Donets and Dnepr to intercept the Soviet penetration, and the Mius line. To achieve this operational design with limited resources at hand, he had to wrestle with Hitler over the necessity of giving up the Lower Don and hence the eastern portion of the Donbas. This became a highly contentious issue that taxed Manstein's powers of patience and persuasion to the outmost.

Whilst Hitler wanted to retain the region for its coal – and deny that resource to the Russians – the Germans could not hold on to it without significant additional forces being made available, and quickly so. What made matters even worse by mid January was the imminent danger of the Red Army forcing a wide breach in the already porous German front from Voroshilovgrad northwards to Voronezh. If they achieved that, then Soviet forces could continue their advance further west to Kharkov, strike south-west over the Donets to the Dnepr crossings or drive to the coast of the Sea of Azov. Achieving the latter was indeed the mission of the South-Western *Front*'s principal mobile group, commanded by Lieutenant General M. M. Popov, who with four weak tank corps (amounting to only 212 tanks) was tasked with achieving a deep penetration of 300 kilometres to Mariupol in order to block any German withdrawal from the Donbas.[54]

The only ray of hope for the German defence was the SS Panzer Corps (with three powerful panzer grenadier divisions) now in transit from France, due to complete its assembly around Kharkov by the middle of February. Yet that corps was neither sufficiently strong to close the 'gap', nor would it be available in time to secure the Lower Don and Donets. As Manstein saw it, 'The southern wing of the German armies could not close this gap with its own forces if it remained on the Lower Don. Nor could it go on fighting there in isolation if the expected reinforcements took a long time to arrive and deployed far to the rear.' In his memoirs, he addressed this dilemma with his trademark, irrefutable military logic:

> The battle being fought by the southern wing and the deployment of new forces must be so attuned to one another in a spatial sense as to become operationally coherent. Either the new forces must be made to deploy swiftly and relatively far to the east, in which case it would be possible for the Army Group to remain on the Lower Don and Donets, or else they could not, and the Army Group would have to be pulled back to join them. If one of these two courses were not taken, the enemy would have an opportunity to cut off the whole southern wing before any reinforcements could make their presence felt.[55]

He then added, as if there was any doubt in the matter, that the Chief of the General Staff, General Zeitzler, had agreed with him. Convincing

Zeitzler was necessary but not sufficient. Manstein needed to argue his case vociferously with Hitler: it was simply not possible to hold on to the Don–Donets 'salient' with the forces at the disposal of Army Group Don.

In early February, the operational situation deteriorated dramatically under the impact of Operation GALLOP. On Manstein's north-eastern flank, west of Voroshilovgrad, Soviet forces had crossed the Middle Donets on a broad front. If they had wheeled sharp left and attacked south-eastwards from the vicinity of Slavyansk, they would have unhinged the Mius line, which Army Detachment Hollidt had yet to occupy. Meanwhile, on his south-eastern front, the enemy increased its pressure on Fourth Panzer Army covering the passage of First Panzer Army over the Don at Rostov. Manstein now feared for the security of the Dnepr crossings much further to the west and demanded the release of further reinforcements from OKH to protect them. On 3 February, he presented his assessment of recent developments in a detailed estimate of the situation.

Two telephone conversations between Manstein and Zeitzler the next day exemplify their mutual exasperation with Hitler, despite the formal tone. In the morning, Manstein called: 'I now reckon with the launch shortly of an [enemy] attack over the Don to the north.' Zeitzler replied:

> I have received the extensive estimate of the situation (of 3. 2.) from the Field Marshal and regard it as quite excellent. I am exceptionally grateful to the Field Marshal for it.
>
> *Manstein:* If something decisive doesn't happen soon, the situation here will only get more serious. The enemy will redeploy further forces from Stalingrad towards Kursk and to the south.
>
> *Zeitzler:* I completely agree with the assessment of the Field Marshal. One cannot win a war with will alone.
>
> *Manstein:* Inform the Führer once more that I really must have freedom of manoeuvre in order to command. He always thinks that I demand it only to be able to retreat more quickly. The opposite is the case: I need it in order to plan well in advance.

Manstein phoned again that evening: 'The situation has developed precisely as we predicted it would.'

> *Zeitzler:* At noon today, I gave yesterday's estimate of the situation by the Field Marshal to the Führer.... [He] views the current situation very optimistically. He believes that the Russians, after such long offensive operations, must soon run out of puff. Therefore it is more than ever

important to hold on hard. I replied that, in my opinion, that moment is not by any means to be expected yet. I am of the view that the proposal of the Field Marshal is inevitably required and there is absolutely no scope left for any wavering.

Manstein: Absolutely. The longer one waits, the worse it gets. If the Führer doesn't trust me, then he must seek another.

Zeitzler: The same applies to me.[56]

On the morning of 6 February, Hitler responded to the mounting pressure from his Chief of the General Staff by sending his personal Condor aircraft to bring Manstein to Rastenburg, East Prussia, for the evening briefing. As Manstein conceded, the long overdue head-to-head meeting may also have come about at the instigation of Hitler's principal staff officer Schmundt, who had recently visited Headquarters Army Group Don.

Shortly after his arrival at the Rastenburg airfield, Manstein conferred with Hitler for four hours around the map table. The meeting started in dramatic fashion. Stahlberg described the scene as Schmundt announced loudly, 'Gentlemen – the Führer':

> The waiting men fell silent and Hitler gave them his angled salute without speaking. He glanced round once, then shook hands with Field Marshal von Manstein only. There was a paralysed silence in the room.
>
> What I then witnessed was a masterstroke of Hitlerian psychology: 'Gentlemen,' he began, 'first I would like to say a word about Stalingrad. I alone bear responsibility for Stalingrad. And now,' turning to General Zeitzler, 'the current situation in the East, please.'[57]

Not surprisingly in the wake of recent developments, the atmosphere that evening remained unusually cold at the Führer's *Wolfsschanze* headquarters. As Engel recorded, 'it was a dour, icy talk, partially in a larger group, but mostly smaller circle. In a refreshing manner v. M[anstein] put forward clear demands: withdraw to the Mius, more units to the front, evacuate the Donets region.'[58]

Manstein, moreover, wanted to raise an important matter other than the conduct of future operations. He wished to induce Hitler into making urgent changes to the structure of the German High Command. As he recalled, 'the outcome of [Hitler's] style of leadership – Stalingrad – gave me adequate reason for raising it.'[59] This was an opportunity too good to be missed. Crucially, however, Manstein would not call on Hitler to resign or to end the war on this or on any subsequent occasion. Accepting the former approach could have been suicidal, his prime interest was in finding a way to run military affairs in a more coherent fashion. Without such a solution, to his mind there would be little prospect of forcing a draw on the Eastern Front.

Judging that the Führer would never stand down as commander-in-chief of the Wehrmacht, Manstein advanced a case for achieving uniformity of command through the appointment of '*one* Chief-of-Staff, whom [Hitler] must trust implicitly and at the same time vest with the corresponding responsibility and authority'. What he implied here was not only an end to the two competing staffs, OKW led by Keitel and OKH by Zeitzler, but also the establishment of a new post of a fully empowered principal military advisor to the Führer. This solution, Manstein considered, 'would not damage his prestige', yet at the same time would 'guarantee an impeccable military command for the future'.[60] Perhaps; he had been propounding similar ideas for the better organization of the German High Command (*Spitzengliederung*) unsuccessfully since 1937.

Hitler would have none of it. He quietly dismissed Manstein's argument by pointing out his previous disappointments with Blomberg and Brauchitsch, and declared that he could not impose a chief of staff above Göring. Engel's record augments Manstein's account:

> To our astonishment F[ührer] listened to it passively. Afterwards a private talk. Schm[undt] found out that v. M[anstein] touched on the subject of the Army High Command, requested a C-in-C East and a Wehrmacht Chief of the General Staff, this latter with the objective of finally getting rid of Keitel out of [the] Führer's HQ.[61]

The sad fact remained that Hitler, even at a moment of acute vulnerability following the debacle at Stalingrad, would not devolve any meaningful responsibility to a senior military figure in a position to challenge him over his conduct of the war. He neither desired nor received independent professional strategic advice from the likes of an Alanbrooke or Marshall. It remained difficult enough for Manstein and his fellow army group commanders to influence and direct business at the operational level.

In fact, Manstein had only raised the sensitive issue of command towards the end of his session with Hitler, having devoted the majority of the time available in seeking freedom of manoeuvre. The central dispute was Manstein's request for permission to withdraw from the Lower Donets and so pull in his eastern flank to the Mius. He knew that gaining such a decision from the Führer would prove no easy task. So first of all he tried to shock him with the gravity of the prevailing situation. He stressed that in trying to hold on to the Donets Basin,

Germany would not only lose that region but also Army Group Don, and, in turn, Army Group A. Thus the only sensible way to 'avert the catastrophe that threatened to overtake us' was to 'abandon part of it at the right moment'. If he expected the Führer to weaken his stance at this point, he was disappointed, so he then proceeded to explain his operational justification yet again to Hitler, who 'listened with the utmost composure'.[62]

Privately, Manstein reported to his wife that his long, four-hour discussion with 'Effendi' was 'very impressive, and incidentally, also quite harmonious'. 'It's such a pity', he wrote, 'that I can't tell you anything about it.' The next day, he alluded to the operational situation: 'As far as my concerns and decisions go, it would be easier if I had more freedom in the latter.'[63] For once, his hope would not remain a distant dream as the Führer would soon have to cut him some much-needed, albeit temporary, slack.

Meanwhile, First Panzer Army was retiring towards the Middle Donets. In Manstein's view, it was essential to initiate immediately the second 'leapfrog' move by transferring Fourth Panzer Army from the Lower Don to the west of First Panzer Army to 'intercept the still not acute, but nonetheless inevitable threat of an enemy envelopment between the Donets and the Dnepr'. Only by this bold manoeuvre, together with the employment of the reinforcements now coming up, would it be possible to 'restore the situation on the German southern wing of the Eastern Front – i.e. the entire stretch of front from the coast of the Sea of Azov to the right wing of Central Army Group'. As the stakes were so high, 'there was not a day to lose' over reaching a decision.[64]

Hitler realized, of course, that any withdrawal of Fourth Panzer Army would mean giving up the exposed Don–Donets salient and the consequent loss of the Donets Basin. For several hours the two exchanged economic and military arguments for and against its retention. Stahlberg considered them to be 'completely at cross-purposes'. Whilst Manstein concerned himself with achieving 'victory between the Don and the Dnieper', in contrast 'Hitler's thoughts were concentrated on ore, coal, and manganese and arms production'. Of his commander-in-chief, he observed that 'Manstein's manner was amazingly carefree, almost as if he were facing a seminar of young trainee General Staff Officers rather than his military superior. But I remember that the atmosphere was frosty.'[65]

Stubbornly, Hitler could not bring himself to make the necessary decision. He next brought climatic conditions into his deliberations, declaring that in the spring thaw the Don would become an 'impassable obstacle over which the enemy could not possibly attack before the summer'. This suggestion represented the last straw for Manstein. He was not willing to risk his army group 'on the hope of a quite unseasonable change of weather'. In the face of the Field Marshal's persistence, the Führer agreed finally to the withdrawal of Army Group Don's exposed eastern front to the *Maulwurf* (mole) position on the Mius.[66]

Manstein supplemented his detailed account of this meeting with Hitler with an explanation of operational level command, comparing his – the necessary – approach with that of the German leader. It remains one of the most instructive pieces of his military advice:

> all considerations of an operational nature are ultimately based – especially when one has lost the initiative to the enemy – on appreciations [estimates of the situation] or hypotheses regarding the course of action which the enemy may be expected to take. While no one can prove beforehand that a situation will develop in such-and-such a way, the only successful military commander is *one who can think ahead*. He must be able to see through the veil in which the enemy's future actions are always wrapped, at least to the extent of correctly judging the possibilities open to both the enemy and himself. The greater one's sphere of command, of course, the further ahead one must think. And the greater the distances to be covered and the formations to be moved, the longer is the interval that must elapse before the decision one has taken can produce tangible results.[67]

He added, not surprisingly, that this sort of long-term thinking was 'not to Hitler's taste'. The Führer, however, was quite capable of planning well in advance when he wanted to, as evidenced by his decision to mount the Ardennes counter-offensive in December 1944. Although Manstein was ultimately successful in extracting the right decision from his supreme commander on this occasion, he had to repeat the process of presenting afresh his operational ideas many times.

In stark contrast to Hitler's strategic gloss and impulsive military decision-making, typically resting on his famous *will*, Manstein, the skilled chess player, always attempted to see through a sequence of operational moves and counter-moves. This approach was as much an art as any science as it depended on getting into the mind of his opponents. Although it was far more an intuitive than a mechanistic process, it also rested on sound estimates of forces, time and space, then and into the future. His frustration at Hitler's inability (or perhaps unwillingness) to think beyond the immediate now spilled over into active criticism. When told by Zeitzler that one of his reports (11 February 1943) had been considered by the Führer to be 'much too far-reaching', Manstein replied tartly that 'it is only right for an army group to think four to eight weeks ahead – unlike the Supreme Command, which never [seems] to look any further than the next three days'.[68] In this regard, he was being unfair to Zeitzler, who tried consistently to represent his views faithfully to Hitler. 'Shooting the messenger', however, has long been a favourite military sport, and not one confined to the German Army and its famous General Staff.

A Crisis Bigger than Stalingrad?

Such was the dynamic nature of the operational situation and the associated requirement for fresh decisions that the next meeting with Hitler followed on 17–19 February. Over the intervening ten days, one emergency was quickly superseded by the next as the Soviet double offensive (Operations GALLOP and STAR) developed momentum and threatened to envelop the entire southern wing of the Eastern Front.

The growing crisis had not even reached a climax when Soviet forces of the Voronezh *Front* in executing Operation STAR by 9 February took Belgorod and Kursk within Army Group B's sector north of Kharkov. Three armies (40th, 69th and 3rd Tank) now converged on that city. To the south, as GALLOP continued, the Soviet 6th Army drove its attack westwards beyond the Northern Donets.[69] Between that enemy axis and the right wing of Army Group Centre, well to the north, lay the battered elements of Army Group B's Second Army to the west of Kursk, together with the newly formed army detachment under General of Mountain Troops Hubert Lanz. This force was now in action in a wide arc strung out east and north-east of Kharkov on over-extended frontages.[70] If the enemy were not halted and the yawning gap closed, then not only Kharkov would be lost but also, far more seriously, armoured spearheads would head for the Dnepr north of Dnepropetrovsk.

The latent danger of being outflanked in great depth, which had so haunted Manstein in recent weeks, was now becoming very real. At its worst extent, if Soviet forces succeeded in forcing the river on a broad front, they could block the approaches to the Crimea and the crossing at Kherson. The result would be the complete envelopment of Army Groups B and Don, and the isolation of Army Group A, stuck fast on its bridgehead on the Kuban peninsula. Thus he called once again for urgent reinforcements to secure the Dnepr (at least six divisions) and further forces to bolster up Army Group B.[71] It was increasingly evident that Manstein now saw himself being responsible not only for his own army group but also for his northern and southern neighbours.

In the light of the acute crisis affecting the southern wing, OKH realized belatedly that an urgent reorganization of the command structure on the Eastern Front was required. Although it considered subordinating Army Group A to Manstein, which would have made sense as that army group now comprised one army only (the Seventeenth), this radical step was not taken. The recent promotion of its commander, Ewald von Kleist, to field marshal on 1 February 1943 may have been a limiting factor. However, Army Group B was disbanded; its Second Army was subordinated to Army Group Centre whilst Army Detachment Lanz was subsumed into Manstein's widened command, retitled Army Group South on 12 February. He recorded in his memoirs that this change was welcome as it allowed his headquarters to 'exercise *exclusive* command at the decisive place and the decisive time'.[72]

None the less, Manstein's most pressing problems remained obtaining urgently required reinforcements and gaining the necessary time to deploy them before being outmanoeuvred by the enemy. He sent a fresh estimate to OKH on 11 February, stressing several points. First of all he complained about the inappropriate correlation and distribution of forces. According to his figures, whereas Army Groups North and Centre were dealing with an enemy superiority of 4:1, Army Groups B and Don – even taking into account recent reinforcements – were facing at least 8:1. Secondly, the differing terrain and tactical conditions needed to be taken into account. Whereas the two army groups to the north (North and Centre) were defending in close country from well-established positions, this was certainly not the case in the south. Apart from the newly arrived SS Panzer Corps, Manstein's depleted divisions had been in hard combat for three months in open country. Finally, and perhaps the most significant argument he could present, was the undeniable fact that the German southern wing had been, and remained, the focus of the Soviet winter campaign. Taking these points together, he felt 'it was inadmissible that we should continue to be left at such numerical disadvantage'.[73]

When Manstein submitted his latest appreciation, powerful Soviet forces now threatened Kharkov directly: from the north, 40th Army; from the east, 69th Army; from the south-east and south, 3rd Tank Army. As the fourth largest city of the Soviet Union and one of its biggest industrial centres, its retention had become a matter of prestige to Hitler. On 13 February, he ordered the city to be held 'at all costs'. Manstein queried this but before he received an answer, events had taken their own course. By 14 February, after heavy fighting on its approaches and suburbs, the city was in acute danger of being encircled. On this occasion, he noted, 'circumstances proved stronger than Hitler's will'. SS General (*Gruppenführer*) Paul Hausser, commander of the SS Panzer Corps defending Kharkov, on 15 February took the unilateral decision to evacuate it against the explicit orders of Hitler and Lanz. Manstein, however, privately agreed with Hausser's action, having already demanded that the SS Panzer Corps be employed offensively rather than being isolated in the city.[74]

In Manstein's opinion, had Hausser been an army general, he would have been court-martialled by Hitler. He declined to make the obvious comparison with the treatment of Count Sponeck who had made a similar decision to withdraw from the exposed Kerch peninsula on the Crimea. Lanz became the scapegoat for the loss of Kharkov; he was replaced by General of Panzer Troops Werner Kempf on the rather unconvincing grounds that, as an armoured officer, he was more suited than Lanz, the mountain infantryman. Far more likely, Lanz's inability to grip the SS Panzer Corps sufficiently was the principal reason for his removal.[75]

On 16 February, the situation took another turn for the worse. Army Group Centre failed to close the gap between west of Kursk and north of Kharkov. Even more worryingly, German intelligence reports now confirmed that Soviet forces were advancing in strength towards Pavlograd and Dnepropetrovsk, exploiting the 150-kilometre-wide hole between Army Detachment Lanz and First Panzer Army. Furthermore, the promised flow of reinforcements had slackened off. The crisis was fast approaching its apogee.

That night Hitler decided to fly to Manstein's newly established headquarters in the industrial centre of Zaporozhye on the Dnepr. His army adjutant, Engel, informed Stahlberg that the Führer would arrive on 17 February and stay for three days. After alerting Colonel Georg Schulze-Büttger, the new operations chief, and putting a series of frantic preparations in hand, Stahlberg thought it wise to check with his commander.[76]

Manstein's immediate response on being told the news was: 'Did you have to wake me up for that?' Just as his ADC was leaving, he asked: 'Tell me, Stahlberg, what does Effendi really want here?' Stahlberg replied: 'It is not for me to judge.' Then he heard Manstein say, as if half asleep, 'Yes, yes, Effendi often has a nose for a propaganda coup.'[77] Perhaps Zeitzler had already talked up the prospects for Manstein's intended counterblow?

At noon on 17 February, two Condor aircraft swooped down over Zaporozhye airfield and landed. Manstein greeted the Supreme Commander, who chatted quietly with him and Busse. Following a short delay whilst SS guards checked Hitler's temporary accommodation, a motorcade of staff cars took the Führer and his accompanying party to the headquarters; a silent local population and cheering members of the German garrison lined the roadsides.

On arrival, Manstein introduced his ADC to Hitler, who shook hands and allowed Stahlberg to take his coat. Stahlberg recalled:

> and at that point I discovered with a shudder that Hitler had very bad breath. As I took his coat there was a savage outburst from the Alsatian bitch and I admit that I was not too happy, faced with her bared teeth and her crouching posture, ready to spring. But ... she turned out to be an extremely well-trained animal. 'Down, Blondi, down!' her master shouted, and Blondi obeyed at once. I hung the coat on the clothes' stand and I could have sworn that in the pockets ... there were two pistols. Alternatively the coat may have had a bullet-proof lining. At all events it was unusually heavy.[78]

Manstein and Stahlberg were then dismissed and later called back to Hitler on the arrival of General Zeitzler, who had been travelling separately.

The conference started that afternoon. With his uncanny eye for detail, Stahlberg observed of Hitler: 'His appearance shocked me. His skin was slack and yellowish, he was unshaven and the lapels of his double-breasted grey uniform tunic were spotted, apparently with food stains. His stance made a disturbing impression on me: his head hanging forward from his shoulders, his stomach projecting without restraint. He looked like a used-up man, a sick man.'[79]

Manstein started his first session with Hitler with a formal review of the situation. From north to south: Army Detachment Lanz had evacuated Kharkov and withdrawn south-westwards; First Panzer Army had halted the enemy in bitter fighting south of the Middle Donets 'but [had] not yet finished him off'; the battle with enemy forces in the Kramatorskaya area 'was still undecided'; and Army Detachment Hollidt had just reached its position on the Mius, 'closely pursued by the enemy'.[80] Manstein omitted to mention his intentions for Hoth's uncommitted Fourth Panzer Army at this stage.

So far so good: the awkward part of the briefing came when Manstein explained his plan of attack to Hitler, designed to not just block but rather slice off the enemy offensive. He intended to launch the SS Panzer

Corps from the area of Krasnograd southwards towards Pavlograd in close concert with Fourth Panzer Army's thrust coming up from the south towards that town. Together, these forces would 'smash the enemy advancing through the broad gap between First Panzer Army and Army Detachment Lanz'. Only on successful completion of this first operation, ensuring that 'there was no further danger that First Panzer Army and Army Detachment Hollidt would be cut off', would he 'proceed to attack in the Kharkov area'.[81]

The Führer disapproved of Manstein's desired sequence of operations. He refused to accept that the enemy pouring through the gap between Army Detachment Lanz and First Panzer Army represented such a serious threat, and feared that any mobile operations between the Dnepr and the Donets would soon get bogged down in the mud. Manstein was right to discern that Hitler wished to recapture Kharkov 'at the earliest possible date, which he hoped would be when the SS Panzer Corps had assembled its full complement of divisions'.[82]

Hitler's opposition to Manstein's intent derived from his predilection for seizing terrain objectives rather than destroying enemy groupings. The army group commander, whose understanding of operational art far exceeded the Führer's, knew that the sounder operational solution – particularly when facing a numerically superior enemy – was to defeat him by manoeuvre rather than conducting a static defence. As the war continued, Hitler's firm desire to hold on to urban centres evolved into a formal policy of Feste Plätze, which immobilized and squandered tens of thousands of German troops in defence of indefensible 'fortresses'.[83]

Manstein was forced to justify his plan once again in painful detail, setting out the rationale for his desired sequence of operations. First, he pointed out that the situation was such that 'a prior condition for any stroke in the direction of Kharkov was the removal of the threat to the Dnepr crossings'. Dramatically, he then produced a trump card: 'Unless the communications across this river are kept open, neither First Panzer Army nor Army Detachment Hollidt will survive.' Furthermore, any operation to retake Kharkov would require 'the co-operation of at least a part of Fourth Panzer Army'. Still Hitler would not agree. So Manstein turned around one of the Führer's arguments against him. Precisely because of the spring thaw that would put an end to mobile operations, it would come first in the area between the Donets and the Dnepr 'before it affected the country around and north of Kharkov'. In this manner, Manstein reasoned that there would still be time to mount the attack on that city after completing the first operation in defeating the enemy advancing between Army Detachment Lanz and First Panzer Army. 'It was more than doubtful, he concluded, whether the two operations could be carried out the other way around.'[84]

Hitler still would not bow to Manstein's logic, and so 'another interminable discussion ensued'. Sensing deadlock, Manstein then played for time and declared that the decision about the committal of the SS Panzer Corps – north or south – could be put off for the next day as the Corps could not be launched in any case before 19 February. He knew, but didn't tell Hitler, that Fourth Panzer Army would not be ready to attack before that day either. Hence it was safe to postpone.[85]

No doubt catching Manstein's mood, Stahlberg summed up the first session with a penetrating assessment of Hitler: '. . . it all seemed to him very risky. . . . He simply would not see that in view of the massive numerical superiority of the Soviets our only chance was to shift decisively to mobile warfare. What constantly astonished me was Hitler's incapacity to learn from such an outstanding military expert as Manstein.'[86]

That evening, as if Manstein did not have enough to contend with, Stahlberg raised the prospect of a Soviet air attack on the headquarters in an attempt to kill Hitler. In response, the Field Marshal

> looked up from his reading, tapped the ash off his cigar and said that I had a vivid imagination. I asked him if my worries were not realistic, but he said that they were quite the opposite. . . . 'My dear Stahlberg,' he began, 'listen carefully. In this war Stalin and Effendi are not going to hurt each other, I am quite sure of that. Well, and if I should be wrong and you right, then you have already solved the problem of our security without my assistance, because you and I are sitting here under Effendi's rooms!'[87]

Whether Hitler was ever targeted in this manner is unknown, but there was no bombing. Perhaps the Soviets felt that their war effort was best served by the German leader's erratic command.

The next day Manstein saw Hitler again in two sessions. He began his morning brief with an update on the situation, which had developed dramatically overnight. Soviet forces had been identified south of Krasnograd and had taken Pavlograd, exploiting the vast breach between Army Detachment Lanz and First Panzer Army. The vital crossings over the Dnepr were now directly threatened. As Stahlberg noted, 'For anyone who has ever witnessed the development of a battle on a military situation map, the tension in the room was indescribable.'[88]

Paradoxically, what appeared as another setback provided Manstein with the ideal opportunity he needed to focus his impending counterblow on the enemy rather than on retaking Kharkov. A report had just come in stating that wheeled units of the SS *Totenkopf* Division were 'completely bogged down between Kiev and Poltava'. For Manstein, this was a lucky break as it 'washed out the northwards stroke to retake Kharkov'. Therefore, 'the only thing to do' now was to 'strike south-eastwards and destroy the enemy advancing through the gap'. Faced with this reality Hitler agreed reluctantly to Manstein committing the SS Panzer Grenadier Division *Das Reich*, as the only available formation of the SS Panzer Corps, in a preliminary operation towards Pavlograd prior to it joining Fourth Panzer Army's attack.

Having forced this urgent tactical decision, Manstein then tried to persuade the Führer 'to consider operations on a long-term basis'. He tried in vain to extract a campaign plan for 1943. Hitler played down Soviet military superiority by restating his view that the enemy was exhausted. When Manstein raised again his demand for operational freedom, Hitler denied it, preferring to discuss economic factors and German armaments production. To Manstein they were living 'in two entirely separate worlds', a sentiment echoed by Stahlberg, who observed 'the debate was endless, but once again they were talking at cross purposes'.[89]

The subsequent session that evening yielded no fresh decisions. It had provoked, however, a remarkable change in Hitler's appearance if not demeanour. Stahlberg saw 'a completely different Hitler' enter the conference room, 'in no way comparable with the man of earlier today and the day before. The drooping, failing figure was suddenly transformed into an upright, brisk and vital apparition.'[90] Drugs may indeed have been at work, but Hitler was by now rather enjoying his visit, despite the gravity of developments on the Eastern Front and in North Africa. In the meantime, he had summoned Field Marshal Ewald von Kleist, commander-in-chief of Army Group A, to join the conference the next day.

During the session with Kleist, according to Manstein, Hitler agreed to transfer troops from the 'adjacent reservoir of forces', which Army Group A represented, to Army Group South. Stahlberg, however, remembered Hitler taunting his subordinates. 'Gentlemen, I observe that there is little point in continuing this conversation, as you have agreed among yourselves.' After witnessing a subsequent spat between the two field marshals over the release of First Panzer Army, Hitler interrupted them, according to Stahlberg: 'That's enough, gentlemen. You see how necessary it is for me to be the one to decide. Please stop quarrelling in front of me now!'[91]

The need to calm things down was underlined by the announcement that Soviet armour (elements of 25th Tank Corps) had reached the railway junction of Sinelnikovo, 60 kilometres to the north-northeast.[92] This report may well have prompted the, Führer's rapid departure that afternoon. According to Manstein, Hitler's visit 'had helped bring home to him the danger of encirclement which immediately threatened the southern wing of the Eastern Front'. Ironically, Hitler's initial opposition to Manstein's counter-offensive meant that Soviet forces advanced westwards ever deeper into the trap prepared for them, albeit the stakes were raised correspondingly.

Finally, on the third day Hitler seemed to grasp what Manstein proposed. Only by resolute offensive action could operational initiative be restored and any hope of establishing a stable front be realized. It involved taking considerable risks on the flanks, most especially in the defence of the Mius line, which had to be stripped of armour. If this position were penetrated, then the Soviets would have almost a clear run to the Dnepr, enveloping the whole of Army Group South in the process.[93]

Manstein was at pains in his memoirs to deny that the real purpose of Hitler's stay had been 'to put some backbone into the Army Group'. Rightly, he defended his reputation: 'I do not think it would be easy to find another headquarters, which, in the teeth of so many crises, clung more stubbornly than our own to its will for victory.'[94] At the time, he confided to his wife that Hitler's visit 'had been very useful'. 'After all,' he observed, 'things appear rather differently when viewed at close hand.' Furthermore, Manstein felt that he had got on well with the Führer but added that 'we view matters from different perspectives so it always takes a considerable time to put forward one's own point of view'. There was also scope for some humour in his family correspondence – no doubt for the benefit of young Rüdiger. Manstein's small dog Knirps had 'put [Hitler's] massive dog [Blondi] to flight on two occasions'. But the strategic, and his personal, situation was never far from the Field Marshal's thoughts: 'According to a Reuter report, Churchill is ill. If he were to drop out, it would be a considerable win for us. According to Zeitzler, a couple of days ago Reuter asserted that I was going to assume supreme command. Clearly a nasty attempt at sowing mistrust.'[95]

The Battle Between the Donets and the Dnepr

No sooner was Hitler out of the way, flying to Vinnitsa on 19 February 1943, than Manstein and his staff issued orders for the counter-offensive:

urgent battle procedure could no longer be postponed. That evening Headquarters Army Group South set out new tasks for the subordinate armies, having confirmed its overall mission:

> Army Group South defends Mius and Maulwurf Line and Donets (North Front) Line to the south of Slaviansk, defeats enemy in the gap between First Panzer Army and Army Detachment Lanz[96] with newly established Fourth Panzer Army and covers simultaneously deep left flank of attacking Fourth Panzer Army with Army Detachment Lanz in the area forward of the Poltava-Akhtyrka Line.[97]

Manstein's counter-offensive, aimed at destroying the Soviet 6th and 1st Guards Armies, together with Popov's Mobile Group, required the employment of virtually all of Army Group South's mobile forces, some seven – rising to ten – army and SS panzer divisions, initially supported by two infantry divisions. As David Glantz has keenly observed, his plan

> relied on an attack by concentrated forces along converging axes of advance. It capitalized on the offensive strength of the SS Panzer Corps' divisions and the synergistic effect of the weaker panzer divisions attacking on adjacent axes along converging lines. In essence, it extracted maximum shock effect from units, many of which were of depleted strength, and the plan relied heavily on the flexibility and imagination of German corps, division, regiment, and battalion commanders and staffs.[98]

The final scheme of manoeuvre (see Map 10) involved four shock groups – from left (west) to right (east): SS, XXXXVIII, LVII and XXXX Panzer Corps – striking Soviet forces in their flanks and rear.[99] Although the numbers of German tanks and assault guns were never high, amounting at the start of the counter-offensive to only 225, they were employed to best effect against the weak, stretched underbellies of Soviet armoured brigades and corps that were running out of ammunition and fuel – becoming increasingly immobile as a result.

There is no need to go into the dense tactical detail of the counter-offensive plan. Within Fourth Panzer Army, the SS Panzer Corps was ordered to thrust south-eastwards from Krasnograd towards Pavlograd, whilst XXXXVIII Panzer Corps would advance northwards from the south. Together with LVII Panzer Corps, these forces would shear the exposed tips of the Soviet 6th Army, prior to continuing the attack towards Lozovoya and Barkenkovo, then exploiting north-eastwards to the Northern Donets. Meanwhile, XXX Panzer Corps of First Panzer Army would attack north from the area of Krasnoarmeysk to destroy the Popov Mobile Group and the right flank of 1st Guards Army.

Subsequently, III Panzer Corps would join in First Panzer Army's operation once freed up from the Mius position.

Whereas both the SS and XXXX Panzer Corps launched their attacks on 20 February, XXXXVIII Panzer Corps, having completed its deployment, crossed its line of departure as soon as it could on the 23rd. Whilst Manstein let his army and corps commanders get on with their battles, he continued to press OKH for reinforcements and clarity over future intentions. 'We require a big solution', he demanded to Zeitzler on the 21st, so that 'we know what we should do at the end of the muddy period'.[100] Yet there was no answer to this legitimate request as neither Hitler nor OKH had a strategic vision for the war in the East.

Further frictions of a more immediate nature came when OKH diverted forces destined for Army Group South to its northern neighbour, Field Marshal von Kluge's Army Group Centre. When, for example, 332nd Infantry Division, destined for Pavlograd, was switched in this manner at Hitler's request, Manstein despaired: 'As far as I am concerned, the Russians can march to Kiev; I cannot prevent it.'[101] On a positive note, his counter-offensive was making remarkable progress. By the evening of the 24th, the three German shock groups had penetrated as far as the line Pavlograd–area south-east of Lozovaya–area south of Barvenkovo, corresponding to an advance of approximately 60 kilometres in the case of XXXXVIII Panzer Corps. Across the front, the German armour had smashed Soviet forces strung out across the snow, eliminating the threat of the mobile groups (Popov's, 25th Tank Corps and 1st Guards Cavalry Corps) once and for all. Manstein now prepared to issue new instructions in order to exploit his startling success and maintain the momentum of the attack.

German aerial reconnaissance had spotted fresh Soviet forces crossing the Northern Donets at Izium to support 6th Army. Vatutin had at last recognized the dire threat to his forces and ordered his South-Western *Front* to assume a defensive posture west of the river. Manstein now intended to 'attack enemy forces still south of the Donets and to destroy them, so creating operational freedom for a thrust into the southern flank of the enemy's Kharkov grouping'.[102] Meanwhile, he recognized the possibility of thrusting deeply over the Northern Donets into the rear of the Soviet forces. As he noted, 'One felt a strong temptation to chase the enemy across the still frozen river and take him in the rear in and west of Kharkov.'[103]

By 28 February, after eight days of fighting, Fourth Panzer Army reported it had captured or destroyed 156 tanks and 178 guns, and had inflicted over 15,000 casualties. Its commander, Colonel General Hermann Hoth, declared to his army group commander on 1 March that the 'attack had gone amazingly well'.[104] For all the tactical gains of both First and Fourth Panzer Armies, however, Manstein kept his feet on the ground. The previous day he had stressed to Zeitzler that 'a fundamental change in the operational situation has yet to be achieved despite the recent successes. Make that quite clear to the Führer.'[105]

By 2 March Manstein was able to review with satisfaction the results of his counter-offensive. Without doubt, the forces of the Soviet South-Western *Front* had received a heavy beating between the Donets and the Dnepr, rendering them temporarily incapable of any further offensive action. But it was certainly no Cannae. For all the fatal casualties inflicted (23,000) and enemy equipment destroyed on this battlefield, including 615 tanks, only relatively small numbers of prisoners were taken (9,000). As he conceded, 'individual Soviet soldiers and units which abandoned their vehicles were left with plenty of room to slip away.... It had not been possible to block the Donets in the enemy's rear, as it was still ice-bound and entirely passable to lightly armed troops on foot.'[106]

The Third Battle of Kharkov

Although its name does not chime with the redolence of Leningrad, Moscow or Stalingrad, the city of Kharkov had the notable distinction of being fought over no fewer than four times during the Second World War. As the second city of Ukraine, and former capital for a brief period between the wars, it had considerable prestige value. Apart from its industry, its military value lay as an important transportation hub and in its widespread logistic facilities. Although Manstein did not want his forces to be dissipated in Kharkov through costly street fighting, the soldiers of the SS Corps had a score to settle, having had to evacuate the city ignominiously in February 1943 during the second battle – an unprecedented stain on their copybook.

On regaining the operational level initiative between the Donets and the Dnepr, Manstein turned his attention to attacking the Voronezh *Front* located in the Kharkov area. As he stressed, the object 'was not the possession of Kharkov but the defeat – and if possible the destruction – of the enemy units located there'. None the less, he admitted that it was inevitable that this city would act as 'a magic stimulus on the fighting troops and less senior command staffs'. He had in mind the SS Panzer Corps, who 'wishing to lay the recaptured city at "its Führer's feet" as a symbol of victory, was eager to take the shortest route there'. Manstein aimed to take Kharkov by *coup de main*, and at all costs, avoid the city 'becoming a second Stalingrad in which our assault forces might become irretrievably committed'.[107] Yet Hitler's influence remained: Zeitzler had reminded him on 7 March 1943 that 'the seizure of Kharkov is very greatly desired by the Führer on political grounds'.[108] To reinforce the point, Hitler returned on 10 March. Manstein reflected once again on the Führer: 'In general [our discussions] were satisfactory, although we think on different levels. Effendi over-emphasises the impact of technology and materiel; ... important as these are, they're only means [to an end].'[109]

Manstein's priority meantime was to smash through the southern wing of the Voronezh *Front* formed by the Soviet 3rd Tank Army on the Berestova River, south-west of Kharkov. North of this army lay three more armies: the 69th, 40th and 38th. Having achieved this initial objective by 5 March, Fourth Panzer Army – now spearheaded by a complete SS Panzer Corps of three divisions – thrust north-eastwards from Krasnograd towards Kharkov (see Map 11). West of the city, as Soviet pressure reduced in response to Hausser's manoeuvre, Army Detachment Kempf attacked. Reinforced with additional infantry, Corps Raus advanced eastwards towards the area north of Kharkov on an axis towards Belgorod. Panzer Grenadier Division *Grossdeutschland* struck with great shock effect, splitting the bulk of 40th Army from 69th Army. To the north, Second Army of Army Group Centre finally applied some pressure on the junction of 38th and 40th Armies.[110] Simultaneously, XXXXVIII, XXXX and III Panzer Corps (the latter two corps from First Panzer Army) surged up to the Donets, clearing a disorganized and demoralized enemy in their wake.

These multiple operations developed into a general pursuit of the enemy. Kharkov fell to the SS Panzer Corps after three days of vicious street fighting on 14 March 1943, one month after its loss, despite Manstein's express orders to avoid the city centre. The last Soviet resistance was crushed at the huge tractor factory complex on the city's eastern outskirts, which he had visited in September 1931. Hausser's troops, in close conjunction with *Grossdeutschland*, then continued their attack northwards, occupying Belgorod on the evening of the 18th. Over the next few days German forces consolidated their positions on the Northern and Middle Donets – the line held before the start of the 1942 summer offensive. Throughout, the Mius position remained firm. By 23 March the spring thaw had set in and mobile operations ceased on both sides.

The capture of Kharkov and Belgorod marked the end of the second phase of Manstein's celebrated counter-offensive. The sharp turn in the weather, the exhaustion and losses of the attacking forces, a deficiency of fresh operational reserves and, above all, the lack of a coherent plan for the Eastern Front meant that his success could not be exploited. Manstein would have liked – in close co-operation with Army Group Centre – to have eliminated the dangerous enemy salient projecting westwards from Kursk. As we shall see, Hitler refused Manstein's repeated requests to conduct this operation as quickly as possible in order to exploit the newly won initiative.

Assessment

Manstein's counter-offensive was a masterstroke of manoeuvre that showed him at his best. It took the form of two sequential battles against a numerically superior but over-extended enemy. The first, conducted between the Donets and Dnepr, was followed by the recapture of Kharkov and the re-establishment of a firm defensive line on the Donets. Both operations were conducted with relatively weak mobile forces, excepting the well-equipped SS Panzer Corps and the separate Panzer Grenadier Division *Grossdeutschland*.

Not unnaturally, the Soviets played down the German success. Marshal A. I. Eremenko complained that Manstein in his memoirs 'had taken casual, inconsequential successes of the Hitlerites on some sectors in late February–early March [1943] and elevated them to the level of outstanding victories that allegedly returned the initiative to the Wehrmacht'.[111] In fact, Soviet overoptimism and significant failures of intelligence (mirroring similar German shortfalls before Stalingrad) contributed in large measure to their defeat. As late as 17 February, the South-Western *Front* failed to understand the German defensive battle, let alone detect any preparations for a counterstroke. One senior staff estimate concluded that 'all information affirms that the enemy will leave the territory of the Don basin and withdraw his forces beyond the Dnepr'.[112] That, of course, would have been a prudent course of action for Manstein to have taken, but Hitler's opposition to such a significant retrograde move would have precluded it. In any case, the Field Marshal wanted to exploit the present, precarious situation to his advantage by fighting a decisive action to the *east* of the river. He confounded his opponents by attacking when he was – by any conventional military thinking – too weak to defend.

General Vatutin had absolutely no inkling of the impending blow when he supported his staff's advice, 'Without a doubt the enemy is hurrying to withdraw his forces from the Donbas across the Dnepr.'[113] His opponent had indeed drawn a veil of secrecy over his plans, by undertaking the absolutely unexpected. When the Soviets observed Hausser's corps withdrawing from Kharkov they perceived this move wrongly as confirmation of a German strategic retreat. Within a week, Manstein's forces had counterattacked, achieving a surprise only surpassed by his *Sichelschnitt* plan.

Manstein's genius not only lay in appreciating that if the Soviet attack could be brought to a state of culmination, there was an opportunity for mounting an operationally decisive counterblow. His extraordinary achievement also lay in the brilliant manner in which he orchestrated it by overcoming Hitler's misgivings, wrong-footing his opponents and snatching a spectacular victory from the jaws of likely defeat. At times he appeared to confound the German High Command as much as the enemy. On the eve of the counterattack in mid February, back at OKH, everything seemed so confused on the map. Heusinger remarked to his subordinate, Johann Adolf Graf von Kielmansegg, who became a prominent general in the Bundeswehr, 'I really don't know how Manstein will make it work.'[114] In the execution of his plan, however, the army group commander was well supported by his highly able subordinate army, corps and divisional commanders, skilled in combined arms operations and imbued with an ethos of *Auftragstaktik*.

For all that it accomplished, the magnitude and manner of the Soviet defeat was unexpected. During the course of the operation, Manstein had observed perceptively that:

> Our war here is gradually becoming a really peculiar affair: at any rate not to be viewed in the normal scheme of things. All together, one could describe it as almost extraordinary. But at the same time one should not let oneself be influenced by momentary situations. Rather, one must keep one's eye firmly set on the wider and bigger picture.

In consequence, he would not allow success to go to his head. Writing home again at the end of February 1943, he noted: 'Despite this victory, I can only hope that we'll continue to judge the situation in a sober manner.'[115]

Manstein's counter-offensive has been closely analysed by military historians and professional soldiers. In many senses his remarkable achievement in the spring of 1943 redeemed his military reputation after the failure to relieve Stalingrad. The strategic consequence of his operation lay not in what he had won, but rather in what he had prevented – the complete disintegration of the Eastern Front. His gifted art of command won through all the doubters and difficulties. Somewhat naively, however, he regarded his battlefield victory as a basis for a political solution, a draw or *'Remisfrieden'*, which never had any chance of being agreed by either Hitler or Stalin. So for all his efforts, his accomplishment in stabilizing the southern wing was but another *lost victory*.[116] Eremenko was right to conclude that 'the initiative was taken over by us definitively and irrevocably at Stalingrad.'[117] Had Stalin concentrated all his forces to exploit this victory, then it is hard to see how even Manstein would have scored his stunning success.

Yet it would be wrong to dilute the Field Marshal's great accomplishment. As one expert analysis concludes:

> One cannot deny the brilliance of von Manstein's operation. In fact, it can now be argued that his winter counterstroke was, in reality, a counteroffensive, since it had strategic rather than just operational significance. This is so because, rather than forestalling a Soviet drive into the Donbas, von Manstein's operations actually thwarted a larger and more ambitious Soviet effort to split the entire German front.[118]

The counter-offensive represented a brief German recovery at the end of a wretched, ruinous winter of defeat. Following the debacle at Stalingrad, it had offered a welcome, fleeting glimpse of victory borne of superior manoeuvre on open field. Paget compared Manstein's feat with Alexander the Great's battle of Gaugamela:

> He had submitted to the envelopment of both his flanks and then changed his front and driven his armour at the hinge of the enemy turning movement. Darius and Stalin had enjoyed about the same numerical superiority, for von Manstein had one division under command for every eight Russian divisions that had been opposed to him. Seldom in the history of war has a more hopeless position been more brilliantly retrieved.[119]

In so doing, he echoed the Field Marshal's own contemporary sentiment: 'There are not many historical examples of such a reversal of fortune from such a difficult situation. Therefore we are very grateful to God and also very proud.'[120]

13

Defeat at Kursk

*'The Russians have learnt a lot since 1941. They are no longer
peasants with simple minds. They have learnt the art of
war from us.'* Colonel General Hermann Hoth[1]

Prelude to Disaster

Along with Stalingrad, the battle of Kursk in July 1943 is regarded as a
turning point not only on the Eastern Front, but also of the Second
World War as a whole.[2] The two previous summer offensives of the
Wehrmacht had resulted in deep penetrations of the Soviet front. This
time, *Stavka* determined to 'meet the enemy attack in a well-prepared
defensive bridgehead; to bleed [the] attacking German groupings dry;
and then to launch a general offensive'.[3] By the use of such language, the
Soviets' aim resembled that of Falkenhayn, the Chief of the German
General Staff, who in early 1916 had resolved infamously to bleed the
'French Army white' by attacking Verdun. As the French had achieved
twenty-seven years before, the Soviet defenders defeated the German
assault, but at terrible cost. Then their twin counter-offensives
(Operations KUTUZOV and RUMIANTSEV) sought to roll the *Ostheer*
back to the Dnepr and beyond. By the end of September, Manstein's
sorely depleted army group had been forced to withdraw behind that
great Ukrainian river.

At Kursk, the German High Command's intention to shorten its front
in the East, to write down the Red Army's reserves and so reduce the
power of the inevitable offensives against Army Groups Centre and
South was denied. So too was the political imperative of gaining an
impressive victory. A major success in the East would have brought
a much-needed psychological fillip to German morale and restored
confidence amongst its allies. Failure proved unforgiving. After the
battle, the 'Wehrmacht no longer had the chance to reverse the military
balance of power'.[4] With no chance of regaining the strategic initiative,
Manstein's cherished goal of achieving a 'draw' died in the process.

Fuelled by Soviet propaganda that hugely exaggerated German losses,
the battle is widely recalled as the 'swan-song' or 'death-ride' of the

German panzer force, culminating in the titanic tank clash at Pro-khorovka in which the 'Tigers burned' in the 'hell of Kursk'.[5] Such myths have fed many popular accounts. In fact, German forces inflicted far greater damage on their opponents than they received: Soviet casualties 'were more than three times higher'.[6] But the Red Army with its growing numerical superiority on the ground and in the air could afford to slug it out in an attritional manner whilst the Wehrmacht could not. Furthermore, the Soviets' quantitative advantage was now being com-plemented by qualitative improvements in organization, training, command and operational art that the Germans, including Manstein, were slow to recognize and to adapt to. So far rather than another German victory *lost*, Kursk was won by a reinforced, re-forming and revitalized Red Army. In sum, nearly two million men, 7,400 tanks and assault guns, and 5,000 aircraft were involved in this one vast general engagement that dwarfed in scale and intensity any battles being fought in the parallel theatre of war in the Mediterranean.[7]

Manstein observed accurately that 'the enemy opposite the two attack-ing armies of Southern Army Group had suffered four times their losses in prisoners, dead and wounded'.[8] The Soviet leadership was not as confident of success before the battle as their subsequent propaganda would suggest. Stalin took no risks in the run-up to the battle, building up a massive preponderance of men and *matériel* to meet and defeat the German attack. Such were the stakes on both sides that no less than 'about fifty per cent of all Soviet and sixty-four per cent of all German armoured forces, including strategic reserves, were concentrated in the Kursk sector'.[9]

After Kursk, the initiative passed irrevocably to the Soviet Union: Germany remained on the back foot on the Eastern Front thereafter. With the possible exception of the Ardennes winter counter-offensive of 1944/45, never again would the Wehrmacht assemble such a powerful striking force, its soldiers and airmen so hopeful of success prior to the battle and so bitterly disappointed at their failure. With the Allied landings on Sicily on 10 July 1943, the long-awaited Second Front in Europe had opened: Germany was forced to divert further forces to Italy and fight a costly campaign there until the end of the war.

Analysis of Kursk, together with its prelude and aftermath, has been augmented recently by major studies.[10] In the light of this new research it is now possible to re-evaluate Manstein's role in the planning and conduct of the battle, examining his performance as an army group commander in this critical episode of the Second World War. Readers of *Lost Victories* are short-changed with a very abridged version, representing only one-fifth of the author's original German text.[11] This omission goes some way to explain why some Anglo-American commentators have failed to challenge Manstein's account. He claimed that breaking off the battle at its climax on 13 July was 'tantamount to throwing a victory away', but conceded 'the last German offensive in the east ended in a fiasco'. After Kursk, the *Ostheer* generally, and Army Group South in particular, was hard pressed to maintain itself in the field. Wearing down 'the enemy's offensive capacity' became, in Manstein's words, 'the whole essence of the struggle'.[12] It proved a prolonged but ultimately forlorn quest.

The Missed Opportunity?

One of the biggest questions posed in any study of Kursk is the rationale for the continued delays in mounting the German attack during the period May–June 1943. According to Manstein, there was a missed opportunity in March or April. A week before Kharkov fell, he was despairing of OKH's planning, urging Zeitzler to think strategically. Their cool exchange of 7 March 1943 speaks volumes for the lack of clarity over future intentions and the absence of any effective military advice to Hitler or direction from him:

> *Manstein*: It's important to know now what OKH is thinking about in terms of the big picture.
>
> *Zeitzler*: First of all, rehabilitation of the mobile troops.
>
> *Manstein*: That's not much! If all we want to do is to defend, then I must employ all available troops on the front. But I am too weak to defend across the whole front and enemy penetration is inevitable.... Either I conduct offensive blows in close conjunction with the right flank of Army Group Centre and thereby retain the initiative, or I must remain defensive and be forced again on to the back-foot accordingly. After all, I cannot defend a 700 kilometre-long front with 25 divisions. Think about the situation of Sixth Army and its encirclement. Either I keep the initiative in my grasp, or I cannot hope to hold such an exposed bend [the Donets].
>
> *Zeitzler*: The ideas of the Field Marshal completely correspond to mine. Therefore we must do all we can to receive additional formations.[13]

Manstein did not forsake his attention on Kursk, but perversely Hitler gave higher priority to the less important task of clearing the enemy from its remaining bridgeheads on the Donets.

On 8 March, Manstein phoned Zeitzler again and pressed for

reinforcements: 'For further operations we need an additional sixteen divisions.' Headquarters Army Group South war diary records that the Chief of the General Staff then 'laughed'. Manstein, clearly irritated by this jocular interjection, responded: 'I mean that seriously. You'll receive it in writing today. Everything now depends on not letting the initiative pass out of our hands.' Once again he urged Zeitzler to get Second Army of Army Group Centre to strike: 'it should be ordered to attack Akhtyrika' rather than 'pushing in' the enemy on its right flank.[14]

Hitler returned to Zaporozhye on 10 March for a major conference as Manstein's victory at Kharkov seemed assured. It involved no fewer than sixteen field marshals and generals from the army and Luftwaffe, the attendance list reading like a 'Who's Who' of the Eastern Front.[15] For Stahlberg, the sudden reappearance of the Führer at Manstein's headquarters was nothing but a 'propaganda coup' to associate the German leader – 'the greatest commander of all time' – with the 'outcome of these last successful operations in the East'. Not surprisingly, Hitler was pleased with the prominent role of the SS Panzer Corps and his beloved Leibstandarte in the attack towards Kharkov. During the ensuing discussion, Stahlberg observed that 'Manstein's thoughts were less with the battle now nearing its close than with the future planning of the war in Russia.'[16]

Manstein records that he tried to impress Hitler with his view of 'how operations should be conducted at the end of the muddy season, which was now setting in'.[17] He recommended once more that the German Army should exploit its superior mobility and command capability by fighting a battle of manoeuvre, rather than defending from static positions. The Field Marshal tried again to win Hitler round to the idea of another 'backhand' blow by luring Soviet forces into attacking and then striking them decisively in the flanks in a counter-offensive. Discussion then turned to the Kursk 'balcony', as Manstein described it, and to the alternate possibility of a 'forehand' attack to eliminate it, thus saving frontage and generating new reserves (see Map 12). On departure, Hitler did not commit himself except to stress once again the importance of retaining the Donbas.

Three days later Hitler flew to Headquarters Army Group Centre near Smolensk, where Kluge had assembled his army commanders. The Führer outlined his ideas for an attack on the Kursk salient. His audience was sceptical, concerned about the 'weakness of the German divisions, the imbalance of armoured forces and the Soviet echeloned defensive system that was already in evidence'.[18]

On 13 March, OKH issued Operation Order No. 5, 'Instructions for the conduct of combat during the next months', which provided the genesis of Operation CITADEL. It assumed that the Russians would 'resume their attack at the end of the winter and the mud period after a period of refitting and reconstitution' and declared that 'the time has come for us to attack in as many sectors of the front as possible before he does'. Army Group South was tasked to bring 'the entire Mius front ... as well as the Donets front' to 'the highest degree of defensive readiness', and to prepare for offensive operations. Specifically,

A strong panzer army is to be formed on the northern flank of the army group immediately and no later than mid-April so that it will be ready for commitment at the end of the mud period, before the Russian offensive. The objective of this offensive is the destruction of enemy forces in front of Second Army by attacking north out of the Kharkov area in conjunction with an attack group from Second Panzer Army.[19]

Notwithstanding these orders, Manstein remained frustrated by OKH's lack of urgency and foresight. Although Kharkov had been retaken on 14 March, much to Hitler's satisfaction, there remained the more important operational goals of retaining the initiative and defeating Soviet forces at their weakest. Hence on 18 March the commander of Army Group South opined to Zeitzler: 'The Russians in front of our left wing and Army Group Centre's right wing are not capable of doing very much. I believe that Army Group Centre could now take Kursk without difficulty.' When Zeitzler replied that the 'Führer would like an operation from Chugayev [towards] Izium', Manstein objected tersely:

We wish that as well, and we would like to do a lot more! But that would require greater forces than currently I have at my disposal. Please tell the Führer: if he gave me the divisions being continuously redeployed from the West, then I could carry out [such] operations with deep objectives. At the moment, I can't because the available forces for such a mission are too weak. Right now, we shall clean up the west bank of the Donets. All further plans on the left wing depend on the co-operation of Second Army.[20]

Over the next few days, the argument swayed back and forth about the need to extend operations towards Kursk.

On the morning of 20 March, Manstein demanded an immediate continuation of the counter-offensive. 'Today and tomorrow we're clearing up the west bank of the Donets and are sending out strong reconnaissance probes from Belgorod to the north and northwest. Obviously an operation towards Kursk now presents itself, but that won't be possible without the co-operation of Army Group Centre.' At 17.45 hours the next day came the Führer's decision: 'Stop the intended operation in the direction of Kursk and start preparing an operation to the south-east.'[21]

From Manstein's perspective, an apparently golden opportunity to remove the Kursk salient, saving a substantial length of front (over 200 kilometres) and regenerating much needed operational level reserves was lost. There is no simple explanation for Hitler's refusal to allow Manstein to exploit northwards and to direct Kluge's Army Group Centre to attack eastwards towards Kursk. The most obvious reasons were the lack of fresh forces and the *rasputitsa*. But Hitler remained concerned about the loss of the Donbas industrial region, his old hobby-horse. Therefore, as we have seen, the Führer had been pressing Manstein hard to clear the east bank of the Donets. Eventually these plans (PANTHER and HABICHT) were given up in favour of CITADEL, but were retained to support the attack on Kursk as deception operations.[22]

Another reason could have been more personal. One can surmise that having given Manstein exceptional operational freedom to conduct his Kharkov counter-offensive, Hitler did not wish to inflate his awkward subordinate's success. Perhaps in the German dictator's twisted mind it would have risked promoting a victorious Manstein into a position of greater military authority. Goebbels may have blacked the Field Marshal around this time, as evidenced by his diary entry of 11 March 1943 following Hitler's visit to Headquarters Army Group South: '[the Führer] does not seem to know how infamously Manstein behaved towards him'.[23] Goebbels, with Himmler, continued to undermine the Field Marshal until he was dismissed from command at the end of March 1944. Hitler may also have been worried that closer co-operation between Army Groups Centre and South might have increased calls for an overarching Commander-in-Chief *Ost*, thus undermining his direct control of operations.

In the meantime, however, there were perhaps some more practical grounds for Hitler's refusal to sanction an immediate offensive towards Kursk. By the third week of March, German casualties, particularly in Hausser's SS Panzer Corps, had mounted alarmingly, many troops having been squandered during the bitter street fighting in Kharkov.[24] Furthermore, the Red Army was reinforcing the Kursk region with fresh formations, including 1st Guards Tank Army, to an extent that Manstein was not aware of.[25] Therefore, in continuing the counter-offensive it is just as likely that German armour would have been blocked by Soviet forces as being stuck in the mud. Equally importantly, Army Group Centre was fully preoccupied during March in conducting Operation

BUFFALO, its carefully staged withdrawal from the exposed Rhzev salient. This highly successful retrograde manoeuvre released Ninth Army under Colonel General Walther Model for an offensive role in Operation CITADEL. Meanwhile, Second Army, to Manstein's immediate north, never had sufficient striking power to thrust towards Kursk.

Towards the end of March, Manstein received a visit from Guderian at Zaporozhye, who six weeks before had been appointed by Hitler as 'Inspector-General of Armoured Troops' to rectify grave deficiencies in the condition of the German armoured force. Guderian was particularly interested in gathering lessons on the recent employment of *Grossdeutschland* and SS *Leibstandarte Adolf Hitler* Divisions' Tiger battalions in the recapture of Kharkov, a victory won, Manstein's visitor later noted, 'by using armoured formations in the correct operational way'. Guderian knew Manstein well enough to form an accurate comparison between the Field Marshal and the Führer:

> I once again realised what a pity it was that Hitler could not tolerate the presence of so capable and soldierly a person as Manstein in his environment. Their characters were too opposed: on the one hand Hitler, with his great will-power and his fertile imagination: on the other Manstein, a man of most distinguished military talents, a product of the German General Staff Corps, with a sensible, cool understanding, who was our finest operational brain.[26]

Initial Planning Considerations

On 30 March 1943, Manstein returned to Germany on sick leave to attend to growing problems with his eyesight. At the University Eye Clinic in Breslau (now Wrocław in Poland) a cataract was diagnosed. His specialist, a Professor Dieter in SS uniform, as Stahlberg recorded, determined that a tonsillectomy would arrest the problem. The operation duly took place and the Field Marshal went home to Liegnitz to rest.[27] Over a five-week period, Model and von Weichs stood in for him as army group commander. As Manstein was by nature not inclined to remain inactive by pottering around at home, he kept in close touch by letter over military developments with his trusty chief of staff, Busse.

Most significantly, on 15 April Hitler had issued through OKH Operation Order No. 6, which detailed the plan for CITADEL. The Führer laid immense store on the operation, declaring 'the attack is of the utmost importance', which 'must be executed quickly'. Moreover,

It must seize the initiative for us in the spring and summer. Therefore,

all preparations must be conducted with great circumspection and enterprise. The best formations, the best weapons, the best commanders, and
great stocks of ammunition must be committed in the main axes. Each
commander and each man must be impressed by the decisive significance
of this offensive. The victory at Kursk must be a beacon to the entire
world.

As is often the case, striving for the 'best' turned out to be the 'enemy of
the good'. By ensuring the 'best', Hitler proceeded to undermine two
essential prerequisites of success stated in his order, namely: 'We must
ensure that the element of surprise is preserved and the enemy kept in
the dark as to when the attack will begin'; and that 'The attack forces
are concentrated on a narrow axis, in order to provide local overwhelming
superiority of all attack means.'[28]

By attempting to ensure a sufficiency for the latter precondition,
which would take time, any delay in mounting the operation would
imperil the former. Furthermore, any postponement would benefit the
Soviets more than their opponents as they would be able to build up
their defences within the Kursk bulge and elsewhere more quickly
than the Germans could reinforce their attacking forces. Above all,
Soviet production of aircraft, armour and artillery far exceeded that
of its enemy. Ominously, Operation Order No. 6 had stated an 'earliest
date' for the attack as 3 May, implying it could slip well beyond
that.

From Liegnitz, Manstein was fully aware of the implications of such
a step. On 18 April, he wrote a letter to Zeitzler (but designed to be
brought to Hitler's attention) highlighting that the 'earlier that CITADEL
can begin, the less likely that a major enemy offensive on the Donets
will take place'. He also stressed that '*everything* must now be devoted
to ensuring the success of CITADEL, because a victory there would
compensate for any temporary setbacks on other sectors of the Army
Group's front'.[29] His language here betrayed the central dilemma posed
in the planning and execution of the offensive. In 1943, the *Ostheer*
simply was not powerful enough to provide the necessary forces to launch
a major offensive towards Kursk and to defend strongly elsewhere. Risks,
therefore, had to be taken in other sectors in order to generate sufficient
mobile forces for the attack. Perhaps more should have been taken, as
in the run-up to the Ardennes offensive.

Manstein always regarded the *forehand* stroke (an attack from present
positions) represented by CITADEL as inferior to another *backhand* blow
(a counterattack having yielded ground intentionally) such as the one he

conducted in exemplary manner between the Donets and the Dnepr. He had advanced again the operational idea of 'drawing the enemy westwards towards the Lower Dnepr' and then smashing them in the flank to 'suffer the same fate on the Sea of Azov as he had in store for us on the Black Sea'. Hitler did not agree, holding firm, in Manstein's words, to 'his belief that we must fight for every foot of ground' and shrinking 'from the risks which the proposed operation would assuredly entail'. More damningly, the Field Marshal felt that the German dictator 'did not trust himself to cope with them, for in spite of having a certain eye for tactics, he still lacked the ability of a great captain'.[30]

In the original German edition of *Lost Victories*, however, Manstein conceded a major disadvantage of this course of action. After all, in the spring of 1943 it 'was far from certain whether the enemy would do us the favour of opening the battle with an offensive'. Furthermore, 'if the Western Powers supported a Soviet offensive' (he implied here the opening of a second front), then 'perhaps Stalin could afford to wait'.[31] Although he did, Stalin required much persuasion to wait for the German offensive rather than get his blow in first.

Within the Soviet High Command, a wide-ranging debate on strategy had taken place. Should the winter's operations be continued into the spring or, in anticipation of a powerful German counterblow, would it be preferable to adopt an initial defensive posture within the context of a later summer offensive? Stalin's instincts were for the former. The consensus of the Red Army generals was for the latter, championed by Zhukov. The possibility of the Germans attempting to bite off the Kursk salient in a pincer attack was obvious to all. The Soviet general's skill, however, lay in reading German intentions more precisely, telegraphed by the deployment and concentration of armoured forces to the north and south of Kursk. As early as 8 April he had predicted that the enemy would strike towards that city and urged caution accordingly. Zhukov wrote:

> I do not consider it necessary for our troops to mount a preventive offensive in the next few days. It will be better if we wear the enemy out in defensive action, destroy his tanks, and then, taking in fresh reserves, by going over to an all-out offensive, we will finish off the enemy's main grouping.[32]

On 12 April – three days *before* the issue of German Operation Order No. 6 – Stalin met with his senior military advisors: Zhukov, Vasilevsky and Antonov. Major General S. M. Shtemenko of the General Staff's Operational Directorate recorded the outcome of this conference:

Ultimately it was decided to concentrate our main forces in the Kursk area, to bleed the enemy forces here in a defensive operation, and then to switch to the offensive and achieve their full destruction. To provide against eventualities, it was considered necessary to build deep and secure defences along the whole strategic front, making them particularly powerful in the Kursk sector.[33]

Behind the Central and Voronezh *Fronts* tasked with the defence of Kursk, Stalin ordered the creation of a new strategic reserve, the Steppe *Front* (see Map 13). Under command of Colonel General I. S. Konev, this huge force of over half a million men consisted of five rifle armies and a tank army, together with one tank, two mechanized and three cavalry corps. This was a richness of plenty of which the Wehrmacht could only dream. In particular, Lieutenant General P. A. Rotmistrov's 5th Guards Tank Army with nearly 1,000 tanks would represent a trump card in the coming battle. Further, the Soviets massed four air armies in a determined bid to wrest air superiority from the Luftwaffe and to inflict as much damage as possible to German armour.

Within the Kursk salient and into the strategic depth to the east, Soviet defensive planning and preparations were ambitious and thorough. As the *General Staff Study* noted:

To create the most stable defence capable of countering massed attacks by large tank groupings, front commanders were ordered to create no fewer than five or six defensive lines [blocking] the most important axes. In addition, the eastern bank of the Don [some 200 kilometres east of Kursk] (the so-called 'state defensive line') was prepared for defence and, subsequently, Steppe Military District forces constructed a line [midway to the Don] along the eastern shores of the Kshen and Oskol Rivers in the sector from Livny to Novyi Oskol.[34]

Within the Kursk bulge, the result of Soviet labours was a veritable labyrinth of fortified villages and field fortifications (blockhouses, strong points and trench systems), wire obstacles and minefields, all covered by observed fire. In the most vulnerable sections of both the Central and Voronezh *Fronts*, Soviet sappers had laid as many as 1,500 anti-tank and 1,700 anti-personnel mines per kilometre.[35]

In the Central *Front*'s sector, the presumed main German axis towards Kursk was defended by the Soviet 13th Army. Its twelve rifle divisions were deployed on a narrow frontage of 32 kilometres in three echelons, reinforced by a tank brigade and five tank regiments. Here the forward defence of the salient was at its most dense: 4,500 men, 45 tanks and 104 guns per kilometre. In contrast, within the Voronezh *Front* across the critical frontages of 6th and 7th Guards Armies, fourteen rifle divisions defended a sector 100 kilometres wide in two echelons. Here the force density was less: 2,500 men, 42 tanks and 59 guns per kilometre. So a German breakthrough operation might have appeared easier to achieve here than in the north. Yet the Soviet defences contained further depth and very significant counterattack potential. In addition to the armies, reinforcing tank brigades and regiments forming the *fronts'* first echelons, there were both *front* reserves and mobile shock groups. Facing Manstein's attacking force, these additional enemy troops included 69th Army and 35th Guards Rifle Corps together with 1st Tank Army, 54th and 2nd Guards Tank Corps and a host of tank, mechanized and motorized brigades, anti-tank rifle battalions and mortar regiments. All these Soviet units were carefully sited with well-rehearsed counter-attack options.[36]

German planning for CITADEL, meanwhile, had identified a number of objectives other than pinching off the Kursk bulge. Apart from encircling a considerable enemy grouping, by shortening the front it would free up German forces for employment elsewhere. The second goal was to draw Soviet operational reserves into the battle and to destroy them, thus setting the conditions for further, limited, offensives other than at Kursk. There was never any realistic prospect of mounting a grand armoured drive to the Don and wheeling north to Moscow as Stalin and his General Staff feared. Yet it was beyond doubt, in Manstein's opinion, that the risks of the forehand blow increased in direct proportion to 'the amount of time given to the enemy to reconstitute his beaten forces'.[37] Any delay in CITADEL, moreover, gave the Soviets more time to prepare their defences and to build up fresh reserves. In the case of the Steppe *Front*, it was to be employed as offensively as possible.

Manstein prepared to return to his headquarters on 4 May 1943 in good time for an anticipated D-Day of the Kursk operation in the middle of that month. On the eve of his planned departure, Busse arrived in Liegnitz to inform his commander-in-chief that he had been summoned to meet with Hitler in Munich the next day. Apart from Manstein, also present were Kluge, Zeitzler, Guderian and Jeschonnek.[38]

Hitler had begun to have doubts as to the success of CITADEL, having proposed previously on 18 April to Zeitzler an alternative scheme of manoeuvre involving the combined forces of Army Groups Centre and South undertaking a frontal assault on an easterly thrust towards Kursk instead of the 'pincer' attack. His Chief of the General Staff convinced him that adjusting the deployment of the troops concerned would cause further, intolerable delay.[39] A massive, concentrated, cleaving blow along an unexpected axis might have generated sufficient penetration and shock effect to rupture the Soviet defence. That said, it would have been difficult to disguise the necessary redeployment and hence achieve operational level surprise. It was, however, precisely the trick the Soviets employed a year later in Operation BAGRATION that led to the crushing defeat of Army Group Centre.

A more tactical objection to CITADEL had come from Model, who in a written submission (26 April) had warned Hitler about the growing strength of the Soviet defences facing him, now some 20 kilometres in depth. According to his biographer, the commander of Ninth Army, 'Buttressed by aerial photographs of prepared Soviet antitank positions and trench lines', argued that the offensive 'should be postponed by at least a month, during which time his army would have to receive the reinforcements thus far lacking'.[40] He was pushing on an open door as Hitler was sympathetic to any delay. As Guderian explained to Manstein on the morning of 4 May before their meeting with Hitler, the Führer wished to enhance the striking power of the attack with an increased level of armoured support. He had in mind here the employment of heavy armour (Tiger tanks and Ferdinand tank destroyers) and not least the new medium tank, the as yet combat-unproven and still unreliable Panther, the German answer to the T-34. In addition, he wished to wait out developments in the Mediterranean theatre before confirming CITADEL.

During the main, four-hour conference on the afternoon of 4 May, the Führer opened proceedings by explaining why he wished to postpone the attack. He raised Model's reservations about the Soviet defences; he was worried about the force ratios; and recent German attacks had demonstrated that it was not possible to penetrate a deeply echeloned position without strong fire support. He then asked for the views of his audience on the practicality of the operation.

Manstein was the first to speak. He could not avoid observing that 'an early success in the East was desirable and required' in view of the wider political and military situation. His own forces 'were weak, especially in infantry' in relation to those of the enemy. Postponing the start of the operation would only bring success 'if further infantry divisions were allocated to him'. More specifically, success in the East must be achieved 'before Tunis falls' and the 'western powers open a new front'. Further, any delay would mean 'an increased threat to the Mius-Donets-Front. At the moment, the Russians there are probably not capable of mounting an attack, but in June they would certainly be,' he continued. Finally, it was questionable whether the 'rise in own troops would compensate for the monthly production of Russian armour, recovery in morale and building of defensive positions'.[41]

Manstein's own account added some important detail. He maintained that 'however tempting a further reinforcement of our armoured forces' was, an 'immediate attack was required'. If a postponement were to ensue, then his army group 'needed additional infantry divisions in order to overcome the enemy positions'. In conclusion, he felt that CITADEL would be 'no easy undertaking', adding that one must hold firm to the decision of launching an offensive soon.[42]

The commander of Army Group Centre, Kluge, irritated by the report of his subordinate's downbeat assessment, spoke out strongly against any adjournment. Manstein recalled his colleague protesting: 'Model's description of a twenty-kilometre deep defensive position is exaggerated.' By waiting, Germany 'could be put on to the back-foot' and have to 'redeploy forces away from CITADEL'. Hitler, who had already rejected Manstein's request for additional infantry by stating that the additional armoured forces would have to replace them, then responded to Kluge's comments. In his view, Colonel General Model was 'fully positive' in his briefing; the pessimist in the matter was none other than 'himself' – the Führer.

Guderian's version of the exchange is interesting in several key respects. Quite apart from confirming that Kluge spoke *after* Manstein rather than the other way about, he recalled: 'Manstein, as often when face to face with Hitler, was not at his best. His opinion was that the attack would have had a good chance of succeeding in April; now its success was doubtful.' The Inspector-General of Armoured Troops also remembers Manstein stating 'he would need a further two full-strength divisions'. Then he plunged his knife: '[Hitler] then repeated his question', but 'unfortunately received no very clear answer' from Manstein. According to his account, which is confirmed by the war diary, Guderian then voiced his own opinion following Kluge, who had spoken 'unambiguously in favour of Zeitzler's plan'. In contrast, he declared that the Kursk attack was 'pointless'. Specifically, if Germany attacked following the plan of the Chief of the General Staff [Zeitzler], 'we were certain to suffer heavy tank casualties, which we would not be in a position to replace in 1943'. Furthermore, he pointed out that the new Panthers, on whose performance Zeitzler (and by implication Hitler) 'was relying so heavily, were still suffering from the many teething problems inherent in all new equipment'.[43]

For his part, Manstein recalls that the Inspector-General of Armoured Troops suggested that all armoured forces should be amassed on one attack sector to generate 'crushing superiority', whether by Army Groups South or Centre, a proposal not mentioned at all by Guderian but one recorded nevertheless in the war diary. Colonel General Jeschonnek then agreed with Guderian. A concentration of ground effort in one place could be supported by all available aircraft. Furthermore, the grouping of enemy air power indicated preparations for a large-scale Soviet attack on Army Group South. Any delay to CITADEL would not bring any significant reinforcements to the Luftwaffe, merely two groups of Stukas.

In closing, Hitler repeated his arguments for a delay until 10 June, stating that the 'possible increase in Soviet armour would be compensated for by the technical superiority of the additional Tigers, Panthers and Ferdinands', but he could not provide any further infantry divisions.[44] Hitler dismissed his audience by concluding that he would consider the timing of the Kursk offensive once more. As other studies have noted, the doubts of his military subordinates may have 'had the unintended effect of strengthening his resolve' in delaying the attack.[45] Whatever, it is difficult to escape the impression that the post-war accounts of the surviving participants of the conferences were self-serving.

The Fatal Interlude

On 11 May, CITADEL was called off until 12 June as the two army group commanders had feared. Two days later, nearly a quarter of a million Axis forces in Tunisia capitulated on the Cape Bon peninsula, a military disaster on the scale of Stalingrad. Meanwhile, the promised reinforcements of armour trickled towards the Eastern Front, prompting several more delays of the attack until it was finally fixed on 25 June for 5 July 1943. During this interlude, the Soviet defences grew ever stronger, whilst German attempts to camouflage their intentions with deception measures, including telegraphing an attack (Operation PANTHER) from the Donets area by the use of concentrations of dummy tanks, failed to fool their opponents.

During the long weeks of waiting in May and June, Manstein supervised the operational planning and training of his subordinate formations, undertaking frequent tours of the 'front'. On 10 May, for example, he visited Hoth's headquarters at Bogodukhov, west of Kharkov. The army commander had brought together General of Panzer Troops Otto von Knobelsdorff (XXXXVIII Panzer Corps) and his subordinate divisional commanders, including such famous names as Balck

(*Grossdeutschland*) and Choltitz (11th Panzer). This meeting led to a free-ranging, open discussion between experts as to the ways and means of the coming offensive. Because of a lack of infantry, Manstein had already decided to commit his armour to an overwhelming initial assault, relying on the supporting infantry to protect the flanks of the panzer spearheads. He declared to his audience that 'The attack will not be easy! The main battle will begin when own troops have penetrated the [enemy's] first position.' Yet even in mid May, Manstein was having some nagging doubts as to the Germans' ability to penetrate the Soviets' first line of defence, stressing to his formation commanders the importance of planning and rehearsing the attack 'down to the last detail'; the imperative of concentrating air and artillery support effectively; the requirement to 'employ heavy tanks in the first assault'; and to practise the suppression of Soviet anti-tank nests in the attack with artillery. In closing, he reminded his officers of the need to keep the 'enemy big picture in mind', and warned them prophetically to 'expect strong enemy air activity'.[46]

The next day (11 May) he was in Kharkov visiting Hausser's SS Panzer Corps, where the three commanders of the SS panzer grenadier divisions (*Leibstandarte*, *Reich* and *Totenkopf*) updated him on their combat strengths and concerns. After Hausser presented his outline plan for the attack, Manstein warned his SS subordinates about the growing strength of the Soviet defences: 'Formations should assume that the enemy will continue to develop his positions in depth and to the front. Don't make light of the attack: rather, reconnoitre and prepare for it thoroughly.'[47]

During such visits, Manstein managed to confer with the vast majority of his subordinate commanders down to divisional level. Unlike the over-energetic Model of Ninth Army, however, he trusted his people sufficiently to let them plan the tactical detail of their operations and remained responsive to their own proposals as to the commitment of forces. Rather than mandating schemes of manoeuvre down to regimental level, his direction was more of a general nature, focusing on training and other preparations. In hindsight, however, Manstein missed some of the eventual errors of army, corps and divisional plans that would lead to the grave difficulties in the German assault. We shall return to these later, but as is often the case in war, it is not only the enemy who can frustrate best intentions.

Back at army group headquarters, Manstein had some time on his hands. Using his initiative, Stahlberg called for his horses from Liegnitz. The Field Marshal and his ADC galloped together across the open steppe south of Zaporozhye for an hour each day. Manstein rode 'a rangy, thoroughbred grey in the prime of life', and Stahlberg's horse 'was also a sheer joy to ride'. Notice of the pair's riding habits soon came to Hitler's attention. According to Stahlberg, his cousin Henning von Tresckow had informed him, 'lately Hitler has flown into a violent rage several times when Manstein's name has been mentioned'. Furthermore, it had been reported that on being told about Manstein's and his ADC's activities, the Führer had commented, 'it would be an easy matter to have a partisan ambush get rid of them both'.⁴⁸ In response to this threat, Manstein's ADC arranged that motorized military police escort the pair, but after the Field Marshal had questioned what was going on, the afternoon jaunts on the saddle came to an abrupt end.⁴⁹

Perhaps fuelled by time spent thinking whilst horse-riding, Manstein's concerns about the looming offensive remained unabated. On 1 June, he wrote to Zeitzler, giving him his latest appreciation of the situation. In comparison with the original timing of the attack in mid May, 'prospects for CITADEL had not improved'. In addition to the growing strength of Soviet defences and forces within the Kursk bulge, 'the threat to Donets and Mius had increased considerably'. But CITADEL would require all available forces, bringing with it the possibility of crises elsewhere. In any event, 'CITADEL remained a difficult attack with limited chances of success' and could only represent a 'partial blow'. Manstein concluded realistically: 'The battle in the East, in view of the enemy's reserves could not be won with the present level of forces.' It would 'require further reserves from OKH'.⁵⁰

Zeitzler was also surprisingly candid in his own assessment of CITADEL: 'The Russians must now have a really clear picture of our force groupings, intentions and resultant axes of our main thrusts. [Our] attack will not only have to overcome much more established positions, but confront a well-prepared and largely refreshed enemy.'⁵¹ Yet the existing OKH plan for a pincer attack on Kursk would remain.

Meanwhile, over the period 3–5 June 1943, Manstein directed the main war game prior to CITADEL. Run over three consecutive morning periods in each of his panzer corps headquarters (XXXXVIII, II SS and III), *Planspiel Zitadelle* was designed to synchronize the army group's scheme of manoeuvre. Towards the end of the month, Manstein hosted a big demonstration of armoured forces near Belgorod for the benefit of a visiting Turkish delegation, led by the Chief of the General Staff, Colonel General Cemil Cahit Toydemir. Army Detachment Kempf was entrusted with the planning and execution of the event, known as the *Türkenübung*. Its highlight was an exciting firepower display involving the 503rd Heavy Tank Battalion, equipped with the latest Tiger tanks, and all the other modern weaponry of the combined arms battle.[52]

Away from the Eastern Front, Germany's military planners were increasingly preoccupied with reinforcing Italy. On 18 June, the OKW Operations Staff submitted a strategic estimate to Hitler. Reflecting the growing probability that the Kursk attack would overlap with the start of the anticipated Allied offensive in the Mediterranean (coincidentally, one of Manstein's main concerns raised with Hitler on 4 May), it recommended that 'until the situation had been clarified, CITADEL should be cancelled and that a strong operational reserve at the disposal of the Supreme Command should be constituted both in the East and in Germany'. The same day, 'although he appreciated the point of view of OKW', Hitler resolved that CITADEL should 'definitely be carried out' on the 3rd, then subsequently postponed to 5 July.[53]

Notwithstanding the decision to proceed with the attack, the growing strength of the Soviet forces and their defences within the Kursk bulge continued to concern the German chain of command. Within OKH and Headquarters Army Groups Centre and South, the assessment of the enemy *within* the salient was pretty accurate. German intelligence, however, had scant understanding of what lay behind in the strategic depth. Having failed to detect the defensive preparations of the Steppe Military District, it had 'little idea about the size, composition, mechanized capabilities, or offensive potential of General Konev's force' – a fatal shortcoming.[54]

The omission of Stalin's most powerful strategic reserve is highly significant for two reasons. First, together with the positions at Kursk, Soviet defences had a total depth of 300 kilometres, far beyond the Germans' imagination. Secondly, as we shall see, when committed offensively on 12 July, Rotmistrov's 5th Guards Tank Army blunted and blocked Manstein's attack at the culmination of the battle at Prokhorovka. Although this Soviet armoured force was mauled in that action, its contribution to the Soviet defensive victory was none the less decisive.

The reports of OKH department 'Foreign Armies East' under the leadership of Gehlen had become increasingly pessimistic in the run-up to the battle. In mid June it had reported that a German attack in the area of Kursk would meet no less than '138 infantry divisions, 64 tank brigades and over 2,350 tanks'.[55] Three weeks later, on the eve of CITADEL, Gehlen concluded prophetically:

The Russians have awaited our attack in the anticipated sectors for weeks; through their energetic development of deeply echeloned positions and appropriate deployment of troops, they have done everything to block our thrust quickly. It is therefore most unlikely that the German attack will achieve a break-through.... I consider the planned operation as a really grave error, which will revenge itself greatly.[56]

So neither of the two essential preconditions for the success of CITADEL was present: there appeared next to no chance now of achieving operational surprise or in gaining sufficient tactical superiority to achieve a breakthrough, let alone conducting deep manoeuvre thereafter.

What, in retrospect, appears so obvious as an unwarranted gamble was not that clear at the time. After all, previous German Blitzkrieg offensives had been successful, and the undeniable triumph of Manstein's counter-offensive in February/March in saving the southern wing of the Eastern Front – although the circumstances were quite different to those now pertaining at Kursk – had led to a revival of German confidence. So it was not entirely fanciful for Wehrmacht commanders to believe that they would prevail again at Kursk, particularly if they were minded institutionally to overestimate their own forces' capabilities and to underestimate those of their enemy. Thus notwithstanding the depressing intelligence, Manstein recalled that although 'our attack would be difficult', it nevertheless 'would lead to success'. He admitted being more doubtful about whether an enemy offensive could be held in the Donets area. 'Yet we remained convinced', he assured his readers, that 'we could have coped with such a crisis after a victory at Kursk. Indeed, perhaps we could have derived an even larger victory from it.'[57]

Manstein noted in his memoirs that one might reasonably question why the army group commanders concerned did not declare unequivocally to Hitler that as the attack no longer made any sense, it should not be carried out. He conceded it 'may have been an error' not to have raised such objections more forcefully at the time.[58]

Final Deployment Plans

The OKH plan for CITADEL, authored by Zeitzler, was designed as a classic double envelopment. Soviet forces within the Kursk bulge would be trapped and destroyed by powerful concentric attacks from the north and south, with the heaviest available air and tank support, converging in the vicinity of Kursk. One of the last German manoeuvres conducted on this grand scale was the encirclement of Kiev in September 1941 by two panzer groups, which perhaps had given some inspiration for the Kursk operation, as might the traditional Cannae thinking and teaching of the German General Staff. Nearly two years later, however, the Wehrmacht now faced a much better organized and led Red Army, with apparently inexhaustible reserves of manpower and equipment, expecting and well prepared for the German attack. In the face of Soviet superiority at Kursk, there was little chance of the German forces conducting anything more than a preventive operational level strike before the inevitable Soviet summer offensive was unleashed. Whether it could delay or disrupt seriously this 'avalanche' remained to be seen. The unfavourable odds that the German armed forces faced are explained by analysing their deployment plans.

Within Army Group Centre, Lieutenant General Rudolf Schmidt's weak Second Panzer Army, an armoured force only in name consisting of three corps with fourteen infantry divisions and a sole panzer division in army reserve, defended the northern and eastern fronts of the Orel bulge.[59] Therein lay one of the basic flaws in the operational design of CITADEL: the best (and obvious) way for the Soviets to disrupt any German attack on the Orel–Kursk axis was to squeeze out the Orel salient by their own counter-offensive, which indeed happened. Manstein was therefore justified in drawing attention to this shortcoming in his memoir, stating that Second Panzer Army should have been sufficiently reinforced with infantry (and presumably with additional armour and artillery) to meet the inevitability of a Soviet attack, so 'preventing the enemy from achieving a quick success in the rear of Ninth Army'. In his view, further reinforcements were also required in both Model's army and in his own army group in order to ensure a clean break through the Soviet defences. He considered that the forces required could have been drawn from 'the so-called OKW theatres of war such as Norway, France and the Balkans, and through a timely evacuation of North Africa'. Yet Hitler was not prepared to accept the risks involved in denuding these areas and stake all on CITADEL.[60]

Model's Ninth Army was tasked with conducting the northern arm of attack on the Orel–Kursk axis. It was organized into five corps of which three panzer corps (XXXXI, XXXXVII and XXXXVI with four panzer and seven infantry divisions) were to conduct the main blow, supported by an infantry corps (XXIII) advancing on the left flank whilst his final corps (XX) secured his right. In reserve, he held back *Korpsgruppe Esebeck* with two panzer and one panzer grenadier divisions. Of a grand total of twenty-one divisions, only fourteen were engaged in the initial attack. Model decided to commit his infantry formations first, relying on these supported by heavy tanks (Tiger), tank destroyers (Ferdinand) and lighter assault guns (StG III) to force the defences of the Soviet 70th and 13th Armies, prior to releasing his panzer divisions.[61] Of his infantry formations, which were all below their established strength, only one was rated 'fully fit for all types of offensive operations'. In total, he had 988 tanks, tank destroyers and assault guns at his disposal for employment in the north, supported by 917 guns or rocket launchers and 640 combat aircraft of 1st *Fliegerdivision*.[62] Much to his chagrin, all of the promised new Mark V Panthers went to Army Group South.

South of Ninth Army lay Colonel General Walther Weiss's Second Army (not to be confused with Second Panzer Army), which lined the western extremity of the Kursk bulge from Sevsk to south of Sumy with two infantry corps (a total of eight divisions) supported by only 100 self-propelled anti-tank guns on an extended sector of over 200 kilometres, a true economy of force mission.[63] None the less, this army continued to fix a Soviet force considerably larger than its own.

Manstein's army group received the following mission in Hitler's Operational Directive No.6: 'Army Group South will jump off with strongly concentrated forces from the Belgorod–Tomarovka line, break through the Prilepy–Oboyan line, and link up with the attacking armies of Army Group Centre east of Kursk.'[64] Forming the southern pincer on the Belgorod–Oboyan–Kursk axis, Manstein's attacking force of Fourth Panzer Army (*left*) and Army Detachment Kempf (*right*) was much stronger than Model's, certainly in armour. Excluding army group reserves (only two divisions), it comprised nine panzer or panzer grenadier and seven infantry divisions.

Hoth's Fourth Panzer Army constituted the main effort of Army Group South. Consisting of one infantry (LII) and two panzer corps (XXXXVIII and II SS), it was strongly reinforced by heavy tanks and assault guns. This shock grouping constituted the cream of the German armoured force. It included the lavishly equipped *Grossdeutschland* and the three SS panzer grenadier divisions, each of which had on average half as many again more tanks and assault guns than the 'standard' army panzer divisions. *Grossdeutschland* was the strongest German armoured formation that took part in the battle, having been reinforced by 10th Panzer Brigade equipped with 200 unproven Panthers.

Hoth's army was required to attack from a line of departure astride Tomarovka to north-west Belgorod and punch through the Soviet 6th Guards Army, towards Kursk. He employed LII Corps in the west with two assaulting infantry divisions (255th and 332nd) to secure his left flank. His main attack would be conducted on a narrow frontage (25 kilometres) towards his first objective, Oboyan, some 50 kilometres distant to the north and roughly halfway to Kursk. On this axis, his principal thrust was to be conducted by XXXXVIII Panzer Corps, with two-thirds of 167th Infantry, 3rd and 11th Panzer Divisions and *Grossdeutschland*. On a parallel axis to its right was II SS Panzer Corps, with its three heavy panzer grenadier divisions, and one-third of 167th Infantry Division. Together, these twin mailed fists comprised nearly 1,100 tanks and assault guns. According to his chief of staff, Hoth resolved that the direct attack on Oboyan should 'not be interpreted literally'. Acknowledging the increasing strength of Soviet forces in that area, and more particularly, the growing threat to his eastern flank, Hoth had decided well before the attack that 'following our penetration of the enemy's defensive belt, II SS Panzer Corps would not advance north across the [river] Psel but veer sharply northeast toward Prokhorovka to destroy the Russian tank forces we expected to find there'.[65] Manstein concurred. It would mean that Hoth would strike to the north-east and not advance solely northwards towards Oboyan as the Soviet defenders expected. The snag was that this scheme of manoeuvre would risk dissipating Fourth Panzer Army's armour on two divergent axes unless XXXXVIII Corps conformed to its right neighbour. Overall, it was a risk worth taking if – and this was a very big if – Kempf could provide sufficient support from the south in advancing rapidly towards Prokhorovka.

Army Detachment Kempf was tasked with 'offensive screening' to the east and north-east of Fourth Panzer Army's attack. He was assigned two corps for this mission, III Panzer and XI Corps (Corps Raus) with three panzer (6th, 7th and 19th) and three infantry divisions (106th, 168th and 320th) between them.[66] His third corps (XXXXII) had a purely defensive function guarding the Northern Donets Front. The army detachment had two main tasks on breaking out from the sector Belgorod–Volchansk through 7th Guards Army's positions. Whilst Corps Raus secured a defensive front facing east along the river Korocha, a tributary of the Northern Donets, tight on its left flank III Panzer Corps would pivot around Belgorod and thrust in the general direction of Skorodnoye, 70 kilometres to the north-east.

Taking the final plans of Fourth Panzer Army and Army Detachment Kempf together, there was now an opportunity to co-ordinate closely the assaults of II SS and III Panzer Corps as the inner wings of the army group attack that would converge on Prokhorovka. If the breakthrough towards Kursk succeeded, the shock groups of his attacking armies were, in Manstein's words, 'to take part in the defeat of the enemy's operational reserves rushing there'.[67] There were, however, several imponderables in this design: would there be sufficient forces available successively to pierce the Soviet defences, to exploit into the enemy's depth and then to fight a decisive encounter battle whilst protecting throughout the resultant exposed flanks?

Following his front inspection of 10–12 May 1943, Manstein deduced the requirement for a set-piece, phased operation in the face of the enemy's growing defences and reserves. On 18 May he issued specific direction to his army, corps and divisional commanders. Sequentially, the attack would involve: breaking through the enemy's forward positions by a deliberate, combined arms attack with strong air and artillery support followed by fast exploitation to, and through, the second position using the normal attack methods of the panzer divisions; then battle in open ground against the enemy's operational reserves.[68] Surprisingly, he did not explain what the role of his own, limited operational reserve would be.

Superficially, there would appear to be an important difference between the operational designs of Manstein's two armies. Hoth was required to conduct a frontal assault on the enemy's main defences on an entirely expected axis, as was Model's Ninth Army in the north. Not surprisingly Hoth had informed Manstein that 'breaking through the Russian defensive system would be difficult, costly and time-consuming', mirroring the army group commander's own assessment.[69] Kempf, on the other hand, was required to penetrate the shoulder of the Voronezh *Front*'s defences that was nominally less well protected. Although utilizing a less likely avenue of approach, it proved an even tougher nut to crack. The Soviet 7th Guards Army had established very strong defences east and south-east of Belgorod on the Lipovyi and Northern Donets rivers respectively. Furthermore, strong operational level Soviet reserves, including the rifle divisions and anti-tank reserves of 69th Army, stood by to reinforce this particular sector.

Manstein had chosen a different approach from that adopted by Model in the north. In a similar manner – but in quite different circumstances – to Guderian at Sedan in May 1940, he had opted to employ armour rather than infantry in order to achieve a decisive breakthrough of the enemy's defences. It was not just a matter of having insufficient infantry and artillery available to use traditional tactics of attacking a well-established enemy. Manstein, Hoth and Kempf all reckoned on gaining sufficient penetration of the Soviets' first position by the concentrated employment of armour in forging an unstoppable battering ram. Such would be the momentum of this mass panzer attack that it would be able not only to punch through the enemy's rear positions, but also to destroy his armoured reserves beyond in a meeting engagement.

In total, Manstein had 1,377 tanks and assault guns at his disposal, supported by 1,134 artillery pieces or rocket launchers and 732 combat aircraft of VIII *Fliegerkorps*.[70] In addition, he held an army group reserve (XXIV Panzer Corps) ready to support the attack. In comparison with the plentiful Soviet strategic and operational reserves, Manstein's force was a modest grouping of 17th Panzer Division and 5th SS Panzer Grenadier Division *Wiking*, reinforced on 7 July by 23rd Panzer Division, together comprising only 181 tanks and assault guns.[71] The corps also held thirteen infantry battalions. The army group commander envisioned his reserve corps being employed with III Panzer Corps once the latter had reached open terrain. Both corps would then manoeuvre to defeat the anticipated operational level counterattack by Soviet tank reserves. But OKH held a 'string' on the employment of XXIV Corps: in other words, Manstein had to seek and receive permission to commit it, a fatal drawback in his plan. The lack of true reserves at both army group and army levels was a significant shortcoming in Army Group South's scheme of manoeuvre, which was never satisfactorily addressed.

Despite his armoured strength and assured close air support, Manstein was rightly concerned about shortfalls in artillery and his lack of infantry. He had assessed that he needed two further full-strength infantry divisions in order to mount the attack, which were never made available. By taking risks during the battle on 9 July, he was able to extract 198th Division, held as a reserve at the Donets front, and feed it into Kempf's attack. Yet he also needed further reserves of armour to call on. OKH could not provide any more; already, 70 per cent of the *Ostheer*'s armour had been concentrated for the operation at Kursk. In consequence, all other sectors of the Eastern Front had been stripped of tank support – including Manstein's thin front of over 600 kilometres along the Donets and Mius, defended by First Panzer and Sixth Armies respectively, with a total of twenty-one divisions. Significantly, there remained no strategic reserve such as the Soviets held in their Steppe *Front*, either to reinforce offensive success at Kursk or to counter a Soviet offensive. All available forces in the East had been staked on Operation CITADEL, which had all the hallmarks of a gambler's last defiant throw.

Astonishingly, on 5 July 1943 the Wehrmacht attacked with a marked inferiority of forces in all categories. Grouping together forces in both the Kursk and Orel sectors, the Soviet defenders outnumbered their opponents in manpower by 3.2:1; in armour by 3:1; in artillery by 5:1; and in aircraft 4.3:1.[72] German hubris in launching CITADEL in complete reversal of the military maxim that an attacker should outnumber the defender by at least 3:1 overall, seeking to achieve local superiorities of double that or more, may seem – in hindsight – beyond belief. Yet what was the alternative to attacking at Kursk if no ground could be sacrificed for manoeuvre? Surely the inevitable Soviet summer offensive would have come soon enough with even greater force? Despite their legitimate concerns, German senior commanders, including Manstein, were convinced that they had no alternative but to attack. They understood that it would be an exceptionally tough battle, but they had prepared well, and their forces, particularly the armoured formations, were rested and well equipped. Manstein declared in his memoirs, 'as far as Headquarters Army Group South was concerned, we acknowledged that our attack would be difficult, but were convinced that it would lead to success'.[73] This statement perhaps best explains why he never demanded vigorously the cancellation of Operation CITADEL, for all the delays and lack of infantry. Whereas in previous German offensives Soviet forces had crumbled as a result of Blitzkrieg, insufficient attention was now paid to the ability of their opponents to learn from past experience – an enduring lesson of war.

Just before the launch of the offensive, Manstein was due to fly to Bucharest to present Marshal Antonescu with a ceremonial Crimea Shield in Gold on the anniversary of the fall of Sevastopol. This visit was designed as a strategic deception measure to veil the date of the impending German attack. At the last moment, the flight to Rumania was postponed when Hitler summoned all his principal air and ground commanders for CITADEL to his headquarters in East Prussia.

As had become by now the Führer's customary style, this meeting was not a conference, rather an opportunity for Hitler 'to give a lecture', as Manstein recalled. The Führer reminded his audience that 'a successful operation would have a positive effect on Germany's allies and on the homeland'.[74] He then announced that the offensive would be launched on 5 July and justified his decision – correctly in Manstein's opinion – that Germany could not wait until the enemy attacked, perhaps in the winter or after the onset of the Second Front.

For his part, Manstein used the event to request the recall of Field Marshal von Richthofen from the Mediterranean theatre to reassume command of Fourth Air Fleet for CITADEL. Not that he had anything against his newly appointed successor, General of Flak Artillery Otto Dessloch, but Manstein and Richthofen had co-operated very closely since the recapture of the Kerch peninsula fourteen months before. Together they had seen through the highs and lows of Sevastopol and Stalingrad, and integrated air and land operations most effectively during the spring counter-offensive of 1943. The commander of Army Group

South was rightly concerned about the break-up of this proven team, which Corum has described as 'one of the most effective military partnerships of World War II'.[75] Manstein's bid was declined abruptly by Göring who, in Manstein's opinion, was 'not prepared to admit how critical the personality [of an airman] such as Richthofen was in commanding combat air formations'.[76]

Manstein flew from Rastenburg to Bucharest on 2 July 1943 and presented the Golden Crimea Shield to his friend Antonescu. The official ceremonies had begun with the German Field Marshal laying a wreath at the national memorial to the fallen as 'solemn music played'.[77] The next day, Manstein was back in Zaporozhye while 'journalists, diplomats and agents in the gossipy Rumanian capital were still radioing the news of [his] visit'.[78]

The Doomed Attack

On the eve of the attack on 4 July, Manstein and his battle staff joined their forward command post. It was located in a command train, *Steppenreiter*, hidden away in a woodland siding near Kharkov. Manstein did not remain passively in his train, for he used it as a mobile headquarters. As he wrote, not only did the train provide comfortable working and living conditions, but it allowed him to undertake on many occasions 'a long journey along the front, to visit staffs and troops of a particular sector by day, and then to travel on by night to the next'.[79]

Unfortunately, as Allied commanders such as Montgomery found out to their cost during the campaign in north-west Europe, this method of forward command, for all its advantages of proximity to the fighting troops, separated a ground force commander from his supporting airmen. Whereas the headquarters of General Dessloch's Fourth Air Fleet was based in the small town of Murafa, 60 kilometres west of Kharkov, the headquarters of VIII *Fliegerkorps*, which provided direct support to Fourth Panzer Army and Army Detachment Kempf, was located at Mikoyanovka, south of Belgorod. None the less, co-operation between the Luftwaffe and German land forces during CITADEL proved extremely effective, due in large measure to the excellent air liaison teams that were embedded in all German formation headquarters down to divisional level.

One of the German vulnerabilities was the dense concentration of aircraft, particularly those supporting Manstein's army group. In sixteen airfields around Kharkov and on strips as far forward as Belgorod, Luftwaffe machines were exposed to a pre-emptive Soviet strike. At first

light on 5 July, pre-warned about the imminent German assault by
Werther's intelligence and the German preliminary moves the previous
day, streams of Soviet bombers from the 17th Air Army attacked. They
were met in the air by swarms of Messerschmitt Me109s that had been
alerted just in time by fighter directors equipped with the Freya radar
system. A turkey shoot developed in which the Russians lost over 400
aircraft in one day, and 200 the next.[80] This was the first, and only, piece
of really good news that Manstein had on the opening of the offensive.
Over the ensuing week, further great air battles took place. The Luftwaffe continued to have a technical edge, employing newly developed
bomblet munitions against Soviet ground targets for the first time, but
could not be strong enough everywhere to prevent Soviet aircraft from
making dangerous raids on German armour and troop concentrations.
As Manstein had predicted, CITADEL was turning out to be as much an
air as a tank battleground. He sorely missed Richthofen, particularly
when ground attack aircraft allocated to his army group were switched
to support Ninth Army at the height of the attack, reinforcing failure
rather than success.

In the north, Model's attack had quickly become bogged down in the
Soviet defensive system. Taking huge casualties, his forces achieved a
maximum penetration of 14 kilometres by the close of 6 July. Three days
later his assault had culminated on the high ground at Olkhovatka, only
19 kilometres forward of his army's line of departure. Despite receiving
the lion's share of close air support in recent days, the Soviet resistance
had been formidable. In consequence, his infantry and tank losses were
becoming unsustainable. All Model's worst fears about the extraordinary
difficulty of the operation had come true. He was poised to commit his
final armoured reserves on 12 July in a desperate bid to break through
the remaining lines of the Soviet defence and advance towards Kursk. In
response to a massive Soviet attack that same day against the German
Second Panzer Army's exposed position in the Orel bulge, however,
Headquarters Army Group Centre ordered Model to turn around his
armour to face the new threat. This redeployment closed down his
offensive towards Kursk for good.

In the south, although they got off to a bad start, Manstein's armies
fared relatively better. Despite all the planning and rehearsals, basic
mistakes were made, particularly by XXXXVIII and III Panzer Corps.
Grossdeutschland's attack almost foundered when 10th Panzer Brigade
ran into a minefield and its novice, unwieldy Panther detachments struggled to fight an effective combined arms battle. Significantly, the brigade
had arrived at the beginning of July – far too late to take part in the

preliminary training and the new tanks proved highly unreliable.[81] On the left flank of Breith's corps, 6th Panzer Division failed to cross the Donets in strength and was pulled out and inserted behind 7th Panzer on the far right, thereby reducing at a stroke the flank protection available to II SS Panzer Corps. All units were surprised by the effectiveness of the Red Army's tactical deception measures and by the tenacity of its defence, which despite Manstein's and Hoth's warnings, still came as an unpleasant shock. That said, there was some significant progress in Army Group South.

Although there was general disappointment in the slow rate of advance, particularly by Kempf's corps on the right flank, Hoth's armour had broken through the first and second enemy positions after two exceptionally intense days of battle. But as Manstein commented, 'penetrating the enemy system of defences proved difficult. Particularly noticeable was the lack of infantry divisions for the first breakthrough operation, as was the relative weakness in artillery to support the attack.'[82] Knobelsdorff's XXXXVIII Panzer Corps had failed to reach its first day's objective, the crossings of the river Psel south of Oboyan, but had torn out large chunks of the Soviet defence. Hausser's II Panzer Corps had made the most progress, penetrating 25 kilometres in one and a half days, but taking heavy losses in the process.

Common to all three attacking panzer corps was the growing pressure of Soviet counterattacks into their flanks, which had become ever more extended as the panzer spearheads bit ever deeper into the Soviet defences. The problem was confounded by the gap that had opened up between Hausser's right flank and Breith's left flank – both of which were under heavy attack. Motorized infantry formations, heavily reinforced with anti-tank detachments, held ready behind the assaulting divisions would have been ideal for this task. Yet there was no second echelon as Hoth and Kempf had committed all their divisions in their initial assault, and no army group reserves yet available to assist.

Already by 6 July, the second day of the attack, Manstein had sensed that he had insufficient forces. He phoned Zeitzler accordingly and requested the immediate release of XXIV Panzer Corps – 'otherwise it won't work'. But he was disappointed then, as he was to be the next day with the very same demand: the Führer remained concerned about the risk to the Donets. Manstein complained that 'one must accept that risk in order to ensure success'. On 8 July, the Field Marshal again pressed his case to Zeitzler for the release of the panzer corps. Eventually, on 9 July, the fifth day, he asked the Chief of the General Staff to inform the Führer that the battle could not be won without XXIV Panzer Corps.

That brought only a partial result: whilst the concentration of the corps near Kharkov was authorized, it remained an 'OKH reserve'.[83] In other words, Manstein could not utilize it without gaining prior permission. It was never granted.

Although its precious armour and infantry would have represented useful assets to Manstein, whether the employment of XXIV Corps early on or later in the battle would have made any appreciable difference to its outcome is a matter of conjecture. In any event, the striking power that should have been available at the tips of the German armoured lances was dissipated in protecting its shafts, so blunting fatefully the power of the attack. The deeply constructed Soviet defensive system delayed the German advance sufficiently to give Soviet commanders time to reorganize their defences and to bring up fresh reserves. This proved to be the defining pattern of the battle. As Glantz and House have remarked, at Kursk, the Soviet Union 'learned to integrate combined arms forces into a mix that proved lethal for the attacking Germans'.[84]

Continuing pressure on XXXXVIII Panzer Corps' left flank resulted in a marked loss of momentum in Knobelsdorff's attack. His original scheme of manoeuvre had foreseen *Grossdeutschland* and 11th Panzer Divisions attacking abreast on the main axis towards Oboyan, with 3rd Panzer Division providing a secondary axis to the left. This division was in turn supported by the trailing 255th and 332nd Infantry Divisions of LII Corps. On 10 July, *Grossdeutschland* had to wheel to the south-west to 'clean up the enemy on the left flank'. Throughout the next day, the crews of 11th Panzer Division waited impatiently for the departed formation to return so that the two divisions could resume their drive to the north.

By this time Manstein had recognized that his main effort was constituted by Hausser's corps, which would provide the spearhead of his advance towards Kursk, and on 9 July gave it priority for close air support. However, in a mirror image of the problem affecting Knobelsdorff, Hausser had to commit half his force (*Das Reich* and 167th Infantry Division) to protecting his open right flank. That left only the *Leibstandarte* and *Totenkopf* Divisions available for the advance north. Including *Grossdeutschland* and 11th Panzer Divisions, this armoured grouping might have had sufficient striking power for a combined thrust on Oboyan and Kursk. Yet the growing threat to the east had to be dealt with, as Hoth had predicted well before the battle.

Army Group South's scheme of manoeuvre had begun to unravel further with the slow progress of III Panzer Corps. This meant that it neither protected Fourth Panzer Army's right flank nor was able to intercept Soviet strategic reserves.

Manstein does not appear to have made any critical decisions during the first four days of the operation, having approved Hoth's fateful orders on 9 July to stabilize both flanks of his army and to direct Hausser towards Prokhorovka. The first and second phases of Manstein's battle were fought out largely at corps level and below. He remained quietly confident, despite the uneven progress of his advance and mounting casualties, particularly in his infantry and panzer grenadier regiments. It was clear that the enemy was taking a beating and was throwing in its tactical and operational reserves fast and furious (including 1st Tank Army, 2nd and 5th Guards Tank Corps) in a desperate attempt to stem the German tide. Yet had Manstein reacted too late to events, or had he realized belatedly that a thrust towards Kursk was no longer practical as a result of the difficulties his and Model's forces were facing? Manstein's memoirs are silent on this issue.

The first operational level crisis came on 10 July when Kempf reported that III Panzer Corps could not make any further headway. It had 'stuck' 19 kilometres forward of the Donets, but far to the south of II SS Panzer Corps. Manstein met Kempf at his headquarters at Novo Bavaria on the morning of 10 July. The Field Marshal ordered the continuation of the attack, having previously reinforced Kempf with 198th Infantry Division, a reserve hurriedly brought up from the Donets front in trucks, releasing 7th Panzer Division from defensive tasks.

A more fundamental review of the attack came on 11 July, when Manstein met with Kempf and Hoth at the former's headquarters to hold a council of war. According to Busse, the Field Marshal asked, 'Should the attack be continued, considering the condition of the troops, the ever-increasing strength of the Russians, and – particularly – the fact that Ninth Army's assault had ground to a complete halt by 9 July?' Kempf recommended suspension. Hoth, on the other hand, 'advocated a continuation of the operation with the more limited objective of destroying the Red Army units south of the Psel river by a co-ordinated attack by both armies'. Manstein was inclined once again to share Hoth's opinion and reserved his decision pending going forward to consult with Breith. On return, Manstein confirmed that his army group would continue offensive operations.[85]

Late on 11 July, Breith broke through the second Soviet line of defence and his three panzer divisions plunged at last into open ground. Meanwhile, both II SS and XXXXVIII Panzer Corps were involved that day in heavy defensive fighting, beating off all Soviet attacks. This was surely the moment to bring up XXIV Panzer Corps, if it could be released. But as Hausser prepared to attack Prokhorovka the next day, Vatutin assembled fresh forces in order to destroy both Fourth Panzer Army and Army Detachment Kempf by a well-co-ordinated attack. Manstein likewise issued orders for the continuation of operations albeit with a much more limited objective than that originally intended at the outset of CITADEL. He determined that the best course open was to defeat the enemy formations already in contact and those expected over the next few days, so achieving freedom of manoeuvre for subsequent operations. At the very least, German forces would then be able to return to their original line of departure, having inflicted as much damage as possible to the Red Army during the battle.[86]

Specifically, Manstein directed that whilst the right wing of III Panzer Corps should continue to thrust towards Korodscha, its left wing should turn north-west and – in close co-operation with the right wing of II SS Corps – should envelop and destroy the enemy's 69th Army that lay in between.[87] Even more ambitiously, Manstein and Hoth determined that the mass of XXXXVIII and II SS Panzer Corps should reassume the offensive, cross the Psel east of Oboyan, then wheel to the west and destroy the enemy in the west part of the Kursk bulge in a battle of reversed front.[88] Subsequently this plan was developed as Operation ROLAND. In order to protect this manoeuvre from enemy attack from the north and east, Army Detachment Kempf would need to be reinforced with XXIV Corps.

Although historical attention on the events of 12 July 1943 has focused on the famous tank action at Prokhorovka, all three of Manstein's attacking corps (XXXXVIII, II SS and III Panzer) were involved in ferocious, largely defensive, fighting that day and the next. Whilst Hausser's SS troopers smashed the tank and mechanized corps of 5th Guards Tank Army in a confused, swirling encounter battle to the immediate west of Prokhorovka, Knobelsdorff's tank crews and grenadiers on the north and left flanks of Fourth Panzer Army held off equally determined Soviet counterattacks from 1st Tank Army and other formations. Manstein and his subordinate commanders all the way down to sub-unit level held their nerve, mastered one local crisis after the next and stood their ground. Although German casualties continued to rise alarmingly, particularly in the hard-pressed panzer grenadier and infantry regiments, tank and assault-gun strengths had held up surprisingly well. His panzer and panzer grenadier divisions, although tired and battered, were all available to continue the offensive on 14 July. In addition, his only operational reserve, XXIV Panzer Corps, although still under a string from OKH, now stood ready west of Kharkov. Other than this corps, Manstein had nothing left to throw into the battle. As he could not afford to take any further risk on the threatened Donets and Mius fronts, he could not touch his sole remaining mobile formation, 16th Panzer Grenadier Division. It remained in reserve in the south.

Operation CITADEL was fast approaching its culmination. At this most critical moment, Manstein was called away from the battle on the morning of 13 July to attend a conference with the Führer in East Prussia, along with Kluge. From his perspective, Manstein was absolutely right to reflect that 'Hitler should either have come forward to both army group headquarters – or if the strategic situation did not permit his absence – to send the Chief of the General Staff.' But that was not the German leader's style. In any case, events far away from Kursk had intervened. Hitler now wished to call off CITADEL in consequence of the successful Allied landings on Sicily (10 July) and the threat of an imminent Italian collapse.

Before Manstein got to hear about Hitler's rationalization of strategy, his diversion to East Prussia took on a near-farcical dimension. According to Stahlberg, he and the Field Marshal left Kharkov prematurely and arrived at Lötzen on the morning of the 13th far too early for the conference with the Führer that evening. Such are the petty frictions of war. They were taken to the OKH guesthouse, and with time on their hands, decided to go for a swim in the hot summer sun. As neither had a suitable costume, they decided to go skinny-dipping in the Mauersee. And who should be waiting for them on return at the lake's shore? None other than Field Marshal Erwin Rommel, recalled from Italy to be present at Hitler's big conference, the first and only time that Manstein and he met.[89]

That evening, Hitler explained the strategic situation facing the Reich. 'Most likely, Sicily would be lost, and the next step of the enemy could be a landing in the western Balkans or in lower Italy,' Manstein recalled. To meet this threat, 'fresh armies were required'. As the only available source was the Eastern Front, CITADEL would have to be called off. Kluge agreed: Ninth Army, having already lost 20,000 men, could not make any more progress and all mobile forces were committed to dealing with the crisis in Second Panzer Army's sector. 'For this reason', Kluge concluded, 'its attack could neither be continued nor resumed later.'[90]

Manstein pleaded for the attack to continue. 'After the defensive successes of the previous days against practically all the enemy's operational reserves thrown into the battle', he argued, 'victory is very close.' If only Ninth Army 'could continue to fix the enemy to its front, and perhaps later resume its attack', then Manstein proposed to destroy finally the enemy already in contact with his forces. He then outlined his modified plan (Operation ROLAND) to swing towards the west with Fourth Panzer Army. At the very least, if Ninth Army could not reassume its operations in CITADEL once it had restored the situation in the Orel salient, then Army Group South would have to 'clear up' the situation in order to gain 'free air' – in other words, attack the enemy sufficiently hard in order to disengage.[91]

When Kluge confirmed that there was absolutely no question of Ninth Army reassuming offensive operations, Hitler confirmed his intention to break off CITADEL, having taken into account the urgent need to transfer forces to the Mediterranean. Furthermore, in the face of the looming Soviet offensive against the Donets area, he denied Army Group South the employment of XXIV Corps. The only crumb of good news that Manstein could take back to his headquarters was that the Führer approved his proposal to destroy enemy forces to the army group's front in order to establish the appropriate conditions to break contact and withdraw.[92]

Before Manstein could fly back to the battle the next morning, he – along with Rommel and Kluge – returned to spend the night in the OKH guesthouse. According to Stahlberg's account, 'There was good French red wine and gradually tongues were loosened.' Kluge was the first to go to bed, and on departure stated: 'Manstein, the end will be bad, and I repeat what I told you earlier: I am prepared to serve under you.' Manstein, Rommel and Stahlberg were left in the room and drank some more wine. Rommel forecast a catastrophic end to the Third Reich: the whole house of cards would collapse. Manstein did not agree; he felt that Hitler would give up the Supreme Command before the end came. Rommel countered: 'He will never give up the Supreme Command. I obviously know him better than you do, Herr von Manstein.' Manstein then rose to retire, whereupon Rommel declared: 'I too am prepared to serve under you.'[93]

Manstein's forces conducted modest attacks for the next three days, but did not execute the ROLAND plan. The XXIV Corps remained unemployed in the Kharkov area. When OKH ordered the release of II SS Panzer Corps and *Grossdeutschland* on 17 July, it spelled the end of CITADEL. All that had been gained at such cost was given up to no appreciable gain.

Assessment

In concluding his brief chapter in *Lost Victories*, Manstein offered no detailed explanation for the failure of Kursk. In the German original, he highlighted the omission of surprise, the insufficiency of forces and the successive delays in launching the offensive. There was not even a hint of self-criticism of the army group or subordinate formation plans. 'The lack of success,' he opined, cannot be put down to the 'performance of the troops or in their command'. Furthermore, rather then giving any credit to the skill and tenacity of the Soviet defenders, he stressed that 'a comparison of casualties on both sides shows how superior our troops were in capability to the opposition'.[94]

His chief of staff echoed some of these sentiments, stressing that the 'spirit, bearing, and selfless devotion of the men were beyond praise'. However, Busse took serious issue with the overall design for battle, observing critically that forcing 'the enemy into an open battle by means of a breakthrough [operation] was an erroneous decision'. There were, in his view, sufficient panzer and panzer grenadier divisions available to gain a major victory, 'but only if they succeeded in reaching open terrain'. Part of the Germans' difficulties lay in the lack of infantry divisions (a concern that Manstein and he had raised repeatedly in the run-up to the offensive), which in turn led to over-extended flanks in the assaulting mobile formations and a dissipation of their fighting power. Above all, the fateful delays in launching the attack solely benefited the enemy: 'Time worked for the Red Army in every respect', hence 'all the dark forebodings of OKH and the combat commanders came true'. Busse agreed with his army group commander: 'CITADEL failed because it was carried out with insufficient forces, considering the late timing of the operation.'[95]

Busse also supported Manstein over the superiority of the 'backhand' manoeuvre as opposed to the 'forehand' approach. He considered that the Soviets would have attacked in the summer of 1943 'regardless of whether we did them the favour of making the first move'. That year, he maintained, 'could have taken a different turn had the Red Army been made to expend its forces in a direct assault on our unbroken front, backed up by powerful mobile reserves'. Yet the fact remained that Hitler and OKH, with the acquiescence of Kluge and Manstein, had decided on an offensive solution, one that turned out to be hopelessly ambitious. Furthermore, neither Manstein nor his faithful chief of staff acknowledged that mistakes in their own planning could have contributed to the severe difficulties that their forces faced during the opening phase and subsequent conduct of the attack. It took one of their corps commanders, Raus, in retrospect to put his finger on a fundamental military truth that his superiors, including Kempf, ignored. One of the reasons for the failure of the operation 'included the adherence to a battle plan that had been formulated in anticipation of other events and conditions'.[96] Hoth and Manstein, and by implication Busse, were also applicable to varying degrees of this telling criticism. Significantly, Manstein failed to offer any retrospective analysis of his intent or scheme of manoeuvre, or those of his army commanders.

The battle of Kursk was not of Manstein's conception; it is hard not to conclude that he never identified personally with its purpose and planning. For all his concerns about the lack of forces and the time delays, he never enunciated a clear operational idea that balanced the two competing imperatives of seizing terrain (pinching out the bulge to shorten the front) and defeating the enemy's forces (particularly his operational and strategic reserves). As Newton has observed, it was Hoth rather than he who first recognized the need to deal with these reserves 'as a prerequisite for attempting major territorial gains'. Whilst Manstein deferred to Hoth when it came to the need to adjust the original plan to fight a general engagement in the vicinity of Prokhorovka, he failed to adjust both Hoth's and Kempf's planning to ensure that the army group's attention remained focused on this critical action at the decisive point. Furthermore, he should have ensured that his attacking armies had sufficient tactical and operational reserves available to feed into the battle in order to reinforce initial success, the location of which could never be predicted with sufficient certainty when confronted by a well-organized and determined enemy. Manstein's and his subordinates' faith in their own abilities, perhaps justified on recent past experience, had led to this dangerous overconfidence.

Newton's criticism that 'Erich von Manstein was a strategist, first and foremost, rather than a tactician' is an inaccurate generalization, for Manstein's forte was neither strategy nor tactics, but rather operational art.[97] Yet his uncanny sixth sense for operational level matters deserted him at Kursk. In his three-phase design for battle, he failed to predict the need to defeat heavy Soviet counterattacks on the Germans' exposed, over-extended flanks by tactical and operational reserves. This was a fight that had to be won quickly if there was to be any hope of meeting the Soviet strategic reserves in open ground on reasonably favourable terms. Had he more closely supervised his subordinates' planning and decisions in battle, then some of the problems in Knobelsdorff's and Breith's initial attacks might have been avoided, and perhaps the wide separation between Hoth's and Kempf's armies could have been narrowed. Relying as they do on hindsight, such criticisms may appear rather unfair. As we have seen, Manstein was a firm believer in trusting his subordinates. On this occasion, however, it would appear that he had given them rather too much latitude, particularly in respect of the strong-willed Hoth.[98]

Manstein deduced a vital lesson from the battle for the Dnepr later in 1943: 'that even when forced to resort to operational expedients, one should never for a moment disregard the fundamental idea on which one's own conduct of operations is based'.[99] Whereas one can identify such an overarching operational concept in all his major operations before Kursk, one can search long and hard for that special hallmark of generalship at CITADEL. Hence the final scheme of manoeuvre of Army Group South was never greater than the sum of the parts of the subordinate armies, who fought largely independent, bitterly contested battles.

In passing, Glantz and House offer a succinct explanation for the Soviet success, which brings much needed balance to the largely self-serving German accounts:

> [It] required remarkable self-confidence for Vatutin, Rokossovsky and the other Soviet commanders to wait calmly while the German juggernaut prepared to do its worst. When the worst came, Soviet numerical superiority, the stubborn tenacity of the Soviet soldier, the improved combat skill of his commanders, and the Soviets' ability to sustain staggering losses spelled doom for Citadel.[100]

Manstein's memoir surely would have been all the better had he, just the once, acknowledged that he had been outfought at Kursk by a superior enemy. For all the odds that were stacked against the German forces under his command, he may have sensed that the battle did not represent the finest chapter in his military career. It was without doubt a Soviet victory, one with which he never fully came to terms.

14

Fighting on Two Fronts

*'As long as I remain at this post ... I must have the chance
to use my own head.'*[1] Erich von Manstein

Confronting the Hydra

'When CITADEL was called off', Manstein wrote, 'the initiative in the
Eastern theatre of war finally passed to the Russians.'[2] Nine months of
near continuous fighting followed in which the Red Army pushed
German forces steadily back to the Polish and Rumanian borders. He
remained in command of Army Group South until dismissed by Hitler
at the end of March 1944 as he 'now appeared in need of a rest'.[3] The
reality was different. Urged by Goebbels and Himmler, the Führer
parted company with the Field Marshal because he could no longer
afford to make public concessions to a highly talented but increasingly
awkward subordinate.

Manstein faced two closely interrelated challenges. On one hand, he
conducted a series of bitterly contested defensive battles against superior
Soviet forces in the most threatened sector of the Eastern Front. These
involved withdrawal from the Donets–Mius Line and Kharkov, a fighting
retreat to the Dnepr, the abandonment of Kiev and subsequent loss of
the western Ukraine. On the other, was an equally sapping, personal
dispute with Hitler to gain freedom of manoeuvre and to establish a new
command structure for the *Ostheer*. In both spheres, he was unsuccessful.
'The struggle to get operational needs recognized in time', he observed,
'was the decisive feature of the 1943–44 campaign on the German side.'[4]

Army Group South bore the brunt of Soviet offensives on the Eastern
Front that lasted without significant interruption from CITADEL to early
May 1944. Whilst he succeeded in preventing another military disaster
on the scale of Stalingrad, Manstein only managed to slow down the
remorseless Soviet onslaught. His army group remained always 'on the
back foot in relation to the measures of the enemy'. Therefore it 'could
not prevent the successes of a [numerically] superior enemy; rather it
could merely limit their operational consequences'. Accordingly, his

operations were characterized by a 'system of expedients'. Manstein's defensive concept depended on 'concentrating forces from one less threatened sector to another as required in order to block an enemy penetration, or when possible, to inflict a counter-blow'.[5] However proactively these measures were taken at the tactical level, Manstein's command remained primarily *reactive* at the operational level against an enemy growing in capability.

Hitler and Manstein failed to concede the fact that the Red Army had now come of age. The four *Fronts* pitched against Army Groups South and A were handled with great skill.[6] Their major operations were planned meticulously, employing deception and security measures that regularly fooled German intelligence. Backed with *matériel* aplenty, Soviet forces acted largely at will across Manstein's over-extended front. At the same time, his enemy's technique grew ever more sophisticated. By establishing overwhelming local superiority at the chosen decisive point, supported by air and massed artillery fire, Soviet armour penetrated routinely into the depth of the German defence. These spearheads could no longer be defeated quickly and disaster often beckoned. In consequence, Manstein's meagre reserves of armour were shuttled from one flank to the other in order to master one crisis whilst the next was already brewing. As much as he could juggle his forces, he could never rest them adequately and prepare for new tasks.

Typically executed against the odds, Manstein's operations demanded great sacrifice of the forces under his command. His armies bled in the process. German infantry formations were largely immobile; their inadequate artillery and logistic support remained horse-powered. A sprinkling of assault guns and self-propelled tank-destroyers provided the only rocks of the defence. Depleted infantry units rarely gained any respite from combat or received adequate replacements to refill their thinned-out ranks. New recruits rushed to the front lacked sufficient training and experience to survive for long. By August 1943, Manstein recorded, 'divisional casualties were already alarmingly high, and two divisions had broken down completely as a result of continuous over-strain'.[7] At the end of his tenure in command, the fighting power of Army Group South was so diminished that OKH had to order the break-up of no less than eight infantry divisions.[8] Despite the impressive gains in German armaments production in the second half of 1943, replacements of wheeled and tracked vehicles could not keep pace with continual losses. As a result, Manstein's panzer and panzer grenadier divisions fought with tank and assault-gun strengths well below their establishments, and were organized typically as regimentally sized battle groups (*Kampfgruppen*). In comparison with the infantry, by and large they retained a qualitative edge over their opponents.

Whilst the Red Army also suffered grievously, it could regenerate itself successively in a manner that the Wehrmacht could not. Despite the hammering they received at Kursk, the Soviet forces engaged – particularly the tank and mechanized corps – were quickly brought back up to strength whilst rifle formations remained weak on re-entering battle.[9] As Manstein remarked bitterly, 'In fact, we confronted a hydra: for every head cut off, two new ones appeared to grow.'[10] Across this vast battlefield, the local population endured terrible privations. Large tracts of the Ukraine bore the marks and tears of the infamous German policy of 'scorched earth' that became a central charge at Manstein's war crimes trial in 1949.[11]

Meanwhile, Manstein's relationship with Hitler remained professional but increasingly strained. Over time, he tried the Führer's patience with his repeated demands for additional forces and freedom of action. Despite his best advocacy, he never obtained sufficient operational leeway to manoeuvre in the flexible manner and to the end he desired – to fight the Russians to a standstill. Any small concessions or reinforcements he extracted from Hitler were usually either too modest or too late to be effective. In the bigger strategic scheme, any tactical successes scored would only delay, rather than thwart, the inevitable Soviet advance.

Despite all the pressures on him, Manstein remained surprisingly optimistic about the military situation. He resisted all attempts of the German resistance to involve him in decapitating the regime as, in a position of senior command, he considered it irresponsible to let down his soldiers fighting at the front to an uncertain fate. Although he remained outwardly loyal to the Führer, he knew many of those plotting against Hitler. Individuals such as Erich Fellgiebel, Henning von Tresckow and Eberhard Finckh were close associates. He did not betray them. Of his chief of operations, Colonel Georg Schulze-Büttger, he wrote for many: 'This especially capable officer and man of fine character [was] unfortunately one of the many victims' in the bloody aftermath of the plot of 20 July 1944.[12]

Fighting Withdrawal to the Dnepr: Further Wrangling with Hitler

As Operation CITADEL closed down on 17 July 1943, the Red Army launched its anticipated offensives against the German Sixth Army on the Mius and the First Panzer Army on the Middle Donets. Although the attacks of the Southern and South-Western *Fronts* were held by employing his only reserves, including XXIV Panzer Corps that had remained uncommitted during CITADEL, Manstein considered that the situation would not remain stable if substantial Soviet bridgeheads on these rivers were left intact. As there were no fresh forces at hand, he stripped his northern wing of armour in order 'to iron things out in the Donets area'. In so doing, he had failed to realize that the Soviet operations in the south were diversions. Compounding this error, he assumed that the Soviet forces struck in the battle of Kursk had been given 'so much punishment' that 'we could count now on a breathing space in this part of the front'. In this estimation he made, in his own words, a 'disastrous' decision as 'the enemy took the offensive there earlier than we had expected'.[13]

The massive Soviet Belgorod–Kharkov offensive (Operation RUMIANTSEV) launched on 3 August 1943 that led to the loss of these two cities caught Manstein's forces completely off balance, setting a pattern of operations in which the *Ostheer* danced to the Red Army's tune. The fact that a short, sharp German counterattack (30 July–2 August) in the south restored the Mius front temporarily was irrelevant, as the principal threat to the integrity of the southern wing of the Eastern Front remained on Manstein's northern flank. Although no doubt he took some pleasure from being named again in the *Wehrmachtsberichte* of 4 August 1943, stirring words of personal recognition could not relieve the pressure.[14]

A major Soviet penetration on Manstein's northern flank would not only threaten cohesion with Army Group Centre but also risk the destruction of both Army Groups South and A by deep envelopment. Indeed, the aim of RUMIANTSEV was to achieve just that by advancing through Kharkov to Dnepropetrovsk and then wheeling down to the Black Sea coast.[15] Despite the renewed threats to German positions on the Donets and Mius, and subsequently to the Dnepr bend to the west, Manstein attempted to hold true to the principle 'that the Army Group's northern wing was operationally more important'.[16]

In the meantime, the Soviets had recuperated at a pace and scale that the Germans could scarcely imagine. Manstein was not alone in misjudging their extraordinary recovery since CITADEL. Throughout this period Hitler was convinced that the Red Army would soon run out of steam. Yet the battle of Kursk had only delayed *Stavka* from launching a series of offensives that rippled across much of the Eastern Front in the second half of 1943, involving a succession of skilfully placed and well-timed operational blows that ruptured the German defence. Operation RUMIANTSEV is a case in point. On the first day of attack, the

Soviet 5th Guards Tank Army penetrated 26 kilometres astride the vulnerable boundary between Fourth Panzer Army and Army Detachment Kempf.[17] Two days later, Soviet forces seized Belgorod and Orel (the latter as part of Operation KUTUZOV), prompting Stalin to order a celebratory artillery salute in Moscow.

By 8 August, to the north-west of Kharkov, a gap of 55 kilometres had opened up between Fourth Panzer Army and Army Detachment Kempf. To an alarmed Manstein, the way appeared open for the enemy to 'drive through to Poltava and onwards to the Dnepr'.[18] On that day of crisis, Zeitzler appeared at Headquarters Army Group South. Having highlighted the imminent threat to his two northern armies, Manstein urged his guest to take urgent decisions to prevent the destruction of the German southern wing. He proposed two courses of action. The first was to 'evacuate the Donets area forthwith in order to release forces for the Army Group's northern wing and at least hold the Dnepr in the south'. The alternative was to reinforce on a scale that took Zeitzler completely by surprise. Manstein demanded the speedy transfer of no less than twenty divisions: ten 'from other fronts to those of Fourth Panzer Army and Central Army Group's Second Army adjoining it in the north' and 'a further ten to set in motion towards the Dnepr'.[19] In fact, the situation required a combination of both measures: shortening the front and receiving substantial reinforcements. Moreover, he needed to add depth to his defence by establishing a strong position on the Dnepr, the construction of which he had argued for since February 1943.

Manstein lamented in his memoir that 'no effective action' was taken as a result of Zeitzler's visit.[20] This was not quite the case. On 11 August, Hitler very belatedly authorized work to start on the *Ostwall* (Eastern Wall). By the end of that month, Army Group South had received five additional infantry divisions and one armoured. These reinforcements, which would have proved extremely useful prior to CITADEL, now proved woefully insufficient to stem the Russian juggernaut. Operation RUMIANTSEV had yet to run its bloody course. Fourth Panzer Army and Army Detachment Kempf battled to survive, giving ground to superior Soviet forces whose pressure was unrelenting.[21]

Within a week of the start of the Soviet operation, Manstein had assembled two strong counterattack groups: III Panzer Corps, including SS panzer grenadier divisions *Das Reich* and *Totenkopf* brought up by rail from the Mius front, and XXIV Corps, which included *Grossdeutschland* returned from Army Group Centre. Whilst the Germans were able to stabilize the situation temporarily in Fourth Panzer Army's sector through a series of costly tank engagements around Bogodukhov and

Akhtyrka (12–17 August), Kharkov remained threatened with encirclement, as was Army Detachment Kempf charged with its defence. Although Hitler had demanded on 12 August that the 'city be held at all costs', Manstein 'had no intention of sacrificing an army' for it.[22]

On 16 and 18 August, Malinovsky's South-Western and Tolbukhin's Southern *Fronts* launched a powerful offensive against the Middle Donets and Mius. The Soviet Donbas–Melitopol operation was not a mere diversion: its aim was to 'speed up the destruction of the German First Panzer and Sixth Armies and to liberate the Donets Basin'.[23] By this time, Manstein had already drawn the majority of German armour to the north. He had not anticipated a renewed offensive erupting so soon in the south. With no reserves available to reinforce this freshly endangered wing, it is hardly surprising that he recorded 22 August as 'very much a day of crisis'. Sixth Army was 'not able to restore the situation'. Whilst First Panzer Army had managed to bring the enemy attack 'to a standstill . . . it, too, was coming to the end of its strength'.[24] That day Kharkov was abandoned, so ending the fourth and final battle for the Ukrainian industrial centre during the Second World War.

By 27 August, Operation RUMIANTSEV had petered out and Manstein was able to establish a 'fairly continuous front from Kharkov to Sumy'.[25] Fourth Panzer and Eighth Armies remained intact, licking their wounds, proud that they had halted the Soviet offensive. Although the Voronezh and Steppe *Fronts* had together lost a quarter of a million men in the Belgorod–Kharkov operation, the Red Army could afford to accept such staggering losses of attrition whilst the *Ostheer* could not. Manstein reported to OKH on 20/21 August that his thirty-eight infantry and fourteen armoured divisions had been reduced in fighting power to the equivalent of eighteen and six respectively. For a casualty total of 133,000 men, he had only received 33,000 replacements that month.[26]

Apart from the mounting butcher's bill, Manstein had wider concerns. Although his northern flank now enjoyed a brief respite, the situation on the southern 'became more perilous than ever'. Therefore he either needed further forces in this sector or freedom of manoeuvre to establish a shorter line to the rear. His 'categorical demand' to this effect resulted in Hitler flying out to Vinnitsa on 27 August to meet him and his army commanders. This meeting was the first of a series of four over the next three weeks. Manstein was in no mood to pull his punches, stressing to the Führer that 'while the Donets area could not be held with the forces now available', the 'far greater danger for the German southern wing as a whole lay on the northern wing of [the] Army Group'. In the long run,

Eighth and Fourth Panzer Armies would be unable 'to prevent the enemy from breaking through to the Dnepr'.

Manstein then gave Hitler two choices: either reinforce Army Group South with 'not less than twelve divisions' or 'abandon the Donets area to release forces'. Hitler 'remained entirely objective throughout the discussion', according to Manstein. He agreed that the army group 'must be afforded vigorous support' and promised to provide 'whatever formations could possibly be spared from the sectors of Northern and Central Army Groups'.[27] On this occasion, Manstein was inclined to take the Führer at his word. Yet the enemy always has a vote. The previous day (26 August) Rokossovsky's Central *Front* had unleashed an offensive against Second Army. This development only added to the pressure on Army Group Centre's defence as both Fourth and Ninth Armies were still struggling to contain earlier Soviet attacks. As a result, Kluge could not release even a single division. So nothing came of Hitler's pledges.

The conference at Vinnitsa was to demonstrate again to Manstein that Hitler would give assurances that he was not in a position to keep. Meanwhile, the operational situation took several further turns for the worse. In the south, Sixth Army's position became untenable under heavy Soviet pressure. By 31 August it had been authorized to fall back on to the 'Tortoise Position', thus starting the evacuation of the Donets area that Manstein had long requested. Hitler reluctantly gave him permission to withdraw Sixth Army and the right wing of First Panzer Army. This limited concession 'served only to preserve the southern wing from defeat', Manstein commented ruefully. Had the Führer's decision been made 'a few weeks earlier', he maintained, then 'the Army Group would have been in a position to fight the battle on its southern wing more economically'.[28]

After CITADEL, the increasing gravity of the operational situation made it evident to both Kluge and Manstein that something had to be done. They saw the necessity for a radical change to the high command of Germany's armed forces to improve the chances of military success leading to an 'acceptable' outcome of the war. In his memoirs, Manstein says he asked Field Marshal von Kluge to accompany him to East Prussia so that they could act together in confronting Hitler.[29] Yet the meeting of 3 September was very much a joint initiative. Although Manstein makes no mention of it, Kluge had sounded him out beforehand by means of an emissary, Colonel Rudolph-Christoph Freiherr von Gersdorff, a member of the resistance.

According to Gersdorff, before he set off for Zaporozhye, Kluge instructed him to inform Field Marshal von Manstein that 'after a *coup d'état*' he would 'offer him the post of Chief of the Wehrmacht General Staff – in other words the combined staffs of the army, navy and Luftwaffe'.[30] On departure, Tresckow gave Gersdorff letters for Manstein from Goerdeler and Popitz, who both implored Germany's generals to take action against Hitler, under the strict proviso that he was only to hand the letters over if he were sure about the Field Marshal's reaction.[31]

Kluge, nicknamed 'Clever Hans', if not the brightest general in the German Army had a good, solid reputation. Although sympathetic to the opposition against Hitler, despite Tresckow's best efforts he had not committed himself fully. None the less, he wished to gain wider support. He was astute in understanding Manstein's psyche and strategic perspective. In view of recent events, including their discussion with Rommel, he knew – no doubt urged by Tresckow – that his comrade-in-arms would be extremely interested in discussing the high command of the Wehrmacht. So Gersdorff communicated Kluge's thoughts on this issue. Simply put, 'the collapse of the Eastern Front is only a question of time due to the conflict between OKW and OKH and Hitler's dilettantish style of command'. Gersdorff recalled that Manstein agreed: 'I'm of the same opinion entirely, but I am not the right man to say this to Hitler. He now regards me with distrust. Only Rundstedt and Kluge could undertake this mission.'[32]

Although Manstein did not document verbatim his conversation with Gersdorff in his private diary, his entry of 8 August 1943 lists his deliberations on Kluge's questions. Some excerpts reveal his dangerously frank position on Hitler:

a) *View on foreign policy.* In my opinion, there is no possibility of peace at the moment because the enemy believes that victory is close at hand ...

b) *Question of internal difficulties.* Whether these exist, I cannot judge. In principle, the Army has nothing to do with such things. It has its oath and duty of obedience, and will always be that part [of society?] that remains ever loyal. Any thought that military commanders should meddle in questions of political leadership would mean the undermining of the military chain of command ... In any case, Hitler is the only man who enjoys the trust of the people and the soldiers, and whom they believe in. No other would have this [support].

c) *Question of military command.* There is no doubt that the current situation is the result of errors in command. However, one can fully exclude the possibility of Hitler giving up supreme command. On the other hand, a sensible command structure is urgently required and must be achieved through presentation to the Führer.... We must achieve [a situation in which] the Führer listens to his advisors, and does not [try to] command everything himself. His task as Führer and commander is at a higher level.

[With reference to] the request from Kluge to present these matters of military command to Hitler. I cannot do this myself, since foreign propaganda is making me out to be the man who wants to assume high command.[33]

To his last comment, Manstein added a revealing footnote: 'Zeitzler had informed me that the English Agency Reuter [*sic*] had claimed a couple of days before that I was going to be appointed to overall command. An attempt, then, to sow mistrust.'[34]

What Manstein did not record was the more candid exchange that then took place, if Gersdorff's memory – thirty years after the event – can be trusted. 'Perhaps you and the other field marshals should go to Hitler and hold a pistol to his chest,' he suggested provocatively. Allegedly, Manstein countered with a pithy remark that has gone down in popular history to exemplify his attitude to any military opposition: 'Prussian field-marshals do not mutiny.' If Hitler were removed, the war could no longer be fought, let alone won, he explained to his visitor. Gersdorff then changed tack, raising Kluge's proposal about the post of Chief of a Wehrmacht General Staff. Manstein's reported reply was of priceless ambiguity, tinged with ambition: 'Please convey my thanks to Field Marshal von Kluge for the trust he places in me. Tell him that Field Marshal von Manstein will always stand loyally at the disposal of the legitimate state authority.'[35]

There remains doubt as to the accuracy of Gersdorff's record, particularly the latter part. As one German writer has pointed out, it is hard to imagine that Manstein would have been so open with an officer whom he barely knew.[36] Perhaps Kluge's envoy had been less specific during the meeting, and then embellished his subsequent account along the lines of what he would have wished to have said – if not heard. That said, Manstein not only confirmed some aspects of the visit when giving evidence at Nuremberg, but also revealed his position:

Now, afterwards, it has become clear to me that several other attempts to contact me were made, apparently to sound me out. On one occasion, General von Gersdorff visited me and, as he told me afterwards, he had letters on him from Goerdeler, I believe, and Popitz, which he was supposed to show me if he got the impression that I could be enlisted for a *coup d'état*. As it was always my point of view, however, that the removal or the assassination of Hitler during the war would lead to chaos, he never showed me these letters. That they were supposed to be feelers is something that became clear to me only afterwards. I had never, therefore, made a promise to anyone to participate in such affairs.[37]

In his memoirs, Manstein sustained his equivocal attitude to the resistance:

As one responsible for an army group in the field I did not feel that I had the right to contemplate a *coup d'état* in wartime because in my own view it would have led to an immediate collapse of the front and probably chaos inside Germany. Apart from this, there was always the question of the military oath and the admissibility of murder for political motives.

He explained further,

As I said at my trial: "No senior military commander can for years on end expect his soldiers to lay down their lives for victory and then precipitate defeat by his own hand." We had not, to my mind, reached the point where such action had to be regarded as the only possible solution.[38]

Manstein did not harbour openly any sense of moral outrage at the crimes committed in the East; nor did he ever concede the fact that many millions of German lives – soldiers and civilians – let alone those of the enemy might have been spared had Hitler been removed in 1943 or 1944.

At the time, Manstein was far from convinced that the war would be lost and that Hitler should be removed. None the less, as the stifling Ukrainian summer drew to a close in 1943, he overcame his doubts about challenging Hitler again on the organization of the Wehrmacht's high command. On 2 September, prior to meeting Hitler with Kluge the next day, Manstein had sent a starkly worded memorandum to Zeitzler: 'If the arrival of reinforcements from other theatres is delayed until our Western opponents commit themselves to a landing on the Continent, we shall be too late in the East.' Apparently, the Chief of the General Staff showed this note to Hitler, who in turn 'fumed with rage and averred that all Manstein was interested in doing was conducting ingenious operations and justifying himself in the war diary'.[39]

On arrival at the Führer's headquarters, it was soon clear that Hitler was not going to make any concessions to Kluge and Manstein whatsoever in rationalizing the command arrangements of Germany's armed forces. According to Manstein's account, Hitler declared that transferring OKW's theatres to Zeitzler, empowering the Chief of the General Staff, would 'make no difference or improvement to the overall conduct of the war'.[40] Thus the lack of effective co-ordination between OKW, responsible for all theatres of war other than the East, and OKH solely for the latter, would remain. Likewise, the Führer would not appoint a commander-in-chief East to direct the four army groups (North, Centre, South and A) defending the Eastern Front. For Army Group South, no further forces could be spared. So both Kluge and Manstein returned to their respective headquarters empty-handed.

The longer-term significance of the meeting was an acceleration of the breakdown in relations between Hitler and Manstein; their differences grew ever sharper over the next six months as mutual understanding and trust declined inexorably. There had never been any bonhomie between them; now an icy formality pervaded all discussions.

In the meantime, nothing changed to improve the position of Army Group South. Manstein's growing exasperation is well illustrated by his message to OKH on 7 September, in which he insisted that 'decisive action must be taken urgently' if his army group 'were to remain in control of the situation'.[41] Such language did little to endear him to Hitler, who was getting increasingly rattled by developments on the southern and central sectors of the Eastern Front. Persistent requests for permission to withdraw did little to improve his mood. At Rastenburg, the Führer's toadies nicknamed Manstein 'Field Marshal Backwards'. As Zeitzler recalled, Hitler mocked his subordinates: 'My generals only wish to manoeuvre rearwards: so much for their renowned operational art.'[42]

On 8 September Hitler made his third and final visit to Manstein's headquarters at Zaporozhye. Field Marshal Kleist and Colonel General Ruoff, commanders-in-chief of Army Group A and Seventeenth Army respectively, were summoned to attend. In his presentation, Manstein tried to confine himself to operational issues, having been rebuffed by the Führer only five days before on matters of command. So he set out his army group's situation in painstaking detail.

On the right, southern, wing his forces would soon be 'compelled to retire behind the Dnepr'. Hitler accepted reluctantly that some withdrawal was required. He authorized Manstein to pull Sixth and First Panzer Armies back to an intermediate line (the Panther position) from Melitopol on the Black Sea coast to the Dnepr bend near Zaporozhye. To sustain the northern wing, fresh forces were still required. The Führer agreed that a corps should be assembled by Army Group Centre on the boundary with Fourth Panzer Army; four additional divisions would safeguard the Dnepr crossings. As significantly, within Army Group A, the Kuban bridgehead would at last be evacuated. With any luck, several of Seventeenth Army's divisions would soon be available for redistribution to more needy sectors of the front. When Manstein saw Hitler off at the airfield, he 'repeated his promise of reinforcements before getting into his machine'.[43]

Manstein had learned through painful previous experience that Hitler was one to change his mind and reverse decisions abruptly. So his staff wasted no time in issuing orders to First Panzer and Sixth Armies to go over to mobile defensive tactics. Both armies were to conduct a battle of delay, trading ground for time until a firm position could be reached. For his two northern armies, Manstein hoped that with the promised reinforcements, it would 'still be possible to halt the enemy forward' of the Dnepr in the vicinity of Poltava.[44]

Yet nothing further of benefit to Army Group South came from the Führer's assurances. Manstein felt compelled to write to Hitler the next day (9 September), mounting an unambiguous challenge to his strategic direction (or rather lack of it):

> The Army Group has been reporting ever since the end of the winter battles that it would not be able to defend its front with the forces at its disposal and has repeatedly called, without success, for a radical adjustment of forces within the Eastern Front or between the latter and other theatres of war.

Sensing that he was writing again in a manner that had so annoyed Hitler recently, he made it clear that his motive 'in making these statements is not to fix *ex post facto* responsibility for developments in the east but to ensure that in future the necessary action is taken in good time'.[45]

Despite this stiffly worded letter and Zeitzler's representations, the promised reinforcements never materialized. Hitler feared (rightly) that Army Group Centre was threatened by renewed attack and (falsely) that it was not in a position to withdraw to the Upper Dnepr. Thus *Stavka* had succeeded in fixing the German High Command, preventing it from rebalancing its defence in the East on a firm position. In consequence, Fourth Panzer Army was 'threatened by envelopment from the north and being pushed away from Kiev to the south'. Manstein immediately recognized the criticality of the situation, understanding that 'such a development would not only preclude the establishment of a new front behind the Dnepr, but also put the Army Group in imminent danger of encirclement'. With this crisis about to break, Manstein reported to OKH on 14 September, declaring with unmistakable clarity that his headquarters 'would be compelled the following day to order even [the] northern wing to retire behind the river on both sides of Kiev'.[46]

Hitler was not one to receive such a thinly veiled ultimatum from a subordinate, even if he were a field marshal. In reply, OKH directed Headquarters Army Group South not to issue the order until the commander-in-chief had discussed it with the Führer. Manstein, whose exasperation had reached a new level, replied that 'such a meeting would be pointless' unless he could speak to Hitler privately with only Zeitzler in attendance. This condition was agreed. On 15 September, Manstein flew to Rastenburg yet again.

The Field Marshal was in combative mood: his presentation to the Führer was uncompromising. He painted a picture of grave crisis that not only affected his army group, but also had fatal implications for the whole of the Eastern Front, stressing that it was 'very doubtful whether Fourth Panzer Army would get back over the Dnepr'. There were two key issues at stake. It was not just a matter of there being insufficient forces to defend the front. The current predicament was as much a consequence of orders not being obeyed: Army Group Centre had not handed over any troops yet. Manstein declared boldly: 'Mein Führer, it is quite intolerable that a transfer of formations that the Supreme Command itself had acknowledged to be urgently necessary has not been enforced.'

Then came the rub: 'I, at any rate, am confident that my own orders will get carried out.'[47] With such a defiant remark, Field Marshal von Manstein was lucky not to have been sacked on the spot. That would come in less than six months' time. In the interim, Hitler still needed him because the fate of the whole Eastern Front – and most certainly its southern wing – hung by a thread. That can be the only explanation for Hitler's apparent acceptance of such open criticism of his leadership. But behind the scenes, it was a further nail in Manstein's coffin, for no dictator can tolerate such censure. As Manstein observed neatly, 'the moment he gives way, his dictatorship ends'.[48]

Hitler agreed to direct Army Group Centre to furnish four divisions and promised that Army Group South would be reinforced by the equivalent of thirty-two infantry battalions in order to refresh its weakened infantry formations. More importantly, Manstein had managed to extract from the Führer a decision to withdraw to the Dnepr. He had gained this important victory through prolonged and robust negotiation over the last three weeks. Hitler had finally bowed to the inevitable in the face of Soviet strategic superiority borne of inherent German weakness on the Eastern Front. Furthermore, with the Allied landings on mainland Italy, and perceived threats to the Balkans and even France, the Führer had neither ready reserves nor ways to generate them without being prepared to give up occupied territory in one theatre in order to reinforce another. As ever, he was not willing to do so.

On return to Headquarters Army Group South that evening (15 September 1943), Manstein issued orders for a general retirement 'to a line running from Melitopol along the Dnepr to a point above Kiev and thence along the Desna'.[49] At last he could make this vital move.

Scorched Earth: The Withdrawal Behind the Dnepr

Manstein's withdrawal of Army Group South behind the Dnepr was conducted under continual threat from Soviet air and land forces (see Map 14). At the time, the Germans probably overestimated the forces facing them as the Red Army's armoured spearheads had been worn down by the recent fighting and its logistic lines were stretched. None the less, weakened Soviet mobile forces pressed their pursuit as vigorously as they could.[50] Hence the challenge that Manstein and his embattled troops faced was far from enviable. As he explained, the retreat 'executed in the face of unremitting pressure from a far superior enemy probably represents the most difficult operation performed by the Army Group throughout the 1943/44 campaign'.[51]

On paper, Sixth Army on the extreme right flank had the simplest manoeuvre to conduct, pulling back its two southern corps into prepared positions north of Melitopol. However, it was chased across the Nogaisk Steppe by Tolbukhin's Southern *Front*, undoing all that Manstein's Eleventh Army had achieved in September 1941. Less its northern corps that entered the Zaporozhye bridgehead, Sixth Army transferred to Army Group A. Meanwhile, Seventeenth Army withdrew from the Kuban peninsula into the Crimea. From his perspective, Manstein's remaining three armies faced the following problem:

> From a front of 700 kilometres in length they had to converge on a maximum of five Dnepr crossings. Having once crossed the Dnepr, however, they had to form another defensive front as wide as their previous one, and be fully deployed again before the enemy could gain a foothold on the southern bank. It was this process of concentrating the entire forces of each army on one or at most two crossing points that gave the enemy his big chance. Apart from anything else, he could

exploit the period in which the Germans were being fed back through Dnepropetrovsk, Kremenchug, Cherkassy, Kanev and Kiev crossing points in order to take the river in his stride in between.[52]

In order to impede the enemy's advance and thereby facilitate the German withdrawal, Manstein applied Hitler's policy of 'scorched earth', one which he noted 'the Soviets had adopted during their retreats in previous year'. That argument, however, yielded little legitimacy during his war crimes trial six years later in Hamburg. As an occupying power, Germany was required to protect the local population. Unsurprisingly, Manstein was at pains to stress that 'all the measures on the German side were conditioned by *military necessity*'.[53]

So what was involved? Manstein explained that within a 20–30-kilometre zone forward of the Dnepr, 'everything which might enable the enemy to go straight over the river on a broad front was destroyed or evacuated. This included anything affording cover or accommodation for Soviet troops in an assembly area opposite our Dnepr defences.' More controversially, the policy required the elimination of 'anything that might ease their supply problem, particularly in the way of food'. On top of this, the zone 'was to be emptied of all provisions, economic goods and machinery which could assist Soviet war production'. Within his army group, Manstein assured his readers that this latter measure was 'confined to essential machinery, horses and cattle'. Furthermore, 'on instructions of the Supreme Command', the civil population was evacuated in order to prevent the Soviets from conscripting all able-bodied males and directing the remaining population to carry out military works.[54]

Manstein conceded that 'scorched earth' caused the Soviet people 'a great deal of misfortune and hardship', but in his view, it bore 'no comparison to the terror-bombing suffered by the civil population in Germany or what happened later in Germany's eastern territories'. On this matter, he remained unrepentant during his trial and thereafter. During wartime, the Germans' actions handed the Soviet Union a huge propaganda coup that only fuelled the soldiers' thirst for revenge. Vatutin, commander of the Voronezh *Front* and one of Manstein's principal opponents, exhorted his troops to press forward to the Dnepr with the battle cry: 'They are burning our bread, we must attack.'[55] So it became a desperate race to the river.

As an experienced commander, Manstein understood only too well the risks involved in undertaking a withdrawal, in which tight control by the staff and iron discipline within formations are essential prerequisites for success. A breakdown in either would imperil the operation and, at worst, turn it into a disorganized rout. Hence his direction to Army Group South emphasized that 'all orders and decisions must give priority to the principle that as long as units remain intact they will overcome every difficulty, whereas no withdrawal can be carried out with troops who have lost their fighting strength or stability'.[56] Hoth, Manstein's most able army commander, appreciated this imperative equally well, stating to his corps commanders on 18 September 1943: 'The withdrawal of the army is one of the most difficult tasks it can be given. It must be mastered. If this doesn't happen, the consequences are unthinkable. It must succeed.' There can be no doubt that Manstein's subordinates were determined to make the best of the situation. As Hoth concluded his briefing, 'The Panzer Army has resolved to get its formations back over the Dnepr, without losing a man or a weapon.'[57]

By 30 September, Manstein's armies – all weakened but essentially intact – had re-established themselves on the Dnepr line. They had not prevented, however, Soviet spearheads from seizing bridgeheads on the right bank. Despite the lack of bridging equipment, Soviet forces had managed to use a multitude of crossing means – by ferrying, rafting and simply swimming – to storm across thinly guarded sectors. It was a triumph of technical improvisation, tactical skill and military will. In contrast, the German defenders – some demoralized – had insufficient time and resources to reinforce the natural obstacle of the Dnepr (800–1,200 metres wide at Kremenchug) to best advantage. The lack of fortification was to prove a fatal omission, a product of Hitler giving priority to the Atlantic Wall and his enduring opposition to giving troops a safe rear position to fall back on.[58] Army Group South on its own initiative had reinforced the major bridgeheads of Zaporozhye, Dnepropetrovsk, Kremenchug and Kiev, but the sectors in between received little effort. Front-line German infantry strength had declined to such an extent that many gaps remained.

In Manstein's view, the withdrawal represented 'an immense technical achievement', involving the evacuation of 200,000 wounded, 2,500 trains to shift German equipment and requisitioned Soviet property, and not least in extracting many hundreds of thousands of 'Russian civilians who had attached themselves to us'. Moreover, 'far from being forcibly abducted, these people received every possible help from the German Armies' and 'were allowed to take along everything, including horse and cattle, which could possibly accompany them'.[59] The operation only succeeded, in Manstein's opinion, thanks to the 'versatile leadership of the army commanders and the magnificent attitude of the troops'.[60]

Concluding the withdrawal on 29 September, he honoured his command with an order of the day:

> Soldiers of Army Group South!
>
> After weeks of heavy attacks and defensive battles, the armies of the army group have withdrawn across the Dnepr to face the enemy again in a more suitable position. The enemy, who has been vanquished by you whether in defence or in counterattack, could not prevent this man-oeuvre.... That the enemy, in spite of his strength, could not stop us from what we wanted to do in view of the overall situation, guarantees us that we'll be able to master new tasks.
>
> Signed von Manstein
> Field Marshal[61]

Despite questions over the scorched earth policy, to which we shall return later, there is little doubt that Manstein's hasty withdrawal was well planned and conducted. No better praise comes from Field Marshal Carver, who judged that the operation was 'a feat of military skill and resolution at all levels, from Army Group Headquarters down to the troops in the front line, which it is doubtful if any other Army could have equalled.'[62]

Manstein could not afford for one moment to rest on his laurels. The Soviets had gained several important bridgeheads across the Dnepr, including those either side of Kiev, and near Dnepropetrovsk.[63] The fact that their parachute (*desant*) operations had failed in the vicinity of Bukrin on 24/25 September was an unfortunate setback, but did not alter the reality of their firm lodgements on the far (right) bank of the Dnepr. Disappointingly for the weary German troops, there was neither a for-midable *Ostwall* on which to base their defence, nor sufficient armoured reserves available to respond to anything more than a local crisis. A bitter fight for the Dnepr line with inadequate resources soon commenced.

In mid September Manstein moved his headquarters from Zaporozhye to Kirovograd, behind the Dnepr bend, and at the beginning of October further back to Vinnitsa, the Führer's former General Headquarters (see Map 15). Here the commander and staff of Army Group South enjoyed the amenity of the *Werwolf* complex's offices and living quarters in wooden huts, 'simply built but tastefully furnished'.[64] Stahlberg recalled:

> The Field Marshal took over Hitler's former residence.... [The] suite at the back of the house contained a beautiful living-room and study, bedroom and bathrooms.... [He] used the 'Führer' house only to live in,

keeping our offices in one of the other houses and using Hitler's big room to sit in with his 'small circle' only in the evenings.

Manstein's ADC also fondly remembered the Field Marshal's 'reddish-brown, long-haired dachshund, an attractive and entertaining dog called Knirps'. Stahlberg even trained the animal to 'raise his right paw before he was given a titbit', the Hitler salute![65] There was precious little time for such light relief as the operational situation would soon worsen. In any case, Manstein used the opportunity in Vinnitsa, a large health resort, to visit the military hospitals located in the city's hotels and spas.

The Fight for the Dnepr and Kiev

Manstein knew that a renewed Soviet offensive was inevitable, sensing correctly that Kiev would be a prime objective. The difficulty was that he did not know either where or when the main blow would come. He could not risk denuding his southern wing, including the Zaporozhye bridgehead, which Hitler insisted on retaining. As he had insufficient troops to cover the Dnepr, let alone establish powerful reserves, there was no possibility of dislodging the Soviets from their existing bridge-heads. In view of the inherent weakness of his defence, Manstein reported to OKH that it was doubtful whether the river 'could be held for any length of time'.[66]

The Red Army took great pains to disguise its battle preparations in order to keep the Germans guessing for as long as possible about the timing, axis and strength of any attack. In the run-up to the Kiev 'Strategic Offensive Operation', whose initial aim was the liberation of the Ukrainian capital, Vatutin knew from recent experience that Manstein's forces would resist strongly. A witness of his Military Soviet (council of war) held on 28 October 1943 recalled him – on reading the latest intelligence reports that indicated increased German reconnaissance efforts – assessing his opponent:

> Manstein is now ranting and raving, demanding accurate information about Soviet troops and the concentration of our striking force. He is a cunning, clever, vicious and dangerous enemy. The Hitlerites still have a fair number of combat effective divisions, including tank formations. The coming battle will be fierce ... [67]

So the stage was set for an intense struggle for the Dnepr and Kiev, one that would engulf ultimately the entire frontage of Army Group South and push it back to Ukraine's western borders over the next six months.

By early November 1943, it was evident to Manstein that Kiev would soon fall and his northern flank would be turned. Unless hindered, a Soviet offensive in this area would lead to the envelopment of his army group and Army Group A; strategic disaster would certainly follow. So he needed to reinforce Fourth Panzer Army in order to stabilize the situation through a powerful counterblow. As the only reinforcements (three panzer divisions) soon available were destined on Hitler's orders to the Lower Dnepr, he had to gain permission from OKH to redeploy them to the more threatening sector in the north. These formations, together with whatever could be spared from his southern wing, including, he planned, XXXX Panzer Corps from First Panzer Army, would then form the counterattack force. As no decision came, on 7 November Manstein flew to the Führer's headquarters to force the issue in person.

The ensuing meeting with Hitler proved another unsatisfactory encounter. In some regards Manstein was hoist with his own petard. He had suggested recently – as 'an operational expedient' – that XXXX Panzer Corps should mount a surprise attack southwards out of the Nikopol bridgehead, 'driving into the flank of the enemy pursuing Sixth Army'. If successful, this counterstroke would not only 'enable Sixth Army to form a front forward of the Dnepr and to maintain contact with Seventeenth Army', now isolated in the Crimea, but also eliminate the threat to the right rear of First Panzer Army.[68] This clever idea was 'vintage Manstein': ever one on the look-out for a suitable opportunity to seize the operational initiative. On this occasion it would build on a recent local victory by XXXX Panzer Corps in defeating an enemy thrust at Krivoi Rog – 'a neat success,' he noted.[69] In the event, the planned attack could not be executed because Sixth Army had been forced to withdraw much more quickly to the west than anticipated. In the meantime, the proposed operation had fired Hitler's imagination. As a result, the Führer remained convinced that the Lower Dnepr could be held and the promised counterblow could still be delivered.

When Manstein outlined his plans for reinforcing his northern wing, Hitler was not prepared to forgo 'this first opportunity' to retain the Crimea. As Manstein recalled further, the Führer considered that any success achieved by Army Group South at Kiev 'could be so effective that the armour up there would become free in time to help the southern wing'. Manstein and Hitler then locked horns in a robust exchange of views similar to previous ones in which the Field Marshal would advance operational level, military arguments that would be countered immediately by the Führer raising wider strategic, predominantly economic, matters. In earlier debates, Hitler had feared the loss of coal production in the Donbas. Now it was 'vitally necessary to our war economy to retain Nikopol's manganese'. As for the Crimea, and this must have riled Manstein who had spent so much effort leading Eleventh Army in its capture (less Sevastopol) almost exactly two years before, 'the enemy must not be allowed to regain [it] as a basis for aerial warfare against the Rumanian oilfields'.

Against these familiar arguments, Manstein sensed he was facing checkmate. But he was too skilled a player to relinquish the contest at this critical point, and so made another move. 'The risk on our northern wing', he declared, 'was now becoming too great.' Specifically, 'If things were to go badly for Fourth Panzer Army, then sooner or later the fate of Army Groups South and A would be sealed.' In response, Hitler noted the risk. But it was one that had to be accepted: he 'would shoulder the responsibility'. At that moment Manstein might have felt the game was up, but perhaps to his surprise, the Führer conceded that Fourth Panzer Army indeed needed reinforcements. Those forthcoming included two recently refitted, experienced formations, 1st Panzer Division and the SS *Leibstandarte*, together with a newly raised 25th Panzer Division. There was a price to be paid, however. On Hitler's orders, First Panzer Army was required to remain on its 'perilous position on the Dnepr bend'.[70]

For the present, Manstein had to be content with the results he had obtained. In the background, however, Hitler's entourage continued to scheme against him. Goebbels recorded in his diary, 'As I learn from Berlin, the Führer received Manstein at G.H.Q. [General Headquarters]. Contrary to expectations, the interview is said to have passed off well, and it is assumed that Manstein is to remain in post. I regard this as a grave disaster.' To rub salt into the wound, he also noted that 'Himmler was especially opposed to Manstein, whom he regards as a first-class defeatist. The crisis in the southern sector of the Eastern Front would not have had to become so serious had a man of real calibre been in Manstein's place.'[71] However absurd and unjust such criticism, Manstein's days in command were now numbered.

Even though many operational setbacks can be anticipated, some well in advance, there is never a guarantee that planned countermeasures will take effect in sufficient time. Dire military situations, in a similar fashion to painful economic crises, have a nasty habit of getting a lot worse before they get better, if at all. Fourth Panzer Army's predicament in November 1943 is a vivid example. According to Manstein, Hoth's army with eleven weakened infantry divisions – each now down to regimental (brigade) strength – and two depleted panzer divisions stood little chance of holding its ground against Vatutin's First Ukrainian *Front* with up to twenty rifle divisions, four tank corps and a cavalry corps in its first echelon.[72]

Yet Vatutin's success did not rest solely on force of numbers. As we have seen, he had considerable respect for Manstein, but he was an equally canny and skilled operator. After failing to break out of his bridgehead at Velikii Bukrin, just below Kiev, he amended his plan cleverly. He heavily reinforced a much smaller foothold north of the city at Liutezh in such swampy terrain that the Germans had not considered it a viable jumping-off point. In a textbook operation of developing an unexpected axis under the strictest operational security, he first fed 5th Guards Tank Corps into the Liutezh bridgehead, defended by elements of 38th Army, then the whole of Rybalko's 3rd Tank Army regrouped secretly from Bukrin, together with significant reinforcements of infantry and artillery.

On 1 November, Vatutin's 27th and 40th Armies began offensive operations in the area of the Bukrin bridgehead, which the Germans assumed was the main axis of attack. Mobile reserves, including SS *Das Reich*, were brought up accordingly to contain it. Then, completely out of the blue, on 3 November 38th Army, supported by 2nd Air Army, sprung from the Liutezh bridgehead and overwhelmed a totally astounded German defence.[73] It was a masterpiece of deception.

Soon the First Ukrainian *Front* had not only enlarged its lodgement on the right bank of the Dnepr, but also exploited this remarkable success expeditiously with the committal of 3rd Tank Army, which cut the Kiev–Zhitomir road. By the evening of 5 November elements of 38th Army had fought their way into the northern suburbs of Kiev. In order to avoid the loss of VII Corps, Manstein was forced to order the evacuation of the city, which fell next morning. Its capture was a most significant milestone in the improving Soviet fortunes, which was duly celebrated with a general salute in Moscow. It marked a triumphant conclusion to the Second Period of the Great Patriotic War. Zhukov proudly signalled Stalin: 'Immensely happy to report that the task set by you to liberate our beautiful city of Kiev, capital of the Ukraine, has been accomplished by the troops of the 1st Ukrainian Front. The city has been completely cleared of the Nazi invaders.'[74]

Without delay, Rybalko's tank army fanned out in a wide arc to the north-west, west and south-west towards Korosten, Zhitomir and Fastov respectively. In the process, Manstein noted that Fourth Panzer Army 'was torn into three widely separated groups'.[75] The Soviet offensive had driven a broad and deep salient that not only threatened to divide Army

Groups Centre and South, but also acted as a powerful springboard for the continuation of the offensive. Particularly dangerous, in Manstein's opinion, was the Soviet thrust to the south-west that risked cutting off his left, western, flank.

Manstein, renowned in the German Army as being *krisenfest* (calm in crisis), kept his head. He assembled the strongest possible counterattack force to destroy the Soviet armoured spearheads and to drive the enemy back behind the Dnepr. Although he never made the direct comparison in his memoirs, it is reasonable to suppose that he wished to repeat his spectacular successes of February and March, which had resulted in the destruction of three Soviet armies and was neatly rounded off with the recapture of Kharkov and Belgorod. This time, Kiev would be the principal prize. Yet the circumstances in late autumn were very different from those of the preceding spring. On this occasion, Vatutin's troops had yet to outreach their logistics; Soviet infantry was more plentifully equipped with anti-tank weapons and their tank units were much better handled in combined arms teams. It proved a much tougher fight accordingly.

The German counterattack was mounted by XXXXVIII Panzer Corps under the command of Balck, with Mellenthin as his chief of staff; they together proved a very accomplished pair. The latter wrote of his boss: 'He was one of our most brilliant leaders of armour; indeed, if Manstein was Germany's greatest strategist during World War II, I think Balck has strong claims to be regarded as our finest field commander.'[76]

As XXXXVIII Panzer Corps formed up (six panzer and one infantry divisions[77]), the situation south-west of Kiev deteriorated. Manstein was forced to order a preliminary attack on Fastov in order to keep the corps' assembly area free. The committal of the green 25th Panzer Division ended in disaster. 'Instead of leading to the recapture of Fastov junction', Manstein wrote, 'this undertaking caused a psychological setback to troops who were fighting their first action in the east.' Mellenthin was more graphic: 'Unused to any fighting the troops streamed back in great disorder.' He summed up the episode well: 'The experience of the 25th Panzer Division proved once again that while veteran troops can outmanoeuvre the Russians, yet untrained units have little chance against them.'[78] The Red Army had indeed become a force to be reckoned with.

The main counterattack launched on 15 November fared much better and Zhitomir was retaken. Further north, Korosten was recaptured, reopening the railway link with Army Group Centre. Subsequent counterattacks mounted in December dented the First Ukrainian *Front*'s flank, but did not lead to a decisive victory, let alone restore Kiev to German occupation. Casualties were considerable on both sides.

Manstein's claims as to the damage inflicted on the Soviet forces ('two-thirds of the infantry divisions involved, as well as four tank, one mechanized and one cavalry corps ... were seriously weakened'[79]) may be disputed, but the fact remains that by 25 December the heavily reinforced First Ukrainian *Front* had resumed its offensive with a massive surprise attack. Unknown to German intelligence, much of the weight of the German counterattack had fallen on Vatutin's deception force rather than on his main shock grouping. So rather like Kursk, any gains were short-lived and the irrepressible Russian hydra, as Manstein commented, 'lost no time in sprouting new heads'.[80]

Hitler demanded a scapegoat for the loss of Kiev and found one in Hoth, who had commanded his army with distinction over the previous eighteen months. Manstein fought for his retention, insisting that 'the loss of the Dnepr front had been due to the superior strength of the enemy and the run-down state of our own divisions rather than to errors in the leadership of the army', but his interjection with the Führer was to no avail.[81] He much regretted the departure of an officer for whom he had the greatest respect. Hoth, he wrote, 'represented his views clearly and firmly. His manner of command was characterized by great flexibility in difficult situations.'[82]

The planning of the German counterattack against the Kiev salient was not without controversy in the battle of the memoirs. Mellenthin claims that XXXXVIII Corps' plan was to 'use this powerful force to advance from Fastov directly towards Kiev, thus cutting in towards the base of the huge salient, hamstringing any further Russian advance to the west, and perhaps trapping and destroying very considerable forces'. He then blames the new commander of Fourth Panzer Army, General Erhard Raus, for regarding this plan as 'too ambitious'. Moreover, Raus felt it was essential to recapture Zhitomir first before turning against Kiev. Hence 'our idea of a lightning thrust far into the rear of the Russian masses was discarded in favour of an operation which was essentially orthodox in nature'. In his defence, Raus makes clear that he did not assume command until the second attack (6 December), and agreed his scheme of manoeuvre for this operation with Manstein.[83] As the latter makes no mention of planning a direct thrust to Kiev, there remains some doubt as to the accuracy of Mellenthin's record.[84]

Resistance to Hitler

A month before the resumption of the Soviet winter offensive from the Kiev salient, it had become clear to Manstein that the whole Dnepr front was at risk. There was no time to relax anywhere. The enemy had still uncommitted reserves and was at liberty to choose where next to strike. As there was 'no question of releasing forces from the Army Group's operationally decisive northern wing for a supporting action in the Dnepr bend', an operational breakthrough in the south was inevitable. On 20 November, Manstein highlighted to OKH:

> The Army Group would have to get through the winter holding a front which far exceeded the resources of its almost exhausted divisions. It would not have enough reserves to take effective action against any major enemy attacks, particularly if called upon to do so at several places at once. Operationally, therefore, the Army Group would remain completely at the enemy's mercy – a particularly dangerous state of affairs in view of the reduced fighting power of its own formations.

He concluded that a successful continuation of this unequal struggle needed a 'sufficiency of hard-hitting reserves'. Without these, he forecast, 'the Army Group could not last the winter'.[85] It was to prove a very apposite warning. Whether Germany could prevail under Hitler remained equally questionable.

Although not recorded in Manstein's memoir, one last attempt was made by the German opposition to win him for their cause. On 25 November 1943, Tresckow visited Headquarters Army Group South in Vinnitsa prior to assuming his new post as Chief of Staff Second Army. According to his biographer, he tried to persuade the Field Marshal that Hitler's actions would lead to Germany's certain downfall. The Führer was 'not teachable', he maintained. 'We, on the other hand, have it in our power to stop him in our tracks. If we don't do it, no one will.' To underline the point, his visitor added, 'We have the responsibility. Responsibility applies to us.'[86]

In common with the previous attempts by Stauffenberg and Gersdorff to win him over, Manstein would not be turned by such arguments. Against all his previous experience, he still thought he could convince Hitler to change course. He rejected the use of force to remove the Führer, believing it would lead to a collapse at the front and certain defeat. During a second discussion later that day, Manstein and Tresckow could not resolve their differences. In the margins of one of these tense meetings, it is reported that a member of Manstein's general staff, (Colonel) Hans-Adolf von Blümroder, heard Manstein raising his voice: 'For God's sake, Tresckow, give me a rest from your stupid politicking!'[87]

Whilst a British prisoner of war, Manstein set out his views on the plot to overthrow Hitler in rebutting an account of his final meeting with Tresckow given by one of the co-conspirators, Fabian von Schlab-rendorff. In his book *Offiziere gegen Hitler* (Officers against Hitler), he had claimed that the Field Marshal was 'incapable of coming to a decision' and that his 'whole body had shaken'. In a lengthy note, Manstein declared in response:

> I stress, that as long as I was in command, neither I nor Busse, nor Schulze-Büttger, regarded the war in the East as hopeless. We were convinced, despite Hitler's defective command, that we would succeed in breaking the offensive power of the Russians forward of the Reich's borders. Notwithstanding Hitler, we had always managed to avoid a debacle on our front.... A *coup d'état* with the murder of Hitler would in any event lead to defeat with the present consequences. Continuing the fight under his command could still have led to a draw.... Tresckow presented the point of view that [this situation] could not [be allowed] to go on any more.... I said, the only way out was ... to convince Hitler to at least give up command in the East, if not in an official but in a de facto manner, and appoint a responsible Chief of the General Staff. I added that he would hardly choose me, as [good relations] between us would not last for long.
>
> The conversation with Tresckow was purely about the question of changing military command. Tresckow did not raise any other arguments, such as political or moral ones. I did not have reason to either, as my head was full of military concerns ...
>
> I really had no reason to tremble 'with my whole body' on his opening remarks, quite apart from the fact that it did not match my nature. Tresckow did not inform me of his plans. I had my clear position. There-fore the issue that 'he could not convince me of giving a clear yes' never came up.
>
> Whether my standpoint was right or wrong, is not the matter under discussion here; rather, whether I refused to come to a decision out of cowardice or feebleness, or let matters rest in veiled speech. That was not the case. I don't know why Tresckow didn't talk to me in a more open manner. But he knew very well, whatever happened, that I would never let the Army down.[88]

This remained Manstein's position throughout his trial, and in writing his memoirs. He never committed himself to the resistance because he was never asked directly. Had he been, he would have refused on principle.

One Crisis after the Next

At the turn of the year, and throughout the first quarter of 1944, Manstein faced one crisis after the next, with few options except to withdraw, regroup, then mount a limited, spoiling attack with his scarce mobile reserves to delay the next pulse of the Soviet offensive. His final period in command was marked by a steadily deteriorating relationship with the Führer, which could only end with one result: the famous Field Marshal would have to take his leave.

By late December 1943 a considerable proportion of Manstein's precious armoured reserves had been consumed in the recent, costly battles to the west of Kiev. On Christmas Eve 1943, Manstein spent some time with the regiments of 20th Panzer Grenadier Division held ready behind the threatened northern front. It was here that he received the first news of the First Ukrainian *Front*'s offensive towards Zhitomir, with subsidiary axes towards Fastov and Korosten. By the time he had rushed back to Vinnitsa, the situation was grimmer than he had suspected. On what appeared to be the main axis, the principal Soviet shock grouping consisted of 38th, 1st Guards and 1st Tank Armies, amounting to over eighteen infantry divisions and six tank or mechanized corps. To add to this very significant threat, German intelligence (for once) had picked up the assembly of a reconstituted 3rd Tank Army with up to six tank or mechanized corps behind 60th and 13th Armies advancing on Korosten. Manstein perceived accurately that 'this concentration of mobile forces implied that the enemy intended to supplement the breakthrough towards Zhitomir with a far-flung outflanking movement by way of Korosten'.[89]

It was now quite clear within Headquarters Army Group South that there was a distinct possibility of the southern wing of the Eastern Front being cut off and forced to withdraw to the south-west, leaving a gaping hole in the *Ostheer*'s defence. To prevent this calamity, on 25 December Manstein signalled OKH that Fourth Panzer Army needed to be 'radically reinforced'. Further, he demanded freedom of action to evacuate the Dnepr bend in order to release 'at least five or six divisions' to the north. Such was the severity of the Soviet threat in this sector, he reported, that 'the time for attempting to master the situation on the Army Group's northern wing by such isolated measures as the transfer of single divisions is now past'.[90] Indeed it was: the whole of his army group faced envelopment and potential destruction.

As Manstein recalled, the overall situation was similar to that which had prevailed during the previous winter. Then, as now, the only possible salvation lay in 'castling' First Panzer Army from the right to the left wing of his army group to form a new counterattack force. He proposed to effect this redeployment by giving up the eastern part of the Dnepr bend and pulling back the front to a line from Nikopol to Krivoi Rog. By shortening his defence in the south he estimated that he could save up to twelve divisions, half to First Panzer Army for its new mission, with the other six benefiting Sixth Army. The latter, now back under his command, would have an extended front on taking over the former positions of First Panzer Army.

In the absence of any decisions from OKH by 28 December, Manstein ordered initial moves the next day. As he had not received Hitler's permission to evacuate the exposed Dnepr bend, he could not put his entire plan in motion. Whilst procrastination at Supreme Command level continued, the situation deteriorated further. A ray of hope came with the promise of three further divisions by OKH. Hitler's scorn for Manstein, however, had become more vocal. His heated exchanges with Jodl and Zeitzler over this period betray considerable frustration over the manner in which Army Group South was being run and fast consuming reinforcements, from his viewpoint, to little apparent benefit.

On 28 December 1943, the Führer declared: '[Manstein] was very impressed, of course, by the unlucky fellow, Hoth, outside Kiev. We learn about this bit by bit, how devastatingly this man has worked. It has been a source of defeatism of the worst kind.' Later in the conversation, Hitler mocked Manstein's proposed measures to stem the Soviet advance: 'He should not speak of a "counter operation", but call it by the right name: running away.' The Führer's venom continued unabated: 'The fact that some of his troops are very demoralized is related to the spirit that they absorb from above.'

Hitler believed Manstein had made insatiable demands for more troops: 'No other front sector has received as much as Field Marshal von Manstein has received, although his ratio of forces is not worse than anywhere else. It's because of his frame of mind that not only is there no positive mood but there's a totally negative mood coming from his headquarters.' As for Manstein's latest signal, 'What is written in the telegram is all a fantasy.... He won't get any more forces from the Crimea – aside from the fact that it's none of Manstein's business anyway.' The next day (29 December), the Führer added to his previous criticisms: '[Manstein] acts like a stepchild. In reality, he's the only one who has received anything.' Zeitzler, uncharacteristically, agreed: 'He basically devours everything.'[91] In the face of such criticism, however unjust, the only surprising matter is that Hitler retained Manstein for another three months.

The New Year brought no relief. Manstein's most serious military challenge remained in the north, where there was a yawning gap with Army Group Centre. Now Fourth Panzer Army was in danger of being outflanked on both wings. By early January, Raus's army had been forced to retire to a weakly defended, patchy line – certainly not a coherent front – 70 kilometres east of Vinnitsa, running north towards Berdichev, then turning west to the former Soviet–Polish border (see Map 16). At the same time, a fresh Soviet offensive was tying down Eighth and Sixth Armies to the south, hindering the regrouping of forces to assist Fourth and First Panzer Armies. These unwelcome developments prompted Manstein to fly to Hitler on 4 January in an attempt to convince him 'of the need for a radical transposition of forces from the right to the left wing of the army group'.[92]

At General Headquarters, Manstein started his presentation with an operational overview, stressing the critical situation on his northern wing. Two planned counterattacks involving III and XXVI Panzer Corps from the east and north-west respectively 'offered no solution' in the long term. 'If the position here were not cleared up once and for all,' he maintained, 'the entire southern wing of the Eastern Front would be in mortal peril.'[93] To prevent this disaster, he proposed evacuating the Dnepr bend completely and withdrawing to a line stretching from the lower reaches of the Bug northwards to the present battle positions of Fourth Panzer Army, saving a considerable frontage in the process. Further forces, he suggested, could be generated by abandoning the Crimea and redeploying Seventeenth Army.

In response, Hitler resorted to his by now all-too-familiar wider strategic arguments. Manstein recalled that he 'categorically refused to evacuate the Dnepr bend or to give up Nikopol.... The resultant loss of the Crimea would provoke a change of heart in Turkey, as well as in Bulgaria and Rumania.' Fresh forces were neither available from other sectors of the Eastern Front, nor from other theatres of war. In consequence, argued Hitler, the only course of action open was 'to play for time until things clarified in the west and our new formations were ready to go into action'. In view of the gravity of the operational situation, Manstein was not impressed by this flat rejoinder. He felt it was imperative that 'a new army be swiftly assembled behind the northern wing of the Army Group, roughly in the region of Rovno, to meet the threat of a large-scale envelopment'.[94] Understanding that there was nothing further to be gained in the large forum of the Führer's daily conference, he asked to speak to Hitler in private. In his memoirs, Manstein left a graphic description of his last, doomed attempt to effect radical change 'in the handling of military affairs'.

The briefing room emptied, leaving only Hitler, Manstein and Zeitzler. Hitler invited the Field Marshal to speak. He cut to the quick: 'One thing we must be clear about, *mein Führer*, is that the extremely critical situation we are now in cannot be put down to the enemy's superiority alone, great though it is. It is also due to the way in which we are led.'

Although Manstein did not record an immediate reply, he bequeathed a striking impression of 'the wordless struggle of will that played out between us within a few seconds':

> As I spoke these words, Hitler's expression hardened. He stared at me with a look which made me feel he wished to crush my will to continue. I cannot remember a human gaze ever conveying such willpower. In his otherwise coarse face, the eyes were probably the only attractive and certainly the most expressive feature, and now they were boring into me as if to force me to my knees. At the same moment, the notion of an Indian snake-charmer flashed through my mind, and I realized that those eyes must have intimidated many a man before me.[95]

Manstein did not pause for breath, and continued with his demands, made on two previous occasions, for urgent changes in Germany's military leadership.

Once again he called for the appointment of a 'thoroughly responsible Chief of the General Staff on whose advice alone' Hitler should rely for military policy. Hitler refused to budge on this issue, as 'he alone' could determine the balance of forces between one theatre and another. As for establishing a Commander-in-Chief East, who, in Manstein's opinion, should 'enjoy full independence within the framework of grand strategy', this proposal only aggravated Hitler's increasing ire. As he had stated often before, no other individual in the Reich would have his authority. After all, 'Even I cannot get the Field Marshals to obey me,' he shouted. 'Do you imagine', he then asked Manstein, 'that they would obey you more readily? If it comes to the worst, I can dismiss them. No one else would have the authority to do that.'

The vast majority of German generals would have bitten their lips at this point. But Manstein ventured a bold reply to the effect that *his* orders were always carried out. Hitler made no further comment, bringing the meeting to a brusque close. There is little doubt that Manstein's card was marked as a result. All in all, the incident was a curious replay of Manstein's earlier complaints about other army groups not obeying Hitler's orders.

Once again the Field Marshal left Hitler empty-handed. He rationalized his failure by stressing the weaknesses in the dictator's personality. 'His unwillingness to hand over to a soldier was probably due in part to his exaggerated faith in his powers,' Manstein noted. 'Not even in private would he admit to having made mistakes or to being in need of a military adviser.'[96] The only documented instance of him assuming responsibility for any significant failure, which Manstein had recorded earlier in his memoirs, was in the shadow of Stalingrad.

During January 1944, as the situation across his front worsened without respite, Manstein's frustration with the Supreme Command grew in direct proportion. He continued to fire off angry letters of complaint to Zeitzler and Hitler to no effect other than to increase the latter's distrust of the Field Marshal. His language began to betray a contempt that was becoming mutual. Although he had 'operational right' on his side, he could not make any headway against the strategic stubborn opposition of the Führer, who declined to give any clear direction other than to defend the indefensible, leading to an 'impossible state of affairs'. This situation led to one particularly sharp letter that month to OKH, in which Manstein hammered home his point as if he were the commandant of a war college addressing his students:

> If any leadership is to be successful, it must be based on a harmonious co-ordination of policy at all levels, which is dependent on clear directives from the top and a unanimous appreciation of the situation obtaining on the enemy's side. The Army Group cannot merely think from one day to the next. It cannot make do with a directive to hold on regardless when at the very same time it sees the enemy preparing to force the issue by an outflanking movement which it has no means of opposing.... If the Supreme Command remains dumb as well as deaf to the conclusions drawn by the Army Group in its own limited sphere of activity, a co-ordinated policy will be quite out of the question.[97]

This unambiguous riposte remained unanswered, as did a subsequent letter to Hitler, which all added more fuel to the fire when Manstein saw Hitler again on 27 January at General Headquarters.

Hitler had summoned all his army group and army commanders, together with other senior officers, to give them a pep-talk on the need for National Socialist education in the army. Manstein was not one well disposed to listen to a political diatribe at a time when his army group was fighting for its life between the Dnepr and the Bug. So when Hitler declared that 'If the end should come one day, it should really be the field marshals and generals who stand by the flags to the last', Manstein's patience with the Supreme Commander finally broke. This was an insult too far. By his own admission, the 'blood rushed to his head' and he cried out: 'And so they will, *mein Führer!*' The totally unexpected interruption threw Hitler off his train of thought. 'With an icy glare in my direction', Manstein recalled, he said: 'Thank you, Field Marshal von Manstein.' This unprecedented exchange brought Hitler's address to 'a somewhat abrupt conclusion.'[98]

Manstein must have sensed that the Führer was not going to let him get away with such a public interjection, amounting to a challenge to his authority. A little while later, when having a cup of tea with Zeitzler, he was summoned to see Hitler in the presence of Keitel. The anticipated reprimand came soon enough: 'Field Marshal, I cannot allow you to interrupt me when I am addressing the generals. You yourself would not tolerate such behaviour from your own subordinates.'

Now it was Manstein's turn to fall silent, for he had no reply. That would have been the end of the matter if Hitler had not reproached him on another issue. 'By the way, a few days ago you sent me a paper on the situation. I suppose your idea was to justify yourself to posterity in the war diary.' This was an old hobby horse of Hitler's – one that had flared up the previous September. Manstein did not let this unfair accusation remain unanswered. He explained that personal communications to the head of state did not get filed in the war diary. Indeed, the letter in question had gone by courier via the Chief of the General Staff. Then he chanced his hand: 'Please excuse me if I now use an English expression. All I can say with regard to your opinion is that *I* am a gentleman.'[99]

There was silence. After a dramatic pause, Hitler answered: 'Thank you very much.' In this manner, the Field Marshal was curtly dismissed. Although the Führer was pleasant enough to him during the evening conference, Manstein knew that he would never be forgiven for the incident earlier in the day. Hitler's negative attitude to the Field Marshal may well have been influenced by overseas reporting about the difficulties between the two. The front cover of *Time* magazine (10 January 1944) illustrated Manstein with the subtitle: 'Retreat may be masterly, but victory is in the opposite direction.'

The Final Engagements

On his return on 28 January to army group headquarters, Manstein could not afford to dwell on the matter. There was yet another crisis that demanded all his powers to master. Soviet forces had broken the Dnepr fronts of both First Panzer and Eighth Armies. As a result, two

corps (XXXXII and XI) had been encircled in the area south-west
of Cherkassy. Somewhat confusingly, Manstein's account and German
military history more generally refers to the ensuing battle of the
'Cherkassy Pocket'. The 'sack' was in fact centred on Korsun with its
vital airfield, Cherkassy lying well outside the ring of encirclement.[100]
The action turned out to be one of high drama, in which German troops
managed to break out, unlike Stalingrad, but taking very heavy losses in
the process. Once again, it proved to be a battle of wills between Hitler
and Manstein, revealing an ever-deepening cleft of opinion in the
conduct of operations, and another unequal struggle for the German
forces involved.

Stavka planners had identified the exposed German salient, stretching
in the north for 40 kilometres south-east of Kanev along the Dnepr
towards Cherkassy, with exposed western and eastern flanks about 70
kilometres long, as a vulnerable prize. Destruction of the German forces
here would not only remove a large part of Eighth Army, but also open
the path to the envelopment of Manstein's southern wing, and with it,
Army Group A. Despite Manstein's frequent urging, Hitler had forbidden any withdrawal as he wished to retain the 'Fortress on the Dnepr'
as a springboard for the recapture of Kiev. On 24 January, Vatutin's First
Ukrainian *Front* attacked from the north-west whilst Konev's Second
Ukrainian *Front* thrust from the south-east. Armoured spearheads of the
two *fronts* – 6th Tank and 5th Guards Tank Armies respectively – linked
up near the town of Zvenigorodka on 28 January, trapping approximately
50,000 Germans in six weakened divisions and an independent brigade.[101]
Command of the encircled forces was vested in the commander of XI
Corps, General of Artillery Wilhelm Stemmermann.

There was now an opportunity for the Soviet forces to seal off the
pocket and wheel their main attacks into the operational depth of Manstein's army group with devastating consequences. Luckily for him, the
Soviets had overestimated the numbers of German troops encircled and
proceeded methodically in the eradication of the pocket, gaining him
precious time to mount a relief attack. But Hitler's ambitions were far
greater. On this occasion, the Führer's imagination sprung all reality: he
designed not only to encircle the encircling Soviet forces, but also to
drive on Kiev.

On paper, up to nine panzer divisions, a heavy panzer regiment and
an infantry division were available for the operation, organized into two
assault groups based on III and XXXXVII Panzer Corps. Because most
of these forces were still fixed in action elsewhere, the first relief attacks
conducted by the weaker XXXXVII Panzer Corps failed, coming to an

abrupt halt in the snow and then the mud, well south of the shrinking pocket. The stronger III Panzer Corps launched its main attack from the west on 11 February, but despite its best efforts, this operation ground to a halt on the 15th.[102] Running short of fuel, and fighting against superior Soviet forces in atrocious weather, German armour, with Bäke's Heavy Panzer Regiment in the van, could not make any further headway. Manstein was now faced with a similar situation to that pertaining at Stalingrad. The relieving force was firmly stuck and the only escape for 'Group Stemmermann' lay in breaking out towards III Panzer Corps' positions, up to 13 kilometres to the south-west.

There was no time for hesitation. Without waiting for Hitler's permission, Manstein gave the order to break out during the night of 16/17 February. As he sat in his command train, moved forward to Uman, it was a nervous occasion for the Field Marshal. But it proved a terrifying one for the exfiltrating troops running the gauntlet of Russian guns, tanks and machine-gun fire. Leaving the vast majority of the seriously wounded and almost all their heavy equipment behind, according to German accounts 'about 30,000 men' managed to fight their way through the Soviet lines. Stemmermann fell during the break-out attempt, which turned into a massacre as dawn broke. At best, it was a narrow escape for the lucky and certainly no victory despite the German propaganda describing it as such. Manstein put a brave face on the battle:

> It had thus been possible to spare both corps the fate suffered by Sixth Army at Stalingrad. In this case too, Hitler had called for the pocket to be held, but in the end he had consented retrospectively to the break-out operations by the Army Group. . . . The six and a half liberated divisions obviously had to be pulled out of the line for the time being. However, this loss of fighting power, though it further complicated the Army Group's position, was to a great extent counter-balanced by the joy of having saved at least the fighting men of the two corps.[103]

The fact that he had ordered the break-out in such a manner that his order could not have been countermanded by OKH undoubtedly saved XI and XXXXII Corps from complete destruction, but did little to improve relations with Hitler. It remains debatable, moreover, whether Manstein should have ordered an earlier relief attack aimed at a weaker point of the Soviet ring of encirclement. Had he done so, which would have gone against Hitler's intent, perhaps a greater proportion of the encircled force could have been rescued. It was a point not lost on the Field Marshal.

Matters had now come to a head. As Manstein concentrated his efforts at Korsun, Soviet attacks crumbled his flanks. In the north 1st Ukrainian *Front* seized Rovno and Lutsk, gaining favourable jumping-off positions for subsequent operations into the rear of Army Group South. Concentric blows by 3rd and 4th Ukrainian *Fronts* in the south eliminated the exposed salient on the Dnepr bend and collapsed the Nikopol bridgehead. By the beginning of March 1944 multiple Soviet offensives had cleared the Dnepr River line (see Map 16). With thirty-three weak divisions, Army Group South was not able to defend its 850-kilometre front. It was now vulnerable to defeat in detail in the wide plains of the western Ukraine.[104]

The onset of the *rasputitsa* at the beginning of the month had not led to a cessation of Soviet offensive operations. Indeed, the Red Army reinforced its efforts against the southern wing of the Eastern Front by threatening Manstein's left flank with its First Belorussian *Front*. Faced now with the attacks of five *fronts*, Manstein's armies were in danger of penetration, then envelopment and, even worse, encirclement. Under very heavy enemy pressure, in mid March he was forced to order a general withdrawal behind the Bug, but even that river could not be held. Then there was no alternative but to fall back yet further on the Dnestr, which Hitler opposed adamantly. Manstein's requests that OKH establish two new armies with '15–20 divisions in the area of Lvov' to defend Galicia remained a dream, for there were no such reserves available. In any case, Hitler had declared the West to be his strategic priority over the East; whatever the Wehrmacht could muster it was inadequate for a multi-front war against the Soviet Union and its Western Allies.

It was at this critical stage that Manstein was summoned to Obersalzberg on 19 March in order to witness the handing over of a declaration of loyalty to Hitler, signed by Germany's senior generals, Manstein included. Yet again, there was no meeting of minds. The Führer refused to concede any freedom of manoeuvre to his generals. Quite the contrary, his recently published directive on 'fixed places' (*feste Plätze*), which were to be defended to the last man, had led to the useless sacrifice of Tarnopol.[105] This policy was to lead to many more disasters. Manstein returned to his headquarters to face his biggest crisis since Stalingrad, the encirclement of First Panzer Army, a challenge far exceeding that at Korsun. It was to prove his ultimate test in command.

After Korsun, Manstein perceived belatedly the growing threat to his left flank in the sector between Fourth and First Panzer Armies in the vicinity of Proskurov and ordered a regrouping of forces to fill the gap. The deployment of III (weakened by its recent operation) and XXXXVIII Panzer Corps was insufficient to block 1st Ukrainian *Front*'s ambitious offensive that opened on 4 March, directed towards Cher-novtsy near the Rumanian border. Zhukov had assumed *front* command following the shooting of Vatutin by Ukrainian nationalist partisans. Spearheaded by Katukov's 1st Tank Army, Zhukov's forces broke through the German defences and advanced into the depth of Army Group South as Manstein had feared, crossing the Dnestr without pause on 24 March. Simultaneously, Konev's 2nd Ukrainian *Front* had launched its Uman–Botoshany operation, capturing Vinnitsa on 10 March and reaching the Dnestr on 21 March. First Panzer Army with twenty-one weak divisions was now loosely encircled in a pocket, centred on the city of Kamenets-Podolsk.

Having failed to obtain Hitler's permission to withdraw First Panzer Army in good time, Manstein now faced an operational catastrophe on the scale of Stalingrad. He had no option but to focus all his efforts on rescuing the entrapped army in what appeared to be an equally hopeless situation. The easiest direction for break-out appeared to be to the south towards Rumania, the course of action favoured by the army commander, General of Armoured Troops Hans-Valentin Hube.[106] Manstein dis-agreed, arguing that a break-out to the west would be advantageous for both tactical and operational reasons, judging that it would cut the Soviet lines of communications rather than hit the enemy's main armoured groupings on the Dnestr, where it faced destruction. Above all, a westerly break-out represented a surprise, the decisive factor in his estimate. It would also lead to the re-establishment of a coherent army group defence in which First Panzer Army was required to fill an indispensable sector north of the Carpathians.

With this in mind, Manstein gave Hitler a direct ultimatum at noon on 24 March. He reported that unless he received appropriate direction by 15.00 hours he would order First Panzer Army to break out. Manstein recalled the response:

> At 16.00 hours we received the Solomon-like reply that the Führer agreed to the fundamental idea of First Panzer Army's clearing its com-munications to the west but still insisted that it should mainly continue to hold the present front between the Dnestr and Tarnopol. Where the army was to find the forces to drive west and clear its communications zone of the enemy was quite beyond us.

As he pointed out in his memoirs, the situation was uncannily similar to that at Stalingrad in December 1942, when Hitler had been prepared to let Sixth Army break out but insisted that it at the same time hold on to the city. Then as now, the only salvation of the encircled army lay in it breaking out. Manstein argued the point on the phone vociferously with Zeitzler, who replied that Hitler 'did not grasp the full gravity of the situation'.[107] Later that evening the Field Marshal received a summons to report to the Führer the next day. He took the precaution beforehand of issuing a warning order to Hube to prepare to break out to the west.

Manstein's Dismissal

Early in the morning of 25 March, Manstein flew from his headquarters – now in Lvov – to arrive at the Berghof in time for the midday conference. Manstein explained to the Führer where First Panzer Army had to break out, and demanded that Fourth Panzer Army be reinforced so that it could link up from the opposite direction. With Hitler's refusal to understand that a breakthrough of First Panzer Army to the west meant that necessarily it must withdraw its eastern front, Manstein's patience was sorely tried. The Führer broke it by holding the Field Marshal personally responsible for the unfavourable situation in which Army Group South now found itself. A 'sharp exchange' then took place in which the two – in the presence of an audience – rehearsed old arguments as to who deserved the blame for events since Operation CITADEL.

Hitler asserted that all Army Group South did was 'manoeuvring', and in making one withdrawal after another. Manstein replied that 'things had been bound to turn out that way', as 'you [Hitler] have detained our forces on the southern wing to hold the Donets and Dnepr areas instead of letting us strengthen our northern wing'.[108] The wrangling continued. Finally, Manstein insisted that orders be issued to First Panzer Army that day in order to ensure a successful break-out. Hitler rejected this demand and ordered a further session with the Field Marshal that evening.

Manstein now decided to act. He requested General Schmundt to inform Hitler that he considered 'it futile to remain in command of the Army Group' unless the Führer accepted his recommendations. If Hitler could not approve his actions, then Manstein 'requested command of Southern Army Group to be entrusted to somebody else'. As if he did not have enough on his plate, he received a call from Busse telling him that Hube had requested urgent permission to move *south* across the Dnestr rather than to the west. Manstein directed that his subordinate should carry out the break-out as ordered: he was still in command!

At Hitler's evening conference, Manstein was surprised by the Führer's changed mood and response. He informed the Field Marshal that he had 'been thinking the matter over again and agree with your plan to make First Panzer Army fight its way out to the west'. 'With great reluctance', Hitler continued, 'I have decided to provide an SS Panzer Corps' for Fourth Panzer Army's relief attack. Exploiting Hitler's more positive attitude, Manstein ventured to propose that Eighth Army should come under command of Army Group A, and further, that a unified command should be set up 'to cover all forces on the southern wing, including the allied armies'. As to his first recommendation, it chimed with an identical one from Kleist, and was implemented without delay. Nothing was heard again of the second. Manstein flew back to Army Group South the next day and conferred with General Raus about Fourth Panzer Army's future operations.

Events then moved quickly. On the morning of 30 March, Manstein was picked up by Hitler's Condor aircraft, already with Kleist on board, and flown to the Obersalzberg. A telephone call to Zeitzler at Lvov airfield revealed the purpose of the surprise flight: both Kleist and Manstein were being relieved of their commands. Manstein recorded his final meeting with the Führer:

> Saw the Führer in the evening. After handing me the Swords to my Knight's Cross, he announced that he had decided to place the Army Group in other hands (Model's), as the time for grand-style operations in the east, for which I had been particularly qualified, was now past. All that counted now, he said, was to cling stubbornly to what we held. This new style of leadership must be inaugurated under a new name and a new symbol. Hence the change in command of the Army Group, whose name he also intended to alter.[109]

Although he knew about the scheming behind his back, Manstein considered that Hitler's decision to dismiss him was primarily based on the incident of 25 March. His final words to the Führer were cryptic: 'I trust, *mein Führer*, that the step you have taken today will not have any untoward effect.'[110] This Parthian shot could be interpreted as something along the lines of 'without me, don't expect the military situation to improve'. It did not.

Manstein's fall from grace had many grounds and a long gestation. Hitler had long disliked him personally but respected his military ability, remaining courteous throughout their many difficult exchanges. Amongst the reasons for the Führer's distaste of the Field Marshal was his profound dislike of the German-Prussian officer class, typified by the aristocracy's dominance of the General Staff. There was a dark hatred here, borne not necessarily of envy but rather of deep-seated mistrust.

Manstein was not politically reliable, having shown little sympathy for National Socialism as a popular movement.

In the military field, as the German official history of this period now stresses, the Führer could no longer tolerate an intelligent, confident and challenging personality who was of 'superior operational talent'.[111] Hitler and Manstein had completely different views on the planning and conduct of operations. The Führer never appreciated the sophistication and potential of his difficult field marshal's 'backhand' manoeuvres within a defensive campaign that required an understanding of a sequence of operational moves and blows. As with *Sichelschnitt*, four years before, Hitler could often see the 'opening' but not necessarily grasp the dynamics of the underpinning operational idea. If the time for *Operieren* (operational manoeuvre) was over, so must Manstein leave.

The removal of Manstein was a combined act of despair and revenge: having been forced to concede earlier decisions, Hitler's patience had run out. The final parting came through the Führer's pride and prejudice. Germany's enemies could breathe a sigh of relief with the departure of the Wehrmacht's most capable and dangerous commander.

15

The Last Battles

*'The soul of our defence was Field Marshal von Manstein, the
ablest of our military commanders.'* Siegfried Westphal[1]

Gardening Leave

Manstein's departure from Army Group South was a journey into the
unknown, but hardly into obscurity. Within fourteen months, with
decisive Allied success on all fronts, the war in Europe would be over and
the Field Marshal would be interned by the British Army as a prisoner of
war. His personal destiny was emblematic for his nation: from victor to
vanquished. The once mighty were humbled; their world would be turned
upside down in the Armageddon of Germany's total defeat. Then the
reckoning would follow, in which the cruel and murderous actions of the
Nazi aggressor would be exposed to the world. Manstein became the
Wehrmacht's unofficial champion when he appeared at the IMT at
Nuremberg to defend the honour of the German General Staff and High
Command and to deny any complicity in war crimes.

On handing over to Model on 2 April 1944, Manstein left his former
headquarters a disappointed and frustrated man, a departure made all
the more poignant with the presentation of the Crimean Shield that had
adorned his personal Ju52 since the capture of Sevastopol some twenty
months before. Yet there was also relief from the pressures of command:
no longer would he have to fight Hitler incessantly to obtain decisions
that were well within a field marshal's competence to take for himself.
He still kept a close interest in military events and held a sense of shared
responsibility for the increasingly bad news from the front. Initially, he
hoped to return soon to active duty following medical treatment and
subsequent recuperation. After all, had not the Führer indicated that he
was already pencilled in as Commander-in-Chief West to replace his old
boss Rundstedt? Meanwhile, his loyal staff requested postings away from
his former headquarters. With the exception of Busse, who remained
with Model for some months to provide continuity, these were all
granted.[2]

The operation on Manstein's right eye to remove a cataract led to many complications, not least to an infection that threatened loss of his sight. During his painful recovery at home in Liegnitz, he spent much of his time in a darkened room or wearing dark glasses. In order to remain current with the operational situation, he sent Stahlberg out on tours to various headquarters to gather information. On return, his ADC would describe military developments to the Field Marshal. Stahlberg was 'astonished again and again by his geographical knowledge. All the maps ... were in his head – he could have been a champion at "blind chess" had he so wished'. They discussed the war in Italy, which 'excited him greatly.' Manstein had little regard for either the Axis or the Allied style of command in this theatre of war. Stahlberg got the distinct impression that he 'had no time for his fellow Field Marshal Kesselring'. Of the Allied generalship, he declared: 'Those gentlemen in Italy command like pipsqueaks! ... If they think that they must fight in Italy, they should look for one decisive battle in the Po valley.'[3] Fair enough, but the Allied armies in Italy would have a hard fight in penetrating the Gothic Line beforehand.

Still requiring rest and with no new appointment in the offing, in May 1944 Manstein undertook a period of convalescence in the Weisser Hirsch military sanatorium in the eponymous suburb of Dresden, a city then largely untouched by the war. Slowly he regained his sight and strength, awaiting patiently the call to arms, but none came. Attempts by Guderian and the Army Personnel Office to have the Field Marshal reappointed amounted to nothing: Hitler always refused each proposal. We now know that the Führer had expressed severe doubts as to Manstein's suitability some nine months before his dismissal. 'I don't trust Kleist and Manstein', he had told Schmundt in mid July 1943. They were 'clever, intelligent chaps, but not National Socialists'. Hitler now put his hopes in the 'younger ones'. Commanders such as 'Rommel, Model and Schörner' were the men that he liked, those with 'fingertip-feeling, energy and drive'.[4]

In 1944, the new generation had taken up post and Manstein was left on the sidelines, kicking his heels in the *Führerreserve*, a reserve pool of commanders. When Rundstedt was sacked in July following the Allied invasion of Normandy, Kluge rather than Manstein was appointed as Commander-in-Chief West, much to the latter's disappointment. His frustration must have been complete when Kluge, associated with the 20 July plot, was dismissed by Hitler in August, and none other than Rundstedt was reappointed in early September.[5] By then it must have been abundantly clear that Manstein was never going to assume another command under Hitler.

Meantime, Stahlberg retained his very close links to the military chain of command and to the resistance. On a trip to Berchtesgaden on 11 July, he learned from General Fellgiebel that an assassination attempt on Hitler was imminent: 'Stahlberg, you have come just at the right moment. Stauffenberg is at the Berghof with the bomb in his briefcase. Manstein will be free of his oath at any moment. He must know now. When will you be seeing him?'[6] During the course of his visit, Stahlberg met Stauffenberg, who enquired after Manstein. The ADC intimated that there was no change in the Field Marshal's position since their meeting at Taganrog on 26 January 1943.

On returning to Liegnitz, Stahlberg determined to alert his field marshal. According to his account, he raised the matter whilst travelling on the autobahn between Liegnitz and Breslau in Manstein's staff car, an elegant and powerful pre-war Mercedes 540 K coupé. On this particular occasion, the good Sergeant Sakolowski had been left behind, warning Stahlberg not to drive too quickly on the poor-quality fuel then available. At the steering wheel, the ADC remarked: 'Sir, I feel it is my duty to report that today or within the next few days the Führer will be killed.' After a long pause, Manstein replied, 'Say that again!' Stahlberg repeated his statement. Then followed an intermittent conversation with many silences; the Field Marshal closed the matter as they neared their destination: 'Stahlberg, what the two of us know now is quite something.'[7]

With this warning in mind, Manstein decided to take summer leave on the Baltic. He accepted his ADC's suggestion that they should stay in a seafront hotel, the Seeschloss at the resort of Bansin on the island of Usedom. The fact that it was close to the secret test site at Peenemünde was entirely coincidental, but one of its frequent guests was none other than Wernher von Braun, the designer of the V2 rocket. In Stahlberg's opinion, the real reason for the trip was to construct an 'extremely conspicuous alibi'.[8] Keeping his distance in this manner was a rather naive assumption since no place in occupied Europe was beyond the reach of the Gestapo. Perhaps what mattered most was that Manstein was seen not to be anywhere conveniently close to Berlin, and certainly nowhere in the vicinity of any member of the opposition.

The happy summer days enjoying the Baltic sun and sea were shattered on 20 July by the early evening news of the failed attempt to take Hitler's life. On Manstein's behalf, Stahlberg took a grave risk in phoning Fellgiebel at the Führer's *Wolfschanze* headquarters to obtain detailed information. The reply was blunt: 'Everything is as you have just heard on the radio. I have nothing to add. My regards to the Field Marshal. And farewell!'⁹

Later that evening Hitler spoke to the nation, declaring

> a tiny clique of ambitious, ruthless officers who were also criminal lunatics forged a plot to get rid of me, and together with me virtually to wipe out the staff of the German Wehrmacht Command.... I regard [my survival] as confirmation of my mission from Providence to pursue my life's goal as I have done up to now ...¹⁰

The opposition's attempt to kill Hitler and install a new government, codenamed Operation VALKYRIE, had failed spectacularly.

In the circumstances there was nothing that Manstein could do to help. As Stahlberg's cousin had predicted the *coup d'état* had failed, but the attempt was necessary in order to redeem something of Germany's honour. Shortly after, Henning von Tresckow, the principal organizer of the military opposition to Hitler, committed suicide, sacrificing, in Stahlberg's view, 'his own life in order to save what could be saved'. As Hitler had sworn, 'This time the account will be settled in accordance with National Socialist practice!'¹¹ The show trials of the People's Court and the executions soon began.

At home in Liegnitz, it became obvious that the Manstein residence in the Holteistrasse was under Gestapo surveillance.¹² Fortunately for the Field Marshal and his family, he was spared the terrible fate that awaited Rommel, who was forced by Hitler to commit suicide. The 'Desert Fox' had been implicated in the plot, but had neither prior knowledge of, nor involvement with, Stauffenberg's bomb. Although Manstein had not been drawn into VALKYRIE, and had refused consistently to have anything whatsoever to do with any coup attempt, the fact remained that three prominent members of the resistance (Stauffenberg, Tresckow and Gersdorff) had met with him. It is hardly surprising, then, that Stahlberg noted that his field marshal 'was growing uneasy'.¹³ His restlessness was a combination of professional inactivity and not least concern for his dependants and the victims of Hitler's bloody revenge.

Still without a new appointment, at the end of August Manstein turned to Guderian, who had now taken over from Zeitzler as Chief of the General Staff. The Field Marshal's letter summed up all his pent-up dissatisfaction. 'You will understand', he wrote, 'how unbearable it is for me to sit around with nothing useful to do, particularly in a small town such as Liegnitz, where naturally everyone asks why I'm staying at home with the war on.' 'I must assume', he continued, 'that the Führer is not considering me for an appointment.'[14] Manstein went on to ask Guderian for assistance on a delicate matter that has since fuelled controversy. As one critical commentator has it, 'After Manstein became convinced the Führer would not recall him to save the Reich, he displayed his grasp of strategy and politics by taking the substantial honorarium he received from Hitler as well as the family savings and buying an estate in East Prussia in October 1944.'[15] This is not so.

The facts are that Manstein made a number of enquiries as to how he should purchase a smallholding in Pomerania or Silesia, but never got close to choosing a specific property let alone signing a contract for one. In his letter to Guderian he stressed that he was not seeking a gift, but rather Hitler's permission to proceed. 'I would be very grateful,' he concluded, 'if you could raise my request with the Führer at a suitable moment. . . . No one is better qualified than you to appreciate my position of forced inactivity.'[16] Manstein intended to draw on his wife's inheritance and his own funds, which had accumulated considerably as a result of Hitler's generous supplementary payments that all senior officials and officers received, some 4,000 Reichsmark (RM) monthly, continuing during retirement.[17] Unlike Kluge, who had received a cheque for RM 250,000 on his 60th birthday in October 1942, or Kleist who obtained nearly RM 200,000 for the purchase of an estate in November of that year, there is no evidence of Manstein being rewarded in this manner. What he did eventually receive on 17 October 1944, on Hitler's instructions, was permission from the Führer to buy a property and advice from the Reich Ministry of Food and Agriculture as to how to go about it.[18]

With hindsight, Manstein's preferred location for a country retreat remains odd. Stahlberg had suggested that it would be preferable to look for something suitable in Schleswig-Holstein or Westphalia, a much more sensible choice, but the Field Marshal had set his heart on East Pomerania, an area which he had so much enjoyed as a battalion commander in Kolberg. 'If Pomerania were lost,' he explained to his ADC, 'we would all be lost.'[19] In the late summer of 1944, although he had realized there was no longer any chance of a stalemate peace settlement, Manstein did not foresee the destruction of Germany and the loss of all its eastern provinces. On 20 July, for example, no foreign army had breached the Reich's borders of 1937. By this time, however, the Allies were breaking out of Normandy in the West and Army Group Centre was being destroyed in the East. He still assumed, rather naively given the Allies' insistence on Germany's unconditional surrender, a result similar to the end of the First World War – defeat certainly, but not dismemberment. By the autumn of 1944, however, the writing was on

Erich von Manstein, aged 11 years, 1898. (Manstein archive)

ABOVE RIGHT On promotion to Lieutenant, 27 January 1907. (Manstein archive)

RIGHT With cousin (adoptive sister) Martha and adoptive parents Georg and Hedwig von Manstein, 1906. (Manstein archive)

Battalion Adjutant, 3rd Foot Guards, on his horse Frechdachs, 1911. (Manstein archive)

RIGHT Captain in the General Staff, First World War. (Manstein archive)

Manstein (head circled) with the commander and staff of 213rd Infantry Division, Reduit de Chenay (north-east of Reims), June 1918. (Manstein archive)

Wedding to Jutta-Sibylle von Loesch on 10 June 1920 at Lorzendorf, Kreis Namslau, Silesia. (Manstein archive)

Frau von Manstein with children (left to right) Gisela, Rüdiger and Gero, c.1930. (Manstein archive)

Frau Jutta-Sibylle von Manstein, 1937.
(Manstein archive)

RIGHT On the eve of the French
campaign, May 1940. (Manstein archive)

Commanding General LVI Corps (Motorized), Summer 1941.
(Manstein archive)

Manstein with Major General Erich Brandenberger, commander 8th Panzer Division, summer 1941. (Bundesarchiv)

Manstein relaxing on his favourite horse, Osman. (Manstein archive)

With General Franz Mattenklott, Commanding General XXXXII Corps, Crimea, autumn 1941. (Manstein archive)

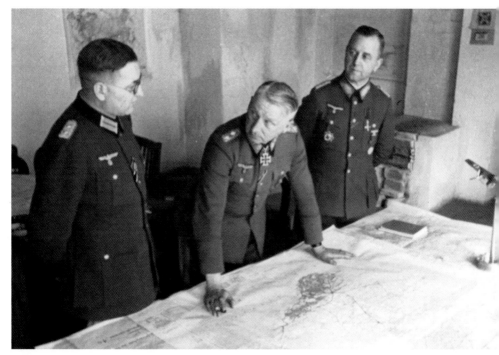

Manstein with his principal staff, Colonel Theodor Busse (left) and Major General Otto Wöhler (right), in his Eleventh Army tactical headquarters at Sarabus, near Simferopol, Crimea. (Manstein archive)

With senior quartermaster Colonel Friedrich-Wilhelm Hauck (left) and Eleventh Army administrator Dr. Rabus (right) at Simferopol, winter 1941–1942. (Manstein archive)

Manstein consulting with Colonel General Wolfram Baron von Richthofen,
Commanding General VIII Fliegerkorps, May 1942. (Manstein archive)

Observing the battle for Kerch, May 1942. (Manstein archive)

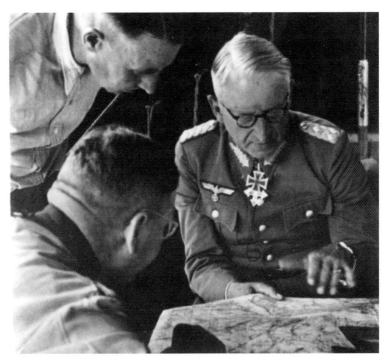

Visiting the headquarters of 50th Infantry Division during the siege of Sevastopol, June 1942. (Manstein archive)

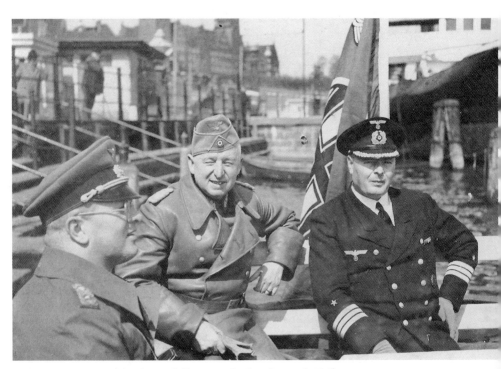

Touring Sevastopol harbour following the battle, early July 1942. (Manstein archive)

Presentation to Marshal Ion Antonescu, *Conducător* ('Leader') of Rumania, summer 1942. (Manstein archive)

Manstein with his old friend Colonel General Ernst Busch, autumn 1942. (Manstein archive)

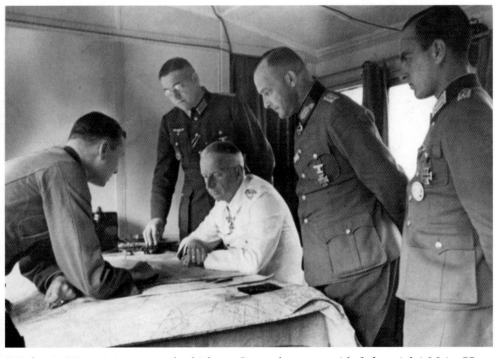

Briefing in Manstein's command vehicle, 20 September 1942, with (left to right) Major Hans Eismann, Chief of Intelligence; Colonel Theodor Busse, Chief of Operations; Major General Friedrich Schulz, Chief of Staff, and Lieutenant 'Pepo' Specht, ADC. (Manstein archive)

Manstein's last meeting with his son Gero, shortly before the latter's death on 29 October 1942. (Manstein archive)

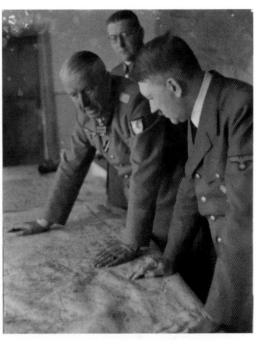

Colonel General von Manstein, summer 1942. (Manstein archive)

Discussions with the Führer, Adolf Hitler, at Headquarters Army Group South, Zaporozhye, February 1943. (Manstein archive)

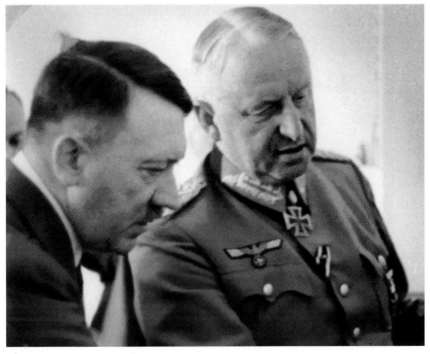

Field Marshal von Manstein with Hitler, September 1943. (Manstein archive)

A cordial farewell to the Führer at Zaporozhye airfield, September 1943. (Manstein archive)

The Field Marshal, baton in hand, with General of Armoured Troops Erhard Raus, 12 May 1943. (Manstein archive)

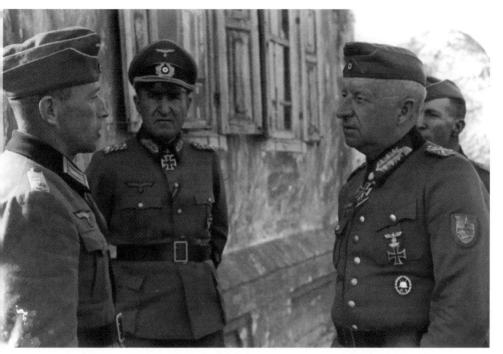

Manstein quizzing a regimental commander; General Raus looks on, May 1943.
(Manstein archive)

Manstein, accompanied by Busse, at the funeral of Major General Walther von
Hünersdorff, 19 July 1943; also in the picture is the diminutive Colonel General
Hermann Hoth. (Celle Military Museum, courtesy Mr Colin Albert)

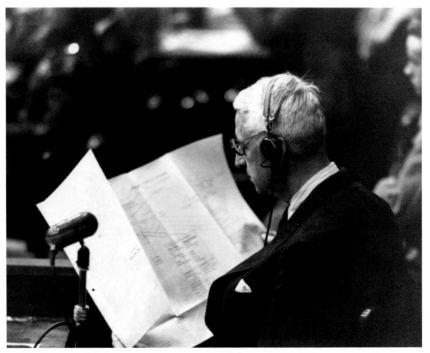

Witness at Nuremberg, 9 August 1946. (Manstein archive)

Manstein with Field Marshal Gerd von Rundstedt and their British interpreter (in battledress), c.1948. (Imperial War Museum, HU 44887)

Manstein in the dock at Hamburg, August 1949. (Imperial War Museum, HU 42740)

BELOW In the garden of the military prison at Werl. With Manstein (bare-chested) are, left to right, General of Artillery Curt Gallenkamp, Lieutenant General Kurt Wolff and Colonel General Eberhard von Mackensen. (Photo courtesy *After the Battle*)

The Field Marshal and Frau von Manstein on the official day of his release at Allmendingen (near Ulm), 7 May 1953. (Manstein archive)

The Field Marshal on his 80th birthday, 24 November 1967, with the Inspector of the Bundeswehr, General Ulrich de Mazière. (Manstein archive)

Manstein in his twilight years with his old friends Walter Wenck (sitting) and Theodor Busse (standing). (Manstein archive)

the wall. The Western Allied forces had cleared most of France and Belgium; East Prussia was threatened and the Red Army had bridgeheads on the Vistula in Poland. The Soviet offensive in January 1945 would propel it to Küstrin on the Oder and within 90 kilometres of Berlin. Manstein's dreams of a country estate in the East vanished in the process, and all his savings were lost at the end of the war.

In the meantime, Manstein devoted himself to visiting family friends, corresponding with former comrades, writing notes for his memoirs and engaging in good works. He set up a charitable fund for the orphan children of soldiers who had fallen or had been severely wounded whilst serving in Eleventh Army in the Crimea. By the sale of illustrated albums such as 'We Conquered the Crimea', up to fifty children per division were presented with a savings book of RM 500.[20] His only duty in uniform was to attend on 7 October 1944 at Tannenberg the state funeral of Schmundt, who had died of his wounds from Stauffenberg's bomb. Otherwise, although technically still on duty as a field marshal, usually he wore plain clothes – a silent protest at his lack of military employment.

On 18 January 1945, Manstein accompanied by his wife and son made his last trip to Frau von Manstein's Silesian home in Lorzendorf in Kreis Namslau. The happy occasion was the marriage of Stahlberg's brother Hans-Conrad to one of Jutta-Sibylle von Manstein's nieces, the 19-year-old Maria von Loesch.[21] As the bridal pair was betrothed at the registry office in nearby Buchelsdorf, Manstein undertook an excursion in his car in a quest to buy some fabric of pre-war quality in a shop in Reichtal, across the former German–Polish border. On the way there he encountered an army general who reported to the Field Marshal that 'they were far and wide the only German soldiers around, only ten kilometres distant from a Russian tank spearhead that in all probability would thrust to the Oder by the evening'.[22] According to the young bride's account, on returning to Lorzendorf, Manstein announced his grim news to the assembled wedding party in a 'hoarse, almost emotionless voice, as if he were making one of his dry jokes that he so loved to make'.[23] He made it quite clear that he and his family would have to leave straight after the meal: it wouldn't do to have a field marshal captured by the Russians.

After the church ceremony, the wedding feast 'with all the candles lit, was festive, the food good and abundant'.[24] None the less it was a surreal occasion and conversation was muted. Outside, as the short winter's day drew to a close, Maria recalled, 'one could hear in the distance the clanking of tank tracks on the hard frozen ground'. The Russians were coming! Manstein urged everyone to get a move on. With no time for lengthy speeches, the Field Marshal raised his glass: 'Even in this hour we think of our fighting troops and of our Führer!'[25] There was an icy silence as the harsh reality of the situation sank in. The priest sitting opposite Manstein remembered him remarking, 'Yes, now that our land here has become a battle zone, we'll find out soon enough what that means.'[26] A telephone call from Namslau suddenly interrupted proceedings: there was a possibility of catching the last train for Breslau. With not a moment to lose, the wedding party abruptly left their food and drink on the table, and took immediately by car and sledge to the station, squeezing into a carriage crammed full with wounded.

The whole of Silesia was now threatened by the rapid advance of Soviet troops. On 22 January 1945 came the order to evacuate Breslau, excepting the military garrison that held out in the soon encircled 'fortress city' to the war's end. In compliance with instructions from General Headquarters, the Mansteins prepared to leave Liegnitz.[27] They obtained temporary accommodation with family friends in Berlin whilst awaiting advice on what to do next.

Stahlberg records that on the morning of 29 January, Manstein suddenly announced his desire to speak to Hitler.[28] Although he did not have an appointment, he decided to appear in person in the Reich Chancellery in the Vossstrasse. Picking their way through the damaged, partially roofless, staterooms, the Field Marshal and his ADC managed to find the entrance to the underground bunker. They were left there in an undignified fashion and told to wait: half an hour later a guard announced that Hitler 'was not receiving'. No one else was authorized to speak, not even one of the Führer's adjutants.

Manstein, speechless with anger, stormed out of the *Reichskanzlei*. No doubt he recalled his eventful discussion with Hitler in that very building about the campaign against France. The rebuttal four years later was the final insult to one who had served Germany so well. Manstein left no record of his motives in undertaking this abortive visit. Perhaps he hoped that he would have his 'moment' with the Führer. A possibility suggested by Stahlberg is that he wished to offer his services for the apocalyptic 'last battle', which Hitler had described a year before.[29] Alternatively, with the undignified flight from Silesia so fresh in mind, might not the Field Marshal have wished to advise the Supreme Commander to end the war before all was lost? One can only speculate what would have happened had a meeting taken place. It is highly unlikely, however, that the Führer would have seen sense at well past the eleventh hour from an individual he had dismissed ten months before.[30]

During his brief sojourn in the capital, Manstein sought and obtained permission from OKH to take up residence in Achterberg on the western end of the Bergen training area near Dorfmark, on the Lüneburg Heath, the former home of Fritsch.

'In Achterberg', wrote Manstein's surviving son Rüdiger, then 15 years old, 'there was calm and order, as if in peacetime, in unbelievable contrast to recent experiences.' Only the sight of 'Allied bombers flying continuously above us' reminded one that there was still a war on.[31] Over the coming weeks and months, the main house and adjoining buildings became a rallying point or resting place for friends, relations and former estate workers from Silesia. Manstein's mother-in-law, old Frau Amaly von Loesch, had led one trek out herself, but did not turn up in Achterberg until July. Manstein's married daughter Gisela Lingenthal, who cycled from Berlin when heavily pregnant, found her parents and brother gone when she arrived in May shortly after the German surrender.[32]

There was a simple reason for the Mansteins' precipitate departure. The country idyll in Achterberg was threatened when the British Second Army crossed the Weser on 9 April and its spearheads thrust north-east towards Hamburg; to the south, an advance guard of the American Ninth Army had taken Hannover on the 10th. As Manstein determined not to fall into Allied hands before any capitulation, he and his family had to move again post-haste. The Field Marshal's last refuge was Schleswig-Holstein. On the journey there, on 19 April, he made a brief stop in Hamburg.

In the proud, battered Hanseatic city, the Field Marshal visited the headquarters of Army Group North-West, under command of his old friend Busch. The latter had been sacked following the destruction of Army Group Centre the previous summer but since rehabilitated, unlike Manstein. As the two field marshals and close comrades-in-arms discussed the desperate situation, none other than Albert Speer joined them. His report of conditions inside Hitler's bunker was dramatic: 'In the office a trembling sick man sits under the portrait of Frederick the Great, scarcely listening to his visitor.' More disconcertingly for the German population, the Führer ordered him to 'ensure that all major factories in the German Reich are destroyed before the arrival of the enemy'. Speer explained that he was undermining Hitler's mad policy of scorched earth, urging non-compliance wherever he went.[33]

Before leaving Hamburg, Manstein allowed himself one last luxury. He asked Stahlberg where they could have a good lunch in a first-class restaurant. His trusty ADC, always good for such advice and having undertaken business training in the city before the war, suggested the Ehmke in the Gänsemarkt, still open in the almost completely destroyed town centre. As Stahlberg recalled, the elegant establishment justified its fine reputation that day as they sat down to some splendid fare in a private room, served by frock-coated waiters. It was an incongruous scene in the last confused weeks of the Second World War.

The Mansteins' final home until the war's end and subsequent place of temporary internment was a grand country residence on the Baltic coast, near Oldenburg in Holstein. Gut Weissenhaus was a 'lovely big house', Stahlberg recalled, 'its ground floor stuffed to bursting ... with the stocks of the Kiel Landesmuseum.'[34] The owners, Clemens Graf Platen and his wife, looked after the Mansteins and many others as well.

As the war drew to a close, the Field Marshal nearly returned to military command. On 1 May, German state radio announced that Hitler had died 'heroically' in Berlin – in fact, he had committed suicide the day before. His successor as head of state was Grand Admiral Karl Dönitz, who even before the Führer's demise had thought of re-employing Manstein. In his memoirs, he recorded:

> Towards the end of April, just before my appointment, Field Marshals von Bock and Manstein had paid me a visit, and we discussed the military situation. Manstein had laid particular emphasis on the necessity of withdrawing the armies on the Eastern Front to positions in the vicinity of the British and American fronts. This coincided entirely with my own views. On May 1, I therefore gave orders that von Manstein was to be contacted at once. It had been my intention to invite him to replace Keitel as Chief of Staff [of OKW]. We failed, however, to contact him, and so Supreme Headquarters remained under the direction of Keitel and Jodl.[35]

As a result, Manstein remained unemployed through the friction of war when his rare talents were needed urgently. His son has suggested that 'representatives of a former era' such as Himmler, Ribbentrop, Keitel and Jodl were still powerful influences on Dönitz in his provisional headquarters in Plön, subsequently evacuated to Flensburg.[36] With advisors such as these, it appears hardly surprising that the new German president did not appoint Manstein as Chief of OKW. In fact, Dönitz had no time for either Himmler or Ribbentrop and declined to include them in his new government. Of Jodl, he 'formed a very high opinion of [his] clarity of thought'.[37]

The Admiral would have been well served by Manstein in negotiating the capitulation, seeking to prevent as many soldiers as possible of the Army of the East from becoming Russian prisoners of war. Other than that, even for an individual of the Field Marshal's ability, authority and reputation, it was now far too late to have brought about a significant change to the military situation. The only thing to be done was to bring the war to a close as expeditiously as possible with a minimum loss of further life.

Before the end, a local tragedy occurred. On 3 May, Manstein had invited the retired Field Marshal von Bock, living with his family near by in Lensahn, to tea at the Weissenhaus to discuss the inevitable capitulation. Ominously, as Stahlberg awaited the arrival of the guests, he observed Royal Air Force fighters swooping across the sky. A few minutes later he heard 'the clatter of their machine guns'. Bock's car had been struck: his wife and daughter died on the spot; the Field Marshal, mortally wounded, was transported to the nearby Oldenburg hospital. On establishing the casualty's location, Manstein and Stahlberg drove immediately there and found him, very heavily bandaged and only barely able to talk. Bock asked Manstein to look after his 16-year-old stepson, Dinnies von der Osten. His visitor agreed. He then gasped his last words: 'Manstein, save Germany.'[38] Again, it was a call too late.

Bock died a few hours later, at the very same time as Dönitz's envoy, Admiral Hans Georg von Friedburg, was negotiating an armistice at Field Marshal Montgomery's tactical headquarters, south of Lüneburg. A day later, at 18.30 hours, Friday, 4 May 1945, he signed an instrument of surrender affecting all German armed forces in Holland, north-west Germany, Schleswig-Holstein and in Denmark. All hostilities ceased at 08.00 hours the next day: the war in this part of Europe was at last over.

That Saturday, 5 May, Manstein asked Stahlberg to compose a personal letter in English to Montgomery, stating his location and putting himself at the disposal of the Commander-in-Chief of 21st Army Group. Before dawn on Sunday morning, 6 May, Stahlberg set off with Graf Platen for the British lines in Manstein's staff car, and via a hearty breakfast and lunch at various intervening stops to pick up escorts, arrived at Monty's headquarters later that afternoon. After a long wait, Stahlberg reported to a 'small, wiry, athletic figure in an open-necked shirt, displaying no badges of rank or decoration'. The famous British commander replied via a staff officer. After another long delay, a letter was produced, 'requesting Field Marshal von Manstein to stay at Weissenhaus until further notice and await any other news there'. Platen and Stahlberg returned in darkness, armed with a safe conduct pass to get them back across the Elbe.[39]

Had Dönitz appointed Manstein as Chief OKW in lieu of Keitel, it is reasonable to suppose that he might have sent him – Germany's leading soldier – to negotiate the surrender with Montgomery, or later with Eisenhower. One can only imagine the scene: the tall, aristocratic

German, in best field grey wearing full decorations with his field marshal's interim baton in hand, being addressed by the shorter, ascetic
Anglo-Irishman, dressed as casually as possible in his khaki jacket and
bleached corduroy trousers, with his trademark twin-badged black beret,
strictly against regulations, and hands clenched tightly behind his back.
Would the jaunty Monty have chipped at Manstein in the tongue-
lashing manner he inflicted on the real German emissaries at his Tactical
Headquarters: 'Who are you? ... I have never heard of you. ... What do
you want?'[40]

Or instead of this carefully rehearsed theatre, had it come down to
polite conversation in Monty's caravan, would not the occasion have
been held in a more correct manner? Whatever, both soldiers of equal
rank, rightly proud of what they had achieved in their careers, would
have done their duty as they had always done in the best interests of
their respective countries. Sadly for history, the two famous field marshals
never met. What would each have thought of the other? They were both
opposite and alike: their nations' best operational brains.

Monty nearly caught a cold over the handling of the German generals,
including Manstein. Early on 6 May 1945, he had reported to London his
intention to collocate temporarily senior commanders and staff echelons
(Busch, Blaskowitz and Blumentritt) with his army group and subordinate army headquarters in order to supervise the surrender. In
typically Monty fashion, he felt that this 'method of running the show
will be the quickest way of getting a move on and of dealing with the
very complex problems that lie ahead'. Whilst this represented a wise
and pragmatic step, putting 'the surplus members, including the Commanding Generals' into prisoner-of-war (POW) cages was not. It elicited
a furious and prescient response from Churchill later that day: 'Why is
it necessary to put the commanding generals into Prisoners of War
cages? Have we no facilities for observing the ordinary distinctions of
military rank pending any war charges that may be afterwards formulated
against individuals?' Monty took this admonishment in good spirit and
replied on 7 May: 'Much regret that para[graph] 3 of M 578 was loosely
worded and of course I would not put commanding generals into cages
as we have special arrangements for Senior Officers.'[41]

During the immediate post-war occupation period, Montgomery was
quartered in the magnificent seventeenth-century mansion of Schloss
Ostenwalde, a short car ride away from his main headquarters in Bad
Oeynhausen, near Minden. He never desired to call for Manstein, who
remained in internment in the Weissenhaus, escaping special attention
for the moment.[42] The British Field Marshal had little time for Germans

individually, but was seized of his new mission to put the country back on to its feet. Monty was not unsympathetic to Germany's plight, declaring in London on 23 May 1945 to the assembled members of the Control Commission, 'Between us we have to re-establish civil control, and to govern, a country which we have conquered and which has become sadly battered in the process' in order 'to enable the [people] to live decently, and without disorder and disease'.[43] For millions of Germans including Manstein and his family, however, basic survival was all that mattered. For the general population at 'Hour Zero', food, accommodation and employment were all terribly short; their future prospects under occupation were uncertain at best.

Rüdiger von Manstein stresses that his father was well treated by the British Army in the months immediately following the German surrender. Indeed, he retained certain privileges associated with his rank. Constrained within Prohibited Zone 'F', one of the 'captivity peninsulas' into which millions of German prisoners were herded, Manstein was allowed to live with his wife and son in his private guest rooms in the Weissenhaus, retain his staff car and driver, and keep his personal weapon. The only irritating slight was the theft of his much-prized field marshal's baton by a plundering British soldier, in crass contravention of good order and military discipline.[44] On his word of honour, Manstein was able to travel outside the restricted zone for medical treatment. Not only did complications arise again in his eye, but he also had a very dangerous, life-threatening abscess as a result of a bad injection.

Although he was a suspected typhoid case, Manstein's fair treatment came to an abrupt halt on 26 August 1945. Without any explanation he was hauled out of a hospital in Heiligenhafen, a coastal town not far from Oldenburg in Holstein, by British military police, never the most subtle element of an army. The arrest came totally out of the blue. Despite the protests of the British and German medical staff, who declared the Field Marshal unfit to travel, he was taken to a POW camp near Lüneburg. So began Manstein's detention that lasted to his release in May 1953, eight and a half years later.[45] By this time, Alexander Stahlberg regarded his duty as ADC as finished. Having obtained his release papers, he had no cause to remain interned with the Field Marshal whom he had served loyally for two and a half years. According to Maria Stahlberg, who visited the Mansteins at the Weissenhaus, her uncle was not at all impressed by the sudden departure of her brother-in-law.[46] The war, however, was over and Manstein had no claim on an ADC in captivity.

Witness at Nuremberg: Preparing the Defence

Now held under much closer confinement behind barbed wire, Manstein kept himself busy in the Lüneburg POW camp by making wooden chairs. Occasionally he was able to speak to his wife, disguised as a farm labourer, at the camp's perimeter fence. He remained interned there until summoned on 18 October 1945 together with Brauchitsch, a fellow inmate, to Headquarters British Army of the Rhine at Bad Oeynhausen.[47]

The next day they were taken to Nuremberg and detained in the 'Nazi' city's relatively undamaged Palace of Justice. This was the site of the trial of the Major War Criminals before the IMT, which tried twenty-one of the most important surviving military and civilian leaders of Nazi Germany. In parallel to the cases brought against these individuals, Göring, Keitel, Jodl, Raeder and Dönitz being the prominent military figures, also prosecuted were six groups and organizations. The latter included 'the General Staff and OKW'. Manstein was called to give evidence for the defence of this grouping, and as such landed in the witness rather than the criminal wing of the prison. In accordance with the London Agreement of 8 August 1945, which had set up the procedures for the IMT, individuals and organizations were to be tried under three broad categories: 'crimes against peace', 'war crimes' and 'crimes against humanity'.[48]

Supreme Court Justice Robert H. Jackson was the American chief counsel for the prosecution. His first deputy was William J. Donovan, a Medal of Honor recipient in the First World War, who became the Director of the Office of Strategic Services (OSS) in the Second. In preparing his case, Donovan wished to gain a German perspective on the development of the German Army from the end of the First World War to 1945. He turned to a lawyer, Dr Leverkuehn (who assisted at Manstein's trial in 1949), for advice, who then approached Field Marshal Walther von Brauchitsch to take on this task. In turn, the former commander-in-chief of the army called on Field Marshal von Manstein, Colonel General Franz Halder, General of Artillery Walter Warlimont and General of Cavalry Siegfried Westphal to assist. Interestingly, there was neither naval nor air force input. For the latter, Field Marshal Albert Kesselring, a cellmate of Manstein, would have been available. In the event, Manstein and Westphal wrote a large proportion of the 134-page typescript. Whilst this pair authored the sections 1920–1938 and Autumn 1942 to 1945, Brauchitsch and Halder covered the intervening period with Warlimont – Jodl's deputy – adding detail on OKW. As their work started, Manstein was faced with a sharp change in his environment.

In contrast with a British camp, prison life at Nuremberg – even as a witness – was far harsher. As Manstein complained in a letter to his wife,

> none of the rules of the Geneva Convention relating to prisoners of war are being applied here.... All officers who arrived in uniform had their badges of rank ripped off. As Westphal and another protested, they were put into solitary confinement and had to starve for two days. I'm glad that I'm wearing civilian clothes.

But the Field Marshal's first impressions were not all negative. He also wrote that 'the American soldiers [the prison guards] generally behave well'. He went on to praise the medical treatment as far as it went, but noted that he was not allowed to visit an eye specialist, for his sight was still impaired. Pretty greetings cards from his wife cheered him up, as did his harmonious relations with Westphal: 'Neither of us allow our heads to hang, rather we take fate as it comes, for we are not in a position to change it.... Above all, despite everything, both of us still have a laugh together, which is of great value.'[49]

Working conditions for writing 'The German Army 1920–1945' were a little better than life in a four-man cell: the five senior officers laboured under extreme time pressure in a spare room of the court. The one concession they enjoyed was being left undisturbed by the guards, which they had made a condition for their participation. Having no access to official records, the team discussed issues and then wrote from memory. Leverkuehn came to visit from time to time. The work reached a crisis when Donovan demanded an advance copy, and was disappointed not to find 'the guilty names'. Initially, there was indecision amongst the writing team as to how to react. Manstein and Westphal, however, were convinced that it was not their job to make the work of the prosecution any easier. Their view was accepted and the document was duly completed on 19 November 1945 without incriminating any individual.

Overall, the generals' treatise gave a clear and convincing rationale for a 'clean' Wehrmacht whose members were abused by the Führer, who had won and spent the trust of the German people. Failures in the conduct of operations had their prime source in the misjudgements of Hitler. It would be far too simplistic and inaccurate, however, to dismiss the document as a complete whitewash. It remains of historical value, providing much background and context for Manstein's and his colleagues' defence. Of specific interest are the perspectives and themes picked up during the cross-examination of Manstein and others the following summer, and subsequently at Manstein's trial. Furthermore, there is a clear link between the arguments set out in 'The German Army 1920–1945' and those presented in his memoirs.

It can be hardly disputed that 'Hitler neither trusted the General Staff nor the generals'.[50] Conversely, however, the document failed to offer a convincing view as to why so many in the armed forces – and especially those within the senior ranks – trusted Hitler, particularly in the run-up to, and during the early years of the war.[51] The Führer, of course, was not present at Nuremberg so could not defend himself. Hence it was convenient to highlight his shortcomings and to minimize any impression of military enthusiasm and support for his policies. Significantly, the authors stressed the increasing politicization of the Wehrmacht during the war years. 'As Hitler assumed the command of the army in December 1941, he informed the Chief of the General Staff that the "principal task of a commander-in-chief is to educate the army in National Socialism. I know of no army general with whom I can entrust this task. Therefore I have decided to take over command myself".'[52] Of course, the Wehrmacht was not synonymous with the *Heer* – the Luftwaffe had been politicized from its founding.

The *Kommissarbefehl* was dismissed lightly on the grounds that it was not distributed by OKH, and that Brauchitsch had issued supplementary instructions demanding correct behaviour by the troops.[53] A more surprising statement came in the supposedly excellent co-operation between OKW and OKH, which jars with Manstein's memoirs.[54] With his own uncomfortable experience in mind, he highlighted the severe constraints under which army group commanders had to operate. For example, they were not informed about developments outside their own areas of responsibility, and under these circumstances 'could not make any professionally reasoned proposals for the conduct of strategy'. More particularly within their own spheres, they 'stood in perpetual battle with Hitler over intentions of command', which over time led to 'increasingly difficult relations with the Supreme Commander'.[55] In a passage describing the conduct of operations from 1943 onwards Manstein wrote:

> Critical for this development in the Eastern theatre of war was the inadequate command at the highest operational level. One body of troops after the other was sacrificed for the sole principle of fighting for every foot of ground. The lack of any real reserves made things worse. The ratio of forces was usually 7:1 to the Russians' advantage. All warnings to the effect that the German armed forces were spent were ignored.[56]

The authors also covered the German administration of occupied territories, and hence addressed the issue of war crimes, a central charge against the General Staff and OKW. Their aim here was to absolve the German Army of any collective responsibility. Concerning combat against 'partisans and bands', it was quite clear that incidents of 'severe retribution should not be denied', but when such cases were brought to the attention of superiors, 'they were investigated'.[57] The destruction that accompanied the evacuation of occupied areas under 'scorched earth' policies was justified on the grounds of military necessity and carried out under the 'general laws pertaining to the conduct of war'.[58] The IMT would not be so convinced.

The 'Brauchitsch' group of generals concluded with some observations on the military opposition to Hitler. It is fair to suppose that Manstein, as a deeply religious man, added: 'Officers who were brought up as Christians – and this was the vast majority, particularly in the older generation' could not 'break their oath to their Supreme Commander, let alone kill him'. The final apologia was a rationalization of the German Army's inability to dispose of Hitler: 'Since the last [First World] War, the Army had been brought up to keep itself apart from politics. Now, in the hour of greatest danger, it possessed neither the men nor the means by which to take over the political leadership of the nation.'[59] One suspects that Manstein spoke not only for the members of the General Staff, but also for the vast majority of those who had served in the Wehrmacht.

What was the value of the document? According to Colonel Telford Taylor, associate prosecution counsel for the United States, it 'proved worthless for Donovan's purpose, as he himself saw, since it pointed the finger of blame for Germany's sorry state at Hitler and away from the army, and attributed no individual responsibility to Keitel or Jodl.'[60] For the defence, however, the generals' report provided a useful framework on which to build a convincing, if not compelling, case.

Having completed their written work in exculpation of the German Army, Manstein and his fellow witnesses now awaited the prosecution case against the General Staff and OKW. It was opened on 4 January 1946 by Telford Taylor. He addressed the Tribunal, stating that 'the indictment seeks a declaration of criminality, under Articles 9 to 11 of the Charter, against six groups and organizations; and the last one listed in the indictment is a group described as the General Staff and the High Command of the German Armed Forces'.[61] He continued:

> It is not the Prosecution's position that every member of this group was a wicked man or that they were all equally culpable. But we will show that this group not only collaborated with Hitler and supported the

essential Nazi objectives, but we will show that they furnished the one thing which was essential and basic to the success of the Nazi program for Germany; and that was skill and experience in the development and use of armed might.[62]

Taylor, an experienced US Army lawyer and intelligence officer, and later a noted military historian of the Second World War, had a smooth turn of phrase and put his powers of rhetoric to good use at Nuremberg, accusing the 'generals, like Hitler' of 'wanting to aggrandize Germany at the expense of neighbouring countries and were prepared to do so by force or threat of force'. Notching up his oratory, he declared:

> the Nazis offered the generals the chance of achieving much that they wished to achieve by expanding German armies and German frontiers; and so, as we will show, the generals climbed onto the Nazi bandwagon. They saw it was going in their direction for the present. No doubt they hoped later to take over the direction themselves. In fact, as the proof will show, ultimately it was the generals who were taken for a ride by the Nazis. Hitler, in short, attracted the generals to him with the glitter of conquest and then succeeded in submerging them politically; and, as the war proceeded, they became his tools. But if these military leaders became the tools of Nazism, it is not to be supposed that they were unwitting or that they did not participate fully in many of the crimes which we will bring to the notice of the Tribunal. The willingness – and, indeed, the eagerness – of the German professional officer corps to become partners of the Nazis, will be fully developed.[63]

Taylor's opening plea continued in such detail that it required part of another day's hearing, 7 January 1946, to complete.

In the meantime, Manstein would not rest. He worked long hours assisting the principal defence counsel, Dr Laternser, in proposing various tactics and arguments to be employed. By the spring of 1946 he had produced several hundred pages of material loosely titled 'Contributions to the Defence of the General Staff'. It says much for the Field Marshal's determination and energy that he achieved so much despite the primitive working conditions and his poor eyesight.

Manstein's deliberations are quoted extensively by his son in *Soldat im 20. Jahrhundert*.[64] Suffice it to say, the Field Marshal used his time at Nuremberg well in anticipating the potential lines of enquiry that the prosecution would employ, and in preparing a convincing set of responses. His main concern with regard to 'crimes against peace' was to demonstrate that Hitler, rather than OKW, OKH or more widely the General Staff, was responsible for planning and waging wars of aggression. Laternser and Manstein recognized the risk, if the defence were unsuccessful, that 'thousands of members of the General Staff, whatever position in which they served, would be automatically condemned by a guilty verdict without any further trial'.[65]

In his notes, Manstein concluded: 'In accordance with constitutional law, the decision over war and peace was Hitler's. . . . The military commanders neither provoked nor recommended war. They tried to resist decisions as to going to war where and as far as they could.' As for the military, 'There was no law that allowed for the removal of obligatory obedience if acts of war breached international treaties.' As fundamentally, in his view, it should not be permissible to condemn soldiers as criminals for doing their duty. Hitherto, waging war has never been a crime in law.[66] Manstein was convinced that the General Staff and OKW would be found not guilty of being a criminal body, because they constituted neither a group nor an organization. After all, their planning activities were similar in nature to those conducted in every other country.[67] His anticipation was to prove correct, but it would be many months before the Tribunal would come to that finding.

With regard to the alleged war crimes by the military, Manstein was emphatic in his written considerations. 'German commanders from the beginning to the end fought against the armed forces of the enemy according to military law,' he declared. More particularly, in view of the accusations by the prosecution, he maintained that the 'proper attitude of German military commanders towards enemy soldiers was reflected in their stance to civilian populations in occupied areas'. Manstein explained his position as follows, which in principle remains as valid for today's complex operating environment as it did during the Second World War:

> The commander-in-chief, who bears a heavy responsibility for fighting at the front, has only one interest, namely that rear areas remain quiet. To achieve this, he will do all in his power to keep the local population at peace, as far as one can in war. This cannot be achieved by harsh measures. He knows only too well that these will lead to reactions by the enemy [people], and these in turn to repression that finally leads to insurrection. . . . On the other hand, it's obvious that open resistance in the rear of an army cannot be tolerated.

Yet it is clear that Manstein had convinced himself that the German military – and he meant here its three armed services (army, air force and navy) and not the *Waffen* SS – had conducted themselves by and large correctly throughout the Second World War. That considerable numbers of German units and formations had been engaged in assisting or committing war crimes, since proven beyond all reasonable doubt, according to his son was beyond his 'moral comprehension' and lay outside his direct experience.[68] Manstein was in defiant denial when he concluded his notes for Dr Laternser:

> Indisputably the Second World War – on both sides – caused severe transgressions against the laws of armed conflict. Certainly it displayed appalling manifestations with respect to humanity as a result of its total character. Certainly the norms of international law ... were broken many times. However, this can in no way be traced back to the plans of German military commanders. As far as they had to obey orders, which contravened previous views [of law], they found themselves in the same position as those tasked in other countries with bombing campaigns.[69]

Meanwhile, among the defendants and witnesses, Manstein became an individual of special interest to an American psychiatrist, Dr Leon Goldensohn. His observations of the Field Marshal, only recently published, offer a fascinating picture of a

> tall man, about six foot in height, well developed and well nourished. He wears a black patch over the right eye, which has been operated upon for a cataract several years ago. He has been the main organizer of the defence of the General Staff and the driving spirit behind the other field marshals and generals imprisoned in Nuremberg. It was Manstein who delegated various roles to these officers in the preparation of the defence of the General Staff.[70]

Apart from Westphal, corroboration of Manstein's pivotal role in organizing the witnesses and in planning a campaign for the defence came from Kleist. The latter told Goldensohn:

> [He] has assigned us each a section ... and each of us has completed his section and more. All of this material was given to Manstein, who, in turn, delivered it to Dr Laternser. Now we sit around doing nothing, except for Manstein, who has in a way assumed the responsibility for the defence of the General Staff and the Army.

Goldensohn then enquired about his fellow field marshal's method. The psychiatrist recorded:

> I cautiously asked Kleist what Manstein had assigned to him and in general what the nature of his testimony in defence of the General Staff

would be. Kleist smiled craftily, and replied with an attitude as if to say, 'Wouldn't you like to know?' He did say, however, 'I am answering certain questions that Manstein is devising and we divided these questions among us. Certain of us, like Halder, Brauchitsch, Westphal, Wilhelm List, Wilhelm Ritter von Leeb, Rundstedt, Guenther Blumentritt, and so on, will each take the responsibility for answering certain charges and explaining certain aspects of the military situation.'[71]

The moral and practical leadership that Manstein exercised over his colleagues is demonstrated by Kleist's response when Goldensohn pressed him on the nature of the orders issued by Keitel. 'Were they not contrary to the international code of ethics?' he asked. 'I am here as a witness for the General Staff and Army, and that is almost the crucial point of our defence,' Kleist replied. He continued: 'It is something that the prosecution will, without doubt, dwell on, and I must think this over rather carefully and talk to Manstein before I express any official position on Keitel's orders.'[72]

The next discussion concerned Field Marshal Paulus, who had appeared as a surprise witness at Nuremberg, and the destruction of Sixth Army at Stalingrad. 'Did this loss of life depress you at the time?' Goldensohn enquired. 'Of course,' Manstein responded. 'For myself, as a leader with the responsibility for 100,000 people, the spiritual burden was very great. But I blame Paulus to a certain extent for not taking some responsibility himself and breaking out to the rear before he was encircled, despite Hitler's wishes.' 'On the other hand', Manstein continued, 'I agreed with Hitler that once Paulus was encircled, he should stand ground and fight as he did, despite the loss of life, because if he had capitulated, it would have meant the defeat of Germany then and there.'[73] There was little hint of comradeship or sympathy with his former subordinate.

Goldensohn then switched his line of questioning to the Führer. 'What was your general feeling about Hitler?' Manstein replied: 'He was an extraordinary personality. He had a tremendously high intelligence and an exceptional willpower.' Then came an extraordinary question: 'Was this willpower directed toward good, or evil?' 'It's hard to say,' declared the Field Marshal. '. . . I suppose at the time it can be said that his willpower served both bad and good purposes.' Then Manstein's interviewer changed tack. 'When did you first believe that Hitler had no moral scruples?' 'After the war was over . . . after I heard about all the things that had happened.' Manstein continued: 'The first sight of Hitler's lack of morality was his behaviour after July 20, 1944, with the subsequent trials, hangings, *et cetera*. And later when I heard about the annihilation of the Jews.'[74] So Manstein appeared to forget the murders associated with the Röhm crisis of 1934, the Nuremberg race laws, and not least the invasions of Czechoslovakia and Poland. In sum, he tried to make it clear that he knew nothing about the crimes perpetrated by the Nazis until very late in the day. Not surprisingly, Goldensohn challenged this position.

Surely Manstein must have been aware of the activities of the *Einsatzkommandos* in the Crimea? In response, the Field Marshal 'looked slightly uncomfortable but remained cool and indifferent'. He then admitted that 'Ohlendorf's Einsatzgruppe was in my district. I heard that here for the first time.... What they did, I never knew.' He then elaborated: 'I never personally saw or reliably heard of the shootings of the Jews en masse by these *Einsatzkommandos*. Such installations [*sic*] were not under my command and in reality I could not do anything about them.'[75] The Field Marshal had touched on the crux of the matter that would dominate his subsequent cross-examinations at the witness stand at Nuremberg and at his trial in Hamburg, three years later. The prosecution would seek to establish the degree of complicity with the *Einsatzgruppen* by Headquarters Eleventh Army and its commander-in-chief. What did he know, what did he do and what could, or should, he have done to prevent or mitigate those shocking crimes? In many respects, therefore, Goldensohn's interview of 14 June 1946 was but a rehearsal for dealing with some very awkward questions that were bound to return.

Witness at Nuremberg: Manstein's Evidence

Manstein's oral evidence at Nuremberg began on the 199th day of the hearings on Friday, 9 August 1946 and ended on the morning of Monday, the 12th. Following Brauchitsch, he was Dr Laternser's second and principal witness. During the first, afternoon, session, Manstein answered a number of uncontroversial questions about his role in the General Staff and during his period of divisional command prior to the outbreak of the war. The really interesting, and most revealing, part of his testimony came on Saturday morning, 11 August, when defence counsel asked him about the war in Russia.

Dr Laternser: You received the Commissar Order, did you not?
Von Manstein: Yes.
Dr Laternser: What attitude did you adopt with reference to that order?

Von Manstein: It was the first time I found myself involved in a conflict between my soldierly conceptions and my duty to obey. Actually, I ought to have obeyed, but I said to myself that as a soldier I could not possibly co-operate in a thing like that, and I told the commander of the army group under which I came at the time, as well as the commander of the armoured group, that I would not carry out such an order, which was against the honour of a soldier.

In practice, the order was not carried out. My divisional commanders, who had already received the order independently from me in the Reich, shared my views and, apart from that, the commissars, as good fighters, defended themselves to the last and in many cases shot themselves before being taken prisoner, or they removed their insignia of rank and could not be identified by the troops. The troops, who inwardly disliked the order intensely, certainly did not look for the commissars amongst the prisoners.[76]

Significantly, amongst the seventeen charges raised against Manstein at his war crimes trial in 1949, one involved the implementation of the Commissar Order within his command.

Having confirmed the names of Manstein's superior commanders, Laternser then asked Manstein about he how he reconciled his disobedience in this case with his 'conception of the military duty to obey'. Their carefully rehearsed exchange built on complex argument continued:

Von Manstein: In itself military obedience is, of course, unconditional, indivisible, but during wars there have always been cases where higher military leaders did not obey an order or carried it out differently. That is part of the higher responsibility which a high military leader bears. No army leader can be expected to join a battle when he knows he is bound to lose.

In these questions, that is to say, operational questions, there is in practice in the final analysis a certain right to deviate from orders given, which, however, must be confirmed by success. In the German Army particularly that independence of lower-ranking leaders has always been strongly emphasized.[77]

The situation is quite different in the case of orders which deal with actions on the part of all soldiers. In such cases, disobedience on the part of the small man [*sic*] can be dealt with by means of punishment. If the higher leader, however, has disobeyed orders in such cases, then he undermines not only his own authority but discipline as a whole, and thereby endangers military success. In such cases, it is more binding on the higher leader than it is on the soldier and lower-ranking leader, because he, the higher man, should be an example.

Dr Laternser: Did you not undermine discipline by this disobedience of yours?[78]

Von Manstein: No, not in this case, because the troops felt the same as I did. In other words, the soldierly feelings which we had instilled into our troops opposed the political will imposed upon them by Hitler.[79]

The defence counsel continued to give Manstein ample opportunity to explain the harsh and unforgiving operating conditions of the war in the East, including the reasons for the 'scorched earth' policy.

Dr Laternser: Was this destruction necessary for the carrying out of the war?

Von Manstein: As far as this retreat beyond the Dnieper is concerned I have to answer that question absolutely in the affirmative. The situation was such that if we could not bring the Soviet armies to a halt at the Dnieper and if they were able to continue their breakthrough and their advance, the war was lost. The Dnieper had not been fortified. Hitler had forbidden it when we proposed it earlier. The work had only just begun. There were not sufficient troops to hold the Dnieper line against a heavy attack. If, therefore, the Russian attack could not be halted on account of disrupted Russian lines of supply, it could be assumed that in the autumn of 1943 the fighting in the southern part of the Eastern Front would be decided, and the war in the East would end unfavourably for us. In such cases only the highest leaders could in the last analysis decide what would be achieved operationally by military necessity. The lower leader lacks the ability to judge; he can only see the necessities of his sector and therefore cannot have the right to reject such decisions.[80]

Laternser raised later the accusation that German forces had looted in occupied territories. Manstein gave a robust response. Alluding to 'scorched earth' again, he stated:

We had the strictest orders in the Army against looting, and rigorous action was taken against looters. The individual soldier was not allowed to requisition, but only troop units, and then only what the unit needed for the feeding of the troops within ration allotments. On the other hand in 1943 we co-operated in bringing back goods which were especially needed by us for carrying on the war. But by an express order of mine that was limited in the Ukraine to grain, oilseeds, some small quantity of metal, and a small number of cattle which could be driven along with us. However, all this was not looting private property; it was a State requisitioning State property.[81]

The distinction between private and state property would have been a semantic one to the Ukrainian population who relied on farm animals for their existence. In fact, the 'small number' of cattle amounted to tens, if not hundreds, of thousands. In September 1943, for example, 80,000 cattle were driven 'herd after herd' across the Dnepr at Kremenchug.[82] Manstein's memory could be selective if required.

The questioning continued. Manstein made it clear that he knew next to nothing about the concentration camps. Then the defence counsel enquired about the true nature of the war.

> *Dr Laternser:* As a soldier of the old tradition, how do you explain the shootings with which the Prosecution has charged the German war leaders as a crime against humanity?
>
> *Von Manstein:* Beginning in 1941 with the Soviet campaign, this last war was, one might say, fought from two points of view. The first was the military conduct of the war which we, the soldiers, were carrying through, and the other was – incidentally on both sides – the ideological conduct of the war which we soldiers were not carrying out, but was determined by other factors.
>
> *Dr Laternser:* You said 1941?
>
> *Von Manstein:* Yes, it is my view that the Polish war and the war in the West and the campaigns in Norway and in the Balkans were still carried out in a purely military manner as long as the fighting was going on. The other side, that is the ideological side of the war, started, in my opinion, with the campaign against the Soviet Union, and it was then extended to the other occupied territories by those who conducted this type of war.
>
> *Dr Laternser:* But then, who was conducting this ideological fight on the part of Germany?
>
> *Von Manstein:* We soldiers did not wage this ideological war. In my opinion it was waged by Hitler together with some of his closest collaborators, and a limited number of accomplices.[83]

Hans Ohlendorf, commander of *Einsatzgruppe* D, had given evidence to the Tribunal on 3 January 1946 that was particularly damaging. He had implied that Manstein, as commander-in-chief of Eleventh Army, was well aware of the liquidation of the Jews. He claimed, for example, that an order from the headquarters of this army 'was sent to Nikolaiev stating that liquidations were to take place only at a distance of not less than 200 kilometres from the headquarters of the commanding general'. Further, 'In Simferopol the army command requested the *Einsatzkommandos* in its area to hasten the liquidations, because famine was threatening and there was a great housing shortage.'[84] Laternser tried to get to the bottom of this horrific crime, and as Goldensohn before him, enquired about the *Einsatzgruppen*.

'What did you know about the tasks given to these groups?' he asked. Manstein replied: 'All I knew about the tasks of these *Einsatzgruppen* was that they were organized to prepare for the political administration; that is to say, to carry out the political screening of the population in the occupied territories of the East, and they were acting on special instructions under Himmler's responsibility.' The Field Marshal denied that he knew about the intention to exterminate Jews. 'No, I never heard of that; in fact, as the witness Ohlendorf has said, this order was given orally by Himmler directly to the *Einsatzgruppen*.' As already related in an earlier chapter, Laternser asked Manstein to explain why he could not recall the murder of 90,000 Jews. The Field Marshal evaded the question by pointing out the geographical area involved, one mostly not under his responsibility. Dr Laternser then asked: 'But could you have helped hearing about it if in the Crimea, for instance, several hundred Jews were murdered?'[85]

Manstein answered again to the contrary. He explained that he occupied a succession of tactical headquarters in the combat zone. In the Crimea, when based at Sarabus (Gvardeyskoye) north of the capital Simferopol, subordinates such as Eleventh Army's chief quartermaster (Colonel Finckh) only reported to him on 'essential matters'. Otherwise, he was fully occupied 'by the worries of the battle and that, quite rightly, only the essential points of other matters were reported'.[86] Hence, he implied, as commander-in-chief he did not have sufficient time to concern himself with complex issues of occupation when still fighting a war.

It would appear that Dr Laternser kept some of his most telling questions until towards the end of his examination in an effort to give Manstein an opportunity to highlight the constraints under which he held his command, including the need to obey orders. Following a brief exchange on the Field Marshal's very limited interaction with Nazi civilian officials Koch, Rosenberg and Sauckel, Laternser asked, 'Field Marshal, why did you, as a high military leader, tolerate all these violations of international law and laws of humanity?'

Von Manstein: ... in my military province, I did not tolerate such things, and whatever happened in the ideological struggle outside of my sphere, we did not get to know about. It was taking place outside of our sphere of influence and knowledge, and we had neither the power nor the right to prevent it, apart from the fact that we never knew of all the abominations which have since been disclosed.

Dr Laternser: Were you of the opinion that for reasons of military obedience you had to tolerate everything, or rather co-operate in everything?

Von Manstein: The military duty to obey is without doubt binding and indivisible. The right or duty to disobey I would say does not exist for the soldier. There may be a moral duty which would apply, for instance, in such cases as the execution of Jews.[87]

Until now Dr Laternser had been doing all the interviewing. Then the bulk of the cross-examination was taken up by Colonel Telford Taylor. Having asked Manstein about the Commissar Order, he switched his attention to the operations of the *Einsatzgruppen* and the infamous Reichenau Order.

Col. Taylor: Did the commanding generals on the Eastern Front submit special instructions to the troops which support this program to liquidate the Jews and the commissars?

Von Manstein: No, that is quite out of the question.

Col. Taylor: Did General Reichenau issue such an instruction?

Von Manstein: No, I only know of one order of General Reichenau, which has been brought up in court, and in which he discusses fighting in the East. This order was sent to us on Hitler's instructions as an example. I personally turned down the order and did not apply it in any way in the orders I issued, and I know of no other commander who attached any weight to it.[88]

It was the first time that Manstein put a foot wrong at the Tribunal, for Taylor had damning evidence ready to catch the Field Marshal out. When asked again about what action he took on receipt of the Reichenau Order, Manstein's response was 'I did nothing about it and I considered such an order as quite beside the point, because I wanted to fight in a military manner and in no other way.' Manstein was digging himself an ever-deeper hole from which there would be no escape. Taylor went swiftly for the kill: 'Will you look at this order, Witness, and tell us if that is not a document issued out of your headquarters and signed with your facsimile signature, on 20 November 1941?'

The prosecution counsel then produced the incriminating order (already quoted in Chapter 10), observing that its resemblance with Reichenau's was 'striking and the date is about the same'.[89] As the document was then read out, the court listened in stunned silence. Manstein kept his cool and answered calmly, 'I must say that this order escapes my memory entirely. According to the signature and particularly what is contained in the last part, I must assume that the order is genuine and has been issued by me.' He attempted then to deflect the impression that he had misled the IMT. He stated:

> I had quite forgotten the Reichenau order until it appeared amongst the documents here, and I have no recollection especially of this order of mine. After all, that is not surprising, because that is a number of years ago, and during these years I have signed hundreds, if not thousands of orders, and I cannot possibly remember every detail.

Taylor was not going to let the Field Marshal off the hook with such a lame excuse. 'Did you sign a lot of orders like this one? Is that why you have such difficulty remembering it?' Manstein retorted:

> No. I certainly have not signed a lot of orders like this one, but I have signed a lot of other orders. Above all, I had to write and read a large number of reports and if I forgot this order, a fact which I admit, it is not surprising. I only know that this order, at any rate, as opposed to the Reichenau order, very strongly emphasizes the demands which I made for decent behaviour on the part of my soldiers. That, after all, is the important point.

Taylor then quizzed him further about the Reichenau and his own order, asking Manstein whether he wrote the second part and not the first, which the Field Marshal had implied. A surprising answer followed: 'I did not write the order at all myself. Very probably the order was shown to me in draft and then I signed it.' There then followed an exchange about the purpose of the Manstein order, which concluded as follows:

> *Col. Taylor:* Witness, isn't it true that this order is very carefully drawn up so that troops would understand and, we shall say, sympathize with what the *Einsatzkommandos* were doing in the way of mass execution of Jews?
> *Von Manstein:* You mean my order?
> *Col. Taylor:* Yes.
> *Von Manstein:* No. There can be no question that I at any time urged my troops, even between the lines, to co-operate in such methods. How could I have concluded by stressing the soldier's honour?

Col. Taylor: My Lord, the Prosecution has no further questions of this
witness.

The President: We will adjourn now.[90]

Taylor remained unconvinced about the veracity of the Field Marshal's
evidence about the *Einsatzgruppen*. In his memoir of the IMT he wrote:

> I did not for a moment believe Manstein's claim that he knew nothing of
> the massacres. I did not expect to make him confess his knowledge, but
> rather to show how absurd it was to suppose that murder groups moved
> through the army's front and rear lines without being noticed or that an
> alert commander would not want to know what these unusual armed
> units sponsored by Himmler were doing.[91]

Following the revelation of the order of 20 November 1941 and associated cross-examination, the prosecution considered Manstein's credibility 'shattered'. Apparently, Dr Laternser told Taylor's associate Walter
Rapp, 'if he had known of the document he would never have called
Manstein as a witness'.[92] That may be so, but the fact remains that
Laternser went on to be a prominent member of the Field Marshal's
defence team in Hamburg.

After a break on Sunday, 11 August, the hearing continued on Monday,
12 August 1946. Major General G. A. Alexandrov, assistant prosecutor
for the USSR, took over from Taylor. He continued to probe about the
activities of *Einsatzgruppe* D. The key allegations, which returned to
haunt Manstein at his trial, were first, the supply of watches to Eleventh
Army from Jews who had been shot, and secondly, whether members of
the army had attended such executions.

> *Gen. Alexandrov:* Do you know that these facts were brought out here in
> Court by the witness Ohlendorf? Do you think that Ohlendorf testified
> falsely here when relating these facts?
>
> *Von Manstein:* I know Ohlendorf's testimony and I remember he said that
> soldiers had participated in executions near Simferopol. But he also
> said that he did not know for certain what soldiers they were. He
> thought they were probably mostly subsidiary technical units, that is,
> not regular troops of my army. In any event, while I was in the Crimea
> I never heard that any soldier participated in the execution of Jews.
>
> *Gen. Alexandrov:* I would like you to answer my question. Do you call
> Ohlendorf's testimony false or do you consider it correct?
>
> *Von Manstein:* I assume that he made a mistake. At any rate, I am quite
> certain that regular units of my army did not participate in these

executions of Jews. What he means by subsidiary technical units, I do not know.

Alexandrov proceeded to grill Manstein on the treatment of prisoners of war before returning to the Reichenau Order, developing his American colleague's enquiries about the Field Marshal's own order of 20 November 1941.

The Russian challenged the Field Marshal on whether 'such decrees' could only be explained by 'the fact that their authors were not generals brought up in the military tradition, but generals brought up in the Hitlerite tradition'. Manstein had to be asked twice before he grasped its impact, or perhaps he was cleverly playing for time in order to formulate a convincing response. He stressed that the order was composed in two parts, differentiating between the two as follows:

> Part One, which deals with the necessity of safeguarding the rear against attack, et cetera, and with the alertness of soldiers, contains some ideas about the meaning of this struggle. When the order speaks of the extermination of the system, then it means the political system, and not human beings, it means exactly what is today meant when the other side speaks of the extermination of National Socialism. Part Two, I would, say contains my own ideas, it states what has to be done positively, and it also states quite clearly that the soldiers must avoid all arbitrary action, and that any violation of soldierly honour will be punished. I believe that this order is evidence of the fact that I conducted the fight as a soldier, and not as a politician.[93]

This was Manstein's last key statement before the Tribunal, which attempted to provide further separation between a conventional, clean war fought by the army against a uniformed opponent and the 'ideological war' waged by other elements such as the SD against partisans and the local population, including the Jews. It remained to be seen whether he would be successful in achieving this objective.

Nuremberg: The Judgement

Monday, 30 September 1946 was the day of judgement on the General Staff and OKW. The Tribunal held that 'no declaration of criminality should be made in respect of the General Staff and High Command'. It found that it was neither a group nor organization, which 'must be more than this collection of military officers'. So far, so good for Manstein and the other generals. But then came the damning finding. The Tribunal 'has heard much evidence as to the participation of these officers in planning and waging aggressive war, and in committing war crimes and crimes against humanity. The evidence is, as to many of them, clear and convincing.' The ire of the judges continued:

[These individuals] have been responsible in large measure for the miseries and suffering, that have fallen on millions of men, women and children. They have been a disgrace to the honourable profession of arms. Without their military guidance the aggressive ambitions of Hitler and his fellow-Nazis would have been academic and sterile. Although they were not a group falling within the words of the Charter, they were certainly a ruthless military caste.[94]

With such language, it is clear that the General Staff and OKW – as a body – were found not guilty on a technicality. Many of its members were fellow travellers of Nazism. As they shared in Hitler's triumphs, so should they also bear responsibility for the worst excesses of National Socialism and grievous offences conducted in its name. That certainly was implied in the judgement. Manstein, for one, did not see it that way at all. He wrote to his wife on 2 October 1946:

that at Nuremberg the General Staff was not declared as criminal has given me great satisfaction. So during my ten months of work for the defence, I have been able to give the army, my life's work, one last service. This battle for its honour was conducted with such passion unlike any one hitherto.

He could not entirely ignore, however, the negative qualifications that accompanied the judgement. 'They were to be expected, but did not alter anything,' he added.[95]

Westphal was in no doubt as to the value of Manstein's contribution. He concluded his account of the main trial at Nuremberg by writing: 'Without the comprehensive support, which he provided throughout for the defence, it would have been difficult to have achieved our objective. Manstein's phenomenal memory, his extraordinary work drive and his ingenious impetus were simply indispensable for our defence.'[96]

With the indictment failing against the General Staff as a collective body, Manstein had indeed won his last battle, but it proved a Pyrrhic victory individually. His cross-examination and those of other witnesses provided the foundation for subsequent proceedings, including those laid against him at his trial three years later in Hamburg. In particular, the 'terrier' Telford Taylor was unrelenting in his quest to see senior commanders such as Manstein convicted. The American prosecutor was convinced that the Field Marshal had lied in maintaining his ignorance about the murderous activities conducted by *Einsatzgruppe* D. Moreover, Taylor was concerned that the 'first steps towards the revival of German militarism' had taken place at the Tribunal. In his closing address he had argued:

> The German General Staff have had plenty of time to think since the spring of 1945, and it well knows what is at stake here. The German militarists know that their future strength depends on re-establishing the faith of the German people in their military powers and in disassociating themselves from the atrocities which they committed in the service of the Third Reich.[97]

Between the beginning of 1947 and the end of 1949, the staff of the American Office of Chief-of-Counsel for War Crimes (OCCWC), with Taylor as its driving force, conducted twelve further trials at Nuremberg. Although Manstein was not brought to account in these 'Subsequent Nuremberg Proceedings', Taylor considered that with new evidence having come to light, the cases against Manstein and Rundstedt were 'overwhelming'; indeed, they were the strongest against any potential defendants.[98] So Manstein was not off the hook after the IMT. He went on to face no fewer than seventeen charges of war crimes at his eventual trial in Hamburg in 1949, in preparation of which Taylor had done much of the groundwork before passing the case over to the British authorities.

Within a wider strategic context, however, Manstein's old friend General Walther Wenck was probably right to reflect nearly thirty years after Nuremberg that without a successful defence of the General Staff, in all probability there would have been no Bundeswehr and thus no German contribution to Euro-Atlantic security.[99] If one accepts this hypothesis, Manstein, for all the subsequent allegations he had to face during his trial, had indeed done his country a valuable service. He had none the less fed assiduously the myth of a clean Wehrmacht and offered no atonement for its misdeeds. In this sense, Taylor was right about Manstein, both the man and his purpose.

16

Crime and Punishment

'Revenge is, of all satisfactions, the most costly and long drawn out; retributive persecution is, of all politics, the most pernicious.' Winston Churchill[1]

Island Farm

Following his cross-examination at the IMT, at the end of August 1946 Manstein was transferred back into the custody of the United Kingdom. From Nuremberg, he was sent via the 'London District Cage', a former interrogation centre that housed the War Crimes Investigation Unit (WCIU) in Kensington Palace Gardens, to Special Camp No. 11 near Bridgend in Wales.[2] During the Second World War, Island Farm, as it is more commonly termed, was famous for the largest escape attempt by German prisoners of war in Great Britain.[3] Since early January 1946 nearly two hundred senior German officers from all three services and the *Waffen* SS had been detained in the camp. The most prominent was Field Marshal von Rundstedt, who had been joined there by his son, Hans Gerd, on compassionate grounds. On being removed temporarily from his comfortable surroundings to the witness wing at the IMT, the old field marshal had described the living conditions in Nuremberg as a 'pig sty'.[4] Returning to Bridgend, Rundstedt was delighted to re-enter 'his Hotel Island Farm', according to the camp intelligence officer and interpreter, Captain Ted Lees.[5]

Manstein was admitted to Island Farm on 2 September 1946 as British prisoner of war No. B33419. He lived in a one-storey block – the most comfortable hut available – with two other field marshals, Brauchitsch and Rundstedt, together with the latter's son.[6] At his disposal was a room with bed, desk and chair; only Rundstedt was given the additional privilege of a separate study and bedroom. The senior officers shared communal ablutions and ate in the generals' dining room. An orderly was also available for part of the day.[7] Not surprisingly, Manstein's first impressions of the camp were extremely positive. Shortly after his arrival, he wrote to Jutta-Sibylle:

It's very reasonable here. I particularly enjoy the freedom of movement in the camp. We live in stone barrack huts with heating! After ten months in Nuremberg one really values the luxuries of a bed with covers, a comfortable chair, flowers, a laid table in a dining hall and a knife and fork to eat with, not just a metal bowl and a spoon. The food is simple but sufficient, certainly more than you're getting in Germany. All this and the lack of the atmosphere of hate that pervaded Nuremberg, is an obvious blessing. It's very agreeable to receive all the main English newspapers. Also a library is available.[8]

Manstein obtained permission to plant and tend a small garden. Unlike the junior rank orderlies, who had to work six hours a day on nearby farms, he had time on his hands. On their word of honour, the senior prisoners were allowed to walk outside the wire into town. As one local account recalls, 'it was not unusual to see these generals and field marshals in Bridgend, out for a stroll, buying a sandwich, or feeding the ducks in the river'.[9] As at Nuremberg, Manstein soon got into a daily routine, which he described in a letter home: 'I am healthy, and the weeks fly by quickly. I spend the morning with clearing up and reading. After lunch, I go for an hour's walk. In the afternoon, I read or write.'[10]

Amongst his fellow prisoners of war was General Frido von Senger und Etterlin, who had commanded 17th Panzer Division during the abortive attack to relieve Stalingrad in December 1942.[11] In his memoirs, he left a revealing perspective on the composition of the Germans at Island Farm:

> The officers split themselves into three groups. The first, which I joined, aimed at drawing up a balance-sheet, clearing-up obscurities and coming to conclusions. Its members were long standing opponents of the régime, whose attitude towards it had been clear before the collapse. Membership of this group was not an easy matter for those inmates of the camp who had waited until after the collapse before criticising the Hitler régime; they would not admit that its shortcomings had been previously discernible. A number of generals in this category nevertheless found their way into the group, but many others refrained from joining it for the reasons given. The latter were far more numerous, and they probably reflected the attitude of the average German in his own country. Lastly, the third group consisted of die-hard followers of Hitler, who understandably kept away from any discussions on the subject.[12]

Senger und Etterlin left no hint as to which group Manstein belonged in, but it is safe to assume that the second is more likely than the first. He might have had the Field Marshal in mind when he wrote that a 'not altogether unjustified reproach was levelled at the generals because their opposition to the régime developed only as a result of their belief that they would have avoided Hitler's mistakes and might therefore have won the war'. Alternatively, Manstein could have been among the 'other opponents, who, while attributing the defeat to Hitler's incompetence, had no understanding of the need for the statesman's political control of the military, and who nevertheless objected to the régime on moral grounds'. Senger und Etterlin felt that this latter standpoint was 'particularly attributable to the tradition-bound Prussian officers, with their marked Lutheran outlook'.[13]

Manstein remained very much his own man: fiercely independently minded and therefore hard to stereotype. He kept himself away from the majority of the other prisoners and led his own life as best he could, usually taking solitary walks. Of Manstein's former associates, apart from his fellow field marshals and Colonel General Strauss, there was occasional company in General of Infantry Günther Blumentritt, who had served with him in Poland and was later Rundstedt's chief of staff in the West, and General of Infantry Friedrich Herrlein from his old 3rd Foot Guards days.

Despite the inevitable restrictions, conditions at Island Farm were much better than those encountered at the cramped and cold Grizedale Hall near Ambleside in the Lake District, where many of the German generals, including Rundstedt, had been held before being moved south to the Glamorgan coast. The new camp was run by 'two successive commandants, both carefully selected, both personifying the British gentleman – polite, sympathetic and courteous, in short [they were] disarming towards many an inmate.'[14] As press officer, Senger und Etterlin wrote weekly reports in German, and was, in his own words, 'able to exert a certain amount of educational influence'. One can presume that Manstein would not have needed such stimulus, but certainly he would have subscribed to his fellow officer's notion that it was necessary to encourage 'men of good will' towards the 'way back'. In other words, 'back to the normality of civil and civic life, back to a respect for essential moral standards, back to law and order – for this was the only possible basis for the new life of our own nation with the community of nations.'[15]

Manstein's fellow field marshals reacted differently in custody. Rundstedt isolated himself, only conversing with his close friend Blumentritt, and 'wrote no historical papers and took little interest in the future'. Fellow inmate Lieutenant General Kurt Dittmar described Brauchitsch to Captain B. H. Liddell Hart as 'the most active and thoughtful of the older prisoners'.[16] In making this assessment, Dittmar may not have been aware of Manstein's literary efforts that probably exceeded all others' at Island Farm. The Field Marshal rarely rested intellectually, devoting much of his time to drafting two books: *Der Weg zum Weltfrieden* (The Way Towards World Peace) and *Die andere Seite* (The Other Side).[17] He rehearsed his thinking in extensive correspondence with his wife. In February 1947, for example, he addressed why National Socialism had been so popular with so many Germans. 'The more one concerns oneself with this question,' he wrote, 'the more one comes to the following results.' He then explained: 'That this illness broke out especially [in Germany] and brought with it such evil manifestations, lay in the overall political, social and economic development.'[18]

There is little doubt that the lengthy re-examination of recent historical events had a cathartic effect on Manstein – it helped to clear his mind (if not wipe his memory) of the grim negatives of Hitler's Third Reich and allowed him to think much more positively towards a brighter future for Germany. Although the propositions he expounded were to some extent overtaken by events, he never regretted the effort involved. Corresponding some years later whilst serving his sentence in Germany, he remarked to his wife: 'Don't worry if nothing comes from the writing now, or not even in the immediate future. Occupying myself with these questions, after all, has consumed many hours of imprisonment and made many problems clearer to me. It has served to keep my brain active.'[19]

Manstein deliberated over the unification of Europe, the pressing need for a rapprochement between Germany and France, and eventually one with Russia. In this manner, he anticipated the Treaty of Rome (1957), the Élysée Treaty concluded by Charles de Gaulle and Konrad Adenauer (1963), and Germany's later *Ostpolitik* of the 1960s and 1970s. In a letter to Dr Christoph Freiherr von Imhoff, a personal friend who had served with him in the Crimea, he declared that 'we Europeans need to find a new form of democracy. In foreign policy terms it can only be achieved through the amalgamation of [nation states] to larger units; economically, there is in any case no alternative.' He went on to propose: 'The first necessary step would be the union of Germany–France–Benelux under the patronage of England. If this first step were achieved, then northern European and later Mediterranean countries would join.'[20] In an equally prescient passage in 'The Way Towards World Peace', he concluded:

The natural place of Germany is within the framework of a 'United Europe'. She can only assume it when she is accepted as an equal and free partner, and when her unity and self-sufficiency are recognized as for others. The final reconciliation between France and Germany is the prerequisite for a 'United Europe'. It requires from both a line being drawn under the past, the sacrifice of forgetting and the courage of trust. Germany is ready for this. In joining a 'United Europe', Germany must also strive for friendly relations with the East. It will be her task to build a bridge between East and West.[21]

Manstein was neither politician nor futurologist but he was able to forecast with remarkable accuracy the direction and thrust of German foreign policy over the next thirty years and more. In this respect, he was certainly no narrow-minded Prussian *Junker*. Although as a senior commander of the Wehrmacht he had a 'past' that would be exposed at his trial, his principal interest at Island Farm lay in thinking about Germany's future place in the world.

Manstein and other senior officers at the camp had ample occasion to reminisce on the war. Unlike their American allies, however, the British did not run a comprehensive military history programme to engage former Wehrmacht commanders in discussing and writing up their wartime experiences. Whereas the United States Army Europe Historical Division ran a special camp at Allendorf near Marburg in Western Germany for this purpose, no attempt was made to employ the senior German officers held at Island Farm in a similar manner. Although the American programme, which eventually was co-ordinated by Colonel General (Retired) Franz Halder, can be questioned for providing its German authors with an ideal opportunity to rehabilitate themselves by rewriting history in their favour, the lack of an equivalent British scheme represented a wasted opportunity.[22] It reflected not only an enduring tightness of resources, but also a paucity of official interest in recording, documenting and publishing pertinent lessons of operations from whatever source.[23]

One individual, working largely on a freelance basis, attempted to fill the gap from 1945 to 1947. Based on lengthy discussions with German generals held in Grizedale Hall, spread over no less than fifteen visits, Liddell Hart published the first edition of his famous *The Other Side of the Hill* in January 1948. Much to his chagrin, he was denied access to Island Farm until March 1948, but was allowed to write to the prisoners of war.[24] As Senger und Etterlin remarked, the British author was 'well-disposed towards the Germans'.[25] Perhaps rather too much so: with hindsight it is tempting to criticize him for his gullibility. He portrayed the German generals as 'essentially technicians, intent on their professional job, and with little idea of things outside it. It is easy to see how Hitler hoodwinked and handled them and found them good instruments up to a point.'[26] Although he grouped Manstein as one of the 'Soldiers in the Shadow', he was fulsome in his praise of the Field Marshal, describing him as probably the 'ablest of all the German generals'. 'That was the verdict of most with whom I discussed the war,' he added, 'from Rundstedt downwards.'[27]

Liddell Hart had such an open affection and admiration for the German generals that he became their champion. In his memoirs, Manstein left no comment on his relationship with the British writer. The correspondence between the two, however, was considerable: they were in regular contact for much of the period 1948–51 and their close connection was maintained thereafter. The Field Marshal certainly made an enduring impression on Liddell Hart, who supported him faithfully during his trial and its aftermath, and facilitated later the publication of the English edition of *Lost Victories*.[28]

Notwithstanding his appearance at Nuremberg and the latent threat of follow-up prosecutions, Manstein had good reason to believe that he would escape a war crimes trial. As the months at Island Farm wore on, there seemed no urgency on the part of the British government to progress the issue. The arrival of Dr Otto John at the camp in October 1946, however, was an ominous development. John, a colourful and highly controversial figure in modern German history, had been a member of the resistance to Hitler. He escaped via Spain and Portugal to Britain after the failed *Attentat*, and then worked for the British propaganda radio station '*Soldatensender* Calais'. After the war, he turned up as an observer at Nuremberg and ran on behalf of the British Control Office for Germany and Austria a screening commission at Island Farm.[29]

As Manstein informed his wife, John's activity was designed to sieve the prisoners on the basis of 'whether they could demonstrate credibly a democratic heart; whether they belonged to the grey mass; or whether they should be regarded as wild Nazis or dangerous.'[30] Rather than conduct formal interrogations, John's approach was far more subtle. In Manstein's case, 'an interesting discussion' about the events of 20 July 1944 took place during a quiet seaside walk overlooking the Bristol Channel. According to John's account, whilst chatting and smoking on the sand dunes for several hours, Manstein 'insisted that no one had approached him to bring him into the anti-Hitler conspiracy, and in any case he would not have agreed to join'. Furthermore, the Field Marshal considered the defeat by Soviet forces avoidable, and 'felt himself to be the best qualified to halt the advance of the Red Army into Germany, if only Hitler had handed over supreme command of the entire Eastern Front in good time'.[31]

The results of John's screening into three categories of A (opponent of the Nazi regime), B (politically indifferent) and C (convinced supporter of the regime) were made known in September 1947. The field marshals, all on the Central Registry of War Crimes and Security Suspects (CROWCASS) list, were excluded from this classification. With the exception of thirty-nine officers, including Brauchitsch, Manstein, Rundstedt and Strauss, all the prisoners of war were due to be released in 1948. John's activities 'in co-operation with the enemy' did not make him especially popular amongst the German military. Manstein was convinced that his retention at Island Farm was down to Otto. The latter's appearance at Manstein's trial in Hamburg as an interpreter and assistant to the prosecution only added to his disapprobation. Notwithstanding the political sifting, Manstein remained optimistic about his chances of escaping conviction. Writing to his wife, he considered that if it ever came to a trial, 'and if real justice were to be applied', then 'it could only end with a not-guilty verdict'.[32]

Around this time, it would appear that Manstein and Rundstedt fell out. The grounds for their antipathy are not clear, but Ted Lees ventured an opinion that Rundstedt considered that Manstein 'still had too much of a Nazi stance'.[33] Anyway, the two field marshals were separated when Manstein, suffering from renewed cataract problems and suspected diabetes, was transferred in early October 1947 to No. 99 Military Hospital at Shugborough Park, Great Haywood, near Stafford. Brauchitsch, who had been there since April with stomach trouble, now had some senior company.

Meanwhile, the United States had decided to prosecute at Nuremberg fourteen admirals and generals in the so-called High Command Trial.[34] The accused included Manstein's former chief of staff in Eleventh Army and subordinate army commander, General of Infantry Otto Wöhler. According to correspondence with his wife in early 1948, Manstein tried to appear as a witness on his associate's behalf. He understood that his attendance was being blocked by the British government.[35] The reality, however, was far more complicated. At that time, the Cabinet had yet to decide how to deal with the German generals: to transfer them to the Americans, to undertake a British trial or simply to release them. On 10 April, Telford Taylor had signalled the British Judge Advocate General's (JAG) office requesting that Brauchitsch, Manstein and Strauss appear as witnesses at the High Command Trial. Only two days later the Overseas Reconstruction Committee, mindful of the need to restore confidence in Western Allied Zones in Germany, had decided that war crimes should not be pursued after 1 September 1948.

The days at Island Farm were numbered: it was to close in July. When the majority of the prisoners, including Senger und Etterlin, departed on 12 May 1948 for Germany and release, the three remaining field marshals in British custody were not included. Kept in the dark as to their fate, they had been transferred to No. 231 Prisoner of War Hospital at Redgrave Park in Suffolk, near Diss. In a letter to Liddell Hart, Rundstedt felt that their future was 'very gloomy and uncertain'. As his biographer has noted, the only compensation was the sympathetic regime.[36]

On 16 July, Brauchitsch and Strauss, both ill, were taken by hospital ship to Germany and then transferred to No. 6 PW Hospital, Munsterlager, near Lüneburg. Manstein and Rundstedt, assessed fit, were transported by train on 22 July to London and then flown to Nuremberg. On arrival, they ran into a bizarre situation. Although the Americans wished to arraign them as defence witnesses for the High Command Trial then in progress, they were unwilling to do so if the individuals concerned were not aware of their imminent indictment. Although, as we shall see, the British Cabinet had decided to prosecute the 'German generals' on 5 July, they had informed neither the public, nor crucially, the accused. The Presiding Judge issued a court order to the effect that since the potential witnesses were likely to be tried by the British, they should be given twenty-four hours to decide whether they were prepared to testify or not. On 28 July, perhaps sensing the disadvantage of giving evidence without adequate legal advice and preparation, both Manstein and Rundstedt declared that they would not appear for the defence. It must have been a hard decision for Manstein as he was now not able to speak on behalf of Wöhler.[37] The two field marshals were promptly despatched to Munsterlager to join Brauchitsch and Strauss.

Manstein did not enjoy his brief return to Nuremberg and its tight custody one bit. Writing a couple of weeks later to Liddell Hart from Munsterlager, he complained: 'The housing, food and medical treatment were good. But we were strictly isolated from everyone, always a guard (a Negro) in the room of each of us. Although I have never been an adherent of the silly theory of "*Herrenrasse*" [master race], this method of putting a Negro as guard at one's bedside seems a perverseness of taste.'[38]

On arrival at the British camp, he had received a further shock. After the comparatively comfortable life in Island Farm, conditions were much harsher. The senior officers were isolated from the other prisoners of war and kept under continual observation, as at Nuremberg. As his son has described it, 'only the atmosphere of hate was absent'.[39] In his letter to Liddell Hart, Manstein had written:

> You will understand that we are deeply depressed by such treatment. Three years after the war we are still prisoners of war, although none of us [was] in command when the war finished.... If there be any true case against us, there would surely have been time enough during these three years to tell us something about it and to have made the necessary investigations. The prolonged uncertainty of our future as to the time of our further confinement is a torture not only for ourselves but even heavier for our wives.[40]

The Decision to Prosecute

The decision to prosecute Manstein for war crimes was made by the British Cabinet, following a long period of vacillation.[41] The Nuremberg judgement relating to the German General Staff had included a key recommendation: 'Where the facts warrant it, these men should be brought to trial so that those among them who are guilty of these crimes should not escape punishment.'[42] Acting on this remit, United States investigators, led by Telford Taylor, compiled an extensive 82-page dossier of evidence on the senior German officers held in British custody. Passed to the British Attorney General in August 1947, it exposed apparently strong evidence from German operations on the Eastern Front that appeared to incriminate heavily Manstein, as well as Rundstedt, Brauchitsch and Strauss. In contrast, senior officers within the British Army of the Rhine and the British Military Government in Germany were firmly opposed to any trials in the face of Soviet hostility and the need to garner West German support against any potential aggression. This view reflected an assessment of the German domestic situation at a time when the Soviet government was holding out promises of a unified, neutral state. Hence the demands of geopolitics, as much as the requirements of justice, drove decision-making over those suspected of war crimes.

Meanwhile, on 17 June 1948, the Secretary of State for War, Emmanuel Shinwell, submitted a memorandum to Cabinet setting out arguments for and against prosecution. Noting that 'public opinion at home and abroad may be critical of our letting them go free', he argued: 'We ought not to let senior officers who incited the commission of war crimes go unscathed.' Against this, he stressed: 'There is the time, expense and man-power involved in staging these further trials of senior officers who have already been in our hands for nearly three years.' He concluded, 'it is not worth while, at this date, undertaking the heavy task of attempting to bring these generals to trial.'[43] Even Field Marshal Montgomery had indirectly questioned the wisdom of proceeding against the German field marshals. In a speech on 9 July 1948 in Paris at a luncheon of the Franco-British Association, he had averred that the Nuremberg trials had made the waging of unsuccessful war a crime, 'for the generals of the defeated side are tried and then hanged'.[44]

Notwithstanding Shinwell's submission, the Attorney General, Sir Hartley Shawcross, who, it will be recalled, was the principal British prosecutor at Nuremberg, remained strongly in favour of a war crimes trial. Given the American evidence and calls for extradition from the Poles and Russians, the Cabinet – after a considered discussion on 5 July 1948 – decided it had no option but to mount a trial or otherwise face inevitable international condemnation. The Secretary of State for Foreign Affairs, Ernest Bevin, produced the most compelling argument for prosecution: 'Although we had not given specific undertakings to the Soviet and Polish governments that we would bring these officers to trial, we had allowed these Governments to understand that it was on this basis that we declined to hand them over.' 'From the international point of view', Mr Bevin continued, 'it was necessary that these officers who were fit to be tried should be brought to trial as soon as possible.'[45]

When the Foreign Secretary came to the Commons on 22 September 1948 to announce that the four senior German officers had been returned to Germany under British military custody for trial, there was dissent in the House.[46] Mr Reginald Paget (Labour, Northampton) asked: 'Is there any reason why these men should not be given bail while they are awaiting their trial? They have now been incarcerated for three years; surely it is time that they were given bail while awaiting trial?' In response, the Foreign Secretary quipped: 'If every poor prisoner was incarcerated in the same way as these men have been then he would not have much complaint.' Richard Stokes (Labour, Ipswich) interjected: 'But it is three years.' Mr Bevin was not in the least sympathetic: 'I do not understand this protest. I regret the delay in bringing them to trial. That I acknowledge. I think it should have been done earlier.'[47] Other members raised further concerns but the Cabinet had decided and acted: there was to be no turning back.

Amenities at Munsterlager, meantime, only improved after a campaign in the British press orchestrated by Liddell Hart. Manstein had complained to him on 11 August 1948 about being placed in solitary confinement in a 'tormenting manner of custody'. It provoked the British military historian to write to the editor of the *Manchester Guardian*. Quoting extracts of Manstein's letter, Liddell Hart asked: 'Is there no end to this judicial torturing process? It is repulsive to our decent human instincts and our traditions, especially when applied to old and sick men.'[48] Further letters of protest followed in *The Times* and the *Daily Telegraph* that month. When the government announced on 27 August that the generals would be prosecuted, Manstein heard about it on the BBC radio news. The initial storm of protest culminated on 3 September 1948 with a letter to *The Times* signed by nine politicians and writers that concluded: 'The decision suddenly announced, three and a quarter years after the German surrender, to try these men as war criminals makes the whole affair not less but more indecent.'[49]

Following such objections, the government eased conditions of custody at Munsterlager. Liddell Hart was able to report this news to readers of *The Times* on 21 September 1948, having received a letter of thanks from Manstein. He had written on behalf of the field marshals and their wives, expressing their gratitude 'to all those who had interceded in such a magnanimous manner in our favour, and at the same time in favour of the British feeling of justice and humanity'.[50] Even the wives were now able to support their husbands, joining them on transfer to 94th (Hamburg) British Military Hospital in the suburb of Barmbek.

That autumn, Manstein's old friend Theodor Busse arrived in Hamburg. He soon set about enlisting the agreement of former soldiers to come forward as potential witnesses.[51] Busse worked closely with the Field Marshal and his lawyers, reprising his former chief-of-staff function, taking on a pivotal role in co-ordinating the strategy for the defence. Very much still in awe of his wartime superior, at the end of 1948 he wrote enthusiastically of Manstein to a former subordinate, retired Colonel Boehringer: 'He is still very much the Old Man. Unbowed and ready for a fight. It's disgraceful that such an exceptional, irreproachable man is being hauled before a judge.'[52]

In October, Richard Stokes visited the German generals in Hamburg. On his return, he raised their plight in a debate in the House of Commons on 26 October, declaring: 'I believe that those who feel as I do represent a large body of opinion in this country and elsewhere when I say that the whole thing is entirely repugnant to our sense of fair play.' He was supported by General Sir George Jeffreys (Conservative, Petersfield), who considered 'we have treated these distinguished German officers very shabbily and in a way entirely unworthy of our great country, the traditions of our fighting services and of our previous records in many wars'.

In reply, the Under-Secretary of State for War, Mr Michael Stewart, explained the government's decision to bring the German generals to trial. The first reason, he stressed, was the 'extreme gravity of the offences'; secondly, 'subordinates of these men have been brought to trial, convicted and punished for offences similar to those alleged against these four men'; and thirdly, 'His Majesty's Government are under a very clear obligation to hand these men over to certain other Governments, Allies of ours in the recent war, unless we bring them to trial before a British tribunal.' The minister's comments cut little ice in the House. The last words in the debate fell to Reginald Paget: 'The trial of these Germans ... offends every sense of good taste in this country. It is something which has, at last, really roused the people in this country to a sense of indecency. Surely, it is not, even now, too late to stop?'[53]

Two days later the stakes were raised when the leader of His Majesty's Opposition and of the Conservative Party, Winston Churchill, attacked the government in the Commons. Noting 'we should put no needless obstacles in the way of a reconciliation with Germany', he deplored 'the harsh and wrongful procedure which the Foreign Secretary has authorised towards the aged German generals'. Britain's wartime leader described the forthcoming trial as an 'act of administrative and political stupidity and of judicial impropriety, equally repugnant to humanitarian and soldierly sentiment', and called for clemency:

> Revenge is, of all satisfactions, the most costly and long drawn out; retributive persecution is, of all politics, the most pernicious. Our policy, subject to the exceptional cases I have mentioned, should henceforth be to draw the sponge across the crimes and horrors of the past – hard as that may be – and look for the sake of our salvation, towards the future.

Churchill then made his most telling political point. Reminding the House of the international context in which any trial would take place, he thundered: 'There can be no revival of Europe without the active and loyal aid of all the German tribes.'[54] It now remained to be seen whether the field marshals were fit enough to stand trial.

A succession of British Army and Home Office medical boards had come to differing conclusions, serving only to delay proceedings. It remains debatable whether there was any attempt made during the medical screening to block the prosecutions. There were certainly suspicions, but claims of foul play by British Army doctors under direction from the chain of command have never been proven.[55] In the event, a practically blind Brauchitsch had succumbed to a heart attack on 18 October 1948, aged 67.

On 10 March 1949, a joint board of two experienced medical officers of the British prison service and two army doctors examined the three surviving senior officers held in Hamburg. Finding Manstein 'alert and co-operative' and 'well' apart from 'his longstanding eye condition', they concluded that:

he is fit to stand trial, and that he will remain fit to instruct his Defence Counsel during such a trial, also to give evidence if he wishes, be cross-examined and follow proceedings in court. We do not consider that there is any serious probability that he will collapse or break down under the strain of the trial.

Rundstedt and Strauss were deemed unfit to stand for trial. Prompted by these fresh medical reports, on 28 March 1949 Shinwell recommended that 'all further proceedings against Rundstedt and Strauss' should be abandoned, but Manstein alone should be tried.[56]

On 5 May 1949, the Cabinet discussed the German officers' medical conditions again (based on a further medical inquiry by the Lord Chancellor) and confirmed that whilst Rundstedt and Strauss should now be freed, the prosecution against Manstein would stand. The date of the Cabinet meeting was opportune as the Bishop of Chichester, the Right Reverend George Bell, had requested a debate on German war crimes in the House of Lords that very afternoon. The noble prelate explained:

My Lords, the Motion which stands in my name raises issues of justice, humanity and political wisdom. It affects the Germans, for the future of the new West German Republic, and indeed of Germany.... But still more this Motion affects ourselves, and our reputation for justice and humanity; and on that ground in particular I plead against a further continuance of trials in any form, including the prosecution of the three German Generals.

In the ensuing debate, the Bishop received strong support from a number of peers, not least from Lord Maurice Hankey. In response, the Lord Chancellor opined: 'In making up my mind as to what advice to give, I must have regard to the gravity of the crime. If the accusations are true, [Manstein] is one of the major war criminals of the whole war.... He is accused of breaches of the usages of war, with the murder on a huge scale of vast numbers of people.'[57]

Manstein alone would appear in the dock despite the best efforts of both Houses of Parliament to have proceedings stopped.[58] Rundstedt died in 1953, aged 77. Strauss, for all his 'highly emotional state and the evidence of progressive and extensive coronary disease' that had ruled out his prosecution, lived on to the ripe old age of 93.[59]

Whilst the political debate and decision-making ran its course in the United Kingdom, Manstein remained held in Hamburg, with Jutta-Sybille and at times son Rüdiger for company. The Mansteins were allowed to roam the confines of the hospital complex under minimal supervision. British units stationed in northern Germany provided the security force, the task representing a pleasant distraction from more mundane training and occupation duties. Paget recalled that the guards found Manstein 'a difficult customer'. He was a stickler for military correctness: 'Everything had to be exactly right or there was a row.' Yet Manstein earned the respect of his warders as if they were members of his own staff. They proved 'one and all strong partisans of the defence, delighted when things went well and indignant when decisions went against us'.[60]

Whilst the Field Marshal had been given a statement of the charges against him on 1 January 1949, he was not served with a complete charge sheet until 24 May, receiving a final, amended version on 14 July 1949. It was an extremely lengthy document of forty typed pages, comprising seventeen separate charges with 174 counts in total.[61] As Paget recalled, the charges 'were summarised by a reporter who said that the prosecution had collected everything that occurred in the Eastern war and thrown it at von Manstein's head'. There was more than a grain of truth in this observation. As pertinently, Paget noted: 'What von Manstein was actually supposed to have done and what law or custom was alleged to have been contravened, was left quite vague.'[62] We shall return to the details of the charges later, but Manstein's greatest problem prior to the trial's start on 24 August 1949 was assembling his defence and paying for it.

Manstein's German defence team was funded by public subscription, organized by retired Lieutenant General Hans von Donat.[63] The Field Marshal was represented by Dr Hans Laternser, with whom he had co-operated so closely at Nuremberg over the General Staff, and Dr Paul Leverkuehn. The latter, who had lived in both Britain and America and thus was familiar with those countries' legal systems, was convinced none the less that a British counsel was necessary to provide a fully effective defence. As he explained in a letter to The Times of 11 July 1949:

> It is the view of my colleague and myself that without the assistance of British counsel we cannot ensure that von Manstein will receive an adequate defence. The court is a British court composed of British officers acting in accordance with British procedure and British rules of evidence,

with neither of which we are familiar. The British technique of cross-examination is something quite foreign to continental lawyers. Moreover, in our view only British counsel (and preferably British counsel who have served in the British forces) are fully competent to understand the psychology of a court of this nature.

The result of this appeal was a subscription organized by Lord de L'Isle and Dudley and General Lord Bridgeman, with the public support of Lords Simon and Hankey.[64] Winston Churchill was one of the first to subscribe, donating £25. The impressive sum of £1,620 was raised within a month.[65]

In seeking a suitable counsel, Leverkuehn turned to Paget, who was at first not minded to take on the case. 'Professionally', he wrote, 'it does one little good to be involved in a notorious case which one is almost bound to lose.' But when Leverkuehn pressed him again, Paget accepted. Regarding the 'matter as being political rather than judicial', he declined to accept a fee for his services.[66] Paget travelled to Hamburg in August 1949, where he joined his junior, Sam Silkin, a former wartime lieutenant colonel in the British Army with experience in war crimes trials against the Japanese. The fact that Silkin, a Jew, 'fought so hard for von Manstein', Paget recalled, 'deeply impressed the German public'.[67] The third member of the British element of the defence team was Bill Croome, a former intelligence officer who by sheer coincidence had been operating against Leverkuehn during the war. Now former enemies were co-operating closely in the common service of justice.

The combined British and German legal team was supported by Busse, whom Paget described as a 'tower of strength on all military matters ... devoting himself without reward to the defence of his chief'. Dr Alfred Schacht, who had served as an artillery officer under Manstein's command, assisted Dr Leverkuehn and became the defence team's managing clerk. Paget was generous in his praise of Schacht: 'He had an immense capacity for finding documents and was probably the best international lawyer of the lot of us.' The whole team, the British lawyer stressed, 'regarded the defence of von Manstein as a crusade, and were prepared to work all hours, day in and day out. This we had to do.'[68]

Paget's first impression on meeting Manstein in Hamburg paints an unconventional picture of a former Wehrmacht senior commander:

I was surprised both by his appearance and his personality. Had I not known he was a Field-Marshal, I should have guessed that he was the Principal of a University. His intellectual quality was the first thing to strike one, together with a curious, rather academical fussiness....

[Manstein] had adopted a frigid and forbidding personality through which humour and humanity would break suddenly and surprisingly. I think that in this quality lay his undoubted capacity to inspire love in his subordinates.[69]

As there was scant time for Paget to prepare for the trial, it was essential for him to get to know his client. He told Manstein that he was only defending him as it was 'contrary to the honour of my country' if the Field Marshal were to be 'denied the defence he desired'. In reply, Manstein opened his heart to his new British counsel:

I am not particularly concerned as to what happens to me; in any event my life is over. I am concerned for my honour and the honour of the German army I led. Your soldiers know that when they met us we fought like honourable soldiers. You have been convinced by Bolshevik propaganda that in Russia we fought like savages. That is untrue. In a terribly hard war we maintained firm discipline and fought honourably. I am determined to defend the honour of the German army.[70]

Manstein's comments are revealing but did not elicit written comment from Paget. They portray an individual determined, above all, to protect the 'honour' of the German soldiers who had fought and died for him – a self-appointed task he had initiated at Nuremberg, which would continue throughout his trial at Hamburg and remain an important, if not the key, theme expressed in his memoirs. A crucial matter in the trial, therefore, would be to establish how reliable and credible Manstein would be in defending that honour.

Conduct of the Trial

From the official side, preparation for the trial in the broad format of a British general court martial proceeded as Operation MARCO. Lieutenant General Sir Frank Simpson, serving in Chester as General Officer Commanding Western Command, was appointed president at short notice. Field Marshal Slim, Chief of the Imperial General Staff, informed him 'how sorry I am to ask you to do what may well be a tedious and unpleasant duty'.[71] So it turned out. Alongside Simpson on the panel were six members ranging in rank from major general to colonel.[72] Judge Advocate Hon. Charles Arthur Collingwood, a county court judge, advised the court on points of law and summarized the evidence at its end. Senior prosecuting counsel was Sir Arthur Strettell Comyns Carr KC; his junior was Frederick Elwyn-Jones (Labour MP for Plaistow), supported by the German émigré lawyer Frederick Honig. Colonel Gerald Draper and Major S. Smith from the Directorate of Army Legal Services, together with Otto John and a large support staff, completed the prosecution team.[73]

The court was held in the main concert hall of Hamburg's Curio House from 23 August to 19 December 1949.[74] A plaque on an external wall today recalls that the building was used in 1946–48 by a British military court for conducting trials against 'members of the SS who were responsible for crimes in the Neuengamme concentration camp'. There is no reminder of the Manstein trial, presumably to prevent the Curio House from becoming a shrine for German militarism. During the sixty-two days of proceedings, the courtroom was open to members of the press and public, except for two when sessions were held in camera. Paget recalled that Manstein was an 'erect and dignified figure' in the dock, adding that 'the doddering almost blind old Field-Marshal was as much a figment of the journalistic imagination as the jackbooted spectators'. In the German gallery looking down into the hall sat his wife, 'an inconspicuous little woman in dark severe clothes'.[75]

On the first day, Paget mounted a serious challenge to the jurisdiction of the court. The main thrust of his submission was that the Royal Warrant of 18 June 1945, under which military courts had been set up for the trial of war criminals, was in itself illegal, and hence the present court had no jurisdiction. Specifically, Paget held that Manstein was still a prisoner of war and that his protected status under international law could not be altered at the discretion of his captors. Secondly, in his view, the Warrant breached Article 63 of the Geneva Convention by not following its provision that 'a sentence shall be pronounced on a prisoner of war only by the same tribunals and in accordance with the same procedure as in the case of prisoners belonging to the armed forces of the detaining power'.[76] Paget went on to point out that the Royal Warrant denied a prisoner a trial by his peers in rank. He then argued that it allowed hearsay evidence to be presented which, if accepted, would make a fair trial impossible, resulting in a grave miscarriage of justice. The defence counsel concluded his speech with an impassioned appeal to the honour and integrity of the military members of the court:

> What Field-Marshal von Manstein asks for is to be treated as a soldier. He asks for that which you yourselves would demand if you were in his position. He asks to be tried by his peers in rank. He asks that his life, his liberty and his military honour be afforded that same protection which you would demand for your own. Your nation and army have, in the

course of centuries, evolved by judicial experience a system of court-martial governed by rules of evidence and procedure which you have found necessary for the protection of accused persons. To be so tried is your right. I humbly submit it also the right of your enemy.[77]

In response, Comyns Carr argued that Manstein was no longer a prisoner of war and the provisions protecting him in that case did not extend to those suspected of war crimes. Manstein, he argued, was 'discharged from the status of prisoner of war and from the Wehrmacht', and then 'confined as a prisoner awaiting trial as a war criminal'. The prosecution dismissed any notion that the trial would not be conducted fairly, and in a typically baffling turn of legal phraseology Comyns Carr concluded: 'It is not to be assumed in the least that merely because the Royal Warrant lays down a different method of proof ... it is not from that circumstance to be supposed for one moment that a trial will be any less fair than a trial conducted under our ordinary rules of evidence.'[78]

The court accepted the prosecution counsel's complex assurances and rejected Paget's submission. Proceedings therefore continued the next day with the Judge Advocate reading out in turn the charges listed in the indictment. As reported in *The Times*, at the end of each, Manstein 'stood up, removed his earphones, and answered "Not Guilty"'.[79] Comyns Carr then opened the case for the prosecution with an address that lasted two days.[80] After summarizing Manstein's career during the war, he quoted the IMT Judgement on the General Staff to implicate the Field Marshal by association:

> The contemporary German militarism flourished briefly with its recent ally, National Socialism, as well as or better than it had in the generals of the past. Many of these have made a mockery of the soldier's oath of obedience to military orders. When it suits their purpose they say they had to obey; when confronted with Hitler's brutal crimes which are shown to have been within their general knowledge, they say they disobeyed. The truth is they actively participated in all these crimes, or sat silent and acquiescent, witnessing the commission of crimes on a scale larger and more shocking than the world has ever had the misfortune to know. This must be said.[81]

In drawing attention to Manstein's attendance at Hitler's address to his generals at Obersalzberg on 22 August 1939 prior to the Polish campaign, Comyns Carr argued that it was clear 'that anyone attending that Hitler conference must have been fully forewarned of the brutal character of the war which Germany was about to launch on Poland'. In the same vein, he blasted Manstein: 'The accused gave himself unsparingly for almost 5 years of Hitler's campaigns to the service of this barbarous policy and was one of its principal executants.'[82] This one sentence summarized effectively the entire case against the Field Marshal.

The first three charges concerned crimes that had been committed in Poland between September and October 1939 when Manstein was serving as Chief of Staff of Army Group South, and latterly, as Commander-in-Chief East. The *first charge* detailed twenty-three counts (one of which had been withdrawn) of killing and maltreatment of Polish citizens by SS troops, army troops, units of the Security Service of the SS (SD) and police units. Within the total of 1,209 killings it included the shooting of twenty-two Jewish citizens in the village square of Końskie, referred to in an earlier chapter. An equally shocking event was the deportation of Polish Jews from Eastern Upper Silesia across the river San, and the prevention of their return. In consequence, 'large numbers of Polish Jews, including women and children, were drowned or shot to death by troops'. Whereas the first charge alleged that Manstein had 'authorised and permitted' such actions, the *second* accused him of 'deliberately and recklessly' disregarding his duty 'to take such steps within his power' to prevent the killing and maltreatment as specified in the first charge.

Unsurprisingly, the press covering the trial quoted the most sensational and damning material produced by the prosecution. *The Times*, for example, reported one horrific passage from a document entitled 'Germany's crimes in Poland' concerning the San:

> The Gestapo stood on the bank and drove the Jews into boats. Many did not get on board and were carried away by the current. Women in the water held their children above their heads to prevent them from drowning and screamed for help. The Gestapo shot into the struggling mass of people. The blood of those hit spurted in all directions and coloured the river blood red.[83]

Of all the 'Polish' counts, the crimes committed at the San were the most incriminating as the prosecution alleged that Manstein, as army group chief of staff, had specifically 'added his own gloss to the order [of OKH] and said the floating back to Eastern Upper Silesia of Jewish refugees will be prevented with all possible means'.[84]

In summing up the first and second charges, Comyns Carr submitted that 'the accused knew and could not have been ignorant of these grave and widespread atrocities against Polish civilians. Instead of taking steps to stop them, in the case of the San river episode, by his own order he made matters worse for the victims. Well knowing that these abominations (a) were contemplated from the outset of the war and (b) were perpetrated when the war started, he permitted them to continue.'[85] The *third charge* against Manstein concerned six counts of maltreatment or killing of Polish prisoners of war.

The remaining fourteen charges related to crimes conducted in the Soviet Union (the so-called 'Russian' charges), during which Manstein was either an army or an army group commander as opposed to the chief of staff of an army group. The prosecution reminded the court about the distinction between the duties of the two appointments: 'The responsibility of a commander, is of course, greater than that of his chief of staff, and you will have to consider both in this case, remembering, however, that insofar as the responsibility of the accused as a chief of staff during the Polish campaign may be minimised, his responsibility as a commander during the Russian campaign will be increased.'[86] This was a fair point that lessened the burden on Manstein over the first three charges, on which he was to be ultimately acquitted, but would reinforce it inevitably on the remainder.

The *fourth charge* accused Manstein of deliberately and recklessly disregarding his duty by failing to ensure the humane treatment of Soviet prisoners of war, and, in consequence, large numbers died or were handed over to units of the SD to be killed. Across the eleven counts, it was alleged that 7,393 individuals 'died or were shot dead by said forces'. The prosecution held that the 'fate of the prisoners-of-war of the 11th Army under the Defendant was determined by his deliberate neglect on the one hand, and the ruthless execution of certain basic orders of the High Command, conceived in the same spirit, on the other hand'.

The *fifth charge* alleged that Manstein had 'permitted the continued operation of orders of the German High Command and himself issued an order dated 20th September 1941, the combined effect of such orders being that members of the Soviet Armed Forces when captured were illegally to be treated as partisans, guerrillas, *francs-tireurs* or terrorists and were illegally to be killed without trial'. Eight specific counts were raised within this charge. The prosecution claimed that the term 'partisan' was given the 'widest possible meaning' and that it was 'left to the discretion of the individual officers whether a captured member of the Russian Armed Forces was to be considered a prisoner-of-war or to be shot as a partisan'.[87]

The *sixth charge* accused Manstein in a similar manner to that of the fifth in 'permitting the continued operation of orders of the High

Command of the German Army and himself issued orders on 17th and 27th November 1941' which resulted in Soviet prisoners of war being 'compulsorily recruited into units of the German Armed Forces under his command'. By the time of the trial, one out of the three counts raised within this charge had been withdrawn. The prosecution, having reminded the court that 'Articles 23 and 45 of the Hague Convention expressly prohibit any compulsion to be used on subjects of the hostile country to participate in the operations of war against their own country', then accused Manstein of having done so. It was claimed that he had 'ordered Soviet prisoners-of-war to be enlisted and drafted into his field formations, fighting the very army or regiment to which they had belonged a little while before'.[88]

The *seventh charge* concerned the 'compulsory employment by forces' under Manstein's command 'of Soviet prisoners-of-war on prohibited and dangerous work'. Out of the original sixteen counts, ten involved the misemployment of Soviet prisoners in the construction of defensive positions and field works during the retreat to the Dnepr and battles for Western Ukraine in the period July 1943–February 1944. Earlier, within Eleventh Army during the period January–September 1942, the prosecution alleged that '43,782 prisoners-of-war' were employed in the supply service and '13,198' were employed on the 'construction of quarters and defence positions for the troops of the Defendant', all involving employment of 'purely military nature'.[89]

The *eighth charge* listed fifteen counts of summary executions by army units of political commissars and their lower ranking 'politruks', or transfer to the SD leading to their deaths, in pursuit of the Commissar Order. The prosecution stressed not only that it was 'criminal and vicious', but also 'to German generals trained in the Staff College brought up in the tradition of military honour', the order 'could only appear as clearly contrary to the rules of warfare, morality and soldierly decency'. The implication was clear enough: the defendant had to answer not only for the crimes but also for the breach of this code.[90]

The ninth to twelfth charges, which formed the core of the prosecution's case, concerned the murder of the Jews by *Einsatzgruppe* D and by army troops, primarily on the Crimea. In the *ninth charge*, Manstein was accused with twenty-three counts of ordering, authorizing and permitting the mass extermination by this *Einsatzgruppe* of 'Jews, Gypsies, Krimtschaks and other citizens of the U.S.S.R. by shooting, hanging, gassing, drowning and other methods of killing at divers places within the area of his command'.[91] The scale of this mass murder was shocking. According to one count, between 16–30 September 1941, '22,467 Jews and others ... were killed ... at or near Nikolajew or Cherson'. To give a further example, it was alleged that 'between 16th November and 15th December 1941, 21,185 citizens of the U.S.S.R., including 17,645 Jews, 2,504 Krimtschaks and 824 Gypsies were killed by units of *Einsatzgruppe* D at or near Simferopol, Eupatoria, Aluschta [*sic*], Karasubasar and Feodosia'.[92]

In the *tenth charge*, which complemented the ninth, Manstein was accused of 'deliberately and recklessly' disregarding 'his duty as a military commander to ensure public order and safety and to respect family honour and rights and individual life', which in consequence led to the murderous actions by *Einsatzgruppe* D listed in the previous charge. The *eleventh charge* listed seventeen counts of the transfer by troops under Manstein's command of Soviet citizens to *Einsatzgruppe* D, which 'as the accused well knew, would and did result in the killing of large numbers of' such individuals.

Having presented the ninth, tenth and eleventh charges, the prosecution then described to the court the organization and role of the *Einsatzgruppen*, with particular reference to the activities of *Einsatzgruppe* D and its subordinate *Einsatzkommandos* on the Crimea. Comyns Carr explained:

> The brutality, horror and ruthlessness of these forms of death produced by the SS are vividly described by eye-witnesses whose evidence will be before the Court. Although these mass killings were carried out by the Einsatzgruppe it will be the case for the Prosecution that they would not have been possible had it not been for certain assistance given to Einsatzgruppe D by the 11th Army and later Army Group DON, and that the killings were everywhere carried out by the Einsatzgruppe with the knowledge of the Army which from time to time exercised supervision and control over the movements of the Einsatzgruppe and on at least one occasion directly ordered a mass extermination.

The prosecuting counsel then drove his point home by claiming that Manstein knew 'from start to finish' of the 'murderous activities' of the *Einsatzgruppe*. Furthermore, their actions could not have been carried out 'without his consent and indeed his co-operation'. Rather than preventing these horrors, 'instead he assisted them in flagrant violation of all human decency, as well as of Regulations 43 and 46 of the Hague Convention.'[93]

Notwithstanding the gravity of the three previous charges, the *twelfth charge* was perhaps even graver in that Manstein was accused *directly* of instigating and inciting troops under his command – as opposed to those of *Einsatzgruppe* D – 'to commit acts of brutality against Jewish citizens of the U.S.S.R.'. Amongst the worst of seven counts were the alleged killings between 1–3 December 1941 of 'about 2,500 Jewish citizens ... at Kertsch' [*sic*], and between 15–30 June 1942, of 'all the Jewish inhabitants then still in Kertsch'.

The *thirteenth charge*, similarly shocking, accused Manstein of 'enjoining the killing of civilians, citizens of the U.S.S.R, for offences alleged to have been committed by persons other than the said civilians and not by them or any of them, in consequence of which numerous civilians were so killed by units under his command'. The most serious of six counts referred to the killing between 1–31 January 1942 of 'about 1300 civilians ... at or near Eupatoria'. The Field Marshal was accused in the *fourteenth charge* of issuing, distributing and executing specific orders 'which were illegal in that they provided for the execution of civilians, citizens of the U.S.S.R: (i) without trial; (ii) for merely being suspect of having committed offences, and in particular of having engaged in partisan activities; (iii) for having committed acts which did not amount to punishable offences', and then listed seven counts.

The *fifteenth charge* concerned the 'compulsory labour by male and female citizens ... for the purpose of carrying out military operations or work directly connected therewith'. The construction of fortifications and positions and the digging of entrenchments in battle areas were itemized in twenty-five separate counts over the period January 1943 to February 1944. As no evidence was produced for the latter two counts by the time of the trial these were withdrawn.

The *sixteenth charge* listed fourteen counts (one was withdrawn) of 'deportation of male and female civilians ... for forced labour outside the U.S.S.R.'. In total, this involved the transportation of tens of thousands of individuals to the Reich. The final, *seventeenth charge*, accused Manstein whilst his 'Army Group was in retreat' of issuing orders to 'deport civilian inhabitants of the territories occupied by the German Armed Forces under his command, to seize their cattle and foodstuffs and to destroy their houses as well as all other objects of economic value which could not be seized'. In thirteen counts over the period September–December 1943, it was alleged that tens of thousands of 'persons, horned cattle, sheep, horse-drawn vehicles and horses and numerous other animals', together with tens of thousands of tons of wheat were forcibly removed.

With regard to the latter charge, the prosecution summed up its case by linking Manstein's operations with the 'scorched earth' policy that accompanied it, neatly illustrating the controversial nature of his military performance on the Eastern Front:

The retreat of von Manstein's forces from the Caucasus and the Don, first to the Donets and then through the Donets basin to the Dnieper and across it, has sometimes been described as a masterpiece of strategy. In fact he staved off a fate which eventually overcame his armies in spring 1944 for a year, by ruthlessly destroying anything fit for human use or habitation, driving the civilian population made homeless by the destruction of all the houses and buildings into the open without food or clothing, on treks over hundreds of miles, marching and working for the German armies ten hours a day, an operation during which thousands of innocent civilians must have perished through hunger and exposure, apart from those who were shot because they tried to escape deportation.[94]

Comyns Carr finished his opening speech with a powerful indictment of Manstein's tenure in command, which had included 'daily illegalities of every conceivable description and every type of brutality'. He pulled no punches in highlighting:

These are samples of a continuous record of crimes of every kind, probably without parallel in history. On any view the responsibility for them rests heavily upon the accused; that is so even if he should succeed in persuading you that he was simply the capable soldier – no doubt he was that – and that he was too busy to attend to such matters as wholesale murders and mass ill-treatment going on in the areas of his several commands over a series of years. That would be no defence in our submission. Our submission, however, to you is that obviously on this evidence, entirely documentary and from German sources and incontrovertible, that was not the position at all. Too often will we show not only his knowledge but his active participation in these awful crimes for any such lenient view to be taken. We are bound to put him before you as a ruthless criminal.[95]

The prosecution then completed its case by reading out the wealth of evidence it had assembled, which took twenty days in court. As one reporter observed during this period, the '61-year-old field-marshal listened quietly today during the reading of masses of documents describing atrocities. When especially brutal passages were read he fidgeted with his papers or sighed deeply.'[96]

A particularly awkward moment came when Manstein was confronted, as at Nuremberg, with his order of the day of 20 November 1941 when in command of Eleventh Army in the Crimea. The *New York Herald* reported: 'Erich von Manstein shifted uneasily when the prosecution showed him a copy of the document.'[97] As three years before at the IMT, the Field Marshal initially professed complete ignorance. 'I have to state that I have no recollection whatsoever of the document,' he protested. When his memory was tweaked, however, Manstein admitted that he had instructed his Ic to 'draft an order somewhat similar to the one by General von Reichenau'. He then claimed that he had amended his subordinate's submission, and went on to point out that 'the sentence "has to be exterminated" refers to the system and not to human beings'.[98] None the less the liquidation of the Jews had taken place within the area of operations of Eleventh Army.

Manstein knew he was standing on extremely shaky ground at this point of the prosecution's case, which, if accepted by the court, would scar him as complicit with genocide. This was the most damaging charge, but he had been here before. In a letter to his wife, *composed three years earlier* – following his cross-examination by Telford Taylor at Nuremberg – he had written:

Then they showed me an order of the day, issued by Eleventh Army. It was obviously intended to demonstrate my untrustworthiness. The first part was a kind of propaganda order that I never liked, but which apparently has been presented by the Ic and then signed by me. I simply could no longer remember it. But in the second part I had explicitly insisted against any arbitrariness or violation of soldiers' honour. Therefore the order of the day certainly must be seen in positive light.[99]

On being questioned at Hamburg whether Jews had been shot as a result of his order of the day, Manstein maintained that 'Soldiers, who happened to be eyewitnesses to such occurrences, did not report them to me at the time. Had I received such a report, I would have intervened immediately.'[100] The court would believe him on this charge.

In his book about the trial, Paget conceded the prosecution's opening speech was a tour de force. With the completion of the presentation of its evidence, it was now the business of the defence, he wrote, 'to ensure by the end of the trial the court would remember the [prosecution's] speech for one thing only, the enormous gap between the accusations against von Manstein and evidence produced to support them.'[101]

Leaving the specific charges briefly to one side, and now looking back over sixty years, it is clear that the key questions for the court to assess were as follows. First, it had to conclude on the degree of Manstein's responsibility for, or complicity in, the various crimes that had been committed in breach of international law. Was it correct, however, for his defence counsel to assume that 'If Manstein had anything to do with those crimes it was merely as one who either passed on the orders received from above, or knowing that the orders had been given, allowed his troops to obey them'? What, then, was his accountability? Simply put, what exactly did Manstein know: did he in fact order actions that violated the 'Laws and Usages of War' or not? And if he were not the originator of any war crimes, did he acquiesce to others' wrongdoings? Finally, had he done so, was he in any position to prevent them being carried out even if he had objected to them?

Bearing in mind his duties as a commander, who is accountable for the actions of his troops, it became imperative for the defence to demonstrate that he was ignorant of the crimes that took place within his nominal area of responsibility. Yet, as the Deputy Judge Advocate General stated in his advice to the confirming officer following the trial and sentence, '[It is not] a defence to say that the accused knew nothing about what was going on if in fact his ignorance of the true position were solely due to a lack of supervision.'[102] Further, was Manstein accountable whatsoever for the actions of troops not under his command but within that zone? This latter point as to his vicarious liability became one of the most important questions of law within the trial. It formed a central plank of the prosecution's case which tried, *inter alia*, to hold Manstein responsible for the murderous actions of the *Einsatzgruppe* on the Crimea and to question the credibility of his protestations of ignorance about these.

During the first week in court a significant issue arose that got to the crux of the case against Manstein. It concerned the admissibility of the documentary evidence given by the 'Landsberg prisoners', indicted officers of *Einsatzgruppe* D under the command of Ohlendorf, held under American custody pending confirmation of sentence. In January 1949, a British military legal commission had taken evidence from these individuals that had implicated Manstein. Silkin argued that the court should be extremely guarded in hearing the evidence of men who 'on their own admission had committed murders and were under sentence of death'. They had 'every interest in the world', he maintained, 'to try to push their crimes on to somebody else.' The court's ruling on this point came as a disappointment to the defence: the written evidence would stand but Ohlendorf and the other 'accomplices' would not be brought to Hamburg for cross-examination. Paget, not for the last time in the trial, momentarily lost his cool and asserted that the Landsberg prisoners 'had kept themselves alive by giving evidence'. Comyns Carr protested against 'the aspersion which Mr Paget had unwarrantably chosen to cast on the Americans, and I hope it may be withdrawn'.[103] This angry exchange set the tone for the trial in which passions on either side ran high.

Thereafter, the prosecution remained convinced that *Einsatzgruppe* D had 'worked hand-in-glove' with Manstein's Eleventh Army, and claimed that the Field Marshal should have stopped their murderous operations. Depositions by Karl Braune and Heinz Schubert, subordinates of Ohlendorf, read out in court by Elwyn-Jones, indicated that Eleventh Army had offered logistic support in the liquidation of Jews in Simferopol before Christmas 1941, but had ruled out the direct involvement of soldiers in the shooting.[104] The prosecution closed its presentation of evidence on 13 September 1949. In response, the defence then applied for an adjournment of a fortnight to complete the preparation of its case. This period was granted by the court, which was subsequently extended to three weeks.

The opening speech for the defence commenced on Wednesday, 5 October. Paget pointed out the challenges the defence was facing. 'Indeed, it may be a hopeless task', he declared, '. . . on the basis of this Royal Warrant procedure . . . no general who ever commanded an army could obtain his acquittal from his conquerors.'[105] His main objection, however, lay in the application of the 'post-hostilities Nuremberg law'. As he maintained in his book, Paget submitted that 'the acts alleged against von Manstein were not criminal by international law'.

The senior defence counsel then dealt with the issue of superior orders. At this stage of proceedings, it is fair to say that, in the light of the Nuremberg judgements, Paget may have surprised the court with his argument:

> There is no legal limit whatsoever to the duty of a general officer to obey. The question as to whether an order does or does not conform to international law is the concern of the Government, it is not the concern of the commanding general. The order may be in flagrant conflict with international law; it may involve the murder of civilians or of neutrals but it is still the duty of a general officer to obey.

This submission reflected Paget's central proposition that it was 'fundamentally unjust to apply the penalties of international law to individuals; the nation takes the consequences'. Paget saw no contradiction in accepting that it is the duty of a *subordinate* officer to disobey an illegal order. In this case, it 'must be plain to the subordinate that the order is one which the superior had no authority to give'. A sovereign government, he argued, 'has authority to give any orders, including orders to infringe international law'.[106] He implied that Manstein, as a senior general officer, had no option but to obey.

In turning to the charges, they constituted, in his view, 'an indictment of the German army commanded by Hitler, not of acts which von Manstein is alleged to have done'.[107] Paget then criticised the rules of evidence pertaining to the court, objecting in particular to the use of hearsay evidence, which 'is more likely to mislead than to guide'. With regard to the mass of documents that the prosecution had quoted, 'which the accused has never seen', he warned the court that they should not act on them 'if there is any possible explanation that is consistent with innocence'. Moreover, 'everything possible should be assumed in his favour upon such documents'.[108]

Paget's approach in attempting to undermine both the application of 'Nuremberg law' and the value of the prosecution evidence being presented was, of course, music to Manstein's ears and to those of his supporters. As one news reporter described the scene, 'After the court had adjourned, Manstein warmly shook hands with Mr Paget, grasping both his hands vigorously and thanking him for his speech.'[109] After Paget concluded his speech, some fourteen and a half hours spread over three days, his colleagues Silkin, Laternser and Leverkuehn completed a detailed analysis of the documentary evidence that took a further seven days.

On Friday, 21 October, Manstein was called to give evidence in his own defence. He appeared as a witness for ten and a half days, the latter seven of which were under cross-examination. In a well-prepared statement the Field Marshal outlined his upbringing, early career, the rise of Nazism and Hitler's regime before the Second World War. He then described in more detail the campaigns he fought from the time he assumed command of Eleventh Army on 17 September 1941 to his dismissal on 31 March 1944 as commander-in-chief of Army Group South.[110]

Manstein was candid in his observations. He described the Nazi persecution of the Church, the Jews and the aristocracy as repulsive; he was disgusted by the 'behaviour of many of the Nazi party chiefs' and was shocked especially by 'Göring's greed and showing off'.[111] But he admitted to being greatly impressed by Hitler at first: 'I regarded him in no way as militarily incapable.' Manstein continued by saying that Hitler had accepted his proposal for an offensive in the West through the Ardennes, which was 'entirely sensible of him'. Yet later, when under the Führer's direct command in the East as commander-in-chief of an army group, 'I came to realise that we had entirely different views as to command in war, and that Hitler lacked in many respects the necessary qualities to make him a senior commander.' Driving his point home, the Field Marshal stressed that Hitler 'wanted to fight for every foot of ground, and regarded the only decisive matter in command as the will to fight'. He did not consider command in war an art form, 'under whose principles the campaigns in Poland and France had been won'. 'This was the difference', Manstein explained, between the views of a '[professional] soldier and a political fanatic'.[112]

The Field Marshal's evidence was a treatise of skilfully crafted self-vindication designed in a similar manner to the one he had constructed with Dr Laternser at Nuremberg: the fatal decisions in the conduct of the war and the guilt for the crimes associated with it lay with Hitler – and not with his surviving principal commanders.

Paget gave a glowing description of his client's commanding demeanour in court: 'His personality in the witness box was extremely effective. His answers were vigorous and bold. When he produced his operational maps and explained his campaigns the attention of the court was humble.' Furthermore, he 'went into the witness box to defend not himself but the German army. He resolutely defended every order which the army had accepted and carried out. He stood by every subordinate whose action was reasonably within his orders.'[113] The court, however, did not necessarily share the defence counsel's opinion. The deputy president, Major General Ashton Wade, stated of the Field Marshal: 'His appearance in the dock, dressed in a sober suit, during the early stages of the trial was that of a middle-aged successful doctor, lawyer or academic. He displayed little emotion and made copious notes.' Under cross-examination, 'to start with Manstein continued to give long and voluble answers to every question, and it was not until the seventh day under gruelling examination on the question of the maltreatment of prisoners that he started to stumble on his replies and appeared to lose a measure of self-confidence'. On the killing of the 1,300 partisans – or civilians who had taken up arms – after the Soviet landing at Eupatoria, Wade highlighted: 'Manstein's attitude was revealed under cross-examination when he stated, "It was immaterial to me whether they were shot during the action or afterwards. Our situation was far too serious for me to bother about it."'[114]

Manstein was followed by sixteen witnesses over the period 4–22 November, including General of Armoured Troops Erich Brandenburger, who had led 8th Panzer Division within Manstein's LVI Corps during the opening attack on the Soviet Union. He confirmed that his corps commander had forbidden the application of the Commissar Order, and in consequence it was never carried out. The defence's main effort, however, was to refute the most incriminating of the charges, numbers nine to twelve. To this end, it called key members of Manstein's

Eleventh Army staff including his chief quartermaster, Colonel Friedrich Wilhelm Hauck, and his head of anti-partisan operations, Konrad Stephanus.[115] Both denied that Manstein had any knowledge of, let alone any involvement in, the killings of Jews.

Most significantly, Hauck assumed personal responsibility for providing logistic assistance to the SD in Simferopol, and maintained that he had done so without informing Manstein. His evidence, held in camera on the forty-fourth day of proceedings (9 November) proved critical to the Field Marshal's defence. Hauck was emphatic in stating:

> On the question of the Jews, I never ascertained the views of the Commander-in-Chief, because I never exchanged one word with him on the subject of the Jews, nor did he ever exchange a word with me on the subject.... A report from me would not have altered matters in the slightest for the SD was not subordinate to the Commander-in-Chief.... I had decided not to tell the Commander-in-Chief about the activities of the SD.[116]

The Roman Catholic Chaplain of Eleventh Army, Stefan Gmeiner, and Manstein's then chief of operations, Theodor Busse, both stated that they had no knowledge of any massacres.[117] Paget raised a rather odd point in his book, claiming that his 'witnesses generally would have been more impressive had they been less obviously devoted to Manstein', but he 'doubted if this really mattered very much because Manstein himself had been so obviously truthful'.[118] Whether the court actually believed him would be shown in their verdict.

Paget opened his final speech on the fifty-first day, Wednesday, 23 November. The next morning, Manstein approached his counsel and requested: 'Don't let Sir Arthur start his speech today. I really can't bear the prospect of having to listen to that man on my birthday.' Accordingly, Paget wound up his speech on Manstein's sixty-second birthday 'precisely at the normal time for the court to rise'.[119] In a passionate appeal to the court, Paget had claimed that 'The political purpose of this trial has been to condemn the reputation of the German army and of its greatest commander. It has failed utterly!' His peroration concluded with:

> Nobody in this court imagines that Manstein is a bad man. He was beloved of his soldiers and staff. That at least this trial has made obvious. Nobody questions that he possesses every conventional and domestic virtue. The uttermost that is put against him is that he executed the will of his commander-in-chief. But that is the crime of Germany.... What the prosecution seeks to say is 'Unless you prove that you had no part in

the crimes for which you are already being punished as a German, you shall receive exceptional and extraordinary punishment'. That is fundamentally unjust. That is fundamentally totalitarian. For to impose upon an individual symbolic atonement for the crime of a nation is to deny the individual. Sir, I ask for the acquittal of von Manstein because I believe that acquittal will be honourable to my country.

Manstein's reaction to Paget's touching words was human enough: he cried freely. He grasped his counsel's hand and declared: 'You who were my enemy have taken years of bitterness from my heart.... This has been a lovely birthday.'[120] That was the last Paget saw of his client. As a busy MP and barrister he did not remain in Hamburg to hear the prosecution's closing speech.

Over three days, Comyns Carr reiterated the case against Manstein: he was guilty on all charges. Above all, he could have, and should have, taken action to stop the SD in its murderous activities. Whether he would have been successful in so doing was not the point; he had not done so and therefore effectively had supported the liquidation of the Jews. He concluded his speech with a direct rejection of Paget's strategy: 'I ask you to ignore the political considerations and to say that this accused is guilty under which he has been charged.'[121]

After the prosecution's closing speech, the court adjourned for three weeks to provide the Judge Advocate with sufficient time to prepare his summing up, a complex task bearing in mind the mass of documentary evidence and fifty days of proceedings in court he had to review, and not least consider the vexed questions as to the application of international law developed at Nuremberg.

Summing Up, Verdict and Sentence

Judge Collingwood began his speech on Monday, 12 December 1949, the beginning of the last full week of the trial. As reported in *The Times*, 'Manstein listened attentively all day', and 'the public galleries were filled'. The Judge Advocate administered his first piece of advice to the members: '... there have been not a few occasions in this court when ... [it] has been invited to regard the indictment as a political one. It is, of course, nothing of the kind, and it goes without saying that you will not so regard it.' In so doing he took a swipe at Paget's controversial strategy of defence which had attempted to portray it as such.

He dealt next with the defence's plea of deference to higher authority. 'Obedience to an unlawful order', he stressed, 'did not absolve the perpetrator of a war crime.' Likewise, he advised the court 'to reject the theory that military necessity overrode all the rules of war.'[122] In this vital point, his direction could not have been clear enough. The overall effect of his advice was to uphold the Nuremberg Principles, confirming that the Hague Convention applied in the German war against the Soviet Union, whether or not the Russians complied, and to reject the defence's submissions to the contrary.

Over the following four days, the Judge Advocate continued to review in a comprehensive and painstaking manner the evidence for and against each charge. He highlighted the crucial issue as to whether Manstein knew of the mass slaughter of the Jews within the area of his command in the Crimea, and, if so, whether he took sufficient steps to prevent it. He reminded the court that the Field Marshal had said under cross-examination that he done nothing because he was ignorant of what was happening. But could the court believe, he asked, that there 'was a conspiracy of silence among the officers around Manstein?'

He then dealt with the evidence taken on commission from the 'Landsberg prisoners', under sentence of death. In a key piece of legal direction, he warned the court not to take this evidence, which was that of accomplices, without corroboration by independent evidence tending to implicate Manstein. Without directing its opinion, Justice Collingwood left it to the court to decide whether there was proof that Manstein had allowed the *Einsatzgruppe* to seize and murder civilians, or whether he had instigated his troops to acts of brutality against the Jews, of which limited evidence had been offered. Further, it was up to the court to determine whether the Field Marshal had authorized his subordinates to execute civilians without trial for non-punishable offences, or simply on suspicion as partisans.

By Friday, 16 December, the sixty-first of the proceedings, the Judge Advocate had reached the final three charges. His treatment of the destruction of property under the 'scorched earth' policy is indicative of his scrupulously even-handed approach in the best traditions of his appointment. As Paget conceded freely, 'Nothing could have been fairer than the manner with which he dealt with the facts'.[123] Quoting Article 23(g) of the 1907 Hague Convention, namely 'It is especially forbidden to destroy or seize the enemy's property, unless such destruction or seizure be imperatively demanded by the necessities of war', Justice Collingwood instructed the court:

> In coming to a conclusion on this question as to whether the destruction caused by the Accused was excusable on this ground [of military necessity],

it is essential that you should view the situation through the eyes of the Accused and look at it at the time when the events were actually occurring. It would not be just or proper to test the matter in the light of subsequent events, or to substitute an atmosphere of calm deliberation for one of urgency and anxiety. You must judge the question from this standpoint; whether the accused having regard to the position in which he was and the conditions prevailing at the time acted under the honest conviction that what he was doing was legally justifiable.

He advised further that if, 'in regard to any particular instance of seizure or destruction, you are left in doubt upon the matter, then the Accused is entitled to have that doubt in his favour'. This guidance chimed with his line on all the charges, reflecting the enduring principle in English criminal law (and by extension, British military law) that the benefit of the doubt goes to the defendant. He brought balance to his advice by reminding the court that the documents the prosecution had presented

tend to show that so far from this destruction being the result of impera-tive necessities of the moment, it was really the carrying out of a policy planned a considerable time before, a policy which the Accused had in fact been prepared to carry out on two previous occasions and now was carrying out in its entirety and carrying out irrespective of any question of military necessity.

So Manstein was not let off the hook over the application of the 'scorched earth' policy. In his final remarks, the Judge Advocate again reminded the court of the burden of proof. 'As to every allegation, [it] is on the prosecution and never leaves it.' He concluded his summing up by saying:

As Counsel of the Defence said in his opening address, some of these are horrible charges, many of them are charges against the honour of a man who has risen high in the honourable profession which is yours and was his. It is only in the presence of the evidence which leaves you with no alternative as reasonable men that you can convict him of such charges. On the other hand, if the evidence leaves you with no reasonable doubt at all in respect of any of these charges, then your duty is that imposed upon you by the oath that was administered at the beginning of this trial.

The President then adjourned the court to consider its findings over the weekend and reassemble on Monday, 19 December to present them.

On the final, sixty-second, day of proceedings, the President announced that the accused was *not guilty* of eight charges.[124] Unsurprisingly, the Field Marshal avoided conviction for crimes committed by others in Poland (*Charges 1–3*); he was, after all, serving then as a chief of staff and not as a responsible commander-in-chief. The court found him not guilty of forcing Soviet prisoners of war into the Wehrmacht (*Charge 6*), and, more crucially, of the most damning of crimes, including mass murder, committed predominantly by the SD – but also by German Army troops – against Jews, gypsies and communists (*Charges 9, 11 and 12*). Equally significantly, Manstein was also found not guilty of the shooting of civilians as 'partisans' (*Charge 14*) although his subordinates were held to be so accountable in the OKW trial.

Manstein was found *guilty* on nine charges: the seventh, fifteenth and sixteenth without amendment; and the remaining six as amended (*Charges 4, 5, 8, 10, 13 and 17*). The changes in the wording of these latter charges had the effect of reducing the culpability of the Field Marshal. The most prominent example was the striking of the words 'deliberately and recklessly' from the fourth and tenth charges. Overall, this changed the character of Manstein's conviction from crimes of commission to those of *omission*.

The Field Marshal was sentenced to eighteen years of imprisonment. Both Ashton Wade and Otto John thought that the severity of the punishment was due to Manstein's denial of the charges. But it was not in his nature to offer contrition for crimes that he believed he was not responsible for.

As the close of the trial approached, Slim had written to Simpson observing that 'It has been a long and tedious business and I am very grateful for you having taken it on'.[125] He was rewarded with the 'Kermit Roosevelt' lecture tour of the United States in 1950. Such were the spoils of the victorious and the fate of the vanquished. Manstein's conviction surprised his counsel. Paget had been confident that the court would acquit him. In his opinion, his client had 'abundantly proved himself not only a great soldier but a decent humane man. I thought that his personality had overcome the technicalities of the Royal Warrant that had seemed to make acquittal impossible.'[126]

Epilogue

'Manstein is and will remain a hero amongst his people. He was the architect of their victory and the Hector of their defeat ...' Reginald Paget[1]

Imprisonment

Reaction to Manstein's sentence varied according to national, political and private perspectives. Paget was appalled, and wrote immediately to his client on 19 December 1949: 'I cannot tell you how distressed I was for you on hearing the news today. I can only say that I personally regard it as a most unjust sentence, and I shall continue to do my upmost to get a remission.'[2] The newspapers were mixed in their response. In reporting the outcome of the trial, *The Times* informed its readers that 'the defence intends to file a petition with the reviewing authority, Lieutenant-General Keightley, arguing the case again on points of law and asking for a reduction in sentence'.[3] The next day it noted that German newspapers had debated the extent to which 'responsibility for the execution of orders attaches to the commander in the field', and whether 'a different set of morals and rules must apply in dealings with the Russians as opposed to the western Powers'. Other German papers had argued that the severity of Manstein's sentence 'will help to revive nationalism, and therefore militarism, but the opposite could be argued equally'. As significantly, the report concluded: 'the sentence gives the answer to Russian criticism some time ago that the trial was a mockery'.[4]

On conclusion of his trial, Manstein was transported from Hamburg to the Allied Prison in the small Westphalian town of Werl, 30 kilometres east of Dortmund, which housed – among other 'ordinary' prisoners – the war criminals convicted by British military courts.[5] After a short period in the inmates' hospital for treatment of a broken collar bone, he was allocated a cell in the VIP area – the top floor of Wing B in Building 1. In writing to his wife shortly after his arrival, he expressed surprise at his sentence and hoped that Mr Paget would achieve a revision. He then reassured Jutta-Sibylle:

You should know that I don't rail against my fate. I accept it as a duty which I must bear with decency for our beloved Germany and for my soldiers to whom my heart belongs. Whatever I did, I did it for those who fought and died under my command. And I don't regret that, even now when I, innocent, have to suffer for it.[6]

On New Year's Day 1950, Manstein typed a long letter to Paget, presenting a detailed critique of the judgement and setting out grounds for a petition. On a personal note, he thanked his counsel: 'The fact of my condemnation being so hard cannot diminish my feelings of gratefulness towards you but only increase it. ... Even if I had to spend, according to the sentence, all my life in this prison, not a single day will pass without my remembering you with deep gratefulness and full admiration.'[7] Manstein wrote again to Paget on 11 January 1950, praising his defence: 'Your fight for true justice and your attitude towards a member of a former enemy nation is one of the finest and greatest experiences of my life. An experience I will never forget and which compensates me for all the bitterness of my previous captivity.'[8]

Manstein got into his stride in complaining about his conviction with a comprehensive letter of mid January 1950 to Liddell Hart. Such correspondence was the Field Marshal's method of letting off steam and rationalizing his fate. 'You will feel how strong my disillusion was about the sentence against me,' he wrote. It had come so unexpected. 'After the brilliant final speech of Mr Paget we all were convinced that there would be an honourable acquittal.' Manstein revealed his intense frustration with the outcome of the trial by stressing:

> In fact it is difficult to understand, how today the application of the rules of Nuremberg, which are the result of hate and revenge and of a total misunderstanding of the realities of modern warfare and especially of a war against the Soviet Union, could overrule once more common sense, soldierly thinking and above all the realities of the last war.

Later in the same letter he returned to this issue, declaring, 'I don't understand how a court, composed of high-ranking soldiers, could follow the Judge Advocate in this way, which denies all realities of modern warfare and especially the conditions under which the German army had to fight in Russia against the Bolsheviks.' He continued hammering home his point, maintaining:

> It may be said, that it was my crime to serve under Hitler. But I was not serving Hitler; I was serving my country in its greatest danger! I had the duty to help my soldiers in their heavy fighting against an enemy, who

himself didn't acknowledge any rule or usage of war. I have frankly told the court that I have considered some measures taken by my government as justified under the conditions of modern warfare and with regard to the activities of the other side. That applies for example to the taking of reprisals (which the prosecution wrongly defines as the killing of hostages), to the evacuation of the population, to the labour of prisoners of war, to the shooting of partisans including commissars, who were members of partisan-organisations. In fact, it seems to me to be very questionable even under the Hague rules whether these measures were indeed illegal or not, the Hague rules being very vague. Also I don't understand how these matters should be illegal, if the destroying of undefended cities, the killing of their inhabitants by bombing is acknowledged by the necessities of war.

From this statement, it is absolutely clear that Manstein did not concede any wrong or accept any guilt whatsoever either for his actions as a commander or for those of his subordinates. Anticipating an obvious question from his correspondent, the Field Marshal added:

Perhaps it is necessary to add one remark with regard of the question of the Jews killed by the SD. I have told the court that, if I had had the knowledge of these horrible facts, I should have made every attempt to prevent them. But there can't be any doubt that the result only would have been my dismissal.[9]

Manstein's letter to Liddell Hart provides clear documentary proof that he had few regrets about his role in Hitler's war of aggression against the Soviet Union. Whether he knew anything about the murders of the Jews remains unproven, so the court was right to give him the benefit of doubt on this charge. However, it would appear that neither the IMT judgement at Nuremberg nor his conviction at Hamburg caused him either to reconsider his position or accept any personal liability for the crimes conducted within his area of operations. It was precisely this lack of contrition that had led the Deputy President of the court, Major General Ashton Wade, to conclude:

By the end of the cross-examination any feelings I had of sympathy towards Manstein had been replaced by disgust at the manner in which he appeared to be hiding behind his subordinates and relying on the plea of superior orders. I could not help comparing his attitude with that taken by Kesselring at his trial. ... [He] never attempted to evade responsibility for events which took place in the area of his Command.[10]

It is reasonable to assume that Wade, with his previous experience as chairman of the Review of Sentences (Europe) Board, involving meetings with convicted generals such as Field Marshal Albert Kesselring and Colonel General Nikolaus von Falkenhorst, both serving life imprisonment, had made a strong impression on him prior to the trial in Hamburg. It is also probable that he took a hard line accordingly with Manstein, becoming a powerful and compelling voice within the court in pressing for a guilty verdict and calling for a long sentence. By his own admission, Wade was inclined to see a 'streak of cruelty indigenous to the German race'.[11]

Meanwhile, Manstein's letter to Liddell Hart had crossed with the military historian's letter to *The Times* of 11 January 1950, in which he highlighted the extent to which the Field Marshal has been cleared of the charges against him, noting that only 'two of the original 17 were sustained'. He emphasized that 'von Manstein never initiated any policy of brutality, and was acquitted on having "instigated and incited the troops under his command to commit acts of brutality" – the most important points in any accusation of war crimes'. Furthermore, 'It is evident that von Manstein took the initiative in mitigating inhumane measures. One may hope, not least for our own reputation, that we shall be led to show a similar sense of humanity in mitigating the savage sentence inflicted on him.'[12] By his action, it is clear that Liddell Hart sought to influence publicly the confirmation of Manstein's sentence. Wade was incensed by the letter, deploring in particular Liddell Hart's accusation that the Field Marshal's condemnation 'appears a glaring example either of gross ignorance or gross hypocrisy'. In this respect, he found this criticism of the court 'quite astonishing and offensive'.[13]

It is doubtful whether the officer responsible, Lieutenant General Sir Charles Keightley, General Officer Commanding-in-Chief, British Army of the Rhine, paid any attention to Liddell Hart's plea. The advice from his Deputy Judge Advocate General, Brigadier Lord Russell of Liverpool, however, was uncompromising. In his detailed note on Manstein's preliminary petition of 2 January 1950, Russell acknowledged that 'the sentence awarded by the Court may, on the face of it, appear excessive'. He went on to state:

> Nevertheless, you will doubtless bear in mind, when considering whether or not there should be some remission of sentence, that the accused was convicted of the eighth and thirteenth charges, the second of which alleged the unlawful shooting of over two thousand hostages without trial

which, according to international law, is murder. You may think that the sentence awarded by the Court is justified by the conviction upon these two charges.[14]

Russell's legal opinion on the final petition was similarly adamant. Taking the tenth charge, for example, he analysed Manstein's submission that 'the exterminations could not be *in consequence* [emphasis as in original] of any disregard of duty by the Petitioner, as is alleged in the charge, unless they could have been prevented by him'. Although Russell thought the contention 'sound', he considered 'the Court were entitled to find [that] von Manstein could have prevented the massacres in the charge had he so minded'.

Russell then applied a further argument, again presuming Manstein's knowledge about the executions, which had not been fully exposed during the trial. He observed that the 'localities in which it was alleged ... that thousands of Soviet citizens were massacred were all situated within the Army area in which a very fluid battle was being fought'. In his view, however, Manstein had failed to exploit a loophole in the instructions covering the attachment of the *Einsatzgruppen*, 'whereby he could keep the *Einsatzgruppen* outside his Army area on the pretext that their presence would interfere with military operations'. Russell then played his most powerful card:

> Doubtless, had he taken this course the Petitioner would have had to reckon with Hitler to whom Himmler would have at once appealed, but there was ample evidence given at the trial by the accused himself that when he differed from his Führer on matters of high *military* importance, he was perfectly prepared to make a stand. That he did not do so on this issue raises a strong inference which the Court were entitled to draw, namely that it was only because he did not consider the mass murder of a hundred thousand Russians was worth a quarrel with Hitler.

With this strength of view, it is hardly surprising that Russell concluded: '... this petition discloses no adequate grounds for refusing confirmation of any of the findings in this case'.[15]

In the event, on 24 February 1950 Keightley confirmed the guilty verdicts but reduced Manstein's sentence from eighteen to twelve years without explanation. The Field Marshal was immediately informed by a member of Keightley's staff who had travelled to Werl. In writing to Paget the next day, Manstein considered the reduction of sentence: ' ... it remains inexplicable how the C-in-C could confirm the findings at all after considering the petition you have drawn up in such a convincing manner. The only explanation to me is the supposition that he was bound to do so by higher orders.'[16]

Manstein soon settled down into a steady routine at Werl. He found the atmosphere 'humane', and sensed in those with whom he had to deal, whether comrade or member of the prison staff, 'a feeling of respect, understanding and a will to help'.[17] The regime for the German generals was considerably more relaxed than that for lower-ranking prisoners, let alone common criminals. They were permitted to mix freely during the day, and messed together for lunch. As a special privilege, the prison governor, Lieutenant Colonel E. R. Vickers, allowed them to tend a small garden where they were permitted to grow fresh vegetables, mingle with each other and get some fresh air. Although they were entitled to receive a visitor only every six weeks, it has been suggested that Vickers 'turned a blind eye to food parcels smuggled into the prison'.[18] Manstein's daughter, Gisela Lingenthal, confirms this lenient approach. She recalled making many such visits: 'It wasn't very difficult to bring father some drink and other supplies into the prison as the guards only conducted the most cursory of searches. I used to hide brandy miniatures under my coat on the way in and take pages of his draft memoirs with me on the way out.'[19]

Apart from gardening, Manstein's principal occupation – as at Island Farm – was his writing. Whilst Kesselring assisted the research of the US Army Historical Division as well as penning his memoirs, Manstein refused to co-operate with the Americans, preferring to concentrate solely on his own work.[20] Initially he wrote about his trial with a view to getting a book published by either Leverkuehn or Busse, but from May 1950 onwards he concentrated on drafting his wartime experiences. A real bonus came when he received permission to call for and receive military historical material.[21] Although the products of any research were not allowed to leave the prison, let alone be published, Manstein, as we have seen, got round this restriction through lax security.

Obtaining Manstein's Release

Manstein's eventual release in May 1953 was as much a political decision as the determination to bring him to trial in the first place. Those involved in pressing for his discharge on the German side came from many walks of life. In addition to the former generals, including Busse, Heusinger, Speidel and Westphal, whose loyalty and persistence were unflagging, were members of the clergy, and a wide range of journalists and politicians. From the latter, both Federal President Theodor Heuss and president of the Bundestag Hermann Ehlers called for Manstein's sentence to be reviewed.[22] Most prominently, Chancellor Konrad Adenauer became involved when release of the Germans held under Allied sentence became a de facto prerequisite of West German rearmament. He had stated in mid 1950 that two of the necessary conditions for such action were 'cessation of the defamation of the German soldier and a satisfactory settlement of sentences for war crimes'.[23] So it was not merely a matter of requesting an act of goodwill or mercy from the Western Allies. It had far more to do with restoring the honour of Germany, its military and population, and rearming Germany to meet the Soviet threat, itself a highly contentious matter. Centre (FDP) and centre-right (CDU) parties held that the imprisonment of the generals was unjust, and advocated either revision or release. More widely, in German public opinion, the term *Kriegsverurteilte* (war convicted) was much preferred over *Kriegsverbrecher* (war criminals).

Meanwhile, working as 'technical advisors' within the *Amt Blank* (the office of Theodor Blank, the disguised forerunner of the West German Ministry of Defence), former Generals Speidel and Heusinger understood only too well the importance of obtaining a 'solution' if West Germany were to enter the Atlantic Alliance and to build an officer corps within its new armed forces, the Bundeswehr.[24] As *The Times* reported in late 1950, one of the first matters for discussion between senior representatives of the Amt Blank and their Allied opposite numbers was 'the rehabilitation of the honour of the German soldier, which must be the foundation of the equality of rights of an eventual German contingent in a European army'.[25]

Within the United Kingdom, Liddell Hart remained a pivotal force in arguing the German generals' case, along with Reginald Paget. Later, Winston Churchill, re-elected as prime minister after the General Election in October 1951, returned to the charge. During the early 1950s, Liddell Hart undertook a series of tours to West Germany where he had ample opportunity to gauge the opinion of ex-soldiers concerning the Allies' war crimes trials. It became quickly apparent to him that reaching a public consensus on rearmament within Germany was highly dependent on 'solving' the problem of the generals. Even given a political decision towards rearmament, it would be difficult to recruit a new German Army of twelve divisions as long as totemic figures such as Kesselring and Manstein remained in prison. The importance of Liddell

Hart's role is demonstrated by his reception by Adenauer on 9 June 1952 in Bonn, during which the main topic of discussion was the matter of the imprisoned generals.[26]

Manstein, still confined within Werl, was not inactive in advancing his release. In a letter home, he set out his position as follows:

> It all concerns the question of honour and the equality for the German soldier. In other words, a quite fundamental matter. Of course, the destiny of Germany – whether it joins the West and contributes to its defence or not – cannot hang on our personal destiny, but is very much dependent on the question of honour, on justice and on equality.

The Field Marshal even managed to place an anonymous letter in the *Frankfurter Allgemeine Zeitung* in February 1952, in which he rehearsed his case again: 'In truth, this question is all about three matters: law and justice, equal rights for Germany and the honour of the German nation.'[27] This by now had become an all too familiar call.

Yet for all the German pressure, whether political or from the public relations campaign orchestrated by his many supporters in the media, the decision to release Manstein could only be made in London by the British government. An attempt in late 1950 by Sir Ivone Kilpatrick, the British member of the Allied High Commission for West Germany, to undertake a review of the sentences of the German prisoners received only lukewarm support from the Foreign Office. It was made clear in a memorandum to Cabinet that 'No special treatment will be accorded to Manstein.' However, the same document noted 'the strong feeling in Germany against war crimes trials and convictions'. With this in mind, it conceded, 'whilst we clearly must not allow ourselves to be deflected from doing what is just and right ... we have a strong interest in mitigating public resentment in Germany'.[28] Perversely, the Cabinet decided in May 1951 to strip the High Commissioner's powers of clemency because 'it would be wrong for him to be guided by German opinion' in any reduction of sentences.[29]

The correspondence pages of *The Times* continued to attract letters about Manstein's trial and sentence. In September 1951, Paget struck home with:

> I do not believe that any decent Englishmen would serve in an army as the comrades of men who were imprisoning Field-Marshals Alexander and Montgomery. German ex-soldiers have made it plain that they will not serve while we imprison men like Kesselring and Manstein. ... If we want German soldiers in our European army we must distinguish between

German soldiers and Nazi politicians and we must recognize that the German soldiers fought decently for their country. We must distinguish between those who initiated the atrocities and those who did no more than obey military orders, and we must grant to the latter an honourable discharge: for unless we do these things no decent German will join the European army.[30]

In paraphrasing his defence of Manstein at Hamburg within the new context of German rearmament, no doubt Paget felt he was doing his former client a useful service. As a matter of coincidence, the barrister's account of the trial had just been published. His criticisms of the competence of the court and the Judge Advocate drew a furious reaction from Sir Hartley Shawcross, President of the Board of Trade, who took the unusual step of issuing a formal statement. He wrote:

> As one who was Attorney-General at the time I feel it right to repudiate the criticisms made by Mr Paget and to express my regret that he should have thought fit to make them. ... [The Judge Advocate] discharged his function with great fairness and outstanding patience. Indeed the trial was conspicuous for the latitude allowed to the defence.

In response, Paget suggested cheekily that the minister should read his book, for 'I think it may do him good'.[31]

Manstein would have to wait for nearly a year before any real progress would be made on his behalf. There were many false dawns; high hopes were dashed when no release came prior to Christmas. At the beginning of 1952, the British High Commissioner had stressed that it 'would be "monstrous" if the case of Manstein were singled out for special consideration just because he had many friends to support his cause'.[32] In the background, however, in a neat reversal of respective positions, the Churchill government rather than its independently minded plenipotentiary in Germany, was quietly designing a cunning scheme to rid themselves of the war criminals issue once and for all. It involved counting Manstein's years of detention as a prisoner of war prior to his sentence, then applying a remission of a third for good behaviour, and finally, in any case of doubt, declaring him too ill to remain imprisoned. By this reckoning, he could assume release in May 1953 if not earlier, based on a total of eight years' 'sentence' served since the German surrender.

During 1952, conditions in Werl steadily improved, including a very welcome relaxation of postal restrictions. A further relief came when Manstein's wife received financial support from the German government and was assured of a widow's pension. However, Jutta-Sibylle's health was deteriorating to such an extent that Manstein was granted compassionate leave 'on his word of honour' to be at her side during a serious operation in Freudenstadt, where they had holidayed during the 1930s.[33] In June, Manstein was examined by a psychiatrist at Werl to establish his fitness to stay in confinement. The trouble was he was in too good physical and mental shape to trigger an immediate medical discharge. As the Field Marshal described the situation, 'I was not exactly the right type for a psychiatrist, and I'm not really a suitable candidate to pretend that I've had a nervous collapse.'[34] In August 1952, the British authorities granted Manstein medical parole, which allowed him to undergo specialist treatment for a cataract in a Kiel private clinic. Professor Dieter, who had successfully treated the Field Marshal's right eye in Breslau in the spring of 1944, would now perform a second operation on his left. His transfer was conditional on the acceptance of strict conditions of avoiding any external contacts and publicity.

The operation at the end of October went well and Manstein managed to stay in Kiel until February 1953 with the blessing of the British authorities. Their generosity of spirit was extended when he was allowed to take a period of extended convalescence in the small community of Allmendingen, about 30 kilometres west of Ulm, where his wife had taken up temporary residence with relations in the Schloss der Freiherren von Freyberg. Although money remained very tight, it was fitting that Manstein should serve the final part of his 'sentence' in such convivial and friendly patrician surroundings. Had Manstein been extradited to Russia, imprisonment would have been much more uncomfortable, and it is highly unlikely he would have ever been seen alive again.

On 7 May 1953, Manstein was 'released' from house arrest, after exactly eight years of detention and imprisonment. It was an occasion of great joy not only to Manstein and his family, but also to Allmendingen as a whole. The burgomaster gave the local schoolchildren a day off and organized a festive procession through the town.[35] Manstein thanked the assembled inhabitants for the friendly support extended to his wife during his imprisonment, and remarked magnanimously: 'Let us not think of the sufferings of the past but rather of the future. Our hope lies in the reconciliation of nations and the unity of Europe.'[36] It could have been a diplomat or politician, even Adenauer, speaking.

Over the next few weeks, Manstein received a flood of greetings and best wishes from old friends and acquaintances: a particular honour came with a handwritten note of kind regards from the German chancellor. A final line was drawn under his sentence when he was invited to pay

an official visit to Headquarters British Army of the Rhine in Bad
Oeynhausen, the very place where nearly eight years before he had
begun his extended journey under detention to Nuremberg, Bridgend,
Munsterlager, Hamburg and Werl. Through this act of reconciliation,
as his son later remarked, 'The political problems of the past should
neither adversely affect co-operation between forces in the future nor
spoil relationships between members of both armies.'[37] This was a significant step, and one unthinkable in 1945. With Germany's accession
to NATO and the founding of the Bundeswehr in 1955, British and
German troops would stand alongside each other in the common defence
of Germany against potential Soviet aggression until the fall of the Berlin
Wall in November 1989. Manstein would have a significant role in the
design of the new German armed forces required to conduct 'forward
defence' close to the Inner German Border. In the meantime, the only
sting in the tail was that he had to complete the bureaucratic process of
'denazification', which was concluded in August 1953 with the desired
exoneration.

Memoirs

Following the Field Marshal's release in Allmendingen, the Mansteins
remained for a short time in rural Württemberg before joining their son
in Essen. By this time, Rüdiger von Manstein had become a successful
businessman working for Siemens, which was expanding rapidly during
Germany's economic miracle of the 1950s. The Field Marshal's itinerant
life continued with subsequent moves to Bonn and Münster in Westphalia (not to be confused with Munster in Lower Saxony) before he was
able to settle down at last in 1958 near Munich in the district of Bad
Tölz-Wolfratshausen. With the money earned from his memoirs,
Manstein was able to afford to build a comfortable house in the small
settlement of Irschenhausen, now in the municipality of Icking, whose
beautiful setting had so enchanted D. H. Lawrence before the First
World War.[38]

Manstein's writings, of course, were not the steamy stuff of *Sons and
Lovers*! His immediate concern was to complete his wartime memoirs,
Lost Victories. Published in 1955 under its original German title, *Verlorene
Siege*, it was a runaway success, although not escaping criticism for the
author's treatment of Stalingrad and resistance to Hitler. Preparation of
the English edition, on which the Field Marshal's enduring international
reputation mainly rests, depended considerably on the support of Liddell
Hart.

In October 1955, the British military historian visited the Mansteins in Essen. The Field Marshal asked him to help 'to arrange for an English translation of the book, as well as to write a short foreword to it'.   On return to England, Liddell Hart engaged the London publishers Methuen via their literary advisor, the classical scholar Dr E. V. Rieu. In his letter, he not only attempted to negotiate royalties on behalf of the Field Marshal, but he also stressed that 'Manstein's memoirs are better written than Guderian's, and of wider interest'.[39] By chance, Methuens had already approached Manstein's German publisher, Athenäum Verlag of Bonn, and clinched a deal. Suffice it to say that by spring 1957, Anthony Powell had abridged and translated most of *Verlorene Siege*, and had written to Liddell Hart to seek agreement on the wording of the blurb well before the book had been completed.[40] Methuens' editor, John Cullen, offered Liddell Hart the princely sum of 25 guineas for an introduction, and requested advice on the book's title, as 'Lost Victories', in his opinion, might 'annoy at least some English reviewers'.[41] Liddell Hart replied via Anthony Powell, suggesting the following alternatives: 'War of Forfeits', 'Illusionary Victories', 'Vanishing Victories' and 'False Victories'. Wisely, Methuen stuck to the literal translation, ensuring that the symbolic *Lost Victories* title remained on the front cover.[42]

By early 1958, the translation was nearly complete, incorporating Liddell Hart's foreword, in which he extolled Manstein's career. It concluded: 'That ended the active career of the Allies' most formidable military opponent – a man who combined modern ideas of mobility with a classical sense of manoeuvre, a mastery of technical detail and great driving power.' No hyperbole was intended; far from it, for such language flowed smoothly from the author of works such as *Great Captains Revealed*, *The Ghost of Napoleon* and *Strategy: the Indirect Approach*. At least Liddell Hart had not placed an endorsement of his own work as he had done in the English-language edition of Heinz Guderian's autobiography, *Panzer Leader*. Meanwhile, Cullen confided to Liddell Hart that Powell's abridgement had ended up as 'less than 20%', although permission had been received from the author to cut the text 'by some 25%'. The only possible point of disagreement was the very much foreshortened Chapter 14 on the battle of Kursk, 'but it was Manstein's own suggestion'.[43] After all, that episode hardly represented the Field Marshal's finest hour. *Lost Victories* was finally published in London in May 1958, following serialization in the *Sunday Dispatch*.

The reviews in Britain were overwhelmingly positive. Whilst the *Daily Telegraph* commented almost exclusively on Manstein's account of the German system of command, *The Sunday Times* provided a well-balanced assessment: 'On the whole the author succeeds not only in making a damning exposure of Hitler's shortcomings as Supreme Commander but also in being fair to him. Yet he does not always escape the temptation to explain away the army's mistakes by overstating the case against the Führer.' The *Listener* was more effusive. It concluded that *Lost Victories*

> rises to its finest from the moment of the encirclement of Paulus at Stalingrad. Just because it is detailed and shirks no problems – in his anxiety to enforce what he has to say the Field-Marshal is occasionally led to repetition – one cannot for a moment promise those who like easy reading that they will get it here. On the other hand, no intelligent, even if uninstructed, reader will put the book down without having achieved a clearer view of the nature of the fighting in those wide spaces.

The *Journal* of the Royal United Services Institute considered the memoirs as 'among the most interesting which a senior officer has contributed to the literature of the Second World War'.[44]

The most powerful critique, however, came from Paul Johnson in London's *Evening Standard* under the banner, 'The Manstein Myth: Don't Blame the Generals'. He considered that the memoirs constituted 'a formidable contribution' to the myth that 'had the [German] generals been allowed to control strategy . . . Russia would have been subdued and Germany would have remained dominant on the European mainland'.[45]

In the autumn of 1958, *Lost Victories* was published in the United States by Henry Regnery of Chicago, receiving ecstatic reviews. The *Baltimore Evening Sun*, for example, considered that Manstein had provided 'an extraordinarily sharp portrait' of Hitler, and concluded that 'this is one of the best of the World War II memoirs, from either side of the front line'. One of the most authoritative appraisals came from Brigadier General S. L. A. Marshall, former chief combat historian of the U. S. Army. 'No higher commander', he wrote of Manstein in the *New York Times*, 'was more useful to Hitler, pulled more of his irons out of the fire, or contributed more of his brain to undertakings from which arose the myth of Hitler's military genius.' '[Manstein's] book', he continued, 'beautifully reflects the imaginative approach and administrative competence of a truly extraordinary military mind. His campaigns were always tough; the odds grew increasingly against him, and he in turn increased in stature, even as he was given heavier responsibility.'[46]

Manstein's achievements were richly commended in the influential *Military Review*, the in-house academic journal of the American army: 'Reading the significant military account of this outstanding soldier is a worthwhile and rewarding endeavour. For the professional military reader interested in the requirements of higher command this book offers a wealth of primary source material.'[47] This glowing assessment, written at the height of the Cold War, reflected the US Army's enduring fascination with the Wehrmacht's defensive successes against the Red Army. Significantly, there was no mention of war crimes in any of the American reviews.

The second volume of Manstein's memoirs, *Aus einem Soldatenleben 1887–1939 (From a Soldier's Life)* was published in Germany in 1958. After a brief sketch of his childhood and early military career, Manstein provided a detailed commentary on the Reichswehr, the rise of Hitler and the founding of the new Wehrmacht. Whilst *Lost Victories* with its high drama of war remains in print, and has been translated into many languages, its prequel 'did not find the same echo' according to his son, despite it covering such significant political and military events between the wars.[48] None the less, it remains an important source of information about the period.

Apart from his memoirs, Manstein penned a number of other pieces in the 1950s. His close association with Liddell Hart led to a chapter 'The Development of the Red Army, 1942–45' in the British historian's study of the Soviet Army, published in 1956. Although Manstein acknowledged the 'Soviet command had learnt a great deal during the first years of the war', and had concentrated its armoured forces well (in the German manner, of course) from the summer of 1943, he stressed that Soviet commanders were 'never compelled to fight against superior numbers'. Nor were they 'asked to win a victory against an enemy superior in numbers'.[49]

In addition, he wrote four articles for the United States *Marine Corps Gazette* over the period November 1955 to April 1957: 'German Operational Planning for the Campaign in the West'; 'The Campaign in the Crimea 1941–42'; 'Operational Citadel: A Study in Command Decision'; and 'Defensive Operations in Southern Russia 1943–44'. There was little in the first two that had not been explained previously in *Lost Victories;* the third, however, provided a complete chapter for the abridged English edition. The fourth, with its commentary by Liddell Hart, is the most revealing. It offered its author a further opportunity to stress that defeat on the Eastern Front 'did not rest solely on the many-fold superiority of forces which the enemy could place in the field, but also in the basic errors committed by the German Supreme Command'. Manstein spared no criticism of the Führer by concluding:

Hitler's principle, that every foot of ground had to be defended, in the hope that the Soviets would bleed themselves white in their attacks, would have had a certain justification if such a defence could have been conducted with sufficient forces. With the [divisional] frontages that existed this was not possible. ... [Hitler's direction] not only led to renewed crises and the danger of encirclement, but also vastly deprived the German side of the capability (by dissipating its strength) which lay in the superiority of its troops and commanders to conduct a mobile war of strategic movement.[50]

During the Cold War, the contemporary lesson was clear. What linked Manstein's assessment of the Red Army and his critique of Hitler's military strategy was the need to establish a credible defence of Western Europe against Soviet attack, based on sufficiently strong and flexibly commanded NATO forces to which West Germany must contribute.

Forging a New Army

A comprehensive description and assessment of Manstein's role in the development of the Bundeswehr during the mid 1950s would demand a separate study. Contrary to a recent claim that his appointment as advisor to the West German government was 'more symbolic than real', Manstein's role was significant on two counts.[51] As might be expected from an individual of such experience, his professional contribution was valuable and widely respected. Secondly, his work certainly did not harm his speedy rehabilitation within German society. Over twenty-five years before, as a colonel in the *Truppenamt*, he had made radical proposals for the Reichswehr that had borne fruit in Hitler's Wehrmacht. Now he would have a fresh opportunity to bring his views to bear in the organization of a completely new German Army. Manstein did so as much out of personal conviction as by any official invitation. Although retired, he felt he should not remain on the sidelines and evade a responsibility in assisting the security of his country.[52] The key issue concerning the Field Marshal was the structure of the land forces that the new Federal Republic would assign to NATO.

During the autumn of 1955, the Amt Blank invited Manstein with ten other former senior officers to a conference in Oestrich, near Mainz. The object of the event was to solicit opinion on the draft plans for the formation of the German Army. Generals Alfred Heusinger and Hans Röttiger presented the official position, which foresaw the establishment of twelve divisions similar in strength and structure to those of the old Wehrmacht, reinforced by corps and army level troops.

Manstein criticized these proposals. In the context of a future conflict scenario in Europe that might involve NATO forces fighting without the benefit of air superiority, and one in which the employment of tactical nuclear weapons could not be excluded, he considered the 'old' structure as too inflexible. Instead he recommended that each of the divisions be organized into three strong independent brigades, which would be easier to command and more self-sufficient in combat. These new combined-arms formations would represent the lowest 'operational units'. In his concept, which was radical for the time, he was looking forward rather than harking back to a comfortable past. Coincidentally, the U.S. Army was shortly to adopt quite another structural solution in the form of the 'Pentomic Division', so named for being split into five semi-autonomous fighting units, but abandoned it in the early 1960s. As it turned out, the American, British and West German armies eventually would implement structures similar to those of the Field Marshal's design. As Wenck pointed out, 'as ever Manstein was marching at the head of military progress'.[53]

Manstein's ideas received a mixed reception at Oestrich, and were rejected outright by the Amt Blank. Undeterred, the Field Marshal developed his concept, drew on the advice of his friends Wenck and Westphal, and produced a formal paper that he sent to Heusinger in early November 1955. In his covering letter, he acknowledged that 'you certainly won't have much pleasure initially in reading my proposal because it means knocking the previous planning on the head'. Appealing to his former assistant in the *Truppenamt*, Manstein wrote on: 'I request sincerely that you read the proposal fully impartially, and recall how we in our "T1 days" rejected Keitel's mobilization plan at the very last moment and forced through a solution that matched the situation.'[54]

Manstein raised four main objections to the structure developed by the Amt Blank under Heusinger's direction. First, he explained, the 'proportion of army troops to operational formations is unhealthy, and the number of the latter is too small'. Secondly, 'the organization of the basic formations does not match the requirements of future war. They are insufficiently agile, meeting neither operational nor tactical level requirements.' Thirdly, the 'strength of the individual staffs and unit establishments should be reduced from "desirable" to the "essential minimum", in order to create a reasonably flexible force with the best possible proportion of combat troops to supporting ones'. Fourthly, Manstein believed that the existing programme for the raising of the army 'is not expedient on military grounds, is inappropriate for military-political reasons, and pays insufficient attention to the possibility of political development'.[55]

Manstein's solution to these problems built on his ideas presented at Oestrich. Within the armed forces of the new Bundeswehr (army, navy and air force), he noted that the peacetime establishment of the army *(Heer)* was capped at 366,000 men, of which 157,700 were allocated to army troops, leaving only 208,000 for the front-line brigades and divisions. Instead of six armoured (panzer) and six armoured infantry (panzer grenadier) divisions, he proposed that eight of the former and four of the latter should be raised, giving four balanced corps (structured 2:1). Each of the divisions would be expanded to include three powerful brigades rather than two battle groups of up to three battalions as envisaged at the time.[56] In the Field Marshal's conception, the armoured brigade would contain no less than two each of armoured, armoured infantry and artillery battalions, together with separate rifle, engineer, anti-aircraft and anti-tank battalions – in total around 7,500 men, a mini division in all but name. The armoured infantry brigade (7,300 men) was similarly organized with three 'grenadier' battalions and only one tank.

According to his proposals, the new divisions would be about 25,000 strong. Notable throughout the proposed structure was the paucity of logistic support, which was concentrated at divisional level and above. Manstein was only able to increase the number of combat units (eighteen tank, five armoured infantry and ten artillery battalions) by making deep cuts in army troops, particularly within the support area. He justified taking risk here (only 10 per cent of the logistic and engineer troops would be active) by assuming that there would be sufficient warning time to mobilize them. Although Manstein's ideas were never fully implemented, the balanced 'square' armoured brigade of two tank and two armoured or mechanized infantry battalions became standardized within the German and British Armies by the 1970s.

Manstein's last major contribution to the development of the Bundeswehr came in June 1956, when he was invited to present a report on the length of conscript service to the defence committee of the Bundestag. He was assisted in this study by retired generals Reinhardt, Busse and Sixt. The Field Marshal spoke on 20 June 1956 and pressed his case for eighteen months' service based on the requirement to build up an effectively led and well-trained force with sufficient deterrent value. Notwithstanding the possibility of nuclear weapons being used by either NATO or the Warsaw Pact, in his view the Bundeswehr could never be strong enough conventionally. With this in mind, Manstein proposed the formation of additional forces, based on experienced reservists, to protect rear areas.[57] Again this was an idea well ahead of its time. It was implemented much later in the form of the *Heimat-schutzbrigaden* (home defence brigades). In the event, the first Bundeswehr conscripts served only twelve months; their successors had to serve eighteen! Manstein concluded his address, and as such his last formal contribution to the new army, as follows: 'As much as we might regret from many points of view the requirement that the Federal Republic must re-arm again, in view of her particularly precarious situation, nothing should be spared within the art of the possible to achieve her security.'[58]

The Last Farewells

In 1966, Manstein's wife of forty-six years died after a series of long illnesses. Jutta-Sibylle was buried in Dorfmark, near Bad Fallingbostel, the adopted home of her displaced Silesian kin, the von Loesch family. Her bereaved husband, who was utterly devoted to his wife, was looked after by two housekeepers, and by his loyal friends and close relations. Manstein's twilight years in Irschenhausen were taken up principally with reading and correspondence, and in meeting regularly his close former Wehrmacht colleagues, Busse, Westphal and Wenck.

The Bundeswehr celebrated the Field Marshal's eightieth birthday in November 1967 with style and substance. During the run-up to his 'round' anniversary, a grand beating retreat (*grosser Zapfenstreich*) was held in his honour at the Combat Arms School in Munster on the occasion of the annual reunion of armoured troops. On the big day, the *Generalinspekteur* (Chief of Defence Staff) General Ulrich de Maizière visited Manstein at Irschenhausen, conveying the collective greetings of the Bundeswehr. A choir from the army officers' school in Munich entertained the Field Marshal and the many guests from far and wide with old soldiers' songs.[59]

The highlight of the event was undoubtedly the presentation of a Festschrift entitled *Nie Ausser Dienst* (*Never Retired*) that not only included laudatory passages from former generals and colleagues such as Heusinger, Busse and Wenck, but also contained a more critical essay from a prominent German military historian, Dr Andreas Hillgruber. Hence de Maizière highlighted in his introduction that 'Erich von Manstein's path, so uniform it may appear to run, is full of variety, as are the contributions to this book'. Despite their differences, he maintained that all the authors recognized 'his honourableness, his superior intellect and his achievements as a military commander'.[60]

In his presentation speech at the Manstein home, the *Generalinspekteur* spared no praise for the Field Marshal, which embraced the words:

> With confidence we can concur with Liddell Hart's external and independent judgement that you were the most capable German military commander of the Second World War. ... [Afterwards] you appeared in front of a victor's court, as representative of many soldiers; you then accepted your sentence and imprisonment, withstanding indomitably all disappointments and injustice. The Bundeswehr thanks you for all the valuable advice and help that you provided at the request of the government and parliament during its preparatory and build-up years.[61]

Manstein's eighty-fifth birthday was marked by a visit by de Maizière's successor, Admiral Armin Zimmermann, who brought personal greetings and thanks from the Federal minister of defence and from the members of the Bundeswehr more generally. A military band played in the garden.

After this high point, Manstein's health deteriorated markedly in his eighty-sixth year. Over the Whit weekend of 1973, his condition worsened. During the night of 9/10 June, Manstein succumbed to a cerebral apoplexy. He was buried on 15 June 1973 alongside his wife in the village graveyard at Dorfmark. The funeral with full military honours was attended not only by family, friends and other invited guests, but also by 'hundreds of former and still active soldiers', according to his son. The Bundeswehr contingent, led in person by Admiral Zimmermann, included a band and an honour guard from *Panzerlehrbrigade* 9, based in nearby Munster. A young panzer officer, Leutnant Erhard Drews, commanded the platoon-sized detachment. Thirty-six years later, he recalled the event: 'It was a hot summer's day, which I remember well. Because there were so many high-ranking guests to greet formally, my right arm ached so long as I held my salute. It was a very dignified and special occasion that made a really big impression on me, as I'm sure it did on everyone else.'[62]

At the funeral service in the overflowing village church, Theodor Busse delivered the eulogy. His heartfelt remarks on behalf of his closest friend must have struck many a chord with those present:

> This genial soldier and great military commander was a nobleman in the truest sense of the word – an example to us in every respect. Daring, and quick in thought and deed – hard on himself – undemanding as a person –

modest even during the times of his greatest successes – steadfast in the face of setbacks of destiny that he had to withstand – chivalrous to the enemy – considerate to all who were entrusted to him. That's what he meant for us – so will he live on for us.

To work for him and with him was a joy and a gain. His subordinates trusted him unreservedly and followed gladly in the wake of his superior and decisive leadership. On this basis he could fully apply his exceptional ability, achieving his great victories and mastering apparently hopeless crises.[63]

At Manstein's burial place, the last words of farewell were spoken by Admiral Zimmermann: 'The soldiers of the Bundeswehr take their leave from Field Marshal Erich von Lewinski, called von Manstein. A long military life, shaped by a chivalrous attitude, unerring professional judgement, sense of responsibility and the spirit of service to the public good, has come to an end.' The *Generalinspekteur* then paraphrased the Field Marshal's career before concluding with the equally moving words: 'The soldiers of the Bundeswehr bow before Field Marshal von Manstein, who departs into eternity. For us, the memory of him remains a valuable legacy.'[64]

The obituaries of Manstein were mixed, reflecting a more critical public approach to the Wehrmacht since the publication of his memoirs. In the United Kingdom, *The Times* summed up neatly his military achievement by stating that when 'Hitler removed him from command', it 'removed from the path of the Russians and her allies the most formidable obstacle in their advance to victory'. It also commented on his period of imprisonment, which represented 'penalty and retribution for his failure, in common with most of his fellow generals, to make a firm and timely stand against the Nazi regime and its abuses, despite the disapproval he early and often showed'.[65] As was to be expected, the left-leaning German *Spiegel* magazine was much more critical of the Field Marshal. 'He embodied both the degeneration and downfall of the Prussian-German military cast. He assisted in the march to catastrophe – misled by his blind sense of duty.' The boot went in further. 'In Russia he incited his soldiers to fight a racial war with the cry: "the Judaic-Bolshevik system must be eradicated once and for all".'[66]

A Military Life Reviewed

Marcel Stein titled his critical account of Manstein, with its particular emphasis on his alleged war crimes, *The Janus Head*. Superficially, this catching strap line appears to have merit. Even the most fleeting Internet survey of the Field Marshal will reveal two very contrasting faces of the man: one, the most gifted German operational brain of the Second World War; the other, a convicted war criminal who had much to answer for. But the real picture is far more complex: over time, 'good' and 'bad' can never look in opposite directions from one single, fixed position in history. Manstein's life is one of contradiction and paradox.

The Field Marshal's career, which encompassed service to the Kaiser's Army, the Reichswehr, the Wehrmacht, and after an interlude of eight years in British custody, advice to the nascent Bundeswehr, was in many ways emblematic for many other German soldiers, perhaps thousands. But what made it so special was that Manstein as a military commander not only enjoyed the respect and confidence of his peers and the enduring trust of his troops for his various triumphs, but also was highly regarded by friends and foes alike for his intellect, judgement and adroit decision-making in both victory and defeat. He was a devout Christian and supported the Wehrmacht chaplaincy within his army and army group.[67] Although he never achieved the 'cult status' of Rommel, unwittingly crafted by a poorly led British Desert Army, Manstein was by far his superior at the operational level in the much wider and darker canvas of war on the Eastern Front. As such, Manstein deserves far greater recognition.

Set against this record of achievement, however, if not his refusal to support the resistance to Hitler, are his alleged war crimes. From today's perspective of exposure and recrimination against the Wehrmacht, a much less rosy picture of the individual emerges. Recent academic research indicates a degree of complicity with the SD that was never proven at his trial. Where he failed, in the eyes of his detractors, was to show sufficient moral courage and integrity when confronted by illegal orders and by the murderous actions of the SD – which he denied ever knowing about – or when informed of such crimes by members of the resistance to the Führer. Manstein's well-rehearsed argument that a successful *Attentat* was bound to end in collapse at the front and civil war within Germany cannot be disproved, but he never reconciled in his own mind the limits to personal loyalty when national honour is at stake. Likewise, he never subscribed to Tresckow's view that the attempt must be made to depose Hitler whether it had any chance of success or not.

Yet where he thought that the reputation of the German Army was being threatened in tribunals after the war he was prepared to protect it tenaciously, often to the extent of disputing the indisputable, such as the German Army's involvement – predominantly by assisting the SD – in the liquidation of the Jews in the Crimea. Acknowledgement of complicity, let alone any form of atonement, would have undermined his fundamental position: to defend the honour of the German Army *at all costs*. With twenty-first-century hindsight and with the benefit of detailed research, of course, it is easy to cast doubt on the veracity of Manstein's evidence at Hamburg and condemn him for his failure to protect the lives of Jews and others in the Soviet Union. He was given the benefit of the doubt in court, but that reservation must remain.

Notwithstanding the judgements at both the International and American tribunals at Nuremberg, Manstein became the very personification – if not a scapegoat – of the Wehrmacht under trial for its cruel misdeeds during the Second World War, particularly on the Eastern Front. He paid a bitter price for his determination to protect his name and that of his soldiers in his sentence at Hamburg. Despite its apparent severity, he was lucky, however, to be tried by a British military court and not be extradited to the Soviet Union to face probable execution.

Manstein's case reflects the very serious moral dilemmas that face a senior commander in war when confronted with unethical, if not illegal, political direction. In this regard, the crucial issue is to consider what practical options were available to him when commanding his army and army group. When in high command during wartime, neither protest nor resignation provides an easy and reliable method of opposition. At what level, for example, is a field commander entitled to confront his commander-in-chief if he disagrees with the latter's orders?[68] Manstein offered to resign many times, but was refused by Hitler until their final parting at the end of March 1944. A commander, as with any man at the front, has a duty and responsibility to 'soldier on' until relieved. In a 'free' country, with safeguards to protect the rights of the individual, he can refuse an illegal order and submit a formal complaint. One course open to Manstein was to join the plot to kill Hitler. The extent to which he was informed of the intended *Attentat* it remains unclear, but had he been asked directly, which remains a hotly disputed matter, there is little doubt that he would have refused to support it.

As a highly professional and accomplished general staff officer and talented operational commander (there remains no contradiction here in the German Army today), Manstein had the priceless ability to anticipate the actions of his opponent, to manoeuvre decisively and to foresee intuitively how best to exploit the resulting situation. An accomplished bridge and chess player, he was always thinking several moves ahead. As with fellow great captains such as Frederick the Great, Napoleon Bonaparte or Robert E. Lee, he was not immune from mistake and misjudgement, but he was nevertheless remarkably and similarly successful for most of his operations and battles. His talents were well summarized in *The Listener*'s review of *Lost Victories:*

> [Manstein] was at home in all types of military activity: a first-class creative staff officer, a dashing and skilled leader of an infantry corps, a thunderbolt when fighting an armoured corps, although he was a guardsman and had no special training in that arm. But it was 'above the corps level', as an army commander and still more as an army group commander that his eye for an opening and his skill in using one revealed his true greatness as a soldier.[69]

Where Manstein foundered was in combating a superior military system that could afford to apply and sustain force in a manner he could not compensate for, demonstrated by the disastrous turn of events on the Eastern Front from Kursk onwards. It was not, as he often thought, just a matter of confronting superior Soviet numbers on the battlefield, nor was defeat solely the consequence of being tied to a fixed, static defence by Hitler. Manstein's blind spot – one common amongst the German generals – was often to underestimate the cunning, flexibility and resolve of the Soviet forces opposing him, and the ability of their leadership on occasion to deceive him, such as at Kiev in November 1943.

Operational level manoeuvre, in which Manstein had few peers, if it has to have any chance of realizing a lasting strategic victory in conventional war must be based on the right, eclectic mix of intelligence, time, space and forces, and indeed luck. A winning operational design is framed by strategy, moreover, and not the other way about. Without the necessary ideas and tools of war, men, machines and other *matériel*, imaginatively and firmly applied, no military campaign let alone a war can be won. Manstein was nearly always short of resources, and thrived in crisis. But fortune not only favours the bold, it also blesses more predictably the well prepared and well supplied. It can never be emphasized enough that no amount of tactical or operational virtuosity (such as Manstein excelled in) can reverse the overall strategic odds or correct basic errors of policy.

The irony and tragedy of Manstein's military success is that it often masked the fundamental weaknesses of Germany's war effort that was outfought strategically as much on factory floors as on fields of battle. All the German sacrifice, the blood of millions let towards meeting the designs of Hitler's criminal wars of aggression – to accept the *lex post facto* Nuremberg Principles – was for naught. No war can be fought and won on a shoestring, whether it is legitimate or not. Hitler's was manifestly not so, a matter that Manstein conveniently ignored until presented with the brutal facts at Nuremberg.

Rising in rank from second lieutenant to field marshal in thirty-five and a half years, although the uniforms changed as ruling regimes came and went, Manstein was trapped throughout his career in a severely illiberal, authoritarian military hierarchy deeply imbued with Prussian-German virtues of honour, loyalty and obedience. Undue deference to the sovereign figure, whether Kaiser Wilhelm II or Hitler, an inherent distrust of democracy at home and a contempt of Bolshevism abroad, are all charges that can be levelled at countless thousands of Germans, Manstein included. Where he broke the mould from the vast majority of his fellow generals was in his ability to argue his case well operationally, and to take on the Führer in the military, though distinctly not in the political, sphere. He showed here a single-mindedness of purpose and robustness of approach that many contemporary senior military leaders, who are rather too politically attuned for the good of their commands, could profitably learn from. With the possible exceptions of his overly optimistic initial assessment of Sixth Army at Stalingrad and his failure to press home his well-founded objections to Operation CITADEL, Manstein gave consistently sound military advice to Hitler. The German supreme commander dismissed the Field Marshal when he realized that his awkward subordinate had seen through him. No dictator can accept sustained criticism, particularly when it becomes public within the echelons of high command.

What of Manstein the man? As an individual, he was widely read, well spoken and good-mannered, as one would expect from one of his background and class. He was interested in art and music, and was above all, a good family man. As a commander, he had his fair share of qualities and faults, although the balance was well towards the former. He was ambitious, bordering on the arrogant, impatient with the slow and intolerant of the less gifted. If he was conceited at times, he kept his vanity under better wraps than Montgomery, whose titanic military ego can scarcely be surpassed. Like his British counterpart, he could be ruthless when required, but his dismissals – or the removals in which he had a close hand (von Sponeck, Lanz and Kempf) – were few and far between. The numbers involved were not exceptional for any army of the Second World War.

On the overwhelmingly positive side, he was articulate verbally and on paper (qualities he shared with Eisenhower), proved himself as an exceptionally good trainer (on a par with Montgomery), possessed an outstanding operational mind, and was consistently steady and calm in crisis. He was as bold tactically as Patton or Rommel, but always kept the bigger, operational picture foremost in mind. Rushing around for activity's sake was not his style: he always focused on achieving not only the task at hand but also the one after next. Although a dedicated planner, he was none the less easily recognized by his troops. He pressed well forward into battle – typically without helmet or bodyguard – to inform his decision-making. He was able to communicate easily with the German *Landser* in the combat zone, often getting out of his staff car to share a cigarette with soldiers near or at the front. He cared deeply for his troops, seeking opportunities to visit the wounded whenever he could. Ironically, the lie of château-generalship was fuelled by his own memoirs, which dwelled too much on the pleasing architecture of France.

His staff was devoted to him, as demonstrated by the roll call of former subordinates who testified on his behalf at Hamburg and who paid their last respects at Dorfmark. He inspired trust and confidence within his command, and widely beyond it. With close intimates, he provided cultured and pleasant company, on and off duty. He did not court publicity and in any case – with the exception of his victory at Sevastopol – the victories of his corps, army or army group were never exploited by the Goebbels' propaganda machine in the manner of Rommel's *Afrika Korps* or *Panzerarmee Afrika*. He was good with the Rumanians for the most part, although they tried him sorely in the Crimea; he struck up a particularly close relationship with their leader, Marshal Ion Antonescu. In this respect Manstein was atypical amongst the senior members of the Wehrmacht, who tended to regard their brother allies-in-arms with scarcely disguised disdain, no doubt taking their cue from Hitler.

In sum, Manstein's life spans the arc between triumph and tragedy, an iconic figure that basked in victory and remained unbowed in defeat. His military achievements were unsurpassed by any German commander of the Second World War. His methods of command, and above all, his brilliant operational ideas, remain rightly as the objects of professional military study today. Although a patriot, his misfortune, along with many millions of fellow Germans, was to serve blindly a criminal regime, whose inherently flawed strategy and terrible wrongdoings he only recognized belatedly. As a senior and well-respected commander-in-chief, he was in a position to question Hitler militarily, which he did repeatedly, but not to challenge him politically. He was never minded to do so, for that lay not in his Prussian blood. He rejected any thought of mutiny, when his soldiers were fighting tenaciously for their *Vaterland*.

After the Second World War Manstein was held to account for many

of the crimes committed on the Eastern Front. Yet to portray him as a
wholly innocent victim of victors' justice would be as unfair and unjust
as to forget the cruel destiny of the millions who did not survive. His
fate, after all, was eight years' imprisonment followed by rehabilitation
as one of the founding fathers of the Bundeswehr in the Cold War, when
a line was drawn under the Wehrmacht's complicity in murder. So he
was neither a Hector nor an Achilles, but deserves none the less to be
remembered if not revered as one of the leading soldiers of the twentieth
century. There is still much to learn from him.

Table of Ranks

Prussian-German	American	British
Fähnrich	Cadet	Officer Cadet/Under Officer
Leutnant	Second Lieutenant	Second Lieutenant
Oberleutnant	First Lieutenant	Lieutenant
Hauptmann	Captain	Captain
Major	Major	Major
Oberstleutnant	Lieutenant Colonel	Lieutenant Colonel
Oberst	Colonel	Colonel
Generalmajor	Brigadier General	Brigadier
Generalleutnant	Major General	Major General
General (der Infanterie etc.)	Lieutenant General	Lieutenant General
Generaloberst	General	General
Generalfeldmarschall	General of the Army	Field Marshal

Chronology of Erich von Manstein

24 November 1887	Born in Berlin, son of General der Artillerie Eduard von Lewinski (1829–1906) and Helene von Lewinski (née von Sperling) (1847–1910). Adopted by his mother's childless sister Hedwig (1852–1925), married to General der Infanterie Georg von Manstein (1844–1913).
1894	Educated at the Strasbourg Lycée.
Easter 1900	Cadet at Plön then Berlin-Lichterfelde (1902–1906). Also served in the Corps of Pages at court of Kaiser Wilhelm II. *Abitur,* 1906.
6 March 1906	Entered active service as a Fähnrich in 3. Garde-Regiment zu Fuß (3rd Prussian Foot Guards), Berlin.
27 January 1907	Promoted Leutnant (with seniority back-dated to 14 June 1905).
1 January–30 June 1910	Seconded to the Military Gymnastics Institute, Wünsdorf, south of Berlin.
1 July 1911	Battalion adjutant and military court officer, 3. Garde-Regiment zu Fuß.
1 October 1913	Entered the War Academy in Berlin for General Staff training.
19 June 1914	Promoted Oberleutnant.
2 August 1914	Regimental adjutant, 2. Garde-Reserve-Infantry-Regiment; fought in Belgium and Eastern Front.
17 November 1914	Severely wounded on the Eastern Front.
17 June 1915	General Staff officer, Army Group Gallwitz in Poland and Serbia.
24 July 1915	Promoted Hauptmann.
19 August 1915	Adjutant, Twelfth Army, Poland and Serbia.
22 January 1916	Staff officer, Eleventh Army on Verdun Front.
July 1916	Staff officer, First Army on the Somme.
1 October 1917	Operations officer (Ia), 4th Cavalry Division in Courland, Estonia.
4 May 1918	Operations officer (Ia), 213th (Assault) Reserve Division on the Western Front.
7 January 1919	Held strength 3. Garde-Regiment zu Fuß pending appointment in the Reichswehr.
14 February 1919	General Staff officer, Grenzschutz Ost (Frontier Defence Command East) at Breslau.

10 June 1919	Personal assistant to General von Lossberg, Chairman, Commission for the Future Army.
13 August 1919	General Staff officer, Gruppenkommando 2, Kassel.
10 June 1920	Married Jutta-Sibylle von Loesch at Loerzendorf, Kreis Namslau, Silesia.
24 April 1921	Birth of daughter Gisela.
1 October 1921	Officer Commanding, 6th Company, 5th Infantry Regiment, Angermünde.
31 December 1922	Birth of son Gero, killed in action on 29 October 1942 at Lake Ilmen, northern Russia.
1 October 1923	General Staff officer at Wehrkreis II (Stettin). Instructor in tactics and military history.
1 October 1924	General Staff officer at Wehrkreis IV (Dresden). Instructor as above.
1 October 1927	General Staff officer, Infantry Leader IV, Magdeburg.
1 February 1928	Promoted Major (with seniority of 1 February 1927).
1 October 1929	Branch chief, Operations Branch of the *Truppenamt*, Berlin.
19 November 1929	Birth of son Rüdiger.
1 April 1931	Promoted Oberstleutnant.
1 October 1932	Commanding Officer IInd (Jäger) Battalion, 4th Infantry Regiment, Kolberg.
1 December 1933	Promoted Oberst.
1 February 1934	Chief of Staff Wehrkreis III, Berlin.
1 July 1935	Head of 1st (Operations) Directorate of the Army General Staff, Berlin.
1 October 1936	Promoted Generalmajor.
6 October 1936	Oberquartiermeister I (deputy chief of staff) to General der Artillerie Ludwig Beck, Chief of the Army General Staff.
4 February 1938	General Officer Commanding 18th Infantry Division at Liegnitz. Retained in previous post until 31 March 1938 during the incorporation of Austria into the German Reich.
1 April 1938	Promoted Generalleutnant.
Sept–Oct 1938	Recalled temporarily into the General Staff as Chief of Staff Twelfth Army during the occupation of the Sudetenland.
May–August 1939	Seconded on a part-time basis to 'Arbeitsgruppe Rundstedt' for planning of the Polish Campaign.
18 August 1939	Chief of Staff of Army Group South (Generaloberst Gerd von Rundstedt) during the Polish campaign.
22 October 1939	Chief of Staff of Army Group A (Rundstedt) in the West (Koblenz).
15 February 1940	Commanding General, XXXVIII Army Corps. Led corps during the French campaign, May–June 1940.
1 June 1940	Promoted General der Infanterie.
July–Sept 1940	Preparations and training for Operation SEA LION. Followed by garrison duties in France.
15 February 1941	Commanding General, LVI Army Corps (Motorized). Engaged in the invasion of the Soviet Union from 22 June 1941.

13 September 1941	Commander-in-Chief, Eleventh Army, in Rundstedt's Army Group South in Russia.
7 March 1942	Promoted Generaloberst (back-dated to 1 January 1942).
1 July 1942	Promoted Generalfeldmarschall after successful capture of Sevastopol.
22 November 1942	Commander-in-Chief, Army Group Don (renamed Army Group South in February 1943) in Russia.
30 March 1944	Relieved of command by Hitler and transferred to the *Führerreserve* (senior officers' reserve pool). Returned home to Liegnitz and remained unemployed for the remainder of the Second World War.
January– *April 1945*	In response to the advancing Red Army, flight with family from Silesia via Berlin and Lower Saxony to Schleswig-Holstein.
8 May 1945	Interned by the British Army in Schleswig-Holstein, Restricted Area F.
23 August 1945	Taken into custody from a military hospital at Heiligenhafen as a prisoner of war and transferred to Munsterlager, near Lüneburg.
18 September 1945	Leading defence witness for the German General Staff at the International Military Tribunal, Nuremberg. Returned to British military custody, late August 1946.
2 September 1946	Transferred to Island Farm Special Camp 11 at Bridgend, via the London District Cage.
October 1947	Transferred to No. 99 Military Hospital at Shugborough Park, Great Haywood, near Stafford.
30 April 1948	Transferred to No. 231 Prisoner of War Hospital at Redgrave Park near Diss, Suffolk.
16 August 1948	Transferred to Munsterlager after a short return to Nuremberg. Subsequently transferred to British Military Hospital, Hamburg, in December 1948.
23 August 1949	Commencement of trial by a British military court at Hamburg as a war criminal.
19 December 1949	Sentenced to 18 years' imprisonment, later reduced to 12 years. Transferred to British Military Prison, Werl, East Westphalia.
Aug 1952–May 1953	Medical parole in Kiel and Allmendingen, near Stuttgart.
7 May 1953	Release from house arrest at Allmendingen.
Summer 1956	Worked as an external expert consultant on conscription and the development of the Bundeswehr on behalf of the defence committees of the Bundestag and Bundesrat, Bonn.
1958	Settled in Irschenhausen (now Icking), near Munich.
1966	Death of Jutta-Sibylle von Manstein.
10 June 1973	Died at Irschenhausen, Bavaria.
15 June 1973	Military funeral at Dorfmark, near Bad Fallingbostel, Lower Saxony.

Decorations and Awards

First World War

Prussian Royal Hohenzollern House Order, Knight's Cross with Swords
Prussian Iron Cross, 1st Class (1914) with 1939 Bar
Prussian Iron Cross, 2nd Class (1914) with 1939 Bar
Württemberg Friedrich Order, Knight 1st Class with Swords
Schaumburg-Lippe Cross for Faithful Service
Hamburg Hanseatic Cross
Cross of Honour for Combatants 1914–1918
Wound Badge in Black – First World War award

Second World War

Knight's Cross of the Iron Cross: 19 July 1940
Oakleaves to the Knight's Cross of the Iron Cross (No. 209): 14 March 1943
Swords to the Knight's Cross of the Iron Cross (No. 59): 30 March 1944
Medal for the Winter Campaign in Russia 1941/1942 ('East Medal')
Crimea Shield in Gold (special version of the standard bronze shield worn only by
    Manstein and Romanian Marshal Ion Antonescu)

Miscellaneous and Foreign Awards

German Armed Forces Long Service Award, 3rd Class (12-year Service Medal)
German Armed Forces Long Service Award, 1st Class (25-year Service Cross)
Austrian Military Merit Cross, 3rd Class with War Decoration
Turkish War Medal ('Iron Crescent')
Romanian Order of Michael the Brave, 2nd Class: 16 July 1942 (Royal Decree No.
    2029)
Romanian Order of Michael the Brave, 3rd Class: 25 November 1941 (Royal
    Decree No. 3258)
Bulgarian Order of St Alexander, 2nd Class, a pre-Second World War award without
    Swords

Selected Writings and Publications

Die andere Seite [*The Other Side*] and *Der Weg zum Weltfrieden* [*The Way to World Peace*], unpublished manuscripts, 1946–1948.

Verlorene Siege (Bonn: Athenäum Verlag, 1955). Published in English as *Lost Victories* in the United Kingdom and United States in 1958. *Verlorene Siege* was also translated and published in France, Spain, Argentina, the Former Republic of Yugoslavia and in the Soviet Union.

'German Operations Planning for the Campaign in the West', *Marine Corps Gazette*, November 1955, 39, 11, pp. 42–52.

'The Campaign in the Crimea 1941–42', *Marine Corps Gazette*, May 1956, 40, 5, pp. 32–47.

'Operation Citadel', *Marine Corps Gazette*, August 1956, 40, 8, pp. 44–47.

'The Development of the Red Army, 1942–45', in B.H. Liddell Hart, ed., *The Soviet Army* (London: Weidenfeld & Nicolson, 1956) pp. 140–152.

'Defensive Operations in Southern Russia 1943–1944', *Marine Corps Gazette*, April 1957, 41, 4, pp. 40–53.

Aus Einem Soldatenleben 1887–1939 (*From a Soldier's Life, 1887–1939*), (Bonn: Athenäum Verlag, 1958).

Acknowledgements

This book would not have been possible without the interest, advice and support of many family members, friends, colleagues and staff of various military and academic institutions, who together have encouraged and sustained me during my research, writing and revision over a five-year period. Notwithstanding their advice, I remain responsible for all opinions stated and for any errors of fact.

I would like to extend my sincere thanks to the Trustees of the Liddell Hart Centre for Military Archives, King's College London, for permission to quote from material for which they hold the copyright. In this regard I am very grateful to Professor Brian Holden Reid, former Resident Historian at the Staff College, Camberley, and Head of War Studies Department at King's, for sponsoring me and advising me at various times from the very inception of this book. Likewise, in Germany I owe great debts of gratitude to the director and members of staff of the *Bundes-Archiv Militär-Archiv* (BA-MA, Federal German Military Archive), Freiburg; the *Militärgeschichtliches Forschungsamt* (MGFA, German Military Historical Research Office), Potsdam; and the *Institut für Zeitgeschichte* (IfZ), Munich. In the United Kingdom, I thank the staff of the Royal Engineers Museum, Library and Archive, Chatham; the Ministry of Defence Library, Whitehall, London; the Prince Consort Library, Aldershot; and the libraries of the Royal Military Academy, Sandhurst, and Defence Academy, Shrivenham. Back in Germany, I received enormous assistance from the Command Library, Rheindahlen; and, last but not least, from the municipal library of Mönchengladbach, who sourced the majority of the German-language texts quoted.

I am particularly grateful to Herr Rüdiger von Manstein and his sister, Frau Gisela Lingenthal, who have put family papers freely at my disposal and kindly given me permission to quote from them. They have also answered my many questions about their father's career, life and times, and provided the majority of the photographs contained in this book. Also in Germany, my long-standing mentor, General Helge Hansen, who arranged my introduction to the Manstein family, has been a great source of military wisdom and support. Major General (Ret'd) David T. Zabecki PhD has given much friendly advice and facilitated my research trips to the BA-MA in Freiburg. In addition, I am grateful to Colonel Dr Hans Ehlert, former director of the MGFA, and to his colleagues Professor Rolf-Dieter Müller, Colonel Dr Winfried Heinemann and Colonel (Ret'd) Karl-Heinz Frieser for their specialist insights. Herr Horst-Karl Guenther-Luebbers has been enthusiastic in providing support. I have also received valuable information from Hans-Adam, Freiherr von Hammerstein-Gesmold; Herr Egbert von Schulzendorff and family in Dorfmark; and from Dr Christian Hartmann of the IfZ.

In the United Kingdom, I would like to thank especially Mr Charles Dick, former Head of the Conflict Studies Research Centre (CSRC) of the Defence Academy for giving me access to his extensive private library, for his expert advice on the Red Army and Soviet military doctrine, and for commenting constructively on all my draft chapters. Without his input this book would be much the poorer. Similarly, I am grateful to Lieutenant General Sir John Kiszely, former Commandant of the Defence Academy, and to Mr Eric Morris, who have read parts of my manuscript, giving generously of their time in the process. Miss Irene Klymchuk, formerly of the Advanced Research and Assessment Group (ARAG) at the Defence Academy, has read several chapters and provided a number of translations from the Russian. For the cartographic support, I thank Mrs Barbara Taylor not only for her advice on mapping products but more particularly for her superb artwork in the sixteen colour maps included in this book. Mrs Susan Hawthorne of Brynteg School, Bridgend, assisted me with my research into Island Farm Special Camp No. 11. Mr John Harding, formerly of Historical Branch (Army), helped me considerably in my early research into the Manstein trial. I am grateful to Judge Jeff Blackett for giving me access to the files of his office (the Judge Advocate General) and for advising on some points of law. Additionally, I thank his colleague, Judge Michael Hunter, for lending me other reference material. Most recently, I have had useful discussions on war crimes with Mr Dan Saxon, Senior Prosecuting Trial Attorney at the International Criminal Tribunal for the former Yugoslavia, and with Miss Emma Browne.

In the Ukraine, where I have travelled extensively on the track of Manstein, I am grateful for the kind support from General of the Army Vitalii Radetsky, Commandant of the Ukrainian National Defence University (UNDU) in Kiev; General of the Army Ivan Svida, commander-in-chief of Ukrainian Armed Forces; and Colonel (Ret'd) Sergei Sidorov, senior lecturer of military history at UNDU. I owe much to my Kiev-based intrepid interpreter and researcher, Miss Ksenia Verzhbytska, who has assisted me on several field trips, advised me on Russian terminology and provided translations of many former Soviet wartime accounts. In the Crimea, I am also grateful to Eduard Rogovskiy for guiding me on a number of occasions around Sevastopol and Simferopol, as I am to Sergei Sidorov for taking me to Feodosia and Kerch.

In the United States, I thank Colonel David Glantz, a leading expert on the Eastern Front and author of numerous standard works on the Red Army and the Great Patriotic War, for his expert comments; I also acknowledge the encouragement and counsel from Mr Rick Atkinson, a Pulitzer Prize winner and noted historian of the Second World War.

Back in Britain, Professors Richard Holmes, Gary Sheffield and Christopher Bellamy, together with Mr Chris Donnelly, have all been very helpful and free with their academic advice. I received friendly interest and support from Michael Orr (Hon. Sec.) and other fellow members of the British Commission for Military History, including Seb Cox, Charles Messenger and John Peaty. General Sir David Richards has encouraged me considerably in the writing of the book, as have Air Marshal Sir Stuart Peach RAF and Lieutenant Generals Sir Nick Parker and Sir Richard Shirreff.

Amongst my former colleagues, I would like to thank Majors Kingsley Donaldson and Donald Smith, Captains Adrian Pask and Rich Roberts; and Mr Colin Gordon, Herr Martin Hajduk and Mr Renn Lang, who have either accompanied me in the

Ukraine or assisted in various ways in Germany. Kingsley Donaldson, Adrian Pask and Ksenia Verzhbytska share the honour of rediscovering Manstein's observation point on El Buron above the Sevastopol battlefield, and helped me confirm his headquarters locations in the Crimea, all defining moments in the preparation of the book.

I would also like to acknowledge the support I have received throughout from my London agent, Robert Dudley, and from my editors at Weidenfeld & Nicolson: initially, Ian Drury, then Alan Sampson; and more recently from Keith Lowe, who has accompanied the book to publication over the last eighteen months.

Finally, within my own family both my daughters Catharine and Stephanie have read chapters and contributed to the bibliography; my son Stuart assisted with the photographic research. My greatest thanks of all, however, goes to my long-suffering wife, Sigi, for her patient forbearance and enduring assistance throughout the 'Manstein' period of *our* lives: whether checking translations, correcting my German correspondence, proof-reading the draft English text and not least for putting up cheerfully with long periods of separation whilst I have been engaged in this project at home and abroad. I could not have asked for greater understanding or personal support: she has made the greatest sacrifice.

April 2010   *Mungo Melvin, Windsor*

Notes

Prologue

1. Quoted by Erich von Manstein, *Lost Victories* (London: Methuen, 1958), ed. and trans. Anthony G. Powell, p. 259. Originally published in German under the title *Verlorene Siege* by Athenäum Verlag, Bonn, in 1955.

2. As explained in a later chapter, Manstein's previous attempts to storm Sevastopol in November and December 1941 had failed miserably with heavy casualties. Throughout the intervening period, the Red Navy had continued to control the Black Sea and reinforce the port, bringing in a steady stream of fresh troops and supplies.

3. The very significant contribution of German air power to the defeat of Soviet forces in the Crimea is detailed in Joel S. A. Hayward, *Stopped at Stalingrad: The Luftwaffe and Hitler's Defeat in the East 1942–1943* (Lawrence: University Press of Kansas, 1998), Chapters 2–4.

4. German losses in the East between 22 June 1941 and 10 September 1942 amounted to no fewer than 336,349 killed, 1,226,941 wounded and 75,990 missing, a total 1,639,280; see General Franz Halder in *The Halder War Diary 1939–1942*, ed. Charles Burdick and Hans-Adolf Jacobsen (London: Greenhill Books, 1988), p. 669.

5. Manstein, *Lost Victories*, p. 259.

6. In the Soviet Union (and in today's Russian Federation and other former Soviet states) the Second World War is referred to as the 'Great Patriotic War'. I am grateful to Ksenia Verzhbytska for drawing my attention to a poem by Vasily Lebedev Kumach, which became one of the most famous Russian songs of the war. It includes the words: 'Let the noble rage/Well up like a wave/It is people's war/It is holy war.'

7. Manstein, *Lost Victories*, p. 280.

8. *Time*, 'Retreat may be masterly, but victory is in the opposite direction', vol. XLIII, no. 2, 10 January, 1944, p. 30.

9. Recalled by Rudolf-Cristoph Freiherr von Gersdorff, *Soldat im Untergang* (Frankfurt am Main: Ullstein, 1977), p. 135. Manstein's alleged statement has gone down into popular history; this conversation is analysed in Chapter 14.

10. Personal communication to the author by Manstein's surviving son, Rüdiger von Manstein, 19 June 2009.

11. There is a rapidly expanding literature in both German and English. Three recent studies include: Geoffrey P. Megargee,

War of Annihilation: Combat and Genocide on the Eastern Front, 1941 (Lanham, Md: Rowman & Littlefield, 2006); Wolfram Wette, *The Wehrmacht: History, Myth, Reality* (Cambridge, Mass.: Harvard University Press, 2007, originally published as *Die Wehrmacht–Feindbilder, Vernichtungskrieg, Legenden* (Frankfurt am Main: S. Fischer Verlag, 2002), Dieter Pohl, *Die Herrschaft der Wehrmacht; Deutsche Militärbesatzung und einheimische Bevölkerung in der Sowjetunion 1941–1944* (Munich: R. Oldenbourg Verlag, 2008). For a wider view, see Rolf-Dieter Müller and Hans-Erich Volkmann (eds.), *Die Wehrmacht: Mythos und Realität* (Munich: R. Oldenbourg Verlag, 1999).

12. Sir James Butler, editor of the British official *History of the Second World War*, reminds us that contemporary official records must, of course, carry far greater authority than the statements of individuals made after the event and subject to intentional or unintentional distortion, though statements of the latter kind have their use and interest: see J. R. M Butler's foreword to Ronald Wheatley, *Operation Sea Lion: German Plans for the Invasion of England 1939–1942* (Oxford: Clarendon Press, 1958), p. v.

13. Dwight D. Eisenhower, *Crusade in Europe* (Garden City, NY: Doubleday, 1948); Omar N. Bradley, *A Soldier's Story* (New York: Henry Holt, 1951); Field Marshal The Viscount Montgomery of Alamein, *The Memoirs* (London: Collins, 1958).

14. Marshal Sergei Sokolov, USSR Minister of Defence, *Battles Hitler Lost and the Soviet Marshals Who Won Them* (New York: Jove Books, 1988); *The Memoirs of Marshal Zhukov* (London: Johnathan Cape, 1971); (first published in the USSR under the title *Reminiscences and Ruminations by Novosty Press, Moscow, 1969)*, pp. 423–424. V. I. Chuikov, *The Battle for Stalingrad* (New York: Holt, Rinehart & Wilson, 1964) and *The End of the Third Reich* (Moscow: Progress Publishers, 1978).

15. Kenneth Macksey has written unreferenced biographies of Kesselring and Guderian. His revised *Guderian: Panzer General* (2nd edn.) (London: Greenhill Books and Mechanicsburg, Pa: Stackpole Books, 2003) remains particularly useful.

16. Siegfried Westphal, *The German Army in the West* (London: Cassell, 1951) [originally published in Germany under the title *Heer in Fesseln* in 1950], p. 32. General Frederick von Mellenthin stated: 'All who knew Field Marshal von Manstein, or had any dealings with him in war or peace, admired his rare ability, and that was especially the feeling of those who served under him. Certainly good fortune often smiled on him, but it is well to remember that fortune favours only the most capable in the long run. And without doubt Manstein was among the most capable of soldiers. He was truly a great general.' See F. W. von Mellenthin, *German Generals of World War II As I Saw Them* (Norman: University of Oklahoma Press, 1977), pp. 38–39.

17. Quoted by Guido Knopp and Jörg Müllner, 'The Strategist – Erich von Manstein', trans. Angus McGeoch, in Guido Knopp (ed.),

Hitler's Warriors (Stroud: Sutton, 2005), p. 131.

18. B. H. Liddell Hart, *The Other Side of the Hill, Germany's Generals their rise and fall, with their own account of military events 1939–1945* (London: Cassell 1948), revised and enlarged edition published in 1951, p. 94. [Page reference to Macmillan Papermac edition, 1993.]

19. Recent detractors of Manstein include: Oliver von Wrochem, *Erich von Manstein: Vernichtungskrieg und Geschichtspolitik* (Paderborn: Schöningh, 2006) and Marcel Stein, *Field Marshal von Manstein, The Janus Head: A Portrait* (Solihull: Helion, 2007).

20. The first part of R. T. Paget, *Manstein: His Campaigns and His Trial* (London: Collins, 1951) is biographical. Apart from Stein's and Wrochem's recent studies, see also Benoît Lemay, *Erich von Manstein: Le stratège de Hitler* (Paris: Librairie Académique Perrin, 2006).

21. I have borrowed this approach from Brian Holden Reid, *Robert E. Lee* (London: Weidenfeld & Nicolson, 2005), pp. 22–23, in which he distinguishes carefully between his subject and the cause of the Confederacy.

22. For more detail on 'military genius', see Carl von Clausewitz, *On War*, ed. and trans. Michael Howard and Peter Paret (New York: Everyman's Library, 1993), Book One, Chapter 3.

1. Son of Prussia

1. Described by Alexander Stahlberg, *Bounden Duty* (London: Brassey's, 1990), pp. 400–406.

2. This description of Manstein's early life is drawn largely from the first volume of his memoirs, *Aus einem Soldatenleben 1887–1939* (Bonn: Athenäum Verlag, 1958), augmented by Joachim Engelmann, *Manstein: Stratege und Truppenführer* (Friedberg: Podzun-Pallas-Verlag, 1981). Additional sources include the privately published manuscript of Martha von Sperling-Manstein, *Aus einer Kindheit vor der Jahrhundertwende* (Allmendingen, March 1996) and other personal papers from the von Manstein and von Sperling families.

3. David Fraser, *Frederick the Great* (London: Penguin, 2000), pp. 352–355 and 493.

4. Gordon A. Craig, *The Politics of the Prussian Army 1640–1945* (Oxford: University Press, 1964), p. 30.

5. Prussian and German military ranks above the rank of colonel up to the end of the Second World War did not match those of the British or United States Armies. There was no rank of brigadier or brigadier general. A German lieutenant general (*Generalleutnant*), for example, often only equated to a British or US major general; a general of infantry, artillery or engineers to a lieutenant general; and a colonel general to a (full) general. A *General-Feldmarschall*, as Manstein became in July 1942, did equate to 'five-star' British field marshal or US General of the Army. There were no fixed ranks for appointments, either. A divisional commander could equally well be either a *Generalmajor* or a *Generalleutnant*.

6. Manstein, *Aus einem Soldatenleben*, p. 14.

7. Ibid., p. 13.
8. Ibid., p. 16–17.
9. Ibid., p. 17.
10. Manstein's wife was a source of indefatigable support to him in the inter-war years, throughout the Second World War, and during his subsequent internment, imprisonment and retirement. Manstein outlived her by seven years, after a marriage of forty-six years (1920–66). In marked contrast, Montgomery's marriage to his treasured wife, Betty, was short-lived. She died in 1937 from blood poisoning after only ten years of matrimony.
11. Sperling-Manstein, pp. 62, 86–88; 99.
12. Manstein, *Aus einem Soldatenleben*, p. 21.
13. An extract from 'Der Weg zum Weltfrieden' is contained in Erich von Manstein, *Soldat im 20. Jahrhundert*, ed. Rüdiger von Manstein and Theodor Fuchs (Bonn: Bernard & Graefe Verlag, 1997), pp. 255–268.
14. This state of affairs represents a piece of unifying historic symbolism quite evident to some but a perplexing, tax-wasting merry-go-round for others. See *The Times* (26 April 2006), p. 13: 'EU travelling circus comes to town and loses £105m for taxpayer. The French city of Strasbourg may have been fleecing the European Parliament for 25 years ...'
15. The sequence of classes for Manstein was completion of the *Unter-* and *Obertertia* (Lower and Upper Third years) at Plön, followed by the *Unter-* and *Obersekunda* (Lower and Upper Second) and then the *Unter-* and *Oberprima*, which culminated with the *Abitur* (leaving examination) at

Gross-Lichterfelde in Berlin.
16. Sperling-Manstein, p.130.
17. The cadet schools were closed in 1920 under the terms of the Treaty of Versailles. The *Hauptkadettenanstalt* in Berlin-Gross-Lichterfelde then became an educational institute of the Weimar Republic until the SS took it over in 1933 as a barracks for the Führer's bodyguard, the SS *Leibstandarte Adolf Hitler*. Many of the buildings were destroyed in 1945, but the site was redeveloped during the Allied occupation of Berlin as the Andrews Barracks of the United States Army. In 1994 it became a site of the Federal German Archive, and now houses the archives of the former German Democratic Republic.
18. For a detailed account of von Rundstedt's life, including his military education, see Charles Messenger, *The Last Prussian: A Biography of Field Marshal Gerd von Rundstedt 1875–1953* (London: Brassey's, 1991). See also Günther Blumentritt, *Von Rundstedt: The Soldier and the Man* (London: Odhams Press, 1952).
19. The *Abitur* remains the highest level of German school-leaving certificate. It represents the broad equivalent of British A-levels but is nearer in concept to the French Baccalaureate.
20. A notable exception was Douglas Haig, field marshal and commander of the British Expeditionary Force on the Western Front from December 1915, who had attended Oxford University (Brasenose College) in the early 1880s.
21. Heinz Guderian, *Panzer Leader* (London: Michael Joseph, 1952), p. 16.

22. Manstein, *Aus einem Soldatenleben*, p. 22.

23. Ibid., pp. 22–23. It is not clear which institutions Manstein had in mind here. Whilst the British Army had no direct equivalent for schoolboys – the job of producing the nation's future leaders being left to the major public schools – the nearest parallel in Britain was probably the Royal Naval College at Osborne on the Isle of White, the entry age for which was 12 years. The college at Osborne ran from 1903–21 as the junior department of the Royal Naval College at Dartmouth. Boys stayed at Osborne for two or three years before transferring to Dartmouth at 14 or 15. The most famous cadets included the royal princes Edward and Albert, the future kings Edward VIII and George VI, and Earl Louis Mountbatten.

24. See John C. G. Röhl, *The Kaiser and His Court: Wilhelm II and the Government of Germany* (Cambridge: University Press, 1994), pp. 70–106, for a detailed description of the German court, including detailed lists of precedence and the costs involved.

25. Manstein, *Aus einem Soldatenleben*, p. 34.

26. Sperling-Manstein, pp. 123–124.

27. Manstein, *Aus einem Soldatenleben*, p. 35.

28. A point made by Eckard Michels, *Der Held von Deutsch-Ostafrika: Paul von Lettow-Vorbeck* (Paderborn: Ferdinand Schöningh, 2008), p. 48.

29. Manstein, *Aus einem Soldatenleben*, p. 42.

30. Manstein states incorrectly (*Aus einem Soldatenleben*, p. 44) that the famous earthquake took place a 'couple of years' after his brief visit to Messina. In fact, it took place less than three months later on 28 December 1908.

31. Engelmann, *Manstein: Stratege und Truppenführer*, p. 19.

32. For example, see General Bronsart von Schellendorf, *The Duties of the General Staff* (trans. for the General Staff, War Office) (London: His Majesty's Stationery Office, 1905).

33. For an account of the evolution of the staff ride as a training method, see Brigadier R. A. M. S. Melvin, 'Contemporary Battlefield Tours and Staff Rides: A Military Practitioner's View', *Defence Studies*, vol. 5, no.1 (March 2005), pp. 59–80.

34. Cited by Michels, p. 55.

35. See Jehuda L. Wallach, *The Dogma of the Battle of Annihilation* (Westport, Conn. and London: Greenwood Press, 1986), pp. 103–106.

36. Messenger, p. 12. Messenger's research on German general staff training at the beginning of the twentieth century rests on the Edmonds papers held in the Liddell Hart Centre for Military Archives (LHCMA).

37. See Johannes Hürter, *Hitlers Heerführer: Die deutschen Oberbefehlshaber im Krieg gegen die Sowjetunion 1941/42* (Munich: R. Oldenbourg Verlag, 2007), pp. 55–57, for a description of the *Kriegsakadamie*.

38. Macksey, *Guderian*, p. 7.

39. Manstein, *Aus einem Soldatenleben*, p. 7.

40. Significantly, the tradition of safeguarding sufficient time for individual study and self-development has been preserved in the German Armed Forces Command and Staff College (the

Führungsakademie) at Hamburg today, an example that British and American staff colleges would do well to emulate.

41. The German military's institutional lack of attention to strategy is highlighted eloquently by Williamson Murray in his foreword to Geoffrey P. Megargee, *Inside Hitler's High Command* (Lawrence: University Press of Kansas, 2000), pp. x–xi: '[The Germans] worshipped at the altar of operational manoeuvre to the exclusion of wider strategy. They seemed to believe that everything would run into place if they could just win enough battles, but they failed to recognize the economic, political, or geographical limits on the ability to do so.'

42. BA-MA, MSg 1/1830. 'Erinnerungen an Feldmarschall von Manstein als dessen 1. Ordonnanzoffizier' (undated), pp. 14–15.

43. Letter held in the private possession of Rüdiger von Manstein.

44. The development of German war planning prior to 1914, including the reality behind the so-called Schlieffen Plan, is covered in detail by Hew Strachan, *The First World War*, vol. i, *To Arms* (Oxford: University Press, 2001), pp. 163–180.

45. See Barbara Tuchman, *August 1914* (London: Constable, 1962), pp. 247–249. Further details are given in the Bryce Report of the Committee on Alleged German Outrages (12 May 1915). Commissioned by the British Government, the committee of Viscount James Bryce (a former British ambassador in Washington) was hardly neutral in its composition, if not in its findings. Regarded as credible in the United States, however, it did much to damage Germany's reputation there and in the wider international community. For a more recent study, see John Horne and Alan Kramer, *German Atrocities, 1914: A History of Denial* (New Haven and London: Yale University Press, 2001), pp. 30–35 and 97–98.

46. J. W. Wheeler-Bennett, *Hindenburg: The Wooden Titan* (London: Macmillan, 1936), p. 16.

47. East Prussia is now divided between Poland and the Russian Kaliningrad *Oblast*. Modern place names are as follows: Elbing, Elbąg (Poland); Allenburg, Druzhba; Wehlau, Snamensk (both in Kaliningrad *Oblast*).

48. Quoted by Engelmann, *Manstein: Stratege und Truppenführer*, pp. 21–22.

49. Meanwhile, Manstein's place as adjutant in 2nd Guards Reserve Regiment was taken by Friedrich Herrlein, a younger brother officer of the prestigious 3rd Foot Guards.

50. Manstein, *Aus einem Soldatenleben*, pp. 44–45.

51. See David T. Zabecki, 'Fritz von Lossberg' in Major General David T. Zabecki (ed.), *Chief of Staff: The Principal Officers Behind History's Great Commanders*, vol. 1, *Napoleonic Wars to World War I* (Annapolis, RI: U.S. Naval Institute, 2008), pp. 174–186. I am very grateful to Major General (Ret'd) Zabecki PhD for bringing his research on Lossberg to my attention.

52. Introduced on 1 December 1916. See Timothy T. Lupfer, 'The Dynamics of Doctrine: The

Changes in German Tactical Doctrine during the First World War', *Leavenworth Papers*, no. 4, US Army Command and Staff College, July 1981, pp. 11–21.

53. Manstein, *Aus einem Soldatenleben*, pp. 53–54. Manstein omits to give any geographical detail, but during the course of the battle the French – at huge cost – had managed by 5 May 1917 to capture a 4-km stretch of front along the Chemins des Dames ridge.

54. Letter held in the private possession of Rüdiger von Manstein.

55. Sir John Wheeler-Bennett, *Brest-Litovsk: the Forgotten Peace, March 1918* (London: W. W. Norton 1969), pp. 93 and 257.

56. The Germany Army's new offensive doctrine, *The Attack in Position Warfare* (1 January 1918) is described by Lupfer, pp. 41–46.

57. A very comprehensive monograph on Ludendorff's attempt to win the war in the west is David T. Zabecki, *The German 1918 Offensives* (London and New York: Routledge, 2006).

58. BA-MA, PH 81/453.213. Infanterie-Division Abt. Ia Nr. 97/VI pers. Div.St.Qu., Ende Juni 1918: 'Gefechtsbericht für die Durchbruchsschlacht westlich Reims 27. Mai-18. Juni 1918'.

59. Letter held in the private possession of Rüdiger von Manstein.

60. The significance of the battle and the events of 18 July 1918 in particular are explained in Steven H. Newton, *Hitler's Commander: Field Marshal Walther Model–Hitler's Favorite General* (Cambridge, Mass: De Capo Press, 2006), pp. 37–40; but also see Gary Sheffield, *Forgotten Victory* (London: Headline, 2001), pp. 198–202, who provides strong evidence to the effect that 'Amiens marks a true turning point in the Western Front'. Von Lossberg, incidentally, considered the shock of 18 July 1918 as the more significant.

61. Newton, *Hitler's Commander*, p. 41.

62. Ernst Jünger, *Storm of Steel*, trans. Michael Hofmann (London: Allen Lane, 2003), pp. 275–276. First published in German as *In Stahlgewittern* in 1920, Jünger revised his work successively. Hofmann's admirable new translation is based on the edition contained in *Sämtliche Werke*, vol.1, *Der Erste Weltkrieg* (Stuttgart: Klett-Cotta, 1978).

2. A Rising Star: The Reichswehr Years

1. Colonal General Hans von Seeckt, founder and commander of the Reichswehr (1919–26). Quoted by James S. Corum, *The Roots of Blitzkrieg: Hans von Seeckt and German Military Reform* (Lawrence: University Press of Kansas, 1992), p. 31.

2. The American 1st Infantry Division had taken part in the famous 'race to Sedan' during the last two weeks of the war. See Robert H. Ferrell, *America's Deadliest Battle: Meuse-Argonne 1918* (Lawrence: University Press of Kansas, 2007), pp. 139–142.

3. Manstein, *Aus einem Soldatenleben*, p. 60.

4. BA-MA, PH 8 1/511. Gruppe Soden Generalkommando V. Reservekorps K.H.Qu., den 11.11.1918. 'Demobilmachungs- und Rückzugsbefehle der 213. Infanterie-Division, Mai-Dez 1918.'

5. Most of the operational staff work held in BA-MA file PH 8 1/511 reflects this.

6. Manstein, *Aus einem Soldatenleben*, p. 61.

7. John W. Wheeler-Bennett, *The Nemesis of Power: The German Army in Politics 1918–1945*, 2nd edn. (London: Palgrave Macmillan, 2005), p. 27; John W. Wheeler-Bennett, *Hindenburg: The Wooden Titan* (first pub. 1936) (London: Macmillan, 1967), p. 209.

8. Manstein, *Aus einem Soldatenleben*, p. 62.

9. Signed by Wilhelm II at Amerongen, the Netherlands, on 28 November 1918.

10. Manstein, *Aus einem Soldatenleben*, p. 51.

11. EK [Iron Cross] II, 5 October 1914; EK I, 13 November 1915; Ritterkreuz [Knight's Cross] des Königlichen Hausordens von Hohenzollern mit Schwertern, 22 April 1918.

12. In comparison, the first time Field Marshal Montgomery ever served in a corps, army or army group headquarters was when he commanded one during the Second World War, reflecting not only a traditional British focus on regimental duty in small wars but also a lack of emphasis on professional staff development, an enduring anti-intellectual bias.

13. Strictly speaking, one should differentiate consistently between the *Reichsheer* and the *Reichswehr*. Most Germans associated their army with the *Reichswehr* and Manstein referred to the *Reichswehr* rather than the *Reichsheer* throughout his memoirs. Following the example of its subject, this biography therefore uses *Reichswehr* rather than *Reichsheer*.

14. After serving on the Western Front as chief of staff of a corps, von Seeckt was employed on the Eastern Front successively as chief of staff to General von Mackensen's Eleventh Army in the victorious summer campaign of 1915 against the Russians in Galicia; as chief of staff of von Mackensen's Austro-Bulgarian-German army group, which defeated Serbia in the autumn of 1915; as chief of staff of the Austrian Archduke Josef's army group, which fought the Russians and Rumanians in the summer and autumn of 1916. See Corum, *The Roots of Blitzkrieg*, pp. 26–29, for further biographic details.

15. Wheeler-Bennett, *The Nemesis of Power*, pp. 85–87.

16. Manstein, *Aus einem Soldatenleben*, p. 46.

17. Wheeler-Bennett, *The Nemesis of Power*, p. 45.

18. Corum, *Roots of Blitzkrieg*, p. 171.

19. Quoted by Hans Kohn, *The Mind of Germany* (London: Macmillan, 1965), p. 310.

20. Martin Kitchen, *A Military History of Germany from the Eighteenth Century to the Present Day* (London: Weidenfeld & Nicolson, 1975), p. 237.

21. Ibid., pp. 234–236.

22. Manstein, *Aus einem Soldatenleben*, p. 67. Manstein may have been confusing July 1919 with the French reoccupation of the Rhineland in 1923, in which colonial troops were prominent.

23. Ibid., pp. 69–70.

24. Ibid., pp. 74–76.

25. Ibid., pp. 77–78.

26. Ibid., p. 47.

27. Of Jutta-Sibylle's one elder and four younger brothers, two fell

during the Second World War. Her eldest brother, Konrad, died in March 1940 as a result of the severe wounds he had received during the campaign in Poland the previous September. Konrad's son, Hans-Friedrich, fostered by the Mansteins throughout the war, was killed in action in April 1945 as a 17-year-old tank gunner. Such was the fate and tragedy of so many German families – and of many other nations too – that cut across all classes and generations.

28. Quoted by John Lee, *The Warlords: Hindenburg and Ludendorff* (London: Weidenfeld & Nicolson, 2005), p. 36. In his translated memoirs, *Out of My Life* (London: Cassell, 1920), p. 57, Hindenburg noted simply: 'I found in my wife a loving mate who shared with me loyally and untiringly my joys and sorrows, my cares and labours. She presented me with a son and two daughters.' That was it. In contrast, Hindenburg characterized famously his relations with his chief of staff General Ludendorff as being a 'happy marriage' (p. 84) and described their work together in great detail.

29. Manstein, *Aus einem Soldatenleben*, p. 49.

30. Walther von Schultzendorff, 'Der Mensch und der Soldat: Erich von Manstein' in *Nie Ausser Dienst: [Festschrift] Zum achtzigsten Geburtstag von Generalfeldmarschall Erich von Manstein*, (Köln: von der Markus Verlagsgesellschaft, 1967), p. 17.

31. Manstein, *Aus einem Soldatenleben*, p. 50.

32. The full quote attributed to Samuel Johnson is: 'Norway, too, has noble prospects; and Lapland

is remarkable for prodigious noble wild prospects. But, Sir, let me tell you, the noblest prospect which a Scotchman ever sees is the high road that leads him to England!' Quoted in James Boswell, *Life of Dr Johnson* (1791). Entry for 6 July 1763.

33. Manstein, *Aus einem Soldatenleben*, p. 85.

34. Franz von Gaertner, *Die Reichswehr in der Weimarer Republik: Erlebte Geschichte* (Darmstadt: Fundus Verlag, 1969), p. 83.

35. Corum, *The Roots of Blitzkrieg*, p. 47, makes the pertinent observation that as a result of there being no Allied limit on the number of NCOs, in 1922 the Reichswehr had 17,940 senior NCOs (sergeants and above) and 30,740 junior NCOs (lance corporals and corporals). Thus, when taking the 4,000 officers into account, more than half of the remaining structure (96,000) comprised either junior or senior NCOs.

36. '*Nicht ein Söldnerheer, sondern ein Führerheer.*' Quoted by Wheeler-Bennett, *The Nemesis of Power*, p. 101.

37. Manstein, *Aus einem Soldatenleben*, p. 86.

38. Ibid.

39. Corum, *Roots of Blitzkrieg*, pp. 39–40.

40. *Heeresdienstvorschrift* 487, *Führung und Gefecht der verbundenen Waffen*. Part 1 was published in September 1921; Part 2 in June 1923. For all his valuable analysis, Corum's translation of this publication as 'Leadership and Battle with Combined Arms' is clumsy: 'leadership' is best expressed in German as '*Menschenführung*'; battle by 'Schlacht'. Matthias

Strohn, 'Hans von Seeckt and His Vision of a "Modern Army"', *War in History*, 2005, 12 (3), p. 326, perhaps renders it less literarily but more neatly as 'Leadership and Command of Combined Arms'. In his article, Strohn gives a useful modern German perspective of the achievement of von Seeckt.

41. For a reliable English translation, see *On the German Art of War: Truppenführung*, ed. and trans. Bruce Condell and David T. Zabecki (London and Boulder, Colo.: Lynne Rienner Publishers, 2001).

42. There is much more to an army's make-up than its *conceptual* component, one of the principal foundations of fighting power. It and the *physical* component (organization, training and logistics) have to be underpinned by a *moral* component in which command, leadership and cohesion all have important parts to play. For all the emphasis on modernization, an army's history and heritage remain important in instilling the right spirit and in retaining traditional virtues. Unsurprisingly, the Reichswehr strove to retain various links to the imperial army of the First World War. Many aspects of dress were maintained, including the field grey uniform and the iconic coal-scuttle steel helmet, the *Stahlhelm*. More significantly, affiliations to the recently disbanded imperial regiments were fostered. Each unit had to keep the history, heritage and spirit of a former regiment alive, acting as the 'bearer of tradition' (*Traditionsträger*) in a nationwide military association.

43. Manstein, *Aus einem Soldatenleben*, p. 87.

44. Corum, *Roots of Blitzkrieg*, pp. 89–94.

45. Personal communication from Rüdiger von Manstein to the author, 3 July 2009.

46. Manstein, *Aus einem Soldatenleben*, pp. 90–91.

47. Ibid., p. 91.

48. Ibid., pp. 91–92. Manstein's description of general staff trips has an enduring quality. The present author, when undertaking German general staff training in the mid 1980s, on various tours experienced a similar mixture of operational theory, practical tactics and 'cultural visits', together with the odd diversion to a local hostelry to take stock of the day's training.

49. Manstein, *Aus einem Soldatenleben*, pp. 92–93.

50. Author's interview with Gisela Lingenthal at Bad Honnef on 4 March 2007.

51. *Chef der Heeresleitung*.

52. Adolf Heusinger, 'Der Unbequeme Operative Kopf: Ein Gespräch über Generalfeldmarschall v. Manstein' in *Nie Ausser Dienst*, p. 36.

53. After the Second World War Kammhuber became the first General Inspector of the Luftwaffe in 1956.

54. Manstein, *Aus einem Soldatenleben*, pp. 108–109. Kurt Freiherr von Hammerstein-Equord (1878–1943) is said to have advised: 'Keep yourself free of detail. Keep a few clever people for that. But give yourself a lot of time to think about matters and to be clear yourself. Make sure that your thoughts are carried out. Only in this way can you command correctly.' Quoted from the family history of Hans-

Adam Freiherr von Hammerstein, to whom I am grateful for supplying this information.

55. Soviet Army doctrine expounded in *Field Regulations (Provisional)* 1936 (PV-36) likewise had a forward-looking and enduring quality, and in many respects (such as in the handling of armoured forces) was more advanced than its German counterpart.

56. The need for combined arms co-ordination in the execution of the attack was later detailed in *Truppenführung* §329–348 (pp. 92–98).

57. The so-called *A-[Aufstellungs-] Heer*, corresponding to the army to be raised in the future, as opposed to a standing army.

58. Letter written on 23 March 1930 in Berlin. Quoted in Wilhelm Keitel, *General Feldmarschall: Verbrecher oder Offizier, Erinnerungen, Briefe, Dokumente des Chefs des Oberkommandos der Wehrmacht* ed. Walter Görlitz (Schnellbach: Verlag Siegfried Bublies, 1998), pp. 56–57.

59. Manstein, *Aus einem Soldatenleben*, p. 119.

60. Ibid., p. 121. Manstein was referring here to Article 2 of the Annex to the Hague Convention (IV), 'Regulations Respecting the Laws and Customs of War on Land'. See Adam Roberts and Richard Guelff (eds.), *Documents on the Laws of War*, 3rd edn. (Oxford: University Press, 2000), p. 73.

61. Manstein, *Aus einem Soldatenleben*, p. 135.

62. Ibid., p. 139.

63. Ibid., pp. 140–141. I am grateful to Ksenia Verzhbytska for supplying details of General Yegorov and his wife.

64. Ibid., p. 141.

65. Ibid., pp. 141–142.

66. See Shimon Naveh's excellent essay on Tukhachevsky in Harold Shukman (ed.), *Stalin's Generals* (London: Weidenfeld & Nicolson, 1993), pp. 255–273. Manstein *(Aus einem Soldatenleben*, pp. 142–143) also left an amusing anecdote. In addition to his professional talents, Tukhachevsky was clearly a charmer and womanizer. When at the opera to see a performance of Tchaikovsky's *Queen of Spades (Pique Dame)*, Manstein observed him with his escort. 'But it was not the same lady we had met at dinner with the Voroshilovs,' he noted. Seeking explanation, 'We were told that Tukhachevsky had two wives. When he was invited by the ambassador, it was always enquired as to which of the two one should expect.'

67. Letter reproduced in the guidebook of the Berlin-Karlshorst Museum, *Erinnerungen an einen Krieg (Memories of a War)* (Berlin: Jovis Verlagsbüro, 1997), p. 65. I am grateful to Irene Klymchuk for providing a translation.

68. Manstein, *Aus einem Soldatenleben*, p. 158.

69. Keitel, p. 60, for example, noted: 'Western, in other words European, Russia resembles a huge building site.... The Red Army is at the centre of the state, and springboard for the highest offices in the land.'

70. 'Philosophy and Tactics of Armoured Warfare', a Summary Report of a conference of tactical warfare during the period 19 to 22 May 1980 hosted by the BDM Corporation under the auspices of the Director of Net Assessment, Office of the Secretary of Defense, p. 11.

3. Serving Under Hitler

1. Manstein, *Aus einem Soldatenleben*, p. 179. All references to Manstein in this chapter are to this memoir unless otherwise stated.
2. Bismarck's speech of December 1876, quoted by W. N. Medlicott, *Bismarck and Modern Germany* (London: English Universities Press, 1965), p. 125.
3. No less a German national hero than Graf August-Wilhelm Neidhardt von Gneisenau had commanded the fortress in close co-operation with Joachim Nettelbeck, the town's mayor, on whose autobiography the film script was based.
4. Field Marshal Viscount Slim, *Defeat into Victory* (London: Cassell, 1952), p. 3.
5. Manstein p. 160.
6. Ibid., p. 161.
7. Author's interview with Gisela Lingenthal at Bad Honnef on 4 March 2007.
8. Manstein, p. 162.
9. Ibid., p. 163
10. This much oversimplified summary of the major political events of 1932–33 serves only to provide some context for Manstein's recollections and observations. For a detailed analysis, there is a vast literature to choose from. For a perspective on the Reichswehr's involvement, see, for example, F. L. Carsten, *The Reichswehr and Politics 1918–1933* (Oxford: Clarendon Press, 1966), pp. 364–405; Craig, *The Politics of the Prussian Army*, pp. 427–467; Wheeler-Bennett, *The Nemesis of Power*, pp. 182–286. Good general accounts are contained in Ian Kershaw, *Hitler 1889–1936: Hubris* (London: Allen Lane, 1998), pp.

379–427; Richard J. Evans, *The Coming of the Third Reich* (London: Penguin, 2004), pp. 247–349; Anthony Read, *The Devil's Disciples* (London: Pimlico, 2004), pp. 223–272. An authoritative German account is given by Ralf Georg Reuth, *Hitler: Eine politische Biographie* (Munich: Piper Verlag, 2003), pp. 235–303.
11. Manstein, p. 173.
12. Ibid., p. 174.
13. Ibid., p. 177.
14. Ibid., pp. 178–179.
15. Quoted by John Tolland, *Adolf Hitler* (Toronto: Ballantine, 1977), pp. 424–425.
16. Manstein, p. 178.
17. Ibid., p. 179.
18. Evans, p. 381.
19. Manstein, pp. 185–186.
20. Kershaw, *Hubris*, p. 505.
21. Klaus-Jürgen Müller, *Das Heer und Hitler: Armee und nationalsozialistisches Regime 1933–1940* (Stuttgart: Deutsche Verlags-Anstalt, 1969) [2nd edn, 1988], p. 83.
22. Both Manstein's covering letter and memorandum are reproduced in full as Document 4 in Müller, *Das Heer und Hitler*, pp. 593–598, from which all quotations are taken.
23. Knopp (ed.), *Hitler's Warriors*, p. 139.
24. Klaus-Jürgen Müller, *Generaloberst Ludwig Beck: eine Biographie* (Paderborn: Schöningh, 2009), p. 143.
25. Müller, *Das Heer und Hitler*, pp. 594 and 596. I am grateful to Rüdiger von Manstein for reminding me of the wider context of his father's protest.
26. Manstein, pp. 186–187. Additional information from an interview conducted on 4 March 2007 with

Gisela Lingenthal at Bad Honnef.

27. Manstein, p. 198.

28. Fritsch was appointed as commander-in-chief of the army in June 1935, and promoted to colonel general on 20 April 1936, Hitler's birthday.

29. Manstein, p. 208.

30. Kershaw, *Hubris*, p. 519.

31. Manstein, p. 209.

32. Ibid., pp. 211–212.

33. Read, pp. 220–221.

34. Craig, p. 465.

35. Manstein, p. 214.

36. Craig, p. 479.

37. Manstein, p. 215.

38. Carsten, pp. 310–311 and Kershaw, *Hubris*, p. 525.

39. Manstein, p. 216.

40. Ibid., pp. 216–218.

41. In the famous Ulm court case of September 1930, in which young lieutenants were prosecuted on account of spreading National Socialist thinking, their complaints about the slow promotion system – 'people know nothing of the tragedy of the four words "twelve years as subalterns" ' – in the Reichswehr aroused much public sympathy. See Wheeler-Bennett, *Nemesis of Power*, pp. 213–220.

42. Manstein, pp. 220–222.

43. Siegfried Westphal, *Erinnerungen* (Mainz: v. Hase & Koehler Verlag, 1975), pp. 55 and 60–61.

44. Manstein, pp. 223–226. Manstein described Model as a '*Hecht im Karpfenteich*'.

45. Ibid., p. 227.

46. Ibid., p. 229.

47. In painting the political scene, I have drawn here extensively on the analysis by Richard Bussel, *Nazism and War* (London: Weidenfeld & Nicolson, 2004), pp. 52–58. Hitler's text is reproduced in Wilhelm Treue, 'Hitlers

Denkschrift zum Vierjahresplan 1936', *Vierteljahrshefte für Zeitgeschichte*, vol. 3 (1955).

48. Quoted by Klaus-Jürgen Müller, *Armee und Drittes Reich 1933– 1939: Darstellung und Dokumentation* (Paderborn: Schöningh, 1987), p. 102.

49. Manstein, p. 229. In some respects the evidence points strongly otherwise. For example, Fritsch is recorded in the Hossbach Memorandum as ordering a study during the winter of 1937 into an attack into Czechoslovakia, and specifically to investigate the overcoming of the Czech border defences.

50. Ibid. But also see Müller's detailed analysis in *Beck*, pp. 238–240, which suggests that a strategic offensive against Czechoslovakia was in fact planned in Case Green, contrary to Manstein's memoir.

51. Heusinger, 'Der Unbequeme Operative Kopf', p. 37.

52. Müller, *Beck, Biographie*, p. 236.

53. On 3 April 1939 Hitler issued a directive on war preparations enclosing a document containing details of the projected attack on Poland '*Fall Weiss*' (Case White).

54. Müller, *Beck, Biographie*, pp. 240– 243.

55. Macksey, *Guderian*, p. 64.

56. Liddell Hart wrote laudatory forewords to the English editions of both Guderian's *Panzer Leader* and Manstein's *Lost Victories*.

57. Manstein, p. 241. No English translation can reflect fully the alliteration, idiom or nuance of the original German: '*Wenn dabei der Chef des Generalstabs, General Beck, hinsichtlich der den Panzerverbänden zubilligenden Erfolge mehr Wasser in den Wein Guderians schüttete, als berechtigt war, so lag dies in seiner*

Natur, die das "Wägen" vielleicht etwas zu stark vor das "Wagen" zu stellen, geneigt war.'

58. The 'light' armoured divisions were based on former cavalry concepts of operation but did not prove themselves in the Polish campaign of September 1939. All were converted to panzer divisions by 1940 with the exception of 15th Light Division that was deployed to North Africa in April 1941 as part of Rommel's Afrika Korps. It was converted later to a panzer division.

59. For example, Montgomery's 21st Army Group in Normandy on 1 August 1944 contained eight independent armoured or tank brigades as well as five armoured divisions (three British, one Canadian and one Polish), excluding the specialist 79th Armoured Division. Data from Major L. F. Ellis, *Victory in the West*, vol. i, *The Battle of Normandy* (London and Nashville: The Imperial War Museum and The Battery Press, 1993), pp. 521–532.

60. Manstein's account is given in *Aus einem Soldatenleben*, pp. 243–250.

61. Manstein (*Aus einem Soldatenleben*, p. 249) recalled the precise words that in German betray a kinder tone from Beck than an English translation might otherwise indicate: *'Na, mein lieber Manstein, diesmal haben Sie aber fehlgeschossen!'* Hitler addressed Manstein courteously as 'Herr General' or 'Herr Feldmarschall', rather than 'Manstein'. Note that the use of surnames between superior and subordinate was usual in the Reichswehr and Wehrmacht and remained so in the Bundeswehr long after its foundation in 1955. Nowadays, a

typical salutation to equals or subordinates would be 'Herr Schmidt', for example. To superiors 'Herr Oberst' or 'Herr General' is typical.

62. Additional details of the development of the assault gun are taken from Franz Kurowski and Gottfried Tornau, *Sturmgeschütze – Die Panzer der Infanterie* (Würzburg: Flechsig Verlag, 2008), pp. 9–14.

63. *Author's Note:* I have deliberately translated the German term *Abteilung* as 'detachment' in order not to cause confusion by using either the word 'regiment' or 'battalion'.

64. Kurowski and Tornau, pp. 19–26.

65. Ibid., p. 18.

4. At the Very Centre of Power

1. Manstein, *Aus einem Soldatenleben*, p. 318. Unless otherwise stated, all quotes from Manstein in this chapter are taken from this memoir.

2. So that there is no misunderstanding, Manstein bought the house from another individual who had purchased the property from Elisabeth Bergner in 1934. I am grateful to Rüdiger von Manstein for clarifying this issue.

3. An observation made by Knopp, *Hitler's Warriors*, p. 141.

4. Author's interview with Gisela Lingenthal at Bad Honnef on 4 March 2007.

5. Figures extracted from Documents M725a and M725b in Karl-Volker Neugebauer, *Grundzüge der deutschen Militärgeschichte*, Band 2, Arbeits- und Quellenbuch (Freiburg: Rombach Verlag, 1993), p. 317.

6. Author's interview with Rüdiger

von Manstein at Icking, near Munich, on 1 October 2006.

7. Engelmann, *Manstein: Stratege und Truppenführer*, p. 39.

8. Author's interview with Rüdiger von Manstein at Icking, near Munich, on 1 October 2006.

9. Author's interview with Gisela Lingenthal at Bad Honnef on 4 March 2007.

10. Quoted by Knopp (ed.), *Hitler's Warriors*, pp. 144–145; confirmed in interview on 4 March 2007.

11. Manstein, p. 254.

12. Ibid., p. 256.

13. Ibid., p. 257.

14. The equivalent post to the British Military Secretary.

15. Manstein, pp. 257–258.

16. Ibid., p. 238.

17. The British Army never had the necessary manpower to build a substantial field force on the scale of the German Army. Churchill often complained about the lack of fighting troops, demanding a 'leaner army'. See David Fraser, *And We Shall Shock Them: The British Army in the Second World War* (London: Hodder & Stoughton, 1983), p. 86, and David French, *Raising Churchill's Army: The British Army and the War against Germany 1919–1945* (Oxford: University Press, 2000), p. 186.

18. Manstein, p. 238.

19. Ibid., p. 239.

20. For a detailed description and analysis of the Hossbach Memorandum, see Ian Kershaw, *Hitler: 1936–1945 Nemesis* (London: Penguin, 2001), pp. 46–51.

21. Manstein, p. 240.

22. Karl-Volker Neugebauer, 'Die Wehrmacht im nationalsozialistischen Regime' in *Grundzüge der deutschen Militärgeschichte*, vol. 1, *Historischer Überblick* (Freiburg: Rombach Verlag, 1993), pp. 352–355.

23. Notwithstanding the variable quality of the force, the magnitude of the achievement is reflected in the figures. At the time of the mobilization in August 1939, the German Army possessed 53 'active' divisions forming the first 'wave'. Sixteen further divisions of fully trained reservists made up the second wave; 21 divisions of partially trained reservists or older age class reservists from the First World War constituted a third wave, with a further 14 divisions assembled from other units and formations bringing up the fourth wave. In addition to this deployable field army of 104 divisions, a replacement army (*Ersatzheer*) of nearly a million men remained in the Reich to recruit, train and hold men for future use, and to guard the homeland. See Karl-Volker Neugebauer, op. cit., p. 356

24. A summary of the paper is reproduced in Manstein and Fuchs, *Soldat im 20. Jahrhundert*, pp. 385–388. The full text of the memorandum that Manstein drafted for Fritsch's signature in August 1937 is given in Keitel, *General Feldmarschall*, pp. 157–181.

25. Manstein and Fuchs, p. 386.

26. Manstein, p. 284.

27. Ibid., p. 285.

28. Ibid., p. 291.

29. Müller, *Beck*, pp. 297–298.

30. Manstein, pp. 299–301. The dismissal of Blomberg and Fritsch is documented comprehensively. Detailed accounts are given by Wheeler-Bennett, *The Nemesis of Power*, pp. 363–374, and Walter

Goerlitz, *History of the German General Staff 1657–1945* (London and New York: Praeger, 1953), pp. 312–319. A condensed but slightly different interpretation of events is given by Richard Overy, *The Dictators* (London and New York: W. W. Norton, 2004), pp. 478–480. See also Kershaw, *Nemesis*, pp. 51–60.

31. Apart from Blomberg and Fritsch, Manstein *(Aus einem Soldatenleben*, pp. 316–317) lists the following individuals who were retired on an involuntary basis: General Ritter von Leeb (commander-in-chief of Group 3); General Ewald von Kleist and General Baron [Kress] von Kressenstein (commanding generals of VIII and XII Corps respectively); General von Niebelschütz (inspector of education and training); and General von Pogrell (inspector of cavalry). Goerlitz, op. cit., p. 318, adds further details including that General Lutz, commander of armoured troops, was also retired. Wheeler-Bennett, op. cit., p. 373, adds the names of: [Gerd] von Rundstedt, [Günther] von Kluge, [Georg] von Küchler, [Maximilian] von Weichs and [Erwin] von Witzleben. There remains some dispute as to the overall numbers of dismissed or transferred. Magnus Brechten, *Die Nationalsozialistische Herrschaft 1933–1939* (Darmstadt: Wissenschaftliche Buchgesellschaft, 2004), p. 143, states that twelve generals (other than Blomberg and Fritsch) were retired and changes were made in fifty-one other posts; Wheeler-Bennett states that 'sixteen high-ranking generals were relieved and forty-four others were transferred

to other duties'.

32. *Verordnung über das Heiraten der Angehörigen der Wehrmacht* of 1 April 1936, Sub-Paragraph 3b.

33. Manstein, p. 297.

34. The complex relationship between Blomberg and Keitel is explained by Wheeler-Bennett, *Nemesis of Power*, p. 364, and by Keitel, quoted in Leon Goldensohn and Robert Gellately (eds.), *The Nuremberg Interviews* (London: Pimlico, 2006), p.164. First published in the USA by Knopf, Borzoi Books, in 2004. Keitel left a more detailed account in his memoirs, including noting that his daughter Nona was friendly with Blomberg's daughter Sibylle and his son got engaged to her sister Dorle. For example, both Blomberg girls spent Christmas 1937 with the Keitels whilst their father was otherwise distracted with Erna Gruhn. See here Keitel, p. 128.

35. Walter Warlimont, *Inside Hitler's Headquarters 1939–45* (London: Weidenfeld & Nicolson, 1964), p. 13. First published in Germany under the title *Im Hauptquartier der Deutschen Wehrmacht 1939–1945* by Bernard und Graefe, Frankfurt am Main, 1962.

36. Goldensohn, p. 167. As an historical record, the edited transcript of Goldensohn's recorded interviews of nineteen defendants (including Keitel) at Nuremberg and fourteen witnesses (including Manstein) is invaluable, but the worth of the editorial contribution and notes is rather brought into doubt by a considerable number of inaccuracies, not least in confusing in two places the appointments of Field Marshal Werner von

Blomberg and Colonel General
Baron Werner von Fritsch, who
until their dismissals in early 1938
were Minister of War/
Commander-in-Chief of Armed
Forces and Commander-in-Chief
of the German Army respectively.
37. Manstein, *Lost Victories*, p. 153.
38. Keitel, p. 144.
39. See Hinrich Baumann, *Die
Heidmark Wandel einer Landschaft:
Die Geschichte des
Truppenübungsplatzes Bergen*
(Walsrode: J. Gronemann, 2005),
pp. 232–235, for a description of
Fritsch's association with
Achterberg.
40. Manstein, pp. 302–304.
41. Ibid., p. 305.
42. Ibid., p. 306.
43. Keitel, p. 142.
44. Wheeler-Bennett, *The Nemesis of
Power*, p. 373, and Craig, *The
Politics of the Prussian Army*, p. 496.
45. An English translation of the
announcement is given by
Wheeler-Bennett, p. 372: 'From
henceforth [ran the Führer's
decree], I exercise personally the
immediate command over the
whole armed forces. The former
Wehrmacht Office in the War
Ministry becomes the High
Command of the Armed Forces
[OKW], and comes immediately
under my command as my military
staff. At the head of the Staff of the
High Command stands the former
chief of the Wehrmacht Office
[Keitel]. He is accorded the rank
equivalent to that of a Reich
Minister. The High Command of
the Armed Forces also takes over
the functions of the War Ministry,
and the Chief of the High
Command exercises, as my deputy,
the powers hitherto held by the
Reich War Minister.'

46. Manstein's daughter, Gisela
Lingenthal, disputes this version
of events. She distinctly recalls her
father learning of his dismissal in a
newspaper (in other words on 5
February 1938) and going out
immediately to buy a top hat as he
had become a civilian – interview
of 4 March 2007 in Bad Honnef.
47. Manstein, p. 318.
48. Ibid.
49. Ibid., p. 319.
50. See Knopp (ed.), *Hitler's Warriors*,
p. 143. Gisela Lingenthal
confirmed this account to the
present author – interview of 4
March 2007 in Bad Honnef.
51. Manstein, p. 323.
52. Ibid., p. 324.

5. To War Again

1. Recorded by General of Artillery
Franz Halder on 22 August 1939.
See *The Halder War Diary*, p. 31.
2. Principally from Gisela
Lingenthal, *Als Mutter ein Kind
war*; Joachim Engelmann, *Die 18.
Infanterie- und Panzergrenadier-
Division 1934–1945* (Friedberg:
Podzun-Pallas-Verlag, 1984).
3. As one of the first new formations
of the rapidly expanding German
Army, its proper designation as
18th Infantry Division was not
declared until 15 October 1935.
On 16 March 1935 the German
government proclaimed the
introduction of general military
service (conscription) and the
expansion of the peacetime army
of twelve army corps and thirty-six
divisions (*Gesetz für den Aufbau der
Wehrmacht*) in full breach of the
Treaty of Versailles. The army's
established strength would grow to
550,000 men, five and a half times
the Treaty limit. The German

armed forces and people supported the restoration of military sovereignty *(Wehrhoheit)*. For further background, see Wheeler-Bennett, *The Nemesis of Power*, pp. 337–338; Ian Kershaw, *Hubris*, pp. 549–555.

4. Lingenthal, p. 73.

5. Ibid., p. 75.

6. The *Königsgrenadier-Regiment*, whose colonel-in-chief had been Kaiser Wilhelm II. The regiment was still referred to by its traditional name before the Second World War.

7. Details of the dispositions of 18th Division are taken from Engelmann, pp. 5, 21 and 38; and Werner Haupt, *Die deutschen Infanterie-Divisionen* (Eggolsheim: Dörfler Verlag, 2005), pp. 71–72. The divisional reconnaissance battalion was raised in 1939; companies of the machine-gun battalion were absorbed later into the three infantry regiments. In addition, Manstein's command extended beyond that of a 'first wave' regular infantry division, manned by a mixture of professional officers, non-commissioned officers and conscripts, the latter serving for two years. He was also responsible for a number of supplementary *(Ergänzung)* infantry battalions and artillery batteries that trained older age groups of reservists with years of birth from 1901 to 1913. This pool of personnel provided the German Army's 'Reserve II', which was destined to man the new divisions of the second to fourth waves of the army on mobilization.

8. Manstein, *Aus einem Soldatenleben*, p. 334. The 'first general staff officer' was the Ia, chief of operations and *de facto* chief of

staff. Mauritz Freiherr von Strachwitz und Gross-Zauche (1898–1953) ended the Second World War as a lieutenant general, commanding a division. He died in Soviet captivity.

9. Engelmann, *Die 18. Infanterie- und Panzergrenadier-Division 1934–1945* (Friedberg: Podzun-Pallas-Verlag, 1984), p. 39.

10. Manstein, *Lost Victories*, p. 21.

11. Quoted by Roland Kopp in 'Die Wehrmacht feiert. Kommandeurs-Reden zu Hitlers 50. Geburtstag am 20. April 1939', *Militärgeschichtlichen Zeitschrift* 62 (2003), vol. 2, p. 512 (Document No. 7).

12. Ibid., pp. 509–534.

13. Manstein, *Aus einem Soldatenleben*, p. 352.

14. See Klaus-Jürgen Müller (ed.), *General Ludwig Beck, Studien und Dokumente zur politisch-militärischen Vorstellungswelt und Tätigkeit des Generalstabschefs des deutschen Heeres 1933–1938* (Boppard am Rhein: Harald Boldt Verlag, 1980).

15. Ibid., p. 525.

16. Ibid., pp. 537–541.

17. The precise date and place of the conversation with Beck, or more likely, with a third party that prompted Manstein's paper, are not recorded, but it is reasonable to assume it was probably in mid July 1938 in Berlin. He was not one to dwell for long on such matters.

18. Manstein, *Aus einem Soldatenleben*, p. 336. The full text of Manstein's paper to Beck is reproduced by Müller, *Das Heer und Hitler*, Document 42, pp. 656–665. The original document is contained in the Nachlass Beck, BA-MA, H 08–28/4.

19. This point is also made by

Kershaw, *Nemesis*, p. 103.

20. Müller, *Beck, Biographie*, pp. 353–354.
21. The text of Beck's letter is reproduced in Müller, *Das Heer und Hitler*, Document 43, p. 665.
22. In his memoirs, Manstein (*Aus einem Soldatenleben*, pp. 336–337) could not cite the exact date but recalled erroneously that it was 'the end of August', and so implied that the meeting took place *after* Beck's resignation, which Hitler had accepted on 18 August. In fact, as annotated on Beck's (unsent) letter to him, Manstein visited Beck in Berlin on 9 August 1938, in other words *between* his leave in Sylt and duty trip to Berchtesgaden.
23. Manstein, *Aus einem Soldatenleben*, p. 337.
24. According to his memoirs, Manstein refrained from telling Hitler that the most popular exhibits on show were none other than two depictions of the Führer, including the famous image of him wearing armour, sitting on a horse and carrying a flag! Manstein is presumably referring here to '*Der Bannerträger*' [*The Standard Bearer*], a famous idealized portrait of Hitler as a knight in shining armour by Hubert Lanzinger, which was displayed in the *Haus der Deutschen Kunst* (House of German Art) in Munich in its 1938 summer exhibition.
25. Manstein, *Aus einem Soldatenleben*, pp. 338–339.
26. Ibid., p. 340.
27. Ibid., p. 341.
28. Golo Mann, *Deutsche Geschichte des 19. und 20. Jahrhunderts* (Frankfurt am Main: S. Fischer Verlag, 1992), p. 886: '*Der deutsche Widerstand gegen Hitler hat im August und*

September 1938 seine höchste Dichtigkeit erreicht.'
29. Manstein, *Aus einem Soldatenleben*, pp. 341–343.
30. Mann, p. 949.
31. Manstein, *Aus einem Soldatenleben*, p. 340.
32. Ibid., pp. 345–346.
33. According to Manstein, this group first assembled at Neuhammer on 12 August 1939 and Rundstedt joined them 'in mid August'. BA-MA, RH 19 I/5, *Kriegstagebuch der Heeresgruppe Süd in Polen 1939* [War Diary of Army Group South in Poland 1939], p. 4, confirms the *final* assembly of the working staff at Neuhammer on that date, which was then expanded into an army group staff on 18 August in Munich, prior to its move (less commander-in-chief and chief of staff) to Neisse on 21 August 1939. However, Blumentritt's team had been hard at work developing the army group plan for many months before following OKH's instructions. It is hardly conceivable that Manstein did not have his hand in the scheme of manoeuvre, and the same goes for Rundstedt who, according to normal German convention, would have had to approve the plan prior to its submission to OKH. Further, by the same military tradition, it is doubtful that Rundstedt would have done so without consulting his designate chief of staff, Manstein. Documents preserved in the German Military Archive confirm that Blumentritt had already produced a draft army group deployment plan on 20 May 1939, and that Manstein's signature was on *Arbeitsstab* instructions dated 29 June 1939. See BA-MA, RH 19

I/9, *Arbeitsstab Rundstedt.* The two key documents are: 'Arbeitsstab Rundstedt Ia Nr. 1/39 g. Kdos. Berlin, den 20. Mai 1939 Entwurf Aufmarschanweisung "Weiss"' [Draft Deployment Instruction 'White'] signed by Blumentritt; and 'Stab Rundstedt, 28 Juni 1939' [untitled], signed by Manstein, which ordered that the former directive would take effect on 20 August 1939.

34. Manstein, *Lost Victories*, p. 23. *Author's Note:* I have amended the 'grand tactics' of the English translation to 'operational art', which reflects the original German: '*Er* [Rundstedt] *war ein operativ glänzend begabter Soldat*'. See Manstein, *Verlorene Siege*, p. 13.

35. Westphal, *Erinnerungen*, p. 73.

36. Manstein, *Lost Victories*, p. 22, and Günther Blumentritt, *Von Rundstedt*, p. 47.

37. Manstein, *Lost Victories*, p. 28.

38. Ibid., p. 29.

39. *The Halder War Diary*, p. 31

40. Ibid., p. 29

41. Horst Rohde, 'Hitler's First Blitzkrieg and its Consequences for North-eastern Europe' in *Germany and the Second World War*, vol. 11 (Oxford: Clarendon Press, 1991), p. 75.

42. Gerhard Engel, *At the Heart of the Reich: The Secret Diary of Hitler's Army Adjutant* (London: Greenhill Books, 2005), p. 72. Originally published as *Heeresadjutant bei Hitler 1938–1943*, ed. Hildegard von Kotze (Stuttgart: Deutsche Verlags-Anstalt, 1974). Diary entry for 22 August 1939.

43. Manstein, *Lost Victories*, p. 30.

44. Ibid., p. 31

45. Helmuth Greiner, *Die Oberste Wehrmachtführung 1939–1943* (Wiesbaden: Limes Verlag, 1951), p. 40.

46. Meanwhile, Manstein's command of 18th Division had lapsed on 25 August 1939. Major General (later, Lieutenant General) Friedrich-Carl Cranz led it throughout the ensuing Polish and French campaigns.

47. Blumentritt, p. 47, and Manstein, *Lost Victories*, p. 47.

48. Manstein ibid., pp. 43–45

49. Figures from Manstein, ibid., pp. 34–35. See also Horst Rohde, 'Hitlers erster "Blitzkrieg" und seine Auswirkungen auf Nordosteuropa' in *Das Deutsche Reich und der Zweite Weltkrieg*, Band 2, *Die Errichtung der Hegemonie auf dem Europäische Kontinent* (Stuttgart: Deutsche Verlags-Anstalt, 1979), p. 111.

50. Horst Rohde, ibid., p. 85. See also BA-MA, RH 19 I/5, Kriegstagebuch der Heeresgruppe Süd [Army Group South War Diary].

51. BA-MA, RH 19 I/5, pp. 11–13: Heeresgruppe Süd Ia Nr. 390/39 g.Kdos., Neisse-Heiligkreuz, den 30.8.39, 13.00 Uhr, Heeresgruppenbefehl Nr. 1 [Army Group Order No. 1].

52. Hans von Luck, *Panzer Commander* (New York: Praeger, 1989), p. 20.

53. Manstein, *Lost Victories*, p. 48.

54. Manstein to his wife, 1 September 1939. Letter held in the private possession of Rüdiger von Manstein.

55. Ibid., 23 September 1939. Letter held in the private possession of Rüdiger von Manstein.

56. BA-MA, RH 19 I/5, pp. 26–27: Heeresgruppe Süd Ia, Neisse, den 3.9.39, An O.K.H., Gen.St.d.H. Op. Abt. Beurteilung der Lage [Estimate of the Situation], signed

by Manstein.

57. Manstein, letter to his wife, 5 September 1939. Letter held in the private possession of Rüdiger von Manstein.

58. Manstein, *Lost Victories*, p. 56.

59. Ibid., pp. 57–58.

60. Manstein, letters to his wife, 8 and 14 September 1939. Letters held in the private possession of Rüdiger von Manstein.

61. Manstein, *Lost Victories*, pp. 58–59.

62. *The Halder War Diary*, p. 61. Entry for 24 September 1939.

63. See the account, for example, in Jochen Böhler, *Der Überfall: Deutschlands Krieg gegen Polen* (Frankfurt am Main: Eichborn, 2009), pp. 171–176.

64. Manstein, letter to his wife, 26 September 1939. Letter held in the private possession of Rüdiger von Manstein.

65. Ibid., 27 September 1939.

66. Ibid., 3 October 1939.

67. Blumentritt, p. 53.

68. Manstein, *Lost Victories*, p. 50.

69. The date of Heusinger's visit as 15 October 1939 is given in Manstein, *Lost Victories*, p. 63; and *Verlorene Siege*, p. 59. In his letter to his wife of 13 October 1939, however, Manstein recorded: 'Heusinger appeared today with a written confirmation of that which Stülpnagel had already announced. According to this, we won't need to remain here very long.'

70. Manstein, *Lost Victories*, p. 63. The present author has lightly amended Powell's translation here.

71. Ibid., p. 62.

72. As Blumentritt noted (p. 54), 'It was a war without fixed positions, with continuous change between attack, defence, outflanking, elusion and counter-attack. There

were perpetually new and surprising situations, swiftly fluctuating results and no rest for troops or staffs by day, and most certainly not by night. It was a campaign which conformed particularly to the operational and tactical plans of Rundstedt – a war of successive changes. His Chief of Staff, the able General von Manstein, was particularly adapted to this campaign.'

73. Kershaw, *Nemesis*, pp. 240–241.

74. Wrochem, *Erich von Manstein*, p. 46

75. Manstein, *Verlorene Siege*, p. 53. By an odd twist of fate, an imposing memorial to Fritsch stands today only a short distance away from the official residence of the British brigade and garrison commander in Bergen-Hohne, Hopp House, at the edge of Hohne Camp.

76. Ibid., pp. 53–54. Manstein wrote to his wife on 19 September 1939, 'As I came back home [to the headquarters], the news was that Dico had fallen a couple of days before. You can imagine how hard this was for me after such a long friendship. And then came your letter about Konrad.... Death would have been easier for him. One can only hope that after all perhaps it won't remain so bad.' Letter held in the private possession of Rüdiger von Manstein.

77. Manstein, *Verlorene Siege*, pp. 54–55.

78. Ibid., p. 44.

79. See Rainer Rother, *Leni Riefenstahl: The Seduction of Genius* (London and New York: Continuum, 2002) [first pub. in German by Henschel, Berlin, in 2000 as *Leni Riefenstahl: Die Verführung des Talents*, pp. 127–133, for a detailed description of

the event and the post-war controversy that surrounded it. Another perspective is given by Steven Bach, *Leni: The Life and Work of Leni Riefenstahl* (London: Little, Brown, 2007), pp. 187–192.

80. Manstein, *Verlorene Siege*, p. 44.

81. Wrochem, p. 47. Böhler (p. 195) names the officer concerned as Reserve Lieutenant Bruno Kleinmichel.

82. Manstein, *Lost Victories*, pp. 179–180; *Verlorene Siege*, pp. 176–177.

83. Recounted to the present author by General (Retired) Helge Hansen, whose father was Keitel's adjutant (military assistant) at the time.

84. Engel, p. 80. Diary entry for 18 November 1939.

85. Müller, *Das Heer und Hitler*, pp. 435–438.

86. Rohde, p. 126.

87. From a wide literature, for example, see Müller and Volkmann (eds.), Die *Wehrmacht*.

88. Witness statement of 12 August 1946. *Trial of the Major War Criminals Before the International Military Tribunal* (Nuremberg, 1948), vol. 21, p. 10.

6. Architect of Victory

1. Quoted by Engel, *At the Heart of the Reich*, p. 87.

2. The narrative of this section is based on Manstein's account given in the original German edition of his war memoirs, *Verlorene Siege*, augmented by further material contained in his personal war diary and letters to his wife in the private possession of his son, Rüdiger von Manstein. Where no previous or satisfactory translation exists, material has been translated into English by the present author.

Some of the analysis contained in this chapter is developed from that previously published by Mungo Melvin, 'The German View', in Brian Bond and Michael Taylor (eds.), *The Battle for France & Flanders Sixty Years On* (Barnsley: Leo Cooper, 2001), pp. 207–226. The literature on the Fall of France is very extensive. In addition to personal memoirs such as Manstein's and the British and German official histories, particularly useful works for the study of the campaign include: Alistair Horne, *To Lose a Battle: France 1940* (London: Macmillan, 1969); Jeffrey A. Gunsberg, *Divided and Conquered* (Westport, Conn.: Greenwood Press, 1979); Robert A. Doughty, *The Breaking Point: Sedan and the Fall of France, 1940* (Hamden, Conn.: Archon, 1990); Ernest R. May, *Strange Victory* (New York: Hill & Wang, 2000). Robert M. Citino's meticulously researched *Quest for Decisive Victory: From Stalemate to Blitzkrieg in Europe 1899–1940* (Lawrence: University Press of Kansas, 2002) provides useful detail and context. Philip Warner's *The Battle of France, 1940* (London: Simon & Schuster, 1990) is a thoroughly readable account but lacks references. One of the best overall accounts is given by Hugh Sebag-Montefiore, *Dunkirk: Fight to the Last Man* (London: Penguin, 2007), which is much wider in scope than the title would suggest. For the German perspective, see Liddell Hart, *The Other Side of the Hill*; Hans-Adolf Jacobsen, *Fall Gelb: Der Kampf um den deutschen Operationsplan zur Westoffensive 1940* (Wiesbaden: Franz Steiner, 1971); Florian K. Rothbrust,

Guderian's XIXth Panzer Corps and the Battle of France: Breakthrough in the Ardennes, May 1940 (Westport, Conn: Praeger, 1990); and not least *The Halder War Diary*. The most authoritative modern German analysis is contained in Karl-Heinz Frieser's *The Blitzkrieg Legend: The 1940 Campaign in the West* (Annapolis, Md.: Naval Institute Press, 2005), originally published as *Blitzkrieg-Legende* (Munich: R. Oldenbourg Verlag, 1995).

3. The origin of the term 'sickle-cut' is not clear. Frieser, *Blitzkrieg Legend*, p. 74, suggests that Manstein's use of *Sichelbewegung* (sickle-movement) was adapted by Halder after the Second World War into *Sichelschnitt*. Meanwhile, in *Their Finest Hour* (London: Cassell, 1949), p. 53, Churchill had described the advancing columns of German armour as 'hideous, fatal scythes [that] encountered little or no resistance once the front had been broken'. However, the German translation of scythe is *Sense*; sickle is *Sichel*.

4. *The Halder War Diary* (p. 142), includes a note dated 22 January 1940 about personnel changes including the requirement to get von Rundstedt's opinion of Manstein, and a note of 26 January (p. 196) about 'Manstein, Commanding General', which indicates a new appointment was being considered. Halder's entry of 31 January indicates that the decision on selecting Manstein's relief (von Sodenstern) was made on 1 February, apparently in consultation with Keitel. Doubts were to creep in later on – see *The Halder War Diary*, p. 260.

5. Corroborating evidence for Manstein's influence on Schmundt is contained in Engel's diary. His entry for 4 February 1940 *(At the Heart of the Reich*, p. 86) records that: 'Schmundt was at Koblenz where he spoke to the C-in-C, Manstein and Blumentritt. He returned very impressed by a long discussion with Manstein who had expressed great reservations with regard to the proposed OKH operational plan. Schmundt was very excited and told me that whilst with Manstein, he had ascertained that Manstein's plan contained the same opinion regarding the best concentration of forces, albeit in a considerably more precise form, as that continually advocated by the Führer. He had also spoken to Blumentritt whose ideas coincided with those of Manstein, except that Blumentritt was more cautious although very critical of Halder.'

6. Engel (p. 86) recorded on 5 February 1940: 'Schmundt suggested summoning Manstein to hear his ideas. F.[ührer] agreed at once but ordered both Schmundt and me not to mention this proposed conference to the C-in-C [von Brauchitsch] or Halder.'

7. Lieutenant Generals Geyr von Schweppenburg, Schmidt, Reinhardt and Stumme attended with Manstein as corps commanders (designate), together with Erwin Rommel, who had been newly appointed on 15 February 1940 to command 7th Panzer Division.

8. Manstein, Personal War Diary, Book 2. Entry for 17 February 1940 cited in Manstein and Fuchs, *Soldat im 20. Jahrhundert*, p. 141.

9. On 16 February 1940, HMS *Cossack* had cornered the German tanker and supply ship *Altmark* in the Jøssingfjord and boarded it,

releasing 299 British merchant seamen who had been captured following the sinking of their vessels by the German pocket battleship, the *Admiral Graf Spee*, in the South Atlantic during the previous autumn. This incident may have prompted Hitler to advance his plans for the invasion of Norway, believing (rightly in the event) that Britain would not respect Norwegian neutrality. Indeed, Winston Churchill, as First Lord, had stiffened the resolution of the Admiralty to direct the captain of *Cossack*, Captain P. L. Vian, to board the *Altmark* should she and her escorting Norwegian warships prove unco-operative. See S. W. Roskill, *The Navy at War 1939–1945* (London: Collins, 1960), pp. 57–58.

10. Present author's translation of *Verlorene Siege*, p. 119.
11. Manstein, *Lost Victories*, p. 105.
12. Manstein, Personal War Diary, Book 2a. Entry for 24 October 1939.
13. Emphasis as in the original.
14. Manstein, Personal War Diary, Book 2a. Entry for 24 October 1939.
15. Author's adaptation of the former Tsarist officer A. A. Svechin's succinct description of the operational level cited by David M. Glantz and Jonathan M. House, *When Titans Clashed: How the Red Army Stopped Hitler* (Lawrence: University Press of Kansas, 1995), p. 8; a full reference to Svechin is contained at p. 332, fn 7.
16. Müller, *Beck, Biographie*, p. 394.
17. For a detailed description of Hitler's political manoeuvrings at this time and the military opposition to his plans, see

Kershaw, *Nemesis*, pp. 262–279
18. Various contradictory figures are given by different sources. Much depends on whether French forces outside France in North Africa and elsewhere are counted in. See Raymond Cartier, *Der Zweite Weltkrieg* (Munich: Piper, 1967), pp. 53 and 57; May, pp. 471–480. Frieser, *Blitzkrieg Legend*, p. 36, states that France 'had 104 divisions manning the northeast front'. I am grateful to Charles Dick for his assistance on clarifying this matter.
19. Frieser, p. 36.
20. General of Infantry Karl Heinrich Stülpnagel was the German military governor for occupied France (1942–44) and was close to the inner circle of the resistance to Hitler. After his troops achieved initial successes in rounding up Gestapo and SS forces in Paris on 20 July 1944, he was forced to concede failure. A botched attempt at suicide was followed by trial and sentence to death.
21. Manstein, *Verlorene Siege*, p. 317. Marcel Stein, *Feldmarschall von Manstein: Der Januskopf* (Bissendorf: Biblio Verlag, 2004), also draws attention to this observation (p. 307), but falsely quotes '*dann fand [Hitler] alsbald solche aus dem politischen oder militärischen Bereich*' rather than '*dann fand [Hitler] alsbald solche aus dem politischen oder wirtschaftlichen Bereich*'. The English translation of *Verlorene Siege* by Anthony G. Powell is flawed in that it renders '*mit seinem operativen Ansichten*' as 'with his opinions on strategy'. In numerous places throughout *Verlorene Siege* '*operative*' is mistranslated as 'strategic' in *Lost Victories* rather than 'operational'.

But to be fair, when Powell undertook the translation (1956–58), the operational level of war was unrecognized in Britain and the United States. The contemporary term 'grand tactics', however, could not convey the full force of '*operativ*'. Hence when Manstein (as in this passage) is making a distinction between operational and strategic, Powell's translation can be misleading.

22. Letter dated 31 October 1939.
23. English translation taken from H. R. Trevor-Roper (ed.), *Hitler's War Directives 1939–1945* (Edinburgh: Birlinn, 2004), p. 50, first published by Sidgwick & Jackson in 1964.
24. Manstein, Personal War Diary, Book 2a. Entry for 28 October 1939.
25. Letter dated 29 October 1939.
26. Whilst the German reader of *Lost Victories* gets a full version of the OKH plan of 19 October as an appendix, and a key extract of the plan of 29 October, the reader of the English edition gets neither. This is not necessarily a major handicap as Manstein gives a full description of the development of the campaign plan in his main text – but either way the reader must beware: Manstein rather suggests that the final, executed, plan was very much of his design. His place in military history largely rests on this notion. The weight of evidence suggests that whereas Manstein argued vociferously for a new plan that would reflect a switch of main effort to the centre (and thus from Army Group B to Army Group A) whilst Army Group C continued to face the Maginot Line in the south, others, including Hitler and Halder, also played key

parts in its evolution. That said, the germ of a brand-new operational idea was indeed Manstein's and his later representation to Hitler swung the Führer and thus OKH behind it.
27. See L. F. Ellis, *The War in France and Flanders 1939–1940* (London: HMSO, 1953), p. 341. Ellis concedes, however, that 'how much [Rundstedt] owed to his Chief of Staff (Manstein) cannot be known'.
28. Within the German Army, the responsibility of the senior general staff officer in a formation headquarters (typically its chief of staff) to advise the commander and to share the decision-making (*Mitverantwortung*) is a traditional characteristic of the General Staff. In 1939 the Chief of the General Staff, General of Artillery Franz Halder, removed this responsibility in *The Handbook for General Staff Duties in War*. But the duty of the general staff officer to advise and, if necessary, to press his commander for a timely decision remains part of the Bundeswehr's doctrine today. Thus a German general staff officer retains typically more responsibility than his Allied counterpart. See Christian Millotat, *Das Preussisch-Deutsche Generalstabssystem* (Bonn: Bundesministerium der Verteidigung, undated), p. 56. Further information on Halder's perspective and role is described in H[ildegard] Gräfin von Schall-Riaucour, *Generaloberst Franz Halder, Generalstabschef 1938–1942* (Beltheim-Schnellbach: Lindenbaum Verlag, 2006), pp. 104–112.
29. Manstein, *Verlorene Siege*, p. 64.
30. Letters dated 4 November and 4 December 1939.

31. Translated by the present author from *Anlage* [Appendix] 3 to Manstein, *Verlorene Siege*, p. 625.

32. The historian Correlli Barnett has compared Manstein's plan favourably with Ludendorff's great MICHAEL offensive of March 1918, which sought to defeat the British Army on the Western Front by envelopment of its southern flank. Whilst it is perhaps an exaggeration to describe *Sichelschnitt* as a 'successful replay of MICHAEL', there are some similarities but none the less many differences. Operation MICHAEL, for all its success in achieving an unprecedented breakthrough of the British Fifth Army, was not the product of an integrated operational idea. Ludendorff, in stark contrast to Manstein, focused almost exclusively on breaking through the Allied line as opposed to setting the appropriately deep operational objectives. See Correlli Barnett, *The Swordbearers: Supreme Command in the First World War* (London: Cassell, 2000), pp. 284–289.

33. On German intelligence in 1940, see May's *Strange Victory* and Williamson Murray and Allan R. Millett, *A War to be Won: Fighting the Second World War* (Cambridge, Mass. and London: Belknap Press of Harvard University Press, 2000), p. 23: 'Their almost exclusive focus on the battlefield led German generals to minimize the importance of strategy, to believe naively that logistics would take care of themselves and that intelligence was only of value in the immediate help it would provide combat units.' A harsh, but none the less largely valid judgement.

34. Manstein, *Verlorene Siege*, p. 626.

35. Ibid., p. 105.

36. German military terminology evolved during the course of the Second World War and is a pitfall for the unwary as much post-war literature uses titles that were in place at the *end* of the war, but which did not necessarily exist at the beginning. Manstein's memoirs were no exception, as he referred throughout to panzer corps whether or not they were so titled. In 1939–42, army corps comprising armoured or motorized forces, or a combination of both, were distinguished from standard infantry corps with the designation (mot.), short for motorized. These were only retitled as panzer corps in 1942. Groups of such corps were already known as panzer groups (*Panzergruppe*) in 1941, later termed panzer armies in 1942.

37. Manstein, *Verlorene Siege*, p. 106.

38. Hitler's remark to Jodl on 9 November 1939, cited but not referenced by Macksey in *Guderian*, p. 98.

39. Translated by the present author from Manstein, *Verlorene Siege*, p. 106. Anthony G. Powell's translation is flawed potentially here in at least two areas. With respect to the likely going of Fourth Army in relation to the Meuse, *abwärts* is mistaken for *aufwärts* (upstream) and is thus rendered incorrectly as 'further up' rather than 'downstream' (*Lost Victories*, p. 109). Secondly, Powell makes an emendation to the original text, changing 'H.Gr B' [Army Group B] to 'Army Group A', which at first sight makes more sense. However, Manstein may indeed have been crediting Hitler

with the thought of either extending the front of Army Group B southwards towards Sedan (but thus pinching out Army Group A) or, much more credibly, of regarding the 'opening' at Sedan as a means to unhinge the French defence of the Meuse so enabling German forces of Army Group B, including its southernmost army (the Fourth), to cross further north. This second line of reasoning is supported by Manstein's later interpretation of Hitler's view, correctly translated by Powell at p. 111 of *Lost Victories* as: 'I think [Hitler] must have been primarily concerned with the reinforcement of our Army Group's armour as a means of opening up the line of the Meuse at Sedan in the interest of Army Group B.'

40. Heinz Guderian, *Panzer Leader* (London: Futura, 1974), p. 89.

41. Manstein, *Lost Victories*, p.109.

42. Manstein, *Verlorene Siege*, pp. 633–637. Annex 6 is one of the many useful documents missing from the English edition.

43. Letter dated 19 November 1939.

44. There is one possible exception to this within the British Army of the Second World War. Colonel, acting Major General, 'Chink' Dorman-Smith was chief of staff to General Sir Claude Auchinleck, Commander-in-Chief Middle East until sacked in August 1942. He is credited by some with having inspired Operation COMPASS, the spectacular British offensive that destroyed the Italian Tenth Army over the period December 1940–February 1941.

45. Manstein, *Lost Victories*, pp. 113–114; *Verlorene Siege*, pp. 111–112. Powell has translated 'following

the hare' as 'To wait and see "which way the cat jumped".' The Allied forces were more 'running hares' than 'jumping cats'!

46. In the event, Fourth Army was switched from Army Group B to A. Eighteenth Army remained in Army Group B and formed the extreme northern wing of the German offensive and struck into the Netherlands.

47. The so-called Maginot Line 'Extension' parallel to the Franco-Belgian frontier provided a loose form of fortifications based on a string of bunkers constructed on a lesser scale than at the Maginot Line proper.

48. Manstein, *Aus einem Soldatenleben*, p. 241

49. Manstein, *Lost Victories*, p. 118. Emphasis as in original.

50. Jodl Diary, 17 February 1940. Quoted by Frieser, *The Blitzkrieg Legend*, p. 75.

51. For detailed descriptions of the Mechelen incident and its consequences, see Cartier, pp. 60–65; and Sebag-Montefiore, *Dunkirk*, pp. 26–37.

52. See Bryan Perrett, *Lightning War: A History of Blitzkrieg* (London: Granada, 1985), p. 108: 'Manstein, coldly hostile, made reference to the "well known negative attitude of OKH.... Brauchitsch was prepared to take bullying from Hitler, but not from his subordinates.'

53. Details of the German approach to war-gaming are contained in General Rudolf Hofmann, *War Games*, MS # P-094, trans. P. Luetzendorf (United States Army Europe Historical Division, 1952).

54. *The Halder War Diary*, pp. 95–96

55. Manstein, *Lost Victories*, p. 120.

56. Guderian, p. 90.

57. See Ellis, *The War in France*, pp. 340–342, quoting Jodl's diary from *Trial of the Major War Criminals*, vol. 27, Document No. 1809-PS, Appendix II, p. 397.

58. *The Halder War Diary*, p. 99.

59. Guderian, p. 91.

60. Montgomery, *The Memoirs*, p. 56.

61. For a comparison of German and British approaches (albeit for 1944), see R.A.M.S. Melvin, 'The German View' in John Buckley (ed.), *The Normandy Campaign 1944 – Sixty Years On* (London: Routledge, 2006), pp. 22–34.

62. Schall-Riaucour, p. 202, fn 51.

63. Frieser, *Blitzkrieg Legend*, p. 75.

64. Ibid., pp. 74–75.

7. A Glorious Summer

1. Manstein, *Lost Victories*, p. 139.

2. Engel, *At the Heart of the Reich*, p. 87. Entry for 19 February 1940.

3. According to the mission of the corps, divisions and army troops such as reinforcing artillery, air defence, engineer and supply units would be subordinated on a temporary basis.

4. Details of each exercise are contained in BA-MA, RH 24–38/12, 'Planspiele 1–6'.

5. Entries in BA-MA, RH 24–38/2, Generalkommando XXXVIII. Corps Kriegstagebuch 1 (KTB1). The divisions inspected were the 161st, 162nd, 197th, 206th and 213th.

6. The contemporary British Army term was General Staff Officer Grade (GSO1). Neither German nor British divisions had 'chiefs of staff' by title during the Second World War, although the Ia and the GSO1 had this function to a large extent.

7. F. W. von Mellenthin, *Schach dem Schicksal* (Osnabrück: Biblio Verlag, 1989), p. 79.

8. BA-MA, MSg 1/1830. Graf, 'Erinnerungen', p. 5.

9. General of Cavalry Ewald von Kleist commanded XXII Army Corps (Motorized) that was transformed into '*Gruppe v. Kleist*' on 6 March 1940, and later termed '*Panzergruppe Kleist*'. See Frieser, *The Blitzkrieg Legend*, p. 102, and note 7, p. 383.

10. Full details are contained in Frieser, *The Blitzkrieg Legend*, p. 101, in the diagram, 'Organization of Army Group A, 10 May 1940'.

11. Ibid., p. 96

12. Ibid., p. 96–97.

13. Ibid., p. 81–82.

14. Ibid., p. 99.

15. As a member of the OKW staff, Lieutenant Colonel Zeitzler had had a prominent role in the planning of Case Green, the invasion of Czechoslovakia in 1938. He replaced Halder as Chief of the German General Staff in September 1942.

16. This halt order had resulted in a tense disagreement between Kleist and Guderian on 17 May, and the latter's request to be relieved of command. The timely intervention and mediation of List, under whose command Kleist's panzer group had been placed on 15 May, resulted in Guderian's reinstatement.

17. Army Group A War Diary entry for 17 May 1940, quoted by Frieser, *The Blitzkreig Legend*, p. 257. Original source: BA-MA, RH 19 I/37, p. 121.

18. *The Halder War Diary*, p. 149.

19. Army Group A's daily situation report of 02.30 hours on 22 May 1940 shows that on 21 May, Headquarters XXXVIII Corps

was responsible for co-ordinating the movement of 81st, 82nd, 290th, 292nd, 293rd and 298th Infantry Divisions and the Police Division. See Klaus-Jürgen Thies, *Der Zweite Weltkrieg im Kartenbild*, Band 3, *Der Westfeldzug 10. Mai bis 25. Juni 1940* (Osnabrück: Biblio Verlag, 1994), p. 20.

20. BA-MA, MSg 1/1830. Graf, 'Erinnerungen', p. 7.

21. Manstein, *Lost Victories*, p. 130; *Verlorene Siege*, p. 127.

22. Rommel's 7th Panzer Division had experienced only a minor setback at the hands of Major General Martel's improvised 'Frankforce' (two tank battalions and two infantry battalions supported by reconnaissance and anti-tank units) and elements of 3rd French Light Mechanized Division. The action at Arras is well documented: see, for example, Frieser's detailed analysis (pp. 275–290).

23. Halder had conceived the hammer and anvil analogy, recording on 25 May 1940 that 'I wanted to make AGp.A the hammer and AGp.B the anvil in this operation. Now B will be the hammer and A the anvil. As AGp.B is confronted with a consolidated front, progress will be slow and casualties high. The air force, on which all hopes are pinned, is dependent on the weather.' *The Halder War Diary*, p. 165.

24. BA-MA, RH 24–38/2, KTB1. Entry for 24.5.1940.

25. The garrisons were formed from elements of 35th and 37th Brigades of the hapless 12th (Eastern) Division. This Territorial Army division, together with its two sister formations, 23rd (Northumbrian) and 46th (North Midland and West Riding)

Divisions, was employed primarily to provide a labour force rather than to fight. These incomplete divisions had no integral artillery and had not undergone any serious training prior to deploying to France in April 1940. The 12th Division's isolated and unsupported infantry brigades stood no chance in action against a first-class panzer division with powerful close air support.

26. Manstein, *Lost Victories*, p. 132; *Verlorene Siege*, p. 130.

27. Ellis, *The War in France*, p. 260. The view of the divisional commander, Major General R. Evans, contained in the War Diary of 1st (British) Armoured Division, was more critical: 'Thus nothing was achieved in an operation that used Cruiser Tanks in the role of I[nfantry] Tanks against prepared defences, piecemeal, with no Inf. or Arty. Support. There had been insufficient time to prepare for battle and tank crews had had no proper sleep since landing in France. As a result of the engagement the tank strength of units – except 9 L[ancers] who were not engaged – was reduced 25% by enemy action and a further 25% due to mechanical breakdown during the hurried approach march during which there had been no opportunity for maintenance.' Quoted in Cabinet Office Historical Section Narrative (undated), *The Fighting in the Saar and South of the Somme*, p. 28.

28. Manstein records that on 29 May at Abbeville 'strong British armour broke into a number of German positions and caused heavy losses not only in killed and wounded, but also, as was later discovered, in

prisoners'. See *Lost Victories*, p. 133; *Verlorene Siege*, p. 131.

29. BA-MA, MSg 1/1830. Graf, 'Erinnerungen', p. 8.

30. Manstein, *Lost Victories*, p. 132. BA-MA, RH 24–38/2, KTB1. Entry for 27.5.1940, 22.30 hours. Brinkforth received an Iron Cross Second Class immediately and received his Knight's Cross finally on 7 March 1941, the very first private soldier in the German Army to be so recognized. His biography, including details of the action on 27 May 1940, is at: http://www.ritterkreuztraeger-1939-45.de/Infanterie/B/BrBrinkforth-Hubert.htm accessed on 6 June 2009.

31. Unsurprisingly, the *Bartholomew Report* (London: The War Office, 1940) was concerned primarily with lessons to be gained from *defensive* operations. It included a number of recommendations (p. 3) about anti-tank defence, including 'all ranks must be taught to adopt aggressive tactics against any tanks which succeed in penetrating our positions; they should be hunted and ambushed by day and stalked and harried by night, relentlessly and tirelessly until they have been destroyed'. The Report did, however, emphasize the need for offensive spirit: 'The key to success against the German is to hit him and to hit him hard at every opportunity.... Moreover the German dislikes being attacked and this may be the weak spot in his armour.' There was no suggestion of any lessons to be learned from the failings in combined arms tactics and command of troops shown in the British counterattacks at Arras and the Somme bridgeheads, a painful

omission in the light of subsequent experience against the Afrika Korps in the Western Desert.

32. BA-MA, RH 24–38/2, KTB1. Entry for 2.6.1940.

33. Manstein had held predominantly general staff posts throughout the First World War. His appointments commanding troops at company, battalion and divisional level were all held during the inter-war years.

34. For details of these three divisions, see Haupt, *Die deutschen Infanterie-Divisionen*, pp. 25–28; 115–116 and 169–172.

35. The English translation in Manstein, *Lost Victories* (p. 134), renders this as '30 miles wide on each side of Picquigny', which by simple observation of the map, let alone by comparison with the sectors and tasks of the neighbouring corps, is impossible. The XXXVIII Corps' *entire frontage* was 20 km long. Liddell Hart spotted this error too late after publication of the English edition, alerting translator Anthony Powell on 4 May 1959: it has remained uncorrected in all subsequent English editions. See LHCMA, LH (von Manstein) 9/25/45.

36. Condell & Zabecki, *On the German Art of War: Truppenführung*, p. 91, Paragraph 326: 'The width of an infantry division supported on both flanks and conducting a main frontal attack against prepared defences should not exceed 3,000 metres.' [Originally published as the German Army's *Heeresdienstvorschrift* 300 in 1933 (Part 1) and 1934 (Part 2).]

37. Manstein, *Lost Victories*, p. 135.

38. Ibid., pp. 135–136.

39. Manstein incorrectly identifies this

location as 'Arraines'. For a
description of Rommel's attack, see
David Fraser, *Knight's Cross*
(London: HarperCollins, 1993),
pp. 194–198. Subsequently,
Rommel avoided roads when
necessary by adopting a novel
cross-country formation for his
division, the *Flächenmarsch*
(literally: 'area march').

40. Manstein, *Lost Victories*, p. 136.
41. '*Was heute leicht ist, kann morgen
Ströme von Blut kosten.*' Hermann
Balck, *Ordnung im Chaos*
(Osnabrück: Biblio Verlag, 1981),
p. 270.
42. Manstein, *Lost Victories*, p. 138;
Verlorene Siege, p. 136, states Coisy
rather than Oissy surely in error.
Coisy lies 5 km to the north of
Amiens, just off *Route Nationale* 25
towards Doullens. Oissy, on the
other hand, is 8 km south-west of
Picquigny, on the D156 – the
logical axis of advance of 46th
Division.
43. Manstein, *Lost Victories*, pp. 137–
138; *Verlorene Siege*, p. 137.
44. *Truppenführung*, p. 18, Paragraph 8.
45. General Sir Archibald Wavell,
Generals and Generalship (London:
The Times, 1941), p. 15. From the
second of three Lees Knowles
Lectures delivered by Wavell at
Trinity College, Cambridge, in
1939.
46. BA-MA, RH 24–38/2, KTB1.
Entry for 6.6.1940.
47. Manstein, *Lost Victories*, p. 137.
48. *Truppenführung*, p. 116, Paragraph
415: 'From the very moment the
enemy begins to retreat, the
subordinate commanders who are
closest to the enemy initiate the
pursuit, immediately and without
waiting for orders. They must act
boldly and independently. All
weaknesses of the withdrawing

enemy must be exploited.'
49. Manstein (*Verlorene Siege*, p. 138)
states that XXXVIII Corps was
approximately 70 km from the
Seine. This represents a
conservative figure. Other sources,
including German daily situation
maps, indicate that forward
elements of both 6th and 46th
Divisions were already
approaching Gournay-en-Bray, 40
km north-east of the Seine crossing
at Les Andelys. Rommel,
meanwhile, reached the Seine
south of Rouen during the early
hours of 9 June. As he prepared to
cross the river at Elbeuf at 03.00
hours, the French blew the Seine
bridges (Fraser, *Knight's Cross*, pp.
199–200).
50. *The Halder War Diary*, p. 191.
Entry for 10 June 1940.
51. As a norm, a division needs a
minimum of two, preferably three,
crossing points over a major river.
Routinely, the German Army in
the Second World War had the
capacity to provide one fixed
crossing per division, with little
margin for the unforeseen.
Although the German bridging
equipment was technically sound,
as one might expect, there was
never enough *matériel* to go round.
Nor was there anything to match
the flexibility of the Bailey
bridging system that the British
Army employed in 1943–45.
52. Manstein, *Verlorene Siege*, p. 142.
For some reason Powell cut out
the relevant sentence in *Lost
Victories*, p. 143.
53. Ellis, *The War in France*, pp. 289–
293.
54. BA-MA, RH 24–38/2, KTB1.
Entry for 12.6.1940.
55. Trevor-Roper (ed.), *Hitler's War
Directives*, p. 72.

56. Manstein, *Verlorene Siege*, p. 144. In *Lost Victories*, p. 145, Powell mistranslated '*eine motorisierte Vorausabteilung*' as 'a motorized reconnaissance battalion'.

57. Manstein, *Lost Victories*, p. 145.

58. *Truppenführung*, p. 18, Paragraph 9.

59. Manstein *Lost Victories*, p. 146. Manstein's account is confirmed in BA-MA, MSg 1/1830. Graf, 'Erinnerungen', pp. 10–11.

60. BA-MA, RH 24–38/2, KTB1. Entries for 17 and 18.6.1940.

61. Ibid. Entry for 19.6.1940.

62. Ibid. Entry for 20.6.1940.

63. The German ideological commitment is highlighted by Williamson Murray in his foreword to Megargee's detailed study, *Inside Hitler's High Command*, p. ix: '... arguments about the efficacy of German tactical and operational virtuosity must also contain a recognition that German soldiers were willing to take extremely high casualties to accomplish their mission.'

64. BA-MA, MSg 1/1830. Graf, 'Erinnerungen', p. 9.

8. From France to Russia

1. The castle of Serrant lies 15 km west of Angers in the small commune of St Georges-sur-Loire and 7 km north of Chalonnes.

2. Manstein, *Lost Victories*, p. 147.

3. Ibid.

4. Ibid., p. 149.

5. Horne, *To Lose a Battle*, p. 652, supplemented by other sources.

6. BA-MA, RH 24–38/18. XXXVIII. A.K., Kriegstagebuch Nr. 2 (KTB2). Entry for 26.6.1940.

7. Ibid. Entries for 26.6.1940, 23.00 hours, and 27.6.1940, 18.00 hours respectively.

8. Ibid. Entries for 27 and 28.6.1940 refer.

9. Westphal, *The German Army in the West*, p. 85.

10. Max Hastings, 'Why Resistance Mattered': book review of Matthew Cobb, *The Resistance* (London: Simon & Schuster, 2009) in *The Sunday Times*, 7 June 2009.

11. This remains a most controversial point. See, for example, Alan Clarke, *Barbarossa: The Russian-German Conflict* (London: Cassell, 2005) [originally published in 1965], p. 193: '[A]trocities were so commonplace that no man coming fresh to the scene could stay sane without acquiring a protective veneer of brutalisation.' Omer Bartov's *Hitler's Army* (New York: Oxford University Press, 1991) gives a comprehensive treatment of the subject.

12. Manstein, *Lost Victories*, p. 151.

13. Kershaw, *Hitler: Nemesis*, p. 299.

14. *The Halder War Diary* p. 210. Halder's entry for 19 June 1940 included a brief note on the projected organization of the 'Future Army', including 20 armoured and 10 motorized divisions; 6 mountain and 26 infantry divisions.

15. Kershaw, *Hitler: Nemesis*, pp. 303–304; Reuth, *Hitler: Eine politische Biographie*, pp. 483–484.

16. See William L. Shirer, *The Rise and Fall of the Third Reich* (London: Secker & Warburg, 1960), pp. 753–755, for an account of Hitler's speech of 19 July 1940.

17. The full list of nine army promotions from *Generaloberst* (colonel general) to *General-feldmarschall* (field marshal) was: Wilhelm Keitel and Walther von Brauchitsch; Gerd von Rundstedt,

Fedor von Bock and Wilhelm Ritter von Leeb (commanders-in-chief of Army Groups A, B and C respectively); Erwin von Witzleben, Hans-Günther von Kluge, Walther von Reichenau and Wilhelm List (commanders-in-chief of the First, Fourth, Sixth and Twelfth Armies respectively). Of the Luftwaffe, three senior officers were promoted to field marshal: *General der Flieger* Albert Kesselring (commander of *Luftflotte* 2); *Generaloberst* Erhard Milch (*Generalinspekteur der Luftwaffe*) and Hugo Sperrle (commander of *Luftflotte* 3). Of other prominent generals, Guderian was promoted from *General der Panzertruppe* (general of armoured troops) to colonel general on the same day (19 July 1940) as was Halder.

18. Manstein, *Lost Victories*, p. 150.

19. Wheatley, *Operation Sea Lion*, pp. 35–36. The best (and technically very detailed) German view is given by Peter Schenk, *Invasion of England 1940* (London: Conway Maritime Press, 1990) (first pub. in 1987 as *Landung in England* by Oberbaum Verlag, Berlin).

20. Alistair Horne (pp. 653–654), for example, criticizes the fact that 'Hitler and the planners of genius who had created *Sichelschnitt* had in reality thought no further ahead than Falkenhayn [the German Chief of the General Staff in 1916 who had proposed the offensive at Verdun]; no contingency had been prepared whereby a tottering Britain might be invaded immediately after success had been achieved in France. By mid July, when the first O.K.H. plan was drafted, it was already too late.'

21. Wheatley, pp. 3–13.

22. BA-MA, MSg 1/1830. Graf, 'Erinnerungen', pp. 11–12.

23. The original OKH plan for Operation SEA LION was overambitious: under command of Rundstedt's Army Group A, Colonel General Ernst Busch's Sixteenth Army (six divisions) would land between Ramsgate and Bexhill in Kent, whilst Ninth Army (four divisions) under Colonel General Adolf Strauss would land between Brighton and the Isle of Wight. In addition, three divisions of Field Marshal Walther von Reichenau's Sixth Army would prepare to land at Lyme Bay between Weymouth and Lyme Regis. This first wave of thirteen divisions landing within the first three days (an initial level of effort never achieved by Allied forces in any theatre of war), would have been supported by no less than nine armoured or motorized divisions in a second wave, with a further nine infantry divisions planned for a third wave, together with eight divisions held in OKH reserve as a potential fourth wave. Two airborne formations (the Luftwaffe's 7th Parachute and the German Army's 22nd Air Landing Divisions) were also available for early employment.

24. Details of the proposed organization and tactical employment of Manstein's corps are given in Schenk, pp. 286–300.

25. Close air support was to be provided by the 228 dive-bombers of Lieutenant General Baron Wolfram von Richthofen's VIII *Fliegerkorps* (with whom Manstein was later to develop a very close working relationship on the Eastern Front) and by about 320 bombers and 60 dive-bombers of

General Ulrich Grauert's
I *Fliegerkorps*.

26. Winston Churchill, *The Second World War*, vol. ii, *Their Finest Hour* (London: Cassell, 1949), p. 221.

27. Technical details of the German submersible and amphibious tanks are given by Schenk, pp. 107–114.

28. Quoted by Telford Taylor, *The Breaking Wave: The German Defeat in the Summer of 1940* (London: Weidenfeld & Nicolson, 1967), p. 254.

29. BA-MA, MSg 1/1830. Graf, 'Erinnerungen', p. 12.

30. Manstein, *Lost Victories*, p. 152.

31. Manstein, *Verlorene Siege*, p. 151.

32. BA-MA, RH 24–38/18. Entry for 12.9.1940.

33. *The Halder War Diary*, p. 257.

34. BA-MA, RH 24–38/18. Entry for 7.10.1940, 10.20 hours.

35. Manstein, *Lost Victories*, pp. 152–171.

36. Ibid., pp. 154–155.

37. Ibid., p. 156.

38. Manstein, *Lost Victories*, p. 156.

39. Ibid., pp. 157–162.

40. Ibid., p. 162.

41. Ibid., pp. 162–163.

42. Ibid., p. 164.

43. Ibid., p. 165.

44. Emphasis as given in the German language original edition and the English translation. See Manstein, *Verlorene Kriege*, p. 169, and *Lost Victories*, p. 169.

45. Ibid.

46. Ibid., p. 170.

47. Of note, military historians and retired officers from both Britain and Germany took part in a major war game at the Royal Military Academy Sandhurst in 1979. The results indicated that a German invasion would have been defeated with heavy casualties once the Royal Navy and Royal Air Force had intervened decisively. Casualties on both sides, however, would have been extremely heavy.

48. The best detailed study on this question is contained in Douglas Porch, *Hitler's Mediterranean Gamble: The North African and Mediterranean Campaigns in World War II* (London: Weidenfeld & Nicolson, 2004).

49. The publication of *Lost Victories* is described in the Epilogue.

50. Manstein, *Lost Victories*, p. 163, fn 1.

51. LHCMA, LH (von Manstein) 9/24/45. Colin Young, 'Manstein invades us over coffee', *Sunday Dispatch*, 25 May, 1958.

52. Manstein, *Lost Victories*, p. 171.

53. Such mechanized forces, which the Germans described as 'fast' or mobile troops, remained very much in a minority within the German Army. The vast majority of the formations fielded throughout the Second World War were horse-drawn infantry divisions.

54. BA-MA, Pers 6/33, Personalakte Gen Feldmarschall von Manstein, Folio 11, Armee-Oberkommando 9, A.H.Qu., den 17. März 1941.

55. Trevor-Roper (ed.), *Hitler's War Directives*, p. 49.

56. Manstein, *Lost Victories*, p. 175.

57. See *The Halder War Diary*, pp. 345–346; and Hürter, *Hitlers Heerführer*, pp. 1–13, for a detailed description and analysis of Hitler's address of 30 March 1941.

58. Quoted by Megargee, *War of Annihilation*, p. 38.

59. Translated from BA-MA, RH 24–56/8, Folio 4, Anlage 11 zu Gen.Kdo.LVI.A.K.(mot), Ia op. Nr. 210/41 g.Kdos. v. 12.6.41, Section I, Paragraphs 1 and 2.

60. JAG Archives, London:

DJAG/15418/972/BAOR dated 16 January 1950 – 'Military Court (War Crimes) Trial Fritz Erich von Lewinski (called von Manstein)', p. 11.

61. For a comprehensive study of the Commissar Order, see Felix Römer, *Der Kommissarbefehl: Wehrmacht und NS-Verbrechen an der Ostfront 1941/42* (Paderborn: Ferdinand Schöningh, 2008). For Römer's assessment of Manstein's attitude, as reflected in his evidence to the International Military Tribunal, see p. 514.

62. Manstein, *Lost Victories*, p. 179.

63. Ibid., p. 180.

64. Ibid.

65. For example, see BA-MA, RH 27–8/9, War Diary of 8th Panzer Division, entry for 18.6.41, 10.00 hrs: '... *Ferner wurde besprochen die Behandlung der roten Funktionäre und Soldaten usw.*' ('Further, the handling of Red functionaries and soldiers et cetera was discussed.')

66. BA-MA, RH 21-4/272. For an analysis of the impact of the Commissar Order, see Hürter, pp. 393–404.

67. Manstein, letter to his wife, 20 July 1941. Letter held in the private possession of Rüdiger von Manstein.

68. Manstein, *Lost Victories*, p. 175. For evidence of the Wehrmacht's collusion with the SD and other agents of repression, there is a growing literature. See, for example, Wette, *The Wehrmacht*.

69. Manstein, *Lost Victories*, pp. 176–177.

70. Critical to the planning and conduct of any campaign is the correct identification of the enemy's centre of gravity – his primary source of power from which his strength stems. At the strategic level, was it areas of economic significance or the capital city, not only a national transportation hub but the political core of Communist power? If it were the latter, then Moscow should have been given priority from the outset.

71. Glantz and House, *When Titans Clashed*, p. 33. See also, for example, the analysis in John Erickson, *The Road to Stalingrad* (London: Weidenfeld & Nicolson, 1975); Richard Overy, *Russia's War* (London: Penguin, 1999); and Christopher Bellamy, *Absolute War* (London: Macmillan, 2007).

72. On 22 June 1941, the German Army employed nineteen panzer divisions and ten motorized infantry divisions on the Eastern Front, of which only three panzer and two motorized divisions, together with a motorized SS division, were subordinated to Fourth Panzer Group. Hence the vast majority of the mobile divisions were concentrated in the other three panzer groups, the Second and Third in Army Group Centre, and the First in Army Group South.

9. Panzer Corps Commander

1. Manstein, Personal War Diary, Entry for 24 June 1941.

2. In June 1941, the Germans estimated the Red Army's active strength as 170 rifle and 33.5 cavalry divisions, 46 tank and motorized and 7–8 airborne brigades. In fact, the real figures were 196 rifle, 13 cavalry, 61 tank and 31 motorized divisions, together with 16 airborne brigades. Excluding separate brigades amounting to 133 division

equivalents, the Red Army had fielded by 1 December 1941 a total of 483 rifle, 73 tank, 31 motorized and 101 cavalry divisions. I am grateful to Charles Dick for supplying this data.

3. Glantz and House, *When Titans Clashed*, p. 35: 'The 3d Mechanized Corps in Lithuania possessed 460 tanks, of which 109 were of the new KV-1 and T-34 designs.' Each mechanized corps contained two tank divisions and a motorized infantry division.

4. Manstein, *Lost Victories*, p. 181.

5. Place names are a sensitive political issue in the Baltic states, with many locations having historical German (or Polish) and Russian names in addition to modern Estonian, Latvian and Lithuanian ones. For example, Daugavpils (Latvian) is known in German as Dünaburg, in Russian as Dvinsk and in Lithuanian as Daugpils. Within the Kaliningrad *Oblast*, however, Russian names now prevail over German; hence Kaliningrad rather than Königsberg.

6. Manstein, *Lost Victories*, p. 179.

7. Manstein's account was criticized severely by Walter Chales de Beaulieu in his *Der Vorstoss der Panzergruppe 4 auf Leningrad – 1941* (Neckargemünd; Kurt Vowinckel Verlag, 1961). De Beaulieu, Hoepner's chief of staff, declared (p. 145) that the descriptions in *Verlorene Siege* were of 'little value for military historical research'.

8. Manstein, Personal War Diary. Entry for 18 June 1941.

9. Manstein, *Lost Victories*, p. 180; and BA-MA, RH 27-8/9, 8th Panzer Division War Diary, entries for 16–20.6.41.

10. BA-MA, RH–21-4/16, Folio 188.

Der Befehlshaber der Panzergruppe 4, Tagesbefehl am 21.6.1941.

11. Ibid., entry for 22 June 1941.

12. Manstein, letter to his wife, 9 July 1941. Letter held in the private possession of Rüdiger Manstein.

13. Manstein, *Lost Victories*, p. 180.

14. BA-MA, RH 24-56/8, HQ LVI Corps War Diary, Folio 4, Anlage 11 zu Gen.Kdo.LVI.A.K.(mot) Ia op. Nr. 210/41 g.Kdos. v. 12.6.41, 'Richtlinien für das Verhalten der Truppe in Rußland' [= OKW Guidelines for the behaviour of troops in Russia], Paragraph 3.

15. The Soviet tank actions against XXXXI Corps are described in Bellamy, *Absolute War*, pp. 188–189, and Erickson, *The Road to Stalingrad*, p. 143; see also the detailed account by Erhard Raus in *Panzer Operations: The Eastern Front Memoir of General Raus, 1941–1945*, ed. and trans. Steven H. Newton (Cambridge, Mass: De Capo Press, 2003), pp. 21–34.

16. Manstein, Personal War Diary. Entry for 24 June 1941.

17. Ibid., entry for 24 June 1941.

18. Manstein, *Lost Victories*, p. 184.

19. Ibid., p. 186. See also Zhukov, *Memoirs*, pp. 260–261, for a brief Soviet account of the battle of the Dvina. He describes Lelyushenko's corps as undertaking a 'bold counter-offensive, delivering a blow at the 56th German Motorized Corps and checking its advance'. It can be inferred that the armoured formation Manstein mentioned was 46th Tank Division, commanded by Colonel A. Koptsov, 'a hero of Khalkhin-Gol', the scene of Zhukov's great victory against the Japanese in 1939.

20. Megargee, *War of Annihilation*, p.

70, implies that LVI Corps at Daugavpils took action against Jews accused of sabotage, quoting from Förster 'Securing Living Space', p. 1,204.

21. Manstein, *Lost Victories*, p. 185.

22. *The Halder War Diary*, p. 428.

23. Manstein, *Lost Victories*, p. 185.

24. BA-MA, RH 24–56/6, HQ LVI Corps War Diary, Folio 2, Der Befehlshaber der Panzergruppe 4, Gr. H. Qu., den 1. 7. 1941, An die Herren Kommandierenden Generäle des XXXXI. und LVI. A.K.

25. See Martin van Creveld, *Supplying War: Logistics from Wallenstein to Patton* (Cambridge: University Press: 1977), pp. 158–162, for a description of the transport and supply problems that bedevilled Army Group North's operations.

26. *The Halder War Diary*, p. 443.

27. Manstein, *Lost Victories*, p. 186.

28. Russian Army *Field Regulations (Provisional)* of 1936, a tactical manual with underpinning operational level thinking, stated at Paragraph 9: 'Modern technical means of combat make possible the simultaneous defeat of the enemy's combat formation[s] throughout the entire depth of his deployment. Opportunities have greatly increased for rapid regrouping, the surprise envelopment of the enemy and seizure of his rear areas and cutting his lines of retreat.' Paragraph 181 developed this theme with: 'The mission of deep-acting tank groups is to penetrate into the rear of the enemy's main forces to destroy their reserves and headquarters.' I am grateful to Charles Dick in bringing this reference to my attention and in supplying the translation.

29. See George S. Patton, *War As I Knew It* (Boston: Houghton Mifflin, 1947), pp. 354–355: 'Commanders and their staffs should visit units two echelons below their own, and their maps should be so kept. ... The more senior the officer who appears with a very small unit at the front, the better the effect is on the troops. If some danger is involved in the visit, its value is enhanced. ... Corps and Army commanders must make it a point to be physically seen by as many individuals of their command as possible – certainly by all combat soldiers.'

30. Manstein, *Lost Victories*, pp. 189–190.

31. Ibid., p. 190.

32. Ibid., p. 203; *Verlorene Siege*, p. 205.

33. Manstein, *Lost Victories*, pp. 191–192.

34. Manstein, Personal War Diary. Entries for the dates stated in the text; for the mine incident, see *Verlorene Siege*, p. 203.

35. Manstein, *Lost Victories*, pp. 187–188; Personal War Diary. Entries for 2 and 7 July 1941.

36. Manstein, Personal War Diary. Entry for 10 July 1941.

37. *The Halder War Diary*, pp. 420–421.

38. Manstein, *Lost Victories*, pp. 192–193.

39. BA-MA, RH 24–56/6, LVI Corps War Diary, Folio 3, Der Kommandierende General des LVI.A.K.(mot.), K.H.Qu. 14.7.41., An den Befehlshaber der Panzergruppe 4 Herrn Generaloberst Hoepner.

40. BA-MA, RH 24–56/6, LVI Corps War Diary, Folio 4, Der Befehlshaber der Panzergruppe 4, Gr. H. Qu., den 15.7.1941., An Herrn Kommandierenden

General des LVI. A.K. Herrn
General der Infanterie v. Manstein.

41. See David M. Glantz, *Before
Stalingrad: Barbarossa: Hitler's
Invasion of Russia 1941* (Stroud:
Tempus Publishing, 2003), p. 95,
for further details.

42. Zhukov, *Memoirs*, p. 277.

43. Manstein, *Lost Victories*, pp. 194–
196; Personal War Diary. Entries
for 14–18 July 1941. See also
Bellamy, p. 251; Erickson, *The
Road to Stalingrad*, p. 183.

44. Manstein, *Lost Victories*, p. 196;
Personal War Diary. Entry for 18
July 1941. Manstein was mistaken
in thinking that Voroshilov was a
front commander at the time. He
had met Voroshilov in 1931 (see
Chapter 2, p. 55) as Commissar for
War (renamed Defence in 1934), a
post he retained until being sacked
by Stalin in May 1940. Although
his performance in many functions
during the Great Patriotic War
was lamentable, he was one of the
Soviet Union's greatest survivors,
having been removed from post
many times but escaping the firing
squad, and then to become nominal
president of the USSR (1954–60).
His biographer summed him up
well as the 'legendary Red Marshal
who possessed neither strategic
thinking, nor operational vision,
nor organizational ability ... an
"Emperor with no clothes".'
(Dmitri Volkogonov in Harold
Shukman (ed.), *Stalin's Generals*, p.
317.) One of the great ironies of
the Soviet Union was that the
prestigious General Staff Academy
in Moscow was named after
Voroshilov.

45. Manstein, Personal War Diary.
Entry for 16 July 1941; BA-MA,
RH 24–56/6, LVI Corps War
Diary, Folio 5–7, Der

Kommandierende General des
LVI.A.K.(mot.), K.Gef.St.,
16.7.41., An Herrn Befehlshaber
der Panzergruppe 4.

46. Manstein, Personal War Diary.
Entry for 17 July 1941.

47. BA-MA, RH 24–56/6, LVI Corps
War Diary, Folio 9–10, Der
Kommandierende General des
LVI.A.K.(mot.), K.Gef.St.,
22.7.41., An den Befehlshaber der
Panzergruppe 4 Herrn
Generaloberst Hoepner.

48. Manstein, letter to his wife, 22 July
1941. Letter held in the private
possession of Rüdiger von
Manstein.

49. Manstein, Personal War Diary.
Entry for 25 July 1941. Although
Gero von Manstein was the son of
a senior officer he none the less
had to start his military career in
common with every other German
Army recruit as a soldier and prove
himself worthy for promotion to a
non-commissioned officer before
he could be considered for a
commission.

50. Manstein, *Lost Victories*, p. 198.

51. See *The Halder War Diary*, p. 487:
'Hoepner, von Manstein, and
Reinhardt concur that the area
between Lake Ilmen and Lake
Peipus is unsuited to operations of
armoured units. All we can do at
Lake Ilmen is to attack with the
infantry while keeping in readiness
the armour not yet committed (von
Manstein's corps) for a follow-up
where infantry has cleared the
path.'

52. BA-MA, RH 24–56/6, LVI Corps
War Diary, Folios 16–18,
Generalkommando
LVI.A.K.(mot.), Der
Kommandierende General,
K.Gef.St., 31.7.41., An den Herrn
Befehlshaber der Panzergruppe 4.

Manstein, Personal War Diary. Entries for 31 July, 2 and 4 August 1941.

53. Manstein, *Lost Victories*, p. 198. Guderian's maxim is often slightly mistranslated (including by Anthony G. Powell) as 'Don't spatter: Boot 'em.' In modern colloquial German the equivalent expression is more often: *'Nicht Kleckern, sondern klotzen'*. Either way, the sense is 'Stop messing about with half measures'. See *Oxford–Duden German Dictionary* (Oxford: University Press, 2005), p. 418.

54. Manstein, letter to his wife, 14 August 1941. Letter held in the private possession of Rüdiger von Manstein.

55. Ibid., 30 July 1941. Letter held in the private possession of Rüdiger von Manstein.

56. Manstein, *Lost Victories*, p. 199; Personal War Diary, Entries for 15 and 16 August 1941.

57. BA-MA, RH 21-4/14, Fourth Panzer Group War Diary, Folio 226. Entry for 15 August 1941, 18.00 hours.

58. Erickson, p. 187. David M. Glantz, *Forgotten Battles of the German Soviet War (1941–1945)*, vol. I, *The Summer-Fall Campaign (22 June–4 December 1941)* (privately published, 1999), pp. 51–59.

59. Manstein, *Lost Victories*, pp. 200–201; Personal War Diary. Entries for 19–23 August 1941.

60. BA-MA, RH 24-56/6, LVI Corps War Diary, Folios 35–37, Generalkommando LVI.A.K.(mot.), Der Kommandierende General, K.G.St., 29.8.7.41., An den Herrn Oberbefehlshaber der 16. Armee.

61. Ibid., Folios 38–39, Der Oberbefehlshaber der 16. Armee,

A.H.Qu., 30.8.1941. Zum Bericht vom 29.8.41: An den Herrn Kommandierenden General des LVI. A.K.

62. Ibid., Folios 40–41, Der Kommandierende General des LVI. A.K., den 2.9.41.

63. Manstein, *Lost Victories*, pp. 201–202; Personal War Diary. Entries for 5–12 September 1941. Manstein's memoir contradicts his first entry for 12 September that indicates 3rd Motorized Division would be subordinated to Fourth Army whilst LVI Corps, finally, would receive 8th Panzer Division for a 'new and very fine task'.

64. Manstein, Personal War Diary. Second entry for 12 September 1941.

65. BA-MA, Pers 6/33, Personalakte Gen Feldmarschall von Manstein, Folio 12, Kommando der Panzergruppe 4, Gr.H.Qu., den 13. Sept. 1941.

10. The Campaign in the Crimea

1. Dietrich von Choltitz, *Soldat unter Soldaten* (Zürich: Europa Verlag, 1951), p. 127.

2. Carl von Clausewitz, *On War*, pp. 133 and 117.

3. BA-MA, RH 20-11/489. Eleventh Army War Diary, entry for 13.30 hours, 12.9.1941.

4. See Chapter 9 of Manstein's *Lost Victories*. Until recently, Hayward, *Stopped at Stalingrad* and Porter Randall Blakemore's *Manstein in the Crimea: The Eleventh Army Campaign, 1941–1942* (Ann Arbor, Mich., University Microfilms International, 1989) were the best sources in English. Pending the publication of C. J. Dick's new study, see David M. Glantz, *Forgotten Battles of the German-*

Soviet War (1941–1945), vol. II.,
*The Winter Campaign (5 December
1941–April 1942)* (privately
published: 1999); and David M.
Glantz with Jonathan M. House,
To the Gates of Stalingrad, vol. 1,
*Soviet-German Combat Operations,
April–August 1942* (Lawrence:
University Press of Kansas, 2009).
Robert Forczyk, *Sevastopol 1942:
Von Manstein's Triumph* (Oxford:
Osprey, 2008) provides better
detail than C. G. Sweeting, *Blood
and Iron: The German Conquest of
Sevastopol* (Washington, DC:
Potomac Books, 2004). From a
German perspective, the novel by
Christoph von Imhoff, *Die Festung
Sewastopol* (Stuttgart: Veria Verlag,
1953) brings to life many of the
principal personalities. Franz
Kurowski, *Sevastopol: Der Angriff
auf die stärkste Festung der Welt*
(Wölfersheim-Berstadt: Podzun-
Pallas-Verlag, 2002) gives a
number of German unit accounts.
For the Soviet side, see the very
detailed – as yet untranslated –
account by A. V. Basov, *Crimea in
the Great Patriotic War 1941–1945*
(Moscow: Nayuka, 1987). In
addition, see Vladimir V. Karpov,
The Commander, trans. Yuri S.
Shirokov and Nicholas Louis
(London: Brassey's, 1987), which is
a considerably condensed
biography of Manstein's principal
opponent, Major General I. E.
Petrov, commander of the Soviet
Coastal Army. A 'slightly
shortened' version of Karpov's
book is given in: *Der General und
Ich* (Berlin: Militärverlag der
Deutschen Demokratischen
Republik, 1989).
5. Manstein, *Lost Victories*, p. 204.
6. In this and subsequent chapters,
original Russian rather than
modern Ukrainian spellings are
used.
7. Glantz, *Before Stalingrad*, pp. 127–
129.
8. Manstein, *Lost Victories*, p. 208.
9. Research in the Federal Military
Archive (BA-MA) reveals that
many of the letters and estimates
of the situation by Eleventh Army
sent to Headquarters Army Group
South (subsequently Army Group
A) over the period September 1941
to July 1942 were written by
Manstein himself; with typical
German thoroughness his pencil
drafts have been preserved
carefully and archived alongside the
typed final versions.
10. BA-MA, RH 20–11/489.
Headquarters Eleventh Army War
Diary, September 1941: Notes of
staff briefing opposite entries for
19.9 and 20.9.41: [Point] 5.
*'Zuschauen bei Judenerschiessungen
ist eines Offz. Unwürdig.'* [Point] 6.
[Obscured] *'Keine Scheu vor neuem
O.B., er ist ein Freund der
ungezwungenen Unterhaltung'*
[subsequently pasted over, perhaps
on Manstein's instructions].
11. Paget, *Manstein: His Campaigns and
His Trial*, pp. 35–36.
12. Manstein, *Lost Victories*, p. 222.
13. In the Supplement to Hitler's
Directive No. 34. See Trevor-
Roper (ed.), *Hitler's War Directives*,
p. 93.
14. Trevor-Roper, p. 95. Hitler
entertained the wildest dreams for
the Crimea. As the future *Gau
Gotenland*, it would become the
Greater German Reich's place in
the sun linked to Berlin by a grand
trans-European, 3,000-km-long
autobahn and wide-gauge railway.
The Tsar's former summer palace
at Livadia next to Yalta would
become the Führer's retirement

home, and to make the region fit for Hitler and his élite, the Crimea would be cleared of all ethnic Russians, Tatars and Ukrainians and be settled with 'pure' Germans. See Bernd Wegner, 'Die Kämpfe auf der Krim', *Der Globale Krieg: Die Ausweitung zum Weltkrieg und der Wechsel der Initiative 1941–1943* [Das deutsche Reich im Zweiten Weltkrieg, vol. 4] (Stuttgart: Deutsche Verlags-Anstalt, 1990), p. 840; see also Norman Rich, *Hitler's War Aims: The Establishment of the New Order* (London: André Deutsch, 1974), p. 383: 'In memory of the German Ostrogoths who had first civilized this great land, the German Crimea was to be called Gotenland, the city of Sevastopol was to be renamed Theoderichshafen, and Simferopol was to be called Gotenburg.'

15. Once the home of the German settler and nature reserve pioneer family, the Falz-Feins. It remains an important nature reserve today.

16. BA-MA, RH 20–11/489. Eleventh Army War Diary. Entry for 18 September 1941, 19.15 hours.

17. Paget, pp. 37–38.

18. Manstein, *Lost Victories*, p. 211.

19. From Ishun in the north-west to the capital city and central pivot of Simferopol is 110 km. From here, 86 km distant lies Yalta on the southern coast whilst the major port of Sevastopol is 71 km to the south-west. From Simferopol, the port of Feodosia lies 120 km to the east, Kerch a further 120; Yevpatoriya (more commonly transliterated as Eupatoria) is 64 km to the west.

20. Eleventh Army's order of battle

consisted of some eight and a half German divisions. XXX Corps: 72nd and 22nd Infantry Divisions, together with the reinforced motorized brigade SS *Leibstandarte Adolf Hitler*; XXXXIX Corps: 1st and 4th Mountain Divisions plus 170th Infantry; LIV Corps: 46th and 73rd Infantry Divisions; 50th Infantry Division remained under the army's direct command initially.

21. Manstein, *Lost Victories*, p. 210.

22. Ibid.

23. Glantz, *Before Stalingrad*, p. 153.

24. Manstein, *Lost Victories*, p. 210.

25. Ibid.

26. Ibid., p. 212.

27. *On the German Art of War: Truppenführung*, § 315, p. 88.

28. Leutnant Dittrich, 'Tataren-Graben und Perekop' in *Wir Erobern die Krim* (Neustadt/Weinstrasse: Pfälzische Verlagsanstalt, 1943), pp. 19–22.

29. Manstein, *Lost Victories*, p. 214

30. Manstein, Personal War Diary. Entry for 28 September 1941.

31. Manstein, *Lost Victories*, p. 215.

32. Paget, p. 38.

33. Blakemore, p. 58.

34. BA-MA, N/507–92. Der Oberbefehlshaber der 11. Armee, A.H.Qu, den 4.10.41.

35. See *Die Wehrmachtsberichte 1939–1945*, Band 1, 1. September 1939 bis 31. Dezember 1941 (Munich: Deutscher Taschenbuch Verlag, 1985), p. 694. Interestingly, the Soviet losses reported by OKW are significantly fewer than those given in Manstein's memoirs (Manstein's figures are in parentheses): 64,325 (106,362) prisoners of war; 126 (212) tanks; and 519 (672) artillery pieces. The discrepancy probably reflects a degree of double-counting within

the three Axis armies involved (German First Panzer and Eleventh Armies, Third Rumanian Army).

36. BA-MA, N/507–92. A.H.Qu., den 15. Oktober 1941 Ia Nr. 4080/41 geh.Kdos. *Operationen Krim–Kertsch.*

37. Manstein, *Lost Victories*, p. 217.

38. Ibid., p. 219.

39. BA-MA, N/507–92. Der Oberbefehlshaber der 11. Armee, A.H.Q., den 20.10.41. *An den Herrn Chef des Generalstabes der Heeresgruppe Süd!*

40. Manstein, Personal War Diary. Entry for 22 October 1941.

41. Manstein, *Lost Victories*, p. 220. Manstein was referring here to the Clausewitzian notion of culmination. German doctrine was specific on this matter. See *Truppenführung*, § 324, p. 91: 'As a rule, every attack passes through a series of crises until it reaches the point of culmination. It is critical that the commander recognises this point, and possesses the ability to make a decision to immediately exploit the success with all available means, or to prevent failure.'

42. See Mark Axworthy, *Third Axis: Fourth Ally* (London: Arms & Armour Press, 1995), p. 67. The Rumanian forces under the command of Colonel Radu Korne, grouped as the 'Korne Motorized Detachment', comprised 6th Motorized Regiment and 5th Mechanized Squadron of 8th Cavalry Brigade, which included a number of R1 light tanks. I am grateful to Charles Dick for bringing this reference to my attention.

43. Manstein, Personal War Diary. Entry for 30 September 1941. In fact, Manstein would have to wait until April 1942 before he was reinforced temporarily by 22nd Panzer Division for the recapture of the Kerch peninsula. For the majority of the campaign on the Crimea, Eleventh Army possessed only three detachments (battalion equivalents) of tracked assault guns to provide close-in armoured support for the hard-pressed infantry divisions and regiments, notwithstanding the frequent Soviet reports of heavy tank attacks on Sevastopol.

44. BA-MA, N/507–92. Der Oberbefehlshaber der 11. Armee, A.H.Q., den 30. Oktober 1941, An Heeresgruppenkommando Süd. *Absicht für Weiterführung der Krim-Operationen.*

45. I. A. Laskin, *On the Way to the Turning Point* (Moscow: Voenizdat, 1977), pp. 34–36. I am grateful to Ksenia Verzhbystka for finding and translating this quote.

46. *The Halder War Diary*, p. 555. Entry for 10 November 1941.

47. Manstein, Personal War Diary. Entries for 9 and 11 November 1941.

48. I thank Ksenia Verzhbystka for tracking down the whereabouts of Sarabus (later named Ostriakovo in honour of the eponymous Soviet airman and hero), which lies today near the rail junction of Gvardeyskoye, 24 km north of Simferopol. The former school building still survives, its flaking pink plaster hinting of better times long ago.

49. Manstein, *Lost Victories*, p. 221.

50. Paget, p. 37.

51. Friedrich-August von Metzsch, *Die Geschichte der 22. Infanterie-Division 1939–1945* (Kiel: Verlag Hans-Henning Podzul, 1952), p. 33.

52. German casualty figures and estimate of Soviet losses are taken from BA-MA, N/507–92, Armee-Oberkommando 11 Ia, A.H.Qu., den 9. November 1941, *Weiterführung Operation Krim und Heeresgruppe Süd*, pp. 1 and 5. In contrast, Soviet statistics after the war put the overall loss figure for the period to 16 November 1941 at 63,860. Figures of the losses of the Maritime (Coastal) and 51st Armies and of the Sevastopol Defence Region are from G. F. Krivosheyev (ed.), *Soviet Casualties and Combat Losses in the Twentieth Century* (London: Greenhill Books, 1997), p. 107. I am grateful to Charles Dick for giving me this source.

53. Karpov, *Der General und Ich*, pp. 128–138.

54. Quoted by Catherine Merridale, *Ivan's War: The Red Army 1939–1945*, paperback edn. (London: Faber and Faber, 2006), p. 72.

55. Erickson, *Road to Stalingrad*, pp. 112–113.

56. The Sevastopolskogo Oboronitelnogo Raiona (SOR).

57. Behind this stood the main defensive zone, some 35 km in length and 4–6 km in depth, with up to 90 km of wire obstacles and 130 fire positions in October, rising to 270 by December 1941.

58. Karpov, *Der General und Ich*, p. 135. Matching the energy and ingenuity of the famous Lieutenant Colonel Eduard Todleben, who had frustrated Allied attempts for nearly a year to capture Sevastopol during the Crimean War, equally enterprising modern Soviet engineers under the command of General A. F. Khrenov and Colonel G. P. Kedrinski had blasted new positions into the rocks and laid tens of thousands of mines throughout the area.

59. Ibid., p. 130.

60. Manstein, *Lost Victories*, p. 241.

61. Charges 4–13 inclusive and Charge 16, of a total of seventeen served on Manstein on 14 July 1949.

62. Samuel W. Mitcham, *Hitler's Field Marshals and Their Battles* (Guild Publishing, 1988), pp. 120–121.

63. BA-MA, RH 20–11/489. Eleventh Army War Diary. Entry for 19 November 1941.

64. Armeeoberkommando 11, Abt. Ic/AO Nr. 2379/41 geh., A.H.Qu. den 20.11.1941. The German original is reprinted in Gerd R. Ueberschär and Wolfram Wette (eds.), *Der deutsche Überfall auf die Sowjetunion 'Unternehmen Barbarossa' 1941* (Munich: Fischer-Taschenbuch-Verlag, 1991), p. 343. The English translation is taken from the official record given in *The Trial of the Major War Criminals*, vol. 21, pp. 641–643.

65. *The Trial of the Major War Criminals*, vol. 21, p. 644.

66. See Manstein, Personal War Diary, Entries for 19 and 20 November 1941; Eleventh Army KTB entry for 19 November 1941 also mentions staff work on Operation WINTER GAME.

67. The significance (and severity) of this crime was highlighted by Martin Gilbert, *The Holocaust: The Jewish Tragedy* (London: Collins, 1986), p. 210: 'Reichenau's directive was copied by General von Manstein who issued it in the Crimean city of Simferopol nine days before the killing of 4,500 Jews at the Crimean port of Kerch, and three weeks before the murder of 14,300 Jews in Simferopol itself.'

68. *The Trial of the Major War Criminals*, vol. 21, p. 645.

69. See Wrochem, *Erich von Manstein*, pp. 63–78. His research shows that not only *Einsatzgruppe* D was involved in anti-partisan operations, but also German Army units *Geheime Feldpolizei* 647 and *Feldgendarmerie-Abteilung (mot.)* 683. These specialist military police units worked closely with the Ib and Ic staff branches of Headquarters Eleventh Army and with *Korück* 553, the headquarters responsible for administering and securing the army's rear area.

70. Meant here is First Panzer Army.

71. Charges 9, 11–12 and 14. See Chapter 16.

72. Manstein, *Verlorene Siege*, pp. 235–236. This section describing Manstein's deliberations over the first major assault on Sevastopol is missing from the English edition.

73. Manstein, Personal War Diary. Entry for 17 October 1941. See also *Lost Victories*, p. 223.

74. Trevor-Roper, p. 108.

75. Karpov, *The Commander*, p. 72.

76. Both *Verlorene Siege*, p. 238, and *Lost Victories*, p. 223, give the date as 17 October in error. Manstein's Personal War Diary entry for 17 December confirms this latter date as the correct one by noting 'Finally I succeeded in convincing Reich[enau] that we should retain 170. Div.'

77. Manstein, *Lost Victories*, p. 224.

78. Metzsch, pp. 34–35.

79. Karpov, *The Commander*, pp. 78–80.

80. Choltitz, pp. 114–115.

81. Ibid.

82. Extract from a list of eight points given in: BA-MA, RH 20–11/455, Der Oberbefehlshaber der 11. Armee, A.H.Qu., den 7. Januar 1942, an die Kommandierende Generale, Divisions-

Kommandeure, Oberquartiermeister.

83. Glantz, *Forgotten Battles*, vol. ii., p. 118.

84. Manstein, *Lost Victories*, p. 225.

85. Ibid, p. 226.

86. Ibid. Note that the English edition wrongly refers to '46th Infantry Regiment' rather than 46th Infantry Division in one instance on this page (cf. *Verlorene Siege*, p. 241).

87. The Eleventh Army War Diary gives a running narrative of nine pages for 29 December 1941 (the daily average is less than a page) describing how this fast-moving situation developed.

88. *The Halder War Diary*, p. 595.

89. It was Field Marshal Reichenau, Commander-in-Chief Army Group South, rather than Manstein, who intervened on the strength of Hitler's notorious 'Halt' order (the *Durchhaltebefehl*) of 26 December 1941 that forbade any retirement without the Führer's express approval.

90. See Eberhard Einbeck, *Das Exempel Sponeck* (Bremen: Carl Schünemann Verlag, 1970), pp. 36–45, for details of Sponeck's court martial. Manstein's account of the 'tragic case' of Sponeck is not given in *Lost Victories*. See *Verlorene Siege*, pp. 243–245, for an explanation of his decision-making on the matter.

91. BA-MA, RH 20–11/489. Eleventh Army War Diary. Entry for 4 January 1942.

92. Manstein, *Verlorene Siege*, pp. 248–249; Wrochem, pp. 55–57.

93. Manstein, *Lost Victories*, p. 227.

94. Karpov, *The Commander*, p. 82.

95. As quoted by Glantz, *Forgotten Battles*, vol. ii, p. 127, Kozlov replied obsequiously: 'I will fully

exploit all means of the military and civil fleet. Comrade Stalin, I will direct all my energies at the fulfilment of your order. I hope to fulfil the missions. I am taking the liberty to report that I am not inclined to glance behind and will try to vindicate that.' The conversation ended with 'Good luck and I wish you success. We shake your hand. Stalin, Vasilevsky.'

96. Manstein, Personal War Diary. Entry for 14 January 1942.

97. Manstein, *Lost Victories*, p. 228.

98. Manstein, *Verlorene Siege*, p. 247.

99. BA-MA, RH 20–11/489. Eleventh Army War Diary. Entry for 4 January 1942.

100. Manstein, Personal War Diary. Entry for 16 January,1942.

101. Ibid. Entries for 18 and 21 February 1942. The comment on 'losing the Crimea or the Crimea *and* Eleventh Army' reflected General von Sodenstern's (Chief of Staff, Army Group South) conversation with Halder, reported to Manstein and noted in his Personal War Diary on 4 January 1942.

102. The new '*Leichte*', subsequently described as '*Jäger*' (light infantry) divisions were similar in equipment and structure to a mountain division. It had nothing in common with the part armoured, part cavalry formations of the late 1930s that took part in the invasion of Poland before being restructured as panzer divisions.

103. Manstein, *Lost Victories*, p. 230. The mistake of employing a green armoured division with inadequate training was repeated in November 1943 when 25th Panzer Division attacked Fastov. See Chapter 14, p. 403.

104. Ibid., p. 231.

105. Trevor-Roper, pp. 117–118.

106. Manstein, *Lost Victories*, p. 231.

107. See Basov, Appendix 2.

108. Manstein, Personal War Diary. Entry for 17 April 1942.

109. Ibid.

110. Manstein, *Lost Victories*, p. 238.

111. Manstein, Personal War Diary. Entry for 19 April 1942.

112. Quoted by Hayward, p. 73.

113. Manstein, *Lost Victories*, p. 235.

114. Ibid., p. 236.

115. After the failure of the January battles, *Stavka* had sent two representatives to supervise Kozlov's work: Commissar of First Rank L. Z. Mekhlis, the chief of the Red Army's Main Political Directorate and deputy chief of the General Staff; and his assistant, Major General P. P. Vechnyi. According to David Glantz, not only were both individuals 'close cronies of Stalin', but they were also 'universally feared and loathed by many in the Red Army officer corps'.

116. Manstein, *Lost Victories*, p. 236.

117. Ibid., p. 237.

118. Erickson, *Road to Stalingrad*, p. 348.

119. Local guides maintain that the Germans used poison gas in liquidating most of their opponents based in the Adzhimushkai quarries. This claim has not been substantiated. For a discussion of the *possible* use of chemical weapons by both sides during the campaign on the Crimea, see Christopher Bellamy, *Absolute War: Soviet Russia in the Second World War* (London: Pan Books, 2008), pp. 458–461.

120. Manstein, *Lost Victories*, p. 237.

121. *Die Wehrmachtsberichte 1939–1945*, Band 2: 1. Januar 1942 bis 31. Dezember 1943, p. 134. The report also gave due

acknowledgement to the crucial role that air power had played in the German-Rumanian success, highlighting the contributions of Colonel Generals Löhr and Freiherr von Richthofen.

122. Hayward, p. 85.
123. Glantz and House, *To the Gates of Stalingrad*, vol. 1, p. 77.
124. Manstein, *Lost Victories*, pp. 243–244.
125. Ibid.
126. BA-MA, RH 20–11/464a. Generalkommando XXX A.K. Abt. Ia Nr. 152/42 g. Kdos. Kps. Gef. Std., den 1.6.1942, p. 11, Paragraph 18.
127. See BA-MA, RH 20–11/464a. Armeeoberkommando 11, Abt. Ia Nr. 2304/42 geh. Kdos. A. K. Qu., den 30. Mai 1942. *Betr.:* 'Störfang', Paragraph 7. In this supplementary instruction for *Störfang*, Manstein ordered a number of strictly tactical actions aimed at confusing the enemy as to the precise deployment for the attack.
128. The principal Soviet formations were: 2nd, 25th, 95th, 172nd, 345th and 388th Rifle Divisions; 40th (dismounted) Cavalry Division; and 7th, 8th and 79th Marine Infantry Brigades. In addition, 9th Marine Infantry Brigade was shipped in as a reinforcement. See Basov, p. 328, for full details.
129. BA-MA, RH 20–11/464a. File Note dated 4.6.1942. 'XXX A.K.: 13 Pz. III (½ Pz. Abt. 300); LIV A.K.: Teile Pz. Abt. 300. Beute Pz. Kp. 223.'
130. Ibid., Paragraph 1: 'Keinesfalls darf die Masse der 24. Div. [LIV Corps] in einem aussichtslosen Waldkampf ostwärts Gajtani festgelegt werden.'
131. BA-MA, RH 20–11/464b.

132. BA-MA, RH 20–11/465a. Unreferenced Table, 'Artillery on the Sevastopol Front as at 6.6.42':

Artillery Pieces

[Sector]	North	Middle	South	
Light	154	57	95	306
Heavy	114	65	78	257
Super-Heavy (excepting Karl and Dora)	46	—	2	48
Total	314	122	175	611

Nebeltruppe (Mortars and Rocket Launchers):

	North Corps	South Corps	
10 cm	22	—	22
15 cm	216	96	312
28/32 cm	318	102	420
Total	556	198	754

LIV Corps had in support some 64 per cent of the total artillery effort, including that of the *Nebeltruppe*, whereas XXX Corps had 27 per cent and the Rumanian Mountain Corps only 9 per cent. These figures mask the fact that LIV Corps had forty-six out of forty-eight super-heavy guns and mortars firing in direct support of its operations.

133. Manstein, *Lost Victories*, p. 245.
134. Ibid., p. 246.
135. M. V. Avdeev, *At the Bluest Sea* (Moscow: DOSAAF, 1968). General of Aviation Mikhail Vasilievich Avdeev, Hero of the Soviet Union, was one of the legendary pilots of the Great Patriotic War. I am grateful to

Ksenia Verzhbytska for finding
and translating this reference.

136. Manstein, *Lost Victories*, p. 247.

137. Manstein, *Verlorene Siege*, p. 271.

138. Laskin, pp. 108–109.

139. Karpov, *The Commander*, pp. 86–87.

140. Manstein, *Lost Victories*, pp. 248–
249.

141. BA-MA, RH 20–11/464a.
Armeeoberkommando 11 Abt. Ia
Nr.2475/42 geh.
Vorgesch.Gef.Stand, den 8.6.42.

142. BA-MA, RH 20–11/465b.
[Letter] 9.6.42 [An] Generaloberst
Halder, Chef des Genst. des
Heeres. Ia Nr. 2516/42 geh.

143. Apart from 46th Infantry Division,
reinforcements closer to hand
were found on the Kerch
peninsula. These included 4th
Rumanian Infantry Division and a
tank battalion from 204th Panzer
Regiment. Manstein ordered these
units into the battle for Sevastopol
on 8 and 9 June 1942 respectively.

144. Manstein, *Lost Victories*, p. 250.

145. BA-MA, RH 20–11/460.
Headquarters Eleventh Army War
Diary. Entries for 22, 23 and 28
June 1942.

146. On 12 June, he visited the
headquarters of both the
Rumanian and XXX Corps,
receiving briefings of the situation
at 1st and 18th Rumanian
Divisions, then at the headquarters
of 72nd, 28th Light and 170th
Divisions, meeting in one day all
seven commanders and their staffs.
The round of intense battlefield
visits continued unabated.
Returning to LIV Corps on 14
June, he visited 50th and 22nd
Divisions and then went in turn to
the headquarters of five infantry
regiments (65th, 437th, 436th,
213th and 16th Infantry in that
order). On 15 June, Manstein

visited headquarters 72nd Division
and XXX Corps. He returned to
the south on the 21st for a briefing
from 170th Division and a
conference at the corps
headquarters, and was back again
the next day to see 50th Division.

147. BA-MA, RH 20–11/460.
Headquarters Eleventh Army War
Diary. Ibid., entries for 12 and 14
June 1942. The average casualty
figure is taken from the Army
Casualty Return, which includes a
breakdown by division up to and
including 13 June 1942. See RH
20–11/465a.

148. The present author has found no
evidence to support Robert
Forczyk's (*Sevastopol 1942*, p. 21)
assertion that Manstein 'spent
much of the siege of Sevastopol at
his comfortable requisitioned
castle on the Black Sea coast'.

149. BA-MA, RH 20–11/460.
Headquarters Eleventh Army War
Diary. Entry for 7 June 1942, 17.00
hours.

150. BA-MA, RH 20–11/465a.
Armeekommando 11 Abt. Ia nr.
2664/42 geh. A.H.Qu., den 20.
Juni 1942. Zeit: 14.30 Uhr.
*Vorbefehl für die Fortführung des
Angriffs auf den inneren
Festungsbereich.*

151. Ibid., Sub-Paragraph 6a.

152. Manstein, *Lost Victories*, p. 245.

153. Ibid., p. 257.

154. Choltitz, p. 127.

155. BA-MA, RH 20–11/489.
Headquarters Eleventh Army War
Diary. Entry for 4 January 1942.

156. Wegner, 'Die Kämpfe auf der
Krim', pp. 850–852.

11. The Vain Struggle for Stalingrad

1. Manstein, *Verlorene Siege*, p. 287.

2. For details of Hitler's Directive No. 43 'Continuation of operations from the Crimea' dated 11 July 1942 and Directive No. 45 'Continuation of "Operation Brunswick [Braunschweig]"' dated, 23 July 1942 see Trevor-Roper (ed.), *Hitler's War Directives*, pp. 124–127 and 129–131 respectively. As a result of the diversion of Eleventh Army to Leningrad, Army Group A received only a corps headquarters (XXXXI) and a division (the 46th), together with some Rumanian forces as reinforcements.

3. The 50th Infantry Division remained to garrison the Crimea; 22nd Division was sent to Crete; the 72nd was transferred to Army Group Centre. Manstein retained only four divisions in Eleventh Army: the 24th, 132nd and 170th Infantry Divisions and 28th Light Division (one fewer than the five originally specified in Directive No. 45).

4. Manstein, *Lost Victories*, pp. 260–261.

5. German doctrine (*Truppenführung*, §24) also stressed that 'Unit integrity should be maintained as far as possible.' See Condell and Zabecki, *On the German Art of War: Truppenführung*, pp. 20–21.

6. Manstein, *Lost Victories*, p. 261.

7. The argument between Hitler and Halder is narrated in detail by Warlimont, *Inside Hitler's Headquarters*, including the Führer's devastating broadside: 'Colonel-General Halder, how dare you use language like that to me! Do you think you can teach me what the man at the front is thinking? What do you know about what goes on at the front? Where were you in the First World War?'

8. Manstein, *Lost Victories*, pp. 261–262.

9. Ibid., Chapter 11, 'Hitler as Supreme Commander'.

10. Manstein, *Lost Victories*, p. 275.

11. A much more common nickname of derision for Hitler was 'GröFaZ', '*Grösster Feldherr aller Zeiten*' – 'the greatest general of all time'. Apart from his letters to his wife, three examples of Manstein's use of 'Effendi' are given by his final ADC. See Stahlberg, *Bounden Duty*, pp. 262, 273 and 377. First published in German under the title *Die Verdammte Pflicht: Erinnerungen 1932 bis 1945* by Ulstein Verlag, Berlin and Frankfurt am Main, in 1987. Stahlberg's memoirs add much colour and interesting detail on Manstein's life from this point on until the end of the war, but there remains some doubt as to their accuracy in places.

12. Warlimont, p. 254.

13. Manstein, *Lost Victories*, p. 276.

14. Ibid., p. 278.

15. Bellamy, *Absolute War*, pp. 386–388.

16. Manstein, *Lost Victories*, p. 264.

17. Glantz and House, *When Titans Clashed*, p. 132 and p. 345, fn 8.

18. Manstein, *Lost Victories*, p. 267.

19. Two issues remained unexplored in Manstein's memoirs. First, had Eleventh Army not been at hand in the north, would the integrity of Eighteenth Army specifically and Army Group North more generally have been threatened? Secondly, had it been available in the south in support of operations of either Army Groups A or B, as Manstein implied, would its presence have made any appreciable difference?

20. Quoted by Evan Mawdsley, *Thunder in the East: The Nazi-Soviet War 1941–1945* (London: Hodder Arnold 2005), pp. 167–168. The full translated text of Stalin's Order No. 227 is given as Document 2 in Geoffrey Roberts, *Victory at Stalingrad* (Harlow: Pearson Educational, 2002), pp. 203–210.

21. I am grateful to Ksenia Verzhbytska for clarifying these terms for me.

22. Simon Sebag Montefiore, *Stalin: The Court of the Red Tsar* (London: Weidenfeld & Nicolson, 2003), p. 436.

23. Quoted by Vasily Grossman in *A Writer at War: Vasily Grossman with the Red Army 1941–1945*, ed. and trans. Antony Beevor and Luba Vinogradova (London: Harvill Press, 2005), p. 176.

24. Manstein, *Lost Victories*, p. 287.

25. Ibid., p. 269.

26. *The Memoirs of Field-Marshal Keitel*, ed. Walter Görlitz and trans. David Irving (London: William Kimber, 1965), p. 165. Originally published in Germany by Musterschmidt-Verlag, Göttingen, 1961.

27. A comment recalled by Halder, quoted by Christian Hartmann, *Halder – Generalstabschef Hitlers* (Paderborn: Schöningh, 1991), p. 304.

28. Since serving with Manstein in Headquarters Army Group A in Koblenz (described in Chapter 6), Tresckow had become the Ia (operations officer) of Army Group B, retitled Centre on Commencement of Operation BARBAROSSA on the Eastern Front, serving successively under Field Marshals Fedor von Bock and Günther von Kluge.

29. The letter is reproduced by Hans Breithaupt, *Zwischen Front und Widerstand* (Bonn: Bernard & Graefe Verlag, 1994). Manstein had considerable support within the army. In December 1941, his former subordinate, Bernhard von Lossberg, suggested to Jodl that the strategic direction of the war be handed over by Hitler to an 'outstanding soldier' such as Manstein. Quoted by Megargee, *Inside Hitler's High Command*, p. 147.

30. Breithaupt, p. 183.

31. Reflecting the Red Army's due diligence to time and space calculations in synchronizing offensive operations, the attack of the South-Western *Front* with 140 km to cover to Kalach was launched one day ahead of the Stalingrad *Front* with only 90 km of advance.

32. There is a huge literature on Stalingrad generally, and much on the planning of Operation URANUS specifically. In particular: Erickson, *The Road to Stalingrad*, pp. 464–472; Glantz and House, *When Titans Clashed*, pp. 130–134; Bellamy, pp. 507–537; Mawdsley, pp. 155–162; Anatoliy G. Chor'kov, 'Die sowjetische Gegenoffensive bei Stalingrad' in Jürgen Förster, *Stalingrad: Ereignis – Wirkung – Symbol* (Munich: Piper, 2002), pp. 55–61; Antony Beevor, *Stalingrad* (London: Viking, 1998), pp. 239–265. An official Soviet view is given in Louis C. Rotundo (ed.), *Battle for Stalingrad: The 1943 Soviet General Staff Study* (London: Pergamon-Brassey's, 1989). A psychological analysis is contained in Geoffrey Jukes, *Hitler's Stalingrad Decisions* (Berkeley:

University of California Press, 1985). Other useful accounts are given in Walter Kerr, *The Secret of Stalingrad* (London: Macdonald & Jane's, 1978) and Roberts, *Victory at Stalingrad*. The most comprehensive source from a German perspective is contained in Manfred Kehrig, *Analyse und Dokumentation einer Schlacht* (Munich: Deutsche Verlags-Anstalt, 1979), together with Heinz Magenheimer's detailed study, *Stalingrad* (Selent: Pour le Mérite – Verlag für Militärgeschichte, 2007). Guido Knopp, *Stalingrad: Das Drama* (Munich: Bertelsmann, 2002) adds detail. Michael K. Jones, *Stalingrad: How the Red Army Triumphed* (Barnsley: Pen & Sword, 2007) provides a human face of the battle. For a comprehensive account of the associated air operations, see Hayward, *Stopped at Stalingrad*, pp. 183–310. Finally, Torsten Diedrich's biography, *Paulus: Das Trauma von Stalingrad* (Paderborn: Schöningh, 2008) gives a sympathetic, but none the less objective, view of Sixth Army's commander-in-chief.

33. Manfred Kehrig, 'Die 6. Armee im Kessel von Stalingrad', in Förster (ed.), *Stalingrad*, p. 76.
34. Warlimont, p. 255.
35. Hayward, p. 216.
36. Manstein, *Lost Victories*, p. 267.
37. Ibid., pp. 267–268; *Verlorene Siege*, pp. 297–298. Note that the English edition states erroneously that Manstein visited Hitler *before* Specht's funeral, not the other way about.
38. Manstein, *Lost Victories*, pp. 268–269.
39. Hayward, p. 216.

40. Manstein, *Lost Victories*, p. 271.
41. Ibid., p. 269.
42. Quoted by Hayward, p. 260.
43. F. W. Mellenthin, *Panzer Battles: A Study of the Employment of Armour in the Second World War* (London: Cassell, 1955), p. 171.
44. Manstein, *Lost Victories*, p. 271.
45. The total of Axis troops trapped in the pocket remains disputed, according to assumptions varying between 200,000 and 300,000. Manstein maintained that the actual number was closer to the lower figure whereas most authorities now consider 250,000 to be a safe estimate.
46. Manstein, *Lost Victories*, p. 295.
47. Kershaw, *Nemesis*, p. 540: '[Hitler] again held out the prospect of imminent victory at Stalingrad. "I wanted to take it and, you know, we are modest: we have it."'
48. Helmut Heiber (ed.), *Hitler and His Generals: Military Conferences 1942–1945* (New York: Enigma Books, 2003), pp. 29–30. First published in 1962 under the title *Hitlers Lagebesprechungen: Die Protokollfragmente seiner militärischen Konferenzen 1942–1945* by the Insitut für Zeitgeschichte, Munich. Note the slightly different wording of Hitler's remarks on 12 December 1942 given by Bellamy, p. 539.
49. Adolf Heusinger, *Befehl im Widerstreit* (Tübingen and Stuttgart: Rainer Wunderlich Verlag, 1950), p. 220.
50. Details from: BA-MA, RH 19-VI, Kriegstagebuch [War Diary] Nr. 1 Oberkommando der Heeresgruppe Don/Süd (20 November 1942–23 March 1943), entry for 21.11.1942, p. 1–2 (4–5). Note that this war diary carries two page-numbering systems.

(Henceforth described as 'Army Group Don/South Main War Diary'.)

51. Manstein, *Lost Victories*, p. 294.

52. Captain Gerhard Dengler, Sixth Army. Quoted by Knopp, *Stalingrad*, p. 261.

53. Apart from Magenheimer, one of the most authoritative critiques of Manstein is contained in Joachim Wieder, *Stalingrad und die Verantwortung des Soldaten* (Munich: Nymphenburger Verlagshandlung, 1962), pp. 133–174. A revised edition, under the co-authorship of Heinrich Graf von Einsiedel, was published in German in 1993, the English translation of which, under the title *Stalingrad: Memories and Reassessments*, was first published by Arms & Armour Press in 1995. References in this book are taken from the Cassell Military Paperbacks edition of 2002, pp. 133–178. An equally critical analysis has been undertaken by Marcel Stein, *Feldmarschall von Manstein: Der Januskopf*, pp. 117–176. Unless otherwise stated, quotes are taken from the English edition, *Field Marshal von Manstein, The Janus Head*, pp. 115–170.

54. HQ Army Group Don War Diary. Untimed entry for 21.11.1942, p. 3(6).

55. A rough estimate indicates that two armour-heavy corps, deeply echeloned, were required to attack towards Stalingrad with a further corps protecting each flank. In addition, a reserve would have had to be found, and not least sufficient forces to mount a credible deception attack on a separate axis.

56. Manstein, *Lost Victories*, pp. 318–319.

57. The author has been unable to locate a copy of the original signal. The quoted wording reflects that given in Headquarters Army Group Don War Diary, untimed entry for 21 November 1942, but from the location of the entry it is probable that the signal was sent on or after 18.00 hours that day. Manstein's own recollection of the signal, given in his memoirs, is a much clearer request to Army Group B that 'Sixth Army be instructed to withdraw forces quite ruthlessly from its defence fronts in order to keep its rear free at the Don crossing at Kalach' (*Verlorene Siege*, p. 327; *Lost Victories*, p. 295).

58. Stahlberg, pp. 207–210.

59. Manstein, *Lost Victories*, p. 309.

60. Assuming no diversions, the completed route was Vitebsk to Smolensk (139 km)–Starobelsk (1,331 km)–Rostov-on-Don (453 km)–Novocherkassk (51 km), a total of 1,974 km. I am grateful to Donald Smith for providing this information, drawn from contemporary Russian sources.

61. Stahlberg, p. 212.

62. For an armoured train in winter this was average going. German Army doctrine prescribed an average speed of 30 km per hour.

63. Stahlberg, pp. 212–213. There is some evidence that Stahlberg conflated a number of memories of rail journeys accompanying the Field Marshal into this long passage south. Manstein mentions the first use of his Serbian 'Salonwagen', for example, in a letter to his wife on 12 February 1943. Letter held in the possession of Rüdiger von Manstein.

64. Ibid., p. 214.

65. HQ Army Group Don War Diary. Entry for 09.30 hrs, 24.11.1942, p. 4(7).

66. Hayward, pp. 234–237.
67. Hans-Detlef Herhudt von Rohden, *Die Luftwaffe ringt um Stalingrad* (Wiesbaden: Limes Verlag, 1950), p. 29.
68. As Charles Dick has pointed out to the present author, the operational level outer ring of encirclement, created by Operation LITTLE SATURN, was not launched until 16 December. So there was an imperative to act quickly, reinforcing the view that the best time for Sixth Army to break out was 'as soon as possible'.
69. HQ Army Group Don War Diary. Untimed entry, 24.11.1942, p. 7(10).
70. Stahlberg, p. 215.
71. Manstein, *Lost Victories*, p. 309. Hitler's adjutant, Major Gerhard Engel, recorded the discussion between Hitler, Göring and Zeitzler: 'Z[eitzler] was doubtful, thought that 300 (or 500) tonnes would not be enough, talked about the weather situation and losses. However Reichsmarschall [Göring] was enormously strong, said he would fly in any weather conditions. Demyansk and other cases had proved it possible. We were horrified at his optimism, which is not shared even by the Luftwaffe General Staff. F[ührer] was enthusiastic about the Reichsmarschall, who would deliver the goods as he had done in the past. There was no chicken-heartedness with him as there was in many Army circles.' Engel, *At the Heart of the Reich*, p. 143.
72. HQ Army Group Don War Diary. Entry for 24.11.1942, pp. 7–8, 10–11): 'Sixth Army can still break out to the South-west, the safe direction. Remaining [in Stalingrad], given its supply position (particularly with regard to ammunition and fuel) represents an extreme risk. [Nevertheless,] so long as there remains the prospect of sufficient supplies, at least with armour-piercing ammunition, infantry ammunition and fuel, CinC cannot agree to a break-out. The supply situation is critical! The situation will be restored with forces being brought up by the beginning of December.... As a last resort, the break-out of Sixth Army will be required, particularly if the deployment of new forces cannot be achieved in the face of strong enemy pressure.'
73. Magenheimer, *Stalingrad*, p. 259.
74. Diedrich, pp. 257–258.
75. Mainstein, Personal War Diary, Book 4. Entry for 25 November 1942.
76. Engel, p. 143.
77. Manstein, *Lost Victories*, p. 309.
78. Quoted by Knopp, *Stalingrad*, p. 215; Manstein, Personal War Diary, Book 4. Entry for 27 November 1942.
79. Ibid.
80. Stahlberg, p. 217.
81. Manstein, *Verlorene Siege*, pp. 649–651; *Lost Victories*, pp. 551–554.
82. HQ Army Group Don War Diary. Entry for 08.00 hrs, 28.11.1942, p. 13 (16).
83. Manstein, *Lost Victories*, p. 314. One further explanation for Manstein's decision not to fly into Stalingrad on 28 November 1942 is that he wished to remain in his headquarters to supervise the estimate of the situation and production of the outline plan for the relief himself, which was very much his style.
84. Manstein, letter to his wife of 14 February 1943. Letter held in the

possession of Rüdiger von
Manstein.

85. For similar criticism of Manstein,
see Stein, pp. 147–149.

86. HQ Army Group Don War Diary.
Entry for 28.11.1942, p. 21 (24).

87. Ibid., p. 26 (29).

88. Manstein, *Lost Victories*, p. 334.

89. Ibid., p. 329.

90. Sixth Army's break-out force was
planned to consist of elements of
14th Panzer, 3rd and 29th
Motorized Infantry Divisions,
with in all about 100–120 tanks.
(HQ Army Group Don War
Diary, p. 49, entry for 1.12.1942,
21.20 hours).

91. For a description of Operation
SATURN, see David M. Glantz,
*From the Don to the Dnepr: Soviet
Offensive Operations December
1942–August 1943* (London: Frank
Cass, 1991), pp. 10–15.

92. In view of this grouping, a link-up
with Sixth Army would have
required two full-strength panzer
corps (at least six mobile divisions)
in deep echelon. Additional troops
would have been necessary to
secure the flanks of the main attack
(perhaps a corps each) and another
corps to mount a credible
deception operation on an
alternative axis.

93. Kerr, p. 232.

94. Manstein, *Lost Victories*, pp. 325–
326.

95. Ibid., p. 327.

96. Ibid.

97. Ibid., p. 559.

98. Raus, *Panzer Operations* , pp. 137–
184.

99. The reinforced 11th Panzer
Regiment of 6th Panzer Division,
under its expert commander,
Colonel Walther von
Hünnersdorff, conducted two
battles and advanced 70 km on the
first day. On the next (13
December), the division skilfully
destroyed a superior Soviet
grouping at Verkhniy-Kumskiy
that threatened its left flank. In a
helter-skelter 'revolving battle',
Raus's division succeeded in
'breaking the enemy's armoured
backbone' and winning 'a
temporary superiority in tanks', but
lost valuable time and hence
momentum in the process.

100. Glantz, *From the Don to the Dnepr*,
pp. 15–17.

101. John Erickson, 'Malinkovsky', in
Shukman (ed.), *Stalin's Generals*, p.
120.

102. For a detailed account of this
action, see Horst Scheibert, ... *bis
Stalingrad 48 km: Der
Entsatzversuch 1942* (Eggolsheim:
Dörfler Verlag, 2003).

103. General Frido von Senger und
Etterlin, *Neither Fear nor Hope*
(London: Macdonald, 1963), p. 75.
First published in German in 1960
under the title *Krieg in Europa* by
Kiepenheuer & Witsch, Cologne
and Berlin.

104. Manstein, *Lost Victories*, p. 335.

105. Ibid., p. 560.

106. Engel, p. 144.

107. Manstein, *Lost Victories*, pp. 562–
563.

108. See, for example, the critique by
Arthur Schmidt on 18 February
1960 of Walter Görlitz's study of
Field Marshal Paulus contained in
BA-MA, N/547/21 (Nachlass
Hauck).

12: A Brief Glimpse of Victory

1. The title of Chapter 12 is drawn
from Manstein, *Lost Victories*, p.
367, and the introductory quote
from p. 438.

2. The Latin original (*Audentis*

fortuna iuvat) is the motto of the Allied Rapid Reaction Corps, the British framework NATO High Readiness Force (Land), whose headquarters were established in 1992 in Bielefeld, Germany, before moving in 1994 to Mönchengladbach near Düsseldorf. In the summer of 2010 it is due to move to Innsworth, near Gloucester, in southern England.

3. Manstein, *Lost Victories*, p. 289. There has been a monument, a metal cross, to the German fallen at Stalingrad since 1999 with the consecration of the military cemetery at Rossoschka, near the former airfield at Gumrak.

4. Quoted by Herodotus, *The Histories*, (trans.) Aubrey de Sélincourt (London: Penguin, 1996), p. 446.

5. Manstein, *Lost Victories*, p. 349.

6. Stalin had dissipated the Soviet offensive effort by launching Operation MARS. Had even greater forces been available for SATURN, then an even greater defeat than Stalingrad could have been inflicted on the German Army.

7. An observation by Marshal of the Soviet Union Sergei Akhromeyev, quoted by Heinz Magenheimer, *Hitler's War: Germany's Key Strategic Decisions 1940–1945* (London: Cassell, 1999) p.168.

8. For the wider purpose and impact of the speech, see Albert Speer, *Inside the Third Reich* (London: Weidenfeld & Nicolson, 1970), pp. 354–355. (Page references to Phoenix paperback edition, 1955.)

9. Zhukov, *Memoirs*, pp. 423–424.

10. Manstein, *Lost Victories*, p. 350.

11. Ibid., p. 351.

12. Engel, *At the Heart of the Reich*. Entry for 28 December 1942, p. 146.

13. Zhukov, *Memoirs*, p. 422.

14. Manstein, *Lost Victories*, pp. 353–354.

15. Glantz, *From the Don to the Dnepr*, p. 82.

16. Manstein, *Lost Victories*, p. 354.

17. Speer, p. 299 '... even at the height of the military successes in 1940 and 1941 the level of armaments production of the First World War was not reached. During the first year of the war in Russia, production figures were only a fourth of what they had been in the autumn of 1918.'

18. Manstein, *Lost Victories*, p. 354.

19. Ibid.

20. Ibid., p. 358.

21. Ibid., p. 359.

22. Ibid., p. 365.

23. Ibid., p. 386: As Manstein explained, the 'Quartermaster-General's "sub-directorates" at army groups were headed by older staff officers who ran their formations' supply and transport services in accordance with direct instructions from the central directorate'.

24. Ibid., p. 361. There is, however, no corroboration of this remark in his chief of operation's own account. See Theodor Busse, 'Der Winterfeldzug 1942 in Südrussland' in *Nie Ausser Dienst*: p. 54, which confirms only that Manstein offered his resignation on 5 January 1943.

25. Balck, *Ordnung im Chaos*, p. 439.

26. Manstein, *Lost Victories*, p. 361.

27. Stahlberg, *Bounden Duty*, pp. 239–247. This account has been paraphrased uncritically in a recent biography of Stauffenberg: Hans Bentzien, *Claus Schenk Graf von Stauffenberg: Der Täter und seine Zeit* (Berlin: Das Neue Berlin

Verlagsgesellschaft, 2004), pp. 237–245.

28. Manstein, Personal War Diary, Book 4. Entry for 26 January 1943.

29. Peter Hoffmann, *The History of the German Resistance 1939–1945*, 3rd English edn. (Montreal: McGill-Queen's University Press, 1996), p. 320.

30. Colonel Eberhard Finckh was a close friend of Stauffenberg. He was also an active member of the resistance and was executed after the failure of the 20 July plot.

31. Breithaupt, *Zwischen Front und Widerstand*, pp. 61–64.

32. Ibid., p. 64.

33. Manstein, Personal War Diary, Book 4. Entry for 27 January 1943.

34. Manstein, letters to his wife, 2 and 4 February 1943. Both letters are held in the private possession of Rüdiger von Manstein.

35. Glantz, *From the Don to the Dnepr*, p. 83.

36. Manstein, *Lost Victories*, p. 371.

37. Ibid., p. 372.

38. Clausewitz, *On War*, p. 443.

39. In chess this is a castling move, known in German as *Rochade*. In German accounts, therefore, it is often termed as Manstein's *Rochade*.

40. Two major international conferences addressed the subject: the *1984 Art of War Symposium*, 'From the Don to the Dnepr: Soviet Offensive Operations – December 1942 to August 1943', held at the Center for Land Warfare, US Army War College, 26–30 March 1984 (which became the basis for Glantz's book, *From the Don to the Dnepr*); and the *Military History Symposium* 'Training in Operational Level Thinking from War Experiences as presented in Manstein's Counter Attack of Spring 1943', held at the German Armed Forces Command and Staff College, Hamburg, 9 September 1986. Glantz's text is common to both conferences. For a good example of the theses written by staff college students, see: Hauptmann Erich H. Könen, 'The Operational Ideas of Manstein with Respect to the Use of Space, Gaining the Initiative, Creating Freedom of Action and the Choice between Offensive and Defensive Operations' (30 November 1987).

41. General Sir Nigel Bagnall, for example, attended the US Army War College symposium in March 1984, which included Generals Balck and von Mellenthin as guest speakers. For an account of this conference, see von Mellenthin, *Schach dem Schicksal*, pp. 247–248. Bagnall also visited Balck that year in Stuttgart, Germany, as his former ADC, Captain (now Lieutenant General) Simon Mayall, has confirmed with the present author.

42. Manstein, *Lost Victories*, p. 370.

43. Glantz, *From the Don to the Dnepr*, pp. 88–89.

44. The land masses by country in square kilometres are: Ukraine 603,500; Poland 312,685; United Kingdom 242,900.

45. Manstein, *Lost Victories*, pp. 369–370; *Verlorene Siege*, pp. 399–400.

46. Ibid., respectively pp. 382–383 and 413–414. *Author's Note:* I have diverged here from Anthony Powell's translation as '*Führung*' in this context is much better rendered in military English as 'Command'.

47. See Manstein, *Lost Victories*, p. 284.

48. Manstein, *Lost Victories*, p. 382. Any variations from the Powell

translation are deliberate. In particular, '*Aufträge*' in Manstein's original has been rendered here as 'missions', not tasks.

49. Ibid., p. 383.

50. Ibid.

51. Ibid.

52. Ibid., p. 380.

53. Ibid., respectively p. 387 and p. 418.

54. Glantz, *From the Don to the Dnepr*, pp. 88 and 93.

55. Manstein, *Lost Victories*, pp. 400–401.

56. BA-MA, RH VI/43, Anlage 1 zum KTB HGr Don/Süd (4.2.-23.3. 1943), pp. 3 and 4. Entries for 4.2.1943, 11.00 hours and 18.55 hours respectively.

57. Stahlberg, p. 253. In his account, Stahlberg implies that the evening briefing and the meeting between Manstein and Hitler started between 21.00 and 22.00 hours. The Army Group Don War Diary confirms that the meeting took place between 17.00 and 21.00 hours, which was followed by a further hour (21.00–22.00 hours) when Busse joined. See BA-MA, RH 19 VI/43, p. 6, entries for 6.2.1943.

58. Engel. Entry for 7 February 1943, p. 147.

59. Manstein, *Lost Victories*, p. 407.

60. Ibid., p. 407; *Verlorene Siege*, p. 438. *Author's Note:* I have not followed Powell's translation of '*einwandfreie militärische Führung*' as 'salutary military leadership'; rather, I have used 'impeccable military command'.

61. Engel. Entry for 7 February, pp. 147–148.

62. Manstein, *Lost Victories*, p. 409.

63. Manstein, letters to his wife, 9 and 10 February 1943. Both letters are held in the private possession of Rüdiger von Manstein.

64. Manstein, *Lost Victories*, p. 409.

65. Stahlberg, p. 253.

66. Manstein, *Lost Victories*, pp. 410–413.

67. Ibid., p. 409.

68. Ibid., p. 422. The war diary provides confirmation only of Zeitzler's remark, not Manstein's response. See BA-MA, RH 19 VI/43, p. 13. Entry for 14.2.1943, 11.20 hours: 'Zeitzler: *Der Führer empfindet die Lagebeurteilung des Herrn Feldmarschall vom 11.2. als etwas weitgehend.*'

69. Glantz, *From the Don to the Dnepr*, pp. 170–172.

70. At the beginning of February 1943, Army Detachment Lanz (subsequently Kempf from 20 February) defended a 150-km front on the Oskol River to the east of the Northern Donets. It consisted of an improvised Corps 'Cramer' [later, 'Raus'], comprising 168th Infantry Division (plus remnants of the Hungarian 10th, 13th and 23rd Infantry Divisions) and Panzer Grenadier Division *Grossdeutschland*; SS Panzer Grenadier Division *Das Reich* (minus), and 298th and 320th Infantry Divisions. The remainder of the SS Panzer Corps was assembling to the west of Kharkov. The composition of the army detachment changed frequently thereafter as the Soviets took Kharkov (10–16 February) and the Germans subsequently retook the city (10–14 March) and recaptured Belgorod (18 March 1943).

71. See BA-MA, RH 19 VI/43, p. 8. Entry for 9.2.1943, 17.10 hours.

72. Italics as in the original. See Manstein, *Lost Victories*, p. 421. At the time, however, Manstein appeared to be less enthusiastic

about subsuming Army Group B (with Army Detachment Lanz) and even less so in taking over command of Second Army or other forces from Army Group Centre. The war diary is unambiguous in this respect 'I don't find it a particularly happy situation if an army group has 5 armies subordinated to it. Army Group B needs to be brought back, potentially with an Army Front [*sic*] over A and B [Manstein omits here to mention South!]. I would never have taken Army Group B out.' BA-MA, RH 19 VI/43, p. 26. Entry for 24.2.1943, 19.45 hours.

73. Manstein, *Lost Victories*, p. 419.

74. This particular battle for Kharkov (the second of four during the Second World War) during the period 10–16 February 1943 is described in detail by Glantz, *From the Don to the Dnepr*, pp. 171–179.

75. An abrupt exchange between Manstein and Lanz on 15 February 1943 captures the weak position of the latter. '*Manstein:* How high are the casualties of the SS formations? *Lanz:* I don't know. They fight well, but it is difficult to command these formations. They don't provide reports and are exceptionally independent. Most of the time one learns of an event that is already out of date. *Manstein:* You must enforce better reporting. Where is the *Leibstandarte* now? *Lanz:* At Alexejevka, in combat there. *Manstein:* Report this evening quite clearly: Enemy, Own Task Organization and Losses.' BA-MA, RH 19 VI/43, p. 16. Entry for 15.2.1943, 17.10 hours.

76. Schulze-Büttger had just taken over from Busse, who had been promoted to major general on becoming Manstein's new chief of staff. He was adjutant (ADC) to General Ludwig Beck until 1938, when Manstein first came across him. They later served together in Headquarters XXXVIII Corps during the second half of 1940. He joined the resistance and became an important intermediary for Henning von Tresckow in Headquarters Army Group Centre and then South. After the unsuccessful assassination attempt of 20 July 1944, Schulze-Büttger was arrested, sentenced to death by the People's Court on 13 October 1944 and killed the same day in Berlin-Plötzensee.

77. When Manstein was in a bad mood, Stahlberg noted, 'He liked to give Hitler this oriental title.' See Stahlberg, pp. 260–262.

78. Ibid., p. 266.

79. Ibid., p. 270.

80. Manstein, *Lost Victories*, p. 424.

81. Ibid.

82. Ibid.

83. See Trevor-Roper (ed.), *Hitler's War Directives*, pp. 161–162. Führer Order No. 11 of 8 March 1944, entitled 'Commandants of Fortified Areas *[feste Plätze]* and Battle Commandants', dictated: 'The "Fortified Areas" will fulfil the function of fortresses in former historical times. They will ensure that the enemy does not occupy these areas of decisive operational importance. They will allow themselves to be surrounded, thereby holding down the largest possible number of enemy forces, and establishing conditions favourable for successful counter-attacks.'

84. Manstein, *Lost Victories*, p. 425.

85. Ibid.

86. Stahlberg, p. 271.

87. Ibid., p. 273.

88. Ibid., p. 274.

89. Manstein, *Lost Victories*, pp. 425–427; Stahlberg, pp. 273–275.

90. Stahlberg, p. 275.

91. Ibid., pp. 278–279.

92. Manstein, *Lost Victories*, pp. 420 and 423.

93. This point is also made by Dana V. Sadarananda, *Beyond Stalingrad: Manstein and the Operations of Army Group Don* (Westport, Conn,: Greenhill, 1990), p. 117.

94. Manstein, *Lost Victories*, p. 428.

95. Manstein, letters to his wife, 19 and 20 February 1943. Both letters are held in the private possession of Rüdiger von Manstein.

96. General Lanz was relieved by General Kempf on 20 February 1943. Henceforth the Army Detachment was renamed 'Kempf'.

97. Quoted by General (Ret'd) Dr Ferdinand Maria von Senger und Etterlin, 'Gegenschlagoperation der Heeresgruppe Süd, 17.–25. Februar 1943' in *Hamburg Military Historical Symposium Proceedings*, p. 145.

98. Glantz, *From the Don to the Dnepr*, p. 124.

99. In addition, III Panzer Corps joined First Panzer Army's attack whilst LVII Panzer Corps supported Fourth Panzer Army.

100. BA-MA, RH 19 VI/43, p. 22. Entry for 21.2.1943, 16.35 hours.

101. Ibid., p. 22. Entry for 21.2.1943, 11.00 hours.

102. Dr Ferdinard Maria von Senger und Etterlin, p. 155.

103. Manstein, *Lost Victories*, p. 432.

104. BA-MA, RH 19 VI/43, p. 29. Entry for 1.3.1943, 11.00 hours.

105. Ibid., p. 29. Entry for 28.2.1943, 19.10 hours.

106. Manstein, *Lost Victories*, p. 433.

107. Ibid., p. 435.

108. BA-MA, RH 19 VI/43, p. 35. Entry for 7.3.1943, 11.05 hours.

109. Manstein, letter to his wife, 10 March 1943. Letter held in the private possession of Rüdiger von Manstein.

110. Glantz, *From the Don to the Dnepr*, pp. 203–205.

111. Marshal A. I. Eremenko, *Stalingrad* (Moscow: Voenizdat, 1961), p. 467. I am grateful to Ksenia Verzhbytska for supplying this reference and translation.

112. Glantz, *From the Don to the Dnepr*, p. 120.

113. Ibid.

114. Recalled by Kielmansegg on 9 September 1986. See Dieter Ose (ed.), *Wehrgeschichtliches Symposium Proceedings* (Bonn: March 1987), p. 184.

115. Manstein, letters to his wife, 22 and 28 February 1943 respectively. Both letters are held in the private possession of Rüdiger von Manstein.

116. Friedhelm Klein and Karl-Heinz Frieser, 'Mansteins Gegenschlag am Doneč; Operative Analyse des Gegenangriffs der Heeresgruppe Süd im Februar/März 1943', *Militärgeschichte*, 9 (1999), p. 18.

117. Eremenko, p. 467.

118. David M. Glantz and Jonathan M. House, *The Battle of Kursk* (Kansas: University of Kansas Press, 1999), p. 261.

119. Paget, *Manstein: His Campaigns and His Trial*, p. 52.

120. Manstein, letter to his wife, 14 March 1943. Letter held in the private possession of Rüdiger von Manstein.

13. Defeat at Kursk

1. Quoted by Mark Healy, *Kursk 1943: The Tide Turns in the East*

(Oxford: Osprey, 1993), p. 90.

2. The most detailed Soviet description is contained in David M. Glantz (ed.) and Harold S. Orenstein (trans.), *The Battle for Kursk 1943: The Soviet General Staff Study* (London and Portland, Oreg.: Frank Cass, 1999). This work, originally entitled 'Collection of Materials for the Study of War Experience', No. 11, was published by the Military Publishing House of the People's Commissariat of Defence, Moscow, in 1944. The best modern accounts of the battle are given by Walter S. Dunn, *Kursk: Hitler's Gamble, 1943* (Westport, Conn.: Praeger, 1997) and Glantz and House, *The Battle of Kursk*. Healy's recent *Zitadelle: The German Offensive against the Kursk Salient 4–7 July 1943* (Stroud: The History Press, 2008) is much better researched than his Osprey account. For a succinct strategic review, see Magenheimer, *Hitler's War*, pp. 202–215; and for greater detail, Steven H. Newton, *Kursk: The German View* (New York: Da Capo, 2002), which comprises a series of accounts by a number of the senior German officers involved. Bernd Wegner's strategic overview, 'Von Stalingrad nach Kursk', and Karl-Heinz Frieser's detailed operational analysis 'Die Schlacht im Kursker Bogen', both contained in *Das Deutsche Reich und der Zweite Weltkrieg*, vol. 8, *Die Ostfront 1943/44* (Munich: Deutsche Verlags-Anstalt, 2007), represent the most definitive analyses to date from a German perspective. The most reliable data is contained in Frieser's study, together with Niklas Zetterling and Anders Frankson, *Kursk 1943:*

A Statistical Analysis (London: Frank Cass, 2000), noting there are some inconsistencies between the two.

3. *Kursk: Soviet General Staff Study*, p. 28.

4. Magenheimer, *Hitler's War*, p. 214.

5. See, for example, Kurt Pfötsch, *Die Hölle von Kursk: SS-Grenadiere 1943 im Kampf* (Selent: Pour le Mérite, 2008).

6. Zetterling and Frankson, p. 136. See their detailed analysis of casualties in Chapter 8, 'The Cost of the Battle', pp. 111–131. From the data presented, the 'exchange rate' for tanks and assault guns (total losses) was even higher to the advantage of the Germans, at least 5:1.

7. The figures extracted from the totals for CITADEL are given by Frieser, p. 100.

8. Manstein, *Lost Victories*, p. 449.

9. Ibid., p. 212.

10. Notably the contributions by Dunn, Glantz, Zetterling and Frankson, and Frieser.

11. Compare Chapter 14 of *Lost Victories* (6½ pages) with that of *Verlorene Siege* (33½ pages); both editions include a one-page map, notably without any reference to the Steppe *Front*.

12. Manstein, *Lost Victories*, p. 450.

13. BA-MA, RH 19 VI/43, p. 37. Entry for 7.3.1943, 18.00 hours.

14. Ibid., p. 38. Entry for 8.3.1943, 10.45 hours.

15. KTB HQ Army Group South. BA-MA, RH 19-VI/41, p. 86. Apart from Hitler and Manstein, those present included: Field Marshal von Kleist, Commander-in-Chief Army Group A; Field Marshal von Richthofen, Commander-in-Chief Fourth Air Fleet; Colonel General Ruoff,

Commander-in-Chief
Seventeenth Army; General of
Infantry Zeitzler, Chief of the
General Staff; General of Cavalry
von Mackensen, Commander-in-
Chief First Panzer Army; General
of Armoured Troops Kempf,
Commander-in-Chief Army
Detachment Kempf; General
Hollidt, Commander-in-Chief,
Sixth Army; five Luftwaffe
generals; Major Generals Busse,
Schmundt and Fangohr. In
addition to Busse, other members
of Manstein's staff attended.

16. Stahlberg, *Bounden Duty*, pp. 290–
293.

17. Manstein, *Lost Victories*, p. 436.

18. Bodo Scheurig, *Alfred Jodl:
Gehorsam und Verhängnis*
(Schnellbach: Verlag Siegfried
Bublies, 1999), pp. 225–226.

19. OKH/GenSt d H/OpAbt (vorg-St)
Nr. 430 163/43 g. KdosChefs
dated 13 March 1943. Reproduced
by Glantz and House, *The Battle of
Kursk*, Appendix E, pp. 354–355.

20. BA-MA, RH 19 VI/43, p. 42.
Entry for 18.3.1943 (no time
given).

21. Ibid., pp. 43–45. Entries for
20.3.1943, 11.05 hours; 21.3.1943,
17.45 hours.

22. Glantz and House, *The Battle of
Kursk*, p. 23.

23. Warlimont, *Inside Hitler's
Headquarters*, p. 312.

24. On 11 May 1943, the commanders
of the SS Divisions *Leibstandarte
Adolf Hitler* and *Das Reich* reported
that they had lost 6,000 and 5,000
men respectively during recent
fighting (February to May). BA-
MA, RH VI/45, p. 95.

25. Glantz and House, *The Battle of
Kursk*, p. 14.

26. Guderian, *Panzer Leader*, p. 302.

27. Ibid., p. 295.

28. OKH, GenStdH, Op.Abt (I) Nr.
430246/43 g. KdosChefs, Führer
Headquarters dated 15 March
1943. Reproduced by Glantz and
House, *The Battle of Kursk*, Annex
F, pp. 356–358.

29. Manstein, *Verlorene Siege*, p. 488.

30. Manstein, *Lost Victories*, p. 446.

31. Manstein, *Verlorene Siege*, p. 483.

32. Glantz and House, *The Battle of
Kursk*, p. 29.

33. Ibid., p. 30.

34. *Kursk: Soviet General Staff Study*, p.
10.

35. Frieser, 'Die Schlacht im Kursker
Bogem', p. 103. Frieser states that
the Soviet artillery density in the
Central *Front* was as high as 125
guns per kilometre at the points of
main effort for the defence.

36. *Kursk: Soviet General Staff Study*,
pp. 10–21; Glantz and House, *The
Battle of Kursk*, pp. 62–68.

37. Manstein, *Verlorene Siege*, p. 485.

38. Wegner, 'Von Stalingrad nach
Kursk', p. 75. Additionally present
were Major General Schmundt,
Hitler's Chief Adjutant and Head
of Army Personnel, and Colonel
Walther Scherff, the Führer's
special representative for Military
History at OKW. A summary of
discussion at the meeting is given
in the Headquarters Army Group
South War Diary, which was
reproduced from the dictated
notes of Major General Busse. See
BA-MA, RH-19 VI/45, pp. 80–
82. Manstein's later memoir differs
in sequence and content in some
respects from this contemporary
source.

39. There is some implied evidence
that Manstein toyed with this idea.
It came up a number of times in
discussion. Busse and Zeitzler
discussed it again on 2 June 1943,
but agreed to reject this operation

'for the same reasons as set out in the recent past'. BA-MA, RH-19 VI/45, p. 124.

40. Steven H. Newton, *Hitler's Commander* p. 219.

41. BA-MA, RH-19 VI/45, p. 81.

42. Manstein, *Verlorene Siege*, p. 491.

43. Guderian, pp. 306–307.

44. Manstein, *Verlorene Siege*, p. 492.

45. Glantz and House, *The Battle of Kursk*, p. 55.

46. BA-MA, RH-19 VI/45, pp. 92–93.

47. Ibid., p. 96.

48. Stahlberg, pp. 299–301.

49. Engelmann, *Manstein: Stratege und Truppenführer*, p. 142, suggests that Manstein still tried to find the time for a daily ride on his favourite mount 'Osman' 'in order to offset the mental pressure he was under by getting some much needed physical exercise and diversion'.

50. BA-MA, RH 19-VI/45, pp. 120–121. Reflected in Manstein, *Verlorene Siege*, p. 494.

51. Ibid., pp. 122–124.

52. Stahlberg, pp. 301–302: '[We observed] an attack the like of which had not occurred in this war. We felt as if we were on one of Frederick the Great's observation hilltops. Heavy and light artillery opened the "battle", reconnaissance Panzers roared to and fro across the terrain, engineers with flame-throwers set part of the prairie grass alight, armoured personnel carriers rolled along, spewing out crowds of soldiers firing non-stop.' Hitler had invited the 'Turkish Officer Committee' to visit the Eastern Front and the English Channel coastal defences between 25 June 1943 and 7 July 1943.

53. Warlimont, p. 333.

54. Glantz and House, *The Battle of Kursk*, p. 74. Interestingly, Manstein's account of Kursk and the map of the battle contained in *Lost Victories* (both the German and English editions) fail to include the Steppe *Front*.

55. FHO (I), Statistische Aufstellung vom 15.6.1943, BA-MA, RH-2/2089, p. 97. Quoted by Wegner, p. 77, fn. 99.

56. Informal document with Gehlen's initials, 4.7.1943, BA-MA, RH-2/2586, with a (contemporary?) handwritten note: 'I have briefed the Chief of the General Staff with my assessment. Externally, the opinion of the Führer must be represented.' Quoted by Wegner, p. 77, fn. 100.

57. Manstein, *Verlorene Siege*, p. 495.

58. Ibid., p. 494.

59. In addition there were two security divisions. The Ninth Army reserve, 5th Panzer Division, had 102 tanks. A second panzer division (the 8th), an OKH reserve, arrived on 12 July 1943 with 101 tanks.

60. Manstein, *Verlorene Siege*, p. 505.

61. Of his armoured formations, Model committed only 20th Panzer Division in his initial assault.

62. Frieser, 'Die Schlacht', pp. 87–88. Of the armour in Ninth Army, on 5 July 1943 there were 599 combat-ready tanks (of which only 26 were Tigers); 90 Ferdinand tank destroyers; and 299 assault guns.

63. Manstein, *Verlorene Siege*, p. 486, mentions erroneously that Second Army had nine divisions.

64. Glantz and House, *The Battle of Kursk*, p. 356.

65. Quoted by Newton, *Kursk*, p. 78.

66. Grouped as follows (north to south facing the Donets); III Panzer Corps: 106th Infantry, 6th, 19th

and 7th Panzer Divisions; Corps Raus: 106th and 320th Infantry Divisions.

67. Manstein *Verlorene Siege*, pp. 486–487.

68. BA-MA, RH 21-4/104 Kriegstagebuch Oberkommando der 4. Panzerarmee (25.3.43–31.7.43), p. 98.

69. Quoted by Newton, *Kursk*, p. 79.

70. Frieser, 'Die Schlacht', pp. 88, 91 and 93. Of Army Group South's inventory of armoured fighting vehicles at the start of the attack (*excluding* XXIV Panzer Corps) there were 409 Panzer III, 426 Panzer IV, 200 Panzer V (Panther) and 102 Panzer VI (Tiger) tanks, together with 240 assault guns.

71. Zetterling and Frankson, p. 31.

72. Force ratios (as at 5 July 1943) presented by Frieser, 'Die Schlacht', p. 101. From Zetterling and Frankson, excluding the Orel sector, the Soviet preponderance is reduced to manpower, 2.45:1; armour, 2.09:1 artillery, 4.23:1; air, 1.93:1. I am grateful to Charles Dick for bringing this discrepancy between the data to my attention.

73. Manstein, *Verlorene Siege*, p. 495.

74. Ibid., p. 496.

75. James S. Corum, *Wolfram von Richthofen: Master of the German Air War* (Lawrence: University Press of Kansas, 2008), p. 13.

76. Ibid., p. 497.

77. Stahlberg, pp. 304–305; Manstein, *Verlorene Siege*, p. 497; BA-MA, RH 19-VI/45, p. 153. From the three accounts there is some contradiction over flights and dates concerning Manstein's visit to Bucharest.

78. Paul Carell, *Scorched Earth: Hitler's War on Russia*, vol. 2 (London: Harrap, 1970), p. 25.

79. Manstein, *Verlorene Siege*, p. 498.

80. Ibid., pp. 62–66.

81. On 7 July 1943, 76 Panthers of *Grossdeutschland* were in workshops with technical defects. See BA-MA, RH 21-4/104, p. 133.

82. Manstein, *Verlorene Siege*, p. 499.

83. Manstein, Personal War Diary, Book 5. Entries for 6, 7, 8 and 9 July 1943.

84. Glantz and House, *The Battle of Kursk*, p. 269.

85. Quoted by Newton, *Kursk*, p. 22.

86. Ibid., p. 23.

87. Manstein, *Verlorene Siege*, p. 500.

88. Ibid., p. 502.

89. Stahlberg, pp. 307–308.

90. Manstein, *Verlorene Siege*, p. 502.

91. Ibid.

92. Ibid., p. 503.

93. Stahlberg, pp. 309–310.

94. Manstein, *Verlorene Siege*, p. 506.

95. Quoted by Newton, *Kursk*, pp. 24–26.

96. Ibid., p. 59.

97. Ibid., p. 403.

98. Ibid., p. 389.

99. Manstein, *Lost Victories*, p. 485.

100. Glantz and House, *The Battle of Kursk*, p. 272.

14. Fighting on Two Fronts

1. Manstein, *Lost Victories*, p. 453 (letter to Zeitzler).

2. Ibid., p. 450.

3. Manstein, *Verlorene Siege*, p. 545.

4. Manstein, *Lost Victories*, p. 467.

5. Manstein, *Verlorene Siege*, pp. 513–514. Oddly, the whole introductory section to Chapter 15 ('*Führungsfragen*', 'Questions of Command') of over seven pages was cut in translation to two short paragraphs. Thus the context for this important chapter is entirely missing in the English edition.

6. On 20 October 1943, the Voronezh

Front was renamed the 1st
Ukrainian; the Steppe *Front* the
2nd Ukrainian; the South-
Western *Front*, the 3rd Ukrainian;
the Southern *Front*, the 4th
Ukrainian.

7. Manstein, *Lost Victories*, p. 455.
Presumably one of the formations
Manstein was referring to here was
57th Infantry Division. 'Shattered
by sustained artillery fire on 18
August 1943' with 'most of its
officers and sergeants killed, the
57th simply ran away'. Glantz and
House, *The Battle of Kursk*,
p. 251.

8. Werner Haupt, *Die Schlachten der
Heeresgruppe Süd* (Friedberg:
Podzun-Pallas-Verlag, 1985), p.
377.

9. Glantz and House, *The Battle of
Kursk*, pp. 245–246.

10. Manstein, *Verlorene Siege*, p. 509.

11. The seventeenth – and final –
charge against Manstein was
'Committing a war crime in that he
in the U.S.S.R., on divers dates
between 16th February 1943 and
1st April 1944, when Commander-
in-Chief of Army Group South
while the said Army Group was in
retreat, in violation of the Laws and
Usages of War issued divers orders
and in particular orders dated 25th
August 1943 and 7th September
1943 to deport civilian inhabitants
of the territories occupied by the
German Armed Forces under his
command, to seize their cattle and
foodstuffs and to destroy their
houses as well as all other objects
of economic value which could not
be seized, in consequence of which
large numbers of men, women and
children, citizens of the U.S.S.R.,
were forcibly deported and
suffered great hardship ...'
Extracted from Charge Sheet of

May 1949, served on 14 July 1949,
p. 37.

12. Manstein, *Verlorene Siege*, pp. 534–
535.

13. Manstein, *Lost Victories*, p. 452.

14. The *Wehrmachtsbericht* of 4 August
1943 read: 'In the battle of the
Mius, infantry and armoured
formations of the Army and
Waffen-SS under the command of
Field Marshal von Manstein and
General of Infantry Hollidt, with
exemplary support of *Luftwaffe*
units led by General of Fliers
Dessloch, have prevented repeated
breakthrough attempts by strong
enemy forces and have destroyed
the enemy that penetrated north of
Kuibyshevo in a spirited
counterattack.' *Die
Wehrmachtsberichte 1939–1945*,
Band 2, 1. Januar 1942 bis 31.
Dezember 1943, p. 532.

15. Glantz and House, *The Battle of
Kursk*, p. 241.

16. Manstein, *Lost Victories*, p. 486.

17. Glantz, *From the Don to the Dnepr*,
p. 261.

18. Manstein, *Lost Victories*, p. 454.

19. Ibid., p. 455.

20. Ibid.

21. The opposing force ratios were 4:1
in men and 8:1 in armour in favour
of the Red Army. 'By the time
Rumiantsev commenced, the
Stavka had concentrated 980,588
men, 12,627 guns and mortars, and
2,439 tanks and self-propelled guns
for the attack. The German
defenders could muster scarcely
210,000 men and approximately
250 tanks and assault guns. Soviet
force superiority in main attack
sectors was even more
pronounced.' Glantz and House,
The Battle of Kursk, p. 246.

22. Manstein, *Lost Victories*, p. 456.

23. David Glantz, *Soviet Military*

Deception in the Second World War (London: Frank Cass, 1989), p. 221. For consistency, the present author has substituted 'First' for '1st' and 'Sixth' for '6th' in the numeration of the German armies concerned.

24. Manstein, *Lost Victories*, p. 456.
25. Ibid., p. 458.
26. Ibid., pp. 457 and 459.
27. Ibid., p. 459.
28. Ibid., p. 460.
29. Ibid.
30. Gersdorff, *Soldat im Untergang*, p. 134.
31. Carl Goerdeler, former Lord Mayor of Leipzig, and Johannes Popitz, former Prussian Minister of Finance, prominent members of the opposition, were executed on 1 March and 2 February 1945 respectively as a result of the failed plot of 20 July 1944.
32. Gersdorff, p. 135.
33. Translated excerpts from Manstein and Fuchs, *Soldat im 20. Jahrhundert*, pp. 184–185.
34. Ibid., p. 185. This would appear to be a repetition of the same report by Zeitzler referred to by Manstein in a letter to his wife on 20 February 1943, quoted in Chapter 12 of this book.
35. Gersdorff, pp. 135–136.
36. See Knopp (ed.), *Hitler's Warriors*, pp. 173–177 for a detailed account and perceptive analysis of Gersdorff's meeting with Manstein; another perspective is given by Bodo Scheurig, *Henning von Tresckow* (Berlin: Propyläen Verlag, 1987), pp. 171–172.
37. Testimony of 10 August 1946. *Trial of the Major War Criminals*, vol. 21.
38. Manstein, *Lost Victories*, pp. 287–288.
39. Ibid., p. 461.
40. Manstein, Lost *Victories*, p. 462.

41. Ibid.
42. BA-MA N/68–80 *Nachlass Zeitzler*. 'Das Ringen um die grossen Entscheidungen im zweiten Weltkrieg', vol. ii., *Abwehrschlachten*, p. 117.
43. Manstein, Lost *Victories*, pp. 463–464.
44. Ibid., p. 464.
45. Ibid., pp. 464–465.
46. Ibid., pp. 465–466.
47. Ibid., pp. 466–467.
48. Evidence given by Manstein at Nuremberg, 10 August 1946. *Trial of the Major War Criminals*, vol. 20, p. 624.
49. Manstein, *Lost Victories*, p. 467. The Desna, the largest tributary of the Dnepr, flows south to Briansk, then south-west to join the Dnepr just above Kiev. This easterly bulge in the front was conditioned by Hitler's refusal to order the withdrawal of Army Group Centre to the upper reaches of the Dnepr to conform to Army Group South's retirement.
50. See Glantz and House, *When Titans Clash*, p. 172: 'The 5th Guards Tank Army, for example, had only 50 of its 500 tanks left after the Belgorod–Khar'kov operation.'
51. Manstein, *Lost Victories*, p. 468.
52. Ibid., p. 469.
53. Ibid. Italics in original.
54. Ibid., p. 470.
55. Quoted by Glantz and House, *When Titans Clash*, p. 172.
56. Manstein, *Lost Victories*, p. 467.
57. BA-MA, RH 21-4/130, War Diary Fourth Panzer Army. Entry for 18.9.43, pp. 240 and 242.
58. BA-MA, N63–80, *Nachlass Zeitzler*. 'Das Ringen um die grossen Entscheidungen im zweiten Weltkrieg', vol. II. *Abwehrschlachten* (undated), pp.

104–105. When Hitler changed his mind about the *Ostwall*, he rounded on Zeitzler: 'I've now given permission for the construction of the Dnepr-position which you've always demanded. But nothing has happened. The troops have nothing to fall back on. You see, it's pointless to give agreement.' When the Chief of the German General Staff replied, 'Yes, of course it is, if given too late', the Führer fell silent.

59. Manstein, *Lost Victories*, p. 471.

60. Ibid., pp. 469 and 471.

61. Quoted by Werner Haupt, *Army Group South: The Wehrmacht in Russia 1941–1945* (Atglen, Pa: Schiffer Military History, 1998), pp. 295–296. Originally published as *Heeresgruppe Süd* by Podzun-Pallas Verlag, Friedburg, in 1985, pp. 332 and 337. The present author has substituted a corrected English translation.

62. Michael Carver, 'Field Marshal Manstein', in Correlli Barnett (ed.), *Hitler's Generals* (London: Weidenfeld & Nicolson, 1989), p. 239.

63. The number of bridgeheads and their size grew. By the end of September 1943, there were twenty-three bridgeheads, some of them over 10 km wide and 1–2 km deep.

64. Manstein, *Lost Victories*, p. 477.

65. Stahlberg, *Bounden Duty*, pp. 311–312.

66. Manstein, *Lost Victories*, p. 473. To underline his point he gave the supporting facts and figures. For the immediate defence of the Dnepr front of 700 km, he had nominally thirty-seven 'divisions'. Each of these was responsible for 20 km, which on paper looked reasonable provided the

formations were at, or near, full strength. Yet the 'average number of soldiers fit for front-line combat duties per division was now only about 1,000 – a figure which would not rise above 2,000 even after the promised replacements had arrived'.

67. *Commanders and Military Leaders of the Great Patriotic War*, vol. 1 (Moscow: Molodaia Gvardia, 1971), pp. 52–53. The memoir is of Colonel General K. V. Krainiukov, who at that time was serving in the Voronezh/First Ukrainian *Front*. I am grateful to Ksenia Verzhbytska for locating and translating this quotation.

68. Manstein, *Lost Victories*, p. 484.

69. Ibid., p. 483.

70. Ibid., pp. 486–487.

71. *The Goebbels Diaries* (ed.) H. R. Trevor Roper (Secker & Warburg, 1978), entry for 8 November 1943, p. 409.

72. Manstein, *Lost Victories*, pp. 487–488.

73. Glantz and House, *When Titans Clash*, p. 173.

74. Zhukov, *Reminiscences and Ruminations*, vol 2, p. 221.

75. Manstein, *Lost Victories*, p. 407

76. Mellenthin, *Panzer Battles*, pp. 251–252.

77. XXXXVIII Corps order of battle: 1st and 7th Panzer Divisions; SS Panzer Division *Leibstandarte Adolf Hitler*; 19th Panzer Division (not available before 18 November); 25th Panzer Division (weakened by losses); SS Panzer Division *Das Reich* (equivalent in strength to a weak battle group); 68th Infantry Division. Mellenthin, *Panzer Battles*, pp. 252–253.

78. Ibid., p. 251.

79. Manstein, *Lost Victories*, p. 490.

80. Ibid., p. 497.

81. Ibid., p. 490.

82. Manstein, *Verlorene Siege*, p. 534.

83. Raus, *Panzer Operations*, pp. 258–261.

84. Mellenthin, *Panzer Battles*, p. 265. Mellenthin's account falls into the trap of confusing tactical gains with operational success. That XXXXVIII Corps through its virtuosity could outmanoeuvre the enemy forces it faced was one matter, but it did not alter the strategic odds in Germany's favour. None the less, Mellenthin was very much of the 'Manstein school', who thought that the war, even by December 1943, 'was by no means lost'. Hitler was of the same opinion, believing the Russians would soon bleed to death. He and others such as Mellenthin who thought that the 'limits of the Soviet manpower were being reached' and that 'the Russians could not continue to suffer these huge losses indefinitely', however, were mistaken. Soviet war production and superior strategy, together with increasingly sophisticated operational techniques, were winning the war on the Eastern Front, not just numbers. Mellenthin complimented the commander of Army Group South by inferring that 'if the German Supreme Command had been controlled by a Manstein instead of a Hitler', the outcome on the Eastern Front might have been different.

85. Manstein, *Lost Victories*, pp. 491–492.

86. Quoted by Scheurig, *Henning von Tresckow*, p. 199, based on information provided by Fabian von Schlabrendorff (see Chapter 10, Note 17, p. 263).

87. Quoted by Guido Knopp and Jörg Müllner, 'The Strategist – Erich von Manstein' in Guido Knopp (ed.) *Hitler's Warriors*, trans. Angus McGeoch (Stroud: Sutton, 2005), p. 177. [The present author has not found any corroboration for this remark.] Blümroder, a general staff officer and later Bundeswehr general, was a loyal supporter of Manstein, assisting him in the compilation of his memoirs after the Second World War. See Manstein, *Verlorene Siege*, p. 8, and *Lost Victories*, p. 18.

88. Undated letter to Fabian von Schlabrendorff; extracts quoted by Manstein and Fuchs, *Soldat im 20. Jahrhundert*, pp. 206–207.

89. Manstein, *Lost Victories*, p. 497.

90. Ibid., p. 498.

91. Helmut Heiber (ed.), *Hitler and His Generals*, pp. 353, 355–356, 363 and 375.

92. Manstein, *Lost Victories*, p. 501.

93. Ibid., p. 502.

94. Ibid., p. 504.

95. Ibid. The translated account of Manstein's private meeting with Hitler is somewhat abridged in *Lost Victories*. See *Verlorene Siege*, pp. 572–573, for the full version.

96. Manstein, *Lost Victories*, p. 505.

97. Ibid., p. 510, and *Verlorene Siege*, pp. 578–579.

98. Manstein, *Lost Victories*, pp. 511–512.

99. Manstein, *Verlorene Siege*, pp. 580–581.

100. Soviet accounts refer to 'Korsun-Shevchenkovskii', the full name of the Korsun locality. For comprehensive descriptions of the battle, see David M. Glantz and Harold S. Orenstein, *The Battle for the Ukraine: The Red Army's Korsun'-Shevchenkovskii Offensive, 1944* (London: Frank Cass, 2003),

an edited translation of a Soviet
General Staff Study; Niklas
Zetterling and Anders Frankson,
*The Korsun Pocket: The Encirclement
and Breakout of a German Army in
the East, 1944* (Philadelphia and
Newbury: Casemate, 2008); Karl-
Heinz Frieser, 'Die
Rückzugsoperationen der
Heeresgruppe Süd', in *Das
Deutsche Reich and der Zweite
Weltkrieg*, vol. 8, pp. 394–416.

101. In the Korsun pocket were six
starkly reduced divisions (57th,
72nd, 88th, 112th and 389th
Infantry Divisions; 5th SS Panzer
Division *Wiking*) together with
Corps Detachment 'B' and the SS
Wallonian Brigade under Leon
Dagrelle, with a total of about forty
tanks and assault guns.

102. The III Panzer Corps assault
grouping was based on 16th and
17th Panzer Divisions, Bäke's
Heavy Panzer Regiment with a
battlegroup of the *Leibstandarte*
protecting the northern flank and
elements of 1st Panzer Division the
southern. Only 149 tanks and
assault guns were available.

103. Manstein, *Lost Victories*, p. 517.

104. Glantz and House, *When Titans
Clash*, p. 188.

105. *Führerbefehl* (Führer's Order) No.
51 of 8 March 1944 required the
defence of all major localities.

106. Hube had commanded a panzer
division and a corps at Stalingrad.
He was flown out on Hitler's orders
and in the summer of 1943 had
conducted a brilliant defence of
Sicily and fought at Salerno. He
assumed command of First Panzer
Army in October 1943. On the
departure of Hoth in December
1943, he was Manstein's most able
army commander.

107. Manstein, *Lost Victories*, p. 538.

108. Ibid., pp. 539–542.

109. Ibid., pp. 544–545.

110. Ibid., p. 546.

111. Frieser, 'Die Rückzugsoperationen
der Heeresgruppe Süd', p. 448.

15. The Last Battles

1. Siegfried Westphal, *Der Deutsche
Generalstab auf der Anklagebank
Nürnberg 1945–1948* (Mainz: v.
Hase & Koehler Verlag, 1978), p.
92.

2. Busse, after a short period in the
'commanders' reserve', assumed
command of 121st Infantry
Division in July 1944.
Command of I Corps and Ninth
Army followed, the latter to the
war's end. He supported Manstein
at Nuremberg and Hamburg.
There was no closer or more loyal
subordinate and friend.

3. Stahlberg, *Bounden Duty*, p. 345.

4. Heusinger, *Befehl in Widerstreit*, p.
262.

5. Field Marshal Model, transferred
from the Eastern Front, assumed
command of Army Group B and
the post of *Oberbefehlshaber West*,
as von Kluge had done, until
Rundstedt reassumed command of
the latter position on 3 September
1944.

6. Stahlberg, p. 356.

7. Ibid., pp. 359–360.

8. Ibid.

9. Ibid., p. 362.

10. Ibid., p. 363.

11. Ibid.

12. As Rüdiger von Manstein notes,
within his family, 'the SS and SD
were [regarded as] dangerous
enemies'. Accordingly, Field
Marshal von Manstein instructed
his children 'to avoid all contact
with members of the SD who lived
in the neighbouring house in

Liegnitz; the same held for members of the Nazi Party. None of them was allowed into our home.' Personal communication to the present author, 6 August 2009.

13. Stahlberg, p. 368.

14. Manstein and Fuchs (eds.), *Soldat im 20. Jahrhundert*, p. 200.

15. Williamson Murray and Allan R. Millett, *A War to be Won*, p. 401.

16. Manstein and Fuchs, p. 200.

17. Gerd R. Ueberschär and Winfried Vogel, *Dienen und Verdienen: Hitlers Geschenke an seine Eliten* (Frankfurt am Main: S. Fischer Verlag, 1999), pp. 103 and 110.

18. Ibid., Dokument 27, p. 238: 'Dotationsfall' Generalfeldmarschall von Manstein. Schreiben von Staatssekretär Backe vom Reichsministerium für Ernährung und Landwirtschaft v. 17.10.1944. Source: BA Berlin, NS 19/904.

19. Stahlberg, p. 363.

20. Manstein and Fuchs, p. 202.

21. Stahlberg, p. 378.

22. Rüdiger von Manstein challenges this account. He recalls his father said that the general concerned had declared that the Russians were 'in Wilum', in other words, still about 60 km distant. This version of events is more credible than Stahlberg's '10 km', as it would have been hardly possible in such circumstances to conduct the wedding ceremony and feast so close to the front. Personal communication to the present author, 6 August 2009.

23. Maria Frisé, *Meine schlesische Familie und ich: Erinnerungen* (Berlin: Aufbau-Verlag, 2004), p. 144. Maria von Loesch's marriage to Hans-Conrad Stahlberg lasted twelve years. In 1957 she married

Adolf Frisé and wrote for many years for the *Frankfurter Allgemeine Zeitung*.

24. Stahlberg, p. 380.

25. Frisé, p. 146.

26. Gottfried Röchling, *Die Vertreibung aus der Heimat* (Lembeck Westfalen: March 1951), reproduced in the entry for Standort Namslau (now Luban in Poland) in the online Lexikon der Wehrmacht, accessed under: http://www.lexikon-der-wehrmacht.de/Kasernen/Wehrkreis08/KasernenNamslau-R.htm on 15 February 2009. Gottfried Röchling was a Protestant minister in Namslau in the period 1930–1945. Also accessible under: http://www.namslau-schlesien.de, the website of the *Namslauer Heimatfreunde* e. V.

27. Manstein and Fuchs, p. 212. The 'retired' field marshals Brauchitsch, Kleist and Busch, then living in Silesia, were similarly affected.

28. Rüdiger von Manstein, who accompanied his parents in Berlin during this period, cannot recall any such visit to Hitler taking place. In particular, he felt he would have remembered his father donning uniform again for such an occasion. Personal communication to the present author, 6 August 2009.

29. Stahlberg, pp. 388–390.

30. Manstein's real opinions as to the state of the war and Hitler in the final months are difficult to determine. Stahlberg (p. 380) recalls him crying out at the wedding banquet of 18 January 1945 at Lorzendorf, 'The end is not yet, not yet.'

31. Manstein and Fuchs, p. 212; see

also Rüdiger von Manstein's account in Hinrich Baumann, *Die Heidmark*, p. 236.

32. Baumann, pp. 548–549.
33. Stahlberg, pp. 396–397. See also Manstein and Fuchs, p. 213.
34. Stahlberg, p. 398.
35. Admiral Karl Dönitz, *Memoirs: Ten Years and Twenty Days*, trans. R. H. Stevens (London: Weidenfeld & Nicolson, 1959), p. 447. First published in German in 1958 under the title *Zehn Jahre und Zwanzig Tage* by Athenäum Verlag, Junker und Dünnhaupt, Bonn.
36. Manstein and Fuchs, p. 214.
37. Dönitz, p. 447.
38. Stahlberg, p. 400.
39. Ibid., pp. 401–406.
40. The present author has drawn this imaginary scene from Nigel Hamilton, *Monty: The Field Marshal 1944–1976* (London: Hamish Hamilton, 1986), pp. 502–503; Alistair Horne with David Montgomery, *The Lonely Leader: Monty 1944–1945* (London: Macmillan, 1994), pp. 336–337.
41. From the Simpson papers deposited in the Royal Engineers Museum, Archive and Library, Royal School of Military Engineering, Chatham. I am grateful to Mrs Rebecca Nash, Chief Curator, for locating this file for me.
42. Montgomery did summon Field Marshal Busch on 11 May 1945, giving him a 'dressing down' for querying orders and delaying their implementation. He recalled in his memoirs: 'I explained that I was making use of him and his headquarters so long as the job of implementing the surrender could be more efficiently carried out by that method. If he did not carry out his orders promptly and efficiently, I would remove him from command and find some other senior German officer to do the job.... He was to understand that the German Army had been utterly defeated in the field and must now accept the consequences of the defeat. After this I had no more trouble with Busch or with any other German commander.' Montgomery, *The Memoirs* (London: Collins, 1958), p. 367. Ironically, had Busch subsequently failed in Monty's eyes, then perhaps Manstein would have replaced him.
43. Hamilton, pp. 541–542.
44. The whereabouts of this stolen trophy remain unknown. Kluge's baton, on the other hand, is on display in the German Armour Museum at Munster. The present author is interested in retrieving Manstein's baton and returning it to his family. Montgomery had issued orders on 6 May 1945 prohibiting such activity. He wrote: 'Looting by individuals, or bodies of individuals, was of course forbidden at any time and I made it clear that any contravention of this order would be tried by court martial, whatever the rank of the individual concerned.' Montgomery, *The Memoirs*, p. 357.
45. Manstein and Fuchs, pp. 217–218. Technically, Manstein's last six months were not in detention as he spent time on medical treatment and subsequent rehabilitation at home prior to his official release.
46. Frisé, p. 165.
47. Headquarters 21st Army Group was renamed Headquarters British Army of the Rhine in August 1945. It remained in Bad Oeynhausen until moving to Mönchengladbach (Rheindahlen), west of Düsseldorf,

in 1954. Forty years later, a new organization was created in its place, the United Kingdom Support Command (Germany), which the present author commanded during the period 2006–2009.

48. The Charter of the International Military Tribunal is set out in Volume 1 of the Nuremberg Trial Proceedings. It consisted of thirty articles grouped into seven sections. Article 6 defined the following crimes: (a) crimes against peace; (b) war crimes; (c) crimes against humanity.

49. Manstein and Fuchs, pp. 219–222.

50. Westphal, *Der Deutsche Generalstab auf der Anklagebank*, p. 45.

51. This would hardly have been in the interests of the writing team. Manstein later gave considerable explanation as to Hitler's attraction to the military in his second memoir, *Aus einem Soldatenleben*, as highlighted in Chapters 3 and 4 of this biography. Within 'Das Deutsche Heer von 1920–1945', however, the seeds are sown. The declaration of German *Wehrfreiheit* – loosely interpreted as 'military sovereignty' – in March 1935, was 'warmly greeted as indicative of the fact that Germany now stood again as an equal in the circle of nations'. (Westphal, *Der Deutsche Generalstab auf der Anklagebank*, p. 40).

52. Westphal, *Der Deutsche Generalstab auf der Anklagebank*, p. 85.

53. Ibid., pp. 64–65.

54. Ibid., p. 50.

55. Ibid., p. 73.

56. Ibid., p. 81.

57. Ibid., p. 77.

58. Ibid., p. 79. '*In der Praxis wurde dieser Befehl [Zerstörungen] nur zum Teil und nur soweit es die militärischen Bedürfnisse erforderten, durchgeführt. Dabei wurden die allgemeinen Gesetze der Kriegsführung beachtet*'. ('In practice, this order [concerning destructions] was only carried out in part, and only as far as military necessity required. In so doing, the general laws of war were observed.')

59. Ibid., pp. 86–87.

60. Telford Taylor, *The Anatomy of the Nuremberg Trials: A Personal Memoir* (New York: Knopf, 1992), p. 180.

61. *Article* 9 of the Charter of the IMT set out: 'At the trial of any individual member of any group or organization the Tribunal may declare (in connection with any act of which the individual may be convicted) that the group or organization of which the individual was a member was a criminal organization.' *Article 10*: 'In cases where a group or organization is declared criminal by the Tribunal, the competent national authority of any Signatory shall have the right to bring individuals to trial for membership therein before national, military or occupation courts. In such case the criminal nature of the group or organization is considered proved and shall not be questioned.' *Article 11*: 'Any person convicted by the Tribunal may be charged before a national, military or occupation court, referred to in Article 10 of this Charter, with a crime other than of membership in a criminal group or organization and such court may, after convicting him, impose upon him punishment independent and additional to the punishment imposed by the Tribunal for participation in the

criminal activities of such group or organization.'

62. *Trial of the Major War Criminals*, vol. 4, pp. 390–392.

63. Ibid., p. 392.

64. Manstein and Fuchs, pp. 229–243.

65. Ibid., p. 233. In fact, the prosecution had never intended to indict all the members of the General Staff, nor implicate them. In his opening statement of 4 January 1946, Colonel Telford Taylor explained: 'There was in the German Army a war academy, and graduates of the war academy were in the branch of service described as the General Staff Corps. They signed themselves, for example, "Colonel in Generalstab" [he meant here *Oberst im Generalstab*]. They functioned largely as adjutants and assistants to the chief staff officers. I suppose there were some thousands of them – two or three thousand, but they are not included in the group. Many of them were officers of junior rank. They are not named in the indictment, and there is no reason and no respect in which they are comprehended within the group as defined.' *Trial of the Major War Criminals*, vol. 4, p. 403.

66. Manstein's view, of course, did not take the Nuremberg Charter into account, and its notion of 'aggressive war'. To be fair, he could not have been expected to anticipate or reflect the 'Nuremberg Principles', which were principles of international law recognized in the Charter of the Nuremberg Tribunal and in the judgement of the Tribunal. They were adopted by the International Law Commission of the United Nations in 1950. Specifically, *Principle VI a. i.*

defined 'Planning, preparation, initiation or waging a war of aggression or a war in violation of international treaties, agreements or assurances' as a punishable crime under international law. Further, *Principle VII* declared: 'Complicity in the commission of a crime against peace, a war crime, or a crime against humanity as set forth in *Principle VI* is a crime under international law.' See the *Report of the International Law Commission Covering its Second Session*, 5 June–29 July 1950, Document A/1316, pp. 11–14.

67. Manstein and Fuchs, pp. 235–236.

68. It is has never been seriously suggested, let alone proven in a court of law, that Manstein was witness to any war crime. The principal charges laid against him, described in Chapter 16, were those of *omission* rather than commission.

69. Manstein and Fuchs, p. 243.

70. Goldensohn and Gellately (eds.), *The Nuremberg Interviews*, p. 351. Goldensohn left detailed interview notes and observations on nineteen defendants and fourteen witnesses, the latter group including Manstein.

71. Ibid., pp. 337–338. Interview of 12 June 1946.

72. Ibid., p. 333.

73. Ibid., pp. 355–356.

74. Ibid.

75. Ibid., p. 357.

76. *Trial of the Major War Criminals*, vol. 20, p. 609.

77. Manstein was referring here to German mission-type orders, the celebrated *Auftragstaktik*.

78. Dr Laternser was referring here to the Commissar Order.

79. *Trial of the Major War Criminals*, vol. 20, p. 610.

80. Ibid., pp. 613–614.
81. Ibid., p. 622.
82. Raus, *Panzer Operations*, p. 254.
83. *Trial of the Major War Criminals*, vol. 20, pp. 615–616.
84. See, in particular, *Trial of the Major War Criminals*, vol. 4, pp. 318–319 and 346–347. Ohlendorf was the chief defendant at the subsequent Nuremberg Trial of the *Einsatzgruppen* (29 September 1947–10 April 1948), charged with crimes against humanity, war crimes and membership in criminal organizations. Ohlendorf pleaded not guilty on all three counts, was found guilty and sentenced to death by hanging. He was executed at Landsberg am Lech, Bavaria, on 7 June 1951.
85. *Trial of the Major War Criminals*, vol. 20, pp. 617–619.
86. Ibid., p. 619.
87. Ibid., pp. 623–625.
88. Ibid., p. 640.
89. Ibid., pp. 641–643.
90. Ibid., pp. 664–666.
91. Taylor, *The Anatomy of the Nuremberg Trials*, pp. 519–520.
92. Ibid., p. 520
93. *Trial of the Major War Criminals*, vol. 21, pp. 10–11.
94. Ibid., vol. 22, p. 522.
95. Quoted by Manstein and Fuchs, p. 245.
96. Westphal, *Der Deutsche Generalstab auf der Anklagebank*, pp. 137–138.
97. Taylor, *The Anatomy of the Nuremberg Trials*, pp. 530–531.
98. See Donald Bloxham, 'Punishing German Soldiers during the Cold War: The Case of Erich von Manstein' in *Patterns of Prejudice*, vol. 33, no. 4 (London: Thousand Oaks, New Delhi: SAGE Publications, 1999), pp. 28–29.
99. Walther Wenck, 'Nie Ausser Dienst', in *Nie Ausser Dienst*, p. 86.

16. Crime and Punishment

1. Speech in the House of Commons, 28 October 1948.
2. For the description of the decision to prosecute the German generals, I am indebted to the account given in Charles Messenger, *The Last Prussian*, Chapters 13 and 14.
3. The site was originally developed in the late 1930s as a dormitory camp for workers at the nearby Royal Ordnance Factory, Bridgend, with sites at Waterton and Brackla. During the war it was used by American forces and later as Prisoner of War Camp 198. It came to fame during the night of 10/11 March 1945, when sixty-six Germans tunnelled out only to be recaptured within a few days. As a precautionary measure all prisoners were transferred to Camp 181 at Carburton, near Worksop in Nottinghamshire. After the war, the camp was refurbished to make it suitable for senior officers. For a description and history of Island Farm, see Susan M. Hawthorne *et al.*, *Island Farm: Special Camp 11 for Prisoners of War* (Bridgend: Brynteg Comprehensive School, 1989) and Jeff Vincent, 'Island Farm Camp', *After the Battle*, no. 67 (1990), pp. 28–39. I am grateful to Mrs Hawthorne for providing me with extracts from her book and updating me on Island Farm since I visited the site in April 2006. There is little to see of the camp today except the sole remaining and semi-derelict Hut 9, from which the Germans tunnelled out during the war. Hut 14, the field marshals' block, is long since demolished. For further details of the camp and its prominent

inmates, see:
http://www.islandfarm.fsnet.co.uk;
http://www.specialcampII.fsnet.co.uk
and http://www.bracklaordnance.
co.uk/island%20farm.htm.

4. Recalled by Siegfried Westphal in
Franz Kurowski, *General der
Kavallerie Siegfried Westphal*
(Würzburg: Flechsig Verlag,
2007), p. 130.

5. Quoted by Matthew Barry
Sullivan, *Thresholds of Peace: Four
Hundred Thousand German
Prisoners and the People of Britain
1944–1948* (London: Hamish
Hamilton, 1979), p. 358.

6. Field Marshal Ewald von Kleist
was held at Island Farm until 3
September 1946. He was then
extradited on war crimes charges
from the United Kingdom to
Yugoslavia, and thence to the Soviet
Union to face conviction on
further charges. He was sentenced
to life imprisonment and died in
Soviet captivity in 1954.

7. For conditions at Island Farm, see:
Hawthorne, pp. 66–79;
Messenger, pp. 243–257; Sullivan,
pp. 348–360. In addition, Otto
John, *Twice Through the Lines: The
Autobiography of Otto John*
(London: Macmillan, 1972),
originally published in German by
Econ Verlag in 1969 under the title
Zweimal kam ich heim, provides
further fascinating detail. See, for
example, pp. 184–188.

8. Manstein, letter to his wife, 4
September 1946. Quoted by
Manstein and Fuchs, *Soldat im 20.
Jahrhundert*, p. 246.

9. Accessed from
http://www.bracklaordnance.
co.uk/island%20farm%20special%
20camp%2011.htm on 2 May
2009.

10. Letter of 1 February 1947.

Manstein and Fuchs, p. 247.

11. Other prominent prisoners held at
Island Farm included: Colonel
General Gotthard Heinrici;
Colonel General Kurt Student
(Luftwaffe); General of Armoured
Troops Hasso von Manteuffel;
Major General Walter Dornberger
(co-designer of the V2 rocket) and
Rear Admiral Hans Voss, the Camp
Liaison Officer.

12. Senger und Etterlin, *Neither Fear
nor Hope*, p. 347. His
differentiation between the
German prisoners of war in three
groups corresponded to the British
official categorization into White,
Grey and Black, the latter being
hardened Nazis.

13. Ibid., p. 349.

14. Ibid, p. 351. The two, equally
sympathetic, commandants were
Major Denis Topham, Grenadier
Guards, who was followed in
September 1947 by Lieutenant
Colonel Charles Clements MC,
4th Hussars. See Messenger, p.
265, and Sullivan, pp. 348–349.

15. Senger und Etterlin, *Neither Fear
nor Hope*, p. 350.

16. Sullivan, p. 357.

17. Neither has been published but
excerpts of the former are
contained in Manstein and Fuchs,
pp. 255–268.

18. Letter of 19 February 1947. Ibid.,
pp. 250–251.

19. Letter of 5 September 1950. Ibid.,
p. 314.

20. Undated letter. Ibid., pp. 253–254.

21. Ibid., p. 268.

22. There was an attempt by John
Wheeler-Bennett, the eminent
historian, then working in the
German Section of the Foreign
Office, to initiate such a
programme. In an internal minute,
he wrote on 6 October 1947: 'It

does not seem entirely just that General Halder, having "sold out" to the Americans, should have the opportunity of establishing a historical monopoly ... it seems a pity to deprive ourselves of what should clearly be material of outstanding historical interest and value.' Quoted by Messenger, p. 259, from PRO FO 371/64474. However, as one modern historian of this period and subject has concluded: 'The writing of military-historical and military-technical reports and studies was not, in fact, greatly encouraged by the British. But they did send considerable numbers of generals to camps in the American zone in 1946 and 1947 to take part in the military history programme being run by the U.S. Army Historical Division.' See Alaric Searle, *Wehrmacht Generals, West German Society, and the Debate on Rearmament 1949–1959* (Greenwood, Conn.: Praeger, 2003), pp. 29–30. For further critical detail on the history programme, see James A. Wood, 'Captive Historians, Captivated Audience: The German Military History Program, 1945–1961,' *The Journal for Military History*, 69 (January 2005), pp. 123–147; and Ronald M. Smelser and Edward J. Davies, *The Myth of the Eastern Front* (Cambridge: University Press, 2007), Chapter 3. German historians have also levelled considerable criticism at the work of the German military authors involved, cautioning against its use as a reliable historical source. See, for example, Müller and Volkmann (eds.), *Die Wehrmacht*, p. 7: 'The seemingly apolitical, factual work fostered the myth of the

professional, apolitical Wehrmacht. . . . [Halder's] plan was simple: to present the Army High Command as Hitler's victim, an instrument abused in the pursuit of a criminal policy.'

23. The lack of a proper United Kingdom Armed Forces Military Historical Research Centre today speaks volumes for this serious institutional deficiency. Whilst the Royal Air Force and Royal Navy continue to run their own separate historical sections, the Army Historical Branch has been subsumed into the Ministry of Defence's 'Corporate Memory' that is nothing more than an archive. Its research and publishing output is minimal. With characteristic German efficiency, the Bundeswehr established its Armed Forces Military Historical Research Office (*Militärgeschichtliches Forschungsamt* (MGFA)) in 1958. It serves today as an exemplar. The armed services of the United States have their own comprehensive historical institutes, as do the French.

24. Alaric Searle, 'A Very Special Relationship: Basil Liddell Hart, Wehrmacht Generals and the Debate on West German Rearmament 1945–1953', *War in History*, 1998, 5 (3), p. 330.

25. Senger und Etterlin, p. 353.

26. B. H. Liddell Hart, *The Other Side of the Hill*. This quote is taken from the Papermac edition of 1993, pp. 7–8.

27. Ibid., p. 94. Liddell Hart wrote in his contemporaneous notes that 'R.[undstedt] evidently thinks [Manstein] the best, though he hesitates to say so definitely'. Quoted by Messenger, p. 241.

28. A strong caution, however, must be applied to the manuscripts of the United States Army's history programme, Liddell Hart's *Other Side of the Hill* and the memoirs written by senior Wehrmacht commanders such as Guderian and Manstein. Invariably and unsurprisingly, such work gives a one-sided German viewpoint. As James A. Wood concluded, moreover (p. 145): 'The writing of historical accounts for the U.S. Army provided former German officers with much more than an opportunity to present the U.S. Army with lessons on fighting the Soviets – it allowed the authors to present the last war as a crusade against Bolshevism rather than a ruthless war of expansion.'

29. For a sympathetic view, see H. R. Trevor-Roper's introduction to Otto John's autobiography, *Twice Through the Lines*. A balanced German perspective is given by Karl-Heinz Janssen, 'Der Fall John', *Die Zeit*, 06.09.1985 Nr 37, accessed under http://www.zeit.de/1985/37/Der-Fall-John on 11 April 2009. John's controversial career continued as President of the Federal Agency for Protection of the Constitution, to which office he had been appointed in October 1951. In West Berlin for the tenth anniversary of 20 July 1944, he fled (or was abducted) under mysterious circumstances to East Berlin. On his return eighteen months later to West Germany he was arrested, tried and convicted of treason, and sentenced to four years' hard labour. He was never rehabilitated.

30. Manstein and Fuchs, p. 269, quoting letters to Manstein's wife of 1 May and 25 July 1947.

31. John, pp. 92–93.

32. Manstein, letter to his wife, 12 October 1947. Quoted by Manstein and Fuchs, p. 270.

33. Related by Messenger, p. 257, with reference to British Channel Four Television programme *Jailed by the British*, screened in two episodes 'Alien Internment' and 'German POWs' on 16 and 23 February 1983 respectively. Messenger omits to mention in which screening Lees made this assertion.

34. The High Command Trial (officially, *The United States of America vs. Wilhelm von Leeb, et al.*) was the last of the twelve trials for war crimes the US authorities held at Nuremberg under the American Military Tribunal.

35. Manstein and Fuchs, p. 270.

36. Rundstedt's letter of 6 May 1948, LH 9/24/77, quoted by Messenger, p. 272.

37. Messenger, pp. 273–274.

38. LHCMA, LH 9/24/158. Letter to the editor of the *Manchester Guardian* of 21 August 1948, 'Imprisoned German Generals', quoting letter from Manstein to Liddell Hart dated 11 August 1948.

39. Manstein and Fuchs, p. 271.

40. Continuation of Manstein's letter to Liddell Hart dated 11 August 1948; extract published on 21 August 1948.

41. In writing this section the present author is indebted to Mr John Harding, formerly of Historical Branch (Army), who wrote a research essay, 'Manstein: His War Crimes Trial and Background' (July 2006). Although I have drawn on Mr Harding's preparatory work, the narrative and conclusions expressed are mine

alone. Manstein's trial is covered comprehensively from a defence – and arguably very partisan – viewpoint in *Manstein: His Campaigns and His Trial*, Part Two, Chapters VIII–XIII, by R. T. Paget. Dr Paul Leverkuehn, *Verteidigung Manstein* (Hamburg: H.H. Nölke Verlag, 1950) provides a factual account. The decision of the court analysed in H. Lauterpacht (ed.), *Annual Digest and Reports of Public International Law Cases Year 1949* (London: Butterworth, 1955) is taken largely from the Deputy Judge Advocate General's summing up. Critical analysis is given in Tom Bower, *Blind Eye to Murder: Britain, America and the Purging of Nazi Germany – A Pledge Betrayed* (London: André Deutsch, 1981); Donald Bloxham, *Genocide on Trial: War Crimes Trials and the Formation of Holocaust History and Memory* (Oxford: University Press, 2001); and in Wrochem, *Erich von Manstein*, Chapter 4.

42. *Trial of the Major War Criminals*, vol. 22, pp. 522–523.

43. National Archives, CAB/29/28 C.P.(48) 151 dated 17 June 1948 – War Crimes: Case of German Generals in British Custody. Memorandum by the Secretary of State for War.

44. Reported in *The Times* on 10 July 1948 and quoted by the Bishop of Chichester in the House of Lords on 5 May 1949.

45. National Archives, CAB/128/13 C.M.(48) 47th Conclusions – Conclusions of Meeting of Cabinet, Monday 5 July 1948.

46. Mr Bevan declared: 'His Majesty's Government were under an obligation to hand over alleged war criminals, against whom a clear prima facie case existed, to the Governments of the countries in which their crimes were committed, unless it was intended to try them before a British tribunal. The decision of His Majesty's Government was taken purely on the merits of the case after being advised that there was a prima facie case against them; and – this is very important – since some of their subordinates had already been tried and convicted of offences which might have proved to have resulted from their orders, His Majesty's Government felt it essential in the interests of justice that further steps should be taken to bring them to trial if the evidence warranted it.' Hansard, 22 September 1948. Retrieved under http://hansard. millbanksystems.com/commons/ 1948/sep/22/foreign affairs on 12 April 2009.

47. Ibid.

48. Continuation of Manstein's letter to Liddell Hart dated 11 August 1948; extract published on 21 August 1948.

49. 'The German Generals', letter to the editor of *The Times* signed by H. N. Brailsford, Michael Foot, Victor Gollancz, J. H. Hudson, R. T. Paget, J. B. Priestley, [Lord] Russell, T. C. Skeffington-Lodge, R. R. Stokes and Leonard Woolf dated 1 September and published on 3 September 1948.

50. 'The German Generals', letter to the editor of *The Times*, published on 21 September 1948.

51. See, for example, Busse's 'standard' five-page letter of 5 June 1949 requesting support at BA-MA, N630/12.

52. BA-MA, N630/13. Letter of 29 December 1948. Quoted by Wrochem, p. 143.

53. Hansard, 26 October 1948, vol. 457 cc57–84: http://hansard.millbanksystems.com/commons/1948/oct/26/germangenerals-trial accessed on 16 April 2009.

54. Ibid., 28 October 1948: http://hansard.millbanksystems.com/commons/1948/oct/28/debate-on-foreign affairs accessed on 16 April 2009

55. Bloxham, *Genocide on Trial*, p. 33, believes there was: ' . . . the variety of opinions suggests that something was amiss (and, as we shall see, the function of medical reasoning after von Manstein's conviction strongly corroborates suspicions of foul play)'.

56. National Archives, CAB/129/34 C.P.(49) 73 dated 28 March 1949 – War Crimes: The German Generals. Memorandum by the Secretary of State for War, pp. 4–5.

57. HL Deb 05 May 1949 vol. 162 cc376–418. Retrieved under http://hansard.millbanksystems.com/lords/1949/may/05/german-war-crimes-trials on 13 April 2009.

58. Lord Hankey subsequently wrote a book condemning the war crimes trials: *Politics, Trials and Errors* (Oxford: Pen-in-Hand, 1950).

59. National Archives, CAB/129/34 C.P.(49) 73 dated 28 March 1949, p. 5.

60. Paget, p. 75.

61. As a primary source, the present author has used a charge sheet of [undated] May 1949, but with a handwritten inscription on the first page: 'Amended. As served 14 July 1949' and signed by 'Maj Gen D.A.L. Wade', the Deputy President of the Court Martial, and deposited as part of his papers in the LHCMA, now in folder von Manstein 3. There is little doubt, moreover, that this charge sheet represents an original document used in court as the specific counts itemized in the seventeen charges are each cross-referenced in manuscript to numbered exhibits of documentary evidence. In LHCMA, von Manstein 6, there are twelve document books, containing a total of 689 numbered documents. Originally, there were no fewer than 184 specified counts amongst the seventeen charges. When the trial began, however, ten of these had been withdrawn for lack of evidence.

62. Paget, p. 73.

63. Wrochem, p. 145, states that from the end of February 1948 to the middle of March 1950, a sum of no less than DM 55,000 was raised.

64. Lord Simon's letter to the editor of *The Times*, dated 18 July, published on 20 July 1949; likewise Lord Hankey's of 23 July, published two days later.

65. *The Times*, 10 August, 1949. Report, 'Von Manstein's Trial: Defence Fund Closed'.

66. Paget, p. 72.

67. Ibid., p. 74.

68. Ibid., pp. 107–108.

69. Ibid., p. 75.

70. Ibid., pp. 75–76.

71. CIGS DO/77 dated 9 August 1949. Simpson Papers.

72. General Sir Frank E. W. Simpson GBE KCB DSO (1899–1986) was a distinguished Royal Engineer and general staff officer. As a lieutenant colonel, he was awarded his DSO for his contribution to the successful withdrawal of the British Expeditionary Force in 1940. After Dunkirk, he was Brigadier General Staff (de facto chief of staff) to Montgomery in V, and later, XII Corps. Appointed

Director of Military Operations in the War Office in 1943 as a major general he kept in very close touch with Montgomery for the rest of the war. His loyalty to his former commander was rewarded when appointed Vice Chief of the Imperial General Staff in 1946 as a lieutenant general. He assumed command of Western Command in March 1948 and was promoted to general in 1950. Slim had selected him as president of the Manstein trial because he was 'one of the more experienced Army commanders'. His last tour was Commandant of the Imperial Defence College. With Simpson, the other six members of the court martial were: Major General D. A. L. Wade, CB OBE MC BA AMIEE, Brigadiers C. A. Dixon OBE and R. B. Lambe, Colonels R. F. Wilson, E. T. Henlop and L. A. Liddell. Paget's accusation that none of the members of the court had any recent operational experience was not supported by any evidence.

73. The prosecuting team was a formidable one of great distinction. Sir Arthur Comyns Carr (1909–65) was a Liberal Party politician and lawyer who had prosecuted in the Tokyo trials against the Japanese. Frederick Elwyn Elwyn-Jones (1900–1989) was a barrister and Labour Party political, who had prosecuted at Nuremberg and later served as both Attorney General (1964–70) and as Lord Chancellor (1974–79). The German refugee, Frederick Honig, had become a prominent barrister-at-law in Britain. Professor Colonel Gerald Draper OBE (1914–1989) of the Directorate of Army Legal

Services became the foremost specialist in the law of armed conflict of his generation in the United Kingdom.

74. The Curio House was erected in 1911 for the 'Society of Friends of the Patriotic Schooling and Education' as a teachers' meeting house. It was named after Johann Carl Daniel Curio, who had founded the society in 1805. Today the building is an office and conference centre complex, housing the practices of doctors, dentists, tax advisors and solicitors, and the Amerika-Zentrum (America Centre).

75. Paget, p. 78.

76. Paget is referring here to the 'Convention relative to the Treatment of Prisoners of War, Geneva, 27 July 1929', which entered into force on 19 June 1931. It was replaced by the third Geneva Convention of 12 August 1949, which entered force on 21 October 1951. All Paget's references are to the 1929 Convention rather than that of 1949.

77. Paget, pp. 202–218.

78. Ibid., pp. 218–225.

79. *The Times*, 25 August 1949. Report, 'Prosecution's Case, From Our Special Correspondent, Hamburg, Aug. 24'.

80. LHCMA, von Manstein 4, Prosecution Opening Speech, 136 pages.

81. Ibid., p. 6. The prosecution quoted here the judgement on the General Staff given on Monday, 30 September 1946. See *Trial of the Major War Criminals*, vol. 22, pp. 521–522.

82. LHCMA, von Manstein 4, Prosecution Opening Speech, p. 34.

83. *The Times*, 31 August 1949. *Reuter*

report, 'Allegations at Trial of von Manstein, Hamburg, Aug. 30'.

84. LHCMA, von Manstein 4, Prosecution Opening Speech, p. 36.

85. Ibid., p. 38.

86. Ibid., p. 4.

87. Ibid., p. 53.

88. Ibid., p. 56.

89. Ibid., p. 62.

90. Ibid., p. 73

91. Ibid., p. 83.

92. LHCMA, von Manstein 3, Charge Sheet, Ninth Charge, counts (a) and (g); pp. 18–19.

93. LHCMA, von Manstein 4, Prosecution Opening Speech, pp. 87 and 90.

94. Quoted by Paget, pp. 103–104.

95. LHCMA, von Manstein 4, Prosecution Opening Speech, p. 135. Also quoted by Paget, p. 104.

96. *The Times*, 30 August 1949. *Reuter* report, 'Polish Civilians Shot in the Streets, Hamburg, Aug. 29'.

97. *New York Herald*, 6 September 1949. Cited by Stein, *The Janus Head*, p. 314.

98. Manstein Trial Proceedings, p. 1930.

99. Manstein, letter to his wife, 21 August 1946. Quoted by Manstein and Fuchs, pp. 244–245.

100. Manstein Trial Proceedings, p. 1932.

101. LHCMA, von Manstein 4, Prosecution Opening Speech, p. 105.

102. JAG Archives, London: DJAG/15418/972/BAOR dated 16 January 1950 – 'Military Court (War Crimes) Trial Fritz Erich von Lewinski (called Manstein)', p. 8.

103. *The Times*, 26 and 27 August 1949. Reports 'From Our Special Correspondent, Hamburg, Aug. 25' and '26' respectively.

104. Reported in *The Times*, 8

September 1949. *Reuter* report, 'Order to Murder Jews in Crimea: Accusation against Manstein, Hamburg, Sept. 7'.

105. Paget, p. 110.

106. Ibid., pp. 116–118.

107. Ibid., p. 123.

108. Ibid., pp. 123–125.

109. *The Times*, 6 October 1949. *Reuter* report, 'Trial of Manstein: Defence Counsel's Speech, Hamburg, Oct. 5'.

110. The text is reproduced in Leverkuehn, pp. 3–8.

111. Ibid., p. 4.

112. Ibid., pp. 4, 7 & 8.

113. Paget, p. 182.

114. Ashton Wade, *A Life on the Line* (Tunbridge Wells: D. J. Costello, 1988), pp. 170–171.

115. Hauck ended the war as a general of artillery; Stephanus as a colonel. The latter became a brigadier general in the Bundeswehr.

116. Institut für Zeitgeschichte (IfZ), München, G29. Quote taken from the court record for the forty-fourth Day, pp. 109, 116 and 126.

117. For further details of defence witnesses' evidence given during this period, corresponding to the forty-first to fiftieth days of proceedings, see Wrochem, pp. 183–197.

118. Ibid., p. 186.

119. Ibid., p. 187.

120. Ibid., pp. 190–192.

121. National Archives FO 1060/1339, p. 3,071. Quoted by Wrochem, p. 189.

122. *The Times*, 13 December 1949. Report, 'Manstein and Rules of War: Summing-Up Begins, From Our Special Correspondent, Hamburg, Dec. 12'.

123. Paget, p. 193.

124. The court's findings are given in FO 1060/1345, 'Trial Shorthand

Notes', p. 3,395. For analysis of the verdict, see Paget, pp. 194–195; Manstein and Fuchs, pp. 286–299; Wrochem, pp. 191–192.

125. Simpson Papers. CIGS/BM/36/3604 dated 12 December 1949.

126. Paget, p. 192.

Epilogue

1. Paget, *Manstein: His Campaigns and His Trial*, p. 191.
2. BA-MA, N 507/3, p. 119.
3. *The Times*, 20 December, 1949. Report, '18 Years for Manstein: Guilty of Nine War Crimes', From Our Special Correspondent, Hamburg, 19 Dec.
4. Ibid., 21 December 1949. Report, 'Germans and the Manstein Trial: Criticism of Sentence', From Our Special Correspondent, Frankfurt, 20 Dec. For a detailed analysis of the press reaction to the outcome of the trial, see Wrochem, *Erich von Manstein*, pp. 199–202.
5. The description of Werl as an Allied Prison and the treatment of its 'VIP' prisoners (ten field marshals and generals, including Field Marshals Kesselring and Manstein) is taken from Helmuth Euler, 'Werl Allied Prison', *After the Battle*, no. 118 (2002), pp. 44–55. In addition, Kesselring left some impressions on prison life at Werl during his detention there (October 1947–July 1952). See *The Memoirs of Field Marshal Kesselring* (London: Greenhill Books, 2007), pp. 311–314.
6. Manstein and Fuchs, *Soldat im 20. Jahrhundert*, p. 309, quoting letters by Manstein to his wife from the period 19 December 1949–5 January 1950.
7. BA-MA, N 507/3, p. 112. A copy

of the complete typewritten letter is at pp. 112–118.

8. Paget, pp. 200–201. Rather strangely with regard to Manstein's letter of 1 January 1950, the later letter opens with: 'Until today I have not been able to write to you and convey my thanks which I could only incoherently express due to the fact that I know very little English. Up to now my broken collar-bone has stopped me from writing and I was not permitted to dictate a letter to one of the typists. Therefore my thanks reach you somewhat tardily.'
9. Letter dated 15 January 1950. LHCMA, LH 9/24/71 Part I, pp. 133, 134, 139–140.
10. Wade, *A Life on the Line*, p. 172.
11. Ibid., p. 175.
12. 'Von Manstein's Trial: The Court's Findings Examined', letter to the editor of *The Times*, dated 7 Jan, published 11 January 1950.
13. Wade, pp. 172–173.
14. JAG Archives, London: DJAG/15418/972/BAOR dated 16 January 1950 – 'Military Court (War Crimes) Trial Fritz Erich von Lewinski (called von Manstein)', p. 25.
15. JAG Archives, London: DJAG/15418/972/BAOR dated 3 February 1950 – 'Military Court (War Crimes) Trial Fritz Erich von Lewinski (called von Manstein)', pp. 6 and 9. In his autobiography, *That Reminds Me* (London: Cassell, 1959), Lord Russell opined (p. 189): 'When giving evidence, von Manstein boasted that whenever he disagreed with Hitler's conduct of the war he used to climb into his aeroplane, fly to the Führer's Headquarters and protest. There was, in my opinion, ample evidence that von Manstein must have

known that the Einsatzgruppe of Ohlendorf was busy exterminating Jews in the field-marshal's Army Area, but there was no evidence that he made any protest, written or otherwise.' I am grateful to Judge Michael Hunter for lending me this volume.

16. BA-MA, N 507/3, p. 124. Letter from Field Marshal von Manstein to Mr Paget dated 25 February 1950.
17. Manstein and Fuchs, p. 313.
18. Euler, p. 51.
19. Author's interview with Gisela Lingenthal on 4 March 2007 at Bad Honnef.
20. Euler, p. 51. Wade (p. 156) recalls visiting Werl in February 1949, when the 'prison governor ushered us into a map-lined room, where to our astonishment Kesselring sat at the head of a long table around which six or seven German generals were seated holding a conference. We were informed that under an agreement between the US and British governments the Field-Marshal and his fellow prisoners were engaged in research for the British and American Military Historical Sections.'
21. Manstein and Fuchs, p. 314
22. Ibid., p. 316.
23. Quoted by Bloxham, 'Punishing German Soldiers during the Cold War', p. 36.
24. Manstein and Fuchs, p. 318.
25. *The Times* 23 December 1950. Report, 'German Defence Contribution: Fixing the Scale', From Our Own Correspondent, Bonn, 22 Dec.
26. Alaric Searle, 'A Very Special Relationship: Basil Liddell Hart, Wehrmacht Generals and the Debate on West German Rearmament 1945–1953', *War in History*, 1998 5 (3), pp. 340–349.
27. Manstein and Fuchs, pp. 318–320.
28. National Archives, CAB/129/44 C.P. (51) 38 dated 6th February, 1951 – 'War Criminals: Memorandum by the Minister of State', pp. 2–4.
29. National Archives, CAB/128/19, C.M (51), 39th Conclusions of Cabinet, Thursday, 31st May, 1951, p. 53.
30. *The Times*, 21 September 1951. Letter to the editor, 'The German Soldier' by R. T. Paget.
31. Ibid., 26 September 1951. Report, 'Trial of Manstein: Sir Hartley Shawcross's Statement'.
32. Ibid., 24 January 1952. Report, 'Britain's Stake in Europe: Sir I. Kirkpatrick's New Emphasis', From Our Own Correspondent, Bonn, 23 Jan.
33. Manstein and Fuchs, p. 321.
34. Ibid., p. 322.
35. Ibid., pp. 322–323.
36. *The Times*, 8 May 1953. Report, 'Von Manstein Free: Expiry of Sentence as War Criminal', From Our Own Correspondent, Bonn, 7 May.
37. Manstein and Fuchs, p. 323. Letter from Konrad Adenauer of 26 May 1953.
38. 'He was struck again by the beauty of Irschenhausen, the pine-woods behind the little house, the sweeping clarity of the Alps in front, the autumn crocuses, the deer jumping up and down to shake off the rain and the squirrels (he joked) hanging themselves out to dry.' From Mark Kinkead-Weekes, *D. H. Lawrence: Triumph to Exile, 1912–1922* (Cambridge: University Press, 1996), p. 91.
39. LHCMA, LH 3/25. Letter to Dr E. V. Rieu dated 20 October 1955.
40. Ibid., LH 9/24/45. Letter to

Captain Liddell Hart dated 22
April 1957.

41. Ibid. Letter to Captain B. H.
Liddell Hart, JC/AMW, dated 25
June 1957.

42. Ibid. Letter dated 8 July 1957.

43. Ibid. Letter dated 16 January 1958.

44. The RUSI reviewer also struck a
more cautious note: 'A flair for
moral philosophy cannot be
expected in every general, but he
must not be astonished that some
awareness of this discipline should
be demanded of him – particularly
when he leads thousands of young
men to fight for a regime whose
innate evilness could have
remained hidden only to the
woefully blind. Manstein's sense of
responsibility expressed itself in an
unusually pronounced feeling of
comradeship with his troops and
the determination to lead them as
competently and successfully as
Hitler would allow.' *RUSI Journal*,
August 1958, vol. CIII, no. 611.

45. LHCMA, LH 9/24/45. Copies of
book reviews published in the
Daily Telegraph and Morning Post,
and in the *Evening Standard* on 29
May; *The Sunday Times* on 1 June;
The Listener on 12 June 1958.

46. Ibid. Copies of reviews published
in the *Baltimore Evening Sun* on 1
October and in the *New York Times*
on 5 October 1958.

47. Reviewed by Major Harry H.
Jackson, *Military Review*, vol. 39,
no. 2, May 1959, p. 112.

48. Manstein and Fuchs, p. 325.

49. Field-Marshal Erich von
Manstein, 'The Development of
the Red Army 1942–45' in B. H.
Liddell Hart (ed.), *The Soviet Army*
(London: Weidenfeld & Nicolson,
1956), pp. 140–52.

50. Field-Marshal Erich von
Manstein, 'Defensive Operations

in Southern Russia 1943–44',
Marine Corps Gazette, April 1957,
41, p. 53.

51. John Zimmermann, *Pflicht zum
Untergang: Die deutsche
Kriegführung im Westen des Reiches
1944/45* (Paderborn: Ferdinand
Schöningh, 2009), p. 453.

52. Manstein and Fuchs, p. 326.

53. Wenck, *Nie Ausser Dienst*, p. 93.

54. BA-MA, BW 2 20193. Letter
dated 4 November 1955.

55. Ibid; Manstein and Fuchs, pp. 329–
330. Manstein's paper on the
structure of the German Army is
reproduced in full as Document 2,
pp. 389–405.

56. In strict contrast to British Army
usage then or since, the German
term *Kampfgruppe* was never fixed
to the battalion group during the
Second World War or
subsequently. It could be as large as
a US Army wartime combat
command or reinforced regimental
combat team. The key character of
the battle group was that it was
'task-organized' for a specific
mission, and had no fixed grouping.

57. Wenck, *Nie Ausser Dienst*, pp. 93–
94.

58. Ibid., p. 95.

59. Manstein and Fuchs, p. 376.

60. General Ulrich de Maizière,
Geleitwort in *Nie Ausser Dienst*, pp.
7–8.

61. Manstein and Fuchs, p. 387.

62. Author's interview with Major
General Erhard Drews, a serving
divisional commander in the
Bundeswehr, on 20 May 2009 at
Colmar.

63. BA-MA, MSg. 1/256, Gedenkrede
für Generalfeldmarschall Erich
von Manstein gehalten am 15. Juni
1973 in der Kirche zu Dorfmark
von General der Infanterie a. D.
Theodor Busse.

64. Manstein and Fuchs, pp. 382–383.
65. LHCMA, von Manstein 10, cutting from *The Times*, 13 June 1973: 'Obituary Field Marshal von Manstein: An outstanding German soldier'.
66. BA-MA, MSg. 1/221. Obituary, *Der Spiegel*, Nr. 25, 18 June 1973.
67. BA-MA, N 507–13, Affidavit of Walter Trepte, retired Wehrmacht chaplain, dated 10 July 1947.
68. An interesting and revealing analysis of this dilemma within a modern context is given by Martin L. Cook, 'Revolt of the Generals: A Case Study in Professional Ethics', *Parameters*, vol. XXXVII, no. 1, Spring 2008, pp. 4–15. I am grateful to David Zabecki for bringing this article to my attention.
69. *The Listener*, 12 June 1958.

Select Bibliography

A. Unpublished Documents, including Archival Sources and Family Papers

Bundesarchiv/Militärarchiv, Freiburg im Breisgau (BA-MA)

a. *Militärgeschichtliche Sammlung* (MSg) [Military historical collection]

MSg1/1830 Rudolf Graf

b. *Nachlässe* (N) [Bequests of documents]

N63 Kurt Zeitzler
N507 Erich von Manstein
N547 Friedrich-Wilhelm Hauck
N630 Theodor Busse

c. *Personalakten* (Pers) [Personal files]

Pers 6/33 Erich von Manstein

d. *Heeresdienststellen* (PH or RH) [Headquarters files of the Prussian Army or *Reichsheer* respectively]

PH 81/453 213rd Infantry Division
RH 19–I Heeresgruppe Süd [Army Group South]
RH 19–VI Heeresgruppe Don/Süd [Army Group Don/South]
RH 20–11 Armeeoberkommando 11 [Eleventh Army]
RH 21–4 Panzeroberkommando 4 [Fourth Panzer Group/Army]
RH 24–38 Generalkommando XXXVIII [XXXVIII Corps]
RH 24–56 Generalkommando LVI [LVI Corps (Motorized)]

e. *Bundeswehr* (BW) [Bundeswehr files]

BW 2 Including correspondence of General Heusinger

Field Marshal Erich von Manstein family memoirs and private papers

a. Held by Herr Rüdiger von Manstein:

Personal war diary of Erich von Manstein
Private family letters
Photograph albums

Martha von Sperling-Manstein, *Aus einer Kindheit vor der Jahrhundertwende* (Allmendingen: March 1996)

b. Held by Frau Gisela Lingenthal:

Als Mutter ein Kind war (undated)

Institut für Zeitgeschichte, Munich (IfZ)

G29   Manstein-Prozess [Manstein trial record]
MA 113   Manstein-Prozess [Manstein trial material]

Liddell Hart Centre for Military Archives, King's College London (LHCMA)

a. Sir James Edmonds papers

b. Sir Basil Liddell Hart papers

c. Documentation relating to the proceedings of the trial of Field Marshal Erich von Manstein

National Archives (formerly the Public Record Office), Kew

FO 371/64474
CAB/29/28
CAB/128/13
CAB/129/34

Judge Advocate General Archive, London

D/JAG/15418/972

Royal Engineers Museum, Library and Archive, Chatham

General Sir Frank Simpson papers

B. Published Primary Sources, including War Diaries and Personal Memoirs

Avdeev, General of Aviation M. V., *At the Bluest Sea* (Moscow: DOSAAF, 1968)
Balck, Hermann, *Ordnung im Chaos* (Osnabrück: Biblio Verlag, 1981)
Beaulieu, Walter Chales de, *Der Vorstoss der Panzergruppe auf Leningrad – 1941* (Neckargemünd: Kurt Vorwinckel Verlag, 1961)
Bradley, Omar N., *A Soldier's Story* (New York: Henry Holt, 1951)
Choltitz, Dietrich von, *Soldat unter Soldaten* (Zürich: Europa Verlag, 1951)
Chuikov, V. I., *The End of the Third Reich* (Moscow: Progress Publishers, 1978)
Chuikov, V. I., *The Battle for Stalingrad* (New York: Holt, Rinehart & Wilson, 1964)
Dittrich, Leutnant, 'Tataren-Graben und Perekop' in *Wir Erobern die Krim!* (Neustadt/Weinstrasse: Pfälzische Verlagsanstalt, 1943)

Dönitz, Admiral Karl, *Memoirs: Ten Years and Twenty Days* (London: Weidenfeld & Nicolson, 1959)

Eisenhower, D., *Crusade in Europe* (Garden City, NY: Doubleday, 1948)

Engel, Major Gerhard, *At the Heart of the Reich: The Secret Diary of Hitler's Army Adjutant* (London: Greenhill Books, 2005)

Eremenko, Marshal A. I., *Stalingrad* (Moscow: Voenizdat, 1961)

Frisé, Maria, *Meine schlesische Familie und ich: Erinnerungen* (Berlin: Aufbau-Verlag, 2004)

Gaertner, Franz von, *Die Reichswehr in der Weimarer Republik: Erlebte Geschichte* (Darmstadt: Fundus Verlag, 1969)

Gersdorff, Rudolf-Cristoph Freiherr von, *Soldat im Untergang* (Frankfurt am Main: Ullstein, 1977)

Goebbels, Joseph, *The Goebbels Diaries*, (ed.) H. R. Trevor-Roper (Secker & Warburg, 1978)

Greiner, Helmuth, *Die Oberste Wehrmachtführung 1939–1943* (Wiesbaden: Limes Verlag, 1951)

Grossman, Vasily, *A Writer at War: Vasily Grossman with the Red Army 1941–1945*, (ed.) Antony Beevor & (trans.) Luba Vinogradova (London: Harvill Press, 2005)

Guderian, Heinz, *Panzer Leader* (London: Michael Joseph, 1952; Futura, 1974)

Halder, General Franz, *The Halder War Diary 1939–1942*, (eds.) Charles Burdick and Hans-Adolf Jacobsen (London: Greenhill Books, 1988)

Hankey, Lord Maurice Pascal Alers, *Politics, Trials and Errors* (Oxford: Pen-in-Hand, 1950)

Heusinger, Adolf, *Befehl im Widerstreit* (Tübingen and Stuttgart: Rainer Wunderlich Verlag, 1950)

Hindenburg, Marshal Paul von, *Out of My Life* (London: Cassell, 1920)

John, Otto, *Twice Through the Lines: The Autobiography of Otto John* (London: Macmillan, 1972)

Keitel, Wilhelm, *General Feldmarschall: Verbrecher oder Offizier, Erinnerungen, Briefe, Dokumente des Chefs des Oberkommandos der Wehrmacht*, (ed.) Walter Görlitz (Schnellbach: Verlag Siegfried Bublies, 1998)

Kesselring, Albert, *The Memoirs of Field Marshal Kesselring* (London: Greenhill Books, 2007)

Laskin, I. A., *On the Way to the Turning Point* (Moskow: Voenizdat, 1977)

Luck, Hans von, *Panzer Commander: The Memoirs of Colonel Hans von Luck* (New York: Praeger, 1989)

Manstein, Erich von, *Aus einem Soldatenleben 1887–1939* (Bonn: Athenäum-Verlag, 1958)

Manstein, Erich von, *Lost Victories* (London: Collins, 1958)

Manstein, Erich von, *Verlorene Siege* (Bonn: Athenäum Verlag, 1955)

Manstein, Erich von, *Soldat im 20. Jahrhundert*, (eds.) Rüdiger von Manstein and Theodor Fuchs (Bonn: Bernard & Graefe Verlag, 1997)

Mellenthin, F. W. von, *German Generals of World War II As I Saw Them* (Norman: University of Oklahoma Press, 1977)

Mellenthin, F. W. von, *Panzer Battles: A Study of the Employment of Armour in the Second World War* (London: Cassell, 1955)

Mellenthin, F. W. von, *Schach dem Schicksal* (Osnabrück: Biblio Verlag, 1989)

Montgomery of Alamein, Field Marshal The Viscount, *The Memoirs* (London: Collins, 1958).

Patton, George S., *War As I Knew It* (Boston: Houghton Mifflin, 1947)

Pfötsch, Kurt, *Die Hölle von Kursk: SS-Grenadiere 1943 im Kampf* (Selent: Pour le Mérite, 2008)

Röchling, Gottfried, *Die Vertreibung aus der Heimat* (Lembeck, Westfalen: March 1951)

Russell of Liverpool, Lord Edward Frederick Langley, *That Reminds Me* (London: Cassell, 1959)

Senger und Etterlin, General Frido von, *Neither Fear nor Hope* (London: Macdonald, 1963)

Speer, Albert, *Inside the Third Reich* (London: Weidenfeld & Nicolson, 1970; Phoenix, 1995)

Stahlberg, Alexander, *Bounden Duty: The Memoirs of a German Officer 1932–1945* (London: Brassey's, 1990)

Taylor, Telford, *The Anatomy of the Nuremberg Trials: A Personal Memoir* (New York: Knopf, 1992)

Other Published Works

Anon., *Berlin-Karlshorst Museum, Erinnerungen an einen Krieg* (Berlin: Jovis Verlagsbüro, 1997)

Anon., *Commanders and Military Leaders of the Great Patriotic War*, vol. 1 (Moscow: Molodaia Gvardia, 1971) [poss. author is Col. Gen. K. V. Krainiukov]

Anon., *Trial of the Major War Criminals before the International Military Tribunal* (IMT) (Nuremberg: IMT, 1948)

Anon., *Die Wehrmachtsberichte 1939–1945*, vol. I, 1 September 1939–31 December 1941 (Munich: Deutscher Taschenbuch Verlag, 1985)

Anon., *Die Wehrmachtsberichte 1939–1945*, vol. II, 1 January 1942–31 December 1943 (Munich: Deutscher Taschenbuch Verlag, 1985)

Axworthy, Mark, *Third Axis: Fourth Ally* (London: Arms & Armour Press, 1995)

Barnett, Correlli (ed.), *Hitler's Generals* (London: Weidenfeld & Nicolson, 1989)

Bartholomew, General Sir William H. et al, *The Bartholomew Committee Final Report* (London: The War Office, 1940) [republished in *British Army Review*, no. 129, Spring 2002, pp. 87–104]

Bartov, Omer, *Hitler's Army* (New York: Oxford University Press, 1991)

Basov, A. V., *Crimea in the Great Patriotic War 1941–1945* (Moscow: Nayuka, 1987)

Baumann, Hinrich, *Die Heidmark Wandel einer Landschaft: Die Geschichte des Truppenübungsplatzes Bergen* (Walsrode: J. Gronemann, 2005)

Beevor, Antony, *Stalingrad* (London: Viking, 1998)

Bellamy, Christopher, *Absolute War: Soviet Russia in the Second World War* (London: Macmillan, 2007; Pan Books, 2008)

Bentzien, Hans, *Claus Schenk Graf von Stauffenberg: Der Täter und seine Zeit* (Berlin: Das Neue Berlin Verlagsgesellschaft, 2004)

Blakemore, Porter Randall, *Manstein in the Crimea: The Eleventh Army Campaign, 1941–1942* (Ann Arbor, Mich.: University Microfilms International, 1989)

Bloxham, Donald, 'Punishing German Soldiers during the Cold War: The Case of Erich von Manstein', *Patterns of Prejudice*, vol. 33, no. 4 (1999)

Bloxham, Donald, *Genocide on Trial: War Crimes Trials and the Formation of Holocaust History and Memory* (Oxford: University Press, 2001)

Blumentritt, Günther, *Von Rundstedt: The Soldier and the Man* (London: Odhams Press, 1952)

Bower, Tom, *Blind Eye to Murder: Britain, America and the Purging of Nazi Germany – A Pledge Betrayed* (London: André Deutsch, 1981)

Brechten, Magnus, *Die Nationalsozialistische Herrschaft 1933–1939* (Darmstadt: Wissenschaftliche Buchgesellschaft, 2004)

Breithaupt, Hans, *Zwischen Front und Widerstand* (Bonn: Bernard & Graefe Verlag, 1994)

Busse, Theodor, 'Der Winterfeldzug 1942 in Südrussland' in *Nie Ausser Dienst* (Cologne: von der Markus Verlagsgesellschaft, 1967)

Bussel, Richard, *Nazism and War* (London: Weidenfeld & Nicolson, 2004)

Carsten, F. L., *The Reichswehr and Politics 1918–1933* (Oxford: Clarendon Press, 1966)

Carver, Michael, 'Field Marshal Manstein' in *Hitler's Generals*, (ed.) Correlli Barnett (London: Weidenfeld & Nicolson, 1989)

Chor'kov, Anatoliy G., 'Die sowjetische Gegenoffensive bei Stalingrad' in *Stalingrad: Ereignis – Wirkung – Symbol*, (ed.) Jürgen Förster (Munich: Piper, 2002)

Churchill, Winston, *The Second World War*, vol. ii, *Their Finest Hour* (London: Cassell, 1949)

Clarke, Alan, *Barbarossa: The Russian-German Conflict* (London: Cassell, 2005)

Clausewitz, Carl von, *On War*, (ed. & trans.) Michael Howard and Peter Paret (New York: Everyman's Library, 1993)

Condell, Bruce and Zabecki, David T. (eds.), *On the German Art of War: Truppenführung* (London and Boulder, Colo.: Lynne Rienner Publishers, 2001)

Cook, Martin L., 'Revolt of the Generals: A Case Study in Professional Ethics', *Parameters*, vol. XXXVII, no. 1, Spring 2008

Corum, James S., *The Roots of Blitzkrieg: Hans von Seeckt and German Military Reform* (Lawrence: University Press of Kansas, 1992)

Corum, James S., *Wolfram von Richthofen: Master of the German Air War* (Lawrence: University Press of Kansas, 2008)

Craig, Gordon A., *The Politics of the Prussian Army 1640–1945* (Oxford: University Press, 1964)

Creveld, Martin van, *Supplying War: Logistics from Wallenstein to Patton* (Cambridge University Press, 1977)

De Mazière, General Ulrich et al., *Nie Ausser Dienst: [Festschrift] Zum achtzigsten Geburtstag von Generalfeldmarschall Erich von Manstein* (Cologne: von der Markus Verlagsgesellschaft, 1967)

Diedrich, Torsten, *Paulus: Das Trauma von Stalingrad* (Paderborn: Schöningh, 2008)

Dunn, Walter S., *Kursk: Hitler's Gamble, 1943* (Westport, Conn.: Praeger, 1997)

Einbeck, Eberhard, *Das Exempel Sponeck* (Bremen: Carl Schünemenn Verlag, 1970)

Ellis, Major L. F., *The War in France and Flanders 1939–1940* (London: HMSO, 1953)

Ellis, Major L. F., *Victory in the West*, vol. i, *The Battle of Normandy* (London and Nashville: The Imperial War Museum and The Battery Press, 1993)

Engelmann, Joachim, *Die 18. Infanterie- und Panzergrenadier-Division 1934–1945* (Friedberg: Podzun-Pallas-Verlag, 1984)

Engelmann, Joachim, *Manstein: Stratege und Truppenführer* (Friedberg: Podzun-Pallas-Verlag, 1981)

Erickson, John, *The Road to Stalingrad* (London: Weidenfeld & Nicolson, 1975)

Evans, Richard J., *The Coming of the Third Reich* (London: Penguin, 2004)

Ferrell, Robert H., *America's Deadliest Battle: Meuse-Argonne 1918* (Lawrence: University Press of Kansas, 2007)

Forczyk, Robert, *Sevastopol 1942: Von Manstein's Triumph* (Oxford: Osprey, 2008)

Förster, Jürgen (ed.), *Stalingrad: Ereignis – Wirkung – Symbol* (Munich: Piper, 2002)

Fraser, David, *And We Shall Shock Them: The British Army in the Second World War* (London: Hodder & Stoughton, 1983)

Fraser, David, *Frederick the Great* (London: Penguin, 2000)

Fraser, David, *Knight's Cross* (London: HarperCollins, 1993)

French, David, *Raising Churchill's Army: The British Army and the War against Germany 1919–1945* (Oxford: University Press, 2000)

Frieser, Karl-Heinz, 'Die Schlacht im Kursker Bogen' in *Das Deutsche Reich und der Zweite Weltkrieg*, vol. 8, *Die Ostfront 1943/44* (Munich: Deutsche Verlags-Anstalt, 2007)

Frieser, Karl-Heinz, 'Die Rückzugsoperationen der Heeresgruppe Süd' in *Das Deutsche Reich und der Zweite Weltkrieg*, vol. 8, *Die Ostfront 1943/44* (Munich: Deutsche Verlags-Anstalt, 2007)

Frieser, Karl-Heinz, with Greenwood, J. T., *The Blitzkrieg Legend: The 1940 Campaign in the West* (Annapolis: Naval Institute Press, 2005)

Gilbert, Martin, *The Holocaust: The Jewish Tragedy* (London: Collins, 1986)

Glantz, David M. (ed.) and Harold S. Orenstein (trans.), *The Battle for Kursk 1943: The Soviet General Staff Study* (London: Frank Cass, 1999)

Glantz, David M. (ed.) and Harold S. Orenstein (trans.), *The Battle for the Ukraine: The Red Army's Korsun'-Shevchenkovskii Offensive, 1944,* (London: Frank Cass, 2003)

Glantz, David M. and House, Jonathan M., *The Battle of Kursk* (Lawrence: University Press of Kansas, 1999)

Glantz, David M. and House, Jonathan M., *When Titans Clashed: How the Red Army Stopped Hitler* (Lawrence: University Press of Kansas, 1995)

Glantz, David M. and House, Jonathan M., *To the Gates of Stalingrad*, vol. I, *Soviet-German Combat Operations, April–August 1942* (Lawrence: University Press of Kansas, 2009)

Glantz, David M., *Before Stalingrad: Barbarossa: Hitler's Invasion of Russia 1941* (Stroud: Tempus Publishing, 2003)

Glantz, David M., *Forgotten Battles of the German-Soviet War (1941–1945)*, vol. I, *The Summer–Fall Campaign (22 June–4 December 1941)*, (privately published, 1999)

Glantz, David M., *Forgotten Battles of the German-Soviet War (1941–1945)*, vol. II, *The Winter Campaign (5 December 1941–April 1942)*, (privately published, 1999)

Glantz, David M., *From the Don to the Dnepr: Soviet Offensive Operations December 1942–August 1943* (London: Frank Cass, 1991)

Glantz, David M., *Soviet Military Deception in the Second World War* (London: Frank Cass, 1989)

Goldensohn, Leon and Gellately, Robert (eds.), *The Nuremberg Interviews: Conversations with the Defendants and Witnesses* (London: Pimlico, 2004)

Goerlitz, Walter, *History of the German General Staff 1657–1945* (London and New York: Praeger, 1953)

Goerlitz, Walter (ed.), *The Memoirs of Field-Marshal Keitel* (London: William Kimber, 1965)

Hamilton, Nigel, *Monty: The Field Marshal 1944–1976* (London: Hamish Hamilton, 1986)

Hartmann, Christian, *Halder – Generalstabschef Hitters* (Paderborn: Schöningh, 1991)

Haupt, Werner, *Die deutschen Infanterie-Divisionen* (Eggolsheim: Dörfler Verlag, 2005)

Haupt, Werner, *Army Group South: The Wehrmacht in Russia 1941–1945* (Atglen, Pa.: Schiffer Military History, 1998)

Haupt, Werner, *Die Schlachten der Heeresgruppe Süd* (Friedberg: Podzun-Pallas-Verlag, 1985)

Hawthorne, Susan M. et al., *Island Farm: Special Camp 11 for Prisoners of War* (Bridgend: Brynteg Comprehensive School, 1989)

Hayward, Joel S. A., *Stopped at Stalingrad: The Luftwaffe and Hitler's Defeat in the East 1942–1943* (Lawrence: University Press of Kansas, 1998)

Healy, Mark, *Kursk 1943: The Tide Turns in the East* (Oxford: Osprey, 1993)

Healy, Mark, *Zitadelle: The German Offensive against the Kursk Salient 4–7 July 1943* (Stroud: The History Press, 2008)

Heiber, Helmut (ed.), *Hitler and His Generals: Military Conferences 1942–1945* (New York: Enigma Books, 2003)

Herodotus, *The Histories* (trans.) Aubrey de Sélincourt (London: Penguin, 1996)

Hoffmann, Peter, *The History of the German Resistance 1939–1945* (Montreal: McGill-Queen's University Press, 1996)

Horne, Alastair with Montgomery, David, *The Lonely Leader: Monty 1944–1945* (London: Macmillan, 1994)

Horne, Alastair, *To Lose a Battle: France 1940* (London: Macmillan, 1969; Penguin, 1979)

Horne, John and Kramer, Alan, *German Atrocities, 1914: A History of Denial* (New Haven and London: Yale University Press, 2001)

Hürter, Johannes, *Hitlers Heerführer: Die deutschen Oberbefehlshaber im Krieg gegen die Sowjetunion 1941/42* (Munich: R. Oldenbourg Verlag, 2007)

Imhoff, Christoph von, *Die Festung Sewastopol* (Stuttgart: Veria Verlag, 1953)

Jones, Michael K., *Stalingrad: How the Red Army Triumphed* (Barnsley: Pen & Sword, 2007)

Jünger, Ernst, *Storm of Steel* (trans.) Michael Hofmann (London: Allen Lane, 2003)

Karpov, Vladimir V., *The Commander*, (trans.) Yuri S. Shirokov and Nicholas Louis (London: Brassey's, 1987)

Kehrig, Manfred, 'Die 6. Armee im Kessel von Stalingrad' in *Stalingrad: Ereignis – Wirkung – Symbol* (ed.) Jürgen Förster (Munich: Piper, 2002)

Kehrig, Manfred, *Stalingrad: Analyse und Dokumentation einer Schlacht* (Munich: Deutsche Verlags-Anstalt, 1974)

Kerr, Walter, *The Secret of Stalingrad* (London: Macdonald & Jane's, 1978)

Kershaw, Ian, *Hitler: 1889–1936 Hubris* (London: Allen Lane, 1998)

Kershaw, Ian, *Hitler: 1936–1945 Nemesis* (London: Penguin, 2001)

Kinkead-Weekes, Mark, *D. H. Lawrence: Triumph to Exile, 1912–1922* (Cambridge: University Press, 1996)

Kitchen, Martin, *A Military History of Germany from the Eighteenth Century to the Present Day* (London: Weidenfeld & Nicolson, 1975)

Klein, Friedhelm and Frieser, Karl-Heinz, 'Mansteins Gegenschlag am Doneč; Operative Analyse des Gegenangriffs der Heeresgruppe Sud im Februar/März 1943', *Militärgeschichte*, 9 (1999)

Knopp, Guido (ed.), *Hitler's Warriors* (Stroud: Sutton, 2005), first published in 1998 by Bertelsmann, Munich, under the title *Hitlers Krieger*

Knopp, Guido, *Stalingrad: Das Drama* (Munich: Bertelsmann, 2002)

Kohn, Hans, *The Mind of Germany* (London: Macmillan, 1965)

Könen, Hauptmann Erich H., 'The Operational Ideas of Manstein with Respect to the Use of Space, Gaining the Initiative, Creating Freedom of Action and the Choice between Offensive and Defensive Operations' (Hamburg: German Armed Forces Command and Staff College, Dissertation, 30 November 1987)

Kurowski, Franz and Tornau, Gottfried, *Sturmgeschütze – Die Panzer der Infanterie* (Würzburg: Flechsig Verlag, 2008)

Kurowski, Franz, *General der Kavallerie Siegfried Westphal* (Würzburg: Flechsig Verlag, 2007)

Kurowski, Franz, *Sevastopol: Der Angriff auf die stärkste Festung der Welt* (Wölfersheim-Berstadt: Podzun-Pallas-Verlag, 2002)

Lauterpacht, H. (ed.), *Annual Digest and Reports of Public International Law Cases Year 1949* (London: Butterworth, 1955)

Lee, John, *The Warlords: Hindenburg and Ludendorff* (London: Weidenfeld & Nicolson, 2005)

Leverkuehn, Dr Paul, *Verteidigung Manstein* (Hamburg: H. H. Nölke Verlag, 1950)

Liddell Hart, B. H., *The Other Side of the Hill* (London: Papermac, 1993) [orig. pub. London: Cassell, 1948]

Macksey, Kenneth, *Guderian: Panzer General* (London: Greenhill and Mechanicsburg, Pa: Stackpole Books, 2003)

Magenheimer, Heinz, *Hitler's War: Germany's Key Strategic Decisions 1940–1945* (London: Cassell, 1999)

Magenheimer, Heinz, *Stalingrad* (Selent: Pour le Mérite – Verlag für Militärgeschichte, 2007)

Mann, Golo, *Deutsche Geschichte des 19. und 20. Jahrhunderts* (Frankfurt am Main: S. Fischer Verlag, 1992)

Mawdsley, Evan, *Thunder in the East: The Nazi-Soviet War 1941–1945* (London: Hodder Arnold, 2005)

Medlicott, W. N., *Bismarck and Modern Germany* (London: English Universities Press, 1965)

Megargee, Geoffrey P., *Inside Hitler's High Command* (Lawrence: University Press of Kansas, 2000)

Megargee, Geoffrey P., *War of Annihilation: Combat and Genocide on the Eastern Front, 1941* (Lanham, Md: Rowman & Littlefield, 2006)

Melvin, Brigadier R. A. M. S., 'Contemporary Battlefield Tours and Staff Rides: A Military Practitioner's View', *Defence Studies*, vol. 5, no.1 (March 2005)

Melvin, Mungo, 'The German View' in *The Battle for France and Flanders Sixty Years On*, (eds.) Brian Bond and Michael Taylor (Barnsley: Leo Cooper, 2001)

Melvin, Mungo, 'The German Perspective' in *The Normandy Campaign 1944 – Sixty Years On*, (ed.) John Buckley (London: Routledge, 2006)

Merridale, Catherine, *Ivan's War: The Red Army 1939–1945* (London: Faber and Faber, 2006)

Messenger, Charles, *The Last Prussian: A Biography of Field Marshal Gerd von Rundstedt 1875–1953* (London: Brassey's, 1991)

Metzsch, Friedrich-August von, *Die Geschichte der 22. Infanterie-Division 1939–1945* (Kiel: Verlag Hans-Henning Podzul, 1952)

Michels, Eckard, *Der Held von Deutsch-Ostafrika: Paul von Lettow-Vorbeck* (Paderborn: Schöningh, 2008)

Mitcham, Samuel W., *Hitler's Field Marshals and Their Battles* (Guild Publishing, 1988)

Montefiore, Simon Sebag, *Stalin: The Court of the Red Tsar* (London: Weidenfeld & Nicolson, 2003)

Montefiore, Hugh Sebag, *Dunkirk: Fight to the Last Man* (London: Viking, 2006)

Müller, Klaus-Jürgen, *Generaloberst Ludwig Beck: eine Biographie* (Paderborn: Schöningh, 2009)

Müller, Klaus-Jürgen, *Armee und Drittes Reich 1933–1939: Darstellung und Dokumentation* (Paderborn: Schöningh, 1987)

Müller, Klaus-Jürgen, *Das Heer und Hitler: Armee und nationalsozialistisches Regime 1933–1940* (Stuttgart: Deutsche Verlags-Anstalt, 1969) [2nd ed., 1988]

Müller, Klaus-Jürgen, (ed.), *General Ludwig Beck, Studien und Dokumente zur politisch-militärischen Vorstellungswelt und Tätigkeit des Generalstabschefs des deutschen Heeres 1933–1938* (Boppard am Rhein: Harald Boldt Verlag, 1980)

Müller, Rolf-Dieter and Volkmann, Hans-Erich (eds.), *Die Wehrmacht: Mythos und Realität* (Munich: R. Oldenbourg Verlag, 1999)

Murray, Williamson and Millett, Allan R., *A War to be Won: Fighting the Second World War* (Cambridge, Mass. and London: Belknap Press of Harvard University Press, 2000)

Neugebauer, Karl-Volker, 'Die Wehrmacht im nationalsozialistischen Regime' in *Grundzüge der deutschen Militärgeschichte*, vol. 1., *Historische Überblick* (Freiburg: Rombach Verlag, 1993)

Neugebauer, Karl-Volker, *Grundzüge der deutschen Militärgeschichte*, vol. 2., *Arbeits- und Quellenbuch* (Freiburg: Rombach Verlag, 1993)

Newton, Steven H., *Hitler's Commander: Field Marshal Walther Model – Hitler's Favorite General* (Cambridge, Mass.: De Capo Press, 2005)

Newton, Steven H., *Kursk: The German View* (New York: Da Capo, 2002)

Ose, Dieter (ed.), *Wehrgeschichtliches Symposium Proceedings* (Bonn: March 1987)

Overy, Richard, *Russia's War* (London: Penguin, 1999)

Overy, Richard, *The Dictators* (London and New York: W. W. Norton, 2004)

Paget, R. T., *Manstein: His Campaigns and His Trial* (London: Collins, 1951)

Pohl, Dieter, *Die Herrschaft der Wehrmacht; Deutsche Militärbesatzung und einheimische Bevölkerung in der Sowjetunion 1941–1944* (Munich: R. Oldenbourg Verlag, 2008)

Porch, Douglas, *Hitler's Mediterranean Gamble: The North African and Mediterranean Campaigns in World War II* (London: Weidenfeld & Nicolson, 2004)

Raus, Erhard, *Panzer Operations: The Eastern Front Memoir of General Raus, 1941–1945*, (ed. and trans.) Steven H. Newton (Cambridge, Mass.: De Capo Press, 2003)

Read, Anthony, *The Devil's Disciples* (London: Pimlico, 2004)

Reid, Brian Holden, *Robert E. Lee* (London: Weidenfeld & Nicolson, 2005)

Reuth, Ralf Georg, *Hitler: Eine politische Biographie* (Munich: Piper Verlag, 2003)

Rich, Norman, *Hitler's War Aims: The Establishment of the New Order* (London: André Deutsch, 1974)

Roberts, Adam and Guelff, Richard (eds.), *Documents on the Laws of War*, 3rd edn. (Oxford: University Press, 2000)

Roberts, Geoffrey, *Victory at Stalingrad: The Battle That Changed History* (Harlow: Pearson Educational, 2002)

Rohde, Horst, *Das Deutsche Reich und der Zweite Weltkrieg*, vol. 2, *Die Errichtung der Hegemonie auf dem Europäische Kontinent* (Stuttgart: Deutsche Verlags-Anstalt, 1979)

Rohden, Hans-Detlef Herhudt von, *Die Luftwaffe ringt um Stalingrad* (Wiesbaden: Limes Verlag, 1950)

Röhl, John C. G., *The Kaiser and His Court: Wilhelm II and the Government of Germany* (Cambridge: University Press, 1994)

Römer, Felix, *Der Kommissarbefehl: Wehrmacht und NS-Verbrechen an der Ostfront 1941/42* (Paderborn: Schöningh, 2008)

Rother, Rainer, *Leni Riefenstahl: The Seduction of Genius* (London and New York: Continuum, 2002)

Rotundo, Louis C. (ed.), *Battle for Stalingrad: The 1943 Soviet General Staff Study* (Pergamon-Brassey's 1989)

Sadarananda, Dana V., *Beyond Stalingrad: Manstein and the Operations of Army Group Don* (Westport, Conn.: Greenhill Books, 1990)

Scheibert, Horst, ... *bis Stalingrad 48km: Der Entsatzversuch 1942* (Eggolsheim: Dörfler Verlag, 2003)

Schellendorf, General Bronsart von, *The Duties of the General Staff*, [trans. for the General Staff, War Office] (London: His Majesty's Stationery Office, 1905)

Schenk, Peter, *Invasion of England 1940* (London: Conway Maritime Press, 1990)

Scheurig, Bodo, *Alfred Jodl: Gehorsam und Verhängnis* (Schnellbach: Verlag Siegfried Bublies, 1999)

Scheurig, Bodo, *Henning von Tresckow – Ein Preuße gegen Hitler* (Berlin: Propyläen Verlag, 1987)

Searle, Alaric, 'A Very Special Relationship: Basil Liddell Hart, Wehrmacht Generals and the Debate on West German Rearmament 1945–1953', *War in History*, 1998, 5, (3)

Searle, Alaric, *Wehrmacht Generals, West German Society, and the Debate on Rearmament 1949–1959* (Greenwood, Conn.: Praeger, 2003)

Sheffield, Gary, *Forgotten Victory* (London: Headline, 2001)

Shirer, William L., *The Rise and Fall of the Third Reich* (London: Secker & Warburg, 1960)

Shukman, Harold (ed.), *Stalin's Generals* (London: Weidenfeld & Nicolson, 1993)

Smelser, Ronald M. and Davies, Edward J., *The Myth of the Eastern Front* (Cambridge: University Press, 2007)

Sokolov, Sergei, *Battles Hitler Lost and the Soviet Marshals Who Won Them* (New York: Jove Books, 1988)

Stein, Marcel, *Feldmarschall von Manstein: Der Januskopf – eine Neubewertung* (Bissendorf: Biblio Verlag, 2004); english edn. *Field Marshal von Manstein – The Janus Head: A Portrait* (Solihull: Helion, 2007)

Strachan, Hew, *The First World War*, vol. i, *To Arms* (Oxford: University Press, 2001)

Strohn, Matthias 'Hans von Seeckt and His Vision of a 'Modern Army', *War in History*, 2005, 12 (3)

Sullivan, Matthew Barry, *Thresholds of Peace: Four Hundred Thousand German Prisoners and the People of Britain 1944–1948* (London: Hamish Hamilton, 1979)

Sweeting, C. G., *Blood and Iron: The German Conquest of Sevastopol* (Washington DC: Potomac Books, 2004)

Taylor, Telford, *The Breaking Wave: The German Defeat in the Summer of 1940* (London: Weidenfeld & Nicolson, 1967)

Thies, Klaus-Jürgen, *Der Zweite Weltkrieg im Kartenbild*, vol. 3, *Der Westfeldzug 10. Mai bis 25. Juni 1940* (Osnabrück: Biblio Verlag, 1994)

Thyen, O., Clark, M., Scholze-Stubenrecht, Werner and Sykes, J. B. (eds.), *Oxford-Duden German Dictionary* (Oxford: University Press, 2005)

Tolland, John, *Adolf Hitler* (Toronto: Ballentine, 1977)

Treue, Wilhelm, 'Hitlers Denkschrift zum Vierjahrsplan 1936', *Vierteljahrshefte für Zeitgeschichte*, vol. 3 (1955)

Trevor-Roper, H. R. (ed.), *Hitler's War Directives 1939–1945* (London: Sidgwick & Jackson, 1964)

Tuchman, Barbara, *August 1914* (London: Constable, 1962)

Ueberschär, Gerd R. and Vogel, Winfried, *Dienen und Verdienen: Hitlers Geschenke an seine Eliten* (Frankfurt am Main: S. Fischer Verlag, 1999)

Wade, Ashton, *A Life on the Line* (Tunbridge Wells: D. J. Costello, 1988)

Wallach, Jehuda L., *The Dogma of the Battle of Annihilation* (Westport, Conn. and London: Greenwood Press, 1986)

Wavell, General Sir Archibald, *Generals and Generalship* (London: *The Times*, 1941)

Wegner, Bernd, 'Die Kämpfe auf der Krim' in *Das deutsche Reich im Zweiten Weltkrieg*, vol. 4, *Der Globale Krieg: Die Ausweitung zum Weltkrieg und der Wechsel der Initiative 1941–1943* (Stuttgart: Deutsche Verlags-Anstalt, 1990)

Wegner, Bernd, 'Von Stalingrad nach Kursk' in *Das Deutsche Reich und der Zweite Weltkrieg*, vol. 8, *Die Ostfront 1943/44* (Munich: Deutsche Verlags-Anstalt, 2007)

Wenck, Walther, 'Nie Ausser Dienst' in *Nie Ausser Dienst* (Cologne: Markus Verlagsgesellschaft, 1967)

Westphal, Siegfried, *Der Deutsche Generalstab auf der Anklagebank Nürnberg 1945–1948* (Mainz: v. Hase & Koehler Verlag, 1978)

Westphal, Siegfried, *Erinnerungen* (Mainz: v. Hase & Koehler Verlag, 1975)

Westphal, Siegfried, *The German Army in the West* (London: Cassell, 1951)

Wette, Wolfram and Ueberschär, Gerd R. (eds.), *Der deutsche Überfall auf die Sowjetunion und 'Unternehmen Barbarossa' 1941* (Munich: Fischer-Taschenbuch-Verlag, 1991)

Wette, Wolfram, *The Wehrmacht, History, Myth, Reality* (Cambridge, Mass.: Harvard University Press, 2007)

Wheatley, Ronald, *Operation Sea Lion: German Plans for the Invasion of England 1939–1942* (Oxford: Clarendon Press, 1958)

Wheeler-Bennett, J. W., *Hindenburg: The Wooden Titan* (London: Macmillan, 1936)

Wheeler-Bennett, J.W., *Brest-Litovsk: the Forgotten Peace, March 1918* (London: W. W. Norton, 1969)

Wheeler-Bennett, J.W., *The Nemesis of Power: The German Army in Politics 1918–1945* (2nd ed.) (London: Palgrave Macmillan, 2005)

Wieder, Joachim and Einsiedel, Heinrich Graf von, *Stalingrad: Memories and Reassessments* (London: Cassell, 2002)

Wieder, Joachim, *Stalingrad und die Verantwortung des Soldaten* (Munich: Nymphenburger Verlagshandlung, 1962)

Wrochem, Oliver von, *Erich von Manstein: Vernichtungskrieg und Geschichtspolitik* (Paderborn: Schöningh, 2006)

Zabecki, David T., *The German 1918 Offensives* (London and New York: Routledge, 2006)

Zabecki, David T. (ed.), *Chief of Staff: The Principal Officers Behind History's Great Commanders*, vol. 1, *Napoleonic Wars to World War I* (Annapolis, RI: US Naval Institute, 2008)

Zetterling, Niklas and Frankson, Anders, *Kursk 1943: A Statistical Analysis* (London: Frank Cass, 2000)

Zetterling, Niklas and Frankson, Anders, *The Korsun Pocket: The Encirclement and Breakout of a German Army in the East, 1944* (Philadelphia and Newbury: Casemate, 2008)

Zhukov, Marshal, *The Memoirs of Marshal Zhukov* (London: Jonathan Cape, 1971) [Orig. pub. as *Reminiscences and Ruminations* (Moscow: Novosty Press, 1969)]

Zimmermann, John, *Pflicht zum Untergang: Die deutsche Kriegführung im Westen des Reiches 1944/45* (Paderborn: Schöningh, 2009)

Index

The index is arranged in a word-by-word order. Military ranks shown are the last held by the individual. Sub-headings for Adolf Hitler and Erich von Manstein appear in alphabetical order.

Carrie
Soto
is
Back

Carrie Soto is Back

Taylor Jenkins Reid

HUTCHINSON
HEINEMANN

1 3 5 7 9 10 8 6 4 2

Hutchinson Heinemann
20 Vauxhall Bridge Road
London SW1V 2SA

Hutchinson Heinemann is part of the Penguin Random House group of companies whose addresses can be found at global.penguinrandomhouse.com

Penguin
Random House
UK

First published in the USA by Ballantine Books in 2022
First published in the UK by Hutchinson Heinemann in 2022

www.penguin.co.uk

A CIP catalogue record for this book is available from the British Library.

ISBN: 9781529152128 (hardback)
ISBN: 9781529152135 (trade paperback)

Book design by Susan Turner

Printed and bound in Great Britain by Clays Ltd, Elcograf S.p.A.

The authorised representative in the EEA is Penguin Random House Ireland,
Morrison Chambers, 32 Nassau Street, Dublin D02 YH68

Penguin Random House is committed to a sustainable future
for our business, our readers and our planet. This book is made from
Forest Stewardship Council® certified paper.

To Brad Mendelsohn, the closest thing I've ever had to a coach

Carrie Soto is Back

CHAN VS. CORTEZ

US Open

September 1994

MY ENTIRE LIFE'S WORK RESTS ON THE OUTCOME OF THIS MATCH.

My father, Javier, and I sit front row center at Flushing Meadows, the sidelines just out of reach. The linesmen stand with their arms behind their backs on either side of the court. Straight in front of us, the umpire presides over the crowd high in his chair. The ball girls crouch low, ready to sprint at a moment's notice.

This is the third set. Nicki Chan took the first, and Ingrid Cortez squeaked out the second. This last one will determine the winner.

My father and I watch—along with the twenty thousand others in the stadium—as Nicki Chan approaches the baseline. She bends her knees and steadies herself. Then she rises onto her toes, tosses the ball in the air, and with a snap of her wrist sends a blistering serve at 126 miles per hour toward Ingrid Cortez's backhand.

Cortez returns it with startling power. It falls just inside the line. Nicki isn't able to get to it. Point Cortez.

I let my eyes close and exhale.

"*Cuidado.* The cameras are watching our reactions," my father says through gritted teeth. He's wearing one of his many panama hats, his curly silver hair creeping out the back.

"Dad, *everyone's* watching our reactions."

Nicki Chan has won two Slam titles this year already—the Australian Open and the French Open. If she wins this match, she'll tie my lifetime record of twenty Grand Slam singles titles. I set that record back in 1987, when I won Wimbledon for the ninth time and established myself as the greatest tennis player of all time.

Nicki's particular style of play—brash and loud, played almost exclusively from the baseline, with incredible violence to her serves and groundstrokes—has enabled her to dominate women's tennis over the past five years. But when she was starting out on the WTA tour back in the late eighties, I found her to be an unremarkable opponent. Good on clay, perhaps, but I could beat her handily on her home turf of London.

Things changed after I retired in 1989. Nicki began racking up Slams at an alarming rate. Now she's at my heels.

My jaw tenses as I watch her.

My father looks at me, his face placid. "I'm saying that the photographers are trying to get a shot of you looking angry, or rooting against her."

I am wearing a black sleeveless shirt and jeans. A pair of tortoise-shell Oliver Peoples sunglasses. My hair is down. At almost thirty-seven, I look as good as I've ever looked, in my opinion. So let them take as many pictures as they want.

"What did I always tell you in junior championships?"

"Don't let it show on your face."

"*Exacto, hija.*"

Ingrid Cortez is a seventeen-year-old Spanish player who has surprised almost everyone with her quick ascent up the rankings. Her style is a bit like Nicki's—powerful, loud—but she plays her angles more. She's surprisingly emotional on the court. She hits a scorcher of an ace past Nicki and hollers with glee.

"You know, maybe it's Cortez who's going to stop her," I say.

My father shakes his head. *"Lo dudo."* He barely moves his lips when he talks, his eye consciously avoiding the camera. I have no doubt that tomorrow morning, my father will open the paper and scan the sports pages looking for his photo. He will smile to himself when he sees that he looks nothing short of handsome. Although he lost weight earlier this year from the rounds of chemo he endured, he is cancer-free now. His body has bounced back. His color looks good.

As the sun beats down on his face, I hand him a tube of sunscreen. He squints and shakes his head, as if it is an insult to us both.

"Cortez got one good one in," my father says. "But Nicki saves her power for the third set."

My pulse quickens. Nicki hits three winners in a row, takes the game. It's now 3–3 in the third set.

My father looks at me, lowering his glasses so I can see his eyes. *"Entonces,* what are you going to do?" he asks.

I look away. "I don't know."

He puts his glasses back on and looks at the court, giving me a small nod. "Well, if you do nothing, that is what you are doing. Nothing."

"Sí, papá, I got it."

Nicki serves wide. Cortez runs and scrambles to catch it on the rise, but it flies into the net.

I look at my father. He wears a slight frown.

In the players' box, Cortez's coach is hunched over in his seat, his hands cupping his face.

Nicki doesn't have a coach. She left her last one almost three years ago and has taken six Slams since then without anyone's guidance.

My dad makes a lot of cracks about players who don't have coaches. But with Nicki, he seems to withhold judgment.

Cortez is bent over, holding her hand down on her hips and try-ing to catch her breath. Nicki doesn't let up. She fires off another serve across the court. Cortez takes off running but misses it.

Nicki smiles.

I know that smile. I've been here before.

On the next point, Nicki takes the game.

"Dammit," I say at the changeover.

My father raises his eyebrows. "Cortez crumbles as soon as she doesn't control the court. And Nicki knows it."

"Nicki's powerful," I say. "But she's also hugely adaptable. When you play her, you're playing somebody who is adjusting on the fly, tailoring their game to your specific weakness."

My father nods.

"Every player has a weak spot," I say. "And Nicki is great at find-ing it."

"Right."

"So what's hers?"

My father is now holding back a smile. He lifts his drink and takes a sip.

"What?" I ask.

"Nothing," my father says.

"I haven't made a decision."

"All right."

Both players head back out onto the court.

"Nicki is just a tiny bit slow," I say, watching her walk to the base-line. "She has a lot of power, but she's not fast—not in her footwork or her shot selection. She's not quite as quick as Cortez, even today. But especially not as quick as Moretti, Antonovich, even Perez."

"Or you," my father says. "There's nobody on the tour right now who is as fast as you were. Not just with your feet, but with your head, *también*."

I nod.

He continues. "I'm talking about getting into position, taking the ball out of the air early, taking the pace off so Nicki can't hit it back with that power. Nobody on the tour is doing that. Not like you did."

"I'd have to meet her power, though," I tell him. "And somehow still maintain speed."

"Which will not be easy."

"Not at my age and not with my knee," I say. "I don't have the jumps I used to have."

"*Es verdad*," my father says. "It will take everything you have to give."

"*If* I did it," I say.

My father rolls his eyes but then swiftly paints another false smile on his face.

I laugh. "Honestly, who cares if they get a picture of you frowning?"

"I'm staying off your back," my father says. "You stay off mine. *¿Lo entendés, hija?*"

I laugh again. "*Sí, lo entiendo, papá.*"

Nicki takes the next game too. One more and it's over. She'll tie my record.

My temples begin to pound as I envision it all unfolding. Cortez is not going to stave off Nicki Chan, not today. And I'm stuck up here in the seats. I have to sit here and watch Nicki take away everything I've worked for.

"Who's going to coach me?" I say. "You?"

My father does not look at me, but I can see his shoulders stiffen. He takes a breath, chooses his words.

"That's for you to answer," he finally says. "It's not my choice to make."

"So, what? I'm gonna call up Lars?"

"You are going to do whatever you want to do, *pichona*," my father says. "That is how adulthood works."

He is going to make me beg. And I deserve it.

Cortez is busting her ass to make the shots. But she's tired. You can see it in the way her legs shake when she's standing still. She nets a return. It's now 30–love.

Motherfucker.

I look around at the crowd. People are leaning forward; some are tapping their fingers. Every one of them seems to be breathing a little faster. I can only imagine what the sportscasters are saying.

The spectators sitting around us are looking at my father and me out of the corner of their eyes, watching my reaction. I'm starting to feel caged.

"If I do it . . ." I say softly. "I want you to coach me. That's what I'm saying, Dad."

He looks at me as Cortez scores a point off Nicki. The crowd holds their breath, eager to see history being made. I might be too if it weren't *my* history on the line.

"Are you sure, *hija*? I am not the man I once was. I don't have the . . . stamina I once did."

"That makes two of us," I say. "You'll be coaching a has-been."

Now it's 40–15. Nicki is at championship point.

"I'd be coaching the greatest tennis player of all time," my father says. He turns to me and grabs my hand. I am staring down forty, but still, somehow, his hands dwarf mine. And just like when I was a child, they are warm and rough and strong. When he squeezes my palm, I feel so small—as if I am forever a child and he is this giant I will have to gaze up at to meet his eye.

Nicki serves the ball. I inhale sharply.

"So you'll do it?" I ask.

Cortez sends it back.

"We might lose . . . badly," I say. "Prove to everyone the Battle Axe can't hack it now. They'd love that. I'd tarnish not only my record but my legacy. It might . . . ruin everything."

Nicki hits a groundstroke.

My father shakes his head. "We cannot ruin everything. Because tennis is not everything, *pichona*."

I am not sure I agree.

Cortez returns the shot.

"Still," I say. "We'd have to work harder together than we ever have. Are you up for that?"

"It would be the honor of my lifetime," my father says. I can tell there are tears forming in his eyes, and I stop myself from looking away. He holds my hand tighter. "To coach you again, *pichona*, I'd die happy."

I try to move past the tender ache taking hold in my chest. "So I guess that decides it, then," I say.

A smile takes over my father's face.

Nicki lobs the ball. It arcs through the air, slowly. The stadium watches as it flies high, then starts its descent.

"I guess I'm coming out of retirement," I say.

The ball looks like it is going to be out. If so, Cortez will delay defeat for the moment.

My father puts his arm around me, hugging me tight. I can barely breathe. He whispers in my ear, "*Nunca estuve más orgulloso, cielo.*" He lets go.

The ball falls, landing just inside the baseline. The crowd is silent as it bounces, high and fast. Cortez has already backed off, thinking it would be long, and it is too late now. It's impossible to return. She lunges forward and misses.

There is no sound for a split second, and then the roar erupts.

Nicki Chan just won the US Open.

Cortez falls to the ground. Nicki throws her fists into the air.

My father and I smile. Ready.

THE
FIRST TIME
AROUND

1955–1965

MY FATHER MOVED TO THE UNITED STATES FROM BUENOS AIRES AT AGE twenty-seven. He had been an excellent tennis player back in Argentina, winning thirteen championships over his eleven-year career. They called him "Javier el Jaguar." He was graceful but deadly.

But, as he would tell it, he went too hard on his knees. His jumps were too high, and he didn't always land properly. As he approached thirty, he knew that they wouldn't hold up for much longer. He retired in 1953—something he never talked to me about without tensing up and eventually leaving the room. Soon after that, he started making plans to come to the United States.

In Miami, he got a job at a fancy tennis club as a hitter, available all day to play with any member who wanted a game. It was a job normally reserved for college students home for the summer—but he did it with the same focus with which he competed. As he told many of the members at that first club, "I do not know how to play tennis without my full heart."

It wasn't long until people started asking him for private lessons. He was known for his commitment to proper form, his high expectations, and the fact that if you listened to *el Jaguar,* you'd probably start winning your matches.

By 1956, he had offers to work as a tennis instructor all over the country. That's how he landed at the Palm Tennis Club in Los Angeles, where he met my mother, Alicia. She was a dancer, teaching the waltz and foxtrot to club members.

My mother was tall and stood taller, wearing four-inch heels wherever she went. She walked slowly, purposefully, and always looked people in the eye. And it was hard to make her laugh, but when she finally did, it was so loud you could hear it through the walls.

On their first date, she told my father that she thought he had tunnel vision when it came to tennis. "It is something you have to grow out of soon, Javier. Or else, how will you learn to be whole?"

My father told her she was out of her mind. Tennis was what *made* him whole.

She responded by saying, "Ah, so you're stubborn too."

Still, he showed up the next day at the end of one of her classes with a dozen red roses. She took them and said thank you, but he noticed she didn't smell them before she set them down. My father got the sense that while he had given flowers to only a few women in his life, my mother had received flowers from dozens of hopeful men.

"Will you teach me the tango?" he said.

She looked at him sideways, not buying for one minute that this Argentine didn't have at least a passing knowledge of the tango. But then she put one hand on his shoulder and another in the air, and said, "Come on, then." He took her hand, and she taught him how to lead her across the dance floor.

My father says he couldn't take his eyes off her; he says he marveled at how easy it was to glide with her across the room.

When they got to the end, my father dipped her and she smiled at him and then said, rather impatiently, "Javier, this is when you kiss me."

Within a few months, he'd convinced her to elope. He told her that he had big dreams for them. And my mother told him his dreams were his own. She didn't need much at all besides him.

The night my mother told him she was pregnant, she sat in his lap in their Santa Monica apartment and asked if he could feel that he held the weight of two people. He teared up as he smiled at her. And then he told her he could feel in his gut that I was a boy, and that I was going to be twice the tennis player he'd ever been.

When I was a baby, my father would bring a high chair to the courts so I could watch him play. He says I would dart my head back and forth, tracking the ball. According to him, my mother would sometimes come and try to take me out of the high chair to sit in the shade or have a snack, but I'd cry until she brought me back to the court.

My father loved to tell the story of the time when I was just barely a toddler and he first put a racket in my hand. He softly tossed the ball to me, and he swears that on that fateful day, I swung and made contact.

He ran back to the house, carrying me on his shoulders, to tell my mother. She smiled at him and continued making dinner.

"Do you understand what I'm telling you?" he said.

My mother laughed. "That our daughter likes tennis? Of course she likes tennis—it's the only thing you've shown her."

"That's like saying Achilles was a great warrior simply because he lived during wartime. Achilles was a great warrior because it was his *destiny* to be one."

"I see. So Carolina is Achilles?" my mother asked, smiling. "And what does that make you, a god?"

My father waved her away. "She's destined," he said. "It is plain as day. With your grace and my strength, she can be the greatest tennis player the world has ever seen. They will tell stories about her one day."

My mother rolled her eyes at him as she began to put dinner on the table. "I would rather she was kind and happy."

"Alicia," my father said as he stood behind my mother and wrapped his arms around her. "No one ever tells stories about that."

I do not remember being told my mother had died. Nor do I remember her funeral, though my father says I was there. As he tells it, my mother was making soup and realized we were out of tomato paste, so she put her shoes on and left me with him in the garage while he was changing the oil in the car.

When she didn't come home, he knocked on our neighbors' door and asked them to watch me while he searched through the streets.

He saw the ambulance a few blocks away and his stomach sank. My mother had been hit by a car when she was crossing the street on her way home.

After my mother's body was buried, my father refused to go into their bedroom. He started sleeping in the living room; he kept his clothes in a hamper by the TV. It went on for months. Whenever I had a bad dream, I'd leave my own bed and walk right to the couch. He was always there, with the TV on, static hissing as he slept.

And then, one day, light flooded into the hallway. Their bedroom door was open, the dust that had long accumulated was off the handle, and everything of my mother's was packed into cardboard boxes. Her dresses, her high heels, her necklaces, her rings. Even her bobby pins. Somebody came to the house and took them all out. And that was it.

There wasn't much left of her. Barely any proof she'd ever lived. Just a few pictures I'd found in my father's top drawer. I took my favorite one and stashed it under my pillow. I was afraid that if I didn't, it would soon be gone too.

For a while after that, my dad would tell me stories about my mother. He'd talk about how she wanted me to be *happy*. That she was *good* and *fair*. But he cried when he told them, and pretty soon, he stopped telling them altogether.

To this day, the only significant memory I have of my mother is hazy. I can't tell what is real and what are the gaps that I've filled in over time.

In my head, I can see her standing in the kitchen over the stove. She is in a maroon dress with a pattern on it, something like polka dots or tiny flowers. I know that her hair is curly and full. My father calls from across the house to me, using the name he had for me then, *"Guerrerita."* But then my mother shakes her head and says, "Don't let him call you a warrior—you are a queen."

Most of the time, I'm absolutely positive that all of this actually happened. But sometimes, it feels so obvious that the entire thing must have been a dream.

What I actually remember most about her is the emptiness she left behind. There was this sense, within the house, that there used to be someone else here.

But now it was just my father and me.

In my first concrete memories, I am young but already annoyed. I am annoyed at all of the other girls' questions: "Where is your mom?" "Why isn't your hair ever brushed?" Annoyed at the teacher's insistence that I speak English without any traces of my father's accent. Annoyed at being told to play nicer during recess, when all I wanted to do was race the other kids across the field or see who could swing highest on the swing set.

I suspected the problem was that I was always the winner. But I could not for the life of me understand why that made people want to play with me *less* instead of more.

Those early memories of trying to make friends are all accompanied by the same twinge of confusion: *I'm doing something wrong, and I don't know what it is.*

When school let out, I used to watch all the other students greet their mothers at pickup. My classmates told their moms about their days, bristled at the squeezes their moms gave them by the car, wiped their mothers' kisses off their cheeks.

I could have watched them for hours. What else did they do with their moms after school? Did they go out for ice cream? Did they go shopping together for those pretty pencil cases some of them had? Where were they all getting those hair bows?

As they drove away, I would dutifully begin my walk two blocks over, to meet my father on the public tennis courts.

I grew up on the court. The public courts after school, the country club courts during the summers and on weekends. I grew up in tennis skirts and ponytails. I grew up sitting in the shade by the sidelines, waiting while my father finished a lesson.

He loomed over the net. His serves were always fluid, his groundstrokes smooth. His opponent, or whomever he was teaching, always looked so chaotic in comparison. My father was unfailingly in control of the court.

In hindsight, I can see that he must have been tense and lonely most days of my young life. He was a widowed single father in a country that was not his home, with no one else to rely on. It seems obvious to me now that my dad was likely stretched so tight he could nearly have snapped.

But if his days were hard, his nights restless, he grew very good at hiding it from me. The time I got to spend with him felt like a gift that other kids didn't get. Unlike them, my time had *purpose;* my father and I were working toward something of *meaning. I* was going to be the best.

Every day after school, when my father was finally done with his paid lessons, he would turn and look at me. "*Vamos,*" he would say. "*Los fundamentos.*" At which point, I would pick up my racket and join him at the baseline.

"Game, set, match: Why do we say this?" my father would ask me.

"Because each time you play, it is a game. You must win the most games to win the set. And then you must win the most sets to win the match," I'd recite.

"In a game, the first point is . . ."

"Fifteen. Then 30. Then 40. Then you win. But you have to win by two."

"When the score is 40–all, what do we call that?"

"Deuce. And if you're at deuce and win a point, that brings you to either advantage-in or advantage-out, depending on whether you're serving or not."

"So how do you win?"

"If you are serving at ad-in, you have to win the next point to win the game. You have to win six games to win the set, but, again, you have to win by two. You can't just win a set 6–5."

"And a match?"

"Women play three sets, men often play five."

"And love? What does it mean?"

"It means nothing."

"Well, it means zero."

"Right, you have no points. Love means nothing."

Having gotten all the answers right, I would get a pat on the shoulder. And then we would practice.

There are many coaches out there who innovate, but that was never my father's style. He believed in the beauty and simplicity of doing something the way it has always been done but better than anyone else has ever done it. "If I had been as committed to proper form as you will be, *hijita*," he would say, "I would still be playing professional tennis." That was one of the only times he told me something that I suspected wasn't true. I knew even then that not many people ever played tennis professionally past age thirty.

"*Bueno, papá,*" I would say as we began our drills.

My entire childhood was drills. Drill after drill after drill. Serves, groundstrokes, footwork, volleys. Serves, groundstrokes, footwork, volleys. Again and again. All summer long, after school, every weekend. My dad and I. Always together. Our little team of two. Proud coach and star student.

I loved that each element of the game had a *wrong* way and a *right* way to execute it. There was always something concrete to strive for.

"*De nuevo,*" my dad would say, as I tried for the fiftieth time that day to perfect my flat serve. "I want both arms coming up at the same speed at the same time."

"*De nuevo,*" he'd say, a grown man crouching down low to get eye-to-eye with me when I was no taller than his hip. "In a pinpoint stance, you must bring your back foot in before you connect."

"*De nuevo,*" he'd say, smiling. "Save that spin for a second serve, *hijita. ¿Entendido?*"

And each time, at the ages of five, six, seven, eight, he'd be met with the same response. "*Sí, papá.*" *Sí, papá. Sí, papá. Sí, papá.*

Over time, my father started peppering his "*De nuevo*" with "*Excelente.*"

I reached every day for those "*excelentes.*" I dreamed about them. I lay in bed at night on my Linus and Lucy sheets, staring at the framed Rod Laver press photo I'd begged my father for, going over my form in my head.

Soon enough, my groundstrokes were strong, my volleys were sharp, my serves were deadly. I was an eight-year-old able to serve from the baseline and hit the small target of a milk carton one hundred times in a row.

People walking by the courts would think they were clever when they called me "Little Billie Jean King," as if I didn't hear it ten times a day.

Soon, my father introduced the idea of strategy.

"A lot of players can win the games they serve," my father would say. "*Decime por qué.*"

"Because a serve is the only time a player can control the ball."

"*¿Y qué más?*"

"If you serve it right, you control the serve and then the return. And even the rally."

"*Exacto.* Holding your game when you serve is the basis of your strategy."

"*Bueno, entiendo.*"

"But most people, they focus all their energy on their serve. They perfect their serve so much, and they forget the most important part."

"The return."

"*Exacto.* Your serve is your defense, but you can *win* games with a good return. If you hold all the games you serve, and your opponent holds all their games, who is going to win the set?"

"The first person to break the other one's service game."

"*Exacto.* If you break their serve in just one game—just one— and you hold all of your own, you will win the set."

"So I have to be a good server and a good returner."

"You have to be what we call an 'all-court player,'" he said. "Great at serving, volleying, groundstrokes, and your return. Okay, let's play."

He always won, day after day. But I kept trying. Match after match, every evening after school, sometimes twice on weekends.

Until one cloudy January afternoon, when the air was just a bit too crisp. All day it had been threatening to do the very thing the Southern California sky had promised to almost never do.

We were tied in the first set when I returned two serves in a row with cross-court forehands that were so fast, my father couldn't get to them.

And for the first time in my young life, I broke his serve.

"*¡Excelente!*" he said with his arms in the air, running over to my side of the court. He spun me in the air.

"I did it!" I said. "I broke your serve!"

"Yes, you did," he told me. "Yes, you did."

About two minutes after I won the set, the sky cracked open and the rain started pouring down. My father put his jacket over my head as we raced to the car.

After we got in and shut the doors, I looked over at him. His face was all lit up even as he shivered from the cold. "*Excelente, pichon-cita,*" he said as he grabbed my hand and squeezed. "*Muy pero muy bien.*" He was still smiling as he turned the key in the ignition and backed out of the parking lot.

From that moment on, though I still couldn't beat him in a match, I set my mind to breaking his serve at least once every day. And I did it.

At the end of every session, my father and I would drive home with two doggie bags of food from the dining room at the club staying warm in my lap. I'd watch the big houses go by as we made our way back to our apartment.

My father would park, and then, before we got out, he'd say, "We did well today. But what are we going to do better tomorrow?"

I'd give him the list I'd been working on the entire way home.

"Get my feet up faster," I'd say. "And keep my wrist down." Or "Make sure I don't pull back too far before I hit the drop volley."

Each night, he would add one more thing I didn't think of. "And keep your eye on the ball, not on your racket." "Follow through on the forehand groundstroke."

Each night, I would nod. *Of course. How could I forget?*

Then we would go inside and eat dinner together in front of the TV. Most of the time it was just the evening news, but I always loved those rare nights when he'd let us watch *The Lucy Show.* Him in his recliner, me on the couch, a pair of TV trays. He would laugh so hard. And so I laughed too.

Later, after I brushed my teeth and put on my pajamas, my father would give me a kiss on the forehead and say, "Good night, my Achilles, the greatest warrior tennis has ever seen."

When the light was off, I would put my hand under my pillow, searching for the photo of my mother that I had taken from my father's dresser.

In it, my mother is lying in a hammock in our backyard, holding me and smiling at the camera. There is an orange tree above us. I am asleep in her arms, her chin is resting on my head, her hand is on my back. Her hair is long and her curls soft. I used to run my finger over the photo, the length of her dress, from her shoulders to her feet.

I would hold the photo to my chest and then tuck it back under my pillow and go to sleep.

One night when I was about eight years old, I went to find the photo and it was gone.

I threw my pillow onto the ground. I jumped off my bed and lifted the mattress onto its side. How could I have lost it, something so important? I started screaming, tears falling down my cheeks.

My father came in and saw me sitting there, red-faced, my eyes wet, my room torn apart. He calmly put my mattress back on the frame and took me in his arms.

"*Pichoncita*," he said. "*No te preocupés.* The photo is fine. I put it back in my dresser. It's time to stop looking at it every night."

"*Pero* I want to look at it every night."

He shook his head and held me tight. "*Cariño,* put it out of your mind. It is too heavy of a weight for you to bear."

1966

BY MY NINTH BIRTHDAY, I'D BEATEN EVERY KID MY AGE AT THE CLUB. SO my father recruited the son of one of the adults he taught to play me, a thirteen-year-old boy named Chris.

"I don't understand why you're allowed to play here," Chris said to me. "You're not a member." We were standing by the net, waiting to start. Our fathers were talking, laughing.

"Neither are you," I said.

"My dad is. Your dad *works* here. Your dad works for *us*."

Our fathers headed in our direction, and Chris groaned. "Can we just get this over with? I don't feel like playing a seven-year-old girl."

I stared at him for a moment, feeling my shoulders tighten. "I'm nine, you moron."

Chris looked at me with his eyes wide, but he didn't say anything else. Something I learned early is that most assholes don't have comebacks.

"All right, kids, best out of three," my dad said.

Chris served first and I crouched, ready. He tossed the ball up and hit it in a slow curve. I smacked it back, cross-court. My point. *Love–15.*

Chris served again. I returned it with a passing shot. *Love–30.*

The next time, I feigned yawning. *Love–40.*

"Game for Carrie," my father said.

Chris's face grew slightly red. I couldn't tell if he was angry or embarrassed. I smiled at him.

The rest of the match was over quick.

On the last serve, I tapped the ball over, unwilling to bother with any topspin or speed. But he still hit it wide.

"You are terrible at tennis," I said to him when I shook his hand.

"Carolina!" my father called out.

"Sorry, but he is," I said. I looked over at Chris. "You are."

I watched Chris glance at his father on the side of the court. His father shook his head and put out the cigarette he'd been smoking, rolling his eyes.

I remember thinking, *That's why you should practice, Chris.*

When we walked off the court, my father put his hand on my shoulder and said, "That was something."

"I didn't even have to try," I said as we headed toward the locker rooms.

"Oh, you made that clear. And you were mean."

"Why should I be nice to him? He called me a seven-year-old."

"People are going to call you a lot of things in your life," he said. "People always call people like us all kinds of things."

"Because we aren't members here?" I asked as I put my things down.

My father stopped in place. "Because we are winners. Do not grow a chip on your shoulder, Carolina," he said. "Do not let what anyone says about you determine how you feel about yourself."

I looked at him.

"If I say your hair is purple, does that mean it's purple?" he asked.

"No, it's brown."

"Does it mean you have to prove to me it's brown?"

I shook my head. "No, you can see it is."

"You are going to be one of the greatest tennis players in the world someday, *cariño*. That is as true as your brown hair. You don't need to show them. You just need to be."

I considered.

"Next time you play a kid like Chris, I expect you to still play a beautiful game of tennis," he said. "Do you understand?"

I nodded. *"Está bien."*

"And we don't cry when we lose, but we also don't gloat when we win."

"Bueno, entiendo."

"You're not playing your opponent, you understand that, yes?"

I stared at him, unsure. But I needed him to believe that I understood everything I was supposed to be—it seemed like an unbearable betrayal of our mission for me to be confused about any of it.

"Every time you get out on that court, you must play a better tennis game than you played the time before. Did you play your best game of tennis today?"

"No," I said.

"Next time, I want you to beat yourself. Every day you must beat the day before."

I sat down on the bench next to me and considered. What my father was proposing was a much, much harder endeavor. But once the thought had been put in my head, I had to rise to it. I could not expel it.

"Entiendo," I said.

"Now go get your things. We are driving to the beach."

"No, Dad," I said. "Please, no. Can't we just go home? Or what if we went out for ice cream? This girl in my class said there is a place that has great ice cream sandwiches. I thought we could go."

He laughed. "We are not going to condition your legs sitting around eating ice cream sandwiches. We can only do that by . . ."

I frowned. "Running in the sand."

"Sí, running in the sand, *entonces vámonos.*"

1968

AFTER ABOUT TWO MORE YEARS OF BEATING EVERY KID IN TOWN, WE got a call from Lars Van de Berg, one of the biggest junior tennis coaches in the country.

He was coaching a fourteen-year-old named Mary-Louise Bryant down in Laguna Beach. Mary-Louise had already started winning junior championships. She'd gotten to the semifinals at Junior Wimbledon that year.

"Lars called because everyone in L.A. is talking about you," my father said as we drove south on the freeway toward Laguna Beach. I was in a white tennis skirt and polo shirt, a cream-colored cardigan on top. I wore new socks and a brand-new blindingly white pair of tennis shoes on my feet.

My father had gone out and bought the whole outfit the week before. He'd washed it all and laid it out for me that morning. When I saw the ruffles on the butt of the tennis underpants for the skirt, I looked at him for a moment, hoping he was not serious. But from the look on his face, it was clear he was. So I put it on.

"He's pretending it's just a friendly match," my father continued. "But he wants to see if you're a threat to Mary-Louise."

There were already whispers about my future. Competing was something I knew I would do soon, the way some kids know they will go to college. And just like college, I got the impression my father was silently working out how to pay for it.

I wriggled in my seat, trying to stop the sweater from chafing my neck. "*Am* I a threat to Mary-Louise?" I asked.

"Yes," my father said.

I rolled down my window and watched the Pacific Ocean fly by.

"I want you thinking of your game plan," my father said. "Mary-Louise is three years older, so you have to assume she's taller, stronger, maybe more confident. How will that affect your strategy? You have five minutes."

"Okay," I said.

My father turned the radio up and focused on the road. Soon enough, traffic slowed considerably and we came to a full stop. I looked out the window, watching kids on the beach, playing in the sand. I saw two girls around my age building a sandcastle.

The gap between myself and girls like that—girls like the ones I went to school with—had always felt significant, but it seemed nearly insurmountable now.

A half second later, we started moving again and I wondered why anyone would want to build anything out of sand, when tomorrow it will be gone, and you'd have nothing to show for your day.

"*Bueno, contame,*" my dad said. "What's your plan?"

"If she's stronger than me, I need to get her up to the net as much as I can, use my angles. And she's probably feeling pretty confident, so I need to shake her, right at the beginning. If I can get her worrying about whether an eleven-year-old is gonna beat her, then an eleven-year-old is gonna beat her."

"*Muy bien*," he said as he lifted his hand, to give me a high five. "My Achilles. Greatest of the Greeks."

I held back a smile as we sped down the freeway.

Mary-Louise won the toss and elected to serve first.

I stood at the baseline and bounced the taut strings of my racket against my palm. I held the grip and turned it over in my hand.

I looked down at my brand-new shoes. I noticed there was a scuff on the toe. So I bent down and rubbed it off.

My father and Lars were on the bench. Lars was over six feet tall, with sandy hair and a smile that never made it to his eyes. He had introduced my father as "the Jaguar" to Mary-Louise in a tone that bothered me.

Mary-Louise was standing across the court, in a white tennis skirt and sweater with a matching headband in her hair. As she stood up, I could see just how tall and lanky she was, her face angular and delicate. Maybe it was the perfect creases in her skirt or the casual way she held her wooden Dunlop Maxply Fort racket, but I could tell that while she and I might both be at home on this court, we would not recognize the rest of each other's worlds.

She smiled at me, and I wondered if she might be the prettiest girl I'd ever seen in my life.

I fostered no illusions that I was beautiful. I was stocky and broad-shouldered, my calves and forearms thicker than those of the other girls in my class. Some of the more popular girls—the ones who wore bows in their hair and cardigans over their dresses, the ones the boys chased at recess—had started calling me names when the teacher wasn't listening.

As I'd walked into class one morning, Christina Williams whispered loudly to Diane Richards, "There she goes. *Boom, boom, boom,*" as if the weight of my steps was shaking the room when I walked to my desk.

The whole class laughed.

"At least I didn't get a D on the math quiz, you loser," I said as I sat down.

The class laughed at that too. But then Christina started crying. My teacher noticed and called us both to the front of the room.

When pressed, Christina cried even harder and denied she'd ever teased me. I kept my head up and admitted what I'd said.

And somehow, the coward went free, and I got sent to the principal's office, who then called my father. He came and picked me up and took me home.

After hearing my side of the story, my father reprimanded me and then made me look in the mirror. He told me I was beautiful. *"Pichona, sos hermosa."*

I scanned my face for a glimpse of what he was talking about. I had my mother's olive skin and green eyes. I had my father's hair color. But my body, my features . . . I could not tell where they came from. I wanted curls like my mother and father both had, I wanted my mother's length, her thin wrists, her perfect nose. I had none of it.

"I look nothing like Mom," I said finally. She had been so undeniably beautiful, her worth written right across her face.

"Yes, you do," he said. "And you are strong like her."

My eyes took in my broad shoulders, my powerful arms. Luckily, I did not need to be pretty. My body was built to wage war.

And thank God, because I was about to use it to crush pretty Mary-Louise Bryant.

Love serving love.

Mary-Louise tossed the ball up in the air and then cut across it with her racket. As I ran for the ball, I thought that my best bet was to take it out of the air quick. But as I got in position, I saw Mary-Louise approach the net. She was assuming I didn't have the power to hit a passing shot. And so, at the last minute, I hit a deep groundstroke. She had to rush her return and hit it into the net.

The first point was mine. *Love serving 15.*

I looked at my father as I made my way back to the baseline. Both he and Lars were watching me, and Lars's eyes were wide. My father was fighting off a smile.

I crouched and waited for her next serve. Mary-Louise's face was tight now. Suddenly, the ball came across the net, fast as a whip. I couldn't return it.

15–all.

Serve after serve stunned me.

30–15.

40–15.

And just like that, she'd won the first game.

I glanced over at my father and saw his brow furrowed. I couldn't tell what he was thinking.

Now it was my serve. I landed each one exactly where I wanted it to go. I was setting up my shots a few strokes ahead. I kept her running all over the court. But every time, she returned it. Our long rallies would inevitably end in her favor.

I stayed alert. I met the ball each time. But regardless of how good my shots were, it just didn't matter.

She took the first set 7–5.

I was exhausted already. My father handed me a towel, not saying a single word. I breathed in deeply. I could not lose; it was not an option.

I thought that by getting that first point off her, I would have thrown her off. But I'd awakened her. I'd given her a reason to play her best.

I had to take away her opportunities to hit winners. I was going to try for aces, each and every serve. It was risky; I could double-fault. But it felt like my only shot.

My first serve was hard and bounced high. She dove for it and hit it out. *15–love.*

I did it again. *30–love.*

I glanced over at my father as I went to pick up the ball, and I saw a smile creep over his face.

I hit another flat serve, but this time I kept it close to the T. It whizzed past her. *40–love.*

I had her. I could feel the tingle in the top of my head and down my back. I could feel the space in between my joints, the fluidity of my muscles. I felt a hum in my bones.

I served the ball low and fast. She returned it with spin that I *understood* innately. I knew where it would go, how it would bounce. I hit it back with the full force of my shoulder. Her return went long.

I went on to win the set. The score was now 1–1, and it would come down to who won the third.

Mary-Louise's first serve on the next game had us rallying back and forth for the point but ended in her hitting a low groundstroke that whizzed past me. I wanted to scream as I saw the ball bounce past my racket. But I knew my father wouldn't stand for that.

Here's the thing about that hum: It can leave just as quickly as it comes.

Mary-Louise took control of the court. She broke my serve, and she held her own. I showed up to the ball. I ran like hell. But it wasn't enough.

When she scored the last point, I fell to my knees. I felt like the world was splitting into pieces. I held on to the ground for a moment and closed my eyes.

When I opened them, Mary-Louise and Lars were by the bench talking calmly and my father was standing over me, offering me his hand.

My father had a warm face with curly dark hair. His eyelashes were long, his eyebrows were full, and his eyes were a soft brown. I had trouble meeting them.

"*Vámonos,*" he said. "We are ready to go."

I stood up and focused my gaze on Mary-Louise. I knew what I had to do. I just had to find the will to do it.

I walked over to her. "You played a beautiful game," I said. I could hear, as I was saying it, that I didn't sound like myself. My voice remained hard and cold, its various melodies not available to me at that moment. I put my hand out for her to shake, and she smiled and took it immediately.

"Carrie," she said. "That was the hardest match I've played in a long time."

"Thank you for saying that," I said. "But you won."

"Still," she said. "I would not have beaten you when I was eleven."

"Thanks," I said. But surely she knew that all that mattered was that I had lost.

My father and I packed up our stuff and walked back to the car. I zipped my racket in its cover and threw it into the back, then sank myself into the front seat.

When my dad got in, I stared at the glove box, trying to hold back the tears that were forming in my eyes.

"*Hablemos,*" he said.

"You shouldn't have made me play her," I said, my voice catching and breaking.

My father shook his head. "*Ni lo intentes,*" he said. "That was not the lesson you should take from this. Try again."

"I hate tennis," I said, and then I kicked the glove box.

"Get your foot off my car," he said. "You know better."

I closed my eyes and tried to breathe. When I opened them, I couldn't look at my father. I looked out the window and watched as, across the street, a woman came out of her house and got her mail. I wondered if she was having a terrible day too. Or maybe her life looked nothing like mine. Maybe she lived free from all this pressure, this sense that she lived or died by how good she was at something. Was she burdened by the need to win everything she did? Or did she live for nothing?

I looked up at my father, but he didn't turn back at first. And that was when I suspected that I had finally failed him, that I had proven myself unworthy of all the faith he had in me.

"Are you done?" he said as he turned to look at me. "With the hysterics?"

"Do you still . . . want to coach me?" I asked.

My father's face contorted in ways I could not read. He shook his head and put his hand on my cheek, wiping away my tears with his thumb. "*Cariño*, how could you ever ask that?" He lowered his gaze until he caught mine. "I am prouder to be your father and your coach today than I have ever been in my life."

"How is that possible?"

"I know you're upset because you lost," he said.

"I *lost*," I said. "Which makes me a *loser*."

Dad shook his head with the smile still on his face. "You are so much like me, *hija*. But listen now, please," he said. "I have been so focused on teaching you how to win that I have not taught you that everybody loses matches."

"I'm not everybody. I'm supposed to be the greatest."

My father nodded. "And you will be. Today you proved that. You played the best you've ever played in your life today."

I looked up at him.

"Have you ever hit that many groundstrokes that bounced *just* in front of the baseline?" he asked.

"No," I said.

"Have you ever served three aces in a row like you did today?"

I started tapping my foot as I listened to him. "No," I said. "My first serve was great today."

"You were on fire, *cariño*," he said. "You ran down the ball almost every shot."

"Yeah, but then I hit it into the net half the time."

"Because you are not yet who you will one day be."

I looked up at him, my guarded heart opening ever so slightly.

"Every match you play, you are one match closer to becoming the greatest tennis player the world has ever seen. You were not born that person. You were born to *become* that person. And that is why you must best yourself every time you get on the court. Not so that you beat the other person—"

"But so that I become more myself," I finished.

"Now you're getting it," my father said. "You played the best tennis you've ever played in your life."

"And you're happy," I said. "With me. Because I played great."

"Because you played *the best* you ever have."

"And every day I will play better and better," I said. "Until one day, I am the greatest."

"Until you've reached the fullest of your potential. That's the most important thing. We don't stop for one second until you are the best you can be," he said. "We don't rest. Until it's finally true. *Algún día.*"

"Because then I will be who I was born to be."

"*Exacto.*"

My father turned back to the steering wheel and put the car in drive. But before he pulled out onto the road, he looked at me one more time. "Do not wonder again, *hija,* if I would stop coaching you," he said. "Do not ever wonder that. *Nunca.*"

I nodded, smiling. I thought I understood perfectly what he was trying to tell me.

"Since today went okay," I said a few moments later, on the drive home, "I was thinking, about what I did. You know, that worked."

My father nodded. "*Contame.*"

I gave him a list of the strategies I'd used, a few of my split-second decisions. And then the last one, "*También,* just before the match, I cleaned the tops of my shoes."

My father raised his eyebrows.

"I think maybe it's a good-luck thing," I said. "You know? Like some of the pros do."

My father smiled. "*Me encanta.*"

"Yeah," I said. "And I think that will help me, you know? I'll just keep getting better and better. Until one day, when I'm good enough to go pro."

1971–1975

AT AGE THIRTEEN, I ENTERED THE JUNIOR CHAMPIONSHIPS. I SHOCKED everyone except my father and myself when I won the SoCal Junior Championships that year and catapulted myself up the rankings.

My first time at Junior Wimbledon, I made it all the way to the quarterfinals. The next year, I made it to the final. Quickly, my father and I came to understand that while I was great on a hard surface and could hold my own on clay, I dominated on grass. Winning Junior Wimbledon went from a dream to a goal.

My father took my already aggressive training schedule and kicked it into its highest gear. We went to every tournament we could, regardless of my school schedule. We flew all over the country.

Also, I noticed that my father took on twice as many clients when we were home. Occasionally, he would return to the house late at night with a bounce in his step that I found puzzling.

At first, I thought that maybe he had a girlfriend. But one night,

I dragged the truth out of him: He'd been hustling blue bloods at the club. He was making hundreds of dollars in a night.

When I asked him why, he said it kept his mind sharp. But I knew the prices for renting out grass courts, and flights to New York and London, and the entry fees for tournaments.

The next time I saw him leave to go play a match, I walked out onto our tiny stoop and called to him just as his hand grabbed the car door handle.

"Are you sure about all of this?" I asked.

He looked up at me. "Never been more sure of anything in my life," he said.

I took a deep breath. "I want to drop out of school and dedicate my full days to tennis."

The Virginia Slims tour was proving to be a significant money-maker for women who went pro. I was already good enough to compete in some of the main draws. He wouldn't need to hustle dupes much longer.

"Not yet," he said. But I could see the corners of his lips turning up. And I could feel the rest of the sentence, though it remained unsaid. *Not yet, but soon.*

Unless I was competing, I was out on the court from eight A.M. every morning until early afternoon.

From about three to five P.M., I took a break to study with a tutor my father had hired from the yellow pages. And then my dad and I went over strategy for about an hour, which would sometimes bleed into dinner.

After that, if I didn't have homework, I could do my own thing for an hour or so, and then I went to bed by ten so that I could be up by five-thirty to run, eat breakfast, and study strategy before getting back to the court at eight.

In the spring of '73, when I was fifteen, my father and I set up shop at Saddlebrook in Florida so that we could play on their grass courts day after day, sharpening every single shot I had in my arsenal, preparing for my third Junior Wimbledon in July.

It was at Saddlebrook that I met Marco.

My father had hired me a hitter named Elena to help me work on my returns. Elena was almost twenty and had an incredible serve. I often wondered, as we played together, why she didn't hone the rest of her game to try to play professionally. But she seemed entirely uninterested. A fact that I was exceedingly unnerved by.

Instead, every day Elena would show up, hit these incredible serves that made me think faster than I'd ever had to before, and then go on her way.

One day a few weeks in, her younger brother, Marco, came by the courts.

Marco was sixteen and over six feet tall, so he was impossible to miss as he stood outside the green chain-link fence, waiting for Elena to be done. Toward the end of our session, I found myself staring at him for the briefest of seconds. He caught my eye, and I quickly turned away.

But after that, he kept coming back to watch.

I did not know what it meant to have a crush—to feel that inexplicable pull toward another person—but by the third day that Marco showed up, I started to feel a lightness in me that was entirely new.

For weeks, Marco would come earlier and earlier to wait for Elena. Sometimes I could feel him watching me, and I would strain to stay focused on my game.

I would will myself not to look at the perfect square of Marco's shoulders, his deep brown hair, the slight pout to his lips, the way he leaned so casually against the fence. I tried not to imagine what his hands would feel like across my back.

"Keep your eye on the ball, Carrie!" my father said to me one afternoon. "C'mon now!" He shook his head. And my heart sank, but I straightened up and finished strong.

After we were done, my father went to go book our next court time. As Elena packed up her things, Marco came onto the court and approached me.

"Hi," he said.

"Hi."

"I'm Marco," he said.

"Carrie."

"I know," he said, smiling. "Everybody here seems to know who you are."

Elena put her kit over her shoulder and gestured that she wanted to go. Marco told her he'd meet her at the car and turned back to me.

"I've wanted to talk to you for a while, but your dad is always around."

"Oh." For a moment, I envisioned him asking me out, and my pulse quickened so intensely that I thought I might pass out.

If he asked me out, what would I even say?

My father had told me earlier in the week to expect double sessions on my backhand and my inside-out forehand. And I'd failed—actually failed—the practice GED my tutor had given me the week before. I'd promised my father I'd study all weekend. Answering yes was entirely impossible. And yet the wish that he would ask grew stronger and stronger in my belly by the second.

"Yeah, so . . ." he said, but then never finished his sentence. I watched his face, desperate to know what he was thinking. I felt a heaviness, a leaded feeling in my hips. I did not even know what it was that I needed so badly from him, but I could feel how much I needed it.

Instead of saying anything further, Marco put one hand against the fence and closed the gap between us. I watched his lips as he leaned his mouth toward mine. When he finally kissed me, I did not hesitate. I kissed him back with my entire body, pressing myself against him, wanting every inch of me to touch every inch of him.

His lips were so soft and his hands felt warm as they traveled from my shoulders down my torso.

I tilted my head back as his mouth went to my neck, and I moaned quietly, forgetting everything except this boy and his hands and how they felt.

And then suddenly, we could hear the crunch of the gravel that was my father walking back up the path. Marco pulled his hands away.

It was over almost as quickly as it had begun. Marco whispered, "I'll see you around," and then took off just as my father came back. My father picked up his racket and stood across the court from me and started calling out the shots he wanted to do.

I hit the ball the same as I always did, but inside, I felt flushed and in possession of my first real secret. It was like opening the front door and letting fresh air into the house.

For the next month, every day after training, Marco would be there. Whenever my father and Elena weren't around, he would kiss me in the corner of the court. I felt embarrassed by how much I looked forward to it, by how desperate I was to feel more of him, how often I thought of him when he was gone.

I felt such an insatiable need for him to touch me, a hunger for his body. It felt exactly like the hunger I felt to win. The sense that at the center of my being there was an unfillable void. There would never be enough matches to win. There would never be enough of Marco.

And it wasn't one-sided. He seemed to need me too. I could tell in the hurried way he grabbed me, in the look on his face when I had to leave. I felt bright and shiny for maybe the first time in my life, glowing with the knowledge that I was wanted.

I'm stunned at what Marco and I got away with in those small pockets of time that spring in Florida, just how far things went. Eventually, we found our way to the back of his parents' old sedan, parked in the far corner of the parking lot.

Marco opened up a whole slice of the world for me, a whole new thing my body could do. And I felt consumed by it. I could torture my body all day—making my muscles so tired that my whole body felt heavy. And then in just a few minutes, Marco could lighten every limb, loosen my chest.

"Are you my boyfriend?" I asked him one afternoon in June,

pulling my shirt down and fixing my hair. The start of Junior Wimbledon was only two short weeks away.

"I don't think so," Marco said. "We don't hang out or anything."

"Well, maybe we could," I said. "After the tournament. It's in a couple weeks, and when it's over, I could convince my dad we should come back here."

"I don't want you to come back here just for me," Marco said as he kissed me on the lips. When he pulled away, he was smiling. I loved his smile—the way his dimples were barely there but I was close enough to see them.

"But if we like each other . . ."

"Sure," he said. "But it's good, how it works now. Where we both do our own thing but then do . . . this." He kissed my neck, and all over again I found myself closing my eyes, on the verge of surrendering.

What little I knew of Marco outside of our time together mystified me. He got Cs in school and didn't play a single sport. His mother and father never kept track of where he was. All he did was play guitar and try to get his band together in his garage to practice. I could barely imagine his world, and yet I could not stop trying.

I liked the way he talked a lot but never said much. That he never took anything seriously. That nothing ever felt like a big deal. Sometimes, I pictured being with him outside that car. I pictured me sitting across the table from him at a restaurant and having him reach his hand out for mine. For other people to see that *he chose me.* "I'm just saying, if we wanted to, we could figure it out," I said.

"It's not like you even have time to go to a party with me or do anything I want to do. You're obsessed with tennis."

"I'm not *obsessed* with anything," I said. "I'm dedicated to winning. And I work hard at that."

"Right," Marco said. "And so let's just keep doing what we're doing."

I did not like his answer, but the next afternoon, I met him right back in that car with a smile on my face.

Maybe Marco and I would never go out to dinner. Maybe I was

not the sort of girl who became a girlfriend at all. Maybe I was the type of girl you kissed when no one was looking and that was it. If that was the case, then fine. I would not demean myself enough to want more. But that did not mean I could not have the rest, that my body did not deserve what he could give it.

When we left Saddlebrook for London, I knew I would probably never see Marco again. But I did not cry. As I watched the plane lift up above the clouds, it seemed obvious to me that there would be other Marcos—that Marcos were easy to find now that I knew to look for them.

But then as the plane leveled out, I glanced back at my father, who was talking to the flight attendant. I couldn't quite make sense of him. I kept staring at his face, trying to understand why he looked so foreign to me now.

There was a space between us that had not ever been there before, a gulf for which there would be no bridge.

Weeks later, I won Junior Wimbledon. I went on to win the next three juniors events. All the coverage started touting me as "the Next Tennis Phenom."

My father cut out the headlines from the sports papers. They said things like UPSTART CARRIE SOTO PROVES UNSTOPPABLE. He put them in frames and hung them up in my bedroom. When they ran an article with the headline IS JAVIER SOTO'S STYLE THE FUTURE OF WOMEN'S TENNIS? he hung that one on the fridge.

Our phone started ringing so often we had to get an answering machine. Journalists wanted interviews; a racket company was offering me an endorsement deal.

And there was also a representative from the Virginia Slims tour. In her message, she suggested that it was time for me to enter the main women's draw.

My father and I looked at each other.

My moment was here.

1975–1976

THE MORNING OF MY FIRST MATCH ON THE VIRGINIA SLIMS TOUR, MY
father gave me a pep talk before I went into the locker rooms. "You
can talk and joke around with the other players if you have to," he
said, "but remember they are not your friends, they are your . . ."

"Enemies."

"Opponents," he said.

"Same thing," I said.

"And like we talked about, everyone will be looking at you, looking to see if you're as good as they've heard. Ignore all that. Just *be*
good—don't try to prove it."

"*Bueno, entiendo.*"

As I turned to go into the locker room, the door swung open and
hit me hard in the shoulder. Out walked Paulina Stepanova.

Eighteen years old, six feet tall, white-blond hair and arms like
cannons—she had come out of nowhere. A baseliner from just outside Moscow, she was the kind of competitor I was not expecting.

She had just joined the tour two months prior and had already gotten to the final in the Australian Open.

As Paulina walked by, she barely looked at me. "*Izvinite menya,* I did not see you there. You are so short."

I gave a tight smile and then turned to my father. "I want to beat her to the ground."

My first year on the tour, I clinched some big titles and quickly turned pro, bringing in tens of thousands of dollars. I was up against some of the biggest names in tennis, women I had looked up to for years, like Amparo Pereira, and players who had long eluded me, like Mary-Louise Bryant. But it was Stepanova the newspapers were talking about.

PAULINA THE POWERFUL DOMINATES THE REST. STEPANOVA STEPS OUT TO DEAFENING APPLAUSE.

Publicly, I kept my face neutral. But afterward, in the hotels and on the long flights, I raged.

"She is in *my way,*" I told my father.

"It is your first year on the tour," he said. "Not everything comes the second you want it. Keep your head down and keep working. You will get there."

I did what he told me. I did *everything* he told me. Extra training sessions, no Sundays off, studying tapes of other opponents' matches. I watched Mary-Louise Bryant up against Tanya McLeod, Olga Zeman vs. Amparo Pereira. I watched tape of Stepanova up against everybody. Even me.

And my father and I adjusted. I learned to take it out of the air earlier with Stepanova, slow the game down against Mary-Louise, come out of the gate strong against Tanya McLeod, try to piss off Pereira.

Throughout '75, I climbed my way up the rankings.

61st

59th

30th
18th
16th
12th
11th

During the fall of '75, I finally got the chance to go head-to-head with Stepanova for a title when the two of us made the final of the Thunderbird Classic. I'd never beaten her in a meaningful tournament before. But as we got to the third set, I felt a groundedness, an energy, and started to sense that familiar hum in my bones.

When the score was 6–6, we went to a tiebreaker. I kept on her. The tiebreaker went to 12–12, but I could see her slowing. She double-faulted, and then I served an ace.

And it was over. I'd won.

Afterward, during my press conference, it was confirmed that my win had officially broken me into the top ten. I was seventeen years old and the number ten player in the world. I smiled when I heard the news. One of the reporters commented, "We are not used to seeing you smile. You should smile more." I immediately pulled my lips tight.

In her post-match, someone asked Stepanova, "You and Carrie Soto have proven to be well-matched competitors. Do you agree?"

She said nothing for a moment and then leaned into the microphone. "My shoulder started aching earlier this morning. I played through the pain, but it took a toll. Carrie would not have won otherwise. She does not have the ability to beat me when I am playing my best."

"Is this a joke?" I said to my father as I watched it on TV. "She was fine! She wasn't injured! What a crock!"

My father insisted I ignore her, and so I tried.

By the end of the year, I was ranked number four. Stepanova was three.

In an interview with *SportsPages,* Paulina was asked how she felt about "Soto vs. Stepanova" becoming a rivalry for the ages. We had gone up against each other in the final of two Slams that year, as well as a number of tournaments around the world. Sportswriters were calling it "the Cold War."

"Carrie Soto, people talk about her a lot now, yes," Stepanova said. "But she needs to lose about ten pounds or so if she wants to win against me when I am not injured. That is not a rivalry."

When I read that quote, I put the magazine down and then kicked a trash can in my hotel suite, sending it across the room and making a dent in the wall.

My father shook his head. "Control yourself, *hija*. You are not competing with her. You are competing with yourself."

"I *am* competing with her," I said. "And I'm losing."

"This is a long game," my father said to me as we were flying back from the Australian Open in 1976, where I'd lost to Stepanova in the semifinals and she'd gone on to win the damn thing.

"I'm done with the long game," I said. The flight attendants had just served us a full breakfast, and my father had devoured his. Mine was untouched. "I need to win every single time I go up against her," I said.

"She is playing better than you right now," he said. "But you are capable of more. That is your secret, that you have even more potential. We will figure it out."

I slammed my window shade up. "I don't want potential. I want wins now."

Despite the fact that I was eighteen, my father put his hand gently on my shoulder and said, "We are Sotos. We do not yell, and we do not throw temper tantrums if we're not good enough. What do we do?"

"We get good enough," I said as I turned my head away from him and settled my gaze out the window. For a moment, I couldn't remember which country we'd left and which we were going to. I looked down, and that was when I remembered we were over the Pacific.

"*Bien*," he said.

A few moments later, I turned back to him. "I'm holding my serve pretty well against her. She's having to win in tiebreakers half the time."

"*Es cierto*," my dad said, not looking up from his magazine.

"But she has more power than me," I said. "I have trouble taking her pace off the ball sometimes. I'm picking the wrong shots."

He was silent.

"You said I'm supposed to be the greatest tennis player of a generation. You said I had to grow into who I would become. What are we going to do? I need you . . ." I said. "I need you to figure it out."

He closed his magazine and looked at me. "*Dame un minuto*. I'm thinking."

He stood up, stretched out his back, and started pacing along the aisle of the plane. Then suddenly he was back. "Your slice."

"My slice?"

"Let's refine it, make it sharper, make it bulletproof. It will take away all of her momentum. We make it deadly and then . . ." He nodded. "That will kill her."

My father and I practiced my slice for months. We made it my very best shot. We perfected it over hours and hours of drills. My angle was brutal. And I knew how and when to implement it.

Amparo Pereira capsized when I used it. Tanya McLeod didn't stand a chance against me anymore. Olga Zeman fell to her knees that summer and cried when I beat her in straight sets. After that match, a reporter asked me on camera what advice I had for the opponents struggling to keep up with me.

I said, "Honestly? Get better at tennis."

That sound bite was played on every single sports show in the country. My father would shake his head every time. "That was unnecessary, Carolina."

"But that's what *I* did," I'd remind him. "Why is everyone so sensitive about the truth?"

"They are calling you 'Cold-Hearted Carrie' now," my dad lamented once.

Nobody liked my style. But who could argue with the results? It wasn't just McLeod and Pereira and Zeman I was taking down.

Stepanova was crumbling. I'd annihilated her with that slice in the semis at Wimbledon. And then two days later, I won my first Grand Slam when I defeated Mary-Louise Bryant in the final.

My first Wimbledon trophy.

The next day after winning, I slept in until eight for the first time in what felt like years. When I woke up, I could hear the television in the living room of the suite, my father delighting in the moment we both had worked so hard for.

"We may just be seeing the beginning of a stunning Wimbledon career," I heard the announcer say as I got out of bed. "Carrie Soto's slice has proven to be a dangerous weapon indeed, as it helped her take down fellow American Mary-Louise Bryant yesterday. And, maybe more notable, it slayed her fiercest rival, Paulina Stepanova, in the semis."

"Although, Brent," the commenter said, "Paulina has gone on record as saying her ankle was giving her trouble."

I marched into the living room and shut the TV off.

US Open 1976.

Stepanova and I were in the semifinals.

I took the first set easily. We were 5–4 in the second. All I had to do was hold the next game and I'd take Stepanova in straight sets, passing through to the final.

I served an ace right on the line. Stepanova stomped her foot. She walked over to the umpire and appealed, but it held. My point.

Stepanova walked back to the baseline, shaking her head. When fans booed on her behalf, she put her hand to her chest and pouted, as if she were the victim of a bad call.

I ignored her and served again, watching it land on the line and then bounce far and high.

Stepanova ran for it, lunging as far as she could. She returned it but landed on the edge of her foot, which buckled under her weight, rolling her ankle.

By the time I hit the ball back over, she was folded over on the ground. A medic came rushing onto the court. Soon he was holding Stepanova up as she started hobbling off. They called a medical time-out.

I sat down and wiped my forehead. I ate a banana. I drank some water. Shortly after, an official came up to me.

"Ms. Stepanova is asking if you would consider a delay."

"What?" I said.

"Her team is requesting more time for her to have her ankle wrapped and assess the injury."

"A delay?" I said, taking another sip of water. "No, absolutely not. If the roles were reversed, she would not grant me a delay in a million years. No."

The man went to tell Stepanova. I looked over at my father in the box. I could tell he understood exactly what had been asked. He nodded at me.

As we made our way back onto the court, Stepanova stared at me with a scowl. I truly could not believe it. What right did she have to be angry?

"If you really are hurt, you should retire," I said. "As you always tell the press, I only beat you when you're injured."

"Never," she spat.

"It just kills you to think I might be better than you, doesn't it?" I said.

She laughed. "You cannot be better than me if I'm always above you in the rankings, *druzhok*."

The crowd was cheering for her. She waved to them as she limped to the baseline.

She was brilliant. She knew she was going to lose this match, but at least now she had the sympathy of the world. She'd somehow seized the moral high ground by implying that I was exploiting her injuries for the win.

She had trapped me.

Fuck it, I thought. If she was insisting on playing, then she had to be willing to play on that ankle. And I was going to go after it.

I sent a thunderous serve right to the far corner of the box, making her run to meet it. When she managed a return, I sent it to the opposite side of the court. I watched her scramble to it, limping. The grimace on her face made it clear she was in agony. I took the point.

I could imagine it—could almost *feel* it—myself. The tenderness of her ankle, the twinging agony that ran through her as she had to turn on it, the awareness that it might buckle again at any moment.

Still, this was match point.

Before Stepanova hobbled back to the baseline, she took a step toward the net and said, "This is the only way you'll win against me. So I hope you enjoy it."

"You understand I'm going to run you into the ground, right?" I said, not bothering to keep my voice low. The cameras were on us; the umpire was watching. "I'm gonna make you run so hard on that ankle you're going to break it in half."

My heart started to bang against my chest. I walked to the baseline. I took a deep breath. And then I served the ball, as fast as a bullet, right to her fucking feet.

She jumped out of the way—falling onto the ground. She was in tears.

"Game, set, and match. Soto."

Half the crowd was cheering, and the other half was booing louder than I'd ever heard before.

In the post-match interview, one of the reporters asked me if I felt bad, going after Stepanova's ankle. I leaned into the microphone and said, "No."

The room went so silent I could hear my own heartbeat.

The next morning, under a headline dubbing the match "The Coldest War," one of the journalists called me "the Battle Axe." Within days, it had become my name.

JANUARY 23, 1979

BY THE TIME I WAS TWENTY, I HAD FOUR SLAM TITLES. TWO WERE AT Wimbledon, one was at the US Open, and I'd beaten Stepanova in the final of the Australian Open in a nearly three-hour battle, one of the longest and most-watched matches in tennis history.

Our rivalry dominated the sports pages. THE COLD WAR CONTINUES ON THE COURT. SOTO WINS SLAMS, BUT STEPANOVA TAKES MORE TITLES. STEPANOVA VS. SOTO GETS UGLY IN LONDON. And yet, in the end-of-the-year rankings, she still took the top spot.

The rivalry had become so popular—and made such good television—that it made my father famous too. The camera loved the handsome Javier Soto. The papers all printed photos of "the Jaguar" sitting proudly in the players' box. One of them was captioned *The man who taught Carrie Soto everything she knows.*

In 1978, he released a book, *Beautiful Fundamentals,* that hit the bestseller lists and quickly became a mainstay of tennis instruction.

There was even a moment when he became a recurring guest on *Johnny Carson*.

People loved him. And he took to it. He seemed satisfied with what we had done together, what we'd accomplished. His dreams had been fulfilled.

Mine had not.

"I should be number one," I said to him as we ate lunch at a tennis club in Florida. I'd just beaten Stepanova in the final at Houston at an Avon Championships event. "At this point, I've earned it."

"Let's enjoy our food, please," my father said.

"I want to hold the record for the most Grand Slams for any player ever," I said, my voice rising. "And I can't do that until I destroy her *every time* we play."

"*Hija* . . ." my father said, a gentle warning. He maintained his insistence that I never make a scene on or off the court. And I did my best, but it required a great effort. And as a result, sportscasters started referring to me as "stiff" and "robotic."

I'd seen more than a few op-eds in sports magazines about how *Carrie Soto acts more like a machine than a woman* and *The Battle Axe never seems to enjoy her wins*. Other players on the tour would mention in interviews that I wasn't very friendly. As if I was supposed to befriend the very same women I was defeating week after week.

I would read tabloids in airports, and whenever my name was mentioned, there was always some crack about how I didn't smile enough.

I can't tell you how many times I flipped through a magazine only to come across someone trashing me in print. I'd hand it to my father so that I wouldn't look at it. But five minutes later, I'd take it back and continue torturing myself.

No matter how good I was on the court, I was never good enough for the public.

It wasn't enough to play nearly perfect tennis. I had to do that and *also* be charming. And that charm had to appear effortless.

I couldn't seem to be *trying* to get them to like me. I could not let anyone ever suspect that I might *want* their approval. I saw the way they wrote about a player like Tanya McLeod, the way they had contempt for her for trying so hard to be cute. I had contempt for it too.

But c'mon. That's an awfully small needle to thread.

And the eye of that needle just got smaller and smaller the more successful I became.

It was okay to win as long as I acted *surprised* when I did and attributed it to luck. I should never let on how much I *wanted* to win or, worse, that I believed I *deserved* to win. And I should never, under any circumstances, admit that I did not believe all of my opponents were just as worthy as I was.

The bulk of the commentators . . . they wanted a woman whose eyes would tear up with gratitude, as if she owed them her victory, as if she owed them everything she had.

I don't know if it had ever been within me to act like that, but by the age of twenty, it was long gone.

And it cost me.

By the time I was a Grand Slam champion, ranked number two in the world, I had fewer endorsement deals than any of the other players in the top ten. I had no real friendships on the tour or elsewhere.

And while I'd slept around a lot, the longest relationship I'd ever had was with an actor I'd been with a few times at the Chateau Marmont when he was filming in L.A.

He was a huge tennis fan. He'd been there when I won Wimbledon the year before. Maybe it was because of that that I had thought he might actually *like* me. But after a few weeks, without warning, he stopped calling.

I convinced myself that he'd lost my number. So I tracked down his agent and tried to leave him a message. Upon hearing his agent's cringing pause, I realized he hadn't lost my number at all.

So I fucking better be ranked number one. What else did I have?

"Stepanova's not as good as I am, Dad," I said. "But she's still squeaking out way more titles than she should, and that's how she's beating me in the end-of-the-year rankings."

"You go weeks at a time where you're ranked number one," he said. "The end-of-the-year ranking is not the best metric."

"I'm supposed to be the greatest *by all metrics*," I said.

My father put his fork down and looked at me as I continued.

"If I am not number one at the end of the year, it is because I did not win enough of the right matches, and thus I am not yet the greatest."

My father frowned. "*Como quieras,* Carolina."

"We need to work *harder,*" I said. "Both of us. We need to be out on the court twice as much. You need to look inside your little bag of tricks and come up with another angle I'm not seeing. Stepanova has gotten quicker now, to keep up with me. Have you noticed that?"

"*Hija,* you are everything we wanted you to be. And time will show that you are the better player," he said. "Stepanova's going to be out in just a few years. She's already ruining her shoulder. And then your reign will be longer."

"If I am number one only after she's done, I'm not the greatest. She is."

"But you will go down in history as the more decorated player."

"I want the record to show that *now.* We need a plan."

My father pushed his plate away. "*Hija,* I don't know how much better you can get."

"What are you talking about?"

"I think I have done you a disservice," my father finally said, looking me in the eye. "I told you from such a young age that you could be the very best. But I never explained to you that it's about aiming for excellence, not about stats."

"What?"

"I am just saying that when you were a child, I spoke in . . . grandiosities. But, Carrie, there is no actual unequivocal greatest in the world. Tennis doesn't work like that. The world doesn't work like that."

"I'm not going to sit here and be insulted."

"How am I insulting you? I am telling you there is no one way to define the greatest of all time. You're focusing right now on rankings. But what about the person who gets the most titles over the span of their career? Are they the greatest? How about the person with the fastest recorded serve? Or the highest paid? I'm asking you to take a minute and recalibrate your expectations."

"Excuse me?" I said, standing up. "Recalibrate my expectations?"

"Carrie," my father said. "Please listen to me."

"No," I said, putting my hands up. "Don't use your calm voice and act like you're being nice. Because you're not. Having someone on this planet who is as good as me—or better—means I have not achieved my goal. If you would like to coach someone who is fine being second, go coach someone else."

I threw my napkin down and walked out of the restaurant. I made my way through the lobby to the parking lot. I was still furious by the time my father caught up to me by my car.

"Carolina, stop, you're making a scene," he said.

"Do you have any idea how hard it is?" I shouted. It felt shocking to me, to hear my own voice that loud. "To give everything you have to something and still not be able to grasp it! To fail to reach the top day after day and be expected to do it with a smile on your face? Maybe I'm not allowed to make a scene on the court, but I will make a scene here, Dad. It is the very least you can give me. Just for once in my life, let me scream about something!"

There were people gathering in the parking lot, and each one of them, I could tell, knew my name. Knew my father's name. Knew exactly what they were witnessing.

"WHAT ARE YOU ALL LOOKING AT? GO ON ABOUT YOUR SAD LITTLE DAYS!"

I got in my convertible and drove away.

. . .

The second I got back to my hotel suite, I sat down on the sofa and grabbed the phone off the side table. I put it in front of me and stared at it for a brief moment before picking up the receiver and dialing.

"Hello?"

"Hi, it's Carrie." My heart rate was rising; I could feel my face flushing. I kept looking at the door, knowing my father could walk through it at any moment.

"The Battle Axe! Finally!" Lars Van de Berg said. "I have left you countless messages."

He'd been calling more and more as Mary-Louise's career began to plateau.

"Yes, well," I said. "It has been a complicated call to return."

"Yes, I'd imagine it is."

"I'm the number two player in the world," I said. I cradled the phone between my ear and my shoulder. I hunched over, my elbows on my knees. "I should be number one."

"I agree," Lars said.

"Javier thinks that being second is a great achievement and I should be proud," I said.

"Well, he is your father. I have three children, and I want, very much, for them to be happy," Lars said. "But sometimes I think being the very best is antithetical to being happy."

"Yes," I said. "*Exactly.*" I stood up and carried the phone with me to my balcony. I watched the palm trees sway in the wind. There was a breeze coming through, and I was thankful for it, despite the January chill in Florida.

"Carrie, listen to me. I am one of the best coaches in women's tennis, you know this. Everyone has known this since I coached Chrissy Salvos to take eight titles in '62. What Mary-Louise and I have done together is truly spectacular, given her ability. But she is not performing at the level I need."

"This would hasten the end of her career," I say. "If you were to leave her now."

"It might. But you cannot worry about that."

"She'd be worried about it, if the situation were reversed. She'd be considering my feelings."

"Yes," he said, then sighed. "She would. And she wonders why she never reached her full potential. Look, I have never coached a player with as much natural talent as you. And as coaches, we can't do our best work without the *perfect* player. I will never know what I am truly capable of until I have the chance to coach someone as good as you. I need you to do my greatest work. I am a sculptor. And you are the finest piece of clay I could ever work with. I saw that back in '68 when you first played Mary-Louise. And I will tell you now what I told your father then: He has done a fine job honing your talent. And I can take it from here."

I looked back at the door of the suite. "What are you going to do that my father has not done?"

"Are you ready to have this conversation now?" he asked.

I stared at the people walking on the streets below me. The cars pulling away from the curb into traffic. The family chatting on the corner while they waited for a walk signal.

"It is the only reason I called," I said.

"Well," he said. "The gap between the player you are today and the player you want to be—"

"I want to be the greatest tennis player in the world," I said.

"That gap is not big. We are talking about that vital half-percent improvement. And that's not found in changing your strategy. It's in shortening the nanosecond of time between getting to the ball and slicing it across the court. It is going to be found in the minute change you make to the angle of your serve. The details are fine, and they are going to get finer. It is going to be nearly imperceptible, the ways we need to change your game. No one will be able to see it from the outside, but Stepanova is going to feel it. Every time she loses to you for the next ten years."

I could feel my pulse in my ears; my face felt hot. "Okay," I said. "How do we do that?"

"Are you cross-training?" he asked.

"I run and do drills."

Lars laughed. "That's not enough. Stepanova is right about one thing—you need to lose at least a couple pounds. We need you doing sprints, lunges, weight training. You can jump higher to hit overheads. You rarely do—it's a weakness in your game, in my opinion. I want to see what happens when you blast off the court into the air. Take out some of Stepanova's lobs before they hit the ground. We start there and see where we get."

"No," I said, shaking my head. "If we are doing this, I need to know right now that you believe I can bury her. That I can be number one."

"If I am your coach and you do not become the number-one-ranked player for the year," he said, "I will be disgusted."

A shield was forming over me, a hard edge. "Okay," I said. "I will call you soon to discuss this more. Don't say a word. To anyone."

When I turned back into my suite, my father was standing by the coffee table.

He was staring at me, his eyes wide and tearing up. I had never seen this version of him before.

"What have you done?" he said softly. His voice was barely a whisper. It cracked as it escaped his mouth. "Carolina."

"I cannot have a coach who is less ambitious for me than I am for myself," I said. My voice was strong and clear despite the fact that I could not look at him.

"You're misunderstanding me if you think that's the case," my father said. "*Y lo sabés.*"

"I *don't* know that," I said.

"*Cariño,* since the time you could hold a racket, I have told you that you have the potential to be extraordinary," Dad said. "I do not know what more ambition a person can have for their child."

"You said you believed I was born to be *the greatest,*" I said. "And now, suddenly, I'm supposed to settle for what I have. For second best."

"That's not what I said. I said that you are already great. That you have achieved everything I dreamed for you."

"Why? Because you've sold enough books now?"

My father's jaw dropped. "How could you say that?"

I didn't respond. He already knew. If a coach needs clay, my father had made me his.

"When I see you play, I see perfection," he said. "I see the player I always believed you could be. So be happy, right here and now. Because of what you have done, who you've become. And not on some condition of being number one."

"But why stop striving *now*, Dad? You've raised me to be *the very best*. That means number one. And I'm not yet. Why are you changing the rules?"

My father sat down in the chair next to him. But I could not sit down.

"At least be honest," I said, shaking my head. "*Decime la verdad, papá.*" My eyes were burning and starting to tear. "Do you not believe I can do it?" I asked him. "Do you not think I can knock her out of first place?"

He closed his eyes and sighed. I stared at him, wiping away the tear that fell out of my eye. "After all this time," I said, "have you given up on me?"

He did not open his eyes. He did not respond.

"*Respondeme,*" I said. "*¿Creés que puedo hacerlo?*"

He threw his hands into the air. "Why won't you listen to what I'm trying to tell you, Carolina?"

I stepped closer to him. My breath slowed; my mouth turned down. "Do you think I can beat her, Dad?" I asked him. "Yes or no."

He finally looked up at me, and I swear my heart started breaking before he even said it. "I do not know."

I closed my eyes and tried to stay upright, but my legs nearly gave out. I sat down, but then just as quickly, I was back on my feet.

"*Te podés ir,*" I said.

I ran to my hotel room door and opened it. "*¡ANDATE DE ACÁ!*" I said to him.

"Carolina," my father said.

"Get out of my room," I said. "We're done."

"Carolina, you cannot be done with your father."

"I'm talking to you as my coach," I said. "Get out."

My father stood, his shoulders low. His eyelids half closed, suddenly heavy. He hung his head.

"*Te amo, hija,*" he said as he walked into the hallway.

I shut the door behind him.

In the morning, I got up and went to the court alone. My father flew home to L.A. later that day.

1979–1982

SOON AFTER, I BEGAN TRAINING WITH LARS SIX DAYS A WEEK, EVEN ON match days. Within a few months, I'd lost three pounds of fat and gained a pound of muscle, almost entirely in my arms and shoulders.

My serve got bigger. I could run half a second faster. My groundstrokes got harder.

But it was my jump that improved the most. Lars had me getting higher than I'd ever gone. Suddenly, I had better angles on my serves, I was taking balls out of the air faster, and I was returning shots that were nearly *unreturnable*. I hadn't seen that big a difference in my performance since the work on my slice. It was now almost impossible to get a ball past me.

By September, I'd beaten Stepanova at the Italian and French Opens, advanced further than her at Wimbledon.

The morning of the first round of the US Open, I went into the locker room seeded second. I knew that if I played Stepanova, it would not be until the final. There were players all around the lockers chatting with one another. I didn't make eye contact.

Suze Carter, a seventeen-year-old player new to the tour, came up to me. "I hope you win," she said. "Everyone's saying that if you take the trophy, there's no way Stepanova can hold on to number one."

Ines Dell'oro, a volleyer who had been around a few years, put her hand on Suze's shoulder. "Don't waste your breath. The Battle Axe doesn't talk to us," she said. "We are beneath her."

I looked at Suze. "Thank you," I said.

And then I looked at Ines. "I am ranked number two. And you are ranked—what? Maybe thirty? So in this case, yes, you are beneath me."

As predicted, Stepanova and I met in the final.

And while the end-of-the-year rankings were still months away, she and I both knew the stakes of the match. It would determine who ended the year number one.

And over the course of two hours and ten minutes, I took the match and championship.

After the cheering and the award ceremony, as I made my way back to the locker room, I saw Lars in the tunnel standing there, grinning. "*Prachtig,* Soto! Great air, just like I taught you," he said. "And now, you will end this year best in the world." He smacked me on my back, and then suddenly he was gone. He'd left to talk to the reporters.

I didn't take a step toward the lockers. I stood there, unmoving. I was waiting for it to feel the way I'd always imagined it would. For someone to hug me and tell me I had vanquished the enemy like the Greeks against Troy . . .

But, of course, there was none of that.

· · ·

That fall, I beat Stepanova at the US Indoor, the Thunderbird Classic, and the Porsche Grand Prix. With her shoulder out of commission at the Emeron Lion Cup, I took her down in straight sets.

In December—having been ranked number one for thirty straight weeks—I flew to Melbourne. The Australian Open started on Christmas Eve. In a little less than a week, the end-of-the-year rankings would come out.

That night, as I sat in my hotel room, hearing Christmas music from the streets below, I finally picked up the phone to call my father. It had been almost eleven months since we had spoken.

"Hello?"

His voice, once such an everyday presence that it was as if it were my own, had been gone from my life. I expected it to sound foreign or strange to me now. But instead, it felt utterly familiar, as if nothing had changed.

"*Hola, papá. Feliz Navidad.*"

The line was quiet for a moment, and I wondered, briefly, if he'd hung up.

"*Feliz Navidad, cariño.* I am so incredibly proud of you."

My chest began to heave, and I could not stop the tears from falling down my face. He was quiet as I caught my breath.

"*Pichona,* you have to know that whatever happens between us, I am always proud of you. Always watching you."

"I miss you," I said.

My dad laughed. "You think I've been having such a grand old time?"

I dried my eyes.

"But you are doing beautifully," he said. "So you keep going. You fight for what you want. Like you always have. And I'll be here for you."

I ended the year as the number-one-ranked player on the women's tour. When it became official, I popped open a bottle of champagne by myself in my hotel room. But then I couldn't bring myself to pour a glass for only one person.

After the Australian Open, I flew to my father's house. When he opened the door, he was holding two glasses of Dom Pérignon. I hugged him and drank the whole glass right there at his door.

Later, I unpacked my bags in his guest room. My father seared steaks on the grill. And we tried to find a new way of speaking.

Should I ask my father why there was a women's razor and an extra toothbrush in his bathroom? Was he going to ask about the tabloid photos that had recently started appearing of me being spotted outside hotels with a few different men?

Instead, our conversations only went as deep as "It feels wetter this winter than in the past, yes?" and "Oh, so you've been drinking Fresca now instead of ginger ale?"

But my second day home, he came into the living room and asked me if I wanted to go out for ice cream sandwiches.

"Ice cream sandwiches?" I said. "What are you talking about?"

"You don't remember when you were a kid and you always wanted an ice cream sandwich or a sundae?"

"That . . . doesn't sound like me."

My father sighed and picked up his car keys. "Come with me, *por favor, hija.*"

I looked at my watch. "I mean, I should get to the courts soon to practice."

"It will take a half hour," he said. "You can spare a half hour."

That afternoon, I sat in the front seat of my father's new Mercedes and ate an ice cream sandwich beside him as we people-watched. "These are good," I said.

He nodded. "I'm sorry I never let you have one."

"No," I said. "I'm better for it."

I could tell from the look on his face that he wasn't sure that was true. And I thought, *See, Dad, this is why you're not my coach anymore.*

But after that, something broke open between us. We went to the movies together. We went out to eat. I bought him a new panama hat. He gave me his old chessboard, "because you must always keep thinking four moves ahead."

On my last day before heading back out on the tour, I was packing when my father came and found me. "I wanted to talk to you about something," he said as I gathered pair after pair of Adidas. They were my biggest endorsement deal after Wilson rackets, and I had been designing a shoe line with them, the Carrie Soto Break Points. While I was not as popular as Stepanova or McLeod, I did have my fans. You couldn't deny that when I was playing, you were going to see a show. And the number of spectators—and thus endorsement deals—were starting to reflect that.

"Okay," I said.

"You're getting higher and higher out there on the court, reaching for Stepanova's lobs."

"Yes, I know," I said. I stopped packing and looked at him. "And it's working. I'm beating her every time now."

"But you're landing hard," he said. "Maybe during clay season it won't be too much of a problem, but on the hard courts coming up . . ."

"I'm landing fine."

"Trust me, I know what I'm talking about. You need to bend your leg more when you land. I'm worried your knee—"

"Lars says it's fine. Without adding in that height, I'd never—"

"I don't want to talk about Lars with you," my dad said.

"And I don't want to talk about my *tennis game* with *you*."

"*Está bien*," my father said. And he left the room.

We talked on the phone every day I was on tour in the early eighties. And we started opening up about things we'd never discussed before.

He finally started talking about my mother, telling me how much he missed her. I told him I thought about her when things around me got too quiet. He told me about the things she had wanted for me.

"She never thought tennis was terribly important," he told me once, when I was in Rome for the Italian Open. "She thought joy was more important."

I laughed. "Winning is joy," I said.

"Exactly, *pichona,* I tried to tell her that. But she was less competitive than you and me. More happy in the moment. And she was so open-minded and accepting about things. She probably would have been fine with all your dating. But, *cariño,* I don't know if I want to see many more of these photos in the magazines of you and your . . . suitors."

I sighed. "I'm having fun. That's all."

I didn't know how to tell my father that these men weren't suitors, that they rarely even called me twice. But I let him assume that it was me who chose not to see them again, instead of the other way around.

I was "the Battle Axe." I was cold. I was a machine. Sure, a lot of them were intrigued by the idea of the sheer power of my body. But I was not the woman that men were looking to bring home to their mothers.

I reminded myself not to fall for the bullshit they peddled. How much they admired me, how I was unlike anyone else they had ever met before. So often there was talk of going on vacation together, ideas of renting a yacht in the south of France, conversations about some imaginary future. I knew I had to ignore the promises they made so casually, the promises I wanted so badly for at least one of them to keep.

"Maybe you can find someone good for you," my father said. "Someone for more than one date."

"It's not that simple, Dad. It's not . . ." I wanted to get off the phone. But at the same time, I did want to tell someone, anyone, the growing fear that had started feeling as if it could corrode the lining of my stomach. *No one wants me.*

"You are picking the wrong men, like that Bowe Huntley. What are you doing being photographed coming out of a hotel with that walking tantrum? He's the number two player in the ATP and he's screaming at the umpire? That's not the guy you pick."

"So then who is the guy I pick?"

"That Brandon Randall is a good one."

Brandon Randall was the number one player in the ATP. They called him "the Nice Guy of Tennis."

"*Sí, claro, papá,*" I said. "I would love to go out on a date with Brandon Randall. But he's married. To Nina Riva, a swimsuit model."

"Mick Riva's kid?" my dad said. "I cannot stand that guy. Oh. Well, someone *like* Brandon, then. A nice guy. Go for a nice guy. Please."

1983

BRANDON RANDALL *WAS* MARRIED. AND HE WAS *NOT* AS NICE A GUY AS my father thought he was.

I know because I went back to his hotel room with him in Paris after the final of the French Open in 1983.

I'd never won the French Open before. It's a clay court, which is the hardest kind for a fast-moving serve-and-volley player like me. Plenty of greats have gone their entire careers without winning it.

But then I defeated Renee Levy in the final that year, and in that moment, I felt the breathtaking joy of knowing I had the rare distinction of claiming each and every Slam.

Brandon and I ran into each other in the elevator the weekend we each took our singles titles. When we stopped on Brandon's floor, he took a step out but then put his arm out to stop the elevator door from closing. He looked me in the eye and said, "Do you want to grab a cocktail in my room? A toast, maybe? To our success."

I searched his face for some clue as to what he wanted—what he was really asking. I wasn't quite sure. But I still said yes.

As he made me a drink, he told me his marriage to Nina was on the rocks. "She doesn't understand me," he said. "Though I get the distinct impression you do."

I am embarrassed by how unoriginal it all was.

In the morning, as we lay underneath the bright white sheets, Brandon told me he thought that I might be the only person in the world who made him feel less alone.

"I try to tell the people around me the pressure I feel, just how low the lows are sometimes. But they can't relate. And I'm kicking myself because it seems so obvious now: Who else but you, my equal, could ever truly understand?"

It was presumptuous of him to call us equals. I had significantly more Slams than he did. Still, I let him compare us.

Lying in his bed, with the sun shining through the big windows, I felt like maybe I wasn't destined to be alone after all. Maybe I was the sort of woman who was so singular, so exceptional, that I could only form a connection with someone like Brandon, someone as driven as me.

I feared it might still end up a one-night thing. But Brandon kept calling. He kept calling! This closeness between us, it continued growing, like a balloon filling with air.

There was a moment, there in the middle of it all—when he and I were together in secret and winning titles and taking Wimbledon side by side—that it felt like fate. I could look back at my own history with men and see that every single one of them had been a domino that had to fall in order to trigger this one.

For the months we were together, I finally belonged to somebody. And it was just as good as I'd made it out to be.

During the summer of 1983, I demolished Paulina Stepanova every time we played each other. Her shoulder, once just an excuse, was now deteriorating rapidly. She'd fallen thirty spots in the rankings.

Just before the US Open, she announced she was retiring. I was shocked that the woman who had once been my greatest adversary would become a footnote.

Upon retirement, Stepanova had only nine Slams to her name. I had twelve. And now she was done.

The morning after the announcement, Brandon called down to room service and had them bring up breakfast. When it arrived, he congratulated me on burying Stepanova once and for all.

"It's over," he said. "There's no more rivalry. There's no question who came out the victor."

I put my hands over my face, my smile so wide I had to contain it.

He kissed me, and I thought, *I have everything.*

Like a complete fucking dope.

We got caught in late July. He left Nina shortly after, and the tabloids reported it all that August—which was when the cruelty of what I was doing became obvious.

It was on the cover of every magazine in the checkout aisle. LOVE–LOVE: BRANDON AND CARRIE SET UP LOVE NEST AT BEVERLY HILLS HOTEL, LEAVING NINA RIVA BROKENHEARTED and BRANDON AND CARRIE TAKE A BATTLE AXE TO NINA RIVA'S HEART.

And yet I didn't end it.

Not when the paparazzi started following us or when *NowThis* showed a photo of Nina crying outside a grocery store in Malibu. Not even when he tried to go back to her and she rejected him. He came crawling back to me, and I stuck with him then too. I was too far gone, too desperate to believe I'd found the real thing.

And after all that, he was the one who ended it when he left me for another woman in December.

It took a while for me to dust myself off. But even then, I couldn't ignore the power of the hatred of the fans in the stands. The tabloid headlines only got worse. Things like CARRIE SOTO: LONELY AT THE TOP. And then, perhaps worst of all, WHO COULD LOVE A BATTLE AXE?

I was used to being disliked, but nothing prepared me for being mobbed by paparazzi as I was coming out of a restaurant, having them casually ask things like "How do you feel about the fact that people think you're a whore?"

I wore sunglasses and baseball caps outside. I ran from anybody with a camera. I hid in hotel rooms. I barely looked up into the crowds at my matches. Sportsade dropped me from their commercials; ticket sales for tournaments were down, and people were reporting that it was my fault.

I felt a million things.

But I felt one thing the strongest: Whatever soft parts of my heart I had tentatively exposed to Brandon, it had been a mistake. I would never again be that type of fool.

1984-1989

A LOT OF PEOPLE HATED ME IN 1984. BUT I KEPT MY HEAD DOWN, AND I took three Grand Slams. I set a record for most weeks at number one. And winning, I've found, does sway a lot of people. I seemed to have won some of their affection back.

In 1985, I took Wimbledon for the third year in a row. In 1986, I won it and the US Open.

Going into Wimbledon in '87, I was twenty-nine years old. Everyone was watching to see if I could win my twentieth Slam and set the record for most singles Slam titles. The papers were all saying that surely I was nearing the end of my career.

I won the final match in straight sets. And there it was. My world record.

Just shy of thirty and I was not just great. But *the greatest*. Of all time.

As I stood there on the court, watching the officials walk toward me with the plate, my entire career flashed in front of me.

Doing drills with my father as a kid. Playing Mary-Louise Bryant. Winning juniors, entering the main draws. Climbing up the rankings, improving my slice, learning that jump, defeating Stepanova once and for all. Domination.

I was now the most decorated tennis player by nearly every measure. Most Grand Slam singles titles ever. Most weeks at number one for any player in the history of the tour. Most singles titles, most aces over the course of a career. Most years ending number one. Highest-paid female athlete of all time.

I was the Carrie Soto I had always believed I could be.

I accepted the trophy that day as I had accepted all the others— my face stoic, my speech short. But this time, as I waved and turned to leave, I had to hobble off the court.

My left knee was killing me. It was often aching and tender all day. I'd get sharp pains when I bent it too far or put too much weight on it. I was getting cortisone shots, but they weren't doing enough. It was beginning to slow me down on the court. And while I'd been able to withstand the pain through sheer force of will up until now, I knew I couldn't do so much longer.

"*Hija,*" my father said over the phone. "You need surgery."

"Stop," I said, my voice clipped.

But I knew he was right. Before the US Open, my knee was so bad that I had to have painkillers injected directly into it, and I still lost in the semis to Suze Carter. Early the next year, I had to pull out of the Australian Open.

I took some time off, and when I came back, I could not get a foothold. In all of '88, I did not win a single title.

Just before the start of Wimbledon in 1989, Lars sat me down at a hotel gym in London.

"It's over, Carrie," he said. "I have done all I can do. You have achieved what you will achieve."

"No, it's not over. I just . . ." I looked down at the floor and then back up at him, ready to admit what I had long been denying. "I need to get the surgery. Then I can come back."

"Come back so you can lose more? Let everyone see the queen is dead?"

I flinched. "The queen is not dead," I said.

Lars nodded his head. "Carrie, your body, your skills, they always had an expiration date. And it is now. You are thirty-one. It is time."

"I don't know about that. Maybe it is. But maybe it's not."

"It is."

I looked him in the eye, starting to sense what was happening. "You already have another player lined up," I said. "You've already decided."

"It does not matter. Your body is done, Carrie," he said. "I do not want to stick around to see what less-than-perfect version of yourself awaits us on the other end of your surgeries. I'm not interested in it."

"I could bounce back. I could have the best parts of my career ahead of me."

"Not in your thirties," he said. "Don't make me humor you about that. If you continue after Wimbledon, it will be without me as your coach."

Lars stood up and left. And I sat there in the stale, cold gym, staring at a stationary bike. My knee ached just thinking about riding it.

Still, I ignored him and entered the main draw at Wimbledon. For the first time in almost ten years, I did not make it to the round of sixteen.

I fell so far in the rankings that I would have been unseeded at the US Open.

"Get surgery and see where you are," my father said on the phone. I was in New York, preparing to enter the Open as a wild card. He was back in L.A., getting settled into the compound I had bought for the two of us. A main house for me, a guest house for him, a pool, and a tennis court. "You won't know if your knee can be rehabilitated unless you try."

"And take the chance I'll lose again? In front of all of them?" I said. "Do you see how much they are loving this? My failure? No. I won't give it to them. No."

"So what are you going to do?" he said.

"I am not discussing this with you," I said. "Ever. It's not for you to say."

"Okay," he said. "*Está bien.*"

Two days later, in August 1989, I pulled out of the US Open and announced my retirement. "I have had a momentous run during a truly outstanding time in the world of tennis," I said as I read my prepared statement at the lectern. "I have achieved everything I set out to achieve. I believe my accomplishments will be remembered in the decades to come. And now, I am done. Thank you."

I did not play a professional match again.

Until now.

THE
COMEBACK

OCTOBER 1994

Three and a half months before Melbourne

I WAKE UP AT SEVEN-FIFTEEN. I DRINK A BLUEBERRY SMOOTHIE AND eat raw unsalted almonds for breakfast. I put on my track pants and a T-shirt. I slip a sweatband across my forehead.

And at eight A.M. on the dot, half a decade after my retirement—and fifteen years since my father last coached me—I step onto my tennis court, prepared to train.

The sun is shining bright against the mountains, and the sky is clear except for the fifty-foot palm trees lining my yard. It is quiet here, even though the frenzy of L.A. traffic is just beyond my gates.

I do not care about the rest of the city. I am focused on *this* court, *this* ground underneath my feet. I will defend my record. I will take down Nicki Chan.

"We begin," my father says. He is in a polo shirt and chinos. Looking at him, I can see he's so much grayer since the last time we were on the court together, skinnier too. But he stands just as tall as he did when I was a child.

"I'm ready," I say. He cannot hold back his smile.

"Three things I want to get a good sense of today," he says.

I bend down and reach for my toes, stretching my legs. "My serve, first," I say as I bounce, grabbing my right foot with both hands, then my left.

My father shakes his head. "No, I'm *telling you* what I want to see—you're not guessing. It's not a quiz."

I stand up and blink at his tone. "Okay."

He sits down on the bench on the side of the court, and I put one foot up beside him and stretch again.

My father starts counting off. "*Uno*," he says, "your serve. By which I mean, I want to know what kind of firepower you still have, I want to see your control."

"*Está bien.*"

"Second is footwork. I want to know: How fast are you getting from one end of the court to the other? How agile can you be?"

"*Perfecto. ¿Qué más?* Endurance?"

He ignores me. "Third, endurance."

I nod.

"Your endurance greatly improved with Lars," my father says. I flinch at the mention of Lars's name. "What did he add to your training to get you there?"

I am not sure how to respond, unsure how to have this conversation with him. "You mean other than the jump?" I finally say.

"We're not putting your knee through too much jumping. You had surgery to fix your ACL and you're not gonna tear it up again—"

"*Bueno, papá. Basta, ya lo entendí.*"

"So what else did he add to your game?" He meets my gaze and holds it. "*Contame.*"

"Cross-training," I say. "You and I always ran, but he added aerobics, calisthenics, weight lifting."

He nods and rolls his eyes. "You train for tennis doing things other than tennis. What a genius."

"You asked. And it worked."

My father nods. "*Bien, bien, bien.*"

We are both quiet for a moment. I can hear the gardener starting a lawn mower at the estate behind mine. "So . . . do you want to do that or . . . ?"

My father nods. "*Sí, estoy pensando.*"

I wait for him to finish his thought. I start rolling my neck.

My father says, "Nicki's going to assume her best bet is to wear you out."

"Anyone playing me is going to assume that. I'm thirty-seven years old. All you have to do is wear out the old lady."

My dad laughs. "You have no idea what it feels like to be old."

"In the grand scheme of things, Dad, sure," I tell him. "But in tennis . . ."

He nods. "So the most important thing we can do for you right now is work on your stamina."

"Yes, agreed."

"So, let's start with—every day—you run ten miles."

I haven't run ten miles in a few years. But fine. "And then we start hitting balls?"

He shakes his head. "And then squats and sprints, plus jump rope for the footwork. I'm assuming that's what you'd do the most with Lars? Then you'll swim, to further condition your muscles but keep it low impact. Then you can have lunch, and then in the afternoon, you hit."

"I'm gonna die," I say.

"Don't whine."

"I am not going to perform a triathlon every day and *not* whine about it," I say.

My father starts to open his mouth, and I stop him. "I'm not a child anymore. Sometimes I'm going to have an opinion. Sometimes, when I'm ten miles and fifty laps in, I'm going to complain. But I'll do what you say, and you deal with my attitude, and maybe one day soon, we'll win another Slam title, *¿Está bien?*"

He looks at me, emotionless for a moment. And then he smiles and holds out his hand. "*Perfecto.*"

. . .

Every day for seven days, I put on my running shoes and take off.

I run as fast as I can as my father rides in a golf cart next to me, yelling, "*¡Más rápido! ¡Más rápido!*"

My feet hit the pavement, over and over and over again. He yells, "If you are not ahead, you are behind!"

"*Sí,*" I say each time. "*Lo sé.*"

"*¡Vamos, más rápido!*" he yells the second he can tell I'm slowing down. "We are not out for a nice jog! We are running to win a title!"

I try to yell back to him from time to time, in whatever language comes to me first. But by the end of ten miles, I stop wasting any extra breath.

The runs are manageable. It is after that, when I'm jumping rope as he stands there barking out things like "*¡Más rápido!*" and "*¡No pares!*" that make me want to scream.

Instead, I focus on the burning of my calves, the ache of my arms.

And then there is the swimming. Lap after lap. As my legs and shoulders start to slow from wear, my father stands on the edge of the pool chanting, "*Usá esos brazos,*" like some sort of military command.

Every day when I come out of the pool, my arms are limp, my legs wobbly. I am a newborn calf, unable to find my footing.

On the seventh day, after my last lap, I can barely get myself up the ladder. Everything hurts—my hamstrings and quads are sore, my shoulders and biceps ache. I wasn't able to stay on my lap pace.

I lie down on the deck, and my father comes over and hands me a towel. He sits beside me.

I look up at him. I can feel his frown before it makes its way to his face.

"How bad is it?" I ask.

My father tilts his head from side to side. "You're half a mile per hour too slow on the runs. Your form needs work. Your swimming is . . ." He inhales deeply. "*Mirá,* considering your age and how long you've been off the court, it's impressive. But you are not where you need to be to win a Slam, *cariño.*"

"*Sí, lo sé.*" I dry my face. I sit up. I shake my head and look up at the sky. It is clear and bright, not a single cloud, not a single impediment.

This whole thing is a fucking joke. A player coming out of retirement after this many years? And I think I'm going to win a Slam? Am I insane?

"I do think you are on the path," he says.

I look up at him.

"You are the hardest-working person I know," he says. "If you decide to dedicate yourself to this, you will do it."

I nod, already resenting that we are starting with the old "effort" chestnut and not the "sheer talent" one. "Thanks."

He bumps me on the shoulder and smiles. "What I'm telling you is even though there is a lot of ground to cover, I believe you can be the greatest in the world again. I have that faith."

I start fiddling with the nails on my left hand. "Yeah?" I ask. "Are you sure?"

"I'm positive. But listen, *hija,*" my father says, putting his arm around my shoulders and squeezing me. "It does not matter if I have faith."

"It does, actually," I say. There is an edge to my voice that startles us both.

My father nods but leaves it at that. Like me, he has no interest in excavating what is long buried.

"Your faith in yourself drove you to the top once. And it can drive you there again," my father says finally.

I know that he is right. For decades, my talent and drive were utterly devastating to those who stood in my wake. If each person is blessed with an individual gift, determination is mine.

"Do *you* think you can beat her?" my father says.

I respond quicker than I intend. "Yes."

"And will you be able to bear it if you don't?"

That one takes me far longer to answer. "No."

He closes his eyes and then nods. "All right," he says, sighing. "Then there is no time to waste."

I SIT DOWN IN A CHAIR IN MY AGENT'S OFFICE, NEXT TO HER FLOOR-TO-ceiling windows. I've been with Gwen for about seven years now.

I signed with her after being at two different agencies run by men who kept telling me to "be reasonable" about things I was already being reasonable about. I took meetings with every agency in town, and then at one, in walked Gwen Davis. She is a Black woman born and raised in L.A. who had been a talent agent at a massive agency, and then pivoted to sports stars and struck out on her own.

"If you need to, I expect you to tell me to fuck off," she said in that first meeting. "And if I need to, I'm going to throw it right back at you. We have to have a relationship that is brutally honest. I'm not interested in being your yes man. It's not worth your time or mine."

I signed with her right then and there.

Today, in her office, I look out over Beverly Hills—the palm trees and wide streets and large lots. From here, I can see the golden crown that sits atop city hall.

I turn toward Gwen as she sits down on the sofa next to me. She's in her late fifties, dressed in a red pantsuit and mules. Sometimes I wonder if she's in the wrong field; she's too striking, too glamorous to be the one behind the scenes.

Ali, her assistant, comes in. Her long black hair is pulled into a bun with a pen, and it is already falling apart. She's in a flannel shirt and black jeans with a pair of boots. Something about the fact that Gwen doesn't care what her assistant wears in the office while she, herself, looks like a runway model makes me like them both even more.

"An herbal tea for you," Ali says as she hands me a mug. "With a muffin I know you won't eat."

I laugh. "I have to be back on the court this afternoon, and I don't even like muffins," I say.

"Next time, I'll get you raw unsalted almonds," Ali says. And I know she's making fun of me, but honestly, I *would* rather have the almonds.

Ali hands Gwen a coffee and then leaves.

Gwen takes a sip from her mug and then looks at me. She raises her eyebrow as she gently sets her mug on the glass table, next to a coffee table book with my face on it. It was released in 1990 and features shots of me at Wimbledon spanning about fifteen years. *Soto on Grass.*

Gwen meets my eye as she leans back on the sofa. "Are you sure about returning?"

"I would not be here if I wasn't sure."

"It's not something to be taken lightly," she adds.

"Do I look like I'm taking it lightly?"

"Well, your sponsorships . . ."

"I know."

"You're supposed to shoot the new Elite Gold campaign this spring."

"I know."

"And Gatorade is running the 'Champions' commercial soon too, with you front and center."

I nod.

"Your Break Points are outselling all other tennis shoes for Adidas right now."

One of the most surprising things about my retirement was that it turned out to be very lucrative. Apparently, when I wasn't around anymore, people forgot how much they disliked me—and remembered how much they liked my shoes.

"I know that too," I say.

"These endorsements are all based on the premise that you are now a legend. That you were one of the *very best* athletes in the world."

"Right, and I'm going to prove that I *still* am."

"But if . . ."

I look her dead in the eye, daring her to say it.

She pivots. "If it's a matter of earning, I think, for you, there is more money to be made as a commentator or a WTA official than as a player. We position you as an elder stateswoman of tennis. That's how we keep you relevant and active."

"First of all, nobody wants to hear what I have to say," I tell her.

Gwen raises her eyebrows, considering, and then nods, conceding the point.

"But second of all, it's not a matter of money. It's a matter of honor."

Gwen reaches out and puts her hand on my arm. "I need you to really think about this, Carrie. *Honor* is . . . sometimes just a nice word for *ego*. And I will always choose money over ego. Personally."

I look at her. "I appreciate your advice, but it's not up for debate."

"I'm just trying to look out for your future," Gwen says, pulling back. She picks up the muffin, tears a piece off, and eats it.

"Gwen, all I've ever had is this game," I say.

She nods. "I know that."

"And now it's about to be ripped from my hands. Leaving me with nothing."

"That's not tr—"

"Yes," I say, cutting her off. "It is true. I cannot let Nicki overtake the record. And I need you on board."

Gwen takes a sip of her coffee, then puts the mug back down. "And you are confident this is the right move?"

"It is the only move. I cannot conceive of any other future."

"Okay," she says. "Then I'm on board. I'm all in."

I can tell from the timid look on her face that she is worried I'm about to lose us both a lot of money. And while I feel a spark of rage at her lack of confidence, I'm smart enough to take the win.

"Thank you," I say. "And get ready to be proven wrong."

"There's nothing to prove me wrong about," she says. "I believe in you. So what's the plan?"

"I'm going to play in all four Slams this year, and I am going to win at least one to reclaim my record."

"So your first year out of retirement, you're confident you can win a Slam?" Gwen says.

"Yes," I say. "I am."

"And what if Nicki wins another one first?"

My shoulders tense, and I try to unclench my teeth. "Let me worry about that."

"Okay," she says. "Understood. And you're not rejoining the full WTA tour?"

I shake my head. "No, I just want to play select tournaments. But I don't know my standing with the ITF or the WTA."

Gwen gets up and hits the intercom on her desk phone. "Ali, can you get someone from ITF or WTA on the line and find out—as coyly as possible, please—whether a player like Carrie would get wild cards at all four Slams if she entered?"

"On it."

Gwen lets go of the intercom. "Okay, what's next? What else do you need?"

"Well, I could use a good hitter, if you have any ideas. Not just someone to rally with. I need someone really high-level. So I can gauge whether I'm ready for the best players."

Gwen nods. "You need someone at the top of the game, some-body who can help you get to where Nicki is."

I wince at the implication that we are that far apart. "Well, Nicki's . . . yeah, someone at top level."

"We can make some calls," Gwen says. "And see who wants to practice with you."

"Okay," I say. "Fine. But not Suze Carter—I can't stand her. Or Brenda Johns. But anyone else is fine. The two of them are just so . . . perky. What about Ingrid Cortez? She keeps giving Nicki a run for her money in the final. Maybe she and I can work together a little."

"Anything else?"

"I need Wilson to send me new rackets. I'll need Adidas to send outfits and new Break Points in this season's colors. Should I hire an assistant again? To book my travel and coordinate hotels?"

"If it's just four tournaments, Ali can do it."

"Okay, thank you."

"But you're packing your own luggage. I'm not your mother."

The joke sits there, heavy in the air for a moment. When your mother is dead, it follows you everywhere—popping up in offhand remarks. I notice them all the time, even if the person speaking doesn't. I can tell that Gwen realizes what she said was insensitive, and I appreciate that she decides to breeze past it. There is nothing worse than having to make someone else feel better that your mom died.

"What's next?" Gwen asks.

But for the briefest of moments, I wonder what my mother would think of me today. If she would be proud of what I'm attempting to do. I don't know the answer. And I realize just how long it's been since I asked myself that question.

Ali knocks on the door and comes in. "Okay! This is exciting. I have our answers."

"Tell me," I say.

"Because you are a former WTA number one and have won all

four Slams previously, you are guaranteed a wild card at any WTA or ITF event you choose."

"Yeah!" I say. "Now we're talkin'."

"You can pick and choose what tournaments you want to enter. We have to file some paperwork, but it will be no problem to get you in as a wild card draw for the Australian Open in three months."

"Will I be seeded?"

"No," Ali says. "All your past points are irrelevant now. You don't have any current ranking to seed from. Until you start winning," she adds, grinning.

I see a flash of myself, three months from now, standing on that green hard court in Melbourne, looking across the net at my opponent, whoever she is going to be. I can almost hear the crowd, can practically feel the sweltering tense air.

It has been such a long time since I've played a tournament. And it's been almost three times as long as that since I've played one unseeded.

It sends a tiny thrill through me, like I'm a teenager again, staring up at a mountain I have yet to scale, each match a step toward the top. It has been so long since I have felt the perfect ache of climbing.

The following statement was released today by Carrie Soto through her agent, Gwen Davis.

For Immediate Release 10/11/1994

CARRIE SOTO IS BACK

I am coming out of retirement for the 1995 season to play all four Grand Slam events—the Australian Open in January, the French Open in May, Wimbledon in June, and the US Open in August—in order to reclaim the world record for most Grand Slam singles titles.

I congratulate Nicki Chan on her accomplishments in women's tennis. But her domination is over.

I'm back.

Soto to Come Out of Retirement to Take On Chan

Los Angeles Daily
October 12, 1994

Women's tennis great Carrie Soto, 37, once known as "the Battle Axe," has announced her intention to come out of retirement in order to defend her Grand Slam singles title record. Force of nature Nicki Chan, 30, has been the leading figure in women's tennis since 1989 when Soto retired, holding a record of twenty Slam titles. Chan, often called "the Beast" by tennis fans, tied that record last month.

Soto has long been a polarizing figure in women's tennis, known for her sharp tongue and her ruthless strategies toward other players on the court. If the former champion were to win a Slam, she would be the oldest woman to do so in the history of the game.

"I welcome her return," Nicki Chan said in a press conference yesterday, after being informed of Soto's decision. "I've looked up to Carrie Soto my entire career. It would be an honor to play her once more."

When asked if she thought Carrie Soto could beat her, Chan appeared amused. "Well," she said. "We are going to see, aren't we?"

SportsNews Network
Wild Sports with Bill Evans
October 12, 1994

Bill Evans: So, we have some drama coming out of the women's tennis world. Jimmy, what is your take here? Carrie "the Battle Axe" Soto is back? What do we make of this?

Jimmy Wallace, editor of *SportsSunday*: It's certainly unexpected.

Evans: "Unexpected" seems like an understatement. Carrie Soto ended her career after a pretty sharp drop in the rankings back in the late eighties.

Wallace: Yes, she did. Though I think she would argue that's on account of her knee. Which has since healed.

Evans: But she's been gone—what—five years now? It's been a big five years in women's tennis.

Wallace: Certainly. And over that period of time we have seen the rise of Nicki Chan.

Evans: And a new type of tennis.

Wallace: Yes, I think that's true. Women's tennis has shifted away from serve and volley. We are seeing more baseliners, more power players. Soto was always a dancer—agile, graceful on the court. Chan is a brute—she's a boxer. She's tough.

Evans: Can the Battle Axe still compete in today's game?

Wallace: We will see. There's something else here that I think it's important to note.

Evans: And what is that?

Wallace: Soto isn't just playing an old style—she herself is old. No woman has won a Slam in her late thirties.

Evans: And here is another question: Do we even want her back? She's not the most . . . well-liked, is she?

Wallace: Well, they don't call her the Battle Axe for nothing.

Evans: So maybe she shows up in Melbourne and gets sent home quickly. And then she does the elegant thing and bows out again.

Wallace: I think that's very possible, Bill. Time will tell. Otherwise, Chan will have to put her down.

MY FATHER HAS BEEN READING TOO MANY SPORTS PAGES AND WATCHING too much news.

"Absurd," my father says, sitting at my breakfast table. "The way they are implying you cannot win."

I sip my smoothie. The coverage bothers me, but I know there's nothing I can do about it. When I decided to play professional tennis, I apparently signed a contract to let people talk shit about me for the rest of my life.

My father continues to read the paper. "I just think they should remember who they are talking about," he says.

"My sentiments exactly," I say.

He turns toward the TV, which is on mute. "Wait," he says, getting up and turning the volume up. "They are talking about you on *Morning in America*."

I look over at the kitchen TV.

News anchor Greg Phillips speaks directly into the camera with an image of me at Wimbledon over his shoulder. I cannot stand him. He's interviewed me at least a dozen times over the years and constantly asks about my skirt lengths. We once got into a spat, back in the eighties, when he said I held the record for most Grand Slam trophies in women's tennis. I corrected him on air, pointing out that I held the most trophies out of *anyone* in tennis.

"You thought she was gone!" Greg says. "But American tennis champion Carrie Soto is returning to women's tennis in order to defend her Grand Slam record. Soto has been retired for over five years and, at the age of thirty-seven, will be the *oldest* tennis player on the circuit. Still, she has made the bold claim that she will win at least one tournament this year, a feat that, should she do it, would make her the first woman in the Open Era to win a Slam title in her late thirties. Regardless of how things go for her, it should prove for a wild year in women's tennis now that the Battle Axe is back!"

I move to turn off the TV as Greg announces a commercial break and the show's logo appears. Then, just as my hand touches the dial, we can hear Greg's voice, plain as day, saying to someone, "C'mon, 'The Battle Axe is back'? We should just say, 'The bitch is back.' That's what she is."

Then comes the sound of a woman gasping, jarring feedback, and dead air as the station cuts away from the hot mic. A second later, the screen changes to a commercial of a teenage boy riffling through the refrigerator, pushing away the "purple stuff" because he wants Sunny D.

I turn off the TV and look at my dad. He looks right back at me, his eyes wide.

Finally, I speak. "Did Greg Phillips just call me a bitch on national television?"

My father's face is flushed; his neck is growing redder by the second.

"He did, didn't he?" I say, frozen in place. "He just called me a bitch."

My father gets up from the table and throws away the newspaper.

"I mean . . ." I say. "I knew they thought it. I just . . . I didn't think they said it out loud."

My father puts one of his hands on each of my shoulders. "*Pichona,*" he says, his voice pleading. "Listen to me carefully."

"It shouldn't surprise me. But . . . it does. Why does it feel different than anything else they've called me?"

"Because it's disrespectful," he says. "And you have earned the right of their respect. But listen closely, *hija*. I am serious."

"*Bueno,*" I say, looking him in the eye.

"Fuck 'em," he says. "You go win every goddamn match and you show them that you don't care what they think, you are not going anywhere."

EARLY NOVEMBER

Two and a half months until Melbourne

MY FATHER AND I ARE ON MY HOME COURT, WORKING ON MY FIRST serve.

"*De nuevo*," he calls out, standing there in his tracksuit on the other side of the net. "*Necesitás ser mucho más rápida, hija.*"

He has put a shopping cart full of tennis balls to my right. I pull one out, ready to serve again. We will be here all day, just like when I was a child. I will aim for that milk carton until my father is satisfied.

Over the month that I have been training, my game has come back to me. I can feel my muscles coming to attention. My speed is picking up; my power is increasing by the day. My serve is fast— sometimes clocking in at over 120 miles per hour. My control and accuracy are excellent. My dad is having a harder and harder time calling out where my serves will land.

But still.

I am not in the same body I was in at age twenty-nine. I am not running as fast. I am tiring more quickly. I am slower to pivot. I can feel the cartilage of my knee sometimes as I bounce. When I'm hitting against a ball machine, I'm not always getting my racket back fast enough. And even when I succeed—it is harder. It is taking more effort to do all of it.

By the second hour of the afternoon these days, I can feel myself begin to tire. My swings are wider and less controlled. My follow-throughs are sloppier. My hits are just a tad softer.

And when that happens, I am quicker to lose my cool. I start missing more shots, growing frustrated, overthinking. It is maddening, working just as hard for a less impressive result. Playing with this body is like trying to cut a steak with a dull blade.

As I stand at the baseline and hit yet another serve over the net, I think about Björn Borg. He was the best male player on the tour in the seventies, but when he came out of retirement three years ago, he couldn't even win a single set. A world champion, the gold standard. Now look at him.

What the fuck was I thinking?

There is a reason that I will be setting a world record if I win a Slam at my age: because no one has ever been able to do it before.

I hit the carton again. I now have not missed in ten serves.

"*¡Excelente!*" my father says as he grabs the carton and moves it to a new spot, farther back. "I want to see four or five, smoked right past me into the corner. *¡Vamos!*"

"*Sí, papá.*"

I toss the ball up in the air and send it flying across the net, right to the top of the carton. It falls once more. I look to my father, but his attention has shifted. Gwen is parking her Benz in my driveway.

I put my racket down, grab a towel, and drink a sip of water as Gwen walks toward us.

"Gwen!" my dad says, his voice booming as he walks toward her, pulling her in for a hug. What is it with hugging? Why would anyone want to press themself up against someone's body to say hello? A wave will do; a handshake is more than enough.

"Javi!" Gwen says, hugging him back.

"You look radiant, as always," my father says.

"Oh, stop it, Javier," Gwen says. And then she turns to me. "I come bearing news."

"Which must be bad, otherwise you would have called," I say.

"Carrie, you don't know that," my dad says.

"No, she's right. I'm here to hand-hold."

I sit down on the bench. "What is it?"

"We are having trouble finding you someone to practice with."

"Seriously?"

Gwen sits next to me. "We called . . . almost everyone on the WTA."

"Surely one of the young players wants to learn a thing or two from me," I say. "Did you point out that the benefits go both ways? What about Ingrid Cortez?"

Gwen's eyes dance around. "Ingrid feels that because she is the number four player in the world, she does not have anything to gain by hitting with you."

My father guffaws. "Her backhand is terrible, and she's giving her opponents opportunities to break serve because of it. She's a child."

"And the rest of the tour?" I ask.

"I think, you know, the women who haven't played you yet are probably a little scared. And the women who have . . ."

"Hate me," I say.

"I think some have held on to some hurt feelings, yes."

"Because I whipped their asses and I'll do it again?" I ask.

"You know you have a way of . . . grinding your opponents down. You know people have not always liked your way of winning."

"Next time I mop the court with someone, I'll remind myself to pretend I'm 'shocked that it went my way' and that it 'could have been anyone's game,'" I say.

Gwen laughs. "Right, but in the meantime, it does not leave us with many options."

I look at my dad. "This is kind of funny, right?" I ask him. "I'm thirty-seven years old, and still no one wants to play with me."

"So we get you a regular hitter," he says. "It's not like we've needed to practice against other professionals before."

"But I want to know how I stack up before I go out there," I tell him. "This isn't like before. This is . . . I need to play against my peers. To see if I still can. I need to do that here on a private court. Before I go out there in front of the world."

Gwen nods.

"Did you ask Nicki?" I say.

"You want me to ask Nicki Chan to hit with you?" Gwen says.

"No," I say.

"Okay, well," Gwen says, "Ali did have one idea."

I look at her and realize she has not driven all the way here to *hold my hand*. She's here to *pitch me* on something. "What is it?"

"I have an old client who is in a similar boat to you," Gwen says.

"Who on earth is in a similar boat to *me*?"

Gwen laughs. "A tennis player I used to work with, who is on the older side of things, trying to give it one last go around the block. And you two might be able to help each other out."

"Who are you talking about? Ilona Heady? She's barely thirty."

"No," Gwen says. "Not Ilona."

"Will Ilona play me?"

"You beat Ilona at Monte Carlo in '88 and then told reporters it was 'embarrassingly easy,' so no, Ilona does not want to play you."

"It *was* embarrassingly easy. I was embarrassed for her. That's *empathy*."

"So who is it?" my dad says.

"Just . . . please get yourself in the right mind space to hear me out."

"Spit it out."

"Bowe Huntley."

I haven't spoken to Bowe Huntley since we slept together in Madrid and he never called me again. "You've got to be kidding me," I say.

"That man is an embarrassment to tennis," my father says. "Yelling at linesmen? Throwing his racket?"

"Bowe has stopped drinking. He got divorced last year. He's in a period of . . . reflection. And, despite what you may think of his tantrums . . . he's a very talented tennis player. Even still. But this is going to be his last year on the ATP."

"He's older than me," I say.

"He's thirty-nine."

"He hasn't won a Slam in almost a decade," I remind her.

"Yes, that's true. Though he does still win a title here and there. And he is a good guy. Truly. He left the agency to go over to YRTA about ten years ago, but we stay in touch. He's not what he seems."

"Yes," my dad says. "I believe Carrie knows him . . . well."

I glare at my father. "All right, keep it to yourself."

Gwen looks at me. "The bottom line is, if it's uncomfortable for you, don't do it. But if you do want a player you can test yourself against . . . Bowe is in."

"You already asked him?"

"I wasn't going to get you on board without knowing if he would do it."

I look at my dad.

"You can just get a hitter," he says. "We can even do two-on-ones, to keep you running around the court."

I consider it. I imagine myself growing more and more confident heading into Melbourne, hitting against amateurs. Only to be clobbered once I'm up against anybody on the circuit. The thought of it knocks the wind out of me.

But I also really don't want to see Bowe Huntley. That knocks the wind out of me too.

"I don't know," I say. "I have to think about it."

• • •

Later that evening, I am in my sweatpants with a seltzer water in my hand, sitting down to watch *ER,* when the phone rings. I mute the television just as the theme song begins.

I put my drink down and pick up the receiver, expecting it to be my father telling me he ran out of toilet paper or shampoo and asking me if I have any.

But it's Bowe.

"Oh, hi," I say.

"Long time," he says.

"Yeah," I say. "I guess it has been."

"Well," he says, "sorry to call so late, but Gwen said you might want to hit together, and I realized if we're doing this, we need to make a plan ASAP."

"You are interrupting my new favorite show, but fine, we can talk."

Bowe laughs. "Are you watching *ER*? What's happening?"

"I don't know, I'm talking to you instead of watching because you think it's all right to call people at ten at night."

"Well, I'll wait," he says.

"You want me to tell you what's happening on *ER*? You can't just turn it on?"

"I'm staying at the home of a nice lady friend I just met who doesn't believe in owning a television."

"Oh, jeez," I say. "I don't know who is worse, you or her." I turn to the TV. "Dr. Lewis is talking to Carter." I pause. "Do you really want me to give you the play-by-play on this entire episode?"

"Sort of," he says. "The rerun won't be until summer."

I sit down on my sofa, crossing my legs. "Okay, fine. Now they have rushed a teenager into an OR. Oh, here we go! Here's George Clooney!"

"Love Dr. Ross."

"I like the one who doesn't put up with the bullshit. What's his name?"

"Benton."

"Yeah, he's my favorite."

"Of course he is," Bowe says.

"Is this really why you called?" I ask. "To have *ER* narrated to you?"

"No," he says. "I want to know if we're doing this thing. Gwen said you weren't fully on board with the idea."

"I just said I wanted to think about it."

"Well, what is there to think about?"

"I don't know, Bowe. That's why I need time."

"You have to *think about* what to *think about*?"

"I'm trying to be thoughtful about everything I'm doing over the next few months."

"Look," he says. "This is a good idea. We can both help each other a lot. You need somebody who can help you get back in fighting shape. I need someone to help me . . .'"

"Remember how to win a match?" I ask.

Bowe is silent for a moment, and then he says, "You are not as charming as you think you are."

"If I remember correctly, you're the one people are supposed to find charming."

"A lot of people *do* find me charming."

"How nice for them."

"I remember this about you—every sentence that comes out of your mouth is like a razor blade."

"Yeah, maybe that's why you slept with me and never called me again."

He laughs. "Bullshit."

"It's what happened."

"It is not. I might have spent a big portion of the eighties drunk and confused about what tournament I was at, but let me make one thing perfectly clear, Soto. Before you left my hotel in Madrid, I said, 'I'll call you.' And you said, 'This can just be what it is.' And I remember that because I thought, *Wow, she's so cool*, and I also thought, *She doesn't want to see me again.*"

"Am I supposed to believe that I left you heartbroken?"

"Not at all. I just don't want you pretending I'm a womanizer, because I'm not."

"You are a womanizer. Everyone knows that."

Bowe is the most fined tennis player in history. But he was once also one of the best. He has eleven Grand Slam titles—mostly from the Australian Open and the US Open in the early eighties. He was one of the best returners I'd ever seen. He was also loud and handsome and intoxicating. And almost all of the women on the WTA tour knew they should stay away from him—which was why none of us did.

"Well, I wasn't just trying to get in your pants is my point."

"Yeah, sure. Regardless, everyone on both tours thinks you're a dick."

"And they call you a bitch, apparently."

I laugh. *The Dick and the Bitch,* coming this fall to NBC."

Bowe laughs, uproariously loud. And I can't help but smile.

"So what do you say, then? Do you want to play together or not?" he asks me. "My ankle is shot. My wrist never really fully recovered from my surgery two years ago. My back is killing me. I'm the oldest guy on the tour. But I still have some fire. And I know you do too. Plus, I know your game, Soto. I know you're the best goddamn player tennis has. I don't care how long you've been off the court. If I can hit a few balls off you—if I can learn from you—I want to."

I look around the room, thinking, trying to come up with a reason to say no. But the truth is, he is my best shot at refining my game in time. And that has to be the most important thing. That has to outweigh everything else. "Fine," I say. "Yes. When are you back in town?"

"I play Frankfurt on Monday; I fly straight home to L.A. after. How about the Sunday I'm back, first thing, we can get started. I'll come to you."

"Sounds like a plan," I say. "Javier will join. And what about you? Who's coaching you now? Still Gardner?"

"Uh, no," he says. "Pete's gone on to Washington Lomal, of all people. It's just me now. No coach."

I let the silence last too long. Bowe chimes in after a few seconds. "It's fine. He stuck by me as long as he could. I know what I am, Soto. I'll see you next week."

After I hang up the phone, I sit there holding on to the receiver, not yet letting it go.

MID-NOVEMBER

Two months until Melbourne

I AM SITTING OUTSIDE ON THE COURT, STRETCHING, AT EIGHT-THIRTY IN the morning.

The air is dewy and brisk. The sun has begun to warm up the day. I keep looking over my shoulder at the driveway, wondering when Bowe will arrive.

My father paces by the sideline. "He's already two minutes late."

"Maybe this whole thing was a mistake," I say.

My father whips his head in my direction. "I thought Bowe was a mistake the second Gwen suggested it."

Another few minutes go by as I stand up and stretch out my shoulders and my arms, glancing at the driveway one more time. My father looks at me. "You're nervous," he says. "But you shouldn't be. You're serving at a speed that the midtier players can't hit. Chan, sure. Cortez or Antonovich, I think so. But that's it. You're quicker than you were even last week. You're disguising your shots beautifully. And that's just off a month and a half of training. You are playing at an elite level already."

I look at him.

"And each day you're getting better," he adds. "Have you noticed that?"

I let go of my shoulder and stand up straighter. He's right. At some point in my career, I'd stopped thinking that way. I let myself focus entirely on stats and records. But that had never been the real goal. I shake my head, recalibrating, stunned for a moment at just how easy it had been for me to forget the most basic ideals I grew up with.

People act like you can never forget your own name, but if you're not paying attention, you can veer so incredibly far away from everything you know about yourself to the point where you stop recognizing what they call you.

"Every day," I say, "I'm playing better than the day before."

My father nods. "So do not live in the future, *cariño*. Don't play the first match in Melbourne months before you've gotten there. We don't know what kind of player you'll be that day."

"I will be two months better of a player than I am today," I say.

A Jeep pulls into the driveway and Bowe gets out. He looks older and grayer than the last time I saw him, weathered—like a leather wallet that has lightened and wrinkled at the folds. He sees us and waves as he heads toward the court.

My father pats me on the back. "Let's see what this thug over here has got left in him. He's already ten minutes late."

"Be nice, Dad."

"I will be perfectly nice to his face, you know that," he says. "But it is my God-given right to complain about him behind his back."

One of the great injustices of this rigged world we live in is that women are considered to be depleting with age and men are somehow deepening.

But Bowe swiftly puts any of my resentments about that to rest. He looks like shit and I take him in straight sets.

When the match is over, he sits on the ground, staring at the racket in his hand. "You demolished me," he says.

"My daughter is one of the very best in the world," my father reminds him.

"Yes, I know," Bowe says. "But still."

My father rolls his eyes and goes inside to get more water. I sit down next to Bowe.

"Today went well for me," I say. "I'm not going to lie."

Bowe looks up. His brown eyes are so big and wide, and his hair is cut close to his head, gray creeping across his temples. His skin is sun-beaten. It has been a big ten years.

"You played well," he says. "You're not all that far from the Carrie I knew."

I am surprised by his magnanimity. I would not possess it in his position.

"Thank you," I say. "There is still a long way to go. Still seems like I'm running through mud out there."

Bowe nods. "I know what you mean."

"And it is not enough to be *good*," I say. "It's not even enough to be great. I have to be . . ."

"You have to be better than you've ever been," Bowe says, "to go up against this crop of women. I've seen some of them. Chan's a killer, but Cortez is deadly too."

"I know," I say, feeling myself tense up.

"Look, I've been in this part of my career for years now. Competing against people half my age, practically. Some of these women you're going to face are twenty years younger than us. They have brand-new knees—fresh from the factory. Brand-new everything, not a stress fracture on them."

"That is not helping—"

"Brand-new hearts too. They haven't been shattered yet, haven't taken a beating over and over. New hearts bounce back faster."

"You're not—"

"You know what my heart is—no, my soul? It's like an old

mattress that's been bounced on so many times that now, if you put your hand on it, it leaves a permanent imprint. That's what my soul is now. Just a big old mattress showing every dent."

"Were you always so good at self-pity?"

Bowe laughs. "Why do you think I drank so much?"

I turn from him and let a tennis ball roll away from me, just watching it drift farther and farther into the court.

I say, "Listen, I can't get better unless you get better. I need to play somebody good, and I need it *now*. So quit it with the crying and try to play the game."

Bowe looks away. "I don't know. It might be better to get someone else. Somebody on the WTA."

I sigh. "It's not that simple." I look at the net, rattling in the breeze, and then back at him. "Nobody on the WTA will play me."

Bowe's eyes go wide. "Are you serious?"

"Bowe, I've heard it enough times; I don't need it from you too. Nobody likes me—I get it."

Bowe catches my gaze. "I always liked you."

I roll my eyes. "Being attracted to me and liking me are two different things."

Bowe looks at me a moment longer. "Huh," he says. "Wow."

"What?"

"I . . . you're right."

"You didn't already know that?" I shake my head. "You're almost forty. How emotionally stunted can you be?"

Bowe looks at me and frowns. But he has the grace to refrain from pointing out that I am throwing stones from my glass house.

"Why are you coming back?" Bowe says. "Why put yourself through this?"

I shrug. "I just can't . . ." I tell him. "I just can't let her have it."

Bowe nods.

"Why are you doing it?" I ask. "Why not quit?"

"I don't know," Bowe says, sighing. "Maybe I should."

"But you haven't. So it must be for some reason."

"I suppose it must," he says. He stands up and wipes the dirt off himself. He reaches his hand out to pull me up, but I stand up on my own.

"Let's go again," he says. "Two out of three. I'm not gonna win any tournaments playing how I played this morning. And quite frankly, neither are you."

"You sure you're ready to play me again?" I ask him as I walk toward the baseline. "Can you suffer the indignity of losing to a woman twice in one day?"

"I told you, Carrie," Bowe says. "You're not as charming as you think you are."

"Okay," I say, shrugging. "But I don't think I'm very charming at all."

Just Because Soto Can Doesn't Mean She Should

By John Fowler

Op-Ed, Sports Section
California Post

Much has been made of Carrie Soto's comeback. In her interview with *SportsPages* last week, Carrie seems to think she has a great chance of winning in Melbourne at the top of next year. "A lot of people think I'm crazy. But I've done exceptional things in my career. Remember that." As if she would ever let us forget.

Soto is just one more in a string of desperate celebrities who cannot live without a spotlight. One would hope by now she would have moved on to starting a family or running her foundation. But no. She's back on the court.

Over the course of my lifetime, I have watched many of the sports I love become commodified into celebrity-industrial-complex machines, churning out champions who turn out to be no role models at all. Tonya Harding and Pete Rose come to mind. And I write this as the nation waits with bated breath to find out what kind of man O. J. Simpson truly is.

It seems the best we can hope for from our legends is that they merely become self-obsessed image-conscious shills for soft drinks, sneakers, and watches.

And who is surprised? This is but the natural consequence of putting athletes on the front of a Wheaties box
all those years ago. When they retire, they cannot stand
to be like the rest of us, seeing our own faces only in
family photos and mirrors. They yearn for yet another
billboard.

Soon, Carrie Soto is sure to show us just exactly what
five years of retirement does to a tennis player's body.
But I'm more interested in what those five years have
done to her brain.

It appears she is today even worse than she was back
then: even more self-absorbed and wickedly ambitious.

If it makes for a good show, then who am I to stand in
the way of the spectacle? But I can tell you this: When
the players set this kind of example in a gentleman's
sport, no one wins.

Why I'm Thankful for Carrie Soto

Letter from the Editor

Helene Johannes
Vivant Magazine

When I was eleven years old, my mother sat me down at the table and explained to me that I was now too old to wrestle in the backyard with my younger brothers.

"It's not appropriate anymore," she said. She had softened the reprimand by making me a warm apple cider. "I need you inside with me from now on, helping with dinner."

That evening, I sat at the kitchen table watching my three little brothers wrestle as I peeled the potatoes.

My mother has long passed away and my brothers and I are all adults now. But I would be lying if I said that the memory of losing my favorite pastime with my brothers—running around in the crisp fall weather, hearing the crunching of leaves as I tackled one of them—didn't ache.

Some men's childhoods are permitted to last forever, but women are so often reminded that there is work to be done.

And yet here is Carrie Soto, daring to play.

I felt a sense of thrill at her announcement last month. And it's not just me; so many of my friends seem to agree. Carrie Soto is living the dream for all of us, coming back for one last go around the block.

As we look ahead to what 1995 may have in store for us, our writers this month have focused on *what's new:* the ingénues, the rookies, and the Young Turks. We have our cover story with breakout star Cameron Diaz, an upcoming look at what's next for Aaliyah, and a conversation with Ethan Hawke and Julie Delpy, the cast of Richard Linklater's upcoming *Before Sunrise.*

But I would like to take the time to also celebrate those of us from the previous generation who are staying in the fight.

We know that Carrie Soto is likely not going to win a single title next year. And it would, perhaps, behoove her to admit it now and spare us all the embarrassment of having to pretend otherwise. One cannot deny the toll age takes on an athlete's body, no matter how unjust. She will be a shadow of the dominant Battle Axe we knew in the eighties. But that is far from the point.

It is her right to have fun, to keep playing. To not help with dinner.

And I, for one, am glad she's exercising it.

DECEMBER 1994

A month and a half before Melbourne

I STOP READING THE SPORTS PAGES FOR NOW. INSTEAD, IN THE MORNINGS as I drink my smoothie and eat my almonds, I read the tabloids. Cindy Crawford and Richard Gere are getting divorced, which sort of shocks me, though I don't know why.

I love gossip magazines. I cannot get enough of the delicious buzz of who is sleeping with who and what they are naming their babies. It is one of the many benefits to my dating life no longer making the covers of the magazines. I can read them at breakfast without fear. One tiny moment of peace in an otherwise grueling day.

After breakfast, every morning, I work out. Then, in the afternoon, I do drills. And then every evening, a little after five P.M., the lights kick on, and Bowe shows up and we play in the cool evening air.

At first, I win almost every time. But he improves quickly, too quickly. Soon, I am only winning when we play two out of three. Bowe starts winning when we play three out of five. An acute reminder that I need to work on my stamina.

Now, today, Bowe is playing the best he's ever played. His serve is sharper, his focus is there. His shots are surprising me. He's broken my serve multiple times today.

"This!" my father shouts to him across the court. "This is the player I wanted to see!"

"What?" Bowe calls out.

"I said this is the player I wanted to see!"

Bowe nods and then serves the ball. I suspect he heard my father the first time and simply hadn't known how to respond.

Bowe and I play until about eight, when he squeezes out a win. I started tripping up in the last set, sending my forehands wide, my backhands into the net.

My father does not need to say anything. I can tell what he's thinking when he catches my eye. If I play this way in the Open, I'm done for.

Bowe packs up his kit.

"So, tomorrow?" he says. We had agreed to one more session before he heads out for the ATP tour. We'll play in Melbourne a bit too, before the tournament starts—acclimate to the weather and the courts. My father has already planned out which days I'll be doing drills and practice matches and resting. He can tell you in December what I'll be doing down to the minute at the end of January.

"Tomorrow it is," I say.

"I'd be open to just hitting drills back and forth, instead of a match," Bowe says. "We both could use some work on our serves. I'm breaking your serve more. I can feel that my backhand is getting more precise. But my own serve . . . I still need . . ."

"You need to work on your first serve for a solid week," my father interjects. "Your form right now is pathetic compared to what you are capable of."

"Dad . . ."

"No, it's fine," Bowe says.

"Of course it's fine!" Javier says. "Because you know I'm right. You should not be using a pinpoint stance. You do not need power. You need precision, you need to—"

"I've used a pinpoint stance my whole life. That's why I can smoke 'em past fuckers like Randall."

"Randall quit tennis seven years ago. And you aren't smoking them past anybody anymore."

"So what's your point?" Bowe says, his voice rising.

"My point is, practice a platform stance. You still have power, somehow. But you have lost your accuracy. You're relying on your second serve way too much. Get your first serve past the net and you will win more."

Bowe looks at my father. And then at me.

"He's right," I say.

"Yeah," Bowe says, grabbing his things and walking off. "I fucking know he's right. I'll see you both tomorrow morning."

As Bowe drives away, I look at my father.

"Why did you do that?" I say. "You're not his coach—you don't even like him."

My father shakes his head from side to side. "He's . . . he's improving significantly just playing against you. And you . . . you're hitting about three to four miles per hour faster on some strokes than just last week. He's throwing shots at you just like ones we can expect from Nicki and Cortez and maybe Antonovich. And you're . . . you're hitting them better than you have all fall, *hija*. Do you see that?"

"So this is . . . it's working," I say.

"Yes," my dad says. "It's working."

The next morning when Bowe shows up, he will barely look at my father.

But on his first serve, he's using a platform stance.

My father stands on the sidelines and clocks it. I can see him hold back a smile.

JANUARY 1995

Melbourne

Less than a week before the beginning of the Australian Open

MY FATHER AND I HAVE BEEN IN MELBOURNE FOR TWO WEEKS NOW.
Bowe has been in and out of town, playing in the Hard Court Championships in Adelaide and the Sydney Outdoor.

I feel a sense of missing out as he goes off to the ATP tour. The
1995 tennis season has begun, and it feels wrong not to be a part of
it. But I am not the player I was fifteen years ago. My best shot at
winning any of these is to stay focused on the Slams.

Every morning, my father and I cross-train until lunch. And then, on
the days when Bowe is in town, he and I play a match in the afternoon.

A fan or two have found us some days, watching us rally back and
forth. But today the crowd has grown significantly. There must be
twenty people hanging around, trying to get a glimpse.

I can't stop glancing at them. I can't keep my eye on the court
like it should be. I miss a few shots.

"Can we tell them to leave?" I ask my father during a changeover.
Bowe is up a set.

"I've already asked them to," my dad says. "I'm not sure what else we can do. Especially because Bowe's pandering to them."

I look at Bowe as he waves and then walks over to the crowd. I watch him sign an autograph and take a picture. His smile is big and wide, nearly brilliant under his baseball cap.

These past weeks he's played a couple great matches in his tournaments. He's lifted himself a few spots in the rankings. It is obvious to me now that there is an element of Bowe's game that I haven't accounted for. When the energy of the crowd is there for him, when eyes are on him, he rises to it.

"C'mon, Soto!" Bowe yells as he makes his way back to the baseline, ready to begin again.

I get in position, and he serves it to me—fast, deadly. An ace.

I look to my father and see that his face is completely blank. I feel my shoulders tense.

So much of my game is coming back, as if my muscles have a long and generous memory. But sometimes I lose control of my swing, or I choose the wrong shots. And that is not a sign of a player who is ready for a Slam.

Bowe hits two more aces past me over the course of three games. When he sends a groundstroke down the center and I mis-hit, I nearly throw my racket. I glance at my father, whose face has grown tighter.

Bowe takes the next game, making it 4–1 in the second set. I want to stop the match. I do not want all these spectators watching me—it's their first sight of me after five years and I am *tanking*. I want to jump out of my skin. On my next serve, I double-fault twice in a row. *Fuck. Fuck. FUCK.*

My father pulls me aside. "What's going on?"

"I don't know."

"You do know."

"I don't want to embarrass myself in front of these people."

"When you get out there, in the first round next week, everyone is going to be watching you."

"Thanks, Dad."

"Get. It. Together," he says. "You did not work this hard for the past four months to choke now."

"I know that!" I say.

"*Hija,* you can either beat the other players out there or you can't. This is when you will find out. But I have never known you to be afraid of the truth."

I take a deep breath. The truth was always in my favor before.

"Let's go!" Bowe yells. "No coaching during a match."

"It's not a real match, Huntley!"

"It is if I'm winning it, Soto!"

Three hours later, Bowe and I are sitting at a bar a few blocks from the arena. Bowe's drinking a seltzer water with lemon. I've ordered an iced tea.

"You didn't have to do that," he says as I pick up my glass. "You can have alcohol in front of me."

"You're not tempted?"

"I'm tempted every day. I just . . . It's not your problem."

"Why did you quit?" I ask.

"Is this therapy?" he says, and then sighs. "I quit because I don't want the life I had when I was drinking. I'm ready for something quieter, less stressful, less dramatic. Less getting arrested for public intoxication, more staying in on Saturday nights."

"It was only once, right?" I say. "You getting arrested?"

"Once was enough for me, thank you," he says.

I am sitting with the sun in my face. The glare is making me squint.

"Do you want to switch spots?" Bowe asks. I shake my head; I have always liked the sun.

I look out into the bright afternoon. I can't stop tapping my foot on the ground. I look back at Bowe. I beat him so easily on my home court just six weeks ago. But now, in Melbourne, when I should be playing even better, he's just destroyed me.

"Are we friends?" I ask him.

Bowe sips his seltzer and raises his eyebrows. He puts his drink down. "I don't know. Maybe we're friends. Maybe we're more colleagues?"

"We spend a lot of time together," I say.

"Working."

"Helping each other out," I offer.

"Because it's good for both of us."

I nod and drink my iced tea.

"You act like you've never had a friend before," Bowe says.

I roll my eyes at him. "I've had a friend before."

Bowe has a glint in his eye. I know that smile, see how devilish it is. "But not many."

"What I'm asking is . . . are we close? Can we tell each other things?"

"I don't know, Soto. I just told you why I'm sober, so maybe. What is it you want to tell me?"

"I want to ask you something. From your point of view . . ." I say. "Why did I tank today?"

"Isn't that for your daddy to tell you?"

"You mean my coach, who happens to be my father?"

Bowe raises his eyebrow.

"Plenty of players are coached by their father."

"Yeah, when they are starting out. You're an adult woman."

I find it interesting that for him, it wasn't a sign of disloyalty back in '79 when I fired my father as my coach. Instead, he thinks it's *childish* to go back to my father now.

"Yeah, well, at least someone wants to coach me," I say.

Bowe's jaw shifts and he nods without saying anything. He takes a sip of his drink, the condensation of the glass dripping onto the table. It's hot outside. It will only get hotter as the tournament goes on. That is a leg up I have on a lot of the other women I'll be playing— I like this heat, this blistering sun.

"Fine. You want my opinion? You slow down in the second set,"

Bowe says. "Still. It's improving, but not much. So I know that the harder I run you around in the first set, the more likely I am to win. Today, that's exactly what I did, and by the second set you were done for."

I'm disappointed in his answer. I already know that my endurance is still my weak spot. My father and I have discussed it, and for the next week, I'll be doing sprints in the mornings to gear up for sustaining my efforts longer.

"Okay," I say. "Thanks."

"Your knee seems fine," he adds. "But you're afraid to lean on it. I can tell when I hit a wide one to your forehand—which is easy to do because you favor your forehand."

I nod again; I already know this. Though it is helpful to hear that he can sense it, which means my opponents might be able to as well.

I look out onto the street, watching people walk by the bar. I wonder how many—if any—of them have tickets to the tournament. If any of them will be in the stands watching me try to make something of all this. How many of them are calling me "the Battle Axe" but meaning "the Bitch."

"But none of that is why you tanked *today*," Bowe continues.

I look back at him. "You've got more?"

"You asked the question."

"Go ahead," I say.

"Your mental game sucks."

"Excuse me? My mental game is great. My shot selection is just as good as it's ever been. I'm still planning winners out three, four shots ahead. And you're barely keeping up with them."

Bowe nods. "Yeah, but that's not what I'm talking about."

"What are you talking about?"

"Back in the eighties, you were so unflappable. You knew you deserved that trophy. You were unafraid."

"That . . . is not true."

"Well, you faked it better. Have you read *The Inner Game of Tennis*?"

"I could write *The Inner Game of Tennis*."

"So that's a no. Because if you had read it, you'd know that you, of all people, could never write it."

"What's that supposed to mean?"

"When you're out there—I mean, I'm not in your head so maybe I'm wrong—but with each mistake you make, it looks like you're getting angrier and angrier. You've got so much on the line. If I can get you off-balance early, I can upset you for the rest of the match."

"I—" I start to disagree with him, but I can't decide which argument to make. That I *don't* do that or that *everyone* does that.

Bowe leans forward on the table and moves his drink out of the way. "This guy, the *Inner Game of Tennis* guy, he talks about two selves. Self 1 and Self 2. Self 1 says, 'C'mon, Huntley! Get it together!' Self 2 is the Huntley who's supposed to be doing the getting it together."

I say, "I get you so far."

"Self 2 is doing all the work, right? Self 2 is going to win you the game. Self 2 is the hero. Self 1 just yells and gets frustrated and gets in the way."

"I see," I say.

"Look, Soto," Bowe says. His voice softens as he leans toward me. "You're a better player, physically, than me right now. You're a phenomenal player; that has not changed."

"Thank you," I say.

"But you do have weaknesses that you haven't faced before," he says. "We are older. Our bodies are different. You can't ignore that just because it's inconvenient."

"But if we both are struggling with that, I should be able to beat you, being the better player."

"The difference is that I've made peace with my limitations and you haven't. I can feel it. I can feel the struggle. I can see it on your face. And because of that, you're easy to manipulate. If I can mess with your head, if I can get you mad at yourself for not being the Carrie Soto you think you should be—I will beat you every time," he says. "And that means Nicki will slaughter you."

I take a sip of my iced tea. But then I can't bring myself to pull the glass away from my mouth. I down the rest in one gulp. And then I glance up.

"Okay," I say. "Thank you for your advice. I appreciate it."

Bowe leans back with his hands up in surrender. "Don't ask if you don't want the answer—"

"I said thank you, didn't I? Fuck."

Bowe laughs. "Yes, you did." He slaps his hand on the table. "All right, I'll bite. Do me now."

"It doesn't have to be tit for tat," I say.

"No, I want to know. I want a win, Carrie," he says. "I want a *big* one. I want to do something this season. I want to . . ." He looks me in the eye but then immediately looks away. "I want to prove I was right to stay in the game this long. If I do something great this season, everyone will say, 'Thank God he stuck around,' instead of . . . what they say now."

"'Why hasn't he given up?'"

"Yes, thank you," Bowe says.

I think about it and then chew a piece of ice left in the bottom of my glass. "You take too long to warm up. If you play somebody like O'Hara or Garcia who comes out of the gate hot, you're gonna be down a set before you know it."

Bowe nods. "I know," he says. "You're right."

"Your serve is better now that you're using the platform stance. But you don't disguise your shots enough. I can always tell where you're going."

"How?" Bowe asks.

"Your right foot turns in or out depending on how wide you're going."

"No, it doesn't," he says, blinking and shaking his head.

"Yes, it does."

"That's insane."

"It's still true."

"Okay," he says. "That's . . . thank you."

"I'm not done. You're way too lazy out there. You should be running down more balls. I can squeak any ball past you just by going wider than you feel like running. Everyone playing you knows you're old. They know your back gives you trouble. The first thing they're gonna do is hit it wide every time. You have to conserve energy, and I get that. But if you actually want to win something, you have to be willing to die to get to the ball, Huntley. And you're not willing to do that. So you're not gonna win any match that matters."

Bowe's jaw clenches; his lips are tight. He looks like he's about to get up from the table. I feel a flash of disappointment, because like most men, he can dish it out but he can't take it.

"It's not my fault if you can't handle the criticism," I say.

Bowe looks down at the table. He stares at the water ring his drink has made on the cardboard coaster advertising a beer he can't drink.

"Thank you," he says, finally, when he looks up at me. "Sincerely. Thank you."

"Oh," I say. "Okay, well . . . yeah, you're welcome."

Bowe leans into the table and keeps his voice low. He says, "I want to fucking win, Carrie. I want the crowd screaming my name. I want to know that for one moment, I am the best in the world. One last time."

I can't help but smile. "You are taking the words right out of my mouth."

Transcript

Sports Australia
SportsLine with Stephen Mastiff

Stephen Mastiff: Pivoting to women's singles for a moment, who are we keeping an eye on here, mate?
Harrison Trawley, editor of *SportsPages Australia*: Well, Nicki Chan, obviously. Everyone is expecting her in the final. But also, I'm looking at Ingrid Cortez, I'm looking at Natasha Antonovich. I'm excited to see some quick, daring moves from her. And I think power hitters like Odette Moretti out of Italy will have a good showing.
Mastiff: I notice you're not mentioning Soto.
Trawley: [*laughs*] No, nobody's looking at Soto for this. But if we want to talk about Americans, I think perhaps Carla Perez could seize the moment.

MID-JANUARY

The night before the Australian Open

MY FATHER AND I ARE SITTING ON THE PATIO OF MY HOTEL SUITE, looking out over the city, discussing the draw, which was announced earlier today. I'm in section 7. In my first match I'll be playing a twenty-two-year-old Czech serve-and-volley player named Madlenka Dvořáková. We are playing day 1 at Rod Laver Arena, the highest-profile court.

"It is not an accident," my father says. "That they have you center court against a low-ranked player. You're unseeded, but they are behind you."

I shake my head. "They just know it will make them money. To keep me in the tournament as long as they can."

I look out over the small slice of Melbourne that we can see from my hotel, including the Yarra River as it crosses through the city. I have sat outside looking at this river so many times in my life—as a rookie, as a challenger, as a champion. Now it's as a comeback. I am both stunned to find myself here again and positively sure I've never left.

"You'll go out there tomorrow," my father says, "and you'll beat her, *no le vas a dar tiempo ni de pensar.*"

I inhale sharply—imagining the opposite of what my father is describing. What if tomorrow I lose in the first round? What if this whole thing is over before it's even begun? The idea of it is so humiliating, I feel nauseated.

The phone rings, and the clang of it startles me. I walk into the bedroom to answer it. "Hello?"

"Good luck tomorrow," Bowe says.

"You too."

"Fucking crush her. Make her bleed."

"Will do," I say. "You too."

"We can do this," Bowe says. "At least, you can. I know it."

"Thank you," I say, almost choking on the words. I am suddenly embarrassed at how transparent the emotion in my voice is. "I guess this is it. No turning back now."

"No, I suppose not," he says. "But you wouldn't turn back even if you could, Soto."

THE 1995 AUSTRALIAN OPEN

WHEN I WAKE UP IN THE MORNING, I FEEL A HUM IN MY BONES THAT I have not felt in years. It is startling, the buzz of unexpected joy.

It is still early as I get out of bed. The sun has not yet risen. I feel a sense of control that I sometimes get when I wake up before the rest of the world. I have the feeling that the day's events are mine to determine, that I hold everything in the palm of my hand.

I get up to get ready for a short run. I throw on dolphin shorts and a T-shirt, a pair of sneakers. I go down to the lobby. But before I can get out the front door of the hotel, the woman behind the check-in desk stops me.

"Ms. Soto?" she says.

"Yes?" I want to get running. "What is it?"

"A package arrived for you," she says.

She hands me a padded envelope with a return address from Gwen. I rip the end off. Inside, there is a gift box not much bigger than a book. On top is a note in Gwen's unmistakable cursive.

If anyone can do this, it is you.
Track One —G.

I open the gift box to see a Discman with a pair of headphones plugged in, a CD already in it. It is Elton John's *Caribou*. I look at the first song and laugh.

"Ms. Soto?" the woman says, clasping her hands together.

"Yes?"

"Would you mind terribly if I asked for an autograph?"

I sigh, but then I remember there are a lot of people who wish I would crawl into a hole right now. So I'll take a kind face over that. "Sure, yes, of course you can," I say.

She hands me a piece of paper and a pen. "Oh, wow, Ms. Soto, this is . . . this is just amazing," she says. "Thank you so much."

I take the pen and I scrawl *Take 'em all down, Carrie Soto* across the paper and hand it back to her.

"Thank you so much, Ms. Soto," she says. "I've been a fan of yours since I was thirteen and you won here back in '85. I was there in the stands with my father. He loves you too."

"You don't mind that I'm an arrogant, ambitious bitch?"

She laughs. "No, I do not," she says.

"I'm going to win today," I tell her.

"I have no doubt," she says.

I nod at her, take the Discman out of the box, and put the headphones on. I tap the desk and smile at her as I make my way back toward the door. I press play and start running out of the lobby.

Instantly, I hear the familiar stinging riff of "The Bitch Is Back."

I run on the sidewalk past the hotel. I breeze past people out for coffee, parents with strollers moseying down the street. When I turn the corner and Elton John gets to the chorus, I know—I can feel it in the way the blood is pumping with intention through my veins— that Madlenka Dvořáková is dead in the water.

· · ·

"All eyes are going to be on your first serve, to see who you are at thirty-seven. Knock the socks off her from the jump," my father says to me just outside the locker room. "Scare her, you hear me? Scare everybody out there."

I nod, staring down at the scuffs on my Break Points. I picked out the white ones with green stripes this morning, to go with my white tank top and tennis skirt.

This moment—my father and me here in the hall, waiting to go out—feels just like it used to. I'm back at war, after years of not knowing how to live during peacetime. This is the only place where I make sense to myself.

I pick up my racket and turn it around in my hand. My whole arm begins throbbing, ready to be used.

I luxuriate, for one moment, in the quiet din of the stadium that filters through the walls. I inhabit the silence of this moment with my father, when we are still asking questions and do not yet have to live with the answers.

"*Te quiero mucho, pichona,*" he says.

I open up my eyes. "I know. I love you too."

"Go out there . . ." He looks me directly in the eye with an intensity I have not seen in years, maybe even since I was a kid. "And show them that the Bitch, the Battle Axe—whatever they want to call you—it doesn't matter. They cannot stop you. And they don't get to decide what your name is. Carrie Soto is back."

I breathe in deep and then wipe the tops of my shoes clean and start walking—one step at a time—onto the court.

SOTO VS. DVOŘÁKOVÁ

1995 Australian Open

First Round

IT IS NOT DEAFENING, BY ANY MEANS, BUT AS I STEP INTO THE ROD Laver Arena I can hear it begin. "Car-rie, Car-rie, Car-rie!"

I look up to see signs with my name on them. *Welcome back, Carrie!* and *The Bitch Is Back!* I smile at the last one, and I point to the young woman holding it.

I can only imagine what the sportscasters are saying in their booths, what delightful euphemisms they are using to describe just how "too old" or "too cocky" they think I am. It will be a pleasure to make them report my win today. I breathe in deeply, ready to make it happen.

Madlenka Dvořáková looks so tiny, so far away. Her long blond hair is pulled back into a bun. She is wearing a navy blue tank and matching tennis skirt. She looks guarded and nervous, and though her right hand grips the racket firmly, I can see the fingers quivering on her left hand.

I win the coin toss.

As I make my way to the baseline, my whole chest starts thumping, my heart beating heavy and strong. The crowd cheers, and I look up into the players' box to see my father taking his seat.

The loudspeaker erupts. "Miss Soto has won the toss and elected to serve first." I can feel the vibrations of it in my sternum and feel myself turn on, every far edge of my body tingling. I hear the next part in my head before it comes over the loudspeaker, the routine as known to me as my own name.

Linesmen, ready.

"Linesmen, ready."

Players play.

"Players play."

I stand on the baseline and hold the ball in my hand. I brush the felt with my thumb, feel the roughness of it in my palm. And then I bounce it, over and over. Until my mind is clear.

I throw the ball up in the air, pull my arm back, and even before I hit the ball I know—*I can feel*—it is a stunner.

It whistles past Dvořáková so fast she barely has time to step toward it. First point is mine.

I feel the roar of the crowd underneath my feet, ringing into my bones. I look to my father, who nods.

I hold the first game.

On the second, the crowd grows wild when I get to break point. They scream when I break Dvořáková's serve, taking the second game.

I hold the third. It is now three games to none.

In the next, Dvořáková gets some fire in her, and she holds the fourth. But she and I both know the set is mine. I win the next three.

"Set is Soto's."

The crowd cheers, some boo. I try not to pay attention. I stay focused. I cannot let up.

Halfway through the second set, Dvořáková's groundstroke is getting weaker, but I am now only getting stronger. Perhaps it is the adrenaline of the fight, or the fact that I've been training even harder since my conversation with Bowe, but I have full control of my power. I am not letting up. I come in for the kill time and again.

I start smiling during the changeovers, nearly giddy. I am delighted by all of these sounds I've missed—the crowd screaming, the ball girls scrambling on and off the court, the linesmen calling shots.

I am winning this thing.

My last serve in the second set flies right past her. I jump into the air and pump my fist as the ball lands clean inside the lines with Dvořáková nowhere near it. My first match back, and it's mine in straight sets.

As the stadium cheers, I catch a glimpse of Dvořáková's face. Her jaw is tight, her head down. She looks completely blindsided by the way I have pummeled her. A twenty-two-year-old ranked in the bottom fifty, not a Slam title to her name, and she assumed she'd take me.

"Who's next?" I call out, racket in hand. I'm not sure anybody in the stands hears me, but it feels so good to scream into the roar of the crowd.

When I walk off the court, my father is standing there in the tunnel, waiting for me.

"*¡Excelente!*" he says. "Absolute perfection. You warrior, you king."

"The first of many," I say to him.

My father smiles but says nothing. His smile grows bigger as he turns and guides me toward the locker room, and soon he's laughing.

"What?" I ask him. "What are you thinking right now?"

"Nothing," he says. "It's just that . . . this is the part I missed the most. Me and you, in the tunnel."

IN MY NEXT MATCH, I BEAT AN AMERICAN I'VE NEVER MET BEFORE, A woman named Josie Flores, in straight sets. When I cinch the match with an ace, I jump into the air and spin. I bounce on both my feet, side to side, and throw my hands up.

In the post-match press conference, I am still jumpy, still pumped. My victories, no matter how early in the tournament, are *undeniable*. And I feel a near absence of worry.

Months of preparing, months of lying awake at night scared. But now the test is here, and I am killing it.

The first few questions are the usual softballs. "How does it feel to be back on the court?" "Did you expect to win your first two matches?" "What is it like to have your father coaching you again?"

I answer honestly. "It feels great to be back out there." "I expect to win every single match I play." "My father and I are both thankful for this opportunity to work together again."

A man in a sweater-vest speaks up. "Carrie, what do you say in response to players like Ingrid Cortez?"

"I'm not sure what you mean."

"This morning in her post-match, she said that you should have stayed on the bench."

This was news to me. I'd seen Ingrid around in the locker rooms—tall and humorless, with white-blond hair and wide shoulders and a lightness in her step that only a teenager can have—but I'd not spoken much to her.

"She says that she had not heard of you, before you came out of retirement," he adds.

"That's ridiculous—everyone in tennis has heard of me. Half of the world has heard of me." I lean away from the microphone, finished speaking. But then I lean back into it. "She can trash-talk however she wants, but let me say this: I'm grateful for every single woman who stood here before me. You don't see me going around asking who the Original 9 are, do you? No, because I know what I owe them. What about Althea Gibson and Alice Marble and Helen Wills? Suzanne Lenglen? Maria Bueno? I know whose shoulders I'm standing on. If Cortez doesn't, that's on her."

"But," he follows up, "is there any truth to her statement? Some people are saying this comeback is a stunt. What's your response?"

I can hear the shuffling of papers and the readjusting of microphones. But all eyes remain on me.

"I've proven so far that my game is outstanding," I say. "So everyone can whine and moan all they want about me being here, but I've earned the right."

Everyone's hands go up. There is a woman, young and focused, standing on the edge of the press corps.

"How are you feeling about the challenge ahead?" she says. "Your return may be controversial, but there are many spectators out there thrilled to see you playing again. It is expected you'll be playing Carla Perez in the next round. She seems to be the first player who could match your power. So . . . how bullish should your fans feel about seeing this run continue? How confident do you feel?"

I smile wide, and it grows into a laugh. "I'm gonna crush Carla Perez and anyone else I play on my way to the final. I am going to hold their beating hearts in my hand."

For a fraction of a second, none of the reporters in the room know quite what to say.

God, I've missed this.

Transcript

SportsHour USA
The Mark Hadley Show

Mark Hadley: . . . and Bowe Huntley appears to be doing better than anticipated. He annihilated Greg Simmons in the first round and even held up against Wash Lomal.

Briggs Lakin: Which is no easy feat, given that coach Peter Gardner left Huntley to work with Lomal. But Huntley came out the victor.

Hadley: Turning to the women's matches, Nicki Chan is sailing through, no surprise. Though we are seeing some pressure on that ankle.

Gloria Jones: She's an intense player. Intense players are prone to injury, we know that. But Nicki seems to have a handle on it.

Hadley: Natasha Antonovich meeting no resistance yet either. Let's talk about Carrie Soto. Some surprises there. Gloria, thoughts? You played her back in the day, did you not?

Jones: I did, Mark. And look, what can be said about Carrie during this tournament except that she's blowing us all away?

Hadley: She's a former world champion. Should we be impressed that she's in the third round? Dvořáková, Flores—these are not hugely formidable opponents she's faced.

Jones: Well, when you consider how many people had written Soto off before she even set foot back on the court, I do think it's impressive, yes.

Lakin: But, Gloria, I'm curious, because I consider you an incredibly gracious player—you were always respectful and polite on the court—so I'd love your take on Soto's attitude right now.

Jones: You mean the "Who's next?" thing?

Lakin: Well, yeah, screaming out "Who's next?" after your first round seems a bit brazen, no?

Jones: Well . . .

Lakin: And then in her match against Josie Flores, she gloated when she won.

Jones: She danced on the court.

Lakin: That's not gloating?

Jones: I don't know. But—

Lakin: If she has to come back, fine, I say. You know, I was one of the people saying from the beginning that it's her right to do it.

Jones: Yes, you did say that. I remember that.

Lakin: But is it not another thing entirely to come back and then act like an animal? "I am going to hold their beating hearts in my hand"? Where is the grace? The poise? This is a sport of ladies and gentlemen.

Jones: I'm not sure I agree with that. But your point, Briggs, I understand. Carrie Soto is a loud, abrasive player. She always has been. If we thought she'd mellow out, we were wrong.

Hadley: Unfortunately, Gloria, I agree with you on that. Looking forward, she's up against Carla Perez. Perez is a tough opponent. Can Carrie hold her own?

Jones: I'm not saying no—

Lakin: I would not bet on her, I'll say that.

I AM SITTING IN MY HOTEL ROOM, WATCHING NICKI PLAY ANDRESSA Machado. She has one set behind her; it's 7–6 in the second. Machado is serving, and Nicki is running all over the court, making every shot. I don't know how running with that much speed and hitting with that much intensity doesn't deplete her.

Nicki gets Machado to match point. Machado serves it low and wide; Nicki runs and hits the backhand with full force. It flies past Machado, sealing the match for Nicki. The crowd cheers. The commentators are fawning over her. "Nicki Chan sails to the third round, as if anyone had any doubt!"

No one but me seems to notice that as Nicki walks off the court, she's favoring her left ankle.

The phone rings, and I assume it's my father. That ankle won't have gotten by him either. But it isn't my father at all, it's Bowe.

"Oh, hi," I say.

"I mopped the floor with Lomal," Bowe says. I can hear his smile through the phone.

"I heard," I say. "Congratulations."

He says, "Congrats on beating Flores."

"Thank you, thank you. She never stood a chance."

"No," he says. "She didn't. But we all knew that, didn't we?"

"Knew what?"

"That you were going to come back and it would be like you never left."

"It might be a little early to say that," I say.

"You have something, Carrie," Bowe says. "You always have."

"And so have you."

"Do you really think that?" he asks.

"Yes," I say. "I do."

Bowe is quiet for a moment—a second too long. "Are you still there?" I ask.

"Yeah, I'm here," he says, but his voice becomes low and quiet, breathy almost. "Carrie, let me come up to your room."

I freeze.

"Carrie?" he says.

"Yeah."

"Did you hear me?"

"Yeah."

"And?"

"That's not what this is," I say. "It's not like that."

"It could be like that," Bowe says. "It was like that before."

"That was more than a decade ago."

"Please do not remind me how long I've been at this."

"I'm just saying . . . things are different now."

"Can't they be different in a good way?" he asks. "Like this time you don't tell me not to call you. Or if you do, I don't listen?"

"Bowe," I say, shaking my head. My heart is racing, and I immediately resent him for making me waste this much angst on something like sex, when I need to focus on my game. "No."

"Okay," he says, his voice sharper now, back to normal. "Message received. I won't ask again."

"Good, please don't."

"Good luck against Perez. I hope I get to see you crush her."

"Who do you play next?" I ask.

"O'Hara."

I inhale a bit too sharply, and he hears me.

"My thoughts exactly," he says.

"You can take him. You can."

"Uh-huh," Bowe says, laughing. "You're starting to sound like my sister. But I want you to sound like Carrie Soto."

I think about it for a minute. "He's going to exhaust you. If he gets you to five sets, you're done for. So don't let him get to five sets. Break his serve early in the first—that's your shot for an upset."

"Yeah," Bowe says. "I was thinking that too. About me being toast if it goes to five."

"So you do it in three," I say.

"Oh, sure, just take O'Hara in straight sets?" Bowe says. "It's that easy, huh?"

"It can be. If you want it bad enough."

"That's not always true, Soto. But thank you. I appreciate the pep talk."

SOTO VS. PEREZ

1995 Australian Open

Third Round

IT IS SCORCHING HOT. I CAN FEEL THE SWEAT ACROSS MY FOREHEAD and on my upper lip. I wipe it away with the towel in my hand as I sit down on the sideline, catching my breath.

On the opposite side of the court is Carla Perez. They call her the Baltimore Baseliner—and sportscasters have long talked about her forehand power. But they've never felt it like I've felt it today. It is devastating, the ball coming at me like a bullet shot from a gun.

She caught me off guard in the first set. But I came back to take the second, meeting her power and keeping my angles sharp. So now we are 5–5 in the third.

I settle in at the baseline. I bounce the ball in place, and then I look over the court to see Carla crouched, waiting.

The sun is behind me—I can feel it on my neck. Which means it's in Carla's eyes. I serve the ball high and fast, knowing Perez will have a hard time tracking it. She loses sight of it, and the ball lands at her feet. She scrambles backward to hit it on the rise. Her return is too wide.

I hold the game, which means I am now only one away from winning the set and the match.

The crowd begins to cheer. I've won many of them over. I can see it when I look up at the stands.

And here's the thing about arena sports—it's not just about how good you are at the game. It's about how good you are at feeling the crowd when they are with you and ignoring the crowd when they aren't.

It's about how swept up you can get in the momentum when winning, but also how defiant you can be when the tide turns against you.

Back in the eighties, I was great when the crowd was with me. But I was also great when they weren't. I did not need their love or their approval. I just needed the goddamn trophy.

Sadly for Carla, she does not have that single-mindedness. Not today.

I'm at break point within six serves.

Carla tosses the ball up into the air and then slams it across the net. It comes barreling toward me. I return it down the sideline, out of her reach.

Suddenly, my father is pumping his fist in the air.

Carla drops her racket onto the ground. I fall back onto the court in relief.

I'm through to the round of sixteen.

AT BREAKFAST THE NEXT MORNING, BOWE IS SITTING OUTSIDE ON THE hotel patio, eating scrambled eggs and toast.

He has a placid look on his face that reminds me of the surface of the ocean—which is to say it looks tranquil, but you know there are sharks mauling baby seals underneath.

I toy with the idea of turning around so that Bowe can't see me.

He lost to O'Hara yesterday. It was not just a defeat but a bloodbath. I saw the recap last night on the sports channels. Briggs Lakin said, "Someone come out here and put Bowe Huntley down."

I can't afford to sit here consoling him. I have a match to focus on. My father is meeting me in the lobby at eight to practice.

"You can at least not stare," Bowe says suddenly, not even lifting his head up but clearly speaking directly to me.

"I wasn't staring," I say. "I was . . . trying to gauge whether you wanted company."

Bowe laughs without a smile. "You were trying to figure out if you could ignore me because you're afraid losing is contagious."

I look at him. He looks handsome in his regular clothes—a pair of jeans and a black pocket T-shirt, his hair combed. It's like seeing an entirely different person.

I pick up my smoothie and walk over to his table. "I'm sorry you lost."

I grab a chair and sit.

"Thank you," he says. "That's kind of you, given that I wouldn't do the same."

"Is that true?"

"One time, after McEnroe lost a match to Borg, I wouldn't even look at him for the rest of clay season, in case he was bad luck."

"And did you win a lot? That clay season?"

He cocks his head. "No."

"I don't actually think luck has much to do with any of this," I say.

Bowe rolls his eyes. "If it wasn't bad luck that got my ass handed to me yesterday, then what was it?" He puts his finger out before I say a word. "Don't answer that."

"It's you," I say. "Luck didn't lose. You lost. Because you didn't break his first service game like I told you to."

"Oh, like it was that fucking easy?"

I shrug. "Could have been. If you used the platform stance Javier told you to use. It had been working for you, and then I looked at the footage from last night and you're using pinpoint again. Like a moron."

Bowe shakes his head. "You're lucky I'm on the first flight out of here. That way I can't stick around to watch you get ripped to shreds by Cortez."

"Oh, fuck off," I say as I get up from the table. "I was just trying to help you."

"Telling me what I *should have done* helps absolutely no one. You know, Carrie, you get a bad rap—but some of it is deserved."

"Or maybe some little boys are too sensitive."

Bowe looks up at me, his eyes narrow. "You are—"

"What?" I say, daring him.

"This whole thing, it's just not worth it," he says. "At all."

"All right, fuck you kindly," I say, and I walk away.

I barely look behind me as my father comes down out of the elevator with my kit. He is scanning the crowd but doesn't spot me until I walk up to him. He has a huge smile on his face.

"Oh," he says. "I didn't see you over there. Were you celebrating?"

"Celebrating?" I ask.

His smile grows wider.

"Nicki Chan tore her ankle up against Antonovich. She's out for the rest of the tournament."

"No way," I say.

My father nods.

"I could take this," I say.

"Yes, you could."

"I am going to take the whole goddamn tournament!" I say. "While she's nursing a bum ankle from her bad form, I can set this whole thing back where it belongs."

"Yes, you can, *cariño*," he says. "But not if you keep standing here bragging about it."

I am in the entryway, just two steps from the court. I can hear the noise of the crowd. I can see, from my narrow vantage point, a sign in the far back of the arena that reads *Take it to the finals, Carrie!*

There are three people standing between Ingrid Cortez and me—the guard, my father, and her coach are acting as the buffer between us. I am glad for it.

Yesterday, she told one of the newspapers, "I expect a swift and decisive victory in my favor. But I will try not to make it too embarrassing for Soto."

I hold my racket in my hand and play with the strings, making sure they are tight. I have seven more in my kit. I bounce a few times on the balls of my feet, wearing my neon pink Break Points and a neon pink sweatband to pull my hair away from my forehead.

My father puts his hand on my shoulder. I can feel the weight of him there, the weight of his belief in me, his excitement.

When I was playing pro the first time around—that decade and a half of clawing my way to the top and staying there for as long as I could—I did not delight enough in the accomplishments. I would win and then move on to the next challenge.

But right now, as I turn back to take another look at the crowd, I know that, in at least one way, I have evolved.

My older self knows that you must stop—in the middle of the chaos—to take in the world around you. To breathe in deeply, smell the sunscreen and the rubber of the ball, let the breeze blow across your neck, feel the warmth of the sun on your skin. In this respect, I love the way the world has aged me.

I inhale and hold the breath; I let it fill my lungs and raise my chest. And then I blow it out, ready to go.

I wipe the tops of my shoes and walk out onto the court.

SOTO VS. CORTEZ

1995 Australian Open

Round of Sixteen

I CROUCH BEHIND THE SERVICE LINE, WAITING FOR INGRID CORTEZ'S first serve.

She is over six feet tall. Her incisors are long and sharp, and when she smiles, she looks like she is about to bite.

She tosses the ball into the air and serves to the far-right edge of the box. I hit a groundstroke back. We rally for the point, and I take it. *Love–15.*

Another serve, another rally. My point. *Love–30.*

I look up at my father and see a small smile on his lips.

Cortez serves again, this time shorter, tighter. I hit it to the baseline. She hits it back soft. I win the point. *Love–40.* I'm already at break point in the first game.

She underestimated me. And it is a thrill to set her straight.

The sun has begun to burn, slow and hot. The crowd mumbles. I look up in the players' box to see my father. He is nodding at me, willing me to take the game. Then I look in the next section over, and Bowe is taking a seat.

He has canceled his flight, I guess. And come here, to watch me play Cortez.

My eyes soften as I look at him. *Sorry,* he mouths. I nod.

I move my eyes back to the court. Cortez serves high, with a top-spin and force that make it hard to predict. Still, I manage to get to the ball on the rise and return it deep to the baseline, a full two feet past her backhand.

The announcer says, "Game is Soto's." Bowe gives me a fist pump.

Over the next nine games, I take the set.

During the changeover, I look over at Cortez. She has talked such a big game of not being afraid of me, and I've pummeled her in the first set. I expect to see some anxiety or concern, a sign that she understands what she's up against now.

Instead, when she catches my eye, she smiles. As if none of this has worried her in the slightest.

During the second set, Cortez's groundstrokes become harder and faster. Her serves sting in my arm as I return them. I adjust quickly, reducing my shots just like I did back in the eighties up against Stepanova. I'm pulling out the Soto Slice.

It works, but she keeps pressing. She won't even take her winners where she can. She lobs the ball back over. Our rallies go sometimes as many as fifteen, sixteen shots.

I overshoot a couple groundstrokes, send a few cross-court backhands a hair too wide. *Fuck.*

The heat bears down on me. I can feel it on my neck and shoulders.

Out of the first five games in the second set, Cortez takes four.

At the changeover, I do not look into the players' box at my father or at Bowe. I bury my head in my towel and think. The momentum has shifted.

Grab control of the court. Don't slow down now.

I go back out there. Cortez gets more intense by the second. I'm trying to hit them back with as much fire as she has. I'm throwing my entire weight into my shoulder, my elbow heavy with the strain of it all. When I return one of her forehands, my racquet cracks in half.

The crowd screams.

As I get a new racket, I breathe out. *If she takes the set, she can take the match back. Don't let her take the match back. Don't do it. Don't do it.*

Cortez takes the second set.

I am breathless, drenched in sweat. My elbow is killing me. My knee has started to twinge. I pour half of the bottle of water over my towel and then put my towel over my head, cooling myself off and blocking the world out.

I have to win the next set. If I don't, the whole thing is over. And the whole thing cannot be over. Not yet.

This is what you've always been good at.

I put the towel down and stand up. I shake my head vigorously, shake the tension out of my arms and shoulders. I focus in. Get back on the court.

I serve the ball with the spin and precision that I am known for. It flies right past Cortez. An ace. The crowd cheers. And I pump my fist. I am clawing my way back.

It's 5–5 in the last set. I wipe the sweat from my face and try to stretch out my legs without telegraphing to Cortez how much my knee is aching. She isn't even sitting down during the changeover. She's bouncing on her toes, as if eager to get right back out there. My gut drops as I watch her—it's all coming into focus now. She ran me around in the second set, let me wear myself out. And now I'm slowing down when she is just getting started.

I squeeze the ball in my hand. How could I have played this so wrong? How could I have been so stupid? So green! *You did exactly*

*what she wanted! And now you're just as tired as everyone expected you
to be!*

I get myself back on the court, and Cortez's shots start coming at
me again, no sign of slowing, running me left to right, playing each
one she can to my backhand, knowing I don't have the energy to run
around the ball to play the forehand.

I run, I hit hard. I get points off her. But it doesn't matter. I can't
break her serve.

We're now at 5–6. If she wins this game, she wins the match.
CARRIE, DO NOT LOSE THIS.

I take the next point. *15–love.*

Her point. *15-all.*

Her point.

Her point.

Match point.

I serve it low. She returns it down the line. *Don't let them all be
right about you.*

I hit a drop shot. I can bring this back from the brink.

She returns it short. It bounces once. I run, but before I can
reach it, it bounces again.

I'm overwhelmed by a downpour of dread—as if the sky has
opened up and rained shame.

Cortez wins. I am done at the 1995 Australian Open.

"YOU GOT TO THE ROUND OF SIXTEEN YOUR FIRST TOURNAMENT BACK, *hija*," my father says. I'm lying in the trainers' room with an ice pack on my knee. "That is something to be proud of!"

"Since when was losing something to be proud of?"

In a moment, I'll have to shower and head to the press room for an interview. Cortez is already in there—gloating, I'm sure. Which is her right. She won, after all.

I'm the fucking loser who has to go out there and face all of them, knowing I've been both outsmarted *and* outplayed. And what makes it worse is that I know, *I know*, that she is not a better tennis player than me. That is the full weight of my failure.

"You have no patience," my father says, shaking his head. "And I know it is not my fault, because I tried to instill it in you. But you still don't understand that you can't have everything the second you want it."

"I'm going to ignore you right now," I say, sitting up and taking the ice pack off. "And go talk to the press about throwing away my chance at a title. But feel free to remember that lecture word for word and give it to me later."

"Carolina—" my father says.

"I'll meet you back at the hotel."

My father keeps talking, but I'm not listening. I walk away, into the locker room—past all the other players—and straight into the shower.

At the post-match press conference, the cameras and reporters are all over me.

"Cortez is a strong opponent, but one who probably could not have beaten you at your height," a female reporter says before I've even sat down. "How does that feel?"

"I did not play my best today. And I have to live with that."

"After three successful matches marking your return," a man says, "does this loss today take you by surprise? What are you feeling in this moment?"

"I am feeling like I played poorly and a bunch of reporters are asking me questions about how it feels to suck. I'm not happy right now. Obviously. I will use it as fuel to play better in the future, as I always have."

"But at some point," another man says, "everyone's game declines. Is that what we are seeing here?"

"Why don't you go ask Dvořáková, Flores, and Perez if they think my game is declining?"

"What will you do now?" a woman asks.

"I will go home and get back to work, ready to win in Paris."

"Yes, but, clay is historically your toughest surface," this woman says. "You've only won the French once, in 1983."

"Yeah, well," I say. "Watch me win it again in '95."

They continue to ask questions, but I get up from the table and walk out the door.

. . .

Back at the hotel, I get in the elevator and head to my room. But as I round the corner, I see Bowe standing in the hallway with his suitcase.

I stop right in my tracks.

"I wasn't sure if you're a 'wants company when they lose' sort of person or an 'everyone get away from me' sort of person," he says.

I say, "I'm an 'everyone get away from me' person."

Bowe nods. "Roger that," he says as he grabs his suitcase. "I'll be going."

I walk toward him. "You didn't have to move your flight," I say.

Bowe looks at his suitcase and then back up at me. "I did, actually," he says. "I . . . I didn't stand a chance against O'Hara. But I wouldn't have stood a chance against any of the players I've beaten in this tournament if it hadn't been for you."

"Practicing together?" I say.

"Yeah," he says. "But also . . . the fact that you're doing this. That you've shown up and said, 'I still have more to do.' Randall's retired, Stepanova's gone. McEnroe. Borg looked like a fool out there, coming back after so many years with his wooden racket. But not you. You look like a mercenary. And it . . . it makes me feel less stupid, I guess. That I'm trying too."

I lean against the wall. He steps closer.

"Don't try to kiss me," I say.

Bowe smiles and shakes his head. "You already told me that. You don't have to keep rejecting me."

"Well," I say. "I'm just saying . . . don't do it."

Bowe nods. "I'm sorry I yelled at you this morning. You were right, about my stance. And my game."

"I . . . could have said it nicer."

"*I Could Have Said It Nicer: The Carrie Soto Story.*"

I laugh. "Where are you headed next?"

Bowe shrugs. "Well, I'm not playing in the Davis Cup, obviously," he says. "But I'm headed to Marseille and San Jose. Then Memphis. And on it goes."

"I miss it a little," I say. "The whole tour. The constant movement and focus. You can't dwell on a loss if you're already on to the next match."

"You could have rejoined the full tour, you know."

I nod, picking at my fingernails, not looking at him. "I'm not good enough yet to dominate the way I'd want to."

"You played well today," he says. "And I'm glad I saw it. I know you didn't get what you wanted, but I'm still blown away by what you accomplished here. So many people are."

"Thanks," I say. And then I stop playing with my fingernails and look up at him, meet his eye. "Thank you."

"So I'll see you at the French, it sounds like," Bowe says, his hand on his suitcase again.

I nod. "I'll be back home trying to get myself in fighting shape until then."

"And I'll be out on the courts trying to pull a rabbit out of a hat."

Bowe puts his hand out for me to shake, and I grab it. I am surprised by how warm it is.

He turns to go.

"Do you even have a room?" I ask. "You were supposed to leave this morning."

"I'll get another one," he says. "Don't worry about it."

There's a pullout sofa in the living area of my suite. But I know that at some point in the night, he would knock on the bedroom door. Or worse yet, I'd slip into his bed on the couch.

When I play out the scenario in fast-forward, I can barely stand to watch it. He'll say something wonderful at some point, and I'll start to believe he means it, despite all evidence to the contrary. And then I'll start to like him or love him or feel something that I swear I've never felt before. And then one day, when I'm in too deep, he'll stop liking me or loving me, for one reason or another. And I'll be left with a hole in my heart.

"All right, then," I say. "Good luck. See you in Paris."

Transcript

SportsHour USA
The Mark Hadley Show

Mark Hadley: And Carrie Soto out before the quarter-finals? What do we make of that?

Gloria Jones: I think it was an excellent showing.

Briggs Lakin: It was what we all knew it would be, which was a failed attempt at a comeback.

Jones: I mean, yes. Ultimately, if she's going to be a contender to win a Slam this year, you'd want to see her get past the round of sixteen.

Lakin: If she can't make it to the final in Melbourne when Nicki Chan's gone home with a bum ankle, she has no shot at a Slam title this year. Especially once the Beast comes back. And you all know I'm no big fan of Chan. I can't get over the grunting. But she is the best player in the world right now. So this was Soto's chance to take a title, and it's over.

Jones: Yes, that last part, I agree with.

Hadley: Look at that! For once, we all agree.

Lakin: Turning to the quarterfinals, I think Cortez can take this thing to the end.

Jones: Absolutely not. Antonovich is going to stop her.

Hadley: Well, Chan's no spring chicken. Who takes the reins after the Beast is done? This could be Cortez's or Antonovich's moment. To take a Slam while she's out. To show us what the future of tennis looks like.

ON THE FLIGHT HOME TO LOS ANGELES, MY FATHER WANTS TO GO OVER what went wrong, how I can do better next time.

"*Sí, pero,* I played poorly, Dad," I say. "I got cocky. I assumed I was back to my old level of playing, and I wasn't. Cortez got the best of me. And now, anyone who saw that match knows that they can run me down."

"*Sí y . . .*" my father says, gesturing his hand toward me to encourage me to keep talking.

"So . . . I need to work on it."

My father smiles. "*We* need to work on it. We need to think through multiple strategies with each player and react more quickly once we understand what they are up to. And we need to get your volley game to the best it's ever been, so you don't have to rely on the groundstrokes, if you feel yourself starting to lose your power." There is a buoyancy to his voice—an excitement—that irritates me.

"Yes, but please stop smiling about it."

"I cannot!" he says, throwing his hands up in the air. "This is an exciting time. It is phase two. We have learned where we can improve, and now we will. The sun is shining, the birds are singing, the world is ours."

We are however many thousand miles up in the air. It is night and there are no birds up here. Only defeat and jet lag in a pressurized cabin.

"Yeah, *está bien,*" I say. "*Está bien.*"

We land and make our way home, where I sleep for twelve hours. I had planned to spend the next day alone in my room with the curtains drawn, ordering expensive pizza. But when I open my eyes, I make myself get up and turn on the television. I want to confirm what I already suspect.

Ingrid Cortez is on my television screen, holding up the Daphne Akhurst Memorial Cup. She's won the goddamn final against Antonovich.

She looks so happy, standing there. Like the young kid she is—so full of joy and life and eagerness. Her face is beaming; her skin is flushed.

When did I lose that? The delight of success? When did winning become something I *needed* in order to survive? Something I did not enjoy having, so much as panic without?

Before I know what I am doing, I am in shorts and a T-shirt, knocking on my father's door at eight-thirty in the morning on a rest day.

He opens the door in his robe and slippers, wiping the crust out of his eyes. But when he sees me, he perks right up.

I say, "Let's play."

"All right," he says. "Let me gather my notes on what we need to work on."

I shake my head. "No. Just me and you. Playing a match. For fun. No drills."

My father smiles and claps his hands in delight. "*¡Me encanta el plan!*"

He puts his hand up, ready for a high five. I laugh and slap it.

"*Dame cinco minutos,*" my dad says. "*Y después jugamos.*"

When he comes out, there is a bounce to his step and a grin on his face. He takes the first serve, and I kick his ass.

FEBRUARY 1995

Three and a half months until Paris

THE SUN IS BARELY IN THE SKY, AND YET I AM STANDING ON THE COURT in front of my father, already warmed up.

"This is," he says, "the beginning of clay season. We put the past behind us. We look forward to Paris. *¿Estamos de acuerdo?*"

"*Sí, está bien,*" I say. The loss in Melbourne still burns. The only thing that will cure it is a win at Roland-Garros.

As the reporters so kindly reminded me, I have only won the French Open once. Twelve years ago. The other nineteen of my Slams have been on hard courts or grass. But Roland-Garros is red clay.

Clay surfaces are softer; they absorb more of the power of the ball. Which means everything about them is slower. Players run slower, the ball bounces slower, and the ball bounces *higher,* too, which gives my opponents more time to react to my shots. Clay cuts into my advantage at almost every juncture. It neutralizes my speed, dulls my accuracy; even my angles don't have quite the same effect.

Clay is not for quick players. It favors the heavy hitters. It is a game of muscle.

Clay is Nicki's surface. And I sincerely hope her ankle's too fucked to play it.

"Are you ready to work?" my father says, holding a tennis ball in his hand.

"Obvio que sí."

He throws the ball at me. I catch it. Then he begins to walk away, toward the driveway.

"What are you doing?" I ask him.

He turns back to me, summoning me with his hand. "Today, *hija*, is an adventure."

I sigh as I begin to follow.

"You can leave your racket and the tennis balls," he says.

I look at him sideways. "Do I need my running shoes?"

He bobs his head from side to side. "No, I do not think so."

"Where are we going?" I ask as he opens the driver's-side door of the green Range Rover I bought him two years ago.

He says, "There are three and a half months until the French Open."

I open the passenger-side door and get in. "Yes, I'm aware."

He turns the ignition. "It's a clay surface . . ."

He puts the car in reverse and turns to look behind him. *Oh no.*

I say, "No. Dad, no. *De ninguna manera.*"

"Carrie, *sí*," he says.

"No, ni lo sueñes, papá."

"Lo siento, pero ya lo estás haciendo."

"What am I? Twelve again? *No necesito hacer esto.*"

"Yes, you do," he says. "It's exactly what you need to do."

I can see a tiny smile erupt on his face as he turns left out of the driveway. To the beach.

I stand there, looking out onto the ocean in Santa Monica, the soft, hot sand under my feet.

"You start here," my dad says. "I'll drive up the coast exactly five miles and meet you there."

I am once again about to run in the fucking sand.

And not wet sand either. Dry, coarse sand that breaks apart under your weight, your feet sinking with each step.

It hurts. Your calves, your hamstrings, your quads, your glutes. All of it.

They make it look way too easy on *Baywatch*.

I look around and sigh. Behind me, teenagers in oversized T-shirts and ripped jeans are walking on the paved path that follows the beach. A few women in neon bike shorts and sports bras glide by on Rollerblades, listening to Walkmans.

What I wouldn't give to run on that track instead of the sand beside it.

I turn my head north, focused on the miles of beach before me.

"*¿Y bien?*" my father says.

Muscle fatigue leads to a lack of agility. You can't hit your marks as accurately. Your shots don't have the same sharpness. You can't get high enough to hit your angles.

He is right. I need to do this.

"*Está bien,*" I say. "Five miles. I'll see you soon."

My father gives me a captain's salute and then gets back in his car. I watch as he makes his way onto PCH and then drives away from me.

I look down at the sand. I take in a deep breath and start jogging.

It is effortless at first; it always is. And then suddenly, my breath is thicker, my legs feel heavier.

Forty minutes in, I am convinced I must have run the whole five miles already. My father is messing with me; he must have driven ten miles out.

My thighs are killing me. I'm panting. But I can't slow down—I have to keep the pace my father gave me. I have to be *able* to do this. This run is something I can control.

The sand is growing hotter, burning the bottoms of my feet. The glare of the sun is blinding. Sweat drenches my forehead, getting in my eyes, soaking my T-shirt.

I clear my mind; I listen to my breath. And for a moment, I stop thinking about the misery of what I'm doing. I think, only, of Nicki Chan.

She is the daughter of Chinese parents, born in London, who picked up a racket at the age of six. A left-handed player, she had an advantage from the beginning. And she was good, maybe even great, at various points throughout her junior career. She turned pro and did fine. I remember playing her. I remember beating her. But then, in 1989, she took half a year off from the tour and completely revamped her game with a coach named Tim Brooks.

Nicki's groundstrokes became brutal, her serve deadly. She no longer played what we call percentage tennis—always hitting the safe shot. Instead, she opted for the wild, risky shots, each one a cannonball, her stamina unparalleled.

In her new incarnation, she's a player who dives for the ball, jumps high into the air. She goes into splits on clay, slides like a baseball player into first base.

Her form isn't always perfect; her shots are sometimes ugly. But she does the one thing we are all out there to do: win.

Unfortunately for her, it's a bitch on her body. She injures herself more often than most players—a twisted ankle, a sprained elbow, a weak knee, a back problem. She is thirty-one now, and it's hard to say how much longer she's got. But there is immense beauty in her game too, the wild desperation of it, the brutality. She is not a dancer. She is a gladiator.

I wonder what she's doing at this exact moment. I wonder if her ankle is healing. Will she be ready for Paris? Or is this the injury that takes her down for good?

Does she know yet which it is? Is she scared? Is she as anxious as I am to see what this year holds? Or is she thrilled by it all?

I hope at least a part of her is thrilled. It is all so thrilling.

"That was abysmal," my father says as I finally approach where he is standing on the beach. "It should have been *at least* ten minutes faster. We come back again *mañana*."

I can barely breathe. *"Bueno,"* I gasp. *"Mañana."*

My life becomes:

Five miles in the sand every other morning.

Forty-yard sprints on the days off.

Hitting against a machine spitting balls at me that are as fast as 80 miles per hour.

Playing against hitters for hours on end.

My father clocking my serves with a radar gun and shaking his head until I hit at least 120 miles per hour.

And then, when the sun begins to set and evening takes hold, watching tape.

My father and I watch my matches in Melbourne to figure out what I could have done better. We watch Cortez, Perez, Odette Moretti, Natasha Antonovich, Suze Carter, Celine Nystrom, Petra Zetov, and Andressa Machado at the IGA Classic in Oklahoma City.

My father's jaw tenses as we watch Natasha Antonovich dominate in the final against Moretti. He doesn't have to say anything— I already know his concern.

Antonovich plays like I used to. She's fast, with a full arsenal of shots. It will not be easy for me to go up against her in Paris, if I have to.

"I think we should go to Indian Wells," my father says as we turn off the TV one night. "See these players up close again, look for their weak spots. Train to defeat them."

"All right," I say. "Sure."

My father stands up to go to his house. "Did you see Bowe got to the quarters in Milan?" he says.

"Yeah," I say, nodding.

"We gotta get you two back on the court. The better he gets, the better you'll play. Until one day, you will play the greatest tennis you've ever played in your life, *pichona*."

"*No lo sé, papá*," I say.

"I'm telling you, *hija*, the greatest match of your career is ahead of you."

It is such a kind thing for him to say—exactly the sort of thing a father like him would tell a daughter like me. Full of heart and love and belief, and maybe a little bit untrue.

MARCH 1995

Three months until Paris

MY FATHER, GWEN, AND I PACK OUR SUITCASES INTO GWEN'S SUV AND head west for Indian Wells.

Gwen is driving, and I am in the passenger seat. TLC is playing on the radio, and Gwen's stereo system makes me feel like they are right here in the car.

My father is in the back seat and falls asleep five minutes after we get onto the 10.

Gwen turns the radio down. "Look," she says, her voice low. "I need to talk to you about something."

"Okay . . ." I say as we drive through downtown L.A.

"Elite Gold wants to pause on the photo shoot and commercials, for now."

I turn to Gwen. "But I made it to the round of sixteen."

She checks her mirrors and moves into the fast lane—which is almost at a standstill. "They were impressed with your showing in

Melbourne. But they said clay is your worst surface and they don't want to run a bunch of commercials about what a legend you are off of two . . ."

"Failures."

"They used the word *defeats*."

"I haven't lost the French Open yet, and they are already counting me out?"

"I told them they were making a mistake. I said, 'You have a contract with the most talked-about athlete of the year. You want to shoot her *now* so that when she wins this summer you have the campaign of the decade.'"

"But they didn't buy it."

"They would rather wait and see."

I kick her car door, and Gwen glares at me. "What the fuck are you doing?"

"Sorry."

"Look, you and I both know Melbourne was the beginning. You will win one by the end of the year."

"Do you really believe that?" I ask her.

"I believe in you. I think if you say something can be done, it will be done."

I close my eyes for a moment and wonder how to tell her how much I needed to hear that. But I cannot find the words.

"So, Bowe," Gwen says, looking at me for a split second before looking back at the road. "How did that all go? He said he got a lot out of it. Was it good? Did it help?"

"It was great, actually," I say. "It was really helpful to have a sparring partner at that level."

Gwen raises her eyebrow. "And that's all?"

I look at her. "I don't know what you're getting at."

"I saw a photo of you two out to dinner in Melbourne. And people are saying he came to your matches. I was wondering if . . ."

I shake my head. "Mind your own business."

"Oh, c'mon!" she says. "I could tell that Bowe maybe still had a thing for you. I could *tell*."

I turn to face the passenger-side window and watch us crawl through traffic. We are passing through the industrial side of Los Angeles at a snail's pace. "You're creating a soap opera in your head."

"I really think you two would be good together. He's rough around the edges, but he's such a good person—just like someone else I know."

"Gwen, give it up."

"I just think it would be nice if you, you know, had someone in your life."

My hand is on the door of the car, and I find myself tightening my fist. "Are you dissatisfied in your own relationship?" I ask. "Is that why you're prying into my mine?"

"I'm not prying. I just want to see you happy. Is that wrong? To think it would do you good to be with someone for a change?"

I want to open the door and jump out on the side of the freeway. "You don't get laid enough, Gwen," I say, keeping my voice low, not wanting to wake up my father. "I'm going to tell Michael he needs to step it up so you get out of my business."

Gwen rolls her eyes and waves me off. "Well, excuse me for wanting you to be loved."

"I'll just call him and tell him now," I say. "That he needs to learn how to satisfy you so you're not trying to live vicariously through me." I pick up her car phone and hit the speed dial, assuming it will be her husband. It starts to ring.

Gwen snatches the phone out of my hand as Michael picks up.

"Hi," she says. "Just letting you know we're off and running, headed out to the . . ."

I stop listening as traffic opens up and we start actually moving on the freeway. I glance at Gwen when she hangs up the phone. "You take shit too far sometimes," Gwen says.

I turn and look out my window as Gwen puts her foot on the gas and speeds us farther down the 10, headed to the desert.

My father is wearing sunglasses and a hat, like he's going to be unrecognizable sitting ten rows back on the ground floor of the venue. We are watching Ingrid Cortez play Madlenka Dvořáková. My father watches every stroke, making notes on both players in a black leather book he bought the other day. He hasn't used a notebook since I was a teenager. I wonder if he's using one now because he's old and doesn't trust his memory—or because I'm old and we can't take any chances.

Dvořáková holds the first set, which is a shock. I clap and cheer. My father turns to me.

"What?" I say.

"You're cheering," he says. "For the worse player."

"I don't like Cortez."

"But she's a phenomenal player. Certainly you respect her game? Her talent?"

"Sure," I say. "I mean, yes. But Dvořáková is working so hard. It's gonna take everything in her to give Cortez a run for her money. So I'm clapping for her, all right?"

He smiles and shakes his head. "You're getting soft in your old age."

I ignore him and look down at the schedule. "Once we watch Cortez for a bit more, we should stop by Perez versus Zetov too," I say. "Gwen is there now, I think."

I am lucky that Gwen is not one to hold a grudge. She was cold to me for the rest of the drive out here, but the next morning, it was as if nothing had happened. I had formulated a few different apologies in my head, but the words never made their way out of my mouth.

My father nods. "And we need to see Antonovich and Moretti tonight."

"Yes, agreed."

"This is fun!" he says. He bumps my shoulder with his. "God, I love this sport."

I bump his shoulder back. I wonder how it feels to be able to love tennis without it threatening to forget you with every passing match.

A COUPLE OF DAYS LATER, I WAKE UP EARLY IN THE RENTAL HOUSE, unable to quiet my mind.

I look at the clock and see that it is just before five. I decide to go for a run.

In the early desert morning, my body is hotter than the crisp air. I run in the center of the road, through the empty neighborhood streets, slow but steady, pounding my feet over the pavement.

If I don't make it far enough in the French Open, I may lose sponsorships.

I do not care about the money. Ever since I paid off the mortgage on my compound, most of my money goes to funding youth centers across the United States and in Argentina through my foundation. I've invested well, so I will still be able to afford to donate without a single other sponsorship.

It's not about profit.

It's about the look on Gwen's face if she has to tell me they're officially pulling out. It's walking onto the court at Wimbledon while the news of my being dropped is hitting the papers. It's about sitting at a table in a restaurant and everyone around me knowing the result of my hubris.

It is about being cut down to size, just as some people have long wanted me to be.

I'd hate to give them the satisfaction.

I run with no attention to where I am going—finding myself standing outside the rental house again before I even realize I've run in a circle.

I take a shower. With my hair still wet, I throw on a pair of jeans and a T-shirt, and I get in the car. I don't know where I'm going— only that I need to move. I drive through the desert—pale red mountains and beige plains, palm trees and strip malls.

What if I've fucked this all up?

I can't let that happen. I have to practice, and I have to plan. I have to work.

My ambition has long felt oppressive. It is not a joy—it is a master that I must answer to, a smoke that descends into my life, making it hard to breathe. It is only my discipline, my willingness to push myself harder, that has been my way through.

But right now, I can feel that my intuition is lacking. I need to be able to improvise, to think faster than I did back in Melbourne, to understand my opponents instinctively.

Before I know what I'm doing, I drive to the arena.

There, I take a seat in the middle of the stands, and I watch.

I watch Nystrom vs. Antonovich. I notice the way Antonovich's serve is accurate to the inch. I watch Moretti vs. Machado. I see the sheer power behind Moretti's groundstrokes. Her forehand is stunning, but her two-handed backhand leaves her open.

When the match is over, I look down at the schedule and let my eye wander to the men's tournaments. Bowe is playing O'Hara again. Now. And so, instead of checking in on Perez vs. Cortez, I head over to another court.

Bowe is wearing navy blue shorts and a white polo. His hair looks a bit shaggy under his navy baseball cap. He is tied two sets to two against O'Hara and up in the fifth. I am surprised, but perhaps I shouldn't be. I can't help but feel some pride in him.

O'Hara is so blond that his hair is almost white, with eyebrows the same. He is a frustrating and uninteresting player, often a moon-baller. He plays percentage tennis to an absurd degree. It's well known that there are big rifts between O'Hara and his coach, Henry Bouchard, for that exact reason. There's no passion in O'Hara's game, no personality.

That's what made Bowe such a compelling player his whole career—whether he won or lost. Back in the eighties, even when he was yelling at the umpire—maybe especially when he was—you knew you were watching a man throw his heart onto the court, a human being with flaws that threatened to do him in. You knew you were watching someone fighting, willing to risk everything.

I have always admired that about him.

Bowe holds the current game. He's up 6–5 in the fifth set. If he breaks O'Hara's serve, he's got the match.

I want it for him—the whole arena wants it for him. You can hear it in the way the crowd quiets. All eyes glued to the court.

For a moment, I smile at the idea that Bowe has no idea I am watching him. It feels vaguely sneaky, oddly intimate.

O'Hara scores. *15–love.*

Then, *15–all.*

30–15.

30–all.

Bowe wipes his brow with his shirtsleeve, fiddles a lot with his hat, bounces a little too fast as he crouches, waiting for the serve. He's wired up and nervous. But I suspect no one else is noticing those things right now. Because Bowe is returning beautifully. I cannot help but beam.

40–30.

Then deuce.

Bowe scores again; it's ad-out. This is break point—it's *match point*. Bowe *has this*. It is *so close*. One more and he wins the match.

O'Hara serves the ball wide and high. Bowe returns it swiftly, hitting the sideline. It's in! I stand up as people begin to cheer all around me.

Then the umpire calls it out.

O'Hara looks shocked. I turn to look at Bowe, who has already ripped his hat off his head. He slams it down on the ground. "ARE YOU KIDDING ME?!" Bowe screams as he marches toward the umpire. "YOU CROOK!"

I can't make out what the umpire is saying.

"YOU'RE A COMPLETE LIAR! YOU DON'T GIVE A SHIT ABOUT THE ART OF THIS GAME."

Multiple officials come onto the court as Bowe starts walking back to the baseline. "YOU DON'T NEED TO CONTROL ME," Bowe yells. "CONTROL THAT ASSHOLE."

O'Hara is laughing at him.

Bowe is throwing his hands up in the air.

I scan the crowd for a moment, unable to look at Bowe as he's being reprimanded by the official. He's going to get a point penalty for the swearing alone. *Oh, Bowe. C'mon.* He'll be that much further from winning now.

There are some young teenage fans in the row in front of me, watching Bowe with rapt attention. I can't decide if I think Bowe is a good influence, standing up against an umpire biased for the opposition, or a terrible influence, a grown man throwing a temper tantrum when things don't go his way. But of course there are no absolute morals or lessons. Only perspectives. One man's bitch is another woman's hero.

As I look through the stands, my eyes land on a woman in a pair of sunglasses and a baseball cap, four rows ahead of me. My heart leaps into my throat.

It's Nicki Chan.

I look at her, trying to convince myself that I'm crazy. But it's clearly her.

Her long, broad body is unmistakable. Her strong, muscular arms. Her wide shoulders. Her long black hair. Nobody ever talks about it much—which is telling—but Nicki Chan is gorgeous. Show-stoppingly gorgeous. A round face with high cheekbones, full lips.

Other women in tennis—blond women with big boobs and long legs—often get modeling contracts at age seventeen. They show up on the cover of men's magazines within a year or so of hitting the court for the first time.

But not thicker women, like me. Or dark-skinned women like Carla Perez or Suze Carter. Not women who are British Chinese, like Nicki, or downright scary in their intensity like her either. Not the women who aren't skinny and white and smiling.

And yet, no matter what type of woman you are, we all still have one thing in common: Once we are deemed too old, it doesn't matter who we used to be.

I watch Nicki for a second too long, wondering why she's here. But the thought pops out of my head the moment she turns her gaze and meets my eye. She looks just as surprised to see me as I am to see her. But she smiles, just a bit. And waves.

There's something sweet about it, unnervingly pure. I try to smile as I wave back.

Then both of us turn to watch what I know, in my gut, is about to happen.

Bowe has lost his point and then some. It's now ad-in. O'Hara only needs one more point to hold the game and destroy Bowe's lead.

He serves the ball—it flies past Bowe at a clip. An ace.

It is now 6–6.

I can't stand to watch him lose this match, so I get up and make my way home.

I am already in the car and turning the ignition on when I realize Nicki is probably at Indian Wells for the same reason I am. Scouting the competition to prepare for the French Open. She could beat my record before I've even taken it back.

I put my head down on the car horn and let it sing through the parking garage.

Motherfucker.

When I get back to the rental house, my father is sitting out by the pool, drinking what appears to be a classic daiquiri. He's making notes in his notebook but looks up when he sees me.

"Where the hell have you been?" he asks.

I throw the car keys on the table and sit next to him, keeping my sunglasses on, slumping into the chair.

"I don't know," I say.

I do not want to tell him I watched Bowe throw a tantrum on the court. And I cannot bring myself to tell him about Nicki.

I cannot bear to tell him just how impossible the task ahead of us feels right now.

Gwen comes out to the pool in a tailored blue dress and heels.

"Wow," I say. "You look great."

"Thank you," she says. "I have an early dinner with the execs from American Express. To see if maybe they want to pick up your contract with Elite Gold, among other things."

"Good God," I say. "Are we already there?"

"No," she says, grabbing her purse. "We're not there at all. But I told you I'm going to make this comeback work. And I'm not taking any chances." She looks me in the eye. "You will be in a credit card commercial this year, come hell or high water."

My father looks at me, raises his eyebrows. And then I look at Gwen.

I'm embarrassed that I'm about to cry because it is so silly. It's just the stupidest goddamn thing under the sun.

"Okay," I say, trying to hold it all in. I turn back around to the pool. "Have fun."

APRIL 1995

Two months before Paris

BY APRIL, AFTER TRAINING A COUPLE MORE MONTHS, MY SERVE IS NOW regularly clocking in at 122 miles per hour.

My feet feel light on the court. My knee feels all right. I feel nimble but mighty, exactly what I need to be for Paris.

"Unbelievable!" "*¡Increíble!*" "*¡Brillante!*" my father says at the end of each session lately, with a brightness in his eyes.

There are entire weeks of the spring when it seems like the craziest thing in the world that I could have doubted myself. I can do this. *This* is what I do.

One evening in early April, my father and I are eating dinner in my kitchen. We have spent the day working on my second serve. It is one of the first days in a long time when I am not exhausted, when hitting at the very best of my abilities did not take everything out of me. I remember this feeling from my twenties—this sense of sheer accomplishment without the weight of the cost. It has eluded me all year, but I finally have it back.

My father and I are eating his grilled chicken.

"It's bone dry," I say. "Why didn't you make chimichurri? Or a white wine sauce? Something?"

"I'd like to see you make dinner," he says.

"I don't cook," I say. "I order takeout. Because if I made chicken, it would taste like this."

The phone rings in the kitchen, and my father gets up.

"It's my phone, Dad," I say. "I'll answer it if I want it answered."

He swats me away with a dish towel.

"Hello?" he says. And then he smiles and turns to me. "It's Bowe."

I bolt up and take the phone from him.

"Hey," I say. "How are you? Nice job in Johannesburg."

"Thank you," Bowe says, but his voice is flat. He got to the third round and went down against Wash Lomal. But I saw the game, and he played beautifully. "Listen, I'm pulling out of Barcelona and Tokyo."

"Oh," I say, resting against the countertop. "Why?"

"My back is starting to hurt, and I want to save my energy. I need to regroup. Need to get ready for Roland-Garros."

"Are you going to play Nice or Monte Carlo?" I ask.

"No," he says. "I'm going to go to Paris now. Set up there, practice on clay."

"Oh," I say. "That's a great idea. Javier and I were thinking of doing the same at Saddlebrook."

"Well," Bowe says. "That's my question. What if you and Javier come to Paris instead and we train together?"

"You want us to come to Paris to train with you?" I ask.

My father hears this and immediately leaps out of his chair and starts nodding. "Tell him yes," my father says. "You need it. You both do. Tell him I have ideas for him. Two words: *Eastern grip*."

I laugh. "Did you get all that?" I say into the phone.

Bowe laughs too. "Every word, sadly. But . . ."

"What?"

"I don't want to know if your dad wants you to come. I want to know if *you* want to come."

I want to win the goddamn French Open with my whole gut. I want to shock every commentator out there who thinks I can't do it. I want to make Elite Gold vomit regret. And then I want them all to sit at my feet and sob, begging for forgiveness.

"Yeah," I say. "Let's do this. Let's train and let's win the French Open together."

Bowe laughs. "It's oddly sweet that you think I can win the French Open. But okay, yeah."

"I guess if we're being honest, I did mean me more than you."

Bowe laughs again, this time wild and delighted. And I can't help but smile.

"There you go. That's the Carrie Soto we all know and love."

My father and I are sitting in first class across the aisle from each other on our flight to Paris. Despite the fact that I am fully reclined and trying to watch the in-flight movie, my father is leaning over the space between us and quizzing me about strategy.

"The plan for Cortez is . . ." he says, after I've answered him about Perez, Moretti, and Antonovich.

"Enough for now," I say. "People could be listening."

My father lowers his voice to a whisper. "The plan for Cortez is . . ." he says again. I notice the older woman sitting next to him. She seems to recognize me but isn't making a fuss about it, which I appreciate.

"The plan for Cortez is *don't be an asshole like last time and spin out,*" I whisper. "Now let me watch the movie."

My father sits back in his seat. "It wasn't exactly the answer I was looking for," he says. "*Pero bueno.*"

He turns back to his tray, looking over his notebook. And then he looks back at me, nagging me again. "Bowe needs to work on his toss," he says. "You agree with me, don't you?"

"Yes," I say, ready to put on my in-flight headphones. They are playing a movie that has Sharon Stone in it and I love her. My dad continues to stare at me, not yet satisfied by my answer.

I sigh. "He's hitting the ball too late on the toss. If he hits it sooner, his angle will be better. On all surfaces, honestly."

My dad snaps his fingers. "Yes!" he says. "*¡Exacto! ¡Gracias!*"

The woman next to him smiles, as if charmed.

"You're welcome. But be smart about how you tell him that."

"A player needs to be open to anything that can make them better," my dad says.

"Obviously, but each player needs to be coached differently."

My father nods, considering. "You think I am coaching him?" he asks.

"Aren't you?"

My father nods again. "Does he think of me as a coach?"

"I don't know, Dad, you need to ask him."

I move to put the headphones on, but he doesn't stop looking at me. "Are the two of you dating?" he says.

I suddenly have the burning desire to eject myself from the plane. "We're not doing this, Dad," I say. "We've never done it. Let's not start now."

"But you are dating him?"

I shake my head and close my eyes. "I'm not dating anyone. You can pretty much always assume that."

"Don't be that way, *pichona*. Please keep your heart open. Please don't close it. Please."

"Dad," I say, holding my breath, losing patience. "Let me watch my movie now." That boy from *What's Eating Gilbert Grape* is in it too, and he is so good. I really want to watch this. The only thing that saves me is the woman next to my father, who finally speaks up.

"Excuse me," she says to him. She looks to be in her sixties, and she is gorgeous. She has big brown eyes and long eyelashes. "Are you Javier Soto?"

I turn away from them, but I'm too nosy not to eavesdrop.

"I am," my father says, putting on his showstopper smile. He would get recognized a lot on the circuit in the seventies. He'd be the center of attention, other coaches and tennis parents and players trying to corner him for advice. When he did his book tour, he was the man of the hour. Everyone wanted to get a little bit of whatever gold dust he had to spread around. It doesn't happen as often anymore.

He sits a bit straighter, pulls back his shoulders, and puts his hand out to her. "Nice to meet you."

"I'm Coral," she says. "I'm a big fan."

"Of my daughter's?" he asks.

"Well, yes, but of you too."

"Of me?" he says.

"Yeah, the Jaguar."

My father blushes. He *blushes*.

"I'm a tennis player," she continues. "I have been all my life. I've always loved what you said about a classic, well-executed game. I loved your book, *Beautiful Fundamentals*."

"Well, thank you," my dad says. "I appreciate it."

I finally put my headphones on and watch the movie, though I've missed a good twenty minutes of the beginning. A few times, I look over to see my dad and Coral laughing together. Or talking back and forth, Coral even touching his forearm.

When the flight attendants serve the meals, I see them trade salt and butter. He gives her his dessert. She smiles sweetly; there is something girlish about the way she accepts it.

At some point after my movie ends, they start playing something called 3 *Ninjas Knuckle Up,* and I doze off to sleep. But I wake up a few hours later, when we are about to land, and I see that my father and Coral are still talking.

She asks him something that I cannot make out for the life of me, and my dad puts his hand on her hand for the briefest of seconds and gives a very slight shake of the head.

As we all stand up to get off the plane, Coral nods at my father and says, "Goodbye, Javier, it's been a pleasure," and then walks away.

Soon, my father is walking faster than me off the concourse and into the airport. I catch up with him quickly, though. "What's the deal?" I say.

He looks at me. "What deal?"

"Did you ask Coral out or what?"

My father scoffs. "No, I did not *ask her out.*"

"Well, why not? Weren't you just telling me to open my heart?"

"I was talking about you, not me," he says as we get onto the escalator. "I have had my love."

When we get to the hotel, the concierge gives me a message from Gwen, telling me to call her, no matter the time. I look at my watch. It's almost midnight in Paris but only afternoon in L.A.

My father and I walk up to my room. I find the phone and call.

"Hi," Ali says. "One second."

I put it on speaker as Gwen picks up the line.

"So," Gwen says.

It's either that Elite Gold is pulling out or Nicki Chan is back in. And I'm not sure which I dread more.

"Chan," Gwen says. "She's playing the French Open."

Ah, fuck. That's the one I hate more. I look at my father, who looks back at me.

"You've got this," Gwen says. "Clay is her surface, but you can take her down."

"Yeah," I say. "Yeah. All right, talk soon."

I hang up the phone and say, "If she takes the French Open . . . before I've been able to win one . . ."

My father nods. "It's not good."

I stand up. "But she's not going to win the French Open."

"No, she's not. You're going to win the French Open."

"Because I am the greatest tennis player of all time."

My dad walks up to me and puts a hand on each of my shoulders. "You are the greatest warrior the world has ever seen."

Transcript

SportsHour USA
The Mark Hadley Show

Mark Hadley: And now that Nicki Chan has announced she will be playing in the French Open—how does that change everyone's prospects?

Gloria Jones: Well, we don't know what sort of player we are going to see. A lot of people are saying she's coming back too soon after her injury. There are rumors she's intent on taking another Slam title to break the tie between her and Soto and she's rushed her return in order to do it.

Briggs Lakin: I have to say, Gloria, I'm hearing the opposite. I'm hearing the Beast is playing the best she's ever played. Meanwhile, Soto's only chance at a Slam was one where she wouldn't have to face Nicki. That was Melbourne. I think it's safe to say, for the Battle Axe, it's all over.

END OF APRIL

One month until the French Open

WE MEET BOWE ON THE PRACTICE COURT AT EIGHT A.M. THERE'S NOT another soul around. He is wearing gym shorts and a white T-shirt, tapping his racket against his shoes. Bright white, they stand out in stark contrast to the burnt orange clay.

"Even with your back bothering you, you've been kicking ass," I say as I make my way onto the court. My father walks just two steps behind me.

"Thank you," Bowe says. "Though I suspect you're fighting at peak level right now. I'm a little scared."

"You should be," I say.

"All right, kids, shall we?" my father says.

Bowe shakes my hand. "May the best player win," he says.

"Don't worry, I will."

"Best of three or five?" my father asks.

I really want to earn it. I really want to run myself into the ground and see what I'm made of. "Five," I say.

He nods. "Here we go."

I serve first, and it's a stunner. Sharp, fast, with a high bounce. "Fuck," Bowe says after he misses it.

"Get used to it."

"Don't worry, I'm sure I will," Bowe says, and I can't help but laugh.

I keep it up but then find myself pulling back, going for the safe shots, worried that I'll run out of steam too quickly. Bowe gets the edge on me and wins the first set, 7–5.

I need to find balance in my game, some ability to go hard and keep going, some power to draw on that will not deplete me. I look over at my father for guidance, but he's making notes in his notebook.

I already know the answer, though. I need better shot selection. I need to go bigger on some shots—really take some risks. And I need to put more of the pressure on Bowe's side of the court. I start lobbing more frequently, constructing longer points.

I take the second set, 6–3. "Uh-oh," I say. "She's coming for ya."

"I'm not worried."

I take the next.

"Ohhhh," I say, teasing him as we stand by the net. "Now it's starting to sting, right? Starting to feel a little pinch?"

"It's out of five, Soto," he says. "I know you're used to two sets giving you the match, but you're playing a man's game now."

"Kindly fuck off."

My father shakes his head.

Bowe takes the fourth. I'm getting tired. My serve is softening.

"Oh shit," Bowe says. "It's anybody's game now, Battle Axe."

"You're both terrible in the fifth set of any match," my father calls out. "So let's not trash-talk until one of you gets *results*."

Our fifth set goes to a tiebreak. Match point is on Bowe's serve, which lands right on the T. I return it with a backhand down the line. It bounces high, and he can't reach it.

"Yes!" I say, pumping my fist. "How do you like that?"

Bowe shakes his head, visibly pissed at himself for handing me that serve.

"You win," he says. "You win this one."

My father nods at me. "I'm going inside for a drink," he says. "See you in ten to talk about what we can do better. I have a lot of notes. For both of you."

Bowe grabs the ball on his side of the net and then meets me over by the bench. I take a long sip of water just as he takes one himself. But we catch each other's gaze.

"How are you?" Bowe says.

"What do you mean?" I ask.

"Chan."

I sit down on the bench. "I feel like I set out to prove that I'm a better player than her. And I got a bit of a break with her ankle in Melbourne, but you know, I did plan on facing her eventually. I want the challenge." This is what I'm telling myself, anyway.

"So it's good, then, her coming back."

I laugh. "Yes," I say. "No. I don't know. Yes, it's good, if I'm as great as I say I am."

"You are," he says. "You'll do it. I'm the one who needs a miracle," he says.

"Maybe," I say, smiling.

"I literally just told you you're doing great. And you can't return the favor?"

"What do you want me to do? Lie? Don't fish for compliments," I say.

"Christ, Carrie," Bowe says. But he's laughing. And I am too. And then suddenly my father is there, his head still in his notebook.

"Carrie, go to the baseline. We need to work harder on your second serve. Huntley, I assume you're staying? I have notes for you, if you want them. Your game is getting better, but you still stink at the net. You could benefit from my expertise."

Bowe rolls his eyes. "The two of you, man," he says to my father and me. "Bulls in a china shop."

"Let's not pretend you're such a prize," my dad says, his eyebrows raised.

"Fine," Bowe says. "I want your notes. I'm here to win, so . . . anything you got, I'm listening."

My father's face lights up. And I'm happy for him, to be back here doing this job that he does so well, this job that has defined him for as long as I can remember.

This is not just *my* comeback.

Soto vs. Huntley, Love?

Sub Rosa Magazine

The word out of Paris is that iconoclast Carrie Soto and former wild child Bowe Huntley might be dating again.

Those who were around for the whirlwind of Soto's and Huntley's respective dominance in the eighties will remember that the two were seen canoodling in Spain back in the day.

Now, almost fifteen years later, it appears they are cuddling up close once again.

Multiple sources say they've seen "the Battle Axe" and "Howlin' Huntley" sparring on the court in preparation for the upcoming French Open.

But we have to think this isn't all business. . . .

MID-MAY

Two weeks until the French Open

IT'S LATE, ALMOST TEN P.M. BOWE AND I ARE ABOUT TWO HOURS INTO A practice match on a court just outside Paris. The court lights are bright. The clay is dense under our feet.

It's just Bowe and me. My father went to bed.

Bowe and I decided to play tonight because, earlier in the day, people had started gathering by the court we were on, trying to catch a glimpse of us. I felt myself getting more and more tight, with all of their eyes on me.

"I need privacy," I told my father in between games. "Clay is my worst surface. I need to get everything ready and in control first, and *then* people can watch me."

Bowe started walking toward us. I gathered he heard the last part of my complaint because he raised his eyebrows at me.

"You're in your head too much," Bowe said, pointing at his temple. "Didn't I tell you that?"

My father frowned at Bowe. "Hi, I missed the meeting where I hired you as assistant coach."

"The two of you comment on my game constantly!" Bowe said.

My father's face did not soften. Bowe put his hands up, giving in. "Fine, you both say whatever thoughts come into your head and I'll be as quiet as a church mouse."

My father nodded. "That'd be best."

Bowe rolled his eyes. "Are we playing or what?"

My father looked at me. "*Practicá sola,*" he said, "*dos días más. Después, tenés que estar lista para jugar con todos los ojos clavados en vos. ¿Entendido?*"

"*Bueno,*" I said. "*Está bien.*"

"*Esta noche, practicá sin mí.*"

My father then grabbed his water and his hat. "*Nos vemos después,*" he said, and headed off, I was sure, to the nearest bistro.

Bowe looked at me. "What was that?"

"You really should learn Spanish," I said.

"So I can understand your father?"

"So you can understand a lot of people. Including me sometimes."

Bowe smirked. "Are we playing now or what?"

I started packing up my kit. "We are not. He said let's do two more days with no one watching me. And then I need to be ready. So, I'm asking you, please, can we pick this match up later today when no one is here? You name the time."

Bowe nodded. "Fine, how about eight? I'll talk to Jean-Marc. I'll make sure no one is here."

"Thank you," I said. "Truly."

As I started to walk away, Bowe called out to me. "Take a moment to consider that I'm right about your mental game."

I turned back to him. "And you, take a moment to shut the fuck up."

Now, in the cool night air with no one around, my game is much better.

"Dammit!" Bowe yells as I win the current game. If I win one more, I'll take the tiebreak set and win the match.

I laugh. "Whose mental game are you worried about now?" I ask. Bowe rolls his eyes.

"Oh, poor baby is losing!" I say.

As I move across the court tonight, I'm feeling confident that I will last longer in Paris against heavy hitters like Cortez than I did back in Melbourne. I am doing *well*.

I serve the ball, and Bowe returns it wide. I get there in time and send a cross-court forehand to the deep corner. He hits a backhand groundstroke. And then I have my two-shot strategy in place. First, an approach shot, an easy return. And then a drop shot.

"It's almost too easy," I say. "Too damn easy."

"Dammit, Carrie," Bowe says, his voice low and flat. "Have a little humility."

"Humility?" I say. I have the ball in my hand, about to serve, but I put it in my pocket.

"You called off the match this afternoon when I was winning," he says. "And now, when you're winning, you're gloating."

"Oh no, here comes the Huntley tantrum."

"I don't throw tantrums," he says. "C'mon. You're playing into that sportscaster crap. And I don't do that with you."

"I mean—"

"I don't yell anymore."

"Oh, come on . . ." I say.

"What?"

"I saw you at Indian Wells. Screaming at the umpire. You called him a crook."

Bowe's face falls. He closes his eyes. "I'm really trying, Carrie. I'm trying so hard to not do the shit I used to do. You think I want to be the guy that screams on the court because he's not winning?" Bowe says. "Of course not. I know I fucked up at Indian Wells with that bad call. But I'm trying. And I wish you didn't have to be *right there* to remind me when I slip up."

I look down at my shoes. They are covered in clay. "I get—"

"And by the way, what right do you have to come to Indian Wells and not tell me?" he says.

"What?"

"You're just sitting there in the stands and you don't tell me you're watching my game? And you didn't even bother to say hi? To wish me luck?"

"What are you, twelve? You need me to wish you luck?" I say.

Bowe shakes his head. "Forget it. I don't know why I bother. Just serve the ball, Carrie. Or are you too nervous now and need to postpone until tomorrow?"

"I'm trying to get myself ready for Roland-Garros, all right? I'm sorry it's not on your exact schedule."

"You're ready now!" he says. "You're playing like it's ten years ago. And somehow you're still acting like 'Oh jeez, am I good enough? I'd hate for anyone to see me unless I'm the greatest in the world.'"

"What do you care?" I ask.

"Because. You're so afraid of losing that you fucked up my whole session today to avoid it."

"No, I didn't."

"Yes!" he says. "You did! I don't have much longer on this tour, Carrie. I don't even know if I can finish the year. I pulled out of other tournaments to protect my back, and to be here, trying to play you in the hardest conditions possible. I want to give myself a real chance of doing something great."

"Of course you're going to finish the year."

Bowe rolls his eyes. "Just serve the ball and let's get this over with."

"You have no chance of winning if that's your attitude," I say.

"I'm begging you to shut up, Soto."

"See? This is your problem. One tiny little thing doesn't go your way and you explode."

"Yeah, well, at least I don't walk away."

"What's that supposed to mean?"

"It means you're a quitter, Carrie. Now serve the ball."

I watch him as he walks back to the baseline. When he gets there, he turns, expecting to see me ready to serve, but instead I am staring at him from the net.

"If you have something to say to me," I say, "then say it."

"I just said it," he says.

I stare at him still.

He deflates. "I just want you to serve the ball," he says.

I start walking backward, still glaring at him as I make my way to the baseline. "Call me a quitter again, asshole. I dare you."

"Serve the ball, Carrie."

With lightning speed, I toss it up in the air and slam it across the court. It flies from my racket straight across the net and into the ground. It bounces out of reach before Bowe gets to it.

"Break point," I say.

"Goddammit," Bowe says as he throws his racket.

I shake my head and start heading toward the bench to drink some water.

Bowe picks up his racket and walks to the bench too. When he gets to me, he has calmed slightly. But the racket in his hand is broken—half the frame hanging by the strings.

I nod toward it. "That's what happens when you don't know how to *control your emotions.*"

"Yeah, maybe I should just quit every time I think I'm losing."

"One time!" I say. "One time! I asked you to reschedule a match because I didn't want people looking at me. One time! And you're so bent out of shape about it that you're gonna wreck your racket? C'mon. You're an adult man. Get ahold of yourself."

"I truly cannot stand," he says as he packs up his other rackets, "to be lectured by you."

"Why not? Who else *should* lecture you? You and I are the same, Bowe. Old and out to prove something. And I'm at least handling it with some dignity."

"You left!" he says, his voice rising. And then he shakes his head and laughs to himself. "You hurt your knee, you lost a couple matches, and you gave up. That's what you did. You're saying we're the same, but we're not. I stuck around. I had the guts to try. I have the guts to lose. You, you just run. Well, guess what, Carrie? People who are actually playing the game *lose*. We all lose. We lose *all the time*. That is life. So we are not the same, Soto. I have courage. You're just good at tennis."

He zips up his kit as I try to get control of my breathing.

"You're mad at me because I retired?" I ask. "Are you serious? What should I have done instead? Hung around and become a joke? Let everyone see me limping to the finish line?"

Bowe looks at me and closes his eyes slowly. He takes a breath. "You act like you've dedicated your life to tennis. But you came back to win, not to play. That's why they're all pissed at you for returning. You've got no heart."

Bowe puts his bag over his shoulder and walks away.

"Who is the quitter now?" I call out. "You're forfeiting this match, you know!"

But Bowe just shakes his head and leaves.

The next morning, Bowe doesn't show up. So it's just my father and me hitting.

"He just decides not to come? Not to practice?" my father asks as we rally a bit to warm up.

I send a soft shot back to him. "*No lo sé.*"

My father frowns. "So you got into a fight, then."

"He doesn't like it when he's told the truth. What do you want me to do?"

My father shakes his head and smiles. "The both of you . . ."

"Hey, I'm here, aren't I?"

My father nods. "I will check up on him later."

"Do whatever you want."

We run drills. My father pulls in a hitter last minute. It's not a vigorous practice. But it keeps me warm. And given how many people are lining up to watch, I realize that if Bowe had come this morning, he'd have gotten the showdown he wanted.

Regardless, I'm putting the ball where I want it. I find myself more and more unbothered by the crowd watching me. They begin growing louder, more engaged, shouting, "Carrie!" and *"Nous t'aimons!"*

With each perfectly executed groundstroke, I try to let their presence bolster me instead of scare me.

I am good. On any surface you put me on, I am good. This is a level of performance that I can allow everyone to see.

But then I notice my father's attention turn toward one of the other courts, as fans all over the complex begin to hum. I look over in their direction. Nicki Chan is signing autographs as she walks onto the court with a hitter.

My father turns and looks at me. When he catches my gaze, there is nothing we need to say. I continue to hit for another few minutes.

"*Vámonos,*" my father says. "That's enough for today."

I nod and start to gather my things. My hitter packs up. The crowd groans, disappointed I'm leaving. I think of Bowe for a moment—how he would react. He would call out something witty to them, walk to the crowd lining up at the fence and sign their tennis balls and make them laugh. There's a woman here with a toddler, and I know that Bowe would give the kid a high five.

But I can't think of how to do it without seeming disingenuous. I don't feel grateful for their attention, and I don't know how to be full of shit. I don't have the foggiest clue what to say to a toddler.

I wave briefly and head out. We have to pass Nicki's court in order to leave the facility. And as we do, I stop and watch her.

She is serving balls straight to her hitter, one screamer after the next. My father whistles low.

Her form is untraditional. Because she is left-handed, a lot of players aren't used to her angles. But she also serves the ball in a stance that breaks most of the rules and in a form that breaks even more. She grunts so loud you can hear her in Brussels. Yet as the ball goes soaring off her racket into the service court, it looks deadly.

And that's not just a turn of phrase. It seriously looks as if it is heading toward the clay so fast, with so much heat on it, that if it got you in the chest it might kill you.

"*Vamos,*" my father says.

I nod but I don't move. I can't seem to take my eyes off her. I've seen her play in person before, but standing right next to her, watching her from maybe fifteen feet away, is . . . It's beautiful to see.

When she finishes with the balls she has next to her, her hitter begins collecting them all, and she looks up and spots us. She waves.

"Hi," she says as she walks toward my father and me. "I tried to catch your eye when you were practicing earlier, but I don't think you saw me." I have to actively resist rolling my eyes. I didn't want a conversation. I just wanted to be a fly on the wall.

"Hi," I say.

When she finally gets to us, she looks at my father. "You're Javier."

"Yes," my father says. "Indeed I am."

"Can I tell you what a pleasure it is to meet you? When I was a child, I used to . . . Well, Carrie, I watched every single one of your matches. I used to have one of your *SportsPages* covers on my wall. Surely I told you this, back on the tour when we met. But . . . well, Javier, I was so jealous that Carrie had you as a father. My own dad barely knows a thing about tennis. He tries, but it's futile. As a kid, I had to find my own coaches. And . . ." Nicki shakes her head, remembering. "I just thought you were the coolest."

My father smiles.

"We should let you practice," I say. "We will see each other soon, I'm sure."

"Oh, most definitely. We absolutely will. But listen," Nicki says as she leans farther toward me. I take a step closer to her, bridging the gap, the fence the only thing between us now. "I want to thank you."

"Thank me?" I ask.

"I don't think I would have worked so hard on my recovery without knowing I had you to compete against. Knowing I'd have to defend my titles."

I don't like how joyful her face looks, how sincere it all seems.

"All right, well," I say. "You know why I'm here. You know what I'm out to do. I'd imagine your intent is the same. So . . . may the best woman win."

Nicki nods. "Until then, Carrie."

Transcript

SportsHour USA
The Mark Hadley Show

Mark Hadley: The French Open starts tomorrow. Gloria, walk us through the women's singles.

Gloria Jones: Well, obviously, we are looking to Nicki Chan—clay is a good surface for her. I think Natasha Antonovich has also shown herself to be very adroit at adapting to a clay surface.

Hadley: The ads for the tournament feature a lot of old clips of Carrie Soto, but let's call it now: Carrie doesn't really have a chance.

Jones: Clay is not where Carrie Soto shines, no. The Battle Axe—which, by the way, is what I have long called her and I believe we *all should* call her unless we call her by her name—is a grass surface player. Not a clay surface player.

Briggs Lakin: Gloria, I think you're alluding to the fact that people are referring to Carrie Soto as "the B word." You and I were talking earlier—or maybe I should be honest and say *disagreeing*—about whether that's appropriate.

Jones: Yes, that's right. I find it offensive.

Lakin: But to play devil's advocate here . . .

Jones: [inaudible]

Lakin: I don't think it's much different than calling her "the Battle Axe." Remember, we all started calling her "the

Battle Axe" because she went after Paulina Stepanova's ankle in the match we still call "the Coldest War" at the US Open in '76. It was ugly and cruel. And there are countless other examples. So I'm sorry, but Carrie Soto *is* a "B word."

And you're saying that when you call her "the Battle Axe" too. You're just using a euphemism.

Jones: I think there's a difference.

Lakin: I know you do. But an athlete's job is not just to win—it's also to be someone we can cheer for. Soto puts no effort into courting public opinion at all. I guess I want to know why we all have to walk on eggshells to pretend Carrie Soto isn't the exact thing she clearly enjoys being?

Hadley: And with that, we'll be right back.

THE 1995
FRENCH
OPEN

THE AIR OF ROLAND-GARROS IS LIKE NO OTHER COURT IN THE WORLD. It is earthy and humid, heavy with the unyielding scent of tobacco. The smoke from the spectators' pipes has accumulated over the years and lives in the very molecules of this place.

As I walk toward the locker room this morning, preparing for my first match, I am struck by how intense the memories are. Each time I've played here comes back to me all at once.

The midseventies, the early eighties. Great wins and crushing losses.

I spent the first five or so years here desperate and frustrated, pushing myself to rise up the ranks. I lost to Stepanova in the semis in '78. I defeated her in the semis in '79, only to lose to Gabriella Fornaci. Lost to Mariana Clayton in '80. Renee Mona in '81. Bonnie Hayes in '82. And then in '83, I finally won the whole thing.

Was I the greatest then—at that very moment? Even though I'd also failed here many times before? Which matters more? The wins or the losses?

Despite how hard I am seeking some unimpeachable label of "greatness," it doesn't really exist. I do know that, on some level.

But then I walk into the locker room, full of players—Antonovich and Cortez talking in the corner, Brenda Johns pulling on her shoes, Carla Perez opening a locker—and suddenly, I am pulled out of my head back into the world I know best.

The world of winners and losers.

SOTO VS. ZETOV

1995 French Open

First Round

I WALK OUT ONTO THE COURT AND HEAR THE CROWD BEGIN TO CHEER.

I look over at Petra Zetov. She's warming up her shoulder, stretching her legs as men in the crowd holler. She's currently ranked the highest of her career, number eighty-nine. But she has a rabid fan base out of proportion to her ranking.

She's stunningly beautiful—tall and thin, blond hair, blue eyes. She's a model for Calvin Klein, does commercials for Diet Coke, and was in a Soul Asylum video.

And she has a burden I have never had. In order to keep getting paid, she has to keep looking beautiful on the court.

I wonder, briefly, if it weighs on her. Or, if, conversely, it frees her from the pressure I live with, the pressure to win.

Either way, it's a prison. Both her beauty and my ability—they've both got an expiration date.

"It is an honor to play you," she says.

I nod.

This will not be hard. I fully admit that I do not have what she has. But it is equally true that she doesn't have what I have.

The coin is tossed; Zetov wins. She elects to serve first, her face bright and hopeful, as if she thinks this bodes well for her, as if she has a real chance.

I take the match in straight sets.

I TAKE OUT CELINE NYSTROM IN THE SECOND ROUND. NICKI DEFEATS Avril Martin.

In the third, Nicki takes down Josie Flores. I beat Andressa Machado.

When I get back to the hotel after the match, I take a shower and open up a book.

I try to calm myself. The round of sixteen is tomorrow afternoon. Tomorrow morning, I will practice with my father. So tonight, this quiet, is my respite.

The book I brought is an unauthorized biography of Daisy Jones and the Six. I'm only reading to see who slept with who, but I can't focus.

The phone rings and I wonder for a moment if it's Bowe.

"Hola, hija."

"Hola, papá."

"Tomorrow morning, eight A.M."

"Yes, *ya lo sé.*"

"Just reminding you. And, I . . . Did you see Bowe's match?"

"Yeah," I say. "He played beautifully." He defeated Nate Water-house in the round of sixteen.

"Maybe the best I've seen him all year." Bowe's now headed to the quarterfinals for the first time in a Slam since 1991.

I haven't spoken to Bowe since our fight. When I hang up with my dad, I keep the phone in my hand. I consider calling Bowe's hotel. My fingers hover over the buttons. But instead, I put down the receiver and go to bed.

"You've beaten Perez before," my father says in the tunnel, right before I set out onto the court. "Just do it again."

I turn back to him. "What?"

"You've beaten her once already," he says. "You can do it again."

"You said Perez," I say.

"Right. So you play to her backhand, keep the pressure on her, hit hard to compensate for the clay. You got this."

"I'm playing Odette Moretti," I say.

"Oh," he says, closing his eyes for a second and then opening them right back up. "Right, right. Sorry. Sorry. Nicki's playing Perez. Right, okay, Moretti. She's got a light arm, keep her at the baseline, she doesn't have the power to keep them bouncing on clay."

I look at my dad for a moment.

"It's time, *hija.* ¡*Vos podés!*" he says.

I bend down and wipe my shoes clean.

SOTO VS. MORETTI

1995 French Open

Round of Sixteen

MORETTI STRIDES ONTO THE COURT IN A WHITE-AND-NAVY-BLUE TENNIS dress, waving to the crowd. She blows kisses to the stands. She is sponsored by Nike, so it's no surprise that she is covered in Swooshes from head to toe. When she turns to look at me, she gives me a big smile.

I nod at her.

She starts strong after winning the toss. But I'm stronger.

15–love becomes 15–all. 30–15 becomes 30–all. Deuces become ad-ins and then back to deuces and ad-outs.

Three hours in, we are now in the third set. 6–6.

The crowd is cheering. I look up at my father, who is sitting elegantly behind a flower box.

It's now my serve. I need to hold this one and break hers. And then I'm on to the quarterfinals.

I close my eyes. *I can do this.*

When I open my eyes again, I am looking directly at Moretti. She hovers over the court, her hips swaying side to side as she waits for my serve.

I breathe in and then serve it straight down the middle. She returns it with a groundstroke to the center. I hit it back, deep and to the far-right corner. She runs for it, fast and hard. There's no way she's gonna make it.

But then she does. And I can't return it.

It's fine. It's fine. I can feel my knee twinging, but I have plenty more to go.

I look up at my father again in the players' box. He catches my eye.

I can feel the hum in my bones, the lightness in my belly. I serve it again, this time just at the line. She dives and misses it.

I hold my game and then begin my assault on her serve. I chip away at her, love–15, love–30. By the time I get to match point, she's exactly where I want her. I set her up so she's on the far side of the court. I return it to her backhand and that's it. She's done.

The crowd roars. I jump up into the air and pump my fist.

Nobody thought I'd last past the round of sixteen, but for the first time in seven years, I have earned my way to the quarterfinals. And as it begins to sink in, I feel myself tearing up.

I keep thinking, *I don't cry on the court. I don't cry on the court.*

But then I think, *Maybe it's a lie that you have to keep doing what you have always done. That you have to be able to draw a straight line from how you acted yesterday to how you'll act tomorrow. You don't have to be consistent.*

You can change, I think. *Just because you want to.*

And so, for the first time in decades, I stand in front of a roaring crowd and cry.

I AM IN THE MEDIC ROOM AFTER THE MATCH, HAVING MY KNEE ICED and my calves massaged. My father is making notes and flipping through the channels, to see if I'll play Cortez or Antonovich in the semis.

But then Bowe appears on the screen. He's live in the press room, sitting slightly hunched over, a baseball cap over his barely dry hair. He has on a blue T-shirt. And the second I catch sight of him, I know he is in physical pain.

"Can you walk us through what happened?" a male reporter asks. "Out on the court today?"

Bowe leans into the microphone. "I tore the cartilage between my ribs during the second set. It was hurting this morning before the match even started, but I ignored it, and now here we are." He winces as he sits back.

"How does it feel to lose today, because of an injury, when you were doing so well?" a woman asks him.

"It feels really great, Patty," Bowe says. "Best day of my life."

My father laughs and I look at him, surprised. "He's grown on me," he says. "He's funny."

"What if he's really hurt?" I say.

My father nods. "Maybe it's a small tear. With a little bit of time . . . he can get back in fighting shape."

"For Wimbledon?"

"No," my dad says. "But maybe by the US Open. If he's still in this thing."

"He won't give up," I say. The trainer comes around and starts massaging my other calf. "He'd rather lose than give up."

My father looks at me and raises his eyebrows. "Yeah, he does have that sense of honor about him."

"So, will you be going home?" a reporter asks Bowe. "You are still currently scheduled to play Queen's Club next month. Will you pull out?"

"I'm pulling out of all my events next month. Focusing on recovery. But . . . I'm not going home. I'm going to stick around and watch Carrie Soto," he says. "I think what she's doing here is remarkable. And I want to be able to say I saw it happen."

That night, after I go back to my hotel room, I lie down on the sofa and try to read the French gossip magazines that Gwen sent over to my hotel. They have some good tidbits about Pam and Tommy Lee, but other than that, it's too difficult trying to piece together, in another language, who all the French celebrities are. I throw the magazine back down onto the coffee table and stare up at the ceiling.

Then I stand up, grab my room key, and walk to the elevator.

Bowe's hotel is two blocks over and soon enough, I'm standing in the lobby asking the concierge to tell him I'm here.

I sit in the lobby, in an overstuffed velvet chair, taking in the shine of the marble floors and the gold fixtures. And then Bowe is in front of me in chinos and a T-shirt, his baseball cap on. He's holding his ribs.

"Hi," I say.

"Hi."

"I was really mean," I say. "The other day."

Bowe nods and bites his lip. "I wasn't great either."

"Are you okay?"

Bowe looks down at his torso. "I honestly do not know."

"What happened?" I saw the replay—the way he twisted and then fell to the ground.

Bowe nods at the elevators, and we head toward them. A young teenage boy and his father sneak into the elevator just as we are about to head up, and I watch their faces as they realize who we are.

"You're—" the teenager says as he begins to point at us. His father immediately pushes his hand down.

"Jeremy, don't point at people," he says, and then turns to us. "I'm sorry."

Bowe waves them off. "Not a problem."

"Congrats," the dad says to me. "Great match today against Moretti."

I say, "Thank you."

"Sorry about Alderton," the dad says to Bowe. "Rough break."

"Thank you, sir."

The doors open, and the boy and his father get off. Bowe and I are now left in the elevator together.

"It's not always so easy," Bowe says. "Standing next to you."

"I'm not going to apologize for it," I say.

"No," Bowe says, shaking his head. "Nor would I want you to."

The elevator opens on his floor. He gestures for me to go first, and we walk into his room.

It is smaller than I expected. He does not have a suite but instead a single bed, not much of a view.

When he closes the door behind us, I turn to look at him. "What is your plan?" I say, pointing to his ribs.

Bowe sits on the edge of his bed, softly. He shakes his head. "I don't know."

I sit next to him. "Are you in a lot of pain?" I ask.

Bowe nods. "It hurts like hell. I can barely breathe without feeling like my chest is ripping open."

"Are you taking anything?"

Bowe shakes his head. "No, and I'm not going to. I didn't kick alcohol just to take up worse stuff. I'll deal with it."

"What did the doctor say?"

Bowe frowns. "I'm out for weeks, at least. Wimbledon's fucked." He shakes his head. "The season is going to be winding down before I'm back on the court."

"I'm sorry," I say. I grab his hand and hold it. He looks down at our hands together, and I pull mine back. "You will be ready for the US Open. I know it. And Wimbledon isn't even your best surface. You're shit at anticipating the ball on grass."

"Yes, thank you," Bowe says. "I'm so glad you're here."

"What I'm saying is that the US Open is your best chance. And you will be better by then."

Bowe nods.

"Plenty of time to fuck shit up."

Bowe laughs.

"I am sorry," I say. "About saying you were embarrassing yourself."

"I shouldn't have lost my cool about any of it," Bowe says. "You play how you want to play—that's your business."

"Sometimes I think you're the only person who's harder to deal with than me," I say.

Bowe rolls his eyes. "Not even close."

I laugh. "You're going to be okay."

"I know, I know," he says. "It's not the end of the world."

I stand up.

"Are you really sticking around?" I ask.

"Yep," he says. "I meant what I told the reporters. I think you can win it, Carrie. I really do."

"I hate," I say, "how much that means to me."

Bowe laughs. "Yeah, look, I get it," he says. "I hate that I care so much what all of you Sotos think of me."

We are quiet for a moment, and then Bowe begins to speak. But before he can get a word out, I say, "I should go."

He looks thrown but quickly nods. "Good night, Soto. Rest up."

My father and I are at the practice courts after a sweltering session against a hitter. I'm drenched in sweat, and my father is sitting on the bench beside me, running through his plan for defeating Natasha Antonovich.

I've never played her before—only seen the devastation of her speed from the seats.

"She's quick," my father says. "The clay barely slows her down. It doesn't present the challenge for her that it does for others."

"So I have to be faster," I say.

My father shakes his head. "No. That is not what I'm saying."

"What do you mean?"

"Do not lose your temper," he says, "when I say this."

"I'm not going to lose my temper."

My father raises his eyebrow at me.

"I won't," I say, shifting my tone. "I promise."

"You are not as quick as she is," he says. "Maybe once you were. At your height, perhaps. But not now. Certainly not on clay."

I can feel my heart start to beat in my chest, my pulse rising.

"You have to be okay with that information, *hija*."

My vision narrows; my mouth tightens.

"You are not the same person you were when you played six years ago, in ways both good and bad. Your body is not the same. Your mind is not the same. You have to acknowledge the areas where you are not as strong," he says. "Even back then, clay was harder for you. We have to accept that. So that we can find another way."

"Go on . . ." I say. I thump my racket against my thigh.

"I don't want you trying to match her speed. What would be a better strategy?"

"I don't know. Just tell me."

"What do you have that she doesn't?"

"Crow's feet?" I say.

My father frowns. *"Dale, hija."*

"Time on the court," I say. "I have at least a decade of playing professional tennis over her."

My father nods. "Exactly."

"Just get to the point," I say. "I don't need the Socratic method."

My father frowns again. "You have always excelled at shot selection and anticipation. You understand where the ball is going, how it will bounce. And you know how to construct a point—three, four, even five returns down the line. You have years of learning this. So let your body—which has done this a thousand times more than she has—guide you. You have instincts she doesn't have yet. Use them."

I sit down next to him. "You're saying play smarter."

"I'm saying control the court. When it's your serve, don't try to prove you can hit as fast. Set up the shots to benefit a slower game, not a quicker one. Because you know you're not the quicker player this time. And be economical in your movements, anticipate where the ball is going. Conserve your energy and let her tire herself out. Antonovich is the rare bird that if this goes three sets, you will probably beat her. Just stay still and slow her down. At every juncture. Even at the changeovers, stretch the time limit. Make her frustrated, make her wait. Don't play for speed. It's not how you win this one."

I am not sure he's right. I'm not sure muscle memory and shot selection is going to bridge the gap between Antonovich's speed and mine. Only me running as fast as possible can do that.

"I . . . I don't know, Dad."

"Carrie, listen to me. I have gone over this in my head a thousand times."

"Dad, I need to get through Antonovich to get to Chan. I *have* to. I can't fail this time."

"I know you feel that way," he says. "Trust me, I know that. That's why I've been up the past two nights, going over old tape in my hotel room. I'm desperate for you. You have to know how much . . ."

I wait for him to finish his sentence, but he seems to have given up on finding the words.

"How much what?"

He sighs. "How much I worry," he says, resting his back against the bench. "I worry about how you will feel if you do not win this match, or the semifinals. Or the final."

I nod.

"I do not want to see the look on your face if it were to come to pass that Chan wins. If she takes your record. I do not think I could bear to see it."

"I know, me neither."

"No, I'm saying I don't think I could bear to see what it would do to *you*," he says. "My feelings won't change one way or another if you win, *hija*. But . . ."

He looks down and then back up at me. "Sometimes I think you don't understand the heartache I feel when I see you lose," he says, catching my eye and not letting go. "Knowing how badly you want it, knowing how much your soul needs it. Sometimes I think it is enough to break me."

"Dad . . ." I say, putting my hand on his shoulder. "I will be okay."

"Is that true?" he asks.

I close my eyes and let my shoulders fall.

There have been so many times in my life when I've lost and it was not okay. Times when I paced in my hotel room for more than twenty-four hours straight; times I didn't sleep or eat for days. After I lost at Wimbledon in '88, I flew home and shut myself in my bedroom and didn't come out for two and a half weeks.

"It is my responsibility to take care of myself," I tell him. "Whether I win or lose. That's on me."

My father shakes his head with a smile. "It will never matter," he says, "whose responsibility is what. My heart hurts when you hurt because *you* are my heart."

I inhale sharply.

"So please, listen to me, and let's work on your first serve, let's work on your shot selection, let's construct some points here, hypothetically, against her."

I nod. I get what he's saying, and he is right about some of it. "Yeah, okay," I say. But I also do need to meet her speed. And if I'm not there yet, I need to spend as much of today as I can getting there. "I'll do your thing, but also, I do need to work on my speed. So let's do both."

My father frowns slightly. "All right."

"Can we get a second ball machine? Having them both coming at me? I'm gonna rise to the occasion. Watch me."

My father nods, and within twenty minutes, I'm hitting balls hurtling at me from both machines. I spend a couple hours at it. Forehand to backhand, up to the net, back at the baseline. I meet the ball time and again.

At the end of the day, as I'm coming off the court, my father raises his eyebrows at me and I shine. I can tell he's impressed, maybe even a little surprised.

"I don't think Antonovich's speed is going to be a problem," I say.

"*Bien, pichona,*" he says.

"It's so close, Dad."

My father pulls me into him, putting his arm around my shoulders and kissing the top of my head. "Go out there tomorrow and take it," he says.

SOTO VS. ANTONOVICH

1995 French Open

Quarterfinals

NATASHA ANTONOVICH IS FIVE ELEVEN AND EXTREMELY THIN. HER visor, shirt, and tennis skirt are all bright white. She elects to serve first without a hint of emotion, her face an arid desert where no smile can grow. *Like I should talk.*

I look up at the stands. My father is staring straight ahead. But next to him is Bowe. He smiles at me.

I look back and crouch down, waiting. Antonovich tosses the ball up into the air.

Her first serve is flat and angry, but it hits just outside the line and I relax. Then the linesman calls it in. I walk up to the line of the service box, ready to fight it. But the dent in the clay shows that it has indeed hit the line, by just a hair.

She's got an ace.

Fuck.

I realign.

She serves another just like it, but right on the T this time, instead of cross-court. I am stunned as I watch the ball get past me again.

The crowd begins cheering. The hairs on the back of my neck start to rise. I roll my shoulders, trying to calm myself down.

Get it together.

I get my head straight. She runs me all over the court, but I meet her there, and then I run her all over too. There are some games when I'm outpacing her. But still, she takes the first set, 6–4.

During the changeover, I wipe my face and my racket. I tap the clay off my shoes. I look up at the players' box to see Bowe and my father talking. Bowe nods as my father gesticulates gently, speaking no doubt in a whisper.

I do not know what they are saying, but I know what I need to do.

I need to get more on Antonovich's level. I need to run as fast as her, take the ball out of the air even quicker.

I close my eyes and breathe in deeply. Antonovich stands in front of me, waiting for my serve. I toss the ball in the air and spin it toward her as fast as I can. I can feel the force of it reverberating up my arm, from the elbow to my shoulder. It sneaks past her.

I pump my fist. *Here we fucking go.*

I do it again, and this time she returns it, but it lands a foot past the baseline. I have got this. I hold the first game in the set.

As the set goes on, both of us are playing at our top levels, and neither one of us can break the other's serve. It's 3–3 and then 3–4 and then 4–4. I serve another game, I hold it. We're at 5–4.

Now it's her serve.

I do not look at my father. I do not want to see the worry in his eyes. I tell myself: *Do not let her win this set. You are either a champion or a fuckup. There is no in-between.*

Antonovich sends a screamer right down the T, and I meet it

with an inside-out forehand. But it hits the tape at the top of the net. *Goddammit.*

If she holds this game and then breaks mine, it's all over. I cannot have all these eyes on me, watching me fail. I cannot be the pathetic bitch they think I am.

But Antonovich just keeps coming. It doesn't matter if I run her around the court—she just glides into position, nicks the ball with the edge of her racket, puts it where she wants it.

We're at 5–5. Then 5–6.

Now she's serving for the match. If I don't break her serve on this game, it's over.

I crouch down low. I move the weight back and forth from one foot to the other. She tosses the ball. This is my moment. My moment to take it all back.

She serves one deep into the corner. I run like hell, even though my knee is starting to ache. I return it into the net.

15–love.

30–love.

40–love.

CARRIE! For fuck's sake, pull it together!

Her serve. Match point.

She sends the ball screaming over. I return it, fast and clean. She hits a groundstroke. I return to her backhand. I can feel the hum in my bones. I can feel this match coming to me—later than I want, but it's here.

Antonovich takes the ball out of the air early. I reach it, return it cross-court. Before I complete my follow-through, she's under it, chipping it over the net. I dive, my chest hitting the ground, sliding with my racket outstretched.

The ball hits the clay and I'm still feet away. It's over.

The crowd erupts for Antonovich. I lie frozen, staring at the dent in the clay where the ball landed.

When I finally get up and dust myself off, I am covered in red clay—my shoes, my knees, my skirt, and tank top are all rust. It is in my hair and in my mouth. It feels like it is in my lungs.

My eye lands on a woman in the crowd a few rows back. She is in her twenties or so, and she's holding a sign that says *Oui, oui, Carrie!*

I cannot bear the sight of her.

"I DIDN'T PLAY MY BEST! SO IF THAT'S WHAT YOU'RE ABOUT TO SAY, Dad . . . don't."

I am standing in the tunnel about to head to the showers. My knee is screaming. I need a massage and ice. I need a lot of things.

Antonovich comes up behind me and passes by. I can feel her trying to catch my eye as she walks into the locker room, but I continue to stare at my father instead.

He is standing against the wall, his eyes closed.

"Carolina," he says. His voice is calm and slow. "Now is the time for perspective. We talked about this."

"Dad!" I say. "Don't pretend that what I did out there was good enough! It wasn't!"

"I understand that you didn't win the match as you'd hoped. . . ."

"Didn't win the match as I'd hoped?" I yell. I can hear the other coaches and players coming down the tunnel, so I pull him into an open room off the corridor. "I just lost my second shot at a title," I say. "I only have four chances!"

"I understand that."

"I think we should all be pretty *fucking* worried that I am not going to be able to do what I set out to do!"

"Do not swear at me. I told you yesterday I was concerned about this possibility."

"I went out there and told everyone that I am the greatest living tennis player, and now I'm proving myself wrong! In front of the entire world!"

My father nods but says nothing.

"You're just going to stand there? Say something!" I shout.

"What do you want me to say?" he asks, throwing his hands in the air.

"Tell me that you can see the colossal fuckup I've just committed! That you know I'm a better player than I was today! That I am as good as I think I am! Or I'm not! If that's what you think! But say something. I've lost my shot at the goddamn French Open, and we both know Nicki's gonna take it! Say something!"

He looks at me and frowns. He begins to pace, shaking his head. There's a folding chair next to a card table, and just when I think he's approaching the chair to sit down, he pulls back and kicks it into the wall. "What do you want from me?" he yells.

"I—"

"You may *not* be the greatest living tennis player anymore!" he says. "I don't know. We don't know! You want me to keep telling you that, but I don't know, Carolina."

"I—"

"I'm not allowed to have any doubts! I'm not allowed to see you as my daughter, as a human being. I'm not allowed to say that years after retirement there *might* be better players now, to express *any uncertainty whatsoever.* So I tell you what you want to hear! So that you have what you need to feel okay. So that you're in my life. Those were the terms you set up! And I live by them! What do you want me to say?"

"I want you to be honest!"

My father shakes his head. "No, you want my honest opinion to be the exact thing you need to hear."

I can feel an ache in my teeth from clenching my jaw. I try to loosen it, but it tightens right back up.

My father looks at me. "Carrie, I do not know how to have an honest conversation with you about your tennis game. Because as good as you are, you have never been able to make peace with failure."

My chest tightens. My eyes feel dry. "And why *the fuck* do you think that is?"

"I think it's because—"

"It's because of you!"

My father shakes his head and looks down at the floor. It's as if he's not disagreeing with me so much as he's disappointed that this was the turn the conversation took so quickly.

But I feel the exact opposite. I feel like it's taken decades to get here.

"You told me I was supposed to be the greatest player in the history of tennis. You said it since the day I was born! You told me it was all I was ever meant to be! And then one day I wasn't anymore. You weren't even sure that I could beat her!" I say.

"Are we talking about Stepanova?" he says.

"I asked you if you thought I could get the number one ranking over her, and you said, 'I don't know.'"

"And you've never forgiven me for it," he says. "I'm paying that price even today."

"You should pay it for the rest of your life!" I say. "For making me believe in myself like that and then pulling the rug out from under me. For giving up on me when things were at their hardest. I never gave up on this. Ever. And you did!"

"Carrie, you asked me if I thought you could take number one from Paulina. And I said I didn't know. Because I didn't. I don't know what the future holds. And I can't promise the world is going to always turn out the way you want it to.

"I owed you that honesty, I thought. So you could assess better— how to grow, how to widen your perspective. It felt like it was time for that. But you didn't want to do that then, and you don't want to do that now.

"I've messed up a lot as your father, and I take responsibility for that. But this one, I'm sorry, only you can solve it. You have to make peace with not being a perfect player," he said.

"That is giving up. I won't do it," I said.

My father shakes his head. "You have to find a way to be right with who you actually are, to face what life is really like. I expected you to figure that out by now. But you haven't. And if you don't, I can't see how you ever get past this . . . this moment. You have accomplished so much, but you are instead so focused on keeping it, rather than going out and finding something else in the world."

He walks toward the door. "Everything we achieve is ephemeral. We have it, and then the next second it's gone. You had that record, and you may lose that record. Or you may defend it now and lose it in two years all over again. I wish you'd accept that."

I shake my head and try to look at him. "I can't."

"Well," he says. "It kills me that I cannot fix that for you, *hija*. But I can't. Nobody else can."

And then, as if the door were the lightest thing in the world, he opens it and walks right through, leaving me there alone.

When I finally make my way back to my floor at the hotel, I come out of the elevator to see Bowe standing in front of my door, signing an autograph for a teenage girl. She walks away before she sees me approaching.

When I get to Bowe, he says, "I wasn't sure if you'd want me here or not. But I figured you wouldn't be shy about telling me to fuck off if you didn't."

I drop my things and hug him. I can feel his surprise, but he quickly puts his arms around me. He does it gently, mindful of his ribs.

"Dust yourself off. Your best surface is just around the bend," he says.

His arms are warm and sturdy. His body is strong. I feel like I could go slack against him and he'd hold me up, that he could bear my weight—the weight of my body, the weight of my failure.

"I was worried people would stop respecting my record if Nicki beat it. But now . . . I'm . . . I'm just ruining my record myself."

I am sitting with my feet on the coffee table, my head resting against the back of the sofa. Bowe is in the chair opposite me, trying to find a position that doesn't hurt his ribs.

"I don't think that's true," he says. "I think people respect the attempt. I think they will respect the attempt even more than the achievement. Which will happen. You will achieve it."

I look at him and frown. "C'mon."

"I'm serious."

I look up at the ceiling. "My father thinks my priorities are all fucked-up."

Bowe laughs softly. "I don't think there is a dad alive who believes in their child more than he believes in you. You see that, right?"

I look at Bowe. "Yeah," I say. "I do."

Bowe leans back slowly. I can tell he is at least feeling better than before. "You're lucky," he says.

"You mean because of my dad?"

"Yeah."

"Didn't your dad play tennis?" I ask. "Isn't that how you started?"

"My uncle," Bowe says. "Yeah. And I was never good enough. Nothing I ever did was good enough. But I just kept trying to please him. And I just kept failing."

"And your parents?"

"They didn't care. My father was a mathematician. My mom is still a math teacher. They didn't understand my obsession with tennis and would have preferred, I think, that I did something a bit more . . . traditional."

"They wanted you to be a doctor or a lawyer?"

"Or a mathematician," Bowe says.

I laugh. "So you're what happens when you don't do what your dad wants, and I'm what happens when you do exactly what your dad wants."

Bowe laughs.

"And now we're both disasters," I say.

Bowe shakes his head. "You're not, Soto. I know you can't see it—because you're one of those annoying kids in school who thinks getting ninety-nine on the test only means you didn't get one hundred."

"It does mean that."

"Yeah, and there you go, ruining the curve for everybody else."

"And everyone hates me."

"I wish you could see it from the outside."

"See what?"

Bowe looks me in the eye and is quiet for a moment. And then he says, *"Eres perfecta, incluso en tu imperfección."*

I sit up, unsure I heard him right. But of course I did. His accent is terrible, but it has knocked the wind out of me just the same.

You are perfect, even in your imperfection.

"How did you put that together?"

"I mean, that's kind of embarrassing to answer."

"Still."

"I found a woman in the lobby of my hotel who spoke Spanish, and I asked her how to help me translate a few things."

"A few things? What else did she translate for you?"

"Well, no," Bowe says. "I can't tell you that."

"Why?"

"Because I just wanted to have a few options in case any of it was relevant."

I stand up and walk over to him. "What were the other options? Did you memorize them all?"

"No," he says. "I tried, but I kept getting them wrong."

"So you wrote them down."

He's still seated, and I'm standing over him. Bowe looks up at me.

"You wrote them down, and they are in your pocket," I say.

"Please don't try to get into my pockets—it's gonna kill my ribs. Seriously, I'm begging you."

There is a past version of me that would have dug into his pockets anyway—that would tell him to deal with the pain. I cringe to remember some of the things I've said to myself—and even to other people—back when I was in my prime. *Man up and play through! Stop being a baby and dominate!*

But I don't want to say any of those things now. I just want to make sure he's not hurting . . . and to see what he's written down.

"Please," I say, my voice low. "Show me."

He frowns and then lifts himself off the chair ever so slightly. He takes a piece of hotel stationery out of his pocket.

"Please don't laugh at me," he says.

I take the paper and open it. There are three Spanish phrases, all written out in his messy handwriting.

You are perfect, even in your imperfection.

You are completely insufferable, and I can't stop thinking about you.

I want the real thing this time.

"You wrote these down? So you could say them to me?"

"Yes."

"If I kiss you, will it hurt?" I ask, moving closer to him.

"What?"

"Your ribs. If I kiss you, will I hurt you?"

"No," he says. "I don't think so."

I put both of my hands on his face and kiss him. He reaches his good arm across my lower back and pulls me toward him.

I've kissed him before, years ago. But this feels both familiar and brand-new, like a good stretch, like a deep breath.

"I don't know what this is," I say. "I don't know if it's the real thing or not."

"I don't care," he says, kissing me again. He grabs at the hem of my T-shirt and the buttons on my jeans.

"I don't want to hurt you."

"I don't care about that either," he says, kissing me again.

"You have to be careful," I say. "Of your ribs."

"Carrie, please," he says, kissing my neck. "Stop worrying."

And so I do.

Later, as the sunlight begins to filter through the window of my hotel room in the early hours of the morning, I wake up to see Bowe asleep next to me.

His hair is sticking up straight in the back, a cowlick let loose at some point in the night. His face, up close, is weathered. There are fine wrinkles around his eyes. I turn away and look out the window, overcome with this awful, sinking feeling. As happy as you are when it starts, you always end up that same amount of sad when it's over.

He begins to stir, his eyes opening slowly and reluctantly. He looks at me and smiles.

He says, "Should we order breakfast?"

"You're going to stay?" I ask.

He sits up, fully awake all of a sudden. "You want me to go?"

"Do you want to go? You can go if you want."

"I don't want to go. I told you that last night. In Spanish."

"Okay," I say.

"So I'm staying?" he says.

"If you want to."

Bowe rolls his eyes and growls. He puts a pillow over his head, but I can still hear him bitching. "You are so annoying," he says. "Just say you like me, for fuck's sake!"

I pull the pillow off his head. I want to say it. I try to make myself.

"What do you want for breakfast?" I say. "I'll call down."

Bowe and I spend the next few days together, walking around Paris. My father, who I still have barely spoken to, stays in his room. Gwen's office booked us all flights home the day after the final.

Tonight, Bowe and I are at a French bistro around the corner from my hotel. The women's final is playing on the television by the bar: Chan vs. Antonovich.

I'm wearing one of Bowe's baseball caps and a pair of sunglasses. We are sitting out on the patio. Part of me wants to run back to the hotel and hide, to not be in public right now. But if people recognize us, they don't acknowledge it. And I want to be here, at this bistro, with Bowe.

We can see the TV from our table. At first, we are both pretending not to watch, but by the time Nicki has won the first set, we have given up all pretenses.

Bowe grabs my hand as the second set begins. I don't pull it away, even when our food arrives. Antonovich takes the second set while we eat our steak frites.

"Maybe Antonovich has a shot," Bowe says.

I frown at him. "I almost wish Cortez had made it past Antonovich in the semis," I say. "I think Cortez could beat Nicki here. But Antonovich . . . I don't know. I don't know."

He nods.

Forty-five minutes later, Nicki takes the third set, 6–4. She drops to the ground, victorious and tearful.

That's the match, that's the tournament, that's my record. Shattered.

Bowe looks at me, but he knows there's nothing to say. We watch as the officials hand Nicki Chan the cup.

All of the coverage is in French, so I only half understand the commentators. But it's clear enough when I hear, "*Elle a maintenant dépásse Carrie Soto . . .* " *She has overtaken Carrie Soto.*

Bowe catches my eye. And for a moment, I feel the nearly irresistible urge to flip the table we are sitting at.

"She deserves it," I say. "She played a brutal match."

Down the sidewalk, I see my father walking toward me. And I know that I'm supposed to be mad at him, or he's supposed to be mad at me. But I don't really care very much at the moment. Rather, I'm overwhelmed by a sense of inevitability: Of course he would come find me.

"Hi," he says as he makes his way to us on the sidewalk patio. He puts one hand on my shoulder and then the other on Bowe's. "You both did a great job here in France."

He looks me in the eye, and I don't look away. It feels as if the two of us are cycling through decades of moments together, everything that's led to this. My unparalleled achievement. Now hers.

"I have not made peace with it," I say. "If that's what you're wondering."

"*Ya lo sé, pichona,*" he says.

I look up at the television. Nicki is crying, her shoulders heaving, actual tears falling down her face.

"Come sit," I say.

My father nods and pulls a chair over to join us.

The waitress comes by, and Bowe orders my father a drink. Dad leans over and whispers in my ear, "Nothing will ever diminish what you did and have done."

I do not want to cry, so I can't really think too hard about whether I believe him. Instead, I take the moment and pin it to my heart, as if it will wait for me to come back to it later.

I smile, and I pat his hand, and then I change the subject.

Bowe, my father, and I spend the night at that table. We drink club sodas and ginger ales. Bowe laments having to drop out of Wimbledon. My dad tells Bowe that he'll coach him full-time for the US Open, if Bowe is healed by then.

Bowe reaches his hand out and they shake on it—and I notice how gently my father moves, so as not to hurt Bowe's ribs.

When it gets late, Bowe pays the check, and my father raises his eyebrows at me—as if to pose the question that I've told him a million times not to ask. I nod: the only answer he'll get. And he looks at me and grins, a simple, bright smile.

For a moment, I'm bowled over by just how old he looks. *When did this happen?* But he looks a happy old, a satisfied old. He's had a lot of heartbreak in his life, and yet there is so much he's gotten right.

Sos mi vida, pichona, my father mouths to me. He taps a finger to his chest, right over his heart.

I smile and rest my head on his shoulder for a split second.

And then we all walk back to the hotel—a walk that feels comfortable and familiar, even though there is so much about it that is new.

The Inevitability of Chan

By Rachel Berger

Op-Ed, Sports Section
California Post

Carrie Soto has made no secret of her intention to prevent Nicki Chan from overtaking her record. So it must have made the cut that much deeper when Chan won last night.

Some have been dismissive of Soto's attempt at a comeback. But I am among the growing number of those who cannot help but marvel at the attempt.

Many have been quick to forget what Carrie Soto has done for women's tennis. She set the bar for many of the things we now take for granted: incredibly fast serves, brilliant matches that broke multiple records at a time. And we have all but lost the most exquisite thing she brought to the sport: the grace of the game.

I do not care how hard Nicki Chan can hit a ground-stroke or how fast her serve can be—she cannot hold a candle to the beauty with which Carrie Soto has played. Each shot executed to perfection, every dive for the ball as graceful as a ballet. So I join Carrie Soto in mourning her loss.

And yet, we cannot deny that the tide has turned.

Carrie Soto is the past. Nicki Chan is the future.

The Queen is dead, long live the Queen.

I WAKE UP TO THE HOTEL PHONE RINGING. BOWE HANDS IT TO ME, half-asleep.

It's Gwen.

"Elite Gold is officially pausing the campaign," she says. "I thought you'd want to know sooner rather than later."

I want to scream or throw the phone or bury my head under my pillow, but I don't. "Okay, I understand."

"AmEx is exploring buying them out, but they haven't committed," she says.

"It's your job to convince them," I say.

"Yes, it is. And it's your job to remember I warned you this could happen. And you told me it was worth the risk."

"Yes," I say. "Yes, I did."

"It will be okay. This will all work out in the end."

"Yeah," I say. But neither of us sounds convinced.

. . .

A few hours later, I do my best to put it behind me as we all get on the plane back to Los Angeles. I switch seats with my father, who has the one next to Bowe. He does not tease me or raise an eyebrow—which I appreciate. He takes my spot two rows ahead.

A couple of college-age girls approach us early in the flight and ask us for our autographs. We agree, but then more people start coming down the aisle.

Soon enough, Bowe starts telling people that he's a Bowe Huntley impersonator, and I stare—mouth half-open—when they actually seem to believe him. I try it on the next woman who comes up, and she just frowns at me and says, "You can't just sign one lousy piece of paper? Unbelievable."

When she storms off, Bowe rolls his eyes and then puts his head on my shoulder. I push it away.

"Everyone on this flight recognizes us," I say.

"So?"

"So when this thing between us goes tits-up, I don't want to have to answer questions about it in a post-match."

Bowe looks at me, his eyebrows high and furrowed. He pinches the bridge of his nose.

"I just mean . . ." I add.

"No, I got it," he says, shifting his weight to the window. "Enough said."

"I'm just saying we don't know what we're doing yet."

"Okay," he says. "I got it. Let's drop it."

He's quiet for an hour or two. But when the flight attendants come by offering chocolates, he wordlessly hands me his.

The plane lands a few hours later, and Bowe reaches for my dad's carry-on from the overhead compartment, despite the fact that it clearly kills his ribs.

"Here you go, Jav," he says.

"Jav?" I say. "You're on a nickname basis now?"

"Of course we are," my dad says. Though he's joking around, he seems tired. "Thanks, B."

"Bowe is already short for Bowen," I say. "You don't need to shorten it again."

My dad waves me off. "Mind your own business, Care."

Bowe laughs, and I throw up my hands.

The line begins to move, and the flight attendants gesture for us to go. The three of us exit the row and get off the plane.

"What is our next meal?" Bowe says. "Is it dinner?"

"It's eleven in the morning, so . . . no," I tell him.

"No need for the attitude," Bowe says. "Just say lunch."

I turn back to look at my father. "Are you hungry, Dad?" I ask, but before I even finish the sentence, I can see he's stopped walking. He's holding up the line of passengers behind him. He's lost all the color in his face.

"Carrie . . ." he says.

"Dad?" I take a step to where he's standing.

He collapses on the jet bridge just before I can catch him.

THE CARDIOLOGIST, DR. WHITLEY, IS A WOMAN WITH CURLY RED HAIR and what appears to be a moral opposition to good bedside manner. She looks up at my father and me. "This is an extreme case of cardio-toxicity," she says.

My father is sitting up in the hospital bed. I'm in a chair next to him. Bowe tried to stay, but we both insisted he go home.

"What does that mean?" I ask.

Dr. Whitley does not look away from my father. "It means you are in stage three heart failure, Mr. Soto. Most likely a side effect of the chemo treatment you had last year."

My father gives the slightest scoff. "What doesn't kill you . . . might still kill you."

I grab his hand and squeeze it, offering him a smile.

"Have you been experiencing light-headedness? Shortness of breath?" she asks.

I answer "No" on his behalf just as my father speaks up. "Yes. Both."

I look at him. "I've been feeling weak too," he adds. "More and more."

"Why didn't you say anything?" I ask.

He ignores me.

"Your oncologist should have told you those were symptoms to watch for," Dr. Whitley says.

"They did," I say. "They did tell us that last year."

Dr. Whitley nods. "If you had spoken up sooner, we could have put you on beta-blockers," she says. "Now the damage is done. You will need surgery to fix the tear and put in a pacemaker."

I stop breathing for a second. I stare straight ahead at the poster on the wall, an ugly still life of a vase of flowers. I try to control my breath and focus as best I can on the mauve plastic picture frame. I swallow, hard. "When do you plan on doing that?" I ask. "The surgery."

Dr. Whitley closes the chart. "Within the next few days. And, Mr. Soto, you will need to stay in the hospital until then. And some time after, as we monitor your progress."

My father shakes his head. "I do not have time for this. We play Wimbledon in three weeks."

"Dad—" I say.

Dr. Whitley's face does not move. "I urge you to listen to the medical advice you're paying for. We have reached a point of life or death."

My father quiets and then nods, and Dr. Whitley leaves the room.

I stand up and wait for the door to close, and then I look at him. "For crying out loud, why didn't you say something?"

"*Eso no es tu problema,*" he says.

"*¡Todos tus problemas son mis problemas!*"

"*Puedo cuidarme solo, Carolina. Sos mi hija, no mi madre.*"

"*¡Sí, y como tu hija, si te mueres, yo soy la que sufre, papá!*"

"*No quiero pelear con vos. Ahora no.*"

I look at him and shake my head. I already know why he didn't say anything, and the reason barely matters now anyway.

His face is pale. He's hooked up to machines. He looks so small. I feel another rush of anger. I press my lips together and close my eyes.

"*Bueno*," I say. "So we will get ready for you to have the surgery, then."

"And I'll recover quickly and be back on the court with you in no time," he says.

"Dad, let's not get into that now."

"There's nothing to get into. This doesn't set us back at all."

"Dad . . ."

"Say they get me in tomorrow for the surgery; it goes well. What's recovery time? A week?" He takes my hand. "This is a minor setback. By July we'll be ready for London."

"*Bueno, papá*," I say.

He picks up the remote control and turns on the television and pretends to watch it. So I sit back in the chair and let him.

Then, suddenly, he's yelling. "I am not missing Wimbledon! We may never have another Wimbledon together, and I will not miss it!"

I put my head in my hands. "*Ya lo sé, papá*," I say.

"The last time we were there, back in '78, I didn't know it was our last. I didn't know that I might never coach you again. And I'm not letting this one slip through my goddamn fingers."

"*Está bien, lo entiendo*," I say. "*Te amo, papá.*"

He looks at me and for the first time in this conversation, he lets a frown take hold in the corners of his mouth. "*Yo también, cariño.*"

And then, after he takes a breath, "*Perdoname, hija. Realmente lo siento.*"

That night, I ask the nurse to help me pull out a cot.

"*De ninguna manera*," my father says to me. He turns to the nurse. "That won't be necessary."

"Dad, I'm not leaving you here alone," I say.

"Has it ever occurred to you I might *like* to be by myself?"

"Dad—"

"Sleep at home, Carrie. Please. And in the morning, please go out onto the court with a ball machine," he says. "Do not stop training. You cannot afford to right now."

"I don't know about—"

"You're playing Wimbledon, Carolina María."

The nurse excuses herself, and I sit down for a moment.

"Por favor, no te pierdas Wimbledon. Por favor."

"Dad, I'm not sure—"

My father breathes out, a long and deep breath. He shakes his head. "Even if—I'm saying *if*—I can't be there," he says.

I have to stop the corners of my mouth from pulling down.

"Pero, por favor, play it one more time. *Te encanta jugar Wimbledon. Por favor, hacelo por mí."*

I cannot imagine leaving him. But I also know, right now, I'm not going to fight him.

"Está bien," I say. *"Lo jugaré."*

"Gracias, ahora, andá. Go home."

He seems so determined. *"Bueno,"* I say, grabbing my bag. "I'll see you in the morning."

"Come see me in the afternoon," he says. "Every day, first you train. And then you can come see me after."

I shake my head as I smile at him. "Okay, I'll come tomorrow after I train." I grab his hand and squeeze it.

"Buena, niña," he says.

I walk down the hall and hit the elevator button.

As I wait, I can see out of the corner of my eye that there is a nurse at the station whose gaze lingers on me. She either knows who I am or is trying to figure out where she recognizes me from. I let her wonder as I get in the empty elevator.

When the doors finally close, I lean my back against the wall. I sink down to the floor. "Please let him leave this hospital," I say. It is barely more than a whimper, and I hate the sound of it.

That night, Bowe comes over, and as I'm falling asleep, he puts his arm around me and says, "Everything is going to be okay."

"Everyone always says that," I tell him. "And no one ever knows if it's true."

A couple of days later, my father goes in for surgery. Instead of staying home and training like he has told me to do, I spend the entire day in the waiting room so I can hear the results the moment the surgeon is done.

When Dr. Whitley comes out, she has no smile on her face. For a moment, I feel as if life as I know it is ending. My chest constricts; the room grows hot. But then she says, "He's doing fine." And suddenly I can breathe again.

"Thank you," I say.

"You should go home," she tells me. "He will probably sleep the rest of the night."

But I don't.

I wait until he's moved to recovery and then fall asleep in the chair beside him. Just hearing his breath is enough to allow me to sleep soundly.

In the morning, when he wakes up, he is groggy and confused. But Dr. Whitley says that his pacemaker is operating properly.

"So when can I go home?" he asks.

Dr. Whitley shakes her head. "You have to stay here and recover. The surgery was long, the repairs have to heal. We need you here for observation."

"For how long?"

"Dad, you need to focus on getting better," I say.

He holds my hand and ignores my words. "How long?" he asks again.

"A week at least," she says. "Maybe more."

"Okay," my dad says with a nod. "I understand."

When the doctors leave, I start to ask my dad if he wants me to bring him anything else from home. But he cuts me off.

"If we can't train together, you are wasting your time on the home court. You need to go to London and practice on grass."

"Dad—"

"No," he says. "You know that I'm right. We would have left for London by now anyway. You need to go on your own."

"I know, Dad, but I'm not leaving for London yet, not with you still in the hospital."

"Yes, you are, and don't fight me on it. I've been thinking about this for days now. This is the new plan."

There is a gentle knock at the door. I see Bowe standing in the doorway, holding a fern and a balloon that says *Get Well Soon.*

"Hey, Jav," he says. "Hope I'm not intruding. I just wanted to check on you."

"Come in, come in," my father tells Bowe, who smiles at me. "Actually, I have a great idea," my dad says. "Bowe can come check on me while you're in London. You'll do that, won't you, Bowe?"

Bowe nods. "Absolutely. As long as you need. With my ribs, I can't play tennis. I have *nothing* to do. You could even argue nothing to live for. So yes. It would be a favor to me if you let me check in on you."

I look at the two of them.

"This is a setup," I say.

"It is not a setup," my father says.

"We discussed it prior to today," Bowe says. "If that's what you're saying."

My father rolls his eyes at Bowe. "Don't give up information that hasn't been directly requested."

"Okay," Bowe says. And then he looks at me and mouths, *Sorry.*

"You agree with me that she needs to go to London to train," my father says to Bowe.

And to that, Bowe's answer is clear and appears perfectly honest. "There's no doubt about it. You know damn well you need to go to London."

I hate that they are right.

That Saturday, I'm in a black town car, headed to the hospital to visit my father one last time before my flight. There's a ticket from LAX to Heathrow in my bag. I can barely believe I'm doing this.

When we pull up to the front entrance, the driver drops me off and tells me he'll be waiting in the hospital parking garage.

None of this feels right.

"You'll practice with a hitter every day and then call me each night to talk about the strategy for the next day," my father says after I give him a hug. "We have this under control."

"Don't worry about all of that right now, Dad," I say. I take his hand. "You have one job right now and that is to get healthy."

My father nods. *"Ya lo sé, pero no es el trabajo que quería."*

"I know."

I rub the back of my father's hand. I can see that the years have gained on him. His skin is papery, his knuckles swollen. The hair on his wrists is nearly fully gray.

"Be well," I say to him. "Do everything the doctors tell you. Be the best patient they have. I'll be home in a little more than a month."

In this moment, it feels absolutely impossible that I could leave. For a moment, I wonder if maybe I never *really* planned on getting on that plane this afternoon. I've just been going through the motions so we'd both feel better.

Of course I can't go. Of course I'm staying.

"I don't know about this, Dad."

"Go play Wimbledon, *cariño.*"

I frown.

"Please," he says. "What would make me happiest is to watch you do something you love. So please, go play tennis. Play it like you used to. Play it like you love it, please. *Hacelo por mí, por mí corazón.*"

"Bowe is coming to the hospital this evening," I say, looking at my watch. "In about an hour. So he can get you anything you need."

"Okay. You're going to be late. So go ahead."

I breathe in deeply. And I kiss him on the head.

"Try to enjoy it, *pichona,*" my father says. "That's the one thing you have forgotten."

JUNE 1995

Three weeks until Wimbledon

AS I GET OFF THE PLANE AT HEATHROW, TWO TEENAGE GIRLS ARE standing with their mother and staring at me. I do not know what comes over me but instead of ignoring them, I wave. Their eyes go wide and they each wave back, their mouths agape. I laugh.

When I get into my car at the airport, I ask the driver to take me to my hotel by way of Wimbledon. He gives me a nod. And something about the way his eyes pass over me in the rearview mirror, the way he holds back a smile on his face, I can tell he is excited to do it.

I look out the window as we begin to drive. I watch the buildings and British billboards pass, until we finally reach the outskirts of the All England Lawn Tennis Club.

"Did you want to stop?" he says.

"No, thank you," I say. I just enjoy the sight of it—seeing the park and the courts fly by my window. I like gazing up at the ivy growing over the building at the front entrance. I feel the most like myself just outside that arena. As if I fully embody my own promise.

It is an unparalleled pleasure to be as good at something as I have been at playing Wimbledon.

I miss my father.

"You hold the record," my driver says as he catches my eye in the rearview mirror again. "Don't you now?"

"Which one?" I ask.

"Most Wimbledon wins. Men's or women's."

"Yes," I say. "I do."

He nods and puts his eyes back on the road. "Good on ya."

I check in to my hotel and unpack. I open the curtains and look out over the Thames and the Waterloo Bridge. The city is busy with cars and people—it is, after all—four P.M. in London. But I need to get some rest.

Ali has booked me courts to practice double sessions for the next three weeks. I requested different hitters each time. I need to be able to practice with all types of players.

I watch red double-decker buses cross the bridge, and I consider the biggest hurdle to my game: I need to get my mind right.

I take a shower. Scalding hot, so scorching it reddens the skin of my chest and legs. And then I call my father's room at the hospital.

Bowe answers.

"Hi," I say. "How is he?"

Bowe whispers his response. "He's sleeping now. But he's good. How are you?"

"I'm all right." I look at myself in the mirror of the bathroom as we talk. My hair is wet and pulled back; the white robe around me is bulky and warm. All I can focus on are the bags under my eyes—like two soft bruises. I can blame jet lag and age but also: When I'm alone, I cry.

"It feels weird being here without him," I say. "Or without you, to be honest."

"That's nice of you to say."

"I'm worried I won't find anyone to hit off of who is as good as you."

"Oh," Bowe says. And then he laughs.

"What?"

"No, nothing. Listen, your dad made these notes, and he'll be pissed if I don't relay them."

"Okay."

"He said, 'Spend tomorrow remembering the joy of grass. Do not play to win or to find perfection. Play to observe yourself and the ball.'"

"That's good advice," I say.

"He is, unfortunately, quite good at this," Bowe says.

And now I laugh. "Yes, I suppose he is."

We hang up the phone; I pull the curtains closed and put my eye mask on. I lie down on the gigantic bed.

The windows are thick, and the walls are thick too. My room is about as private and expansive as it gets in central London. And so, despite it being afternoon in a bustling city, things are eerily quiet.

I keep imagining my father coming over from the next room, knocking on my door to tell me he just had a brilliant idea. Or him bothering me to complain about a photo of him printed in the newspaper. Or some other thing that I would be annoyed by, as I tell him I want to go to sleep.

But he is not here.

I don't know when I finally doze off. But when I wake the next morning, I am rested.

I brush my teeth, put on my sweats, grab my kit. The hum is in my bones.

I head out to the courts. Alone.

My father was absolutely right. I have needed to feel the specific crispness of grass.

The hitter I'm playing this morning is named Bridget. She's fast but not terribly powerful. And yet, still, I feel a thrill as I run from sideline to sideline, up and back from the net to the baseline. It is such a joy to play on grass. I relish the snap, the speed, the low bounces, the unpredictability, the strategy. It is an entirely different game—lawn tennis.

And I fucking love it.

At the end of the session, Bridget says, "I fear I did not give you much of a run for your money." I have sweat on my forehead and upper lip. She's drenched through her tank top.

"That's all right," I say. "You did your best."

Her face tightens, and then she makes her way out. I sit down on the bench and drink some water. I begin running through what I want to work on with the ball machine—which shots I'll start with. My slice, in particular, needs some sharpening.

I take stock of my grass game. My footwork feels good. My serves are sharp. I'm putting the ball where I want it. I've come such a long way since Melbourne.

Still, even on grass, I'm probably not as fast as Antonovich. So if I do come up against her again, I will have to find another way to offset her speed. But that's what I'm here to do.

I look down at my yellow sneakers on the green turf. Maybe this whole season has been leading here. Maybe I just needed to come back to Wimbledon.

I stand up, trying to find one of the facility managers to get a ball machine. But when I scan the area, I see Nicki Chan walking past my court.

I pretend not to see her at first, but it soon becomes clear she's not the type to let me get away with that. Why are people like this? Honestly. Let's all just walk by each other all day and not stop to small-talk.

"Carrie," she says, smiling, extending her hand.

"You practice here?" I ask. "I would have thought you'd—"

Nicki shakes her head. "This place is a bit quieter. And I needed some focus. I booked a court out here for the next few weeks until we all head over to Wimbledon Park. You did too, then?"

"Yep."

Nicki laughs. "We both had the same good idea. All right, well," she says. "Maybe one of these days we can grab a drink."

"Maybe," I say. "I mean, no, I'm probably not going to do that."

Nicki laughs again. And I find it irritating, that laugh. It feels performative, like some false unflappability. "You know what somebody on the tour told me about you back in the day?" she asks.

"Oh great, here we go."

"No, no, it's not bad. Just . . . she said that you seem tough, you seem cold. But really, you're one of those players who keep to themselves because you feel conflicted when you have to kick somebody's ass."

"I just think it keeps it a lot simpler . . . to not care too much for anybody."

Nicki nods. "I understand."

"You don't feel that way?" I ask.

Nicki shakes her head. "I'd wreck my best friend in cold blood on national television."

The next morning, I'm awake at four. I can't stand to lie here, turning from one side to the other, fluffing the pillow, staring at the ceiling, thinking about Paris.

How I fucked it all up.

Handed Nicki that record.

I get out of bed and go into the living room. Ali put the matches I requested on VHS tapes and sent them over. I shuffle through the box until I find the one I need.

Soto vs. Antonovich.

My chest tightens as I put the tape in the machine and press play.

It's painful to watch. I hate how helpless I am to prevent what I know will happen onscreen. But it is my only way of ensuring that it does not happen again.

Right from the jump, I'm fast but I'm sloppy. My pace is so hurried, I'm not setting up my angles. I'm running for shots I know I can't get.

I have to will myself not to turn off the television.

The second set, I'm just plainly making bad choices. Not disguising my shots well. Hitting a groundstroke right to her. Sending a slice way too short. I'm choking. Just choking out there.

All because I'm trying to prove to Antonovich that she's not faster than me. When I can see it so clearly on the tape.

She is faster than me. That's exactly what she is.

I head down to the courts hours earlier than I'd planned. There is no one there. I've got the place to myself. And so I start hitting against the ball machine.

Part of what I love about a grass surface is how it requires such quick thinking. Other players may be able to run faster from one side of the court to the other. They might even be able to hit the ball so it moves faster across the net. But what I have always been good at, the challenge I have always taken pleasure in rising to, is thinking on my feet on a tennis court.

You have to ask and answer a series of questions in rapid succession: Where is the ball going? What way will it bounce when it hits? How do I want to hit it back? And where do I need to be standing in order to do that?

When I was a child, my father focused on the fundamentals—the stances, the form.

Look at the ball, turn, swing.

Look, turn, swing.

Look, turn, swing.

Look, turn, swing.

With a serve, it was legs bent, arms up, toss, hit, follow through.

Legs, arms, toss, hit, follow.

Legs, arms, toss, hit, follow.

Legs, arms, toss, hit, follow.

Hour after hour, day after day, the same drills. Sometimes not even hitting an actual ball but just doing the motions, feeling the routine of it. My dad would even make me do it in front of a mirror, watching each movement in my body as I flowed through the form.

I remember getting so frustrated at the repetition—the sheer boredom. My father made me practice long after I'd perfected it. And I would rail against him when I was a kid, but he would not be swayed from his plan, even one session.

"Do you think about breathing?" he asked me one afternoon on the courts when I was complaining. "You are breathing, with your lungs, every second you are alive, no?"

"Yes," I said.

"But do you think about it?"

"No, my body just does it."

"Think about how little else you could do if you had to think about how to breathe every time you did it."

"Okay . . ."

"I want your form to be like breathing. Right now, *hijita,* you are still doing it with your mind," he told me. "We will not stop until you have done it so many times, your body does it without thinking. Because then, you'll be free to think of everything else."

I don't know if I understood it then or just resolved to do as I was told. But when I joined the junior circuits and then the WTA, and I looked at the other women I was playing, I could see how slowly most other players reacted.

My father had crammed my forms, my stances, my strokes into my mind with such repetition that it made its way into my cells. It lived in my muscles and joints.

It's true, still, today.

And so, with every ball that comes at me, my mind remains free to run through every single shot I have in my arsenal, to consider the flaws in the court. I can better anticipate a bad bounce, or find a shot my opponent isn't expecting.

And then comes the moment when I make contact with the ball—and in that split second, muscle memory takes over.

Grass has always been perfect for that type of play.

As I stand here on the court, up against the ball machine, meeting each ball after the bounce, I am fluid. My body is just doing this. It is almost as if I'm not even here. This grace, this flow, this effortlessness—*this* is 1983 me.

When the machine runs out of balls for the fourth time, I stop. All hundred of them are strewn about on the other side of the court.

I am sweating and breathless. I look at my watch. I've been out here almost three hours—but I would have sworn it was twenty minutes. And for one brief moment, it feels like I am Carrie Soto.

"Hello."

I turn to find Nicki watching me through the fence, one hand gripping the grate. *Goddammit.*

"Oh. Hi."

"I came this early to avoid you," Nicki says, laughing.

"Sorry, been out here since about five A.M."

Nicki nods. "It is stunning," she says. "Watching you play."

I walk toward her. "Yeah, well, I am very good."

Nicki laughs again. "Yes, you are. The beauty of your form is . . . it's breathtaking. I remember it always being that way. You could see it even on TV back in the day. Just now, as I was spying a bit . . ." She shakes her head. "It's gorgeous tennis."

How am I supposed to respond to that? "A drink, tonight," I hear myself say. "If you still want. At the Savoy."

Nicki nods. "I'll be there."

Later that afternoon, I'm on the phone in the living room of my suite, looking out the window. "*No sé, papá, pero* . . . I just . . . I'm feeling that hum. I'm feeling like this could be it. This one could be mine."

His voice is small. "It will be, *hija*," he says. I keep pressing my ear harder into the receiver, as if by pressing hard enough, I can force myself through the line and be right next to him. "It will be."

"How are you feeling?"

"*Bien, bien. Pero* do not worry about me. Bowe is coming later this morning. I'm going to demolish him in another round of chess."

"And what does Dr. Whitley say?"

"She says everything is great. Stop worrying," he says.

"Okay," I say. "*Está bien.*"

I don't say what I'm thinking. *You are all I have.*

When I get down to the American Bar at the Savoy, Nicki is already there. She's talking to the bartender, who slides over a cocktail glass.

There's something so casually confident about Nicki, so unbothered. We're in an elegant bar and she's wearing a pair of black jeans and a T-shirt with a pair of Doc Martens. Her long hair hangs down her back.

Nicki waves to me, and I make my way over to the bar. She's drinking what seems to be gin with a twist.

"Absolut and soda, please," I say to the bartender, who nods but then looks back up at me. "Are you Carrie Soto?" she says.

I look at Nicki, who smiles as she takes a sip of her gin.

"Yeah," I say.

"Wow, big fan of yours," she says. "I mean, I don't know much about tennis, but I love your sneakers."

I laugh. "Well, good, I'm glad to hear it."

She heads down the bar, and Nicki laughs, shaking her head. "I've been sitting here talking to that beautiful woman for at least ten minutes, and somehow she doesn't recognize me. Even though my tennis shoes are better than yours, by the way."

Her line is with Nike. They are called 130s—a reference to the fact that she once hit a serve that clocked in at 130 miles per hour. They are the *second* bestselling women's tennis shoe in the UK.

"It appears she disagrees," I say.

"It's not that I *want* to be recognized, mind you," she says. "But if she's going to recognize you and not me . . . well, c'mon."

"You know," I say, sitting down, "I once showed up to cut a ribbon at a tennis center named after me in Arizona, and the woman at the front door wouldn't let me in because I wasn't on the list."

Nicki laughs and takes another sip of her drink. "It's a weird life."

"Yes, it is."

"I'm not always sure I like it."

My drink arrives, and I take a sip of it. "Not always much to like."

"Isn't it strange? How you get into this because you like to hit a ball around a court . . . ? And then, suddenly, you don't belong to yourself anymore? As if it's okay for people to call you 'the Beast' just because you're strong? And they can comment on your clothes and your hair? And make racist comments and pretend they are just joking? Just wait until they find out I'm a lesbian."

Nicki looks at me out of the corner of her eye, as if expecting me to spit out my cocktail. But I have long suspected she is gay, and I couldn't care less. Romantic relationships are so goddamn impossible, I'm honestly impressed with anyone who can keep one going at all.

Though, it's occurring to me now, that probably doesn't account for how hard it is for her to deal with the world's hang-ups about it. Or how hard it must be to decide who to confide in.

And she confided in me. And fuck if it doesn't make me like her more. *Goddamn her.*

"You don't have to tell me how shitty the press are. You're talking to a woman referred to as 'the Bitch,'" I remind her.

Nicki laughs. "I just wanted to play the game. And now, instead, I'm shooting TV commercials and telling twelve-year-old girls to believe in their dreams and agreeing to be a guest host on breakfast television. It just feels like . . . so many things get in the way of the actual point."

I look at her, and then I look down. I turn the glass. "Once you retire, then it's *only* about the TV commercials. And the charity functions and playing to the crowd for exhibition games. And the real tennis just sort of goes. Poof. Gone."

Nicki frowns. "No, I don't believe that."

I shrug. "Believe whatever you want."

"When I retire, I want to take up at my place in the Cotswolds and quit all the rest. Just spend my days playing on my court in the countryside."

"But against who?" I say. "There's no one to play except maybe other retirees. You're not gonna play the neighborhood girl—that's not fun. And you're not going to play anyone in the WTA, because they are busy on tour. And they certainly don't want to be beaten by you. The exhibition games are all right, but they are just for show—there's no real intensity. There's no one to play in any serious way. I swear there were days I'd wake up and my right hand would be jittery, wondering where the racket was."

Nicki nods. "So that's why you're back, then? Your right hand is jittery?"

"No," I say, shaking my head. "I came back to destroy you."

Nicki cackles so loud that people turn and stare. When she quiets, she leans in toward me. "I don't buy it for a second," she says, smiling. "It's about more than that."

"No, I'm dead serious. I want my fucking record back."

"Of course," Nicki says. "Of course you do. Who wouldn't?"

"And you took it."

"I didn't *take* it," Nicki says. "I earned it. The same way you did. But just one more Slam than you." She winks at me and then takes a drink.

"You haven't had to go up against anyone great," I say. "In the past six years, there's been almost nobody who can hold a candle to you."

"Exactly."

"Give me a break. It's easier to win when you don't have a Stepanova. Or somebody like Mary-Louise Bryant, who started out so stunning. Or me, even. The field has been leveled for you. It's not the same as the way I set the record."

Nicki shakes her head. "You sound like every pundit on ESPN."

"What?" I say. "Are you kidding me? Every sportscaster in the world is tripping over themself to crown you the best!"

"That's how it may seem to you. But what I hear—over and again—is that even when I beat your record, it's not good enough. I will never be Carrie Soto. I'll never be as graceful as you. I've never had a truly formidable opponent. Yes, I'm good on clay and hard court, but 'Carrie Soto reigns in London.' This is my hometown, but somehow it still belongs to you."

She takes another sip of her gin. "And then," she adds, "just when it looks like I'm finally going to silence them all, it becomes 'Wow! Carrie Soto is back!' And they all do cartwheels over you."

"I mean this from the bottom of my heart: Are you fucking high?" I say.

Nicki laughs.

"Try being told—over and over and over again—that if you do manage to win anything this year, you will set a record for being the oldest bitch to ever do it."

Nicki laughs. "Yes, I'm sure it's terribly awful to know that if you win Wimbledon, you will set two records and match mine."

My fists clench. It takes everything I have not to slam my hand on the bar and remind her who had that record first, who *made* that record. *There is no you without me.*

But I have no leg to stand on anymore. I lost it back in Paris.

"Do you have any idea," I say, "how hard it is to work your entire life toward one goal—*one goal*—and then to have someone else come in and try to take it away?"

Nicki looks at me, incredulous. "Yes!" she says. "In fact, I do."

I look at her and realize what I've just said. I cannot help but laugh, and neither can Nicki.

"God, you must hate me," I say. "I would. I would hate me."

Nicki downs the rest of her glass. "I don't hate you. I told you before. I'm thankful."

"Yeah. I'm sure."

"I'm serious," Nicki says. "I can't fight unless I have something to fight against. And I like fighting. I like it even more than winning."

"I . . ." I say. "Okay."

"Without you, I wouldn't have much left to fight against. It would be like trying to knock out a deflated punching bag. And without me, you'd be back home, shooting a commercial for Gatorade, would you not?"

I huff, knowing she's right. "Yeah, maybe. Yes."

"But instead, we're here, training, living for something bigger than the two of us."

I take a sip of my vodka soda. And consider her. "I'm not sure I ever thought of it that way with Paulina," I say.

"Stepanova?" Nicki says, rolling her eyes. "Who would? She faked injuries every time she was down, and then the one time she actually messes up her ankle, she doesn't have the courage to either retire or play through."

"Thank you!" I say.

"Crocodile tears, the whole lot of them."

"Yes!"

"She was not a worthy opponent for you."

"That's what I said from the beginning!"

"But I am," Nicki says, her eyes focusing in on me.

I look at her. "I guess that's what remains to be seen, doesn't it?" I say.

"Yes, I believe it does."

Nicki throws down thirty pounds and stands up. She pats me on the shoulder. "What time are you practicing tomorrow?"

"I don't know," I say. "Depends on whether I can sleep."

"All right. Well, work hard. I want to know, when I beat you, that you were playing at your best. I want to know that I can beat the greatest tennis player of all time. I need it. And I need the world to see it."

"Feel free to fuck right off with that bullshit," I say.

Nicki laughs. "It is only by playing you at your best that I can get better," she says. "Just like you up against Stepanova with that slice all those years ago. I'm the best player in the WTA. I need someone else—someone great—to push me up against the ropes. And here you come back, just in time. Just for me."

"Not for you," I say.

"Right, for you," she says. "I'm just the excuse you needed."

She's right, despite how it irritates me. I was never really done before. I was always going to do this: show up and fight one last time.

"Either way, one of us is the catalyst for the other reaching their greatest height yet."

"All right," I say. "Good night, Nicki."

"Good night, mate."

"I'm not your mate," I say, shaking my head. "I may have had a drink with you, but we are not mates."

"We *are* mates," Nicki says. "And that's good—do you know why?"

"Why?"

"Because if you'd made a few mates during your time in the WTA the first go-round, I don't think you would have had such a jittery right hand these past few years."

I look up at her and it's clear she meant to cut, but I can't tell whether she knows how deep the knife just went in.

"All right," I say. "That's my cue to leave."

The bartender pops her head up. Her eyes go wide, looking at the two of us. "Wait, are you Nicki Chan?"

Nicki smiles wide and lopsided, a dimple forming. "Why, yes, I am," she says. "Number one in the world. Record holder for the most Grand Slam singles ever."

"And yet she's only won Wimbledon twice," I say to the bartender. "Isn't that funny?"

Two days before the start of Wimbledon, I find out that my father is being released from the hospital, and I breathe out so completely that I wonder how long I've been holding that breath. When the draft comes in, I call him at home to discuss.

"Read it to me," my father says over the phone.

"I play Cami Dryer in the first round," I say, looking at the pages that had been faxed to my hotel earlier today. I throw myself down on the sofa.

"Piece of cake, she can't anticipate," my dad says. "Hit your marks, you'll be fine. Who is after that?"

I gauge who is likely to win the other match. "Probably Lucy Cameron."

"She's easy to ruffle," my dad says.

I look up at the ceiling. "Yeah, I was thinking the same thing. Break her early and I'm probably good. Then after that it's . . ." I pull the chart up to my eyeline for a second. "Martin or Nystrom."

"It will be Nystrom, most likely," my dad says.

"No way," I say. I'm up now, pacing. "Martin is the better player."

"Martin has had a lot of trouble in the past adjusting her game to grass. She plays too far back on the court. It will be Nystrom, unless Martin has gotten a better coach."

"Well, Nystrom I can take. Her volley game is good, but her serve is shit—I can break her in the first game."

"Exactly. Next?"

"Could be Johns."

"Slow as an ox," my dad says. "She can't keep up. If she gets to you, just keep the ball moving quick. If you set the pace from the jump and don't let up, she's out."

"Yeah, you're right."

"Who's next?"

"Don't you think you should be relaxing?" I say.

"No, I don't," my father says. "Not while my daughter prepares for Wimbledon. Now, who is next?"

"Probably Moretti," I say. "By the looks of it."

"Who else could it be?" he says.

"Maybe Machado."

"I'd put money on Machado," he says.

"Why?"

"She's an underestimated player, but she adjusts very quickly. Moretti only has one mode of play: power. Machado has more shots. I think it's Machado."

"So then what do I do?" I say.

"If it does end up Moretti, she's not strong on the run, so keep her there and her game will fall apart. If it's Machado . . . I think you stay economical at the beginning, play percentage tennis. If you win the first set, you're well on your way. If you don't, you have to win the next two sets, but you're not as tired as she is."

"Okay," I say. "Sure."

"Who's next?"

I look at the chart. "Uh, hard to say," I tell him. I look out the window at the river. "Could be Antonovich, though."

My father is quiet for a moment.

I turn my attention back to the phone. "But I have a plan for Antonovich."

"What's your plan?"

"She's faster than me, and she's good on grass," I say.

He pauses and then says, "Okay."

"So I follow your advice from Paris. I don't try to match her speed. I won't win that game. If anything, I slow the game down."

"Sí, es un buen plan . . ."

"But I've played on Wimbledon grass my whole life, so I know better than anyone where that ball is going."

"That's right."

"So I disguise my shots, don't let her figure out where I'm going. I aim for brown spots in the grass, I watch for bad bounces. If I can get her to three sets, I will win. Because by that point, I'll have run far less than her."

My father takes a deep breath and then lets it out. "Yes, I like it."

"Is it what you would have said?"

"I'd add this: She's going to anticipate that you have something to prove after last time. She'll be expecting that you're coming in hot. So hold back, and make it seem like you're giving it your best, until she realizes you're only getting started."

"Okay," I say. "Yes. That will work."

It is what Cortez did to me in Melbourne.

"And then?" my dad asks. "Who's next?"

"Chan."

"No Cortez?"

"Chan will defeat Cortez in the semis when I'm up against Antonovich."

"All right, so assuming I've called these correctly—which is absolutely impossible . . ."

I laugh.

"In two weeks, you're standing there holding a tenth silver plate."

"That easy, huh?"

"Not easy at all, *pichona,*" he says. "But if anyone can do it, you can. And I'll be watching it all from right here."

"*Gracias, papá.*"

"Bowe wants to talk to you," he says. "He's taking the phone from me—he's literally taking it out of my hands."

"Hi," Bowe says. His voice is warm, and I wish he were here with me instead of thousands of miles away.

"Hi," I say. "How are your ribs?"

"Fine," Bowe says. "Better. Your father and I are a real pair over here."

"Thank you for what you're doing. I don't think I could stand to be *here* if you weren't *there.*"

"Don't mention it, honestly," he says. "But, hey, listen, I wanted to ask you something."

"Okay . . ." I'm worried he's going to ask me if I want him to visit or how things will be between us when I get back. And I don't want to have to think about that right now.

"Have you given any thought to the Self 1, Self 2 thing?" he asks.

"What?"

"All that strategy you and your dad were talking about . . ."

"Yeah?"

"Look, you're a better player than almost anyone on the court. And I don't just mean over the course of your career. I mean right now."

"I hope that's true. I don't know. I need it to be true—let's say that."

I stand at the window and watch a Thames riverboat tour float by. My father and I did that tour once, when I was barely a teenager and we were here for my first Junior Wimbledon. I fell asleep, and later he told me all the history about the Tower of London that I'd missed. "Next time, stay awake," my dad said. "You are getting to see the world, *pichona*. It's an opportunity so few people have." Even then, I didn't know how to tell him that I was too tired, that sightseeing was a luxury that I didn't have, never wanted. What we were doing took all of me; there wasn't anything left over.

"It is true—you're the best out there. But that's the problem," Bowe says. "You need to *know it* instead of needing to *prove it*. You need to quiet Self 1 and let Self 2 do its thing."

"Okay," I say. "Okay."

"I know you don't want to take advice from me—" Bowe begins. But I stop him.

"Yes, I do," I say. "I do want to take advice from you." I sit down at the window and grab a piece of hotel stationery and a pen to make notes for myself. He is right. I do need to calm down, to listen to my instincts. I need to get the voice in my head to shut up. "Go ahead," I say. "Tell me more. I'm listening."

It is the morning of my first match, facing Cami Dryer. I've gone for a run and I'm just getting out of the shower when there is a knock at my door.

I wrap myself in my robe and answer. I'm expecting room service with my breakfast, but when I open the door, it's Gwen. I take it all in—her in front of me in a green velvet suit and a big, bright smile on her face.

"Hi," she says.

The sight of her makes my shoulders relax. Before I know what I'm doing, I throw myself into her arms.

She squeezes me tight and then lets go. "All right. That's enough of that, until you get dressed."

I pull her into my suite.

"You're here," I say. "I had no idea you were coming."

"Ali and I both flew in to surprise you. She's back at the hotel."

"Wow," I say.

"You know I love London. And I love you. And so here I am."

I suddenly feel my voice quivering, and I get control of myself. "That's kind of you."

"Yeah, well, you know I need my yearly strawberries and cream."

When I come back out after getting dressed, she's set herself up in my living room, and she's already on her cellphone, scolding someone. She finishes her call and looks at me. The intensity of her gaze makes me sit straighter.

"How are you?" she says, frowning.

"Well . . . I feel better than I've felt in years."

Gwen nods. "Great. Good. I love that."

"But . . . playing without my dad here . . . I don't know."

Gwen nods.

"It feels like the late eighties all over again. Playing without my dad, when the whole point was to do this *with* my dad. For us to have one last season together."

Gwen grabs my hand and squeezes it. "So go win it and bring him back the trophy."

WIMBLEDON
1995

IN THE ENTRANCE HALL AT CENTRE COURT AT WIMBLEDON, THERE IS an inscription just above the double doors that lead out to the grass. It is from the poem "If—" by Rudyard Kipling.

IF YOU CAN MEET WITH TRIUMPH AND DISASTER
AND TREAT THOSE TWO IMPOSTORS JUST THE SAME

It has never resonated with me. Every time I have walked onto the courts at Wimbledon, I have considered triumph to be paramount. And when I have held it in my hands, it has not felt like an impostor at all.

But as Gwen and I walk into the hall this morning, she says, "I've always loved that quote."

"You know," I say as we head to the clubhouse, "I read the whole poem years ago, to try to understand the inscription better. But it didn't help. I do remember thinking the first line of the poem made more sense to me than that line. But now I can't even remember what it is."

Gwen smiles. "'If you can keep your head when all about you / Are losing theirs and blaming it on you.'"

I look at her. "Yeah, that's it. What, were you an English major or something?"

Gwen pulls her head back. "Yes."

"Wait, really?"

"Yes. I got my BA from Stanford before going to UCLA for my MBA."

"Oh," I say. "I didn't know that. That's cool." I never officially finished high school, never set foot on a college campus. And I am convinced sometimes that, despite all my accomplishments, this lack of sophistication shows in ways I'm unaware of.

"Not sure how cool it is. It doesn't often come in handy that I know the entirety of 'If—' by Rudyard Kipling."

"Well, I still think it's impressive," I say as I head toward the dressing room.

"All right," Gwen says, "I'm going to make some calls, and I'll see you in the players' box."

"Okay," I say.

"Good luck, Carolina," she says.

I cannot help but smile. "Thank you."

I start to walk away, but then I turn back.

"Hey," I say, calling to her. "Thank you for being here. And for supporting me in this, from the beginning. The whole year. Even though it's crazy."

Gwen smiles. "Do you know what part of 'If—' is actually relevant right now? To this moment? 'If you can make one heap of all your winnings / And risk it on one turn of pitch-and-toss, / And lose, and start again at your beginnings / And never breathe a word about your loss.'"

She must be messing with me. Surely she knows she's just described my greatest fear. But no, I can tell from the look on her face that she sincerely thinks that I'm that brave, that I am doing this because I am okay with losing big. Not because I am terrified of losing at all.

And it stuns me silent, for a moment: just how vast the gap is between who I am and how people see me.

I am so much smaller than the Carrie Soto in Gwen's head.

SOTO VS. DRYER

Wimbledon 1995

First Round

AS I STEP OUT ONTO THE COURT, I FEEL THE SUN BLAZING DOWN. I hear the commotion of the crowds. I look up to see stands full of well-dressed Brits with large hats and fascinators. I am flooded with the comfort of the scent of Wimbledon—fresh-cut grass and Pimm's and lemon.

I am home.

I bounce on my toes, feeling the grass and dirt beneath my white Break Points.

I look across the court at Cami Dryer. She is young, not even eighteen.

I smile and shake her hand as we come together at the net.

She is adorable—all perky and eager. She shakes my hand with an excitement that reminds me of myself when I was younger. And I feel this sudden contentment deep within my gut.

You could not pay me enough money to go back to being seventeen. When I was seventeen, my talent was all potential and no proof. The world was a giant set of unknowns, barely any past to pull from.

I am so grateful, right now, for every match and every win and every loss and every lesson that I have behind me. It feels so good, right now, to be thirty-seven years old. To have figured at least *some* things out.

To know the ground underneath my feet.

Poor Cami Dryer doesn't know what is about to hit her. She wins the coin toss and calls first serve. I get into position and take her in two sets.

Transcript

BBC Sports Radio London
SportsWorld with Brian Cress

And in women's tennis it's been nearly a fortnight of stunning wins and crushing losses.

London's own Nicki Chan has sailed through each of her matches. As have favorites such as Ingrid Cortez and Natasha Antonovich. Meanwhile, it's been a hair-raiser for firebrand Carrie Soto. She has clawed her way through the five rounds—beating Brits Cami Dryer and Lucy Cameron in the first and second, Swede Celine Nystrom in the third, and the Baltimore Baseliner Carla Perez in the round of sixteen.

She's now defeated Italian Odette Moretti in the quarterfinals.

Bringing her to the semifinals, where she and Russian phenom Natasha Antonovich will go head-to-head.

Transcript

SportsHour USA
The Mark Hadley Show

Mark Hadley: And wow, Carrie Soto.

Gloria Jones: Carrie is headed to the semifinals! At this point, the fact that she is still a force of nature is undeniable. Briggs, call her whatever you want, but you have to admit this is fun to watch. This is a player giving audiences a rip-roaring good show as she fights her way to the finish.

Briggs Lakin: Look, I am the first to admit when I'm wrong. I said earlier this year that Carrie wouldn't make it to Wimbledon, and I stand corrected. But in hindsight, it seems obvious, doesn't it? Of course this was Soto's move. Of course Wimbledon would be her only real shot at a title this year.

Hadley: And can she do it? Gloria?

Jones: I think it's going to be hard. She now has the three best players in the game ahead of her. She will go up against Antonovich next. This is Carrie's best surface, but this is also Antonovich's.

Lakin: In some ways, it's an interesting match, these two. Natasha Antonovich, her style of play—the quick pace, the great volleys—owes a lot to Carrie Soto. We saw that back in Paris. I said, "Natasha is the new Carrie." It's almost as if this is Carrie's chance to play her old self on her best surface.

Jones: If Carrie wants to prove there is only one Carrie Soto, well, this is the chance.

I AM SITTING IN THE LOCKER ROOM WITH MY EYES CLOSED, LISTENING to the waves of my breath. I pick up my cellphone and dial my dad.

He doesn't miss a beat.

"Don't think about strategy now," he says. "The time for that is over. This is the time for instinct."

"I know," I say, taking in a deep breath. "I know."

"You are prepared. Trust your preparation."

"I know."

"Don't listen to Self 1," he says.

I laugh without opening my eyes. "You've been listening to Bowe."

"Be Self 2."

"Don't think," I say. "Just act."

"Don't think," my father says. "Just *play*."

SOTO VS. ANTONOVICH

Wimbledon 1995

Semifinals

NATASHA ANTONOVICH HOVERS ON THE OTHER SIDE OF THE COURT, adjusting her visor. She's steady now, both feet firmly on the baseline. But we both know the second she wants to, she'll go flying across this court.

She hits a kick serve. It bounces high, and I hit it back over the net. I watch her dive, but it bounces too low for her to get it.

Love–15.

I smile up at Gwen and Ali in the players' box as I walk back to the baseline.

I know my father is watching. I know Bowe is with him. I know they are cheering for me, even if I can't hear them.

Less than an hour later, I'm at break point on the first set. I'm up six games to five. It's her serve.

She sends a fast flat one my way, and I race to it. I notice she hasn't moved toward the center of the court. She's anticipating a cross-court forehand.

I take the ball out of the air quick, sending it right down the line. She dives hard for it, slides across the grass. She can't return it.

The first set is mine.

I see Gwen applauding, Ali hollering. I wonder if Bowe is cheering in front of the television.

But I do not need to imagine my father's reaction. I know he is clapping and smiling ear to ear, for once unworried that the cameras will get an unflattering picture of him.

Antonovich catches up faster than I'd like. She's starting to read my serve. I need to do a better job of disguising my ball toss.

And I need to do it quick, because I'm not getting any more aces off her. I can see her gaining confidence as she starts returning more and more of my junk shots too.

We are now tied 6–6 in the second set.

She's serving for the set. She sends three kick serves in a row, and each one bounces differently. It knocks me out of my flow.

The second set is hers.

It's the final set, 4–4.

I'm sweating down my back, across my forehead, on the backs of my knees. There's a flutter—an unrest—in my stomach. I can barely hear the crowd. The dominating sound is the propulsive and angry *whoosh* of my pulse in my own ears.

My knee is burning.

My strategy is shot. I had hoped to run Antonovich down, but the games are happening too fast. We have such short rallies that I can't wear her out.

During the changeover, I sit down to drink my water. I breathe in deeply and close my eyes. I have to rethink my strategy here.

Antonovich has settled into the game. She is anticipating better. She is moving smarter.

I need a way to get her on the run again, to unnerve her.

When I stand up, I find myself looking into the players' box to meet my father's eye. But of course he isn't there. Instead, Gwen and Ali are smiling at me.

What would he say? I give myself the briefest of seconds before I walk back onto the court.

Slow the game down.

I walk out onto the court and get into position, my own voice churning through my head. *Do not let this slip through your fingers, Soto. You're so goddamn close. And if you fuck this one up, you'll be zero and three.*

My hand tenses around the racket.

I am afraid.

I am afraid of losing. I am afraid of how it will look to the world. I'm afraid of this match being the last match my father ever sees me play. I am afraid of ending this all on a loss. I am afraid of so much.

I loosen my grip on the racket. I clear my mind. I let go. I have to.

Instead of racing to serve the next one, I take a moment on the baseline. I imagine myself serving the ball. I imagine how it will feel in my calves to get up high on my toes, I imagine the swing of my arm, the way my ribs will follow the line of my shoulder.

My body knows what to do. Now I just have to let it do it.

When I open my eyes, I see her crouched in place, waiting. My eye goes right to her feet. I'm going to piss her off. I toss the ball in the air and serve the first shot of the game so that it will bounce straight to her toes. She has to jump out of the way, and she misses it.

Ace. *15–love.*

She walks back to position, shaking her head.

It's working. This time, I wait as long as I can to serve the next one. I bounce the ball over and over, not indicating when I might finally toss it. Then I hit the exact same serve again. She gets in position better, but she still can't return it.

30–love.

She bites her bottom lip, clenches her fist, crouches down. I wait again, hold off on serving until the last second. I serve it short, so that it bounces just over the net. She dives for it and misses. *40–love.*

On the next serve, I hit the net. As I set up for the second serve, I see her visibly relax, assuming my second serve will be safer.

Instead, I angle it to the corner. She returns it, but then I hit it back down the opposite line and it goes whistling right past her.

Game is mine. Now we're 5–4. If I break her serve on this one, I win the match.

I watch her crack her knuckles as she goes back to the baseline. Maybe up against another player she'd be less nervous. It is her serve, after all.

But I am Carrie Soto. Break points are my moment. The evidence of it is branded all over my feet.

I can tell Antonovich's muscles are tight. She did not think she would be here—the match this close, a loss to me threatening her 1995 season.

Her first serve is fast and hot. It has more fire on it than anything she's hit so far. Still, I take the point. *Love–15.*

She stomps back to the baseline. And then hits her racket against the ground before catching herself.

I smile. She's mad. She's so mad.

On the next serve, she footfaults. Then nets it. *Love–30.*

I wink at her. Her face grows tighter.

On the next one, we rally and then she lobs it too high and the ball lands behind the baseline.

Match point.

I can do this. I am doing this. I just have to trust myself.

She hits a high kick serve. I get it on the rise. She returns it fast, exactly like I hoped. Here it is. I take it out of the air early and quick—a drop shot, right over the net.

It lands with such a beautiful, sweet, delicious thud.

Antonovich cannot get to it. She falls to the ground.

I leap into the air and shout. Gwen and Ali stand in their seats. The crowd roars.

I look right at the TV cameras for a brief second, knowing my father is looking right back at me.

Finally, over the loudspeaker come the words I have waited to hear.

"Carrie Soto advances to the championship final."

MY FATHER IS SHOUTING AT ME THROUGH THE PHONE. "YOU WERE incomparable! You were dynamic. You were *interesting* today, *hija*. Interesting! You played in a way that kept us all glued to the TV."

I laugh as I sit down on the couch. The phone was ringing the moment I got in the door. I've barely had time to put my things down. "Thanks, Dad."

"I am not exaggerating! Let me tell you something. . . . At the end of the third set, you two were neck and neck. I watched you at the changeover. I saw you thinking it through. And I *knew*. I said to Bowe, I said, 'She's got it.' And you did. Oh, he was so proud of you. He was beaming."

"Where is he?" I ask.

"He waited around for you to call, but there's only so long the man wants to spend in an old guy's house. Don't worry. He and I talked at length about your brilliance today. I told him, I said, 'She goes after what she wants on the court but not in real life. In real life, you have to be patient.'"

"What are you even talking about? And stop, you don't need to be discussing me with him."

"Oh, Carrie, that ship has sailed. He comes every day, and after we are done playing chess and discussing his strategy for the US Open, what do you think we are going to do? Talk about the weather? This is Los Angeles. It's sunny."

"He's coming every day?" I ask. I look over the room service menu as if I don't know already that I'm going to order grilled chicken.

"Yeah, every day. He brings me breakfast and stays until after lunch. Or he brings me lunch and stays until after dinner. Honestly, it makes sense to me why he's here all the time. Did you know his own father was embarrassed he was a tennis player instead of a professor or something?"

"I know a little."

"Imagine! Imagine having your head that far up your own ass that you're embarrassed your son is a champion."

"All right, all right," I say.

"I like him, Carrie. Even with all those tantrums."

"I can tell."

"No, I like him for you. I think this thing is *verrrry* interesting, you two."

"Dad, cut it out."

"And he thinks so too."

"STOP IT OR I WILL GET OFF THE PHONE," I say.

"*Bueno, pero tengo razón,*" he says. "When does Chan play?"

"Tonight. Soon." I look at my watch. "Any second now, actually."

"*Ay,*" he says. I hear him start to wrestle around for the remote. I can hear the TV turning on. So I sit down and turn on mine. I flip through the channels until I see that the match is just beginning.

Nicki stands tall and sturdy on the court. Her tennis whites are crisp and bright, a tennis skirt and tank top. Her shoes are her own 130s, bright white.

I watch her, bouncing on the balls of her feet, stretching out her shoulder, standing at the baseline. She has a huge smile on her face, like she's living for this moment.

Ingrid Cortez's face is all business.

"This is it," my dad says. "Chan wins this, and then you beat her. And suddenly, it's a whole different story."

"I know," I say, watching her first serve. "I had a drink with her the other night. I . . . liked her."

Nicki hits her first serve. My shoulder starts to sting just watching Cortez return it.

"You didn't talk strategy, did you?" my father says.

"Dad, give me a little credit."

"You know what I say about making friends out of your opponents."

"Honestly," I say, sighing, "no, I don't. Because you just told me to never do it."

"Well, yeah," he says. "*Exacto, hija*. But if you do—don't talk strategy, don't tell them how you felt about your last game, don't tell them your fears, don't tell them your strengths either. And you sure as hell never tell them how much it hurts you to lose."

"Oh, is that all?" I say. Nicki and Ingrid are still rallying for the point.

"Don't tell them what you had for breakfast either," he says. "They could use it against you."

"You sound insane."

"Every genius sounds insane."

Nicki hits a groundstroke to Cortez's backhand, and Cortez misses it. First point Nicki.

"Oh wow," my dad says. "These two."

"They are well matched," I say.

"Two of the greatest in the world," my dad says. "Duking it out for who gets to play you."

I laugh and then sit back on the couch and put my feet up.

My father and I stay on the phone throughout the entire match. Multiple times he worries about the long-distance charges, but I refuse to let him get off the call. We watch and we analyze. Sometimes we are stunned silent at the tension between Nicki and Cortez. It is a close one. Cortez is up, then Nicki is up. Both of them are breaking each other's serves. Cortez slides across the court at one point and skins her knee. Then Nicki steps wrong on her ankle.

"Ouch," I say.

"What is she doing?" my dad says. "Landing like that on her bad ankle? She can't keep playing like this and stay in the game many more years."

"I know."

It's the third set. 5–5. Anybody's match.

On Cortez's serve, Nicki is limping on her way back to the baseline after each point. Cortez holds the game.

"She plays through it, which is impressive," my dad says. "It's not stopping her. But I wish I could just reach through the TV and tell her she's shortening her career."

When it's Nicki's turn to serve, she can't get the height she needs. I gasp when Cortez gets to 30–40. Match point.

"Oh no," my dad says.

On the next serve, Cortez returns it right on the sideline. Nicki can't run fast enough.

"Oh no," my dad says again.

It's over.

I can feel my heart drop as Nicki falls to her knees onto the grass.

"No, that can't be," my father says.

I close my eyes in disbelief.

I am not playing Nicki in the final. I'm playing Ingrid Cortez.

"Actually," my father says, "this is fabulous."

I can barely hold back my tone. "Why is it fabulous? It's not fabulous! I wanted to play Nicki. *Now.* I wanted to put this whole thing to rest."

"Nonsense," my father says. "You will beat Cortez—she is the more predictable player. You already played her in Melbourne."

"And lost."

"But now you know what to do. And she will go down just like Antonovich did the second time. This is great news," my father says. "This is it. This is your next Slam."

The night before the final, I toss and turn.

I lie awake, staring at the shadows on the ceiling, thinking about what tomorrow holds.

The more I think about how important it is that I go to sleep, the more impossible it becomes. The harder I chase it, the more it eludes me.

I get up and check the time. It's early evening in L.A. I think about calling my father. But, instead, I dial Bowe.

"Hi," I say.

"Oh," he says. "Hello."

I say, "I can't sleep," just as he says, "You should be sleeping."

Bowe doesn't say anything else for a moment, but the silence between us feels easy.

"Do you often find it hard to sleep before a big match?" Bowe asks.

"No," I say. "Almost never."

"Not even against Stepanova in '83?"

"No, I slept like a baby that night. I'd worn my body down with so much training, I could barely stay awake."

Bowe is quiet again. "So which self is keeping you awake?" he asks, finally.

It clicks right into place. "Okay," I say. "I get it."

"Let your thoughts go," he says.

"All right, I'll try."

"What did Coach say?"

I laugh. "I didn't call him."

Bowe whistles like a cowboy. "Wow, you called me instead?"

"Yeah," I say. "I think maybe I needed you to tell me that. I knew that you would."

"Or," he says, "and I'm just taking a stab here, maybe you also have a thing for me."

"Would you cut it out?" I say.

"Oh, for fuck's sake," he says. "All right, go to bed. Glad I could help."

"Thank you," I say.

"Yeah, yeah."

"No, Bowe, I'm serious. Thank you."

"Sleep well, Carrie. You have this."

When I get back in bed, I watch the moon as it hangs over the river. I stare at the gentle sway of the curtains. I do my best not to think about Cortez in Melbourne. Not to think of the moment I lost the match. The drop in my stomach. The sheer shame of it.

Instead, I close my eyes and think of the sound of a tennis ball. The *thunk* of a good bounce. The *pop* of a drive volley. The *tap* of a drop shot. The honest-to-God exquisite soundtrack of a great rally. *Pop, thunk, pop.*

All I can do, I understand for one startlingly clear second, is play my grass game and be okay with the outcome.

Impossible.

Transcript

BBC Sports Radio London
SportsWorld with Brian Cress

All eyes are watching as Carrie Soto and Ingrid Cortez go head-to-head in the championship final at Wimbledon today. Both players have shown incredible resolve here in London. Carrie Soto, thirty-seven, has shocked everyone by making it to the final. And Ingrid Cortez, at the age of eighteen, defeated powerhouse Nicki Chan in the semis this week in order to earn her spot up against the Battle Axe.

Soto lost to Cortez in Melbourne earlier this season. But she has been gaining momentum all year and has won Wimbledon nine times previously. Still, betting odds are putting Cortez ahead by 3 to 2.

It will be, no doubt, a rousing event—the Rookie vs. the Comeback.

When asked, Carrie Soto said, quote, "I am eager to get on the court and show Ingrid Cortez why I've long dominated at Wimbledon," unquote. Ingrid Cortez said this morning, quote, "I beat her in Melbourne. I'll beat her again today," unquote. Oof. Harsh words for such ladies. Watch out, gents.

In just a few hours, we will know the victor.

SOTO VS. CORTEZ

Wimbledon 1995

Final

I AM STANDING AT CENTRE COURT. THE GRASS, WHICH JUST TWO SHORT weeks ago was a lively green, is now pale and bone dry. I inhale and take in the distinct and glorious sight of the Wimbledon final court. I hold back the smile on my face.

Ingrid Cortez is standing on the opposite side of the net, fixing her sweatband. Her golden hair shines in the sun; her long limbs hover delicately at the baseline.

She smiles at me. It's not so much a friendly gesture as a baring of teeth.

I adjust my visor. I close my eyes.

Then I toss the ball into the air and open up the court with a flat first serve that fires right over the net, wide to her backhand.

We rally for the point until I hit a slice that she can't return.

First point mine.

I look up to the stands at Gwen and Ali. And then, in the royal box, I see Princess Diana.

Once my eye lands on her, it is hard to look away. She is wearing a pale yellow dress and blazer, and she is, as always, the most elegant woman I've ever seen.

I know that so many people across the world feel a kinship with her. But right now, mine feels especially sharp. I want to win, today, with her here. I want to say to her, *They can't make us go away just because they are done with us.*

I refocus as I set for my next serve.

I take a breath. Before I even know what I am doing, my left arm tosses the ball as my right arm comes up to meet it. The ball goes screaming past Cortez's racket and bounces just inside the sideline. An ace.

I don't bother to smile at Cortez, to even give her the satisfaction of my satisfaction. I show nothing, as if this is nothing. Beating her is nothing to me.

But the truth is, I can feel the hum beginning in my bones.

I take the set.

At the end of the second set, we go to a tiebreaker.

The championship and the record are in the palm of my hand.

But I can feel myself tightening up as victory gets closer; the hum starts to fade into the background.

Cortez takes the tiebreaker.

Third set, 5–4. I'm up, but it's Cortez's serve next.

For a moment, as Cortez begins her toss, I have this flash of wanting it all to be over, wanting to see how it all ends.

Will I do it?

If I win, do I feel at peace knowing Nicki and I are tied again? Does elation run through me as I look around and understand that at age thirty-seven, I am now the oldest woman to ever win Wimbledon? That I have set a new record for the most titles here? Does it fill some sort of hole in my heart? Does it make it all worth it?

Or.

Or do I lose my shot at taking my record back this year?

Is this match the one in which Ingrid Cortez cements her own type of domination in women's tennis, winning in Melbourne and London in the same year—just as I did for the first time back in '81?

Is this Cortez's day or is it mine? I just want to know.

But as she starts to serve, I remember that if I want to win, I have to *hit the fucking ball.*

It comes speeding across the court. I close my eyes for the briefest of seconds and let my body take over. I can't help but let a smile break out on my face as I feel the sheer, undying, intoxicating thrill of pulling my arm back and then smashing my racket into the ball.

It hits the sideline just where I placed it and bounces off the court.

"Point is Soto's."

Cortez is smart and she is agile. She can put herself in position to make whatever shot she wants. But the ball surprised her on that point. And that is because she has not played Wimbledon as often as I have. She may know intellectually that the grass changes over the course of the match, but she doesn't understand it like I do.

She has to *think* about it. I don't.

I *know* this court. I know the bad bounces. I know the wind. I know the stickiness under my feet in this humidity.

After all, this is my grass.

And it is time for Ingrid Cortez to get off my lawn.

She serves it, I return, she hits it into the net. *Love–30.*

I aim straight for a pale spot where the grass is worn away, just beyond the net. It bounces fast and straight sideways. Cortez dives to return it, but her angle is desperate. It doesn't make it over the net.

And here we are. *Championship point.*

My father is watching. Bowe is with him. Gwen and Ali are here. And I wonder, for a brief second, if my mom is seeing this. Wherever she is. If she's proud of me.

I *know* Nicki Chan is watching. It's probably killing her.

I shake them all out of my head and breathe.

Cortez serves the ball, and it flashes, yellow, as it barrels across the court. I watch it curve—the seams spinning so fast they blur—over the net and into the service box. I pull my arm back, ready to strike.

And now, I do not want to fast-forward through the next moment at all. I want to experience every second of this.

I hit the ball cross-court; she returns it down the line. I take it right out of the air with a backhand drive volley, and I move up to the net.

The ball bounces just at her feet. She chips it over. I hit a drop shot, aiming for a spot of dirt. It lands flat, bouncing low and to the side.

Cortez dives for it, but it's too late. The ball bounces again.

Cortez gasps. Her mouth goes wide; her hands go up to her face in disbelief.

For one stunning moment, I can *see* the crowd screaming for me before I can hear them. And then the thunderous roar kicks in and overtakes me. I fall onto my butt and then onto my back as I drop my racket and look up at the sky. I lie there and I can feel the ground vibrating underneath me.

My tenth Wimbledon.

My twenty-first Slam.

The crowd continues to scream. I stand up as the announcers declare me the winner of the 109th annual Wimbledon Championships. I feel as if I can hear my father cheering. I can hear Bowe clapping. The whole stadium is going wild.

But I cannot hear anything as clearly as the sound of my own voice, begging me: *Let this be enough.*

Transcript

SportsHour USA
The Mark Hadley Show

Mark Hadley: And what do we make of this? A shocking upset, a stunning victory for our American, Carrie Soto.

Briggs Lakin: I'm here eating my words, Mark. She pulled out a scorcher of a win.

Gloria Jones: This is what we have seen with Carrie Soto from the beginning of her career. She is relentless. She does not stop. She will not be counted out.

Hadley: And what a match she gave us.

Jones: What a tournament, I say. Not just a match. Look, as tennis fans—certainly as a player who had to play Carrie a few times back in my day—I can tell you that what we all show up for is the beauty of the game. The sheer joy of a great match. And Cortez and Soto gave us that today.

Lakin: Soto, in particular, stunned with that last game. She's the oldest player to ever win Wimbledon, and it was hours into the match. She had to be tired. And yet, now, you understand why she's known as the break point champion.

Hadley: She's given us quite a show this season.

Lakin: If you told me this time last year that Carrie Soto would be winning Wimbledon and Nicki Chan wouldn't even make the final, I'd have thought you'd lost your mind. But here we are.

Jones: Never underestimate Carrie Soto. And to any other women out there, wondering if they are too old to play tennis, let the Battle Axe be all the evidence you need to get in the game.

Hadley: Uh-oh, Gloria, are you considering a return to the sport?

Jones: [*laughs*] Absolutely not. You couldn't pay me to train again, Mark. But that's what's all the more impressive, if you ask me. We had a saying back when I was on the tour. "Carrie Soto is human. But she's superhuman." And I'd say she's proven that tonight.

ALONE IN MY HOTEL SUITE, I PUT MY GOWN ON. IT'S BLACK SATIN AND sleeveless, floor length, though there is a slit cut high to my thigh.

Gwen picked it out for me when we went shopping this afternoon. I can see she made a good choice.

I leave my room and make my way down to the lobby. I'm meeting Gwen here so we can head out to the Wimbledon Champions Ball, at a hotel near Buckingham Palace.

It's almost midnight, and the party is only just about to begin. We all have been waiting—*I have been waiting*—for the men's final to end. The party can't start until then.

The finalists were Andrew Thomas and Jadran Petrovich, neither one of whom would set a record by winning. We live in a world where exceptional women have to sit around waiting for mediocre men.

Petrovich finally takes the fifth set just after eleven P.M., and apparently *now* we are all allowed to celebrate.

In the lobby, I see Gwen arrive in a bright red strapless dress, her hair pulled back, her lips crimson red.

"Wow," I say. "You look good."

"To you as well," she says. And then she grabs my arm and escorts me to the ball.

Just as in years past, there is a horde of people here. They are all coming in and out, trying to find me, trying to shake my hand, trying to tell me that all along, they knew I would succeed.

Board members of the ITF are asking me if I will consider continuing on in the sport after the US Open. One of the directors of the WTA asks if I will join the full tour. A head of the All England Club tells me that he knew from the moment I announced my return that I would win Wimbledon.

"Isn't this nice?" I say to Gwen through gritted teeth. "A whole room full of fair-weather friends."

Gwen laughs. "That is one thing I have always loved about you," she says. "You are the rare star who doesn't like the smell of bullshit."

Not long after we arrive, I get stuck talking to a woman who is some sort of duchess.

"A rather exceptional win you've accomplished," she says to me, taking a restrained sip of her drink.

"Thank you," I say. "I'm quite proud."

"Yes," she says. "And at such an age. It's impressive. I quite admire your fighting spirit. You have that American virtue, don't you? That dogged obstinance—even in the face of indignity."

Gwen can see my face and nods at me slowly, encouraging me not to tell this woman to go fuck herself. "Ah, yes," I say, keeping my tone light. "Well, it was oh-so tempting to roll over and die once I turned thirty, but somehow my *American obstinance* persists."

Suddenly, Gwen's hand is on my arm, and I'm being dragged away.

"Just smile and nod," Gwen says. "How hard is that?"

"Very," I say. "I hate half these people. I hate half of all people."

Gwen leads me through the room. "You love Wimbledon," she says.

"I love London and I love winning," I say. "But I don't care about any of these idiots who thought I was crazy for trying this in the first place."

Gwen keeps us moving, and I can see now that she's ushering me toward Jadran Petrovich—with whom I am going to have to take a photo. I pull her to a stop, ever so briefly.

"The only people who thought I could come back were my father and Bowe," I say. "That's whose opinion I care about. And yours, because you have stood by me every single moment."

Gwen smiles. "Well, I have always admired your American obstinance."

"Thank you for supporting me. And for being here," I say. "When my father couldn't."

Gwen nods.

"And . . . I'm sorry about Indian Wells. I was . . . rude."

"You mean when I gently asked you about your dating life and you acted like a brat?"

"Yes," I say. "I know you were just trying to . . . care about me. And I'm not an easy person to care for."

Gwen shakes her head. "Yes, you are. You think you're so tough, but you're not, Carrie. I can see right through you. To all the raw, scared bits you think you're hiding."

I look at her. "I hate you," I say.

"Anyway," she says, waving me off. "You were wrong, but you weren't *wrong*. Back in Indian Wells."

I'm not sure what she means.

"Michael and I are getting divorced," she says finally. Before I can ask her how she is or what happened, she says, "We will talk about it later, but, you know, maybe I *was* living vicariously through you for a moment there."

I put my arm on her shoulder. "I'm sorry."

She waves me away.

"Well, I did sleep with Bowe," I say. "So there ya go: There's the gossip you wanted."

Gwen laughs abruptly, tossing her head back and delighting in it all with such force and freedom that multiple people turn their heads to look at us.

"Can we leave?" I say.

Gwen nods. "I'm going to go connect with a few sponsors. You go take the photo with Jadran, and then yeah, let's go."

Ten minutes later, I'm posing with a smile across my face as Jadran Petrovich and I have our photos taken. Once the flashes stop, I congratulate him on winning.

"Thank you, it is exciting. My first," he says.

"It's thrilling," I say. "I remember my first one."

"You have won before," he says.

"Ten times," I say. "Yes."

"Hm," he says. "But it is three sets."

"Excuse me?"

"The match is best of three in the women's. We play best of five. The men's tournament."

"Right."

"So it's not comparable, is it?"

I see Gwen coming to meet me. I look Jadran right in the eye. "I assure you," I say, all smile—fake or not—gone from my face, "if I played you two out of three or three out of five, I would drag you across the court and murder your—"

"All right, that's it," Gwen says as she hooks her arm into mine and hauls me away.

Sometime around three in the morning, Gwen and I are in my hotel suite, opening a second bottle of champagne. Gwen's thrown her heels off and is sitting in the club chair, pouring. I am lying, still in my fancy dress, across the sofa. She hands me my refilled glass.

"You should have let me tell that fucker off," I say.

Gwen shakes her head. "If I let you say all the things you wanted to say in public, your career would be over in about two hours."

"Why do I have to be nice when most of the men aren't? Last year, Jeff Kerr called an umpire a 'dogshit salad,' and he's hawking underwear for Fruit of the Loom."

Gwen shakes her head. "You know damn well there's another set of rules for you. Just like there's even *another* set of rules for me."

I look at her, understanding that as much as I know what it's like to be a woman in this world, I have no idea what it's like to be a Black woman.

"Yeah," I say. "And it's not right."

Gwen shrugs. "Most shit isn't."

I nod. "Good point."

"And look, I know you might not care about all the money you stand to make, because you've already got your villa and your foundation, but I want that money! And what you've done this week will catapult you to the top of everyone's list. The figures people are throwing around now—I could retire off this."

"Oh please, you're not gonna retire," I say as I look up at the ceiling.

"I don't know," she says.

I sit up and stare at her.

"The twins are going to college next year. Michael is leaving. He met someone else, apparently. Her name is Naomi. Which is such a pretty name. And that irritates the shit out of me. And, anyway, I don't know. I'd like to do . . . something. Something big. Something unexpected."

"Like what?" I ask, putting my drink down.

"I don't know yet. But where's my midlife crisis? Aren't I allowed one?"

I nod, considering. "Absolutely you are!"

"Yeah, I am."

"Maybe I'll have one too," I say. "Or maybe this is mine."

"You're still a bit young for it, I'm afraid. You have another crisis in front of you in about ten years."

"Oh, good," I say, laying my head back down. I rest my hands across my chest.

"You should do it," I say. "Retire. And do something crazy. Travel the world or take up deep-sea fishing. Or be one of those people who walk across the country. But you do what calls to you."

"Yeah?" Gwen says. "I really am thinking about it, Carrie. It's not just a joke. I wouldn't be your agent anymore."

"I get that, but . . ." I look away from her, at the lipstick on the empty champagne glass in front of me. "I mean . . . you're not . . . Listen, I don't have a ton of people that I trust. But you . . . you mean something to me. So I don't care if you're not the one who brokers my deals. You're not just that. In my life."

Gwen doesn't say anything. She's turned away and is dabbing a tissue against the underside of her eye.

"Was it okay I said that?" I ask.

"Yeah," Gwen says. "I love that you said that. You're almost a sister to me. My irritating, cocky, pain-in-the-ass little sister." She leans over and grabs my hand and squeezes it. And then she bursts into tears. "Ignore me. I'm just drunk and going through a divorce. It's like being pregnant. You're always one good or bad second away from crying."

"I'm sorry you're getting a divorce," I say. "You always seemed so happy."

"We were and we weren't. But when one person wants to end it, it's over."

"Yeah," I say. "I know."

"I will meet someone else," Gwen says. "That's what I keep remembering. All the good stuff at the beginning. The butterflies and the swooning. I'll get to have that again. And that's a gift."

I think about what she's saying. I think about Bowe and his Spanish phrases, the way he inches toward me, the way he spends each day with my father. So many butterflies, so many things to swoon for.

And I keep them crammed down inside a tiny box in my chest and I forbid them from coming out.

"I think that's brave," I say.

"You came out of retirement, announced a nearly impossible intention, and then achieved it on an international stage," Gwen says. "You're brave."

"No," I say. "Not about what you're talking about. Not about love. I've never felt brave about that."

"Oh, for fuck's sake, Carrie," she says, shaking her head. "You just won Wimbledon at the age of thirty-seven—when no one thought you could do it. And now you're going to sell yourself short on the easy stuff?"

"It doesn't seem easy to me at all," I say.

Gwen stands up and puts her hand on my shoulder. "Falling in love is really quite simple," she says. "You want to know the secret? It's the same thing we are all doing about life every single day."

I look to her.

"Forget there's an ending."

I wake up hungover, my makeup smeared all over my face. I've slept in my dress.

My flight is scheduled for midmorning, so I get up and pack my things. I take a shower. I inhale three ibuprofen. I check the time and try to convert it to Pacific Daylight Time but give up. And then, just as I am about to dry my hair, there's a knock on the door.

"One second!" I call out, putting my robe back on.

I open the door to find a bellman holding a bizarre-looking bouquet of flowers. Most of them are bright pink and spiky, but between them all are tiny gold blooms that look like buttons. It is an unusual and interesting bouquet. Every aspect of it unexpected.

I suspect they aren't from my father; he would have sent roses. And I let myself imagine, briefly, that they are from Bowe. But the idea seems too indulgent, too embarrassing.

"Thank you," I say, and I tip the bellman. After he leaves, I put the vase on the coffee table and search for the card. Maybe Gwen got up early and sent them.

Brava, Soto! Take a breath and fill your lungs with your
victory, friend. I promise there will not be another one. See you
in New York. XO, Chan

P.S. The pink flowers are amaranth, which represent
immortality—what we're fighting for, after all. And the yellow
are tansy. They are said to represent a declaration of war. Fun,
right?

Ugh. I hate that I like Nicki Chan.

MY FATHER IS WAITING FOR ME IN THE DRIVEWAY WHEN MY CAR PULLS in. His color is back, and he looks healthy and strong.

The moment he sees me, he beams. It's a smile so big that it takes over his face. I'm not sure I've seen him smile like this in decades. The sight is enough to knock me over. I drop my things and run to him.

He holds me so close I think he might snap my bones. My dad has always had this same smell—a smell I've been fond of my entire life. I always assumed it was his natural scent. Until one day, as a teenager, I wandered into the fragrance section of the pharmacy and smelled English Leather.

I'm embarrassed to say that, for a second, it mystified me—how could a drugstore bottle what my father smelled of? And then I realized the answer was much more mundane. My father wore drugstore cologne.

But right now, in this moment, I love this drugstore cologne more than I love the smell of Wimbledon grass or California oranges or the rubber of a freshly popped can of tennis balls. This drugstore cologne is my home.

"I have never, never been prouder, *cielo*," he says when he finally lets me go.

"I know," I say. "I'm the oldest woman to ever win a singles Slam. And I've tied Nicki. If I beat her at the US Open, I'll have done everything I set out to do."

My father shakes his head. "That's not what I'm talking about."

"What do you mean?"

"Have you rewatched the match?" he asks me.

"No," I say. "Should I?"

"It was a beautiful game, *pichona*. Every shot was loose but perfect. You were there. You were present. It was tennis at its finest and it was *your* tennis at its finest and I have never been more proud of the player you are."

"Thanks, Dad," is about all I can croak out.

"And do you know what else?" he says. "The whole third set, you were smiling. Smiling!"

"I like winning."

My father shakes his head. "No, you were happy," he says. "Just playing like when you were a kid. I saw it with my own eyes. It was joy."

Later that night, after I have unpacked, my father and I go over everything the doctors said when he was released from the hospital. He implores me not to worry anymore and then heads back to his own house.

I take a shower and put on a T-shirt and a pair of sweatpants. I comb my hair. But I don't feel settled. I pick up the phone and dial.

"Hey, it's me," I say. And then I wonder why I think I can do that—act like I am the most important person who could possibly call him.

"How are you, champion?" Bowe says. His voice has changed. It sounds different, even from when we spoke so often in London. It is quieter, heavier, breathier.

"I'm good," I say. "I'm really good. How are you feeling? How are your ribs?"

"Much better, actually," he says. "I think Javier and I are going to start training again. I've been doing a little bit on my own. But I would be lying if I said I wasn't looking forward to having my hitter back."

I laugh. "Is that me?" I say. "Am I your hitter?"

"I don't know what you are," he says.

"Yeah, me neither. I *am* a little lonely, though," I say.

"Yeah?" Bowe's voice picks up a lightness again, that bounce. I like both versions of him.

"Yeah, a little."

"Well, that I can do something about," he says.

The second half of the summer is a train heading full speed toward Flushing Meadows.

There is not much time between Wimbledon and the US Open. My father has his work cut out for him, training both Bowe and me, day in and day out.

He sits on the bench for my morning training sessions, barking drills at me. After the first day, I buy him a megaphone so he won't strain so hard to yell.

After I go in for lunch and to take a shower and rest, Bowe usually shows up and trains with my father for a few hours. Sometimes, as I'm getting dressed, I watch the two of them in the backyard. Bowe and my father are always either passionately agreeing or disagreeing about what Bowe should work on next. The two of them bicker at full volume—Bowe yelling to be heard over my father's megaphone.

As the days pass by, I can see Bowe's first serve growing more and more bold, his second serve more consistent, all from my window.

Then, every day around three, I get back on the court. And Bowe and I play a match.

Bowe always starts off trash-talking. And then I often trounce him—and my father gives us both a series of pointers for the next day.

At which point, Bowe says he'll see us tomorrow. My father and I have dinner. And then I say I'm going to bed.

But instead, I wait until nine-thirty, when I open my door, and Bowe is always standing on my doorstep.

"Hi."

"Hi."

Every night, I grab his hand and pull him inside and bring him to my bedroom. And every night, he presses himself against me and kisses my neck and makes me wonder if anyone has ever survived jumping off the edge of a cliff.

A month before the US Open, Bowe is lying in my bed in the middle of the night. His arm is cradled perfectly under my neck; his right hand is tracing shapes on my upper arm, and I'm almost asleep.

"Your dad knows what's going on," he says.

"He just thinks you're into me."

"No," Bowe says. "He knows that I'm parking across the street and sleeping here until the morning, when I go home for four hours and then come right back, pretending I've been gone the whole time."

"He doesn't know any of that."

Bowe laughs. "He does. Today after he was done barking orders at me about my backhand, he calmly asked me if I had any idea of my plans after I retire. And when I said I wasn't sure, he said, 'Well, do you think settling down is in your future?'"

I cringe so hard I nearly spasm. "No, he didn't," I say, sitting up. I'm now fully awake. "You must have misunderstood him."

"I assure you, I did not."

"Yes, you did."

"We could tell him the truth," Bowe says, turning onto his side, toward me in bed. He's been sleeping here so consistently that I've started wondering if I should get another nightstand. But I have always had one nightstand, and I can't conceive of being the sort of idiot who would buy a second.

"No, c'mon," I say. "Let's not make anything weird, all right? I want him to train you for the US Open. I want you to win the damn thing. And I want to win it too."

"Of course."

"So we know that we're going to be training together for the next month . . ."

Bowe looks at me, his eyebrows furrowed, as if he cannot tell where my train of thought is headed.

"But who knows if we'll even be sleeping together tomorrow."

Bowe pulls his arm away from me. "You're fucking impossible," he says, rolling onto his back. "Absolutely impossible."

"What are we doing, Bowe?" I say.

"I don't know," he says. "You won't tell me."

"*You* tell *me*."

"I don't know!" he says.

"See? You don't have a plan. You don't know what you want."

"I do know what I want," he says. "I'm here, aren't I? You fucking rejected me back in '82 and took up with Randall, of all people. You rejected me back in Melbourne. You all but rejected me back in Paris. And still, I'm here, every night, any second that you want me. I know exactly what I want, Carrie. I've made it clear."

I watch him throw his head back on the bed. And I let myself believe for a moment that maybe he means it. Maybe this time, maybe this man, means it.

"Just forget it," he says. And then he turns his back to me and fluffs his pillow angrily. And I smile to myself because you don't fluff a pillow you're not planning to sleep on.

• • •

Bowe and I both take Sundays off from training. We need one day to recuperate. And sometimes, in the morning, I'll watch tapes with my dad. But in the afternoons, even I need a break from tennis, and I can tell that my dad does not know what to do with himself.

Bowe starts coming over in the afternoons to play chess with my father on Sundays. Then it evolves into the two of them going to Blockbuster together and renting war movies.

They pop popcorn and watch the movies in our home theater, pausing every few minutes to talk about historical references to World War I or II or Vietnam. And I normally sit in the lounger in the same room, only half paying attention.

I've never realized until now that my dad is into war movies. But in hindsight, it's painfully obvious that he would be drawn to them.

One Sunday, the two of them catch me tearing up at the very end of the movie, when the sergeant salutes his captain.

AUGUST 1995

Two weeks before the US Open

I AM RUNNING SPRINTS ACROSS THE COURT, TRAINING HARDER THAN
ever.

"*¡De nuevo!*" my father says as I stop short at his feet.

"*Sí, papá.*"

Bowe has a wild card for the US Open. But I do not need a wild
card or to qualify, because I am now ranked twelfth in the world.

Twelfth. A delicious, enticing number, with the capacity to carry
a boatload of fuck-yous.

When I am done with another sprint, I look at my father for what
to do next. But instead of sending me to the baseline, he pats the
spot on the bench beside him.

"*¿Qué pasa?*" I say, sitting down.

"I see a change in you that I can't quite describe, since Wimbledon. You're . . . freer."

"I'm less afraid," I say. "Of losing."

"Because you've made your peace with it?" he asks.

"Because it's unlikely."

My father laughs. "Well, then you need to keep that with you, heading into New York. Especially up against Chan. New York is her best court."

I nod.

"And I think we both know that I can't go with you."

We've spoken *around* it for weeks—that he is not yet healthy enough to travel. "I know."

"I will be watching," he says. "I can't wait to see you take that record back. Probably right out of her hands."

I breathe in deeply, trying to push down the grief that is blooming in my chest.

"I'll just be doing it from here," he says. "Instead of in the stands."

"Yeah," I say. "Of course."

"You will go and win the US Open, and then you can retire again and come home, and we can throw a party," he says.

"You make it sound so easy."

"It is not easy," he says. "But you will do it."

"And if I don't?"

My father looks at me and narrows his eyes, trying to gauge my reaction.

"I don't need you to guess what I want to hear," I say. "I just want the truth. If I don't win, then what?"

"Well, if you don't win the US Open, I don't care. That's the truth."

I erupt in laughter. "Unreal."

"You said you wanted the truth. It will be no different to me if you win or you lose. It won't affect me at all."

"I mean, it matters a little," I say.

"To you, maybe. But to me? It was never the point."

I put my head on his shoulder and absorb what he's saying. I look up at the bright, unending L.A. sky, palm trees swaying in the breeze.

"He's in love with you," my father finally says.

I don't pull away. I don't even flinch.

"And he knows you're a better player than he is," my dad says. "I was always worried about that with you. Because the only person who could ever understand you would be another player. But how many players would be okay knowing they were second place? He takes to it well, though. Which is about the highest compliment I can think of. I'm not sure there is a greater strength."

"Playing second to a woman?" I ask.

My father winks at me. "Feeling secure, even knowing you are not the best."

I feel both sides of that sword, the compliment and the sharp edge meant for me.

"He is a good guy," I say.

My father nods. "Even if he is sneaking into your house every night like some sort of *pirata*."

I laugh. "Well, that's on me," I say. "I'm not . . . I don't know if there's any future there, and I don't want to make it too much of a thing."

"So you push it away, because it's easier to pretend you don't want it," my dad says.

I look at him.

"Please," he says, pulling me under his shoulder. "Open your heart the tiniest bit, *pichona*. Being married to your mother changed my life. She made me feel joy. She gave me purpose. We became a family. Tennis is nothing compared to that."

"But then she was gone. And you were left with such . . . heartache. And I don't . . . I don't know how to do that . . . to live that way," I say.

"If you did not know how to do something on the court, it would not stop you from figuring it out." He grabs my hand. "I was so broken when your mother died that I buried my heart in the earth. And I taught you to as well. I thought I was showing you how to move on, but I was showing you how to never open up to anybody. I taught you the wrong thing. But I've told you that now, and it's on you to fix it. Okay?"

"Yeah, Dad," I say. "I already knew it. But thank you."

"I know you did. Sometimes, you're much smarter than me. So much stronger too. You're like a bright diamond, one shiny, tough . . ."

"Bitch," I offer.

My dad laughs. "Okay, sure. One shiny, tough bitch."

I laugh, and he pulls me back to him. "*Te amo, cielo.* Being your father is the best thing that has ever happened to me. My Achilles. Greatest of the Greeks."

"Dad . . ." I say.

"No," he says. "Just accept it. Let me feel it and say it. You're the meaning of my life."

That afternoon, Bowe comes over and we play a set with my father barking at us from the sidelines through his megaphone.

"Bowe, get higher up on your toes when you make contact," he says. "And Carrie, don't get lazy on that follow-through!"

Bowe squeaks out a win against me—he's getting better and better, almost by the hour, lately. And it stings to fall just short of him.

At the end of the session, my father gives me a few pointers, but it is Bowe he's focused on. "I think you need a more open stance," he says as Bowe zips his racket into its case. "So your weight is on the right foot as you prepare to move for the return."

"I told you I'm not messing with my footwork now," Bowe says. "Not when it feels right and feels intuitive. I just beat one of the greatest players in the world with my stance. C'mon."

"Good is the enemy of great," my father says.

Bowe looks at me and then my father. "Spoken like a Soto."

Bowe puts his kit over his shoulder, and my father starts discussing dinner.

"See you all tomorrow," Bowe says, waving goodbye as he heads toward his car. I watch him go, so casually, with no expectations.

I look at my father, who looks back at me, incredulous.

Oh, fine.

"Bowe!" I call out.

He turns around.

"Stay for dinner," I say.

Bowe looks at both my father and me. "Really?"

"Yeah," I say. "Yes."

I walk toward him and take his kit off his shoulder. "Stay. Please."

He watches me take his racket bag and put it down on the bench. When I catch his eye, I can tell that he wants to ask me many different questions. But I have just one simple, precarious answer. "I want you to stay."

He smiles. "Okay," he says.

He claps his hands together and says, "All right, let's do this. What are we having? Javier, don't even try me with the steak or the salty food right now. You know what? Why don't I fire up the grill and make chicken?"

My dad laughs. And then he begins walking to my house with Bowe and me. Bowe walks up ahead of us, ever so briefly. And my father puts his arm around me.

"*Siempre supe que no hay montaña que no puedas escalar, paso a paso.*"

I have always known there is no mountain you cannot climb, one step at a time.

Bowe makes dinner, and we eat outside. They play a game of chess while I look up at the stars. My dad hugs me good night. And nobody pretends Bowe is going home tonight.

Bowe and I go inside. I start doing the dishes, and Bowe comes up behind me. He kisses me and I laugh. He says he loves my laugh, and then he says, "Can I say that? Can I say I love your laugh?"

And I say, "I don't know. I mean, I guess yes. Sure."

I can see my father's living room window from my kitchen. I watch as his light goes off.

Bowe grabs my waist and spins me toward him.

And I wonder for a moment why I have spent all my time worried about losing things, when there is so much here.

· · ·

When Bowe and I wake up in the morning, instead of sneaking out, he goes downstairs in his underwear and makes me a blueberry smoothie. I drink it while he makes himself a black coffee. When we're done, he picks up the paper and goes into the den. I go out onto the court.

I stretch my legs. As I start on my shoulders, I look at my watch. It's three past eight.

Where is my dad?

My heart drops through my belly.

I run toward my father's front door. I put my hand on the door-knob and I turn it.

There he is. Lying on one of his sofas, with the TV on ESPN.

Here but gone.

And all that escapes from my mouth is a hushed yelp. *"Papá."*

FROM THEN ON, EVERYTHING FEELS LIKE THOSE MOMENTS JUST BEFORE you wake in the morning. I am not asleep but somehow still dreaming, the world an ambiguous combination of reality and hallucination.

At some point, I am standing on my father's front stoop, staring at my sneakers when somebody—I can't tell if he's an EMT or someone from the coroner's office—comes to find me. I look over and realize Bowe is at my side, holding my hand.

"Your father had another heart attack last night and passed away, most likely sometime between eleven and one A.M.," the man says.

"Yeah, no shit, genius!" I hear myself shout.

Bowe pulls me into his arms.

I think someone gives me a sedative.

. . .

Gwen comes over with dinner. Bowe tries to make me eat something. When I look at him, I can't figure out why Bowe Huntley is in my house, why he is the one beside me.

Gwen tells me this is going to make the news soon. "I'll do my best to hold it all off until you're ready."

I tell her I don't care who knows. Hiding it won't fix it.

Bowe feeds me lunch and dinner and breakfast the next morning. I know that because I can see the dishes piled up around me in my bed.

I see my own face on the television and see Greg Phillips reporting that "Javier Soto, father and coach of Carrie Soto, has died unexpectedly. He was not with his daughter at Wimbledon this past July, and some speculated it was due to health concerns. But he was expected to be with Carrie in New York next week for the US Open."

Bowe tells me later that I threw the remote at the TV and cracked the screen.

In the paper, they print a picture of him from the early seventies at the French Open. He looks young and handsome in his polo shirt and panama hat. He would have loved it. I try to tear it out of the paper to save it, but I accidentally rip it.

At some point, Bowe gets in bed and holds me. He makes me smoothies every morning. He always gives me the wrong type of straw, but I don't know how to tell him without screaming at him and I don't want to scream at him.

I walk into the bathroom, thinking Bowe is in the shower. But instead, I find him sitting on the edge of the tub, with the shower running. When he sees me, he looks up and his eyes are bloodshot. He stands up and asks me if I am okay.

I wonder when he is going to leave. I'd have left by now.

"I'm not going anywhere," he says, even though I can't tell if I said any of that out loud.

After my father's funeral and the reception, Gwen is packing up all the food as I stand there in the kitchen, not moving. She's telling me about all the times my dad made her laugh.

"Can you please, for the love of God, shut up?" I say.

She stops putting cheese slices into Tupperware and looks at me. I say, "I'm sorry."

She takes my hand, but hers is cold and I want her to let go of me. But I also know that even if I ask her to, she won't.

Bowe goes out onto the court every day. Sometimes I watch him from my window.

He comes inside after a particularly grueling session with a hitter. "How are you?" he says, breathless.

"How the fuck do you think I'm doing?" I say.

I look down and see I'm wearing my father's slippers. And I don't remember when I put them on.

Later, I ask Bowe if I should drop out of the US Open, and he tells me I already know the answer. But he's wrong. I do not.

I am in a T-shirt and pair of Bowe's boxers when Bowe comes into the room and tells me he's scheduled to play Franco Gustavo. I'm scheduled to play Madlenka Dvořáková in the first round in New York.

I hear my father's voice. "*Ah, será fácil.* You can whoop her ass." I turn to see him, but he's not there.

I am standing in the middle of my living room, looking at all the flowers people sent. The house is overflowing with blooms that are starting to die.

So many people have *sent* something but not come by. Which is more than I would have done for any of them.

The phone rings as I am lying in bed, and I don't answer it. But I can tell by the way the ringing stops that Bowe has picked it up.

He comes in a few moments later.

"It's Nicki," he says. "Chan."

"I don't want to talk to her," I say. But then I take the phone from his hand anyway.

"Hi."

"I'm so sorry, Carrie," Nicki says.

"Thank you."

"Listen, I want to tell you something. . . . If you don't play the US Open, I will consider bowing out as well."

I can't quite process the rest of what she's saying until she adds, "Just let me know what you're thinking. I want it to be a clean win. I want a fair fight."

"Honestly, Nicki," I say, "it just doesn't matter very much."

Nicki laughs, like I am making a joke.

My first moment of clarity is the following day—when I finally get up the guts to go into my father's house.

I stand in the same spot where I stood when I found him. I look at his things: his remote controls and the half-filled water glasses, his magazines and his books lined up on the shelf, his movies stacked to the side, his leather chairs, his panama hats.

I pick up one of his hats. It smells like English Leather and shampoo, earthy and human.

I wonder if this is how he felt when my mother died: flattened by the impossibility and yet inevitability of tomorrow. I am suddenly so tired, no match for the heaviness of gravity. I look at the floor and it calls to me, as strong as a magnet.

I lie down on the carpet of the home I bought for my father. The gift I gave him. And I do not get up for what feels like hours.

I am so angry at myself for thinking he'd be okay.

Don't I know better? Didn't I learn this lesson earlier than most? That the world doesn't care about you? That it will take the one thing you need, rip it right from your arms?

Grief is like a deep, dark hole. It calls like a siren: *Come to me, lose yourself here.* And you fight it and you fight it and you fight it, but when you finally do succumb and jump down into it, you can't quite believe how deep it is. It feels as if this is how you will live for the rest of your life, falling. Terrified and devastated, until you yourself die.

But that is the mirage.

That is grief's dizzying spell.

The fall isn't never-ending. It does have a ground floor.

Today, I cry for so long that I finally feel the floor under my feet. I find the bottom. And while I know the hole will be there forever, at least for now, I feel as if I can live inside it. I have learned its boundaries and its edges.

I stand up and feel ready to leave my father's house. But as I walk toward the door, I notice a notebook on the kitchen counter. It's the one he started keeping this year, full of all his coaching notes.

I walk into the kitchen, and I pick it up. It is a black leather book, as unassuming as can be. The front says *Carrie.*

I flip through it and see that every page is devoted to a player in the WTA—with stats and plays, strategies—for how to beat them.

Players like Dvořáková and Flores and Martin and Carter and Zetov, they take up maybe half a page. Perez and Moretti and Nystrom and Machado each get more. And then there are multiple pages on Antonovich and Cortez.

Nicki Chan takes up the entire back half of the book.

He's clearly rewatched some of her games, made notes on how she performed against every other player. He's compared our serves and groundstrokes. Our shots. Our stances. Our forms.

And at the top of the last page, he's written in all capital letters *CARRIE CAN BEAT HER.*

His handwriting is a mess, and there are whole sentences I can't read. He has shown no concern for legibility, or whether any of it would make sense to anyone but him. Which is how I know this isn't a book he wrote *to me.* He wrote it for himself. This was his plan for New York.

I hold the book to my chest. I inhale sharply. When my mother died, there was almost nothing of her left. And as hard as I tried, I couldn't summon her. I couldn't hold on.

But there is still a huge piece of my father here. There is still work for him to do. This is one last tournament with my dad. I am holding it in my hands.

And I am going to fucking win it.

"Gwen," I say into the phone. I am in my kitchen, getting blueberries out of the refrigerator. "I'm going. Confirm with the USTA."

"You're sure about this?" she asks.

"Yeah," I say. "I'll fly out with Bowe."

"All right, I'll call you back."

I hang up the phone and walk upstairs, where Bowe is reading the same book I've seen him carrying around for days. I finally register the title. *How to Go on Living When Someone You Love Dies.*

"Hi," I say.

He puts the book down and sits up. "Hi."

I stare at Bowe as he waits for me to say more. He is in a heather gray Henley T-shirt and a pair of jeans. His hair is a mess. His stubble has grown in quite a bit.

He is here. He has not left.

"I'm going to New York with you," I say. "I'm playing the US Open."

"Okay," Bowe says, nodding. "Yes, great."

"My dad would like that," I say. "If I did that."

"I completely agree."

I walk toward him and put my arms around his torso, lean my head against his chest. Here is someone else who knew my father, someone else who knows what I have lost, someone who lost something too.

"I'm gonna go and I'm going to win the whole goddamn thing," I say, pulling back.

"I love it," Bowe says, nodding and smiling. "Yes, I'm gonna do that too."

Both of us laugh, and I don't have a shred of guilt for feeling joyful without my father on this earth. This is the tiniest beginning of a terrible, beautiful whole new life.

THE MORNING OF MY MATCH AGAINST DVOŘÁKOVÁ, THERE IS A KNOCK
at the door of my hotel suite, and Bowe answers it. Gwen comes in
holding a blueberry smoothie.

"I didn't know you were coming," I say.

Gwen smiles softly. "Yes, you did, honey," she says. "It's okay. I'm
here." She hands me the smoothie.

Bowe is gathering my kit and my clothes. But when I watch him
do it, I realize I didn't do any of the packing. He did it all back in L.A.
And now he is doing it all here.

So far this morning, as well as asking Gwen to get the smoothie,
he's woken me up, called down for almonds, run the shower, put me
in it, and then when I just stood there, he got in with me and washed
my hair.

"You're playing Dvořáková?" Gwen says.

"Yeah."

Gwen looks at Bowe. "And you're playing Gustavo?"

Bowe nods. "If I win, I'll play Ortega, probably. And then maybe Griffin or Bracher. But, you know, when I lose, that's it for me."

"You're retiring," Gwen says.

"Yeah. I'm done. I'm ready to be done."

Gwen nods. "And are you retiring?" she says, looking at me. "After this?"

I don't have an answer. I can barely consider this afternoon.

"Okay," Gwen says. "We'll prepare for all scenarios."

Bowe returns to whatever he's doing and then pops his head back up a second later. "Oh, don't forget your notebook."

He hands it to me, and I breathe in. I've read every line of it over and over again since I first found it. I fell asleep reading it last night. I read the page on Dvořáková three times this morning alone. I look at my watch. I'm playing her in a matter of hours.

"What is that?" Gwen says.

I open my mouth to explain, but I can't. I can't get the words out.

"Jav put it together," Bowe says. "His coaching plan. So Carrie's gonna follow it and win."

Gwen nods. "I love it."

"Do you want to see it?" I say.

"Your coaching plan that your father gave you?" Gwen says. "You don't have to share that with me. Or with anyone if you don't want to."

"I want to," I say. "Check it out."

I crack the book open, and I take her through each page. When we get to Dvořáková, Gwen and I read through it together.

Since Carrie beat her back in Melbourne, she's gotten stronger. Her base-line work is better. But she wants to be a power baseliner so bad, even though she's better at serve and volley. Keep her playing at the baseline. It will thrill her, but she won't be able to keep up.

I start to feel that hum in my bones. It feels small, right now, like a nascent flame. But I know it will grow. I know soon it will roar.

Gwen looks up at me. "You've got this," she says.

"Yeah," I say. "Plus, my dad didn't write it down, but Dvořáková is intimidated by me. I've beaten her every time I've played her so far. So if I don't let her get a foothold at the beginning, I think she'll go down like a house of cards."

Gwen nods. "You're a smart one," she says.

"Thanks. Taught by the best."

Gwen holds my hand and gives it a squeeze. "Yes, you were. And you've absorbed it all."

"Thank you."

I get up as she keeps flipping through the pages.

"There's a lot on Chan," she says.

"Yeah, I have to study that section."

"Well," she says, "I'll be in the players' box for each and every match, all right?"

I nod. And then Gwen kisses me on the cheek and hugs Bowe goodbye and leaves.

I turn to Bowe. He is holding up a navy tank top and a white tennis skirt. He has put my yellow Break Points on the bed.

"I fucked up. I forgot socks," he says. "When I was packing your things."

"We will get some on the way," I say. "It's gonna be fine."

THE 1995
US OPEN

I STAND IN THE LOCKER ROOM, SURROUNDED BY OTHER PLAYERS—
Martin and Carter are laughing in the corner. Zetov and Perez are
ignoring each other. Antonovich comes in and smiles and greets
everyone. When Perez sees me, she gives me a pat on the shoulder.
Flores tells me she's sorry for my loss. I say thank you.

When Madlenka Dvořáková walks in, we catch each other's eye.
She looks so childlike in her white dress, her hair pulled back in two
braids. We give each other a nod, and then I shut my locker and
make my way to the training room.

It's oddly quiet in here, just me and a few trainers. I take in the
delicious solitude as I have my knees and elbows taped. But then,
when I'm having my calves massaged, Nicki Chan walks in.

She's smiling sweetly, greeting the trainers she recognizes with a
levity I find puzzling. It is as if it is any other day to her—and not the
first day of a two-week tournament in which she might just break
another record or lose it altogether.

When she sits down next to me, I speak up. "Always so chipper."

"Yes," she says as she sits down on the bench next to mine. "It's rather annoying, isn't it? People tell me that all the time." She laughs as the trainer begins taping her foot. I make a mental note to run her around the court, if I get the chance. Her ankle has to be hurting. She has to stop going so hard on it.

"Thank you for calling," I say, my voice low. "The other day."

Nicki nods. "Of course."

"It was . . . kind of you."

"Like I said," she says, waving me off, "I want to skin you alive and eat your heart for breakfast." She smiles at me and winks. "But I want to know I did it when you were at your strongest."

I nod. "I get it," I say. "And you will get your chance. And you will fail. And everything will go back to the way it should be." I switch positions as one of the trainers starts massaging my forearms.

Nicki keeps her eyes focused entirely on watching the trainer wrap her foot. But her next words are aimed squarely at me. "I don't think you've ever understood what I can do. What I am doing."

"I do," I say. "I see it."

"I am better than you," she says.

"Give me a break, Nicki."

"You think that if this was 1982, I wouldn't stand a chance against you," Nicki continues.

"I *know* that if this was 1982, you wouldn't stand a chance against me," I say. "Because it's 1995, and you don't stand a chance against me."

Nicki scoffs. "You just can't see it."

"How good you are?" I say. "I see how good you are."

"You don't respect what I've done for tennis the way I respect what you've done."

"What have you done that I haven't done?"

Nicki turns and looks at me. Her gaze is heavy. "I'm the first Asian woman to ever win Wimbledon. The first woman like me to do *almost any of the things* I've done in tennis—hitting these records. Because we both know tennis doesn't make it easy for those of us who aren't blond and blue-eyed."

"Yes," I say, nodding. "Absolutely."

"I've increased the fastest serve recorded in tennis. Tennis is a quicker game now, since I served at 132 miles per hour. Now almost every player on the WTA is serving faster than we all were even ten years ago. My forehand *averages* 81 miles per hour. You can't come close to me on that either. So pay me a little respect, Soto. I've won the US Open more than any woman in tennis history, including you. My forehand and backhand groundstrokes have more spin than any other female player ever—last year I topped two thousand revolutions per minute. I am currently the highest-paid female athlete in the world. For someone like me, do you understand what that means? And I've spent the most weeks at number one—which is currently three hundred and seventeen. You only have three hundred and—"

"Nine," I say.

"Right."

"So you just go around memorizing your stats?" I say, even though I know I'm being a hypocrite.

Nicki laughs. "This matters to me, Carrie. Putting my whole soul into this game matters to me. These tournaments matter. I've dedicated my life to this."

"Well, so have I," I say.

"And you had your chance to shine—you were given that opportunity."

"I *took* it," I say. "It wasn't given to me. Nobody wanted *me* to be the face of women's tennis. They still don't. I had to demand it. Just like I am doing now. So if you want it, you're going to have to take it from me."

"No," Nicki says. "That's what you don't seem to get. I *have* taken it from you. *I* have the record. And if *you* want it, you're going to have to take it from *me*."

I stare at her, and she continues.

"I am the best player women's tennis has seen," she says. "And I deserve to be recognized for it."

"You are recognized for it," I say. "Constantly."

Nicki shakes her head. "No, by *you*. By the person I've respected my entire life. The woman I've looked up to."

There is no smile on her face anymore. Not even the hint of one. I look over at the TV. It's playing sports commentary with the sound off. The closed captioning says they are talking about Nicki and me right now.

"I see it," I say, finally looking at her. "Me hating it is me seeing it."

Nicki sighs. "Okay, Soto. I guess I can't squeeze blood from a stone."

"Look, what do you want from me?"

Nicki looks me in the eye.

"Don't worry about what I say," I tell her. "Pay attention to what I *do*. I'm back, aren't I? I'm playing here today. That's how good you are."

The trainer is done. I stand up. I walk past Nicki and put my hand on her shoulder.

"Good luck," I say. "I'm rooting for you up until the last second when I play you."

Nicki smiles. "You should be so lucky."

I put my hand out for her to shake. And she takes it.

Transcript

SportsNews Network
Wild Sports with Bill Evans

Bill Evans: It is the first day of this year's US Open, and Nicki Chan started it off by absolutely *crushing* journeyman Suze Carter this morning. Natasha Antonovich, Ingrid Cortez, Carla Perez, Odette Moretti, Josie Flores, Whitney Belgrade, Erica Staunton, and more are all heading into the second round. And now in the afternoon, Wimbledon champion and all-out sensation Carrie Soto goes up against rookie Madlenka Dvořáková here in the first round at Flushing Meadows. It is just two weeks since her father and coach, Javier Soto, died. Carrie has said she is playing in his honor.

There's a lot of talk about who will come out the victor over the next couple weeks. But we know one thing for sure: There may be one hundred twenty-eight players competing for that trophy, but all eyes are focused on just two of them.

Nicki Chan and Carrie Soto have made no secret of their rivalry. Each of these incomparable women wants that title and the record that comes with it.

Who will it be? The Beast or the B-I-T-C-You-Know-What?

It is sure to be a nail-biter. Stay with us over the next two weeks as we find out who makes it to the final.

SOTO VS. DVOŘÁKOVÁ

1995 US Open

First Round

I AM STANDING IN THE TUNNEL. I LEAN DOWN AND WIPE THE DIRT OFF my yellow Break Points. I remember the words my father wrote down. *Keep her playing at the baseline. It will thrill her, but she won't be able to keep up.*

I breathe in deeply. Here we go.

The second my feet hit the court, the crowd cheers. They cheer so loudly I can barely hear myself think.

I know what the sportscasters are saying. They are telling all the people at home that I've just lost Dad, that I am out here playing my first match without him.

I expect the roar to die down, but it doesn't. The crowd keeps cheering as I set up my things. It is almost eerie—the way their voices ring through the air, the way the howl of it echoes throughout the arena. Their sound is a deep rumble, shaking the net.

I look up all around me—thousands of people stomping and

calling. I wave in a wide circle through each section, and I watch as people in the crowd start standing up.

Bowe and Gwen are in the players' box. Gwen is clapping. Bowe catches my eye, and we look at each other as each section stands, rising like a tide.

They are clapping for my father. For this one moment of time, it feels as if everyone in the arena misses Javier Soto as much as I do.

A tear leaves my eye. I wipe it away.

Poor Dvořáková. She stands no chance. It's over in fifty-one minutes.

Transcript

SportsRadio Nation with Grant Trumbull

Grant Trumbull: We are here with the editor of *SportsSunday,* Jimmy Wallace, to talk about what's going on at the US Open. Jimmy, give us the lay of the land here. Start with the men's game.

Jimmy Wallace: Well, there's no story coming out of men's tennis quite like that of Bowe Huntley.

Trumbull: He's soaring.

Wallace: There was nobody—and I mean *nobody*—favoring Bowe Huntley as we came into this tournament.

Trumbull: This is his last, is it not?

Wallace: All of us were saying, "The guy's retiring, he's the oldest one on the court, his salad days are long behind him."

Trumbull: And he had to pull out of Wimbledon with an injury.

Wallace: He tore the cartilage in his ribs back in May at the French. This was not a player anyone was betting on.

Trumbull: And yet.

Wallace: [*laughs*] And yet! Huntley comes out onto the court in the first round and just pummels Franco Gustavo. Takes him in straight sets. Still, we're all thinking, "Okay, but it won't happen again."

Trumbull: And we were wrong.

Wallace: Dead wrong. He takes Ortega in the second round, again in straight sets. Then Bracher. Then Mailer.

Trumbull: And now he's in the quarterfinals.

Wallace: He's in the quarterfinals. At the age of forty! And let me tell you, the crowd is with him in these matches. I haven't seen a crowd this energized in years. You know I'm a skeptic, Grant.

Trumbull: [*laughs*] You're a believe-it-when-you-see-it kind of guy.

Wallace: But Huntley's got me on the edge of my seat. He's got me rooting for him. I don't know how this ends, but I'll tell you it's a hell of a show.

Transcript

SportsHour USA
The Mark Hadley Show

Mark Hadley: I'm cleaning my glasses over here, disbelieving what I'm seeing. Bowe Huntley just beat Wimbledon champion Jadran Petrovich in the quarterfinals of the US Open?

Briggs Lakin: I wouldn't just say he beat him. Huntley demolished him. It was *embarrassing* for Petrovich. He's ranked two in the world, and Huntley took him down hard.

Gloria Jones: That last serve was simply stunning.

Hadley: Let's get into Huntley's serve—I want to talk about that. It wasn't official, but there's been talk over this past year that Bowe Huntley was being coached by the late Javier Soto. Have either of you heard anything about this?

Jones: I have, yes. We've been seeing Carrie Soto and Bowe Huntley together a lot these past few months. There's an assumption that they are dating. Obviously, we don't know.

Lakin: I mean, we know.

Jones: No one has confirmed anything.

Lakin: I don't need anyone to confirm for me that two plus two equals four.

Jones: [*laughs*] There are many people who say Bowe Huntley and Javier Soto were working together before the French Open. So it stands to reason they may have still been working together when Javier Soto passed away just a few short weeks ago.

Hadley: So maybe Javier Soto is behind this turn in Bowe Huntley.

Jones: Maybe he was.

Hadley: He certainly did beautiful work with Carrie Soto, didn't he?

Jones: That he did. And let's take a moment, if we can. We all expect greatness from Carrie, but she's just lost her father, she's lost her coach. And now we are on the eve of the semifinals and she's handily defeated *every single opponent in front of her.* That includes Odette Moretti, who she beat in the quarterfinals just a few hours ago today.

Lakin: She's shown a lot of heart this tournament.

Jones: Javier Soto was a great coach, a coach for the ages. And I think we're seeing that in this tournament. I think we are seeing, in Bowe Huntley and Carrie Soto, what Javier Soto was best at. The "beautiful fundamentals," as he would say.

Lakin: Well said, Gloria. Absolutely.

HUNTLEY VS. MATSUDA

1995 US Open

Semifinals

GWEN AND I ARE SITTING IN THE PLAYERS' BOX. I AM CHECKING MY watch because I need to leave soon for my own match. But I can't quite tear myself away just yet.

It's the fifth set, 3–5. Bowe is behind, but he can still get back in it if he holds this game and breaks Matsuda's serve on the next one.

He looks at me and smiles.

This morning at breakfast, I was reading *NowThis* in an attempt to clear my mind. The front cover was about this pop star who left this rock star, and I wanted to know if it was true she'd been sleeping with this actor. But when I opened up the magazine, it was my face that was staring back at me.

There was a photo of Bowe and me on the court from the week before. They had caught us kissing.

I closed the magazine, almost reflexively. And then I opened it back up.

In the photo, we are both in shorts and T-shirts. He is wearing his navy blue hat. He has his arm around my lower back, pulling me toward him, and I have to look up to meet his lips.

I didn't know the paparazzi were there. I wouldn't have kissed him if I had. But instead of feeling horrified to have it printed in the magazine for all the world, all I could see was just how grotesquely happy I look in it.

Bowe walked by and glanced over my shoulder. From the look on his face, I could tell he'd already seen it.

"What do you think?" he asked.

I stared at the photo a moment longer. "We look happy," I said, finally.

And Bowe smiled. "Yeah," he said. "I think so too."

Bowe holds the game; it's now 4–5. During the changeover, he comes up to the players' box and winks at me. I smile at him and wink back. I am once again a fool.

Bowe gets back to the baseline. The pressure is on him now. If he does not win this game, it is the last professional match of his career. But you wouldn't know it looking at him. He's waving to the crowd, laughing as they cheer for him, lifting his hands up to encourage them all.

Last night, he told me he would like to make it to the final. "This is all I've ever wanted out of this year. To do something great like this. I never thought I'd get this far, and now I have," he said in the quiet of the night. "So why not dream further?"

But today, right before he went into the locker room, he told me the opposite. "I never thought I'd get this far, and now I have," he said. "So the rest is all icing on the cake."

Matsuda serves a fast one. It lands at Bowe's feet, and Bowe jumps backward to return it. It lands just over the net. Matsuda scrambles for it and misses.

Love–15.

Bowe smiles. The crowd cheers. It's clear that all the cheering annoys Matsuda. And so in between serves, Bowe looks at the crowd, pumping them up to cheer louder. Matsuda shakes his head, sends off another blistering serve.

Bowe lunges for it but hits it into the net.

15–all.

I check my watch again. I have to go.

15–30.

30–all.

30–40.

Deuce.

Advantage Matsuda.

Deuce.

I have to go.

Advantage Bowe.

Deuce.

Advantage Matsuda.

Deuce.

I'm late to warm up.

Advantage Matsuda.

Deuce.

Advantage Matsuda.

Bowe's tired. I don't know if Matsuda can tell, if the crowd can tell, but I can. He's not up as high on his serve. I will him some strength, a burst of energy. Just two points in a row can save this game and maybe take him to the final.

Deuce.

Advantage Matsuda.

Matsuda sends another serve to Bowe's feet. This time, Bowe runs back as fast as he can. He gets into position, gets his racket on the ball. But then it hits the net.

My heart falls. It's over.

Bowe stands still on the court and closes his eyes. I watch his chest rise and fall. He nods and opens his eyes.

The crowd is oddly quiet for the end of a match. They wanted it for him. But it is Matsuda who is going to the final.

Bowe Huntley has retired.

I watch his face for signs of distress or grief—though I'm smart enough to know that grief will take various shapes over the next few months, maybe years. Still, his face now shows only a smile and wet eyes. Not a tantrum in sight.

I wish my father were here to see this. To witness what Bowe has done here at the US Open. He would have cheered the loudest.

Bowe waves to the crowd.

Suddenly, the whole stadium is on their feet, including me. They are screaming so loud for him that it pierces my ears. He waves to each section, nodding as he does.

Matsuda shakes his hand and then hangs back. He gives Bowe the moment.

Bowe looks at me and smiles. I smile back. Bowe turns to the crowd and lifts both of his fists above his head. And then waves goodbye.

He comes right to me, and I lean over from the players' box to talk to him.

"Beautiful run," I say. "A beautiful end to a stunning career."

"I love you," he says.

My eyes go wide.

"Sorry if that makes you cringe," he adds, taking my hand.

I thought if this moment ever came I wouldn't be able to look at him, but it's easy. It's terrifying how easy it is. "It's okay," I say. "I already knew. My dad told me."

He laughs. "It's that obvious, huh?"

"No," I say. "Or maybe. I don't know. Do you need me to say it back?"

"No," he says. "I know who you are. And you're late to warm up."

"Are you okay?" I ask, hugging him. "You're sure?"

"Yeah, I'm sure."

"Okay, I'm going. But I do too, you know. What you said."

"I know," he says.

"That obvious, huh?" I joke.

"Not really, Carrie," he says, laughing. "But you have your tells."

SOTO VS. CORTEZ

1995 US Open

Semifinals

IT'S THE THIRD SET. I'M TWO GAMES AWAY FROM CLINCHING THIS thing.

I'm not tired yet. But Cortez is angry. I can feel it when she starts smacking the tuft off the ball.

She wants to get to the final. She's probably got a chip on her shoulder about London. She's used it to push her forward, and I respect that.

I keep thinking about my father's notebook.

Cortez is irritable and cocky. She does not like losing. She does not like believing someone has bested her. Piss her off and she will start messing up. Very familiar.

I knew he meant me. But as I stand across the net from her now, I can see that Cortez and I are perhaps even more alike than I'd realized. Cutting and relentless, bloodthirsty. Cold but passionate. Needing to win because we cannot bear to lose.

Knock Cortez off her game, make her upset. She's a confident player; undermine her confidence and you will cut her down.

If my father is right and Cortez's mental game is like mine, then I know what I need to do.

I need to hit as many aces as possible. I need to not even give her the chance to fight for the point. If I shut her out of my service games completely, she'll get exasperated and desperate. She'll start making mistakes.

Yes, I think I know Ingrid Cortez very well. The downside of perfectionism is that you are so used to getting it right, you completely collapse when you get it wrong.

And it will not be me who collapses today.

To serve aces, you have to be bold. You have to risk hitting the net or going wide. You have to play like you're not afraid. I can do that.

I toss the ball and whip it right into the far corner of the service box. Cortez can't touch it. *15–love.*

I keep at it. Soon, I've held the game.

Cortez's shoulders tense and her hands turn to fists with every point I chip off her. Each time she walks back to the baseline, she shakes her head at herself and looks at her coach.

I hold steady. And soon I'm at match point.

Cortez bounces the ball at her feet, gearing herself up for the toss.

I feel a wash of affection for her. She is so young. She still has so much time to do all the things she wants to do. But going to the final of the '95 US Open will not be one of them.

She serves a screamer—hard and fast with a quick drop. I run backward, ready for it. I take it on the rise, a forehand cross-court. She returns it with a groundstroke wide to my backhand.

The ball comes at me. I pull my racket back and take it out of the air before the bounce, send it back wide to her forehand.

She runs for it, but it bounces hard and then spins farther off court. She dives, hitting the ground at the same time the ball lands softly out of her reach.

The crowd erupts. Bowe shoots up out of his seat. I see that Gwen is hollering. I fall to my knees, the hard court scraping my skin. I am not proud, as much as I am grateful.

Ahí vamos, papá, I think. *A la final.*

THAT EVENING, BOWE, GWEN, AND I SIT IN MY HOTEL SUITE, IN FRONT of the television. I'm acting calm, but I can feel the stress gathering in my knees. I'm trying to stretch them out.

Bowe's back is killing him, so he's watching TV from the floor with his legs up the wall. Gwen's the only one of us able to sit properly.

Nicki is playing Antonovich in the semis. She's now serving for the match.

"We want Chan to win," Gwen says. "Right? I'm just confirming I'm rooting for the right thing here. It's not an easy one."

I nod, reaching for my toes. I can feel my hamstrings and the backs of my knees sing. "Yeah, we want Chan."

Nicki serves a kick serve. Antonovich returns. Nicki hits a groundstroke, bouncing just at the baseline and then into the stands. Nicki can anticipate the ball better than almost anyone I know.

"Fuck, she's good," I say.

Bowe nods. "She is."

"And she's got no coach," I say. "She doesn't have that magic in her back pocket, like I've had all these years. She's doing this all herself."

Nicki serves another, fast and ugly, like she's dropping a bomb.

"Nicki's gonna take it," I say.

Nicki serves, jumping big and landing hard on the court as she follows it through. I'm not sure Antonovich can reach it. But then somehow Antonovich gets high up and manages to smash it back before she falls onto the court.

Bowe sits up. Gwen is leaning toward the TV. I get to my feet.

Nicki's head looks up as the ball arches across the net. She's running backward watching it. Antonovich, still on the court, is staring at it.

The ball soars through the air and careens down as Nicki rushes for it. It hits *inches* past the sideline. It's out.

Natasha Antonovich pounds her arms on the court.

Nicki jumps into the air.

So here it is. Soto vs. Chan.

I WAKE UP THE NEXT MORNING. THE SUN IS SHINING; THE AIR IS COOL. It is a perfect day to win the US Open.

Bowe is already up, despite the early hour. And when I come out into the living area, he is reading the paper. Beside him is a blueberry smoothie and a jar of unsalted almonds.

"Good morning, record breaker," he says.

"You know better than to say shit like that before I've actually broken a record."

Bowe shakes his head. "No, look," he says. He shows me the paper he's reading. The headline says SOTO VS. CHAN GUARANTEED TO BREAK MULTIPLE RECORDS.

I pick up the paper and read through the article. Among other facts of tonight's match, I learn that between Nicki and me, *one* of us will be the oldest to win the US Open in the Open Era. Nicki, at almost thirty-two, will beat out Margaret Court by nine months. If I take it, I'll beat Margaret Court by almost seven years.

I am officially the oldest player to make the women's singles final of the US Open. I also stand to break the record for most aces in a tournament, and it is looking like Soto vs. Chan will create a new record for viewership numbers.

One record they don't know about yet: Gwen called me last night to tell me AmEx has offered to buy out my contract with Elite Gold. And since Elite Gold now wants to *keep* my contract, AmEx is offering me the largest endorsement fee for any tennis player—male or female—in history.

I told her I'm directing every dollar to my youth center funds. Gwen said she'd donate too.

"I mean, I can do that and still retire off this check," Gwen told me.

I laughed and told her to go for it.

"I'm going to do it, Carrie," she said, her voice now serious. "I'm going to tell my partners I'm retiring next year. Officially."

"Good for you," I told her.

Now I hand the article back to Bowe.

"So many statistics," I say. "Good God. It is exactly what my dad said all those years ago. You just pick one randomly and decide that's the one you're committed to. But when you take a step back, how can you say one means more than another?"

Bowe sips his coffee and nods. "Still," he says. "'Most Slams' means something to a lot of us, let's not kid ourselves. You are defending the one that means the most to you."

I take a breath. "Yeah," I say. "But it didn't ever mean as much to my dad. My dad just wanted me to play beautiful tennis."

Bowe smiles. "And look at that," he says. "You do."

Walking through the tunnel, I can just see the edges of the court. The crowd is already loud. The lights are on, barely brighter than the evening air. When I get to the opening, I pull my shoulders down. I roll my neck. I wipe my shoes.

I inhale sharply. I let the air leave my body like a deflating balloon. I am loose. I am ready.

There is a guard standing behind me. And then I hear footsteps.

"Nicki," I say.

She's wearing a white shirt and a navy blue skirt. Her Nike 130s are white with a blue Swoosh. "Carrie."

"You feeling all right?" I say. "How's your ankle? How's your back? Any injuries I should exploit?"

Nicki laughs. "Unfortunately for you, I'm feeling one hundred percent."

"Good," I say. "The win will be sweeter."

Nicki shakes her head. "I read an interview with you years ago, when I was still a kid," she says. "Where you said your father called you 'Achilles.'"

"Yeah," I say. "The greatest of the Greeks."

"I was always jealous of that. That sense of destiny you seemed to have. Do you remember what Achilles said to Hector after Hector killed Patroclus?"

It has been a long time since I've actually read *The Iliad*. I shake my head.

She smiles. "He says, 'There can be no pacts between men and lions. I will make you pay in full for the grief you have caused me.'"

SOTO VS. CHAN

1995 US Open

Final

Too many people, possibly even Nicki, believe that Nicki is new tennis. That my Carrie is old tennis. They don't realize I taught Carrie to play any tennis. So Carrie should start wild and powerful, start with a splash. Make it clear, from the beginning, that whatever version of Carrie Nicki prepared for, she didn't prepare for this.

I win the toss and elect to serve first.

Nicki's forehand is brutal, so everyone serves to her backhand. Not me. My first serve is low, short, fast, and wide to her forehand. She has to scramble to meet the ball. She returns it just past the net. I chip it back. She doesn't get under it in time. *15–love.*

Nicki looks at me and nods calmly.

I hold the first game.

. . .

Her first serve comes at me like it was shot from a gun—exactly as I knew it would. I return it right to her backhand. She returns it deep. I send it back with a drive volley, pulling her up closer to the net.

> *Nicki succeeds by getting people to play her type of tennis. Carrie can meet her at that level, but Nicki cannot meet Carrie at hers. Carrie should lure Nicki into Carrie's kind of tennis—the kind of tennis where a centimeter matters. I believe the best Carrie will beat the best Nicki. And that means* GET HER TO THE NET.

Nicki runs up to meet my shot and makes it just in time. But her return is too long. The first point in her service game is mine. *Love–15.*

Still, she holds the game.

We each hold our games—neither able to break the other. 1–1 becomes 2–2. 2–2 becomes 3–3, 4–4, 5–5.

At 6–6, we move to a tiebreaker.

Nicki clobbers me with her serves. On my serves, she hammers her returns. The tiebreak quickly gets to 0–4, Nicki's favor. I have to adjust.

I try cutting off the pace of the ball, hitting slices, stopping her short. It works quickly, and I am unyielding until she gets the hang of it.

Now we're 4–4.

5–5.

6–6 in the tiebreaker.

The crowd is beginning to rumble.

Nicki hits a winner past me, bringing her to 6–7. But she's got to win by two.

It's my serve, and I send a fast shot right at her heels. She misses it. 7–7.

Minutes later, Nicki is up 12–11. It's her serve.

I stare at her, watching her toss, trying to guess where it's going. By now I can see that she does have a small tell. She holds her shoulder ever so slightly lower when she's going cross-court.

I watch her, see her shoulder high. I know she's sending it down the line, to my forehand.

It whistles through the air so fast it's gone by the time I hear it. I reach wide, but I can't snag it. *Fuck.* The crowd screams.

At 13–11 in the tiebreak, the first set is hers.

I haven't been looking at anyone during the changeovers. Not Gwen, not Bowe, not Ali. Not the crowd. I keep my head down. I focus on drinking water, drying my face, keeping my father in my head. I only want to hear his voice right now.

> *If Nicki wins the first set, Carrie has a better chance of winning the second. We can use Nicki's confidence—her arrogance???—against her here. And we should. Stay the course. Keep at it. Don't change it up. If we don't take the first set, we can win the second.*

The second set begins. I move her up to the net. I hit the balls low and soft so she can't get as much power off them.

We trade games. 1–1. 2–2. 3–3.

But soon, Nicki starts getting the hang of it. She is staying closer to the net, hitting with more control. Our rallies go ten, twelve, sometimes fifteen times back and forth.

Nobody breaking anyone's serve.

It begins to feel like a perfect rhythm—the ball back and forth, the two of us meeting it. No unforced errors, no mistakes. Perfect execution. Just a dance.

There are times I am looking at the ball and other times I am watching her. I can feel her watching me. I know, as I'm swinging, that she can see the skill in what I'm doing. I can barely take my eyes off the gorgeous brutality of her power. She swings with such concentrated force, screaming as she does it.

I zero in on the yellow dot as it barrels toward me time and again. I feel the ease of my arm pulling back, over and over, my racket gliding on in the follow-through.

I'm playing the best goddamn game I can, moment by moment, shot by shot.

When it's 5–6, her serve, it's time to knock her out. I volley it back to her; she runs up to the net. And just when it seems as if she has settled into this fast, volleying tennis, I hit a flat crushing groundstroke past her.

And then I do it again, and again. Just when she hangs back, I send a drop shot. Just when she thinks I'm pulling up short, I hit it long. It's her serve but she's on the run, one step behind me, trying to catch up. *30–40.*

And now here I am. The moment in which I know I can take the set. Break point.

If Carrie gets to break point, she will convert it to a win. She is great at turning momentum into points. Nicki is a good defensive player—players rarely get to break point against her anymore. And she's a fan of Carrie, she knows Carrie. She knows Carrie lives at break point. We just need to get Carrie to break point once every set. And the rest will fall into place.

Nicki serves the ball. It goes right up against the line but lands inside, bounces high. I jump and hit a smash overhead.

She takes it out of the air early. And I can tell she's expecting a groundstroke return; the ball has too much fire on it for me to try a softer shot. But rather than send it cross-court, I go for the winner. I send it right down the line, along the sideline. She has to rush across the court to get her hands on it. I watch her running, and I can see her ankle roll a bit as she slides.

And she's too late. The ball bounces once, and she can't save it. When she stands up, I can tell her ankle hurts. And thank God, because both my knees, especially my bad one, are starting to ache.

"Set is Soto's," I hear over the loudspeaker as the crowd jumps out of their seats. Everyone begins to scream.

I smile at Nicki, expecting a smile back. But she looks pissed, on the verge of throwing her racket. I don't blame her. I've been there. She thought the match would be hers by now.

But I'm stealing it out of her hands.

This is fun, I think. *How did I forget this is so fucking fun?*

I sit down on the chair and wipe my face dry. I take a drink of water. I look over at Nicki, who will not look at me, her jaw clenched. She unscrews the top of a Gatorade and takes a big swig. If I had to guess, her ankle is swelling. Clouds have started to settle in over the arena. It cools the air, and I am grateful.

Gwen catches my eye. She points at me, right at my chest.

I tap my flat palm to my heart and point back at her.

The deciding set. Nicki's serves get faster, harder. They come at me with a whistle. It is startling. But I don't worry myself with trying to outdo her. My serves are accurate down to the inch. They are sniper shots.

Nicki's playing at full capacity right now. She's fast and watching my tosses. I have to keep my serves unpredictable and sharp.

1–1 to 2–2, 2–2 to 3–3. When I take the ball low, she gets under it. When she goes deep, I get there. When I go short, she pulls up.

She is breathing heavily. I am sweating.

The crowd is going wild with every rally, screaming at every winner.

4–4. 5–5.

My dad was right. The third set is when Nicki plays her hardest.

When she slams another groundstroke past me, I return it just in time, only to see her setting up for another. I am in awe of the firepower of her arm. The way it crushes the ball when it makes contact. I've never seen power like this. Certainly not with this much intuition about where the ball is going, what the ball will do.

My left knee is twinging, my right knee not far behind. I'm breathing harder than when I was running on sand all those months ago. Sweat is pouring off my face. The sky is getting darker. But I'm not letting up. And neither is she. I can tell by the way her eyes have lost their brightness, her shoulders have tightened. Even her gait seems angry as she limps away from the net after every point.

Nicki Chan is a great player. But not great enough to destroy me as quickly as she wanted.

On her next service game, Nicki starts serving so fast it feels like a blitz.

I can feel the fatigue in my legs. They are starting to give out, my thighs quivering when I squat. My knees are screaming. She shuts me out of the game.

I can barely hold her off on my service game. But I do.

It's now 6–6 in the third set. We're going to another tiebreak.

And then lightning cracks, and the sky roars. I look up at the clouds, and rain starts falling.

Gwen, Bowe, and Ali all rush into the locker room during the delay.

"Guys," I say. "I'm fine. I've got this."

"You are dominating!" Gwen says. It is the most intense I've ever seen her. "Raining sheer motherfucking terror!"

I laugh. "Thank you."

Bowe smiles. "She's right."

I lock eyes with him and smile. "I have to stay focused on winning the tiebreak. Do we know how long the delay will be?"

Ali speaks up. "The storm is passing already. They don't think more than twenty minutes."

"In that case, everyone get out of here," I say. And then I add, "Please."

Bowe grabs my shoulder and squeezes it, then escorts the two of them out. He turns back to me at the last second.

"This is a beautiful match," he says. "An absolutely *beautiful* match."

He doesn't wait for my response. He just taps the doorframe and leaves.

Suddenly, it is so quiet around me that I can hear the churn of the pipes in the walls.

I try to think of what my father would say to me right now. I open my locker and look through the notebook. I read his notes again. He says nothing about a tiebreak for the third set. I flip through the pages, searching for something—anything—but there's nothing I haven't already read.

What would he say if he were here? What would he have written in this book if he'd had more time? There are still things I need to know; there is still advice I need to get from him. There is more to do together.

I run through strategies—start slow, let her get tired; come out fast, don't let her get a foothold; go for the big serves; now's not the time for big serves—desperately trying to assess which one sounds the most like him.

But . . . I don't know. I don't know what he would say.

I feel as if the wind has been knocked out of me. From this moment forward, I do not have him with me. I do not know what he would be thinking. I do not know any more of his strategy, his plan. His logic. His advice. Because he is gone. And he will never be back. I have come to the end.

Suddenly, I feel as if the pain is enough to level me.

I pick up the notebook and put it back in the locker. If I win this tiebreak, it will be because I know how to beat her on my own. And if I don't, it will be because she is the better player. This is the test I asked for.

The door opens, and Nicki comes in.

"I was waiting in the training room," she says. "I didn't want to see you."

"Oh."

"But now it's gonna be at least another ten."

"Okay."

She sits down next to me on the bench. She doesn't say anything for a long time. And neither do I. I just sit next to her with my eyes closed, trying to control my breathing, trying to ignore the pain in my knees.

"This should be mine already," Nicki says, finally.

I open my eyes and look at her. "Well, it's not, sunshine."

Nicki shakes her head. "You are the best player I have ever played, then and now," she says. "You bitch."

I laugh.

"I'm trying to be funny to hide how much I hate you with every atom in my body," she says. I check her face, and she's not smiling.

"Don't hate me," I say. "It is a waste of your time."

Nicki huffs.

"You're playing some of the best tennis I've ever seen you play," I tell her. "Thanks to me."

She rolls her eyes. "Okay, Soto."

I add, "You deserve every single place you claim in history."

Nicki looks me in the eye. "I am going to beat you."

"No," I tell her. "You are not."

Nicki laughs, despite herself. A coordinator comes in and tells us they are preparing for us to head back out. We both stand up, and Nicki puts her hand on my shoulder.

"Playing you this year . . . beating these records—with Carrie Soto, against Carrie Soto—it's been a dream come true."

I look her in the eye and nod, unsure quite how to tell her that this match has meant the same for me.

"And now I'm going to shoot an arrow right into your heel so I can say I was the one who finally took down Achilles."

And *that* I instantly have the words for: "I'd like to see you fucking try."

The tiebreaker begins.

A point for Nicki, a point for me.

For Nicki. For Nicki.

For me. For me. For Nicki.

Around and around in circles. It is the most fun I've had in years.

This will be the last tournament that I will ever play. And I can't help but enjoy it.

I did not pick up a racket to grow tense and weary and afraid of failing. I picked it up to feel the joy of smashing a ball as hard as I can. I picked it up to spend time with my dad.

This is it. My last moment of what he and I started together. This match. This tiebreaker. I could live in it forever.

Me. Then Nicki.

Then me. Then Nicki.

Then me. Then Nicki. Then me.

I serve my sharpest, most deadly serve, trying to get an ace off her. But she returns it just as fast. And I can't match her power now. Her point.

Nicki serves maybe the fastest serve I've ever seen in my life. But I gear up and return it. She hits a smash so high I have to leap into the air despite my knees. But I jump higher than I think I've ever jumped before, and I manage to graze the ball with my racket, somehow landing it where she can't reach. My knee is killing me now, but it's my point.

I serve it, and she returns with a groundstroke. I hit a cross-court backhand and watch as it bounces in. But she's too far from it. No one can get across the court in the time she has, certainly not with her ankle. I watch as the ball flies over the net. Nicki is running too fast. I can tell. She's going to overshoot. But the ball bounces lower than I think it's going to.

It shouldn't have bounced that low. It's a fresh ball, and I sent it over hard. But sometimes you get a bad bounce, and the ball doesn't do what it's supposed to. And usually, in those moments, the returner misses the shot.

But not Nicki. Not now. Somehow she saw it happening before it happened. She meets the ball outside the line and skids across the court as she drops low to her knees. She leans back, overextended, and gets under the ball just as it's flying past her, her shin already bleeding from the skid.

She turns ever so slightly and returns it with a shot I can't touch.

Her point. It's now 16–15.

And for the first time, I know something as terrifying as it is freeing.

Nicki Chan might just understand the ball better than I do.

She serves the ball again, whipping it at me. I return it so deep it hits at the baseline and then bounces high off the court. Nicki jumps into the air and returns it with a lob.

It glides, slowly, above us. I watch it as gravity brings it back toward the ground. I move two steps to the right, one step back. I hedge my footing, staying on my toes, ready to run whenever it lands. My left knee feels like steel grinding against steel. The pain rings through me, reverberating, absorbing into every part of my body.

I do not care.

The ball descends toward the court. I have to decide whether to hit it before the bounce or get it on the rise. I cycle through my options, all my shots. And then, instead of choosing, I just let my arms fly.

I take it out of the air, quick—send it careening back. Nicki starts running.

I might beat her today. If that ball is in and she misses it, I can beat her today.

But that will not change the fact that she is *incomparable*. And she will win another Slam in '96. And then probably another, if she goes easier on her ankle.

And what am I going to do? Keep coming back to try to take it from her? Keep holding on for dear life to what I should have let go of long ago? Is that what I want my life to be? Trying to deny what Nicki Chan is?

Where is the beauty in that?

My shot arches toward her, over the net. Nicki's running deep. The ball goes past her. She's not going to get it.

I can feel myself winning this thing and then letting go of it all. Letting her take the rest from here on out. I am ready for that. I am ready to give it to her. To let her have it. Finally.

But as I watch, the ball lands one centimeter past the baseline.

The linesman calls it out.

I can't quite believe what I'm seeing. Nicki screams into the sky, both arms outstretched. The crowd is up on their feet, cheering.

I just lost the tiebreak. I just lost the match.

I can barely catch my breath.

I don't slam down my racket. I don't scream. I don't bury my face in my hands. I just look at Bowe.

Nicki Chan has won the US Open.

I lost. The match and my record, twice in one year.

I wait for the skies to open up and shame to rain down on me. I wait for my belly to split in half. For the grief to overtake me. But . . . it doesn't come.

Bowe is smiling. And Gwen has her arms out, waiting to give me a hug. Ali is clapping wildly, even though I lost.

And the thing I don't understand is that I still feel that hum. That hum in my bones. That sense of weightlessness and groundedness. That sense that the day is mine. That I can do anything.

Nicki Chan looks at me. And I smile at her.

I am no longer the greatest tennis player in the world.

For the first time in my life, I can be . . . something else.

One Year Later

CHAN VS. CORTEZ

1996 US Open

Final

IT'S 5–4 IN THE DECIDING SET. IF NICKI BREAKS CORTEZ'S SERVE ON this last game, she will set a new record.

I am sitting in the players' box. Bowe is next to me. Nicki's parents are on the other side of us. Her new girlfriend, who *cannot stand me,* is sitting with a tight smile on her face in the corner.

I watch as Nicki returns Cortez's heavy forehand with a slice. I nod. The Soto Slice was the first thing I taught her.

"You need to improve your volleys, your short game. That's how I almost beat you back in New York," I said, on our first day on the courts together.

"I don't need a volley game when my baseline game is as good as it is," she said.

"You will never win Wimbledon again with just your baseline game, and you know it. You're gonna give up one-fourth of all Slams a year because you don't want to perfect your volley?" I said. "Now, come on, *de nuevo!*"

Nicki frowned but then did what I told her to. Just like she did when I made her start going easier on her ankle—so she could extend her career a few years. She gets pissed and mouths off, but I can tell she's always listening to me, even if she doesn't act like it.

It makes me laugh—how often my father must have seen my own frown, knowing I'd still do what he said.

And now, here we are—coach and player—at the 1996 US Open, me sitting here in the stands, helpless to do anything but hope she can harness all the new skills we've worked on.

My God, how hard it must have been for my father to do this. To sit here, a ball of nerves, knowing that all of the control was in my hands. He could not think for me on the court, he could not hit the ball for me. He just had to have faith that I could play the way he'd taught me.

What a gift it is, to be able to guide someone to a point and then let them finish it themself. To give someone all the knowledge you have and then pray they use it right. It's a skill I am learning, one I am determined to perfect.

Nicki's now at break point. Which means she is at championship point.

She looks up at me. I nod at her. She nods back, a small smile erupting across her face.

If she takes the next point, she'll win the US Open and hit a record-breaking twenty-three Slams—a feat that, just a few short years ago, was unheard of. But that's Nicki for you. Unstoppable. Raising the bar for absolutely everyone.

Cortez tosses the ball into the air and sends it screaming over the net. Nicki starts backing up, stepping into position.

"She's got it," Bowe says, quietly under his breath. I stare straight ahead, bouncing my knees. He grabs my hand to calm me.

I sit forward, praying with all my might, as Nicki pulls back and swings—

ACKNOWLEDGMENTS

I loved creating Carrie Soto with all of my heart and I only got to do it because of readers. So thank you, to every single person who picked up *Malibu,* or *Daisy,* or *Evelyn,* or *One True Loves* and any of the books that came before it. Thank you for showing up for these characters.

This is a story of a woman who often acts like she does it all on her own but, in fact, benefits greatly from the talented people around her. And because of that, I've dedicated this book to my manager, Brad Mendelsohn, who was the first member of the incredible team I have now—and directly and indirectly led me to the wildly talented people mentioned here whom I am incredibly fortunate to work with.

Thank you to my editor, Jennifer Hershey. You understood Carrie and pushed me to bring her fully to life with all of her flaws. I'm so thankful to you for your commitment to her. And to my agent, Theresa Park, thank you for seeing the joy and fun in this book and feeling it alongside me.

To the team at Ballantine—Kara Welsh, Kim Hovey, Susan Corcoran, Jennifer Garza, Allyson Lord, Quinne Rogers, Taylor Noel, Maya Franson, Paolo Pepe, Elena Giavaldi, Erin Kane, and Sydney Shiffman. I cannot believe I got so lucky as to be published by such a talented and powerful publishing house. Thank you for your passion and all of the effort that goes into getting these books into people's hands. It doesn't happen without you.

To the PFLM team—Emily Sweet, Andrea Mai, Abigail Koons, Anna Petkovich, Kathryn Toolan, Jen Mecum, and Charlotte Gillies. I would not be able to do any of this without your insights. You all are invaluable, and I consider your expertise paramount to my success.

Carisa Hays and Hayley Shear, thank you for always having my back. Each and every time.

Julian Alexander, you are always such a bright spot on every Zoom! Thank you for your faith in me. And to Ailah Ahmed and the entire team at Hutchinson Heinemann, I cannot tell you what it means to have such a phenomenal, robust team behind my work in the UK.

Leo Teti, you have saved me! This book needed you, and I am so grateful to have had you in my corner.

Stuart Rosenthal and Sylvie Rabineau, thank you for being there—calm, cool, and collected—for every curveball that gets thrown our way.

Kari Erickson, I don't think I would have gotten through 2021 without you. And I certainly wouldn't have been able to get this book ready in time. Your insights, thoughtfulness, and conscientiousness have become indispensable. Thank you.

I wrote this book during a pandemic. And I could not have done that without the people closest to me stepping up to help with child-care. I have said it before but I don't think I can ever say it enough: This book does not exist without my mother-in-law, Rose, and my grandmother-in-law, Sally, stepping in to spend time with my daughter. I cannot do it alone. And I do not have to. I thank you for that. Thank you to my brother, Jake, for talking me through it all, even the parts that have no easy answers.

And thank you to my peanuts. I can't make any decisions without you all so I'm very grateful that one of you is always there, at any reasonable hour eastern time, to help me through it all.

Of course, I have never written a book without you, Alex Jenkins Reid. It's not just because you watch our daughter. Or that you help me to remember that these things are only books, after all. It is because you also help me figure out when I should listen to what other people are telling me and when to go with my gut. It is an incredible skill, to understand when you are right and when you are wrong. You have helped me to see it as clearly as I can. And in so doing, you've helped me become more myself than I have ever been before.

And lastly, to Lilah. You've heard me talk about Carrie Soto for a while now. You've patiently listened to me try to figure her out. And you had a very good idea for the title of this book, which I almost used. So, I don't know, maybe you're a writer. But let me tell you something: You are capable of so many amazing things. I hope, as you grow older, that this gives you a sense of peace. I, for so much of my life, have had something to prove. But I think you have a real chance of knowing you don't have to prove a single thing to anyone. If it should come to pass that you feel the need to go do something big, to go be the greatest there ever was, I will stand by you for that journey. I will be there, cheering you on, for anything you go out there and do. But just know that, to me, you showed up perfect. You don't have to prove a single thing.

ABOUT THE AUTHOR

Taylor Jenkins Reid is the *New York Times* bestselling author of eight novels, including *Malibu Rising, Daisy Jones & The Six* and *The Seven Husbands of Evelyn Hugo*. She lives in Los Angeles with her husband and their daughter.

taylorjenkinsreid.com
Instagram: @tjenkinsreid

ABOUT THE TYPE

This book was set in Fairfield, the first typeface from the hand of the distinguished American artist and engraver Rudolph Ruzicka (1883–1978). Ruzicka was born in Bohemia (in the present-day Czech Republic) and came to America in 1894. He set up his own shop, devoted to wood engraving and printing, in New York in 1913 after a varied career working as a wood engraver, in photoengraving and banknote printing plants, and as an art director and freelance artist. He designed and illustrated many books, and was the creator of a considerable list of individual prints—wood engravings, line engravings on copper, and aquatints.